ECE/TRANS/301 (Vol. I)

ECONOMIC COMMISSION FOR EUROPE

Committee on Inland Transport

European Agreement concerning the International Carriage of Dangerous Goods by Inland Waterways (ADN)

including the Annexed Regulations, applicable as from 1 January 2021

Volume I

UNITED NATIONS
New York and Geneva, 2020

Requests to reproduce excerpts or to photocopy should be addressed to the Copyright Clearance Center at copyright.com.

All other queries on rights and licenses, including subsidiary rights, should be addressed to:

United Nations Publications,
405 East 42nd Street, S-09FW001,
New York, NY 10017,
United States of America.
Email: permissions@un.org;
website: https://shop.un.org.

The designations employed and the presentation of material on any map in this work do not imply the expression of any opinion whatsoever on the part of the United Nations concerning the legal status of any country, territory, city or area or of its authorities, or concerning the delimitation of its frontiers or boundaries.

United Nations publication issued by the United Nations Economic Commission for Europe.

ECE/TRANS/301

ISBN: 978-92-1-139182-4
eISBN: 978-92-1-005131-6

ISSN: 2411-8583
eISSN: 2411-8591

Sales number: E.20.VIII.3

Complete set of two volumes
Volumes I and II not to be sold separately

United Nations Economic Commission for Europe (UNECE)

The United Nations Economic Commission for Europe (UNECE) is one of the five United Nations regional commissions, administered by the Economic and Social Council (ECOSOC). It was established in 1947 with the mandate to help rebuild post-war Europe, develop economic activity and strengthen economic relations among European countries, and between Europe and the rest of the world. During the Cold War, UNECE served as a unique forum for economic dialogue and cooperation between East and West. Despite the complexity of this period, significant achievements were made, with consensus reached on numerous harmonization and standardization agreements.

In the post-Cold War era, UNECE acquired not only many new member States, but also new functions. Since the early 1990s the organization has focused on assisting the countries of Central and Eastern Europe, Caucasus and Central Asia with their transition process and their integration into the global economy.

Today, UNECE supports its 56 member States in Europe, Central Asia and North America in the implementation of the 2030 Agenda for Sustainable Development with its Sustainable Development Goals (SDGs). UNECE provides a multilateral platform for policy dialogue, the development of international legal instruments, norms and standards, the exchange of best practices and economic and technical expertise, as well as technical cooperation for countries with economies in transition.

Offering practical tools to improve people's everyday lives in the areas of environment, transport, trade, statistics, energy, forestry, housing, and land management, many of the norms, standards and conventions developed in UNECE are used worldwide, and a number of countries from outside the region participate in UNECE's work.

UNECE's multisectoral approach helps countries to tackle the interconnected challenges of sustainable development in an integrated manner, with a transboundary focus that helps devise solutions to shared challenges. With its unique convening power, UNECE fosters cooperation among all stakeholders at the country and regional levels. The United Nations Economic Commission for Europe (UNECE) is one of the five United Nations regional commissions, administered by the Economic and Social Council (ECOSOC). It was established in 1947 with the mandate to help rebuild post-war Europe, develop economic activity and strengthen economic relations among European countries, and between Europe and the rest of the world. During the Cold War, UNECE served as a unique forum for economic dialogue and cooperation between East and West. Despite the complexity of this period, significant achievements were made, with consensus reached on numerous harmonization and standardization agreements.

In the post-Cold War era, UNECE acquired not only many new member States, but also new functions. Since the early 1990s the organization has focused on analyses of the transition process, using its harmonization experience to facilitate the integration of central and eastern European countries into global markets.

UNECE is the forum where the countries of western, central and eastern Europe, Central Asia and North America – 56 countries in all – come together to forge the tools of their cooperation. That cooperation concerns economic cooperation and integration, statistics, environment, transport, trade, sustainable energy, forestry and timber, housing and land management and population. The Commission offers a regional framework for the elaboration and harmonization of conventions, norms and standards. The Commission's experts provide technical assistance to the countries of South-East Europe and the Commonwealth of Independent States. This assistance takes the form of advisory services, training seminars and workshops where countries can share their experiences and best practices.

Transport in UNECE

The UNECE Sustainable Transport Division is the secretariat of the Inland Transport Committee (ITC) and the ECOSOC Committee of Experts on the Transport of Dangerous Goods and on the Globally Harmonized System of Classification and Labelling of Chemicals. The ITC and its 17 working parties, as well as the ECOSOC Committee and its sub-committees are intergovernmental decision-making bodies that work to improve the daily lives of people and businesses around the world, in measurable ways and with concrete actions, to enhance traffic safety, environmental performance, energy efficiency and the competitiveness of the transport sector.

The ECOSOC Committee was set up in 1953 by the Secretary-General of the United Nations at the request of the Economic and Social Council to elaborate recommendations on the transport of dangerous goods. Its mandate was extended to the global (multi-sectoral) harmonization of systems of classification and labelling of chemicals in 1999. It is composed of experts from countries which possess the relevant expertise and experience in the international trade and transport of dangerous goods and chemicals. Its membership is restricted in order to reflect a proper geographical balance between all regions of the world and to ensure adequate participation of developing countries. Although the Committee is a subsidiary body of ECOSOC, the Secretary-General decided in 1963 that the secretariat services would be provided by the UNECE Transport Division.

ITC is a unique intergovernmental forum that was set up in 1947 to support the reconstruction of transport connections in post-war Europe. Over the years, it has specialized in facilitating the harmonized and sustainable development of inland modes of transport. The main results of this persevering and ongoing work are reflected, among other things, (i) in 58 United Nations conventions and many more technical regulations, which are updated on a regular basis and provide an international legal framework for the sustainable development of national and international road, rail, inland water and intermodal transport, including the transport of dangerous goods, as well as the construction and inspection of road motor vehicles; (ii) in the Trans-European North-south Motorway, Trans-European Railway and the Euro-Asia Transport Links projects, that facilitate multi-country coordination of transport infrastructure investment programmes; (iii) in the TIR system, which is a global customs transit facilitation solution; (iv) in the tool called For Future Inland Transport Systems (ForFITS), which can assist national and local governments to monitor carbon dioxide (CO_2) emissions coming from inland transport modes and to select and design climate change mitigation policies, based on their impact and adapted to local conditions; (v) in transport statistics – methods and data – that are internationally agreed on; (vi) in studies and reports that help transport policy development by addressing timely issues, based on cutting-edge research and analysis. ITC also devotes special attention to Intelligent Transport Services (ITS), sustainable urban mobility and city logistics, as well as to increasing the resilience of transport networks and services in response to climate change adaptation and security challenges.

In addition, the UNECE Sustainable Transport and Environment Divisions, together with the World Health Organization (WHO) – Europe, co-service the Transport Health and Environment Pan-European Programme (THE PEP).

Finally, as of 2015, the UNECE Sustainable Transport Division is providing the secretariat services for the Secretary General's Special Envoy for Road Safety, Mr. Jean Todt.

INTRODUCTION

The European Agreement concerning the International Carriage of Dangerous Goods by Inland Waterways (ADN) done at Geneva on 26 May 2000 under the auspices of the United Nations Economic Commission for Europe (UNECE) and the Central Commission for the Navigation of the Rhine (CCNR) entered into force on 28 February 2008.

The Agreement itself and the annexed Regulations, in their original version, were published in 2001 under the symbol ECE/TRANS/150. That publication also contains the Final Act of the Diplomatic Conference held in Geneva from 22 to 26 May 2000 during which the Agreement was adopted as well as the text of a Resolution adopted by the Conference.

At the time of the preparation of the present publication, the Agreement had eighteen Contracting Parties: Austria, Belgium, Bulgaria, Croatia, Czech Republic, France, Germany, Hungary, Luxembourg, Netherlands, Poland, Republic of Moldova, Romania, Russian Federation, Serbia, Slovakia, Switzerland and Ukraine. Other member States of UNECE whose territory contains inland waterways, other than those forming a coastal route, may also become Contracting Parties to the Agreement by acceding to it, on condition that the inland waterways are part of the network of inland waterways of international importance as defined in the European Agreement on Main Inland Waterways of International Importance (AGN).

The Regulations annexed to the ADN contain provisions concerning dangerous substances and articles, provisions concerning their carriage in packages and in bulk on board inland navigation vessels or tank vessels, as well as provisions concerning the construction and operation of such vessels. They also address requirements and procedures for inspections, the issue of certificates of approval, recognition of classification societies, monitoring, and training and examination of experts.

With the exception of the provisions relating to the recognition of classification societies, which have been applicable since the entry into force of the Agreement, the annexed Regulations did not become applicable until twelve months after the entry into force of the Agreement, namely on 28 February 2009 (see Article 11 (1) of the Agreement).

Before the entry into force of the Agreement, updates of the annexed Regulations were carried out regularly by a Joint Meeting of Experts of the UNECE and CCNR. These updates were adopted by the Administrative Committee of the ADN at its first session which was held in Geneva on 19 June 2008 (see document ECE/ADN/2, paragraphs 13 to 16).

Subsequently, the secretariat has published consolidated versions under the symbol ECE/TRANS/203 ("ADN 2009"), ECE/TRANS/220 ("ADN 2011"), ECE/TRANS/231 ("ADN 2013"), ECE/TRANS/243 ("ADN 2015"), ECE/TRANS/258 ("ADN 2017") and ECE/TRANS/276 ("ADN 2019").

At its twenty-fourth session (Geneva, 31 January 2020), the ADN Administrative Committee requested the secretariat to publish a new consolidated edition of ADN ("ADN 2021") incorporating all agreed corrections and amendments to enter into force on 1 January 2021. The amendments and corrections can be found in the following documents: ECE/ADN/54, ECE/ADN/54/Corr.1, ECE/ADN/54/Add.1, ECE/TRANS/WP.15/AC.2/70, annexes II and III, ECE/TRANS/WP.15/AC.2/72, annexes II and III and ECE/TRANS/WP.15/AC.2/74, annex III.

The annexed Regulations contained in the present publication are the consolidated version which takes account of these updates and which is applicable from 1 January 2021.

It should be noted that, according to Directive 2008/68/EC of the European Parliament and of the Council of 24 September 2008 on the inland transport of dangerous goods, as amended, member States of the European Union, have to, with the exclusion of the derogations provided for in Article 1, paragraph 3 of the Directive, apply these annexed Regulations as well as Article 3 (f) and (h) and Article 8, paragraphs 1 and 3 of the ADN to the national and international transport between member States of dangerous goods by inland waterways on their territory.

All requests for information relating to the application of the ADN should be addressed to the relevant competent authority.

Additional information can be found on the website of the UNECE Sustainable Transport Division at the following address:

www.unece.org/trans/danger/publi/adn/adn_e.html

This site, updated on a continuous basis, contains links to the following information:

- ADN Agreement (excluding the annexed Regulations);

- Corrections to the ADN Agreement (excluding the annexed Regulations);

- Status of the Agreement;

- Depositary notifications;

- Country information (competent authorities, notifications);

- Multilateral agreements;

- Special authorizations;

- Equivalences and derogations;

- Classification societies;

- Accident reports;

- Catalogue of questions;

- Harmonized model checklists;

- Publication details (Corrigenda);

- ADN 2021 (files);

- Amendments to ADN 2019;

- ADN 2019 (files);

- Previous versions of ADN;

- Historical information.

TABLE OF CONTENTS

VOLUME I

Table of contents (cont'd)

Table of contents (cont'd)

EUROPEAN AGREEMENT CONCERNING THE INTERNATIONAL CARRIAGE OF DANGEROUS GOODS BY INLAND WATERWAYS (ADN)

THE CONTRACTING PARTIES,

DESIRING to establish by joint agreement uniform principles and rules, for the purposes of:

(a)   increasing the safety of international carriage of dangerous goods by inland waterways;

(b)   contributing effectively to the protection of the environment, by preventing any pollution resulting from accidents or incidents during such carriage; and

(c)   facilitating transport operations and promoting international trade,

CONSIDERING that the best means of achieving this goal is to conclude an agreement to replace the "European Provisions concerning the International Carriage of Dangerous Goods by Inland Waterways" annexed to resolution No. 223 of the Inland Transport Committee of the Economic Commission for Europe, as amended,

HAVE AGREED as follows:

CHAPTER I

GENERAL PROVISIONS

Article 1

Scope

1.   This Agreement shall apply to the international carriage of dangerous goods by vessels on inland waterways.

2.   This Agreement shall not apply to the carriage of dangerous goods by seagoing vessels on maritime waterways forming part of inland waterways.

3.   This Agreement shall not apply to the carriage of dangerous goods by warships or auxiliary warships or to other vessels belonging to or operated by a State, provided such vessels are used by the State exclusively for governmental and non-commercial purposes. However, each Contracting Party shall, by taking appropriate measures which do not impair the operations or operational capacity of such vessels belonging to or operated by it, ensure that such vessels are operated in a manner compatible with this Agreement, where it is reasonable in practice to do so.

Article 2

Regulations annexed to the Agreement

1. The Regulations annexed to this Agreement shall form an integral part thereof. Any reference to this Agreement implies at the same time a reference to the Regulations annexed thereto.

2. The annexed Regulations include:

    (a) Provisions concerning the international carriage of dangerous goods by inland waterways;

    (b) Requirements and procedures concerning inspections, the issue of certificates of approval, recognition of classification societies, derogations, special authorizations, monitoring, training and examination of experts;

    (c) General transitional provisions;

    (d) Supplementary transitional provisions applicable to specific inland waterways.

Article 3

Definitions

For the purposes of this Agreement:

(a) "*vessel*" means an inland waterway or seagoing vessel;

(b) "*dangerous goods*" means substances and articles the international carriage of which is prohibited by, or authorized only on certain conditions by, the annexed Regulations;

(c) "*international carriage of dangerous goods*" means any carriage of dangerous goods performed by a vessel on inland waterways on the territory of at least two Contracting Parties;

(d) "*inland waterways*" means the navigable inland waterways including maritime waterways on the territory of a Contracting Party open to the navigation of vessels under national law;

(e) "*maritime waterways*" means inland waterways linked to the sea, basically used for the traffic of seagoing vessels and designated as such under national law;

(f) "*recognized classification society*" means a classification society which is in conformity with the annexed Regulations and recognized, in accordance with the procedures laid down in these Regulations, by the competent authority of the Contracting Party where the certificate is issued;

(g) "*competent authority*" means the authority or the body designated or recognized as such in each Contracting Party and in each specific case in connection with these provisions;

(h) "*inspection body*" means a body nominated or recognized by the Contracting Party for the purpose of inspecting vessels according to the procedures laid down in the annexed Regulations.

CHAPTER II

TECHNICAL PROVISIONS

Article 4

Prohibitions on carriage, conditions of carriage, monitoring

1. Subject to the provisions of Articles 7 and 8, dangerous goods barred from carriage by the annexed Regulations shall not be accepted for international carriage.

2. Without prejudice to the provisions of Article 6, the international carriage of other dangerous goods shall be authorized, subject to compliance with the conditions laid down in the annexed Regulations.

3. Observance of the prohibitions and the conditions referred to in paragraphs 1 and 2 shall be monitored by the Contracting Parties in accordance with the provisions laid down in the annexed Regulations.

Article 5

Exemptions

This Agreement shall not apply to the carriage of dangerous goods to the extent to which such carriage is exempted in accordance with the annexed Regulations. Exemptions may only be granted when the quantity of the goods exempted, or the nature of the transport operation exempted, or the packagings, ensure that transport is carried out safely.

Article 6

Sovereign right of States

Each Contracting Party shall retain the right to regulate or prohibit the entry of dangerous goods into its territory for reasons other than safety during carriage.

Article 7

Special regulations, derogations

1. The Contracting Parties shall retain the right to arrange, for a limited period established in the annexed Regulations, by special bilateral or multilateral agreements, and provided safety is not impaired:

    (a) that the dangerous goods which under this Agreement are barred from international carriage may, subject to certain conditions, be accepted for international carriage on their inland waterways; or

    (b) that dangerous goods which under this Agreement are accepted for international carriage only on specified conditions may alternatively be accepted for international carriage on their inland waterways under conditions different from those laid down in the annexed Regulations.

    The special bilateral or multilateral agreements referred to in this paragraph shall be communicated immediately to the Executive Secretary of the Economic Commission for Europe, who shall communicate them to the Contracting Parties which are not signatories to the said agreements.

2. Each Contracting Party shall retain the right to issue special authorizations for the international carriage in tank vessels of dangerous substances the carriage of which in tank vessels is not permitted under the provisions concerning carriage in the annexed Regulations, subject to compliance with the procedures relating to special authorizations in the annexed Regulations.

3. The Contracting Parties shall retain the right to authorize, in the following cases, the international carriage of dangerous goods on board vessels which do not comply with conditions established in the annexed Regulations, provided that the procedure established in the annexed Regulations is complied with:

    (a) The use on a vessel of materials, installations or equipment or the application on a vessel of certain measures concerning construction or certain provisions other than those prescribed in the annexed Regulations;

    (b) Vessel with technical innovations derogating from the provisions of the annexed Regulations.

Article 8

Transitional provisions

1. Certificates of approval and other documents prepared in accordance with the requirements of the Regulations for the Carriage of Dangerous Goods in the Rhine (ADNR), the Regulations for the Carriage of Dangerous Goods on the Danube (ADN-D) or national regulations based on the European Provisions concerning the International Carriage of Dangerous Goods by Inland Waterways as annexed to resolution No. 223 of the Inland Transport Committee of the Economic Commission for Europe or as amended, applicable at the date of application of the annexed Regulations foreseen in Article 11, paragraph 1, shall remain valid until their expiry date, under the same conditions as those prevailing up to the date of such application, including their recognition by other States. In addition, these certificates shall remain valid for a period of one year from the date of application of the annexed Regulations in the event that they would expire during that period. However, the period of validity shall in no case exceed five years beyond the date of application of the annexed Regulations.

2. Vessels which, at the date of application of the annexed Regulations foreseen in Article 11, paragraph 1, are approved for the carriage of dangerous goods on the territory of a Contracting Party and which conform to the requirements of the annexed Regulations, taking into account where necessary, their general transitional provisions, may obtain an ADN certificate of approval under the procedure laid down in the annexed Regulations.

3. In the case of vessels referred to in paragraph 2 to be used exclusively for carriage on inland waterways where ADNR was not applicable under domestic law prior to the date of application of the annexed Regulations foreseen in Article 11, paragraph 1, the supplementary transitional provisions applicable to specific inland waterways may be applied in addition to the general transitional provisions. Such vessels shall obtain an ADN certificate of approval limited to the inland waterways referred to above, or to a portion thereof.

4. If new provisions are added to the annexed Regulations, the Contracting Parties may include new general transitional provisions. These transitional provisions shall indicate the vessels in question and the period for which they are valid.

Article 9

Applicability of other regulations

The transport operations to which this Agreement applies shall remain subject to local, regional or international regulations applicable in general to the carriage of goods by inland waterways.

CHAPTER III

FINAL PROVISIONS

Article 10

Contracting Parties

1. Member States of the Economic Commission for Europe whose territory contains inland waterways, other than those forming a coastal route, which form part of the network of inland waterways of international importance as defined in the European Agreement on Main Inland Waterways of International Importance (AGN) may become Contracting Parties to this Agreement:

    (a)   by signing it definitively;

    (b)   by depositing an instrument of ratification, acceptance or approval after signing it subject to ratification, acceptance or approval;

    (c)   by depositing an instrument of accession.

2. The Agreement shall be open for signature until 31 May 2001 at the Office of the Executive Secretary of the Economic Commission for Europe, Geneva. Thereafter, it shall be open for accession.

3. The instruments of ratification, acceptance, approval or accession shall be deposited with the Secretary-General of the United Nations.

Article 11

Entry into force

1. This Agreement shall enter into force one month after the date on which the number of States mentioned in Article 10, paragraph 1, which have signed it definitively, or have deposited their instruments of ratification, acceptance, approval or accession has reached a total of seven.

    However, the annexed Regulations, except provisions concerning recognition of classification societies, shall not apply until twelve months after the entry into force of the Agreement.

2. For any State signing this Agreement definitively or ratifying, accepting, approving or acceding to it after seven of the States referred to in Article 10, paragraph 1, have signed it definitively or have deposited their instruments of ratification, acceptance, approval or accession, this Agreement shall enter into force one month after the said State has signed it definitively or has deposited its instrument of ratification, acceptance, approval or accession.

    The annexed Regulations shall become applicable on the same date. In the event that the term referred to in paragraph 1 relating to the application of the annexed Regulations has not expired, the annexed Regulations shall become applicable after expiry of the said term.

Article 12

Denunciation

1. Any Contracting Party may denounce this Agreement by so notifying in writing the Secretary-General of the United Nations.

2. Denunciation shall take effect twelve months after the date of receipt by the Secretary-General of the written notification of denunciation.

Article 13

Termination

1. If, after the entry into force of this Agreement, the number of Contracting Parties is less than five during twelve consecutive months, this Agreement shall cease to have effect at the end of the said period of twelve months.

2. In the event of the conclusion of a world-wide agreement for the regulation of the multimodal transport of dangerous goods, any provision of this Agreement, with the exception of those pertaining exclusively to inland waterways, the construction and equipment of vessels, carriage in bulk or tankers which is contrary to any provision of the said world-wide agreement shall, from the date on which the latter enters into force, automatically cease to apply to relations between the Parties to this Agreement which become parties to the world-wide agreement, and shall automatically be replaced by the relevant provision of the said world-wide agreement.

Article 14

Declarations

1. Any State may, at the time of signing this Agreement definitively or of depositing its instrument of ratification, acceptance, approval or accession or at any time thereafter, declare by written notification addressed to the Secretary-General of the United Nations that this Agreement shall extend to all or any of the territories for the international relations of which it is responsible. The Agreement shall extend to the territory or territories named in the notification one month after it is received by the Secretary-General.

2. Any State which has made a declaration under paragraph 1 of this article extending this Agreement to any territory for whose international relations it is responsible may denounce the Agreement in respect of the said territory in accordance with the provisions of Article 12.

3. (a) In addition, any State may, at the time of signing this Agreement definitively or of depositing its instrument of ratification, acceptance, approval or accession or at any time thereafter, declare by written notification addressed to the Secretary-General of the United Nations that this Agreement shall not extend to certain inland waterways on its territory, provided that the waterways in question are not part of the network of inland waterways of international importance as defined in the AGN. If this declaration is made subsequent to the time when the State signs this Agreement definitively or when it deposits its instrument of ratification, acceptance, approval or accession, the Agreement shall cease to have effect on the inland waterways in question one month after this notification is received by the Secretary-General.

   (b) However, any State on whose territory there are inland waterways covered by AGN, and which are, at the date of adoption of this Agreement, subject to a mandatory regime under international law concerning the carriage of dangerous goods, may declare that the implementation of this Agreement on these waterways shall be subject to compliance with the procedures set out in the statutes of the said regime. Any declaration of this nature shall be made at the time of signing this Agreement definitively or of depositing its instrument of ratification, acceptance, approval or accession.

4. Any State which has made a declaration under paragraphs 3 (a) or 3 (b) of this article may subsequently declare by means of a written notification to the Secretary-General of the United Nations that this Agreement shall apply to all or part of its inland waterways covered by the declaration made under paragraphs 3 (a) or 3 (b). The Agreement shall apply to the inland waterways mentioned in the notification one month after it is received by the Secretary-General.

Article 15

Disputes

1. Any dispute between two or more Contracting Parties concerning the interpretation or application of this Agreement shall so far as possible be settled by negotiation between the Parties in dispute.

2. Any dispute which is not settled by direct negotiation may be referred by the Contracting Parties in dispute to the Administrative Committee which shall consider it and make recommendations for its settlement.

3. Any dispute which is not settled in accordance with paragraphs 1 or 2 shall be submitted to arbitration if any one of the Contracting Parties in dispute so requests and shall be referred accordingly to one or more arbitrators selected by agreement between the Parties in dispute. If within three months from the date of the request for arbitration the Parties in dispute are unable to agree on the selection of an arbitrator or arbitrators, any of those Parties may request the Secretary-General of the United Nations to nominate a single arbitrator to whom the dispute shall be referred for decision.

4. The decision of the arbitrator or arbitrators appointed under paragraph 3 of this article shall be binding on the Contracting Parties in dispute.

Article 16

Reservations

1. Any State may, at the time of signing this Agreement definitively or of depositing its instrument of ratification, acceptance, approval or accession, declare that it does not consider itself bound by Article 15. Other Contracting Parties shall not be bound by Article 15 in respect of any Contracting Party which has entered such a reservation.

2. Any Contracting State having entered a reservation as provided for in paragraph 1 of this article may at any time withdraw such reservation by notifying in writing the Secretary-General of the United Nations.

3. Reservations other than those provided for in this Agreement are not permitted.

Article 17

Administrative Committee

1. An Administrative Committee shall be established to consider the implementation of this Agreement, to consider any amendments proposed thereto and to consider measures to secure uniformity in the interpretation and application thereof.

2. The Contracting Parties shall be members of the Administrative Committee. The Committee may decide that the States referred to in Article 10, paragraph 1 of this Agreement which are not Contracting Parties, any other Member State of the Economic Commission for Europe or of the United Nations or representatives of international intergovernmental or non-governmental organizations may, for questions which interest them, attend the sessions of the Committee as observers.

3. The Secretary-General of the United Nations and the Secretary-General of the Central Commission for the Navigation of the Rhine shall provide the Administrative Committee with secretariat services.

4. The Administrative Committee shall, at the first session of the year, elect a Chairperson and a Vice-Chairperson.

5. The Executive Secretary of the Economic Commission for Europe shall convene the Administrative Committee annually, or at other intervals decided on by the Committee, and also at the request of at least five Contracting Parties.

6. A quorum consisting of not less than one half of the Contracting Parties shall be required for the purpose of taking decisions.

7. Proposals shall be put to the vote. Each Contracting Party represented at the session shall have one vote. The following rules shall apply:

    (a) Proposed amendments to the Agreement and decisions pertaining thereto shall be adopted in accordance with the provisions of Article 19, paragraph 2;

    (b) Proposed amendments to the annexed Regulations and decisions pertaining thereto shall be adopted in accordance with the provisions of Article 20, paragraph 4;

    (c) Proposals and decisions relating to the recommendation of agreed classification societies, or to the withdrawal of such recommendation, shall be adopted in accordance with the procedure of the provisions of Article 20, paragraph 4;

    (d) Any proposal or decision other than those referred to in paragraphs (a) to (c) above shall be adopted by a majority of the Administrative Committee members present and voting.

8. The Administrative Committee may set up such working groups as it may deem necessary to assist it in carrying out its duties.

9. In the absence of relevant provisions in this Agreement, the Rules of Procedure of the Economic Commission for Europe shall be applicable unless the Administrative Committee decides otherwise.

Article 18

Safety Committee

A Safety Committee shall be established to consider all proposals for the amendment of the Regulations annexed to the Agreement, particularly as regards safety of navigation in relation to the construction, equipment and crews of vessels. The Safety Committee shall function within the framework of the activities of the bodies of the Economic Commission for Europe, of the Central Commission for the Navigation of the Rhine and of the Danube Commission which are competent in the transport of dangerous goods by inland waterways.

Article 19

Procedure for amending the Agreement, excluding the annexed Regulations

1. This Agreement, excluding its annexed Regulations, may be amended upon the proposal of a Contracting Party by the procedure specified in this article.

2. Any proposed amendment to this Agreement, excluding the annexed Regulations, shall be considered by the Administrative Committee. Any such amendment considered or prepared during the meeting of the Administrative Committee and adopted by it by a two-thirds majority of the members present and voting shall be communicated by the Secretary-General of the United Nations to the Contracting Parties for their acceptance.

3. Any proposed amendments communicated for acceptance in accordance with paragraph 2 shall come into force with respect to all Contracting Parties six months after the expiry of a period of twenty-four months following the date of communication of the proposed amendment if, during that period, no objection to the amendment in question has been communicated in writing to the Secretary-General of the United Nations by a Contracting Party.

Article 20

Procedure for amending the annexed Regulations

1. The annexed Regulations may be amended upon the proposal of a Contracting Party.

   The Secretary-General of the United Nations may also propose amendments with a view to bringing the annexed Regulations into line with other international agreements concerning the transport of dangerous goods and the United Nations Recommendations on the Transport of Dangerous Goods, as well as amendments proposed by a subsidiary body of the Economic Commission for Europe with competence in the area of the transport of dangerous goods.

2. Any proposed amendment to the annexed Regulations shall in principle be submitted to the Safety Committee, which shall submit the draft amendments it adopts to the Administrative Committee.

3. At the specific request of a Contracting Party, or if the secretariat of the Administrative Committee considers it appropriate, amendments may also be proposed directly to the Administrative Committee. They shall be examined at a first session and if they are deemed to be acceptable, they shall be reviewed at the following session of the Committee at the same time as any related proposal, unless otherwise decided by the Committee.

4. Decisions on proposed amendments and proposed draft amendments submitted to the Administrative Committee in accordance with paragraphs 2 and 3 shall be made by a majority of the members present and voting. However, a draft amendment shall not be deemed adopted if, immediately after the vote, five members present declare their objection to it. Adopted draft amendments shall be communicated by the Secretary-General of the United Nations to the Contracting Parties for acceptance.

5. Any draft amendment to the annexed Regulations communicated for acceptance in accordance with paragraph 4 shall be deemed to be accepted unless, within three months from the date on which the Secretary-General circulates it, at least one-third of the Contracting Parties, or five of them if one-third exceeds that figure, have given the Secretary-General written notification of their objection to the proposed amendment. If the amendment is deemed to be accepted, it shall enter into force for all the Contracting Parties, on the expiry of a further period of three months, except in the following cases:

(a) In cases where similar amendments to other international agreements governing the carriage of dangerous goods have already entered into force, or will enter into force at a different date, the Secretary-General may decide, upon written request by the Executive Secretary of the Economic Commission for Europe, that the amendment shall enter into force on the expiry of a different period so as to allow the simultaneous entry into force of these amendments with those to be made to such other agreements or, if not possible, the quickest entry into force of this amendment after the entry into force of such amendments to other agreements; such period shall not, however, be of less than one month's duration.

(b) The Administrative Committee may specify, when adopting a draft amendment, for the purpose of entry into force of the amendment, should it be accepted, a period of more than three months' duration.

Article 21

Requests, communications and objections

The Secretary-General of the United Nations shall inform all Contracting Parties and all States referred to in Article 10, paragraph 1 of this Agreement of any request, communication or objection under Articles 19 and 20 above and of the date on which any amendment enters into force.

Article 22

Review conference

1. Notwithstanding the procedure provided for in Articles 19 and 20, any Contracting Party may, by notification in writing to the Secretary-General of the United Nations, request that a conference be convened for the purpose of reviewing this Agreement.

    A review conference to which all Contracting Parties and all States referred to in Article 10, paragraph 1, shall be invited, shall be convened by the Executive Secretary of the Economic Commission for Europe if, within a period of six months following the date of notification by the Secretary-General, not less than one fourth of the Contracting Parties notify him of their concurrence with the request.

2. Notwithstanding the procedure provided for in Articles 19 and 20, a review conference to which all Contracting Parties and all States referred to in Article 10, paragraph 1, shall be invited, shall also be convened by the Executive Secretary of the Economic Commission for Europe upon notification in writing by the Administrative Committee. The Administrative Committee shall make a request if agreed to by a majority of those present and voting in the Committee.

3. If a conference is convened in pursuance of paragraphs 1 or 2 of this article, the Executive Secretary of the Economic Commission for Europe shall invite the Contracting Parties to submit, within a period of three months, the proposals which they wish the conference to consider.

4. The Executive Secretary of the Economic Commission for Europe shall circulate to all the Contracting Parties and to all the States referred to in Article 10, paragraph 1, the provisional agenda for the conference, together with the texts of such proposals, at least six months before the date on which the conference is to meet.

Article 23

Depositary

The Secretary-General of the United Nations shall be the depositary of this Agreement.

IN WITNESS WHEREOF the undersigned, being duly authorized thereto, have signed this Agreement.

DONE at Geneva, this twenty-sixth day of May two thousand, in a single copy, in the English, French, German and Russian languages for the text of the Agreement proper, and in the French language for the annexed Regulations, each text being equally authentic for the Agreement proper.

The Secretary-General of the United Nations is requested to prepare a translation of the annexed Regulations in the English and Russian languages.

The Secretary-General of the Central Commission for the Navigation of the Rhine is requested to prepare a translation of the annexed Regulations in the German language.

ANNEXED REGULATIONS

PART I

General provisions

CHAPTER 1.1

SCOPE AND APPLICABILITY

1.1.1   **Structure**

The Regulations annexed to ADN are grouped into nine parts. Each part is subdivided into chapters and each chapter into sections and subsections (see table of contents). Within each part the number of the part is included with the numbers of the chapters, sections and subsections, for example Part 2, Chapter 2, section 1 is numbered "2.2.1".

1.1.2   **Scope**

1.1.2.1   For the purposes of Article 2 paragraph 2 (a) and Article 4 of ADN, the annexed Regulations specify:

    (a)   dangerous goods which are barred from international carriage;

    (b)   dangerous goods which are authorized for international carriage and the conditions attaching to them (including exemptions) particularly with regard to:

          –   classification of goods, including classification criteria and relevant test methods;

          –   use of packagings (including mixed packing);

          –   use of tanks (including filling);

          –   consignment procedures (including marking and labelling of packages and placarding and marking of vehicles and wagons embarked, the marking of vessels as well as documentation and information required);

          –   provisions concerning the construction, testing and approval of packagings and tanks;

          –   use of means of transport (including loading, mixed loading and unloading).

1.1.2.2   For the purposes of Article 5 of ADN, section 1.1.3 of this chapter specifies the cases in which the carriage of dangerous goods is partially or totally exempted from the conditions of carriage established by ADN.

1.1.2.3   For the purposes of Article 7 of ADN, Chapter 1.5 of this part specifies the rules concerning the derogations, special authorizations and equivalences for which that article provides.

1.1.2.4   For the purposes of Article 8 of ADN, Chapter 1.6 of this part specifies the transitional measures concerning the application of the Regulations annexed to ADN.

1.1.2.5   The provisions of ADN also apply to empty vessels or vessels which have been unloaded as long as the holds, cargo tanks or receptacles or tanks accepted on board are not free from dangerous substances or gases, except for the exemptions for which section 1.1.3 of these Regulations provides.

1.1.3   **Exemptions**

1.1.3.1   *Exemptions related to the nature of the transport operation*

The provisions laid down in ADN do not apply to:

(a)   the carriage of dangerous goods by private individuals where the goods in question are packaged for retail sale and are intended for their personal or domestic use or for their leisure or sporting activities provided that measures have been taken to prevent any leakage of contents in normal conditions of carriage. When these goods are flammable liquids carried in refillable receptacles filled by, or for, a private individual, the total quantity shall not exceed 60 litres per receptacle and 240 litres per cargo transport unit. Dangerous goods in IBCs, large packagings or tanks are not considered to be packaged for retail sale;

(b)   *(Deleted)*

(c)   the carriage undertaken by enterprises which is ancillary to their main activity, such as deliveries to or returns from building or civil engineering sites, or in relation to surveying, repairs and maintenance, in quantities of not more than 450 litres per packaging, including intermediate bulk containers (IBCs) and large packagings, and within the maximum quantities specified in 1.1.3.6. Measures shall be taken to prevent any leakage of contents in normal conditions of carriage. These exemptions do not apply to Class 7.

Carriage undertaken by such enterprises for their supply or external or internal distribution does not fall within the scope of this exemption;

(d)   the carriage undertaken by the competent authorities for the emergency response or under their supervision, insofar as such carriage is necessary in relation to the emergency response, in particular carriage undertaken to recover dangerous goods involved in an incident or accident and move them to the nearest appropriate safe place;

(e)   emergency transport under the supervision of the competent authorities intended to save human lives or protect the environment provided that all measures are taken to ensure that such transport is carried out in complete safety;

(f)   the carriage of uncleaned empty static storage vessels which have contained gases of Class 2, groups A, O or F, substances of Class 3 or Class 9 belonging to packing group II or III or pesticides of Class 6.1 belonging to packing group II or III, subject to the following conditions:

All openings with the exception of pressure relief devices (when fitted) are hermetically closed;

Measures have been taken to prevent any leakage of contents in normal conditions of carriage; and

The load is fixed in cradles or crates or other handling devices or to the vehicle, container or vessel in such a way that they will not become loose or shift during normal conditions of carriage.

This exemption does not apply to static storage vessels which have contained desensitized explosives or substances the carriage of which is prohibited by ADN.

NOTE: For radioactive material see also 1.7.1.4.

1.1.3.2   *Exemptions related to the carriage of gases*

The provisions laid down in ADN do not apply to the carriage of:

(a)   (*Reserved*)

(b)   (*Reserved*)

(c)   gases of Groups A and O (according to 2.2.2.1), if the pressure of the gas in the receptacle or tank at a temperature of 20 °C does not exceed 200 kPa (2 bar) and if the gas is not a liquefied or a refrigerated liquefied gas. This includes every kind of receptacle or tank, e.g. also parts of machinery and apparatus;

   NOTE: This exemption does not apply to lamps. For lamps see 1.1.3.10.

(d)   gases contained in the equipment used for the operation of the vessel (e.g. fire extinguishers), including spare parts;

(e)   (*Reserved*)

(f)   gases contained in foodstuffs (except UN 1950), including carbonated beverages;

(g)   gases contained in balls intended for use in sports; and

(h)   (*Deleted*)

1.1.3.3   *Exemptions related to dangerous goods used for the propulsion of vessels, vehicles, wagons or non-road mobile machinery carried, for the operation of their special equipment, for their upkeep or for their safety*

The requirements of ADN do not apply to substances used

–   for the propulsion of vessels, vehicles, wagons or non-road mobile machinery carried[1],

–   for the upkeep of vessels,

–   for the operation or upkeep of their permanently installed special equipment,

–   for the operation or upkeep of their mobile special equipment used during carriage or intended to be used during carriage, or

–   to ensure safety,

and which are carried on board in the packaging, receptacle or tanks intended for use for this purpose.

---

[1]   *For the definition of non-road mobile machinery see paragraph 2.7 of the Consolidated Resolution on the Construction of Vehicles (R.E.3) (United Nations document ECE/TRANS/WP.29/78/Rev.3) or Article 2 of Directive 97/68/EC of the European Parliament and of the Council of 16 December 1997 on the approximation of the laws of the Member States relating to measures against the emission of gaseous and particulate pollutants from internal combustion engines to be installed in non-road mobile machinery (Official Journal of the European Communities No. L 059 of 27 February 1998).*

1.1.3.4   *Exemptions related to special provisions or to dangerous goods packed in limited or excepted quantities*

       ***NOTE:** For radioactive material see also 1.7.1.4.*

1.1.3.4.1   Certain special provisions of Chapter 3.3 exempt partially or totally the carriage of specific dangerous goods from the requirements of ADN. The exemption applies when the special provision is referred to in Column (6) of Table A of Chapter 3.2 against the dangerous goods entry concerned.

1.1.3.4.2   Certain dangerous goods may be subject to exemptions provided that the conditions of Chapter 3.4 are met.

1.1.3.4.3   Certain dangerous goods may be subject to exemptions provided that the conditions of Chapter 3.5 are met.

1.1.3.5   *Exemptions related to empty uncleaned packagings*

       Empty uncleaned packagings (including IBCs and large packagings) which have contained substances of Classes 2, 3, 4.1, 5.1, 6.1, 8 and 9 are not subject to the conditions of ADN if adequate measures have been taken to nullify any hazards. Hazards are nullified if adequate measures have been taken to nullify all hazards of Classes 1 to 9.

1.1.3.6   *Exemptions related to quantities carried on board vessels*

1.1.3.6.1   In the event of the carriage of dangerous goods in packages, the provisions of ADN other than those of 1.1.3.6.2 are not applicable when the gross mass of all the dangerous goods carried does not exceed 3,000 kg and for the individual classes does not exceed the quantity that is indicated in the Table below:

Class	Substances or articles in packages	Exempted quantities in kg:	
All	**Carriage in tanks, of any Class**		**0**
1	Substances and articles of Class 1		0
2	Substances and articles of Class 2, groups T, TF, TC, TO, TFC or TOC, according to 2.2.2.1.3 and Aerosols of groups C, CO, FC, T, TF, TC, TO, TFC and TOC according to 2.2.2.1.6;		0
	Substances and articles of Class 2 of group F in accordance with 2.2.2.1.3 or; Aerosols of group F according to 2.2.2.1.6;	300	
	Any other substances of Class 2	3000	
3	Substances and articles of Class 3, Packing Group I	300	
	Any other substances of Class 3	3000	
4.1	Substances and articles of Class 4.1 for which a danger label of model No. 1 is required in column (5) of Table A of Chapter 3.2;		0
	Any other substances and articles of Class 4.1, Packing Group I	300	
	Any other substances and articles of Class 4.1	3000	
4.2	Substances and articles of Class 4.2, Packing Group I	300	
	Any other substances and articles of Class 4.2	3000	

Class	Substances or articles in packages	Exempted quantities in kg:
4.3	Substances and articles of Class 4.3, Packing Group I	300
	Any other substances and articles of Class 4.3	3000
5.1	Substances and articles of Class 5.1, Packing Group I	300
	Any other substances and articles of Class 5.1	3000
5.2	Substances and articles of Class 5.2 for which a danger label of model No. 1 is required in column (5) of Table A of Chapter 3.2;	0
	Any other substances and articles of Class 5.2	3000
6.1	Substances and articles of Class 6.1, Packing Group I	0
	Any other substances and articles of Class 6.1	3000
6.2	Substances and articles of class 6.2, Category A	0
	Any other substances and articles of Class 6.2	3000
7	Substances and articles of Class 7 under UN Nos. 2908, 2909, 2910 and 2911	3000
	Any other substances and articles of Class 7	0
8	Substances and articles of Class 8, Packing Group I	300
	Any other substances and articles of Class 8	3000
9	All substances and articles of Class 9	3000

1.1.3.6.2   The carriage of exempted quantities according to 1.1.3.6.1 is, however, subject to the following conditions:

(a)   The obligation to report in accordance with 1.8.5 remains applicable;

(b)   The requirements of sections 1.10.1, 1.10.2 and 1.10.3 apply to packages bearing UN Nos. 2910 and 2911 of Class 7 if the activity level (per package) exceeds the A_2 value;

(c)   Packages, except vehicles and containers (including swap bodies), shall comply with the requirements for packagings referred to in Parts 4 and 6 of ADR or RID; the provisions of Chapter 5.2 concerning marking and labelling are applicable;

(d)   The following documents shall be on board:

      –   the transport documents (see 5.4.1.1); they shall concern all the dangerous goods carried on board;

      –   the stowage plan (see 7.1.4.11.1);

(e)   The goods shall be stowed in the holds.

This provision does not apply to goods loaded in:

      –   closed containers;

      –   sheeted vehicles or sheeted wagons;

(f)   Goods of different class shall be separated by a minimum horizontal distance of 3 m. They shall not be stowed on top of each other.

This provision does not apply to:

– closed containers;

– sheeted vehicles or sheeted wagons;

(g)   For seagoing and inland navigation vessels, where the latter carry only containers, the above requirements under (e) and (f) shall be considered to have been met if the provisions of the IMDG Code regarding stowage and separation are met and if this particular is recorded in the transport document.

1.1.3.6.3 and 1.1.3.6.4   *(Reserved)*

1.1.3.6.5   For the purposes of this sub-section, dangerous goods exempted in accordance with 1.1.3.1 (a), (b) and (d) to (f), 1.1.3.2 to 1.1.3.5, 1.1.3.7, 1.1.3.9 and 1.1.3.10 shall not be taken into account.

1.1.3.7   *Exemptions related to the carriage of electric energy storage and production systems*

The provisions laid down in ADN do not apply to electric energy storage and production systems (e.g., lithium batteries, electric capacitors, asymmetric capacitors, metal hydride storage systems and fuel cells):

(a)   installed in a means of transport, performing a transport operation and destined for its propulsion or for the operation of any of its equipment;

(b)   contained in an equipment for the operation of this equipment used or intended for use during carriage (e.g. a laptop computer), except for equipment such as data loggers and cargo tracking devices attached to or placed in packages, overpacks, containers or load compartments which are only subject to the requirements in 5.5.4.

1.1.3.8   *(Reserved)*

1.1.3.9   *Exemptions related to dangerous goods used as a coolant or conditioner during carriage*

When used in vehicles or containers for cooling or conditioning purposes, dangerous goods that are only asphyxiant (which dilute or replace the oxygen normally in the atmosphere) are only subject to the provisions of section 5.5.3.

1.1.3.10   *Exemptions related to the carriage of lamps containing dangerous goods*

The following lamps are not subject to ADN provided that they do not contain radioactive material and do not contain mercury in quantities above those specified in special provision 366 of Chapter 3.3:

(a)   Lamps that are collected directly from individuals and households when carried to a collection or recycling facility;

NOTE: *This also includes lamps brought by individuals to a first collection point, and then carried to another collection point, intermediate processing or recycling facility.*

(b)   Lamps each containing not more than 1 g of dangerous goods and packaged so that there is not more than 30 g of dangerous goods per package, provided that:

    (i)   the lamps are manufactured according to a certified quality management system;

        NOTE: ISO 9001 may be used for this purpose.

and

    (ii)   each lamp is either individually packed in inner packagings, separated by dividers, or surrounded with cushioning material to protect the lamps and packed into strong outer packagings meeting the general provisions of 4.1.1.1 of ADR and capable of passing a 1.2 m drop test;

(c)   Used, damaged or defective lamps each containing not more than 1 g of dangerous goods with not more than 30 g of dangerous goods per package when carried from a collection or recycling facility. The lamps shall be packed in strong outer packagings sufficient for preventing release of the contents under normal conditions of carriage meeting the general provisions of 4.1.1.1 of ADR and that are capable of passing a drop test of not less than 1.2 m;

(d)   Lamps containing only gases of Groups A and O (according to 2.2.2.1) provided they are packaged so that the projectile effects of any rupture of the lamp will be contained within the package.

NOTE: Lamps containing radioactive material are addressed in 2.2.7.2.2.2 (b).

1.1.4   Applicability of other regulations

1.1.4.1   *General*

The following requirements are applicable to packages:

(a)   In the case of packagings (including large packagings and intermediate bulk containers (IBCs), the applicable requirements of one of the international regulations shall be met (see also Part 4 and Part 6);

(b)   In the case of containers, tank-containers, portable tanks and multiple element gas containers (MEGCs), the applicable requirements of ADR, RID or the IMDG Code shall be met (see also Part 4 and Part 6);

(c)   In the case of vehicles or wagons, the vehicles or wagons and their load shall meet the applicable requirements of ADR or of RID, as relevant.

NOTE: For the marking, labelling, placarding and orange plate marking, see also Chapters 5.2 and 5.3.

1.1.4.2   *Carriage in a transport chain including maritime, road, rail or air carriage*

1.1.4.2.1   Packages, containers, bulk-containers, portable tanks and tank-containers and MEGCs, which do not entirely meet the requirements for packing, mixed packing, marking, labelling of packages or placarding and orange plate marking, of ADN, but are in conformity with the requirements of the IMDG Code or the ICAO Technical Instructions shall be accepted for carriage in a transport chain including maritime or air carriage subject to the following conditions:

(a)   If the packages are not marked and labelled in accordance with ADN, they shall bear marks and danger labels in accordance with the requirements of the IMDG Code or the ICAO Technical Instructions;

(b)   The requirements of the IMDG Code or the ICAO Technical Instructions shall be applicable to mixed packing within a package;

(c)   For carriage in a transport chain including maritime carriage, if the containers, bulk-containers, portable tanks, tank-containers or MEGCs are not marked and placarded in accordance with Chapter 5.3 of these Regulations, they shall be marked and placarded in accordance with Chapter 5.3 of the IMDG Code. In such case, only 5.3.2.1.1 of these Regulations is applicable to the marking of the vehicle itself. For empty, uncleaned portable tanks, tank-containers and MEGCs, this requirement shall apply up to and including the subsequent transfer to a cleaning station.

This derogation does not apply in the case of goods classified as dangerous goods in classes 1 to 9 of ADN and considered as non-dangerous goods according to the applicable requirements of the IMDG Code or the ICAO Technical Instructions.

1.1.4.2.2   When a maritime, road, rail or air transport operation follows or precedes carriage by inland waterway, the transport document used or to be used for the maritime, road, rail or air transport operation may be used in place of the transport document prescribed in 5.4.1 provided that the particulars it contains are in conformity with the applicable requirements of the IMDG Code, ADR, RID or the ICAO Technical Instructions, respectively except that, when additional information is required by ADN, it shall be added or entered at the appropriate place.

NOTE: *For carriage in accordance with 1.1.4.2.1, see also 5.4.1.1.7. For carriage in containers, see also 5.4.2.*

1.1.4.3   *Use of IMO type portable tanks approved for maritime transport*

IMO type portable tanks (types 1, 2, 5 and 7) which do not meet the requirements of Chapters 6.7 or 6.8 of ADR, but which were built and approved before 1 January 2003 in accordance with the provisions of the IMDG Code (Amdt. 29-98) may continue to be used provided that they meet the applicable periodic inspection and test provisions of the IMDG Code[2]. In addition, they shall meet the provisions corresponding to the instructions set out in columns (10) and (11) of Table A in Chapter 3.2 and the provisions of Chapter 4.2 of ADR. See also 4.2.0.1 of the IMDG Code.

1.1.4.4 and 1.1.4.5   *(Reserved)*

---

[2]   *The International Maritime Organization (IMO) has issued "Revised guidance on the continued use of existing IMO type portable tanks and road tank vehicles for the transport of dangerous goods" as circular CCC.1/Circ.3. The text of this guidance can be found on the IMO website at: www.imo.org.*

1.1.4.6   *Other regulations applicable to carriage by inland waterway*

1.1.4.6.1   In accordance with article 9 of ADN, transport operations shall remain subject to the local, regional or international requirements generally applicable to the carriage of goods by inland waterway.

1.1.4.6.2   Where the requirements of these Regulations are in contradiction with the requirements referred to in 1.1.4.6.1, the requirements referred to in 1.1.4.6.1 shall not apply.

1.1.5   **Application of standards**

Where the application of a standard is required and there is any conflict between the standard and the provisions of ADN, the provisions of ADN take precedence. The requirements of the standard that do not conflict with ADN shall be applied as specified, including the requirements of any other standard, or part of a standard, referenced within that standard as normative.

CHAPTER 1.2

DEFINITIONS AND UNITS OF MEASUREMENT

1.2.1   **Definitions**

NOTE: This section contains all general or specific definitions.

For the purposes of these regulations:

A

Accommodation means spaces intended for the use of persons normally living on board, including galleys, food stores, lavatories, washrooms, bathrooms, laundries, halls, alleyways, etc., but excluding the wheelhouse;

ADR means the Agreement concerning the International Carriage of Dangerous Goods by Road;

Aerosol, see *Aerosol dispenser*;

Aerosol dispenser means an article consisting of any non-refillable receptacle meeting the requirements of 6.2.6 of ADR made of metal, glass or plastics, and containing a gas, compressed, liquefied or dissolved under pressure, with or without a liquid, paste or powder, and fitted with a release device allowing the contents to be ejected as solid or liquid particles in suspension in a gas, as a foam, paste or powder or in a liquid state or in a gaseous state;

Animal material means animal carcasses, animal body parts, foodstuffs or feedstuffs derived from animals;

Approval

Multilateral approval, for the carriage of radioactive material, means approval by the relevant competent authority of the country of origin of the design or shipment, as applicable, and by the competent authority of each country through or into which the consignment is to be carried;

Unilateral approval, for the carriage of radioactive material, means an approval of a design which is required to be given by the competent authority of the country of origin of the design only. If the country of origin is not a Contracting Party to ADN, the approval shall require validation by the competent authority of a Contracting Party to ADN (see 6.4.22.8 of ADR);

ASTM means the American Society for Testing and Materials (ASTM International, 100 Barr Harbor Drive, PO Box C700, West Conshohocken, PA, 19428-2959, United States of America);

Auto-ignition temperature (EN 13237:2011) means the lowest temperature determined under prescribed test conditions of a hot surface on which a flammable substance in the form of a gas/air or vapour/air mixture ignites.

Autonomous protection systems means all devices which are intended to halt incipient explosions immediately and/or to limit the effective range of an explosion and which are separately made available on the market for use as self-contained systems. This includes flame arresters, high velocity vent valves, deflagration safe vacuum valves and devices for the safe depressurization of cargo tanks capable of withstanding a deflagration (see also *Flame arrester, High velocity vent valve, Vacuum valve, Devices for the safe depressurization of cargo tanks* and *Deflagration*);

B

Bag means a flexible packaging made of paper, plastics film, textiles, woven material or other suitable material;

Battery-vehicle means a vehicle containing elements which are linked to each other by a manifold and permanently fixed to this vehicle. The following elements are considered to be elements of a battery-vehicle: cylinders, tubes, bundles of cylinders (also known as frames), pressure drums as well as tanks destined for the carriage of gases as defined in 2.2.2.1.1 with a capacity of more than 450 litres;

Battery-wagon means a wagon containing elements which are linked to each other by a manifold and permanently fixed to a wagon. The following elements are considered to be elements of a battery wagon: cylinders, tubes, bundles of cylinders (also known as frames), pressure drums as well as tanks intended for gases of Class 2 with a capacity greater than 450 litres;

Bilge water means oily water from the engine room bilges, the peak, the cofferdams and the double-hull spaces;

Biological/technical name means a name currently used in scientific and technical handbooks, journals and texts. Trade names shall not be used for this purpose;

Body (for all categories of IBC other than composite IBCs) means the receptacle proper, including openings and closures, but does not include service equipment;

Boil-off means the vapour produced above the surface of a boiling cargo due to evaporation. It is caused by heat ingress or a drop in pressure;

Box means a packaging with complete rectangular or polygonal faces, made of metal, wood, plywood, reconstituted wood, fibreboard, plastics or other suitable material. Small holes for purposes of ease of handling or opening or to meet classification requirements, are permitted as long as they do not compromise the integrity of the packaging during carriage;

Breathing apparatus (ambient air-dependent filter apparatus) means an apparatus which protects the person wearing it when working in a dangerous atmosphere by means of a suitable filter. For such apparatuses, see for example European standard EN 136:1998. For the filters used, see for example European standard EN 14387:2004 + A1:2008;

Breathing apparatus (self-contained) means an apparatus which supplies the person wearing it when working in a dangerous atmosphere with breathing air by means of pressurized air carried with him or by means of an external supply via a tube. For such apparatuses, see for example European standard EN 137:2006 or EN 138:1994;

Bulk container means a containment system (including any liner or coating) intended for the carriage of solid substances which is in direct contact with the containment system. Packagings, intermediate bulk containers (IBCs), large packagings and tanks are not included.

A bulk container is:

–   of a permanent character and accordingly strong enough to be suitable for repeated use;

–   specially designed to facilitate the carriage of goods by one or more means of transport without intermediate reloading;

– fitted with devices permitting its ready handling;

– of a capacity of not less than 1.0 m^3.

Examples of bulk containers are containers, offshore bulk containers, skips, bulk bins, swap bodies, trough-shaped containers, roller containers, load compartments of vehicles or wagons;

NOTE: This definition only applies to bulk containers meeting the requirements of chapter 6.11 of ADR.

Closed bulk container means a totally closed bulk container having a rigid roof, sidewalls, end walls and floor (including hopper-type bottoms). The term includes bulk containers with an opening roof, side or end wall that can be closed during carriage. Closed bulk containers may be equipped with openings to allow for the exchange of vapours and gases with air and which prevent under normal conditions of carriage the release of solid contents as well as the penetration of rain and splash water;

Flexible bulk container means a flexible container with a capacity not exceeding 15 m^3 and includes liners and attached handling devices and service equipment;

Sheeted bulk container means an open top bulk container with rigid bottom (including hopper-type bottom), side and end walls and a non-rigid covering;

Bulkhead means a metal wall, generally vertical, inside the vessel and which is bounded by the bottom, the side plating, a deck, the hatchway covers or by another bulkhead;

Bulkhead (watertight) means

– In a dry cargo vessel: a bulkhead constructed so that it can withstand water pressure with a head of 1.00 metre above the deck but at least to the top of the hatchway coaming;

– In a tank vessel: a bulkhead constructed to withstand a water pressure of 1.00 metre above the deck;

Bundle of cylinders (frame) means an assembly of cylinders that are fastened together and are interconnected by a manifold and carried as a unit. The total water capacity shall not exceed 3,000 litres except that bundles intended for the carriage of toxic gases of Class 2 (groups starting with letter T according to 2.2.2.1.3) shall be limited to 1,000 litres water capacity.

C

Capacity of shell or shell compartment, for tanks, means the total inner volume of the shell or shell compartment expressed in litres or cubic metres. When it is impossible to completely fill the shell or the shell compartment because of its shape or construction, this reduced capacity shall be used for the determination of the degree of filling and for the marking of the tank;

Cargo area means the whole of the following spaces on board tank vessels:

Space below deck:

The space between two vertical planes perpendicular to the centre-line plane of the vessel, which comprises cargo tanks, hold spaces, cofferdams, double-hull spaces and double bottoms; these planes normally coincide with the outer cofferdam bulkheads or hold end bulkheads.

Space above deck: the space which is bounded:

– Athwart, by ships vertical planes corresponding to the side plating;

– Fore and aft, by vertical planes at the height of the outer cofferdam bulkheads/hold end bulkheads;

– Upwards, by a horizontal plane 2.50 m above deck.

The boundary planes fore and aft are referred to as the 'boundary planes of the cargo area';

Cargo piping, see *Piping for loading and unloading*;

Cargo pump-room means a service space where the cargo pumps and stripping pumps are installed together with their operational equipment;

Cargo residues means liquid cargo which cannot be pumped out of the cargo tanks or piping by means of the stripping system;

Cargo tank means a tank which is permanently attached to the vessel and intended for the carriage of dangerous goods.

Cargo tank design:

(a) *Pressure cargo tank* means a cargo tank independent of the vessel's hull, built according to dedicated recognised standards for a working pressure ≥ 400 kPa;

(b) *Closed cargo tank* means a cargo tank connected to the outside atmosphere through a device preventing unacceptable internal overpressure or underpressure;

(c) *Open cargo tank with flame arrester* means a cargo tank connected to the outside atmosphere through a device fitted with a flame arrester;

(d) *Open cargo tank* means a cargo tank in open connection with the outside atmosphere.

Cargo tank type:

(a) *Independent cargo tank* means a cargo tank which is permanently built in, but which is independent of the vessel's structure;

(b) *Integral cargo tank* means a cargo tank which is constituted by the vessel's structure itself and bounded by the outer hull or by walls separate from the outer hull;

(c) *Cargo tank with walls distinct from the outer hull* means an integral cargo tank of which the bottom and side walls do not form the outer hull of the vessel or an independent cargo tank;

(d) *Membrane tank* means a cargo tank which consists of a thin liquid-tight and gastight layer (membrane) and insulation supported by the adjacent inner hull and inner bottom structure of a double hull vessel.

Cargo tank (discharged) means a cargo tank which after unloading may contain some residual cargo.

Cargo tank (empty) means a cargo tank which after unloading contains no residual cargo but may not be gas free.

Cargo tank (gas free) means a cargo tank which after unloading does not contain any residual cargo or any measurable concentration of dangerous gases and vapours.

Cargo transport unit means a vehicle, a wagon, a container, a tank-container, a portable tank or an MEGC;

Carriage means the change of place of dangerous goods, including stops made necessary by transport conditions and including any period spent by the dangerous goods in vessels, vehicles, wagons, tanks and containers made necessary by traffic conditions before, during and after the change of place.

This definition also covers the intermediate temporary storage of dangerous goods in order to change the mode or means of transport (transshipment). This shall apply provided that transport documents showing the place of dispatch and the place of reception are presented on request and provided that packages and tanks are not opened during intermediate storage, except to be checked by the competent authorities;

Carriage in bulk means the carriage of an unpackaged solid which can be discharged;

NOTE: *Within the meaning of ADN, the carriage in bulk referred to in ADR or RID is considered as carriage in packages.*

Carrier means the enterprise which carries out the transport operation with or without a transport contract;

CDNI means Convention on the Collection, Storage and Reception of Waste Generated during Navigation on the Rhine and Other Inland Waterways;

CEVNI means the UNECE European Code for Inland Waterways;

CGA means the Compressed Gas Association (CGA, 14501 George Carter Way, Suite 103, Chantilly, VA 20151, United States of America);

CIM means the Uniform Rules Concerning the Contract of International Carriage of Goods by Rail (Appendix B to the Convention concerning International Carriage by Rail (COTIF)), as amended;

Classification society (recognized) means a classification society which is recognized by the competent authorities in accordance with Chapter 1.15;

Classification of explosion hazardous areas (see Directive 1999/92/CE[1])

Zone 0:   areas in which dangerous explosive atmospheres of gases, vapours or sprays exist permanently or during long periods;

Zone 1:   areas in which dangerous explosive atmospheres of gases, vapours or sprays are likely to occur occasionally;

Zone 2:   areas in which dangerous explosive atmospheres of gases, vapours or sprays are likely to occur rarely and if so for short periods only;

See also *Classification of zones*

Classification of zones: this classification (see diagram) applies to tank vessels when the list of substances on the vessel according to 1.16.1.2.5 contains substances for which explosion protection is required in column (17) of Table C of Chapter 3.2.

---

[1]   *Official Journal of the European Communities No. L 23 of 28 January 2000, p.57.*

Zone 0 comprises:

 – Inside all cargo tanks, tanks for residual products, receptacles for residual products and receptacles for slops, and pipings containing cargoes or cargo vapours, including their equipment, as well as pumps and compressors.

Zone 1 comprises:

 – All spaces located below deck in the cargo area not part of zone 0.

– Closed spaces on deck within the cargo area.

– The deck in the cargo area over the entire width of the vessel to the outer cofferdam bulkheads.

– Up to a distance of at least 1.60 m to the "boundary planes of the cargo area", the height above the deck is 2.50 m, but at least 1.50 m above the highest piping carrying cargoes or cargo vapours.

Adjacent (fore and aft) to the outermost cargo tank bulkheads, the height is 0.25 m above deck.

If the ship is built with hold spaces or a cofferdam/part of a cofferdam is arranged as a service space, the adjacent height (fore and aft) to the "boundary plane of the cargo area" is 1.00 m above deck (see diagram).

– Every opening in zone 0 except the high velocity vent valves/safety valves of pressurized cargo tanks shall be surrounded by a cylindrical ring whose inner radius is that of the opening, the outer radius is equal to that of the opening plus 2.50 m and the height is 2.50 m above the deck and 1.50 m above the piping.

For openings with a diameter of less than 0.026 m (1"), the distance to the outer cofferdam bulkhead may be reduced to 0.50 m, provided it is ensured that such an opening is not opened to the atmosphere within this distance.

– A cylindrical area surrounding the high velocity vent valve/safety valve of pressurized cargo tanks with a radius of 3.00 m up to a height of 4.00 m above the opening of the high velocity vent valve/safety valve of pressurized cargo tanks.

– Around ventilation inlets of service spaces fitted with a ventilation system located in the cargo area, a zone included in a portion of a sphere with a radius of 1.00 m.

Zone 2 comprises:

 – On the deck in the cargo area, a zone extending 1.00 m upwards and sidewards longitudinally from zone 1.

– On the fore deck and the aft deck, an area 7.50 m in length across the entire width of the vessel and adjacent to the "boundary plane of the cargo area". Between the lateral side of the vessel and the protection wall, the length and height of this area equals the dimensions of the lateral side of the protection wall. Elsewhere, the height in zone 2 is 0.50 m.

This area is not part of zone 2 if the protection wall extends from one side of the vessel to the other and there are no openings.

–   An area of 3.00 m extending around zone 1 encompassing the high velocity vent valves/safety valves of pressure cargo tanks.

–   Around the ventilation inlets of service spaces fitted with a ventilation system located in the cargo area, a zone included in a hemispherical shell with a radius of 1.00 m extending around zone 1;

Classification of zones for tank vessels

High velocity vent valve

Protective coaming, gas- and
liquid-tight: h: ≥ 0.075 m

Outer cargo tank bulkhead

Outer cofferdam bulkhead
End bulkhead of the hold space

Boundary plane of the cargo
area

Protection wall; gas and liquid tight, h: ≥ 1.00 m
above the adjacent cargo tank deck

≥ 1.00 m

Mobile
wheelhouse

Boundary plane of
the cargo area

Zone 0

Zone 1

Zone 2

3.00 m

3.00 m

3.00 m

4.00 m

3.00 m

2.50 m

2.50 m

1.50 m

> 2.50 m, > 1.50 m

> 6.00 m

1.00 m

1.00 m

1.00 m

> 1.00 m

2.50 m

0.50 m

7.50 m

0.50 m

7.50 m

-22-

Cofferdam not serving as service space

Zone 0

Zone 1

Zone 2

Boundary plane of the cargo area

≥ 1.00 m

Mobile wheelhouse

Protection wall; gas- and liquid-tight, h: ≥ 1.00 m above the adjacent cargo tank deck

Protective coaming; gas- and liquid-tight: h ≥ 0.075 m

Outer cargo tank bulkhead

Outer cofferdam bulkhead

End bulkhead of the hold space

1.00 m

0.60 m

2.50 m

7.50 m

0.50 m

1.00 m

0.60 m

2.50 m

7.50 m

0.50 m

1.00 m

Bulkhead forming outer wall of accommodation

Protection wall not forming outer wall of accommodation

Tank vessel with hold space/service space in cofferdam

Zone 0
Zone 1
Zone 2

Boundary plane of the cargo area

Mobile wheelhouse

≥ 1.00 m

Protection wall; gas- and liquid-tight, h: ≥ 1.00 m above the adjacent cargo tank deck

1.00 m

2.50 m

0.60 m

7.5 m

0.50 m

1.00 m

0.50 m

0.50 m

7.50 m

1.00 m

Protective coaming; gas- and liquid-tight:
h ≥ 0.075 m

Outer cargo tank bulkhead

Outer cofferdam bulkhead
End bulkhead of the hold space

Bulkhead forming outer wall of accommodation

Bulkhead not forming outer wall of accommodation

Closed bulk container, see *Bulk container;*

Closed container, see *Container;*

Closed-type sampling device means a device penetrating through the boundary of the cargo tank or through the piping for loading and unloading but constituting a part of a closed system designed so that during sampling no gas or liquid may escape from the cargo tank;

Closed vehicle means a vehicle having a body capable of being closed;

Closed wagon means a wagon with sides and a fixed or movable roof.

Closure means a device which closes an opening in a receptacle;

CMNI means the Convention on the Contract for the Carriage of Goods by Inland Waterway (Budapest, 22 June 2001).

CMR means the Convention on the Contract for the International Carriage of Goods by Road (Geneva, 19 May 1956), as amended;

Cofferdam means an athwartship compartment which is bounded by watertight bulkheads and which can be inspected. The cofferdam shall extend over the whole area of the end bulkheads of the cargo tanks. The bulkhead not facing the cargo area (outer cofferdam bulkhead) shall extend from one side of the vessel to the other and from the bottom to the deck in one frame plane;

Collective entry means an entry for a defined group of substances or articles (see 2.1.1.2, B, C and D);

Combination packaging means a combination of packagings for carriage purposes, consisting of one or more inner packagings secured in an outer packaging in accordance with 4.1.1.5 of ADR;

NOTE: *The term "inner packaging" used for combination packagings shall not be confused with the term "inner receptacle" used for composite packagings.*

Competent authority means the authority or authorities or any other body or bodies designated as such in each State and in each specific case in accordance with domestic law;

Compliance assurance (radioactive material) means a systematic programme of measures applied by a competent authority which is aimed at ensuring that the requirements of ADN are met in practice;

Composite IBC with plastics inner receptacle means an IBC comprising structural equipment in the form of a rigid outer casing encasing a plastics inner receptacle together with any service or other structural equipment. It is so constructed that the inner receptacle and outer casing once assembled form, and are used as, an integrated single unit to be filled, stored, transported or emptied as such;

NOTE: *Plastics material, when used in connection with inner receptacles for composite IBCs, is taken to include other polymeric materials such as rubber.*

Composite packaging means a packaging consisting of an outer packaging and an inner receptacle so constructed that the inner receptacle and the outer packaging form an integral packaging. Once assembled it remains thereafter an integrated single unit; it is filled, stored, carried and emptied as such;

NOTE: The term "inner receptacle" used for composite packagings shall not be confused with the term "inner packaging" used for combination packagings. For example, the inner of a 6HA1 composite packaging (plastics material) is such an inner receptacle since it is normally not designed to perform a containment function without its outer packaging and is not therefore an inner packaging.

Where a material is mentioned in brackets after the term "composite packaging", it refers to the inner receptacle.

Compressed natural gas (CNG) means a compressed gas composed of natural gas with a high methane content assigned to UN No. 1971;

Confinement system, for the carriage of radioactive material, means the assembly of fissile material and packaging components specified by the designer and agreed to by the competent authority as intended to preserve criticality safety;

Consignee means the consignee according to the contract for carriage. If the consignee designates a third party in accordance with the provisions applicable to the contract for carriage, this person shall be deemed to be the consignee within the meaning of ADN. If the transport operation takes place without a contract for carriage, the enterprise which takes charge of the dangerous goods on arrival shall be deemed to be the consignee;

Consignment means any package or packages, or load of dangerous goods, presented by a consignor for carriage;

Consignor means the enterprise which consigns dangerous goods either on its own behalf or for a third party. If the transport operation is carried out under a contract for carriage, consignor means the consignor according to the contract for carriage. In the case of a tank vessel, when the cargo tanks are empty or have just been unloaded, the master is considered to be the consignor for the purpose of the transport document;

Containment system, for the carriage of radioactive material, means the assembly of components of the packaging specified by the designer as intended to retain the radioactive material during carriage;

Container means an article of transport equipment (lift van or other similar structure):

– of a permanent character and accordingly strong enough to be suitable for repeated use;

– specially designed to facilitate the carriage of goods, by one or more means of transport, without breakage of load;

– fitted with devices permitting its ready stowage and handling, particularly when being transloaded from one means of transport to another;

– so designed as to be easy to fill and empty;

– having an internal volume of not less than 1 m^3, except for containers for the carriage of radioactive material.

In addition:

Closed container means a totally enclosed container having a rigid roof, rigid side walls, rigid end walls and a floor. The term includes containers with an opening roof where the roof can be closed during transport;

Large container means:

(a) a container which does not meet the definition of a small container;

(b) in the meaning of the CSC, a container of a size such that the area enclosed by the four outer bottom corners is either

    (i) at least 14 m^2 (150 square feet) or

    (ii) at least 7 m^2 (75 square feet) if fitted with top corner fittings;

Open container means an open top container or a platform based container;

Sheeted container means an open container equipped with a sheet to protect the goods loaded;

Small container means a container which has an internal volume of not more than 3 m^3;

A swap body is a container which, in accordance with European Standard EN 283 (1991 edition) has the following characteristics:

− from the point of view of mechanical strength, it is only built for carriage on a wagon or a vehicle on land or by roll-on roll-off ship;

− it cannot be stacked;

− it can be removed from vehicles by means of equipment on board the vehicle and on its own supports, and can be reloaded;

NOTE: *The term "container" does not cover conventional packagings, IBCs, tank-containers, vehicles or wagons. Nevertheless, a container may be used as a packaging for the carriage of radioactive material.*

Control temperature means the maximum temperature at which an organic peroxide, the self-reactive substance or the polymerizing substance can be safely carried;

Conveyance means, with respect to the carriage by inland waterway, any vessel, hold or defined deck area of any vessel; for carriage by road or by rail, it means a vehicle or a wagon;

Crate means an outer packaging with incomplete surfaces;

Criticality safety index (CSI) assigned to a package, overpack or container containing fissile material, for the carriage of radioactive material, means a number which is used to provide control over the accumulation of packages, overpacks or containers containing fissile material;

Critical temperature means the temperature above which the substance cannot exist in the liquid state;

Cryogenic receptacle means a transportable thermally insulated receptacle for refrigerated liquefied gases of a water capacity of not more than 1,000 litres (see also *Open cryogenic receptacle*);

CSC means the International Convention for Safe Containers (Geneva, 1972) as amended and published by the International Maritime Organization (IMO), London;

Cylinder means a transportable pressure receptacle of a water capacity not exceeding 150 litres (see also *Bundle of cylinders (frame)*);

D

Damage control plan means the plan indicating the boundaries of the watertight compartments serving as the basis for the stability calculations, in the event of a leak, the trimming arrangements for the correction of any list due to flooding and the means of closure which are to be kept closed when the vessel is under way;

Dangerous goods means those substances and articles the carriage of which is prohibited by ADN, or authorized only under the conditions prescribed therein;

Dangerous reaction means:

(a)   combustion or evolution of considerable heat;

(b)   evolution of flammable, asphyxiate, oxidizing or toxic gases;

(c)   the formation of corrosive substances;

(d)   the formation of unstable substances; or

(e)   dangerous rise in pressure (for tanks and cargo tanks only);

Deflagration means an explosion which propagates at subsonic speed (see EN 13237:2011);

Degassing means an operation with the aim of lowering the concentration of dangerous gases and vapours in empty or unloaded cargo tanks by emitting them to the atmosphere or to reception facilities;

Demountable tank means a tank, other than a fixed tank, a portable tank, a tank-container or an element of a battery-vehicle or a MEGC which has a capacity of more than 450 litres, is not designed for the carriage of goods without breakage of load, and normally can only be handled when it is empty; or a tank designed to fit the special apparatus of a wagon but which can only be removed from it after dismantling the means of attachment;

Design, for the carriage of radioactive material, means the description of fissile material excepted under 2.2.7.2.3.5 (f), special form radioactive material, low dispersible radioactive material, package or packaging which enables such an item to be fully identified. The description may include specifications, engineering drawings, reports demonstrating compliance with regulatory requirements, and other relevant documentation;

Design life, for composite cylinders and tubes, means the maximum life (in number of years) for which the cylinder or tube is designed and approved in accordance with the applicable standard;

Design pressure means the pressure on the basis of which the cargo tank or the residual cargo tank has been designed and built;

Detonation means an explosion which propagates at supersonic speed and is characterized by a shock-wave (see EN 13237:2011);

Device for the safe depressurization of cargo tanks means a manually operated or remote-operated device which is mounted in such a way as to allow the cargo tanks to be depressurized in safety. When the list of substances on the vessel according to 1.16.1.2.5 contains substances for which explosion protection is required in column (17) of Table C of Chapter 3.2, the device shall be deflagration safe and capable of withstanding steady burning for the most critical substance in the vessel substance list. The deflagration safety shall be tested according to international standard ISO 16852:2016[2] and evidence of compliance with the applicable requirements (e.g., conformity assessment procedure according to Directive 2014/34/EU,[3] the IECEx System,[4] ECE/TRADE/391[5] or at least equivalent) shall be supplied. The deflagration safety may be ensured by an integrated flame arrester plate stack capable of withstanding steady burning or a flame arrester capable of withstanding steady burning (protection against deflagrations);

Diameter (for shells of tanks) means the internal diameter of the shell;

Dose rate means the ambient dose equivalent or the directional dose equivalent, as appropriate, per unit time, measured at the point of interest;

Drum means a flat-ended or convex-ended cylindrical packaging made out of metal, fibreboard, plastics, plywood or other suitable materials. This definition also includes packagings of other shapes, e.g. round, taper-necked packagings or pail-shaped packagings. *Wooden barrels* and *jerricans* are not covered by this definition.

E

EC Directive means provisions decided by the competent institutions of the European Community and which are binding, as to the result to be achieved, upon each Member State to which it is addressed, but shall leave to the national authorities the choice of form and methods;

Emergency temperature means the temperature at which emergency procedures shall be implemented in the event of loss of temperature control;

Electrical apparatus protected against water jets means an electrical apparatus so designed that water, projected by a nozzle on the enclosure from any direction, has no damaging effects. The test conditions are specified in the IEC publication 60529, minimum degree of protection IP55;

EN (standard) means a European standard published by the European Committee for Standardization (CEN) (CEN – Avenue Marnix 17, B-1000 Brussels);

Enterprise means any natural person, any legal person, whether profit-making or not, any association or group of persons without legal personality, whether profit-making or not, or any official body, whether it has legal personality itself or is dependent upon an authority that has such personality;

Equipment (see Directive 2014/34/EU[3]) means electrical or non-electrical machines, apparatus, fixed or mobile devices, control components and instrumentation thereof and detection or prevention systems which, separately or jointly, are intended for the generation, transfer, storage, measurement, control and conversion of energy and/or the processing of material and which are capable of causing an explosion through their own potential sources of ignition.

Equipment and articles which are assigned a UN number and transported as cargo are not included;

---

[2] *Identical to EN ISO 16852:2016*

[3] *Official Journal of the European Union No. L 96 of 29 March 2014, p. 309.*

[4] *http://iecex.com/rules.*

[5] *A Common Regulatory Framework for Equipment Used in Environments with an Explosive Atmosphere, United Nations, 2011.*

Equipment category (see Directive 2014/34/EU[3]) means the classification of equipment to be used within explosion hazardous areas determining the requisite level of protection to be ensured.

Equipment category 1 comprises equipment designed to be capable of functioning in conformity with the operational parameters established by the manufacturer and ensuring a very high level of protection.

Equipment in this category is intended for use in areas in which explosive atmospheres caused by mixtures of air and gases, vapours or mists or by air/dust mixtures are present continuously, for long periods or frequently.

Equipment in this category must ensure the requisite level of protection, even in the event of rare incidents relating to equipment, and is characterized by means of protection such that:

– Either, in the event of failure of one means of protection, at least one independent second means provides the requisite level of protection; or

– Or the requisite level of protection is assured in the event of two faults occurring independently of each other.

Equipment of category 1 according to Directive 2014/34/EU[3] is marked as II 1 G. Such equipment corresponds to EPL[6] 'Ga' according to IEC 60079-0.

Equipment of category 1 is suitable for use in zones 0, 1 and 2.

Equipment category 2 comprises equipment designed to be capable of functioning in conformity with the operational parameters established by the manufacturer and of ensuring a high level of protection.

Equipment in this category is intended for use in areas in which explosive atmospheres caused by mixtures of air and gases, vapours or mists or by air/dust mixtures are likely to occur occasionally.

The means of protection relating to equipment in this category ensure the requisite level of protection, even in the event of frequently occurring disturbances or equipment faults which normally have to be taken into account.

Equipment of category 2 according to Directive 2014/34/EU[3] is marked as II 2 G. Such equipment corresponds to EPL[6] 'Gb' according to IEC 60079-0.

Equipment category 2 is suitable for use in zones 1 and 2.

Equipment category 3 comprises equipment designed to be capable of functioning in conformity with the operating parameters established by the manufacturer and ensuring a normal level of protection.

Equipment in this category is intended for use in areas in which explosive atmospheres caused by mixtures of air and gases, vapours or mists or by air/dust mixtures are unlikely to occur or, if they do occur, are likely to do so only infrequently and for a short period only.

Equipment in this category ensures the requisite level of protection during normal operation.

---

[3]   *Official Journal of the European Union No. L 96 of 29 March 2014, p. 309.*
[6]   *The letters EPL mean: Equipment Protection Level.*

Equipment of category 3 according to Directive 2014/34/EU[3] is marked as II 3 G. Such equipment corresponds to EPL[6] 'Gc' according to IEC 60079-0.

Equipment of category 3 is suitable for use in zone 2.

Equipment intended for use in explosion hazardous areas means electrical and non-electrical equipment where measures are taken to prevent the equipment's own ignition sources becoming effective. Such equipment shall comply with the requirements for use within the respective zone. It shall be tested according to the type of protection and evidence of compliance with the applicable requirements (e.g., conformity assessment procedure according to Directive 2014/34/EU,[3] the IECEx System,[4] ECE/TRADE/391[5] or at least equivalent) shall be supplied;

Equipment protection level (EPL[6] (see IEC 60079-0)) means the level of protection assigned to equipment based on its likelihood of becoming a source of ignition.

EPL 'Ga':

Equipment with a 'very high' level of protection. Such equipment corresponds to equipment category 1 according to Directive 2014/34/EU.[3]

Equipment with the 'Ga' level of protection is suitable for use in zones 0, 1 and 2.

EPL 'Gb':

Equipment with a 'high' level of protection. Such equipment corresponds to equipment category 2 according to Directive 2014/34/EU.[3]

Equipment with the 'Gb' level of protection is suitable for use in zones 1 and 2.

EPL 'Gc':

Equipment with an 'enhanced' level of protection. Such equipment corresponds to equipment category 3 according to Directive 2014/34/EU.[3]

Equipment with the 'Gc' level of protection is suitable for use in zone 2;

Escape boat means a specially designed directly accessible boat designed to withstand all identified hazards of the cargo and to evacuate the people in danger;

Escape device (suitable) means a respiratory protection device, designed to cover the wearer's mouth, nose and eyes, which can be easily put on and which serves to escape from a danger area. For such devices, see for example European standard EN 13794:2002, EN 402: 2003, EN 403: 2004 or EN 1146:2005;

Escape route means a safe route from danger towards safety or to another means of evacuation;

Evacuation boat means a manned and specially equipped boat called in for rescuing people in danger or evacuating them within the minimum safe period of time provided by a safe haven or a safe area;

---

[3] *Official Journal of the European Union No. L 96 of 29 March 2014, p. 309.*
[6] *The letters EPL mean: Equipment Protection Level.*
[4] *http://iecex.com/rules.*
[5] *A Common Regulatory Framework for Equipment Used in Environments with an Explosive Atmosphere, United Nations, 2011.*

Exclusive use, for the carriage of radioactive material, means the sole use, by a single consignor, of a conveyance or of a large container, in respect of which all initial, intermediate and final loading and unloading and shipment are carried out in accordance with the directions of the consignor or consignee where so required by ADN;

Explosion means a sudden reaction of oxidation or decomposition with an increase in temperature or in pressure or both simultaneously (see EN 13237:2011);

Explosion group/subgroup means a grouping of flammable gases and vapours according to their maximum experimental safe gaps (standard gap width, determined in accordance with specified conditions) and minimum ignition currents, and of electrical apparatus intended to be used in a potentially explosive atmosphere (see EN IEC 60079-0:2012), installations, equipment and self-contained protection systems. For self-contained protection systems, the explosion group II B is subdivided into subgroups;

Explosion hazardous areas means areas in which an explosive atmosphere may occur of such a scale that special protection measures are necessary to ensure the safety and health of the persons affected (see Directive 1999/92/CE[1]). Explosion hazardous areas are classified into zones by frequency of occurrence and duration of the presence of an explosive atmosphere.

See also *Classification of explosion hazardous areas, Explosion protection, Classification of zones* - for tank vessels and *Protected area* - for dry cargo vessels;

Explosion protection means all of the requirements which have to be met and means which have to be taken to avoid damage caused by explosions.

This includes:

Organizational measures such as, for example:

(a)   Determining explosion hazardous areas (classification of zones): in which an explosive atmosphere consisting of a mixture with air of flammable gases, vapours or sprays is likely to occur:

  (i)   continuously or for long periods or frequently (zone 0);

  (ii)   occasionally in normal operation (zone 1); or

  (iii)   exceptionally or only briefly (zone 2);

           (see Directive 1999/92/CE[1]).

(b)   Prevention of ignition sources (use of low-sparking hand-tools, no smoking, use of personal protective equipment including dissipative shoes, non-isolating gloves, etc.);

(c)   Drafting of working instructions.

---

[1]   *Official Journal of the European Communities No. L 23 of 28 January 2000, p.57.*

And technical requirements such as, for example:

(a)   Use of installations and equipment proven to be appropriate for use in the different explosion hazardous areas;

(b)   Use of autonomous protection systems;

(c)   Monitoring of potentially explosive atmospheres by the use of gas detection systems and gas detectors;

Explosion range means the range of the concentration of a flammable substance or mixture of substances in air, within which an explosion can occur, respectively the range of the concentration of a flammable substance or mixture of substances in mixture with air/inert gas, within which an explosion can occur, determined under specified test conditions;

Explosive atmosphere means a mixture of air with gases, vapours or mists flammable in atmospheric conditions, in which the combustion process spreads after ignition to the entire unconsumed mixture (see EN 13237:2011);

F

Fibreboard IBC means a fibreboard body with or without separate top and bottom caps, if necessary an inner liner (but no inner packagings), and appropriate service and structural equipment;

Filler means any enterprise

(a)   which fills dangerous goods into a tank (tank-vehicle, tank wagon, demountable tank, portable tank or tank-container) or into a battery-vehicle, battery-wagon or MEGC; or

(b)   which fills dangerous goods into a cargo tank; or

(c)   which fills dangerous goods into a vessel, a vehicle, a wagon, a large container or small container for carriage in bulk;

Filling pressure means the maximum pressure actually built up in the tank when it is being filled under pressure; (see also *Calculation pressure*, *Discharge pressure*, *Maximum working pressure (gauge pressure)* and *Test pressure*);

Filling ratio means the ratio of the mass of gas to the mass of water at 15 °C that would fill completely a pressure receptacle fitted ready for use (capacity);

Filling ratio (cargo tank): Where a filling ratio is given for a cargo tank, it refers to the percentage of the volume of the cargo tank which may be filled with liquid during loading;

Fixed tank means a tank having a capacity of more than 1,000 litres which is permanently attached to a vehicle (which then becomes a tank-vehicle) or to a wagon (which then becomes a tank-wagon) or is an integral part of the frame of such vehicle or wagon;

Flame arrester means a device mounted in the vent of part of an installation or in the interconnecting piping of a system of installations, the purpose of which is to permit flow but prevent the propagation of a flame front. The flame arrester shall be tested according to the international standard ISO 16852:2016[2] and evidence of compliance with the applicable requirements (e.g., conformity assessment procedure according to Directive 2014/34/EU,[3] the IECEx System,[4] ECE/TRADE/391[5] or at least equivalent) shall be supplied;

Flame arrester plate stack means the part of the flame arrester the main purpose of which is to prevent the passage of a flame front;

Flame arrester housing means the part of a flame arrester the main purpose of which is to form a suitable casing for the flame arrester plate stack and ensure a mechanical connection with other systems;

Flammable component (for aerosols) means flammable liquids, flammable solids or flammable gases and gas mixtures as defined in Notes 1 to 3 of sub-section 31.1.3 of Part III of the Manual of Tests and Criteria. This designation does not cover pyrophoric, self-heating or water-reactive substances. The chemical heat of combustion shall be determined by one of the following methods ASTM D 240, ISO/FDIS 13943: 1999 (E/F) 86.1 to 86.3 or NFPA 30B;

Flash-point (Fp) means the lowest temperature of a liquid at which its vapours form a flammable mixture with air;

Flexible bulk container, see *Bulk container,*

Flexible IBC means a body constituted of film, woven fabric or any other flexible material or combinations thereof, and if necessary, an inner coating or liner, together with any appropriate service equipment and handling devices;

Frame (Class 2), see *Bundle of cylinders*;

Fuel cell means an electrochemical device that converts the chemical energy of a fuel to electrical energy, heat and reaction products;

Fuel cell engine means a device used to power equipment and which consists of a fuel cell and its fuel supply, whether integrated with or separate from the fuel cell, and includes all appurtenances necessary to fulfil its function;

Full load means any load originating from one consignor for which the use of a vehicle, of a wagon or of a large container is exclusively reserved and all operations for the loading and unloading of which are carried out in conformity with the instructions of the consignor or of the consignee;

NOTE: *The corresponding term for radioactive material is "exclusive use".*

---

[2] *Identical to EN ISO 16852:2016.*

[3] *Official Journal of the European Union No. L 96 of 29 March 2014, p. 309.*

[4] *http://iecex.com/rules.*

[5] *A Common Regulatory Framework for Equipment Used in Environments with an Explosive Atmosphere, United Nations, 2011.*

G

Gas (for the purposes of Class 2) means a substance which:

(a) at 50 °C has a vapour pressure greater than 300 kPa (3 bar); or

(b) is completely gaseous at 20 °C under standard pressure of 101.3 kPa;

Otherwise, *Gases* means gases or vapours;

Gas cartridge, see *Small receptacle containing gas*;

Gas detection system means a steady state monitoring system with direct-measuring sensors capable of detecting in time significant concentrations of flammable gases at concentrations below their (LEL) and capable of activating the alarms when a limiting value is exceeded. It has to be calibrated at least for n-Hexane. The threshold level of the sensors shall be set at not more than 10% of the LEL of n-Hexane.

It shall be certified according to IEC/EN[7] 60079-29-1:2016 and, with electronically driven systems, also according to EN 50271:2010. If it is used in explosion hazardous areas, it shall also comply with the requirements for use in the zone concerned and evidence of such compliance (e.g., conformity assessment procedure according to Directive 2014/34/EU,[3] the IECEx System,[4] ECE/TRADE/391[5] or at least equivalent) shall be supplied;

Gas detector means a portable device allowing measurement of any significant concentration of flammable gases below the LEL and which clearly indicates the concentration of such gases. Gas detectors may be designed for measuring flammable gases only, but also for measuring both flammable gases and oxygen. This device shall be so designed that measurements are possible without the necessity of entering the spaces to be checked.

The maximum detection level of the sensors is 5% of the LEL of the most critical substance in the vessel substance list for tank vessels or the cargo for dry cargo vessels. The flammable gas detector shall be certified according to IEC/EN[7] 60079-29-1:2016. If it is used in explosion hazardous areas, it shall also comply with the requirements for use in the zone concerned and evidence of such compliance (e.g., conformity assessment procedure according to Directive 2014/34/EU,[3] the IECEx System,[4] ECE/TRADE/391[5] or at least equivalent) shall be supplied;

GESAMP means the Joint Group of Experts on the Scientific Aspects of Marine Environmental Protection. IMO publication: "The Revised GESAMP Hazard Evaluation Procedure for Chemical Substances Carried by Ships", GESAMP Reports and Studies No. 64, IMO, London, 2002.

In applying the GESAMP model for the purposes of the present Regulations, the reference temperature for the relative density, vapour pressure and water solubility is 20°C. The reference relative density to be used to differentiate between floating substances ("floater") and substances that sink ("sinker") is 1,000 (corresponding to the water density in inland waterways of 1000 kg/m^3);

GHS means the eighth revised edition of the Globally Harmonized System of Classification and Labelling of Chemicals, published by the United Nations as document ST/SG/AC.10/30/Rev.8;

---

[7] *IEC/EN means: This standard is available as an IEC standard and as a European standard.*
[3] *Official Journal of the European Union No. L 96 of 29 March 2014, p. 309.*
[4] *http://iecex.com/rules.*
[5] *A Common Regulatory Framework for Equipment Used in Environments with an Explosive Atmosphere, United Nations, 2011.*

H

Handling device (for flexible IBCs) means any sling, loop, eye or frame attached to the body of the IBC or formed from the continuation of the IBC body material;

Hermetically closed tank means a tank that:

– is not equipped with safety valves, bursting discs, other similar safety devices or vacuum valves; or

– is equipped with safety valves preceded by a bursting disc according to 6.8.2.2.10 of ADR, but is not equipped with vacuum valves.

A tank intended for the carriage of liquid substances with a calculation pressure of at least 4 bar or intended for the carriage of solid substances (powdery or granular) regardless of its calculation pressure is also considered hermetically closed if:

– it is equipped with safety valves preceded by a bursting disc according to 6.8.2.2.10 of ADR and vacuum valves, in accordance with the requirements of 6.8.2.2.3 of ADR; or,

– it is not equipped with safety valves, bursting discs or other similar safety devices, but is equipped with vacuum valves, in accordance with the requirements of 6.8.2.2.3 of ADR;

Highest class may be assigned to a vessel when:

– the hull, inclusive of rudder and steering gear and equipment of anchors and chains, complies with the rules and regulations of a recognized classification society and has been built and tested under its supervision;

– the propulsion plant, together with the essential auxiliary engines, mechanical and electrical installations, have been made and tested in conformity with the rules and regulations of this classification society, and the installation has been carried out under its supervision, and the complete plant was tested to its satisfaction on completion;

High-velocity vent valve means a pressure relief valve designed to have nominal flow velocities which exceed the flame velocity of the explosive mixture, thus preventing flame transmission. When the vessel substance list according to 1.16.1.2.5 contains substances for which explosion protection is required in column (17) of Table C of Chapter 3.2, this pressure relief device shall be tested in accordance with international standard ISO 16852:2016[2] and evidence of compliance with the applicable requirements (e.g., conformity assessment procedure according to Directive 2014/34/EU,[3] the IECEx System,[4] ECE/TRADE/391[5] or at least equivalent) shall be supplied;

Hold means a part of the vessel which, whether covered by hatchway covers or not, is bounded fore and aft by bulkheads and which is intended to carry goods in packages or in bulk. The upper boundary of the hold is the upper edge of the hatchway coaming. Cargo extending above the hatchway coaming shall be considered as loaded on deck;

Hold (discharged) means a hold which after unloading may contain some dry cargo remains;

Hold (empty) means a hold which after unloading contains no dry cargo remains (swept clean);

---

[2]   *Identical to EN ISO 16852:2016*

[3]   *Official Journal of the European Union No. L 96 of 29 March 2014, p. 309.*

[4]   *http://iecex.com/rules.*

[5]   *A Common Regulatory Framework for Equipment Used in Environments with an Explosive Atmosphere, United Nations, 2011.*

Hold space means an enclosed part of the vessel which is bounded fore and aft by watertight bulkheads and which is intended only to carry cargo tanks independent of the vessel's hull.

Holding time means the time that will elapse from the establishment of the initial filling condition until the pressure has risen due to heat influx to the lowest set pressure of the pressure limiting devices (s) of tanks intended for the carriage of refrigerated liquefied gases;

NOTE: *For portable tanks, see 6.7.4.1 of ADR.*

Hose assemblies means hoses, which are integrated or welded on both sides into hose fittings; hose fittings shall be integrated so that it is only possible to loosen them with a tool.

Hose fittings means couplings and connection elements of hoses.

Hoses means flexible tubular semi-finished products of elastomers, thermoplastics or stainless steel composed of one or several coatings and liners.

I

IAEA means the International Atomic Energy Agency (IAEA), (IAEA, P.O. Box 100 – A-1400 Vienna);

IAEA Regulations for the Safe Transport of Radioactive Material means one of the editions of those Regulations, as follows:

(a)   For the 1985 and 1985 (as amended 1990) editions: IAEA Safety Series No. 6;

(b)   For the 1996 edition: IAEA Safety Series No. ST-1;

(c)   For the 1996 (revised) edition: IAEA Safety Series No. TS-R-1 (ST-1, Revised);

(d)   For the 1996 (as amended 2003), 2005 and 2009 editions: IAEA Safety Standards Series No. TS-R-1;

(e)   For the 2012 edition: IAEA Safety Standards Series No. SSR-6;

(f)   For the 2018 edition: IAEA Safety Standards Series No. SSR–6 (Rev.1);

IBC see *Intermediate bulk container*;

IBC Code means the International Code for the Construction and Equipment of Ships carrying Dangerous Chemicals in Bulk, published by the International Maritime Organization (IMO);

ICAO means the International Civil Aviation Organization (ICAO, 999 University Street, Montreal, Quebec H3C 5H7, Canada);

ICAO Technical Instructions means the Technical Instructions for the Safe Transport of Dangerous Goods by Air, which complement Annex 18 to the Chicago Convention on International Civil Aviation (Chicago 1944) published by the International Civil Aviation Organization (ICAO) in Montreal;

Identification number means the number for identifying a substance to which no UN number has been assigned or which cannot be classified under a collective entry with a UN number.

These numbers have four figures beginning with 9;

IEC means the International Electrotechnical Commission;

IMDG Code means the International Maritime Dangerous Goods Code, for the implementation of Chapter VII, Part A, of the International Convention for the Safety of Life at Sea, 1974 (SOLAS Convention), published by the International Maritime Organization (IMO), London;

IMO means the International Maritime Organization (IMO, 4 Albert Embankment, London SE1 7SR, United Kingdom);

IMSBC Code means the International Maritime Solid Bulk Cargoes Code of the International Maritime Organization (IMO);

Inner packaging means a packaging for which an outer packaging is required for carriage;

Inner receptacle means a receptacle which requires an outer packaging in order to perform its containment function;

Inspection body means an independent monitoring and verification body certified by the competent authority;

Instruction means transmitting know-how or teaching how to do something or how to act. This transmission or teaching may be dispensed internally by the personnel;

Intermediate bulk container (IBC) means a rigid, or flexible portable packaging, other than those specified in Chapter 6.1 of ADR, that:

(a)   has a capacity of:

    (i)   not more than 3 m^3 for solids and liquids of packing groups II and III;

    (ii)   not more than 1.5 m^3 for solids of packing group I when packed in flexible, rigid plastics, composite, fibreboard and wooden IBCs;

    (iii)   not more than 3 m^3 for solids of packing group I when packed in metal IBCs;

    (iv)   not more than 3 m^3 for radioactive material of Class 7;

(b)   is designed for mechanical handling;

(c)   is resistant to the stresses produced in handling and transport as determined by the tests specified in Chapter 6.5 of ADR;

(see also *Composite IBC with plastics inner receptacle, Fibreboard IBC, Flexible IBC, Metal IBC, Rigid plastics IBC* and *Wooden IBC*)

NOTE 1: *Portable tanks or tank-containers that meet the requirements of Chapter 6.7 or 6.8 of ADR respectively are not considered to be intermediate bulk containers (IBCs).*

NOTE 2: *Intermediate bulk containers (IBCs) which meet the requirements of Chapter 6.5 of ADR are not considered to be containers for the purposes of ADN.*

Intermediate packaging means a packaging placed between inner packagings or articles and an outer packaging;

International regulations means ADR, ICAO-TI, IMDG Code, IMSBC Code or RID.

ISO (standard) means an international standard published by the International Organization for Standardization (ISO) (ISO, 1, rue de Varembé, CH-1204, Geneva 20);

J

Jerrican means a metal or plastics packaging of rectangular or polygonal cross-section with one or more orifices.

L

Large container, see *Container;*

Large packaging means a packaging consisting of an outer packaging which contains articles or inner packagings and which:

(a)   is designed for mechanical handling;

(b)   exceeds 400 kg net mass or 450 litres capacity but has a volume of not more than 3 m³;

Remanufactured large packaging means a metal or rigid plastics large packaging that:

(a)   Is produced as a UN type from a non-UN type; or

(b)   Is converted from one UN design type to another UN design type.

Remanufactured large packagings are subject to the same requirements of ADR that apply to new large packagings of the same type (see also design type definition in 6.6.5.1.2 of ADR);

Reused large packaging means a large packaging to be refilled which has been examined and found free of defects affecting the ability to withstand the performance tests; the term includes those which are refilled with the same or similar compatible contents and are carried within distribution chains controlled by the consignor of the product;

Large salvage packaging means a special packaging which

(a)   is designed for mechanical handling; and

(b)   exceeds 400 kg net mass or 450 litres capacity but has a volume of not more than 3 m³;

into which damaged, defective, leaking or non-conforming dangerous goods packages, or dangerous goods that have spilled or leaked are placed for purposes of carriage for recovery or disposal;

LEL: see *Lower explosion limit;*

Life boat (i.e. ship's boat) means an onboard boat in transport, rescue, salvage and work duties;

Light-gauge metal packaging means a packaging of circular, elliptical, rectangular or polygonal cross-section (also conical) and taper-necked and pail-shaped packaging made of metal, having a wall thickness of less than 0.5 mm (e.g. tinplate), flat or convex bottomed and with one or more orifices, which is not covered by the definitions for drums or jerricans;

Limited explosion risk electrical installations and equipment means electrical installations and equipment which, during normal operation, do not cause sparks or exhibits surface temperatures which are above 200 °C, including e.g.:

–   three-phase squirrel cage rotor motors;

–   brushless generators with contactless excitation;

– fuses with an enclosed fuse element;

– contactless electronic apparatus;

or means electrical installations and equipment with at least an enclosure protected against water jets (protection rating IP55 or higher) which during normal operation do not exhibit surface temperatures above 200 °C;

Liner means a tube or bag inserted into a packaging, including large packagings or IBCs, but not forming an integral part of it, including the closures of its openings;

Liquefied natural gas (LNG) means a refrigerated liquefied gas composed of natural gas with a high methane content assigned to UN No. 1972;

Liquefied petroleum gas (LPG) means a low pressure liquefied gas composed of one or more light hydrocarbons which are assigned to UN 1011, UN 1075, UN 1965, UN 1969 or UN 1978 only and which consists mainly of propane, propene, butane, butane isomers, butene with traces of other hydrocarbon gases.

NOTE 1: *Flammable gases assigned to other UN numbers shall not be regarded as LPG.*

NOTE 2: *For UN No. 1075 see NOTE 2 under 2F, UN No. 1965, in the table for liquefied gases in 2.2.2.3.*

Liquid means a substance which at 50° C has a vapour pressure of not more than 300 kPa (3 bar) which is not completely gaseous at 20° C and 101.3 kPa, and which:

(a)   has a melting point or initial melting point of 20° C or less at a pressure of 101.3 kPa, or

(b)   is liquid according to the ASTM D 4359-90 test method or

(c)   is not pasty according to the criteria applicable to the test for determining fluidity (penetrometer test) described in 2.3.4;

NOTE: *"Carriage in the liquid state" for the purpose of tank requirements means:*

– Carriage of liquids according to the above definition, or

– Solids handed over for carriage in the molten state;

Loader means any enterprise which:

(a)   Loads packaged dangerous goods, small containers or portable tanks into or onto a conveyance or a container; or

(b)   Loads a container, bulk-container, MEGC, tank-container or portable tank onto a conveyance; or

(c)   Loads a vehicle or a wagon into or onto a vessel;

Loading means all actions carried out by the loader, in accordance with the definition of loader;

Loading instrument: A loading instrument consists of a computer (hardware) and a programme (software) and offers the possibility of ensuring that in every ballast or loading case:

–   the permissible values concerning longitudinal strength as well as the maximum permissible draught are not exceeded; and

–   the stability of the vessel complies with the requirements applicable to the vessel. For this purpose intact stability and damage stability shall be calculated.

Lower explosion limit (LEL) means the lowest concentration of the explosion range at which an explosion can occur;

M

Management system, for the carriage of radioactive material, means a set of interrelated or interacting elements (system) for establishing policies and objectives and enabling the objectives to be achieved in an efficient and effective manner;

Manual of Tests and Criteria means the seventh revised edition of the Manual of Tests and Criteria, published by the United Nations (ST/SG/AC.10/11/Rev.7);

Mass density shall be expressed in kg/m^3. In the event of repetition, the number alone shall be used;

Mass of package means gross mass of the package unless otherwise stated. The mass of containers, tanks, vehicles and wagons used for the carriage of goods is not included in the gross mass;

Master means a person as defined in Article 1.02 of the European Code for Inland Waterways (CEVNI);

Maximum capacity means the maximum inner volume of receptacles or packagings including intermediate bulk containers (IBCs) and large packagings expressed in cubic metres or litres;

Maximum net mass means the maximum net mass of contents in a single packaging or maximum combined mass of inner packagings and the contents thereof expressed in kilograms;

Maximum normal operating pressure, for the carriage of radioactive material, means the maximum pressure above atmospheric pressure at mean sea-level that would develop in the containment system in a period of one year under the conditions of temperature and solar radiation corresponding to environmental conditions in the absence of venting, external cooling by an ancillary system, or operational controls during carriage;

Maximum permissible gross mass, means

(a)   (for IBCs) the mass of the IBC and any service or structural equipment together with the maximum net mass;

(b)   (for tanks) the tare of the tank and the heaviest load authorized for carriage;

NOTE: *For portable tanks, see Chapter 6.7 of ADR.*

Maximum working pressure means the maximum pressure occurring in a cargo tank or a residual cargo tank during operation. This pressure equals the opening pressure of high velocity vent valves or pressure relief valves;

Means of evacuation means any means that can be used by people to move from danger to safety as follows:

Dangers that have to be taken into account are:

– For class 3, packing group III, UN 1202, second and third entry and for classes 4.1, 8 and 9 on tank vessels: leakage at the manifold;

– For other substances of class 3 and class 2 and for flammable substances of class 8 on tank vessels: fire in the area of the manifold on the deck and burning liquid on the water;

– For class 5.1 on tank vessels: oxidizing substances in combination with flammable liquids may cause an explosion;

– For class 6.1 on tank vessels: toxic gases around the manifold and in the direction of the wind;

– For dangerous goods on dry cargo vessels: dangers emanating from the goods in the cargo holds;

MEGC, see *Multiple-element gas container*;

MEMU, see *Mobile explosives manufacturing unit;*

Metal hydride storage system means a single complete hydrogen storage system, including a receptacle, metal hydride, pressure relief device, shut-off valve, service equipment and internal components used for the carriage of hydrogen only;

Metal IBC means a metal body together with appropriate service and structural equipment;

Mobile explosives manufacturing unit (MEMU) means a unit, or a vehicle mounted with a unit, for manufacturing and charging explosives from dangerous goods that are not explosives. The unit consists of various tanks and bulk containers and process equipment as well as pumps and related equipment. The MEMU may have special compartments for packaged explosives;

NOTE: *Even though the definition of MEMU includes the expression "manufacturing and charging explosives" the requirements for MEMUs apply only to carriage and not to manufacturing and charging of explosives.*

Multiple-element gas container (MEGC) means a unit containing elements which are linked to each other by a manifold and mounted on a frame. The following elements are considered to be elements of a multiple-element gas container: cylinders, tubes, pressure drums or bundles of cylinders as well as tanks for the carriage of gases as defined in 2.2.2.1.1 having a capacity of more than 450 litres;

NOTE: *For UN MEGCs, see Chapter 6.7 of ADR.*

N

Naked light means a source of light using a flame which is not enclosed in a flameproof enclosure;

Net explosive mass (NEM) means the total mass of the explosive substances, without the packagings, casings, etc. *(Net explosive quantity (NEQ), net explosive contents (NEC), net explosive weight (NEW)* or *net mass of explosive contents* are often used to convey the same meaning.);

Neutron radiation detector means a device that detects neutron radiation. In such a device, a gas may be contained in a hermetically sealed electron tube transducer that converts neutron radiation into a measureable electric signal;

N.O.S. entry (not otherwise specified entry) means a collective entry to which substances, mixtures, solutions or articles may be assigned if they:

(a)   are not mentioned by name in Table A of Chapter 3.2, and

(b)   exhibit chemical, physical and/or dangerous properties corresponding to the Class, classification code, packing group and the name and description of the n.o.s. entry;

Not readily flammable means a material which is not in itself readily flammable or whose outer surface at least is not readily flammable and limits the propagation of a fire to an appropriate degree.

In order to determine flammability, the IMO procedure, Resolution A.653(16), or any equivalent requirements of a Contracting State are recognized;

O

Offshore bulk container means a bulk container specially designed for repeated use for carriage to, from and between offshore facilities. An offshore bulk container is designed and constructed in accordance with the guidelines for the approval of offshore containers handled in open seas specified by the International Maritime Organization (IMO) in document MSC/Circ.860;

Oil separator vessel means an open type N tank-vessel with a dead weight of up to 300 tonnes, constructed and fitted to accept and carry oily and greasy wastes from the operation of vessels. Vessels without cargo tanks are considered to be subject to Chapters 9.1 or 9.2;

Oil sludge means residual hydrocarbons from the normal operation of seagoing ships, e.g. residues from the treatment of fuel or lubricating oils for main or auxiliary machinery, waste oil obtained by separation from oil filtering installations, oily residues collected in pits and residues of hydraulic and lubricating oils;

NOTE: *In ADN, the definition of MARPOL also includes residues resulting from the treatment of bilge water on board sea-going vessels.*

Oily and greasy wastes from the operation of the vessel means used oils, bilge water and other oily or greasy wastes, such as used grease, used filters, used rags, and receptacles and packagings for such wastes;

Open container, see *Container;*

Open cryogenic receptacle means a transportable thermally insulated receptacle for refrigerated liquefied gases maintained at atmospheric pressure by continuous venting of the refrigerated liquefied gas;

Open vehicle means a vehicle the platform of which has no superstructure or is merely provided with side boards and a tailboard;

Open wagon means a wagon with or without side boards and a tailboard, the loading surfaces of which are open.

Opening pressure means the pressure referred to in column (10) of Table C of Chapter 3.2 at which the pressure relief valves/high-velocity vent valves open. For pressure tanks the opening pressure of the safety valve shall be established in accordance with the requirements of the competent authority or a recognized classification society;

OTIF means Intergovernmental Organisation for International Carriage by Rail (OTIF, Gryphenhübeliweg 30, CH-3006 Bern);

Outer packaging means the outer protection of the composite or combination packaging together with any absorbent materials, cushioning and any other components necessary to contain and protect inner receptacles or inner packagings;

Over-moulded cylinder means a cylinder intended for the carriage of LPG with a water capacity not exceeding 13 l made of a coated welded steel inner cylinder with an over-moulded protective case made from cellular plastic, which is non-removable and bonded to the outer surface of the steel cylinder wall;

Overpack means an enclosure used (by a single consignor in the case of radioactive material) to contain one or more packages, consolidated into a single unit easier to handle and stow during carriage;

Examples of overpacks:

(a)   a loading tray such as a pallet, on which several packages are placed or stacked and secured by a plastics strip, shrink or stretch wrapping or other appropriate means; or

(b)   an outer protective packaging such as a box or a crate;

Oxygen measuring system means a steady-state monitoring device capable of detecting in time any significant reduction of oxygen content of the air and capable of activating the alarms in case the oxygen concentration reaches 19.5% by volume.

This device shall be tested according to the European standard IEC/EN[7] 50104:2010. If it is used in explosion hazardous areas, it shall also comply with the requirements for use in the zone concerned and evidence of such compliance (e.g., conformity assessment procedure according to Directive 2014/34/EU,[3] the IECEx System,[4] ECE/TRADE/391[5] or at least equivalent) shall be supplied.

An oxygen measuring system may also be designed as part of a combination measuring system for measuring both flammable gases and oxygen;

Oxygen meter means a portable device allowing measuring of any significant reduction of the oxygen content of the air. An oxygen meter may either be a device for measuring oxygen only or part of a combination device for measuring both flammable gases and oxygen. This device shall be so designed that measurements are possible without the necessity of entering the spaces to be checked. It shall be tested according to IEC/EN[7] 50104:2010. If it is used in explosion hazardous areas, it shall also comply with the requirements for use in the zone concerned and evidence of such compliance (e.g., conformity assessment procedure according to Directive 2014/34/EU,[3] the IECEx System,[4] ECE/TRADE/391[5] or at least equivalent) shall be supplied.

---

[7]   *IEC/EN means: This standard is available as an IEC standard and as a European standard.*

[3]   *Official Journal of the European Union No. L 96 of 29 March 2014, p. 309.*

[4]   *http://iecex.com/rules.*

[5]   *A Common Regulatory Framework for Equipment Used in Environments with an Explosive Atmosphere, United Nations, 2011.*

P

Package means the complete product of the packing operation, consisting of the packaging or large packaging or IBC and its contents prepared for dispatch. Except for the carriage of radioactive material, the term includes receptacles for gases as defined in this section as well as articles which, because of their size, mass or configuration may be carried unpackaged or carried in cradles, crates or handling devices.

The term does not apply to goods which are carried in bulk in the holds of vessels, nor to substances carried in tanks in tank vessels.

On board vessels, the term also includes vehicles, wagons, containers (including swap bodies), tank-containers, portable tanks, battery-vehicles, battery-wagons, tank vehicles, tank wagons and multiple element gas containers (MECGs).

NOTE: *For radioactive material, see 2.2.7.2, 4.1.9.1.1 and Chapter 6.4 of ADR.*

Packaging means one or more receptacles and any other components or materials necessary for the receptacles to perform their containment and other safety functions (see also *Combination packaging, Composite packaging, Inner packaging, Intermediate bulk container (IBC), Intermediate packaging, Large packaging, Light-gauge metal packaging, Outer packaging, Reconditioned packaging, Remanufactured packaging, Reused packaging, Salvage packaging* and *Sift-proof packaging)*;

Packer means any enterprise which puts dangerous goods into packagings, including large packagings and intermediate bulk containers (IBCs) and, where necessary, prepares packages for carriage;

Packing group means a group to which, for packing purposes, certain substances may be assigned in accordance with their degree of danger. The packing groups have the following meanings which are explained more fully in Part 2:

Packing group I   :   Substances presenting high danger;

Packing group II   :   Substances presenting medium danger; and

Packing group III :   Substances presenting low danger;

NOTE: *Certain articles containing dangerous goods are assigned to a packing group.*

Partly closed-type sampling device means a device penetrating through the boundary of the cargo tank or through the piping for loading and unloading such that during sampling only a small quantity of gaseous or liquid cargo can escape into the open air. As long as the device is not used it shall be closed completely;

Piping for loading and unloading (cargo piping) means all piping which may contain liquid or gaseous cargo, including pipes, hose assemblies, connected pumps, filters and closure devices.

Portable tank means a multimodal tank having, when used for the carriage of gases as defined in 2.2.2.1.1, a capacity of more than 450 litres in accordance with the definitions in Chapter 6.7 of ADR or the IMDG Code and indicated by a portable tank instruction (T-Code) in Column (10) of Table A of Chapter 3.2 of ADR;

Portable tank operator, see *Tank-container/portable tank operator*;

Possibility of cargo heating means a cargo heating installation in the cargo tanks using a heat insulator. The heat insulator may be heated by means of a boiler on board the tank vessel (cargo heating system in accordance with 9.3.2.42 or 9.3.3.42) or from shore;

Pressure drum means a welded, transportable pressure receptacle of a water capacity exceeding 150 litres and of not more than 1,000 litres (e.g. cylindrical receptacles equipped with rolling hoops, spheres on skids);

Pressure relief device means an automatically activated safety valve the purpose of which is to protect the cargo tank against unacceptable excess internal pressure;

Pressure receptacle means a collective term that includes cylinders, tubes, pressure drums, closed cryogenic receptacles, metal hydride storage systems, bundles of cylinders and salvage pressure receptacles;

Pressures means for tanks, all kinds of pressures (e.g. working pressure, opening pressure of the high velocity vent valves, test pressure) shall be expressed as gauge pressures in kPa (bar); the vapour pressure of substances, however, shall be expressed as an absolute pressure in kPa (bar);

Pressurized gas cartridge, see *Aerosol dispenser*;

Protected area means the whole of the following spaces on board of dry cargo vessels:

(a)   the hold or holds (when anti-explosion protection is required, zone 1);

(b)   the space situated above the deck (when anti-explosion protection is required, zone 2), bounded:

    (i)   athwartships, by vertical planes corresponding to the side plating;

    (ii)   fore and aft, by vertical planes corresponding to the end bulkheads of the hold; and

    (iii)   upwards, by a horizontal plane 2.00 m above the upper level of the load, but at least by a horizontal plane 3.00 m above the deck.

Protected IBC (for metal IBCs) means an IBC provided with additional protection against impact, the protection taking the form of, for example, a multi-layer (sandwich) or double-wall construction, or a frame with a metal lattice-work casing.

Protection wall, gas- and liquid-tight means a gas- and liquid-tight wall on deck at the height of the boundary plane of the cargo area preventing gases from entering areas outside the cargo area;

Protective coaming, liquid-tight means a liquid-tight coaming on deck at the height of the outer cargo tank bulkhead (see zoning diagram), but at a maximum distance of 0.60 m to the outer cofferdam bulkhead or hold end bulkheads, which prevents liquid from entering the fore and aft parts of the vessel. The connection between the protective coamings and the spill coaming shall be liquid tight;

Protective gloves means gloves which protect the wearer's hands during work in a danger area. The choice of appropriate gloves shall correspond to the dangers likely to arise (see for example European standards EN 374-1:2016, EN 374-2:2015 or EN 374-4:2013). In the case of dangers caused by electrostatic charging/discharging, they shall meet the requirements of standard EN 16350:2015;

Protective goggles, protective masks means goggles or face protection which protects the wearer's eyes or face during work in a danger area. The choice of appropriate goggles or masks shall correspond to the dangers likely to arise. For protective goggles or masks, see for example European standard EN 166:2001;

Protective shoes (or protective boots) means shoes or boots which protect the wearer's feet during work in a danger area. The choice of appropriate protective shoes or boots shall correspond to the dangers likely to arise, especially those caused by electrostatic charging/discharging, and meet the requirements of international standard ISO 20345:2012 or ISO 20346:2014;

Protective lining (for tanks) means a lining or coating protecting the metallic tank material against the substances to be carried;

NOTE: *This definition does not apply to a lining or coating used only to protect the substance to be carried.*

Protective suit means a suit which protects the wearer's body during work in a danger area. The choice of appropriate suit shall correspond to the dangers likely to arise. For protective suits, see for example, ISO 13688:2013. In case of dangers caused by electrostatic charging/discharging, see also European standard EN 1149-5:2008.

Q

Quality assurance means a systematic programme of controls and inspections applied by any organization or body which is aimed at providing confidence that the safety prescriptions in ADN are met in practice.

R

Radiation detection system means an apparatus that contains radiation detectors as components;

Radioactive contents, for the carriage of radioactive material, mean the radioactive material together with any contaminated or activated solids, liquids, and gases within the packaging;

Reception facility means a stationary or mobile facility for receiving gases and vapours during degassing of empty or unloaded cargo tanks and piping for loading and unloading;

Receptacle (Class 1) includes boxes, cylinders, cans, drums, jars and tubes, including any means of closure used in the inner or intermediate packaging;

Receptacle means a containment vessel for receiving and holding substances or articles, including any means of closing. This definition does not apply to shells (see also *Cryogenic receptacle, Inner receptacle, Rigid inner receptacle* and *Gas cartridge*);

Receptacle for residual products means an intermediate bulk container or tank-container or portable tank intended to collect residual cargo, washing water, cargo residues or slops which are suitable for pumping. The receptacle shall be approved according to ADR, RID or the IMDG Code and authorized for the substance concerned. The maximum permissible capacity of an intermediate bulk container is 3 m³, and that of a tank-container or portable tank is 12 m³;

Receptacle for slops means a fire resistant receptacle capable of being closed with a lid intended to collect slops which are unsuitable for pumping. The receptacle shall be approved according to ADR, RID or the IMDG Code and authorized for the substance concerned. The maximum permissible capacity is 450 *l*. It should be easy to handle and marked "SLOP" (character height: 0.10 m);

Recycled plastics material means material recovered from used industrial packagings that has been cleaned and prepared for processing into new packagings;

Reel (Class 1) means a device made of plastics, wood, fibreboard, metal or other suitable material comprising a central spindle with, or without, side walls at each end of the spindle. Articles and substances can be wound on to the spindle and may be retained by side walls;

Relative density (or specific density) describes the ratio of the density of a substance to the density of pure water at 3.98 °C (1000 kg/m³) and is dimensionless;

Remanufactured large packaging see *Large packaging*;

Rescue winch means a device for hoisting persons from spaces such as cargo tanks, cofferdams and double-hull spaces. The device shall be operable by one person;

Residual cargo means liquid cargo remaining in the cargo tank or cargo piping after unloading without the use of the stripping system;

Reused large packaging see *Large packaging*;

RID means Regulations concerning the International Carriage of Dangerous Goods by Rail, Appendix C of COTIF (Convention concerning International Carriage by Rail);

Rigid inner receptacle (for composite IBCs) means a receptacle which retains its general shape when empty without its closures in place and without benefit of the outer casing. Any inner receptacle that is not rigid is considered to be flexible;

Rigid plastics IBC means a rigid plastics body, which may have structural equipment together with appropriate service equipment;

S

Safe area means a designated, recognisable area outside the cargo area which can be readily accessed by all persons on board. The safe area provides protection against the identified hazards of the cargo by a water spray system for at least 60 minutes. The safe area can be evacuated during an incident. A safe area is not acceptable when the identified danger is explosion;

Safe haven means a designated, recognisable, readily accessible module (fixed or floating) capable of protecting all persons on board against the identified hazards of the cargo for at least sixty minutes during which communication to the emergency and rescue services is possible. A safe haven can be integrated into the wheelhouse or into the accommodation. A safe haven can be evacuated during an incident. A safe haven on board is not acceptable when the identified danger is explosion. A safe haven on board and a floating safe haven outside the ship are certified by a recognized classification society. A safe haven on land is constructed according to local law;

Safety adviser means a person who, in an undertaking the activities of which include the carriage, or the related packing, loading, filling or unloading, of dangerous goods by inland waterways, is responsible for helping to prevent the risks inherent in the carriage of dangerous goods;

Safety valve means a spring-loaded device which is activated automatically by pressure the purpose of which is to protect the cargo tank against unacceptable excess internal pressure or negative internal pressure (see also, *High velocity vent valve*, *Pressure-relief device* and *Vacuum valve*);

SADT see *Self-accelerating decomposition temperature*;

Salvage packaging means a special packaging into which damaged, defective, leaking or non-conforming dangerous goods packages, or dangerous goods that have spilled or leaked are placed for purposes of carriage for recovery or disposal;

Salvage pressure receptacle means a pressure receptacle with a water capacity not exceeding 3 000 litres into which are placed damaged, defective, leaking or non-conforming pressure receptacle(s) for the purpose of carriage e.g. for recovery or disposal;

Sampling opening means a closable opening of a cargo tank with a diameter of not more than 0.30 m. When the vessel substance list according to 1.16.1.2.5 contains substances for which explosion protection is required in column (17) of Table C of Chapter 3.2, it shall be deflagration safe, capable of withstanding steady burning for the most critical substance in the vessel substance list and so designed that the opening period will be as short as possible and that it cannot remain open without external intervention.

The deflagration safety shall be tested according to international standard ISO 16852:2016[2] and evidence of compliance with the applicable requirements (e.g., conformity assessment procedure according to Directive 2014/34/EU,[3] the IECEx System,[4] ECE/TRADE/391[5] or at least equivalent) shall be supplied. The deflagration safety may be ensured by an integrated flame arrester plate stack capable of withstanding steady burning or a flame arrester capable of withstanding steady burning (protection against deflagrations);

SAPT see *Self-accelerating polymerization temperature;*

Self-accelerating decomposition temperature (SADT) means the lowest temperature at which self-accelerating decomposition may occur in a substance in the packaging, IBC or tank as offered for carriage. The SADT shall be determined in accordance with the test procedures given in Part II, Section 28 of the Manual of Tests and Criteria;

Self-accelerating polymerization temperature (SAPT) means the lowest temperature at which self-accelerating polymerization may occur with a substance in the packaging, IBC or tank as offered for carriage. The SAPT shall be determined in accordance with the test procedures established for the self-accelerating decomposition temperature for self-reactive substances in accordance with Part II, section 28 of the Manual of Tests and Criteria;

Service life, for composite cylinders and tubes, means the number of years the cylinder or tube is permitted to be in service;

Service space means a space which is accessible during the operation of the vessel and which is neither part of the accommodation nor of the cargo tanks, with the exception of the forepeak and after peak, provided no machinery has been installed in these latter spaces;

Settled pressure means the pressure of the contents of a pressure receptacle in thermal and diffusive equilibrium;

Sheeted bulk container, see *Bulk container;*

Sheeted container, see Container;

Sheeted vehicle means an open vehicle provided with a sheet to protect the load;

---

[2]   *Identical to EN ISO 16852:2016*
[3]   *Official Journal of the European Union No. L 96 of 29 March 2014, p. 309.*
[4]   *http://iecex.com/rules.*
[5]   *A Common Regulatory Framework for Equipment Used in Environments with an Explosive Atmosphere, United Nations, 2011.*

Sheeted wagon means an open wagon provided with a sheet to protect the load;

Sift-proof packaging means a packaging impermeable to dry contents, including fine solid material produced during carriage;

Slops means a mixture of cargo residues with washing water, rust or sludge which may or may not be suitable for pumping;

Small container, see *Container;*

Small receptacle containing gas (gas cartridge) means a non-refillable receptacle having a water capacity not exceeding 1000 ml for receptacles made of metal and not exceeding 500 ml for receptacles made of synthetic material or glass, containing, under pressure, a gas or a mixture of   gases. It may be fitted with a valve;

SOLAS means the International Convention for the Safety of Life at Sea, 1974, as amended;

Solid means:

(a)   a substance with a melting point or initial melting point of more than 20 °C at a pressure of 101.3 kPa; or

(b)   a substance which is not liquid according to the ASTM D 4359-90 test method or which is pasty according to the criteria applicable to the test for determining fluidity (penetrometer test) described in 2.3.4;

Spill coaming means a coaming on deck of the vessel parallel to the side plating with closable openings, to prevent spillage of liquids overboard. The connection to the protective coamings, if installed, shall be liquid tight;

STCW means the International Convention on Standards of Training, Certification and Watchkeeping for Seafarers, 1978, as amended.

Steady burning means combustion stabilized for an indeterminate period (see ISO 16852:2016[2]);

Stripping system (efficient) means a system according to Annex II of CDNI for complete draining, if possible, of the cargo tanks and stripping the cargo piping except for the cargo residues;

Supply installation (bunkering system) means an installation for the supply of vessels with liquid fuels;

Supply vessel means an open type N tank vessel with a dead weight of up to 300 tonnes, constructed and fitted for the carriage and delivery to other vessels of products intended for the operation of vessels;

Swap-body, see *Container.*

---

[2]   *Identical to EN ISO 16852:2016*

T

Tank means a shell, including its service and structural equipment. When used alone, the term tank means a tank-container, portable tank, demountable tank, fixed tank or tank wagon as defined in this section, including tanks forming elements of battery-vehicles, battery wagons or MEGCs (see also *Demountable tank, Fixed tank, Portable tank and Multiple-element gas container);*

NOTE: *For portable tanks, see 6.7.4.1 of ADR.*

Tank-container means an article of transport equipment meeting the definition of a container, and comprising a shell and items of equipment, including the equipment to facilitate movement of the tank-container without significant change of attitude, used for the carriage of gases, liquid, powdery or granular substances and, when used for the carriage of gases as defined in 2.2.2.1.1 having a capacity of more than 0.45 m³ (450 litres);

NOTE: *IBCs which meet the requirements of Chapter 6.5 of ADR are not considered to be tank-containers.*

Tank-container or portable tank operator means any enterprise in whose name the tank-container or portable tank is operated;

Tank for residual products means a permanently built-in tank intended to collect residual cargo, washing water, cargo residues or slops which are suitable for pumping;

Tank record means a file containing all the important technical information concerning a tank, a battery-vehicle, a battery wagon or an MEGC, such as certificates referred to in 6.8.2.3, 6.8.2.4 and 6.8.3.4 of ADR;

Tank swap body is considered to be a tank-container;

Tank-vehicle means a vehicle built to carry liquids, gases or powdery or granular substances and comprising one or more fixed tanks. In addition to the vehicle proper, or the units of running gear used in its stead, a tank-vehicle comprises one or more shells, their items of equipment and the fittings for attaching them to the vehicle or to the running-gear units;

Tank vessel means a vessel intended for the carriage of substances in cargo tanks;

Tank wagon means a wagon intended for the carriage of liquids, gases, powdery or granular substances, comprising a superstructure, consisting of one or more tanks and their equipment and an underframe fitted with its own items of equipment (running gear, suspension, buffing, traction, braking gear and inscriptions).

NOTE: *Tank wagon also includes wagons with demountable tanks.*

Technical name means a recognized chemical name, or a recognized biological name where relevant, or another name currently used in scientific and technical handbooks, journals and texts (see 3.1.2.8.1.1);

Temperature class means a grouping of flammable gases and vapours of flammable liquids according to their ignition temperature; and of the electrical apparatus intended to be used in the corresponding potentially explosive atmosphere according to their maximum surface temperature (*see EN 13237:2011*);

Test pressure means the pressure at which a cargo tank, a residual cargo tank, a cofferdam or the loading and unloading piping shall be tested prior to being brought into service for the first time and subsequently regularly within prescribed times;

Through or into, for the carriage of radioactive material, means through or into the countries in which a consignment is carried but specifically excludes countries "over" which a consignment is carried by air provided that there are no scheduled stops in those countries;

Toximeter means a (trans)portable device allowing measuring of any significant concentration of toxic gases and vapours. The device has to comply with standard EN 45544-1:2015, EN 45544-2:2015, EN 45544-3:2015 and EN 45544-4:2016 or with standard ISO 17621:2015.

If this device is used in explosion hazardous areas it shall be in addition suitable to be used in the respective zone and it has to be proven that the applicable requirements are fulfilled (e.g. conformity assessment procedure according to Directive 2014/34/EU,[3] the IECEx System,[4] or to ECE/TRADE/391[5] or at least equivalent).

This device shall be so designed that such measurements are possible without the necessity of entering the spaces to be checked.

Training means teaching instruction, courses or apprenticeships dispensed by an organizer approved by the competent authority;

Transport index (TI) assigned to a package, overpack or container, or to unpackaged LSA-I or SCO-I or SCO-III, for the carriage of radioactive material, means a number which is used to provide control over radiation exposure;

Transport unit means a motor vehicle without an attached trailer, or a combination consisting of a motor vehicle and an attached trailer;

Tray (Class 1) means a sheet of metal, plastics, fibreboard or other suitable material which is placed in the inner, intermediate or outer packaging and achieves a close-fit in such packaging. The surface of the tray may be shaped so that packagings or articles can be inserted, held secure and separated from each other;

Tube means a transportable pressure receptacle of seamless or composite construction having a water capacity exceeding 150 litres and of not more than 3,000 litres;

Types of protection

Electrical equipment (see IEC 60079-0:2014 or at least equivalent);

  EEx (d): flameproof enclosure (IEC 60079-1:2014 or at least equivalent);

  EEx (e): increased safety (IEC 60079-7:2016 or at least equivalent);

  EEx (ia) and EEx (ib): intrinsic safety (IEC 60079-11:2012 or at least equivalent);

  EEx (m): encapsulation (IEC 60079-18:2014 or at least equivalent);

  EEx (p): pressurized apparatus (IEC 60079-2:2015 or at least equivalent);

  EEx (q): powder filling (IEC 60079-5:2015 or at least equivalent);

---

[3]   *Official Journal of the European Union No. L 96 of 29 March 2014, p. 309.*
[4]   *http://iecex.com/rules.*
[5]   *A Common Regulatory Framework for Equipment Used in Environments with an Explosive Atmosphere, United Nations, 2011.*

Non-electrical equipment (see ISO 80079-36:2016 or at least equivalent);

EEx (fr): flow restricting enclosure (EN 13463-2:2005 or at least equivalent);

EEx (d): flameproof enclosure (EN 13463-3:2005 or at least equivalent);

EEx (c): constructional safety (ISO 80079-37:2016 or at least equivalent);

EEx (b): control of ignition source (EN 13463-6:2005 or at least equivalent);

EEx (k): liquid immersion: (EN 13463-8:2003 or at least equivalent);

Type of vessel

Type G: means a tank vessel intended for the carriage of pressurized or refrigerated gases.

Type C: means a tank vessel intended for the carriage of liquids. The vessel shall be of the flush-deck/double-hull type with double-hull spaces, double bottoms, but without trunk. The cargo tanks may be formed by the vessel's inner hull or may be installed in the hold spaces as independent tanks.

Type N: means a tank vessel intended for the carriage of liquids.

Closed Type N: a tank vessel intended for the carriage of liquids in closed cargo tanks.

Open type N: a tank vessel intended for the carriage of liquids in open cargo tanks.

Open Type N: with flame arrester :a tank vessel intended for the carriage of liquids in open cargo tanks whose openings to the atmosphere are equipped with a flame arrester capable of withstanding steady burning.

Sketches (as example)

Type G:

Type G   Cargo tank design 1,
          Type of cargo tank 1
          (also by flush-deck)

Type G   Cargo tank design 1,
          Type of cargo tank 1
          (also by flush-deck)

Type G   Cargo tank design 2,
          Type of cargo tank 1
          (also by flush-deck)

Type G   Cargo tanks design 2,
          Type of cargo tank 4

Type C:

Type C   Cargo tank design 2,
             Type of cargo tank 2

Type C   Cargo tank design 1,
             Type of cargo tank 1

Type C   Cargo tank design 2
             Type of cargo tank 1

Type N:

Type N Cargo tank design 2, 3 or 4
             Type of cargo tank 2

Type N Cargo tank design 2, 3 or 4
             Type of cargo tank 2

Type N Cargo tank design 2, 3 or 4
             Type of cargo tanks 1
             (also by flush-deck)

Type N Cargo tank design 2, 3 or 4
             Type of cargo tank 3
             (also by flush-deck)

Type N Cargo tank design 2, 3 or 4
             Type of cargo tank 1
             (also by flush-deck)

U

UEL: see *Upper explosion limit;*

UIC means the International Union of Railways (UIC, 16 rue Jean Rey, F-75015 Paris, France);

Ullage opening means a closable opening of the residual cargo tanks with a diameter of maximum 0.10 m. The ullage opening shall be designed in such a way that it is possible to determine the degree of filling by the use of gauging rods;

Undertaking, see *Enterprise*;

UNECE means the United Nations Economic Commission for Europe (UNECE, Palais des Nations, 8-14 avenue de la Paix, CH-1211 Geneva 10, Switzerland);

Unloader means any enterprise which:

(a)   Removes a container, bulk-container, MEGC, tank-container or portable tank from a conveyance; or

(b)   Unloads packaged dangerous goods, small containers or portable tanks out of or from a conveyance or a container; or

(c)   Discharges dangerous goods from a cargo tank, tank-vehicle, demountable tank, portable tank or tank-container; or from a battery-wagon, battery-vehicle, MEMU or MEGC; or from a conveyance for carriage in bulk, a large container or small container for carriage in bulk or a bulk container;

(d)   Removes a vehicle or a wagon from a vessel;

Unloading means all actions carried out by the unloader, in accordance with the definition of unloader;

UN Model Regulations means the Model Regulations annexed to the twenty-first revised edition of the Recommendations on the Transport of Dangerous Goods published by the United Nations (ST/SG/AC.10/1/Rev.21);

UN number means the four-figure identification number of the substance or article taken from the United Nations Model Regulations;

UN Regulation means a regulation annexed to the Agreement concerning the adoption of uniform technical prescriptions for wheeled vehicles equipment and parts which can be fitted and or used on wheeled vehicles and the conditions for reciprocal recognition of approvals granted on the basis of these prescriptions (1958 Agreement, as amended);

Upper explosion limit (UEL) means the highest concentration of the explosion range at which an explosion can occur;

V

Vacuum design pressure means the vacuum pressure on the basis of which the cargo tank or the residual cargo tank has been designed and built;

Vacuum-operated waste tank means a fixed or demountable tank primarily used for the carriage of dangerous wastes, with special constructional features and/or equipment to facilitate the filling and discharging of wastes as specified in Chapter 6.10 of ADR. A tank which fully complies with the requirements of Chapter 6.7 or 6.8 of ADR is not considered to be a vacuum-operated waste tank;

Vacuum valve means an automatically activated safety valve the purpose of which is to protect the cargo tank against unacceptable negative internal pressure. When the list of substances on the vessel according to 1.16.1.2.5 contains substances for which explosion protection is required in column (17) of Table C of Chapter 3.2, it shall be deflagration safe against atmospheric explosions of the most critical substance in the list of substances. The deflagration safety shall be tested according to international standard ISO 16852:2016[2] and evidence of compliance with the applicable requirements (e.g., conformity assessment procedure according to Directive 2014/34/EU,[3] the IECEx System,[4] ECE/TRADE/391[5] or at least equivalent) shall be supplied. The deflagration safety may be ensured by an integrated flame arrester plate stack or a flame arrester (protection against deflagrations);

Vapour return piping (on shore) means a pipe of the shore facility which is connected during loading or unloading to the vessel's venting piping;

Vehicle means any vehicle covered by the definition of the term vehicle in the ADR (see *Battery-vehicle, Closed vehicle, Open vehicle, Sheeted vehicle* and *Tank-vehicle)*;

Venting piping (on board) means a pipe of the vessel's installation connecting one or more cargo tanks to the vapour return piping during loading or unloading. This pipe is fitted with safety valves protecting the cargo tank(s) against unacceptable internal overpressure or vacuums;

Vessel means an inland navigation vessel or a seagoing vessel.

Vessel record means a file containing all the important technical information concerning a vessel or a barge such as construction plans and documents about the equipment;

W

Wagon means a rail vehicle without its own means of propulsion that runs on its own wheels on railway tracks and is used for the carriage of goods (see also *battery-wagon, closed wagon, open wagon, sheeted wagon and tank wagon)*;

Wastes means substances, solutions, mixtures or articles for which no direct use is envisaged but which are transported for reprocessing, dumping, elimination by incineration or other methods of disposal;

Water film means a deluge of water for protection against brittle fracture;

Water spray system means an on-board installation that, by means of a uniform distribution of water, is capable of protecting all the vertical external surfaces of the ship's hull fore and aft, all vertical surfaces of superstructures and deckhouses and deck surfaces above the superstructures, engine rooms and spaces in which combustible materials may be stored. The capacity of the water spray system for the area to be protected should be at least 10 l/m^2 per minute. The water spray system shall be designed for full-year use. The spray system should be operable from the wheelhouse and the safe area;

Watertight means a structural component or device so fitted as to prevent any ingress of water;

Weathertight means a structural component or device so fitted that in normal conditions it allows only a negligible quantity of water to penetrate;

---

[2] *Identical to EN ISO 16852:2016*

[3] *Official Journal of the European Union No. L 96 of 29 March 2014, p. 309.*

[4] *http://iecex.com/rules.*

[5] *A Common Regulatory Framework for Equipment Used in Environments with an Explosive Atmosphere, United Nations, 2011.*

Wooden barrel means a packaging made of natural wood, of round cross-section, having convex walls, consisting of staves and heads and fitted with hoops;

Wooden IBC means a rigid or collapsible wooden body, together with an inner liner (but no inner packaging) and appropriate service and structural equipment;

Working pressure means the settled pressure of a compressed gas at a reference temperature of 15 °C in a full pressure receptacle.

NOTE: *For tanks, see Maximum working pressure.*

1.2.2   Units of measurement

1.2.2.1   The following units of measurement[a] are applicable in ADN:

Measurement of	SI Unit[b]	Acceptable alternative unit	Relationship between units
Length	m (metre)	-	-
Area	m^2 (square metre)	-	-
Volume	m^3 (cubic metre)	l [c] (litre)	$1\ l = 10^{-3}$ m^3
Time	s (second)	min. (minute)	1 min. = 60 s
		h (hour)	1 h = 3 600 s
		d (day)	1 d = 86 400 s
Mass	kg (kilogram)	g (gramme)	1g = 10^{-3} kg
		t (ton)	1 t = 10^3 kg
Mass density	kg/m^3	kg/l	1 kg/l = 10^3 kg/m^3
Temperature	K (kelvin)	°C (degree Celsius)	0° C = 273.15 K
Temperature difference	K (kelvin)	°C (degree Celsius)	1° C = 1 K
Force	N (newton)	-	1 N = 1 kg.m/s^2
Pressure	Pa (pascal)		1 Pa = 1 N/m^2
		bar (bar)	1 bar = 10^5 Pa
Stress	N/m^2	N/mm^2	1 N/mm^2 = 1 MPa
Work		kWh (kilowatt hours)	1 kWh = 3.6 MJ
Energy	J (joule)		1 J = 1 N.m = 1 W.s
Quantity of heat		eV (electronvolt)	1 eV = 0.1602 H 10^{-18}J
Power	W (watt)	-	1 W = 1 J/s = 1 N.m/s
Kinematic viscosity	m^2/s	mm^2/s	1 mm^2/s = 10^{-6} m^2/s
Dynamic viscosity	Pa.s	mPa.s	1 mPa.s = 10^{-3} Pa.s
Activity	Bq (becquerel)		
Dose equivalent	Sv (sievert)		

[a] *The following round figures are applicable for the conversion of the units hitherto used into SI Units.*

Force
1 kg	*= 9.807 N*	
1 N	*= 0.102 kg*	

Stress
1 kg/mm^2	*= 9.807 N/mm^2*	
1 N/mm^2	*= 0.102 kg/mm^2*	

Pressure
1 Pa	*= 1 N/m^2*	*= 10^{-5} bar*	*= 1.02 H10^{-5} kg/cm^2*	*= 0.75 H10^{-2} torr*
1 bar	*= 10^5 Pa*	*= 1.02 kg/cm^2*	*= 750 torr*	
1 kg/cm^2	*= 9.807 H10^4 Pa*	*= 0.9807 bar*	*= 736 torr*	
1 torr	*= 1.33 H10^2 Pa*	*= 1.33 H10^{-3} bar*	*= 1.36 H10^{-3} kg/cm^2*	

Energy, Work, Quantity of heat
1 J	*= 1 N.m*	*= 0.278 H10^{-6} kWh*	*= 0.102 kgm*	*= 0.239 H10^{-3} kcal*
1 kWh	*= 3.6 H10^6 J*	*= 367 H10^3 kgm*	*= 860 kcal*	
1 kgm	*= 9.807 J*	*= 2.72 H10^{-6} kWh*	*= 2.34 H10^{-3} kcal*	
1 kcal	*= 4.19 H10^3 J*	*= 1.16 H10^{-3} kWh*	*= 427 kgm*	

Power
1 W	*= 0.102 kgm/s*	*= 0.86 kcal/h*	
1 kgm/s	*= 9.807 W*	*= 8.43 kcal/h*	
1 kcal/h	*= 1.16 W*	*= 0.119 kgm/s*	

Kinematic viscosity
1 m^2/s	*= 10^4 St (Stokes)*	
1 St	*= 10^{-4} m^2/s*	

Dynamic viscosity

$1\ Pa.s$	$=$	$1\ N.s/m^2$	$=$	$10\ P\ (poise)$	$=$	$0.102\ kg.s/m^2$
$1\ P$	$=$	$0.1\ Pa.s$	$=$	$0.1\ N.s/m^2$	$=$	$1.02\ H\,10^{-2}\ kg.s/m^2$
$1\ kg.s/m^2$	$=$	$9.807\ Pa.s$	$=$	$9.807\ N.s/m^2$	$=$	$98.07\ P$

[b] *The International System of Units (SI) is the result of decisions taken at the General Conference on Weights and Measures (Address: Pavillon de Breteuil, Parc de St-Cloud, F-92 310 Sèvres).*

[c] *The abbreviation "L" for litre may also be used in place of the abbreviation "l" when a typewriter cannot distinguish between figure "1" and letter "l".*

The decimal multiples and sub-multiples of a unit may be formed by prefixes or symbols, having the following meanings, placed before the name or symbol of the unit:

Factor		Prefix	Symbol
1 000 000 000 000 000 000	$= 10^{18}$	quintillion	exa	E
1 000 000 000 000 000	$= 10^{15}$	quadrillion	peta	P
1 000 000 000 000	$= 10^{12}$	trillion	tera	T
1 000 000 000	$= 10^{9}$	billion	giga	G
1 000 000	$= 10^{6}$	million	mega	M
1 000	$= 10^{3}$	thousand	kilo	k
100	$= 10^{2}$	hundred	hecto	h
10	$= 10^{1}$	ten	deca	da
0.1	$= 10^{-1}$	tenth	deci	d
0.01	$= 10^{-2}$	hundredth	centi	c
0.001	$= 10^{-3}$	thousandth	milli	m
0.000 001	$= 10^{-6}$	millionth	micro	μ
0.000 000 001	$= 10^{-9}$	billionth	nano	n
0.000 000 000 001	$= 10^{-12}$	trillionth	pico	p
0.000 000 000 000 001	$= 10^{-15}$	quadrillionth	femto	f
0.000 000 000 000 000 001	$= 10^{-18}$	quintillionth	atto	a

NOTE: $10^{9} = 1$ *billion is United Nations usage in English. By analogy, so is* $10^{-9} = 1$ *billionth.*

1.2.2.2   Unless expressly stated otherwise, the sign "%" in ADN represents:

(a)   In the case of mixtures of solids or of liquids, and also in the case of solutions and of solids wetted by a liquid, a percentage mass based on the total mass of the mixture, the solution or the wetted solid;

(b)   In the case of mixtures of compressed gases, when filled by pressure, the proportion of the volume indicated as a percentage of the total volume of the gaseous mixture, or, when filled by mass, the proportion of the mass indicated as a percentage of the total mass of the mixture;

(c)   In the case of mixtures of liquefied gases and dissolved gases, the proportion of the mass indicated as a percentage of the total mass of the mixture.

1.2.2.3   Pressures of all kinds relating to receptacles (such as test pressure, internal pressure, safety valve opening pressure) are always indicated in gauge pressure (pressure in excess of atmospheric pressure); however, the vapour pressure of substances is always expressed in absolute pressure.

1.2.2.4   Where ADN specifies a degree of filling for receptacles, this is always related to a reference temperature of the substances of 15 °C, unless some other temperature is indicated.

CHAPTER 1.3

TRAINING OF PERSONS INVOLVED IN THE CARRIAGE
OF DANGEROUS GOODS

1.3.1 **Scope and applicability**

Persons employed by the participants referred to in Chapter 1.4, whose duties concern the carriage of dangerous goods, shall be trained in the requirements governing the carriage of such goods appropriate to their responsibilities and duties. Employees shall be trained in accordance with 1.3.2 before assuming responsibilities and shall only perform functions, for which required training has not yet been provided, under the direct supervision of a trained person. Training requirements specific to security of dangerous goods in Chapter 1.10 shall also be addressed.

NOTE 1: With regard to the training for the safety adviser, see 1.8.3 instead of this section.

NOTE 2: With regard to expert training, see Chapter 8.2 instead of this section.

NOTE 3: For training with regard to Class 7, see also 1.7.2.5.

1.3.2 **Nature of the training**

The training shall take the following form, appropriate to the responsibility and duties of the individual concerned.

1.3.2.1 *General awareness training*

Personnel shall be familiar with the general requirements of the provisions for the carriage of dangerous goods.

1.3.2.2 *Function-specific training*

1.3.2.2.1 Personnel shall be trained, commensurate directly with their duties and responsibilities in the requirements of the regulations concerning the carriage of dangerous goods. Where the carriage of dangerous goods involves a multimodal transport operation, the personnel shall be aware of the requirements concerning other transport modes.

1.3.2.2.2 The crew shall be familiarized with the handling of fire-extinguishing systems and fire-extinguishers.

1.3.2.2.3 The crew shall be familiarized with the handling of the special equipment referred to in 8.1.5.

1.3.2.2.4 Persons wearing self-contained breathing apparatus shall be physically able to bear the additional constraints.

They shall:

– in the case of devices operating with pressurized air, be trained in their handling and maintenance;

– in the case of devices supplied with pressurized air through a hose, be instructed in their handling and maintenance. The instruction shall be supplemented by practical exercises.

1.3.2.2.5 The master shall bring the instructions in writing referred to in 5.4.3 to the attention of the other persons on board to ensure that they are capable of applying them.

1.3.2.3   *Safety training*

Commensurate with the degree of risk of injury or exposure arising from an incident involving the carriage of dangerous goods, including loading and unloading, personnel shall be trained in the hazards and dangers presented by dangerous goods.

The training provided shall aim to make personnel aware of the safe handling and emergency response procedures.

1.3.2.4   The training shall be periodically supplemented with refresher training to take account of changes in regulations.

1.3.2.5   *Working instructions concerning explosion protection*

The safety training referred to in 1.3.2.3 shall be supplemented by working instructions concerning explosion protection.

1.3.3   **Documentation**

Records of training received according to this Chapter shall be kept by the employer and made available to the employee or competent authority, upon request. Records shall be kept by the employer for a period of time established by the competent authority. Records of training shall be verified upon commencing a new employment.

CHAPTER 1.4

SAFETY OBLIGATIONS OF THE PARTICIPANTS

1.4.1   **General safety measures**

1.4.1.1   The participants in the carriage of dangerous goods shall take appropriate measures according to the nature and the extent of foreseeable dangers, so as to avoid damage or injury and, if necessary, to minimize their effects. They shall, in all events, comply with the requirements of ADN in their respective fields.

1.4.1.2   When there is an immediate risk that public safety may be jeopardized, the participants shall immediately notify the emergency services and shall make available to them the information they require to take action.

1.4.1.3   ADN may specify certain of the obligations falling to the various participants.

If a Contracting Party considers that no lessening of safety is involved, it may in its domestic legislation transfer the obligations falling to a specific participant to one or several other participants, provided that the obligations of 1.4.2 and 1.4.3 are met. These derogations shall be communicated by the Contracting Party to the secretariat of the United Nations Economic Commission for Europe which will bring them to the attention of the Contracting Parties.

The requirements of 1.2.1, 1.4.2 and 1.4.3 concerning the definitions of participants and their respective obligations shall not affect the provisions of domestic law concerning the legal consequences (criminal nature, liability, etc.) stemming from the fact that the participant in question is e.g. a legal entity, a self-employed worker, an employer or an employee.

1.4.2   **Obligations of the main participants**

NOTE 1: Several participants to which safety obligations are assigned in this section may be one and the same enterprise. Also, the activities and the corresponding safety obligations of a participant can be assumed by several enterprises.

NOTE 2: For radioactive material see also 1.7.6.

1.4.2.1   *Consignor*

1.4.2.1.1   The consignor of dangerous goods is required to hand over for carriage only consignments which conform to the requirements of ADN. In the context of 1.4.1, he shall in particular:

(a)   ascertain that the dangerous goods are classified and authorized for carriage in accordance with ADN;

(b)   furnish the carrier with information and data in a traceable form and, if necessary, the required transport documents and accompanying documents (authorizations, approvals, notifications, certificates, etc.), taking into account in particular the requirements of Chapter 5.4 and of the tables in Part 3;

(c)   use only packagings, large packagings, intermediate bulk containers (IBCs) and tanks (tank-vehicles, demountable tanks, battery-vehicles, MEGCs, portable tanks, tank-containers, tank wagons and battery wagons) approved for and suited to the carriage of the substances concerned and bearing the marks prescribed by one of the international Regulations, and use only approved vessels or tank-vessels suitable for the carriage of the goods in question;

(d)   comply with the requirements on the means of dispatch and on forwarding restrictions;

(e)   ensure that even empty uncleaned and non-degassed tanks (tank-vehicles, demountable tanks, battery-vehicles, MEGCs, portable tanks, tank-containers, tank wagons and tank vehicles) or empty uncleaned vehicles and bulk containers are placarded, marked and labelled in accordance with Chapter 5.3 and that empty uncleaned tanks are closed and present the same degree of leakproofness as if they were full.

1.4.2.1.2   If the consignor uses the services of other participants (packer, loader, filler, etc.), he shall take appropriate measures to ensure that the consignment meets the requirements of ADN. He may, however, in the case of 1.4.2.1.1 (a), (b), (c) and (e), rely on the information and data made available to him by other participants.

1.4.2.1.3   When the consignor acts on behalf of a third party, the latter shall inform the consignor in writing that dangerous goods are involved and make available to him all the information and documents he needs to perform his obligations.

1.4.2.2   *Carrier*

1.4.2.2.1   In the context of 1.4.1, where appropriate, the carrier shall in particular:

(a)   ascertain that the dangerous goods to be carried are authorized for carriage in accordance with ADN;

(b)   ascertain that all information prescribed in ADN related to the dangerous goods to be carried has been provided by the consignor before carriage, that the prescribed documentation is on board the vessel or if electronic data processing (EDP) or electronic data interchange (EDI) techniques are used instead of paper documentation, that data is available during transport in a manner at least equivalent to that of paper documentation;

(c)   ascertain visually that the vessels and loads have no obvious defects, leakages or cracks, missing equipment, etc.;

(d)   ascertain that a second means of evacuation in the event of an emergency from the vessel side is available, when the landside installation is not equipped with a second necessary means of evacuation;

NOTE: Before loading and unloading, the carrier shall consult the administration of the landside installation on the availability of means of evacuation.

(e)   verify that the vessels are not overloaded;

(f)   ensure that, within the explosion hazardous areas on board the vessel, only electrical and non-electrical installations and equipment that meet the requirements for use in the relevant zone are used;

(g)   provide the master with the required instructions in writing and ascertain that the prescribed equipment is on board the vessel;

(h)   ascertain that the marking requirements for the vessel have been met;

(i)   ascertain that during loading, carriage, unloading and any other handling of the dangerous goods in the holds or cargo tanks, special requirements are complied with;

(j)   ascertain that the vessel substance list in accordance with 1.16.1.2.5 complies with Table C of chapter 3.2 including the modifications made to it;

(k)   complete his section of the checklist referred to in 7.2.3.7.2.2 prior to the degassing of empty or unloaded cargo tanks and piping for loading and unloading of a tank vessel to a reception facility;

(l)   complete his section of the checklist referred to in 7.2.4.10 prior to the loading and unloading of the cargo tanks of a tank vessel.

Where appropriate, this shall be done on the basis of the transport documents and accompanying documents, by a visual inspection of the vessel or the containers and, where appropriate, the load.

1.4.2.2.2   The carrier may, however, in the case of 1.4.2.2.1 (a) and (b), rely on information and data made available to him by other participants. In the case of 1.4.2.2.1 (c) he may rely on what is certified in the "container/vehicle packing certificate" provided in accordance with 5.4.2.

1.4.2.2.3   If the carrier observes an infringement of the requirements of ADN, in accordance with 1.4.2.2.1, he shall not forward the consignment until the matter has been rectified.

1.4.2.2.4   *(Reserved)*

1.4.2.2.5   *(Reserved)*

1.4.2.3   *Consignee*

1.4.2.3.1   The consignee has the obligation not to defer acceptance of the goods without compelling reasons and to verify, before, during or after unloading, that the requirements of ADN concerning him have been complied with.

In the context of 1.4.1, he shall in particular:

(a)   *(Deleted)*

(b)   carry out in the cases provided for by ADN the prescribed cleaning and decontamination of the vessels;

(c) to (h)   *(Deleted)*

1.4.2.3.2 and 1.4.2.3.3   *(Deleted)*

1.4.3   Obligations of the other participants

A non-exhaustive list of the other participants and their respective obligations is given below. The obligations of the other participants flow from section 1.4.1 above insofar as they know or should have known that their duties are performed as part of a transport operation subject to ADN.

1.4.3.1   *Loader*

1.4.3.1.1   In the context of 1.4.1, the loader has the following obligations in particular:

(a)   He shall hand the dangerous goods over to the carrier only if they are authorized for carriage in accordance with ADN;

(b)   He shall, when handing over for carriage packed dangerous goods or uncleaned empty packagings, check whether the packaging is damaged. He shall not hand over a package the packaging of which is damaged, especially if it is not leakproof, and there are leakages or the possibility of leakages of the dangerous substance, until the damage has been repaired; this obligation also applies to empty uncleaned packagings;

(c)   He shall comply with the special requirements concerning loading and handling;

(d)   He shall, after loading dangerous goods into a container comply with the requirements concerning placarding, marking and orange-coloured plates conforming to Chapter 5.3;

(e)   He shall, when loading packages, comply with the prohibitions on mixed loading taking into account dangerous goods already in the vessel, vehicle, wagon or large container and requirements concerning the separation of foodstuffs, other articles of consumption or animal feedstuffs;

(f)   He shall ascertain that the landside installation is equipped with one or two means of evacuation from the vessel in the event of an emergency;

(g)   *(Reserved)*

1.4.3.1.2   The loader may, however, in the case of 1.4.3.1.1 (a), (d) and (e), rely on information and data made available to him by other participants.

1.4.3.2   *Packer*

In the context of 1.4.1, the packer shall comply with in particular:

(a)   the requirements concerning packing conditions, or mixed packing conditions; and

(b)   when he prepares packages for carriage, the requirements concerning marking and labelling of the packages.

1.4.3.3   *Filler*

In the context of 1.4.1, the filler has the following obligations in particular:

Obligations concerning the filling of tanks (tank-vehicles, battery-vehicles, demountable tanks, portable tanks, tank-containers, MEGCs, tank wagons and battery wagons):

(a)   He shall ascertain prior to the filling of tanks that both they and their equipment are technically in a satisfactory condition;

(b)   He shall ascertain that the date of the next inspection for tanks has not expired;

(c)   He shall only fill tanks with the dangerous goods authorized for carriage in those tanks;

(d)   He shall, in filling the tank, comply with the requirements concerning dangerous goods in adjoining compartments;

(e)   He shall, during the filling of the tank, observe the permissible degree of filling or the permissible mass of contents per litre of capacity for the substance being filled;

(f)   He shall, after filling the tank, ensure that all closures are in a closed position and that there is no leakage;

(g)   He shall ensure that no dangerous residue of the filling substance adheres to the outside of the tanks filled by him;

(h)   He shall, in preparing the dangerous goods for carriage, ensure that the placards, marks, orange-coloured plates and labels are affixed in accordance with Chapter 5.3.

Obligations concerning the bulk loading of dangerous solids in vehicles, wagons or containers:

(i)   He shall ascertain, prior to loading, that the vehicles, wagons and containers, and if necessary their equipment, are technically in a satisfactory condition and that the carriage in bulk of the dangerous goods in question is authorized in these vehicles, wagons or containers;

(j)   He shall ensure after loading that the orange plates and placards or labels prescribed are affixed in accordance with the requirements of Chapter 5.3 applicable to such vehicles, wagons or containers;

(k)   He shall, when filling vehicles, wagons or containers with dangerous goods in bulk, ascertain that the relevant provisions of Chapter 7.3 of RID or ADR are complied with.

Obligations concerning the filling of cargo tanks:

(l)   (*Reserved*)

(m)   He shall complete his section of the checklist referred to in 7.2.4.10 prior to the loading of the cargo tanks of a tank vessel;

(n)   He shall only fill cargo tanks with the dangerous goods accepted in such tanks;

(o)   He shall, when necessary, issue a heating instruction in the case of the carriage of substances whose melting point is 0 °C or higher;

(p)   He shall ascertain that during loading the trigger for the automatic device for the prevention of overfilling switches off the electric line established and supplied by the on-shore installation and that he can take steps against overfilling;

(q)   He shall ascertain that the landside installation is equipped with one or two means of evacuation from the vessel in the event of an emergency;

(r)   He shall ascertain that, when prescribed in 7.2.4.25.5 and when explosion protection is necessary according to column (17) of Table C of Chapter 3.2, there is a flame-arrester in the vapour return piping to protect the vessel against detonations and flame-fronts from the landward side;

(s)   He shall ascertain that the loading flows conform to the loading and unloading instructions referred to in 9.3.2.25.9 or 9.3.3.25.9 and that the pressure at the connecting-point of the vapour return piping and the venting piping is not greater than the opening pressure of the pressure relief valve/high velocity vent valve;

(t)   He shall ascertain that the joints provided by him for the connecting flange of the ship/shore connections of the loading and unloading piping consist of a material which is not susceptible to be damaged by the cargo or causes a decomposition of the cargo nor forms harmful or dangerous components with it;

(u)   He shall ascertain that during the entire duration of loading a permanent and appropriate supervision is assured.

Obligations concerning the bulk loading of dangerous solids in vessels:

(v)   When special provision 803 applies, shall guarantee and document, using an appropriate procedure, that the maximum permissible temperature of the cargo is not exceeded and shall provide instructions to the master in a traceable form;

(w)   He shall only load the vessel with dangerous goods the bulk carriage of which is authorized in that vessel;

(x)   He shall ascertain that the landside installation is equipped with one or two means of evacuation from the vessel in the event of an emergency.

1.4.3.4   *Tank-container/portable tank operator*

In the context of 1.4.1, the tank-container/portable tank operator shall in particular:

(a)   ensure compliance with the requirements for construction, equipment, inspections, tests and marking;

(b)   ensure that the maintenance of shells and their equipment is carried out in such a way as to ensure that, under normal operating conditions, the tank-container/portable tank satisfies the requirements of ADR, RID or the IMDG Code until the next inspection;

(c)   have an exceptional check made when the safety of the shell or its equipment is liable to be impaired by a repair, an alteration or an accident.

1.4.3.5 and 1.4.3.6   *(Reserved)*

1.4.3.7   **Unloader**

1.4.3.7.1   In the context of 1.4.1, the unloader shall in particular:

(a)   Ascertain that the correct goods are unloaded by comparing the relevant information on the transport document with the information on the package, container, tank, MEMU, MEGC or conveyance;

(b)   Before and during unloading, check whether the packagings, the tank, the conveyance or container have been damaged to an extent which would endanger the unloading operation. If this is the case, ascertain that unloading is not carried out until appropriate measures have been taken;

(c)   Comply with all relevant requirements concerning unloading and handling;

(d)   Immediately following the unloading of the tank, conveyance or container:

(i)   Ensure the removal of any dangerous residues which have adhered to the outside of the tank, conveyance or container during the process of unloading; and

(ii)   By unloading of packages, ensure the closure of valves and inspection openings;

(e)   Ensure that the prescribed cleaning and decontamination of the conveyances or containers is carried out;

(f)   Ensure that the containers, vehicles and wagons, once completely unloaded, cleaned and decontaminated, no longer display the placards, marks and orange-coloured plates that had been displayed in accordance with Chapter 5.3;

(g)   Ascertain that the landside installation is equipped with one or two means of evacuation from the vessel in the event of an emergency;

Additional obligations concerning the unloading of cargo tanks:

(h)   Complete his section of the checklist referred to in 7.2.4.10 prior to the unloading of the cargo tanks of a tank vessel;

(i)   Ascertain that, when a connection to the venting piping is required and when explosion protection is required according to column (17) of Table C of Chapter 3.2, there is a flame arrester in the vapour return pipe to protect the vessel against detonations and flame-fronts from the landward side;

(j)   Ascertain that the unloading flows conform to the instructions on loading and unloading flows referred to in 9.3.2.25.9 or 9.3.3.25.9 and that the pressure at the connecting-point of the vapour return piping and the venting piping or the gas return pipe does not exceed the opening pressure of the pressure relief valve/high velocity vent valve;

(k)   Ascertain that the gaskets provided by him for the connecting flange of the ship/shore connections of the loading and unloading piping consist of a material which will not be damaged by the cargo nor causes a decomposition of the cargo nor forms harmful or dangerous components with it;

(l)   Ascertain that during the entire duration of unloading a permanent and appropriate supervision is assured;

(m)   Ascertain that, during unloading by means of the on-board pump, it is possible for the shore facility to switch it off;

1.4.3.7.2   If the unloader makes use of the services of other participants (cleaner, decontamination facility, etc.) or of the pumps of the vessel he shall take appropriate measures to ensure that the requirements of ADN have been complied with.

1.4.3.8   *Reception facility operator*

1.4.3.8.1   In the context of 1.4.1, the reception facility operator shall in particular:

(a)   Complete his section of the checklist referred to in 7.2.3.7.2.2 prior to the degassing of empty or unloaded cargo tanks and piping for loading and unloading of a tank vessel;

(b)   Ascertain that, when prescribed in 7.2.3.7.2.3, there is a flame arrester in the piping of the reception facility which is connected to the degassing vessel, to protect the vessel against detonations and passage of flames from the side of the reception facility.

CHAPTER 1.5

SPECIAL RULES, DEROGATIONS

1.5.1 **Bilateral and multilateral agreements**

1.5.1.1   In accordance with Article 7, paragraph 1 of ADN, the competent authorities of the Contracting Parties may agree directly among themselves to authorize certain transport operations in their territories by temporary derogation from the requirements of ADN, provided that safety is not compromised thereby. The authority which has taken the initiative with respect to the temporary derogation shall notify such derogations to the Secretariat of the United Nations Economic Commission for Europe which shall bring them to the attention of the Contracting Parties.

NOTE: "Special arrangement" in accordance with 1.7.4 is not considered to be a temporary derogation in accordance with this section.

1.5.1.2   The period of validity of the temporary derogation shall not be more than five years from the date of its entry into force. The temporary derogation shall automatically cease as from the date of the entry into force of a relevant amendment to these annexed Regulations.

1.5.1.3   Transport operations on the basis of these agreements shall constitute transport operations in the sense of ADN.

1.5.2 **Special authorizations concerning transport in tank vessels**

1.5.2.1 *Special authorizations*

1.5.2.1.1   In accordance with paragraph 2 of Article 7 of ADN, the competent authority shall have the right to issue special authorizations to a carrier or a consignor for the international carriage in tank vessels of dangerous substances, including mixtures, the carriage of which in tank vessels is not authorized under these Regulations, in accordance with the procedure set out below.

1.5.2.1.2   The special authorization shall be valid, due account being taken of the restrictions specified therein, for the Contracting Parties and on whose territory the transport operation will take place, for not more than two years unless it is repealed at an earlier date. With the approval of the competent authorities of these Contracting Parties, the special authorization may be renewed for a period of not more than one year.

1.5.2.1.3   The special authorization shall include a statement concerning its repeal at an earlier date and shall conform to the model contained in subsection 3.2.4.1.

1.5.2.2 *Procedure*

1.5.2.2.1   The carrier or the consignor shall apply to the competent authority of a Contracting Party on whose territory the transport operation takes place for the issue of a special authorization.

The application shall conform to the model contained in subsection 3.2.4.2. The applicant shall be responsible for the accuracy of the particulars.

1.5.2.2.2   The competent authority shall consider the application from the technical and safety point of view. If it has no reservations, it shall draw up a special authorization in accordance with the criteria contained in subsection 3.2.4.3 and immediately inform the other competent authorities involved in the carriage in question. The special authorization shall be issued only when the authorities concerned agree to it or have not expressed opposition within a period of two months after receiving the information. The applicant shall receive the original of the special authorization and keep a copy of it on board the vessel(s) involved in the carriage in question. The competent authorities shall immediately communicate to the Administrative Committee the applications for special authorizations, the applications rejected and the special authorizations granted.

1.5.2.2.3   If the special authorization is not issued because doubts or opposition have been expressed, the Administrative Committee shall decide whether or not to issue a special authorization.

1.5.2.3   *Update of the list of substances authorized for carriage in tank vessels*

1.5.2.3.1   The Administrative Committee shall consider all the special authorizations and applications communicated to it and decide whether the substance is to be included in the list of substances in these Regulations, authorized for carriage in tank vessels.

1.5.2.3.2   If the Administrative Committee enters technical or safety reservations concerning the inclusion of the substance in the list of substances of these Regulations authorized for carriage in tank vessels or concerning certain conditions, the competent authority shall be so informed. The competent authority shall immediately withdraw or, if necessary, modify the special authorization.

1.5.3   Equivalents and derogations (Article 7, paragraph 3 of ADN)

1.5.3.1   *Procedure for equivalents*

When the provisions of these Regulations prescribe for a vessel the use or the presence on board of certain materials, installations or equipment or the adoption of certain construction measures or certain fixtures, the competent authority may agree to the use or the presence on board of other materials, installations or equipment or the adoption of other construction measures or other fixtures for this vessel if, in line with recommendations established by the Administrative Committee, they are accepted as equivalent.

1.5.3.2   *Derogations on a trial basis*

The competent authority may, on the basis of a recommendation by the Administrative Committee, issue a trial certificate of approval for a limited period for a specific vessel having new technical characteristics departing from the requirements of these Regulations, provided that these characteristics are sufficiently safe.

1.5.3.3   *Particulars of equivalents and derogations*

The equivalents and derogations referred to in 1.5.3.1 and 1.5.3.2 shall be entered in the certificate of approval.

CHAPTER 1.6

TRANSITIONAL MEASURES

1.6.1   **General**

1.6.1.1   Unless otherwise provided, the substances and articles of ADN may be carried until 30 June 2021 in accordance with the requirements of ADN applicable up to 31 December 2020.

1.6.1.2   *(Deleted)*

1.6.1.3   The transitional measures of 1.6.1.3 and 1.6.1.4 of ADR and RID, or falling within the scope of 4.1.5.19 of the IMDG Code, concerning the packaging of substances and articles of Class 1, are also valid for carriage subject to ADN.

1.6.1.4   *(Deleted)*

1.6.1.5 to 1.6.1.7   *(Reserved)*

1.6.1.8   Existing orange-coloured plates which meet the requirements of sub-section 5.3.2.2 applicable up to 31 December 2004 may continue to be used provided that the requirements in 5.3.2.2.1 and 5.3.2.2.2 that the plate, numbers and letters shall remain affixed irrespective of the orientation of the vehicle or wagon are met.

1.6.1.9   *(Reserved)*

1.6.1.10   *(Deleted)*

1.6.1.11 and 1.6.1.12   *(Reserved)*

1.6.1.13   *(Deleted)*

1.6.1.14   IBCs manufactured before 1 January 2011 and conforming to a design type which has not passed the vibration test of 6.5.6.13 of ADR or which was not required to meet the criteria of 6.5.6.9.5 (d) of ADR at the time it was subjected to the drop test, may still be used.

1.6.1.15   IBCs manufactured, remanufactured or repaired before 1 January 2011 need not be marked with the maximum permitted stacking load in accordance with 6.5.2.2.2 of ADR. Such IBCs, not marked in accordance with 6.5.2.2.2 of ADR, may still be used after 31 December 2010 but must be marked in accordance with 6.5.2.2.2 of ADR if they are remanufactured or repaired after that date. IBCs manufactured, remanufactured or repaired between 1 January 2011 and 31 December 2016 and marked with the maximum permitted stacking load in accordance with 6.5.2.2.2 of ADR in force up to 31 December 2014 may continue to be used.

1.6.1.16 to 1.6.1.20   *(Deleted)*

1.6.1.21 to 1.6.1.23   *(Reserved)*

1.6.1.24 and 1.6.1.25   *(Deleted)*

1.6.1.26   Large packagings manufactured or remanufactured before 1 January 2014 and which do not conform to the requirements of 6.6.3.1 of ADR regarding the height of letters, numerals and symbols applicable as from 1 January 2013 may continue to be used. Those manufactured or remanufactured before 1 January 2015 need not be marked with the maximum permitted stacking load in accordance with 6.6.3.3 of ADR. Such large packagings not marked in accordance with 6.6.3.3 of ADR may still be used after 31 December 2014 but must be marked in accordance with 6.6.3.3 of ADR if they are remanufactured after that date. Large packagings manufactured or remanufactured between 1 January 2011 and 31 December 2016 and marked with the maximum permitted stacking load in accordance with 6.6.3.3 of ADR in force up to 31 December 2014 may continue to be used.

1.6.1.27   Means of containment integral to equipment or machinery containing liquid fuels of UN Nos. 1202, 1203, 1223, 1268, 1863 and 3475 constructed before 1 July 2013, which do not conform to the requirements of paragraph (a) of special provision 363 of Chapter 3.3 applicable as from 1 January 2013, may still be used.

1.6.1.28   *(Deleted)*

1.6.1.29   Lithium cells and batteries manufactured according to a type meeting the requirements of sub-section 38.3 of the Manual of Tests and Criteria, Revision 3, Amendment 1 or any subsequent revision and amendment applicable at the date of the type testing may continue to be carried, unless otherwise provided in ADN.

Lithium cells and batteries manufactured before 1 July 2003 meeting the requirements of the Manual of Tests and Criteria, Revision 3, may continue to be carried if all other applicable requirements are fulfilled.

1.6.1.30 to 1.6.1.32   *(Deleted)*

1.6.1.33   Electric double layer capacitors of UN No. 3499, manufactured before 1 January 2014, need not be marked with the energy storage capacity in Wh as required by sub-paragraph (e) of special provision 361 of Chapter 3.3.

1.6.1.34   Asymmetric capacitors of UN No. 3508, manufactured before 1 January 2016, need not be marked with the energy storage capacity in Wh as required by sub-paragraph (c) of special provision 372 of Chapter 3.3.

1.6.1.35 to 1.6.1.37   *(Reserved)*

1.6.1.38   Contracting Parties may continue to issue training certificates for dangerous goods safety advisers conforming to the model applicable until 31 December 2016, instead of those conforming to the requirements of 1.8.3.18 applicable from 1 January 2017, until 31 December 2018. Such certificates may continue in use to the end of their five year validity.

1.6.1.39 and 1.6.1.40   *(Deleted)*

1.6.1.41   Notwithstanding the requirements of ADN applicable as from 1 January 2017, large packagings conforming to the packing group III performance level in accordance with special packing provision L2 of packing instruction LP02 of 4.1.4.3 of ADR applicable until 31 December 2016 may continue to be used until 31 December 2022 for UN No. 1950.

1.6.1.42   (Deleted)

1.6.1.43   Vehicles registered or brought into service before 1 July 2017, as defined in special provisions 388 and 669 of Chapter 3.3, and their equipment intended for use during carriage, which conform to the requirements of ADN applicable until 31 December 2016 but containing lithium cells and batteries which do not conform to the provisions of 2.2.9.1.7 may continue to be carried as a load in accordance with the requirements of special provision 666 of Chapter 3.3.

1.6.1.44 Undertakings which participate in the carriage of dangerous goods only as consignors and which did not have to appoint a safety adviser on the basis of the provisions applicable until 31 December 2018 shall, by derogation from the provisions of 1.8.3.1 applicable from 1 January 2019, appoint a safety adviser no later than 31 December 2022.

1.6.1.45 Contracting Parties may, until 31 December 2020, continue to issue training certificates for dangerous goods safety advisers conforming to the model applicable until 31 December 2018, instead of those conforming to the requirements of 1.8.3.18 applicable from 1 January 2019. Such certificates may continue in use to the end of their five-year validity.

1.6.1.46 The carriage of machinery or equipment not specified in this annex and which happen to contain dangerous goods in their internal or operational equipment and which are therefore assigned to UN Nos. 3363, 3537, 3538, 3539, 3540, 3541, 3542, 3543, 3544, 3545, 3546, 3547 or 3548, which was exempted from the provisions of ADN according to 1.1.3.1 (b) applicable until 31 December 2018, may continue to be exempted from the provisions of ADN until 31 December 2022 provided that measures have been taken to prevent any leakage of contents in normal conditions of carriage.

1.6.1.47 *(Deleted)*

1.6.2 Pressure receptacles and receptacles for Class 2

The transitional measures of sections 1.6.2 of ADR and RID are also valid for transport operations subject to ADN.

1.6.3 Fixed tanks (tank-vehicles and tank wagons), demountable tanks, battery vehicles and battery wagons

The transitional measures of sections 1.6.3 of ADR and RID are also valid for transport operations subject to ADN.

1.6.4 Tank-containers, portable tanks and MEGCs

The transitional measures of sections 1.6.4 of ADR and RID or of section 4.2.0 of the IMDG Code, depending on the case, are also valid for transport operations subject to ADN.

1.6.5 Vehicles

The transitional measures of section 1.6.5 of ADR are also valid for transport operations subject to ADN.

1.6.6 Class 7

The transitional measures of sections 1.6.6 of ADR and RID or of section 6.4.24 of the IMDG Code are also valid for transport operations subject to ADN.

1.6.7 Transitional provisions concerning vessels

1.6.7.1 *General*

1.6.7.1.1 For the purposes of Article 8 of ADN, section 1.6.7 sets out general transitional provisions in 1.6.7.2 (see Article 8, paragraphs 1, 2 and 4) and supplementary transitional provisions in 1.6.7.3 (see Article 8, paragraph 3).

1.6.7.1.2   In this section:

(a)   "Vessel in service" means

–   A vessel according to Article 8, paragraph 2, of ADN;

–   A vessel for which a certificate of approval has already been issued according to 8.6.1.1 to 8.6.1.4;

In both cases vessels that, as from 31 December 2014, have been without a valid certificate of approval for more than twelve months shall be excluded;

(b)   "N.R.M." means that the requirement does not apply to vessels in service except where the parts concerned are replaced or modified, i.e. it applies only to vessels which are **n**ew (as from the date indicated), or to parts which are **r**eplaced or **m**odified after the date indicated; the date of presentation for first inspection for obtaining a certificate of approval shall be decisive for nomination as a new vessel; where existing parts are replaced by spare or replacement parts of the same type and manufacture, this shall not be considered a replacement 'R' as defined in these transitional provisions.

Modification shall also be taken to mean the conversion of an existing type of tank vessel, a type of cargo tank or a cargo tank design to another type or design at a higher level.

When in the general transitional provisions in 1.6.7.2 no date is specified after "N.R.M.", it refers to N.R.M. after 26 May 2000. When in the supplementary transitional provisions in 1.6.7.3, no date is specified, it refers to N.R.M. after 26 May 2000.

(c)   "Renewal of the certificate of approval after the ..." means that when a vessel has benefitted from the transitional measure in paragraph (b) the requirement shall be met at the next renewal of the certificate of approval following the date indicated. If the certificate of approval expires during the first year after the date of application of these Regulations, the requirement shall be mandatory only after the expiry of this first year.

(d)   Requirements of Chapter 1.6.7 applicable on board vessels in service are only valid if N.R.M. is not applicable.

1.6.7.2   *General transitional provisions*

1.6.7.2.1   *General transitional provisions for dry cargo vessels*

1.6.7.2.1.1   Vessels in service shall meet:

(a)   the requirements of paragraphs mentioned in the table below within the period established therein;

(b)   the requirements of paragraphs not mentioned in the table below at the date of application of these Regulations.

The construction and equipment of vessels in service shall be maintained at least at the previous standard of safety.

1.6.7.2.1.1 Table of general transitional provisions: Dry cargo

Paragraphs	Subject	Time limit and comments
7.1.2.19.1	Vessels necessary to provide propulsion Adaptation to the new requirements in 9.1.0.12.4, 9.1.0.40.2, 9.1.0.51 and 9.1.0.52	N.R.M. from 1 January 2019 Renewal of the certificate of approval after 31 December 2034 Until that date, the following requirements apply to vessels in service: In a pushed convoy or a side-by-side formation, where at least one vessel is required to be in possession of a certificate of approval for the carriage of dangerous goods, all vessels of the convoy or side-by-side formation shall be provided with an appropriate certificate of approval. Vessels not carrying dangerous goods shall comply with the requirements of the following sections, subsections and paragraphs: 1.16.1.1, 1.16.1.2, 1.16.1.3, 7.1.2.5, 8.1.5, 8.1.6.1, 8.1.6.3, 8.1.7, 9.1.0.0, 9.1.0.12.3, 9.1.0.12.5, 9.1.0.17.2, 9.1.0.17.3, 9.1.0.31, 9.1.0.32, 9.1.0.34, 9.1.0.41, 9.1.0.52.7, 9.1.0.56, 9.1.0.71 and 9.1.0.74.
7.1.3.41	Smoking	N.R.M. From 1 January 2019 Renewal of the certificate of approval after 31 December 2020
7.1.3.51.1	Non-electrical installations and equipment	N.R.M. From 1 January 2019 Renewal of the certificate of approval after 31 December 2024
7.1.3.51.5	Disconnection of installations and equipment marked in red	N.R.M. From 1 January 2019 Renewal of the certificate of approval after 31 December 2034
7.1.3.51.5	Installations and equipment generating surface temperatures of above 200 °C	N.R.M. From 1 January 2019 Renewal of the certificate of approval after 31 December 2034
7.1.4.53	Lighting appliances in explosion hazardous areas of zone 2	N.R.M. From 1 January 2019 Renewal of the certificate of approval after 31 December 2022
8.1.2.2 (e) – (h)	Documents which must be carried on board	N.R.M. From 1 January 2019 Renewal of the certificate of approval after 31 December 2020
8.6.1.1 8.6.1.2	Changes to certificate of approval	N.R.M. from 1 January 2019 Renewal of the certificate of approval after 31 December 2018

1.6.7.2.1.1 Table of general transitional provisions: Dry cargo		
Paragraphs	Subject	Time limit and comments
9.1.0.12.1	Ventilation of holds	N.R.M. Renewal of the certificate of approval after 31 December 2018 Until then, the following requirements apply on board vessels in service: Each hold shall have appropriate natural or artificial ventilation; for the carriage of substances of Class 4.3, each hold shall be equipped with forced-air ventilation; the appliances used for this purpose must be so constructed that water cannot enter the hold.
9.1.0.12.3	Ventilation of accommodation and wheelhouse	N.R.M. From 1 January 2019 Renewal of the certificate of approval after 31 December 2034
9.1.0.12.3	Ventilation of service spaces	N.R.M. Renewal of the certificate of approval after 31 December 2018 .
9.1.0.12.3	Equipment in the accommodation, wheelhouse and service spaces where surface temperatures can be higher than those mentioned under 9.1.0.51 or where electrical installations and equipment which do not meet the requirements of 9.1.0.52.1 are used	N.R.M. From 1 January 2019 Renewal of the certificate of approval after 31 December 2034
9.1.0.12.4	Ventilation inlets	N.R.M. From 1 January 2019 Renewal of the certificate of approval after 31 December 2034
9.1.0.12.5	Ventilators used in the protected area and hold ventilators which are arranged in the air flow: Temperature class and explosion group	N.R.M. From 1 January 2019 Renewal of the certificate of approval after 31 December 2034
9.1.0.17.2	Gas-tight openings facing holds	N.R.M. Renewal of the certificate of approval after 31 December 2018 Until then, the following requirements apply on board vessels in service: Openings of accommodation and the wheelhouse facing the holds must be capable of being tightly closed.

1.6.7.2.1.1 Table of general transitional provisions: Dry cargo		
Paragraphs	Subject	Time limit and comments
9.1.0.17.3	Entrances and openings in the protected area	N.R.M. Renewal of the certificate of approval after 31 December 2018 Until then, the following requirements apply on board vessels in service: Openings of engine rooms and service spaces facing the holds must be capable of being tightly closed.
9.1.0.31.2	Air intakes of engines	N.R.M. Renewal of the certificate of approval after 31 December 2034
9.1.0.32.2	Open ends of the air pipes not less than 0.50 m above the open deck	N.R.M. Renewal of the certificate of approval after 31 December 2018
9.1.0.34.1	Position of exhaust pipes	N.R.M. Renewal of the certificate of approval after 31 December 2018
9.1.0.35	Stripping pumps in the protected area	N.R.M. Renewal of the certificate of approval after 31 December 2018 Until then, the following requirements apply on board vessels in service: In the event of the carriage of substances of Class 4.1, UN No. 3175, of all substances of Class 4.3 in bulk or unpackaged and polymeric beads, expandable, of Class 9, UN No. 2211, the stripping of the holds may only be effected using a stripping installation located in the protected area. The stripping installation located above the engine room must be clamped.
9.1.0.40.1	Fire extinguishers, two pumps, etc.	N.R.M. Renewal of the certificate of approval after 31 December 2018
9.1.0.40.2	Fire extinguishing systems permanently fixed in engine rooms	N.R.M. Renewal of the certificate of approval after 31 December 2034
9.1.0.41 in conjunction with 7.1.3.41	Fire and naked light	N.R.M. Renewal of the certificate of approval after 31 December 2018 Until then, the following requirements apply on board vessels in service: Outlets of funnels shall be located not less than 2 m from the nearest point on hold hatchways. Heating and cooking appliances shall be permitted only in metal-based accommodation and wheelhouses. However: - Heating appliances fuelled with liquid fuels having a flashpoint above 55 °C shall be permitted in engine rooms; - Central-heating boilers fuelled with solid fuels shall be permitted in spaces situated below deck and accessible only from the deck.

1.6.7.2.1.1 Table of general transitional provisions: Dry cargo		
Paragraphs	Subject	Time limit and comments
9.1.0.51	Temperature of outer parts of engines and of their air inlets and exhaust ducts	N.R.M. From 1 January 2019 Renewal of the certificate of approval after 31 December 2034
9.1.0.52.1	Electrical installations, equipment and appliances located outside the protected area	N.R.M. From 1 January 2019 Renewal of the certificate of approval after 31 December 2034 Until that date, the following requirements are applicable on board vessels in service: It shall be possible to isolate the electrical equipment in the protected area by means of centrally located switches except where: - In the holds it is of a certified safe type corresponding at least to temperature class T4 and explosion group II B; and - In the protected area on the deck it is of the limited explosion risk type. The corresponding electrical circuits shall have control lamps to indicate whether or not the circuits are live. The switches shall be protected against unintended unauthorized operation. The sockets used in this area shall be designed so as to prevent connection or disconnection except when they are not live. Submerged pumps installed or used in the holds shall be of the certified safe type at least for temperature class T4 and explosion group II B.
9.1.0.52.1	Electrical installations in operation during a stay in the immediate vicinity of or within an onshore assigned zone	N.R.M. From 1 January 2019 Renewal of the certificate of approval after 31 December 2034
9.1.0.52.2	Installations and equipment marked in red	N.R.M. from 1 January 2019 Renewal of the certificate of approval after 31 December 2034
9.1.0.52.5	Failure of the power supply for the safety and control equipment	N.R.M. from 1 January 2019 Renewal of the certificate of approval after 31 December 2024
9.1.0.53.5	Movable electric cables (sheathed, type H 07 RN-F)	N.R.M. from 1 January 2019 Renewal of the certificate of approval after 31 December 2034 Until that date, the following provisions apply on board vessels in service: Until that date, movable electric cables (sheathed, type H 07 RN-F) must comply with IEC 60245-4:1994
9.1.0.53.6	Non-electrical installations and equipment within the protected area	N.R.M. from 1 January 2019 Renewal of the certificate of approval after 31 December 2034
9.2.0.31.2	Air intakes of engines	N.R.M. Renewal of the certificate of approval after 31 December 2034

1.6.7.2.1.1 Table of general transitional provisions: Dry cargo		
Paragraphs	Subject	Time limit and comments
9.2.0.34.1	Position of exhaust pipes	N.R.M. Renewal of the certificate of approval after 31 December 2018
9.2.0.41 in conjunction with 7.1.3.41	Fire and naked light	N.R.M. Renewal of the certificate of approval after 31 December 2018 Until then, the following requirements apply on board vessels in service: Outlets of funnels shall be located not less than 2 m from the nearest point on hold hatchways. Heating and cooking appliances shall be permitted only in metal-based accommodation and wheelhouses. However: - Heating appliances fuelled with liquid fuels having a flashpoint above 55 °C shall be permitted in engine rooms; - Central-heating boilers fuelled with solid fuels shall be permitted in spaces situated below deck and accessible only from the deck.

1.6.7.2.1.2 and 1.6.7.2.1.3   *(Deleted)*

1.6.7.2.1.4   For a vessel or a barge whose keel was laid before 1 July 2017 and which does not conform to the requirements of 9.x.0.1 concerning the vessel record, the retention of files for the vessel record shall start at the latest at the next renewal of the certificate of approval.

1.6.7.2.2   *General transitional provisions for tank vessels*

1.6.7.2.2.1   Vessels in service shall meet:

(a)   the requirements of paragraphs mentioned in the table below within the period established therein;

(b)   the requirements of paragraphs not mentioned in the table below at the date of application of these Regulations.

The construction and equipment of vessels in service shall be maintained at least at the previous standard of safety.

1.6.7.2.2.2 Table of general transitional provisions: Tank vessels		
Paragraphs	Subject	Time limit and comments
1.2.1	Cargo area Spatial extent above the deck	N.R.M. from 1 January 2019 Renewal of the certificate of approval after 31 December 2034 Until that date, the following requirements are applicable on board vessels in service: The spatial extent corresponds to a rectangular pyramidal frustum with the following dimensions: Floor area: from board to board and from outer cofferdam bulkhead to outer cofferdam bulkhead Angle of slope of the short sides: 45° Angle of slope of the long sides: 90° Height: 3.00 m Spatial extent of zone 1 corresponds to the cargo area above the deck
1.2.1	Classification in zones Zone 1 Spatial extent	N.R.M. from 1 January 2019 Renewal of the certificate of approval after 31 December 2034 Until that date, the following requirements are applicable on board vessels in service: the spatial extent of zone 1 corresponds to a rectangular pyramidal fustrum with the following dimensions: Floor area: from board to board and from outer cofferdam bulkhead to outer cofferdam bulkhead Angle of slope of the short sides: 45° Angle of slope of the long sides: 90° Height: 3.00 m
	Zone 2 Spatial extent:	N.R.M. from 1 January 2019 Renewal of the certificate of approval after 31 December 2034
1.2.1	Device for the safe depressurization of cargo tanks Deflagration safety Test according to ISO 16852:2016/Proof of conformity with applicable requirements	N.R.M. from 1 January 2019 Renewal of the certificate of approval after 31 December 2034 The deflagration safety shall be tested according to EN 12874:2001 including the manufacturer's confirmation under Directive 94/9/EC on board vessels built or modified from 1 January 2001 or if the safe pressure-relief device for the cargo tanks has been replaced since 1 January 2001. In other cases, they shall be of a type approved by the competent authority for the use prescribed.

1.6.7.2.2.2 Table of general transitional provisions: Tank vessels		
Paragraphs	Subject	Time limit and comments
1.2.1	Flame arrester · Test according to ISO 16852:2016 or EN ISO 16852:2016	N.R.M. from 1 January 2019 Renewal of the certificate of approval after 31 December 2034 Until that date, the following requirements are applicable on board vessels in service: Flame arresters shall be: - Tested according to ISO 16852:2010 or EN ISO 16852:2010 if they have been replaced since 1 January 2015 or are on board vessels built or modified since 1 January 2015; - Tested according to EN 12874:2001 if they have been replaced since 1 January 2001 or are on board vessels built or modified since 1 January 2001; - Of a type approved by the competent authority for the use prescribed if they were replaced before 1 January 2001 or are on board vessels built or modified before 1 January 2001.
1.2.1	Flame arrester Proof of conformity with applicable requirement	N.R.M. from 1 January 2019 Renewal of the certificate of approval after 31 December 2034
1.2.1	Gas detection system Test according to IEC 60079-29-1:2016 and EN 50271:2010	N.R.M. from 1 January 2019 Renewal of the certificate of approval after 31 December 2024
1.2.1	Gas detector Test according to IEC 60079-29-1:2016	N.R.M. from 1 January 2019 Renewal of the certificate of approval after 31 December 2020
1.2.1	High velocity vent valve Test according to ISO 16852:2016 or EN ISO 16852:2016/Proof of conformity with applicable requirements	N.R.M. from 1 January 2019 Renewal of the certificate of approval after 31 December 2034 Until that date, the following requirements are applicable on board vessels in service: High velocity vent valves shall be - Tested according to ISO 16852:2010 or EN ISO 16852:2010, including the manufacturer's confirmation in line with Directive 94/9/EC or equivalent, if they have been replaced since 1 January 2015 or are on board vessels built or modified since 1 January 2015. - Tested according to EN 12874:2001, including the manufacturer's confirmation in line with Directive 94/9/EC or equivalent, if they have been replaced since 1 January 2001 or are on board vessels built or modified since 1 January 2001. - Of a type approved by the competent authority for the use prescribed if they were replaced before 1 January 2001 or are on board vessels built or modified before 1 January 2001.

1.6.7.2.2.2 Table of general transitional provisions: Tank vessels		
Paragraphs	Subject	Time limit and comments
1.2.1	Hold spaces	N.R.M. For Type N open vessels whose hold spaces contain auxiliary appliances and which are carrying only substances of Class 8, with remark 30 in column (20) of Table C of Chapter 3.2. Renewal of the certificate of approval after 31 December 2038.
1.2.1	Limited explosion risk electrical apparatus	N.R.M. Renewal of the certificate of approval after 31 December 2034 Until then, the following requirements apply on board vessels in service: Limited explosion risk electrical apparatus is: - Electrical apparatus which, during normal operation, does not cause sparks or exhibit surface temperatures exceeding 200 °C; or - Electrical apparatus with a spray-water protected housing which, during normal operation, does not exhibit surface temperatures above 200 °C.
1.2.1	Oxygen measuring system Test according to EN 50104:2010	N.R.M. from 1 January 2019 Renewal of the certificate of approval after 31 December 2020
1.2.1	Oxygen meter Test according to EN 50104:2010	N.R.M. from 1 January 2019 Renewal of the certificate of approval after 31 December 2020
1.2.1	Sampling opening Deflagration safety Test according to ISO 16852:2016 or EN ISO 16852:2016 /Proof of conformity with applicable requirements	N.R.M. from 1 January 2019 Renewal of the certificate of approval after 31 December 2034 The deflagration safety of the sampling opening shall be: - Tested according to ISO 16852:2010 or EN ISO 16852:2010, including the manufacturer's confirmation under Directive 94/9/EC or equivalent, if the sampling opening has been replaced since 1 January 2015 or is on board a vessel built or modified since 1 January 2015. - Tested according to EN 12874:2001, including the manufacturer's confirmation under Directive 94/9/EC or equivalent, if the sampling opening has been replaced since 1 January 2001 or is on board a vessel built or modified since 1 January 2001. - Of a type approved by the competent authority for the use prescribed if the sampling opening was replaced before 1 January 2001 or is on board a vessel built or modified before 1 January 2001.

1.6.7.2.2.2 Table of general transitional provisions: Tank vessels		
Paragraphs	Subject	Time limit and comments
1.2.1	Vacuum valve	N.R.M. from 1 January 2019
	Deflagration safety	Renewal of certificate of approval after 31 December 2034
	Test according to standard EN ISO 16852:2016	The deflagration safety shall be tested according to EN 12874:2001 including the manufacturer's confirmation under Directive 94/9/EC or equivalent on board vessels built or modified from 1 January 2001 or if the vacuum valve has been replaced since 1 January 2001.
	Proof of conformity with applicable requirements	In other cases, they shall be of a type approved by the competent authority for the use prescribed.
7.2.2.6	Calibration of gas detection system for n-Hexane	N.R.M. from 1 January 2019 Renewal of the certificate of approval after 31 December 2020
7.2.2.19.3	Vessels used for propulsion Adaptation to new provisions Provisions of 9.3.3.12.4, 9.3.3.51 and 9.3.3.52.1 to 9.3.3.52.8	N.R.M. from 1 January 2019 Renewal of certificate of approval after 31 December 2034 Until that date, the following requirements apply to vessels in service: Vessels moving a pushed convoy or a side-by-side formation shall comply with the requirements of the following sections, subsections and paragraphs: 1.16.1.1, 1.16.1.2, 1.16.1.3, 7.2.2.5, 8.1.4, 8.1.5, 8.1.6.1, 8.1.6.3, 8.1.7, 9.3.3.0.1, 9.3.3.0.3.1, 9.3.3.0.5, 9.3.3.10.1, 9.3.3.10.4, 9.3.3.12.4 (a) except the wheelhouse, 9.3.3.12.4 (b) except for the t90 response time, 9.3.3.12.4 (c), 9.3.3.12.6, 9.3.3.16, 9.3.3.17.1 to 9.3.3.17.4, 9.3.3.31.1 to 9.3.3.31.5, 9.3.3.32.2, 9.3.3.34.1, 9.3.3.34.2, 9.3.3.40.1 (although a single fire or ballast pump is sufficient), 9.3.3.40.2, 9.3.3.41, 9.3.3.50.1 (c), 9.3.3.50.2, 9.3.3.51, 9.3.3.52.6, 9.3.3.52.7, 9.3.3.52.8, 9.3.3.56.5, 9.3.3.71 and 9.3.3.74, when at least one vessel of the convoy or side-by-side formation is carrying dangerous goods. The requirement of 9.3.3.10.4 may be met by fitting vertical protection walls not less than 0.50 m in height. Vessels moving only type N open tank vessels do not have to meet the requirements of paragraphs 9.3.3.10.1, 9.3.3.10.4 and 9.3.3.12.6. These derogations shall be specified in the certificate of approval or the provisional certificate of approval as follows: "Permitted derogations": "Derogation from 9.3.3.10.1, 9.3.3.10.4 and 9.3.3.12.6; the vessel may only move type N open tank vessels.".
7.2.2.19.4	Vessels of the formation for which explosion protection is required	N.R.M. from 1 January 2019 Renewal of the certificate of approval after 31 December 2034

1.6.7.2.2.2 Table of general transitional provisions: Tank vessels		
Paragraphs	Subject	Time limit and comments
7.2.3.20.1	Ballast water Prohibition against filling cofferdams with water	N.R.M. Renewal of the certificate of approval after 31 December 2038 Until then, the following requirements apply on board vessels in service: Cofferdams may be filled with water during unloading to provide trim and to permit residue-free drainage as far as possible. When the vessel is underway, cofferdams may be filled with ballast water only when cargo tanks are empty.
7.2.3.20.1	Proof of stability in the event of a leak connected with ballast water	N.R.M. for Type G and Type N vessels. Renewal of the certificate of approval after 31 December 2044.
7.2.3.31.2	Motor vehicles only outside the cargo area	N.R.M. for Type N vessels. Renewal of the certificate of approval after 31 December 2034 Until then, the following requirement applies on board vessels in service: the vehicle shall not be started on board.
7.2.3.41	Smoking	N.R.M. from 1 January 2019 Renewal of the certificate of approval after 31 December 2020
7.2.3.51.4	Disconnection of non-electrical installations and equipment marked in red	N.R.M. From 1 January 2019 Renewal of the certificate of approval after 31 December 2034
7.2.3.51.5	Surface temperature where T4, T5 or T6 are required	N.R.M. From 1 January 2019 Renewal of the certificate of approval after 31 December 2020
7.2.4.22.3	Sampling from other openings	N.R.M. for Type N open vessels. Renewal of the certificate of approval after 31 December 2018 Until then, on board vessels in service, cargo tank covers may be opened during loading for control and sampling.

1.6.7.2.2.2 Table of general transitional provisions: Tank vessels		
Paragraphs	Subject	Time limit and comments
8.1.2.3 (r), (s), (t), (v)	Documents which must be carried on board	N.R.M. from 1 January 2019 Renewal of the certificate of approval after 31 December 2020 Until that date, in addition to the documents required in accordance with 1.1.4.6, the following documents are required: (a) A plan indicating the boundaries of the cargo area and the location of the electrical equipment installed in that area; (b) A list of the machinery, appliances or other electrical equipment referred to in (a) above, including the following particulars: Machinery or appliance, location, type of protection, type of explosion protection, testing body and approval number; (c) A list of or general plan indicating the electrical equipment located outside the cargo area which may be operated during loading, unloading or degassing. The documents listed above shall bear the stamp of the competent authority issuing the certificate of approval.
8.1.2.3 (u)	Documents which must be carried on board Plan with classification of zones	N.R.M. from 1 January 2019 Renewal of the certificate of approval after 31 December 2034
8.1.6.3	Verification of the oxygen measuring system	N.R.M. from 1 January 2019 Renewal of the certificate of approval after 31 December 2020
8.1.7.2	Installations, equipment and autonomous protection systems, testing of installations, equipment and autonomous protection systems as well as compliance with the documents referred to in 8.1.2.3 (r) to (v) in respect of the situation on board	N.R.M. from 1 January 2019 Renewal of the certificate of approval after 31 December 2020
8.1.7.2	Marking of installations and equipment to be used in explosion hazardous areas as well as of autonomous protection systems	N.R.M. From 1 January 2019 Renewal of the certificate of approval after 31 December 2024
8.6.1.3 8.6.1.4	Change to certificate of approval	N.R.M. from 1 January 2019 Renewal of the certificate of approval after 31 December 2018

1.6.7.2.2.2 Table of general transitional provisions: Tank vessels		
Paragraphs	Subject	Time limit and comments
9.3.2.0.1 (c) 9.3.3.0.1 (c)	Protection of venting piping against corrosion	N.R.M. from 1 January 2001 Renewal of the certificate of approval after 31 December 2034
9.3.1.0.3 (d) 9.3.2.0.3 (d) 9.3.3.0.3 (d)	Fire-resistant materials of accommodation and wheelhouse	N.R.M. Renewal of the certificate of approval after 31 December 2034
9.3.3.8.1	Continuation of class	N.R.M. for Type N open vessels with flame arresters and Type N open vessels. Renewal of the certificate of approval after 31 December 2044. Until then, the following requirements apply on board vessels in service: Except where otherwise provided, the type of construction, the strength, the subdivision, the equipment and the gear of the vessel shall conform or be equivalent to the construction requirements for classification in the highest class of a recognized classification society.
9.3.1.10.1 9.3.2.10.1 9.3.3.10.1	Penetration of gases and liquids into the wheelhouse Windows that can be opened	N.R.M. from 1 January 2019 Renewal of the certificate of approval after 31 December 2024
9.3.1.10.2 9.3.2.10.2 9.3.3.10.2	Height of protective coaming	N.R.M. from 1 January 2019 Renewal of the certificate of approval after 31 December 2020
9.3.1.10.3 9.3.2.10.3 9.3.3.10.3	Protection wall	N.R.M. from 1 January 2019 Renewal of certificate of approval after 31 December 2024
9.3.1.10.4 9.3.2.10.4 9.3.3.10.4	Door coamings, etc.	N.R.M. Renewal of the certificate of approval after 31 December 2034 Until then, the following requirements apply on board vessels in service, with the exception of Type N open vessels: This requirement may be met by fitting vertical protection walls not less than 0.50 m in height. Until then, on board vessels in service less than 50.00 m long, the height of 0.50 m may be reduced to 0.30 m in passageways leading to the deck.
9.3.1.11.1 (b)	Ratio of length to diameter of pressure cargo tanks	N.R.M. Renewal of the certificate of approval after 31 December 2044
9.3.3.11.1 (d)	Limitation of length of cargo tanks	N.R.M. Renewal of the certificate of approval after 31 December 2044

1.6.7.2.2.2 Table of general transitional provisions: Tank vessels		
Paragraphs	Subject	Time limit and comments
9.3.1.11.2 (a)	Arrangement of cargo tanks Distance between cargo tanks and side walls Height of saddles	N.R.M. for Type G vessels whose keels were laid before 1 January 1977. Renewal of the certificate of approval after 31 December 2044
9.3.1.11.2 (a)	Arrangement of cargo tanks Distance between cargo tanks and side walls Height of saddles	N.R.M. Renewal of the certificate of approval after 31 December 2044 Until then, the following requirements apply on board vessels in service whose keels were laid after 31 December 1976: Where tank volume is more than 200 m^3 or where the ratio of length to diameter is less than 7 but more than 5, the hull in the tank area shall be such that, in the event of a collision, the tanks remain intact as far as possible. This requirement shall be considered as having been met where, in the tank area, the vessel: - is double-hulled with a distance of at least 80 cm between the side plating and the longitudinal bulkhead - or is designed as follows: (a) Between the gangboard and the top of the floorplates there shall be side stringers at regular intervals of not more than 60 cm; (b) The side stringers shall be supported by web frames spaced at intervals of not more than 2.00 m. The height of the web frames shall be not less than 10% of the depth and in any event not less than 30 cm. They shall be fitted with a face plate made of flat steel having a cross section of not less than 15 cm^2; (c) The side stringers referred to in (a) shall have the same height as the web frames and be fitted with a face plate made of flat steel having a cross section of not less than 7.5 cm^2.
9.3.1.11.2 (a)	Distance between suction wells and floor plates	N.R.M. Renewal of the certificate of approval after 31 December 2044
9.3.1.11.2 (b) 9.3.2.11.2 (b) 9.3.3.11.2 (a)	Cargo tank fastenings	N.R.M. Renewal of the certificate of approval after 31 December 2044
9.3.1.11.2 (c) 9.3.2.11.2 (c) 9.3.3.11.2 (b)	Capacity of suction well	N.R.M. Renewal of the certificate of approval after 31 December 2044
9.3.1.11.2 (d) 9.3.2.11.2 (d)	Side struts between the hull and the cargo tanks	N.R.M. from 1 January 2001 Renewal of the certificate of approval after 31 December 2044

1.6.7.2.2.2 Table of general transitional provisions: Tank vessels		
Paragraphs	Subject	Time limit and comments
9.3.3.11.2 (d)	Side struts between the hull and the cargo tanks	N.R.M. from 1 January 2019 Renewal of the certificate of approval after 31 December 2044
9.3.1.11.3 (a)	End bulkheads of cargo area with "A-60" insulation. Distance of 0.50 m from cargo tanks to end bulkheads	N.R.M. Renewal of the certificate of approval after 31 December 2044
9.3.2.11.3 (a) 9.3.3.11.3 (a)	Width of cofferdams of 0.60 m Hold spaces with cofferdams or "A-60" insulated bulkheads Distance of 0.50 m from cargo tanks in hold spaces	N.R.M. Renewal of the certificate of approval after 31 December 2044 Until then, the following requirements apply on board vessels in service: Type C: minimum width of cofferdams: 0.50 m; Type N: minimum width of cofferdams: 0.50 m; on board vessels with a deadweight of up to 150 t: 0.40 m; Type N open: cofferdams shall not be required on board vessels with a deadweight up to 150 t and oil separator vessels: The distance between cargo tanks and end bulkheads of hold spaces shall be at least 0.40m.
9.3.3.11.4	Penetrations through the end bulkheads of hold spaces	N.R.M. from 1 January 2005 for Type N open vessels whose keels were laid before 1 January 1977. Renewal of the certificate of approval after 31 December 2044.
9.3.3.11.4	Distance of piping in relation to the bottom	N.R.M. from 1 January 2005 Renewal of the certificate of approval after 31 December 2038
9.3.3.11.4	Shut-off devices of the loading and unloading piping in the cargo tank from which they come	N.R.M. from 1 January 2005 Renewal of the certificate of approval after 31 December 2018
9.3.3.11.6 (a)	Form of cofferdam arranged as a pump room	N.R.M for Type N vessels whose keels were laid before 1 January 1977. Renewal of the certificate of approval after 31 December 2044.
9.3.3.11.7	Distance between the cargo tanks and the outer wall of the vessel	N.R.M. after 1 January 2001 Renewal of the certificate of approval after 31 December 2038
9.3.3.11.7	Width of double hull	N.R.M. after 1 January 2007 Renewal of the certificate of approval after 31 December 2038
9.3.1.11.7	Distance between the suction well and the bottom spaces	N.R.M. after 1 January 2003 Renewal of the certificate of approval after 31 December 2038

1.6.7.2.2.2 Table of general transitional provisions: Tank vessels		
Paragraphs	Subject	Time limit and comments
9.3.3.11.8	Arrangement of service spaces located in the cargo area below decks	N.R.M. for Type N open vessels. Renewal of the certificate of approval after 31 December 2038.
9.3.1.11.8 9.3.3.11.9	Dimensions of openings for access to spaces within the cargo area	N.R.M. Renewal of the certificate of approval after 31 December 2018
9.3.1.11.8 9.3.2.11.10 9.3.3.11.9	Interval between reinforcing elements	N.R.M. Renewal of the certificate of approval after 31 December 2044
9.3.2.12.1 9.3.3.12.1	Ventilation openings in hold spaces	N.R.M. from 1 January 2003 Renewal of the certificate of approval after 31 December 2018
9.3.1.12.2 9.3.3.12.2	Ventilation systems in double-hull spaces and double bottoms	N.R.M. Renewal of the certificate of approval after 31 December 2018
9.3.1.12.3 9.3.2.12.3 9.3.3.12.3	Height above the deck of the air intake for service spaces located below deck	N.R.M. Renewal of the certificate of approval after 31 December 2018
9.3.1.12.4 9.3.2.12.4 9.3.3.12.4	Ventilation of the wheelhouse	N.R.M. from 1 January 2019 Renewal of the certificate of approval after 31 December 2024
9.3.1.12.4 9.3.2.12.4 9.3.3.12.4	Equipment in the accommodation, wheelhouse and service spaces where surface temperatures can be higher than those mentioned in 9.3.x.51 (a)	N.R.M. from 1 January 2019 Renewal of the certificate of approval after 31 December 2034
9.3.1.12.4 9.3.2.12.4 9.3.3.12.4	Equipment in the wheelhouse where surface temperatures can be higher than those mentioned in 9.3.x.51 (a) or involving the use of electrical equipment which does not meet the requirements of 9.3.x.52.1	N.R.M. from 1 January 2019 Renewal of the certificate of approval after 31 December 2034

1.6.7.2.2.2 Table of general transitional provisions: Tank vessels		
Paragraphs	Subject	Time limit and comments
9.3.1.12.4 9.3.3.12.4	Electrical installations and equipment used during loading, unloading, degassing and when in the immediate vicinity of or within an onshore assigned zone	N.R.M. From 1 January 2019 Renewal of the certificate of approval after 31 December 2034 Until that date, on board type G and type N vessels whose keels were laid before 1 January 1977, all electrical equipment except the lighting installations in accommodation, radio telephone installations in the accommodation and the wheelhouse and combustion engine control appliances, shall meet the following requirements: Generators, engine, etc.: IP 13 protection mode Switchboards, switches near entrances to accommodation, etc.: IP23 protection mode Appliances, etc.: IP 55 protection mode
9.3.1.12.4 9.3.2.12.4 9.3.3.12.4	Non-electrical installations and equipment used during loading, unloading, degassing and when in the immediate vicinity of or within an onshore assigned zone	N.R.M. From 1 January 2019 Renewal of the certificate of approval after 31 December 2034
9.3.1.12.4 (b) 9.3.2.12.4 (b) 9.3.3.12.4 (b)	Gas detection system: T90-time	N.R.M. From 1 January 2019 Renewal of the certificate of approval after 31 December 2034
9.3.1.12.4 9.3.2.12.4 9.3.3.12.4	Alarms outstanding	N.R.M. From 1 January 2019 Renewal of the certificate of approval after 31 December 2024
9.3.1.12.6 9.3.2.12.6 9.3.3.12.6	Distance between ventilation inlets in the wheelhouse and the cargo area	N.R.M. From 1 January 2019 Renewal of the certificate of approval after 31 December 2034
9.3.1.12.6 9.3.2.12.6 9.3.3.12.6	Distance between ventilation openings of accommodation and service spaces and the cargo area	N.R.M. from 1 January 2003 Renewal of certificate of approval after 31 December 2034
9.3.1.12.6 9.3.2.12.6 9.3.3.12.6	Permanently installed devices according to 9.3.x.40.2.2 (c)	N.R.M. from 1 January 2003 Renewal of certificate of approval after 31 December 2018
9.3.1.13 9.3.3.13	Stability (general)	N.R.M. Renewal of the certificate of approval after 31 December 2044
9.3.3.13.3 paragraph 2	Stability (general)	N.R.M. from 1 January 2007 Renewal of the certificate of approval after 31 December 2044

1.6.7.2.2.2 Table of general transitional provisions: Tank vessels		
Paragraphs	Subject	Time limit and comments
9.3.1.14 9.3.3.14	Stability (intact)	N.R.M. Renewal of the certificate of approval after 31 December 2044
9.3.1.15	Stability (damaged condition)	N.R.M. Renewal of the certificate of approval after 31 December 2044
9.3.3.15	Stability (damaged condition)	N.R.M. after 1 January 2007 Renewal of the certificate of approval after 31 December 2044
9.3.1.16.1 9.3.3.16.1	Distance of openings of engine rooms from the cargo area	N.R.M. Renewal of the certificate of approval after 31 December 2044
9.3.3.16.1	Internal combustion engines outside the cargo area	N.R.M. for Type N open vessels. Renewal of the certificate of approval after 31 December 2034.
9.3.1.16.2 9.3.3.16.2	Hinges of doors facing the cargo area	N.R.M. for vessels whose keels were laid before 1 January 1977 where alterations would obstruct other major openings. Renewal of the certificate of approval after 31 December 2034.
9.3.3.16.2	Engine rooms accessible from the deck	N.R.M. for Type N open vessels. Renewal of the certificate of approval after 31 December 2034.
9.3.1.17.1 9.3.3.17.1	Accommodation and wheelhouse outside the cargo area	N.R.M. for vessels whose keels were laid before 1 January 1977, provided that there is no connection between the wheelhouse and other enclosed spaces. Renewal of the certificate of approval after 31 December 2044. Renewal of the certificate of approval after 31 December 2044 for vessels up to 50 m in length whose keels were laid before 1 January 1977 and whose wheelhouses are located in the cargo area even if it provides access to another enclosed space, provided that safety is ensured by appropriate service requirements of the competent authority.
9.3.3.17.1	Accommodation and wheelhouse outside the cargo area	N.R.M. for Type N open vessels. Renewal of the certificate of approval after 31 December 2044.
9.3.1.17.2 9.3.2.17.2 9.3.3.17.2	Arrangement of entrances and openings of forward superstructures	N.R.M. Renewal of the certificate of approval after 31 December 2044
9.3.1.17.2 9.3.2.17.2 9.3.3.17.2	Entrances facing the cargo area	N.R.M. for vessels up to 50 m in length whose keels were laid before 1 January 1977, provided that gas screens are installed. Renewal of the certificate of approval after 31 December 2044.

1.6.7.2.2.2 Table of general transitional provisions: Tank vessels		
Paragraphs	Subject	Time limit and comments
9.3.3.17.2	Entrances and openings	N.R.M. for Type N open vessels. Renewal of the certificate of approval after 31 December 2044.
9.3.1.17.4 9.3.3.17.4	Distance of openings from the cargo area	N.R.M. Renewal of the certificate of approval after 31 December 2044.
9.3.3.17.5 (b), (c)	Approval of shaft passages and displaying of instructions	N.R.M. for Type N open vessels. Renewal of the certificate of approval after 31 December 2018.
9.3.1.17.6 9.3.2.17.6 9.3.3.17.6	Distance between the ventilation inlets in the pump-room and the wheelhouse	N.R.M. From 1 January 2019 Renewal of the certificate of approval after 31 December 2034

9.3.1.17.6
9.3.3.17.6
	Pump-room below deck	N.R.M.
		Renewal of the certificate of approval after 31 December 2018
		
		Until then, the following requirements apply on board vessels in service:
		Pump-rooms below deck shall
		- meet the requirements for service spaces:
		  - for Type G vessels: 9.3.1.12.3
		  - for Type N vessels: 9.3.3.12.3
		- be equipped with a gas detection system referred to in 9.3.1.17.6 or 9.3.3.17.6

9.3.1.17.6 9.3.2.17.6 9.3.3.17.6	Oxygen measuring system Minimum value for the alarm	N.R.M. From 1 January 2019 Renewal of the certificate of approval after 31 December 2020
9.3.1.17.6 9.3.2.17.6 9.3.3.17.6	Alarms outstanding	N.R.M. From 1 January 2019 Renewal of the certificate of approval after 31 December 2024
9.3.2.20.1 9.3.3.20.1	Access to cofferdams or cofferdam compartments	N.R.M. from 1 January 2015 Renewal of the certificate of approval after 31 December 2034
9.3.2.20.2 9.3.3.20.2	Intake valve	N.R.M. Renewal of the certificate of approval after 31 December 2018
9.3.3.20.2	Filling of cofferdams with pump	N.R.M. for Type N open vessels. Renewal of the certificate of approval after 31 December 2018.
9.3.2.20.2 9.3.3.20.2	Filling of cofferdams within 30 minutes	N.R.M. Renewal of the certificate of approval after 31 December 2018

1.6.7.2.2.2 Table of general transitional provisions: Tank vessels		
Paragraphs	Subject	Time limit and comments
9.3.2.20.4 9.3.3.20.4	Explosion group/subgroup	N.R.M. From 1 January 2019 Renewal of the certificate of approval after 31 December 2020
9.3.1.21.3 9.3.2.21.3 9.3.3.21.3	Marking on each level gauge of all permissible maximum filling levels of cargo tanks	N.R.M. from 1 January 2015 Renewal of the certificate of approval after 31 December 2018
9.3.3.21.1 (b)	Liquid level gauge	N.R.M. from 1 January 2005 for vessels of Type N open with flame-arresters and those of Type N open. Renewal of the certificate of approval after 31 December 2018. Until then, on board vessels in service fitted with gauging openings, such openings shall: - Be arranged so that the degree of filling can be measured using a sounding rod; - Be fitted with an automatically-closing cover.
9.3.3.21.1 (g)	Sampling opening	N.R.M. for Type N open vessels. Renewal of the certificate of approval after 31 December 2018.
9.3.2.21.1 (g) 9.3.3.21.1 (g)	Explosion group/subgroup	N.R.M. From 1 January 2019 Renewal of certificate of approval after 31 December 2020
9.3.1.21.4 9.3.2.21.4 9.3.3.21.4	Liquid-level alarm device independent from the liquid-level gauge	N.R.M. Renewal of the certificate of approval after 31 December 2018
9.3.1.21.5 (a) 9.3.2.21.5 (a) 9.3.3.21.5 (a)	Socket close to the shore connections of the loading and unloading piping and switching off of vessel's pump	N.R.M. Renewal of the certificate of approval after 31 December 2018
9.3.1.21.7 9.3.2.21.7 9.3.3.21.7	Alarms outstanding	N.R.M. From 1 January 2019 Renewal of the certificate of approval after 31 December 2024
9.3.1.21.7 9.3.2.21.7 9.3.3.21.7	Vacuum or over-pressure alarms in cargo tanks for the carriage of substances without remark 5 in column (20) of Table C of Chapter 3.2	N.R.M. from 1 January 2001 Renewal of the certificate of approval after 31 December 2018
9.3.1.21.7 9.3.2.21.7 9.3.3.21.7	Temperature alarms in cargo tanks	N.R.M. from 1 January 2001 Renewal of the certificate of approval after 31 December 2018
9.3.1.22.1 (b)	Height of cargo tank openings above the deck	N.R.M. Renewal of the certificate of approval after 31 December 2044

1.6.7.2.2.2 Table of general transitional provisions: Tank vessels		
Paragraphs	Subject	Time limit and comments
9.3.3.22.1 (b)	Cargo tank openings 0.50 m above the deck	N.R.M. Renewal of the certificate of approval after 31 December 2044 for vessels whose keels were laid before 1 January 1977.
9.3.1.22.4	Prevention of spark-formation by closure devices	N.R.M. from 1 January 2003 Renewal of the certificate of approval after 31 December 2018
9.3.1.22.3 9.3.2.22.4 (a) 9.3.3.22.4 (a)	Position of exhaust outlets of pressure relief valves/high velocity vent valves above the deck	N.R.M. Renewal of the certificate of approval after 31 December 2018
9.3.2.22.4 (a) 9.3.3.22.4 (e)	Set pressure of relief valve/high-velocity vent valve	N.R.M. Renewal of the certificate of approval after 31 December 2018
9.3.2.22.4 (e) 9.3.3.22.4 (d)	Explosion group/subgroup	N.R.M. From 1 January 2019 Renewal of certificate of approval after 31 December 2020
9.3.3.23.2	Test pressure for cargo tanks	N.R.M. for vessels whose keels were laid before 1 January 1977, for which a test pressure of 15 kPa (0.15 bar) is required. Renewal of the certificate of approval after 31 December 2044. Until then, a test pressure of 10 kPa (0.10 bar) shall be sufficient.
9.3.3.23.2	Test pressure for cargo tanks	N.R.M. for oil-separator vessels in service before 1 January 1999. Renewal of the certificate of approval after 31 December 2044. Until then, a test pressure of 5 kPa (0.05 bar) is sufficient.
9.3.3.23.3	Test pressure for piping for loading and unloading	N.R.M. for oil-separator vessels in service before 1 January 1999. Renewal of the certificate of approval at the latest by 1 January 2039. Until then, a test pressure of 400 kPa (4 bar) is sufficient.
9.3.2.25.1 9.3.3.25.1	Shut-down of cargo pumps	N.R.M. Renewal of the certificate of approval after 31 December 2018
9.3.1.25.1 9.3.2.25.1 9.3.3.25.1	Distance of pumps, etc. from accommodation, etc.	N.R.M. Renewal of the certificate of approval after 31 December 2044
9.3.1.25.2 (d) 9.3.2.25.2 (d)	Position of loading and unloading piping on deck	N.R.M. Renewal of the certificate of approval after 31 December 2044
9.3.1.25.2 (e) 9.3.2.25.2 (e) 9.3.3.25.2 (e)	Distance of shore connections from accommodation, etc.	N.R.M. Renewal of the certificate of approval after 31 December 2034

1.6.7.2.2.2 Table of general transitional provisions: Tank vessels		
Paragraphs	Subject	Time limit and comments
9.3.2.25.2 (i)	Piping for loading and unloading, and venting piping, shall not have flexible connections fitted with sliding seals.	N.R.M. from 1 January 2009 Vessels in service having connections with sliding seals may no longer transport substances with toxic or corrosive properties (see column (5) of Table C of Chapter 3.2, hazards 6.1 and 8) following the renewal of the certificate of approval after 31 December 2008. Vessels in service shall not have flexible connections fitted with sliding seals following the renewal of the certificate of approval after 31 December 2018
9.3.3.25.2 (h)	Piping for loading and unloading, and venting piping, shall not have flexible connections fitted with sliding seals	N.R.M. from 1 January 2009 Vessels in service having connections with sliding seals may no longer transport substances with corrosive properties (see column (5) of Table C of Chapter 3.2, hazard 8) following the renewal of the certificate of approval after 31 December 2008. Vessels in service shall not have flexible connections with sliding seals following the renewal of the certificate of approval after 31 December 2018.
9.3.2.25.8 (a)	Ballasting suction pipes located within the cargo area but outside the cargo tanks	N.R.M. Renewal of the certificate of approval after 31 December 2018
9.3.2.25.9 9.3.3.25.9	Loading and unloading flow	N.R.M. from 1 January 2003 Renewal of the certificate of approval after 31 December 2018
9.3.3.25.12	9.3.3.25.1 (a) and (c), 9.3.3.25.2 (e), 9.3.3.25.3 and 9.3.3.25.4 (a) are not applicable for Type N open with the exception of Type N open carrying corrosive substances (see Chapter 3.2, Table C, column (5), hazard 8)	N.R.M. Renewal of the certificate of approval after 31 December 2018 This time limit concerns only Type N open vessels carrying corrosive substances (see Chapter 3.2, Table C, column (5), hazard 8).
9.3.2.26.2 9.3.3.26.2 (b)	Explosion group/subgroup	N.R.M. From 1 January 2019 Renewal of certificate of approval after 31 December 2020
9.3.1.31.2 9.3.2.31.2 9.3.3.31.2	Distance of engine air intakes from the cargo area	N.R.M. Renewal of the certificate of approval after 31 December 2044
9.3.1.31.5 9.3.2.31.5 9.3.3.31.5	Temperature in the engine room	N.R.M. Renewal of the certificate of approval after 31 December 2018 Until then, the following requirements apply on board vessels in service: The temperature in the engine room shall not exceed 45 °C.

1.6.7.2.2.2 Table of general transitional provisions: Tank vessels		
Paragraphs	Subject	Time limit and comments
9.3.3.34.1	Exhaust pipes	N.R.M. Renewal of the certificate of approval after 31 December 2018
9.3.1.35.1 9.3.3.35.1	Stripping and ballast pumps in the cargo area	N.R.M. Renewal of the certificate of approval after 31 December 2034
9.3.3.35.3	Suction pipes for ballasting located within the cargo area but outside the cargo tanks	N.R.M. Renewal of the certificate of approval after 31 December 2018
9.3.1.35.4	Stripping installation of the pump-room outside the pump-room	N.R.M. from 1 January 2003 Renewal of the certificate of approval after 31 December 2018
9.3.1.40.1 9.3.2.40.1 9.3.3.40.1	Fire extinguishing systems, two pumps, etc.	N.R.M. Renewal of the certificate of approval after 31 December 2018
9.3.1.40.2 9.3.2.40.2 9.3.3.40.2	Fixed fire extinguishing system in engine room	N.R.M. Renewal of the certificate of approval after 31 December 2034
9.3.1.41.1 9.3.3.41.1	Outlets of funnels located not less than 2 m from the cargo area	N.R.M. Renewal of the certificate of approval after 31 December 2044 for vessels whose keels were laid before 1 January 1977.
9.3.3.41.1	Outlets of funnels	N.R.M. at the latest by 1 January 2039 for oil-separator vessels
9.3.3.42.2	Cargo heating system	N.R.M for Type N open vessels. Renewal of the certificate of approval after 31 December 2034. Until then, the following requirements apply on board vessels in service: This can be achieved by one oil separator fitted to the condensed water return pipe.
9.3.1.51 (a) 9.3.2.51 (a) 9.3.3.51 (a)	The surface temperature of non-electrical installations and equipment shall not exceed 200 °C	N.R.M. From 1 January 2019 Renewal of the certificate of approval after 31 December 2034
9.3.1.51 (b) 9.3.2.51 (b) 9.3.3.51 (b)	Surface temperature of outer parts of engines and of their air inlets and exhaust ducts	N.R.M. Renewal of the certificate of approval after 31 December 2018 Until then, the following requirements apply on board vessels in service: The temperature of outer parts shall not exceed 300 °C.

1.6.7.2.2.2 Table of general transitional provisions: Tank vessels		
Paragraphs	Subject	Time limit and comments
9.3.1.52.1 9.3.2.52.1 9.3.3.52.1	Electrical installations and equipment of the limited explosion risk type	N.R.M. Renewal of certificate of approval after 31 December 2034 Until that date, the following documents are required for electrical equipment used during loading, unloading and degassing of vessels in service whose keels were laid after 1 January 1995: 9.3.1.52.3, 9.3.2.52.3 and 9.3.3.52.3 of the version of ADN in force until 31 December 2018
9.3.1.52.1 9.3.3.52.1	Electrical installations and equipment of the limited explosion risk type	N.R.M. Renewal of the certificate of approval after 31 December 2034 Until that date, on board vessels whose keels were laid before 1 January 1977, all electrical equipment except the lighting installations in the accommodation, radio telephone installations in the accommodation and the wheelhouse and combustion engine control appliances in use during loading, unloading and degassing shall meet the following requirements: Generators, engines, switchboards, lighting, etc.: IP 13 protection mode Appliances, etc.: IP 55 protection mode
9.3.3.52.1	Electrical installations and equipment in operation during a stay in the immediate vicinity of or within an onshore assigned zone	N.R.M. from 1 January 2019 for open Type N vessels Renewal of certificate of approval after 31 December 2034
9.3.3.52.2	Electrical installations and equipment/echo sounding devices	N.R.M. for Type N open vessels. Renewal of the certificate of approval after 31 December 2034.
9.3.3.52.3	Electrical installations and equipment: marking in red	N.R.M. from 1 January 2019 for open Type N vessels Renewal of certificate of approval after 31 December 2034
9.3.1.52.3 9.3.2.52.3 9.3.3.52.3 last sentence	Disconnection of such electrical installations and equipment from a centralized location	N.R.M. Renewal of the certificate of approval after 31 December 2034
9.3.1.52.4 9.3.2.52.4 9.3.3.52.4	Visual and audible alarm	N.R.M. Renewal of the certificate of approval after 31 December 2034
9.3.3.52.6	Shutting down multipolar switch for continuously driven generator	N.R.M. for Type N open vessels Renewal of the certificate of approval after 31 December 2034
9.3.3.52.9	Permanently fitted sockets	N.R.M. for Type N open vessels Renewal of the certificate of approval after 31 December 2034

1.6.7.2.2.2 Table of general transitional provisions: Tank vessels		
Paragraphs	Subject	Time limit and comments
9.3.3.52.10	Accumulators located outside the cargo area	N.R.M. for Type N open vessels. Renewal of the certificate of approval after 31 December 2034.
9.3.1.53.1 9.3.2.53.1 9.3.3.53.1	Type and location of electrical installations and equipment intended to be used in explosion hazardous areas Zone 0, Zone 1	N.R.M. from 1 January 2019 Renewal of certificate of approval after 31 December 2034 Until that date, the following requirements are applicable: (a) In cargo tanks and piping for loading and unloading, only measuring, regulation and alarm devices of the EEx (ia) type of protection may be installed. (b) Electrical equipment on deck in the cargo area and the measuring, regulation and alarm apparatus, motors driving essential equipment such as ballast pumps in the cofferdams, double-hull spaces, double bottoms, hold spaces and service spaces below deck in the cargo area shall be checked and approved by the competent authority with respect to the safety of operation in an explosive atmosphere, for example, intrinsically safe apparatus, flameproof enclosure apparatus, apparatus protected by pressurization, powder filling apparatus, apparatus protected by encapsulation and increased safety apparatus. (c) In the cofferdams, double-hull spaces, double bottoms, hold spaces and service spaces below deck in the cargo area, the lighting appliances must have the "flame-proof enclosure" or "apparatus protected by pressurization" type of protection. (d) The control and protective equipment of the equipment referred to in (a), (b) and (c) above shall be located outside the cargo area if they are not intrinsically safe. For the selection of electrical equipment, the explosion groups and temperature classes assigned to the substances carried in the list of substances shall be taken into consideration (see columns (15) and (16) of Table C of Chapter 3.2). Until that date, the following requirements apply on board vessels in service whose keels were laid before 31 December 1977: Until that date, the following conditions shall be met during loading, unloading and degassing on board vessels having non-gastight wheelhouse openings (e.g. doors, windows, etc.) in the cargo area:

1.6.7.2.2.2 Table of general transitional provisions: Tank vessels		
Paragraphs	Subject	Time limit and comments
		(a) All electrical equipment to be used in the wheelhouse shall be of a limited explosion-risk type, i.e., it shall be so designed that there is no sparking and the temperature of its outer surface does not rise above 200 °C during normal operation, or it shall be of a type protected against water jets and designed in such a way that its surface temperature may not exceed 200 °C during normal operation. (b) Electrical equipment which does not meet the requirements of (a) above shall be marked in red and it shall be possible to switch it off by means of a central switch.
9.3.1.53.1 9.3.2.53.1 9.3.3.53.1	Type and location of electrical installations and equipment intended to be used in explosion hazardous areas Zone 2	N.R.M. from 1 January 2019 Renewal of the certificate of approval after 31 December 2034
9.3.1.53.1 9.3.2.53.1 9.3.3.53.1	Temperature class and explosion group of non-electrical installations and equipment	N.R.M. From 1 January 2019 Renewal of the certificate of approval after 31 December 2034
9.3.1.53.1 9.3.2.53.1 9.3.3.53.1	Temperature class and explosion group of electrical installations and equipment	N.R.M. From 1 January 2019 Renewal of the certificate of approval after 31 December 2034
9.3.1.53.2 9.3.3.53.2	Metallic sheaths for all electric cables in the cargo area	N.R.M. for vessels whose keels were laid before 1 January 1977. Renewal of the certificate of approval after 31 December 2034.
9.3.3.53.2	Metallic sheaths for all electric cables in the cargo area	N.R.M. by 1 January 2039 at the latest for oil-separator vessels.
9.3.1.53.5 9.3.2.53.5 9.3.3.53.5	Movable electric cables (sheathed, type H 07 RN-F)	N.R.M. from 1 January 2019 Renewal of the certificate of approval after 31 December 2034 Until that date, the following provisions apply on board vessels in service: Until that date, movable electric cables (sheathed, type H 07 RN-F) must comply with IEC 60245-4:1994
9.3.1.60 9.3.2.60 9.3.3.60	A spring-loaded non-return valve shall be fitted. The water shall meet the quality of drinking water on board.	N.R.M. Renewal of the certificate of approval after 31 December 2018

1.6.7.2.2.3   Transitional provisions concerning the application of the requirements of Table C of Chapter 3.2 to the carriage of goods in tank vessels.

1.6.7.2.2.3.1 to 1.6.7.2.2.3.3   *(Deleted)*

1.6.7.2.2.4   *(Deleted)*

1.6.7.2.2.5   For a vessel or a barge whose keel was laid before 1 July 2017 and which does not conform to the requirements of 9.3.X.1 concerning the vessel record, the retention of files for the vessel record shall start at the latest at the next renewal of the certificate of approval.

1.6.7.3   *Supplementary transitional provisions applicable to specific inland waterways*

Vessels in service to which the transitional provisions of this subsection are applied shall meet:

–   the requirements of paragraphs and subparagraphs mentioned in the table below and in the table of general transitional provisions (see 1.6.7.2.1.1 and 1.6.7.2.2.1) within the period established therein;

–   the requirements of paragraphs and subparagraphs not mentioned in the table below or in the table of general transitional provisions at the date of application of these Regulations.

The construction and equipment of vessels in service shall be maintained at least at the previous standard of safety.

Table of supplementary transitional provisions		
Paragraph	Subject	Time limit and comments
9.1.0.11.1 (b)	Holds, common bulkheads with oil fuel tanks	N.R.M. The following requirements apply on board vessels in service: Holds may share a common bulkhead with the oil fuel tanks, provided that the cargo or its packaging does not react chemically with the fuel.
9.1.0.92	Emergency exit	N.R.M. The following requirements apply on board vessels in service: Spaces the entrances or exits of which are partly or fully immersed in damaged condition shall be provided with an emergency exit not less than 0.075 m above the damage waterline.
9.1.0.95.1 (c)	Height of openings above damage waterline	N.R.M. The following requirements apply on board vessels in service: The lower edge of any non-watertight openings (e.g. doors, windows, access hatchways) shall, at the final stage of flooding, be not less than 0.075 m above the damage waterline.

Table of supplementary transitional provisions		
Paragraph	Subject	Time limit and comments
9.1.0.95.2 9.3.2.15.2	Extent of the stability diagram (damaged condition)	N.R.M. The following requirements apply on board vessels in service: At the final stage of flooding the angle of heel shall not exceed: 20° before measures to right the vessel; 12° following measures to right the vessel.
9.3.3.8.1	Classification	N.R.M. for Type N open vessels with flame arresters and Type N open vessels. Renewal of the certificate of approval after 31 December 2044.
9.3.1.11.1 (a) 9.3.2.11.1 (a) 9.3.3.11.1 (a)	Maximum capacity of cargo tanks	N.R.M. The following requirements apply on board vessels in service: The maximum permissible capacity of a cargo tank shall be 760 m^3.
9.3.2.11.1 (d)	Length of cargo tanks	N.R.M. The following requirements apply on board vessels in service: The length of a cargo tank may exceed 10 m and 0.2 L.
9.3.1.12.3 9.3.2.12.3 9.3.3.12.3	Position of air inlets	N.R.M. The following requirements apply on board vessels in service: The air inlets to be positioned at least 5.00 m from the safety-valve outlets
9.3.2.15.1 (c)	Height of openings above damage waterline	N.R.M. The following requirements apply on board vessels in service: The lower edge of any non-watertight openings (e.g. doors, windows, access hatchways) shall, at the final stage of flooding, be not less than 0.075 m above the damage waterline.
9.3.2.20.2 9.3.3.20.2	Filling of cofferdams with water	N.R.M. The following requirements apply on board vessels in service: Cofferdams shall be fitted with a system for filling with water or inert gas.
9.3.1.92 9.3.2.92	Emergency exit	N.R.M. The following requirements apply on board vessels in service: Spaces the entrances or exits of which are partly or fully immersed in damaged condition shall be provided with an emergency exit not less than 0.075 m above the damage waterline.

1.6.7.4 *Transitional provisions concerning the transport of substances hazardous to the environment or to health*

1.6.7.4.1 *Transitional provisions: vessels*

Supply vessels and oil separator vessels in service on 1 January 2009 with a dead weight on 1 January 2007 of less than 300 tonnes may continue to transport the substances they were authorized to carry on 31 December 2008 until 31 December 2038.

1.6.7.4.2 *(Deleted)*

1.6.7.5 *Transitional provisions concerning the modification of tank vessels*

1.6.7.5.1 For vessels for which a modification of the cargo area, in order to achieve a Type N double-hull vessel, has been accomplished before 31 December 2018, the following conditions apply:

(a) The modified or new cargo area shall comply with the provisions of these regulations. Transitional provisions under 1.6.7.2.2 may not be applied for the cargo area;

(b) The vessel parts outside of the cargo area shall comply with the provisions of these regulations. However, transitional provisions under 1.6.7.2.2 for 1.2.1, 9.3.3.0.3 (d), 9.3.3.51.3, 9.3.3.52.4 last sentence, applicable until 31 December 2018, may be applied;

(c) If goods which require explosion protection are entered in the list of substances on the vessel according to 1.16.1.2.5, accommodation and wheelhouses shall be equipped with a fire alarm system according to 9.3.3.40.2.3;

(d) The application of this sub-section shall be entered in the certificate of approval under No. 13 (Additional observations).

1.6.7.5.2 Modified vessels may continue to be operated beyond 31 December 2018. The time limits stipulated in the transitional provisions under 1.6.7.2.2 for 1.2.1, 9.3.3.0.3 (d), 9.3.3.51.3, 9.3.3.52.4 last sentence, applicable until 31 December 2018, shall be observed.

1.6.7.6 *Transitional provisions concerning the transport of gases in tank vessels*

Tank vessels in service on 1 January 2011 with a pump room below deck may continue to transport the substances listed in the following table until the renewal of the certificate of approval after 1 January 2045.

UN No. or ID No.	Class and classification code	Name and description
1005	2, 2TC	AMMONIA, ANHYDROUS
1010	2, 2F	1,2-BUTADIENE, STABILIZED
1010	2, 2F	1,3-BUTADIENE, STABILIZED
1010	2, 2F	BUTADIENE STABILIZED or BUTADIENES AND HYDROCARBON MIXTURE, STABILIZED, having a vapour pressure at 70 °C not exceeding 1.1 MPa (11 bar) and a density at 50 °C not lower than 0.525 kg/l
1011	2, 2F	BUTANE
1012	2, 2F	1-BUTYLENE
1020	2,2A	CHLOROPENTAFLUOROETHANE (REFRIGERANT GAS R 115)
1030	2,2F	1,1-DIFLUOROETHANE (REFRIGERANT GAS R 152a)
1033	2,2F	DIMETHYL ETHER
1040	2,2TF	ETHYLENE OXIDE WITH NITROGEN up to a total pressure of 1 MPa (10 bar) at 50 °C
1055	2,2F	ISOBUTYLENE
1063	2,2F	METHYL CHLORIDE (REFRIGERANT GAS R 40)
1077	2,2F	PROPYLENE
1083	2,2F	TRIMETHYLAMINE, ANHYDROUS
1086	2,2F	VINYL CHLORIDE, STABILIZED
1912	2,2F	METHYL CHLORIDE AND METHYLENE CHLORIDE MIXTURE
1965	2,2F	HYDROCARBON GAS MIXTURE, LIQUEFIED, N.O.S., (MIXTURE A)
1965	2,2F	HYDROCARBON GAS MIXTURE, LIQUEFIED, N.O.S., (MIXTURE A0)
1965	2,2F	HYDROCARBON GAS MIXTURE, LIQUEFIED, N.O.S., (MIXTURE A01)
1965	2,2F	HYDROCARBON GAS MIXTURE, LIQUEFIED, N.O.S., (MIXTURE A02)
1965	2,2F	HYDROCARBON GAS MIXTURE, LIQUEFIED, N.O.S., (MIXTURE A1)
1965	2,2F	HYDROCARBON GAS MIXTURE, LIQUEFIED, N.O.S., (MIXTURE B)
1965	2,2F	HYDROCARBON GAS MIXTURE, LIQUEFIED, N.O.S., (MIXTURE B1)
1965	2,2F	HYDROCARBON GAS MIXTURE, LIQUEFIED, N.O.S., (MIXTURE B2)
1965	2,2F	HYDROCARBON GAS MIXTURE, LIQUEFIED, N.O.S., (MIXTURE C)
1969	2,2F	ISOBUTANE
1978	2,2F	PROPANE
9000		AMMONIA, ANHYDROUS, DEEPLY REFRIGERATED

1.6.8   **Transitional provisions concerning training of the crew**

1.6.8.1   The responsible master and the person responsible for the loading or unloading of a barge shall be in possession of a certificate of special knowledge with the entry "The holder of this certificate has participated in an 8-lesson stability training" before 31 December 2019.

The condition for this entry is participation in a basic course required by the Regulations in force after 1 January 2013 or participation in a basic refresher course that, in derogation from 8.2.2.5, comprises 24 lessons of 45 minutes, including eight lessons devoted to the subject of stability.

Until 31 December 2018, the expert on the carriage of gases (as referred to in 8.2.1.5) does not have to be the responsible master (as referred to in 7.2.3.15) but can be any member of the crew when the type G tank vessel is only carrying UN No. 1972. In this case, the responsible master shall have attended the specialization course on gases and shall also have followed an additional training on the carriage of liquefied natural gas (LNG) in accordance with 1.3.2.2.

1.6.8.2   Instead of issuing certificates of special knowledge of ADN in accordance with 8.2.2.8.2 and 8.6.2, Contracting Parties may, until 31 December 2021, issue certificates according to the model applicable until 31 December 2018. Such certificates shall be valid until the expiry of their validity of five years.

1.6.9   **Transitional provisions concerning recognition of classification societies**

1.6.9.1   *(Deleted)*

CHAPTER 1.7

GENERAL PROVISIONS CONCERNING RADIOACTIVE MATERIAL

1.7.1   **Scope and application**

NOTE 1: In the event of a nuclear or radiological emergency during the carriage of radioactive material, provisions as established by relevant national and/or international organizations, shall be observed to protect persons, property and the environment. This includes arrangements for preparedness and response established in accordance with the national and/or international requirements and in a consistent and coordinated manner with the national and/or international emergency arrangements.

NOTE 2: The arrangements for preparedness and response shall be based on the graded approach and take into consideration the identified hazards and their potential consequences, including the formation of other dangerous substances that may result from the reaction between the contents of a consignment and the environment in the event of a nuclear or radiological emergency. Guidance for the establishment of such arrangements is contained in "Preparedness and Response for a Nuclear or Radiological Emergency", IAEA Safety Standards Series No. GSR Part 7, IAEA, Vienna (2015); "Criteria for Use in Preparedness and Response for a Nuclear or Radiological Emergency", IAEA Safety Standards Series No. GSG-2, IAEA, Vienna (2011); "Arrangements for Preparedness for a Nuclear or Radiological Emergency", IAEA Safety Standards Series No. GS-G-2.1, IAEA, Vienna (2007), and "Arrangements for the Termination of a Nuclear or Radiological Emergency", IAEA Safety Standards Series No. GSG-11, IAEA, Vienna (2018).

1.7.1.1   ADN establishes standards of safety which provide an acceptable level of control of the radiation, criticality and thermal hazards to people, property and the environment that are associated with the carriage of radioactive material. These standards are based on the 2018 edition of the IAEA Regulations for the Safe Transport of Radioactive Material. Explanatory material can be found in "Advisory Material for the IAEA Regulations for the Safe Transport of Radioactive Material (2018 Edition)", Safety Standard Series No. SSG-26 (Rev.1), IAEA, Vienna (2019).

1.7.1.2   The objective of ADN is to establish requirements that shall be satisfied to ensure safety and to protect people, property and the environment from harmful effects of ionizing radiation during the carriage of radioactive material. This protection is achieved by requiring:

(a)   Containment of the radioactive contents;

(b)   Control of external dose rate;

(c)   Prevention of criticality; and

(d)   Prevention of damage caused by heat.

These requirements are satisfied firstly by applying a graded approach to contents limits for packages and vehicles and to performance standards applied to package designs depending upon the hazard of the radioactive contents. Secondly, they are satisfied by imposing conditions on the design and operation of packages and on the maintenance of packagings, including a consideration of the nature of the radioactive contents. Thirdly, they are satisfied by requiring administrative controls including, where appropriate, approval by competent authorities. Finally, further protection is provided by making arrangements for planning and preparing emergency response to protect people, property and the environment.

1.7.1.3   ADN applies to the carriage of radioactive material by inland waterways including carriage which is incidental to the use of the radioactive material. Carriage comprises all operations and conditions associated with and involved in the movement of radioactive material; these include the design, manufacture, maintenance and repair of packaging, and the preparation, consigning, loading, carriage including in-transit storage, unloading and receipt at the final destination of loads of radioactive material and packages. A graded approach is applied to the performance standards in ADN that are characterized by three general severity levels:

(a)   Routine conditions of carriage (incident free);

(b)   Normal conditions of carriage (minor mishaps);

(c)   Accident conditions of carriage.

1.7.1.4   The provisions laid down in ADN do not apply to any of the following:

(a)   Radioactive material that is an integral part of the means of transport;

(b)   Radioactive material moved within an establishment which is subject to appropriate safety regulations in force in the establishment and where the movement does not involve public roads or railways;

(c)   Radioactive material implanted or incorporated into a person or live animal for diagnosis or treatment;

(d)   Radioactive material in or on a person who is to be transported for medical treatment because the person has been subject to accidental or deliberate intake of radioactive material or to contamination;

(e)   Radioactive material in consumer products which have received regulatory approval, following their sale to the end user;

(f)   Natural material and ores containing naturally occurring radionuclides (which may have been processed), provided the activity concentration of the material does not exceed 10 times the values specified in Table 2.2.7.2.2.1, or calculated in accordance with 2.2.7.2.2.2 (a) and 2.2.7.2.2.3 to 2.2.7.2.2.6. For natural materials and ores containing naturally occurring radionuclides that are not in secular equilibrium the calculation of the activity concentration shall be performed in accordance with 2.2.7.2.2.4;

(g)   Non-radioactive solid objects with radioactive substances present on any surfaces in quantities not in excess of the limit set out in the definition for "contamination" in 2.2.7.1.2.

1.7.1.5   *Specific provisions for the carriage of excepted packages*

1.7.1.5.1   Excepted packages which may contain radioactive material in limited quantities, instruments, manufactured articles or empty packagings as specified in 2.2.7.2.4.1 shall be subject only to the following provisions of Parts 5 to 7:

(a)   The applicable provisions specified in 5.1.2.1, 5.1.3.2, 5.1.5.2.2, 5.1.5.2.3, 5.1.5.4, 5.2.1.10, 5.4.1.2.5.1 (f) (i) and (ii), 5.4.1.2.5.1 (i), 7.1.4.14.7.3.1, 7.1.4.14.7.4.3, 7.1.4.14.7.5.1 to 7.1.4.14.7.5.4 and 7.1.4.14.7.7; and

(b)   The requirements for excepted packages specified in 6.4.4 of ADR;

except when the radioactive material possesses other hazardous properties and has to be classified in a class other than Class 7 in accordance with special provision 290 or 369 of Chapter 3.3, where the provisions listed in (a) and (b) above apply only as relevant and in addition to those relating to the main class.

1.7.1.5.2   Excepted packages are subject to the relevant provisions of all other parts of ADN.

1.7.2   Radiation protection programme

1.7.2.1   The carriage of radioactive material shall be subject to a radiation protection programme which shall consist of systematic arrangements aimed at providing adequate consideration of radiation protection measures.

1.7.2.2   Doses to persons shall be below the relevant dose limits. Protection and safety shall be optimized in order that the magnitude of individual doses, the number of persons exposed and the likelihood of incurring exposure shall be kept as low as reasonably achievable, economic and social factors being taken into account within the restriction that the doses to individuals be subject to dose constraints. A structured and systematic approach shall be adopted and shall include consideration of the interfaces between carriage and other activities.

1.7.2.3   The nature and extent of the measures to be employed in the programme shall be related to the magnitude and likelihood of radiation exposures. The programme shall incorporate the requirements in 1.7.2.2, 1.7.2.4, 1.7.2.5 and 7.5.11 CV33 (1.1) of ADR. Programme documents shall be available, on request, for inspection by the relevant competent authority.

1.7.2.4   For occupational exposures arising from transport activities, where it is assessed that the effective dose either:

(a)   is likely to be between 1 mSv and 6 mSv in a year, a dose assessment programme via work place monitoring or individual monitoring shall be conducted; or

(b)   is likely to exceed 6 mSv in a year, individual monitoring shall be conducted.

When workplace monitoring or individual monitoring is conducted, appropriate records shall be kept.

NOTE: For occupational exposures arising from transport activities, where it is assessed that the effective dose is most unlikely to exceed 1mSv in a year, no special work patterns, detailed monitoring, dose assessment programmes or individual record keeping need be required.

1.7.2.5   Workers (see 7.1.4.14.7, NOTE 3) shall be appropriately trained in radiation protection including the precautions to be observed in order to restrict their occupational exposure and the exposure of other persons who might be affected by their actions.

1.7.3 **Management system**

1.7.3.1 A management system based on international, national or other standards acceptable to the competent authority shall be established and implemented for all activities within the scope of ADN, as identified in 1.7.1.3, to ensure compliance with the relevant provisions of ADN. Certification that the design specification has been fully implemented shall be available to the competent authority. The manufacturer, consignor or user shall be prepared:

(a) To provide facilities for inspection during manufacture and use; and

(b) To demonstrate compliance with ADN to the competent authority.

Where competent authority approval is required, such approval shall take into account and be contingent upon the adequacy of the management system.

1.7.4 **Special arrangement**

1.7.4.1 Special arrangement shall mean those provisions, approved by the competent authority, under which consignments which do not satisfy all the requirements of ADN applicable to radioactive material may be transported.

NOTE: Special arrangement is not considered to be a temporary derogation in accordance with 1.5.1.

1.7.4.2 Consignments for which conformity with any provision applicable to radioactive material is impracticable shall not be transported except under special arrangement. Provided the competent authority is satisfied that conformity with the radioactive material provisions of ADN is impracticable and that the requisite standards of safety established by ADN have been demonstrated through means alternative to the other provisions of ADN, the competent authority may approve special arrangement transport operations for a single consignment or a planned series of multiple consignments. The overall level of safety in carriage shall be at least equivalent to that which would be provided if all the applicable requirements of ADN had been met. For international consignments of this type, multilateral approval shall be required.

1.7.5 **Radioactive material possessing other dangerous properties**

In addition to the radioactive and fissile properties, any subsidiary hazard of the contents of the package, such as explosiveness, flammability, pyrophoricity, chemical toxicity and corrosiveness, shall also be taken into account in the documentation, packing, labelling, marking, placarding, stowage, segregation and carriage, in order to be in compliance with all relevant provisions for dangerous goods of ADN.

1.7.6 **Non-compliance**

1.7.6.1 In the event of non-compliance with any limit in ADN applicable to dose rate or contamination,

(a) The consignor, carrier, consignee and any organization involved during carriage who may be affected, as appropriate, shall be informed of the non-compliance by:

(i) by the carrier if the non-compliance is identified during carriage; or

(ii) by the consignee if the non-compliance is identified at receipt;

(b)   The consignor, carrier or consignee, as appropriate shall:

  (i)   take immediate steps to mitigate the consequences of the non-compliance;

  (ii)   investigate the non-compliance and its causes, circumstances and consequences;

  (iii)   take appropriate action to remedy the causes and circumstances that led to the non-compliance and to prevent a recurrence of the causes and circumstances similar to those that led to the non-compliance; and

  (iv)   communicate to the competent authority(ies) on the causes of the non-compliance and the corrective or preventive actions taken or to be taken;

(c)   The communication of the non-compliance to the consignor and competent authority(ies), respectively, shall be made as soon as practicable and it shall be immediate whenever an emergency exposure situation has developed or is developing.

CHAPTER 1.8

CHECKS AND OTHER SUPPORT MEASURES TO ENSURE COMPLIANCE WITH SAFETY REQUIREMENTS

1.8.1   **Monitoring compliance with requirements**

1.8.1.1   *General*

1.8.1.1.1   In accordance with Article 4, paragraph 3 of ADN, Contracting Parties shall ensure that a representative proportion of consignments of dangerous goods carried by inland waterways is subject to monitoring in accordance with the provisions of this Chapter, and including the requirements of 1.10.1.5.

1.8.1.1.2   Participants in the carriage of dangerous goods (see Chapter 1.4) shall, without delay, in the context of their respective obligations, provide the competent authorities and their agents with the necessary information for carrying out the checks.

1.8.1.2   *Monitoring procedure*

1.8.1.2.1   In order to carry out the checks provided for in Article 4, paragraph 3 of ADN, the Contracting Parties shall use the checklist developed by the Administrative Committee.[*] A copy of this checklist shall be given to the master of the vessel. Competent authorities of other Contracting Parties may decide to simplify or refrain from conducting subsequent checks if a copy of the checklist is presented to them. This paragraph shall not prejudice the right of Contracting Parties to carry out specific measures or more detailed checks.

1.8.1.2.2   The checks shall be random and shall as far as possible cover an extensive portion of the inland waterway network.

1.8.1.2.3   When exercising the right to monitor, the authorities shall make all possible efforts to avoid unduly detaining or delaying a vessel.

1.8.1.2.4   Checklists used by the authorities of Contracting Parties shall be drawn up at least in the language of the issuing country and also, if that language is not French, English or German, in French, English or German.[1]

1.8.1.3   *Infringements of the requirements*

Without prejudice to other penalties which may be imposed, vessels in respect of which one or more infringements of the rules on the transport of dangerous goods by inland waterways are established may be detained at a place designated for this purpose by the authorities carrying out the check and required to be brought into conformity before continuing their journey or may be subject to other appropriate measures, depending on the circumstances or the requirements of safety.

1.8.1.4   *Checks in companies and at places of loading and unloading*

1.8.1.4.1   Checks may be carried out at the premises of undertakings, as a preventive measure or where infringements which jeopardize safety in the transport of dangerous goods have been recorded during the voyage.

---

[*]   *Note by the secretariat: The model of the checklist can be found on the United Nations Economic Commission for Europe website (http://www.unece.org/trans/danger/danger.html).*

[1]   *The checklist is not included in the documents to be kept on board according to 8.1.2.1.*

1.8.1.4.2   The purpose of such checks shall be to ensure that safety conditions for the transport of dangerous goods by inland waterways comply with the relevant laws.

1.8.1.4.3   *Sampling*

Where appropriate and provided that this does not constitute a safety hazard, samples of the goods transported may be taken for examination by laboratories recognized by the competent authority.

1.8.1.4.4   *Cooperation of the competent authorities*

1.8.1.4.4.1   Contracting Parties shall assist one another in order to give proper effect to these requirements.

1.8.1.4.4.2   Serious or repeated infringements jeopardizing the safety of the transport of dangerous goods committed by a foreign vessel or undertaking shall be reported to the competent authority in the Contracting Party where the certificate of approval of the vessel was issued or where the undertaking is established.

1.8.1.4.4.3   The competent authority of the Contracting Party where serious or repeated infringements have been recorded may ask the competent authority of the Contracting Party where the certificate of approval of the vessel was issued or where the undertaking is established for appropriate measures to be taken with regard to the offender or offenders.

1.8.1.4.4.4   The latter competent authority shall notify the competent authorities of the Contracting Party where the infringements were recorded of any measures taken with regard to the offender or offenders.

1.8.2   **Administrative assistance during the checking of a foreign vessel**

If the findings of a check on a foreign vessel give grounds for believing that serious or repeated infringements have been committed which cannot be detected in the course of that check in the absence of the necessary data, the competent authorities of the Contracting Parties concerned shall assist one another in order to clarify the situation.

1.8.3   **Safety adviser**

1.8.3.1   Each undertaking, the activities of which include the consigning or the carriage of dangerous goods by inland waterways, or the related packing, loading, filling or unloading shall appoint one or more safety advisers, hereinafter referred to as "advisers", for the carriage of dangerous goods, responsible for helping to prevent the risks inherent in such activities with regard to persons, property and the environment.

NOTE: *This obligation does not apply to reception facility operators.*

1.8.3.2   The competent authorities of the Contracting Parties may provide that these requirements shall not apply to undertakings:

(a)   the activities of which concern:

     (i)   The carriage of dangerous goods fully or partially exempted according to the provisions of 1.7.1.4 or of chapters 3.3, 3.4 or 3.5;

     (ii)   Quantities per transport unit, wagon or container not exceeding those referred to in 1.1.3.6 of ADR or RID;

     (iii)   When (ii) above is not relevant, quantities per vessel not exceeding those referred to in 1.1.3.6 of these Regulations.

(b)   the main or secondary activities of which are not the carriage or the related packing, filling, loading or unloading of dangerous goods but which occasionally engage in the national carriage or the related packing, filling, loading or unloading of dangerous goods posing little danger or risk of pollution.

1.8.3.3   The main task of the adviser shall be, under the responsibility of the head of the undertaking, to seek by all appropriate means and by all appropriate action, within the limits of the relevant activities of that undertaking, to facilitate the conduct of those activities in accordance with the requirements applicable and in the safest possible way.

With regard to the undertaking's activities, the adviser has the following duties in particular:

–   monitoring compliance with the requirements governing the carriage of dangerous goods;

–   advising his undertaking on the carriage of dangerous goods;

–   preparing an annual report to the management of his undertaking or a local public authority, as appropriate, on the undertaking's activities in the carriage of dangerous goods. Such annual reports shall be preserved for five years and made available to the national authorities at their request.

The adviser's duties also include monitoring the following practices and procedures relating to the relevant activities of the undertaking:

–   the procedures for compliance with the requirements governing the identification of dangerous goods being transported;

–   the undertaking's practice in taking account, when purchasing means of transport, of any special requirements in connection with the dangerous goods being transported;

–   the procedures for checking the equipment used in connection with the carriage, packing, filling, loading or unloading of dangerous goods;

–   the proper training of the undertaking's employees, including on the changes to the Regulations, and the maintenance of records of such training;

–   the implementation of proper emergency procedures in the event of any accident or incident that may affect safety during the carriage, packing, filling, loading or unloading of dangerous goods;

–   investigating and, where appropriate, preparing reports on serious accidents, incidents or serious infringements recorded during the carriage, packing, filling, loading or unloading of dangerous goods;

–   the implementation of appropriate measures to avoid the recurrence of accidents, incidents or serious infringements;

–   the account taken of the legal prescriptions and special requirements associated with the carriage of dangerous goods in the choice and use of sub-contractors or third parties;

–   verification that employees involved in the consigning, carriage, packing, filling, loading or unloading of dangerous goods have detailed operational procedures and instructions,

–   the introduction of measures to increase awareness of the risks inherent in the carriage, packing, filling, loading and unloading of dangerous goods;

- the implementation of verification procedures to ensure the presence on board means of transport of the documents and safety equipment which must accompany transport and the compliance of such documents and equipment with the regulations;

- the implementation of verification procedures to ensure compliance with the requirements governing packing, filling, loading and unloading;

- the existence of the security plan indicated in 1.10.3.2.

1.8.3.4 The safety adviser may also be the head of the undertaking, a person with other duties in the undertaking, or a person not directly employed by that undertaking, provided that that person is capable of performing the duties of adviser.

1.8.3.5 Each undertaking concerned shall, on request, inform the competent authority or the body designated for that purpose by each Contracting Party of the identity of its adviser.

1.8.3.6 Whenever an accident affects persons, property or the environment or results in damage to property or the environment during carriage, packing, filling, loading or unloading carried out by the undertaking concerned, the safety adviser shall, after collecting all the relevant information, prepare an accident report to the management of the undertaking or to a local public authority, as appropriate. That report shall not replace any report by the management of the undertaking which might be required under any other international or national legislation.

1.8.3.7 A safety adviser shall hold a vocational training certificate, valid for transport by inland waterways. That certificate shall be issued by the competent authority or the body designated for that purpose by each Contracting Party.

1.8.3.8 To obtain a certificate, a candidate shall undergo training and pass an examination approved by the competent authority of the Contracting Party.

1.8.3.9 The main aims of the training shall be to provide candidates with sufficient knowledge of the risks inherent in the carriage packing, filling, loading or unloading of dangerous goods, of the applicable laws, regulations and administrative provisions and of the duties listed in 1.8.3.3.

1.8.3.10 The examination shall be organized by the competent authority or by an examining body designated by the competent authority. The examining body shall not be a training provider.

The examining body shall be designated in writing. This approval may be of limited duration and shall be based on the following criteria:

- competence of the examining body;

- specifications of the form of the examinations the examining body is proposing, including, if necessary, the infrastructure and organisation of electronic examinations in accordance with 1.8.3.12.5, if these are to be carried out;

- measures intended to ensure that examinations are impartial;

- independence of the body from all natural or legal persons employing safety advisers.

1.8.3.11 The aim of the examination is to ascertain whether candidates possess the necessary level of knowledge to carry out the duties incumbent upon a safety adviser as listed in 1.8.3.3, for the purpose of obtaining the certificate prescribed in subsection 1.8.3.7, and it shall cover at least the following subjects:

(a) Knowledge of the types of consequences which may be caused by an accident involving dangerous goods and knowledge of the main causes of accidents;

(b)   Requirements under national law, international conventions and agreements, with regard to the following in particular:

–   classification of dangerous goods (procedure for classifying solutions and mixtures, structure of the list of substances, classes of dangerous goods and principles for their classification, nature of dangerous goods transported, physical, chemical and toxicological properties of dangerous goods);

–   general packing provisions, provisions for tanks and tank-containers (types, code, marking, construction, initial and periodic inspection and testing);

–   marking and labelling, placarding and orange-coloured plate marking (marking and labelling of packages, placing and removal of placards and orange-coloured plates);

–   particulars in transport documents (information required);

–   method of consignment and restrictions on dispatch (full load, carriage in bulk, carriage in intermediate bulk containers, carriage in containers, carriage in fixed or demountable tanks);

–   transport of passengers;

–   prohibitions and precautions relating to mixed loading;

–   segregation of goods;

–   limitation of the quantities carried and quantities exempted;

–   handling and stowage (packing, filling, loading and unloading - filling ratios - stowage and segregation);

–   cleaning and/or degassing before packing, filling, loading and after unloading;

–   crews, vocational training;

–   vehicle documents (transport documents, instructions in writing, vessel approval certificate, ADN dangerous goods training certificate, copies of any derogations, other documents);

–   instructions in writing (implementation of the instructions and crew protection equipment);

–   supervision requirements (berthing);

–   traffic regulations and restrictions;

–   operational discharges or accidental leaks of pollutants;

–   requirements relating to equipment for transport (vessel).

1.8.3.12   *Examinations*

1.8.3.12.1   The examination shall consist of a written test which may be supplemented by an oral examination.

1.8.3.12.2   The competent authority or an examining body designated by the competent authority shall invigilate every examination. Any manipulation and deception shall be ruled out as far as possible. Authentication of the candidate shall be ensured. The use in the written test of documentation other than international or national regulations is not permitted. All examination documents shall be recorded and kept as a print-out or electronically as a file.

1.8.3.12.3   Electronic media may be used only if provided by the examining body. There shall be no means of a candidate introducing further data to the electronic media provided; the candidate may only answer to the questions posed.

1.8.3.12.4   The written test shall consist of two parts:

(a)   Candidates shall receive a questionnaire. It shall include at least 20 open questions covering at least the subjects mentioned in the list in 1.8.3.11. However, multiple choice questions may be used. In this case, two multiple choice questions count as one open question. Amongst these subjects particular attention shall be paid to the following subjects:

–   general preventive and safety measures;

–   classification of dangerous goods;

–   general packing provisions, including tanks, tank-containers, tank-vehicles, etc.;

–   danger marking, labelling and placarding;

–   information in the transport document;

–   handling and stowage;

–   crew, vocational training;

–   vehicle documents and transport certificates;

–   instructions in writing;

–   requirements concerning equipment for transport by vessel;

(b)   Candidates shall undertake a case study in keeping with the duties of the adviser referred to in 1.8.3.3, in order to demonstrate that they have the necessary qualifications to fulfil the task of adviser.

1.8.3.12.5   Written examinations may be performed, in whole or in part, as electronic examinations, where the answers are recorded and evaluated using electronic data processing (EDP) processes, provided the following conditions are met:

(a)   The hardware and software shall be checked and accepted by the competent authority or by an examining body designated by the competent authority;

(b)   Proper technical functioning shall be ensured. Arrangements as to whether and how the examination can be continued shall be made for a failure of the devices and applications. No aids shall be available on the input devices (e.g. electronic search function), the equipment provided according to 1.8.3.12.3 shall not allow the candidates to communicate with any other device during the examination;

(c)   Final inputs of each candidate shall be logged. The determination of the results shall be transparent.

1.8.3.13   The Contracting Parties may decide that candidates who intend working for undertakings specializing in the carriage of certain types of dangerous goods need only be questioned on the substances relating to their activities. These types of goods are:

–   Class 1;

–   Class 2;

–   Class 7;

–   Classes 3, 4.1, 4.2, 4.3, 5.1, 5.2, 6.1, 6.2, 8 and 9;

–   UN Nos. 1202, 1203, 1223, 3475, and aviation fuel classified under UN Nos. 1268 or 1863.

The certificate prescribed in 1.8.3.7 shall clearly indicate that it is only valid for one type of the dangerous goods referred to in this subsection and on which the adviser has been questioned under the conditions defined in 1.8.3.12.

1.8.3.14   The competent authority or the examining body shall keep a running list of the questions that have been included in the examination.

1.8.3.15   The certificate prescribed in 1.8.3.7 shall take the form laid down in 1.8.3.18 and shall be recognized by all Contracting Parties.

1.8.3.16   *Validity and renewal of certificates*

1.8.3.16.1   The certificate shall be valid for five years. The period of validity of a certificate shall be extended from the date of its expiry for five years at a time where, during the year before its expiry, its holder has passed an examination. The examination shall be approved by the competent authority.

1.8.3.16.2   The aim of the examination is to ascertain that the holder has the necessary knowledge to carry out the duties set out in 1.8.3.3. The knowledge required is set out in 1.8.3.11 (b) and shall include the amendments to the Regulations introduced since the award of the last certificate. The examination shall be held and supervised on the same basis as in 1.8.3.10 and 1.8.3.12 to 1.8.3.14. However, holders need not undertake the case study specified in 1.8.3.12.4 (b).

1.8.3.17   The requirements set out in 1.8.3.1 to 1.8.3.16 shall be considered to have been fulfilled if the relevant conditions of Council Directive 96/35/EC of 3 June 1996 on the appointment and vocational qualification of safety advisers for the transport of dangerous goods by road, rail and inland waterway[2] and of Directive 2000/18/EC of the European Parliament and of the Council of 17 April 2000 on minimum examination requirements for safety advisers for the transport of dangerous goods by road, rail or inland waterway[3] are applied.

---

[2]   *Official Journal of the European Communities, No. L145 of 19 June 1996, page 10.*
[3]   *Official Journal of the European Communities, No. L118 of 19 May 2000, page 41.*

1.8.3.18   *Form of certificate*

Certificate of training as safety adviser for the transport of dangerous goods

Certificate No: ....120...

Distinguishing sign of the State issuing the certificate: ....

Surname: ....

Forename(s): ....

Date and place of birth: ....

Nationality: ....

Signature of holder: ....

Valid until .... for undertakings which transport dangerous goods and for undertakings which carry out related consigning, packing, filling, loading or unloading:

☐ by road   ☐ by rail   ☐ by inland waterway

Issued by: ....

Date: ....   Signature: ....

1.8.3.19 *Extension of the certificate*

Where an adviser extends the scope of his certificate during its period of validity by meeting the requirements of 1.8.3.16.2, the period of validity of a new certificate shall remain that of the previous certificate.

1.8.4 **List of competent authorities and bodies designated by them**

The Contracting Parties shall communicate to the secretariat of the United Nations Economic Commission for Europe the addresses of the authorities and bodies designated by them which are competent in accordance with national law to implement ADN, referring in each case to the relevant requirement of ADN and giving the addresses to which the relevant applications should be made.

The secretariat of the United Nations Economic Commission for Europe shall establish a list on the basis of the information received and shall keep it up-to-date. It shall communicate this list and the amendments thereto to the Contracting Parties.

1.8.5 **Notifications of occurrences involving dangerous goods**

1.8.5.1 If a serious accident or incident takes place during loading, filling, carriage or unloading of dangerous goods, or during degassing of tank vessels on the territory of a Contracting Party, the loader, filler, carrier, unloader, consignee or reception facility operator, respectively, shall ascertain that a report conforming to the model prescribed in 1.8.5.4 is made to the competent authority of the Contracting Party concerned at the latest one month after the occurrence.

1.8.5.2 The Contracting Party shall in turn, if necessary, make a report to the secretariat of the United Nations Economic Commission for Europe with a view to informing the other Contracting Parties.

1.8.5.3 *An occurrence subject to report* in accordance with 1.8.5.1 has occurred if dangerous goods were released or if there was an imminent risk of loss of product, if personal injury, material or environmental damage occurred, or if the authorities were involved and one or more of the following criteria has/have been met:

Personal injury means an occurrence in which death or injury directly relating to the dangerous goods carried has occurred, and where the injury

(a)   requires intensive medical treatment,

(b)   requires a stay in hospital of at least one day, or

(c)   results in the inability to work for at least three consecutive days.

Loss of product means the release of dangerous goods of:

(a)   Classes 1 or 2 or packing group I or other substances not assigned to a packing group in quantities of 50 kg or 50 litres or more;

(b)   Packing group II in quantities of 333 kg or 333 litres or more; or

(c)   Packing group III in quantities of 1,000 kg or 1,000 litres or more.

The loss of product criterion also applies if there was an imminent risk of loss of product in the above-mentioned quantities. As a rule, this has to be assumed if, owing to structural damage, the means of containment is no longer suitable for further carriage or if, for any other reason, a sufficient level of safety is no longer ensured (e.g. owing to distortion of tanks or containers, overturning of a tank or fire in the immediate vicinity).

If dangerous goods of Class 6.2 are involved, the obligation to report applies without quantity limitation.

In occurrences involving radioactive material, the criteria for loss of product are:

(a) Any release of radioactive material from the packages;

(b) Exposure leading to a breach of the limits set out in the regulations for protection of workers and members of the public against ionizing radiation ("Radiation Protection and Safety of Radiation Sources: International Basic Safety Standards", IAEA Safety Standards Series No. GSR Part 3, IAEA, Vienna (2014)); or

(c) Where there is reason to believe that there has been a significant degradation in any package safety function (containment, shielding, thermal protection or criticality) that may have rendered the package unsuitable for continued carriage without additional safety measures.

NOTE: *See the provisions of 7.1.4.14.7.7 for undeliverable consignments.*

Material damage or *environmental damage* means the release of dangerous goods, irrespective of the quantity, where the estimated amount of damage exceeds 50,000 Euros. Damage to any directly involved means of carriage containing dangerous goods and to the modal infrastructure shall not be taken into account for this purpose.

Involvement of authorities means the direct involvement of the authorities or emergency services during the occurrence involving dangerous goods and the evacuation of persons or closure of public traffic routes (roads/railways/inland waterways) for at least three hours owing to the danger posed by the dangerous goods.

If necessary, the competent authority may request further relevant information.

1.8.5.4 *Model report on occurrences during the carriage of dangerous goods*

Report on occurrences during the carriage of dangerous goods in accordance with ADN, section 1.8.5

Report No.:

Carrier/Filler/Consignee/Loader: ....

Official number of vessel: ....

Dry cargo vessel (single-hull, double-hull): ....

Tank vessel (type): ....

Address:

Contact name: .... Telephone: ....

Fax/e-mail: ....

(The competent authority shall remove this cover sheet before forwarding the report)

1. Mode	
Inland waterway …………………………….. …………………………………………………………..	Official number of vessel/name of vessel (optional) …….. …………………………………………………………

2. Date and location of occurrence

Year: ………………………….. Month: …………………….. Day: ……………………….. Time:
………………………………….

☐ Port ☐ Loading/unloading/transhipment facility Location/Country: ………………………………………………. or ☐ Free sector Name of sector: …………………………………………… Kilometre point: …………………………………………… or ☐ Structure such as bridge or guide wall	Comments concerning description of location: …………………………………………………………. …………………………………………………………. Location/Country : …………………………………………………………. ………………………………………………………….

3. Conditions of inland waterway

Water level (reference gauge):
…….

Estimated speed through water:
…….

☐ High water
☐ Low water

4. Particular weather conditions

☐ Rain
☐ Snow
☐ Fog
☐ Thunderstorm
☐ Storm
Temperature: …………°C

5. Description of occurrence

☐ Collision with bank, structure or berthing installation
☐ Collision with another cargo vessel (collision/impact)
☐ Collision with a passenger vessel (collision/impact)
☐ Contact with the waterway bed, whether or not vessel has run aground
☐ Fire
☐ Explosion
☐ Leak/Location and extent of damage (with additional description)
☐ Shipwreck
☐ Capsizing
☐ Technical fault (optional)
☐ Human error (optional)
Additional description of occurrence:
…….
…….
…….
…….

6. Dangerous goods involved

UN Number[1] or Identification number	Class	Packing group if known	Estimated quantity of loss of products (kg or l)[2]	Means of containment in accordance with ADN, 1.2.1[3]	Means of containment material	Type of failure of means of containment[4]

[1] For dangerous goods assigned to collective entries to which special provision 274 applies, also the technical name shall be indicated.	[2] For class 7, indicate values according to the criteria in 1.8.5.3.

| ⁽³⁾ Indicate the appropriate number:
  1 Packaging
  2 IBC
  3 Large packaging
  4 Small container
  5 Wagon
  6 Vehicle
  7 Tank-wagon
  8 Tank-vehicle
  9 Battery-wagon
 10 Battery-vehicle
 11 Wagon with demountable tanks
 12 Demountable tank
 13 Large container
 14 Tank container
 15 MEGC
 16 Portable tank
 17 Dry cargo vessel (single-hull, double-hull)
 18 Tank vessel (type) | ⁽⁴⁾ Indicate the appropriate number:
  1 Loss
  2 Fire
  3 Explosion
  4 Structural failure |

7. Cause of occurrence (if clearly known) (optional)

☐ Technical fault
☐ Faulty load securing
☐ Operational cause
☐ Other:

....

....

....

....

8. Consequences of occurrence

Personal injury in connection with the dangerous goods involved:

☐ Deaths (number: ....)
☐ Injured (number: ....)

Loss of product:

☐ Yes
☐ No
☐ Imminent risk of loss of product

Material/Environment damage:

☐ Estimated level of damage   ≤   50 000 Euros
☐ Estimated level of damage   >   50 000 Euros

Involvement of authorities:

☐   Yes   ☐   Evacuation of persons for a duration of at least three hours caused by the dangerous goods involved
                                ☐   Closure of public traffic routes for a duration of at least three hours caused by the dangerous goods involved

☐   No

If necessary, the competent authority may request further relevant information.

CHAPTER 1.9

TRANSPORT RESTRICTIONS BY THE COMPETENT AUTHORITIES

1.9.1   In accordance with Article 6, paragraph 1 of ADN, the entry of dangerous goods into the territory of Contracting Parties may be subject to regulations or prohibitions imposed for reasons other than safety during carriage. Such regulations or prohibitions shall be published in an appropriate form.

1.9.2   Subject to the provisions of 1.9.3, a Contracting Party may apply to vessels engaged in the international carriage of dangerous goods by inland waterways on its territory certain additional provisions not included in ADN, provided that those provisions do not conflict with Article 4, paragraph 2 of ADN, and are contained in its domestic legislation applying equally to vessels engaged in the domestic carriage of dangerous goods by inland waterways on the territory of that Contracting Party.

1.9.3   Additional provisions falling within the scope of 1.9.2 are as follows:

(a)   Additional safety requirements or restrictions concerning vessels using certain structures such as bridges or tunnels, or vessels entering or leaving ports or other transport terminals;

(b)   Requirements for vessels to follow prescribed routes to avoid commercial or residential areas, environmentally sensitive areas, industrial zones containing hazardous installations or inland waterways presenting severe physical hazards;

(c)   Emergency requirements regarding routing or parking of vessels carrying dangerous goods resulting from extreme weather conditions, earthquake, accident, industrial action, civil disorder or military hostilities;

(d)   Restrictions on movement of vessels carrying dangerous goods on certain days of the week or year.

1.9.4   The competent authority of the Contracting Party applying on its territory any additional provisions within the scope of 1.9.3 (a) and (d) above shall notify the secretariat of the United Nations Economic Commission for Europe of the additional provisions, which secretariat shall bring them to the attention of the Contracting Parties.

CHAPTER 1.10

SECURITY PROVISIONS

NOTE: For the purposes of this Chapter, "security" means measures or precautions to be taken to minimise theft or misuse of dangerous goods that may endanger persons, property or the environment.

1.10.1   **General provisions**

1.10.1.1   All persons engaged in the carriage of dangerous goods shall consider the security requirements set out in this Chapter commensurate with their responsibilities.

1.10.1.2   Dangerous goods shall only be offered for carriage to carriers that have been appropriately identified.

1.10.1.3   Holding areas in trans-shipment zones for dangerous goods shall be secured, well lit and, where possible and appropriate, not accessible to the general public.

1.10.1.4   For each crew member of a vessel carrying dangerous goods, means of identification, which includes a photograph, shall be on board during carriage.

1.10.1.5   Safety checks in accordance with 1.8.1 shall also concern the implementation of security measures.

1.10.1.6   The competent authority shall maintain up-to-date registers of all valid certificates for experts stipulated in 8.2.1 issued by it or by any recognized organization.

1.10.2   **Security training**

1.10.2.1   The training and the refresher training specified in Chapter 1.3 shall also include elements of security awareness. The security refresher training need not be linked to regulatory changes only.

1.10.2.2   Security awareness training shall address the nature of security risks, recognising security risks, methods to address and reduce such risks and actions to be taken in the event of a security breach. It shall include awareness of security plans (if appropriate) commensurate with the responsibilities and duties of individuals and their part in implementing security plans.

1.10.2.3   Such training shall be provided or verified upon employment in a position involving dangerous goods transport and shall be periodically supplemented with refresher training.

1.10.2.4   Records of all security training received shall be kept by the employer and made available to the employee or competent authority, upon request. Records shall be kept by the employer for a period of time established by the competent authority.

1.10.3   **Provisions for high consequence dangerous goods**

NOTE: In addition to the security provisions of ADN, competent authorities may implement further security provisions for reasons other than safety during carriage (see also Article 4, paragraph 1 of the Agreement). In order not to impede international and multimodal carriage by different explosives security marks, it is recommended that such marks be formatted consistent with an internationally harmonized standard (e.g. European Union Commission Directive 2008/43/EC).

1.10.3.1   *Definition of high consequence dangerous goods*

1.10.3.1.1   High consequence dangerous goods are those which have the potential for misuse in a terrorist event and which may, as a result, produce serious consequences such as mass casualties, mass destruction or, particularly for Class 7, mass socio-economic disruption.

1.10.3.1.2   High consequence dangerous goods in classes other than Class 7 are those listed in Table 1.10.3.1.2 below and carried in quantities greater than those indicated therein.

Table 1.10.3.1.2: List of high consequence dangerous goods

Class	Division	Substance or article	Quantity		
			Tank or cargo tank (litres)[c]	Bulk[*/] (kg) [d]	Goods in packages (kg)
1	1.1	Explosives	a	a	0
	1.2	Explosives	a	a	0
	1.3	Compatibility group C explosives	a	a	0
	1.4	Explosives of UN Nos. 0104, 0237, 0255, 0267, 0289, 0361, 0365, 0366, 0440, 0441, 0455, 0456, 0500, 0512 and 0513	a	a	0
	1.5	Explosives	0	a	0
	1.6	Explosives	a	a	0
2		Flammable, non-toxic gases (classification codes including only letters F or FC)	3000	a	b
		Toxic gases (classification codes including letter(s) T, TF, TC, TO, TFC or TOC) excluding aerosols	0	a	0
3		Flammable liquids of packing groups I and II	3000	a	b
		Desensitized explosives	0	a	0
4.1		Desensitized explosives	a	a	0
4.2		Packing group I substances	3000	a	b
4.3		Packing group I substances	3000	a	b
5.1		Oxidizing liquids of packing group I	3000	a	b
		Perchlorates, ammonium nitrate, ammonium nitrate fertilisers and ammonium nitrate emulsions or suspensions or gels	3000	3000	b
6.1		Toxic substances of packing group I	0	a	0
6.2		Infectious substances of Category A (UN Nos. 2814 and 2900, except for animal material) and medical waste of Category A (UN No. 3549)	a	0	0
8		Corrosive substances of packing group I	3000	a	b

*/   *Bulk means bulk in the vessel, or bulk in a vehicle or a container.*

a   *Not relevant.*

b   *The provisions of 1.10.3 do not apply, whatever the quantity is.*

c   *A value indicated in this column is applicable only if carriage in tanks is authorized according to Chapter 3.2, table A, column (10) or (12) of ADR or RID or if letter "T" is indicated in chapter 3.2, table A, column (8) of ADN. For substances which are not authorized for carriage in tanks, the instruction in this column is not relevant.*

d   *A value indicated in this column is applicable only if carriage in bulk is authorized according to Chapter 3.2, table A, column (10) or (17) of ADR or RID, or if letter "B" is indicated in chapter 3.2, table A, column (8) of ADN. For substances which are not authorized for carriage in bulk, the instruction in this column is not relevant.*

1.10.3.1.3   For dangerous goods of Class 7, high consequence radioactive material is that with an activity equal to or greater than a transport security threshold of 3 000 A_2 per single package (see also 2.2.7.2.2.1) except for the following radionuclides where the transport security threshold is given in Table 1.10.3.1.3 below.

Table 1.10.3.1.3: Transport security thresholds for specific radionuclides

Element	Radionuclide	Transport security threshold (TBq)
Americium	Am-241	0.6
Gold	Au-198	2
Cadmium	Cd-109	200
Caesium	Cs-137	1
Californium	Cf-252	0.2
Curium	Cm-244	0.5
Cobalt	Co-57	7
Cobalt	Co-60	0.3
Iron	Fe-55	8000
Germanium	Ge-68	7
Gadolinium	Gd-153	10
Iridium	Ir-192	0.8
Nickel	Ni-63	600
Palladium	Pd-103	900
Promethium	Pm-147	400
Polonium	Po-210	0.6
Plutonium	Pu-238	0.6
Plutonium	Pu-239	0.6
Radium	Ra-226	0.4
Ruthenium	Ru-106	3
Selenium	Se-75	2
Strontium	Sr-90	10
Thallium	Tl-204	200
Thulium	Tm-170	200
Ytterbium	Yb-169	3

1.10.3.1.4   For mixtures of radionuclides, determination of whether or not the transport security threshold has been met or exceeded can be calculated by summing the ratios of activity present for each radionuclide divided by the transport security threshold for that radionuclide. If the sum of the fractions is less than 1, then the radioactivity threshold for the mixture has not been met nor exceeded.

This calculation can be made with the formula:

$$\sum_i \frac{A_i}{T_i} < 1$$

Where:

A_i = activity of radionuclide i that is present in a package (TBq)

T_i = transport security threshold for radionuclide i (TBq).

1.10.3.1.5   When radioactive material possess subsidiary hazards of other classes, the criteria of Table 1.10.3.1.2 shall also be taken into account (see also 1.7.5).

1.10.3.2   *Security plans*

1.10.3.2.1   Carriers, consignors and other participants specified in 1.4.2 and 1.4.3 engaged in the carriage of high consequence dangerous goods (see Table 1.10.3.1.2) or high consequence radioactive material (see 1.10.3.1.3) shall adopt, implement and comply with a security plan that addresses at least the elements specified in 1.10.3.2.2.

1.10.3.2.2   The security plan shall comprise at least the following elements:

    (a)   specific allocation of responsibilities for security to competent and qualified persons with appropriate authority to carry out their responsibilities;

    (b)   records of dangerous goods or types of dangerous goods concerned;

    (c)   review of current operations and assessment of security risks, including any stops necessary to the transport operation, the keeping of dangerous goods in the vessel, tank or container before, during and after the journey and the intermediate temporary storage of dangerous goods during the course of intermodal transfer or transshipment between units;

    (d)   clear statement of measures that are to be taken to reduce security risks, commensurate with the responsibilities and duties of the participant, including:

        –   training;

        –   security policies (e.g. response to higher threat conditions, new employee/employment verification, etc.);

        –   operating practices (e.g. choice/use of routes where known, access to dangerous goods in intermediate temporary storage (as defined in (c)), proximity to vulnerable infrastructure etc.);

        –   equipment and resources that are to be used to reduce risks;

    (e)   effective and up to date procedures for reporting and dealing with security threats, breaches of security or security incidents;

    (f)   procedures for the evaluation and testing of security plans and procedures for periodic review and update of the plans;

    (g)   measures to ensure the physical security of transport information contained in the security plan; and

    (h)   measures to ensure that the distribution of information relating to the transport operation contained in the security plan is limited to those who need to have it. Such measures shall not preclude the provision of information required elsewhere in ADN.

NOTE: Carriers, consignors and consignees should co-operate with each other and with competent authorities to exchange threat information, apply appropriate security measures and respond to security incidents.

1.10.3.3   Operational or technical measures shall be taken on vessels carrying high consequence dangerous goods (see Table 1.10.3.1.2) or high consequence radioactive material (see 1.10.3.1.3) in order to prevent the improper use of the vessel and of the dangerous goods. The application of these protective measures shall not jeopardize emergency response.

NOTE: When appropriate and already fitted, the use of transport telemetry or other tracking methods or devices should be used to monitor the movement of high consequence dangerous goods (see Table 1.10.3.1.2 or 1.10.3.1.3).

1.10.4   Except for radioactive material bearing UN Nos. 2910 and 2911, if the activity level (per package) exceeds the A_2 value, the requirements of 1.10.1, 1.10.2 and 1.10.3 do not apply when the quantities carried in packages on a vessel do not exceed those referred to in 1.1.3.6.1. In addition the provisions of this Chapter do not apply to the carriage of UN No. 2912 RADIOACTIVE MATERIAL, LOW SPECIFIC ACTIVITY (LSA-I) and UN No. 2913 RADIOACTIVE MATERIAL, SURFACE CONTAMINATED OBJECTS (SCO-I).

1.10.5   For radioactive material, the provisions of this Chapter are deemed to be complied with when the provisions of the Convention on Physical Protection of Nuclear Material[1] and the IAEA circular on "Nuclear Security Recommendations on Physical Protection of Nuclear Material and Nuclear Facilities"[2] are applied.

---

[1]   *IAEACIRC/274/Rev.1, IAEA, Vienna (1980).*
[2]   *INFCIRC/225/Rev.5, IAEA, Vienna (2011).*

CHAPTERS 1.11 to 1.14

(Reserved)

CHAPTER 1.15

RECOGNITION OF CLASSIFICATION SOCIETIES

1.15.1   **General**

In the event of the conclusion of an international agreement concerning more general regulations or the navigation of vessels on inland waterways and containing provisions relating to the full range of activities of classification societies and their recognition, any provision of this Chapter in contradiction with any of the provisions of the said international agreement would, in the relations among Parties to this Agreement which had become parties to the international agreement and as from the day of the entry into force of the latter, automatically be deleted and replaced ipso facto by the relevant provision of the international agreement. This Chapter would become null and void once the international agreement came into force if all Parties to this Agreement became Parties to the international agreement.

1.15.2   **Procedure for the recognition of classification societies**

1.15.2.1   A classification society which wishes to be recommended for recognition under this Agreement shall submit its application for recognition, in accordance with the provisions of this Chapter, to the competent authority of a Contracting Party.

The classification society shall prepare the relevant information in accordance with the provisions of this Chapter. It shall produce it in, at least, an official language of the State where the application is submitted and in English.

The Contracting Party shall forward the application to the Administrative Committee unless in its opinion the conditions and criteria referred to in 1.15.3 have manifestly not been met.

1.15.2.2   The Administrative Committee shall appoint a Committee of Experts and determine its composition and its rules of procedure. This Committee of Experts shall consider the proposal; it shall determine whether the classification society meets the criteria set out in 1.15.3 and shall make a recommendation to the Administrative Committee within a period of six months.

1.15.2.3   The Administrative Committee shall examine the report of the experts. It shall decide in accordance with the procedure set out in Article 17, 7(c), within one year maximum, whether or not to recommend to the Contracting Parties that they should recognize the classification society in question. The Administrative Committee shall establish a list of the classification societies recommended for recognition by the Contracting Parties.

1.15.2.4   Each Contracting Party may or may not decide to recognize the classification societies in question, only on the basis of the list referred to in 1.15.2.3. The Contracting Party shall inform the Administrative Committee and the other Contracting Parties of its decision.

The Administrative Committee shall update the list of recognitions issued by Contracting Parties.

1.15.2.5   If a Contracting Party considers that a classification society no longer meets the conditions and criteria set out in 1.15.3, it may submit a proposal to the Administrative Committee for withdrawal from the list of recommended societies. Such a proposal shall be substantiated by convincing evidence of a failure to meet the conditions and criteria.

1.15.2.6   The Administrative Committee shall set up a new Committee of Experts following the procedure set out under 1.15.2.2 which shall report to the Administrative Committee within a period of six months. The classification society shall be informed and invited by the Committee of Experts to comment on the findings.

1.15.2.7   The Administrative Committee may decide, in case of a failure(s) to meet the conditions and criteria in 1.15.3, that the classification society shall have the opportunity to present a plan to address the identified failure(s) within a deadline of six months and to avoid any reoccurrence or, in accordance with Article 17, 7 (c), to withdraw the name of the society in question from the list of societies recommended for recognition.

In such a case the society in question shall immediately be so informed. The Administrative Committee shall also inform all the Contracting Parties that the classification society in question no longer meets the requirements to act as a recognized classification society in the context of the Agreement and shall invite them to take the necessary steps in order to remain in conformity with the requirements of the Agreement.

1.15.3   Conditions and criteria for the recognition of a classification society applying for recognition

A classification society applying for recognition under this Agreement shall meet all the following conditions and criteria:

1.15.3.1   A classification society shall be able to demonstrate extensive knowledge of and experience in the assessment of the design and construction of inland navigation vessels. The society should have comprehensive rules and regulations for the design, construction and periodical inspection of vessels. These rules and regulations shall be published and continuously updated and improved through research and development programmes.

1.15.3.2   Registers of the vessels classified by the classification society shall be published annually.

1.15.3.3   The classification society shall not be controlled by shipowners or shipbuilders, or by others engaged commercially in the manufacture, fitting out, repair or operation of ships. The classification society shall not be substantially dependent on a single commercial enterprise for its revenue.

1.15.3.4   The headquarters or a branch of the classification society authorized and entitled to give a ruling and to act in all areas incumbent on it under the regulations governing inland navigation shall be located in one of the Contracting Parties.

1.15.3.5   The classification society and its experts shall have a good reputation in inland navigation; the experts shall be able to provide proof of their professional abilities.

1.15.3.6   The classification society:

–   shall have sufficient professional staff and engineers for the technical tasks of monitoring and inspection and for the tasks of management, support and research, in proportion to the tasks and the number of vessels classified and sufficient to keep regulations up to date and develop them in the light of quality requirements;

–   shall have experts in at least two Contracting Parties.

1.15.3.7   The classification society shall be governed by a code of ethics.

1.15.3.8   The classification society shall have prepared and implemented and shall maintain an effective system of internal quality based on the relevant aspects of internationally recognized quality standards and conforming to the standards EN ISO/IEC 17020:2012 (except clause 8.1.3) (inspection bodies) and ISO 9001 or EN ISO 9001:2015. The classification society is subject to certification of its quality system by an independent body of auditors recognized by the administration of the State in which it is located.

1.15.4 Obligations of recommended classification societies

1.15.4.1 Recommended classification societies shall undertake to cooperate with each other so as to guarantee equivalence from the point of view of safety of their technical standards which are relevant to the implementation of the provisions of the present Agreement.

1.15.4.2 They shall exchange experiences in joint meetings at least once a year. They shall report annually to the Safety Committee. The secretariat of the Safety Committee shall be informed of those meetings. The opportunity will be given to Contracting Parties to attend the meetings as observers.

1.15.4.3 Recommended classification societies shall undertake to apply the present and future provisions of the Agreement taking into account the date of their entry into force. In response to requests from the competent authority, recommended classification societies shall provide all relevant information regarding their technical requirements.

CHAPTER 1.16

PROCEDURE FOR THE ISSUE OF THE CERTIFICATE OF APPROVAL

1.16.0   For the purposes of this Chapter, "owner" means "the owner or his designated representative or, if the vessel is chartered by an operator, the operator or his designated representative".

1.16.1   Certificate of approval

1.16.1.1   *General*

1.16.1.1.1   Dry cargo vessels carrying dangerous goods in quantities greater than exempted quantities, the vessels referred to in 7.1.2.19.1, tank vessels carrying dangerous goods and the vessels referred to in 7.2.2.19.3 shall be provided with an appropriate certificate of approval.

1.16.1.1.2   The certificate of approval shall be valid for not more than five years, subject to the provisions of 1.16.11.

1.16.1.2   *Format of the certificate of approval, particulars to be included*

1.16.1.2.1   The certificate of approval shall conform to the model 8.6.1.1 or 8.6.1.3 with regard to content, form and layout and include the required particulars, as appropriate. It shall include the date of expiry of the period of validity.

Its dimensions are 210 mm x 297 mm (A4). Front and back pages may be used.

It shall be drawn up in the language or one of the languages of the issuing country. If this language is not English, French or German, the title of the certificate and each entry under items 5, 9 and 10 in the certificate of approval for dry cargo vessels (8.6.1.1) and under items 12, 16 and 17 in the certificate of approval for tank vessels (8.6.1.3) shall also be provided in English, French or German.

1.16.1.2.2   The certificate of approval shall attest that the vessel has been inspected and that its construction and equipment comply completely with the applicable requirements of this Regulation.

1.16.1.2.3   All particulars for amendments to the certificate of approval provided for in these Regulations and in the other regulations drawn up by mutual agreement by the Contracting Parties may be entered in the certificate by the competent authority.

1.16.1.2.4   The competent authority shall include the following particulars in the certificate of approval of double-hull vessels meeting the additional requirements of 9.1.0.80 to 9.1.0.95 or 9.2.0.80 to 9.2.0.95:

"The vessel meets the additional requirements for double-hull vessels of 9.1.0.80 to 9.1.0.95" or "The vessel meets the additional requirements for double-hull vessels of 9.2.0.80 to 9.2.0.95."

1.16.1.2.5   For tank vessels, the certificate of approval shall be supplemented by a list of all the dangerous goods accepted for carriage in the tank vessel, drawn up by the recognized classification society which has classified the vessel (vessel substance list). To the extent required for safe carriage, the list shall contain reservations for certain dangerous goods regarding:

—   the criteria for strength and stability of the vessel; and

—   the compatibility of the accepted dangerous goods with all the construction materials of the vessel, including installations and equipment, which come into contact with the cargo.

Classification societies shall update the vessel substance list at each renewal of the class of a vessel on the basis of the annexed Regulations in force at the time. Classification societies shall inform the owner of the vessel about amendments to Table C of chapter 3.2 which have become relevant in the meantime. If these amendments require an update of the vessel substance list, the owner of the vessel shall request this from a recognized classification society. This updated vessel substance list shall be issued within the period referred to in 1.6.1.1.

The entire vessel substance list shall be withdrawn by the recognized classification society within the period referred to in 1.6.1.1 if, due to amendments to these Regulations or due to changes in classification, goods contained in it are no longer permitted to be carried in the vessel.

The recognized classification society shall without delay, after the delivery to the holder of the certificate of approval, transmit a copy of the vessel substance list to the authority responsible for issuing the certificate of approval and without delay inform it about amendments or withdrawal.

NOTE: When the substance list is available electronically, see 5.4.0.2.

1.16.1.2.6   *(Deleted)*

1.16.1.3   ***Provisional certificate of approval***

1.16.1.3.1   For a vessel which is not provided with a certificate of approval, a provisional certificate of approval of limited duration may be issued in the following cases, subject to the following conditions:

(a)   The vessel complies with the applicable requirements of these Regulations, but the normal certificate of approval could not be issued in time. The provisional certificate of approval shall be valid for an appropriate period but not exceeding three months;

(b)   The vessel does not comply with every applicable requirement of these Regulations, but the safety of carriage is not impaired according to the appraisal of the competent authority.

The one-off provisional certificate of approval shall be valid for an appropriate period to bring the vessel into compliance with the applicable provisions, but not exceeding three months.

The competent authority may request additional reports in addition to the inspection report and may require additional conditions.

NOTE: For the issuance of the final certificate of approval according to 1.16.1.2 a new inspection report according to 1.16.3.1 shall be prepared, which confirms conformity also with all hitherto unfulfilled requirements of these Regulations.

(c)   The vessel does not comply with every applicable provision of these Regulations after sustaining damage. In this case the provisional certificate of approval shall be valid only for a single specified voyage and for a specified cargo. The competent authority may impose additional conditions.

1.16.1.3.2   The provisional certificate of approval shall conform to the model in 8.6.1.2 or 8.6.1.4 with regard to content, form and layout or a single model certificate combining a provisional certificate of inspection and the provisional certificate of approval provided that the single model certificate contains the same information as the model in 8.6.1.2 or 8.6.1.4 and is approved by the competent authority. Its dimensions are 210 mm x 297 mm (A4). Front and back pages may be used.

It shall be drawn up in the language or one of the languages of the issuing country. If this language is not English, French or German, the title of the certificate and each entry under item 5 in the provisional certificate of approval for dry cargo vessels (8.6.1.2) and under item 13 in the provisional certificate of approval for tank vessels (8.6.1.4) shall also be provided in English, French or German.

1.16.1.3.3   For tank vessels, the relief pressure of the safety valves or of the high-velocity vent valves shall be entered in the certificate of approval.

If a vessel has cargo tanks with different valve opening pressures, the opening pressure of each tank shall be entered in the certificate of approval.

1.16.1.4   *Annex to the certificate of approval*

1.16.1.4.1   The certificate of approval and the provisional certificate of approval according to 1.16.1.3.1 (a) shall be complemented by an annex in accordance with the model under 8.6.1.5.

1.16.1.4.2   The annex to the certificate of approval shall include the date from which the transitional provisions according to 1.6.7 may be applied. This date shall be:

(a)   For vessels according to Article 8, paragraph 2 of ADN for which evidence can be provided that they were already approved for the carriage of dangerous goods on the territory of a Contracting Party before 26 May 2000, 26 May 2000;

(b)   For vessels according to Article 8, paragraph 2, of ADN for which evidence cannot be provided that they were already approved for the carriage of dangerous goods on the territory of a Contracting Party before 26 May 2000, the proven date of the first inspection for the issue of an approval for the carriage of dangerous goods on the territory of a Contracting Party or, if this date is not known, the date of issue of the first proven approval for the carriage of dangerous goods on the territory of a Contracting Party;

(c)   For all other vessels, the proven date of the first inspection for the issue of a certificate of approval in the sense of ADN or, if this date is not known, the date of issue of the first certificate of approval in the sense of ADN;

(d)   In derogation to (a) to (c) above, the date of a renewed first inspection according to 1.16.8 if the vessel no longer had a valid certificate of approval as from 31 December 2014 for more than twelve months.

1.16.1.4.3   All approvals for the carriage of dangerous goods issued on the territory of a Contracting Party which are valid as from the date under 1.16.1.4.2 and all ADN certificates of approval and provisional certificates of approval according to 1.16.1.3.1 (a) shall be entered in the annex to the certificate of approval.

Certificates of approval issued before the issuance of the annex to the certificate of approval shall be recorded by the competent authority that issues the annex to the certificate of approval.

1.16.2   **Issue and recognition of certificates of approval**

1.16.2.1   The certificate of approval referred to in 1.16.1 shall be issued by the competent authority of the Contracting Party where the vessel is registered, or in its absence, of the Contracting Party where it has its home port or, in its absence, of the Contracting Party where the owner is domiciled or in its absence, by the competent authority selected by the owner.

The other Contracting Parties shall recognize such certificates of approval.

The Contracting Parties shall communicate to the secretariat of the United Nations Economic Commission for Europe (UNECE) the contact information of the authorities and bodies designated by them which are competent in accordance with national law for the issuance of certificates of approval.

The UNECE secretariat shall bring them to the attention of the Contracting Parties through its website.

1.16.2.2   The competent authority of any of the Contracting Parties may request the competent authority of any other Contracting Party to issue a certificate of approval in its stead.

1.16.2.3   The competent authority of any of the Contracting Parties may delegate the authority to issue the certificate of approval to an inspection body as defined in 1.16.4.

1.16.2.4   The provisional certificate of approval referred to in 1.16.1.3 shall be issued by the competent authority of one of the Contracting Parties for the cases and under the conditions referred to in these Regulations.

The other Contracting Parties shall recognize such provisional certificates of approval.

1.16.2.5   The annex to the certificate of approval shall be issued by the competent authority of a Contracting Party. The Contracting Parties shall assist one another at the time of issuance. They shall recognize this annex to the certificate of approval. Each new certificate of approval or provisional certificate of approval issued in accordance with 1.16.1.3.1 (a) shall be entered in the annex to the certificate of approval. Should the annex to the certificate of approval be replaced (e.g. in case of damage or loss), all existing entries shall be transferred.

1.16.2.6   The annex to the certificate of approval shall be withdrawn and a new annex to the certificate of approval shall be issued if according to 1.16.8 a renewed first inspection takes place, as the validity of the certificate of approval expired, as from 31 December 2014, more than twelve months previously.

The valid date is the date on which the application was received by the competent authority. In this case, only such certificates of approval which have been issued after the renewed first inspection shall be recorded.

1.16.3   **Inspection procedure**

1.16.3.1   The competent authority of the Contracting Party shall supervise the inspection of the vessel. Under this procedure, the inspection may be performed by an inspection body designated by the Contracting Party or by a recognized classification society according to Chapter 1.15. The inspection body or the recognized classification society shall issue an inspection report certifying that the vessel conforms partially or completely to the applicable requirements of these Regulations related to the construction and equipment of the vessel.

1.16.3.2   This inspection report shall contain:

–   Name and address of the Inspection Body or the recognized classification society that carried out the inspection;

–   Applicant of the inspection;

–   Date and place of the inspection;

–   Type of the inspected vessel;

–   Identification of the vessel (name, vessel number, ENI number, etc.);

–   Declaration that the vessel conforms partially or completely to the applicable requirements of ADN on the construction and equipment of the vessel (in the version applicable on the date of the inspection or, if later, on the estimated date of issuance of the certificate of approval);

–   Indication (list, description and references in ADN) of any non-conformities;

–   Used transitional provisions;

–   Used equivalents and derogations from the regulations applicable to the vessel with reference to the relevant recommendation of the ADN Administrative Committee;

–   Date of issuance of the inspection report;

–   Signature and official seal of the inspection body or recognized classification society.

If the inspection report does not ensure that all the applicable requirements referred to in 1.16.3.1 are fulfilled, the competent authority may require any additional information in order to issue a provisional certificate of approval according to 1.16.1.3.1 (b).

The authority which is issuing the certificate of approval may request information about the name of the office and surveyor(s) which carried out the inspection including email and phone number, but this information will not become part of the vessel record.

1.16.3.3   The inspection report shall be drawn up in a language accepted by the competent authority and shall contain all the necessary information to enable the certificate to be drawn up.

1.16.3.4   The provisions of 1.16.3.1, 1.16.3.2 and 1.16.3.3 apply to the first inspection referred to in 1.16.8, to the special inspection referred to in 1.16.9 and to the periodic inspection referred to in 1.16.10.

1.16.3.5   Where the inspection report is issued by a recognized classification society, the inspection report may include the certificate referred to in 9.1.0.88.1, 9.2.0.88.1, 9.3.1.8.1, 9.3.2.8.1 or 9.3.3.8.1.

The presence on board of the certificates issued by the recognized classification society for the purposes of 8.1.2.3 (f) and 8.1.2.3 (o) remains mandatory.

1.16.4   **Inspection body**

1.16.4.1   Inspection bodies shall be subject to recognition by the Contracting Party administration as expert bodies on the construction and inspection of inland navigation vessels and as expert bodies on the transport of dangerous goods by inland waterway. They shall meet the following criteria:

–   Compliance by the body with the requirements of impartiality;

–   Existence of a structure and personnel that provide objective evidence of the professional ability and experience of the body;

–   Compliance with the material contents of standard EN ISO/IEC 17020:2012 (except clause 8.1.3) supported by detailed inspection procedures.

1.16.4.2   Inspection bodies may be assisted by experts (e.g. an expert in electrical installations) or specialized bodies according to the national provisions applicable (e.g. classification societies).

1.16.4.3   The Administrative Committee shall maintain an up-to-date list of the inspection bodies appointed.

1.16.5   **Application for the issue of a certificate of approval**

The owner of a vessel shall deposit an application for a certificate of approval with the competent authority referred to in 1.16.2.1. The competent authority shall specify the documents to be submitted to it. In order to obtain a certificate of approval, at least a valid vessel certificate, the inspection report referred to in 1.16.3.1 and the certificate referred to in 9.1.0.88.1, 9.2.0.88.1, 9.3.1.8.1, 9.3.2.8.1 or 9.3.3.8.1 shall accompany the request.

1.16.6   **Particulars entered in the certificate of approval and amendments thereto**

1.16.6.1   The owner of a vessel shall inform the competent authority of any change in the name of the vessel or change of official number or registration number and shall transmit to it the certificate of approval for amendment.

1.16.6.2   All amendments to the certificate of approval provided for in these Regulations and in the other regulations drawn up by mutual agreement by the Contracting Parties may be entered in the certificate by the competent authority.

1.16.6.3   When the owner of the vessel has the vessel registered in another Contracting Party, he shall request a new certificate of approval from the competent authority of that Contracting Party. The competent authority may issue the new certificate for the remaining period of validity of the existing certificate without making a new inspection of the vessel, provided that the state and the technical specifications of the vessel have not undergone any modification.

1.16.6.4   In cases of the transfer of responsibility to another competent authority according to 1.16.6.3, the competent authority to which the last certificate of approval was returned shall submit on request the annex to the certificate according to 1.16.1.4 to the competent authority that will issue the new certificate of approval.

1.16.7   **Presentation of the vessel for inspection**

1.16.7.1   The owner shall present the vessel for inspection unladen, cleaned and equipped; he shall be required to provide such assistance as may be necessary for the inspection, such as providing a suitable launch and personnel, and uncovering those parts of the hull or installations which are not directly accessible or visible.

1.16.7.2 In the case of a first, special or periodical inspection, the inspection body or the recognized classification society may require a dry-land inspection.

1.16.8 **First inspection**

If a vessel does not yet have a certificate of approval or if the validity of the certificate of approval expired more than twelve months ago, the vessel shall undergo a first inspection.

1.16.9 **Special inspection**

If the vessel's hull or equipment has undergone alterations liable to diminish safety in respect of the carriage of dangerous goods, or has sustained damage affecting such safety, the vessel shall be presented without delay by the owner for further inspection.

1.16.10 **Periodic inspection and renewal of the certificate of approval**

1.16.10.1 To renew the certificate of approval, the owner of the vessel shall present the vessel for a periodic inspection. The owner of the vessel may request an inspection at any time.

1.16.10.2 If the request for a periodic inspection is made during the last year preceding the expiry of the validity of the certificate of approval, the period of validity of the new certificate shall commence when the validity of the preceding certificate of approval expires.

1.16.10.3 A periodic inspection may also be requested during a period of twelve months after the expiry of the certificate of approval. After this period of time, the vessel shall undergo a first inspection in accordance with 1.16.8.

1.16.10.4 The competent authority shall establish the period of validity of the new certificate of approval on the basis of the results of the periodic inspection.

1.16.11 **Extension of the certificate of approval without an inspection**

By derogation from 1.16.10, at the substantiated request of the owner, the competent authority that has issued the certificate of approval may grant an extension of the validity of the certificate of approval of not more than one year without an inspection. This extension shall be granted in writing and shall be kept on board the vessel. Such extensions may be granted only once every two validity periods.

1.16.12 **Official inspection**

1.16.12.1 If the competent authority of a Contracting Party has reason to assume that a vessel which is in its territory may constitute a danger in relation to the transport of dangerous goods, for the persons on board or for shipping or for the environment, it may order an inspection of the vessel in accordance with 1.16.3.

1.16.12.2 When exercising this right to inspect, the authorities will make all possible efforts to avoid unduly detaining or delaying a vessel. Nothing in this Agreement affects rights relating to compensation for undue detention or delay. In any instance of alleged undue detention or delay the burden of proof shall lie with the owner of the vessel.

1.16.13 **Withdrawal, withholding and return of the certificate of approval**

1.16.13.1 The certificate of approval may be withdrawn if the vessel is not properly maintained or if the vessel's construction or equipment no longer complies with the applicable provisions of these Regulations, or if the vessel's highest class according to 9.2.0.88.1, 9.3.1.8.1, 9.3.2.8.1 or 9.3.3.8.1 is not valid.

1.16.13.2   The certificate of approval may only be withdrawn by the authority by which it has been issued.

Nevertheless, in the cases referred to in 1.16.9 and 1.16.13.1 above, the competent authority of the State in which the vessel is staying may prohibit its use for the carriage of those dangerous goods for which the certificate is required. For this purpose it may withdraw the certificate until such time as the vessel again complies with the applicable provisions of these Regulations. In that case it shall notify the competent authority which issued the certificate.

1.16.13.3   Notwithstanding 1.16.2.2 above, any competent authority may amend or withdraw the certificate of approval at the request of the vessel's owner, provided that it so notifies the competent authority which issued the certificate.

1.16.13.4   When an inspection body or a recognized classification society observes, in the course of an inspection, that a vessel or its equipment suffers from serious defects in relation to dangerous goods which might jeopardize the safety of the persons on board or the safety of shipping, or constitute a hazard for the environment, or when the vessel's highest class is not valid, it shall immediately notify the competent authority on behalf of which it acts with a view to a decision to withhold the certificate.

If this authority which decided to withdraw the certificate is not the authority which issued the certificate, it shall immediately inform the latter and, where necessary, return the certificate to it if it presumes that the defects cannot be eliminated in the near future.

1.16.13.5   When the inspection body or the recognized classification society referred to in 1.16.13.4 above ascertains, by means of a special inspection according to 1.16.9, that these defects have been remedied, the certificate of approval shall be returned by the competent authority to the owner.

This inspection may be made at the request of the owner by another inspection body or another recognized classification society. In this case, the certificate of approval shall be returned through the competent authority to which the inspection body or the recognized classification society answers.

1.16.13.6   When a vessel is finally immobilized or scrapped, the owner shall send the certificate of approval back to the competent authority which issued it.

1.16.14   Duplicate copy

In the event of the loss, theft or destruction of the certificate of approval or when it becomes unusable for other reasons, an application for a duplicate copy, accompanied by appropriate supporting documents, shall be made to the competent authority which issued the certificate.

This authority shall issue a duplicate copy of the certificate of approval, which shall be designated as such.

1.16.15   Register of certificates of approval

1.16.15.1   The competent authorities shall assign a serial number to the certificates of approval which they issue. They shall keep a register of all the certificates issued.

1.16.15.2   The competent authorities shall keep copies of all the certificates which they have issued, as well as of the associated vessel substance lists of the recognised classification societies and of all amendments, withdrawals, new issuances and declarations of cancellation of these documents.

PART 2

Classification

(See Volume II)

PART 3

Dangerous goods list, special provisions and exemptions related to limited and excepted quantities

CHAPTER 3.1

GENERAL

(See Volume II)

CHAPTER 3.2

LIST OF DANGEROUS GOODS

3.2.1   **Table A: List of dangerous goods in numerical order**

See Volume II

3.2.2   **Table B: List of dangerous goods in alphabetical order**

See Volume II

3.2.3   **Table C: List of dangerous goods accepted for carriage in tank vessels in numerical order**

3.2.3.1   *Explanations concerning Table C:*

As a rule, each row of Table C of this Chapter deals with the substance(s) covered by a specific UN number or identification number. However, when substances belonging to the same UN number or identification number have different chemical properties, physical properties and/or carriage conditions, several consecutive rows may be used for that UN number or identification number.

Each column of Table C is dedicated to a specific subject as indicated in the explanatory notes below. The intersection of columns and rows (cell) contains information concerning the subject treated in that column, for the substance(s) of that row:

–   The first four cells identify the substance(s) belonging to that row;

–   The following cells give the applicable special provisions, either in the form of complete information or in coded form. The codes cross-refer to detailed information that is to be found in the numbers indicated in the explanatory notes below. An empty cell means either that there is no special provision and that only the general requirements apply, or that the carriage restriction indicated in the explanatory notes is in force;

–   If a cell contains an asterisk, "*", the applicable requirements should be determined by applying 3.2.3.3. The determination of the applicable requirements by applying 3.2.3.3 should take precedence over using the entries for mixtures for which no sufficient data is available.

The applicable general requirements are not referred to in the corresponding cells.

Explanatory notes for each column:

Column (1)   "UN number/identification number"

                 Contains the UN number or identification number:

                 –   of the dangerous substance if the substance has been assigned its own specific UN number or identification number, or

                 –   of the generic or n.o.s. entry to which the dangerous substances not mentioned by name shall be assigned in accordance with the criteria ("decision trees") of Part 2.

Column (2)   "Name and description"

Contains, in upper case characters, the name of the substance, if the substance has been assigned its own specific UN number or identification number or of the generic or n.o.s. entry to which the dangerous substances have been assigned in accordance with the criteria ("decision trees") of Part 2. This name shall be used as the proper shipping name or, when applicable, as part of the proper shipping name (see 3.1.2 for further details on the proper shipping name).

A descriptive text in lower case characters is added after the proper shipping name to clarify the scope of the entry if the classification or carriage conditions of the substance may be different under certain conditions.

Column (3a)   "Class"

Contains the number of the Class, whose heading covers the dangerous substance. This Class number is assigned in accordance with the procedures and criteria of Part 2.

Column (3b)   "Classification code"

Contains the classification code of the dangerous substance.

–   For dangerous substances of Class 2, the code consists of a number and one or more letters representing the hazardous property group, which are explained in 2.2.2.1.2 and 2.2.2.1.3.

–   For dangerous substances or articles of Classes 3, 4.1, 6.1 and 9, the codes are explained in 2.2.x.1.2; [1]

–   For dangerous substances or articles of Class 8, the codes are explained in 2.2.8.1.4.1.

Column (4)   "Packing group"

Contains the packing group number(s) (I, II or III) assigned to the dangerous substance. These packing group numbers are assigned on the basis of the procedures and criteria of Part 2. Certain substances are not assigned to packing groups.

Column (5)   "Dangers"

This column contains information concerning the hazards inherent in the dangerous substance. These hazards are included on the basis of the danger labels of Table A, column (5).

In the case of a chemically unstable substance, the code 'unst.' is added to the information.

In the case of a substance or mixture with CMR properties, the code 'CMR' is added to the information.

---

[1]   *x = the Class number of the dangerous substance or article, without dividing point if applicable.*

CMR is used to indicate substances with long-term effects on health (*carcinogenic, mutagenic or toxic to reproduction*, Categories 1A and 1B in accordance with the criteria of Chapters 3.5, 3.6 and 3.7 of the GHS).

In the case of a substance or mixture hazardous to the aquatic environment, the code 'N1', 'N2' or 'N3' is added to the information. (See 2.2.9.1.10).

In the case of a substance or mixture that floats on the water surface, does not evaporate and is not readily soluble in water or that sinks to the bottom of the water and is not readily soluble, the code 'F' (standing for 'Floater') or 'S' (standing for 'Sinker'), respectively, is added to the information.

Where the information is shown in brackets, only the relevant codes for the substance carried should be used.

Column (6)   "Type of tank vessel"

Contains the type of tank vessel: G, C or N.

Column (7)   "Cargo tank design"

Contains information concerning the design of the cargo tank:

1   Pressure cargo tank

2   Closed cargo tank

3   Open cargo tank with flame arrester

4   Open cargo tank

Column (8)   "Cargo tank type"

Contains information concerning the cargo tank type.

1   Independent cargo tank

2   Integral cargo tank

3   Cargo tank with walls distinct from the outer hull

4   Membrane tank

Column (9)   "Cargo tank equipment"

Contains information concerning the cargo tank equipment.

1   Refrigeration system

2   Possibility of cargo heating

3   Water-spray system

4   Cargo heating system on board

Column (10)   "Opening pressure of the pressure relief valve/high-velocity vent valve in kPa"

Contains information concerning the opening pressure of the pressure relief valve/high-velocity vent valve in kPa.

Column (11)   "Maximum degree of filling (%)"

Contains information concerning the maximum degree of filling of cargo tanks as a percentage.

Column (12)   "Relative density at 20 °C"

Contains information concerning the relative density of the substance at 20 °C. Data concerning the density are for information only.

Column (13)   "Type of sampling device"

Contains information concerning the prescribed type of sampling device.

1   Closed-type sampling device

2   Partly closed-type sampling device

3   Sampling opening

Column (14)   "Pump room below deck permitted"

Contains an indication of whether a pump room is permitted below deck.

Yes   pump room below deck permitted

No   pump room below deck not permitted

Column (15)   "Temperature class"

Contains the temperature class of the substance.

Column (16)   "Explosion group"

Contains the explosion group of the substance.

Values between square brackets indicate the explosion group II B subgroups to be used in selecting the relevant autonomous protection systems (flame arresters, vacuum relief valves, pressure relief valves/high velocity vent valves and devices for safe pressure relief of cargo tanks with integrated flame arrester plate stack).

NOTE:

Where autonomous protection systems for explosion group II B are in place, products in explosion group II A or II B, including subgroups II B3, II B2 and II B1, may be transported.

Where autonomous protection systems for explosion group II B3 are in place, products in explosion subgroups II B3, II B2 and II B1, or in explosion group II A, may be transported.

Where autonomous protection systems for explosion group II B2 are in place, products in explosion subgroups II B2 and II B1, or in explosion group II A, may be transported.

Where autonomous protection systems for explosion group II B1 are in place, products in explosion subgroup II B1 or in explosion group II A may be transported.

Column (17)   "Anti-explosion protection required"

Contains information on protection against explosions.

Yes   anti-explosion protection required

No   anti-explosion protection not required

Column (18)   "Equipment required"

This column contains the alphanumeric codes for the equipment required for the carriage of the dangerous substance (see 8.1.5).

Column (19)   "Number of cones/blue lights"

This column contains the number of cones/blue lights which should constitute the marking of the vessel during the carriage of this dangerous substance.

Column (20)   "Additional requirements/Remarks"

This column contains the additional requirements or remarks applicable to the vessel.

These additional requirements or remarks are:

1.   Anhydrous ammonia is liable to cause stress crack corrosion in cargo tanks and cooling systems constructed of carbon-manganese steel or nickel steel.

     In order to minimize the risk of stress crack corrosion the following measures shall be taken:

     (a)   Where carbon-manganese steel is used, cargo tanks, pressure vessels of cargo refrigeration systems and cargo piping shall be constructed of fine-grained steel having a specified minimum yield stress of not more than 355 N/mm^2. The actual yield stress shall not exceed 440 N/mm^2. In addition, one of the following construction or operational measures shall be taken:

          .1   Material with a low tensile strength

               ($R_m < 410$ N/mm^2) shall be used; or

          .2   Cargo tanks, etc., shall undergo a post-weld heat treatment for the purpose of stress relieving; or

-159-

.3   The transport temperature shall preferably be maintained close to the evaporation temperature of the cargo of -33° C, but in no case above -20° C; or

.4   Ammonia shall contain not less than 0.1% water, by mass.

(b)   When carbon-manganese steel with yield stress values higher than those referred to in (a) above is used, the completed tanks, pipe sections, etc., shall undergo a post-weld heat treatment for the purpose of stress relieving.

(c)   Pressure vessels of the cargo refrigeration systems and the piping systems of the condenser of the cargo refrigeration system constructed of carbon-manganese steel or nickel steel shall undergo a post-weld heat treatment for the purpose of stress relieving.

(d)   The yield stress and the tensile strength of welding consumables may exceed only by the smallest value possible the corresponding values of the tank and piping material.

(e)   Nickel steels containing more than 5% nickel and carbon-manganese steel which are not in compliance with the requirements of (a) and (b) above may not be used for cargo tanks and piping systems intended for the transport of this substance.

(f)   Nickel steels containing not more than 5% nickel may be used if the transport temperature is within the limits referred to in (a) above.

(g)   The concentration of oxygen dissolved in the ammonia shall not exceed the values given in the table below:

t in °C	O_2 in %
-30 and below	0.90
-20	0.50
-10	0.28
0	0.16
10	0.10
20	0.05
30	0.03

2.   Before loading, air shall be removed and subsequently kept away to a sufficient extent from the cargo tanks and the accessory cargo piping by the means of inert gas (see also 7.2.4.18).

3. Arrangements shall be made to ensure that the cargo is sufficiently stabilized in order to prevent a reaction at any time during carriage. The transport document shall contain the following additional particulars:

   (a) Name and amount of inhibitor added;

   (b) Date on which inhibitor was added and expected duration of effectiveness under normal conditions;

   (c) Any temperature limits having an effect on the inhibitor.

   When stabilization is ensured solely by blanketing with an inert gas it is sufficient to mention the name of the inert gas used in the transport document.

   When stabilization is ensured by another measurement, e.g. the special purity of the substance, this measurement shall be mentioned in the transport document.

4. The substance shall not be allowed to solidify; the transport temperature shall be maintained above the melting point. In instances where cargo heating installations are required, they must be so designed that polymerisation through heating is not possible in any part of the cargo tank. Where the temperature of steam-heated coils could give rise to overheating, lower-temperature indirect heating systems shall be provided.

5. This substance is liable to clog the venting piping and its fittings or the fittings of cargo tanks. Careful surveillance should be ensured.

   If a closed-type tank vessel cargo tank is required for the carriage of this substance and explosion protection is necessary or the substance for which explosion protection is necessary is carried in a closed cargo tank, the cargo tank shall conform to 9.3.2.22.4 or 9.3.3.22.4 or the venting piping shall conform to 9.3.2.22.5 (a) or 9.3.2.22.5 (b) or to 9.3.3.22.5 (a) or 9.3.3.22.5 (b).

   This requirement does not apply when the cargo tanks and the corresponding piping are inerted in accordance with 7.2.4.18.

6. When external temperatures are below or equal to that indicated in column (20), the substance may only be carried in tank vessels equipped with a possibility of heating the cargo.

   In addition, in the event of carriage in a closed cargo tank, the venting piping, the safety valves and the flame arresters shall be heatable.

   The temperature of the venting piping, safety valves and flame arresters shall be kept at least above the melting point of the substance.

7. If a closed cargo tank is required to carry this substance or if the substance is carried in a closed cargo tank, the venting piping, the safety valves and the flame arresters shall be heatable.

The temperature of the venting piping, safety valves and flame arresters shall be kept at least above the melting point of the substance.

8. Double-hull spaces, double bottoms and heating coils shall not contain any water.

9. (a) While the vessel is underway, an inert-gas pad shall be maintained in the ullage space above the liquid level.

(b) Cargo piping and vent lines shall be independent of the corresponding piping used for other cargoes.

(c) Safety valves shall be made of stainless steel.

10. *(Reserved)*

11. (a) Stainless steel of type 416 or 442 and cast iron shall not be used for cargo tanks and piping for loading and unloading.

(b) The cargo may be discharged only by deep-well pumps or pressure inert gas displacement. Each cargo pump shall be arranged to ensure that the substance does not heat significantly if the pressure discharge line from the pump is shut off or otherwise blocked.

(c) The cargo shall be cooled and maintained at temperatures below 30° C.

(d) The safety valves shall be set at a pressure of not less than 550 kPa (5.5 bar) gauge pressure. Special authorization is required for the maximum setting pressure.

(e) While the vessel is underway, a nitrogen pad shall be maintained in the ullage space above the cargo (see also 7.2.4.18). An automatic nitrogen supply system shall be installed to prevent the pressure from falling below 7 kPa (0.07 bar) gauge within the cargo tank in the event of a cargo temperature fall due to ambient temperature conditions or to some other reason. In order to satisfy the demand of the automatic pressure control a sufficient amount of nitrogen shall be available on board. Nitrogen of a commercially pure quality of 99.9%, by volume, shall be used for padding. A battery of nitrogen cylinders connected to the cargo tanks through a pressure reduction valve satisfies the intention of the expression "automatic" in this context.

The required nitrogen pad shall be such that the nitrogen concentration in the vapour space of the cargo tank is not less than 45% at any time.

(f) Before loading and while the cargo tank contains this substance in a liquid or gaseous form, it and the corresponding piping shall be inerted with nitrogen.

(g) The water-spray system shall be fitted with remote-control devices which can be operated from the wheelhouse or from the control station, if any.

(h) Transfer arrangements shall be provided for emergency transfer of ethylene oxide in the event of an uncontrollable self-reaction.

12. (a) The substance shall be acetylene free.

(b) Cargo tanks which have not undergone appropriate cleaning shall not be used for the carriage of these substances if one of the previous three cargoes consisted of a substance known to promote polymerisation, such as:

.1 mineral acids (e.g. sulphuric acid, hydrochloric acid, nitric acid);

.2 carboxylic acids and anhydrides (e.g. formic acid, acetic acid);

.3 halogenated carboxylic acids (e.g. chloroacetic acid);

.4 sulphonic acids (e.g. benzene sulphonic acid);

.5 caustic alkalis (e.g. sodium hydroxide, potassium hydroxide);

.6 ammonia and ammonia solutions;

.7 amines and amine solutions;

.8 oxidizing substances.

(c) Before loading, cargo tanks and their piping shall be efficiently and thoroughly cleaned so as to eliminate all traces of previous cargoes, except when the last cargo was constituted of propylene oxide or a mixture of ethylene oxide and propylene oxide. Special precautions shall be taken in the case of ammonia in cargo tanks built of steel other than stainless steel.

(d) In all cases the efficiency of the cleaning of cargo tanks and their piping shall be monitored by means of appropriate tests or inspections to check that no trace of acid or alkaline substance remains that could present a danger in the presence of these substances.

(e) The cargo tanks shall be entered and inspected prior to each loading of these substances to ensure freedom from contamination, heavy rust deposits or visible structural defects.

When these cargo tanks are fitted in type C tank vessels, with cargo tank design 1 and cargo tank type 1, and are in continuous service for these substances, such inspections shall be performed at intervals of not more than two and a half years.

When these cargo tanks are fitted in type G tank vessels, with cargo tank design 1 and cargo tank type 1, and are in continuous service for these substances, such inspections shall be performed during the periodic inspection for the renewal of the certificate of approval according to 1.16.10.

(f) Cargo tanks which have contained these substances may be reused for other cargoes once they and their piping have been thoroughly cleaned by washing and flushing with an inert gas.

(g) Substances shall be loaded and unloaded in such a way that there is no release of gas into the atmosphere. If gas is returned to the shore installation during loading, the gas return system connected to the tank containing that substance shall be independent from all other cargo tanks.

(h) During discharge operations, the pressure in the cargo tanks shall be maintained above 7 kPa (0.07 bar) gauge.

(i) The cargo shall be discharged only by deep-well pumps, hydraulically operated submerged pumps or pressure inert gas displacement. Each cargo pump shall be arranged to ensure that the substance does not heat significantly if the pressure discharge line from the pump is shut off or otherwise blocked.

(j) Each cargo tank carrying these substances shall be ventilated by a system independent from the ventilation systems of other cargo tanks carrying other substances.

(k) Hose assemblies for loading and unloading shall be marked as follows:

"To be used only for the transfer of alkylene oxide."

(l) (*Reserved*)

(m) No air shall be allowed to enter the cargo pumps and cargo piping system while these substances are contained within the system.

(n) Before the shore connections are disconnected, piping containing liquids or gas shall be depressurised at the shore link by means of appropriate devices.

(o) The piping system for cargo tanks to be loaded with these substances shall be separate from the piping system for all other cargo tanks, including empty cargo tanks. If the piping system for the cargo tanks to be loaded is not independent, separation shall be accomplished by the removal of spool pieces, shut-off valves, other pipe sections and by fitting blank flanges at these locations. The required separation applies to all liquid pipes and vapour vent lines and any other connections which may exist such as common inert gas supply lines.

(p)   These substances may be carried only in accordance with cargo handling plans that have been approved by a competent authority.

Each loading arrangement shall be shown on a separate cargo handling plan. Cargo handling plans shall show the entire cargo piping system and the locations for installations of blank flanges needed to meet the above piping separation requirements. A copy of each cargo handling plan shall be kept on board. Reference to the approved cargo handling plans shall be included in the certificate of approval.

(q)   Before loading of these substances and before carriage is resumed a qualified person approved by the competent authority shall certify that the prescribed separation of the piping has been effected; this certificate shall be kept on board. Each connection between a blank flange and a shut-off valve in the piping shall be fitted with a sealed wire to prevent the flange from being disassembled inadvertently.

(r)   During the voyage, the cargo shall be covered with nitrogen. An automatic nitrogen make-up system shall be installed to prevent the cargo tank pressure from falling below 7 kPa (0.07 bar) gauge in the event of a cargo temperature fall due to ambient temperature conditions or to some other reason. Sufficient nitrogen shall be available on board to satisfy the demand of automatic pressure control. Nitrogen of commercially pure quality of 99.9%, by volume, shall be used for padding. A battery of nitrogen cylinders connected to the cargo tanks through a pressure reduction valve satisfies the intention of the expression "automatic" in this context.

(s)   The vapour space of the cargo tanks shall be checked before and after each loading operation to ensure that the oxygen content is 2%, by volume, or less.

(t)   Loading flow

The loading flow (L_R) of cargo tank shall not exceed the following value:

$$L_R = 3600 \times U/t \; (m^3/h)$$

In this formula:

U = the free volume (m^3) during loading for the activation of the overflow prevention system;

T = the time (s) required between the activation of the overflow prevention system and the complete stop of the flow of cargo into the cargo tank;

The time is the sum of the partial times needed for successive operations, e.g. reaction time of the service personnel, the time needed to stop the pumps and the time needed to close the shut-off valves;

The loading flow shall also take account of the design pressure of the piping system.

13. If no stabilizer is supplied or if the supply is inadequate, the oxygen content in the vapour phase shall not exceed 0.1%. Overpressure must be constantly maintained in cargo tanks. This requirement applies also to voyages on ballast or empty with uncleaned cargo tanks between cargo transport operations.

14. The following substances may not be carried in a type N vessel:

    – substances with self-ignition temperatures $\leq 200\ °C$;

    – substances with a flash point $< 23\ °C$ and an explosion range > 15 percentage points;

    – mixtures containing halogenated hydrocarbons;

    – mixtures containing more than 10% benzene;

    – substances and mixtures carried in a stabilized state.

15. Provision shall be made to ensure that alkaline or acidic substances such as sodium hydroxide solution or sulphuric acid do not contaminate this cargo.

16. If there is a possibility of a dangerous reaction such as polymerisation, decomposition, thermal instability or evolution of gases resulting from local overheating of the cargo in either the cargo tank or associated piping system, this cargo shall be loaded and carried adequately segregated from other substances the temperature of which is sufficiently high to initiate such reaction. Heating coils inside cargo tanks carrying this substance shall be blanked off or secured by equivalent means.

17. The melting point of the cargo shall be shown in the transport documents.

18. *(Reserved)*

19. Provision shall be made to ensure that the cargo does not come into contact with water. The following additional requirements apply:

    Carriage of the cargo is not permitted in cargo tanks adjacent to slop tanks or cargo tanks containing ballast water, slops or any other cargo containing water. Pumps, piping and vent lines connected to such tanks shall be separated from similar equipment of tanks carrying these substances. Pipes from slop tanks or ballast water pipes shall not pass through cargo tanks containing this cargo unless they are encased in a tunnel.

20. The maximum permitted transport temperature given in column (20) shall not be exceeded.

21. *(Reserved)*

22. The relative density of the cargo shall be shown in the transport document.

23. The instrument for measuring the pressure of the vapour phase in the cargo tank shall activate the alarm when the internal pressure reaches 40 kPa (0.4 bar). The water-spray system shall immediately be activated and remain in operation until the internal pressure drops to 30 kPa (0.3 bar).

24. Substances having a flash-point above 60 °C which are handed over for carriage or which are carried heated within a limiting range of 15 K below their flash-point shall be carried under the conditions of substance number 9001.

25. Type 3 cargo tank may be used for the carriage of this substance provided that the construction of the cargo tank has been accepted by a recognized classification society for the maximum permitted transport temperature.

26. Type 2 cargo tank may be used for the carriage of this substance provided that the construction of the cargo tank has been accepted by a recognized classification society for the maximum permitted transport temperature.

27. The requirements of 3.1.2.8.1 are applicable.

28. (a) When UN 2448 SULPHUR, MOLTEN is carried, the forced ventilation of the cargo tanks shall be brought into service at latest when the concentration of hydrogen sulphide reaches 1.0%, by volume.

    (b) When during the carriage of UN 2448 SULPHUR, MOLTEN, the concentration of hydrogen sulphide exceeds 1.85%, the boat master shall immediately notify the nearest competent authority.

    When a significant increase in the concentration of hydrogen sulphide in a hold space leads it to be supposed that the sulphur has leaked, the cargo tanks shall be unloaded as rapidly as possible. A new load may only be taken on board once the authority which issued the certificate of approval has carried out a further inspection.

    (c) When UN 2448 SULPHUR, MOLTEN is carried, the concentration of hydrogen sulphide shall be measured in the vapour phase of the cargo tanks and concentrations of sulphur dioxide and hydrogen sulphide in the hold spaces.

    (d) The measurements prescribed in (c) shall be made every eight hours. The results of the measurements shall be recorded in writing.

29. *(Deleted)*

30. When these substances are carried, the hold spaces of open type N tank vessels may contain auxiliary equipment.

31. When these substances are carried, the vessel shall be equipped with a quick closing valve placed directly on the shore connection.

32. In the case of transport of this substance, the following additional requirements are applicable:

(a) The outside of the cargo tanks shall be equipped with insulation of low flammability. This insulation shall be strong enough to resist shocks and vibration. Above deck, the insulation shall be protected by a covering.

The outside temperature of this covering shall not exceed 70 °C.

(b) The hold spaces containing the cargo tanks shall be provided with ventilation. Connections for forced ventilation shall be fitted.

(c) The cargo tanks shall be equipped with forced ventilation installations which, in all transport conditions, will reliably keep the concentration of hydrogen sulphide above the liquid phase below 1.85% by volume.

The ventilation installations shall be fitted in such a way as to prevent the deposit of the goods to be transported.

The exhaust line of the ventilation shall be fitted in such a way as not to present a risk to personnel.

(d) The cargo tank and the hold spaces shall be fitted with outlets and piping to allow gas sampling.

(e) The outlets of the cargo tanks shall be situated at a height such that for a trim of 2° and a list of 10°, no sulphur can escape. All the outlets shall be situated above the deck in the open air. Each outlet shall be equipped with a permanently fixed closing mechanism.

One of these mechanisms shall be capable of being opened for slight overpressure within the tank.

(f) The piping for loading and unloading shall be equipped with adequate insulation. They shall be capable of being heated.

(g) The heat transfer fluid shall be such that in the event of a leak into a tank, there is no risk of a dangerous reaction with the sulphur.

33. The following provisions are applicable to transport of this substance:

Construction requirements:

(a) Hydrogen peroxide solutions may be transported only in cargo tanks equipped with deep-well pumps.

(b)   Cargo tanks and their equipment shall be constructed of solid stainless steel of a type appropriate to hydrogen peroxide solutions (for example, 304, 304L, 316, 316L or 316 Ti). None of the non-metallic materials used for the system of cargo tanks shall be attacked by hydrogen peroxide solutions or cause the decomposition of the substance.

(c)   The temperature sensors shall be installed in the cargo tanks directly under the deck and at the bottom. Remote temperature read-outs and monitoring shall be provided for in the wheelhouse.

(d)   Fixed oxygen monitors (or gas-sampling lines) shall be provided in the areas adjacent to the cargo tanks so that leaks in such areas can be detected. Account shall be taken of the increased flammability arising from the increased presence of oxygen. Remote read-outs, continuous monitoring (if the sampling lines are used, intermittent monitoring will suffice) and visible and audible alarms similar to those for the temperature sensors shall also be located in the wheelhouse. The visible and audible alarms shall be activated if the oxygen concentration in these void spaces exceeds 30% by volume. Two additional oxygen monitors shall also be available.

(e)   The cargo tank venting systems which are equipped with filters shall be fitted with pressure/vacuum relief valves appropriate to closed-circuit ventilation and with an extraction installation should cargo tank pressure rise rapidly as a result of an uncontrolled decomposition (see under m). These air supply and extraction systems shall be so designed that water cannot enter the cargo tanks. In designing the emergency extraction installation account shall be taken of the design pressure and the size of the cargo tanks.

(f)   A fixed water-spray system shall be provided for diluting and washing away any hydrogen peroxide solutions spilled onto the deck. The area covered by the jet of water shall include the shore connections and the deck containing the cargo tanks designated for carrying hydrogen peroxide solutions.

The following minimum requirements shall be complied with:

.1   The substance shall be diluted from the original concentration to a 35% concentration within five minutes from the spillage on the deck;

.2   The rate and estimated size of the spill shall be determined in the light of the maximum permissible loading or unloading rates, the time required to halt the spillage in the event of tank overfill or a pipe or hose assembly failure, and the time necessary to begin application of dilution water with actuation of the alarm at the cargo control location or in the wheelhouse.

(g)   The outlets of the pressure valves shall be situated at least 2 metres above the walkways if they are less than 4 metres from the walkway.

(h)   A temperature sensor shall be installed by each pump to make it possible to monitor the temperature of the cargo during unloading and detect any overheating due to defective operation of the pump.

Servicing requirements:

Carrier

(i)   Hydrogen peroxide solutions may only be carried in cargo tanks which have been thoroughly cleaned and passivated, in accordance with the procedure described under (j), of all traces of previous cargoes, their vapours or their ballast waters. A certificate stating that the procedure described under (j) has been duly complied with must be carried on board.

Particular care in this respect is essential to ensure the safe carriage of hydrogen peroxide solutions:

.1   When a hydrogen peroxide solution is being carried, no other cargo may be carried simultaneously;

.2   Tanks which have contained hydrogen peroxide solutions may be reused for other cargoes after they have been cleaned by persons or companies approved for this purpose by the competent authority;

.3   In the design of the cargo tanks, efforts must be made to keep to a minimum any internal tank structure, to ensure free draining, no entrapment and ease of visual inspection.

(j)   Procedures for inspection, cleaning, passivation and loading for the transport of hydrogen peroxide solutions with a concentration of 8 to 60 per cent in cargo tanks which have previously carried other cargoes.

Before their reuse for the transport of hydrogen peroxide solutions, cargo tanks which have previously carried cargoes other than hydrogen peroxide must be inspected, cleaned and passivated. The procedures described in paragraphs .1 to .7 below for inspection and cleaning apply to stainless steel cargo tanks. The procedure for passivating stainless steel is described in paragraph 8. Failing any other instructions, all the measures apply to cargo tanks and to all their structures which have been in contact with other cargoes.

.1   After unloading of the previous cargo, the cargo tank must be made gasfree and inspected for any remaining traces, carbon residues and rust.

.2   The cargo tanks and their equipment must be washed with clear filtered water. The water used must be at least of the same quality as drinking water and have a low chlorine content.

.3   Traces of the residues and vapours of the previous cargo must be removed by the steam cleaning of the cargo tanks and their equipment.

.4   The cargo tanks and their equipment must then be rewashed with clear water of the quality specified in paragraph 2 above and dried in filtered, oil-free air.

.5   Samples must be taken of the atmosphere in the cargo tanks and these must be analysed for their content of organic gases and oxygen.

.6   The cargo tank must be reinspected for any traces of the previous cargo, carbon residues or rust or odours of the previous cargo.

.7   If the inspection and the other measures point to the presence of traces of the previous cargo or of its gases, the measures described in paragraphs .2 to .4 above must be repeated.

.8   Stainless steel cargo tanks and their structures which have contained cargoes other than hydrogen peroxide solutions and which have been repaired must, regardless of whether or not they have previously been passivated, be cleaned and passivated in accordance with the following procedure:

    .8.1   The new weld seams and other repaired parts must be cleaned and scrubbed with stainless steel brushes, graving tools, sandpaper and polishers. Rough surfaces must be made smooth and a final polishing must be carried out;

    .8.2   Fatty and oily residues must be removed with the use of organic solvents or appropriate cleaning products diluted with water. The use of chlorinated products shall be avoided because these might seriously interfere with the passivation procedure;

    .8.3   Any residues that have been removed must be eliminated and the tanks must then be washed.

(k)   During the transfer of the hydrogen peroxide solutions, the related piping system must be separated from all other systems. Loading and unloading piping used for the transfer of hydrogen peroxide solutions must be marked as follows:

"For Hydrogen Peroxide
Solution Transfer only"

(l)   If the temperature in the cargo tanks rises above 35 °C, visible and audible alarms shall activate in the wheelhouse.

Master

(m)   If the temperature rise exceeds 4 °C for 2 hours or if the temperature in the cargo tanks exceeds 40 °C, the master must contact the consignor directly, with a view to taking any action that might be necessary.

Filler

(n)   Hydrogen peroxide solutions must be stabilized to prevent decomposition. The manufacturer must provide a stabilization certificate which must be carried on board and must specify:

.1   The disintegration date of the stabilizer and the duration of its effectiveness;

.2   Actions to be taken should the product become unstable during the voyage.

(o)   Only those hydrogen peroxide solutions which have a maximum decomposition rate of 1.0 per cent per year at 25 °C may be carried. A certificate from the filler stating that the product meets this standard must be presented to the master and kept on board. An authorized representative of the manufacturer must be on board to monitor the loading operations and to test the stability of the hydrogen peroxide solutions to be transported. He shall certify to the master that the cargo has been loaded in a stable condition.

34.   For type N carriage, the flanges and stuffing boxes of the loading and unloading piping must be fitted with a protection device to protect against splashing.

35.   Only an indirect system for the cargo refrigerating system is permitted for this substance. Direct or combined systems are not permitted.

36.   Merged with remark 35.

37.   For this substance, the cargo tank system shall be capable of resisting the vapour pressure of the cargo at higher ambient temperatures whatever the system that has been adopted for treating the boil-off gas.

38. For an initial boiling point above 60 °C and under or equal to 85 °C as determined in accordance with ASTMD 86-01, the applicable conditions of transport are identical to those stipulated for an initial boiling point under or equal to 60 °C.

39. (a) The joints, outlets, closing devices and other technical equipment shall be of such a sort that there cannot be any leakage of carbon dioxide during normal transport operations (cold, fracturing of materials, freezing of fixtures, run-off outlets etc.).

    (b) The loading temperature (at the loading station) shall be mentioned in the transport document.

    (c) An oxygen meter shall be kept on board, together with instructions on its use which can be read by everyone on board. The oxygen meter shall be used as a testing device when entering holds, pump rooms, areas situated at depth and when work is being carried out on board.

    (d) At the entry of accommodation and in other places where the crew may spend time there shall be a measuring device which lets off an alarm when the oxygen level is too low or when the CO_2 level is too high.

    (e) The loading temperature (established after loading) and the maximum duration of the journey shall be mentioned in the transport document.

40. *(Deleted)*

41. n-BUTYLBENZENE is assigned to the entry UN No. 2709 BUTYLBENZENES (n-BUTYLBENZENE).

42. Loading of refrigerated liquefied gases shall be carried out in such a manner as to ensure that unsatisfactory temperature gradients do not occur in any cargo tank, piping or other ancillary equipment. When determining the holding time (as described in 7.2.4.16.17), it shall be assured that the degree of filling does not exceed 98% in order to prevent the safety valves from opening when the tank is in liquid full condition. When refrigerated liquefied gases are carried using a system according to 9.3.1.24.1 (b) or 9.3.1.24.1 (c), a refrigeration system is not required.

43. It may be that the mixture has been classified as a floater as a precautionary measure, because some of its components meet the relevant criteria.

44. A substance shall only be assigned to this entry where there is measurement data or verified information in accordance with IEC 60079-20-1 or equivalent that allows for an assignment to subgroups II B3, II B2 or II B1 of explosion group II B or explosion group II A.

45. When this substance is received from seagoing vessels as waste related to the operation of the vessel, appropriate measures shall be taken on board the vessels to avoid or minimize, to the extent possible, the exposure of personnel on board to gas/air mixtures escaping from the cargo tanks of the receiving vessel during loading and to ensure the protection of personnel on board during such activities. Appropriate personal protective equipment shall be made available to the employees in question and shall be worn for the duration of the increased exposure.

3.2.3.2   *Table C*

(1) UN No. or substance identification No.	(2) Name and description	(3a) Class	(3b) Classification code	(4) Packing group	(5) Dangers	(6) Type of tank vessel	(7) Cargo tank design	(8) Cargo tank type	(9) Cargo tank equipment	(10) Opening pressure of the pressure relief valve/high velocity vent valve, in kPa	(11) Maximum degree of filling in %	(12) Relative density at 20 °C	(13) Type of sampling device	(14) Pump room below deck permitted	(15) Temperature class	(16) Explosion group	(17) Anti-explosion protection required	(18) Equipment required	(19) Number of cones/blue lights	(20) Additional requirements/Remarks
		3.1.2	2.2	2.1.1.3	5.2.2 / 3.2.3.1	1.2.1 / 7.2.2.0.1	3.2.3.1 / 1.2.1	3.2.3.1 / 1.2.1	3.2.3.1 / 1.2.1	3.2.3.1 / 1.2.1	7.2.4.21	3.2.3.1	3.2.3.1 / 1.2.1	3.2.3.1 / 1.2.1	1.2.1	1.2.1 / 3.2.3.3	1.2.1 / 3.2.3.3	8.1.5	7.2.5	3.2.3.1
1005	AMMONIA, ANHYDROUS	2	2TC		2.3+8+2.1+N1	G	1	1	3		91		1	no	T1 [12]	II A	yes	PP, EP, EX, TOX, A	2	1; 2; 31
1010	BUTADIENES (1,2-BUTADIENE), STABILIZED	2	2F		2.1+unst.	G	1	1			91		1	no	T2 [12]	II B [4)]	yes	PP, EX, A	1	2; 3; 31
1010	BUTADIENES (1,3-BUTADIENE), STABILIZED	2	2F		2.1+unst. + CMR	G	1	1			91		1	no	T2 [12]	II B (II B2 [4)])	yes	PP, EP, EX, TOX, A	1	2; 3; 31
1010	1,2-BUTADIENE, STABILIZED, REFRIGERATED	2	3F		2.1+unst.	G	2	4	1; 3		95		1	no	T2 [12]	II B [4)]	yes	PP, EX, A	1	2; 3; 31
1010	1,3-BUTADIENE, STABILIZED, REFRIGERATED	2	3F		2.1+unst. + CMR	G	2	4	1; 3		95		1	no	T2 [12]	II B (II B2 [4)])	yes	PP, EP, EX, TOX, A	1	2; 3; 31
1010	BUTADIENES STABILIZED or BUTADIENES AND HYDROCARBON MIXTURE, STABILIZED, having a vapour pressure at 70 °C not exceeding 1.1 MPa (11 bar) and a density at 50 °C not lower than 0.525 kg/l (contains less than 0.1% 1.3-butadiene)	2	2F		2.1+unst.	G	1	1			91		1	no	T2 [12]	II B [4)] (II B2 [4)])	yes	PP, EX, A	1	2; 3; 31
1010	BUTADIENES STABILIZED or BUTADIENES AND HYDROCARBON MIXTURE, STABILIZED, REFRIGERATED, having a vapour pressure at 70 °C not exceeding 1.1 MPa (11 bar) and a density at 50 °C not lower than 0.525 kg/l (contains less than 0.1% 1.3-butadiene)	2	3F		2.1+unst.	G	2	4	1; 3		95		1	no	T2 [12]	II B [4)] (II B2 [4)])	yes	PP, EX, A	1	2; 3; 31

-175-

(1)	(2)	(3a)	(3b)	(4)	(5)	(6)	(7)	(8)	(9)	(10)	(11)	(12)	(13)	(14)	(15)	(16)	(17)	(18)	(19)	(20)
UN No. or substance identification No.	Name and description	Class	Classification code	Packing group	Dangers	Type of tank vessel	Cargo tank design	Cargo tank type	Cargo tank equipment	Opening pressure of the pressure relief valve/high velocity vent valve, in kPa	Maximum degree of filling in %	Relative density at 20 °C	Type of sampling device	Pump room below deck permitted	Temperature class	Explosion group	Anti-explosion protection required	Equipment required	Number of cones/blue lights	Additional requirements/Remarks
		2.2	2.2	2.1.1.3	5.2.2 / 3.2.1	1.2.1 / 7.2.2.0.1	3.2.3.1 / 1.2.1	3.2.3.1 / 1.2.1	3.2.3.1 / 1.2.1	3.2.3.1 / 1.2.1	7.2.4.21	3.2.3.1	3.2.3.1 / 1.2.1	3.2.3.1 / 1.2.1	1.2.1	1.2.1 / 3.2.3.3	1.2.1 / 3.2.3.3	8.1.5	7.2.5	3.2.3.1
1010	BUTADIENES, STABILIZED or BUTADIENES AND HYDROCARBON MIXTURE, STABILIZED, having a vapour pressure at 70 °C not exceeding 1.1 MPa (11 bar) and a density at 50 °C not lower than 0.525 kg/l, (with 0.1% or more 1.3-butadiene)	2	2F		2.1+unst. + CMR	G	1	1			91		1	no	T2 [12]	II B[4] (II B2[4])	yes	PP, EP, EX, TOX, A	1	2; 3; 31
1010	BUTADIENES, STABILIZED or BUTADIENES AND HYDROCARBON MIXTURE, STABILIZED, REFRIGERATED, having a vapour pressure at 70 °C not exceeding 1.1 MPa (11 bar) and a density at 50 °C not lower than 0.525 kg/l, (with 0.1% or more 1.3-butadiene)	2	3F		2.1+unst. + CMR	G	2	4	1; 3		95		1	no	T2 [12]	II B[4] (II B2[4])	yes	PP, EP, EX, TOX, A	1	2; 3; 31
1011	BUTANE (contains less than 0.1% 1.3-butadiene)	2	2F		2.1	G	1	1			91		1	no	T2 [12]	II A	yes	PP, EX, A	1	2; 31
1011	BUTANE, REFRIGERATED, (contains less than 0.1% 1.3-butadiene)	2	3F		2.1	G	2	4	1; 3		95		1	no	T2 [12]	II A	yes	PP, EX, A	1	2; 31
1011	BUTANE (with 0.1% or more 1.3-butadiene)	2	2F		2.1+CMR	G	1	1			91		1	no	T2 [12]	II A	yes	PP, EP, EX, TOX, A	1	2; 31
1011	BUTANE, REFRIGERATED, (with 0.1% or more 1.3-butadiene)	2	3F		2.1+CMR	G	2	4	1; 3		95		1	no	T2 [12]	II A	yes	PP, EP, EX, TOX, A	1	2; 31
1012	1-BUTYLENE	2	2F		2.1	G	1	1			91		1	no	T2 [12]	II A	yes	PP, EX, A	1	2; 31
1012	1-BUTYLENE, REFRIGERATED	2	3F		2.1	G	2	4	1; 3		95		1	no	T2 [12]	II A	yes	PP, EX, A	1	2; 31

(1)	(2)	(3a)	(3b)	(4)	(5)	(6)	(7)	(8)	(9)	(10)	(11)	(12)	(13)	(14)	(15)	(16)	(17)	(18)	(19)	(20)
UN No. or substance identification No.	Name and description	Class	Classification code	Packing group	Dangers	Type of tank vessel	Cargo tank design	Cargo tank type	Cargo tank equipment	Opening pressure of the pressure relief valve/high velocity vent valve, in kPa	Maximum degree of filling in %	Relative density at 20 °C	Type of sampling device	Pump room below deck permitted	Temperature class	Explosion group	Anti-explosion protection required	Equipment required	Number of cones/blue lights	Additional requirements/Remarks
	3.1.2	2.2	2.2	2.1.1.3	5.2.2 / 3.2.3.1	1.2.1 / 7.2.2.0.1	3.2.3.1 / 1.2.1	3.2.3.1 / 1.2.1	3.2.3.1 / 1.2.1	3.2.3.1 / 1.2.1	7.2.4.21	3.2.3.1	3.2.3.1 / 1.2.1	3.2.3.1 / 1.2.1	1.2.1	1.2.1 / 3.2.3.3	1.2.1 / 3.2.3.3	8.1.5	7.2.5	3.2.3.1
1020	CHLOROPENTAFLUORO-ETHANE (refrigerant gas R 115)	2	2A		2.2	G	1	1			91			no			no	PP	0	31
1020	CHLOROPENTAFLUORO-ETHANE, REFRIGERATED, (REFRIGERANT GAS R 115)	2	3A		2.2	G	2	4	1; 3		95			no			no	PP	0	31
1030	1,1-DIFLUOROETHANE (REFRIGERANT GAS R 152a)	2	2F		2.1	G	1	1			91		1	no	T1 [12)]	II A	yes	PP, EX, A	1	2; 31
1030	1,1-DIFLUOROETHANE, REFRIGERATED, (REFRIGERANT GAS R 152a)	2	3F		2.1	G	2	4	1; 3		95			no	T1 [12)]	II A	yes	PP, EX, A	1	2; 31
1033	DIMETHYL ETHER	2	2F		2.1	G	1	1			91		1	no	T3	II B (II B2)	yes	PP, EX, A	1	2; 31
1033	DIMETHYL ETHER, REFRIGERATED	2	3F		2.1	G	2	4	1; 3		95		1	no	T3	II B (II B2)	yes	PP, EX, A	1	2; 31
1038	ETHYLENE, REFRIGERATED LIQUID	2	3F		2.1	G	1	1	1		95		1	no	T1 [12)]	II B (II B3)	yes	PP, EX, A	1	2; 31; 42
1038	ETHYLENE, REFRIGERATED LIQUID	2	3F		2.1	G	2	4	1; 3		95			no	T1 [12)]	II B (II B3)	yes	PP, EX, A	1	2; 31; 42
1040	ETHYLENE OXIDE WITH NITROGEN up to a total pressure of 1 MPa (10 bar) at 50 °C	2	2TF		2.3+2.1	G	1	1			91			no	T2 [12)]	II B (II B3)	yes	PP, EP, EX, TOX, A	2	2; 3; 11; 31; 35
1055	ISOBUTYLENE	2	2F		2.1	G	1	1			91		1	no	T2 [1), 12)]	II A	yes	PP, EX, A	1	2; 31
1055	ISOBUTYLENE, REFRIGERATED	2	3F		2.1	G	2	4	1; 3		95		1	no	T2 [1), 12)]	II A	yes	PP, EX, A	1	2; 31
1063	METHYL CHLORIDE (REFRIGERANT GAS R 40)	2	2F		2.1	G	1	1			91		1	no	T1 [12)]	II A	yes	PP, EX, A	1	2; 31

(1)	(2)	(3a)	(3b)	(4)	(5)	(6)	(7)	(8)	(9)	(10)	(11)	(12)	(13)	(14)	(15)	(16)	(17)	(18)	(19)	(20)
UN No. or substance identification No.	Name and description	Class	Classification code	Packing group	Dangers	Type of tank vessel	Cargo tank design	Cargo tank type	Cargo tank equipment	Opening pressure of the pressure relief valve/high velocity vent valve, in kPa	Maximum degree of filling in %	Relative density at 20 °C	Type of sampling device	Pump room below deck permitted	Temperature class	Explosion group	Anti-explosion protection required	Equipment required	Number of cones/blue lights	Additional requirements/Remarks
	3.1.2	2.2	2.2	2.1.1.3	5.2.2 / 3.2.3.1	1.2.1 / 7.2.2.0.1	3.2.3.1 / 1.2.1	3.2.3.1 / 1.2.1	3.2.3.1 / 1.2.1	3.2.3.1 / 1.2.1	7.2.4.21	3.2.3.1	3.2.3.1 / 1.2.1	3.2.3.1 / 1.2.1	1.2.1	1.2.1 / 3.2.3.3	1.2.1 / 3.2.3.3	8.1.5	7.2.5	3.2.3.1
1053	METHYL CHLORIDE, REFRIGERATED, (REFRIGERANT GAS R 40)	2	3F		2.1	G	2	4	1; 3		95		1	no	T1 12)	II A	yes	PP, EX, A	1	2; 31
1077	PROPYLENE	2	2F		2.1	G	1	1			91		1	no	T1 12)	II A	yes	PP, EX, A	1	2; 31
1077	PROPYLENE, REFRIGERATED	2	3F		2.1	G	2	4	1; 3		95		1	no	T1 12)	II A	yes	PP, EX, A	1	2; 31
1033	TRIMETHYLAMINE, ANHYDROUS	2	2F		2.1	G	1	1			91		1	no	T4	II A	yes	PP, EX, A	1	2; 31
1036	VINYL CHLORIDE, STABILIZED	2	2F		2.1+unst.	G	1	1			91		1	no	T2 12)	II A	yes	PP, EX, A	1	2; 3; 13; 31
1036	VINYL CHLORIDE, STABILIZED, REFRIGERATED	2	3F		2.1+unst.	G	2	4	1; 3		95		1	no	T2 12)	II A	yes	PP, EX, A	1	2; 3; 13; 31
1038	ACETAL	3	F1	II	3	N	2	2		10	97	0.83	3	yes	T3	II B4)	yes	PP, EX, A	1	
1039	ACETALDEHYDE (ethanal)	3	F1	I	3+N3	C	1	1			95	0.78	1	yes	T4	II A	yes	PP, EX, A	1	35
1090	ACETONE	3	F1	II	3	N	2	2		10	97	0.79	3	yes	T1 12)	II A	yes	PP, EX, A	1	
1092	ACROLEINE, STABILIZED	6.1	TF1	I	6.1+3+unst.+ N1	C	2	2	3	50	95	0.84	1	no	T3 2)	II B (II B3)	yes	PP, EP, EX, TOX, A	2	2; 3; 5; 23
1093	ACRYLONITRILE, STABILIZED	3	FT1	I	3+6.1+unst.+ N2+CMR	C	2	2	3	50	95	0.8	1	no	T1 12)	II B (II B2)	yes	PP, EP, EX, TOX, A	2	3; 5; 23
1098	ALLYL ALCOHOL	6.1	TF1	I	6.1+3+N1	C	2	2		40	95	0.85	1	no	T2 12)	II B (II B3)	yes	PP, EP, EX, TOX, A	2	

(1) UN No. or substance identification No.	(2) Name and description	(3a) Class	(3b) Classification code	(4) Packing group	(5) Dangers	(6) Type of tank vessel	(7) Cargo tank design	(8) Cargo tank type	(9) Cargo tank equipment	(10) Opening pressure of the pressure relief valve/high velocity vent valve, in kPa	(11) Maximum degree of filling in %	(12) Relative density at 20 °C	(13) Type of sampling device	(14) Pump room below deck permitted	(15) Temperature class	(16) Explosion group	(17) Anti-explosion protection required	(18) Equipment required	(19) Number of cones/blue lights	(20) Additional requirements/Remarks
	3.1.2	2.2	2.2	2.1.1.3	5.2.2/ 3.2.3.1	1.2.1/ 7.2.2.0.1	3.2.3.1/ 1.2.1	3.2.3.1/ 1.2.1	3.2.3.1/ 1.2.1	3.2.3.1/ 1.2.1	7.2.4.21	3.2.3.1	3.2.3.1/ 1.2.1	3.2.3.1/ 1.2.1	1.2.1	1.2.1/ 3.2.3.3	1.2.1/ 3.2.3.3	8.1.5	7.2.5	3.2.3.1
1100	ALLYL CHLORIDE	3	FT1	I	3+6.1+N1	C	2	2	3	50	95	0.94	1	no	T2 12)	II A	yes	PP, EP, EX, TOX, A	2	23
1105	PENTANOLS (n-PENTANOL)	3	F1	III	3	N	3	2			97	0.81	3	yes	T2 12)	II A	yes	PP, EX, A	0	
1106	AMYLAMINE (n-AMYLAMINE)	3	FC	II	3+8	C	2	2		40	95	0.76	2	yes	T4 3)	II A 7)	yes	PP, EP, EX, A	1	
1107	AMYL CHLORIDES (1-CHLOROPENTANE)	3	F1	II	3	C	2	2		40	95	0.88	2	yes	T3	II A	yes	PP, EX, A	1	
1107	AMYL CHLORIDES (1-CHLORO-3-METHYLBUTANE)	3	F1	II	3	C	2	2		45	95	0.89	2	yes	T3	II A	yes	PP, EX, A	1	
1107	AMYL CHLORIDES (2-CHLORO-2-METHYLBUTANE)	3	F1	II	3	C	2	2		50	95	0.87	2	yes	T2 12)	II A	yes	PP, EX, A	1	
1107	AMYL CHLORIDES (1-CHLORO-2,2-DIMETHYL-PROPANE)	3	F1	II	3	C	2	2		50	95	0.87	2	yes	T3 2)	II A	yes	PP, EX, A	1	
1107	AMYL CHLORIDES	3	F1	II	3	C	1	1			95	0.9	1	yes	T3 2)	II A	yes	PP, EX, A	1	27
1108	1-PENTENE (n-amylene)	3	F1	I	3+N3	N	1	1			97	0.64	1	yes	T3	II B 4)	yes	PP, EX, A	1	
1114	BENZENE	3	F1	II	3+N3+C MR	C	2	2	3	50	95	0.88	2	yes	T1 12)	II A	yes	PP, EP, EX, TOX, A	1	6: +10 °C; 17; 23
1120	BUTANOLS (tert-BUTYLALCOHOL)	3	F1	II	3	N	2	2	2	10	97	0.79	3	yes	T1 12)	II A 7)	yes	PP, EX, A	1	7;17
1120	BUTANOLS (sec-BUTYLALCOHOL)	3	F1	III	3	N	3	2			97	0.81	3	yes	T2 12)	II A	yes	PP, EX, A	0	
1120	BUTANOLS (n-BUTYL ALCOHOL)	3	F1	III	3	N	3	2			97	0.81	3	yes	T2 12)	II B (II B2)	yes	PP, EX, A	0	

(1)	(2)	(3a)	(3b)	(4)	(5)	(6)	(7)	(8)	(9)	(10)	(11)	(12)	(13)	(14)	(15)	(16)	(17)	(18)	(19)	(20)
UN No. or substance identification No.	Name and description	Class	Classification code	Packing group	Dangers	Type of tank vessel	Cargo tank design	Cargo tank type	Cargo tank equipment	Opening pressure of the pressure relief valve/high velocity vent valve, in kPa	Maximum degree of filling in %	Relative density at 20 °C	Type of sampling device	Pump room below deck permitted	Temperature class	Explosion group	Anti-explosion protection required	Equipment required	Number of cones/blue lights	Additional requirements/Remarks
	3.1.2	2.2	2.2	2.1.1.3	5.2.2 / 3.2.3.1	1.2.1 / 7.2.2.0.1	3.2.3.1 / 1.2.1	3.2.3.1 / 1.2.1	3.2.3.1 / 1.2.1	3.2.3.1 / 1.2.1	7.2.4.21	3.2.3.1	3.2.3.1 / 1.2.1	3.2.3.1 / 1.2.1	1.2.1	1.2.1 / 3.2.3.3	1.2.1 / 3.2.3.3	8.1.5	7.2.5	3.2.3.1
1123	BUTYL ACETATES (sec-BUTYLACETATE)	3	F1	II	3	N	2	2		10	97	0.86	3	yes	T2 ^{12}	II A ^{7}	yes	PP, EX, A	1	
1123	BUTYL ACETATES (n-BUTYL ACETATE)	3	F1	III	3+N3	N	3	2			97	0.86	3	yes	T2 ^{12}	II A	yes	PP, EX, A	0	
1125	n-BUTYLAMINE	3	FC	II	3+8+N3	C	2	2	3	50	95	0.75	2	yes	T2 ^{12}	II A	yes	PP, EP, EX, A	1	23
1127	CHLOROBUTANES (1-CHLOROBUTANE)	3	F1	II	3	C	2	2	3	50	95	0.89	2	yes	T3	II A	yes	PP, EX, A	1	23
1127	CHLOROBUTANES (2-CHLOROBUTANE)	3	F1	II	3	C	2	2	3	50	95	0.87	2	yes	T3	II A	yes	PP, EX, A	1	23
1127	CHLOROBUTANES (1-CHLORO-2-METHYLPROPANE)	3	F1	II	3	C	2	2	3	50	95	0.88	2	yes	T3	II A	yes	PP, EX, A	1	23
1127	CHLOROBUTANES (2-CHLORO-2-METHYLPROPANE)	3	F1	II	3	C	2	2	3	50	95	0.84	2	yes	T1 ^{12}	II A	yes	PP, EX, A	1	23
1127	CHLOROBUTANES	3	F1	II	3	C	1	1			95	0.89	1	yes	T4 ^{3}	II A	yes	PP, EX, A	1	27
1129	BUTYRALDEHYDE (n-BUTYRALDEHYDE)	3	F1	II	3+N3	C	2	2	3	50	95	0.8	2	yes	T4	II A	yes	PP, EX, A	1	15; 23
1131	CARBON DISULPHIDE	3	FT1	I	3+6.1+N2	C	2	2		50	95	1.26	1	no	T6	II C	yes	PP, EP, EX, TOX, A	2	2; 9; 23
1134	CHLOROBENZENE (phenyl chloride)	3	F1	III	3+N2+S	C	2	2		30	95	1.11	2	yes	T1 ^{12}	II A ^{8}	yes	PP, EX, A	0	
1135	ETHYLENE CHLOROHYDRIN (2-CHLOROETHANOL)	6.1	TF1	I	6.1+3+N3	C	2	2		30	95	1.21	1	no	T2 ^{12}	II A ^{8}	yes	PP, EP, EX, TOX, A	2	

(1) UN No. or substance identification No.	(2) Name and description	(3a) Class	(3b) Classification code	(4) Packing group	(5) Dangers	(6) Type of tank vessel	(7) Cargo tank design	(8) Cargo tank type	(9) Cargo tank equipment	(10) Opening pressure of the pressure relief valve/high velocity vent valve, in kPa	(11) Maximum degree of filling in %	(12) Relative density at 20 °C	(13) Type of sampling device	(14) Pump room below deck permitted	(15) Temperature class	(16) Explosion group	(17) Anti-explosion protection required	(18) Equipment required	(19) Number of cones/blue lights	(20) Additional requirements/Remarks
	3.1.2	2.2	2.2	2.1.1.3	5.2.2 / 3.2.3.1	1.2.1 / 7.2.2.0.1	3.2.3.1 / 1.2.1	3.2.3.1 / 1.2.1	3.2.3.1 / 1.2.1	3.2.3.1 / 1.2.1	7.2.4.21	3.2.3.1	3.2.3.1 / 1.2.1	3.2.3.1 / 1.2.1	1.2.1	1.2.1 / 3.2.3.3	1.2.1 / 3.2.3.3	8.1.5	7.2.5	3.2.3.1
1143	CROTONALDEHYDE, STABILIZED	6.1	TF1	I	6.1+3+unst.+ N1	C	2	2		40	95	0.85	1	no	T3	II B (II B2)	yes	PP, EP, EX, TOX, A	2	3; 5; 15
1145	CYCLOHEXANE	3	F1	II	3+N1	C	2	2	3	50	95	0.78	2	yes	T3	II A	yes	PP, EX, A	1	6: +11 °C; 17
1146	CYCLOPENTANE	3	F1	II	3+N2	N	2	3		10	97	0.75	3	yes	T2 [12]	II A	yes	PP, EX, A	1	
1148	DIACETONE ALCOHOL	3	F1	III	3	N	3	3			97	0.93	3	yes	T1 [12]	II A	yes	PP, EX, A	0	
1150	1,2-DICHLOROETHYLENE (cis-1,2-DICHLOROETHYLENE)	3	F1	II	3+N2	C	2	2	3	50	95	1.28	2	yes	T2 [1],[12]	II A	yes	PP, EX, A	1	23
1150	1,2-DICHLOROETHYLENE (trans-1,2-DICHLOROETHYLENE)	3	F1	II	3+N2	C	2	2	3	50	95	1.26	2	yes	T2 [12]	II A	yes	PP, EX, A	1	23
1153	ETHYLENE GLYCOL DIETHYL ETHER	3	F1	III	3	N	3	2			97	0.84	3	yes	T4	II B (II B2)	yes	PP, EX, A	0	
1154	DIETHYLAMINE	3	FC	II	3+8+N3	C	2	2	3	50	95	0.7	2	yes	T2 [12]	II A	yes	PP, EP, EX, A	1	23
1155	DIETHYL ETHER	3	F1	I	3	C	1	1			95	0.71	1	yes	T4	II B (II B1)	yes	PP, EX, A	1	
1157	DIISOBUTYL KETONE	3	F1	III	3+N3+F	N	3	3			97	0.81	3	yes	T2 [12]	II B [4]	yes	PP, EX, A	0	
1159	DIISOPROPYL ETHER	3	F1	II	3+N2	C	2	2	3	50	95	0.72	2	yes	T2 [12]	II A	yes	PP, EX, A	1	
1160	DIMETHYLAMINE AQUEOUS SOLUTION	3	FC	II	3+8+N3	C	2	2	3	50	95	0.82	2	yes	T2 [12]	II A	yes	PP, EP, EX, A	1	23
1163	DIMETHYLHYDRAZINE, UNSYMMETRICAL	6.1	TFC	I	6.1+3+8+ N2+CMR	C	2	2	3	50	95	0.78	1	no	T3	II B (II B1)	yes	PP, EP, EX, TOX, A	2	23
1165	DIOXANE	3	F1	II	3	N	2	2		10	97	1.03	3	yes	T2 [12]	II B (II B3)	yes	PP, EX, A	1	6: +14 °C; 17

(1) UN No. or substance identification No.	(2) Name and description	(3a) Class	(3b) Classification code	(4) Packing group	(5) Dangers	(6) Type of tank vessel	(7) Cargo tank design	(8) Cargo tank type	(9) Cargo tank equipment	(10) Opening pressure of the pressure relief valve/high velocity vent valve, in kPa	(11) Maximum degree of filling in %	(12) Relative density at 20 °C	(13) Type of sampling device	(14) Pump room below deck permitted	(15) Temperature class	(16) Explosion group	(17) Anti-explosion protection required	(18) Equipment required	(19) Number of cones/blue lights	(20) Additional requirements/Remarks
	3.1.2	2.2	2.2	2.1.1.3	5.2.2 / 3.2.3.1	1.2.1 / 7.2.2.0.1	3.2.3.1 / 1.2.1	3.2.3.1 / 1.2.1	3.2.3.1 / 1.2.1	3.2.3.1 / 1.2.1	7.2.4.21	3.2.3.1	3.2.3.1 / 1.2.1	3.2.3.1 / 1.2.1	1.2.1	1.2.1 / 3.2.3.3	1.2.1 / 3.2.3.3	8.1.5	7.2.5	3.2.3.1
1157	DIVINYL ETHER, STABILIZED	3	F1	I	3+unst.	C	1	1			95	0.77	1	yes	T2[12]	II B	yes	PP, EX, A	1	2; 3
1170	ETHANOL (ETHYL ALCOHOL) or ETHANOL SOLUTION (ETHYL ALCOHOL SOLUTION), aqueous solution with more than 70% alcohol by volume	3	F1	II	3	N	2	2		10	97	0,79 - 0,87	3	yes	T2[12]	II B (II B1)		PP, EX, A	1	
1170	ETHANOL SOLUTION (ETHYL ALCOHOL SOLUTION), aqueous solution with more than 24% and not more than 70% alcohol by volume	3	F1	III	3	N	3	2			97	0,87 - 0,96	3	yes	T2[12]	II B (II B1[4])	yes	PP, EX, A	0	
1171	ETHYLENE GLYCOL MONOETHYL ETHER	3	F1	III	3+CMR	N	2	3	3	10	97	0.93	3	yes	T3	II B (II B2)	yes	PP, EP, EX, TOX, A	0	
1172	ETHYLENE GLYCOL MONOETHYL ETHER ACETATE	3	F1	III	3+N3+CMR	N	2	3	3	10	97	0.98	3	yes	T2[12]	II A	yes	PP, EP, EX, TOX, A	0	
1173	ETHYL ACETATE	3	F1	II	3	N	2	2		10	97	0.9	3	yes	T1[12]	II A	yes	PP, EX, A	1	
1175	ETHYLBENZENE	3	F1	II	3+N3	N	2	2		10	97	0.87	3	yes	T2[12]	II A	yes	PP, EX, A	1	
1177	2-ETHYLBUTYL ACETATE	3	F1	III	3	N	3	2			97	0.88	3	yes	T3	II A[7]	yes	PP, EX, A	0	
1179	ETHYL BUTYL ETHER (ETHYL tert-BUTYL ETHER)	3	F1	II	3+N3	N	2	2		10	97	0.74	3	yes	T2[12]	II A	yes	PP, EX, A	1	
1184	ETHYLENE DICHLORIDE (1,2-dichloroethane)	3	FT1	II	3+6.1+CMR	C	2	2		50	95	1.25	2	no	T2[12]	II A	yes	PP, EP, EX, TOX, A	2	
1188	ETHYLENE GLYCOL MONOMETHYL ETHER	3	F1	III	3+CMR	N	2	3	3	10	97	0.97	3	yes	T3	II B (II B2)	yes	PP, EP, EX, TOX, A	0	

(1) UN No. or substance identification No.	(2) Name and description	(3a) Class	(3b) Classification code	(4) Packing group	(5) Dangers	(6) Type of tank vessel	(7) Cargo tank design	(8) Cargo tank type	(9) Cargo tank equipment	(10) Opening pressure of the pressure relief valve/high velocity vent valve, in kPa	(11) Maximum degree of filling in %	(12) Relative density at 20 °C	(13) Type of sampling device	(14) Pump room below deck permitted	(15) Temperature class	(16) Explosion group	(17) Anti-explosion protection required	(18) Equipment required	(19) Number of cones/blue lights	(20) Additional requirements/Remarks
	3.1.2	2.2	2.2	2.1.1.3	5.2.2 / 3.2.3.1	1.2.1 / 7.2.2.0.1	3.2.3.1 / 1.2.1	3.2.3.1 / 1.2.1	3.2.3.1 / 1.2.1	3.2.3.1 / 1.2.1	7.2.4.21	3.2.3.1	3.2.3.1 / 1.2.1	3.2.3.1 / 1.2.1	1.2.1	1.2.1 / 3.2.3.3	1.2.1 / 3.2.3.3	8.1.5	7.2.5	3.2.3.1
1191	OCTYL ALDEHYDES (2-ETHYLCAPRONALDEHYDE)	3	F1	III	3+N3+F	C	2	2		30	95	0.82	2	yes	T4	II A [7]	yes	PP, EX, A	0	
1191	OCTYL ALDEHYDES (n-OCTALDEHYDE)	3	F1	III	3+N3+F	N	3	3			97	0.82	3	yes	T3	II A	yes	PP, EX, A	0	
1193	ETHYL METHYL KETONE (methyl ethyl ketone)	3	F1	II	3	N	2	2		10	97	0.8	3	yes	T1 [12]	II A	yes	PP, EX, A	1	
1198	FORMALDEHYDE SOLUTION, FLAMMABLE	3	FC	III	3+8+N3	N	3	2			97	1.09	3	yes	T2 [12]	II B	yes	PP, EP, EX, A	0	34
1199	FURALDEHYDES (a-FURALDEHYDE) or FURFURALDEHYDES (a-FURFURYLALDEHYDE)	6.1	TF1	II	6.1+3	C	2	2		25	95	1.16	2	no	T3 [2]	II B (II B1)	yes	PP, EP, EX, TOX, A	2	15
1202	GAS OIL or DIESEL FUEL or HEATING OIL, LIGHT (flash-point not more than 60 °C)	3	F1	III	3+(N1, N2, N3, CMR, F or S)	*	*	*	*	*	*	< 0,85	*	yes			no	*	0	*see 3.2.3.3
1202	GAS OIL complying with standard EN 590:2013 + A1:2017 or DIESEL FUEL or HEATING OIL, LIGHT with flash-point as specified in EN 590:2013 + A1:2017	3	F1	III	3+N2+F	N	4	3			97	0,82 - 0,85	3	yes			no	PP	0	
1202	GAS OIL or DIESEL FUEL or HEATING OIL, LIGHT (flash-point more than 60 °C but not more than 100 °C)	3	F1	III	3+(N1, N2, N3, CMR, F or S)	*	*	*	*	*	*	< 1,1	*	yes			no	*	0	*see 3.2.3.3
1203	MOTOR SPIRIT or GASOLINE or PETROL	3	F1	II	3+N2+C MR+F	N	2	3	3	10	97	0,68 - 0,72 [10]	3	yes	T3	II A	yes	PP, EP, EX, TOX, A	1	
1203	MOTOR SPIRIT or GASOLINE or PETROL, WITH MORE THAN 10% BENZENE	3	F1	II	3+N2+C MR+F	C	*	*	*	*	*		*	yes	T3	II A	yes	*	1	*see 3.2.3.3

(1)	(2)	(3a)	(3b)	(4)	(5)	(6)	(7)	(8)	(9)	(10)	(11)	(12)	(13)	(14)	(15)	(16)	(17)	(18)	(19)	(20)
UN No. or substance identification No.	Name and description	Class	Classification code	Packing group	Dangers	Type of tank vessel	Cargo tank design	Cargo tank type	Cargo tank equipment	Opening pressure of the pressure relief valve/high velocity vent valve, in kPa	Maximum degree of filling in %	Relative density at 20 °C	Type of sampling device	Pump room below deck permitted	Temperature class	Explosion group	Anti-explosion protection required	Equipment required	Number of cones/blue lights	Additional requirements/Remarks
	3.1.2	2.2	2.2	2.1.1.3	5.2.2 / 3.2.3.1	1.2.1 / 7.2.2.0.1	3.2.3.1 / 1.2.1	3.2.3.1 / 1.2.1	3.2.3.1 / 1.2.1	3.2.3.1 / 1.2.1	7.2.4.21	3.2.3.1	3.2.3.1 / 1.2.1	3.2.3.1 / 1.2.1	1.2.1	1.2.1 / 3.2.3.3	1.2.1 / 3.2.3.3	8.1.5	7.2.5	3.2.3.1
1203	MOTOR SPIRIT or GASOLINE or PETROL, WITH MORE THAN 10% BENZENE BOILING POINT ≤ 60 °C	3	F1	II	3+N2+C MR+F	C	1	1			95		1	yes	T3	II A	yes	PP, EP, EX, TOX, A	1	
1203	MOTOR SPIRIT or GASOLINE or PETROL WITH MORE THAN 10% BENZENE 60 °C < BOILING POINT ≤ 85 °C	3	F1	II	3+N2+C MR+F	C	2	2	3	50	95		2	yes	T3	II A	yes	PP, EP, EX, TOX, A	1	23
1203	MOTOR SPIRIT or GASOLINE or PETROL WITH MORE THAN 10% BENZENE 85 °C < BOILING POINT ≤ 115 °C	3	F1	II	3+N2+C MR+F	C	2	2		50	95		2	yes	T3	II A	yes	PP, EP, EX, TOX, A	1	
1203	MOTOR SPIRIT or GASOLINE or PETROL WITH MORE THAN 10% BENZENE BOILING POINT > 115 °C	3	F1	II	3+N2+C MR+F	C	2	2	3	35	95		2	yes	T3	II A	yes	PP, EP, EX, TOX, A	1	
1206	HEPTANES	3	F1	II	3+N1	C	2	2		50	95	0.67 – 0.70	2	yes	T3	II A	yes	PP, EX, A	1	
1208	HEXANES	3	F1	II	3+N2	N	2	3		50	97	0.65 – 0.70	2	yes	T3	II A	yes	PP, EX, A	1	
1208	HEXANES	3	F1	II	3+N2	N	2	3	3	10	97	0.65 – 0.70	2	yes	T3	II A	yes	PP, EX, A	1	
1212	ISOBUTANOL (isobutyl alcohol)	3	F1	III	3	N	3	2	3		97	0.8	3	yes	T2 [12]	II A	yes	PP, EX, A	0	
1213	ISOBUTYLACETATE	3	F1	II	3+N3	C	2	2		10	97	0.87	3	yes	T2 [12]	II A [7]	yes	PP, EX, A	1	
1214	ISOBUTYLAMINE	3	FC	II	3+8+N3	C	2	2		50	95	0.73	2	yes	T2 [12]	II A [7]	yes	PP, EP, EX, A	1	23
1216	ISOOCTENES	3	F1	II	3+N2	N	2	3		10	97	0.73	3	yes	T3	II B (II B1)	yes	PP, EX, A	1	

(1)	(2)	(3a)	(3b)	(4)	(5)	(6)	(7)	(8)	(9)	(10)	(11)	(12)	(13)	(14)	(15)	(16)	(17)	(18)	(19)	(20)
UN No. or substance identification No.	Name and description	Class	Classification code	Packing group	Dangers	Type of tank vessel	Cargo tank design	Cargo tank type	Cargo tank equipment	Opening pressure of the pressure relief valve/high velocity vent valve, in kPa	Maximum degree of filling in %	Relative density at 20 °C	Type of sampling device	Pump room below deck permitted	Temperature class	Explosion group	Anti-explosion protection required	Equipment required	Number of cones/blue lights	Additional requirements/Remarks
	3.1.2	2.2	2.2	2.1.1.3	5.2.2 / 3.2.3.1	1.2.1 / 7.2.2.0.1	3.2.3.1 / 1.2.1	3.2.3.1 / 1.2.1	3.2.3.1 / 1.2.1	3.2.3.1 / 1.2.1	7.2.4.21	3.2.3.1	3.2.3.1 / 1.2.1	3.2.3.1 / 1.2.1	1.2.1	1.2.1 / 3.2.3.3	1.2.1 / 3.2.3.3	8.1.5	7.2.5	3.2.3.1
1218	ISOPRENE, STABILIZED	3	F1	I	3+unst.+N2+CMR	N	1	1			95	0.68	1	yes	T3	II B (II B2)	yes	PP, EP, EX, TOX, A	1	2; 3; 5;16
1219	ISOPROPANOL (isopropyl alcohol)	3	F1	II	3	N	2	2		10	97	0.78	3	yes	T2 12)	II A	yes	PP, EX, A	1	
1220	ISOPROPYLE ACETATE	3	F1	II	3	N	2	2		10	97	0.88	3	yes	T2 12)	II A 7)	yes	PP, EX, A	1	
1221	ISOPROPYLAMINE	3	FC	I	3+8+N3	C	1	1			95	0.69	1	yes	T2 12)	II A 7)	yes	PP, EP, EX, A	1	
1223	KEROSENE	3	F1	III	3+N2+F	N	3	3			97	≤ 0,83	3	yes	T3	II A 7)	yes	PP, EX, A	0	14
1224	KETONES, LIQUID, N.O.S.	3	F1	II	3+(N1, N2, N3, CMR, F or S)	*	*	*	*	*	*		*	yes	T4 3)	II B 4)	yes	*	1	14; 27; *see 3.2.3.3
1224	KETONES, LIQUID, N.O.S.	3	F1	II	3+(N1, N2, N3, CMR, F or S)	*	*	*	*	*	*		*	yes	T4 3)	II B 4) (II B3)	yes	*	1	14; 27; 44 *see 3.2.3.3
1224	KETONES, LIQUID, N.O.S.	3	F1	III	3+(N1, N2, N3, CMR, F or S)	*	*	*	*	*	*		*	yes	T4 3)	II B 4)	yes	*	0	14; 27 *see 3.2.3.3
1224	KETONES, LIQUID, N.O.S.	3	F1	III	3+(N1, N2, N3, CMR, F or S)	*	*	*	*	*	*		*	yes	T4 3)	II B 4) (II B3)	yes	*	0	14; 27; 44 *see 3.2.3.3
1229	MESITYL OXYDE	3	F1	III	3	N	3	2			97	0.85	3	yes	T2 12)	II A	yes	PP, EX, A	0	

-185-

(1)	(2)	(3a)	(3b)	(4)	(5)	(6)	(7)	(8)	(9)	(10)	(11)	(12)	(13)	(14)	(15)	(16)	(17)	(18)	(19)	(20)
UN No. or substance identification No.	Name and description	Class	Classification code	Packing group	Dangers	Type of tank vessel	Cargo tank design	Cargo tank type	Cargo tank equipment	Opening pressure of the pressure relief valve/high velocity vent valve, in kPa	Maximum degree of filling in %	Relative density at 20 °C	Type of sampling device	Pump room below deck permitted	Temperature class	Explosion group	Anti-explosion protection required	Equipment required	Number of cones/blue lights	Additional requirements/Remarks
	3.1.2	2.2	2.2	2.1.1.3	5.2.2 / 3.2.3.1	1.2.1 / 7.2.2.0.1	3.2.3.1 / 1.2.1	3.2.3.1 / 1.2.1	3.2.3.1 / 1.2.1	3.2.3.1 / 1.2.1	7.2.4.21	3.2.3.1	3.2.3.1 / 1.2.1	3.2.3.1 / 1.2.1	1.2.1	1.2.1 / 3.2.3.3	1.2.1 / 3.2.3.3	8.1.5	7.2.5	3.2.3.1
1230	METHANOL	3	FT1	II	3+6.1	N	2	2	3	50	95	0.79	2	yes	T2 12)	II A	yes	PP, EP, EX, TOX, A	2	23
1231	METHYL ACETATE	3	F1	II	3	N	2	2		10	97	0.93	3	yes	T1 12)	II A	yes	PP, EX, A	1	
1235	METHYLAMINE, AQUEOUS SOLUTION	3	FC	II	3+8+N3	C	2	2		50	95		2	yes	T2 12)	II A	yes	PP, EP, EX, A	1	
1243	METHYL FORMATE	3	F1	I	3	C	1	1			95	0.97	1	yes	T2 12)	II A	yes	PP, EX, A	1	
1244	METHYLHYDRAZINE	6.1	TFC	I	6.1+3+8	C	2	2		45	95	0.88	1	no	T4	II C 5)	yes	PP, EP, EX, TOX, A	2	
1245	METHYL ISOBUTYL KETONE	3	F1	II	3	N	2	2		10	97	0.8	3	yes	T1 12)	II A	yes	PP, EX, A	1	
1247	METHYL METHACRYLATE MONOMER, STABILIZED	3	F1	II	3+unst.+N3	C	2	2		40	95	0.94	1	yes	T2 12)	II A	yes	PP, EX, A	1	3; 5; 16
1262	OCTANES	3	F1	II	3+N1	C	2	2		45	95	0.69 – 0.71	2	yes	T3	II A	yes	PP, EX, A	1	
1264	PARALDEHYDE	3	F1	III	3	N	3	2			97	0.99	3	yes	T3	II A 7)	yes	PP, EX, A	0	6: +16 °C; 17
1265	PENTANES, liquid	3	F1	I	3+N2	*	*	*	*	*	*	*	*	yes	*	II A	yes	PP, EX, A	1	14; * see 3.2.3.3
1265	PENTANES, liquid	3	F1	II	3+N2	*	*	*	*	*	*	*	*	yes	*	II A	yes	PP, EX, A	1	14; * see 3.2.3.3
1265	PENTANES, liquid (2-METHYLBUTANE)	3	F1	I	3+N2	N	1	1		50	97	0.62	1	yes	T2 12)	II A	yes	PP, EX, A	1	
1265	PENTANES, liquid (n-PENTANE)	3	F1	II	3+N2	N	2	3		50	97	0.63	3	yes	T3	II A	yes	PP, EX, A	1	
1265	PENTANES, liquid (n-PENTANE)	3	F1	II	3+N2	N	2	3	3	10	97	0.63	3	yes	T3	II A	yes	PP, EX, A	1	

-186-

(1) UN No. or substance identification No.	(2) Name and description	(3a) Class	(3b) Classification code	(4) Packing group	(5) Dangers	(6) Type of tank vessel	(7) Cargo tank design	(8) Cargo tank type	(9) Cargo tank equipment	(10) Opening pressure of the pressure relief valve/high velocity vent valve, in kPa	(11) Maximum degree of filling in %	(12) Relative density at 20 °C	(13) Type of sampling device	(14) Pump room below deck permitted	(15) Temperature class	(16) Explosion group	(17) Anti-explosion protection required	(18) Equipment required	(19) Number of cones/blue lights	(20) Additional requirements/Remarks
		3.1.2	2.2	2.1.1.3	5.2.2 / 3.2.3.1	1.2.1 / 7.2.2.0.1	3.2.3.1 / 1.2.1	3.2.3.1 / 1.2.1	3.2.3.1 / 1.2.1	3.2.3.1 / 1.2.1	7.2.4.21	3.2.3.1	3.2.3.1 / 1.2.1	3.2.3.1 / 1.2.1	1.2.1	1.2.1 / 3.2.3.3	1.2.1 / 3.2.3.3	8.1.5	7.2.5	3.2.3.1
1267	PETROLEUM CRUDE OIL	3	F1	I	3+(N1, N2, N3, CMR, F)	*	*	*	*	*	*		*	yes	T4$^{3)}$	II B$^{4)}$	yes	*	1	14; *see 3.2.3.3
1267	PETROLEUM CRUDE OIL	3	F1	I	3+(N1, N2, N3, CMR, F)	*	*	*	*	*	*		*	yes	T4$^{3)}$	II B$^{4)}$ (II B3)	yes	*	1	14; 44 *see 3.2.3.3
1267	PETROLEUM CRUDE OIL	3	F1	II	3+(N1, N2, N3, CMR, F)	*	*	*	*	*	*		*	yes	T4$^{3)}$	II B$^{4)}$	yes	*	1	14; *see 3.2.3.3
1267	PETROLEUM CRUDE OIL	3	F1	II	3+(N1, N2, N3, CMR, F)	*	*	*	*	*	*		*	yes	T4$^{3)}$	II B$^{4)}$ (II B3)	yes	*	1	14; 44 *see 3.2.3.3
1267	PETROLEUM CRUDE OIL	3	F1	III	3+(N1, N2, N3, CMR, F)	*	*	*	*	*	*		*	yes	T4$^{3)}$	II B$^{4)}$	yes	*	0	14; *see 3.2.3.3
1267	PETROLEUM CRUDE OIL	3	F1	III	3+(N1, N2, N3, CMR, F)	*	*	*	*	*	*		*	yes	T4$^{3)}$	II B$^{4)}$ (II B3)	yes	*	0	14; 44 *see 3.2.3.3
1267	PETROLEUM CRUDE OIL WITH MORE THAN 10% BENZENE	3	F1	I	3+CMR+ F+ (N1, N2, N3)	C	*	*	*	*	*		*	yes	T4$^{3)}$	II B$^{4)}$	yes	*	1	*see 3.2.3.3
1267	PETROLEUM CRUDE OIL WITH MORE THAN 10% BENZENE	3	F1	I	3+CMR+ F+ (N1, N2, N3)	C	*	*	*	*	*		*	yes	T4$^{3)}$	II B$^{4)}$ (II B3)	yes	*	1	44 *see 3.2.3.3
1267	PETROLEUM CRUDE OIL WITH MORE THAN 10% BENZENE	3	F1	II	3+CMR+ F+ (N1, N2, N3)	C	*	*	*	*	*		*	yes	T4$^{3)}$	II B$^{4)}$	yes	*	1	*see 3.2.3.3

-187-

(1)	(2)	(3a)	(3b)	(4)	(5)	(6)	(7)	(8)	(9)	(10)	(11)	(12)	(13)	(14)	(15)	(16)	(17)	(18)	(19)	(20)
UN No. or substance identification No.	Name and description	Class	Classification code	Packing group	Dangers	Type of tank vessel	Cargo tank design	Cargo tank type	Cargo tank equipment	Opening pressure of the pressure relief valve/high velocity vent valve, in kPa	Maximum degree of filling in %	Relative density at 20 °C	Type of sampling device	Pump room below deck permitted	Temperature class	Explosion group	Anti-explosion protection required	Equipment required	Number of cones/blue lights	Additional requirements/Remarks
	3.1.2	2.2	2.2	2.1.1.3	5.2.2 / 3.2.3.1	1.2.1 / 7.2.2.0.1	3.2.3.1 / 1.2.1	3.2.3.1 / 1.2.1	3.2.3.1 / 1.2.1	3.2.3.1 / 1.2.1	7.2.4.21	3.2.3.1	3.2.3.1 / 1.2.1	3.2.3.1 / 1.2.1	1.2.1	1.2.1 / 3.2.3.3	1.2.1 / 3.2.3.3	8.1.5	7.2.5	3.2.1
1257	PETROLEUM CRUDE OIL WITH MORE THAN 10% BENZENE	3	F1	II	3+CMR+ F+ (N1, N2, N3)	C	*	*	*	*	*		*	yes	T4 3)	II B4) (II B3)	yes	*	1	44 *see 3.2.3.3
1257	PETROLEUM CRUDE OIL WITH MORE THAN 10% BENZENE	3	F1	III	3+CMR+ F+ (N1, N2, N3)	C	*	*	*	*	*		*	yes	T4 3)	II B4)	yes	*	0	*see 3.2.3.3
1257	PETROLEUM CRUDE OIL WITH MORE THAN 10% BENZENE	3	F1	III	3+CMR+ F+ (N1, N2, N3)	C	*	*	*	*	*		*	yes	T4 3)	II B4) (II B3)	yes	*	0	44 *see 3.2.3.3
1257	PETROLEUM CRUDE OIL WITH MORE THAN 10% BENZENE INITIAL BOILING POINT ≤ 60 °C	3	F1	I	3+CMR+ F+ (N1, N2, N3)	C	1	1			95		1	yes	T4 3)	II B4)	yes	PP, EP, EX, TOX, A	1	43
1257	PETROLEUM CRUDE OIL WITH MORE THAN 10% BENZENE INITIAL BOILING POINT ≤ 60 °C	3	F1	I	3+CMR+ F+ (N1, N2, N3)	C	1	1			95		1	yes	T4 3)	II B4) (II B3)	yes	PP, EP, EX, TOX, A	1	43; 44
1257	PETROLEUM CRUDE OIL WITH MORE THAN 10% BENZENE INITIAL BOILING POINT ≤ 60 °C	3	F1	II	3+CMR+ F+ (N1, N2, N3)	C	1	1			95		1	yes	T4 3)	II B4)	yes	PP, EP, EX, TOX, A	1	
1257	PETROLEUM CRUDE OIL WITH MORE THAN 10% BENZENE INITIAL BOILING POINT ≤ 60 °C	3	F1	II	3+CMR+ F+ (N1, N2, N3)	C	1	1			95		1	yes	T4 3)	II B4) (II B3)	yes.	PP, EP, EX, TOX, A	1	44
1257	PETROLEUM CRUDE OIL WITH MORE THAN 10% BENZENE INITIAL BOILING POINT ≤ 60 °C	3	F1	III	3+CMR+ F+ (N1, N2, N3)	C	1	1			95		1	yes	T4 3)	II B4)	yes	PP, EP, EX, TOX, A	0	

UN No. or substance identification No. (1)	Name and description (2) 3.1.2	Class (3a) 2.2	Classification code (3b) 2.2	Packing group (4) 2.1.1.3	Dangers (5) 5.2.2/3.2.3.1	Type of tank vessel (6) 1.2.1/7.2.2.0.1	Cargo tank design (7) 3.2.3.1/1.2.1	Cargo tank type (8) 3.2.3.1/1.2.1	Cargo tank equipment (9) 3.2.3.1/1.2.1	Opening pressure of the pressure relief valve/high velocity vent valve, in kPa (10) 3.2.3.1/1.2.1	Maximum degree of filling in % (11) 7.2.4.21	Relative density at 20 °C (12) 3.2.3.1	Type of sampling device (13) 3.2.3.1/1.2.1	Pump room below deck permitted (14) 3.2.3.1/1.2.1	Temperature class (15) 1.2.1	Explosion group (16) 1.2.1/3.2.3.3	Anti-explosion protection required (17) 1.2.1/3.2.3.3	Equipment required (18) 8.1.5	Number of cones/blue lights (19) 7.2.5	Additional requirements/Remarks (20) 3.2.3.1
1267	PETROLEUM CRUDE OIL WITH MORE THAN 10% BENZENE INITIAL BOILING POINT ≤ 60 °C	3	F1	III	3+CMR+F+ (N1, N2, N3)	C	1	1			95		1	yes	T4 [3]	II B[4] (II B3)	yes	PP, EP, EX, TOX, A	0	44
1267	PETROLEUM CRUDE OIL WITH MORE THAN 10% BENZENE 60 °C < INITIAL BOILING POINT ≤ 85 °C	3	F1	II	3+CMR+F+ (N1, N2, N3)	C	2	2	3	50	95		2	yes	T4 [3]	II B[4]	yes	PP, EP, EX, TOX, A	1	23; 38
1267	PETROLEUM CRUDE OIL WITH MORE THAN 10% BENZENE 60 °C < INITIAL BOILING POINT ≤ 85 °C	3	F1	II	3+CMR+F+ (N1, N2, N3)	C	2	2	3	50	95		2	yes	T4 [3]	II B[4] (II B3)	yes	PP, EP, EX, TOX, A	1	23; 38; 44
1267	PETROLEUM CRUDE OIL WITH MORE THAN 10% BENZENE 60 °C < INITIAL BOILING POINT ≤ 85 °C	3	F1	III	3+CMR+F+ (N1, N2, N3)	C	2	2	3	50	95		2	yes	T4 [3]	II B[4]	yes	PP, EP, EX, TOX, A	0	23; 38
1267	PETROLEUM CRUDE OIL WITH MORE THAN 10% BENZENE 60 °C < INITIAL BOILING POINT ≤ 85 °C	3	F1	III	3+CMR+F+ (N1, N2, N3)	C	2	2	3	50	95		2	yes	T4 [3]	II B[4] (II B3)	yes	PP, EP, EX, TOX, A	1	23; 38; 44
1267	PETROLEUM CRUDE OIL WITH MORE THAN 10% BENZENE 85 °C < INITIAL BOILING POINT ≤ 115 °C	3	F1	II	3+CMR+F+ (N1, N2, N3)	C	2	2		50	95		2	yes	T4 [3]	II B[4]	yes	PP, EP, EX, TOX, A	1	
1267	PETROLEUM CRUDE OIL WITH MORE THAN 10% BENZENE 85 °C < INITIAL BOILING POINT ≤ 115 °C	3	F1	II	3+CMR+F+ (N1, N2, N3)	C	2	2		50	95		2	yes	T4 [3]	II B[4] (II B3)	yes	PP, EP, EX, TOX, A	1	44

(1)	(2)	(3a)	(3b)	(4)	(5)	(6)	(7)	(8)	(9)	(10)	(11)	(12)	(13)	(14)	(15)	(16)	(17)	(18)	(19)	(20)
UN No. or substance identification No.	Name and description	Class	Classification code	Packing group	Dangers	Type of tank vessel	Cargo tank design	Cargo tank type	Cargo tank equipment	Opening pressure of the pressure relief valve/high velocity vent valve, in kPa	Maximum degree of filling in %	Relative density at 20 °C	Type of sampling device	Pump room below deck permitted	Temperature class	Explosion group	Anti-explosion protection required	Equipment required	Number of cones/blue lights	Additional requirements/Remarks
	3.1.2	2.2	2.2	2.1.1.3	5.2.2 / 3.2.3.1	1.2.1 / 7.2.2.0.1	3.2.3.1 / 1.2.1	3.2.3.1 / 1.2.1	3.2.3.1 / 1.2.1	3.2.3.1 / 1.2.1	7.2.4.21	3.2.3.1	3.2.3.1 / 1.2.1	3.2.3.1 / 1.2.1	1.2.1	1.2.1 / 3.2.3.3	1.2.1 / 3.2.3.3	8.1.5	7.2.5	3.2.3.1
1267	PETROLEUM CRUDE OIL WITH MORE THAN 10% BENZENE 85 °C < INITIAL BOILING POINT ≤ 115 °C	3	F1	III	3+CMR+ F+ (N1, N2, N3)	C	2	2		50	95		2	yes	$T4^{3)}$	II $B^{4)}$	yes	PP, EP, EX, TOX, A	0	
1267	PETROLEUM CRUDE OIL WITH MORE THAN 10% BENZENE 85 °C < INITIAL BOILING POINT ≤ 115 °C	3	F1	III	3+CMR+ F+ (N1, N2, N3)	C	2	2		50	95		2	yes	$T4^{3)}$	II $B^{4)}$ (II B3)	yes	PP, EP, EX, TOX, A	0	44
1267	PETROLEUM CRUDE OIL WITH MORE THAN 10% BENZENE INITIAL BOILING POINT > 115 °C	3	F1	II	3+CMR+ F+ (N1, N2, N3)	C	2	2		35	95		2	yes	$T4^{3)}$	II $B^{4)}$	yes	PP, EP, EX, TOX, A	1	
1267	PETROLEUM CRUDE OIL WITH MORE THAN 10% BENZENE INITIAL BOILING POINT > 115 °C	3	F1	II	3+CMR+ F+ (N1, N2, N3)	C	2	2		35	95		2	yes	$T4^{3)}$	II $B^{4)}$ (II B3)	yes	PP, EP, EX, TOX, A	1	44
1267	PETROLEUM CRUDE OIL WITH MORE THAN 10% BENZENE INITIAL BOILING POINT > 115 °C	3	F1	III	3+CMR+ F+ (N1, N2, N3)	C	2	2		35	95		2	yes	$T4^{3)}$	II $B^{4)}$	yes	PP, EP, EX, TOX, A	0	
1267	PETROLEUM CRUDE OIL WITH MORE THAN 10% BENZENE INITIAL BOILING POINT > 115 °C	3	F1	III	3+CMR+ F+ (N1, N2, N3)	C	2	2		35	95		2	yes	$T4^{3)}$	II $B^{4)}$ (II B3)	yes	PP, EP, EX, TOX, A	0	44
1268	PETROLEUM DISTILLATES, N.O.S. or PETROLEUM PRODUCTS, N.O.S.	3	F1	I	3+(N1, N2, N3, CMR, F)	*	*	*	*	*	*		*	yes	$T4^{3)}$	II $B^{4)}$	yes	*	1	14; 27 *see 3.2.3.3
1268	PETROLEUM DISTILLATES, N.O.S. or PETROLEUM PRODUCTS, N.O.S.	3	F1	I	3+(N1, N2, N3, CMR, F)	*	*	*	*	*	*		*	yes	$T4^{3)}$	II $B^{4)}$ (II B3)	yes	*	1	14; 27; 44 *see 3.2.3.3

(1)	(2)	(3a)	(3b)	(4)	(5)	(6)	(7)	(8)	(9)	(10)	(11)	(12)	(13)	(14)	(15)	(16)	(17)	(18)	(19)	(20)
UN No. or substance identification No.	Name and description	Class	Classification code	Packing group	Dangers	Type of tank vessel	Cargo tank design	Cargo tank type	Cargo tank equipment	Opening pressure of the pressure relief valve/high velocity vent valve, in kPa	Maximum degree of filling in %	Relative density at 20 °C	Type of sampling device	Pump room below deck permitted	Temperature class	Explosion group	Anti-explosion protection required	Equipment required	Number of cones/blue lights	Additional requirements/Remarks
	3.1.2	2.2	2.2	2.1.1.3	5.2.2 / 3.2.3.1	1.2.1 / 7.2.2.0.1	3.2.3.1 / 1.2.1	3.2.3.1 / 1.2.1	3.2.3.1 / 1.2.1	3.2.3.1 / 1.2.1	7.2.4.21	3.2.3.1	3.2.3.1 / 1.2.1	3.2.3.1 / 1.2.1	1.2.1	1.2.1 / 3.2.3.3	1.2.1 / 3.2.3.3	8.1.5	7.2.5	3.2.3.1
1268	PETROLEUM DISTILLATES, N.O.S. or PETROLEUM PRODUCTS, N.O.S.	3	F1	II	3+(N1, N2, N3, CMR, F)	*	*	*	*	*	*		*	yes	T4[3]	II B[4]	yes	*	1	14; 27 *see 3.2.3.3
1268	PETROLEUM DISTILLATES, N.O.S. or PETROLEUM PRODUCTS, N.O.S.	3	F1	II	3+(N1, N2, N3, CMR, F)	*	*	*	*	*	*		*	yes	T4[3]	II B[4] (II B3)	yes	*	1	14; 27; 44 *see 3.2.3.3
1268	PETROLEUM DISTILLATES, N.O.S. or PETROLEUM PRODUCTS, N.O.S.	3	F1	III	3+(N1, N2, N3, CMR, F)	*	*	*	*	*	*		*	yes	T4[3]	II B[4]	yes	*	0	14; 27 *see 3.2.3.3
1268	PETROLEUM DISTILLATES, N.O.S. or PETROLEUM PRODUCTS, N.O.S.	3	F1	III	3+(N1, N2, N3, CMR, F)	*	*	*	*	*	*		*	yes	T4[3]	II B[4] (II B3)	yes	*	0	14; 27; 44 *see 3.2.3.3
1268	PETROLEUM DISTILLATES, N.O.S. or PETROLEUM PRODUCTS, N.O.S. WITH MORE THAN 10% BENZENE	3	F1	I	3+CMR+F+ (N1, N2, N3)	C	*	*	*	*	*		*	yes	T4[3]	II B[4]	yes	*	1	*see 3.2.3.3
1268	PETROLEUM DISTILLATES, N.O.S. or PETROLEUM PRODUCTS, N.O.S. WITH MORE THAN 10% BENZENE	3	F1	I	3+CMR+F+ (N1, N2, N3)	C	*	*	*	*	*		*	yes	T4[3]	II B[4] (II B3)	yes	*	1	44 *see 3.2.3.3
1268	PETROLEUM DISTILLATES, N.O.S. or PETROLEUM PRODUCTS, N.O.S. WITH MORE THAN 10% BENZENE	3	F1	II	3+CMR+F+ (N1, N2, N3)	C	*	*	*	*	*		*	yes	T4[3]	II B[4]	yes	*	1	*see 3.2.3.3
1268	PETROLEUM DISTILLATES, N.O.S. or PETROLEUM PRODUCTS, N.O.S. WITH MORE THAN 10% BENZENE	3	F1	II	3+CMR+F+ (N1, N2, N3)	C	*	*	*	*	*		*	yes	T4[3]	II B[4] (II B3)	yes	*	1	44 *see 3.2.3.3
1268	PETROLEUM DISTILLATES, N.O.S. or PETROLEUM PRODUCTS, N.O.S. WITH MORE THAN 10% BENZENE	3	F1	III	3+CMR+F+ (N1, N2, N3)	C	*	*	*	*	*		*	yes	T4[3]	II B[4]	yes	*	0	*see 3.2.3.3

(1)	(2)	(3a)	(3b)	(4)	(5)	(6)	(7)	(8)	(9)	(10)	(11)	(12)	(13)	(14)	(15)	(16)	(17)	(18)	(19)	(20)
UN No. or substance identification No.	Name and description	Class	Classification code	Packing group	Dangers	Type of tank vessel	Cargo tank design	Cargo tank type	Cargo tank equipment	Opening pressure of the pressure relief valve/high velocity vent valve, in kPa	Maximum degree of filling in %	Relative density at 20 °C	Type of sampling device	Pump room below deck permitted	Temperature class	Explosion group	Anti-explosion protection required	Equipment required	Number of cones/blue lights	Additional requirements/Remarks
3.1.1	3.1.2	2.2	2.2	2.1.1.3	5.2.2 / 3.2.3.1	1.2.1 / 7.2.2.0.1	3.2.3.1 / 1.2.1	3.2.3.1 / 1.2.1	3.2.3.1 / 1.2.1	3.2.3.1 / 1.2.1	7.2.4.21	3.2.3.1	3.2.3.1 / 1.2.1	3.2.3.1 / 1.2.1	1.2.1	1.2.1 / 3.2.3.3	1.2.1 / 3.2.3.3	8.1.5	7.2.5	3.2.3.1
1268	PETROLEUM DISTILLATES, N.O.S. or PETROLEUM PRODUCTS, N.O.S. WITH MORE THAN 10% BENZENE	3	F1	III	3+CMR+F+ (N1, N2, N3)	C	*	*	*	*	*		*	yes	T4 3)	II B4) (II B3)	yes	*	0	44 *see 3.2.3.3
1268	PETROLEUM DISTILLATES, N.O.S. or PETROLEUM PRODUCTS, N.O.S. WITH MORE THAN 10% BENZENE INITIAL BOILING POINT ≤ 60 °C	3	F1	I	3+CMR+F+ (N1, N2, N3)	C	1	1			95		1	yes	T4 3)	II B4)	yes	PP, EP, EX, TOX, A	1	43
1268	PETROLEUM DISTILLATES, N.O.S. or PETROLEUM PRODUCTS, N.O.S. WITH MORE THAN 10% BENZENE INITIAL BOILING POINT ≤ 60 °C	3	F1	I	3+CMR+F+ (N1, N2, N3)	C	1	1			95		1	yes	T4 3)	II B4) (II B3)	yes	PP, EP, EX, TOX, A	1	43; 44
1268	PETROLEUM DISTILLATES, N.O.S. or PETROLEUM PRODUCTS, N.O.S. WITH MORE THAN 10% BENZENE INITIAL BOILING POINT ≤ 60 °C	3	F1	II	3+CMR+F+ (N1, N2, N3)	C	1	1			95		1	yes	T4 3)	II B4)	yes	PP, EP, EX, TOX, A	1	
1268	PETROLEUM DISTILLATES, N.O.S. or PETROLEUM PRODUCTS, N.O.S. WITH MORE THAN 10% BENZENE INITIAL BOILING POINT ≤ 60 °C	3	F1	II	3+CMR+F+(N1, N2, N3)	C	1	1			95		1	yes	T4 3)	II B4) (II B3)	yes	PP, EP, EX, TOX, A	1	44
1268	PETROLEUM DISTILLATES, N.O.S. or PETROLEUM PRODUCTS, N.O.S. WITH MORE THAN 10% BENZENE 60 °C < INITIAL BOILING POINT ≤ 85 °C	3	F1	II	3+CMR+F+ (N1, N2, N3)	C	2	2	3	50	95		2	yes	T4 3)	II B4)	yes	PP, EP, EX, TOX, A	1	23; 38

(1)	(2)	(3a)	(3b)	(4)	(5)	(6)	(7)	(8)	(9)	(10)	(11)	(12)	(13)	(14)	(15)	(16)	(17)	(18)	(19)	(20)
UN No. or substance identification No.	Name and description	Class	Classification code	Packing group	Dangers	Type of tank vessel	Cargo tank design	Cargo tank type	Cargo tank equipment	Opening pressure of the pressure relief valve/high velocity vent valve, in kPa	Maximum degree of filling in %	Relative density at 20 °C	Type of sampling device	Pump room below deck permitted	Temperature class	Explosion group	Anti-explosion protection required	Equipment required	Number of cones/blue lights	Additional requirements/Remarks
	3.1.2	2.2	2.2	2.1.1.3	5.2.2 / 3.2.3.1	1.2.1 / 7.2.2.0.1	3.2.3.1 / 1.2.1	3.2.3.1 / 1.2.1	3.2.3.1 / 1.2.1	3.2.3.1 / 1.2.1	7.2.4.21	3.2.3.1	3.2.3.1 / 1.2.1	3.2.3.1 / 1.2.1	1.2.1	1.2.1 / 3.2.3.3	1.2.1 / 3.2.3.3	8.1.5	7.2.5	3.2.3.1
1268	PETROLEUM DISTILLATES, N.O.S. or PETROLEUM PRODUCTS, N.O.S. WITH MORE THAN 10% BENZENE 60 °C < INITIAL BOILING POINT ≤ 85 °C	3	F1	II	3+CMR+F+ (N1, N2, N3)	C	2	2	3	50	95		2	yes	T4 3)	II B4) (II B3)	yes	PP, EP, EX, TOX, A	1	23; 38; 44
1268	PETROLEUM DISTILLATES, N.O.S. or PETROLEUM PRODUCTS, N.O.S. WITH MORE THAN 10% BENZENE 85 °C < INITIAL BOILING POINT ≤ 115 °C	3	F1	II	3+CMR+F+ (N1, N2, N3)	C	2	2		50	95		2	yes	T4 3)	II B4)	yes	PP, EP, EX, TOX, A	1	
1268	PETROLEUM DISTILLATES, N.O.S. or PETROLEUM PRODUCTS, N.O.S. WITH MORE THAN 10% BENZENE 85 °C < INITIAL BOILING POINT ≤ 115 °C	3	F1	II	3+CMR+F+ (N1, N2, N3)	C	2	2		50	95		2	yes	T4 3)	II B4) (II B3)	yes	PP, EP, EX, TOX, A	1	44
1268	PETROLEUM DISTILLATES, N.O.S. or PETROLEUM PRODUCTS, N.O.S. WITH MORE THAN 10% BENZENE INITIAL BOILING POINT > 115 °C	3	F1	II	3+CMR+F+ (N1, N2, N3)	C	2	2		35	95		2	yes	T4 3)	II B4)	yes	PP, EP, EX, TOX, A	1	
1268	PETROLEUM DISTILLATES, N.O.S. or PETROLEUM PRODUCTS, N.O.S. WITH MORE THAN 10% BENZENE INITIAL BOILING POINT > 115 °C	3	F1	II	3+CMR+F+ (N1, N2, N3)	C	2	2		35	95		2	yes	T4 3)	II B4) (II B3)	yes	PP, EP, EX, TOX, A	1	44

(1) UN No. or substance identification No.	(2) Name and description	(3a) Class	(3b) Classification code	(4) Packing group	(5) Dangers	(6) Type of tank vessel	(7) Cargo tank design	(8) Cargo tank type	(9) Cargo tank equipment	(10) Opening pressure of the pressure relief valve/high velocity vent valve, in kPa	(11) Maximum degree of filling in %	(12) Relative density at 20 °C	(13) Type of sampling device	(14) Pump room below deck permitted	(15) Temperature class	(16) Explosion group	(17) Anti-explosion protection required	(18) Equipment required	(19) Number of cones/blue lights	(20) Additional requirements/Remarks
		3.1.2	2.2	2.1.1.3	5.2.2 / 3.2.3.1	1.2.1 / 7.2.2.0.1	3.2.3.1 / 1.2.1	3.2.3.1 / 1.2.1	3.2.3.1 / 1.2.1	3.2.3.1 / 1.2.1	7.2.4.21	3.2.3.1	3.2.3.1 / 1.2.1	3.2.3.1 / 1.2.1	1.2.1	1.2.1 / 3.2.3.3	1.2.1 / 3.2.3.3	8.1.5	7.2.5	3.2.3.1
1268	PETROLEUM DISTILLATES, N.O.S. or PETROLEUM PRODUCTS, N.O.S. (NAPHTA) 110 kPa < vp50 ≤ 175 kPa	3	F1	II	3+N2+CMR+F	N	2	3		50	97	0,735	3	yes	T3	II A	yes	PP, EP, EX, TOX, A	1	14
1268	PETROLEUM DISTILLATES, N.O.S. or PETROLEUM PRODUCTS, N.O.S. (NAPHTA) 110 kPa < vp50 ≤ 150 kPa	3	F1	II	3+N2+CMR+F	N	2	3	3	10	97	0,735	3	yes	T3	II A	yes	PP, EP, EX, TOX, A	1	14
1268	PETROLEUM DISTILLATES, N.O.S. or PETROLEUM PRODUCTS, N.O.S. (NAPHTA) vp50 ≤ 110 kPa	3	F1	II	3+N2+CMR+F	N	2	3		10	97	0,735	3	yes	T3	II A	yes	PP, EP, EX, TOX, A	1	14
1268	PETROLEUM DISTILLATES, N.O.S. or PETROLEUM PRODUCTS, N.O.S (BENZENE HEART CUT) vp50 ≤ 110 kPa	3	F1	II	3+N2+CMR+F	N	2	3		10	97	0,765	3	yes	T3	II A	yes	PP, EP, EX, TOX, A	1	14
1274	n-PROPANOL (propyl alcohol, normal)	3	F1	II	3	N	2	2		10	97	0.8	3	yes	T2 [12]	II B (II B1)	yes	PP, EX, A	1	
1274	n-PROPANOL (propyl alcohol, normal)	3	F1	III	3	N	3	2			97	0.8	3	yes	T2 [12]	II B (II B1)	yes	PP, EX, A	0	
1275	PROPIONALDEHYDE	3	F1	II	3+N3	C	2	2	3	50	95	0.81	2	yes	T4	II B (II B2)	yes	PP, EX, A	1	15; 23
1276	n-PROPYL ACETATE	3	F1	II	3+N3	N	2	2		10	97	0.88	3	yes	T1 [12]	II A	yes	PP, EX, A	1	
1277	PROPYLAMINE (1-aminopropane)	3	FC	II	3+8	C	2	2	3	50	95	0.72	2	yes	T2 [12]	II A	yes	PP, EP, EX, A	1	23
1278	1-CHLOROPROPANE (propyl chloride)	3	F1	II	3	C	2	2	3	50	95	0.89	2	yes	T1 [12]	II A	yes	PP, EX, A	1	23

(1) UN No. or substance identification No.	(2) Name and description	(3a) Class	(3b) Classification code	(4) Packing group	(5) Dangers	(6) Type of tank vessel	(7) Cargo tank design	(8) Cargo tank type	(9) Cargo tank equipment	(10) Opening pressure of the pressure relief valve/high velocity vent valve, in kPa	(11) Maximum degree of filling in %	(12) Relative density at 20 °C	(13) Type of sampling device	(14) Pump room below deck permitted	(15) Temperature class	(16) Explosion group	(17) Anti-explosion protection required	(18) Equipment required	(19) Number of cones/blue lights	(20) Additional requirements/Remarks
		2.2	2.2	2.1.1.3	5.2.2 / 3.2.3.1	1.2.1 / 7.2.2.0.1	3.2.3.1 / 1.2.1	3.2.3.1 / 1.2.1	3.2.3.1 / 1.2.1	3.2.3.1 / 1.2.1	7.2.4.21	3.2.3.1	3.2.3.1 / 1.2.1	3.2.3.1 / 1.2.1	1.2.1	1.2.1 / 3.2.3.3	1.2.1 / 3.2.3.3	8.1.5	7.2.5	3.2.3.1
1279	1,2-DICHLOROPROPANE or PROPYL DICHLORIDE	3	F1	II	3+N2	C	2	2		45	95	1.16	2	yes	T1 12)	II A 8)	yes	PP, EX, A	1	
1280	PROPYLENE OXIDE	3	F1	I	3+unst.+N3+CMR	C	1	1			95	0.83	1	yes	T2 12)	II B (II B3)	yes	PP, EP, EX, TOX, A	1	2; 12; 31; 35
1282	PYRIDINE	3	F1	II	3+N3	N	2	2		10	97	0.98	3	yes	T1 12)	II A 8)	yes	PP, EX, A	1	
1289	SODIUM METHYLATE SOLUTION in alcohol	3	FC	III	3+8	N	3	2			97	0.969	3	yes	T2 12)	II A	yes	PP, EP, EX, A	0	34
1294	TOLUENE	3	F1	II	3+N3	N	2	2		10	97	0.87	3	yes	T1 12)	II A	yes	PP, EX, A	1	
1296	TRIETHYLAMINE	3	FC	II	3+8+N3	C	2	2		50	95	0.73	2	yes	T1 12)	II A 8)	yes	PP, EP, EX, A	1	
1300	TURPENTINE SUBSTITUTE	3	F1	III	3+N2+F	N	3	3			97	0.78	3	yes	T3	II B 4)	yes	PP, EX, A	0	
1301	VINYL ACETATE, STABILIZED	3	F1	II	3+unst.+N3	N	2	2		10	97	0.93	2	yes	T2 12)	II A	yes	PP, EX, A	1	3; 5; 16
1307	XYLENES (o-XYLENE)	3	F1	III	3+N2	N	3	3			97	0.88	3	yes	T1 12)	II A	yes	PP, EX, A	0	
1307	XYLENES (m-XYLENE)	3	F1	III	3+N2	N	3	3			97	0.86	3	yes	T1 12)	II A	yes	PP, EX, A	0	
1307	XYLENES (p-XYLENE)	3	F1	III	3+N2	N	3	3			97	0.86	3	yes	T1 12)	II A	yes	PP, EX, A	0	6; +17 °C; 17
1307	XYLENES (mixture with melting point ≤ 0 °C)	3	F1	II	3+N2	N	3	3			97		3	yes	T1 12)	II A	yes	PP, EX, A	1	
1307	XYLENES (mixture with melting point ≤ 0 °C)	3	F1	III	3+N2	N	3	3			97		3	yes	T1 12)	II A	yes	PP, EX, A	0	
1307	XYLENES (mixture with 0 °C < melting point < 13 °C)	3	F1	III	3+N2	N	3	3	2		97		3	yes	T1 12)	II A	yes	PP, EX, A	0	6; +17 °C; 17

(1) UN No. or substance identification No.	(2) Name and description	(3a) Class	(3b) Classification code	(4) Packing group	(5) Dangers	(6) Type of tank vessel	(7) Cargo tank design	(8) Cargo tank type	(9) Cargo tank equipment	(10) Opening pressure of the pressure relief valve/high velocity vent valve, in kPa	(11) Maximum degree of filling in %	(12) Relative density at 20 °C	(13) Type of sampling device	(14) Pump room below deck permitted	(15) Temperature class	(16) Explosion group	(17) Anti-explosion protection required	(18) Equipment required	(19) Number of cones/blue lights	(20) Additional requirements/Remarks
		3.1.2	2.2	2.1.1.3	5.2.2 / 3.2.3.1	1.2.1 / 7.2.2.0.1	3.2.3.1 / 1.2.1	3.2.3.1 / 1.2.1	3.2.3.1 / 1.2.1	3.2.3.1 / 1.2.1	7.2.4.21	3.2.3.1	3.2.3.1 / 1.2.1	3.2.3.1 / 1.2.1	1.2.1	1.2.1 / 3.2.3.3	1.2.1 / 3.2.3.3	8.1.5	7.2.5	3.2.3.1
1541	ACETONE CYANOHYDRIN, STABILIZED	6.1	T1	I	6.1+unst.+N1	C	2	2		50	95	0.932	1	no			no	PP, EP, TOX, A	2	3
1545	ALLYL ISOTHIOCYANATE, STABILIZED	6.1	TF1	II	6.1+3+unst.	C	2	2		30	95	1.02	1	no	T4 3)	II B4)	yes	PP, EP, EX, TOX, A	2	2; 3
1547	ANILINE	6.1	T1	II	6.1+N1	C	2	2		25	95	1.02	2	no			no	PP, EP, TOX, A	2	
1578	CHLORONITROBENZENES, SOLID, MOLTEN (p-CHLORONITROBENZENE)	6.1	T2	II	6.1+N2+S	C	2	1	2	25	95	1.37	2	no	T1 12)	II B (II B3 14))	yes	PP, EP, EX, TOX, A	2	7; 17; 26
1578	CHLORONITROBENZENES, SOLID, MOLTEN (p-CHLORONITROBENZENE)	6.1	T2	II	6.1+N2+S	C	2	1	4	25	95	1.37	2	no			no	PP, EP, TOX, A	2	7; 17; 20: +112°C; 26
1591	o-DICHLOROBENZENE	6.1	T1	III	6.1+N1+S	C	2	2	3	25	95	1.32	2	no			no	PP, EP, TOX, A	0	
1593	DICHLOROMETHANE (methyl chloride)	6.1	T1	III	6.1	C	2	2		50	95	1.33	2	no			no	PP, EP, TOX, A	0	23
1594	DIETHYL SULPHATE	6.1	T1	II	6.1+N2 +CMR	C	2	2		25	95	1.18	2	no			no	PP, EP, TOX, A	2	
1595	DIMETHYL SULPHATE	6.1	TC1	I	6.1+8+N3+ CMR	C	3	2		25	95	1.33	1	no			no	PP, EP, TOX, A	2	
1604	ETHYLENEDIAMINE	8	CF1	II	8+3+N3	N	2	2			97	0.9	3	yes	T2 12)	II A	yes	PP, EP, EX, A	1	6: +12 °C; 17; 34
1605	ETHYLENE DIBROMIDE	6.1	T1	I	6.1+N2 +CMR	C	2	2		30	95	2.18	1	no			no	PP, EP, TOX, A	2	6: +14 °C; 17
1648	ACETONITRILE (methyl cyanide)	3	F1	II	3	N	2	2		10	97	0.78	3	yes	T1 12)	II A	yes	PP, EX, A	1	
1662	NITROBENZENE	6.1	T1	II	6.1+N2	C	2	2	2	25	95	1.21	2	no	T1 12)	II B (II B1)	yes	PP, EP, EX, TOX, A	2	6: +10°C; 17

(1) UN No. or substance identification No.	(2) Name and description	(3a) Class	(3b) Classification code	(4) Packing group	(5) Dangers	(6) Type of tank vessel	(7) Cargo tank design	(8) Cargo tank type	(9) Cargo tank equipment	(10) Opening pressure of the pressure relief valve/high velocity vent valve, in kPa	(11) Maximum degree of filling in %	(12) Relative density at 20 °C	(13) Type of sampling device	(14) Pump room below deck permitted	(15) Temperature class	(16) Explosion group	(17) Anti-explosion protection required	(18) Equipment required	(19) Number of cones/blue lights	(20) Additional requirements/Remarks
		2.2	2.2	2.1.1.3	5.2.2 / 3.2.3.1	1.2.1 / 7.2.2.0.1	3.2.3.1 / 1.2.1	3.2.3.1 / 1.2.1	3.2.3.1 / 1.2.1	3.2.3.1 / 1.2.1	7.2.4.21	3.2.3.1	3.2.3.1 / 1.2.1	3.2.3.1 / 1.2.1	1.2.1	1.2.1 / 3.2.3.3	1.2.1 / 3.2.3.3	8.1.5	7.2.5	3.2.3.1
1663	NITROPHENOLS	6.1	T2	III	6.1+N3+S	C	2	2	2	25	95		2	no	T1 12)	II B (II B3 14))	yes	PP, EP, EX, TOX, A	0	7; 17
1663	NITROPHENOLS	6.1	T2	III	6.1+N3+S	C	2	2	4	25	95		2	no			no	PP, EP, TOX, A	0	7; 17; 20: +65 °C
1664	NITROTOLUENES, LIQUID (o-NITROTOLUENE)	6.1	T1	II	6.1+N2+CMR+S	C	2	2		25	95	1.16	2	no			no	PP, EP, TOX, A	2	
1708	TOLUIDINES, LIQUID (o-TOLUIDINE)	6.1	T1	II	6.1+N1+CMR	C	2	2		25	95	1	2	no			no	PP, EP, TOX, A	2	
1708	TOLUIDINES, LIQUID (m-TOLUIDINE)	6.1	T1	II	6.1+N1	C	2	2		25	95	1.03	2	no			no	PP, EP, TOX, A	2	
1710	TRICHLOROETHYLENE	6.1	T1	III	6.1+N2+CMR	C	2	2		50	95	1.46	2	no			no	PP, EP, TOX, A	0	15
1715	ACETIC ANHYDRIDE	8	CF1	II	8+3	N	2	3	3	10	97	1.08	3	yes	T2 12)	II A	yes	PP, EP, EX, A	1	34
1717	ACETYL CHLORIDE	3	FC	II	3+8	C	2	2		50	95	1.1	2	yes	T2 12)	II A 8)	yes	PP, EP, EX, A	1	23
1718	BUTYL ACIDE PHOSPHATE	8	C3	III	8+N3	N	4	3	3		97	0.98	3	yes			no	PP, EP	0	34
1719	CAUSTIC ALKALI LIQUID, N.O.S.	8	C5	II	8+(N1, N2, N3, CMR, F or S)	*	*	*	*	*	*		*	yes			no	*	0	27; 30; 34 *see 3.2.3.3
1719	CAUSTIC ALKALI LIQUID, N.O.S.	8	C5	III	8+(N1, N2, N3, CMR, F or S)	*	*	*	*	*	*		*	yes			no	*	0	27; 30; 34 *see 3.2.3.3
1738	BENZYL CHLORIDE	6.1	TC1	II	6.1+8+3+N3+CMR+S	C	2	2		25	95	1.1	2	no	T1 12)	II A 8)	yes	PP, EP, EX, TOX, A	2	

(1)	(2)	(3a)	(3b)	(4)	(5)	(6)	(7)	(8)	(9)	(10)	(11)	(12)	(13)	(14)	(15)	(16)	(17)	(18)	(19)	(20)
UN No. or substance identification No.	Name and description	Class	Classification code	Packing group	Dangers	Type of tank vessel	Cargo tank design	Cargo tank type	Cargo tank equipment	Opening pressure of the pressure relief valve/high velocity vent valve, in kPa	Maximum degree of filling in %	Relative density at 20 °C	Type of sampling device	Pump room below deck permitted	Temperature class	Explosion group	Anti-explosion protection required	Equipment required	Number of cones/blue lights	Additional requirements/Remarks
	3.1.2	2.2	2.2	2.1.1.3	5.2.2 / 3.2.3.1	1.2.1 / 7.2.2.0.1	3.2.3.1 / 1.2.1	3.2.3.1 / 1.2.1	3.2.3.1 / 1.2.1	3.2.3.1 / 1.2.1	7.2.4.21	3.2.3.1	3.2.3.1 / 1.2.1	3.2.3.1 / 1.2.1	1.2.1	1.2.1 / 3.2.3.3	1.2.1 / 3.2.3.3	8.1.5	7.2.5	3.2.3.1
1742	BORON TRIFLUORIDE ACETIC ACID COMPLEX, LIQUID	8	C3	II	8	N	4	2			97	1.35	3	yes			no	PP, EP	0	34
1750	CHLORACETIC ACID SOLUTION	6.1	TC1	II	6.1+8+N1	C	2	2	2	25	95	1.58	2	no	T1 12)	II A	yes	PP, EP, EX, TOX, A	2	7; 17
1750	CHLORACETIC ACID SOLUTION	6.1	TC1	II	6.1+8+N1	C	2	1	4	25	95	1.58	2	no			no	PP, EP, TOX, A	2	7; 17; 20:+111°C; 26
1760	CORROSIVE LIQUID, N.O.S.	8	C9	I	8+(N1, N2, N3, CMR, F or S)	*	*	*	*	*	*		*	yes			no	*	0	27; 34 *see 3.2.3.3
1760	CORROSIVE LIQUID, N.O.S.	8	C9	II	8+(N1, N2, N3, CMR, F or S)	*	*	*	*	*	*		*	yes			no	*	0	27; 34 *see 3.2.3.3
1760	CORROSIVE LIQUID, N.O.S.	8	C9	III	8+(N1, N2, N3, CMR, F or S)	*	*	*	*	*	*		*	yes			no	*	0	27; 34 *see 3.2.3.3
1760	CORROSIVE LIQUID, N.O.S. (SODIUM MERCAPTOBENZOTHIAZOLE, 50% AQUEOUS SOLUTION)	8	C9	II	8+N1+F	C	2	2		40	95	1.25	2	yes			no	PP, EP	0	
1760	CORROSIVE LIQUID, N.O.S. (FATTY ALCOHOL, C_{12}-C_{14})	8	C9	III	8+F	N	4	3			97	0.89	3	yes			no	PP, EP	0	34
1760	CORROSIVE LIQUID, N.O.S. (ETHYLENEDIAMINE-TETRAACETIC ACID, TETRASODIUM SALT, 40% AQUEOUS SOLUTION)	8	C9	III	8+N2	N	4	3			97	1.28	3	yes			no	PP, EP	0	34

(1)	(2)	(3a)	(3b)	(4)	(5)	(6)	(7)	(8)	(9)	(10)	(11)	(12)	(13)	(14)	(15)	(16)	(17)	(18)	(19)	(20)
UN No. or substance identification No.	Name and description	Class	Classification code	Packing group	Dangers	Type of tank vessel	Cargo tank design	Cargo tank type	Cargo tank equipment	Opening pressure of the pressure relief valve/high velocity vent valve, in kPa	Maximum degree of filling in %	Relative density at 20 °C	Type of sampling device	Pump room below deck permitted	Temperature class	Explosion group	Anti-explosion protection required	Equipment required	Number of cones/blue lights	Additional requirements/Remarks
		2.2	2.2	2.1.1.3	5.2.2 / 3.2.3.1	1.2.1 / 7.2.2.0.1	3.2.3.1 / 1.2.1	3.2.3.1 / 1.2.1	3.2.3.1 / 1.2.1	3.2.3.1 / 1.2.1	7.2.4.21	3.2.3.1	3.2.3.1 / 1.2.1	3.2.3.1 / 1.2.1	1.2.1	1.2.1 / 3.2.3.3	1.2.1 / 3.2.3.3	8.1.5	7.2.5	3.2.3.1
1764	DICHLOROACETIC ACID	8	C3	II	8+N1	N	3	3			97	1.56	2	yes	T1 12)	II A	yes	PP, EP, EX, A	0	6:+13 °C; 17
1778	FLUOROSILICIC ACID	8	C1	II	8+N3	N	2	3		10	97		3	yes			no	PP, EP	0	34
1779	FORMIC ACID with more than 85% acid by mass	8	CF1	II	8+3+N3	N	2	3		10	97	1.22	3	yes	T1 12)	II A	yes	PP, EP, EX, A	1	6:+12 °C; 17; 34
1780	FUMARYL CHLORIDE	8	C3	II	8+N3	N	2	3		10	97	1.41	3	yes			no	PP, EP	0	8; 34
1783	HEXAMETHYLENEDIAMINE SOLUTION	8	C7	II	8+N3	N	3	2	2		97		3	yes	T4 3)	II A	yes	PP, EP, EX, A	0	7; 17; 34
1783	HEXAMETHYLENEDIAMINE SOLUTION	8	C7	III	8+N3	N	3	2	2		97		3	yes	T3	II A	yes	PP, EP, EX, A	0	7; 17; 34
1789	HYDROCHLORIC ACID	8	C1	II	8	N	2	3		10	97		3	yes			no	PP, EP	0	34
1789	HYDROCHLORIC ACID	8	C1	III	8	N	4	3			97		3	yes			no	PP, EP	0	34
1805	PHOSPHORIC ACID, SOLUTION, WITH MORE THAN 80% (VOLUME) ACID	8	C1	III	8	N	4	3	2		95	> 1,6	3	yes			no	PP, EP	0	7; 17; 22; 34
1805	PHOSPHORIC ACID, SOLUTION, WITH 80% (VOLUME) ACID, OR LESS	8	C1	III	8	N	4	3			97	1,00 - 1,6	3	yes			no	PP, EP	0	22; 34
1814	POTASSIUM HYDROXIDE SOLUTION	8	C5	II	8+N3	N	4	2			97		3	yes			no	PP, EP	0	30; 34
1814	POTASSIUM HYDROXIDE SOLUTION	8	C5	III	8+N3	N	4	2			97		3	yes			no	PP, EP	0	30; 34
1823	SODIUM HYDROXIDE, SOLID, MOLTEN	8	C6	II	8+N3	N	4	1	4		95	2.13	3	yes			no	PP, EP	0	7; 17; 34
1824	SODIUM HYDROXIDE SOLUTION	8	C5	II	8+N3	N	4	2			97		3	yes			no	PP, EP	0	30; 34
1824	SODIUM HYDROXIDE SOLUTION	8	C5	III	8+N3	N	4	2			97		3	yes			no	PP, EP	0	30; 34

(1)	(2)	(3a)	(3b)	(4)	(5)	(6)	(7)	(8)	(9)	(10)	(11)	(12)	(13)	(14)	(15)	(16)	(17)	(18)	(19)	(20)
	3.1.2	2.2	2.2	2.1.1.3	5.2.2 / 3.2.3.1	1.2.1 / 7.2.2.0.1	3.2.3.1 / 1.2.1	3.2.3.1 / 1.2.1	3.2.3.1 / 1.2.1	3.2.3.1 / 1.2.1	7.2.4.21	3.2.3.1	3.2.3.1 / 1.2.1	3.2.3.1 / 1.2.1	1.2.1	1.2.1 / 3.2.3.3	1.2.1 / 3.2.3.3	8.1.5	7.2.5	3.2.3.1
UN No. or substance identification No.	Name and description	Class	Classification code	Packing group	Dangers	Type of tank vessel	Cargo tank design	Cargo tank type	Cargo tank equipment	Opening pressure of the pressure relief valve/high velocity vent valve, in kPa	Maximum degree of filling in %	Relative density at 20 °C	Type of sampling device	Pump room below deck permitted	Temperature class	Explosion group	Anti-explosion protection required	Equipment required	Number of cones/blue lights	Additional requirements/Remarks
1830	SULPHURIC ACID with more than 51% acid	8	C1	II	8+N3	N	4	3			97	1,4 - 1,84	3	yes			no	PP, EP	0	8; 22; 30; 34
1831	SULPHURIC ACID, FUMING	8	CT1	I	8+6.1	C	2	2		50	95	1.94	1	no			no	PP, EP, TOX, A	2	8
1832	SULPHURIC ACID, SPENT	8	C1	II	8	N	4	3			97		3	yes			no	PP, EP	0	8; 30; 34
1846	CARBON TETRACHLORIDE	6.1	T1	II	6.1+N2+S	C	2	2	3	50	95	1.59	2	no			no	PP, EP, TOX, A	2	23
1848	PROPIONIC ACID with not less than 10% and less than 90% acid by mass	8	C3	III	8+N3	N	3	3			97	0.99	3	yes			no	PP, EP	0	34
1863	FUEL, AVIATION, TURBINE ENGINE	3	F1	I	3+(N1, N2, N3, CMR, F)	*	*	*	*	*	*		*	yes	T4[3]	II B[4]	yes	*	1	14; *see 3.2.3.3
1863	FUEL, AVIATION, TURBINE ENGINE	3	F1	I	3+(N1, N2, N3, CMR, F)	*	*	*	*	*	*		*	yes	T4[3]	II B[4] (II B3)	yes	*	1	14; 44 *see 3.2.3.3
1863	FUEL, AVIATION, TURBINE ENGINE	3	F1	II	3+(N1, N2, N3, CMR, F)	*	*	*	*	*	*		*	yes	T4[3]	II B[4]	yes	*	1	14; *see 3.2.3.3
1863	FUEL, AVIATION, TURBINE ENGINE	3	F1	II	3+(N1, N2, N3, CMR, F)	*	*	*	*	*	*		*	yes	T4[3]	II B[4] (II B3)	yes	*	1	14; 44 *see 3.2.3.3
1863	FUEL, AVIATION, TURBINE ENGINE	3	F1	III	3+(N1, N2, N3, CMR, F)	*	*	*	*	*	*		*	yes	T4[3]	II B[4]	yes	*	0	14; *see 3.2.3.3
1863	FUEL, AVIATION, TURBINE ENGINE	3	F1	III	3+(N1, N2, N3, CMR, F)	*	*	*	*	*	*		*	yes	T4[3]	II B[4] (II B3)	yes	*	0	14; 44 *see 3.2.3.3

(1)	(2)	(3a)	(3b)	(4)	(5)	(6)	(7)	(8)	(9)	(10)	(11)	(12)	(13)	(14)	(15)	(16)	(17)	(18)	(19)	(20)
UN No. or substance identification No.	Name and description	Class	Classification code	Packing group	Dangers	Type of tank vessel	Cargo tank design	Cargo tank type	Cargo tank equipment	Opening pressure of the pressure relief valve/high velocity vent valve, in kPa	Maximum degree of filling in %	Relative density at 20 °C	Type of sampling device	Pump room below deck permitted	Temperature class	Explosion group	Anti-explosion protection required	Equipment required	Number of cones/blue lights	Additional requirements/Remarks
	3.1.2	2.2	2.2	2.1.1.3	5.2.2 / 3.2.3.1	1.2.1 / 7.2.2.0.1	3.2.3.1 / 1.2.1	3.2.3.1 / 1.2.1	3.2.3.1 / 1.2.1	3.2.3.1 / 1.2.1	7.2.4.21	3.2.3.1	3.2.3.1 / 1.2.1	3.2.3.1 / 1.2.1	1.2.1	1.2.1 / 3.2.3.3	1.2.1 / 3.2.3.3	8.1.5	7.2.5	3.2.3.1
1863	FUEL, AVIATION, TURBINE ENGINE WITH MORE THAN 10% BENZENE	3	F1	I	3+CMR+ F+ (N1, N2, N3)	C	*	*	*	*	*		*	yes	T4 $^{3)}$	II B $^{4)}$	yes	*	1	*see 3.2.3.3
1863	FUEL, AVIATION, TURBINE ENGINE WITH MORE THAN 10% BENZENE	3	F1	I	3+CMR+ F+ (N1, N2, N3)	C	*	*	*	*	*		*	yes	T4 $^{3)}$	II B $^{4)}$ (II B3)	yes	*	1	44 *see 3.2.3.3
1863	FUEL, AVIATION, TURBINE ENGINE WITH MORE THAN 10% BENZENE	3	F1	II	3+CMR+ F+ (N1, N2, N3)	C	*	*	*	*	*		*	yes	T4 $^{3)}$	II B $^{4)}$	yes	*	1	*see 3.2.3.3
1863	FUEL, AVIATION, TURBINE ENGINE WITH MORE THAN 10% BENZENE	3	F1	II	3+CMR+ F+ (N1, N2, N3)	C	*	*	*	*	*		*	yes	T4 $^{3)}$	II B $^{4)}$ (II B3)	yes	*	1	44 *see 3.2.3.3
1863	FUEL, AVIATION, TURBINE ENGINE WITH MORE THAN 10% BENZENE	3	F1	III	3+CMR+ F+ (N1, N2, N3)	C	*	*	*	*	*		*	yes	T4 $^{3)}$	II B $^{4)}$	yes	*	0	*see 3.2.3.3
1863	FUEL, AVIATION, TURBINE ENGINE WITH MORE THAN 10% BENZENE	3	F1	III	3+CMR+ F+ (N1, N2, N3)	C	*	*	*	*	*		*	yes	T4 $^{3)}$	II B $^{4)}$ (II B3)	yes	*	0	44 *see 3.2.3.3
1863	FUEL, AVIATION, TURBINE ENGINE WITH MORE THAN 10% BENZENE INITIAL BOILING POINT ≤ 60 °C	3	F1	I	3+CMR+ F+ (N1, N2, N3)	C	1	1			95		1	yes	T4 $^{3)}$	II B $^{4)}$	yes	PP, EP, EX, TOX, A	1	43
1863	FUEL, AVIATION, TURBINE ENGINE WITH MORE THAN 10% BENZENE INITIAL BOILING POINT ≤ 60 °C	3	F1	I	3+CMR+ F+ (N1, N2, N3)	C	1	1			95		1	yes	T4 $^{3)}$	II B $^{4)}$ (II B3)	yes	PP, EP, EX, TOX, A	1	43; 44

-201-

(1)	(2)	(3a)	(3b)	(4)	(5)	(6)	(7)	(8)	(9)	(10)	(11)	(12)	(13)	(14)	(15)	(16)	(17)	(18)	(19)	(20)
UN No. or substance identification No.	Name and description	Class	Classification code	Packing group	Dangers	Type of tank vessel	Cargo tank design	Cargo tank type	Cargo tank equipment	Opening pressure of the pressure relief valve/high velocity vent valve, in kPa	Maximum degree of filling in %	Relative density at 20 °C	Type of sampling device	Pump room below deck permitted	Temperature class	Explosion group	Anti-explosion protection required	Equipment required	Number of cones/blue lights	Additional requirements/Remarks
	3.1.2	2.2	2.2	2.1.1.3	5.2.2 / 3.2.3.1	1.2.1 / 7.2.2.0.1	3.2.3.1 / 1.2.1	3.2.3.1 / 1.2.1	3.2.3.1 / 1.2.1	3.2.3.1 / 1.2.1	7.2.4.21	3.2.3.1	3.2.3.1 / 1.2.1	3.2.3.1 / 1.2.1	1.2.1	1.2.1 / 3.2.3.3	1.2.1 / 3.2.3.3	8.1.5	7.2.5	3.2.3.1
1863	FUEL, AVIATION, TURBINE ENGINE WITH MORE THAN 10% BENZENE INITIAL BOILING POINT ≤ 60 °C	3	F1	II	3+CMR+F+(N1, N2, N3)	C	1	1			95		1	yes	T4 [3]	II B [4]	yes	PP, EP, EX, TOX, A	1	
1863	FUEL, AVIATION, TURBINE ENGINE WITH MORE THAN 10% BENZENE INITIAL BOILING POINT ≤ 60 °C	3	F1	II	3+CMR+F+(N1, N2, N3)	C	1	1			95		1	yes	T4 [3]	II B [4] (II B3)	yes	PP, EP, EX, TOX, A	1	44
1863	FUEL, AVIATION, TURBINE ENGINE WITH MORE THAN 10% BENZENE 60 °C < INITIAL BOILING POINT ≤ 85 °C	3	F1	III	3+CMR+F+(N1, N2, N3)	C	2	2	3	50	95		2	yes	T4 [3]	II B [4]	yes	PP, EP, EX, TOX, A	0	23; 38
1863	FUEL, AVIATION, TURBINE ENGINE WITH MORE THAN 10% BENZENE 60 °C < INITIAL BOILING POINT ≤ 85 °C	3	F1	III	3+CMR+F+(N1, N2, N3)	C	2	2	3	50	95		2	yes	T4 [3]	II B [4] (II B3)	yes	PP, EP, EX, TOX, A	0	23; 38; 44
1863	FUEL, AVIATION, TURBINE ENGINE WITH MORE THAN 10% BENZENE 85 °C < INITIAL BOILING POINT ≤ 115 °C	3	F1	III	3+CMR+F+(N1, N2, N3)	C	2	2		50	95		2	yes	T4 [3]	II B [4]	yes	PP, EP, EX, TOX, A	0	
1863	FUEL, AVIATION, TURBINE ENGINE WITH MORE THAN 10% BENZENE 85 °C < INITIAL BOILING POINT ≤ 115 °C	3	F1	III	3+CMR+F+(N1, N2, N3)	C	2	2		50	95		2	yes	T4 [3]	II B [4] (II B3)	yes	PP, EP, EX, TOX, A	0	44

(1)	(2)	(3a)	(3b)	(4)	(5)	(6)	(7)	(8)	(9)	(10)	(11)	(12)	(13)	(14)	(15)	(16)	(17)	(18)	(19)	(20)
UN No. or substance identification No.	Name and description	Class	Classification code	Packing group	Dangers	Type of tank vessel	Cargo tank design	Cargo tank type	Cargo tank equipment	Opening pressure of the pressure relief valve/high velocity vent valve, in kPa	Maximum degree of filling in %	Relative density at 20 °C	Type of sampling device	Pump room below deck permitted	Temperature class	Explosion group	Anti-explosion protection required	Equipment required	Number of cones/blue lights	Additional requirements/Remarks
		2.2	2.2	2.1.1.3	5.2.2 / 3.2.1	1.2.1 / 7.2.2.0.1	3.2.3.1 / 1.2.1	3.2.3.1 / 1.2.1	3.2.3.1 / 1.2.1	3.2.3.1 / 1.2.1	7.2.4.21	3.2.3.1	3.2.3.1 / 1.2.1	3.2.3.1 / 1.2.1	1.2.1	1.2.1 / 3.2.3.3	1.2.1 / 3.2.3.3	8.1.5	7.2.5	3.2.3.1
1863	FUEL, AVIATION, TURBINE ENGINE WITH MORE THAN 10% BENZENE INITIAL BOILING POINT >115 °C	3	F1	III	3+CMR+F+ (N1, N2, N3)	C	2	2		35	95		2	yes	T4[3]	II B[4]	yes	PP, EP, EX, TOX, A	0	
1863	FUEL, AVIATION, TURBINE ENGINE WITH MORE THAN 10% BENZENE INITIAL BOILING POINT >115 °C	3	F1	III	3+CMR+F+ (N1, N2, N3)	C	2	2		35	95		2	yes	T4[3]	II B[4] (II B3)	yes	PP, EP, EX, TOX, A	0	44
1888	CHLOROFORM	6.1	T1	III	6.1+N2+CMR	C	2	2	3	50	95	1.48	2	no			no	PP, EP, TOX, A	0	23
1897	TETRACHLOROETHYLENE	6.1	T1	III	6.1+N2+S	C	2	2		50	95	1.62	2	no			no	PP, EP, TOX, A	0	
1912	METHYL CHLORIDE AND METHYLENE CHLORIDE MIXTURE	2	2F		2.1	G	1	1			91		1	no	T1[12]	II A[8]	yes	PP, EX, A	1	2; 31
1915	CYCLOHEXANONE	3	F1	III	3	N	3	2			97	0.95	3	yes	T2[12]	II A	yes	PP, EX, A	0	
1917	ETHYL ACRYLATE, STABILIZED	3	F1	II	3+unst.+N3	C	2	2		40	95	0.92	1	yes	T2[12]	II B (II B1)	yes	PP, EX, A	1	3; 5
1918	ISOPROPYLBENZENE (cumene)	3	F1	III	3+N2	N	3	3			97	0.86	3	yes	T2[12]	II A[8]	yes	PP, EX, A	0	
1919	METHYL ACRYLATE, STABILIZED	3	F1	II	3+unst.+N3	C	2	2	3	50	95	0.95	1	yes	T2[12]	II B (II B1)	yes	PP, EX, A	1	3; 5; 23
1920	NONANES	3	F1	III	3+N2+F	N	3	3			97	0,70 - 0,75	3	yes	T3	II A	yes	PP, EX, A	0	
1922	PYRROLIDINE	3	FC	II	3+8	C	2	2		50	95	0.86	2	yes	T2[12]	II A[7]	yes	PP, EP, EX, A	1	
1965	HYDROCARBON GAS MIXTURE, LIQUEFIED, N.O.S.	2	2F		2.1 + CMR	G	1	1			91		1	no	T4[3]	II B[4]	yes	PP, EX, A, EP, TOX	1	2; 31

(1) UN No. or substance identification No.	(2) Name and description	(3a) Class	(3b) Classification code	(4) Packing group	(5) Dangers	(6) Type of tank vessel	(7) Cargo tank design	(8) Cargo tank type	(9) Cargo tank equipment	(10) Opening pressure of the pressure relief valve/high velocity vent valve, in kPa	(11) Maximum degree of filling in %	(12) Relative density at 20 °C	(13) Type of sampling device	(14) Pump room below deck permitted	(15) Temperature class	(16) Explosion group	(17) Anti-explosion protection required	(18) Equipment required	(19) Number of cones/blue lights	(20) Additional requirements/Remarks
	3.1.2	2.2	2.2	2.1.1.3	5.2.2 / 3.2.3.1	1.2.1 / 7.2.2.0.1	3.2.3.1 / 1.2.1	3.2.3.1 / 1.2.1	3.2.3.1 / 1.2.1	3.2.3.1 / 1.2.1	7.2.4.21	3.2.3.1	3.2.3.1 / 1.2.1	3.2.3.1 / 1.2.1	1.2.1	1.2.1 / 3.2.3.3	1.2.1 / 3.2.3.3	8.1.5	7.2.5	3.2.3.1
1965	HYDROCARBON GAS MIXTURE, REFRIGERATED, N.O.S.	2	3F		2.1 + CMR	G	2	4	1; 3		95		1	no	T4 $^{3)}$	II B $^{4)}$	yes	PP, EX, A, EP, TOX	1	2; 31
1965	HYDROCARBON GAS MIXTURE, LIQUEFIED, N.O.S., (MIXTURE A)	2	2F		2.1	G	1	1			91		1	no	T4 $^{3)}$	II B $^{4)}$	yes	PP, EX, A	1	2; 31
1965	HYDROCARBON GAS MIXTURE, REFRIGERATED, N.O.S., (MIXTURE A)	2	3F		2.1	G	2	4	1; 3		95		1	no	T4 $^{3)}$	II B $^{4)}$	yes	PP, EX, A	1	2; 31
1965	HYDROCARBON GAS MIXTURE, LIQUEFIED, N.O.S., (MIXTURE A0)	2	2F		2.1	G	1	1			91		1	no	T4 $^{3)}$	II B $^{4)}$	yes	PP, EX, A	1	2; 31
1965	HYDROCARBON GAS MIXTURE, REFRIGERATED, N.O.S., (MIXTURE A0)	2	3F		2.1	G	2	4	1; 3		95		1	no	T4 $^{3)}$	II B $^{4)}$	yes	PP, EX, A	1	2; 31
1965	HYDROCARBON GAS MIXTURE, LIQUEFIED, N.O.S., (MIXTURE A01)	2	2F		2.1	G	1	1			91		1	no	T4 $^{3)}$	II B $^{4)}$	yes	PP, EX, A	1	2; 31
1965	HYDROCARBON GAS MIXTURE, REFRIGERATED, N.O.S., (MIXTURE A01)	2	3F		2.1	G	2	4	1; 3		95		1	no	T4 $^{3)}$	II B $^{4)}$	yes	PP, EX, A	1	2; 31
1965	HYDROCARBON GAS MIXTURE, LIQUEFIED, N.O.S., (MIXTURE A02)	2	2F		2.1	G	1	1			91		1	no	T4 $^{3)}$	II B $^{4)}$	yes	PP, EX, A	1	2; 31
1965	HYDROCARBON GAS MIXTURE, REFRIGERATED, N.O.S., (MIXTURE A02)	2	3F		2.1	G	2	4	1; 3		95		1	no	T4 $^{3)}$	II B $^{4)}$	yes	PP, EX, A	1	2; 31
1965	HYDROCARBON GAS MIXTURE, LIQUEFIED, N.O.S., (MIXTURE A1)	2	2F		2.1	G	1	1			91		1	no	T4 $^{3)}$	II B $^{4)}$	yes	PP, EX, A	1	2; 31

(1) UN No. or substance identification No.	(2) Name and description	(3a) Class	(3b) Classification code	(4) Packing group	(5) Dangers	(6) Type of tank vessel	(7) Cargo tank design	(8) Cargo tank type	(9) Cargo tank equipment	(10) Opening pressure of the pressure relief valve/high velocity vent valve, in kPa	(11) Maximum degree of filling in %	(12) Relative density at 20 °C	(13) Type of sampling device	(14) Pump room below deck permitted	(15) Temperature class	(16) Explosion group	(17) Anti-explosion protection required	(18) Equipment required	(19) Number of cones/blue lights	(20) Additional requirements/Remarks
(1)	3.1.2	2.2	2.2	2.1.1.3	5.2.2/3.2.3.1	1.2.1/7.2.2.0.1	3.2.3.1/1.2.1	3.2.3.1/1.2.1	3.2.3.1/1.2.1	3.2.3.1/1.2.1	7.2.4.21	3.2.3.1	3.2.3.1/1.2.1	3.2.3.1/1.2.1	1.2.1	1.2.1/3.2.3.3	1.2.1/3.2.3.3	8.1.5	7.2.5	3.2.3.1
1965	HYDROCARBON GAS MIXTURE, REFRIGERATED, N.O.S., (MIXTURE A1)	2	3F		2.1	G	2	4	1; 3		95		1	no	T4 [3]	II B [4]	yes	PP, EX, A	1	2; 31
1965	HYDROCARBON GAS MIXTURE, LIQUEFIED, N.O.S., (MIXTURE B)	2	2F		2.1	G	1	1			91		1	no	T4 [3]	II B [4]	yes	PP, EX, A	1	2; 31
1965	HYDROCARBON GAS MIXTURE, REFRIGERATED, N.O.S., (MIXTURE B)	2	3F		2.1	G	2	4	1; 3		95		1	no	T4 [3]	II B [4]	yes	PP, EX, A	1	2; 31
1965	HYDROCARBON GAS MIXTURE, LIQUEFIED, N.O.S., (MIXTURE B1)	2	2F		2.1	G	1	1			91		1	no	T4 [3]	II B [4]	yes	PP, EX, A	1	2; 31
1965	HYDROCARBON GAS MIXTURE, REFRIGERATED, N.O.S., (MIXTURE B1)	2	3F		2.1	G	2	4	1; 3		95		1	no	T4 [3]	II B [4]	yes	PP, EX, A	1	2; 31
1965	HYDROCARBON GAS MIXTURE, LIQUEFIED, N.O.S., (MIXTURE B2)	2	2F		2.1	G	1	1			91		1	no	T4 [3]	II B [4]	yes	PP, EX, A	1	2; 31
1965	HYDROCARBON GAS MIXTURE, REFRIGERATED, N.O.S., (MIXTURE B2)	2	3F		2.1	G	2	4	1; 3		95		1	no	T4 [3]	II B [4]	yes	PP, EX, A	1	2; 31
1965	HYDROCARBON GAS MIXTURE, LIQUEFIED, N.O.S., (MIXTURE C)	2	2F		2.1	G	1	1			91		1	no	T4 [3]	II B [4]	yes	PP, EX, A	1	2; 31
1965	HYDROCARBON GAS MIXTURE, REFRIGERATED, N.O.S., (MIXTURE C)	2	3F		2.1	G	2	4	1; 3		95		1	no	T4 [3]	II B [4]	yes	PP, EX, A	1	2; 31
1969	ISOBUTANE (contains less than 0.1% 1.3-butadiene)	2	2F		2.1	G	1	1			91		1	no	T2 [1), 12]	II A [7]	yes	PP, EX, A	1	2; 31
1969	ISOBUTANE (with 0.1% or more 1.3-butadiene)	2	2F		2.1+ CMR	G	1	1			91		1	no	T2 [1), 12]	II A	yes	PP, EP, EX, TOX, A	1	2; 31

(1) UN No. or substance identification No.	(2) Name and description	(3a) Class	(3b) Classification code	(4) Packing group	(5) Dangers	(6) Type of tank vessel	(7) Cargo tank design	(8) Cargo tank type	(9) Cargo tank equipment	(10) Opening pressure of the pressure relief valve/high velocity vent valve, in kPa	(11) Maximum degree of filling in %	(12) Relative density at 20 °C	(13) Type of sampling device	(14) Pump room below deck permitted	(15) Temperature class	(16) Explosion group	(17) Anti-explosion protection required	(18) Equipment required	(19) Number of cones/blue lights	(20) Additional requirements/Remarks
3.1.2	3.1.2	2.2	2.2	2.1.1.3	5.2.2 / 3.2.3.1	1.2.1 / 7.2.2.0.1	3.2.3.1 / 1.2.1	3.2.3.1 / 1.2.1	3.2.3.1 / 1.2.1	3.2.3.1 / 1.2.1	7.2.4.21	3.2.3.1	3.2.3.1 / 1.2.1	3.2.3.1 / 1.2.1	1.2.1	1.2.1 / 3.2.3.3	1.2.1 / 3.2.3.3	8.1.5	7.2.5	3.2.3.1
1972	METHANE, REFRIGERATED LIQUID or NATURAL GAS, REFRIGERATED LIQUID, with high methane content	2	3F		2.1	G	1	1	1		95		1	no	T1 12)	IIA	yes	PP, EX, A	1	2; 31; 42
1972	METHANE, REFRIGERATED or NATURAL GAS, REFRIGERATED, with high methane content	2	3F		2.1	G	2	4	1; 3		95		1	no	T1 12)	IIA	yes	PP, EX, A	1	2; 31; 42
1978	PROPANE	2	2F		2.1	G	1	1	1		91		1	no	T1 12)	II A	yes	PP, EX, A	1	2; 31
1978	PROPANE, REFRIGERATED	2	3F		2.1	G	2	4	1; 3		95		1	no	T1 12)	II A	yes	PP, EX, A	1	2; 31
1986	ALCOHOLS, FLAMMABLE, TOXIC, N.O.S.	3	FT1	I	3+6.1+ (N1, N2, N3, CMR, F or S)	C	1	1	*	*	95		1	no	T4 3)	II B4)	yes	PP, EP, EX, TOX, A	2	27; *see 3.2.3.3
1986	ALCOHOLS, FLAMMABLE, TOXIC, N.O.S.	3	FT1	I	3+6.1+ (N1, N2, N3, CMR, F or S)	C	1	1	*	*	95		1	no	T4 3)	II B4) (II B3)	yes	PP, EP, EX, TOX, A	2	27; 44 *see 3.2.3.3
1986	ALCOHOLS, FLAMMABLE, TOXIC, N.O.S.	3	FT1	I	3+6.1+ (N1, N2, N3, CMR, F or S)	C	2	2	*	*	95		1	no	T4 3)	II B4)	yes	PP, EP, EX, TOX, A	2	27; *see 3.2.3.3
1986	ALCOHOLS, FLAMMABLE, TOXIC, N.O.S.	3	FT1	I	3+6.1+ (N1, N2, N3, CMR, F or S)	C	2	2	*	*	95		1	no	T4 3)	II B4) (II B3)	yes	PP, EP, EX, TOX, A	2	27; 44 *see 3.2.3.3

(1) UN No. or substance identification No.	(2) Name and description	(3a) Class	(3b) Classification code	(4) Packing group	(5) Dangers	(6) Type of tank vessel	(7) Cargo tank design	(8) Cargo tank type	(9) Cargo tank equipment	(10) Opening pressure of the pressure relief valve/high velocity vent valve, in kPa	(11) Maximum degree of filling in %	(12) Relative density at 20 °C	(13) Type of sampling device	(14) Pump room below deck permitted	(15) Temperature class	(16) Explosion group	(17) Anti-explosion protection required	(18) Equipment required	(19) Number of cones/blue lights	(20) Additional requirements/Remarks
	3.1.2	2.2	2.2	2.1.1.3	5.2.2 / 3.2.3.1	1.2.1 / 7.2.2.0.1	3.2.3.1 / 1.2.1	3.2.3.1 / 1.2.1	3.2.3.1 / 1.2.1	3.2.3.1 / 1.2.1	7.2.4.21	3.2.3.1	3.2.3.1 / 1.2.1	3.2.3.1 / 1.2.1	1.2.1	1.2.1 / 3.2.3.3	1.2.1 / 3.2.3.3	8.1.5	7.2.5	3.2.3.1
1986	ALCOHOLS, FLAMMABLE, TOXIC, N.O.S.	3	FT1	II	3+6.1+ (N1, N2, N3, CMR, F or S)	C	2	2	*	*	95		2	no	T4 [3]	II B [4]	yes	PP, EP, EX, TOX, A	2	27; *see 3.2.3.3
1986	ALCOHOLS, FLAMMABLE, TOXIC, N.O.S.	3	FT1	II	3+6.1+ (N1, N2, N3, CMR, F or S)	C	2	2	*	*	95		2	no	T4 [3]	II B [4] (II B3)	yes	PP, EP, EX, TOX, A	2	27; 44 *see 3.2.3.3
1986	ALCOHOLS, FLAMMABLE, TOXIC, N.O.S.	3	FT1	III	3+6.1+ (N1, N2, N3, CMR, F or S)	C	2	2	*	*	95		2	no	T4 [3]	II B [4]	yes	PP, EP, EX, TOX, A	0	27; *see 3.2.3.3
1986	ALCOHOLS, FLAMMABLE, TOXIC, N.O.S.	3	FT1	III	3+6.1+ (N1, N2, N3, CMR, F or S)	C	2	2	*	*	95		2	no	T4 [3]	II B [4] (II B3)	yes	PP, EP, EX, TOX, A	0	27; 44 *see 3.2.3.3
1987	ALCOHOLS, N.O.S. (tert-BUTANOL 90% (MASS)/METHANOL 10% (MASS) MIXTURE)	3	F1	II	3	N	2	2		10	97		3	yes	T1 [12]	II A	yes	PP, EX, A	1	
1987	ALCOHOLS, N.O.S.	3	F1	II	3+(N1, N2, N3, CMR, F or S)	*	*	*	*	*	*		*	yes	T4 [3]	II B [4]	yes	*	1	14; 27; *see 3.2.3.3
1987	ALCOHOLS, N.O.S.	3	F1	II	3+(N1, N2, N3, CMR, F or S)	*	*	*	*	*	*		*	yes	T4 [3]	II B [4] (II B3)	yes	*	1	14; 27; 44*see 3.2.3.3

(1) UN No. or substance identification No.	(2) Name and description	(3a) Class	(3b) Classification code	(4) Packing group	(5) Dangers	(6) Type of tank vessel	(7) Cargo tank design	(8) Cargo tank type	(9) Cargo tank equipment	(10) Opening pressure of the pressure relief valve/high velocity vent valve, in kPa	(11) Maximum degree of filling in %	(12) Relative density at 20 °C	(13) Type of sampling device	(14) Pump room below deck permitted	(15) Temperature class	(16) Explosion group	(17) Anti-explosion protection required	(18) Equipment required	(19) Number of cones/blue lights	(20) Additional requirements/Remarks
	3.1.2	2.2	2.2	2.1.1.3	5.2.2 / 3.2.3.1	1.2.1 / 7.2.2.0.1	3.2.3.1 / 1.2.1	3.2.3.1 / 1.2.1	3.2.3.1 / 1.2.1	3.2.3.1 / 1.2.1	7.2.4.21	3.2.3.1	3.2.3.1 / 1.2.1	3.2.3.1 / 1.2.1	1.2.1	1.2.1 / 3.2.3.3	1.2.1 / 3.2.3.3	8.1.5	7.2.5	3.2.3.1
1987	ALCOHOLS, N.O.S.	3	F1	III	3+(N1, N2, N3, CMR, F or S)	*	*	*	*	*	*		*	yes	T4 [3]	II B [4]	yes	*	0	14; 27 *see 3.2.3.3
1987	ALCOHOLS, N.O.S.	3	F1	III	3+(N1, N2, N3, CMR, F or S)	*	*	*	*	*	*		*	yes	T4 [3]	II B [4] (II B3)	yes	*	0	14; 27; 44 *see 3.2.3.3
1987	ALCOHOLS, N.O.S. (CYCLOHEXANOL)	3	F1	III	3+N3+F	N	3	3	2		95	0.95	3	yes	T3	II A	yes	PP, EX, A	0	7; 17
1987	ALCOHOLS, N.O.S. (CYCLOHEXANOL)	3	F1	III	3+N3+F	N	3	3	4		95	0.95	3	yes			no	PP	0	7; 17; 20: +46 °C
1989	ALDEHYDES, N.O.S.	3	F1	II	3+(N1, N2, N3, CMR, F or S)	*	*	*	*	*	*		*	yes	T4 [3]	II B [4]	yes	*	1	14; 27; *see 3.2.3.3
1989	ALDEHYDES, N.O.S.	3	F1	II	3+(N1, N2, N3, CMR, F or S)	*	*	*	*	*	*		*	yes	T4 [3]	II B [4] (II B3)	yes	*	1	14; 27; 44 *see 3.2.3.3
1989	ALDEHYDES, N.O.S.	3	F1	III	3+(N1, N2, N3, CMR, F or S)	*	*	*	*	*	*		*	yes	T4 [3]	II B [4]	yes	*	0	14; 27 *see 3.2.3.3
1989	ALDEHYDES, N.O.S.	3	F1	III	3+(N1, N2, N3, CMR, F or S)	*	*	*	*	*	*		*	yes	T4 [3]	II B [4] (II B3)	yes	*	0	14; 27; 44 *see 3.2.3.3
1991	CHLOROPRENE, STABILIZED	3	FT1	I	3+6.1+unst.+CMR	C	2	2	3	50	95	0.96	1	no	T2 [12]	II B (II B3)	yes	PP, EP, EX, TOX, A	2	3; 5; 23

-208-

(1) UN No. or substance identification No.	(2) Name and description	(3a) Class	(3b) Classification code	(4) Packing group	(5) Dangers	(6) Type of tank vessel	(7) Cargo tank design	(8) Cargo tank type	(9) Cargo tank equipment	(10) Opening pressure of the pressure relief valve/high velocity vent valve, in kPa	(11) Maximum degree of filling in %	(12) Relative density at 20 °C	(13) Type of sampling device	(14) Pump room below deck permitted	(15) Temperature class	(16) Explosion group	(17) Anti-explosion protection required	(18) Equipment required	(19) Number of cones/blue lights	(20) Additional requirements/Remarks
	3.1.2	2.2	2.2	2.1.1.3	5.2.2 / 3.2.3.1	1.2.1 / 7.2.2.0.1	3.2.3.1 / 1.2.1	3.2.3.1 / 1.2.1	3.2.3.1 / 1.2.1	3.2.3.1 / 1.2.1	7.2.4.21	3.2.3.1	3.2.3.1 / 1.2.1	3.2.3.1 / 1.2.1	1.2.1	1.2.1 / 3.2.3.3	1.2.1 / 3.2.3.3	8.1.5	7.2.5	3.2.3.1
1992	FLAMMABLE LIQUID, TOXIC, N.O.S.	3	FT1	I	3+6.1+(N1, N2, N3, CMR, F or S)	C	1	1	*	*	95		1	no	T4[3]	II B[4]	yes	PP, EP, EX, TOX, A	2	27; *see 3.2.3.3
1992	FLAMMABLE LIQUID, TOXIC, N.O.S.	3	FT1	I	3+6.1+(N1, N2, N3, CMR, F or S)	C	1	1	*	*	95		1	no	T4[3]	II B[4] (II B3)	yes	PP, EP, EX, TOX, A	2	27; 44 *see 3.2.3.3
1992	FLAMMABLE LIQUID, TOXIC, N.O.S	3	FT1	I	3+6.1+(N1, N2, N3, CMR, F or S)	C	2	2	*	*	95		1	no	T4[3]	II B[4]	yes	PP, EP, EX, TOX, A	2	27; *see 3.2.3.3
1992	FLAMMABLE LIQUID, TOXIC, N.O.S	3	FT1	I	3+6.1+(N1, N2, N3, CMR, F or S)	C	2	2	*	*	95		1	no	T4[3]	II B[4] (II B3)	yes	PP, EP, EX, TOX, A	2	27; 44 *see 3.2.3.3
1992	FLAMMABLE LIQUID, TOXIC, N.O.S	3	FT1	II	3+6.1+(N1, N2, N3, CMR, F or S)	C	2	2	*	*	95		2	no	T4[3]	II B[4]	yes	PP, EP, EX, TOX, A	2	27; *see 3.2.3.3
1992	FLAMMABLE LIQUID, TOXIC, N.O.S	3	FT1	II	3+6.1+(N1, N2, N3, CMR, F or S)	C	2	2	*	*	95		2	no	T4[3]	II B[4] (II B3)	yes	PP, EP, EX, TOX, A	2	27; 44 *see 3.2.3.3

(1)	(2)	(3a)	(3b)	(4)	(5)	(6)	(7)	(8)	(9)	(10)	(11)	(12)	(13)	(14)	(15)	(16)	(17)	(18)	(19)	(20)
UN No. or substance identification No.	Name and description	Class	Classification code	Packing group	Dangers	Type of tank vessel	Cargo tank design	Cargo tank type	Cargo tank equipment	Opening pressure of the pressure relief valve/high velocity vent valve, in kPa	Maximum degree of filling in %	Relative density at 20 °C	Type of sampling device	Pump room below deck permitted	Temperature class	Explosion group	Anti-explosion protection required	Equipment required	Number of cones/blue lights	Additional requirements/Remarks
		2.2	2.2	2.1.1.3	5.2.2 / 3.2.3.1	1.2.1 / 7.2.2.0.1	3.2.3.1 / 1.2.1	3.2.3.1 / 1.2.1	3.2.3.1 / 1.2.1	3.2.3.1 / 1.2.1	7.2.4.21	3.2.3.1	3.2.3.1 / 1.2.1	3.2.3.1 / 1.2.1	1.2.1	1.2.1 / 3.2.3.3	1.2.1 / 3.2.3.3	8.1.5	7.2.5	3.2.3.1
1992	FLAMMABLE LIQUID, TOXIC, N.O.S	3	FT1	III	3+6.1+ (N1, N2, N3, CMR, F or S)	C	2	2	*	*	95		2	no	T4 ³⁾	II B ⁴⁾	yes	PP, EP, EX, TOX, A	0	27; *see 3.2.3.3
1992	FLAMMABLE LIQUID, TOXIC, N.O.S	3	FT1	III	3+6.1+ (N1, N2, N3, CMR, F or S)	C	2	2	*	*	95		2	no	T4 ³⁾	II B ⁴⁾ (II B3)	yes	PP, EP, EX, TOX, A	0	27; 44 *see 3.2.3.3
1993	FLAMMABLE LIQUID, N.O.S.	3	F1	I	3+(N1, N2, N3, CMR, F)	*	*	*	*	*	*		*	yes	T4 ³⁾	II B ⁴⁾	yes	*	1	14; 27 *see 3.2.3.3
1993	FLAMMABLE LIQUID, N.O.S.	3	F1	I	3+(N1, N2, N3, CMR, F)	*	*	*	*	*	*		*	yes	T4 ³⁾	II B ⁴⁾ (II B3)	yes	*	1	14; 27; 44 *see 3.2.3.3
1993	FLAMMABLE LIQUID, N.O.S.	3	F1	II	3+(N1, N2, N3, CMR, F)	*	*	*	*	*	*		*	yes	T4 ³⁾	II B ⁴⁾	yes	*	1	14; 27 *see 3.2.3.3
1993	FLAMMABLE LIQUID, N.O.S.	3	F1	II	3+(N1, N2, N3, CMR, F)	*	*	*	*	*	*		*	yes	T4 ³⁾	II B ⁴⁾ (II B3)	yes	*	1	14; 27; 44 *see 3.2.3.3
1993	FLAMMABLE LIQUID, N.O.S.	3	F1	III	3+(N1, N2, N3, CMR, F)	*	*	*	*	*	*		*	yes	T4 ³⁾	II B ⁴⁾	yes	*	0	14; 27 *see 3.2.3.3
1993	FLAMMABLE LIQUID, N.O.S.	3	F1	III	3+(N1, N2, N3, CMR, F)	*	*	*	*	*	*		*	yes	T4 ³⁾	II B ⁴⁾ (II B3)	yes	*	0	14; 27; 44 *see 3.2.3.3
1993	FLAMMABLE LIQUID, N.O.S. WITH MORE THAN 10% BENZENE	3	F1	I	3+(N1, N2, N3, CMR, F)	C	*	*	*	*	*		*	yes	T4 ³⁾	II B ⁴⁾	yes	*	1	*see 3.2.3.3

(1) UN No. or substance identification No.	(2) Name and description	(3a) Class	(3b) Classification code	(4) Packing group	(5) Dangers	(6) Type of tank vessel	(7) Cargo tank design	(8) Cargo tank type	(9) Cargo tank equipment	(10) Opening pressure of the pressure relief valve/high velocity vent valve, in kPa	(11) Maximum degree of filling in %	(12) Relative density at 20 °C	(13) Type of sampling device	(14) Pump room below deck permitted	(15) Temperature class	(16) Explosion group	(17) Anti-explosion protection required	(18) Equipment required	(19) Number of cones/blue lights	(20) Additional requirements/Remarks
		2.2	2.2	2.1.1.3	5.2.2 / 3.2.3.1	1.2.1 / 7.2.2.0.1	3.2.3.1 / 1.2.1	3.2.3.1 / 1.2.1	3.2.3.1 / 1.2.1	3.2.3.1 / 1.2.1	7.2.4.21	3.2.3.1	3.2.3.1 / 1.2.1	3.2.3.1 / 1.2.1	1.2.1	1.2.1 / 3.2.3.3	1.2.1 / 3.2.3.3	8.1.5	7.2.5	3.2.3.1
1993	FLAMMABLE LIQUID, N.O.S. WITH MORE THAN 10% BENZENE	3	F1	I	3+(N1, N2, N3, CMR, F)	C	*	*	*	*	*		*	yes	T4[3]	II B[4] (II B3)	yes	*	1	44 *see 3.2.3.3
1993	FLAMMABLE LIQUID, N.O.S. WITH MORE THAN 10% BENZENE	3	F1	II	3+(N1, N2, N3, CMR, F)	C	*	*	*	*	*		*	yes	T4[3]	II B[4]	yes	*	1	*see 3.2.3.3
1993	FLAMMABLE LIQUID, N.O.S. WITH MORE THAN 10% BENZENE	3	F1	II	3+(N1, N2, N3, CMR, F)	C	*	*	*	*	*		*	yes	T4[3]	II B[4] (II B3)	yes	*	1	44 *see 3.2.3.3
1993	FLAMMABLE LIQUID, N.O.S. WITH MORE THAN 10% BENZENE	3	F1	III	3+(N1, N2, N3, CMR, F)	C	*	*	*	*	*		*	yes	T4[3]	II B[4]	yes	*	0	*see 3.2.3.3
1993	FLAMMABLE LIQUID, N.O.S. WITH MORE THAN 10% BENZENE	3	F1	III	3+(N1, N2, N3, CMR, F)	C	*	*	*	*	*		*	yes	T4[3]	II B[4] (II B3)	yes	*	0	44 *see 3.2.3.3
1993	FLAMMABLE LIQUID, N.O.S. WITH MORE THAN 10% BENZENE INITIAL BOILING POINT ≤ 60 °C	3	F1	I	3+(N1, N2, N3, CMR, F)	C	1	1			95		1	yes	T4[3]	II B[4]	yes	PP, EP, EX, TOX, A	1	
1993	FLAMMABLE LIQUID, N.O.S. WITH MORE THAN 10% BENZENE INITIAL BOILING POINT ≤ 60 °C	3	F1	I	3+(N1, N2, N3, CMR, F)	C	1	1			95		1	yes	T4[3]	II B[4] (II B3)	yes	PP, EP, EX, TOX, A	1	44
1993	FLAMMABLE LIQUID, N.O.S. WITH MORE THAN 10% BENZENE INITIAL BOILING POINT ≤ 60 °C	3	F1	II	3+(N1, N2, N3, CMR, F)	C	1	1			95		1	yes	T4[3]	II B[4]	yes	PP, EP, EX, TOX, A	1	
1993	FLAMMABLE LIQUID, N.O.S. WITH MORE THAN 10% BENZENE INITIAL BOILING POINT ≤ 60 °C	3	F1	II	3+(N1, N2, N3, CMR, F)	C	1	1			95		1	yes	T4[3]	II B[4] (II B3)	yes	PP, EP, EX, TOX, A	1	44

(1) UN No. or substance identification No.	(2) Name and description	(3a) Class	(3b) Classification code	(4) Packing group	(5) Dangers	(6) Type of tank vessel	(7) Cargo tank design	(8) Cargo tank type	(9) Cargo tank equipment	(10) Opening pressure of the pressure relief valve/high velocity vent valve, in kPa	(11) Maximum degree of filling in %	(12) Relative density at 20 °C	(13) Type of sampling device	(14) Pump room below deck permitted	(15) Temperature class	(16) Explosion group	(17) Anti-explosion protection required	(18) Equipment required	(19) Number of cones/blue lights	(20) Additional requirements/Remarks
	3.1.2	2.2	2.2	2.1.1.3	5.2.2 / 3.2.3.1	1.2.1 / 7.2.2.0.1	3.2.3.1 / 1.2.1	3.2.3.1 / 1.2.1	3.2.3.1 / 1.2.1	3.2.3.1 / 1.2.1	7.2.4.21	3.2.3.1	3.2.3.1 / 1.2.1	3.2.3.1 / 1.2.1	1.2.1	1.2.1 / 3.2.3.3	1.2.1 / 3.2.3.3	8.1.5	7.2.5	3.2.3.1
1993	FLAMMABLE LIQUID, N.O.S. WITH MORE THAN 10% BENZENE INITIAL BOILING POINT ≤ 60 °C	3	F1	III	3+(N1, N2, N3, CMR, F)	C	1	1			95		1	yes	T4 3)	II B 4)	yes	PP, EP, EX, TOX, A	0	
1993	FLAMMABLE LIQUID, N.O.S. WITH MORE THAN 10% BENZENE INITIAL BOILING POINT ≤ 60 °C	3	F1	III	3+(N1, N2, N3, CMR, F)	C	1	1			95		1	yes	T4 3)	II B 4) (II B3)	yes	PP, EP, EX, TOX, A	0	44
1993	FLAMMABLE LIQUID, N.O.S. WITH MORE THAN 10% BENZENE 60 °C < INITIAL BOILING POINT ≤ 85 °C	3	F1	II	3+(N1, N2, N3, CMR, F)	C	2	2	3	50	95		2	yes	T4 3)	II B 4)	yes	PP, EP, EX, TOX, A	1	23; 38
1993	FLAMMABLE LIQUID, N.O.S. WITH MORE THAN 10% BENZENE 60 °C < INITIAL BOILING POINT ≤ 85 °C	3	F1	II	3+(N1, N2, N3, CMR, F)	C	2	2	3	50	95		2	yes	T4 3)	II B 4) (II B3)	yes	PP, EP, EX, TOX, A	1	23; 38; 44
1993	FLAMMABLE LIQUID, N.O.S. WITH MORE THAN 10% BENZENE 60 °C < INITIAL BOILING POINT ≤ 85 °C	3	F1	III	3+(N1, N2, N3, CMR, F)	C	2	2	3	50	95		2	yes	T4 3)	II B 4)	yes	PP, EP, EX, TOX, A	0	23; 38
1993	FLAMMABLE LIQUID, N.O.S. WITH MORE THAN 10% BENZENE 60 °C < INITIAL BOILING POINT ≤ 85 °C	3	F1	III	3+(N1, N2, N3, CMR, F)	C	2	2	3	50	95		2	yes	T4 3)	II B 4) (II B3)	yes	PP, EP, EX, TOX, A	0	23; 38; 44
1993	FLAMMABLE LIQUID, N.O.S. WITH MORE THAN 10% BENZENE 85 °C < INITIAL BOILING POINT ≤ 115 °C	3	F1	II	3+(N1, N2, N3, CMR, F)	C	2	2		50	95		2	yes	T4 3)	II B 4)	yes	PP, EP, EX, TOX, A	1	

Field	(1)	(2)	(3)	(4)	(5)	(6)	(7)
UN No. or substance identification No. (1)	1993	1993	1993	1993	1993	1993	1993
Name and description (2)	FLAMMABLE LIQUID, N.O.S. WITH MORE THAN 10% BENZENE 85 °C < INITIAL BOILING POINT ≤ 115 °C	FLAMMABLE LIQUID, N.O.S. WITH MORE THAN 10% BENZENE 85 °C < INITIAL BOILING POINT ≤ 115 °C	FLAMMABLE LIQUID, N.O.S. WITH MORE THAN 10% BENZENE 85 °C < INITIAL BOILING POINT ≤ 115 °C	FLAMMABLE LIQUID, N.O.S. WITH MORE THAN 10% BENZENE INITIAL BOILING POINT > 115 °C	FLAMMABLE LIQUID, N.O.S. WITH MORE THAN 10% BENZENE INITIAL BOILING POINT > 115 °C	FLAMMABLE LIQUID, N.O.S. WITH MORE THAN 10% BENZENE INITIAL BOILING POINT > 115 °C	FLAMMABLE LIQUID, N.O.S. WITH MORE THAN 10% BENZENE INITIAL BOILING POINT > 115 °C
Class (3a)	3	3	3	3	3	3	3
Classification code (3b)	F1	F1	F1	F1	F1	F1	F1
Packing group (4)	II	III	III	II	II	III	III
Dangers (5)	3+(N1, N2, N3, CMR, F)	3+(N1, N2, N3, CMR, F)	3+(N1, N2, N3, CMR, F)	3+(N1, N2, N3, CMR, F)	3+(N1, N2, N3, CMR, F)	3+(N1, N2, N3, CMR, F)	3+(N1, N2, N3, CMR, F)
Type of tank vessel (6)	C	C	C	C	C	C	C
Cargo tank design (7)	2	2	2	2	2	2	2
Cargo tank type (8)	2	2	2	2	2	2	2
Cargo tank equipment (9)							
Opening pressure of the pressure relief valve/high velocity vent valve, in kPa (10)	50	50	50	35	35	35	35
Maximum degree of filling in % (11)	95	95	95	95	95	95	95
Relative density at 20 °C (12)							
Type of sampling device (13)	2	2	2	2	2	2	2
Pump room below deck permitted (14)	yes	yes	yes	yes	yes	yes	yes
Temperature class (15)	T4 [3]	T4 [3]	T4 [3]	T4 [3]	T4 [3]	T4 [3]	T4 [3]
Explosion group (16)	II B [4] (II B3)	II B [4]	II B [4] (II B3)	II B [4]	II B [4] (II B3)	II B [4]	II B [4] (II B3)
Anti-explosion protection required (17)	yes	yes	yes	yes	yes	yes	yes
Equipment required (18)	PP, EP, EX, TOX, A	PP, EP, EX, TOX, A	PP, EP, EX, TOX, A	PP, EP, EX, TOX, A	PP, EP, EX, TOX, A	PP, EP, EX, TOX, A	PP, EP, EX, TOX, A
Number of cones/blue lights (19)	1	0	0	1	1	0	0
Additional requirements/Remarks (20)	44		44		44		44

-213-

(1)	(2)	(3a)	(3b)	(4)	(5)	(6)	(7)	(8)	(9)	(10)	(11)	(12)	(13)	(14)	(15)	(16)	(17)	(18)	(19)	(20)
UN No. or substance identification No.	Name and description	Class	Classification code	Packing group	Dangers	Type of tank vessel	Cargo tank design	Cargo tank type	Cargo tank equipment	Opening pressure of the pressure relief valve/high velocity vent valve, in kPa	Maximum degree of filling in %	Relative density at 20 °C	Type of sampling device	Pump room below deck permitted	Temperature class	Explosion group	Anti-explosion protection required	Equipment required	Number of cones/blue lights	Additional requirements/Remarks
		2.2	2.2	2.1.1.3	5.2.2 / 3.2.3.1	1.2.1 / 7.2.2.0.1	3.2.3.1 / 1.2.1	3.2.3.1 / 1.2.1	3.2.3.1 / 1.2.1	3.2.3.1 / 1.2.1	7.2.4.21	3.2.3.1	3.2.3.1 / 1.2.1	3.2.3.1 / 1.2.1	1.2.1	1.2.1 / 3.2.3.3	1.2.1 / 3.2.3.3	8.1.5	7.2.5	3.2.3.1
1993	FLAMMABLE LIQUID, N.O.S. (CYCLOHEXANONE/ CYCLOHEXANOL MIXTURE)	3	F1	III	3+F	N	3	3			97	0,95	3	yes	T3	II A	yes	PP, EX, A	0	
1999	TARS, LIQUID, including road oils, and cutback bitumens	3	F1	III	3+S	N	4	3	2		97		3	yes	T3	II A[7]	yes	PP, EX, A	0	
2014	HYDROGEN PEROXIDE, AQUEOUS SOLUTION with not less than 20% but not more than 60% hydrogen peroxide (stabilized as necessary)	5.1	OC1	II	5.1+8+un st.	C	2	2		35	95	1.2	2	yes			no	PP, EP	0	3; 33
2021	CHLOROPHENOLS, LIQUID (2-CHLOROPHENOL)	6.1	T1	III	6.1+N2	C	2	2		25	95	1.23	2	no	T1[12]	II A[7]	yes	PP, EP, EX, TOX, A	0	6: +10 °C; 17
2022	CRESYLIC ACID	6.1	TC1	II	6.1+8+3+S	C	2	2		25	95	1.03	2	no	T1[12]	II A[7]	yes	PP, EP, EX, TOX, A	2	6: +16 °C; 17
2023	EPICHLORHYDRINE	6.1	TF1	II	6.1+3+N3	C	2	2		35	95	1.18	2	no	T2[12]	II B (II B3)	yes	PP, EP, EX, TOX, A	2	5
2031	NITRIC ACID, other than red fuming, with more than 70% acid	8	CO1	I	8+5.1+N3	N	2	3		10	97	1,41-1,48	3	yes			no	PP, EP	0	34
2031	NITRIC ACID, other than red fuming with at least 65% but not more than 70% acid	8	CO1	II	8+5.1+N3	N	2	3		10	97	1,39-1,41	3	yes			no	PP, EP	0	34
2031	NITRIC ACID, other than red fuming, with less than 65% acid	8	CO1	II	8+N3	N	2	3		10	97	1,02-1,39	3	yes			no	PP, EP	0	34
2032	NITRIC ACID, RED FUMING	8	COT	I	8+5.1+6.1+N3	C	2	2		50	95	1,48-1.51	1	no			no	PP, EP, TOX, A	2	
2045	ISOBUTYRALDEHYDE (ISOBUTYL ALDEHYDE)	3	F1	II	3+N3	C	2	2	3	50	95	0.79	2	yes	T4	II A[7]	yes	PP, EX, A	1	15; 23

(1) UN No.	(2) Name and description	(3a) Class	(3b) Classification code	(4) Packing group	(5) Dangers	(6) Type of tank vessel	(7) Cargo tank design	(8) Cargo tank type	(9) Cargo tank equipment	(10) Opening pressure of the pressure relief valve/high velocity vent valve, in kPa	(11) Max. degree of filling in %	(12) Relative density at 20 °C	(13) Type of sampling device	(14) Pump room below deck permitted	(15) Temperature class	(16) Explosion group	(17) Anti-explosion protection required	(18) Equipment required	(19) Number of cones/blue lights	(20) Additional requirements/Remarks
2046	CYMENES	3	F1	III	3+N2+F	N	3	3			97	0.88	3	yes	T2 [12]	II A [7]	yes	PP, EX, A	0	
2047	DICHLOROPROPENES (2,3-DICHLOROPROP-1-ENE)	3	F1	II	3+N2+C MR	C	2	2		45	95	1.2	2	yes	T1 [12]	II A [7]	yes	PP, EP, EX, TOX, A	1	
2047	DICHLOROPROPENES (MIXTURES of 2,3-DICHLOROPROP-1-ENE and 1,3-DICHLOROPROPENE)	3	F1	II	3+N1+C MR	C	2	2		45	95	1.23	2	yes	T2 [1), 12]	II A [7]	yes	PP, EP, EX, TOX, A	1	
2047	DICHLOROPROPENES (MIXTURES of 2,3-DICHLOROPROP-1-ENE and 1,3-DICHLOROPROPENE)	3	F1	III	3+N1+C MR	C	2	2		45	95	1.23	2	yes	T2 [1), 12]	II A [7]	yes	PP, EP, EX, TOX, A	0	
2047	DICHLOROPROPENES (1,3-DICHLOROPROPENE)	3	F1	III	3+N1+C MR	C	2	2		40	95	1.23	2	yes	T2 [1), 12]	II A [7]	yes	PP, EP, EX, TOX, A	0	
2048	DICYCLOPENTADIENE	3	F1	III	3+N2+F	N	3	3	2		95	0.94	3	yes	T1 [12]	II A	yes	PP, EX, A	0	7; 17
2050	DIISOBUTYLENE, ISOMERIC COMPOUNDS	3	F1	II	3+N2+F	N	2	3		10	97	0.72	3	yes	T3 [2]	II A [7]	yes	PP, EX, A	1	
2051	2-DIMETHYLAMINO ETHANOL	8	CF1	II	8+3+N3	N	3	2			97	0.89	3	yes	T3	II A [7]	yes	PP, EP, EX, A	1	34
2053	METHYL ISOBUTYL CARBINOL	3	F1	III	3	N	3	2			97	0.81	3	yes	T2 [12]	II A	yes	PP, EP, EX, A	0	
2054	MORPHOLINE	8	CF1	I	8+3+N3	N	3	2			97	1	3	yes	T3	II A	yes	PP, EP, EX, A	1	34
2055	STYRENE MONOMER, STABILIZED	3	F1	III	3+unst.+N3	N	3	2			97	0.91	3	yes	T1 [12]	II A	yes	PP, EX, A	0	3; 5; 16
2056	TETRAHYDROFURAN	3	F1	II	3	N	2	2		10	97	0.89	3	yes	T3	II B (II B1)	yes	PP, EX, A	1	

(1) UN No. or substance identification No.	(2) Name and description	(3a) Class	(3b) Classification code	(4) Packing group	(5) Dangers	(6) Type of tank vessel	(7) Cargo tank design	(8) Cargo tank type	(9) Cargo tank equipment	(10) Opening pressure of the pressure relief valve/high velocity vent valve, in kPa	(11) Maximum degree of filling in %	(12) Relative density at 20 °C	(13) Type of sampling device	(14) Pump room below deck permitted	(15) Temperature class	(16) Explosion group	(17) Anti-explosion protection required	(18) Equipment required	(19) Number of cones/blue lights	(20) Additional requirements/Remarks
		2.2	2.2	2.1.1.3	5.2.2 / 3.2.3.1	1.2.1 / 7.2.2.0.1	3.2.3.1 / 1.2.1	3.2.3.1 / 1.2.1	3.2.3.1 / 1.2.1	3.2.3.1 / 1.2.1	7.2.4.21	3.2.3.1	3.2.3.1 / 1.2.1	3.2.3.1 / 1.2.1	1.2.1	1.2.1 / 3.2.3.3	1.2.1 / 3.2.3.3	8.1.5	7.2.5	3.2.3.1
2057	TRIPROPYLENE	3	F1	II	3 + N1	C	2	2		35	95	0.744	2	yes	T3	II A	yes	PP, EX, A	1	
2057	TRIPROPYLENE	3	F1	III	3 + N1	C	2	2		35	95	0.73	2	yes	T3	II A	yes	PP, EX, A	0	
2078	TOLUENE DIISOCYANATE (and isomeric mixtures) (2,4- TOLUENE DIISOCYANATE)	6.1	T1	II	6.1+N2+S	C	2	2	2	25	95	1.22	2	no	T1 [12]	II B (II B3 [14])	yes	PP, EP, EX, TOX, A	2	2; 7; 8; 17
2078	TOLUENE DIISOCYANATE (and isomeric mixtures) (2,4- TOLUENE DIISOCYANATE)	6.1	T1	II	6.1+N2+S	C	2	1	4	25	95	1.22	2	no			no	PP, EP, TOX, A	2	2; 7; 8; 17; 20: +112°C; 26
2079	DIETHYLENETRIAMINE	8	C7	II	8+N3	N	4	2			97	0.96	3	yes			no	PP, EP	0	34
2137	CARBON DIOXIDE, REFRIGERATED LIQUID	2	3A		2.2	G	1	1	1		95		1	yes			no	PP	0	31,39
2205	ADIPONITRILE	6.1	T1	III	6.1	C	2	2		25	95	0.96	2	no	T4	II B (II B3 [14])	yes	PP, EP, EX, TOX, A	0	6: 6°C; 17
2206	ISOCYANATES, TOXIC, N.O.S. (4-CHLOROPHENYL ISOCYANATE)	6.1	T1	II	6.1+S	C	2	2	4	25	95	1.25	2	no			no	PP, EP, TOX, A	2	7; 17
2209	FORMALDEHYDE SOLUTION with not less than 25% formaldehyde	8	C9	III	8+N3	N	4	2			97	1.09	3	yes			no	PP, EP	0	15; 34
2215	MALEIC ANHYDRIDE, MOLTEN	8	C3	III	8+N3	N	3	3	2		95	0.93	3	yes	T2 [12]	II B [4]	yes	PP, EP, EX, A	0	7; 17; 25; 34
2215	MALEIC ANHYDRIDE, MOLTEN	8	C3	III	8+N3	N	3	1	4		95	0.93	3	yes			no	PP, EP	0	7; 17; 20: +88 °C; 25; 34
2218	ACRYLIC ACID, STABILIZED	8	CF1	II	8+3+unst. +N1	C	2	2	4	30	95	1.05	1	yes	T2 [12]	II B (II B1)	yes	PP, EP, EX, A	1	3; 4; 5; 17
2227	n-BUTYL METHACRYLATE, STABILIZED	3	F1	III	3+unst.+ N3+F	C	2	2		25	95	0.9	1	yes	T3	II A	yes	PP, EX, A	0	3; 5

(1)	(2)	(3a)	(3b)	(4)	(5)	(6)	(7)	(8)	(9)	(10)	(11)	(12)	(13)	(14)	(15)	(16)	(17)	(18)	(19)	(20)
UN No. or substance identification No.	Name and description	Class	Classification code	Packing group	Dangers	Type of tank vessel	Cargo tank design	Cargo tank type	Cargo tank equipment	Opening pressure of the pressure relief valve/high velocity vent valve, in kPa	Maximum degree of filling in %	Relative density at 20 °C	Type of sampling device	Pump room below deck permitted	Temperature class	Explosion group	Anti-explosion protection required	Equipment required	Number of cones/blue lights	Additional requirements/Remarks
3.1.2	3.1.2	2.2	2.2	2.1.1.3	5.2.2 / 3.2.3.1	1.2.1 / 7.2.2.0.1	3.2.3.1 / 1.2.1	3.2.3.1 / 1.2.1	3.2.3.1 / 1.2.1	3.2.3.1 / 1.2.1	7.2.4.21	3.2.3.1	3.2.3.1 / 1.2.1	3.2.3.1 / 1.2.1	1.2.1	1.2.1 / 3.2.3.3	1.2.1 / 3.2.3.3	8.1.5	7.2.5	3.2.3.1
2238	CHLOROTOLUENES (m-CHLOROTOLUENE)	3	F1	III	3+N2+S	C	2	2		30	95	1.08	2	yes	T1 [12]	II A [7]	yes	PP, EX, A	0	
2238	CHLOROTOLUENES (o-CHLOROTOLUENE)	3	F1	III	3+N2+S	C	2	2		30	95	1.08	2	yes	T1 [12]	II A [7]	yes	PP, EX, A	0	
2238	CHLOROTOLUENES (p-CHLOROTOLUENE)	3	F1	III	3+N2+S	C	2	2		30	95	1.07	2	yes	T1 [12]	II A [7]	yes	PP, EX, A	0	6: +11 °C; 17
2241	CYCLOHEPTANE	3	F1	II	3+N2	N	2	3		10	97	0.81	3	yes	T4 [3]	II A [7]	yes	PP, EX, A	1	
2247	n-DECANE	3	F1	III	3+F	C	2	2		30	95	0.73	2	yes	T4	II A	yes	PP, EX, A	0	
2248	DI-n-BUTYLAMINE	8	CF1	II	8+3+N3	N	3	3				0.76	3	yes	T3	II A [7]	yes	PP, EP, EX, A	1	34
2259	TRIETHYLENETETRAMINE	8	C7	II	8+N2	N	3	3			97	0.98	3	yes	T2 [12]	II B (II B [14])	yes	PP, EP, EX, A	0	6: 16°C; 17; 34
2263	DIMETHYLCYCLOHEXANES (cis-1,4- DIMETHYL-CYCLOHEXANE)	3	F1	II	3	C	2	2		35	95	0.78	2	yes	T4 [3]	II A [7]	yes	PP, EX, A	1	
2263	DIMETHYLCYCLOHEXANES (trans-1,4- DIMETHYL-CYCLOHEXANE)	3	F1	II	3	C	2	2		35	95	0.76	2	yes	T4 [3]	II A [7]	yes	PP, EX, A	1	
2264	N,N-DIMETHYL-CYCLOHEXYLAMINE	8	CF1	II	8+3+N2	N	3	3	3		97	0.85	3	yes	T3	II B [4]	yes	PP, EP, EX, A	1	34
2265	N,N-DIMETHYLFORMAMIDE	3	F1	III	3+CMR	N	2	3	3	10	97	0.95	3	yes	T2 [12]	II A	yes	PP, EP, EX, TOX, A	0	
2266	DIMETHYL-N-PROPYLAMINE	3	FC	II	3+8	C	2	2		50	95	0.72	2	yes	T4	II A [7]	yes	PP, EP, EX, A	1	23
2276	2-ETHYLHEXYLAMINE	3	FC	III	3+8+N3	N	3	2			97	0.79	3	yes	T3	II A [7]	yes	PP, EP, EX, A	0	34

(1)	(2)	(3a)	(3b)	(4)	(5)	(6)	(7)	(8)	(9)	(10)	(11)	(12)	(13)	(14)	(15)	(16)	(17)	(18)	(19)	(20)
UN No. or substance identification No.	Name and description	Class	Classification code	Packing group	Dangers	Type of tank vessel	Cargo tank design	Cargo tank type	Cargo tank equipment	Opening pressure of the pressure relief valve/high velocity vent valve, in kPa	Maximum degree of filling in %	Relative density at 20 °C	Type of sampling device	Pump room below deck permitted	Temperature class	Explosion group	Anti-explosion protection required	Equipment required	Number of cones/blue lights	Additional requirements/Remarks
	3.1.2	2.2	2.2	2.1.1.3	5.2.2 / 3.2.3.1	1.2.1 / 7.2.2.0.1	3.2.3.1 / 1.2.1	3.2.3.1 / 1.2.1	3.2.3.1 / 1.2.1	3.2.3.1 / 1.2.1	7.2.4.21	3.2.3.1	3.2.3.1 / 1.2.1	3.2.3.1 / 1.2.1	1.2.1	1.2.1 / 3.2.3.3	1.2.1 / 3.2.3.3	8.1.5	7.2.5	3.2.3.1
2278	n-HEPTENE	3	F1	II	3+N3	N	2	2		10	97	0.7	3	yes	T3	II B⁴⁾ (II B1)	yes	PP, EX, A	1	
2280	HEXAMETHYLENEDIAMINE, SOLID, MOLTEN	8	C8	III	8+N3	N	3	3	2		95	0.83	3	yes	T3	II B (II B3¹⁴⁾)	yes	PP, EP, EX, A	0	7; 17; 34
2280	HEXAMETHYLENEDIAMINE, SOLID, MOLTEN	8	C8	III	8+N3	N	3	3	4		95	0.83	3	yes			no	PP, EP	0	7; 17; 20: +66 °C; 34
2282	HEXANOLS	3	F1	III	3+N3	N	3	2			97	0.83	3	yes	T3	II A	yes	PP, EX, A	0	
2286	PENTAMETHYLHEPTANE	3	F1	III	3+F	N	3	3			97	0.75	3	yes	T2¹²⁾	II A⁷⁾	yes	PP, EX, A	0	
2288	ISOHEXENES	3	F1	II	3+unst.+N3	C	2	2	3	50	95	0.735	2	yes	T2¹²⁾	II B⁴⁾	yes	PP, EX, A	1	3; 23
2289	ISOPHORONEDIAMINE	8	C7	III	8+N2	N	3	3			97	0.92	3	yes	T2¹²⁾	II A⁷⁾	yes	PP, EP, EX, A	0	6: 14 °C; 17; 34
2302	5-METHYLHEXAN-2-ONE	3	F1	III	3	N	3	2			97	0.81	3	yes	T1¹²⁾	II A	yes	PP, EX, A	0	
2303	ISOPROPENYLBENZENE	3	F1	III	3+N2+F	N	3	3			97	0.91	3	yes	T2¹²⁾	II B (II B1)	yes	PP, EX, A	0	
2309	OCTADIENE (1,7-OCTADIENE)	3	F1	II	3+N2	N	2	3		10	97	0.75	3	yes	T3	II B (II B3)	yes	PP, EX, A	1	
2311	PHENETIDINES	6.1	T1	III	6.1	C	2	2	4	25	95	1.07	2	no			no	PP, EP, TOX, A	0	6: +7 °C; 17
2312	PHENOL, MOLTEN	6.1	T1	II	6.1+N3+S	C	2	2		25	95	1.07	2	no	T1¹²⁾	II A⁸⁾	yes	PP, EP, EX, TOX, A	2	7; 17
2312	PHENOL, MOLTEN	6.1	T1	II	6.1+N3+S	C	2	2	4	25	95	1.07	2	no			no	PP, EP, TOX, A	2	7; 17; 20: +67 °C
2320	TETRAETHYLENEPENTAMINE	8	C7	III	8+N2	N	4	3			97	1	3	yes			no	PP, EP	0	34

(1) UN No. or substance identification No.	(2) Name and description	(3a) Class	(3b) Classification code	(4) Packing group	(5) Dangers	(6) Type of tank vessel	(7) Cargo tank design	(8) Cargo tank type	(9) Cargo tank equipment	(10) Opening pressure of the pressure relief valve/high velocity vent valve, in kPa	(11) Maximum degree of filling in %	(12) Relative density at 20 °C	(13) Type of sampling device	(14) Pump room below deck permitted	(15) Temperature class	(16) Explosion group	(17) Anti-explosion protection required	(18) Equipment required	(19) Number of cones/blue lights	(20) Additional requirements/Remarks
		2.2	2.2	2.1.1.3	5.2.2/3.2.3.1	1.2.1/7.2.2.0.1	3.2.3.1/1.2.1	3.2.3.1/1.2.1	3.2.3.1/1.2.1	3.2.3.1/1.2.1	7.2.4.21	3.2.3.1	3.2.3.1/1.2.1	3.2.3.1/1.2.1	1.2.1	1.2.1/3.2.3.3	1.2.1/3.2.3.3	8.1.5	7.2.5	3.2.3.1
2321	TRICHLOROBENZENES, LIQUID (1,2,4-TRICHLOROBENZENE)	6.1	T1	III	6.1+N1+S	C	2	2	2	25	95	1.45	2	no	T1[12]	II A[7]	yes	PP, EP, EX, TOX, A	0	7;17
2321	TRICHLOROBENZENES, LIQUID (1,2,4-TRICHLOROBENZENE)	6.1	T1	III	6.1+N1+S	C	2	1	4	25	95	1.45	2	no			no	PP, EP, TOX, A	0	7; 17; 20: +95 °C; 26
2323	TRIETHYL PHOSPHITE	3	F1	III	3	N	3	2			97	0.8	3	yes	T3	II B[4]	yes	PP, EX, A	0	
2324	TRIISOBUTYLENE	3	F1	III	3+N1+F	C	2	2		35	95	0.76	2	yes	T2[12]	II B[4]	yes	PP, EX, A	0	
2325	1,3,5-TRIMETHYLBENZENE	3	F1	III	3+N1	C	2	2		35	95	0.87	2	yes	T1[12]	II A[7]	yes	PP, EX, A	0	
2333	ALLYL ACETATE	3	FT1	II	3+6.1	C	2	2		40	95	0.93	2	no	T2[12]	II A[7]	yes	PP, EP, EX, TOX, A	2	
2348	BUTYL ACRYLATES, STABILIZED (n-BUTYL ACRYLATE, STABILIZED)	3	F1	III	3+unst.+N3	C	2	2		30	95	0.9	1	yes	T3	II B (II B1)	yes	PP, EX, A	0	3; 5
2350	BUTYL METHYL ETHER	3	F1	II	3	N	2	2	3	10	97	0.74	3	yes	T4[3]	II B[4]	yes	PP, EX, A	1	
2356	2-CHLOROPROPANE	3	F1	I	3	C	2	2		50	95	0.86	2	yes	T1[12]	II A	yes	PP, EX, A	1	23
2357	CYCLOHEXYLAMINE	8	CF1	II	8+3+N3	N	3	2			97	0.86	3	yes	T3	II A	yes	PP, EP, EX, A	1	34
2362	1,1-DICHLOROETHANE	3	F1	II	3+N2	C	2	2	3	50	95	1.17	2	yes	T2[12]	II A	yes	PP, EX, A	1	23
2370	1-HEXENE	3	F1	II	3+N3	N	2	2		10	97	0.67	3	yes	T3	II B[4]	yes	PP, EX, A	1	

(1)	(2)	(3a)	(3b)	(4)	(5)	(6)	(7)	(8)	(9)	(10)	(11)	(12)	(13)	(14)	(15)	(16)	(17)	(18)	(19)	(20)
	Name and description	Class	Classification code	Packing group	Dangers	Type of tank vessel	Cargo tank design	Cargo tank type	Cargo tank equipment	Opening pressure of the pressure relief valve/high velocity vent valve, in kPa	Maximum degree of filling in %	Relative density at 20 °C	Type of sampling device	Pump room below deck permitted	Temperature class	Explosion group	Anti-explosion protection required	Equipment required	Number of cones/blue lights	Additional requirements/Remarks
	3.1.2	2.2	2.2	2.1.1.3	5.2.2 / 3.2.3.1	1.2.1 / 7.2.2.0.1	3.2.3.1 / 1.2.1	3.2.3.1 / 1.2.1	3.2.3.1 / 1.2.1	3.2.3.1 / 1.2.1	7.2.4.21	3.2.3.1	3.2.3.1 / 1.2.1	3.2.3.1 / 1.2.1	1.2.1	1.2.1 / 3.2.3.3	1.2.1 / 3.2.3.3	8.1.5	7.2.5	3.2.3.1
2381	DIMÉTHYL DISULPHIDE	3	FT1	II	3+6.1	C	2	2		40	95	1.063	2	yes	T2 [12)]	II A	yes	PP, EP, EX, TOX, A	2	
2382	DIMETHYLHYDRAZINE, SYMMETRICAL	6.1	TF1	I	6.1+3+C MR	C	2	2		50	95	0.83	1	no	T4 [3)]	II C [5)]	yes	PP, EP, EX, TOX, A	2	
2383	DIPROPYLAMINE	3	FC	II	3+8+N3	C	2	2		35	95	0.74	2	yes	T3	II A	yes	PP, EP, EX, A	1	
2397	3-METHYLBUTAN-2-ONE	3	F1	II	3	N	2	2		10	97	0.81	3	yes	T1 [12)]	II A [7)]	yes	PP, EX, A	1	
2398	METHYL tert-BUTYL ETHER	3	F1	II	3	N	2	2		10	97	0.74	3	yes	T1 [12)]	II A	yes	PP, EX, A	1	
2404	PROPIONITRILE	3	FT1	II	3+6.1	C	2	2		45	95	0.78	2	no	T1 [9), 12)]	II A [7)]	yes	PP, EP, EX, TOX, A	2	
2414	THIOPHENE	3	F1	II	3+N3+S	N	2	3	2	10	97	1.06	3	yes	T2 [12)]	II A	yes	PP, EX, A	1	
2430	ALKYLPHENOLS, SOLID, N.O.S. (NONYLPHENOL, ISOMERIC MIXTURE, MOLTEN)	8	C4	II	8+N1+F	N	3	1	4		95	0.95	2	yes	T2 [12)]	II A [7)]	yes	PP, EP, EX, A	0	7; 17
2430	ALKYLPHENOLS, SOLID, N.O.S. (NONYLPHENOL, ISOMERIC MIXTURE, MOLTEN)	8	C4	II	8+N1+F	N	3	2			95	0.95	2	yes			no	PP, EP	0	7; 17; 20: +125 °C
2432	N,N-DIETHYLANILINE	6.1	T1	III	6.1+N2	C	2	2		25	95	0.93	2	no			no	PP, EP, TOX, A	0	
2448	SULPHUR, MOLTEN	4.1	F3	III	4.1+S	N	4	1	4		95	2.07	3	yes			no	PP, EP, TOX*, A	0	* Toximeter for H2S; 7; 17; 20: +150°C; 28; 32

(1)	(2)	(3a)	(3b)	(4)	(5)	(6)	(7)	(8)	(9)	(10)	(11)	(12)	(13)	(14)	(15)	(16)	(17)	(18)	(19)	(20)
UN No. or substance identification No.	Name and description	Class	Classification code	Packing group	Dangers	Type of tank vessel	Cargo tank design	Cargo tank type	Cargo tank equipment	Opening pressure of the pressure relief valve/high velocity vent valve, in kPa	Maximum degree of filling in %	Relative density at 20 °C	Type of sampling device	Pump room below deck permitted	Temperature class	Explosion group	Anti-explosion protection required	Equipment required	Number of cones/blue lights	Additional requirements/Remarks
	3.1.2	2.2	2.2	2.1.1.3	5.2.2 / 3.2.3.1	1.2.1 / 7.2.2.0.1	3.2.3.1 / 1.2.1	3.2.3.1 / 1.2.1	3.2.3.1 / 1.2.1	3.2.3.1 / 1.2.1	7.2.4.21	3.2.3.1	3.2.3.1 / 1.2.1	3.2.3.1 / 1.2.1	1.2.1	1.2.1 / 3.2.3.3	1.2.1 / 3.2.3.3	8.1.5	7.2.5	3.2.3.1
2458	HEXADIENES	3	F1	II	3+N3	N	2	2		10	97	0.72	3	yes	T4³⁾	II A⁷⁾	yes	PP, EX, A	1	
2477	METHYL ISOTHIOCYANATE	6.1	TF1	I	6.1+3+N1	C	2	2	2	35	95	1,07¹¹⁾	1	no	T4³⁾	II B⁴⁾	yes	PP, EP, EX, TOX, A	2	7; 17
2485	n-BUTYL ISOCYANATE	6.1	TF1	I	6.1+3	C	2	2		35	95	0.89	1	no	T2¹²⁾	II A	yes	PP, EP, EX, TOX, A	2	
2486	ISOBUTYL ISOCYANATE	6.1	TF1	I	6.1+3	C	2	2		40	95		1	no	T4³⁾	II A	yes	PP, EP, EX, TOX, A	2	
2487	PHENYL ISOCYANATE	6.1	TF1	I	6.1+3	C	2	2		25	95	1.1	1	no	T1¹²⁾	II A	yes	PP, EP, EX, TOX, A	2	
2490	DICHLOROISOPROPYL ETHER	6.1	T1	II	6.1	C	2	2		25	95	1.11	2	no			no	PP, EP, TOX, A	2	
2491	ETHANOLAMINE or ETHANOLAMINE SOLUTION	8	C7	III	8+N3	N	3	2			97	1.02	3	yes	T2¹²⁾	II A⁷⁾	yes	PP, EP, EX, A	0	6: 14°C; 17; 34
2493	HEXAMETHYLENEIMINE	3	FC	II	3+8+N3	N	3	2			97	0.88	3	yes	T3²⁾	II A	yes	PP, EP, EX, A	1	34
2496	PROPIONIC ANHYDRIDE	8	C3	III	8+N3	N	4	3			97	1.02	3	yes			no	PP, EP	0	34
2518	1,5,9-CYCLODODECATRIENE	6.1	T1	III	6.1+F	C	2	2		25	95	0.9	2	no			no	PP, EP, TOX, A	0	
2527	ISOBUTYL ACRYLATE, STABILIZED	3	F1	III	3+unst.	C	2	2		30	95	0.89	1	yes	T2¹²⁾	II B⁹⁾	yes	PP, EX, A	0	3; 5
2528	ISOBUTYL ISOBUTYRATE	3	F1	III	3+N3	N	3	2			97	0.86	3	yes	T2¹²⁾	II A	yes	PP, EX, A	0	
2531	METHACRYLIC ACID, STABILIZED	8	C3	II	8+unst.+N3	C	2	2	4	25	95	1.02	1	yes	T2¹²⁾	II A	yes	PP, EP, EX, A	0	3; 4; 5; 7; 17

(1)	(2)	(3a)	(3b)	(4)	(5)	(6)	(7)	(8)	(9)	(10)	(11)	(12)	(13)	(14)	(15)	(16)	(17)	(18)	(19)	(20)
UN No. or substance identification No.	Name and description	Class	Classification code	Packing group	Dangers	Type of tank vessel	Cargo tank design	Cargo tank type	Cargo tank equipment	Opening pressure of the pressure relief valve/high velocity vent valve, in kPa	Maximum degree of filling in %	Relative density at 20 °C	Type of sampling device	Pump room below deck permitted	Temperature class	Explosion group	Anti-explosion protection required	Equipment required	Number of cones/blue lights	Additional requirements/Remarks
	3.1.2			2.1.1.3	5.2.2/3.2.3.1	1.2.1/7.2.2.0.1	3.2.3.1/1.2.1	3.2.3.1/1.2.1	3.2.3.1/1.2.1	3.2.3.1/1.2.1	7.2.4.21	3.2.3.1	3.2.3.1/1.2.1	3.2.3.1/1.2.1	1.2.1	1.2.1/3.2.3.3	1.2.1/3.2.3.3	8.1.5	7.2.5	3.2.1
2564	TRICHLOROACETIC ACID SOLUTION	8	C3	II	8+N1	C	2	2		25	95	1,62[11]	2	yes	T1[12]	II A[7]	yes	PP, EP, EX, A	0	7; 17; 22
2564	TRICHLOROACETIC ACID SOLUTION	8	C3	III	8+N1	C	2	2		25	95	1,62[11]	2	yes			no	PP, EP	0	22
2574	TRICRESYL PHOSPHATE with more than 3% ortho isomer	6.1	T1	II	6.1+N1+S	C	2	2		25	95	1.18	2	no			no	PP, EP, TOX, A	2	
2579	PIPERAZINE, MOLTEN	8	C8	III	8+N2	N	3	3	2		95	0.9	3	yes			no	PP, EP	0	7; 17; 34
2582	FERRIC CHLORIDE SOLUTION	8	C1	III	8	N	4	3			97	1.45	3	yes			no	PP, EP	0	22; 30; 34
2586	ALKYLSULPHONIC ACIDS, LIQUID or ARYLSULPHONIC ACIDS, LIQUID with not more than 5% free sulphuric acid	8	C3	III	8	N	4	3			97		3	yes			no	PP, EP	0	34
2608	NITROPROPANES	3	F1	III	3	N	3	2	2		97	1	3	yes	T2[12]	II B[7] (II B2)	yes	PP, EX, A	0	
2615	ETHYL PROPYL ETHER	3	F1	II	3	N	2	2		10	97	0.73	3	yes	T4[3]	II A[7]	yes	PP, EX, A	1	3; 5
2618	VINYLTOLUENES, STABILIZED	3	F1	III	3+unst.+N2+F	C	2	2		25	95	0.92	1	yes	T1[12]	II A	yes	PP, EX, A	0	
2651	4,4'-DIAMINO-DIPHENYLMETHANE	6.1	T2	III	6.1+N2+CMR+S	C	2	2	1	25	95	1	2	no			no	PP, EP, TOX, A	0	7; 17
2672	AMMONIA SOLUTION, relative density between 0.880 and 0.957 at 15°C in water, with more than 10% but not more than 35% ammonia (more than 25% but not more than 35% ammonia)	8	C5	III	8+N1	C	2	2	2	50	95	0,88[10] – 0,96[10]	2	yes			no	PP, EP	0	
2672	AMMONIA SOLUTION, relative density between 0.880 and 0.957 at 15°C in water, with more than 10% but not more than 35% ammonia (not more than 25% ammonia)	8	C5	III	8+N3	N	2	2		10	95	0,88[10] – 0,96[10]	2	yes			no	PP, EP	0	34

(1) UN No.	(2) Name and description	(3a) Class	(3b) Classification code	(4) Packing group	(5) Dangers	(6) Type of tank vessel	(7) Cargo tank design	(8) Cargo tank type	(9) Cargo tank equipment	(10) Opening pressure of the pressure relief valve/high velocity vent valve, in kPa	(11) Max. degree of filling in %	(12) Relative density at 20 °C	(13) Type of sampling device	(14) Pump room below deck permitted	(15) Temperature class	(16) Explosion group	(17) Anti-explosion protection required	(18) Equipment required	(19) Number of cones/blue lights	(20) Additional requirements/Remarks
2683	AMMONIUM SULPHIDE SOLUTION	8	CFT	II	8+3+6.1	C	2	2		50	95		2	no	T4 3)	II B 4)	yes	PP, EP, EX, TOX, A	2	15; 16
2693	BISULPHITES, AQUEOUS SOLUTION, N.O.S.	8	C1	III	8	N	4	3			97		3	yes			no	PP, EP	0	27; 34
2709	BUTYLBENZENES	3	F1	III	3+N1+F	N	2	3		35	97	0.87	2	yes	T2 12)	II A 7)	yes	PP, EX, A	0	41
2709	BUTYLBENZENES (n-BUTYLBENZENE)	3	F1	III	3+N1+F	N	3	3			97	0.87	2	yes	T2 12)	II A	yes	PP, EX, A	0	41
2733	AMINES, FLAMMABLE, CORROSIVE, N.O.S. or POLYAMINES, FLAMMABLE, CORROSIVE, N.O.S. (2-AMINOBUTANE)	3	FC	II	3+8+N1	C	2	2	3	50	95	0.72	2	yes	T4 3)	II A 7)	yes	PP, EP, EX, A	1	23
2735	AMINES, LIQUID, CORROSIVE, N.O.S. or POLYAMINES, LIQUID, CORROSIVE, N.O.S.	8	C7	I	8+(N1, N2, N3, CMR, F or S)	*	*	*	*	*	*		*	yes			no	*	0	27; 34 *see 3.2.3.3
2735	AMINES, LIQUID, CORROSIVE, N.O.S. or POLYAMINES, LIQUID, CORROSIVE, N.O.S.	8	C7	II	8+(N1, N2, N3, CMR, F or S)	*	*	*	*	*	*		*	yes			no	*	0	27; 34 *see 3.2.3.3
2735	AMINES, LIQUID, CORROSIVE, N.O.S. or POLYAMINES, LIQUID, CORROSIVE, N.O.S.	8	C7	III	8+(N1, N2, N3, CMR, F or S)	*	*	*	*	*	*		*	yes			no	*	0	27; 34 *see 3.2.3.3
2754	N-ETHYLTOLUIDINES (N-ETHYL-o-TOLUIDINE)	6.1	T1	II	6.1+F	C	2	2		25	95	0.94	2	no			no	PP, EP, TOX, A	2	
2754	N-ETHYLTOLUIDINES (N-ETHYL-m-TOLUIDINE)	6.1	T1	II	6.1+F	C	2	2		25	95	0.94	2	no			no	PP, EP, TOX, A	2	

(1)	(2)	(3a)	(3b)	(4)	(5)	(6)	(7)	(8)	(9)	(10)	(11)	(12)	(13)	(14)	(15)	(16)	(17)	(18)	(19)	(20)
3.1.2	3.1.2	2.2	2.2	2.1.1.3	5.2.2 / 3.2.3.1	1.2.1 / 7.2.2.0.1	3.2.3.1 / 1.2.1	3.2.3.1 / 1.2.1	3.2.3.1 / 1.2.1	3.2.3.1 / 1.2.1	7.2.4.21	3.2.3.1	3.2.3.1 / 1.2.1	3.2.3.1 / 1.2.1	1.2.1	1.2.1 / 3.2.3.3	1.2.1 / 3.2.3.3	8.1.5	7.2.5	3.2.3.1
2754	N-ETHYLTOLUIDINES (N-ETHYL-o-TOLUIDINE and N-ETHYL-m-TOLUIDINE MIXTURES)	6.1	T1	II	6.1+F	C	2	2		25	95	0.94	2	no			no	PP, EP, TOX, A	2	
2754	N-ETHYLTOLUIDINES (N-ETHYL-p-TOLUIDINE)	6.1	T1	II	6.1+F	C	2	2	2	25	95	0.94	2	no			no	PP, EP, TOX, A	2	7; 17
2785	4-THIAPENTANAL (3-METHYLMERCAPTO-PROPIONALDEHYDE)	6.1	T1	III	6.1	C	2	2	2	25	95	1.04	2	no			no	PP, EP, TOX, A	0	
2789	ACETIC ACID, GLACIAL or ACETIC ACID SOLUTION, more than 80% acid, by mass	8	CF1	II	8+3	N	2	3	2	10	95	1,05 with 100% acid	3	yes	T1 [12]	II A [7]	yes	PP, EP, EX, A	1	7; 17; 34
2790	ACETIC ACID SOLUTION, not less than 50% but not more than 80% acid, by mass	8	C3	II	8	N	2	3		10	97		3	yes			no	PP, EP	0	34
2790	ACETIC ACID SOLUTION, more than 10% and less than 50% acid, by mass	8	C3	III	8	N	2	3		10	97		3	yes			no	PP, EP	0	34
2796	BATTERY FLUID, ACID	8	C1	II	8+N3	N	4	3			97	1,00 - 1,84	3	yes			no	PP, EP	0	8; 22; 30; 34
2796	SULPHURIC ACID with not more than 51% acid	8	C1	II	8+N3	N	4	3			97	1,00 - 1,41	3	yes			no	PP, EP	0	8; 22; 30; 34
2797	BATTERY FLUID, ALKALI	8	C5	II	8+N3	N	4	3			97	1,00 - 2,13	3	yes			no	PP, EP	0	22; 30; 34
2810	TOXIC LIQUID, ORGANIC, N.O.S.	6.1	T1	I	6.1+(N1, N2, N3, CMR, F or S)	C	2	2	*	*	95		1	no			no	PP, EP, TOX, A	2	27; *see 3.2.3.3

(1)	(2)	(3a)	(3b)	(4)	(5)	(6)	(7)	(8)	(9)	(10)	(11)	(12)	(13)	(14)	(15)	(16)	(17)	(18)	(19)	(20)
UN No. or substance identification No.	Name and description	Class	Classification code	Packing group	Dangers	Type of tank vessel	Cargo tank design	Cargo tank type	Cargo tank equipment	Opening pressure of the pressure relief valve/high velocity vent valve, in kPa	Maximum degree of filling in %	Relative density at 20 °C	Type of sampling device	Pump room below deck permitted	Temperature class	Explosion group	Anti-explosion protection required	Equipment required	Number of cones/blue lights	Additional requirements/Remarks
(1)	3.1.2	2.2	2.2	2.1.1.3	5.2.2 / 3.2.3.1	1.2.1 / 7.2.2.0.1	3.2.3.1 / 1.2.1	3.2.3.1 / 1.2.1	3.2.3.1 / 1.2.1	3.2.3.1 / 1.2.1	7.2.4.21	3.2.3.1	3.2.3.1 / 1.2.1	3.2.3.1 / 1.2.1	1.2.1	1.2.1 / 3.2.3.3	1.2.1 / 3.2.3.3	8.1.5	7.2.5	3.2.3.1
2810	TOXIC LIQUID, ORGANIC, N.O.S.	6.1	T1	II	6.1+(N1, N2, N3, CMR, F or S)	C	2	2	*	*	95		2	no			no	PP, EP, TOX, A	2	27; *see 3.2.3.3
2810	TOXIC LIQUID, ORGANIC, N.O.S.	6.1	T1	III	6.1+(N1, N2, N3, CMR, F or S)	C	2	2	*	*	95		2	no			no	PP, EP, TOX, A	0	27; *see 3.2.3.3
2811	TOXIC SOLID, ORGANIC, N.O.S. (1,2,3-TRICHLOROBENZENE, MOLTEN)	6.1	T2	III	6.1+S	C	2	2	2	25	95		2	no	T4[3]	II A[7]	yes	PP, EP, EX, TOX, A	0	7; 17; 22
2811	TOXIC SOLID, ORGANIC, N.O.S. (1,2,3-TRICHLOROBENZENE, MOLTEN)	6.1	T2	III	6.1+S	C	2	1	4	25	95		2	no			no	PP, EP, TOX, A	0	7; 17; 20: +92 °C; 22; 26
2811	TOXIC SOLID, ORGANIC, N.O.S. (1,3,5-TRICHLOROBENZENE, MOLTEN)	6.1	T2	III	6.1+S	C	2	2	2	25	95		2	no	T4[3]	II A[7]	yes	PP, EP, EX, TOX, A	0	7; 17; 22
2811	TOXIC SOLID, ORGANIC, N.O.S. (1,3,5-TRICHLOROBENZENE, MOLTEN)	6.1	T2	III	6.1+S	C	2	1	4	25	95		2	no			no	PP, EP, TOX, A	0	7; 17; 20: +92 °C; 22; 26
2815	N-AMINOETHYL PIPERAZINE	8	C7	III	8+N2	N	4	3			97	0.98	3	yes			no	PP, EP	0	34
2820	BUTYRIC ACID	8	C3	III	8+N3	N	2	3		10	97	0.96	3	yes			no	PP, EP	0	34
2829	CAPROIC ACID	8	C3	III	8+N3	N	4	3			97	0.92	3	yes			no	PP, EP	0	34
2831	1,1,1-TRICHLOROETHANE	6.1	T1	III	6.1+N2	C	2	2	3	50	95	1.34	2	no			no	PP, EP, TOX, A	0	23
2850	PROPYLENE TETRAMER	3	F1	III	3+N1+F	N	4	3			97	0.76	2	yes			no	PP	0	
2374	FURFURYL ALCOHOL	6.1	T1	III	6.1+N3	C	2	2		25	95	1.13	2	no			no	PP, EP, TOX, A	0	

(1)	(2)	(3a)	(3b)	(4)	(5)	(6)	(7)	(8)	(9)	(10)	(11)	(12)	(13)	(14)	(15)	(16)	(17)	(18)	(19)	(20)
		3.1.2	2.2	2.1.1.3	5.2.2 / 3.2.3.1	1.2.1 / 7.2.2.0.1	3.2.3.1 / 1.2.1	3.2.3.1 / 1.2.1	3.2.3.1 / 1.2.1	3.2.3.1 / 1.2.1	7.2.4.21	3.2.3.1	3.2.3.1 / 1.2.1	3.2.3.1 / 1.2.1	1.2.1	1.2.1 / 3.2.3.3	1.2.1 / 3.2.3.3	8.1.5	7.2.5	3.2.3.1
2904	PHENOLATES, LIQUID	8	C9	III	8	N	4	2			97	1,13-1,18	3	yes			no	PP, EP	0	34
2920	CORROSIVE LIQUID, FLAMMABLE, N.O.S. (2-PROPANOL AND DODECYLDIMETHYL-AMMONIUM CHLORIDE, AQUEOUS SOLUTION)	8	CF1	II	8+3+F	N	3	3			97	0.95	3	yes	T3	II A	yes	PP, EP, EX, A	1	34;
2920	CORROSIVE LIQUID, FLAMMABLE, N.O.S. (AQUEOUS SOLUTION OF HEXADECYLTRIMETHYL-AMMONIUM CHLORIDE (50%) AND ETHANOL (35%))	8	CF1	II	8+3+F	N	2	3		10	95	0.9	3	yes	T2 [12]	II B	yes	PP, EP, EX, A	1	6:+7°C; 17; 34;
2920	CORROSIVE LIQUID, FLAMMABLE, N.O.S. (AQUEOUS SOLUTION OF HEXADECYLTRIMETHYL-AMMONIUM CHLORIDE (50%) AND ETHANOL (35%))	8	CF1	II	8+3+F	N	2	3		10	95	0,9	3	yes	T2 [12]	II B (II B3)	yes	PP, EP, EX, A	1	6:+7°C; 17; 34; 44
2922	CORROSIVE LIQUID, TOXIC, N.O.S.	8	CT1	I	8+6,1+ (N1, N2, N3, CMR, F or S)	C	2	2	*	*	95		1	no			no	PP, EP, TOX, A	2	27; *see 3.2.3.3
2922	CORROSIVE LIQUID, TOXIC, N.O.S.	8	CT1	II	8+6,1+ (N1, N2, N3, CMR, F or S)	C	2	2	*	*	95		2	no			no	PP, EP, TOX, A	2	27; *see 3.2.3.3

Column headers:
- (1) UN No. or substance identification No.
- (2) Name and description
- (3a) Class
- (3b) Classification code
- (4) Packing group
- (5) Dangers
- (6) Type of tank vessel
- (7) Cargo tank design
- (8) Cargo tank type
- (9) Cargo tank equipment
- (10) Opening pressure of the pressure relief valve/high velocity vent valve, in kPa
- (11) Maximum degree of filling in %
- (12) Relative density at 20 °C
- (13) Type of sampling device
- (14) Pump room below deck permitted
- (15) Temperature class
- (16) Explosion group
- (17) Anti-explosion protection required
- (18) Equipment required
- (19) Number of cones/blue lights
- (20) Additional requirements/Remarks

(1) UN No. or substance identification No.	(2) Name and description	(3a) Class	(3b) Classification code	(4) Packing group	(5) Dangers	(6) Type of tank vessel	(7) Cargo tank design	(8) Cargo tank type	(9) Cargo tank equipment	(10) Opening pressure of the pressure relief valve/high velocity vent valve, in kPa	(11) Maximum degree of filling in %	(12) Relative density at 20 °C	(13) Type of sampling device	(14) Pump room below deck permitted	(15) Temperature class	(16) Explosion group	(17) Anti-explosion protection required	(18) Equipment required	(19) Number of cones/blue lights	(20) Additional requirements/Remarks
		2.2	2.2	2.1.1.3	5.2.2 / 3.2.3.1	1.2.1 / 7.2.2.0.1	3.2.3.1 / 1.2.1	3.2.3.1 / 1.2.1	3.2.3.1 / 1.2.1	3.2.3.1 / 1.2.1	7.2.4.21	3.2.3.1	3.2.3.1 / 1.2.1	3.2.3.1 / 1.2.1	1.2.1	1.2.1 / 3.2.3.3	1.2.1 / 3.2.3.3	8.1.5	7.2.5	3.2.3.1
2922	CORROSIVE LIQUID, TOXIC, N.O.S.	8	CT1	III	8+6.1+(N1, N2, N3, CMR, F or S)	C	2	2	*	*	95		2	no			no	PP, EP, TOX, A	0	27; *see 3.2.3.3
2924	FLAMMABLE LIQUID, CORROSIVE, N.O.S.	3	FC	I	3+8+(N1, N2, N3, CMR, F or S)	C	1	1	*	*	95		1	yes	T4 3)	II B4)	yes	*	1	27; *see 3.2.3.3
2924	FLAMMABLE LIQUID, CORROSIVE, N.O.S.	3	FC	I	3+8+(N1, N2, N3, CMR, F or S)	C	1	1	*	*	95		1	yes	T4 3)	II B4) (II B3)	yes	*	1	27; 44 *see 3.2.3.3
2924	FLAMMABLE LIQUID, CORROSIVE, N.O.S.	3	FC	I	3+8+(N1, N2, N3, CMR, F or S)	C	2	2	*	*	95		1	yes	T4 3)	II B4)	yes	*	1	27; *see 3.2.3.3
2924	FLAMMABLE LIQUID, CORROSIVE, N.O.S.	3	FC	I	3+8+(N1, N2, N3, CMR, F or S)	C	2	2	*	*	95		1	yes	T4 3)	II B4) (II B3)	yes	*	1	27; 44 *see 3.2.3.3
2924	FLAMMABLE LIQUID, CORROSIVE, N.O.S.	3	FC	II	3+8+(N1, N2, N3, CMR, F or S)	C	2	2	*	*	95		2	yes	T4 3)	II B4)	yes	*	1	27; *see 3.2.3.3
2924	FLAMMABLE LIQUID, CORROSIVE, N.O.S.	3	FC	II	3+8+(N1, N2, N3, CMR, F or S)	C	2	2	*	*	95		2	yes	T4 3)	II B4) (II B3)	yes	*	1	27; 44 *see 3.2.3.3
2924	FLAMMABLE LIQUID, CORROSIVE, N.O.S.	3	FC	III	3+8+(N1, N2, N3, CMR, F or S)	*	*	*	*	*	*		*	yes	T4 3)	II B4)	yes	*	0	27; 34 *see 3.2.3.3

(1) UN No. or substance identification No.	(2) Name and description	(3a) Class	(3b) Classification code	(4) Packing group	(5) Dangers	(6) Type of tank vessel	(7) Cargo tank design	(8) Cargo tank type	(9) Cargo tank equipment	(10) Opening pressure of the pressure relief valve/high velocity vent valve, in kPa	(11) Maximum degree of filling in %	(12) Relative density at 20 °C	(13) Type of sampling device	(14) Pump room below deck permitted	(15) Temperature class	(16) Explosion group	(17) Anti-explosion protection required	(18) Equipment required	(19) Number of cones/blue lights	(20) Additional requirements/Remarks
	3.1.2	2.2	2.2	2.1.1.3	5.2.2 / 3.2.3.1	1.2.1 / 7.2.2.0.1	3.2.3.1 / 1.2.1	3.2.3.1 / 1.2.1	3.2.3.1 / 1.2.1	3.2.3.1 / 1.2.1	7.2.4.21	3.2.3.1	3.2.3.1 / 1.2.1	3.2.3.1 / 1.2.1	1.2.1	1.2.1 / 3.2.3.3	1.2.1 / 3.2.3.3	8.1.5	7.2.5	3.2.3.1
2924	FLAMMABLE LIQUID, CORROSIVE, N.O.S.	3	FC	III	3+8+(N1, N2, N3, CMR, F or S)	*	*	*	*	*	*		*	yes	T4 $^{3)}$	II B $^{4)}$ (II B3)	yes	*	0	27; 34 *see 3.2.3.3
2924	FLAMMABLE LIQUID, CORROSIVE, N.O.S. (AQUEOUS SOLUTION OF DIALKYL-(C$_8$-C$_{18}$)-DIMETHYL AMMONIUM CHLORIDE AND 2-PROPANOL)	3	FC	II	3+8+F	C	2	2		50	95	0.88	2	yes	T2 $^{12)}$	II A	yes	PP, EP, EX, A	1	
2927	TOXIC LIQUID, CORROSIVE, ORGANIC, N.O.S.	6.1	TC1	I	6.1+8+ (N1, N2, N3, CMR, F or S)	C	2	2	*	*	95		1	no			no	PP, EP, TOX, A	2	27; *see 3.2.3.3
2927	TOXIC LIQUID, CORROSIVE, ORGANIC, N.O.S.	6.1	TC1	II	6.1+8+ (N1, N2, N3, CMR, F or S)	C	2	2	*	*	95		2	no			no	PP, EP, TOX, A	2	27; *see 3.2.3.3
2929	TOXIC LIQUID, FLAMMABLE, ORGANIC, N.O.S.	6.1	TF1	I	6.1+3+ (N1, N2, N3, CMR, F or S)	C	2	2	*	*	95		1	no	T4 $^{3)}$	II B $^{4)}$	yes	PP, EP, EX, TOX, A	2	27; *see 3.2.3.3
2929	TOXIC LIQUID, FLAMMABLE, ORGANIC, N.O.S.	6.1	TF1	I	6.1+3+(N1, N2, N3, CMR, F or S)	C	2	2	*	*	95		1	no	T4 $^{3)}$	II B $^{4)}$ (II B3)	yes	PP, EP, EX, TOX, A	2	27; 44 *see 3.2.3.3

(1) UN No.	(2) Name and description	(3a) Class	(3b) Classification code	(4) Packing group	(5) Dangers	(6) Type of tank vessel	(7) Cargo tank design	(8) Cargo tank type	(9) Cargo tank equipment	(10) Opening pressure of the pressure relief valve/high velocity vent valve, in kPa	(11) Max. degree of filling in %	(12) Relative density at 20 °C	(13) Type of sampling device	(14) Pump room below deck permitted	(15) Temperature class	(16) Explosion group	(17) Anti-explosion protection required	(18) Equipment required	(19) Number of cones/blue lights	(20) Additional requirements/Remarks
3.1.2	3.1.2	2.2	2.2	2.1.1.3	5.2.2 / 3.2.3.1	1.2.1 / 7.2.2.0.1	3.2.3.1 / 1.2.1	3.2.3.1 / 1.2.1	3.2.3.1 / 1.2.1	3.2.3.1 / 1.2.1	7.2.4.21	3.2.3.1	3.2.3.1 / 1.2.1	3.2.3.1 / 1.2.1	1.2.1	1.2.1 / 3.2.3.3	1.2.1 / 3.2.3.3	8.1.5	7.2.5	3.2.3.1
2929	TOXIC LIQUID, FLAMMABLE, ORGANIC, N.O.S.	6.1	TF1	II	6.1+3+(N1, N2, N3, CMR, F or S)	C	2	2	*	*	95		2	no	T4 3)	II B 4)	yes	PP, EP, EX, TOX, A	2	27; *see 3.2.3.3
2929	TOXIC LIQUID, FLAMMABLE, ORGANIC, N.O.S.	6.1	TF1	II	6.1+3+(N1, N2, N3, CMR, F or S)	C	2	2	*	*	95		2	no	T4 3)	II B 4) (II B3)	yes	PP, EP, EX, TOX, A	2	27; 44 *see 3.2.3.3
2935	ETHYL-2-CHLORO-PROPIONATE	3	F1	III	3	C	2	2		30	95	1.08	2	yes	T4 3)	II A	yes	PP, EX, A	0	
2947	ISOPROPYL CHLOROACETATE	3	F1	III	3	C	2	2		30	95	1.09	2	yes	T4 3)	II A	yes	PP, EX, A	0	
2966	THIOGLYCOL	6.1	T1	II	6.1	C	2	2		25	95	1.12	2	no			no	PP, EP, TOX, A	2	
2983	ETHYLENE OXIDE AND PROPYLENE OXIDE MIXTURE, with not more than 30% ethylene oxide	3	FT1	I	3+6.1+un st.	C	1	1	3	35	95	0.85	1	no	T2 12)	II B (II B3)	yes	PP, EP, EX, TOX, A	2	2; 3; 12; 31; 35
2984	HYDROGEN PEROXIDE AQUEOUS SOLUTION with not less than 8%, but less than 20% hydrogen peroxide (stabilized as necessary)	5.1	O1	III	5.1+unst.	C	2	2	2		95	1.06	2	yes			no	PP	0	3; 33
3077	ENVIRONMENTALLY HAZARDOUS SUBSTANCE, SOLID, N.O.S., MOLTEN, (ALKYLAMINE (C12 to C18))	9	M7	III	9+F	N	4	3			95	0.79	3	yes			no	PP	0	7; 17
3079	METHACRYLONITRILE, STABILIZED	6.1	TF1	I	6.1+3+un st.+ N3	C	2	2		45	95	0.8	1	no	T1 12)	II B 4)	yes	PP, EP, EX, TOX, A	2	3; 5

(1) UN No. or substance identification No.	(2) Name and description	(3a) Class	(3b) Classification code	(4) Packing group	(5) Dangers	(6) Type of tank vessel	(7) Cargo tank design	(8) Cargo tank type	(9) Cargo tank equipment	(10) Opening pressure of the pressure relief valve/high velocity vent valve, in kPa	(11) Maximum degree of filling in %	(12) Relative density at 20 °C	(13) Type of sampling device	(14) Pump room below deck permitted	(15) Temperature class	(16) Explosion group	(17) Anti-explosion protection required	(18) Equipment required	(19) Number of cones/blue lights	(20) Additional requirements/Remarks
	3.1.2	3.1.2	2.2	2.1.1.3	5.2.2 / 3.2.3.1	1.2.1 / 7.2.2.0.1	3.2.3.1 / 1.2.1	3.2.3.1 / 1.2.1	3.2.3.1 / 1.2.1	3.2.3.1 / 1.2.1	7.2.4.21	3.2.3.1	3.2.3.1 / 1.2.1	3.2.3.1 / 1.2.1	1.2.1	1.2.1 / 3.2.3.3	1.2.1 / 3.2.3.3	8.1.5	7.2.5	3.2.3.1
3082	ENVIRONMENTALLY HAZARDOUS SUBSTANCE, LIQUID, N.O.S.	9	M6	III	9+(N1, N2, CMR, F or S)	*	*	*	*	*	*		*	yes			no	*	0	22; 27 *see 3.2.3.3
3082	ENVIRONMENTALLY HAZARDOUS SUBSTANCE, LIQUID, N.O.S. (BILGE WATER, FREE OF SLUDGE)	9	M6	III	9+N2+F	N	4	3			97		3	yes			no	PP	0	
3082	ENVIRONMENTALLY HAZARDOUS SUBSTANCE, LIQUID, N.O.S. (BILGE WATER, CONTAINS SLUDGE)	9	M6	III	9+CMR+N1	N	2	3		10	97		3	yes			no	PP, EP, TOX, A	0	45
3082	ENVIRONMENTALLY HAZARDOUS SUBSTANCE, LIQUID, N.O.S. (OIL SLUDGE)	9	M6	III	9+CMR+N1	N	2	3		10	97		3	yes			No	PP, EP, TOX, A	0	45
3082	ENVIRONMENTALLY HAZARDOUS SUBSTANCE; LIQUID, N.O.S. (HEAVY HEATING OIL)	9	M6	III	9+CMR (N1, N2, F or S)	N	2	3		10	97		3	yes			no	PP	0	
3092	1-METHOXY-2-PROPANOL	3	F1	III	3	N	3	2			97	0.92	3	yes	T3	II B (IIB1)	yes	PP, EX, A	0	
3145	ALKYLPHENOLS, LIQUID, N.O.S. (including C2-C12 homologues)	8	C3	II	8+N3	N	4	3			97	0.95	3	yes			no	PP, EP	0	27; 34
3145	ALKYLPHENOLS, LIQUID, N.O.S. (including C2-C12 homologues)	8	C3	III	8+N3	N	4	3			97	0.95	3	yes			no	PP, EP	0	27; 34
3175	SOLIDS CONTAINING FLAMMABLE LIQUID, N.O.S., MOLTEN, having a flash-point up to 60 °C (2- PROPANOL AND DIALKYL-(C12 to C18)-DIMETHYLAMMONIUM CHLORIDE)	4.1	F1	II	4.1	N	3	3	4		95	0.86	3	yes	T2[12]	II A[7]	yes	PP, EX, A	1	7; 17

(1)	(2)	(3a)	(3b)	(4)	(5)	(6)	(7)	(8)	(9)	(10)	(11)	(12)	(13)	(14)	(15)	(16)	(17)	(18)	(19)	(20)
	3.1.2	2.2	2.2	2.1.1.3	5.2.2 / 3.2.3.1	1.2.1 / 7.2.2.0.1	3.2.3.1 / 1.2.1	3.2.3.1 / 1.2.1	3.2.3.1 / 1.2.1	3.2.3.1 / 1.2.1	7.2.4.21	3.2.3.1	3.2.3.1 / 1.2.1	3.2.3.1 / 1.2.1	1.2.1	1.2.1 / 3.2.3.3	1.2.1 / 3.2.3.3	8.1.5	7.2.5	3.2.3.1
3256	ELEVATED TEMPERATURE LIQUID, FLAMMABLE, N.O.S. with flash-point above 60 °C, at or above its flash-point	3	F2	III	3+(N1, N2, N3, CMR, F or S)	*	*	*	*	*	95		*	yes	T4 [3)]	II B [4)]	yes	*	0	7; 17; 27 *see 3.2.3.3
3256	ELEVATED TEMPERATURE LIQUID, FLAMMABLE, N.O.S. with flash-point above 60 °C, at or above its flash-point	3	F2	III	3+(N1, N2, N3, CMR, F or S)	*	*	*	*	*	95		*	yes	T4 [3)]	II B [4)] (II B3)	yes	*	0	7; 17; 27; 44*see 3.2.3.3
3256	ELEVATED TEMPERATURE LIQUID, FLAMMABLE, N.O.S. with flash-point above 60 °C, at or above its flash-point (CARBON BLACK REEDSTOCK) (PYROLYSIS OIL)	3	F2	III	3+F	N	3	3	2		95		3	yes	T1 [12)]	II B	yes	PP, EX, A	0	7; 17
3256	ELEVATED TEMPERATURE LIQUID, FLAMMABLE, N.O.S. with flash-point above 60 °C, at or above its flash-point (PYROLYSIS OIL A)	3	F2	III	3+F	N	3	3	2		95		3	yes	T1 [12)]	II B	yes	PP, EX, A	0	7; 17
3256	ELEVATED TEMPERATURE LIQUID, FLAMMABLE, N.O.S. with flash-point above 60 °C, at or above its flash-point (RESIDUAL OIL)	3	F2	III	3+F	N	3	3	2		95		3	yes	T1 [12)]	II B	yes	PP, EX, A	0	7; 17
3256	ELEVATED TEMPERATURE LIQUID, FLAMMABLE, N.O.S. with flash-point above 60 °C, at or above its flash-point (MIXTURE OF CRUDE NAPHTHALINE)	3	F2	III	3+F	N	3	3	2		95		3	yes	T1 [12)]	II B	yes	PP, EX, A	0	7; 17

(1) UN No. or substance identification No.	(2) Name and description	(3a) Class	(3b) Classification code	(4) Packing group	(5) Dangers	(6) Type of tank vessel	(7) Cargo tank design	(8) Cargo tank type	(9) Cargo tank equipment	(10) Opening pressure of the pressure relief valve/high velocity vent valve, in kPa	(11) Maximum degree of filling in %	(12) Relative density at 20 °C	(13) Type of sampling device	(14) Pump room below deck permitted	(15) Temperature class	(16) Explosion group	(17) Anti-explosion protection required	(18) Equipment required	(19) Number of cones/blue lights	(20) Additional requirements/Remarks
	3.1.2	2.2	2.2	2.1.1.3	5.2.2 / 3.2.3.1	1.2.1 / 7.2.2.0.1	3.2.3.1 / 1.2.1	3.2.3.1 / 1.2.1	3.2.3.1 / 1.2.1	3.2.3.1 / 1.2.1	7.2.4.21	3.2.3.1	3.2.3.1 / 1.2.1	3.2.3.1 / 1.2.1	1.2.1	1.2.1 / 3.2.3.3	1.2.1 / 3.2.3.3	8.1.5	7.2.5	3.2.3.1
3256	ELEVATED TEMPERATURE LIQUID, FLAMMABLE, N.O.S. with flash-point above 60 °C, at or above its flash-point (CREOSOTE OIL)	3	F2	III	3+N1+F	C	2	2	2	10	95		2	yes	T2 12)	II B	yes	PP, EX, A	0	7; 17
3256	ELEVATED TEMPERATURE LIQUID, FLAMMABLE, N.O.S. with flash-point above 60 °C, at or above its flash-point (Low QI Pitch)	3	F2	III	3+N2+CMR+S	N	3	1	4		95	1,1-1,3	3	yes	T2 12)	II B (II B2)	yes	PP, EP, EX, TOX, A	0	7; 17
3257	ELEVATED TEMPERATURE LIQUID, N.O.S. at or above 100 °C and below its flash-point (including molten metals, molten salts, etc.)	9	M9	III	9+(N1, N2, N3, CMR, F or S)	*	*	*	*	*	95		*	yes			no	*	0	7; 17; 20:+115 °C; 22; 24; 25; 27 *see 3.2.3.3
3257	ELEVATED TEMPERATURE LIQUID, N.O.S. at or above 100 °C and below its flash-point (including molten metals, molten salts, etc.)	9	M9	III	9+(N1, N2, N3, CMR, F or S)	*	*	*	*	*	95		*	yes			no	*	0	7; 17; 20:+225 °C; 22; 24; 27 *see 3.2.3.3
3257	ELEVATED TEMPERATURE LIQUID, N.O.S. at or above 100°C and below its flash-point (including molten metals, molten salts, etc.)	9	M9	III	9+(N1, N2, N3, CMR, F or S)	*	*	*	*	*	95		*	yes			no	*	0	7; 17; 20:+250°C; 22; 24; 27 *see 3.2.3.3
3259	AMINES, SOLID, CORROSIVE, N.O.S. (MONOALKYL-(C12 to C18)-AMINE ACETATE, MOLTEN)	8	C8	III	8	N	4	3	2	*	95	0.87	3	yes			no	PP, EP	0	7; 17; 34
3264	CORROSIVE LIQUID, ACIDIC, INORGANIC, N.O.S.	8	C1	I	8+(N1, N2, N3, CMR, F or S)	*	*	*	*	*	*		*	yes			no	*	0	27; 34 *see 3.2.3.3
3264	CORROSIVE LIQUID, ACIDIC, INORGANIC, N.O.S.	8	C1	II	8+(N1, N2, N3, CMR, F or S)	*	*	*	*	*	*		*	yes			no	*	0	27; 34 *see 3.2.3.3

(1)	(2)	(3a)	(3b)	(4)	(5)	(6)	(7)	(8)	(9)	(10)	(11)	(12)	(13)	(14)	(15)	(16)	(17)	(18)	(19)	(20)
UN No. or substance identification No.	Name and description	Class	Classification code	Packing group	Dangers	Type of tank vessel	Cargo tank design	Cargo tank type	Cargo tank equipment	Opening pressure of the pressure relief valve/high velocity vent valve, in kPa	Maximum degree of filling in %	Relative density at 20 °C	Type of sampling device	Pump room below deck permitted	Temperature class	Explosion group	Anti-explosion protection required	Equipment required	Number of cones/blue lights	Additional requirements/Remarks
	3.1.2	2.2	2.2	2.1.1.3	5.2.2 / 3.2.3.1	1.2.1 / 7.2.2.0.1	3.2.3.1 / 1.2.1	3.2.3.1 / 1.2.1	3.2.3.1 / 1.2.1	3.2.3.1 / 1.2.1	7.2.4.21	3.2.3.1	3.2.3.1 / 1.2.1	3.2.3.1 / 1.2.1	1.2.1	1.2.1 / 3.2.3.3	1.2.1 / 3.2.3.3	8.1.5	7.2.5	3.2.1
3264	CORROSIVE LIQUID, ACIDIC, INORGANIC, N.O.S.	8	C1	III	8+(N1, N2, N3, CMR, F or S)	*	*	*	*	*	*		*	yes			no	*	0	27; 34 *see 3.2.3.3
3264	CORROSIVE LIQUID, ACIDIC, INORGANIC, N.O.S. (AQUEOUS SOLUTION OF PHOSPHORIC ACID AND NITRIC ACID)	8	C1	I	8	N	2	3		10	97		3	yes			no	PP, EP	0	34
3264	CORROSIVE LIQUID, ACIDIC, INORGANIC, N.O.S. (AQUEOUS SOLUTION OF PHOSPHORIC ACID AND NITRIC ACID)	8	C1	II	8	N	4	3			97		3	yes			no	PP, EP	0	34
3264	CORROSIVE LIQUID, ACIDIC, INORGANIC, N.O.S. (AQUEOUS SOLUTION OF PHOSPHORIC ACID AND NITRIC ACID)	8	C1	III	8	N	4	3			97		3	yes			no	PP, EP	0	34
3265	CORROSIVE LIQUID, ACIDIC, ORGANIC, N.O.S.	8	C3	I	8+(N1, N2, N3, CMR, F or S)	*	*	*	*	*	*		*	yes			no	*	0	27; 34 *see 3.2.3.3
3265	CORROSIVE LIQUID, ACIDIC, ORGANIC, N.O.S.	8	C3	II	8+(N1, N2, N3, CMR, F or S)	*	*	*	*	*	*		*	yes			no	*	0	27; 34 *see 3.2.3.3
3265	CORROSIVE LIQUID, ACIDIC, ORGANIC, N.O.S.	8	C3	III	8+(N1, N2, N3, CMR, F or S)	*	*	*	*	*	*		*	yes			no	*	0	27; 34 *see 3.2.3.3
3266	CORROSIVE LIQUID, BASIC, INORGANIC, N.O.S.	8	C5	I	8+(N1, N2, N3, CMR, F or S)	*	*	*	*	*	*		*	yes			no	*	0	27; 34 *see 3.2.3.3

(1)	(2)	(3a)	(3b)	(4)	(5)	(6)	(7)	(8)	(9)	(10)	(11)	(12)	(13)	(14)	(15)	(16)	(17)	(18)	(19)	(20)
UN No. or substance identification No.	Name and description	Class	Classification code	Packing group	Dangers	Type of tank vessel	Cargo tank design	Cargo tank type	Cargo tank equipment	Opening pressure of the pressure relief valve/high velocity vent valve, in kPa	Maximum degree of filling in %	Relative density at 20 °C	Type of sampling device	Pump room below deck permitted	Temperature class	Explosion group	Anti-explosion protection required	Equipment required	Number of cones/blue lights	Additional requirements/Remarks
3.1.2	3.1.2	2.2	2.2	2.1.1.3	5.2.2 / 3.2.3.1	1.2.1 / 7.2.2.0.1	3.2.3.1 / 1.2.1	3.2.3.1 / 1.2.1	3.2.3.1 / 1.2.1	3.2.3.1 / 1.2.1	7.2.4.21	3.2.3.1	3.2.3.1 / 1.2.1	3.2.3.1 / 1.2.1	1.2.1	1.2.1 / 3.2.3.3	1.2.1 / 3.2.3.3	8.1.5	7.2.5	3.2.3.1
3266	CORROSIVE LIQUID, BASIC, INORGANIC, N.O.S.	8	C5	II	8+(N1, N2, N3, CMR, F or S)	*	*	*	*	*	*		*	yes			no	*	0	27; 34 *see 3.2.3.3
3266	CORROSIVE LIQUID, BASIC, INORGANIC, N.O.S.	8	C5	III	8+(N1, N2, N3, CMR, F or S)	*	*	*	*	*	*		*	yes			no	*	0	27; 34 *see 3.2.3.3
3267	CORROSIVE LIQUID, BASIC, ORGANIC, N.O.S.	8	C7	I	8+(N1, N2, N3, CMR, F or S)	*	*	*	*	*	*		*	yes			no	*	0	27; 34 *see 3.2.3.3
3267	CORROSIVE LIQUID, BASIC, ORGANIC, N.O.S.	8	C7	II	8+(N1, N2, N3, CMR, F or S)	*	*	*	*	*	*		*	yes			no	*	0	27; 34 *see 3.2.3.3
3267	CORROSIVE LIQUID, BASIC, ORGANIC, N.O.S.	8	C7	III	8+(N1, N2, N3, CMR, F or S)	*	*	*	*	*	*		*	yes			no	*	0	27; 34 *see 3.2.3.3
3271	ETHERS, N.O.S.	3	F1	II	3+(N1, N2, N3, CMR, F or S)	*	*	*	*	*	*		*	yes	T4 [3]	II B[4]	yes	*	1	14, 27; *see 3.2.3.3
3271	ETHERS, N.O.S.	3	F1	II	3+(N1, N2, N3, CMR, F or S)	*	*	*	*	*	*		*	yes	T4 [3]	II B[4] (II B3)	yes	*	1	14, 27; 44 *see 3.2.3.3
3271	ETHERS, N.O.S. (tert-AMYL-METHYL ETHER)	3	F1	II	3+N1	C	2	2	3	50	95	0.77	2	yes	T2 [12]	II B[4]	yes	PP, EX, A	1	

-234-

(1)	(2)	(3a)	(3b)	(4)	(5)	(6)	(7)	(8)	(9)	(10)	(11)	(12)	(13)	(14)	(15)	(16)	(17)	(18)	(19)	(20)
UN No. or substance identification No.	Name and description	Class	Classification code	Packing group	Dangers	Type of tank vessel	Cargo tank design	Cargo tank type	Cargo tank equipment	Opening pressure of the pressure relief valve/high velocity vent valve, in kPa	Maximum degree of filling in %	Relative density at 20 °C	Type of sampling device	Pump room below deck permitted	Temperature class	Explosion group	Anti-explosion protection required	Equipment required	Number of cones/blue lights	Additional requirements/Remarks
	3.1.2	2.2	2.2	2.1.1.3	5.2.2 / 3.2.3.1	1.2.1 / 7.2.2.0.1	3.2.3.1 / 1.2.1	3.2.3.1 / 1.2.1	3.2.3.1 / 1.2.1	3.2.3.1 / 1.2.1	7.2.4.21	3.2.3.1	3.2.3.1 / 1.2.1	3.2.3.1 / 1.2.1	1.2.1	1.2.1 / 3.2.3.3	1.2.1 / 3.2.3.3	8.1.5	7.2.5	3.2.3.1
3271	ETHERS, N.O.S.	3	F1	III	3+(N1, N2, N3, CMR, F or S)	*	*	*	*	*	*		*	yes	T4 3)	II B4)	yes	*	0	14, 27 *see 3.2.3.3
3271	ETHERS, N.O.S.	3	F1	III	3+(N1, N2, N3, CMR, F or S)	*	*	*	*	*	*		*	yes	T4 3)	II B4) (II B3)	yes	*	0	14; 27; 44 *see 3.2.3.3
3272	ESTERS, N.O.S.	3	F1	II	3+(N1, N2, N3, CMR, F or S)	*	*	*	*	*	*		*	yes	T2 12)	II B4)	yes	*	1	14, 27; *see 3.2.3.3
3272	ESTERS, N.O.S.	3	F1	II	3+(N1, N2, N3, CMR, F or S)	*	*	*	*	*	*		*	yes	T2 12)	II B4) (II B3)	yes	*	1	14, 27, 44 *see 3.2.3.3
3272	ESTERS, N.O.S.	3	F1	III	3+(N1, N2, N3, CMR, F or S)	*	*	*	*	*	*		*	yes	T4 3)	II B4)	yes	*	0	14, 27 *see 3.2.3.3
3272	ESTERS, N.O.S.	3	F1	III	3+(N1, N2, N3, CMR, F or S)	*	*	*	*	*	*		*	yes	T4 3)	II B4) (II B3)	yes	*	0	14; 27; 44 *see 3.2.3.3
3276	NITRILES, TOXIC, LIQUID, N.O.S. (2-METHYLGLUTARONITRILE)	6.1	T1	II	6.1	C	2	2	*	10	95	0.95	2	no			no	PP, EP, TOX, A	2	
3286	FLAMMABLE LIQUID, TOXIC, CORROSIVE, N.O.S.	3	FTC	I	3+6.1+8+ (N1, N2, N3, CMR, F or S)	C	1	1	*	*	95		1	no	T4 3)	II B4)	yes	PP, EP, EX, TOX, A	2	27; *see 3.2.3.3

(1) UN No. or substance identification No.	(2) Name and description	(3a) Class	(3b) Classification code	(4) Packing group	(5) Dangers	(6) Type of tank vessel	(7) Cargo tank design	(8) Cargo tank type	(9) Cargo tank equipment	(10) Opening pressure of the pressure relief valve/high velocity vent valve, in kPa	(11) Maximum degree of filling in %	(12) Relative density at 20 °C	(13) Type of sampling device	(14) Pump room below deck permitted	(15) Temperature class	(16) Explosion group	(17) Anti-explosion protection required	(18) Equipment required	(19) Number of cones/blue lights	(20) Additional requirements/Remarks
3286	FLAMMABLE LIQUID, TOXIC, CORROSIVE, N.O.S.	3	FTC	I	3+6.1+8+ (N1, N2, N3, CMR, F or S)	C	1	1	*	*	95		1	no	T4 [3]	II B [4] (II B3)	yes	PP, EP, EX, TOX, A	2	27; 44 *see 3.2.3.3
3286	FLAMMABLE LIQUID, TOXIC, CORROSIVE, N.O.S.	3	FTC	I	3+6.1+8+ (N1, N2, N3, CMR, F or S)	C	2	2	*	*	95		1	no	T4 [3]	II B [4]	yes	PP, EP, EX, TOX, A	2	27; *see 3.2.3.3
3286	FLAMMABLE LIQUID, TOXIC, CORROSIVE, N.O.S.	3	FTC	I	3+6.1+8+ (N1, N2, N3, CMR, F or S)	C	2	2	*	*	95		1	no	T4 [3]	II B [4] (II B3)	yes	PP, EP, EX, TOX, A	2	27; 44 *see 3.2.3.3
3286	FLAMMABLE LIQUID, TOXIC, CORROSIVE, N.O.S.	3	FTC	II	3+6.1+8+ (N1, N2, N3, CMR, F or S)	C	2	2	*	*	95		2	no	T4 [3]	II B [4]	yes	PP, EP, EX, TOX, A	2	27; *see 3.2.3.3
3286	FLAMMABLE LIQUID, TOXIC, CORROSIVE, N.O.S.	3	FTC	II	3+6.1+8+ (N1, N2, N3, CMR, F or S)	C	2	2	*	*	95		2	no	T4 [3]	II B [4] (II B3)	yes	PP, EP, EX, TOX, A	2	27; 44 *see 3.2.3.3
3287	TOXIC LIQUID, INORGANIC, N.O.S.	6.1	T4	I	6.1+(N1, N2, N3, CMR, F or S)	C	2	2	*	*	95		1	no			no	PP, EP, TOX, A	2	27; *see 3.2.3.3
3287	TOXIC LIQUID, INORGANIC, N.O.S.	6.1	T4	II	6.1+(N1, N2, N3, CMR, F or S)	C	2	2	*	*	95		2	no			no	PP, EP, TOX, A	2	27; *see 3.2.3.3

(1)	(2)	(3a)	(3b)	(4)	(5)	(6)	(7)	(8)	(9)	(10)	(11)	(12)	(13)	(14)	(15)	(16)	(17)	(18)	(19)	(20)
UN No. or substance identification No.	Name and description	Class	Classification code	Packing group	Dangers	Type of tank vessel	Cargo tank design	Cargo tank type	Cargo tank equipment	Opening pressure of the pressure relief valve/high velocity vent valve, in kPa	Maximum degree of filling in %	Relative density at 20 °C	Type of sampling device	Pump room below deck permitted	Temperature class	Explosion group	Anti-explosion protection required	Equipment required	Number of cones/blue lights	Additional requirements/Remarks
	3.1.2	2.2	2.2	2.1.1.3	5.2.2/ 3.2.3.1	1.2.1/ 7.2.2.0.1	3.2.3.1/ 1.2.1	3.2.3.1/ 1.2.1	3.2.3.1/ 1.2.1	3.2.3.1/ 1.2.1	7.2.4.21	3.2.3.1	3.2.3.1/ 1.2.1	3.2.3.1/ 1.2.1	1.2.1	1.2.1/ 3.2.3.3	1.2.1/ 3.2.3.3	8.1.5	7.2.5	3.2.3.1
3287	TOXIC LIQUID, INORGANIC, N.O.S.	6.1	T4	III	6.1+(N1, N2, N3, CMR, F or S)	C	2	2	*	*	95		2	no			no	PP, EP, TOX, A	0	27; *see 3.2.3.3
3287	TOXIC LIQUID, INORGANIC, N.O.S. (SODIUM DICHROMATE SOLUTION)	6.1	T4	III	6.1+CMR	C	2	2		30	95	1.68	2	no			no	PP, EP, TOX, A	0	
3289	TOXIC LIQUID, CORROSIVE, INORGANIC, N.O.S. BOILING POINT > 115 °C	6.1	TC3	I	6.1+8+ (N1, N2, N3, CMR, F or S)	C	2	2	*	*	95		1	no			no	PP, EP, TOX, A	2	27; *see 3.2.3.3
3289	TOXIC LIQUID, CORROSIVE, INORGANIC, N.O.S. BOILING POINT > 115 °C	6.1	TC3	II	6.1+8+ (N1, N2, N3, CMR, F or S)	C	2	2	*	*	95		2	no			no	PP, EP, TOX, A	2	27; *see 3.2.3.3
3295	HYDROCARBONS, LIQUID, N.O.S.	3	F1	I	3+(N1, N2, N3, CMR, F)	*	*	*	*	*	*		*	yes	T4[3]	II B[4]	yes	*	1	14; 27 *see 3.2.3.3
3295	HYDROCARBONS, LIQUID, N.O.S.	3	F1	I	3+(N1, N2, N3, CMR, F)	*	*	*	*	*	*		*	yes	T4[3]	II B[4] (II B3)	yes	*	1	14; 27; 44 *see 3.2.3.3
3295	HYDROCARBONS, LIQUID, N.O.S.	3	F1	II	3+(N1, N2, N3, CMR, F)	*	*	*	*	*	*		*	yes	T4[3]	II B[4]	yes	*	1	14; 27 *see 3.2.3.3
3295	HYDROCARBONS, LIQUID, N.O.S.	3	F1	II	3+(N1, N2, N3, CMR, F)	*	*	*	*	*	*		*	yes	T4[3]	II B[4] (II B3)	yes	*	1	14; 27; 44 *see 3.2.3.3
3295	HYDROCARBONS, LIQUID, N.O.S.	3	F1	III	3+(N1, N2, N3, CMR, F)	*	*	*	*	*	*		*	yes	T4[3]	II B[4]	yes	*	0	14; 27 *see 3.2.3.3

(1) UN No. or substance identification No.	(2) Name and description	(3a) Class	(3b) Classification code	(4) Packing group	(5) Dangers	(6) Type of tank vessel	(7) Cargo tank design	(8) Cargo tank type	(9) Cargo tank equipment	(10) Opening pressure of the pressure relief valve/high velocity vent valve, in kPa	(11) Maximum degree of filling in %	(12) Relative density at 20 °C	(13) Type of sampling device	(14) Pump room below deck permitted	(15) Temperature class	(16) Explosion group	(17) Anti-explosion protection required	(18) Equipment required	(19) Number of cones/blue lights	(20) Additional requirements/Remarks
	3.1.2	2.2	2.2	2.1.1.3	5.2.2 / 3.2.3.1	1.2.1 / 7.2.2.0.1	3.2.3.1 / 1.2.1	3.2.3.1 / 1.2.1	3.2.3.1 / 1.2.1	3.2.3.1 / 1.2.1	7.2.4.21	3.2.3.1	3.2.3.1 / 1.2.1	3.2.3.1 / 1.2.1	1.2.1	1.2.1 / 3.2.3.3	1.2.1 / 3.2.3.3	8.1.5	7.2.5	3.2.3.1
3295	HYDROCARBONS, LIQUID, N.O.S.	3	F1	III	3+(N1, N2, N3, CMR, F)	*	*	*	*	*	*		*	yes	T4 [3]	II B[4] (II B3)	yes	*	0	14; 27; 44 *see 3.2.3.3
3295	HYDROCARBONS, LIQUID, N.O.S. WITH MORE THAN 10% BENZENE	3	F1	I	3+CMR+ (N1, N2, N3)	C	*	*	*	*	*		*	yes	T4 [3]	II B[4]	yes	*	1	*see 3.2.3.3
3295	HYDROCARBONS, LIQUID, N.O.S. WITH MORE THAN 10% BENZENE	3	F1	I	3+CMR+ (N1, N2, N3)	C	*	*	*	*	*		*	yes	T4 [3]	II B[4] (II B3)	yes	*	1	44 *see 3.2.3.3
3295	HYDROCARBONS, LIQUID, N.O.S. WITH MORE THAN 10% BENZENE	3	F1	II	3+CMR+ (N1, N2, N3)	C	*	*	*	*	*		*	yes	T4 [3]	II B[4]	yes	*	1	*see 3.2.3.3
3295	HYDROCARBONS, LIQUID, N.O.S. WITH MORE THAN 10% BENZENE	3	F1	II	3+CMR+ (N1, N2, N3)	C	*	*	*	*	*		*	yes	T4 [3]	II B[4] (II B3)	yes	*	1	44 *see 3.2.3.3
3295	HYDROCARBONS, LIQUID, N.O.S. WITH MORE THAN 10% BENZENE	3	F1	III	3+CMR+ (N1, N2, N3)	C	*	*	*	*	*		*	yes	T4 [3]	II B[4]	yes	*	0	*see 3.2.3.3
3295	HYDROCARBONS, LIQUID, N.O.S. WITH MORE THAN 10% BENZENE	3	F1	III	3+CMR+ (N1, N2, N3)	C	*	*	*	*	*		*	yes	T4 [3]	II B[4] (II B3)	yes	*	0	44 *see 3.2.3.3
3295	HYDROCARBONS, LIQUID, N.O.S. WITH MORE THAN 10% BENZENE INITIAL BOILING POINT ≤ 60 °C	3	F1	I	3+CMR+ (N1, N2, N3, F)	C	1	1			95		1	yes	T4 [3]	II B[4]	yes	PP, EP, EX, TOX, A	1	
3295	HYDROCARBONS, LIQUID, N.O.S. WITH MORE THAN 10% BENZENE INITIAL BOILING POINT ≤ 60 °C	3	F1	I	3+CMR+ (N1, N2, N3)	C	1	1			95		1	yes	T4 [3]	II B[4] (II B3)	yes	PP, EP, EX, TOX, A	1	44

(1)	(2)	(3a)	(3b)	(4)	(5)	(6)	(7)	(8)	(9)	(10)	(11)	(12)	(13)	(14)	(15)	(16)	(17)	(18)	(19)	(20)
UN No. or substance identification No.	Name and description	Class	Classification code	Packing group	Dangers	Type of tank vessel	Cargo tank design	Cargo tank type	Cargo tank equipment	Opening pressure of the pressure relief valve/high velocity vent valve, in kPa	Maximum degree of filling in %	Relative density at 20 °C	Type of sampling device	Pump room below deck permitted	Temperature class	Explosion group	Anti-explosion protection required	Equipment required	Number of cones/blue lights	Additional requirements/Remarks
	3.1.2	2.2	2.2	2.1.1.3	5.2.2 / 3.2.3.1	1.2.1 / 7.2.2.0.1	3.2.3.1 / 1.2.1	3.2.3.1 / 1.2.1	3.2.3.1 / 1.2.1	3.2.3.1 / 1.2.1	7.2.4.21	3.2.3.1	3.2.3.1 / 1.2.1	3.2.3.1 / 1.2.1	1.2.1	1.2.1 / 3.2.3.3	1.2.1 / 3.2.3.3	8.1.5	7.2.5	3.2.3.1
3295	HYDROCARBONS, LIQUID, N.O.S. WITH MORE THAN 10% BENZENE INITIAL BOILING POINT ≤ 60 °C	3	F1	II	3+CMR+ (N1, N2, N3, F)	C	1	1			95		1	yes	T4³⁾	II B⁴⁾	yes	PP, EP, EX, TOX, A	1	
3295	HYDROCARBONS, LIQUID, N.O.S. WITH MORE THAN 10% BENZENE INITIAL BOILING POINT ≤ 60 °C	3	F1	II	3+CMR+ (N1, N2, N3)	C	1	1			95		1	yes	T4³⁾	II B⁴⁾ (II B3)	yes	PP, EP, EX, TOX, A	1	44
3295	HYDROCARBONS, LIQUID, N.O.S. WITH MORE THAN 10% BENZENE INITIAL BOILING POINT ≤ 60 °C	3	F1	III	3+CMR+ (N1, N2, N3, F)	C	1	1			95		1	yes	T4³⁾	II B⁴⁾	yes	PP, EP, EX, TOX, A	0	
3295	HYDROCARBONS, LIQUID, N.O.S. WITH MORE THAN 10% BENZENE INITIAL BOILING POINT ≤ 60 °C	3	F1	III	3+CMR+ (N1, N2, N3)	C	1	1			95		1	yes	T4³⁾	II B⁴⁾ (II B3)	yes	PP, EP, EX, TOX, A	0	44
3295	HYDROCARBONS, LIQUID, N.O.S. WITH MORE THAN 10% BENZENE 60 °C < INITIAL BOILING POINT ≤ 85 °C	3	F1	II	3+CMR+ (N1, N2, N3, F)	C	2	2	3	50	95		2	yes	T4³⁾	II B⁴⁾	yes	PP, EP, EX, TOX, A	1	23; 38
3295	HYDROCARBONS, LIQUID, N.O.S. WITH MORE THAN 10% BENZENE 60 °C < INITIAL BOILING POINT ≤ 85 °C	3	F1	II	3+CMR+ (N1, N2, N3)	C	2	2	3	50	95		2	yes	T4³⁾	II B⁴⁾ (II B3)	yes	PP, EP, EX, TOX, A	1	23; 38; 44
3295	HYDROCARBONS, LIQUID, N.O.S. WITH MORE THAN 10% BENZENE 60 °C < INITIAL BOILING POINT ≤ 85 °C	3	F1	III	3+CMR+ (N1, N2, N3, F)	C	2	2	3	50	95		2	yes	T4³⁾	II B⁴⁾	yes	PP, EP, EX, TOX, A	0	23; 38
3295	HYDROCARBONS, LIQUID, N.O.S. WITH MORE THAN 10% BENZENE 60 °C < INITIAL BOILING POINT ≤ 85 °C	3	F1	III	3+CMR+ (N1, N2, N3)	C	2	2	3	50	95		2	yes	T4³⁾	II B⁴⁾ (II B3)	yes	PP, EP, EX, TOX, A	0	23; 38; 44

(1)	(2)	(3a)	(3b)	(4)	(5)	(6)	(7)	(8)	(9)	(10)	(11)	(12)	(13)	(14)	(15)	(16)	(17)	(18)	(19)	(20)
UN No. or substance identification No.	Name and description	Class	Classification code	Packing group	Dangers	Type of tank vessel	Cargo tank design	Cargo tank type	Cargo tank equipment	Opening pressure of the pressure relief valve/high velocity vent valve, in kPa	Maximum degree of filling in %	Relative density at 20 °C	Type of sampling device	Pump room below deck permitted	Temperature class	Explosion group	Anti-explosion protection required	Equipment required	Number of cones/blue lights	Additional requirements/Remarks
3.1.2	3.1.2	2.2	2.2	2.1.1.3	5.2.2 / 3.2.3.1	1.2.1 / 7.2.2.0.1	3.2.3.1 / 1.2.1	3.2.3.1 / 1.2.1	3.2.3.1 / 1.2.1	3.2.3.1 / 1.2.1	7.2.4.21	3.2.3.1	3.2.3.1 / 1.2.1	3.2.3.1 / 1.2.1	1.2.1	1.2.1 / 3.2.3.3	1.2.1 / 3.2.3.3	8.1.5	7.2.5	3.2.3.1
3295	HYDROCARBONS, LIQUID, N.O.S. WITH MORE THAN 10% BENZENE 85 °C < INITIAL BOILING POINT ≤115°C	3	F1	II	3+CMR+ (N1, N2, N3, F)	C	2	2		50	95		2	yes	T4³⁾	II B⁴⁾	yes	PP, EP, EX, TOX, A	1	
3295	HYDROCARBONS, LIQUID, N.O.S. WITH MORE THAN 10% BENZENE 85 °C < INITIAL BOILING POINT ≤115°C	3	F1	II	3+CMR+ (N1, N2, N3)	C	2	2		50	95		2	yes	T4³⁾	II B⁴⁾ (II B3)	yes	PP, EP, EX, TOX, A	1	44
3295	HYDROCARBONS, LIQUID, N.O.S. WITH MORE THAN 10% BENZENE 85 °C < INITIAL BOILING POINT ≤115°C	3	F1	III	3+CMR+ (N1, N2, N3, F)	C	2	2		50	95		2	yes	T4³⁾	II B⁴⁾	yes	PP, EP, EX, TOX, A	0	
3295	HYDROCARBONS, LIQUID, N.O.S. WITH MORE THAN 10% BENZENE 85 °C < INITIAL BOILING POINT ≤115°C	3	F1	III	3+CMR+ (N1, N2, N3)	C	2	2		50	95		2	yes	T4³⁾	II B⁴⁾ (II B3)	yes	PP, EP, EX, TOX, A	0	44
3295	HYDROCARBONS, LIQUID, N.O.S. WITH MORE THAN 10% BENZENE INITIAL BOILING POINT > 115°C	3	F1	II	3+CMR+ (N1, N2, N3, F)	C	2	2		35	95		2	yes	T4³⁾	II B⁴⁾	yes	PP, EP, EX, TOX, A	1	
3295	HYDROCARBONS, LIQUID, N.O.S. WITH MORE THAN 10% BENZENE INITIAL BOILING POINT > 115°C	3	F1	II	3+CMR+ (N1, N2, N3)	C	2	2		35	95		2	yes	T4³⁾	II B⁴⁾ (II B3)	yes	PP, EP, EX, TOX, A	1	44
3295	HYDROCARBONS, LIQUID, N.O.S. WITH MORE THAN 10% BENZENE INITIAL BOILING POINT > 115 °C	3	F1	III	3+CMR+ (N1, N2, N3, F)	C	2	2		35	95		2	yes	T4³⁾	II B⁴⁾	yes	PP, EP, EX, TOX, A	0	
3295	HYDROCARBONS, LIQUID, N.O.S. WITH MORE THAN 10% BENZENE INITIAL BOILING POINT > 115°C	3	F1	III	3+CMR+ (N1, N2, N3)	C	2	2		35	95		2	yes	T4³⁾	II B⁴⁾ (II B3)	yes	PP, EP, EX, TOX, A	0	44

(1) UN No. or substance identification No.	(2) Name and description	(3a) Class	(3b) Classification code	(4) Packing group	(5) Dangers	(6) Type of tank vessel	(7) Cargo tank design	(8) Cargo tank type	(9) Cargo tank equipment	(10) Opening pressure of the pressure relief valve/high velocity vent valve, in kPa	(11) Maximum degree of filling in %	(12) Relative density at 20 °C	(13) Type of sampling device	(14) Pump room below deck permitted	(15) Temperature class	(16) Explosion group	(17) Anti-explosion protection required	(18) Equipment required	(19) Number of cones/blue lights	(20) Additional requirements/Remarks
		2.2	2.2	2.1.1.3	5.2.2 / 3.2.3.1	1.2.1 / 7.2.2.0.1	3.2.3.1 / 1.2.1	3.2.3.1 / 1.2.1	3.2.3.1 / 1.2.1	3.2.3.1 / 1.2.1	7.2.4.21	3.2.3.1	3.2.3.1 / 1.2.1	3.2.3.1 / 1.2.1	1.2.1	1.2.1 / 3.2.3.3	1.2.1 / 3.2.3.3	8.1.5	7.2.5	3.2.3.1
3295	HYDROCARBONS, LIQUID, N.O.S. CONTAINING ISOPRENE AND PENTADIENE, STABILIZED	3	F1	I	3+inst.+N2+CMR	C	2	2	3	50	95	0,678	1	yes	T4³⁾	II B⁴⁾	yes	PP, EP, EX, TOX, A	1	3
3295	HYDROCARBONS, LIQUID, N.O.S. CONTAINING ISOPRENE AND PENTADIENE, STABILIZED	3	F1	I	3+inst.+N2+CMR	C	2	2	3	50	95	0,678	1	yes	T4³⁾	II B⁴⁾ (II B3)	yes	PP, EX, A	1	3; 44
3295	HYDROCARBONS, LIQUID, N.O.S. (1-OCTEN)	3	F1	II	3+N2+F	N	2	3		10	97	0,71	3	yes	T3	II B⁴⁾	yes	PP, EX, A	1	14
3295	HYDROCARBONS, LIQUID, N.O.S. (POLYCYCLIC AROMATIC HYDOCARBONS MIXTURE)	3	F1	III	3+CMR+F	N	2	3	3	10	97	1,08	3	yes	T1¹²⁾	II A	yes	PP, EP, EX, TOX, A	0	14
3412	FORMIC ACID with not less than 10% but not more than 85% acid by mass	8	C3	II	8+N3	N	2	3		10	97	1.22	3	yes	T1¹²⁾	II A	yes	PP, EP, EX, A	0	6; +12 °C; 17; 34
3412	FORMIC ACID with not less than 5% but less than 10% acid by mass	8	C3	III	8	N	2	3		10	97	1.22	3	yes	T1¹²⁾	II A	yes	PP, EP, EX, A	0	6; +12 °C; 17; 34
3426	ACRYLAMIDE, SOLUTION	6.1	T1	III	6.1	C	2	2		30	95	1.03	2	no	T1¹²⁾	II A	no	PP, EP, TOX, A	0	3; 5; 16
3429	CHLOROTOLUIDINES, LIQUID	6.1	T1	III	6.1+S	C	2	2		25	95	1.15	2	no	T1¹²⁾	II A⁷⁾	yes	PP, EP, EX, TOX, A	0	6; +6 °C; 17;
3446	NITROTOLUENES, SOLID, MOLTEN (p-NITROTOLUENE)	6.1	T2	II	6.1+N2+S	C	2	2	2	25	95	1.16	2	no	T2¹²⁾	II B (II B3¹⁴⁾)	yes	PP, EP, EX, TOX, A	2	7; 17
3446	NITROTOLUENES, SOLID, MOLTEN (p-NITROTOLUENE)	6.1	T2	II	6.1+N2+S	C	2	1	4	25	95	1.16	2	no			no	PP, EP, TOX, A	2	7; 17; 20: +88 °C; 26
3451	TOLUIDINES, SOLID, MOLTEN (p-TOLUIDINE)	6.1	T2	II	6.1+NI	C	2	2	2	25	95	1.05	2	no	T1¹²⁾	II A⁸⁾	yes	PP, EP, EX, TOX, A	2	7; 17

-241-

(1) UN No. or substance identification No.	(2) Name and description	(3a) Class	(3b) Classification code	(4) Packing group	(5) Dangers	(6) Type of tank vessel	(7) Cargo tank design	(8) Cargo tank type	(9) Cargo tank equipment	(10) Opening pressure of the pressure relief valve/high velocity vent valve, in kPa	(11) Maximum degree of filling in %	(12) Relative density at 20 °C	(13) Type of sampling device	(14) Pump room below deck permitted	(15) Temperature class	(16) Explosion group	(17) Anti-explosion protection required	(18) Equipment required	(19) Number of cones/blue lights	(20) Additional requirements/Remarks
	3.1.2	2.2	2.2	2.1.1.3	5.2.2 / 3.2.1	1.2.1 / 7.2.2.0.1	3.2.3.1 / 1.2.1	3.2.3.1 / 1.2.1	3.2.3.1 / 1.2.1	3.2.3.1 / 1.2.1	7.2.4.21	3.2.3.1	3.2.3.1 / 1.2.1	3.2.3.1 / 1.2.1	1.2.1	1.2.1 / 3.2.3.3	1.2.1 / 3.2.3.3	8.1.5	7.2.5	3.2.1
3451	TOLUIDINES, SOLID, MOLTEN (p-TOLUIDINE)	6.1	T2	II	6.1+N1	C	2	2	4	25	95	1.05	2	no			no	PP, EP, TOX, A	2	7; 17; 20: +60 °C
3455	CRESOLS, SOLID, MOLTEN	6.1	TC2	II	6.1+8+N3	C	2	2	2	25	95	1,03 - 1,05	2	no	T1 [12]	II A [8]	yes	PP, EP, EX, TOX, A	2	7; 17
3455	CRESOLS, SOLID, MOLTEN	6.1	TC2	II	6.1+8+N3	C	2	2	4	25	95	1,03 - 1,05	2	no			no	PP, EP, TOX, A	2	7; 17; 20: +66 °C
3463	PROPIONIC ACID with not less than 90% acid by mass	8	CF1	II	8+3+N3	N	3	3	3		97	0.99	3	yes	T1 [12]	II A [7]	yes	PP, EP, EX, A	1	34
3475	ETHANOL AND GASOLINE MIXTURE or ETHANOL AND MOTOR SPIRIT MIXTURE or ETHANOL AND PETROL MIXTURE, with more than 10% but not more than 90% ethanol	3	F1	II	3+N2+C MR+F	N	2	3	3	10	97	0.69 – 0.78 [10]	3	yes	T3	II A	yes	PP, EP, EX, TOX, A	1	
3475	ETHANOL AND GASOLINE MIXTURE or ETHANOL AND MOTOR SPIRIT MIXTURE or ETHANOL AND PETROL MIXTURE, with more than 90% ethanol	3	F1	II	3+N2+C MR+F	N	2	3	3	10	97	0.78 – 0.79 [10]	3	yes	T2 [12]	II B (II B1)	yes	PP, EP, EX, TOX, A	1	
3494	PETROLEUM SOUR CRUDE OIL, FLAMMABLE, TOXIC	3	FT1	I	3+6.1+(N1, N2, N3, CMR, F)	C	*	*	*	*	95		1	no	T4 [3]	II B [4]	yes	PP, EP, EX, TOX, A	2	14 *see 3.2.3.3
3494	PETROLEUM SOUR CRUDE OIL, FLAMMABLE, TOXIC	3	FT1	I	3+6.1+(N1, N2, N3, CMR, F)	C	*	*	*	*	95		1	no	T4 [3]	II B [4] (II B3)	yes	PP, EP, EX, TOX, A	2	14; 44 * see 3.2.3.3

(1) UN No. or substance identification No.	(2) Name and description	(3a) Class	(3b) Classification code	(4) Packing group	(5) Dangers	(6) Type of tank vessel	(7) Cargo tank design	(8) Cargo tank type	(9) Cargo tank equipment	(10) Opening pressure of the pressure relief valve/high velocity vent valve, in kPa	(11) Maximum degree of filling in %	(12) Relative density at 20 °C	(13) Type of sampling device	(14) Pump room below deck permitted	(15) Temperature class	(16) Explosion group	(17) Anti-explosion protection required	(18) Equipment required	(19) Number of cones/blue lights	(20) Additional requirements/Remarks
	3.1.2	2.2	2.2	2.1.1.3	5.2.2 / 3.2.3.1	1.2.1 / 7.2.2.0.1	3.2.3.1 / 1.2.1	3.2.3.1 / 1.2.1	3.2.3.1 / 1.2.1	3.2.3.1 / 1.2.1	7.2.4.21	3.2.3.1	3.2.3.1 / 1.2.1	3.2.3.1 / 1.2.1	1.2.1	1.2.1 / 3.2.3.3	1.2.1 / 3.2.3.3	8.1.5	7.2.5	3.2.3.1
3494	PETROLEUM SOUR CRUDE OIL, FLAMMABLE, TOXIC	3	FT1	II	3+6.1+(N1, N2, N3, CMR, F)	C	*	*	*	*	95		2	no	T4³⁾	II B⁴⁾	yes	PP, EP, EX, TOX, A	2	14 *see 3.2.3.3
3494	PETROLEUM SOUR CRUDE OIL, FLAMMABLE, TOXIC	3	FT1	II	3+6.1+(N1, N2, N3, CMR, F)	C	*	*	*	*	95		2	no	T4³⁾	II B⁴⁾ (II B3)	yes	PP, EP, EX, TOX, A	2	14; 44 *see 3.2.3.3
3494	PETROLEUM SOUR CRUDE OIL, FLAMMABLE, TOXIC	3	FT1	III	3+6.1+(N1, N2, N3, CMR, F)	C	*	*	*	*	95		2	no	T4³⁾	II B⁴⁾	yes	PP, EP, EX, TOX, A	0	14 *see 3.2.3.3
3494	PETROLEUM SOUR CRUDE OIL, FLAMMABLE, TOXIC	3	FT1	III	3+6.1+(N1, N2, N3, CMR, F)	C	*	*	*	*	95		2	no	T4³⁾	II B⁴⁾ (II B3)	yes	PP, EP, EX, TOX, A	0	14; 44 *see 3.2.3.3
9000	AMMONIA, DEEPLY REFRIGERATED	2	3TC		2.1+2.3+8+N1	G	1	1	1; 3		95		1	no	T1¹²⁾	II A	yes	PP, EP, EX, TOX, A	2	1; 2; 31
9000	AMMONIA, ANHYDROUS, DEEPLY REFRIGERATED	2	3TC		2.1+2.3+8+N1	G	2	4	1; 3		95		1	no	T1¹²⁾	II A	yes	PP, EP, EX, TOX, A	2	1; 2; 31
9001	SUBSTANCE WITH A FLASHPOINT ABOVE 60 °C, HEATED within a range of 15 K below the flashpoint	3	F4		3+(N1, N2, N3, CMR, F or S)	*	*	*	*	*	*		*	yes	T4³⁾	II B⁴⁾	yes	*	0	27 *see 3.2.3.3
9001	SUBSTANCE WITH A FLASHPOINT ABOVE 60 °C, HEATED within a range of 15 K below the flashpoint	3	F4		3+(N1, N2, N3, CMR, F or S)	*	*	*	*	*	*		*	yes	T4³⁾	II B⁴⁾ (II B3)	yes	*	0	27; 44 *see 3.2.3.3

(1)	(2)	(3a)	(3b)	(4)	(5)	(6)	(7)	(8)	(9)	(10)	(11)	(12)	(13)	(14)	(15)	(16)	(17)	(18)	(19)	(20)
UN No. or substance identification No.	Name and description	Class	Classification code	Packing group	Dangers	Type of tank vessel	Cargo tank design	Cargo tank type	Cargo tank equipment	Opening pressure of the pressure relief valve/high velocity vent valve, in kPa	Maximum degree of filling in %	Relative density at 20 °C	Type of sampling device	Pump room below deck permitted	Temperature class	Explosion group	Anti-explosion protection required	Equipment required	Number of cones/blue lights	Additional requirements/Remarks
	3.1.2	2.2	2.2	2.1.1.3	5.2.2 / 3.2.3.1	1.2.1 / 7.2.2.0.1	3.2.3.1 / 1.2.1	3.2.3.1 / 1.2.1	3.2.3.1 / 1.2.1	3.2.3.1 / 1.2.1	7.2.4.21	3.2.3.1	3.2.3.1 / 1.2.1	3.2.3.1 / 1.2.1	1.2.1	1.2.1 / 3.2.3.3	1.2.1 / 3.2.3.3	8.1.5	7.2.5	3.2.3.1
9002	SUBSTANCES HAVING A SELF-IGNITION TEMPERATURE ≤ 200 °C, N.O.S.	3	F5		3+(N1, N2, N3, CMR, F or S)	C	1	1	*	*	95		1	yes	T4	II B[4]	yes	*	0	27 *see 3.2.3.3
9002	SUBSTANCES HAVING A SELF-IGNITION TEMPERATURE ≤ 200 °C, N.O.S.	3	F5		3+(N1, N2, N3, CMR, F or S)	C	1	1	*	*	95		1	yes	T4	II B[4] (II B3)	yes	*	0	27; 44 *see 3.2.3.3
9003	SUBSTANCES WITH A FLASH-POINT ABOVE 60 °C BUT NOT MORE THAN 100 °C which are not affected to another class	9	M12		9+(N1, N2, N3, CMR, F or S)	*	*	*	*	*	*		*	yes			no	*	0	27 *see 3.2.3.3
9003	SUBSTANCES WITH A FLASH-POINT ABOVE 60 °C BUT NOT MORE THAN 100 °C which are not affected to another class (ETHYLENE GLYCOL MONOBUTYL ETHER)	9	M12		9+N3+F	N	4	3			97	0.9	3	yes			no	PP	0	
9003	SUBSTANCES WITH A FLASH-POINT ABOVE 60 °C BUT NOT MORE THAN 100 °C which are not affected to another class (2-ETHYLHEXYLACRYLATE)	9	M12		9+N3+F	N	4	3			97	0.89	3	yes			no	PP	0	3; 5; 16;
9004	DIPHENYLMETHANE-4,4'-DIISOCYANATE	9	M12		S	N	2	3	4	10	95	1,21[11]	3	yes			no	PP	0	7; 8; 17; 19
9005	ENVIRONMENTALLY HAZARDOUS SUBSTANCE, SOLID, N.O.S., MOLTEN	9	M12		9+(N2, N3, CMR, F or S)	*	*	*	*	*	95		*	yes			no	*	0	27 *see 3.2.3.3

UN No. or substance identification No.	Name and description	Class	Classification code	Packing group	Dangers	Type of tank vessel	Cargo tank design	Cargo tank type	Cargo tank equipment	Opening pressure of the pressure relief valve/high velocity vent valve, in kPa	Maximum degree of filling in %	Relative density at 20 °C	Type of sampling device	Pump room below deck permitted	Temperature class	Explosion group	Anti-explosion protection required	Equipment required	Number of cones/blue lights	Additional requirements/Remarks
(1)	(2)	(3a)	(3b)	(4)	(5)	(6)	(7)	(8)	(9)	(10)	(11)	(12)	(13)	(14)	(15)	(16)	(17)	(18)	(19)	(20)
	3.1.2	2.2	2.2	2.1.1.3	5.2.2 / 3.2.3.1	1.2.1 / 7.2.2.0.1	3.2.3.1 / 1.2.1	3.2.3.1 / 1.2.1	3.2.3.1 / 1.2.1	3.2.3.1 / 1.2.1	7.2.4.21	3.2.3.1	3.2.3.1 / 1.2.1	3.2.3.1 / 1.2.1	1.2.1	1.2.1 / 3.2.3.3	1.2.1 / 3.2.3.3	8.1.5	7.2.5	3.2.3.1
9006	ENVIRONMENTALLY HAZARDOUS SUBSTANCE, LIQUID, N.O.S.	9	M12		9+(N2, N3, CMR, F or S)	*	*	*	*	*	97		*	yes			no	*	0	27 *see 3.2.3.3

-245-

Notes related to Table C

1) The ignition temperature has not been determined in accordance with a standardized determination procedure; therefore, provisional assignment has been made to temperature class T2 which is considered safe.

2) The ignition temperature has not been determined in accordance with a standardized determination procedure; therefore, provisional assignment has been made to temperature class T3 which is considered safe.

3) The ignition temperature has not been determined in accordance with a standardized determination procedure; therefore, provisional assignment has been made to temperature class T4 which is considered safe.

4) The maximum experimental safe gap (MESG) has not been measured in accordance with a standardized determination procedure; therefore, assignment has been made to explosion group II B which is considered safe.

5) The maximum experimental safe gap (MESG) has not been measured in accordance with a standardized determination procedure; therefore, assignment has been made to explosion group II C which is considered safe.

6) *(Deleted)*

7) The maximum experimental safe gap (MESG) has not been measured in accordance with a standardized determination procedure; therefore, assignment has been made to the explosion group which is considered safe.

8) The maximum experimental safe gap (MESG) has not been measured in accordance with a standardized determination procedure; therefore, assignment has been made to the explosion group in compliance with IEC 60079-20-1.

9) Assignment in accordance with IMO IBC Code.

10) Relative density at 15 °C.

11) Relative density at 25 °C.

12) This temperature class does not apply for the selection of explosion protected installations and equipment. The surface temperature of explosion protected installations and equipment shall not exceed 200 °C.

13) *(Deleted)*

14) No maximum experimental safe gap (MESG) has been determined in accordance with a standardized determination procedure; thus, the substance is provisionally assigned to explosion group II B3, which is considered to be safe.

3.2.3.3   *Flowchart, schemes and criteria for determining applicable special requirements (columns (6) to (20) of Table C)*

**Flowchart for classification of liquids of Classes 3, 6.1, 8 and 9 for carriage
in tanks in inland navigation**

- Flash-point ≤ 100 °C,
- Flash-point > 60 °C and heated to T ≤ 15 K from flash-point,
- Toxic substances (see 2.2.61),
- Corrosive substances (see 2.2.8),
- Elevated temperature liquids at or above 100 °C (UN No. 3257), or
- Substances characterized by acute or chronic aquatic toxicity LC/EC$_{50}$ ≤ 100 mg/l (criteria according to 2.2.9.1.10.2).

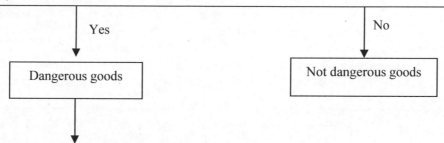

Yes → **Dangerous goods**   No → **Not dangerous goods**

- Flash-point < 23 °C and explosivity range > 15% at 20°C,
- Flash-point < 23 °C and corrosive (see 2.2.8),
- Auto-ignition temperature ≤ 200 °C,
- Toxic substances (see 2.2.61),
- Halogenated hydrocarbons,
- Benzene and mixtures containing more than 10% benzene,
- Substances that may only be transported while stabilized, or
- Substances characterized by acute or chronic 1 aquatic toxicity (N1: criteria according to 2.2.9.1.10.2) and vapour pressure at 50 °C ≥ 1 kPa.

No

Yes → **Vessel of type C
(continued under A)**

- Flash-point < 23 °C and chronic 2 or 3 aquatic toxicity (N2: criteria according to 2.2.9.1.10.2),
- Flash-point < 23 °C and floating on water surface (floater) or sinking to bottom of water (sinker) (criteria according to 2.2.9.1.10.5),
- Corrosive substances (packing group I or II) with vapour pressure at 50 °C > 12.5 kPa,
- Corrosive substances that react dangerously with water,
- Corrosive substances containing gases in solution,
- Acute or chronic toxicity 1 (N1: criteria according to 2.2.9.1.10.2) and vapour pressure at 50°C < 1 kPa, or
- Substances with long-term effects on health - CMR (criteria: Categories 1A or 1B of chapters 3.5, 3.6 and 3.7 of GHS).

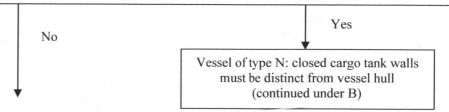

No

Yes → **Vessel of type N: closed cargo tank walls
must be distinct from vessel hull
(continued under B)**

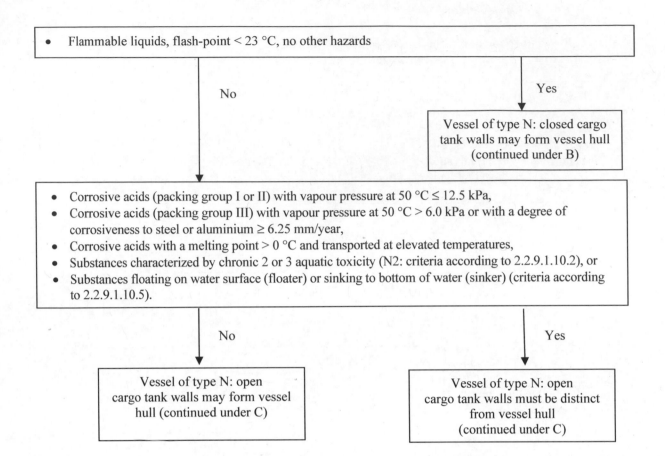

- Flammable liquids, flash-point < 23 °C, no other hazards

No   Yes

Vessel of type N: closed cargo tank walls may form vessel hull (continued under B)

- Corrosive acids (packing group I or II) with vapour pressure at 50 °C ≤ 12.5 kPa,
- Corrosive acids (packing group III) with vapour pressure at 50 °C > 6.0 kPa or with a degree of corrosiveness to steel or aluminium ≥ 6.25 mm/year,
- Corrosive acids with a melting point > 0 °C and transported at elevated temperatures,
- Substances characterized by chronic 2 or 3 aquatic toxicity (N2: criteria according to 2.2.9.1.10.2), or
- Substances floating on water surface (floater) or sinking to bottom of water (sinker) (criteria according to 2.2.9.1.10.5).

No   Yes

Vessel of type N: open cargo tank walls may form vessel hull (continued under C)

Vessel of type N: open cargo tank walls must be distinct from vessel hull (continued under C)

Elevated temperature substances

Irrespective of the above classifications, for substances that must be transported at elevated temperatures, the type of cargo tank shall be determined on the basis of the transport temperature, using the following table:

Maximum transport temperature T in °C	Type N	Type C
T ≤ 80	Integral cargo tank	Integral cargo tank
80 < T ≤ 115	Independent cargo tank, remark 25	Independent cargo tank, remark 26
T > 115	Independent cargo tank	Independent cargo tank

Remark 25 = remark No. 25 in column (20) of the list of substances contained in Chapter 3.2, Table C.

Remark 26 = remark No. 26 in column (20) of the list of substances contained in Chapter 3.2, Table C.

Scheme A: Criteria for cargo tank equipment in vessels of type C

Ascertain which substance/cargo tank characteristics in the first three columns are relevant. Select the applicable row in the relevant column. The cargo tank equipment requirements for C-vessels are then described in this row in the fourth column.

Substance/cargo tank characteristics			Requirements arising
Cargo tank internal pressure at liquid temperature of 30 °C and gaseous phase temperature of 37.8 °C > 50 kPa	Cargo tank internal pressure at liquid temperature of 30 °C and gaseous phase temperature of 37.8 °C ≤ 50 kPa		Cargo tank equipment
Refrigerated			With refrigeration (No. 1 in column (9))
Non-refrigerated	Cargo tank internal pressure at 50 °C > 50 kPa without water spraying	Boiling point ≤ 60 °C	Pressure tank (400 kPa)
	Cargo tank internal pressure at 50 °C > 50 kPa with water spraying	60 °C < boiling point ≤ 85 °C	Pressure relief valve/high velocity vent valve opening pressure: 50 kPa, with water-spraying system (No. 3 in column (9))
	Cargo tank internal pressure at 50 °C ≤ 50 kPa		Pressure relief valve/high velocity vent valve opening pressure as calculated, but at least 10 kPa
		85 °C < boiling point ≤ 115 °C	Pressure relief valve/high velocity vent valve opening pressure: 50 kPa
		Boiling point > 115 °C	Pressure relief valve/high velocity vent valve opening pressure: 35 kPa

Scheme B: Criteria for equipment of vessels of type N with closed cargo tanks

Cargo tank equipment	Class 3, flash-point < 23°C		Corrosive substances	CMR substances
Pressure tank (400 kPa)	175 kPa ≤ $P_{d\,50}$ < 300 kPa without refrigeration			
Pressure relief valve/high velocity vent valve opening pressure: 50 kPa	175 kPa ≤ $P_{d\,50}$ < 300 kPa, with refrigeration (No. 1 in column (9))	110 kPa ≤ $P_{d\,50}$ < 175 kPa without water spraying		
Pressure relief valve/high velocity vent valve opening pressure: 10 kPa	110 kPa ≤ $P_{d\,50}$ < 150 kPa with water spraying (No. 3 in column (9))	$P_{d\,50}$ < 110 kPa	Packing group I or II with $P_{d\,50}$ > 12.5 kPa or reacting dangerously with water or with gases in solution	Pressure relief valve/high velocity vent valve opening pressure: 10 kPa; with water spraying when vapour pressure > 10 kPa (calculation of the vapour pressure according to the formula for column 10, except that $v_a = 0.03$)

Scheme C: Criteria for equipment of vessels of type N with open cargo tanks

As certain which substance/characteristics in the first three columns are relevant. Select the applicable row in the relevant column. The cargo tank equipment requirements for N-vessels with open cargo tanks are then described in this row in the fourth column.

Substance characteristics		Requirements arising
	Flammable substances	Cargo tank equipment
Classes 3 and 9 23 °C ≤ flash-point ≤ 60 °C	Flash-point > 60 °C carried while heated to ≤ 15 K below flash-point or Flash-point > 60 °C, at or above their flash-point	With flame-arrester
Corrosive substances	Acids, transported while heated or flammable substances	
60 °C < flash-point ≤ 100 °C or elevated temperature substances of Class 9	Non-flammable substances	Without flame-arrester

Column (9): Cargo tank equipment for substances transported in a molten state

- **Possibility of heating the cargo (number 2 in column (9))**

  A possibility of heating the cargo shall be required on board:

  - When the melting point of the substance to be transported is + 15 °C or greater,

    or

  - When the melting point of the substance to be transported is greater than 0 °C but less than + 15 °C and the outside temperature is no more than 4 K above the melting point. In column (20), reference shall be made to remark 6 with the temperature derived as follows: melting point + 4 K

- **Heating system on board (number 4 in column (9))**

  A cargo heating system shall be required on board:

  - For substances that must not be allowed to solidify owing to the possibility of dangerous reactions on reheating, and

  - For substances that must be maintained at a guaranteed temperature not less than 15 K below their flash-point

Column (10): Determination of opening pressure of high-velocity vent valve in kPa

For vessels of type C, the opening pressure of the high-velocity vent valve shall be determined on the basis of the internal pressure of the tanks, rounded up to the nearest 5 kPa

To calculate the internal pressure, the following formula shall be used:

$$P_{\max} = P_{Ob\max} + \frac{k \cdot v_a (P_0 - P_{Da})}{v_a - \alpha \cdot \delta_t + \alpha \cdot \delta_t \cdot v_a} - P_0$$

$$k = \frac{T_{D\max}}{T_a}$$

In this formula:

$P_{\max}$	:	Maximum internal pressure in kPa
$P_{Ob\max}$	:	Absolute vapour pressure at maximum liquid surface temperature in kPa
P_{Da}	:	Absolute vapour pressure at filling temperature in kPa
P_0	:	Atmospheric pressure in kPa
v_a	:	Free relative volume at filling temperature compared with cargo tank volume
α	:	Cubic expansion coefficient in K^{-1}
δ_t	:	Average temperature increase of the liquid due to heating in K
$T_{D\max}$	:	Maximum gaseous phase temperature in K
T_a	:	Filling temperature in K
k	:	Temperature correction factor
t_{Ob}	:	Maximum liquid surface temperature in °C

In the formula, the following basic data are used:

P_{Obmax} : At 50 °C and 30 °C

P_{Da} : At 15 °C

P_0 : 101.3 kPa

v_a : 5% = 0.05

δ_t : 5 K

T_{Dmax} : 323 K and 310.8 K

T_a : 288 K

t_{Ob} : 50 °C and 30 °C

Column (11): Determination of maximum degree of filling of cargo tanks

If, in accordance with the provisions under A above:

- Type G is required: 91%; however, in the case of deeply refrigerated substances: 95%

- Type C is required: 95%

- Type N is required: 97%; however, in the case of substances in a molten state and of flammable liquids with 175 kPa $\leq P_{v50} < 300$ kPa: 95%

Column (12): Relative density of substance at 20 °C

These data are provided for information only.

Column (13): Determination of type of sampling device

1 = *closed*:   − Substances to be transported in pressure cargo tanks
      − Substances with T in column (3b) and assigned to packing group I
      − Stabilized substances to be transported under inert gas

2 = *partly closed*:   − All other substances for which type C is required

3 = *open:*   − All other substances

Column (14): Determination of whether a pump-room is permitted below deck

No   − All substances with T in column (3b) with the exception of substances of Class 2

Yes   − All other substances

Column (15): Determination of temperature class

Flammable substances shall be assigned to a temperature class on the basis of their auto-ignition point:

Temperature class	Auto-ignition temperature T of flammable liquids and gases in °C
T1	T > 450
T2	300 < T ≤ 450
T3	200 < T ≤ 300
T4	135 < T ≤ 200
T5	100 < T ≤ 135
T6	85 < T ≤ 100

When anti-explosion protection is required and the auto-ignition temperature is not known, reference shall be made to temperature class T4, considered safe.

Column (16): Determination of explosion group

Flammable substances shall be assigned to an explosion group on the basis of their maximum experimental safe gaps.

The maximum experimental safe gaps shall be determined in accordance with standard IEC 60079-20-1.

The different explosion groups are as follows:

Explosion group	Maximum experimental safe gap in mm
II A	> 0.9
II B	≥ 0.5 to ≤ 0.9
II C	< 0.5

Where self-contained protection systems are in place, the different subgroups for explosion group II B are as follows:

Explosion group/subgroup	Maximum experimental safe gap in mm
II B1	> 0.85 to ≤ 0.9
II B2	> 0.75 to ≤ 0.85
II B3	> 0.65 to ≤ 0.75
II B	≥ 0.5 to ≤ 0.65

When anti-explosion protection is required and the relevant data are not provided, reference shall be made to explosion group II B, considered safe.

Column (17): Determination of whether anti-explosion protection is required

Yes – For substances with a flash-point ≤ 60 °C

– For substances that must be transported while heated to a temperature of less than 15 °C below their flash-point

– For substances that must be transported while heated to a temperature of 15 °C or more below their flash-point and where in column (9) (cargo tank equipment) only a possibility of cargo heating (2) and no cargo-heating system on board (4) is required

– For flammable gases

No – For all other substances

Column (18): Determination of whether personal protective equipment, escape devices, portable gas detectors, portable toximeters or ambient-air-dependent breathing apparatus is required

- PP: For all substances of Classes 1 to 9;

- EP: For all substances
    - of Class 2 with letter T or letter C in the classification code indicated in column (3b),
    - of Class 3 with letter T or letter C in the classification code indicated in column (3b),
    - of Class 4.1,
    - of Class 6.1, and
    - of Class 8,
    - CMR substances of Category 1A or 1B according to chapters 3.5, 3.6 and 3.7 of GHS;

- EX: For all substances for which anti-explosion protection is required;

- TOX: For all substances of Class 6.1,

    For all substances of other classes with T in column (3b),

    For CMR substances of Category 1A or 1B according to chapters 3.5, 3.6 and 3.7 of GHS;

- A: For all substances for which EX or TOX is required

Column (19): Determination of the number of cones or blue lights

For all substances of Class 2 with letter F in the classification code indicated in column (3b):	1 cone/light
For all substances of Classes 3 to 9 with letter F in the classification code indicated in column (3b) and assigned to packing group I or II:	1 cone/light
For all substances of Class 2 with letter T in the classification code indicated in column (3b)	2 cones/lights
For all substances of Classes 3 to 9 with letter T in the classification code indicated in column (3b) and assigned to packing group I or II:	2 cones/lights

Column (20): Determination of additional requirements and remarks

Remark 1: Reference shall be made in column (20) to remark 1 for transport of UN No. 1005 AMMONIA, ANHYDROUS.

Remark 2: Reference shall be made in column (20) to remark 2 for stabilized substances that react with oxygen and for gases for which danger 2.1 is mentioned in column 5.

Remark 3: Reference shall be made in column (20) to remark 3 for substances that must be stabilized.

Remark 4: Reference shall be made in column (20) to remark 4 for substances that must not be allowed to solidify owing to the possibility of dangerous reactions on reheating.

Remark 5: Reference shall be made in column (20) to remark 5 for substances liable to polymerization.

Remark 6: Reference shall be made in column (20) to remark 6 for substances liable to crystallization and for substances for which a heating system or possibility of heating is required and the vapour pressure of which at 20 °C is greater than 0.1 kPa.

Remark 7: Reference shall be made in column (20) to remark 7 for substances with a melting point of + 15 °C or greater.

Remark 8: Reference shall be made in column (20) to remark 8 for substances that react dangerously with water.

Remark 9: Reference shall be made in column (20) to remark 9 for transport of UN No. 1131 CARBON DISULPHIDE.

Remark 10: *No longer used.*

Remark 11: Reference shall be made in column (20) to remark 11 for transport of UN No. 1040 ETHYLENE OXIDE WITH NITROGEN.

Remark 12: Reference shall be made in column (20) to remark 12 for transport of UN No. 1280 PROPYLENE OXIDE and UN No. 2983 ETHYLENE OXIDE AND PROPYLENE OXIDE MIXTURE.

Remark 13: Reference shall be made in column (20) to remark 13 for transport of UN No. 1086 VINYL CHLORIDE, STABILIZED.

Remark 14: Reference shall be made in column (20) to remark 14 for mixtures or N.O.S. entries which are not clearly defined and for which type N is stipulated under the classification criteria.

Remark 15: Reference shall be made in column (20) to remark 15 for substances that react dangerously with alkalis or acids such as sodium hydroxide or sulphuric acid.

Remark 16: Reference shall be made in column (20) to remark 16 for substances that may react dangerously to local overheating.

Remark 17: Reference shall be made in column (20) to remark 17 for substances when reference is made to remark 4, 6 or 7.

Remark 18: *No longer used.*

Remark 19: Reference shall be made in column (20) to remark 19 for substances that must under no circumstances come into contact with water.

Remark 20: Reference shall be made in column (20) to remark 20 for substances the transport temperature of which must not exceed a maximum temperature in combination with the cargo tank materials. Reference shall be made to this maximum permitted temperature immediately after the number 20.

Remark 21: *No longer used.*

Remark 22: Reference shall be made in column (20) to remark 22 for substances for which a range of values or no value of the density is indicated in column (12).

Remark 23: Reference shall be made in column (20) to remark 23 for substances the internal pressure of which at 30 °C is less than 50 kPa and which are transported with water spraying.

Remark 24: Reference shall be made in column (20) to remark 24 for transport of UN No. 3257 ELEVATED TEMPERATURE LIQUID, N.O.S.

Remark 25: Reference shall be made in column (20) to remark 25 for substances that must be transported while heated in a type 3 cargo tank.

Remark 26: Reference shall be made in column (20) to remark 26 for substances that must be transported while heated in a type 2 cargo tank.

Remark 27: Reference shall be made in column (20) to remark 27 for substances for which the reference N.O.S. or a generic reference is made in column (2) and for which the proper shipping names are not already supplemented with the technical name of the goods or additional information concerning the benzene content.

Remark 28: Reference shall be made in column (20) to remark 28 for transport of UN No. 2448 SULPHUR, MOLTEN.

Remark 29: *No longer used.*

Remark 30: Reference shall be made in column (20) to remark 30 for transport of UN Nos. 1719, 1794, 1814, 1819, 1824, 1829, 1830, 1832, 1833, 1906, 2240, 2308, 2583, 2584, 2677, 2679, 2681, 2796, 2797, 2837 and 3320 under the entries for which open type N is required.

Remark 31: Reference shall be made in column (20) to remark 31 for transport of substances of Class 2 and UN Nos. 1280 PROPYLENE OXIDE and 2983 ETHYLENE OXIDE AND PROPYLENE OXIDE MIXTURE of Class 3.

Remark 32: Reference shall be made in column (20) to remark 32 for transport of UN No. 2448 SULPHUR, MOLTEN of Class 4.1.

Remark 33: Reference shall be made in column (20) to remark 33 for transport of UN Nos. 2014 and 2984 HYDROGEN PEROXIDE, AQUEOUS SOLUTION of Class 5.1.

Remark 34: Reference shall be made in column (20) to remark 34 for transport of substances for which hazard 8 is mentioned in column (5) and type N in column (6).

Remark 35: Reference shall be made in column (20) to remark 35 for substances for which complete refrigeration may cause dangerous reactions in the event of compression. This is also applicable if the refrigeration is partly done by compression.

Remark 36: *No longer used.*

Remark 37: Reference shall be made in column (20) to remark 37 for substances for which the cargo storage system must be capable of resisting the full vapour pressure of the cargo at the upper limits of the ambient design temperatures, whatever the system adopted for the boil-off gas.

Remark 38: Reference shall be made in column (20) to remark 38 for mixtures with an initial boiling point above 60 °C or under or equal to 85 °C in accordance with ASTMD 86-01.

Remark 39: Reference shall be made in column (20) to remark 39 for the carriage of UN No. 2187 CARBON DIOXIDE, REFRIGERATED LIQUID of Class 2.

Remark 40: *No longer used.*

Remark 41: Reference shall be made in column (20) to remark 41 for UN No. 2709 BUTYLBENZENES (n-BUTYLBENZENE).

Remark 42: Reference shall be made in column (20) to remark 42 for UN No. 1038 ETHYLENE, REFRIGERATED LIQUID and for UN No. 1972 METHANE REFRIGERATED LIQUID or NATURAL GAS, REFRIGERATED LIQUID, with high methane content.

Remark 43: Reference shall be made in column (20) to remark 43 for all packing group I entries with letter F (flammable) in the classification code indicated in column (3b), and with letter F (floater) in column (5), Dangers.

3.2.4   **Modalities for the application of section 1.5.2 on special authorizations concerning transport in tank vessels**

3.2.4.1   **Model special authorization under section 1.5.2**

Special authorization
under 1.5.2 of ADN

Under 1.5.2 of ADN, the transport in tank vessels of the substance specified in the annex to this special authorization shall be authorized in the conditions referred to therein.

Before transporting the substance, the carrier shall be required to have it added to the list referred to in 1.16.1.2.5 of ADN by a recognized classification society.

This special authorization shall be valid ....
          (places and/or routes of validity)

It shall be valid for two years from the date of signature, unless it is repealed at an earlier date.

Issuing State: ....

Competent authority: ....

Date: ....

Signature: ....

3.2.4.2   **Application form for special authorizations under section 1.5.2**

For applications for special authorizations, please answer the following questions and points.[*] Data are used for administrative purposes only and are treated confidentially.

Applicant

....
(Name)   (Company)

....
(   ) ....

....
(Address)

Summary of the application

Authorization for transport in tank vessels of .... as a substance of Class
....

Annexes
(with brief description)

Application made:

At: ....

Date: ....

Signature: ....
          (of the person responsible for the data)

---

[*]   *For questions not relevant to the subject of the application, write "not applicable".*

1. **General data on the dangerous substance**

1.1   Is it a pure substance ☐, a mixture ☐, a solution ☐ ?

1.2   Technical name (if possible ADN nomenclature or possibly the IBC Code).

1.3   Synonym.

1.4   Trade name.

1.5   Structure formula and, for mixtures, composition and/or concentration.

1.6   Hazard class and, where applicable classification code, packing group.

1.7   UN No. or substance identification number (if known).

2.   **Physico-chemical properties**

2.1   State during transport (e.g. gas, liquid, molten, ...).

2.2   Relative density of liquid at 20 ° C or at the transport temperature if the substance is to be heated or refrigerated during transport.

2.3   Transport temperature (for substances heated or refrigerated during transport).

2.4   Melting point or range ...... °C.

2.5   Boiling point or range ...... °C.

2.6   Vapour pressure at 15 °C ...., 20 °C ...., 30 °C ...., 37.8 °C ...., 50 °C ...., (for liquefied gases, vapour pressure at 70 °C ....), (for permanent gases, filling pressure at 15 °C ....).

2.7   Cubic expansion coefficient ..... K^{-1}

2.8   Solubility in water at 20 °C
       Saturation concentration ...... mg/l

       or

       Miscibility with water at 15 °C

       ☐ Complete   ☐ partial   ☐ none
       (If possible, in the case of solutions and mixtures, indicate concentration)

2.9   Colour.

2.10   Odour.

2.11   Viscosity ..... mm^2/s.

2.12   Flow time (ISO 2431-1996) ....s.

2.13   Solvent separation test ....

2.14   pH of the substance or aqueous solution (indicate concentration).

2.15   Other information.

3. Technical safety properties

3.1   Auto-ignition temperature in accordance with IEC 60079-20-1:2010, EN 14522:2005, DIN 51 794:2003 in °C; where applicable, indicate the temperature class in accordance with IEC 60079-20-1:2010.

3.2   Flash-point

For flash-points up to 175 °C

Closed-cup test methods - non-equilibrium procedure

    Abel method: EN ISO 13736:2008

    Abel-Pensky method: DIN 51755–1:1974 or NF M T60-103:1968

    Pensky-Martens method: EN ISO 2719:2012

    Luchaire apparatus: French standard NF T60-103:1968

    Tag method: ASTM D56-05(2010)

Closed-cup test methods – equilibrium procedure

    Rapid equilibrium procedure: EN ISO 3679:2004; ASTM D3278-96 (2011)

    Closed-cup equilibrium procedure: EN ISO 1523:2002+AC1:2006; ASTM D3941-90 (2007)

For flash-points above 175 °C

    In addition to the above-mentioned methods, the following open-cup test method may be applied:

    Cleveland method: EN ISO 2592:2002; ASTM D92-12.

3.3   Explosion limits:

Determination of upper and lower explosion limits in accordance with EN 1839:2012.

3.4   Maximum safe gap in accordance with IEC 60079-20-1:2010 in mm.

3.5   Is the substance stabilized during transport? If so, provide data on the stabilizer:

    ....

3.6   Decomposition products in the event of combustion on contact with air or under the influence of an external fire:

3.7   Is the substance fire intensifying?

3.8   Abrasion (corrosion) ..... mm/year.

3.9   Does the substance react with water or moist air by releasing flammable or toxic gases? Yes/No. Gases released: ....

3.10   Does the substance react dangerously in any other way?

3.11   Does the substance react dangerously when reheated?
        Yes/no

4.   Physiological hazards

4.1 LD_{50} and/or LC_{50} value. Necrosis value (where applicable, other toxicity criteria in accordance with 2.2.61.1 of ADN).

        CMR properties according to Categories 1A and 1B of chapters 3.5, 3.6 and 3.7 of GHS.

4.2   Does decomposition or reaction produce substances posing physiological hazards? (Indicate which substances where known)

4.3   Environmental properties (see 2.4.2.1 of ADN)

        Acute toxicity:

        LC_{50} 96 hr for fish .... mg/l

        EC_{50} 48 hr for crustacea .... mg/l

        E_rC_{50} 72 hr for algae .... mg/l

        Chronic toxicity:

        NOEC .... mg/l

        BCF .... mg/l or log K_{ow} ....

        Easily biodegradable .... yes/no

5.   Data on hazard potential

5.1   What specific damage is to be expected if the hazard characteristics produce their effect?

        ☐   Combustion

        ☐   Injury

        ☐   Corrosion

        ☐   Intoxication in the event of dermal absorption

        ☐   Intoxication in the event of absorption by inhalation

        ☐   Mechanical damage

        ☐   Destruction

        ☐   Fire

        ☐   Abrasion (corrosion to metals)

        ☐   Environmental pollution

6.   **Data on the transport equipment**

6.1   Are particular loading requirements envisaged/necessary (what are they)?

7.   **Transport of dangerous substances in tanks**

7.1   With which materials is the substance to be carried compatible?

8.   **Technical safety requirements**

8.1   Taking into account the current state of science and technology, what safety measures are necessary in the light of the hazards posed by the substance or liable to arise in the course of the transport process as a whole?

8.2   Additional safety measures

- Use of stationary or mobile techniques to measure flammable gases and flammable liquid vapours.

- Use of stationary or mobile techniques (toximeters) to measure concentrations of toxic substances.

3.2.4.3   Criteria for assignment of substances

A.   Columns (6), (7) and (8): Determination of the type of tank vessel

1.   **Gases** (criteria according to 2.2.2 of ADN)

–   Without refrigeration: type G   pressure

–   With refrigeration: type G   refrigerated

2.   **Halogenated hydrocarbons**

Substances that may only be transported in a stabilized state

Toxic substances (see 2.2.61.1 of ADN)

Flammable (flash-point < 23 °C) and corrosive substances (see 2.2.8 of ADN)

Substances with an auto-ignition temperature ≤ 200 °C

Substances with a flash-point < 23 °C and an explosivity range > 15% at 20 °C

Benzene and mixtures of non-toxic and non-corrosive substances containing more than 10% benzene

Environmentally hazardous substances, aquatic toxicity category Acute 1 or Chronic 1 (group N1 in accordance with 2.2.9.1.10.2 of ADN) and vapour pressure at 50 °C ≥ 1 kPa

–   Cargo tank internal pressure > 50 kPa at the following temperatures: liquid 30 °C, gaseous phase 37.8 °C

●   Without refrigeration: type C   pressure (400 kPa)

●   With refrigeration: type C   refrigerated

–   Cargo tank internal pressure ≤ 50 kPa at the following temperatures: liquid 30 °C, gaseous phase 37.8 °C but with cargo tank internal pressure > 50 kPa at 50 °C

●   Without water spraying: type C   pressure (400 kPa)

●   With water spraying: type C   with pressure relief valve/high velocity vent valve opening pressure of 50 kPa

–   Cargo tank internal pressure ≤ 50 kPa at the following temperatures: liquid 30 °C, gaseous phase 37.8 °C

      with cargo tank internal   type C   with pressure relief
      pressure ≤ 50 kPa at 50 °C   valve/high velocity vent
                                                                valve opening pressure
                                                                as calculated, but at least
                                                                10 kPa

2.1   Mixtures for which type C is required in accordance with the criteria referred to in 2 above but for which certain data are lacking

In cases where the internal pressurization of the tank cannot be calculated owing to a lack of data, the following criteria may be used

– Initial boiling point ≤ 60 °C	type C	(400 kPa)
– 60 °C < initial boiling point ≤ 85 °C	type C	with pressure relief valve/high velocity vent valve opening pressure of 50 kPa and with water spraying
– 85 °C < initial boiling point ≤ 115 °C	type C	with pressure relief valve/high velocity vent valve opening pressure of 50 kPa
– 115 °C < initial boiling point	type C	with pressure relief valve/high velocity vent valve opening pressure of 35 kPa

3.   Substances which are flammable only (see 2.2.3 of ADN)

- Flash-point < 23 °C
  with 175 kPa ≤ Pv 50 < 300 kPa

• Without refrigeration:	closed type N	pressure (400 kPa)
• With refrigeration:	closed type N	refrigerated with pressure relief valve/high velocity vent valve opening pressure of 50 kPa

– Flash-point < 23 °C with 150 kPa ≤ Pv 50 < 175 kPa:	closed type N	with pressure relief valve/high velocity vent valve opening pressure of 50 kPa

- Flash-point < 23 °C
  with 110 kPa ≤ Pv 50 < 150 kPa

• Without water spraying:	closed type N	with pressure relief valve/high velocity vent valve opening pressure of 50 kPa
• With water spraying:	closed type N	with pressure relief valve/high velocity vent valve opening pressure of 10 kPa

– Flash-point < 23 °C with Pv 50 < 110 kPa:	closed type N	with pressure relief valve/high velocity vent valve opening pressure of 10 kPa
– Flash-point ≥ 23 °C but ≤ 60 °C:	open type N	with flame-arrester

– Substances with a flash-point > 60 °C heated to less than 15 K from the flash-point, N.O.S. (...):	open type N	with flame-arrester
– Substances with a flash-point > 60 °C heated to or above the flash-point, N.O.S. (...):	open type N	with flame-arrester

4.   **Corrosive substances (see 2.2.8 of ADN)**

– **Corrosive substances liable to produce corrosive vapours**

● Substances assigned to packing group I or II in the list of substances and having a vapour pressure^2 greater than 12.5 kPa (125 mbar) at 50 °C or	closed type N	cargo tank walls must be distinct from vessel hull; pressure relief valve/high velocity vent valve opening pressure of 10 kPa
● Substances liable to react dangerously with water (for example acid chlorides)		
● Substances containing gases in solution		

– **Corrosive acids:**

● Substances assigned to packing group I or II in the list of substances and having a vapour pressure^2 of 12.5 kPa (125 mbar) or less at 50 °C or	open type N	cargo tank walls must be distinct from vessel hull
● Substances assigned to packing group III in the list of substances and having a vapour pressure^2 of > 6.0 kPa (60 mbar) at 50 °C or	open type N	cargo tank walls must be distinct from vessel hull
● Substances assigned to packing group III in the list of substances because of their degree of corrosiveness to steel or aluminium or	open type N	cargo tank walls must be distinct from vessel hull
● Substances with a melting point greater than 0 °C and transported at elevated temperatures	open type N	cargo tank walls must be distinct from vessel hull
● Flammable substances	open type N	with flame-arresters
● Elevated temperature substances	open type N	with flame-arresters
● Non-flammable substances	open type N	without flame-arresters

---

2   *If the data are available, the sum of the partial pressures of the dangerous substances may be used in place of the vapour pressure.*

–   **All other corrosive substances:**

- Flammable substance   open type N   with flame-arresters

- Non-flammable substances   open type N   without flame-arresters

5.   **Environmentally hazardous substances (see 2.2.9.1 of ADN)**

- Aquatic toxicity Acute 1 or   closed type N   cargo tank walls must
  Chronic 1 (group N1 in   be distinct from vessel
  accordance with 2.2.9.1.10.2)   hull
  and vapour pressure below
  1 kPa at 50 °C

- Chronic 2 and 3 (group N2 in   open type N   cargo tank walls must
  accordance with 2.2.9.1.10.2)   be distinct from vessel
                                                            hull

- Acute 2 and 3 (group N3 in   open type N   _____
  accordance with 2.2.9.1.10.2)

6.   **Substances of Class 9, UN No. 3257**   open type N   independent cargo
                                                                          tanks

7.   **Substances of Class 9, Identification No. 9003**

Flash-point > 60 °C and ≤ 100 °C: open type N   _____

8.   **Substances that must be transported at elevated temperatures**

For substances that must be transported at elevated temperatures, the type of cargo tank shall be determined on the basis of the transport temperature, using the following table:

Maximum transport temperature T in °C	Type N	Type C
T ≤ 80	2	2
80 < T ≤ 115	1 + remark 25	1 + remark 26
T > 115	1	1

1 = cargo tank type: independent tank

2 = cargo tank type: integral tank

Remark 25 = remark No. 25 in column (20) of the list of substances contained in Chapter 3.2, Table C.

Remark 26 = remark No. 26 in column (20) of the list of substances contained in Chapter 3.2, Table C.

9.   **Substances with long-term effects on health - CMR substances (Categories 1A and 1B in accordance with the criteria of chapters 3.5, 3.6 and 3.7 of GHS[3]), provided that they are already assigned to Classes 2 to 9 by virtue of other criteria**

C   carcinogenic

M   mutagenic

---

[3]   *Since there is no official international list of CMR substances of Categories 1A and 1B, pending the availability of such a list, the list of CMR substances of Categories 1A and 1B in Regulation (EC) No 1272/2008 of the European Parliament and of the Council, as amended, shall apply.*

R   toxic to reproduction

closed type N	cargo tank walls must be distinct from vessel hull; pressure relief valve/high velocity vent valve opening pressure of at least 10 kPa, with water-spray system, if the internal pressurization of the tank is more than 10 kPa (calculation of the vapour pressure according to the formula for column 10, except that $v_a = 0.03$)

10.   **Substances that float on the water surface ('floaters') or sink to the bottom of the water ('sinkers') (criteria according to 2.2.9.1.10.5) provided that they are already assigned to Classes 3 to 9 and that type N is required on that basis**

open type N	cargo tank walls must be distinct from vessel hull

B.   **Column (9): Determination of cargo tank equipment**

(1)   Refrigeration system

Determined in accordance with A.

(2)   Possibility of heating the cargo

A possibility of heating the cargo shall be required:

–   When the melting point of the substance to be transported is + 15 °C or greater, or

–   When the melting point of the substance to be transported is greater than 0 °C but less than + 15 °C and the outside temperature is no more than 4 K above the melting point. In column (20), reference shall be made to remark 6 with the temperature derived as follows: melting point + 4 K.

(3)   Water-spray system

Determined in accordance with A.

(4)   Cargo heating system on board

A cargo heating system on board shall be required:

–   For substances that must not be allowed to solidify owing to the possibility of dangerous reactions on reheating, and

–   For substances that must be maintained at a guaranteed temperature of not less than 15 K below their flash-point.

C.   **Column (10): Determination of opening pressure of high-velocity vent valve in kPa**

For vessels of type C, the opening pressure of the high-velocity vent valve shall be determined on the basis of the internal pressure of the tanks, rounded up to the nearest 5 kPa.

To calculate the internal pressure, the following formula shall be used:

$$P_{max} = P_{Ob\,max} + \frac{k \cdot v_a \left(P_0 - P_{Da} \right)}{v_a - \alpha \cdot \delta_t + \alpha \cdot \delta_t \cdot v_a} - P_o$$

$$k = \frac{T_{D\,max}}{T_a}$$

In this formula:

P_{max} : Maximum internal pressure in kPa

P_{Obmax} : Absolute vapour pressure at maximum liquid surface temperature in kPa

P_{Da} : Absolute vapour pressure at filling temperature in kPa

P_0 : Atmospheric pressure in kPa

v_a : Free relative volume at filling temperature compared with cargo tank volume

α : Cubic expansion coefficient in K^{-1}

δ_t : Average temperature increase of the liquid due to heating in K

T_{Dmax} : Maximum gaseous phase temperature in K

T_a : Filling temperature in K

k : Temperature correction factor

t_{Ob} : Maximum liquid surface temperature in °C

In the formula, the following basic data are used:

P_{Obmax} : At 50 °C and 30 °C

P_{Da} : At 15 °C

P_0 : 101.3 kPa

v_a : 5% = 0.05

δ_t : 5 K

T_{Dmax} : 323 K and 310.8 K

T_a : 288 K

t_{Ob} : 50 °C and 30 °C

D. **Column (11): Determination of maximum degree of filling of cargo tanks**

If, in accordance with the provisions under A above:

—	Type G is required:	91%	however, in the case of deeply refrigerated substances: 95%
—	Type C is required:	95%	
—	Type N is required:	97%	however, in the case of substances in a molten state and of flammable liquids with $175\ kPa \leq P_{v50} < 300\ kPa$: 95%.

E. **Column (13): Determination of type of sampling device**

1 = *closed*:   -   Substances to be transported in pressure cargo tanks

                                -   Substances with T in column (3b) and assigned to packing group I

                                -   Stabilized substances to be transported under inert gas.

2 = *partly closed*:   -   All other substances for which type C is required

3 = *open*:   -   All other substances

F. **Column (14): Determination of whether a pump-room is permitted below deck**

No   -   All substances with letter T in the classification code indicated in column (3b) with the exception of substances of Class 2.

Yes   -   All other substances

G. **Column (15): Determination of temperature class**

Flammable substances shall be assigned to a temperature class on the basis of their auto-ignition point:

Temperature class	Auto-ignition temperature T of flammable liquids and gases in °C
T1	$T > 450$
T2	$300 < T \leq 450$
T3	$200 < T \leq 300$
T4	$135 < T \leq 200$
T5	$100 < T \leq 135$
T6	$85 < T \leq 100$

When anti-explosion protection is required and the auto-ignition temperature is not known, reference shall be made to temperature class T4, considered safe.

H. **Column (16): Determination of explosion group**

Flammable substances shall be assigned to an explosion group on the basis of their maximum experimental safe gaps.

The maximum experimental safe gaps shall be determined in accordance with standard IEC 60079-20-1.

The different explosion groups are as follows:

Explosion group	Maximum experimental safe gap in mm
II A	> 0.9
II B	≥ 0.5 to ≤ 0.9
II C	< 0.5

Where self-contained protection systems are in place, the different subgroups for explosion group II B are as follows:

Explosion group/subgroup	Maximum experimental safe gap in mm
II B1	> 0.85 to ≤ 0.9
II B2	> 0.75 to ≤ 0.85
II B3	> 0.65 to ≤ 0.75
II B	≥ 0.5 to ≤ 0.65

When anti-explosion protection is required and the relevant data are not provided, reference shall be made to explosion group II B, considered safe.

I.   Column (17): Determination of whether anti-explosion protection is required

Yes
- For substances with a flash-point ≤ 60 °C

- For substances that must be transported while heated to a temperature of less than 15 K below their flash-point

- For substances that must be transported while heated to a temperature of 15 K or more below their flash-point and where in column (9) (cargo tank equipment) only a possibility of cargo heating (2) and no cargo-heating system on board (4) is required

- For flammable gases

No
- For all other substances

J.   Column (18): Determination of whether personal protective equipment, escape devices, portable gas detectors, portable toximeters or ambient-air-dependent breathing apparatus is required

- PP: For all substances of Classes 1 to 9;

- EP: For all substances

   – of Class 2 with letter T or letter C in the classification code indicated in column (3b);

   – of Class 3 with letter T or letter C in the classification code indicated in column (3b);

   – of Class 4.1;

   – of Class 6.1;

   – of Class 8; and

   for CMR substances of Category 1A or 1B according to chapters 3.5, 3.6 and 3.7 of GHS;[3]

- EX: For all substances for which anti-explosion protection is required;

---

[3]   *Since there is no official international list of CMR substances of Categories 1A and 1B, pending the availability of such a list, the list of CMR substances of Categories 1A and 1B in Regulation (EC) No 1272/2008 of the European Parliament and of the Council, as amended, shall apply.*

- TOX: For all substances of Class 6.1;

  For all substances of other classes with T in column (3b);

  For CMR substances of Category 1A or 1B according to chapters 3.5, 3.6 and 3.7 of GHS;[3]

- A: For all substances for which EX or TOX is required.

K.   **Column (19): Determination of the number of cones or blue lights**

For all substances of Class 2 with letter F in the classification code indicated in column (3b):	1 cone/light
For all substances of Classes 3 to 9 with letter F in the classification code indicated in column (3b) and assigned to packing group I or II:	1 cone/light
For all substances of Class 2 with letter T in the classification code indicated in column (3b):	2 cones/lights
For all substances of Classes 3 to 9 with letter T in the classification code indicated in column (3b) and assigned to packing group I or II:	2 cones/lights

L.   **Column (20): Determination of additional requirements and remarks**

Remark 1: Reference shall be made in column (20) to remark 1 for transport of UN No. 1005 AMMONIA, ANHYDROUS.

Remark 2: Reference shall be made in column (20) to remark 2 for stabilized substances that react with oxygen and for gases for which danger 2.1 is mentioned in column (5).

Remark 3: Reference shall be made in column (20) to remark 3 for substances that must be stabilized.

Remark 4: Reference shall be made in column (20) to remark 4 for substances that must not be allowed to solidify owing to the possibility of dangerous reactions on reheating.

Remark 5: Reference shall be made in column (20) to remark 5 for substances liable to polymerization.

Remark 6: Reference shall be made in column (20) to remark 6 for substances liable to crystallization and for substances for which a heating system or possibility of heating is required and the vapour pressure of which at 20 °C is greater than 0.1 kPa.

Remark 7: Reference shall be made in column (20) to remark 7 for substances with a melting point of + 15 °C or greater.

Remark 8: Reference shall be made in column (20) to remark 8 for substances that react dangerously with water.

Remark 9: Reference shall be made in column (20) to remark 9 for transport of UN No. 1131 CARBON DISULPHIDE.

Remark 10: *No longer used.*

---

[3]   *Since there is no official international list of CMR substances of Categories 1A and 1B, pending the availability of such a list, the list of CMR substances of Categories 1A and 1B in Regulation (EC) No 1272/2008 of the European Parliament and of the Council, as amended, shall apply.*

Remark 11: Reference shall be made in column (20) to remark 11 for transport of UN No. 1040 ETHYLENE OXIDE WITH NITROGEN.

Remark 12: Reference shall be made in column (20) to remark 12 for transport of UN No. 1280 PROPYLENE OXIDE and UN No. 2983 ETHYLENE OXIDE AND PROPYLENE OXIDE MIXTURE.

Remark 13: Reference shall be made in column (20) to remark 13 for transport of UN No. 1086 VINYL CHLORIDE, STABILIZED.

Remark 14: Reference shall be made in column (20) to remark 14 for mixtures or N.O.S. entries which are not clearly defined and for which type N is stipulated under the classification criteria.

Remark 15: Reference shall be made in column (20) to remark 15 for substances that react dangerously with alkalis or acids such as sodium hydroxide or sulphuric acid.

Remark 16: Reference shall be made in column (20) to remark 16 for substances that may react dangerously to local overheating.

Remark 17: Reference shall be made in column (20) to remark 17 for substances when reference is made to remark 4, 6 or 7.

Remark 18: *No longer used.*

Remark 19: Reference shall be made in column (20) to remark 19 for substances that must under no circumstances come into contact with water.

Remark 20: Reference shall be made in column (20) to remark 20 for substances the transport temperature of which must not exceed a maximum temperature in combination with the cargo tank materials. Reference shall be made to this maximum permitted temperature immediately after the number 20.

Remark 21: *No longer used.*

Remark 22: Reference shall be made in column (20) to remark 22 for substances for which a range of values or no value of the density is indicated in column (12).

Remark 23: Reference shall be made in column (20) to remark 23 for substances the internal pressure of which at 30 °C is less than 50 kPa and which are transported with water spraying.

Remark 24: Reference shall be made in column (20) to remark 24 for transport of UN No. 3257 ELEVATED TEMPERATURE LIQUID, N.O.S.

Remark 25: Reference shall be made in column (20) to remark 25 for substances that must be transported while heated in a type 3 cargo tank.

Remark 26: Reference shall be made in column (20) to remark 26 for substances that must be transported while heated in a type 2 cargo tank.

Remark 27: Reference shall be made in column (20) to remark 27 for substances for which the reference N.O.S. or a generic reference is made in column (2) and for which the proper shipping names are not already supplemented with the technical name of the goods or additional information concerning the benzene content.

Remark 28: Reference shall be made in column (20) to remark 28 for transport of UN No. 2448 SULPHUR, MOLTEN.

Remark 29: *No longer used.*

Remark 30: Reference shall be made in column (20) to remark 30 for transport of UN Nos. 1719, 1794, 1814, 1819, 1824, 1829, 1830, 1832, 1833, 1906, 2240, 2308, 2583, 2584, 2677, 2679, 2681, 2796, 2797, 2837 and 3320 under the entries for which open type N is required.

Remark 31: Reference shall be made in column (20) to remark 31 for transport of substances of Class 2 and UN Nos. 1280 PROPYLENE OXIDE and 2983 ETHYLENE OXIDE AND PROPYLENE OXIDE MIXTURE of Class 3.

Remark 32: Reference shall be made in column (20) to remark 32 for transport of UN No. 2448 SULPHUR, MOLTEN of Class 4.1.

Remark 33: Reference shall be made in column (20) to remark 33 for transport of UN Nos. 2014 and 2984 HYDROGEN PEROXIDE, AQUEOUS SOLUTION of Class 5.1.

Remark 34: Reference shall be made in column (20) to remark 34 for transport of substances for which hazard 8 is mentioned in column (5) and type N in column (6).

Remark 35: Reference shall be made in column (20) to remark 35 for substances for which complete refrigeration may cause dangerous reactions in the event of compression. This is also applicable if the refrigeration is partly done by compression.

Remark 36: *No longer used.*

Remark 37: Reference shall be made in column (20) to remark 37 for substances for which the cargo storage system must be capable of resisting the full vapour pressure of the cargo at the upper limits of the ambient design temperatures, whatever the system adopted for the boil-off gas.

Remark 38: Reference shall be made in column (20) to remark 38 for mixtures with an initial boiling point above 60 °C or under or equal to 85 °C in accordance with ASTMD 86-01.

Remark 39: Reference shall be made in column (20) to remark 39 for the carriage of UN No. 2187 CARBON DIOXIDE, REFRIGERATED LIQUID of Class 2.

Remark 40: *No longer used.*

Remark 41: Reference shall be made in column (20) to remark 41 for UN No. 2709 BUTYLBENZENES (n-BUTYLBENZENE).

Remark 42: Reference shall be made in column (20) to remark 42 for UN No. 1038 ETHYLENE, REFRIGERATED LIQUID and for UN No. 1972 METHANE REFRIGERATED LIQUID or NATURAL GAS, REFRIGERATED LIQUID, with high methane content.

Remark 43: Reference shall be made in column (20) to remark 43 for all packing group I entries with letter F (flammable) in the classification code indicated in column (3b), and with letter F (floater) in column (5), Dangers.

PART 4

Provisions concerning the use of packagings, tanks and bulk cargo transport units

CHAPTER 4.1

GENERAL PROVISIONS

4.1.1   Packagings and tanks shall be used in accordance with the requirements of one of the international Regulations, bearing in mind the indications given in the list of substances of these international Regulations, namely:

–   For packagings (including IBCs and large packagings): columns (9a) and (9b) of Chapter 3.2, Table A of RID or ADR, or the list of substances in Chapter 3.2 of the IMDG Code or the ICAO Technical Instructions;

–   For portable tanks: columns (10) and (11) of Chapter 3.2, Table A of RID or ADR or the list of substances in the IMDG Code;

–   For RID or ADR tanks: columns (12) and (13) of Chapter 3.2, Table A of RID or ADR.

4.1.2   The requirements to be implemented are as follows:

–   For packagings (including IBCs and large packagings): Chapter 4.1 of RID, ADR, the IMDG Code or the ICAO Technical Instructions;

–   For portable tanks: Chapter 4.2 of RID, ADR or the IMDG Code;

–   For RID or ADR tanks: Chapter 4.3 of RID or ADR, and, where applicable, sections 4.2.5 or 4.2.6 of the IMDG Code;

–   For fibre-reinforced plastics tanks: Chapter 4.4 of ADR;

–   For vacuum-operated waste tanks: Chapter 4.5 of ADR.

–   For mobile explosive manufacturing units (MEMUs): Chapter 4.7 of ADR.

4.1.3   For carriage in bulk of solids in vehicles, wagons, containers or bulk containers, the following requirements of the international Regulations shall be complied with:

–   Chapter 4.3 of the IMDG Code; or

–   Chapter 7.3 of ADR, taking account of indications in columns (10) or (17) of Table A of Chapter 3.2 of ADR, except that sheeted vehicles and containers are not allowed;

–   Chapter 7.3 of RID, taking account of indications in columns (10) or (17) of Table A of Chapter 3.2 of RID, except that sheeted wagons and containers are not allowed.

4.1.4   Only packagings and tanks which meet the requirements of Part 6 of ADR or RID may be used.

PART 5

Consignment procedures

CHAPTER 5.1

GENERAL PROVISIONS

5.1.1   **Application and general provisions**

This Part sets forth the provisions for dangerous goods consignments relative to marking, labelling, and documentation, and, where appropriate, authorisation of consignments and advance notifications.

5.1.2   **Use of overpacks**

5.1.2.1   (a)   Unless marks and labels required in Chapter 5.2, except 5.2.1.3 to 5.2.1.6, 5.2.1.7.2 to 5.2.1.7.8 and 5.2.1.10, representative of all dangerous goods in the overpack are visible, the overpack shall be:

(i)   marked with the word "OVERPACK". The lettering of the "OVERPACK" mark shall be at least 12 mm high. The mark shall be in an official language of the country of origin and also, if that language is not English, French or German, in English, French or German, unless agreements, if any, concluded between the countries concerned in the transport operation provide otherwise; and

(ii)   labelled and marked with the UN number and other marks, as required for packages in Chapter 5.2 except 5.2.1.3 to 5.2.1.6, 5.2.1.7.2 to 5.2.1.7.8 and 5.2.1.10, for each item of dangerous goods contained in the overpack. Each applicable mark or label only needs to be applied once.

Labelling of overpacks containing radioactive material shall be in accordance with 5.2.2.1.11.

(b)   Orientation arrows illustrated in 5.2.1.10 shall be displayed on two opposite sides of overpacks containing packages which shall be marked in accordance with 5.2.1.10.1, unless the marks remains visible.

5.1.2.2   Each package of dangerous goods contained in an overpack shall comply with all applicable provisions of ADN. The intended function of each package shall not be impaired by the overpack.

5.1.2.3   Each package bearing package orientation marks as prescribed in 5.2.1.10 and which is overpacked or placed in a large packaging shall be oriented in accordance with such marks.

5.1.2.4   The prohibitions on mixed loading also apply to these overpacks.

5.1.3   **Empty uncleaned packagings (including IBCs and large packagings), tanks, MEMUs, vehicles, wagons and containers for carriage in bulk**

5.1.3.1   Empty uncleaned packagings (including IBCs and large packagings), tanks (including tank-vehicles, tank-wagons, battery-vehicles, battery-wagons, demountable tanks, portable tanks, tank-containers, MEGCs, MEMUs), vehicles, wagons and containers for carriage in bulk having contained dangerous goods of the different classes other than Class 7, shall be marked and labelled as if they were full.

NOTE: For documentation, see Chapter 5.4.

5.1.3.2   Containers, tanks, IBCs, as well as other packagings and overpacks, used for the carriage of radioactive material shall not be used for the storage or carriage of other goods unless decontaminated below the level of $0.4 \, Bq/cm^2$ for beta and gamma emitters and low toxicity alpha emitters and $0.04 \, Bq/cm^2$ for all other alpha emitters.

5.1.4   Mixed packing

When two or more dangerous goods are packed within the same outer packaging, the package shall be labelled and marked as required for each substance or article. If the same label is required for different goods, it only needs to be applied once.

5.1.5   General provisions for Class 7

5.1.5.1   *Approval of shipments and notification*

5.1.5.1.1   *General*

In addition to the approval of package designs described in Chapter 6.4 of ADR, multilateral shipment approval is also required in certain circumstances (5.1.5.1.2 and 5.1.5.1.3). In some circumstances it is also necessary to notify competent authorities of a shipment (5.1.5.1.4).

5.1.5.1.2   *Shipment approvals*

Multilateral approval shall be required for:

(a)   the shipment of Type B(M) packages not conforming with the requirements of 6.4.7.5 of ADR or designed to allow controlled intermittent venting;

(b)   the shipment of Type B(M) packages containing radioactive material with an activity greater than $3000 \, A_1$ or $3000 \, A_2$, as appropriate, or 1000 TBq, whichever is the lower;

(c)   the shipment of packages containing fissile materials if the sum of the criticality safety indexes of the packages in a single vessel, vehicle, wagon or container exceeds 50;

(d)   radiation protection programmes for shipments by special use vessels in accordance with 7.1.4.14.7.3.7; and

(e)   the shipment of SCO-III;

except that a competent authority may authorise carriage into or through its country without shipment approval, by a specific provision in its design approval (see 5.1.5.2.1).

5.1.5.1.3   *Shipment approval by special arrangement*

Provisions may be approved by a competent authority under which a consignment, which does not satisfy all of the applicable requirements of ADN may be carried under special arrangement (see 1.7.4).

5.1.5.1.4   *Notifications*

Notification to competent authorities is required as follows:

(a)   Before the first shipment of any package requiring competent authority approval, the consignor shall ensure that copies of each applicable competent authority certificate applying to that package design have been submitted to the competent authority of the country of origin of the shipment and to the competent authority of each country through or into which the consignment is to be carried. The consignor is not required to await an acknowledgement from the competent authority, nor is the competent authority required to make such acknowledgement of receipt of the certificate;

(b)   For each of the following types of shipments:

(i)   Type C packages containing radioactive material with an activity greater than 3000 A_1 or 3000 A_2, as appropriate, or 1000 TBq, whichever is the lower;

(ii)   Type B(U) packages containing radioactive material with an activity greater than 3000 A_1 or 3000 A_2, as appropriate, or 1000 TBq, whichever is the lower;

(iii)   Type B(M) packages;

(iv)   Shipment under special arrangement.

The consignor shall notify the competent authority of the country of origin of the shipment and the competent authority of each country through or into which the consignment is to be carried. This notification shall be in the possession of each competent authority prior to the commencement of the shipment, and preferably at least 7 days in advance;

(c)   The consignor is not required to send a separate notification if the required information has been included in the application for approval of shipment (see 6.4.23.2 of ADR);

(d)   The consignment notification shall include:

(i)   sufficient information to enable the identification of the package or packages including all applicable certificate numbers and identification marks;

(ii)   information on the date of shipment, the expected date of arrival and proposed routeing;

(iii)   the name(s) of the radioactive material(s) or nuclide(s);

(iv)   descriptions of the physical and chemical forms of the radioactive material, or whether it is special form radioactive material or low dispersible radioactive material; and

(v)   the maximum activity of the radioactive contents during carriage expressed in becquerels (Bq) with an appropriate SI prefix symbol (see 1.2.2.1). For fissile material, the mass of fissile material (or of each fissile nuclide for mixtures when appropriate) in grams (g), or multiples thereof, may be used in place of activity.

5.1.5.2   *Certificates issued by the competent authority*

5.1.5.2.1   Certificates issued by the competent authority are required for the following:

    (a)   Designs for:

        (i)   special form radioactive material;

        (ii)   low dispersible radioactive material;

        (iii)   fissile material excepted under 2.2.7.2.3.5 (f);

        (iv)   packages containing 0.1 kg or more of uranium hexafluoride;

        (v)   packages containing fissile material unless excepted by 2.2.7.2.3.5 of the present Regulations or 6.4.11.2 or 6.4.11.3 of ADR;

        (vi)   Type B(U) packages and Type B(M) packages;

        (vii)   Type C packages;

    (b)   Special arrangements;

    (c)   Certain shipments (see 5.1.5.1.2);

    (d)   Determination of the basic radionuclide values referred to in 2.2.7.2.2.1 for individual radionuclides which are not listed in Table 2.2.7.2.2.1 (see 2.2.7.2.2.2 (a));

    (e)   Alternative activity limits for an exempt consignment of instruments or articles (see 2.2.7.2.2.2 (b)).

The certificates shall confirm that the applicable requirements are met, and for design approvals shall attribute to the design an identification mark.

The certificates of approval for the package design and the shipment may be combined into a single certificate.

Certificates and applications for these certificates shall be in accordance with the requirements in 6.4.23 of ADR.

5.1.5.2.2   The consignor shall be in possession of a copy of each applicable certificate.

5.1.5.2.3   For package designs where it is not required that a competent authority issue a certificate of approval, the consignor shall, on request, make available for inspection by the competent authority, documentary evidence of the compliance of the package design with all the applicable requirements.

5.1.5.3   *Determination of transport index (TI) and criticality safety index (CSI)*

5.1.5.3.1   The transport index (TI) for a package, overpack or container, or for unpackaged LSA-I, SCO-I or SCO-III shall be the number derived in accordance with the following procedure:

    (a)   Determine the maximum dose rate in units of millisieverts per hour (mSv/h) at a distance of 1 m from the external surfaces of the package, overpack, container, or unpackaged LSA-I, SCO-I or SCO-III. The value determined shall be multiplied by 100. For uranium and thorium ores and their concentrates, the maximum dose rate at any point 1 m from the external surface of the load may be taken as:

0.4 mSv/h	for ores and physical concentrates of uranium and thorium;
0.3 mSv/h	for chemical concentrates of thorium;
0.02 mSv/h	for chemical concentrates of uranium, other than uranium hexafluoride;

(b) For tanks, containers and unpackaged LSA-I, SCO-I or SCO-III, the value determined in step (a) above shall be multiplied by the appropriate factor from Table 5.1.5.3.1;

(c) The value obtained in steps (a) and (b) above shall be rounded up to the first decimal place (e.g. 1.13 becomes 1.2), except that a value of 0.05 or less may be considered as zero and the resulting number is the TI value.

Table 5.1.5.3.1:   Multiplication factors for tanks, containers and unpackaged LSA-I, SCO-I and SCO-III

Size of load [a]	Multiplication factor
size of load ≤ 1 m^2	1
1 m^2 < size of load ≤ 5 m^2	2
5 m^2 < size of load ≤ 20 m^2	3
20 m^2 < size of load	10

[a]   *Largest cross-sectional area of the load being measured.*

5.1.5.3.2   The TI for each overpack, vessel or cargo transport unit shall be determined as the sum of the TIs of all the packages contained therein. For a shipment from a single consignor, the consignor may determine the TI by direct measurement of dose rate.

The TI for a non-rigid overpack shall be determined only as the sum of the TIs of all the packages within the overpack.

5.1.5.3.3   The criticality safety index for each overpack or container shall be determined as the sum of the CSIs of all the packages contained. The same procedure shall be followed for determining the total sum of the CSIs in a consignment or aboard a vessel or cargo transport unit.

5.1.5.3.4   Packages, overpacks and containers shall be assigned to either category I-WHITE, II-YELLOW or III-YELLOW in accordance with the conditions specified in Table 5.1.5.3.4 and with the following requirements:

(a) For a package, overpack or container, both the transport index and the surface dose rate conditions shall be taken into account in determining which is the appropriate category. Where the transport index satisfies the condition for one category but the surface dose rate satisfies the condition for a different category, the package, overpack or container shall be assigned to the higher category. For this purpose, category I-WHITE shall be regarded as the lowest category;

(b) The TI shall be determined following the procedures specified in 5.1.5.3.1 and 5.1.5.3.2;

(c) If the surface dose rate is greater than 2 mSv/h, the package or overpack shall be carried under exclusive use and under the provisions of 7.1.4.14.7.1.3 and 7.1.4.14.7.3.5 (a) as appropriate;

(d) A package carried under a special arrangement shall be assigned to category III-YELLOW except under the provisions of 5.1.5.3.5;

(e) An overpack or container which contains packages carried under special arrangement shall be assigned to category III-YELLOW except under the provisions of 5.1.5.3.5.

Table 5.1.5.3.4: Categories of packages, overpacks and containers

Conditions		Category
Transport index	**Maximum dose rate at any point on external surface**	
0[a]	Not more than 0.005 mSv/h	I-WHITE
More than 0 but not more than 1[a]	More than 0.005 mSv/h but not more than 0.5 mSv/h	II-YELLOW
More than 1 but not more than 10	More than 0.5 mSv/h but not more than 2 mSv/h	III-YELLOW
More than 10	More than 2 mSv/h but not more than 10 mSv/h	III-YELLOW [b]

[a] *If the measured TI is not greater than 0.05, the value quoted may be zero in accordance with 5.1.5.3.1(c).*
[b] *Shall also be carried under exclusive use except for containers (see Table D in 7.1.4.14.7.3.3).*

5.1.5.3.5 In all cases of international carriage of packages requiring competent authority approval of design or shipment, for which different approval types apply in the different countries concerned by the shipment, the categorization shall be in accordance with the certificate of the country of origin of design.

5.1.5.4 ***Specific provisions for excepted packages of radioactive material of Class 7***

5.1.5.4.1 Excepted packages of radioactive material of Class 7 shall be legibly and durably marked on the outside of the packaging with:

(a) The UN number preceded by the letters "UN";

(b) An identification of either the consignor or consignee, or both; and

(c) The permissible gross mass if this exceeds 50 kg.

5.1.5.4.2 The documentation requirements of Chapter 5.4 do not apply to excepted packages of radioactive material of Class 7, except that:

(a) The UN number preceded by the letters "UN" and the name and address of the consignor and the consignee and, if relevant, the identification mark for each competent authority certificate of approval (see 5.4.1.2.5.1 (g)) shall be shown on a transport document such as a bill of lading, air waybill or CMR, CIM or CMNI consignment note;

(b) If relevant, the requirements of 5.4.1.2.5.1 (g), 5.4.1.2.5.3 and 5.4.1.2.5.4 shall apply;

(c) The requirements of 5.4.2 and 5.4.4 shall apply.

5.1.5.4.3 The requirements of 5.2.1.7.8 and 5.2.2.1.11.5 shall apply if relevant.

5.1.5.5 *Summary of approval and prior notification requirements*

NOTE 1: Before first shipment of any package requiring competent authority approval of the design, the consignor shall ensure that a copy of the approval certificate for that design has been submitted to the competent authority of each country en route (see 5.1.5.1.4 (a)).

NOTE 2: Notification required if contents exceed 3×10^3 A_1, or 3×10^3 A_2, or 1000 TBq (see 5.1.5.1.4 (b)).

NOTE 3: Multilateral approval of shipment required if contents exceed 3×10^3 A_1, or 3×10^3 A_2, or 1000 TBq, or if controlled intermittent venting is allowed (see 5.1.5.1).

NOTE 4: See approval and prior notification provisions for the applicable package for carrying this material.

Subject	UN Number	Competent authority approval required		Consignor required to notify the competent authorities of the country of origin and of the countries en route[a] before each shipment	Reference
		Country of origin	Countries en route[a]		
Calculation of unlisted A_1 and A_2 values	-	Yes	Yes	No	2.2.7.2.2.2 (a), 5.1.5.2.1 (d)
Excepted packages - package design - shipment	2908, 2909, 2910, 2911	 No No	 No No	 No No	-
LSA material[b] and SCO[b] Industrial packages types 1, 2 or 3, non fissile and fissile excepted - package design - shipment	2912, 2913, 3321, 3322	 No No	 No No	 No No	-
Type A packages,[b] non fissile and fissile excepted - package design - shipment	2915, 3332	 No No	 No No	 No No	-
Type B(U) packages,[b] non fissile and fissile excepted - package design - shipment	2916	 Yes No	 No No	 See Note 1 See Note 2	5.1.5.1.4 (b), 5.1.5.2.1 (a) 6.4.22.2 (ADR)
Type B(M) packages,[b] non fissile and fissile excepted - package design - shipment	2917	 Yes See Note 3	 Yes See Note 3	 No Yes	5.1.5.1.4 (b), 5.1.5.2.1 (a), 5.1.5.1.2. 6.4.22.3 (ADR)

Subject	UN Number	Competent authority approval required		Consignor required to notify the competent authorities of the country of origin and of the countries en route[a] before each shipment	Reference
		Country of origin	Countries en route[a]		
Type C packages,[b] non fissile and fissile excepted	3323				5.1.5.1.4 (b), 5.1.5.2.1 (a) 6.4.22.2 (ADR)
- package design		Yes	No	See Note 1	
- shipment		No	No	See Note 2	
Packages for fissile material	2977, 3324, 3325, 3326, 3327, 3328, 3329, 3330, 3331, 3333				5.1.5.2.1 (a), 5.1.5.1.2, 6.4.22.4 (ADR)
- package design		Yes[c]	Yes[c]	No	
- shipment					
- sum of criticality safety indexes not more than 50		No[d]	No[d]	See Note 2	
- sum of criticality safety indexes greater than 50		Yes	Yes	See Note 2	
Special form radioactive material					1.6.6.4 (ADR), 5.1.5.2.1 (a) 6.4.22.5 (ADR)
- design	-	Yes	No	No	
- shipment	See Note 4	See Note 4	See Note 4	See Note 4	
Low dispersable radioactive material					5.1.5.2.1 (a), 6.4.22.5 (ADR)
- design	-	Yes	No	No	
- shipment	See Note 4	See Note 4	See Note 4	See Note 4	
Packages containing 0.1 kg or more of uranium hexafluoride					5.1.5.2.1 (a), 6.4.22.1 (ADR)
- design	-	Yes	No	No	
- shipment	See Note 4	See Note 4	See Note 4	See Note 4	
Special arrangement	2919, 3331				1.7.4.2, 5.1.5.2.1 (b), 5.1.5.1.4 (b)
- shipment		Yes	Yes	Yes	

Subject	UN Number	Competent authority approval required		Consignor required to notify the competent authorities of the country of origin and of the countries en route[a] before each shipment	Reference
		Country of origin	Countries en route[a]		
Approved packages designs subjected to transitional measures	-	See 1.6.6	See 1.6.6	See Note 1	1.6.6.2, (ADR), 5.1.5.1.4 (b), 5.1.5.2.1 (a), 5.1.5.1.2. 6.4.22.9 (ADR)
Alternative activity limits for an exempt consignment of instruments or articles	-	Yes	Yes	No	5.1.5.2.1(e), 6.4.22.7 (ADR)
Fissile material excepted in accordance with 2.2.7.2.3.5 (f)	-	Yes	Yes	No	5.1.5.2.1 (a) (iii), 6.4.22.6 (ADR)

[a]   *Countries from, through or into which the consignment is carried.*

[b]   *If the radioactive contents are fissile material which is not excepted from the provisions for packages containing fissile material, then the provisions for fissile material packages apply (see 6.4.11 of ADR).*

[c]   *Designs of packages for fissile material may also require approval in respect of one of the other items in the table.*

[d]   *Shipments may, however, require approval in respect of one of the other items in the table.*

CHAPTER 5.2

MARKING AND LABELLING

5.2.1   **Marking of packages**

NOTE 1: For marks related to the construction, testing and approval of packagings, large packagings, pressure receptacles and IBCs, see Part 6 of ADR.

NOTE 2:   In accordance with the GHS, a GHS pictogram not required by ADN should only appear in carriage as part of a complete GHS label and not independently (see GHS 1.4.10.4.4).

5.2.1.1   Unless provided otherwise in ADN, the UN number corresponding to the dangerous goods contained, preceded by the letters "UN" shall be clearly and durably marked on each package. The UN number and the letters "UN" shall be at least 12 mm high, except for packages of 30 *l* capacity or less or of 30 kg maximum net mass and for cylinders of 60 *l* water capacity or less when they shall be at least 6 mm in height and except for packages of 5 *l* capacity or less or of 5 kg maximum net mass when they shall be of an appropriate size. In the case of unpackaged articles the mark shall be displayed on the article, on its cradle or on its handling, storage or launching device.

5.2.1.2   All package marks required by this Chapter:

(a)   shall be readily visible and legible;

(b)   shall be able to withstand open weather exposure without a substantial reduction in effectiveness.

5.2.1.3   Salvage packagings, including large salvage packagings, and salvage pressure receptacles shall additionally be marked with the word **"SALVAGE"**. The lettering of the "SALVAGE" mark shall be at least 12 mm high.

5.2.1.4   Intermediate bulk containers of more than 450 litres capacity and large packagings shall be marked on two opposite sides.

5.2.1.5   *Additional provisions for goods of Class 1*

For goods of Class 1, packages shall, in addition, bear the proper shipping name as determined in accordance with 3.1.2. The mark, which shall be clearly legible and indelible, shall be in one or more languages, one of which must be French, German or English, unless any agreements concluded between the countries concerned in the transport operation provide otherwise.

5.2.1.6   *Additional provisions for goods of Class 2*

Refillable receptacles shall bear the following particulars in clearly legible and durable characters:

(a)   the UN number and the proper shipping name of the gas or mixture of gases, as determined in accordance with 3.1.2.

In the case of gases classified under an N.O.S. entry, only the technical name[1] of the gas has to be indicated in addition to the UN number.

In the case of mixtures, not more than the two constituents which most predominantly contribute to the hazards have to be indicated;

(b)   for compressed gases filled by mass and for liquefied gases, either the maximum filling mass and the tare of the receptacle with fittings and accessories as fitted at the time of filling, or the gross mass;

(c)   the date (year) of the next periodic inspection.

These particulars can either be engraved or indicated on a durable information disk or label attached on the receptacle or indicated by an adherent and clearly visible mark such as by printing or by any equivalent process.

NOTE 1: See also 6.2.2.7 of ADR.

NOTE 2: For non refillable receptacles, see 6.2.2.8 of ADR.

5.2.1.7   ***Special marking provisions for radioactive material***

5.2.1.7.1   Each package shall be legibly and durably marked on the outside of the packaging with an identification of either the consignor or consignee, or both. Each overpack shall be legibly and durably marked on the outside of the overpack with an identification of either the consignor or consignee, or both unless these marks of all packages within the overpack are clearly visible.

5.2.1.7.2   For each package, other than excepted packages, the UN number preceded by the letters "UN" and the proper shipping name shall be legibly and durably marked on the outside of the packaging. The marking of excepted packages shall be as required by 5.1.5.4.1.

5.2.1.7.3   Each package of gross mass exceeding 50 kg shall have its permissible gross mass legibly and durably marked on the outside of the packaging.

5.2.1.7.4   Each package which conforms to:

(a)   a Type IP-1 package, a Type IP-2 package or a Type IP-3 package design shall be legibly and durably marked on the outside of the packaging with "TYPE IP-1", "TYPE IP-2" or "TYPE IP-3" as appropriate;

(b)   a Type A package design shall be legibly and durably marked on the outside of the packaging with "TYPE A";

(c)   a Type IP-2 package, a Type IP-3 package or a Type A package design shall be legibly and durably marked on the outside of the packaging with the distinguishing sign used on vehicles in international road traffic[2] of the country of origin of design and either the

---

[1]   *Instead of the proper shipping name or, if applicable, of the proper shipping name of the n.o.s. entry followed by the technical name, the use of the following names is permitted:*
-     *for UN No. 1078 refrigerant gas, n.o.s: mixture F1, mixture F2, mixture F3;*
-     *for UN No. 1060 methylacetylene and propadiene mixtures, stabilized: mixture P1, mixture P2;*
-     *for UN No. 1965 hydrocarbon gas mixture, liquefied, n.o.s: mixture A or butane, mixture A01 or butane, mixture A02 or butane, mixture A0 or butane, mixture A1, mixture B1, mixture B2, mixture B, mixture C or propane.*
-     *for UN No. 1010 Butadienes, stabilized: 1,2-Butadiene, stabilized, 1,3-Butadiene, stabilized.*

[2]   *Distinguishing sign of the State of registration used on motor vehicles and trailers in international road traffic, e.g. in accordance with the Geneva Convention on Road Traffic of 1949 or the Vienna Convention on Road Traffic of 1968.*

name of the manufacturer or other identification of the packaging specified by the competent authority of the country of origin of design.

5.2.1.7.5   Each package which conforms to a design approved under one or more of paragraphs 5.1.5.2.1 of these Regulations, 1.6.6.2.1, 6.4.22.1 to 6.4.22.4 and 6.4.23.4 to 6.4.23.7 of ADR shall be legibly and durably marked on the outside of the package with the following information:

(a)   the identification mark allocated to that design by the competent authority;

(b)   a serial number to uniquely identify each packaging which conforms to that design;

(c)   "Type B(U)", "Type B(M)" or "Type C", in the case of a Type B(U), Type B(M) or Type C package design.

5.2.1.7.6   Each package which conforms to a Type B(U), Type B(M) or Type C package design shall have the outside of the outermost receptacle which is resistant to the effects of fire and water plainly marked by embossing, stamping or other means resistant to the effects of fire and water with the trefoil symbol shown in the figure below.

Basic trefoil symbol with proportions based on a central circle of radius X. The minimum allowable size of X shall be 4 mm.

Any mark on the package made in accordance with the requirements of 5.2.1.7.4 (a) and (b) and 5.2.1.7.5 (c) relating to the package type that does not relate to the UN number and proper shipping name assigned to the consignment shall be removed or covered.

5.2.1.7.7   Where LSA-I or SCO-I material is contained in receptacles or wrapping materials and is carried under exclusive use as permitted by 4.1.9.2.4 of ADR, the outer surface of these receptacles or wrapping materials may bear the mark "RADIOACTIVE LSA-I" or "RADIOACTIVE SCO-I", as appropriate.

5.2.1.7.8   In all cases of international carriage of packages requiring competent authority approval of design or shipment, for which different approval types apply in the different countries concerned by the shipment, marking shall be in accordance with the certificate of the country of origin of the design.

5.2.1.8   *Special marking provisions for environmentally hazardous substances*

5.2.1.8.1   Packages containing environmentally hazardous substances meeting the criteria of 2.2.9.1.10 shall be durably marked with the environmentally hazardous substance mark shown in 5.2.1.8.3 with the exception of single packagings and combination packagings where such single packagings or inner packagings of such combination packagings have:

-        a quantity of 5 *l* or less for liquids; or

-        a net mass of 5 kg or less for solids.

5.2.1.8.2   The environmentally hazardous substance mark shall be located adjacent to the marks required by 5.2.1.1. The requirements of 5.2.1.2 and 5.2.1.4 shall be met.

5.2.1.8.3   The environmentally hazardous substance mark shall be as shown in Figure 5.2.1.8.3.

Figure 5.2.1.8.3

Environmentally hazardous substance mark

The mark shall be in the form of a square set at an angle of 45° (diamond-shaped). The symbol (fish and tree) shall be black on white or suitable contrasting background. The minimum dimensions shall be 100 mm x 100 mm and the minimum width of the line forming the diamond shall be 2 mm. If the size of the package so requires, the dimensions/line thickness may be reduced, provided the mark remains clearly visible. Where dimensions are not specified, all features shall be in approximate proportion to those shown.

NOTE: *The labelling provisions of 5.2.2 apply in addition to any requirement for packages to bear the environmentally hazardous substance mark.*

5.2.1.9   *Lithium battery mark*

5.2.1.9.1   Packages containing lithium cells or batteries prepared in accordance with special provision 188 of Chapter 3.3 shall be marked as shown in Figure 5.2.1.9.2.

5.2.1.9.2   The mark shall indicate the UN number preceded by the letters "UN", i.e. 'UN 3090' for lithium metal cells or batteries or 'UN 3480' for lithium ion cells or batteries. Where the lithium cells or batteries are contained in, or packed with, equipment, the UN number preceded by the letters "UN", i.e. 'UN 3091' or 'UN 3481' as appropriate shall be indicated. Where a package contains lithium cells or batteries assigned to different UN numbers, all applicable UN numbers shall be indicated on one or more marks.

Figure 5.2.1.9.2

Minimum dimension 100 mm

Minimum dimension 100 mm

Lithium battery mark

*   Place for UN number(s)

**   Place for telephone number for additional information

The mark shall be in the form of a rectangle or a square with hatched edging. The dimensions shall be a minimum of 100 mm wide × 100 mm high and the minimum width of the hatching shall be 5 mm. The symbol (group of batteries, one damaged and emitting flame, above the UN number for lithium ion or lithium metal batteries or cells) shall be black on white or suitable contrasting background. The hatching shall be red. If the size of the package so requires, the dimensions may be reduced to not less than 100 mm wide x 70 mm high. Where dimensions are not specified, all features shall be in approximate proportion to those shown.

5.2.1.10   *Orientation arrows*

5.2.1.10.1   Except as provided in 5.2.1.10.2:

-    combination packagings having inner packagings containing liquids;

-    single packagings fitted with vents;

-    cryogenic receptacles intended for the carriage of refrigerated liquefied gases; and

-    machinery or apparatus containing liquid dangerous goods when it is required to ensure the liquid dangerous goods remain in their intended orientation (see special provision 301 of Chapter 3.3),

shall be legibly marked with package orientation arrows which are similar to the illustration shown below or with those meeting the specifications of ISO 780:1997. The orientation arrows shall appear on two opposite vertical sides of the package with the arrows pointing in the correct upright direction. They shall be rectangular and of a size that is clearly visible commensurate with the size of the package. Depicting a rectangular border around the arrows is optional.

Figure 5.2.1.10.1.1   **Figure 5.2.1.10.1.2**

   or

Two black or red arrows on white or suitable contrasting background.

The rectangular border is optional.

All features shall be in approximate proportion to those shown.

5.2.1.10.2   Orientation arrows are not required on:

(a)   Outer packagings containing pressure receptacles except cryogenic receptacles;

(b)   Outer packagings containing dangerous goods in inner packagings each containing not more than 120 ml, with sufficient absorbent material between the inner and outer packagings to completely absorb the liquid contents;

(c)   Outer packagings containing Class 6.2 infectious substances in primary receptacles each containing not more than 50 ml;

(d)   Type IP-2, type IP-3, type A, type B(U), type B(M) or type C packages containing Class 7 radioactive material;

(e)   Outer packagings containing articles which are leak-tight in all orientations (e.g. alcohol or mercury in thermometers, aerosols, etc.); or

(f)   Outer packagings containing dangerous goods in hermetically sealed inner packagings each containing not more than 500 ml.

5.2.1.10.3   Arrows for purposes other than indicating proper package orientation shall not be displayed on a package marked in accordance with this sub-section.

5.2.2   Labelling of packages

5.2.2.1   *Labelling provisions*

5.2.2.1.1   For each article or substance listed in Table A of Chapter 3.2, the labels shown in Column (5) shall be affixed unless otherwise provided for by a special provision in Column (6).

5.2.2.1.2   Indelible danger mark corresponding exactly to the prescribed models may be used instead of labels.

5.2.2.1.3 to 5.2.2.1.5   (*Reserved*)

5.2.2.1.6   Except as provided in 5.2.2.2.1.2, each label shall:

(a)   be affixed to the same surface of the package, if the dimensions of the package allow; for packages of Class 1 and 7, near the mark indicating the proper shipping name;

(b)   be so placed on the package that it is not covered or obscured by any part or attachment to the packaging or any other label or mark; and

(c)   be displayed next to each other when more than one label is required.

Where a package is of such an irregular shape or small size that a label cannot be satisfactorily affixed, the label may be attached to the package by a securely affixed tag or other suitable means.

5.2.2.1.7   Intermediate bulk containers of more than 450 litres capacity and large packages shall be labelled on two opposite sides.

5.2.2.1.8   (*Reserved*)

5.2.2.1.9   *Special provisions for the labelling of self-reactive substances and organic peroxides*

(a)   the label conforming to model No. 4.1 also implies that the product may be flammable and hence no label conforming to model No. 3 is required. In addition, a label conforming to model No. 1 shall be applied for self-reactive substances Type B, unless the competent authority has permitted this label to be dispensed with for a specific packaging because test data have proven that the self-reactive substance in such a packaging does not exhibit explosive behaviour.

(b)   the label conforming to model No. 5.2 also implies that the product may be flammable and hence no label conforming to model No. 3 is required. In addition, the following labels shall be applied:

(i)   a label conforming to model No. 1 for organic peroxides type B, unless the competent authority has permitted this label to be dispensed with for a specific packaging because test data have proven that the organic peroxide in such a packaging does not exhibit explosive behaviour;

(ii)   a label conforming to model No. 8 is required when Packing Group I or II criteria of Class 8 are met.

For self-reactive substances and organic peroxides mentioned by name, the labels to be affixed are indicated in the list found in 2.2.41.4 and 2.2.52.4 respectively.

5.2.2.1.10   *Special provisions for the labelling of infectious substances packages*

In addition to the label conforming to model No. 6.2, infectious substances packages shall bear any other label required by the nature of the contents.

5.2.2.1.11   *Special provisions for the labelling of radioactive material*

5.2.2.1.11.1   Except when enlarged labels are used in accordance with 5.3.1.1.3, each package, overpack and container containing radioactive material shall bear the labels conforming to the applicable models Nos. 7A, 7B or 7C, according to the appropriate category. Labels shall be affixed to two opposite sides on the outside of the package or overpack or on the outside of all four sides of a container or tank. In addition, each package, overpack and container containing fissile material, other than fissile material excepted under the provisions of 2.2.7.2.3.5 shall bear labels conforming to model No. 7E; such labels, where applicable, shall be affixed adjacent to the labels conforming to the applicable model Nos. 7A, 7B or 7C. Labels shall not cover the marks specified in 5.2.1. Any labels which do not relate to the contents shall be removed or covered.

5.2.2.1.11.2   Each label conforming to the applicable model No. 7A, 7B or 7C shall be completed with the following information:

(a)   *Contents*:

(i)   except for LSA-I material, the name(s) of the radionuclide(s) as taken from Table 2.2.7.2.2.1, using the symbols prescribed therein. For mixtures of radionuclides, the most restrictive nuclides shall be listed to the extent the space on the line permits. The group of LSA or SCO shall be shown following the name(s) of the radionuclide(s). The terms "LSA-II","LSA-III", "SCO-I" and "SCO-II" shall be used for this purpose;

(ii)   for LSA-I material, only the term "LSA-I" is necessary; the name of the radionuclide is not necessary;

(b)   *Activity*: The maximum activity of the radioactive contents during carriage expressed in becquerels (Bq) with the appropriate SI prefix symbol (see 1.2.2.1). For fissile material, the total mass of fissile nuclides in units of grams (g), or multiples thereof, may be used in place of activity;

(c)   For overpacks and containers the "contents" and "activity" entries on the label shall bear the information required in (a) and (b) above, respectively, totalled together for the entire contents of the overpack or container except that on labels for overpacks or containers containing mixed loads of packages containing different radionuclides, such entries may read "See Transport Documents";

(d)   *Transport index (TI)*: The number determined in accordance with 5.1.5.3.1 and 5.1.5.3.2 (except for category I-WHITE).

5.2.2.1.11.3   Each label conforming to the model No. 7E shall be completed with the criticality safety index (CSI) as stated in the certificate of approval applicable in the countries through or into which the consignment is carried and issued by the competent authority or as specified in 6.4.11.2 or 6.4.11.3 of ADR.

5.2.2.1.11.4   For overpacks and containers, the label conforming to model No. 7E shall bear the sum of the criticality safety indexes of all the packages contained therein.

5.2.2.1.11.5   In all cases of international carriage of packages requiring competent authority approval of design or shipment, for which different approval types apply in the different countries concerned by the shipment, labelling shall be in accordance with the certificate of the country of origin of design.

5.2.2.1.12   *Special provisions for the labelling of articles containing dangerous goods carried as UN Nos. 3537, 3538, 3539, 3540, 3541, 3542, 3543, 3544, 3545, 3546, 3547 and 3548*

5.2.2.1.12.1   Packages containing articles or articles carried unpackaged shall bear labels according to 5.2.2.1 reflecting the hazards established according to 2.1.5, except that for articles that in addition contain lithium batteries, a lithium battery mark or a label conforming to model No. 9A is not required.

5.2.2.1.12.2   When it is required to ensure articles containing liquid dangerous goods remain in their intended orientation, orientation arrows meeting 5.2.1.10.1 shall be affixed and visible on at least two opposite vertical sides of the package or of the unpackaged article where possible, with the arrows pointing in the correct upright direction.

5.2.2.2   *Provisions for labels*

5.2.2.2.1   Labels shall satisfy the provisions below and conform, in terms of colour, symbols and general format, to the models shown in 5.2.2.2.2. Corresponding models required for other modes of transport, with minor variations which do not affect the obvious meaning of the label, are also acceptable.

> *NOTE*:   *Where appropriate, labels in 5.2.2.2.2 are shown with a dotted outer boundary as provided for in 5.2.2.2.1.1. This is not required when the label is applied on a background of contrasting colour.*

5.2.2.2.1.1   Labels shall be configured as shown in Figure 5.2.2.2.1.1.

Figure 5.2.2.2.1.1

Class/division label

*   *The class or for Classes 4.1, 4.2 and 4.3, the figure "4" or for Classes 6.1 and 6.2, the figure "6", shall be shown in the bottom corner.*

**   *Additional text/numbers/symbol/letters shall (if mandatory) or may (if optional) be shown in this bottom half.*

***   *The class symbol or, for divisions 1.4, 1.5 and 1.6, the division number and for Model No 7E the word "FISSILE" shall be shown in this top half.*

5.2.2.2.1.1.1   Labels shall be displayed on a background of contrasting colour, or shall have either a dotted or solid outer boundary line.

5.2.2.2.1.1.2   The label shall be in the form of a square set at an angle of 45° (diamond-shaped). The minimum dimensions shall be 100 mm x 100 mm. There shall be a line inside the edge forming the diamond which shall be parallel and approximately 5 mm from the outside of that line to the edge of the label. The line inside the edge on the upper half of the label shall be the same colour as the symbol and the line inside the edge on the lower half of the label shall be the same colour as the class or division number in the bottom corner. Where dimensions are not specified, all features shall be in approximate proportion to those shown.

5.2.2.2.1.1.3   If the size of the package so requires the dimensions may be reduced proportionally, provided the symbols and other elements of the label remain clearly visible. Dimensions for cylinders shall comply with 5.2.2.2.1.2.

5.2.2.2.1.2   Gas cylinders for Class 2 may, on account of their shape, orientation and securing mechanisms for carriage, bear labels representative of those specified in this section and the environmentally hazardous substance mark when appropriate, which have been reduced in size, according to the dimensions outlined in ISO 7225:2005, *"Gas cylinders - Precautionary labels"*, for display on the non-cylindrical part (shoulder) of such cylinders.

NOTE: *When the diameter of the cylinder is too small to permit the display of the reduced size labels on the non-cylindrical upper part of the cylinder, the reduced sized labels may be displayed on the cylindrical part.*

Notwithstanding the provisions of 5.2.2.1.6, labels and the environmentally hazardous substance mark (see 5.2.1.8.3) may overlap to the extent provided for by ISO 7225:2005. However, in all cases, the primary hazard label and the figures appearing on any label shall remain fully visible and the symbols recognizable.

Empty uncleaned pressure receptacles for gases of Class 2 may be carried with obsolete or damaged labels for the purposes of refilling or inspection as appropriate and the application of a new label in conformity with current regulations or for the disposal of the pressure receptacle.

5.2.2.2.1.3   With the exception of labels for Divisions 1.4, 1.5 and 1.6 of Class 1, the upper half of the label shall contain the pictorial symbol and the lower half shall contain:

(a)   For Classes 1, 2, 3, 5.1, 5.2, 7, 8 and 9, the class number;

(b)   For Classes 4.1, 4.2 and 4.3, the figure "4";

(c)   For Classes 6.1 and 6.2, the figure "6".

However for label model No. 9A, the upper half of the label shall only contain the seven vertical stripes of the symbol and the lower half shall contain the group of batteries of the symbol and the class number.

Except for label model No. 9A, the label may include text such as the UN number or words describing the hazard (e.g. "flammable") in accordance with 5.2.2.2.1.5 provided the text does not obscure or detract from the other required label elements.

5.2.2.2.1.4   In addition, except for Divisions 1.4, 1.5 and 1.6, labels for Class 1 shall show in the lower half, above the class number, the division number and the compatibility group letter for the substance or article. Labels for Divisions 1.4, 1.5 and 1.6 shall show in the upper half the division number, and in the lower half the class number and the compatibility group letter.

5.2.2.2.1.5   On labels other than those for material of Class 7, the optional insertion of any text (other than the class number) in the space below the symbol shall be confined to particulars indicating the nature of the hazard and precautions to be taken in handling.

5.2.2.2.1.6   The symbols, text and numbers shall be clearly legible and indelible and shall be shown in black on all labels except for:

(a)   the Class 8 label, where the text (if any) and class number shall appear in white;

(b)   labels with entirely green, red or blue backgrounds where they may be shown in white;

(c)   the Class 5.2 label, where the symbol may be shown in white; and

(d)   labels conforming to model No. 2.1 displayed on cylinders and gas cartridges for liquefied petroleum gases, where they may be shown in the background colour of the receptacle if adequate contrast is provided.

5.2.2.2.1.7   All labels shall be able to withstand open weather exposure without a substantial reduction in effectiveness.

5.2.2.2 *Specimen labels*

Label model No.	Division or Category	Symbol and symbol colour	Background	Figure in bottom corner (and figure colour)	Specimen labels	Note
					Class 1 hazard: Explosive substances or articles	
1	Divisions 1.1, 1.2, 1.3	Exploding bomb: black	Orange	1 (black)		** Place for division – to be left blank if explosive is the subsidiary hazard * Place for compatibility group – to be left blank if explosive is the subsidiary hazard
1.4	Division 1.4	1.4: black Numerals shall be about 30 mm in height and be about 5 mm thick (for a label measuring 100 mm × 100 mm)	Orange	1 (black)		* Place for compatibility group
1.5	Division 1.5	1.5: black Numerals shall be about 30 mm in height and be about 5 mm thick (for a label measuring 100 mm × 100 mm)	Orange	1 (black)		* Place for compatibility group
1.6	Division 1.6	1.6: black Numerals shall be about 30 mm in height and be about 5 mm thick (for a label measuring 100 mm × 100 mm)	Orange	1 (black)		* Place for compatibility group

Label model No.	Division or Category	Symbol and symbol colour	Background	Figure in bottom corner (and figure colour)	Specimen labels	Note
				Class 2 hazard: Gases		
2.1	Flammable gases	Flame: black or white (except as provided for in 5.2.2.1.6 (d))	Red	2 (black or white) (except as provided for in 5.2.2.1.6 (d))		-
2.2	Non-flammable, non-toxic gases	Gas cylinder: black or white	Green	2 (black or white)		-
2.3	Toxic gases	Skull and crossbones: black	White	2 (black)		-
				Class 3 hazard: Flammable liquids		
3	-	Flame: black or white	Red	3 (black or white)		-

Label model No.	Division or Category	Symbol and symbol colour	Background	Figure in bottom corner (and figure colour)	Specimen labels	Note
Class 4.1 hazard: Flammable solids, self-reactive substances, polymerizing substances and solid desensitized explosives						
4.1	-	Flame: black	White with 7 vertical red stripes	4 (black)		-
Class 4.2 hazard: Substances liable to spontaneous combustion						
4.2	-	Flame: black	Upper half white, lower half red	4 (black)		-
Class 4.3 hazard: Substances which, in contact with water emit flammable gases						
4.3	-	Flame: black or white	Blue	4 (black or white)		-
Class 5.1 hazard: Oxidizing substances						
5.1	-	Flame over circle: black	Yellow	5.1 (black)		-

Label model No.	Division or Category	Symbol and symbol colour	Background	Figure in bottom corner (and figure colour)	Specimen labels	Note
Class 5.2 hazard: Organic peroxides						
5.2	-	Flame: black or white	Upper half red, lower half yellow	5.2 (black)		-
Class 6.1 hazard: Toxic substances						
6.1	-	Skull and crossbones: black	White	6 (black)		-
Class 6.2 hazard: Infectious substances						
6.2	-	Three crescents superimposed on a circle: black	White	6 (black)		The lower half of the label may bear the inscriptions: "INFECTIOUS SUBSTANCE" and "In the case of damage or leakage immediately notify Public Health Authority" in black colour

Class 7 hazard: Radioactive material

Label model No.	Division or Category	Symbol and symbol colour	Background	Figure in bottom corner (and figure colour)	Specimen labels	Note
7A	Category I – WHITE	Trefoil: black	White	7 (black)		Text (mandatory), black in lower half of label: "RADIOACTIVE" "CONTENTS …" "ACTIVITY …" One red vertical bar shall follow the word: "RADIOACTIVE"
7B	Category II – YELLOW	Trefoil: black	Upper half yellow with white border, lower half white	7 (black)		Text (mandatory), black in lower half of label: "RADIOACTIVE" "CONTENTS …" "ACTIVITY …" In a black outlined box: "TRANSPORT INDEX"; Two red vertical bars shall follow the word: "RADIOACTIVE"
7C	Category III – YELLOW	Trefoil: black	Upper half yellow with white border, lower half white	7 (black)		Text (mandatory), black in lower half of label: "RADIOACTIVE" "CONTENTS …" "ACTIVITY …" In a black outlined box: "TRANSPORT INDEX". Three red vertical bars shall follow the word: "RADIOACTIVE"
7E	Fissile material	-	White	7 (black)		Text (mandatory): black in upper half of label: "FISSILE"; In a black outlined box in the lower half of label: "CRITICALITY SAFETY INDEX"

Label model No.	Division or Category	Symbol and symbol colour	Background	Figure in bottom corner (and figure colour)	Specimen labels	Note
Class 8 hazard: Corrosive substances						
8	-	Liquids, spilling from two glass vessels and attacking a hand and a metal: black	Upper half white, lower half black with white border	8 (white)		-
Class 9 hazard: Miscellaneous dangerous substances and articles, including environmentally hazardous substances						
9	-	7 vertical stripes in upper half: black	White	9 underlined (black)		-
9A	-	7 vertical stripes in upper half: black; battery group, one broken and emitting flame in lower half: black	White	9 underlined (black)		-

CHAPTER 5.3

PLACARDING AND MARKING OF CONTAINERS, BULK CONTAINERS, MEGCs, MEMUs, TANK-CONTAINERS, PORTABLE TANKS, VEHICLES AND WAGONS

NOTE 1: For marking and placarding of containers, MEGCs, tank-containers and portable tanks for carriage in a transport chain including a maritime journey, see also 1.1.4.2.1. If the provisions of 1.1.4.2.1 (c) are applied, only 5.3.1.3 and 5.3.2.1.1 of this Chapter are applicable.

NOTE 2: In accordance with the GHS, a GHS pictogram not required by ADN should only appear in carriage as part of a complete GHS label and not independently (see GHS 1.4.10.4.4).

5.3.1 Placarding

5.3.1.1 *General provisions*

5.3.1.1.1 As and when required in this section, placards shall be affixed to the exterior surface of containers, bulk containers, MEGCs, MEMUs, tank-containers, portable tanks, vehicles and wagons. Placards shall correspond to the labels required in Column (5) and, where appropriate, Column (6) of Table A of Chapter 3.2 for the dangerous goods contained in the container, bulk container, MEGC, MEMU, tank-container, portable tank, vehicle or wagon and shall conform to the specifications given in 5.3.1.7. Placards shall be displayed on a background of contrasting colour, or shall have either a dotted or solid outer boundary line. The placards shall be weather-resistant and shall ensure durable marking throughout the entire journey.

5.3.1.1.2 For Class 1, compatibility groups shall not be indicated on placards if the vehicle or wagon or container or special compartments of MEMUs are carrying substances or articles belonging to two or more compatibility groups. Vehicles or wagons or containers or special compartments of MEMUs carrying substances or articles of different divisions shall bear only placards conforming to the model of the most dangerous division in the order:

1.1 (most dangerous), 1.5, 1.2, 1.3, 1.6, 1.4 (least dangerous).

When 1.5D substances are carried with substances or articles of Division 1.2, the vehicle, wagon or container shall be placarded as Division 1.1.

Placards are not required for the carriage of explosives of Division 1.4, Compatibility Group S.

5.3.1.1.3 For Class 7, the primary hazard placard shall conform to model No. 7D as specified in 5.3.1.7.2. This placard is not required for vehicles, wagons or containers carrying excepted packages and for small containers.

Where both Class 7 labels and placards would be required to be affixed to vehicles, wagons, containers, MEGCs, tank-containers or portable tanks, an enlarged label corresponding to the required label of model No. 7A, 7B or 7C may be displayed instead of placard No. 7D to serve both purposes. In that case, the dimensions shall be not less than 250 mm by 250 mm.

5.3.1.1.4 For Class 9 the placard shall correspond to the label model No. 9 as in 5.2.2.2.2; label model No. 9A shall not be used for placarding purposes.

5.3.1.1.5   Containers, MEGCs, MEMUs, tank-containers, portable tanks, vehicles or wagons containing goods of more than one class need not bear a subsidiary hazard placard if the hazard represented by that placard is already indicated by a primary or subsidiary hazard placard.

5.3.1.1.6   Placards which do not relate to the dangerous goods being carried, or residues thereof, shall be removed or covered.

5.3.1.1.7   When the placarding is affixed to folding panels, they shall be designed and secured so that they cannot unfold or come loose from the holder during carriage (especially as a result of impacts or unintentional actions).

5.3.1.2   *Placarding of containers, bulk containers, MEGCs, tank-containers and portable tanks*

NOTE: This subsection does not apply to swap-bodies, except tank swap bodies carried on vehicles bearing the orange markings stipulated in 5.3.2.

The placards shall be affixed to both sides and at each end of the container, bulk container, MEGC, tank-container or portable tank and to two opposite sides in the case of flexible bulk containers.

When the tank-container or portable tank has multiple compartments and carries two or more dangerous goods, the appropriate placards shall be displayed along each side at the position of the relevant compartments and one placard of each model shown on each side at both ends. If all compartments have to bear the same placards, these placards need to be displayed only once along each side and at both ends of the tank container or portable tank.

5.3.1.3   *Placarding of vehicles and wagons carrying containers, bulk containers, MEGCs, tank-containers or portable tanks*

NOTE: This subsection does not apply to swap-bodies, except tank swap bodies carried on vehicles bearing the orange markings stipulated in 5.3.2.

If the placards affixed to the containers, bulk containers, MEGCs, tank-containers or portable tanks are not visible from outside the carrying vehicles or wagons, the same placards shall also be affixed to both sides and at the rear of the vehicle or to both sides of the wagon. Otherwise, no placard need be affixed on the carrying vehicle or wagon.

5.3.1.4   *Placarding of vehicles for carriage in bulk, wagons for carriage in bulk, tank-vehicles, tank-wagons, battery vehicles, battery-wagons, MEMUs, vehicles with demountable tanks and wagons with demountable tanks*

5.3.1.4.1   Placards shall be affixed to both sides and at the rear of the vehicle, or, for wagons, to both sides.

When the tank-vehicle, tank-wagon, the demountable tank carried on the vehicle or the demountable tank carried on the wagon has multiple compartments and carries two or more dangerous goods, the appropriate placards shall be displayed along each side at the position of the relevant compartments and (vehicles only) one placard of each model shown on each side at the rear of the vehicle. If all compartments have to bear the same placards, these placards need be displayed only once along each side and (vehicles only) at the rear of the vehicle.

Where more than one placard is required for the same compartment, these placards shall be displayed adjacent to each other.

NOTE: When a tank semi-trailer is separated from its tractor to be loaded on board a ship or a vessel, placards shall also be displayed at the front of the semi-trailer.

5.3.1.4.2   MEMUs with tanks and bulk containers shall be placarded in accordance with 5.3.1.4.1 for the substances contained therein. For tanks with a capacity of less than 1 000 litres placards may be replaced by labels conforming to 5.2.2.2.

5.3.1.4.3   For MEMUs carrying packages containing substances or articles of Class 1 (other than of Division 1.4, Compatibility group S), placards shall be affixed to both sides and at the rear of the MEMU.

Special compartments for explosives shall be placarded in accordance with the provisions of 5.3.1.1.2. The last sentence of 5.3.1.1.2 does not apply.

5.3.1.5   *Placarding of vehicles and wagons carrying packages only*

> *NOTE: This sub-section applies also to vehicles or wagons carrying swap-bodies loaded with packages.*

5.3.1.5.1   For vehicles carrying packages containing substances or articles of Class 1 (other than of Division 1.4, Compatibility Group S), placards shall be affixed to both sides and at the rear of the vehicle.

5.3.1.5.2   For vehicles carrying radioactive material of Class 7 in packagings or IBCs (other than excepted packages), placards shall be affixed to both sides and at the rear of the vehicle.

> *NOTE: If a vehicle carrying packages containing dangerous goods of classes other than Classes 1 and 7 is loaded on board a vessel for an ADN journey preceding a voyage by sea, placards shall be affixed to both sides and at the rear of the vehicle. Such placards may remain affixed to a vehicle for an ADN journey following a sea voyage.*

5.3.1.5.3   For wagons carrying packages, placards corresponding to the goods carried shall be affixed to both sides.

5.3.1.6   *Placarding of empty tank-vehicles, tank-wagons, vehicles with demountable tanks, wagons with demountable tanks, battery-vehicles, battery-wagons, MEGCs, MEMUs, tank-containers, portable tanks and empty vehicles, wagons and containers for carriage in bulk*

5.3.1.6.1   Empty tank-vehicles, tank-wagons, vehicles with demountable tanks, wagons with demountable tanks, battery-vehicles, battery-wagons, MEGCs, MEMUs, tank-containers and portable tanks uncleaned and not degassed, and empty vehicles, wagons and containers for carriage in bulk, uncleaned, shall continue to display the placards required for the previous load.

5.3.1.7   *Specifications for placards*

5.3.1.7.1   Except as provided in 5.3.1.7.2 for the Class 7 placard, and in 5.3.6.2 for the environmentally hazardous substance mark, a placard shall be configured as shown in Figure 5.3.1.7.1.

Figure 5.3.1.7.1

Placard (except for Class 7)

The placard shall be in the form of a square set at an angle of 45° (diamond-shaped). The minimum dimensions shall be 250 mm x 250 mm (to the edge of the placard). The line inside the edge shall be parallel and 12.5 mm from the outside of that line to the edge of the placard. The symbol and line inside the edge shall correspond in colour to the label for the class or division of the dangerous goods in question. The class or division symbol/numeral shall be positioned and sized in proportion to those prescribed in 5.2.2.2 for the corresponding class or division of the dangerous goods in question. The placard shall display the number of the class or division (and for goods in Class 1, the compatibility group letter) of the dangerous goods in question in the manner prescribed in 5.2.2.2 for the corresponding label, in digits not less than 25 mm high. Where dimensions are not specified, all features shall be in approximate proportion to those shown. The deviations specified in 5.2.2.2.1, second sentence, 5.2.2.2.1.3, third sentence and 5.2.2.2.1.5 for danger labels also apply to placards.

5.3.1.7.2   The Class 7 placard shall be not less than 250 mm by 250 mm with a black line running 5 mm inside the edge and parallel with it and is otherwise as shown below (Model No. 7D). The number "7" shall not be less than 25 mm high. The background colour of the upper half of the placard shall be yellow and of the lower half white, the colour of the trefoil and the printing shall be black. The use of the word "RADIOACTIVE" in the bottom half is optional to allow the use of this placard to display the appropriate UN number for the consignment.

Placard for radioactive material of Class 7

(No.7D)

Symbol (trefoil): black; Background: upper half yellow with white border, lower half white;
The lower half shall show the word "RADIOACTIVE" or alternatively the appropriate
UN Number and the figure "7" in the bottom corner.

5.3.1.7.3 For tanks with a capacity of not more than 3 m³ and for small containers, placards may be replaced by labels conforming to 5.2.2.2. If these labels are not visible from outside the carrying vehicle or wagon, placards according to 5.3.1.7.1 shall also be affixed to both sides of the wagon or to both sides and at the rear of the vehicle.

5.3.1.7.4 For Classes 1 and 7, if the size and construction of the vehicle are such that the available surface area is insufficient to affix the prescribed placards, their dimensions may be reduced to 100 mm on each side. The dimensions of the placards to be affixed to wagons may be reduced to 150 mm by 150 mm. In this case, the upper dimensions prescribed for the trefoil, lines, figures and letters do not apply.

5.3.2 Orange-coloured plate marking

5.3.2.1 *General orange-coloured plate marking provisions*

5.3.2.1.1 Transport units carrying dangerous goods shall display two rectangular orange-coloured plates conforming to 5.3.2.2.1, set in a vertical plane. They shall be affixed one at the front and the other at the rear of the transport unit, both perpendicular to the longitudinal axis of the transport unit. They shall be clearly visible.

 If a trailer containing dangerous goods is detached from its motor vehicle during carriage of dangerous goods, an orange-coloured plate shall remain affixed to the rear of the trailer. When tanks are marked in accordance with 5.3.2.1.3, this plate shall correspond to the most hazardous substance carried in the tank.

5.3.2.1.2 When a hazard identification number is indicated in Column (20) of Table A of Chapter 3.2 of ADR, tank-vehicles, battery vehicles or transport units having one or more tanks carrying dangerous goods shall in addition display on the sides of each tank, each tank compartment or each element of battery-vehicles, clearly visible and parallel to the longitudinal axis of the vehicle, orange-coloured plates identical with those prescribed in 5.3.2.1.1. These orange-coloured plates shall bear the hazard identification number and the UN number prescribed respectively in Columns (20) and (1) of Table A of Chapter 3.2 of ADR for each of the substances carried in the tank, in a compartment of the tank or in an element of a battery-vehicle.

The provisions of this paragraph are also applicable to tank-wagons, battery-wagons and wagons with demountable tanks. In the latter case the hazard identification number to be used is that indicated in column (20) of table A of Chapter 3.2 of RID. For MEMUs these requirements shall only apply to tanks with a capacity of 1 000 litres or more and bulk containers.

5.3.2.1.3   For tank-vehicles or transport units having one or more tanks carrying substances with UN Nos. 1202, 1203 or 1223, or aviation fuel classed under UN Nos. 1268 or 1863, but no other dangerous substance, the orange-coloured plates prescribed in 5.3.2.1.2 need not be affixed if the plates affixed to the front and rear in accordance with 5.3.2.1.1 bear the hazard identification number and the UN number prescribed for the most hazardous substance carried, i.e. the substance with the lowest flashpoint.

5.3.2.1.4   When a hazard identification number is indicated in Column (20) of Table A of Chapter 3.2 of ADR, vehicles, containers and bulk containers carrying unpackaged solids or articles or packaged radioactive material with a single UN number required to be carried under exclusive use and no other dangerous goods shall in addition display on the sides of each vehicle, container or bulk container, clearly visible and parallel to the longitudinal axis of the vehicle, orange-coloured plates identical with those prescribed in 5.3.2.1.1. These orange-coloured plates shall bear the hazard identification number and the UN number prescribed respectively in Columns (20) and (1) of Table A of Chapter 3.2 of ADR for each of the substances carried in bulk in the vehicle, in the container or in the bulk container or for the packaged radioactive material when required to be carried under exclusive use in the vehicle or in the container.

The provisions of this paragraph are also applicable to wagons for carriage in bulk and full wagon loads comprising packages containing only one substance. In the latter case the hazard identification number to be used is that indicated in Column (20) of Table A of Chapter 3.2 of RID.

5.3.2.1.5   If the orange-coloured plates prescribed in 5.3.2.1.2 and 5.3.2.1.4 affixed to the containers, bulk containers, tank-containers, MEGCs or portable tanks are not clearly visible from outside the carrying vehicle or wagon, the same plates shall also be affixed to both sides of the vehicle or wagon.

NOTE: This paragraph need not be applied to the marking with orange coloured plates of closed and sheeted wagons or vehicles, carrying tanks with a maximum capacity of 3 000 litres.

5.3.2.1.6   For transport units carrying only one dangerous substance and no non-dangerous substance, the orange-coloured plates prescribed in 5.3.2.1.2, 5.3.2.1.4 and 5.3.2.1.5 shall not be necessary provided that those displayed at the front and rear in accordance with 5.3.2.1.1 bear the hazard identification number and the UN number for that substance prescribed respectively in Columns (20) and (1) of Table A of Chapter 3.2 of ADR.

5.3.2.1.7   The requirements of 5.3.2.1.1 to 5.3.2.1.5 are also applicable to empty fixed or demountable tanks, battery-vehicles, tank-containers, portable tanks, MEGCs, tank-wagons, battery-wagons and wagons with demountable tanks, uncleaned, not degassed or not decontaminated, MEMUs, uncleaned as well as to empty vehicles, wagons and containers for carriage in bulk, uncleaned or not decontaminated.

5.3.2.1.8   Any orange-coloured plates which does not relate to dangerous goods carried, or residues thereof, shall be removed or covered. If plates are covered, the covering shall be total and remain effective after 15 minutes' engulfment in fire.

5.3.2.2	*Specifications for the orange-coloured plates*

5.3.2.2.1	The orange-coloured plates shall be reflectorized and shall be of 40 cm base and of 30 cm high; they shall have a black border of 15 mm wide. The material used shall be weather-resistant and ensure durable marking. The plate shall not become detached from its mount in the event of a 15 minutes' engulfment in fire. It shall remain affixed irrespective of the orientation of the vehicle or wagon. The orange-coloured plates may be separated in their middle with a black horizontal line of 15 mm thickness.

If the size and construction of the vehicle are such that the available surface area is insufficient to affix these orange-coloured plates, their dimensions may be reduced to a minimum of 300 mm for the base, 120 mm for the height and 10 mm for the black border. In this case, a different set of dimensions within the specified range may be used for the two orange-coloured plates specified in 5.3.2.1.1.

When reduced dimensions of orange-coloured plates are used for a packaged radioactive material carried under exclusive use, only the UN number is required and the size of the digits stipulated in 5.3.2.2.2 may be reduced to 65 mm in height and 10 mm in stroke thickness.

A non-reflectorized colour is permitted for wagons.

For containers carrying dangerous solid substances in bulk and for tank-containers, MEGCs and portable tanks, the plates prescribed in 5.3.2.1.2, 5.3.2.1.4 and 5.3.2.1.5 may be replaced by a self-adhesive sheet, by paint or by any other equivalent process.

This alternative marking shall conform to the specifications set in this sub-section except for the provisions concerning resistance to fire mentioned in 5.3.2.2.1 and 5.3.2.2.2.

NOTE: The colour of the orange plates in conditions of normal use should have chromaticity coordinates lying within the area on the chromaticity diagram formed by joining the following coordinates:

Chromaticity coordinates of points at the corners of the area on the chromaticity diagram				
x	0.52	0.52	0.578	0.618
y	0.38	0.40	0.422	0.38

Luminance factor of reflectorized colour: β > 0.12.
Luminance factor of non-reflectorized colour (wagons): β ≥ 0.22
Reference centre E, standard illuminant C, normal incidence 45°, viewed at 0°.
Coefficient of reflex luminous intensity at an angle of illumination of 5°, viewed at 0.2°: not less than 20 candelas per lux per m² (not required for wagons).

5.3.2.2.2	The hazard identification number and the UN number shall consist of black digits 100 mm high and of 15 mm stroke thickness. The hazard identification number shall be inscribed in the upper part of the plate and the UN number in the lower part; they shall be separated by a horizontal black line, 15 mm in stroke width, extending from side to side of the plate at mid-height (see 5.3.2.2.3). The hazard identification number and the UN number shall be indelible and shall remain legible after 15 minutes engulfment in fire. Interchangeable numbers and letters on plates presenting the hazard identification number and the UN number shall remain in place during carriage and irrespective of the orientation of the wagon or vehicle.

5.3.2.2.3   *Example of orange-coloured plate with hazard identification number and UN number*

Hazard identification number (2 or 3 figures preceded where appropriate by the letter X, see 5.3.2.3)

UN number (4 figures)

Background orange.
Border, horizontal line and figures black, 15 mm thickness.

5.3.2.2.4   The permitted tolerances for dimensions specified in this sub-section are ± 10%.

5.3.2.2.5   When the orange-coloured plate is affixed to folding panels, they shall be designed and secured so that they cannot unfold or come loose from the holder during carriage (especially as a result of impacts or unintentional actions).

5.3.2.3   ***Meaning of hazard identification numbers***

5.3.2.3.1   The hazard identification number consists of two or three figures. In general, the figures indicate the following hazards:

2   Emission of gas due to pressure or to chemical reaction
3   Flammability of liquids (vapours) and gases or self-heating liquid
4   Flammability of solids or self-heating solid
5   Oxidizing (fire-intensifying) effect
6   Toxicity or risk of infection
7   Radioactivity
8   Corrosivity
9   Risk of spontaneous violent reaction

NOTE*: The risk of spontaneous violent reaction within the meaning of figure 9 includes the possibility following from the nature of a substance of a risk of explosion, disintegration and polymerization reaction following the release of considerable heat or flammable and/or toxic gases.*

Doubling of a figure indicates an intensification of that particular hazard.

Where the hazard associated with a substance can be adequately indicated by a single figure, this is followed by zero.

The following combinations of figures, however, have a special meaning: 22, 323, 333, 362, 382, 423, 44, 446, 462, 482, 539, 606, 623, 642, 823, 842, 90 and 99 (see 5.3.2.3.2 below).

If a hazard identification number is prefixed by the letter "X", this indicates that the substance will react dangerously with water. For such substances, water may only be used by approval of experts.

For substances of Class 1, the classification code in accordance with Column (3b) of Table A of Chapter 3.2, shall be used as the hazard identification number. The classification code consists of:

–   the division number in accordance with 2.2.1.1.5; and

–   the compatibility group letter in accordance with 2.2.1.1.6.

5.3.2.3.2   The hazard identification numbers listed in Column (20) of Table A of Chapter 3.2 of ADR or RID have the following meanings:

20	asphyxiant gas or gas with no subsidiary hazard
22	refrigerated liquefied gas, asphyxiant
223	refrigerated liquefied gas, flammable
225	refrigerated liquefied gas, oxidizing (fire-intensifying)
23	flammable gas
238	gas, flammable corrosive
239	flammable gas, which can spontaneously lead to violent reaction
25	oxidizing (fire-intensifying) gas
26	toxic gas
263	toxic gas, flammable
265	toxic gas, oxidizing (fire-intensifying)
268	toxic gas, corrosive
28	gas, corrosive
285	gas, corrosive, oxidizing

30	flammable liquid (flashpoint between 23 °C and 60 °C, inclusive) or flammable liquid or solid in the molten state with a flashpoint above 60 °C, heated to a temperature equal to or above its flashpoint, or self-heating liquid
323	flammable liquid which reacts with water, emitting flammable gases
X323	flammable liquid which reacts dangerously with water, emitting flammable gases[1]
33	highly flammable liquid (flashpoint below 23 °C)
333	pyrophoric liquid
X333	pyrophoric liquid which reacts dangerously with water[1]
336	highly flammable liquid, toxic
338	highly flammable liquid, corrosive
X338	highly flammable liquid, corrosive, which reacts dangerously with water[1]
339	highly flammable liquid which can spontaneously lead to violent reaction
36	flammable liquid (flashpoint between 23 °C and 60 °C, inclusive), slightly toxic, or self-heating liquid, toxic
362	flammable liquid, toxic, which reacts with water, emitting flammable gases
X362	flammable liquid, toxic, which reacts dangerously with water, emitting flammable gases[1]
368	flammable liquid, toxic, corrosive
38	flammable liquid (flashpoint between 23 °C and 60 °C, inclusive), slightly corrosive or self-heating liquid, corrosive
382	flammable liquid, corrosive, which reacts with water, emitting flammable gases
X382	flammable liquid, corrosive, which reacts dangerously with water, emitting flammable gases[1]
39	flammable liquid, which can spontaneously lead to violent reaction

---

[1]   *Water not to be used except by approval of experts.*

40	flammable solid, or self-reactive substance, or self-heating substance, or polymerizing substance
423	solid which reacts with water, emitting flammable gases, or flammable solid which reacts with water, emitting flammable gases or self-heating solid which reacts with water, emitting flammable gases
X423	solid which reacts dangerously with water, emitting flammable gases, or flammable solid which reacts dangerously with water, emitting flammable gases, or self-heating solid which reacts dangerously with water, emitting flammable gases [1]
43	spontaneously flammable (pyrophoric) solid
X432	spontaneously flammable (pyrophoric) solid which reacts dangerously with water, emitting flammable gases[1]
44	flammable solid, in the molten state at an elevated temperature
446	flammable solid, toxic, in the molten state, at an elevated temperature
46	flammable or self-heating solid, toxic
462	toxic solid which reacts with water, emitting flammable gases
X462	solid which reacts dangerously with water, emitting toxic gases[1]
48	flammable or self-heating solid, corrosive
482	corrosive solid which reacts with water, emitting flammable gases
X482	solid which reacts dangerously with water, emitting corrosive gases[1]

50	oxidizing (fire-intensifying) substance
539	flammable organic peroxide
55	strongly oxidizing (fire-intensifying) substance
556	strongly oxidizing (fire-intensifying) substance, toxic
558	strongly oxidizing (fire-intensifying) substance, corrosive
559	strongly oxidizing (fire-intensifying) substance, which can spontaneously lead to violent reaction
56	oxidizing substance (fire-intensifying), toxic
568	oxidizing substance (fire-intensifying), toxic, corrosive
58	oxidizing substance (fire-intensifying), corrosive
59	oxidizing substance (fire-intensifying), which can spontaneously lead to violent reaction

60	toxic or slightly toxic substance
606	infectious substance
623	toxic liquid, which reacts with water, emitting flammable gases
63	toxic substance, flammable (flashpoint between 23 °C and 60 °C, inclusive)
638	toxic substance, flammable (flashpoint between 23 °C and 60 °C, inclusive), corrosive
639	toxic substance, flammable (flashpoint not above 60 °C) which can spontaneously lead to violent reaction
64	toxic solid, flammable or self-heating
642	toxic solid, which reacts with water, emitting flammable gases
65	toxic substance, oxidizing (fire-intensifying)
66	highly toxic substance
663	highly toxic substance, flammable (flashpoint not above 60 °C)
664	highly toxic solid, flammable or self-heating
665	highly toxic substance, oxidizing (fire-intensifying)
668	highly toxic substance, corrosive
X668	highly toxic substance, corrosive, which reacts dangerously with water[1]
669	highly toxic substance which can spontaneously lead to violent reaction
68	toxic substance, corrosive
687	toxic substance, corrosive, radioactive
69	toxic or slightly toxic substance, which can spontaneously lead to violent reaction

---

[1] *Water not to be used except by approval of experts.*

70	radioactive material
768	radioactive material, toxic, corrosive
78	radioactive material, corrosive

80	corrosive or slightly corrosive substance
X80	corrosive or slightly corrosive substance, which reacts dangerously with water[1]
823	corrosive liquid which reacts with water, emitting flammable gases
83	corrosive or slightly corrosive substance, flammable (flashpoint between 23 °C and 60 °C, inclusive)
X83	corrosive or slightly corrosive substance, flammable (flashpoint between 23 °C and 60 °C, inclusive), which reacts dangerously with water[1]
836	Corrosive or slightly corrosive substance, flammable (flash-point between 23 °C and 60 °C, inclusive) and toxic
839	corrosive or slightly corrosive substance, flammable (flashpoint between 23 °C and 60 °C inclusive) which can spontaneously lead to violent reaction
X839	corrosive or slightly corrosive substance, flammable (flashpoint between 23 °C and 60 °C inclusive), which can spontaneously lead to violent reaction and which reacts dangerously with water[1]
84	corrosive solid, flammable or self-heating
842	corrosive solid which reacts with water, emitting flammable gases
85	corrosive or slightly corrosive substance, oxidizing (fire-intensifying)
856	corrosive or slightly corrosive substance, oxidizing (fire-intensifying) and toxic
86	corrosive or slightly corrosive substance, toxic
88	highly corrosive substance
X88	highly corrosive substance, which reacts dangerously with water[1]
883	highly corrosive substance, flammable (flashpoint between 23 °C and 60 °C inclusive)
884	highly corrosive solid, flammable or self-heating
885	highly corrosive substance, oxidizing (fire-intensifying)
886	highly corrosive substance, toxic
X886	highly corrosive substance, toxic, which reacts dangerously with water[1]
89	corrosive or slightly corrosive substance, which can spontaneously lead to violent reaction

90	environmentally hazardous substance; miscellaneous dangerous substances
99	miscellaneous dangerous substance carried at an elevated temperature.

5.3.3   **Mark for elevated temperature substances**

Tank-vehicles, tank-wagons, tank-containers, portable tanks, special vehicles, special wagons or special containers or specially equipped vehicles, specially equipped wagons or specially equipped containers containing a substance that is carried or handed over for carriage in a liquid state at or above 100 °C or in a solid state at or above 240 °C shall bear on both sides for wagons, on both sides and at the rear for vehicles, and on both sides and at each end for containers, tank-containers and portable tanks, the mark shown in Figure 5.3.3.

---

[1]   *Water not to be used except by approval of experts.*

Figure 5.3.3

Mark for carriage at elevated temperature

The mark shall be an equilateral triangle. The colour of the mark shall be red. The minimum dimension of the sides shall be 250 mm. For tank-containers or portable tanks with a capacity of not more than 3 000 litres and with an available surface area insufficient to affix the prescribed marks, the minimum dimensions of the sides may be reduced to 100 mm. Where dimensions are not specified, all features shall be in approximate proportion to those shown. The mark shall be weather-resistant and shall ensure durable marking throughout the entire journey.

5.3.4   **Marking for carriage in a transport chain including maritime transport**

5.3.4.1   For carriage in a transport chain including maritime transport, containers, portable tanks and MEGCs are not required to carry the orange-coloured plate marking according to section 5.3.2 if they carry the marking prescribed in section 5.3.2 of the IMDG Code, where:

(a)   The proper shipping name of the contents is durably marked on at least two sides:

  –   of portable tanks and MEGCs;

  –   of containers for carriage in bulk;

  –   of containers containing dangerous goods in packages constituting only one substance for which the IMDG Code does not require a placard or the marine pollutant mark;

(b)   The UN number for the goods is displayed in black digits not less than 65 mm high:

  –   either on a white background in the lower half of the placards affixed to the cargo transport unit;

  –   or on an orange rectangular panel not less than 120 mm high and 300 mm wide, with a 10 mm black border, to be placed immediately adjacent to the placard or the marine pollutant marks of the IMDG Code, or, if no placard or marine pollutant mark is prescribed, adjacent to the proper shipping name.

Example of marking for a portable tank carrying acetal, class 3, UN No 1088, according to the IMDG Code

FIRST VARIANT

black flame on
red background

SECOND VARIANT

black flame on
red background

orange background
border and digits in black

5.3.4.2   If portable tanks, MEGCs or containers marked in accordance with 5.3.4.1 are carried on board a vessel loaded on vehicles, only paragraph 5.3.2.1.1 applies to the carrying vehicle.

5.3.4.3   In addition to the placards, orange-coloured plate marking and marks prescribed or permitted by ADN, cargo transport units may carry additional marks, placards and other markings prescribed where appropriate by the IMDG Code, for example, the marine pollutant mark or the "LIMITED QUANTITIES" mark.

5.3.5   *(Reserved)*

5.3.6   Environmentally hazardous substance mark

5.3.6.1   When a placard is required to be displayed in accordance with the provisions of section 5.3.1, containers, bulk containers, MEGCs, tank-containers, portable tanks, vehicles and wagons containing environmentally hazardous substances meeting the criteria of 2.2.9.1.10 shall be marked with the environmentally hazardous substance mark shown in 5.2.1.8.3. This does not apply to the exceptions listed in 5.2.1.8.1.

5.3.6.2   The environmentally hazardous substance mark for containers, bulk containers, MEGCs, tank-containers, portable tanks, wagons and vehicles shall be as described in 5.2.1.8.3 and Figure 5.2.1.8.3, except that the minimum dimensions shall be 250 mm x 250 mm. For tank-containers or portable tanks with a capacity of not more than 3 000 litres and with an available surface area insufficient to affix the prescribed marks, the minimum dimensions may be reduced to 100 mm x 100 mm. The other provisions of section 5.3.1 concerning placards shall apply mutatis mutandis to the mark.

CHAPTER 5.4

DOCUMENTATION

5.4.0   **General**

5.4.0.1   Unless otherwise specified, any carriage of goods governed by ADN shall be accompanied by the documentation prescribed in this Chapter, as appropriate.

NOTE: For the list of documentation to be carried on board vessels, see 8.1.2.

5.4.0.2   The use of electronic data processing (EDP) or electronic data interchange (EDI) techniques as an aid to or instead of paper documentation is permitted, provided that the procedures used for the capture, storage and processing of electronics data meet the legal requirements as regards the evidential value and availability of data during carriage in a manner at least equivalent to that of paper documentation.

5.4.0.3   When the dangerous goods transport information is given to the carrier by EDP or EDI techniques, the consignor shall be able to give the information to the carrier as a paper document, with the information in the sequence required by this Chapter.

5.4.1   **Dangerous goods transport document and related information**

5.4.1.1   *General information required in the transport document*

5.4.1.1.1   *General information required in the transport document for carriage in bulk or in packages*

The transport document(s) shall contain the following information for each dangerous substance, material or article offered for carriage:

(a)   the UN number, preceded by the letters "UN" or substance identification number;

(b)   the proper shipping name supplemented, when applicable (see 3.1.2.8.1) with the technical name in brackets (see 3.1.2.8.1.1), as determined in accordance with 3.1.2.

(c)   –   For substances and articles of Class 1: the classification code given in Column (3b) of Table A of Chapter 3.2.

When, in Column (5) of Table A of Chapter 3.2, label model numbers are given other than 1, 1.4, 1.5 and 1.6, these label model numbers, in brackets, shall follow the classification code;

–   For radioactive material of Class 7: the Class number: "7";

NOTE: For radioactive material with a subsidiary hazard, see also special provision 172 in Chapter 3.3.

–   For lithium batteries of UN numbers 3090, 3091, 3480 and 3481: the Class number "9";

–   For other substances and articles: the label model numbers given in Column (5) of Table A of Chapter 3.2 or applicable according to a special provision referred to in Column (6). When more than one label model number is given, the numbers following the first one shall be given in brackets. For substances and articles for which no label model is given in Column (5) of Table A in Chapter 3.2, their class according to Column (3a) shall be given instead;

(d)   where assigned, the packing group for the substance which may be preceded by the letters "PG" (e.g. "PG II"), or the initials corresponding to the words "Packing Group" in the languages used according to 5.4.1.4.1;

NOTE: For radioactive material of Class 7 with subsidiary hazards, see special provision 172 (d) in Chapter 3.3.

(e)   the number and a description of the packages when applicable. UN packaging codes may only be used to supplement the description of the kind of package (e.g. one box (4G));

NOTE: The number, type and capacity of each inner packaging within the outer packaging of a combination packaging is not required to be indicated.

(f)   the total quantity of each item of dangerous goods bearing a different UN number, proper shipping name or, when applicable, packing group (as a volume or as a gross mass, or as a net mass as appropriate);

NOTE: For dangerous goods in machinery and or equipment specified in these Regulations, the quantity indicated shall be the total quantity of dangerous goods contained therein in kilograms or litres as appropriate.

(g)   the name and address of the consignor;

(h)   the name and address of the consignee(s);

(i)   a declaration as required by the terms of any special agreement.

The location and order in which the elements of information required appear in the transport document is left optional, except that (a), (b), (c) and (d) shall be shown in the order listed above (i.e. (a), (b), (c), (d)) with no information interspersed, except as provided in ADN.

Examples of such permitted dangerous goods descriptions are:

"UN 1098 ALLYL ALCOHOL, 6.1 (3), I" or
"UN1098, ALLYL ALCOHOL, 6.1 (3), PG I"

The information required on a transport document shall be legible.

Although upper case is used in Chapter 3.1 and in Table A of Chapter 3.2 to indicate the elements which shall be part of the proper shipping name, and although upper and lower case are used in this Chapter to indicate the information required in the transport document, the use of upper or of lower case for entering the information in the transport document is left optional.

5.4.1.1.2   *General information required in the transport document for carriage in tank vessels*

The transport document(s) shall contain the following information for each dangerous substance or article offered for carriage:

(a)   the UN number preceded by the letters "UN" or the substance identification number;

(b)   the proper shipping name given in Column (2) of Table C of Chapter 3.2, supplemented, when applicable, by the technical name in parenthesis;

(c)   the data contained in column (5) of Table C of Chapter 3.2. When more than one number is given, the numbers following the first one shall be given in brackets. For substances not mentioned by name in Table C (assigned to a generic entry or a N.O.S. entry and for which the flowchart in 3.2.3.3 is applicable) only the actual dangerous properties of the substance shall be mentioned;

(d)   where assigned, the packing group for the substance, which may be preceded by the letters 'PG' (e.g. 'PG II'), or the initials corresponding to the words 'Packing Group' in the languages used in accordance with 5.4.1.4.1;

(e)   the mass in tonnes;

(f)   the name and address of the consignor;

(g)   the name and address of the consignee(s).

The location and order in which the elements of information required appear in the transport document is left optional, except that (a), (b), (c) and (d) shall be shown in the order listed above (i.e. (a), (b), (c), (d)) with no information interspersed, except as provided in ADN.

Examples of such permitted dangerous goods descriptions are:

**"UN 1203 MOTOR SPIRIT, 3 (N2, CMR, F), II"; or
"UN 1203 MOTOR SPIRIT, 3 (N2, CMR, F), PG II"**

The information required on a transport document shall be legible.

Although upper case is used in Chapter 3.1 and in Table C of Chapter 3.2 to indicate the elements which shall be part of the proper shipping name, and although upper and lower case are used in this Chapter to indicate the information required in the transport document, the use of upper or of lower case for entering the information in the transport document is left optional.

5.4.1.1.3   *Special provisions for wastes*

If waste containing dangerous goods (other than radioactive wastes) is being carried, the proper shipping name shall be preceded by the word "**WASTE**", unless this term is part of the proper shipping name, e.g.:

"UN 1230 WASTE METHANOL, 3 (6.1), II", or
"UN 1230 WASTE METHANOL, 3 (6.1), PG II,", or
"UN 1993 WASTE FLAMMABLE LIQUID, N.O.S. (toluene and ethyl alcohol), 3, II,", or
"UN 1993 WASTE FLAMMABLE LIQUID, N.O.S. (toluene and ethyl alcohol), 3, PG II"

If the provision for waste as set out in 2.1.3.5.5 is applied, the following shall be added to the dangerous goods description required in 5.4.1.1.1 (a) to (d) and (k):

"WASTE IN ACCORDANCE WITH 2.1.3.5.5" (e.g. **"UN 3264, CORROSIVE LIQUID, ACIDIC, INORGANIC, N.O.S., 8, II, WASTE IN ACCORDANCE WITH 2.1.3.5.5"**).

The technical name, as prescribed in Chapter 3.3, special provision 274, need not be added.

5.4.1.1.4   *(Deleted)*

5.4.1.1.5 *Special provisions for salvage packagings, including large salvage packagings, and salvage pressure receptacles*

When dangerous goods are carried in a salvage packaging, including large salvage packaging, or salvage pressure receptacle, the words **"SALVAGE PACKAGING"** or **"SALVAGE PRESSURE RECEPTACLE"** shall be added after the description of the goods in the transport document.

5.4.1.1.6 *Special provision for empty means of containment and for empty cargo tanks of tank vessels*

5.4.1.1.6.1 For empty means of containment, uncleaned, which contain the residue of dangerous goods of classes other than Class 7, the words "EMPTY, UNCLEANED" or "RESIDUE, LAST CONTAINED" shall be indicated before or after the dangerous goods description specified in 5.4.1.1.1 (a) to (d).. Moreover, 5.4.1.1.1 (f) does not apply.

5.4.1.1.6.2 The special provision of 5.4.1.1.6.1 may be replaced with the provisions of 5.4.1.1.6.2.1, 5.4.1.1.6.2.2 or 5.4.1.1.6.2.3, as appropriate.

5.4.1.1.6.2.1 For empty packagings, uncleaned, which contain the residue of dangerous goods of classes other than Class 7, including empty uncleaned receptacles for gases with a capacity of not more than 1000 litres, the particulars according to 5.4.1.1.1 (a), (b), (c), (d), (e) and (f) are replaced with "EMPTY PACKAGING", "EMPTY RECEPTACLE", "EMPTY IBC" or "EMPTY LARGE PACKAGING", as appropriate, followed by the information of the goods last loaded, as described in 5.4.1.1.1 (c).

Example:

"EMPTY PACKAGING, 6.1 (3)".

In addition, in such a case

(a) if the dangerous goods last loaded are goods of Class 2, the information prescribed in 5.4.1.1.1 (c) may be replaced by the number of the class "2".

(b) if the dangerous goods last loaded are goods of Classes 3, 4.1, 4.2, 4.3, 5.1, 5.2, 6.1, 8 or 9, the information of the goods last loaded, as described in 5.4.1.1.1 (c) may be replaced by the words "WITH RESIDUES OF [...]" followed by the class(es) and subsidiary hazard(s) corresponding to the different residues, in the class numbering order.

Example: Empty packagings, uncleaned, having contained goods of Class 3 carried together with empty packagings, uncleaned, having contained goods of Class 8 with a Class 6.1 subsidiary hazard may be referred to in the transport document as:

"EMPTY PACKAGINGS, WITH RESIDUES OF 3, 6.1, 8".

5.4.1.1.6.2.2 For empty means of containment other than packagings, uncleaned, which contain the residue of dangerous goods of classes other than Class 7 and for empty uncleaned receptacles for gases with a capacity of more than 1000 litres, the particulars according to 5.4.1.1.1 (a) to (d) are preceded by **"EMPTY TANK-WAGON"**, **"EMPTY TANK-VEHICLE"**, **"EMPTY DEMOUNTABLE TANK"**, **"EMPTY TANK-CONTAINER"**, **"EMPTY PORTABLE TANK"**, **"EMPTY BATTERY-WAGON"**, **"EMPTY BATTERY-VEHICLE"**, **"EMPTY MEGC"**, **"EMPTY MEMU"**, **"EMPTY WAGON"**, **"EMPTY VEHICLE"**, **"EMPTY CONTAINER"** or **"EMPTY RECEPTACLE"**, as appropriate, followed by the words **"LAST LOAD:"**. Moreover, paragraph 5.4.1.1.1 (f) does not apply.

See example as follows:

"EMPTY TANK-CONTAINER, LAST LOAD: UN 1098 ALLYL ALCOHOL, 6.1 (3), I"
or
"EMPTY TANK-CONTAINER, LAST LOAD: UN 1098 ALLYL ALCOHOL, 6.1 (3), PG I".

5.4.1.1.6.2.3   When empty means of containment, uncleaned, which contain the residue of dangerous goods of classes other than Class 7, are returned to the consignor, the transport documents prepared for the full-capacity carriage of these goods may also be used. In such cases, the indication of the quantity is to be eliminated (by effacing it, striking it out or any other means) and replaced by the words **"EMPTY, UNCLEANED RETURN"**.

5.4.1.1.6.3   (a)   If empty tanks, battery-vehicles, battery wagons and MEGCs, uncleaned, are carried to the nearest place where cleaning or repair can be carried out in accordance with the provisions of 4.3.2.4.3 of ADR or RID, the following additional entry shall be made in the transport document: **"Carriage in accordance with 4.3.2.4.3 of ADR (or RID)"**.

(b)   If empty vehicles, wagons and containers, uncleaned, are carried to the nearest place where cleaning or repair can be carried out in accordance with the provisions of 7.5.8.1 of ADR or RID, the following additional entry shall be made in the transport document: **"Carriage in accordance with 7.5.8.1 of ADR (or RID)"**.

5.4.1.1.6.4   For the carriage of tank wagons, fixed tanks (tank vehicles), wagons with removable tanks, vehicles with demountable tanks, battery-wagons, battery-vehicles, tank-containers and MEGCs under the conditions of 4.3.2.4.4 of ADR or RID, the following entry shall be included in the transport document: **"Carriage in accordance with 4.3.2.4.4 of ADR (or RID)"** as appropriate.

5.4.1.1.6.5   For tank vessels with empty cargo tanks or cargo tanks that have been discharged, the master is deemed to be the consignor for the purpose of the transport documents required. In this case, the following particulars shall be entered on the transport document for each empty cargo tank or cargo tank that has been discharged:

(a)   the number of the cargo tank;

(b)   the UN number preceded by the letters "UN" or the substance identification number;

(c)   the proper shipping name of the last substance carried, the class and, if applicable, the packing group in accordance with 5.4.1.1.2.

5.4.1.1.7   *Special provisions for carriage in a transport chain including maritime, road, rail or air carriage*

For carriage in accordance with 1.1.4.2.1, a statement shall be included in the transport document, as follows: **"Carriage in accordance with 1.1.4.2.1"**.

5.4.1.1.8 and 5.4.1.1.9   (*Reserved*)

5.4.1.1.10   (*Deleted*)

5.4.1.1.11   *Special provisions for the carriage of IBCs, tanks, battery-vehicles, portable tanks and MEGCs after the date of expiry of the last periodic test or inspection*

For carriage in accordance with 4.1.2.2 (b), 4.3.2.3.7 (b), 6.7.2.19.6 (b), 6.7.3.15.6 (b) or 6.7.4.14.6 (b) of ADR (or RID), a statement to this effect shall be included in the transport document, as follows:

"CARRIAGE IN ACCORDANCE WITH 4.1.2.2 (b) of ADR (or RID)",
"CARRIAGE IN ACCORDANCE WITH 4.3.2.3.7 (b) of ADR (or RID)",
"CARRIAGE IN ACCORDANCE WITH 6.7.2.19.6 (b) of ADR (or RID)",
"CARRIAGE IN ACCORDANCE WITH 6.7.3.15.6 (b) of ADR (or RID)"; or
"CARRIAGE IN ACCORDANCE WITH 6.7.4.14.6 (b) of ADR (or RID)" as appropriate.

5.4.1.1.12 and 5.4.1.1.13   (*Reserved*)

5.4.1.1.14   *Special provisions for the carriage of substances carried under elevated temperature*

If the proper shipping name of a substance which is carried or offered for carriage in a liquid state at a temperature equal to or exceeding 100 °C, or in a solid state at a temperature equal to or exceeding 240 °C, does not convey the elevated temperature condition (for example, by using the term **"MOLTEN"** or **"ELEVATED TEMPERATURE"** as part of the proper shipping name), the word **"HOT"** shall immediately precede the proper shipping name.

5.4.1.1.15   *Special provisions for the carriage of substances stabilized by temperature control*

If the word "STABILIZED" is part of the proper shipping name (see also 3.1.2.6), when stabilization is by means of temperature control, the control and emergency temperatures (see 7.1.7) shall be indicated in the transport document, as follows:

"Control temperature: ... °C   Emergency temperature: ... °C".

5.4.1.1.16   *Information required in accordance with special provision 640 in Chapter 3.3*

Where it is required by special provision 640 of Chapter 3.3, the transport document shall bear the inscription **"Special provision 640X"** where "X" is the capital letter appearing after the pertinent reference to special provision 640 in Column (6) of Table A of Chapter 3.2.

5.4.1.1.17   *Special provisions for the carriage of solids in bulk containers conforming to 6.11.4 of ADR*

When solid substances are carried in bulk containers conforming to 6.11.4 of ADR, the following statement shall be shown on the transport document (see NOTE at the beginning of 6.11.4 of ADR):

"Bulk container BK(x)[1] approved by the competent authority of..."

5.4.1.1.18   *Special provisions for carriage of environmentally hazardous substances (aquatic environment)*

When a substance belonging to one of classes 1 to 9 meets the classification criteria of 2.2.9.1.10, the transport document shall bear the additional inscription **"ENVIRONMENTALLY HAZARDOUS"** or **"MARINE POLLUTANT/ ENVIRONMENTALLY HAZARDOUS"**. This additional requirement does not apply to UN Nos. 3077 and 3082 or for the exceptions listed in 5.2.1.8.1.

---

[1]   *(x) shall be replaced with "1" or "2" as appropriate.*

The inscription **"MARINE POLLUTANT"** (according to 5.4.1.4.3 of the IMDG Code) is acceptable for carriage in a transport chain including maritime carriage.

5.4.1.1.19   *Special provisions for carriage of packagings, discarded, empty, uncleaned (UN No. 3509)*

For packagings, discarded, empty, uncleaned, the proper shipping name specified in 5.4.1.1.1 (b) shall be complemented with the words **"(WITH RESIDUES OF [...])"** followed by the class(es) and subsidiary hazard(s) corresponding to the residues, in the class numbering order. Moreover, 5.4.1.1.1 (f) does not apply.

Example: Packagings, discarded, empty, uncleaned having contained goods of Class 4.1 packed together with packagings, discarded, empty, uncleaned having contained goods of Class 3 with a Class 6.1 subsidiary hazard should be referred to in the transport document as:

"UN 3509 PACKAGINGS, DISCARDED, EMPTY, UNCLEANED (WITH RESIDUES OF 3, 4.1, 6.1), 9".

5.4.1.1.20   *Special provisions for the carriage of substances classified in accordance with 2.1.2.8*

For carriage in accordance with 2.1.2.8, a statement shall be included in the transport document, as follows **"Classified in accordance with 2.1.2.8"**.

5.4.1.1.21   *Special provisions for the carriage of UN Nos. 3528, 3529 and 3530*

For carriage of UN Nos. 3528, 3529 and 3530, the transport document, when required according to special provision 363 of Chapter 3.3, shall contain the following additional statement "Transport in accordance with special provision 363".

5.4.1.1.22   *Special provisions for carriage in oil separator vessels and supply vessels*

5.4.1.1.2 and 5.4.1.1.6.5 are not applicable to oil separator vessels or supply vessels.

5.4.1.2   ***Additional or special information required for certain classes***

5.4.1.2.1   *Special provisions for Class 1*

(a)   The transport document shall indicate, in addition to the requirements in 5.4.1.1.1 (f):

– the total net mass, in kg, of explosive contents[2] for each substance or article identified by its UN number;

– the total net mass, in kg, of explosive contents[2] for all substances and articles covered by the transport document.

(b)   For mixed packing of two different goods, the description of the goods in the transport document shall include the UN numbers and names printed in capitals in Columns (1) and (2) of Table A of Chapter 3.2 of both substances or articles. If more than two different goods are contained in the same package in conformity with the mixed packing provisions given in 4.1.10 of ADR special provisions MP1, MP2 and MP20 to MP24, the transport document shall indicate under the description of the goods the UN numbers of all the substances and articles contained in the package, in the form, **"Goods of UN Nos. ..."**.

_____

[2]   *For articles, "explosive contents" means the explosive substance contained in the article.*

(c)   For the carriage of substances and articles assigned to an n.o.s. entry or the entry "0190 SAMPLES, EXPLOSIVE" or packed conforming to packing instruction P101 of 4.1.4.1 of ADR, a copy of the competent authority approval with the conditions of carriage shall be attached to the transport document. It shall be in an official language of the forwarding country and also, if that language is not English, French or German, in English, French or German unless agreements, if any, concluded between the countries concerned in the transport operation provide otherwise.

(d)   If packages containing substances and articles of compatibility groups B and D are loaded together in the same vehicle or wagon in accordance with the requirements of 7.5.2.2 or ADR or RID, the approval certificate of the protective compartment or containment system in accordance with 7.5.2.2, note ^{a} under the table of ADR or RID, shall be attached to the transport document. It shall be in an official language of the forwarding country and also, if that language is not English, French or German, in English, French or German unless agreements, if any, concluded between the countries concerned in the transport operation provide otherwise.

(e)   When explosive substances or articles are carried in packagings conforming to packing instruction P101 of ADR, the transport document shall bear the inscription "**Packaging approved by the competent authority of ...**" (see 4.1.4.1, packing instruction P101).

(f)   *(Reserved)*

(g)   When fireworks of UN Nos. 0333, 0334, 0335, 0336 and 0337 are carried, the transport document shall bear the inscription:

"Classification of fireworks by the competent authority of XX with the firework reference XX/YYZZZZ".

The classification approval certificate need not be carried with the consignment, but shall be made available by the consignor to the carrier or the competent authorities for control purposes. The classification approval certificate or a copy of it shall be in an official language of the forwarding country, and also, if that language is not German, English or French, in German, English or French.

NOTE 1: The commercial or technical name of the goods may be entered additionally to the proper shipping name in the transport document.

NOTE 2: The classification reference(s) shall consist of the ADN Contracting Party in which the classification code according to special provision 645 of 3.3.1 was approved, indicated by the distinguishing sign used on vehicles in international road traffic (XX)^3, the competent authority identification (YY) and a unique serial reference (ZZZZ). Examples of such classification references are:

GB/HSE123456

D/BAM1234.

---

^{3} *Distinguishing sign of the State of registration used on motor vehicles and trailers in international road traffic, e.g. in accordance with the Geneva Convention on Road Traffic of 1949 or the Vienna Convention on Road Traffic of 1968.*

5.4.1.2.2　　　*Additional provisions for Class 2*

(a)　　For the carriage of mixtures (see 2.2.2.1.1) in tanks (demountable tanks, fixed tanks, tank-wagons, portable tanks, tank-containers or elements of battery-vehicles or battery-wagons or of MEGCs), the composition of the mixture as a percentage of the volume or as a percentage of the mass shall be given. Constituents below 1% need not be indicated (see also 3.1.2.8.1.2). The composition of the mixture need not be given when the technical names authorized by special provisions 581, 582 or 583 are used to supplement the proper shipping name;

(b)　　For the carriage of cylinders, tubes, pressure drums, cryogenic receptacles and bundles of cylinders under the conditions of 4.1.6.10 of ADR, the following entry shall be included in the transport document:　**"Carriage in accordance with 4.1.6.10 of ADR"**.

(c)　　*(Reserved)*

(d)　　In the case of tank-wagons, tank-containers or portable tanks carrying refrigerated liquefied gases the consignor shall enter in the transport document the date (or time) by which the actual holding time will be exceeded.

"End of holding time: .... (DD/MM/YYYY)".

5.4.1.2.3　　　*Additional provisions for self-reactive substances and polymerizing substances of Class 4.1 and organic peroxides of Class 5.2*

5.4.1.2.3.1　　For self-reactive substances of Class 4.1 and for organic peroxides of Class 5.2 that require temperature control during carriage (for self-reactive substances or polymerizing substances see 2.2.41.1.17; for organic peroxides, see 2.2.52.1.15; for polymerizing substance see 2.2.41.1.21), the control and emergency temperatures shall be indicated in the transport document, as follows:

"Control temperature: ... °C　　　　　Emergency temperature: ... °C".

5.4.1.2.3.2　　When for certain self-reactive substances of Class 4.1 and certain organic peroxides of Class 5.2 the competent authority has permitted the label conforming to model No. 1 to be dispensed with for a specific packaging (see 5.2.2.1.9), a statement to this effect shall be included in the transport document, as follows: **"The label conforming to model No. 1 is not required"**.

5.4.1.2.3.3　　When organic peroxides and self-reactive substances are carried under conditions where approval is required (for organic peroxides see 2.2.52.1.8, 4.1.7.2.2 and special provision TA2 of 6.8.4 of ADR; for self-reactive substances see 2.2.41.1.13 and 4.1.7.2.2 of ADR, a statement to this effect shall be included in the transport document, e.g. **"Carriage in accordance with 2.2.52.1.8"**. It shall be in an official language of the forwarding country and also, if that language is not English, French or German, in English, French or German unless agreements, if any, concluded between the countries concerned in the transport operation provide otherwise.

A copy of the approval of the competent authority with the conditions of carriage shall be attached to the transport document.

5.4.1.2.3.4　　When a sample of an organic peroxide (see 2.2.52.1.9) or a self-reactive substance (see 2.2.41.1.15) is carried, a statement to this effect shall be included in the transport document, e.g. **"Carriage in accordance with 2.2.52.1.9"**.

5.4.1.2.3.5   When self-reactive substances type G (see Manual of Tests and Criteria, Part II, paragraph 20.4.2 (g)) are carried, the following statement may be given in the transport document: **"Not a self-reactive substance of Class 4.1"**.

When organic peroxides type G (see Manual of Tests and Criteria, Part II, paragraph 20.4.3 (g)) are carried, the following statement may be given in the transport document: **"Not a substance of Class 5.2"**.

5.4.1.2.4   *Additional provisions for Class 6.2*

In addition to the information concerning the consignee (see 5.4.1.1.1 (h)), the name and telephone number of a responsible person shall be indicated.

5.4.1.2.5   *Additional provisions for Class 7*

5.4.1.2.5.1   The following information shall be inserted in the transport document for each consignment of Class 7 material, as applicable, in the order given and immediately after the information required under 5.4.1.1.1 (a) to (c):

(a)   The name or symbol of each radionuclide or, for mixtures of radionuclides, an appropriate general description or a list of the most restrictive nuclides;

(b)   A description of the physical and chemical form of the material, or a notation that the material is special form radioactive material or low dispersible radioactive material. A generic chemical description is acceptable for chemical form. For radioactive material with a subsidiary hazard, see sub-paragraph (c) of special provision 172 of Chapter 3.3;

(c)   The maximum activity of the radioactive contents during carriage expressed in becquerels (Bq) with an appropriate SI prefix symbol (see 1.2.2.1). For fissile material, the mass of fissile material (or mass of each fissile nuclide for mixtures when appropriate) in grams (g), or appropriate multiples thereof, may be used in place of activity;

(d)   The category of the package, overpack or container, as assigned per 5.1.5.3.4, i.e. I-WHITE, II-YELLOW, III-YELLOW;

(e)   The TI as determined per 5.1.5.3.1 and 5.1.5.3.2 (except for category I-WHITE);

(f)   For fissile material:

   (i)   Shipped under one exception of 2.2.7.2.3.5 (a) to (f), reference to that paragraph;

   (ii)   Shipped under 2.2.7.2.3.5 (c) to (e), the total mass of fissile nuclides;

   (iii)   Contained in a package for which one of 6.4.11.2 (a) to (c) or 6.4.11.3 of ADR is applied, reference to that paragraph;

   (iv)   The criticality safety index, where applicable;

(g)   The identification mark for each competent authority certificate of approval (special form radioactive material, low dispersible radioactive material, fissile material excepted under 2.2.7.2.3.5 (f), special arrangement, package design, or shipment) applicable to the consignment;

(h)   For consignments of more than one package, the information required in 5.4.1.1.1 and in (a) to (g) above shall be given for each package. For packages in an overpack, container, or conveyance, a detailed statement of the contents of each package within the overpack, container, or conveyance and, where appropriate, of each overpack, container, or conveyance shall be included. If packages are to be removed from the overpack, container, or conveyance at a point of intermediate unloading, appropriate transport documents shall be made available;

(i)   Where a consignment is required to be shipped under exclusive use, the statement **"EXCLUSIVE USE SHIPMENT"**; and

(j)   For LSA-II and LSA-III substances, SCO-I, SCO-II and SCO-III, the total activity of the consignment as a multiple of A_2. For radioactive material for which the A_2 value is unlimited, the multiple of A_2 shall be zero.

5.4.1.2.5.2   The consignor shall provide in the transport documents a statement regarding actions, if any, that are required to be taken by the carrier. The statement shall be in the languages deemed necessary by the carrier or the authorities concerned, and shall include at least the following information:

(a)   Supplementary requirements for loading, stowage, carriage, handling and unloading of the package, overpack or container including any special stowage provisions for the safe dissipation of heat (see 7.1.4.14.7.3.2), or a statement that no such requirements are necessary;

(b)   Restrictions on the mode of carriage or vehicle or wagon and any necessary routeing instructions;

(c)   Emergency arrangements appropriate to the consignment.

5.4.1.2.5.3   In all cases of international carriage of packages requiring competent authority approval of design or shipment, for which different approval types apply in the different countries concerned by the shipment, the UN number and proper shipping name required in 5.4.1.1.1 shall be in accordance with the certificate of the country of origin of design.

5.4.1.2.5.4   The applicable competent authority certificates need not necessarily accompany the consignment. The consignor shall make them available to the carrier(s) before loading and unloading.

5.4.1.3   *(Reserved)*

5.4.1.4   *Format and language*

5.4.1.4.1   The document containing the information in 5.4.1.1 and 5.4.1.2 may be that already required by other regulations in force for carriage by another mode of carriage. In case of multiple consignees, the name and address of the consignees and the quantities delivered enabling the nature and quantities carried to be evaluated at any time, may be entered in other documents which are to be used or in any other documents made mandatory according to other specific regulations and which shall be on board.

The particulars to be entered in the document shall be drafted in an official language of the forwarding country, and also, if that language is not English, French or German, in English, French or German, unless agreements concluded between the countries concerned in the transport operation, provide otherwise.

5.4.1.4.2   If by reason of the size of the load, a consignment cannot be loaded in its entirety on a single transport unit, at least as many separate documents, or copies of the single document, shall be made out as transport units loaded. Furthermore, in all cases, separate transport documents shall be made out for consignments or parts of consignments which may not be loaded together on the same vehicle by reason of the prohibitions set forth in 7.5.2 of ADR.

The information relative to the hazards of the goods to be carried (as indicated in 5.4.1.1) may be incorporated in, or combined with, an existing transport or cargo handling document. The layout of the information in the document (or the order of transmission of the corresponding data by electronic data processing (EDP) or electronic data interchange (EDI) techniques) shall be as provided in 5.4.1.1.1 or 5.4.1.1.2 as relevant.

When an existing transport document or cargo handling document cannot be used for the purposes of dangerous goods documentation for multimodal transport, the use of documents corresponding to the example shown in 5.4.5 is considered advisable.[4]

5.4.1.5   *Non-dangerous goods*

When goods mentioned by name in Table A of Chapter 3.2, are not subject to ADN because they are considered as non-dangerous according to Part 2, the consignor may enter in the transport document a statement to that effect, e.g.: "**Not goods of Class ...**"

NOTE: *This provision may be used in particular when the consignor considers that, due to the chemical nature of the goods (e.g. solutions and mixtures) carried or to the fact that such goods are deemed dangerous for other regulatory purposes the consignment might be subject to control during the journey.*

---

[4]   *If used, the relevant recommendations of the UNECE United Nations Centre for Trade Facilitation and Electronic Business (UN/CEFACT) may be consulted, in particular Recommendation No. 1 (United Nations Layout Key for Trade Documents) (ECE/TRADE/137, edition 81.3), UN Layout Key for Trade Documents - Guidelines for Applications (ECE/TRADE/270, edition 2002), Recommendation No. 11 (Documentary Aspects of the International Transport of Dangerous Goods) (ECE/TRADE/204, edition 96.1 – currently under revision) and Recommendation No. 22 (Layout Key for Standard Consignment Instructions) (ECE/TRADE/168, edition 1989). Refer also to the UN/CEFACT Summary of Trade Facilitation Recommendations (ECE/TRADE/346, edition 2006) and the United Nations Trade Data Elements Directory (UNTDED) (ECE/TRADE/362, edition 2005).*

5.4.2 Container/vehicle packing certificate

NOTE: For the purposes of this section the term "vehicle" includes wagon.

If the carriage of dangerous goods in a container precedes a voyage by sea, a container/vehicle packing certificate conforming to section 5.4.2 of the IMDG Code[5] shall be provided with the transport document.[6]

The functions of the transport document required under 5.4.1 and of the container/vehicle packing certificate as provided above may be incorporated into a single document; if not, these documents shall be attached. If these functions are incorporated into a single document, the inclusion in the transport document of a statement that the loading of the container or vehicle has been carried out in accordance with the applicable modal regulations together with the identification of the person responsible for the container/vehicle packing certificate shall be sufficient.

NOTE: The container/vehicle packing certificate is not required for portable tanks, tank-containers and MEGCs.

If the carriage of dangerous goods in a vehicle precedes a voyage by sea, a "container/vehicle packing certificate" conforming to section 5.4.2 of the IMDG Code[5,6] may be provided with the transport document.

5.4.3 Instructions in writing

5.4.3.1 As an aid during an accident emergency situation that may occur or arise during carriage, instructions in writing in the form specified in 5.4.3.4 shall be carried in the wheelhouse and shall be readily available.

5.4.3.2 These instructions shall be provided by the carrier to the master in the language(s) that the master and the expert can read and understand before loading. The master shall ensure that each member of the crew and any other person on board concerned understands and is capable of carrying out the instructions properly.

5.4.3.3 Before loading, the members of the crew shall inform themselves of the dangerous goods to be loaded and consult the instructions in writing for details on actions to be taken in the event of an accident or emergency.

5.4.3.4 The instructions in writing shall correspond to the following four-page model as regards its form and contents.

---

[5] *Guidelines for use in practice and in training for loading goods in transport units have also been drawn up by the International Maritime Organization (IMO), the International Labour Organization (ILO) and the United Nations Economic Commission for Europe (UNECE) and have been published by IMO ("IMO/ILO/UNECE Code of Practice for Packing of Cargo Transport Units (CTU Code)").*

[6] *Section 5.4.2 of the IMDG Code (Amendment 39-18) requires the following:*

"5.4.2   Container/vehicle packing certificate

5.4.2.1   When dangerous goods are packed or loaded into any container or vehicle, those responsible for packing the container or vehicle shall provide a "container/vehicle packing certificate" specifying the container/vehicle identification number(s) and certifying that the operation has been carried out in accordance with the following conditions:

.1   The container/vehicle was clean, dry and apparently fit to receive the goods;

.2   Packages, which need to be segregated in accordance with applicable segregation requirements, have not been packed together onto or in the container/vehicle (unless approved by the competent authority concerned in accordance with 7.3.4.1 (of the IMDG Code));

Cont'd on the next page

5.4.3.5   Contracting Parties shall provide the UNECE secretariat with the official translation of the instructions in writing in their national language(s), in accordance with this section. The UNECE secretariat shall make the national versions of the instructions in writing that it has received available to all Contracting Parties.

Footnote 6 (cont'd)

.3   *All packages have been externally inspected for damage, and only sound packages have been loaded;*

.4   *Drums have been stowed in an upright position, unless otherwise authorised by the competent authority, and all goods have been properly loaded, and, where necessary, adequately braced with securing material to suit the mode(s) of transport for the intended journey;*

.5   *Goods loaded in bulk have been evenly distributed within the container/vehicle;*

.6   *For consignments including goods of class 1, other than division 1.4, the container/vehicle is structurally serviceable in accordance with 7.1.2 (of the IMDG Code);*

.7   *The container/vehicle and packages are properly marked, labelled, and placarded, as appropriate;*

.8   *When substances presenting a risk of asphyxiation are used for cooling or conditioning purposes (such as dry ice (UN 1845) or nitrogen, refrigerated liquid (UN 1977) or argon, refrigerated liquid (UN 1951)), the container/vehicle is externally marked in accordance with 5.5.3.6 (of the IMDG Code); and*

.9   *A dangerous goods transport document, as indicated in 5.4.1 (of the IMDG Code) has been received for each dangerous goods consignment loaded in the container/vehicle.*

NOTE: The container/vehicle packing certificate is not required for portable tanks.

5.4.2.2   The information required in the dangerous goods transport document and the container/vehicle packing certificate may be incorporated into a single document; if not, these documents shall be attached one to the other. If the information is incorporated into a single document, the document shall a signed declaration such as "It is declared that the packing of the goods into the container/vehicle has been carried out in accordance with the applicable provisions". This declaration shall be dated and the person signing this declaration shall be identified on the document. Facsimile signatures are acceptable where applicable laws and regulations recognize the legal validity of facsimile signatures.

5.4.2.3   If the container/vehicle packing certificate is presented to the carrier by means of EDP or EDI transmission techniques, the signature(s) may be electronic signature(s) or may be replaced by the name(s) (in capitals) of the person authorized to sign.

5.4.2.4   When the container/vehicle packing certificate is given to a carrier by EDP or EDI techniques and subsequently the dangerous goods are transferred to a carrier that requires a paper container/vehicle packing certificate, the carrier shall ensure that the paper document indicates "Original received electronically" and the name of the signatory shall be shown in capital letters."

INSTRUCTIONS IN WRITING ACCORDING TO ADN
Actions in the event of an accident or incident

In the event of an accident or incident that may occur during carriage, the members of the crew shall take the following actions where safe and practicable to do so:

—   Inform all other persons on board about the emergency and keep them away as much as possible from the danger zone. Alert other vessels in the vicinity;

—   Avoid sources of ignition, in particular, do not smoke, use electronic cigarettes or similar devices or switch on or off any electrical equipment or installation that does not meet the requirements for use in zone 1 (that means no installations or equipment marked in red according to 9.1.0.52.1, 9.3.1.52.2, 9.3.2.52.2 or 9.3.3.52.2) and is not designed for use in emergency response;

—   Inform the appropriate body, giving as much information about the accident or incident and substances involved as possible;

—   Keep the transport documents and the loading plan readily available for responders on arrival;

—   Do not walk into or touch spilled substances and avoid inhalation of fumes, smoke, dusts and vapours by staying up wind;

—   Where appropriate and safe to do so, tackle small/initial fires;

—   Where appropriate and safe to do so, use on-board equipment to prevent leakages into the aquatic environment and contain spillages;

—   Where necessary and safe to do so, secure the ship against drifting;

—   Where appropriate, move away from the vicinity of the accident or incident, advise other persons to move away and follow the advice of the appropriate body;

—   Remove any contaminated clothing and used contaminated protective equipment, dispose of it safely and wash the body by appropriate means;

—   Observe the additional guidance assigned to the hazards of all concerned goods in the following table. For carriage in packages or in bulk, the hazards correspond to the number of the danger label model; for carriage in tank vessels to the data in accordance with 5.4.1.1.2 (c).

Danger labels and placards, description of the hazards	Hazard characteristics	Additional guidance
Additional guidance to members of the crew on the hazard characteristics of dangerous goods by class and on actions to be taken subject to prevailing circumstances		
(1)	(2)	(3)
Explosive substances and articles 1 1.5 1.6	May have a range of properties and effects such as mass detonation; projection of fragments; intense fire/heat flux; formation of bright light, loud noise or smoke. Sensitive to shocks and/or impacts and/or heat.	Take cover but stay away from windows. Steer the vessel as far away as possible from infrastructure and inhabited areas.
Explosive substances and articles 1.4	Slight risk of explosion and fire.	Take cover.
Flammable gases 2.1	Risk of fire. Risk of explosion. May be under pressure. Risk of asphyxiation. May cause burns and/or frostbite. Containments may explode when heated.	Take cover. Keep out of low areas.
Non-flammable, non-toxic gases 2.2	Risk of asphyxiation. May be under pressure. May cause frostbite. Containments may explode when heated.	Take cover. Keep out of low areas.
Toxic gases 2.3	Risk of intoxication. May be under pressure. May cause burns and/or frostbite. Containments may explode when heated.	Use emergency escape mask. Take cover. Keep out of low areas.
Flammable liquids 3	Risk of fire. Risk of explosion. Containments may explode when heated.	Take cover. Keep out of low areas.
Flammable solids, self-reactive substances, polymerizing substances and solid desensitized explosives 4.1	Risk of fire. Flammable or combustible, may be ignited by heat, sparks or flames. May contain self-reactive substances that are liable to exothermic decomposition in the case of heat supply, contact with other substances (such as acids, heavy-metal compounds or amines), friction or shock. This may result in the evolution of harmful and flammable gases or vapours or self-ignition. Containments may explode when heated. Risk of explosion of desensitized explosives after loss of desensitizer.	
Substances liable to spontaneous combustion 4.2	Risk of fire by spontaneous combustion if packages are damaged or contents spilled. May react vigorously with water.	
Substances which, in contact with water, emit flammable gases 4.3	Risk of fire and explosion in contact with water.	Spilled substances should be kept dry by covering the spillages.

Danger labels and placards, description of the hazards	Hazard characteristics	Additional guidance
Additional guidance to members of the crew on the hazard characteristics of dangerous goods by class and on actions to be taken subject to prevailing circumstances		
(1)	(2)	(3)
Oxidizing substances 5.1	Risk of vigorous reaction, ignition and explosion in contact with combustible or flammable substances.	Avoid mixing with flammable or combustible substances (e.g. sawdust).
Organic peroxides 5.2	Risk of exothermic decomposition at elevated temperatures, contact with other substances (such as acids, heavy-metal compounds or amines), friction or shock. This may result in the evolution of harmful and flammable gases or vapours or self-ignition.	Avoid mixing with flammable or combustible substances (e.g. sawdust).
Toxic substances 6.1	Risk of intoxication by inhalation, skin contact or ingestion. Risk to the aquatic environment.	Use emergency escape mask.
Infectious substances 6.2	Risk of infection. May cause serious disease in humans or animals Risk to the aquatic environment.	
Radioactive material 7A 7B 7C 7D	Risk of intake and external radiation.	Limit time of exposure.
Fissile material 7E	Risk of nuclear chain reaction.	
Corrosive substances 8	Risk of burns by corrosion. May react vigorously with each other, with water and with other substances. Spilled substance may evolve corrosive vapours. Risk to the aquatic environment.	
Miscellaneous dangerous substances and articles 9 9A	Risk of burns. Risk of fire. Risk of explosion. Risk to the aquatic environment	

NOTE:
1. *For dangerous goods with multiple risks and for mixed loads, each applicable entry shall be observed.*

2. *Additional guidance shown in column (3) of the table may be adapted to reflect the classes of dangerous goods to be carried and their means of transport.*

3. *Risks see also entries in the transport document as well as Chapter 3.2, Table C, Column (5).*

Additional guidance to members of the crew on the hazard characteristics of dangerous goods, indicated by marks, and on actions to be taken subject to prevailing circumstances		
Mark	Hazard characteristics	Additional guidance
(1)	(2)	(3)
Environmentally hazardous substances	Risk to the aquatic environment.	
Elevated temperature substances	Risk of burns by heat.	Avoid contact with hot parts of the transport unit and the spilled substance.

Equipment for personal and general protection to carry out general actions and hazard specific emergency actions to be carried on board the vessel in accordance with section 8.1.5 of ADN

The equipment required by Chapter 3.2, Table A, Column (9) and Table C, Column (18) shall be carried on board the vessel for all hazards listed in the transport document.

5.4.4   **Retention of dangerous goods transport information**

5.4.4.1   The consignor and the carrier shall retain a copy of the dangerous goods transport document and additional information and documentation as specified in ADN, for a minimum period of three months.

5.4.4.2   When the documents are kept electronically or in a computer system, the consignor and the carrier shall be able to reproduce them in a printed form.

5.4.5.   **Example of a multimodal dangerous goods form**

Example of a form which may be used as a combined dangerous goods declaration and container packing certificate for multimodal carriage of dangerous goods.

MULTIMODAL DANGEROUS GOODS FORM

1. Shipper/Consignor/Sender	2. Transport document number
	3. Page 1 of Pages / 4. Shipper's reference
	5. Freight Forwarder's reference
6. Consignee	7. Carrier (to be completed by the carrier)

SHIPPER'S DECLARATION

I hereby declare that the contents of this consignment are fully and accurately described below by the proper shipping name, and are classified, packaged, marked and labelled/placarded and are in all respects in proper condition for transport according to the applicable international and national governmental regulations.

8. *This shipment is within the limitations prescribed for: (Delete non-applicable)* PASSENGER AND CARGO AIRCRAFT CARGO AIRCRAFT ONLY	9. Additional handling information
10. Vessel/ flight No. and date 11. Port/place of loading	
12. Port/place of discharge 13. Destination	

14. Shipping marks	* Number and kind of packages; description of goods	Gross mass (kg)	Net mass	Cube (m³)

15. Container identification No./ vehicle registration No.	16. Seal number (s)	17. Container/vehicle size & type	18. Tare (kg)	19. Total gross mass (including tare) (kg)

CONTAINER/VEHICLE PACKING CERTIFICATE	21.RECEIVING ORGANIZATION RECEIPT
I hereby declare that the goods described above have been packed/loaded into the container/vehicle identified above in accordance with the applicable provisions ** **MUST BE COMPLETED AND SIGNED FOR ALL CONTAINER/VEHICLE LOADS BY PERSON RESPONSIBLE FOR PACKING/LOADING**	Received the above number of packages/containers/trailers in apparent good order and condition unless stated hereon: RECEIVING ORGANIZATION REMARKS:

20. Name of company	Haulier's name	22. Name of company (OF SHIPPER PREPARING THIS NOTE)
Name/Status of declarant	Vehicle reg. No.	Name/Status of declarant
Place and date	Signature and date	Place and date
Signature of declarant	DRIVER'S SIGNATURE	Signature of declarant

** See 5.4.2.

MULTIMODAL DANGEROUS GOODS FORM

Continuation Sheet

1. Shipper/Consignor/Sender	2. Transport document number	
	3. Page 1 of pages	4. Shipper's reference
		5. Freight Forwarder's reference

14. Shipping marks	* Number and kind of packages; description of goods	Gross mass (kg)	Net mass	Cube (m³)

* FOR DANGEROUS GOODS: you must specify: proper shipping name, hazard class, UN No., packing group (where assigned) and any other element of information required under applicable national and international regulations

CHAPTER 5.5

SPECIAL PROVISIONS

5.5.1   *(Deleted)*

5.5.2   **Special provisions applicable to fumigated cargo transport units (UN 3359)**

5.5.2.1   *General*

5.5.2.1.1   Fumigated cargo transport units (UN 3359) containing no other dangerous goods are not subject to any provisions of ADN other than those of this section.

5.5.2.1.2   When the fumigated cargo transport unit is loaded with dangerous goods in addition to the fumigant, any provision of ADN relevant to these goods (including placarding, marking and documentation) applies in addition to the provisions of this section.

5.5.2.1.3   Only cargo transport units that can be closed in such a way that the escape of gas is reduced to a minimum shall be used for the carriage of cargo under fumigation.

5.5.2.2   *Training*

Persons engaged in the handling of fumigated cargo transport units shall be trained commensurate with their responsibilities.

5.5.2.3   *Marking and placarding*

5.5.2.3.1   A fumigated cargo transport unit shall be marked with a warning mark, as specified in 5.5.2.3.2, affixed at each access point in a location where it will be easily seen by persons opening or entering the cargo transport unit. This mark shall remain on the cargo transport unit until the following provisions are met:

(a)   The fumigated cargo transport unit has been ventilated to remove harmful concentrations of fumigant gas; and

(b)   The fumigated goods or materials have been unloaded.

5.5.2.3.2   The fumigation warning mark shall be as shown in Figure 5.5.2.3.2.

Figure 5.5.2.3.2

* Insert details as appropriate

Fumigation warning mark

The mark shall be a rectangle. The minimum dimensions shall be 400 mm wide x 300 mm high and the minimum width of the outer line shall be 2 mm. The mark shall be in black print on a white background with lettering not less than 25 mm high. Where dimensions are not specified, all features shall be in approximate proportion to those shown.

5.5.2.3.3   If the fumigated cargo transport unit has been completely ventilated either by opening the doors of the unit or by mechanical ventilation after fumigation, the date of ventilation shall be marked on the fumigation warning mark.

5.5.2.3.4   When the fumigated cargo transport unit has been ventilated and unloaded, the fumigation warning mark shall be removed.

5.5.2.3.5   Placards conforming to model No. 9 (see 5.2.2.2.2) shall not be affixed to a fumigated cargo transport unit except as required for other Class 9 substances or articles packed therein.

5.5.2.4   *Documentation*

5.5.2.4.1   Documents associated with the carriage of cargo transport units that have been fumigated and have not been completely ventilated before carriage shall include the following information:

–   "UN 3359, fumigated cargo transport unit, 9", or "UN 3359, fumigated cargo transport unit, class 9";

–   The date and time of fumigation; and

–   The type and amount of the fumigant used.

These particulars shall be drafted in an official language of the forwarding country and also, if the language is not English, French or German, in English, French or German, unless agreements, if any, concluded between the countries concerned in the transport operation provide otherwise.

5.5.2.4.2 The documents may be in any form, provided they contain the information required in 5.5.2.4.1. This information shall be easy to identify, legible and durable.

5.5.2.4.3 Instructions for disposal of any residual fumigant including fumigation devices (if used) shall be provided.

5.5.2.4.4 A document is not required when the fumigated cargo transport unit has been completely ventilated and the date of ventilation has been marked on the warning mark (see 5.5.2.3.3 and 5.5.2.3.4).

5.5.3 **Special provisions applicable to the carriage of dry ice (UN 1845) and to packages and vehicles and containers containing substances presenting a risk of asphyxiation when used for cooling or conditioning purposes (such as dry ice (UN 1845) or nitrogen, refrigerated liquid (UN 1977) or argon, refrigerated liquid (UN 1951) or nitrogen)**

NOTE: In the context of this section the term "conditioning" may be used in a broader scope and includes protection.

5.5.3.1 *Scope*

5.5.3.1.1 This section is not applicable to substances which may be used for cooling or conditioning purposes when carried as a consignment of dangerous goods, except for the carriage of dry ice (UN No. 1845). When they are carried as a consignment, these substances shall be carried under the relevant entry of Table A of Chapter 3.2 in accordance with the associated conditions of carriage

For UN No. 1845, the conditions of carriage specified in this section, except 5.5.3.3.1, apply for all kinds of carriage, as a coolant, conditioner, or as a consignment. For the carriage of UN No. 1845, no other provisions of ADN apply.

5.5.3.1.2 This section is not applicable to gases in cooling cycles.

5.5.3.1.3 Dangerous goods used for cooling or conditioning tanks or MEGCs during carriage are not subject to this section.

5.5.3.1.4 Vehicles, wagons and containers containing substances used for cooling or conditioning purposes include vehicles, wagons and containers containing substances used for cooling or conditioning purposes inside packages as well as vehicles, wagons and containers with unpackaged substances used for cooling or conditioning purposes.

5.5.3.1.5 Sub-sections 5.5.3.6 and 5.5.3.7 only apply when there is an actual risk of asphyxiation in the vehicle, wagon or container. It is for the participants concerned to assess this risk, taking into consideration the hazards presented by the substances being used for cooling or conditioning, the amount of substance to be carried, the duration of the journey, the types of containment to be used and the gas concentration limits given in the note to 5.5.3.3.3.

5.5.3.2 *General*

5.5.3.2.1 Vehicles, wagons and containers in which dry ice (UN 1845) is carried or containing substances used for cooling or conditioning purposes (other than fumigation) during carriage are not subject to any provisions of ADN other than those of this section.

5.5.3.2.2 When dangerous goods are loaded in vehicles, wagons or containers containing substances used for cooling or conditioning purposes any provisions of ADN relevant to these dangerous goods apply in addition to the provisions of this section.

5.5.3.2.3 *(Reserved)*

5.5.3.2.4   Persons engaged in the handling or carriage of vehicles, wagons and containers in which dry ice (UN 1845) is carried or containing substances used for cooling or conditioning purposes shall be trained commensurate with their responsibilities.

5.5.3.3   *Packages containing dry ice (UN 1845) or a coolant or conditioner*

5.5.3.3.1   Packaged dangerous goods requiring cooling or conditioning assigned to packing instructions P203, P620, P650, P800, P901 or P904 of 4.1.4.1 of ADR shall meet the appropriate requirements of that packing instruction.

5.5.3.3.2   For packaged dangerous goods requiring cooling or conditioning assigned to other packing instructions, the packages shall be capable of withstanding very low temperatures and shall not be affected or significantly weakened by the coolant or conditioner. Packages shall be designed and constructed to permit the release of gas to prevent a build-up of pressure that could rupture the packaging. The dangerous goods shall be packed in such a way as to prevent movement after the dissipation of any coolant or conditioner.

5.5.3.3.3   Packages containing dry ice (UN 1845) or a coolant or conditioner shall be carried in well ventilated vehicles, wagons and containers. Marking according to 5.5.3.6 is not required in this case.

Ventilation is not required, and marking according to 5.5.3.6 is required, if:

–   the load compartment is insulated, refrigerated or mechanically refrigerated equipment, for example as defined in the Agreement on the International Carriage of Perishable Foodstuffs and on the Special Equipment to be Used for such Carriage (ATP) and separated from the driver's cab;

–   for vehicles, gas exchange between the load compartment and the driver's cab is prevented.

NOTE: *In this context "well ventilated" means there is an atmosphere where the carbon dioxide concentration is below 0.5% by volume and the oxygen concentration is above 19.5% by volume.*

5.5.3.4   *Marking of packages containing dry ice (UN 1845) or a coolant or conditioner*

5.5.3.4.1   Packages containing dry ice (UN 1845) as a consignment shall be marked "CARBON DIOXIDE, SOLID" or "DRY ICE"; packages containing dangerous goods used for cooling or conditioning shall be marked with the name indicated in Column (2) of Table A of Chapter 3.2 of these dangerous goods followed by the words "AS COOLANT" or "AS CONDITIONER" as appropriate in an official language of the country of origin and also, if that language is not English, French or German, in English, French or German, unless agreements concluded between the countries concerned in the transport operation provide otherwise.

5.5.3.4.2   The marks shall be durable, legible and placed in such a location and of such a size relative to the package as to be readily visible.

5.5.3.5   *Vehicles, wagons and containers containing unpackaged dry ice*

5.5.3.5.1   If dry ice in unpackaged form is used, it shall not come into direct contact with the metal structure of a vehicle, wagon or container to avoid embrittlement of the metal. Measures shall be taken to provide adequate insulation between the dry ice and the vehicle, wagon or container by providing a minimum of 30 mm separation (e.g. by using suitable low heat conducting materials such as timber planks, pallets etc).

5.5.3.5.2   Where dry ice is placed around packages, measures shall be taken to ensure that packages remain in the original position during carriage after the dry ice has dissipated.

5.5.3.6   *Marking of vehicles, wagons and containers*

5.5.3.6.1   Vehicles, wagons and containers containing dry ice (UN 1845) or dangerous goods used for cooling or conditioning purposes that are not well ventilated shall be marked with a warning mark, as specified in 5.5.3.6.2, affixed at each access point in a location where it will be easily seen by persons opening or entering the vehicle, wagon or container. This mark shall remain on the vehicle, wagon or container until the following provisions are met:

(a)   The vehicle, wagon or container has been well ventilated to remove harmful concentrations of dry ice (UN 1845) or coolant or conditioner; and

(b)   The dry ice (UN 1845) or cooled or conditioned goods have been unloaded.

As long as the vehicle, wagon or container is marked, the necessary precautions have to be taken before entering it. The necessity of ventilating through the cargo doors or other means (e.g. forced ventilation) has to be evaluated and included in training of the involved persons.

5.5.3.6.2   The warning mark shall be as shown in Figure 5.5.3.6.2.

Figure 5.5.3.6.2

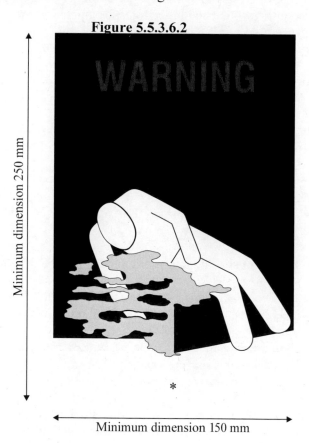

Asphyxiation warning mark for vehicles, wagons and containers

*   Insert the name indicated in column (2) of Table A of Chapter 3.2 or the name of the asphyxiant gas used as the coolant/conditioner. The lettering shall be in capitals, all be on one line and shall be at least 25 mm high. If the length of the proper shipping name is too long to fit in the space provided, the lettering may be reduced to the maximum size possible to fit. For example: "CARBON DIOXIDE, SOLID". Additional information such as "AS COOLANT" or "AS CONDITIONER" may be added.*

The mark shall be a rectangle. The minimum dimensions shall be 150 mm wide x 250 mm high. The word "WARNING" shall be in red or white and be at least 25 mm high.

Where dimensions are not specified, all features shall be in approximate proportion to those shown.

The word "WARNING" and the words "AS COOLANT" or "AS CONDITIONER", as appropriate, shall be in an official language of the country of origin and also, if that language is not English, French or German, in English, French or German, unless agreements concluded between the countries concerned in the transport operation provide otherwise.

5.5.3.7   *Documentation*

5.5.3.7.1   Documents (such as a bill of lading, cargo manifest or CMR/CIM/CMNI consignment note) associated with the carriage of vehicles, wagons or containers containing or having contained dry ice (UN 1845) or substances used for cooling or conditioning purposes and that have not been completely ventilated before carriage shall include the following information:

(a)   The UN number preceded by the letters "UN"; and

(b)   The name indicated in Column (2) of Table A of Chapter 3.2, where appropriate followed by the words "AS COOLANT" or "AS CONDITIONER" in an official language of the country of origin and also, if that language is not English, French or German, in English, French or German, unless agreements, if any, concluded between the countries concerned in the transport operation provide otherwise.

For example: UN 1845, CARBON DIOXIDE, SOLID, AS COOLANT.

5.5.3.7.2   The transport document may be in any form, provided it contains the information required in 5.5.3.7.1. This information shall be easy to identify, legible and durable.

5.5.4   **Dangerous goods contained in equipment in use or intended for use during carriage, attached to or placed in packages, overpacks, containers or load compartments**

5.5.4.1   Dangerous goods (e.g. lithium batteries, fuel cell cartridges) contained in equipment such as data loggers and cargo tracking devices, attached to or placed in packages, overpacks, containers or load compartments are not subject to any provisions of ADN other than the following:

(a)   the equipment shall be in use or intended for use during carriage;

(b)   the contained dangerous goods (e.g. lithium batteries, fuel cell cartridges) shall meet the applicable construction and test requirements specified in ADN; and

(c)   the equipment shall be capable of withstanding the shocks and loadings normally encountered during carriage and shall be safe for use in the dangerous environments to which it may be exposed.

5.5.4.2   When such equipment containing dangerous goods is carried as a consignment, the relevant entry of Table A of Chapter 3.2 shall be used and all applicable provisions of ADN shall apply.

PART 6

REQUIREMENTS FOR THE CONSTRUCTION AND TESTING OF PACKAGINGS, INTERMEDIATE BULK CONTAINERS (IBCS), LARGE PACKAGINGS, TANKS AND BULK CONTAINERS.

CHAPTER 6.1

GENERAL REQUIREMENTS

6.1.1   Packagings (including IBCs and large packagings) and tanks shall meet the following requirements of ADR in respect of construction and testing:

Chapter 6.1:   Requirements for the construction and testing of packagings;

Chapter 6.2:   Requirements for the construction and testing of pressure receptacles, aerosol dispensers, small receptacles containing gas (gas cartridges) and fuel cell cartridges containing liquefied flammable gas;

Chapter 6.3:   Requirements for the construction and testing of packagings for Class 6.2 infectious substances of category A;

Chapter 6.4:   Requirements for the construction, testing and approval of packages and material of Class 7;

Chapter 6.5   Requirements for the construction and testing of intermediate bulk containers (IBCs);

Chapter 6.6   Requirements for the construction and testing of large packagings;

Chapter 6.7   Requirements for the design, construction, inspection and testing of portable tanks and UN multiple-element gas containers (MEGCs);

Chapter 6.8   Requirements for the construction, equipment, type approval, inspections and tests, and marking of fixed tanks (tank-vehicles), demountable tanks and tank-containers and tank swap bodies, with shell made of metallic materials and battery-vehicles and multiple element gas containers (MEGCs);

Chapter 6.9   Requirements for the design, construction, equipment, type approval, testing and marking of fibre-reinforced plastics (FRP) fixed tanks (tank-vehicles), demountable tanks, tank-containers and tank swap bodies;

Chapter 6.10   Requirements for the construction, equipment, type approval, inspection and marking of vacuum-operated waste tanks;

Chapter 6.11   Requirements for the design, construction, inspection and testing of bulk containers;

Chapter 6.12   Requirements for the construction, equipment, type approval, inspections and tests, and marking of tanks, bulk containers and special compartments for explosives of mobile explosive manufacturing units (MEMUs).

6.1.2   Portable tanks may also meet the requirements of Chapter 6.7 or, if appropriate, Chapter 6.9 of the IMDG Code.

6.1.3   Tank-vehicles may also meet the requirements of Chapter 6.8 of the IMDG Code.

6.1.4   Tank wagons, with fixed or demountable tanks and battery-wagons shall meet the requirements of Chapter 6.8 of the RID.

6.1.5   Bodies of vehicles for bulk carriage shall, if necessary, meet the requirements of Chapter 6.11 or of Chapter 9.5 of ADR.

6.1.6   When the provisions of 7.3.1.1 (a) of RID or ADR are applied, the bulk containers shall meet the requirements of Chapter 6.11 of RID or ADR.

PART 7

Requirements concerning loading, carriage, unloading and handling of cargo

CHAPTER 7.1

DRY CARGO VESSELS

7.1.0   **General requirements**

7.1.0.1   The provisions of 7.1.0 to 7.1.7 are applicable to dry cargo vessels.

7.1.0.2 to 7.1.0.99   *(Reserved)*

7.1.1   **Mode of carriage of goods**

7.1.1.1 to 7.1.1.9   *(Reserved)*

7.1.1.10   *Carriage of packages*

Unless otherwise specified, the masses given for packages shall be the gross masses. When packages are carried in containers or vehicles, the mass of the container or vehicle shall not be included in the gross mass of such packages.

7.1.1.11   *Carriage in bulk*

Carriage of dangerous goods in bulk shall be prohibited except where this mode of carriage is explicitly authorized in column (8) of Table A of Chapter 3.2. The code "B" shall then appear in this column.

7.1.1.12   *Ventilation*

The ventilation of holds is required only if it is prescribed in 7.1.4.12 or by an additional requirement "VE …" in column (10) of Table A of Chapter 3.2.

7.1.1.13   *Measures to be taken prior to loading*

Additional measures to be taken prior to loading are required only if prescribed in 7.1.4.13 or by an additional requirement "LO …" in column (11) of Table A of Chapter 3.2.

7.1.1.14   *Handling and stowage of cargo*

During the handling and stowage of cargo additional measures are required only if prescribed in 7.1.4.14 or by an additional requirement "HA …" in column (11) of Table A of Chapter 3.2.

7.1.1.15   *(Reserved)*

7.1.1.16   *Measures to be taken during loading, carriage, unloading and handling of cargo*

The additional measures to be taken during loading, carriage, unloading and handling of cargo are required only if prescribed in 7.1.4.16 or by an additional requirement "IN …" in column (11) of Table A of Chapter 3.2.

7.1.1.17   *(Reserved)*

7.1.1.18   *Carriage in containers, in bulk containers, in intermediate bulk containers (IBCs) and in large packagings, in MEGCs, in portable tanks and in tank-containers*

The carriage of containers, bulk containers, IBCs, large packagings, MEGCs, portable tanks and tank-containers shall be in accordance with the provisions applicable to the carriage of packages.

7.1.1.19   *Vehicles and wagons*

The carriage of vehicles and wagons shall be in accordance with the provisions applicable to the carriage of packages.

7.1.1.20   *(Reserved)*

7.1.1.21   *Carriage in cargo tanks*

The carriage of dangerous goods in cargo tanks in dry-cargo vessels is prohibited.

7.1.1.22 to 7.1.1.99   *(Reserved)*

7.1.2   **Requirements applicable to vessels**

7.1.2.0   *Permitted vessels*

7.1.2.0.1   Dangerous goods may be carried in quantities not exceeding those indicated in 7.1.4.1.4, or, if applicable, in 7.1.4.1.1.2 or 7.1.4.1.1.3:

–   In dry cargo vessels conforming to the applicable construction requirements of 9.1.0.0 to 9.1.0.79; or

–   In seagoing vessels conforming to the applicable construction requirements of 9.1.0.0 to 9.1.0.79, or otherwise to the requirements of 9.2.0 to 9.2.0.79.

7.1.2.0.2   Dangerous goods of classes 2, 3, 4.1, 4.2, 4.3, 5.1, 5.2, 6.1, 7, 8 or 9, with the exception of those for which a No. 1 model label is required in column (5) of table A of Chapter 3.2, may be carried in quantities greater than those indicated in 7.1.4.1.1.2, 7.1.4.1.1.3 and 7.1.4.1.4:

–   In double-hull dry cargo vessels conforming to the applicable construction requirements of 9.1.0.80 to 9.1.0.95; or

–   In double-hull seagoing vessels conforming to the applicable construction requirements of 9.1.0.80 to 9.1.0.95, or otherwise to the requirements of 9.2.0 to 9.2.0.95.

7.1.2.1 to 7.1.2.4   *(Reserved)*

7.1.2.5   *Instructions for the use of devices and installations*

Where specific safety rules have to be complied with when using any device or installation, instructions for the use of the particular device or installation shall be readily available for consultation at appropriate places on board in the language normally spoken on board and also if that language is not English, French or German, in English, French or German unless agreements concluded between the countries concerned in the transport operation provide otherwise.

7.1.2.6 to 7.1.2.18   *(Reserved)*

7.1.2.19   *Pushed convoys and side-by-side formations*

7.1.2.19.1   Where at least one vessel of a convoy or side-by-side formation is required to be in possession of a certificate of approval for the carriage of dangerous goods, all vessels of such convoy or side-by-side formation shall be provided with an appropriate certificate of approval.

Vessels not carrying dangerous goods shall comply with the requirements of the following paragraphs:

1.16.1.1, 1.16.1.2, 1.16.1.3, 1.16.1.4, 7.1.2.5, 8.1.4, 8.1.5, 8.1.6.1, 8.1.6.3, 8.1.7, 8.3.5, 9.1.0.0, 9.1.0.12.3, 9.1.0.12.4, 9.1.0.17.2, 9.1.0.17.3, 9.1.0.31, 9.1.0.32.2, 9.1.0.34, 9.1.0.40.2, 9.1.0.41, 9.1.0.51, 9.1.0.52, 9.1.0.71 and 9.1.0.74.

7.1.2.19.2   For the purposes of the application of the provisions of this Chapter with the exception of 7.1.4.1.1.2, 7.1.4.1.1.3 and 7.1.4.1.4, the entire pushed convoy or the side-by-side formation shall be deemed to be a single vessel.

7.1.2.20 to 7.1.2.99   *(Reserved)*

7.1.3   **General service requirements**

7.1.3.1   *Access to holds, double-hull spaces and double bottoms; inspections*

7.1.3.1.1   Access to the holds is not permitted except for the purpose of loading or unloading and carrying out inspections or cleaning work.

7.1.3.1.2   Access to the double-hull spaces and the double bottoms is not permitted while the vessel is under way.

7.1.3.1.3   If the concentration of gases and vapours given off by the cargo or the oxygen content of the air in holds, double-wall spaces or double bottoms has to be measured before entry, the results of these measurements shall be recorded in writing. The measurement may only be effected by an expert referred to in 8.2.1.2, equipped with suitable breathing apparatus for the substance carried.

Entry into the spaces is not permitted for the purpose of measuring.

7.1.3.1.4   *Carriage of cargo in bulk or without packaging*

If a vessel carries dangerous goods in bulk or without packaging in its holds for which EX and/or TOX appears in column (9) of Table A of Chapter 3.2, the concentration of flammable and/or toxic gases and vapours given off by the cargo in these holds and adjacent holds shall be measured before any person enters these holds.

7.1.3.1.5   Entry into holds where dangerous goods are carried in bulk or without packaging as well as entry into double-hull spaces and double bottoms is only permitted if:

–   the concentration of flammable gases and vapours given off by the cargo in the hold, double hull space or double bottom is below 10% of the LEL, the concentration of toxic gases and vapours given off by the cargo is below national accepted exposure levels, and the percentage of oxygen is between 20 and 23.5 vol %; or

–   the concentration of flammable gases and vapours given off by the cargo is below 10% of the LEL, and the person entering the space wears a self-contained breathing apparatus and other necessary protective and rescue equipment, and is secured by a line. Entry into these spaces is only permitted if this operation is supervised by a second person for whom the same equipment is readily at hand. Another two persons capable of giving assistance in an emergency shall be on the vessel within calling distance.

In deviation of 1.1.4.6, more stringent national legislation on the entry into holds shall take precedence over the ADN.

7.1.3.1.6   *Carriage in packages*

In case of suspected damage to packages, the concentration of flammable and/or toxic gases and vapours given off by the cargo in holds containing dangerous goods of Classes 2, 3, 4.3, 5.2, 6.1 and 8 for which EX and/or TOX appears in column (9) of Table A of Chapter 3.2, shall be measured before any person enters these holds.

7.1.3.1.7   Entry into holds where damage is suspected to packages in which dangerous goods of Classes 2, 3, 4.3, 5.2, 6.1 and 8 are carried as well as entry into double-hull spaces and double bottoms is only permitted if:

–   the concentration of flammable gases and vapours given off by the cargo in the hold, double hull space or double bottom is below 10% of the LEL, the concentration of toxic gases and vapours given off by the cargo is below national accepted exposure levels, and the percentage of oxygen is between 20 and 23,5 vol %; or

–   the concentration of flammable gases and vapours given off by the cargo in the hold is below 10% of the LEL and the person entering the space wears a self-contained breathing apparatus and other necessary protective and rescue equipment and is secured by a line. Entry into these spaces is only permitted if this operation is supervised by a second person for whom the same equipment is readily at hand. Another two persons capable of giving assistance in an emergency shall be on the vessel within calling distance.

In deviation of 1.1.4.6, more stringent national legislation on the entry into holds shall take precedence over the ADN.

7.1.3.2 to 7.1.3.14   *(Reserved)*

7.1.3.15   *Expert on board the vessel*

When dangerous goods are carried, the responsible master shall at the same time be an expert according to 8.2.1.2.

NOTE: Which master of the vessel's crew is the responsible master shall be determined and documented on board by the carrier. If there is no such determination, the requirement applies to every master.

By derogation from this, for the loading and unloading of dangerous goods in a barge, it is sufficient that the person who is responsible for loading and unloading and for ballasting of the barge has the expertise required according to 8.2.1.2.

7.1.3.16   All measurements on board the vessel shall be performed by an expert according to 8.2.1.2, unless provided otherwise in the Regulations annexed to ADN. The results of the measurements shall be recorded in writing in the book according to 8.1.2.1 (g).

7.1.3.17 to 7.1.3.19   *(Reserved)*

7.1.3.20   *Water ballast*

Double-hull spaces and double bottoms may be used for water ballast.

7.1.3.21   *(Reserved)*

7.1.3.22   *Opening of holds*

7.1.3.22.1   Dangerous goods shall be protected against the influences of weather and against spray water except during loading and unloading or during inspection.

This provision does not apply when dangerous goods are loaded in sprayproof containers, IBCs, or large packagings, or in MEGCs, portable tanks, tank-containers, vehicles or wagons which are closed or sheeted.

7.1.3.22.2   Where dangerous goods are carried in bulk, the holds shall be covered with hatch covers.

7.1.3.23 to 7.1.3.30   *(Reserved)*

7.1.3.31   *Engines*

The use of engines running on fuels having a flashpoint equal to or lower than 55 °C (e.g. petrol engines) is prohibited. This provision does not apply to:

–   the petrol-operated outboard motors of lifeboats;

–   the propulsion and auxiliary systems which meet the requirements of Chapter 30 and Annex 8, Section 1 of the European Standard laying down Technical Requirements for Inland Navigation vessels (ES-TRIN) as amended.[1]

If a substance is carried in bulk and has in column (9) of Table A of Chapter 3.2 an entry "EX" then:

–   Outboard motors and their fuel tanks shall be carried on board only outside the protected area; and

–   Mechanical inflation devices, outboard motors and their electrical installations shall be put into operation only outside the protected area.

7.1.3.32   *Oil fuel tanks*

Double bottoms with a height of at least 0.6 m may be used as oil fuel tanks provided that they have been constructed in accordance with Chapters 9.1 or 9.2.

7.1.3.33 to 7.4.3.40   *(Reserved)*

7.1.3.41   *Smoking, fire or naked light*

7.1.3.41.1   Smoking, including electronic cigarettes and other similar devices, fire and naked light are prohibited on board the vessel.

This prohibition shall be displayed on notice boards at appropriate places.

---

[1]   *As available on the website of the Comité Européen pour l'Élaboration de Standards dans le Domaine de Navigation Intérieure – CESNI,* https://www.cesni.eu/en/documents/es-trin/.

The prohibition does not apply in the accommodation or the wheelhouse, provided that their windows, doors, skylights and hatches are closed or the ventilation system is adjusted to guarantee an overpressure of at least 0.1 kPa.

7.1.3.41.2   Heating, cooking and refrigerating appliances shall not be fuelled with liquid fuels, liquid gas or solid fuels.

Cooking and refrigerating appliances may only be used in the accommodation and in the wheelhouse.

7.1.3.41.3   Heating appliances or boilers fuelled with liquid fuels having a flash-point above 55° C which are installed in the engine room or in another suitable space may, however, be used.

7.1.3.42   *Heating of holds*

The heating of holds or the operation of a heating system in the holds is prohibited.

7.1.3.43   *(Reserved)*

7.1.3.44   *Cleaning operations*

The use of liquids having a flash-point below 55° C for cleaning purposes is prohibited.

7.1.3.45 to 7.1.3.50   *(Reserved)*

7.1.3.51   *Electrical and non-electrical installations and equipment*

7.1.3.51.1   The electrical and non-electrical installations and equipment shall be properly maintained.

7.1.3.51.2   The use of movable electric cables is prohibited in the protected area. This provision does not apply to the electric cables referred to in 9.1.0.53.5.

Movable electric cables must undergo visual inspection each time before use. They must be installed in such a way as to ensure that they are not at risk of damage. Connectors must be located outside of the protected area.

The use of electric cables to connect the power network of a vessel to a land-based power network is not permitted:

–   During the loading or unloading of substances that have an entry "EX" in column (9) of Table A of Chapter 3.2; or

–   When the vessel is located immediately adjacent to or within an onshore assigned zone.

7.1.3.51.3   The sockets for connecting the signal lights and gangway lighting and for connecting containers, submerged pumps, hatch cover gantries, or hold fans shall not be live except when the signal lights or the gangway lighting are switched on or when the containers or the submerged pumps or the hatch cover gantries or hold fans are in operation. Connecting or disconnecting shall only be possible when the sockets are not live.

7.1.3.51.4   The electrical installations and equipment in the holds shall be kept switched off and protected against unintentional connection.

This provision does not apply to permanently installed electrical cables passing through the holds, to movable electrical cables connecting containers stowed according to 7.1.4.4.4, or to electrical installations and equipment fulfilling the requirements for use in zone 1.

7.1.3.51.5　During a stay in the immediate vicinity of or within an onshore assigned zone, electrical and non-electrical installations and equipment not fulfilling the requirements of 9.1.0.52.1 or that may have a surface temperature higher than 200 °C (marked in red according to 9.1.0.51 and 9.1.0.52.2) shall be switched off and cooled down to below 200 °C, or the measures mentioned in 7.1.3.51.6 shall be taken.

7.1.3.51.6　7.1.3.51.5 does not apply in accommodation, wheelhouse and service spaces located outside the protected area if:

(a)　The ventilation system is adjusted to guarantee an overpressure of at least 0.1 kPa; and

(b)　The gas detection system is switched on, taking measurements continuously.

7.1.3.51.7　Installations and equipment referred to in 7.1.3.51.5 that have been switched off during loading or unloading or during a stay in the immediate vicinity of or within an onshore assigned zone may only be switched on again when:

(a)　The vessel is no longer in the vicinity of or within the onshore assigned zone; or

(b)　A concentration of less than 10% of the LEL of n-Hexane is reached in the wheelhouse, accommodation and service spaces located outside the protected area.

The results of the measurements shall be recorded in writing.

7.1.3.51.8　If vessels are not able to meet the requirements of 7.1.3.51.5 and 7.1.3.51.6, they are not permitted to remain in the immediate vicinity of or within an onshore assigned zone. The competent authority may allow exceptions in individual cases.

7.1.3.52 to 7.1.3.69　*(Reserved)*

7.1.3.70　***Aerials, lightning conductors, wire cables and masts***

7.1.3.70.1　No part of an aerial for electronic apparatus, no lightning conductor and no wire cable shall be situated above the holds.

7.1.3.70.2　No part of aerials for radiotelephones shall be located within 2.00 m from substances or articles of Class 1.

7.1.3.71 to 7.1.3.99　*(Reserved)*

7.1.4　**Additional requirements concerning loading, carriage, unloading and other handling of the cargo**

7.1.4.1　***Limitation of the quantities carried***

7.1.4.1.1　Single-hull vessels may carry goods of Classes 1, 2, 3, 4.1, 4.2, 4.3, 5.1, 5.2, 6.1, 7, 8 and 9 only in the limited quantities set out in 7.1.4.1.4. This provision also applies to pushed barges and double-hull vessels which do not meet the additional rules of construction in 9.1.0.88 to 9.1.0.95 or 9.2.0.88 to 9.2.0.95.

7.1.4.1.1.1　Where substances and articles of different divisions of Class 1 are loaded in a single vessel in conformity with the provisions for prohibition of mixed loading of 7.1.4.3.3 or 7.1.4.3.4, the entire load shall not exceed the smallest maximum mass given in 7.1.4.1.4 below for the goods of the most dangerous division loaded, the order of precedence being 1.1, 1.5, 1.2, 1.3, 1.6, 1.4.

7.1.4.1.1.2　For pushed convoys and side-by-side formations, the quantity limitations specified in 7.1.4.1.4 apply to each unit. A maximum of 1,100,000 kg is permitted for each unit.

7.1.4.1.1.3   When a vessel is carrying several types of dangerous goods, the total quantity shall not exceed 1,100,000 kg.

7.1.4.1.2   Double-hull vessels meeting the additional construction rules in 9.1.0.88 to 9.1.0.95 or 9.2.0.88 to 9.2.0.95 may carry goods without limitation of the quantity carried, except for:

- goods of Class 1, and

- goods of classes 2, 3, 4.1, 4.2, 4.3, 5.1, 5.2, 6.1, 7, 8 and 9 for which a danger label of model No. 1 is required in column (5) of Table A of Chapter 3.2,

for which the limitations set in 7.1.4.1.1 and 7.1.4.1.1.1 to 7.1.4.1.1.3 apply.

7.1.4.1.3   For activity limits, transport index (TI) limits and criticality safety indices (CSI) in the case of the carriage of radioactive material, see 7.1.4.14.7.

7.1.4.1.4 Quantity limitations

Class	Description	0 kg	90 kg	15,000 kg	50,000 kg	120,000 kg	300,000 kg	1,100,000 kg
1	All substances and articles of Division 1.1, compatibility group A[1]		X					
	All substances and articles of Division 1.1, compatibility groups B, C, D, E, F, G, J or L[2]			X				
	All substances and articles of Division 1.2, compatibility groups B, C, D, E, F, G, H, J or L				X			
	All substances and articles of Division 1.3, compatibility groups C, G, H, J or L[3]						X	
	All substances and articles of Division 1.4, compatibility groups B, C, D, E, F, G or S							X
	All substances of Division 1.5, compatibility group D[2]			X				
	All substances and articles of Division 1.6, compatibility group N[3]						X	
	Empty packaging, uncleaned							X

Note:

[1] *In not less than three batches of a maximum of 30 kg each, distance between batches not less than 10.00 m.*

[2] *In not less than three batches of a maximum of 5,000 kg each, distance between batches not less than 10.00 m.*

[3] *Not more than 100,000 kg per hold. A wooden partition is permitted for subdividing a hold.*

Class	Description	0 kg	90 kg	15,000 kg	50,000 kg	120,000 kg	300,000 kg	1,100,000 kg
2	All goods for which label No. 2.1 is required in column (5) of Table A of Chapter 3.2: total						X	
	All goods for which label No. 2.3 is required in column (5) of Table A of Chapter 3.2: total					X		
	Other goods							X
3	All goods of packing groups I or II for which, in addition to a label of model No. 3, a label of model No. 6.1 is required in column (5) of Table A of Chapter 3.2: total					X		
	Other goods						X	

Class	Description	1,100,000 kg	300,000 kg	120,000 kg	50,000 kg	15,000 kg	90 kg	0 kg
4.1	UN Nos. 3221, 3222, 3231 and 3232: total					X		
	All goods of packing group I;							
	All goods of packing group II for which, in addition to a label of model No. 4.1, a label of model No. 6.1 is required in column (5) of Table A of Chapter 3.2;							
	Self-reactive substances of types C, D, E and F (UN Nos. 3223 to 3230 and 3233 to 3240);							
	All other substances of classification code SR1 or SR2 (UN Nos. 2956, 3241, 3242 and 3251);							
	and desensitized explosive substances of packing group II (UN Nos. 2907, 3319 and 3344): total			X				
	Other goods	X						
4.2	All goods of packing groups I or II for which, in addition to a label of model No. 4.2, a label of model No. 6.1 is required in column (5) of Table A of Chapter 3.2: total		X					
	Other goods	X						
4.3	All goods of packing groups I or II for which, in addition to a label of model No. 4.3, a label of model No. 3, 4.1 or 6.1 is required in column (5) of Table A of Chapter 3.2: total		X					
	Other goods	X						
5.1	All goods of packing groups I or II for which, in addition to a label of model No. 5.1, a label of model No. 6.1 is required in column (5) of Table A of Chapter 3.2: total		X					
	Other goods	X						
5.2	UN Nos. 3101, 3102, 3111 and 3112: total					X		
	Other goods			X				
6.1	All goods of packing group I: total			X				
	All goods of packing group II: total		X					
	All goods carried in bulk							X
	Other goods	X						

Class	Description	0 kg	90 kg	15,000 kg	50,000 kg	120,000 kg	300,000 kg	1,100,000 kg
7	UN Nos. 2912, 2913, 2915, 2916, 2917, 2919, 2977, 2978 and 3321 to 3333	X						
	Other goods							X
8	All goods of packing group I;							
	All goods of packing group II for which, in addition to a label of model No. 8, a label of model No. 3 or 6.1 is required in column (5) of Table A of Chapter 3.2: total						X	
	Other goods							X
9	All goods of packing group II: total						X	
	UN No. 3077, goods carried in bulk and classified as hazardous to the aquatic environment, categories Acute 1 or Chronic 1, in accordance with 2.4.3	X						
	Other goods							X

7.1.4.2   *Prohibition of mixed loading (bulk)*

Vessels carrying substances of Class 5.1 in bulk shall not carry any other goods.

7.1.4.3   *Prohibition of mixed loading (packages in holds)*

7.1.4.3.1   Goods of different classes shall be separated by a minimum horizontal distance of 3.00 m. They shall not be stowed one on top of the other.

7.1.4.3.2   Irrespective of the quantity, dangerous goods for which marking with two blue cones or two blue lights is prescribed in column (12) of Table A of Chapter 3.2 shall not be stowed in the same hold together with flammable goods for which marking with one blue cone or one blue light is prescribed in column (12) of Table A of Chapter 3.2.

7.1.4.3.3   Packages containing substances or articles of Class 1 and packages containing substances of Classes 4.1 or 5.2 for which marking with three blue cones or three blue lights is prescribed in column (12) of Table A of Chapter 3.2 shall be separated by a distance of not less than 12 m from goods of all other classes.

7.1.4.3.4   Substances and articles of Class 1 shall not be stowed in the same hold, except as indicated in the following table:

Compatibility group	A	B	C	D	E	F	G	H	J	L	N	S
A	X	-	-	-	-	-	-	-	-	-	-	-
B	-	X	-	1/	-	-	-	-	-	-	-	X
C	-	-	X	X	X	-	X	-	-	-	2/, 3/	X
D	-	1/	X	X	X	-	X	-	-	-	2/, 3/	X
E	-	-	X	X	X	-	X	-	-	-	2/, 3/	X
F	-	-	-	-	-	X	-	-	-	-	-	X
G	-	-	X	X	X	-	X	-	-	-	-	X
H	-	-	-	-	-	-	-	X	-	-	-	X
J	-	-	-	-	-	-	-	-	X	-	-	X
L	-	-	-	-	-	-	-	-	-	4/	-	-
N	-	-	2/, 3/	2/, 3/	2/, 3/	-	-	-	-	-	2/	X
S	-	X	X	X	X	X	X	X	X	-	X	X

"X"   *indicates that explosive substances or articles of corresponding compatibility groups in accordance with Part 2 of these Regulations may be stowed in the same hold.*

1/   *Packages containing articles assigned to compatibility group B or substances or articles assigned to compatibility group D may be loaded together in the same hold provided that they are carried in closed containers, vehicles or wagons.*

2/   *Different categories of articles of Division 1.6, compatibility group N, may be carried together as articles of Division 1.6, compatibility group N, only when it is proven by testing or analogy that there is no additional risk of sympathetic detonation between the articles. Otherwise they should be treated as hazard Division 1.1.*

3/   *When articles of compatibility group N are carried with substances or articles of compatibility groups C, D or E, the articles of compatibility group N should be considered as having the characteristics of compatibility group D.*

4/   *Packages with substances or articles of compatibility group L may be stowed in the same hold with packages containing the same type of substances or articles of the same compatibility group.*

7.1.4.3.5   For the carriage of material Class 7 (UN Nos. 2916, 2917, 3323, 3328, 3329 and 3330) in Type B(U) or Type B(M) or Type C packages, the controls, restrictions or provisions specified in the competent authority approval certificate shall be complied with.

7.1.4.3.6   For the carriage of material of Class 7 under special arrangement (UN Nos. 2919 and 3331), the special provisions specified by the competent authority shall be met. In particular, mixed loading shall not be permitted unless specifically authorized by the competent authority.

7.1.4.4 *Prohibition of mixed loading (containers, vehicles, wagons)*

7.1.4.4.1   7.1.4.3 shall not apply to packages stowed in containers, vehicles or wagons in accordance with international regulations.

7.1.4.4.2   7.1.4.3 shall not apply to:

–   closed containers;

–   closed vehicles and closed wagons;

–   tank-containers, portable tanks and MEGCs;

–   tank-vehicles and tank-wagons.

7.1.4.4.3   For containers other than those referred to in paragraph 7.1.4.4.1 and 7.1.4.4.2 above the separation distance required by 7.1.4.3.1 may be reduced to 2.40 m (width of container).

7.1.4.4.4   The electrical installations and equipment fitted to the outside of a closed container may be connected with removable electrical cables in accordance with the provisions of 9.1.0.53.5 or be put into operation provided that:

(a)   These electrical installations and equipment are appropriate at least for use in zone 1 and comply with the requirements for temperature class T4 and explosion group II B; or that

(b)   These electrical installations and equipment do not fulfil the requirements referred to in (a), but are sufficiently separated from other containers containing substances of:

–   Class 2 for which a label No. 2.1 is required in column (5) of Table A of Chapter 3.2;

–   Class 3, packing group I or II;

–   Class 4.3;

–   Class 6.1; packing group I or II, with an additional hazard of Class 4.3;

–   Class 8, packing group I, with an additional hazard of Class 3; and

–   Class 8, packing group I or II, with an additional hazard of Class 4.3.

This condition is deemed to be met if no container containing the above-mentioned substances is stowed within an area of cylindrical form with a radius of 2.40 m around the electrical installations and equipment and an unlimited vertical extension.

The requirements of subparagraphs (a) and (b) need not be complied with if containers with the electrical installations or equipment which do not meet the requirements for use in explosion hazardous areas and the containers containing the above-mentioned substances are stowed in separate holds.

Examples of stowage and segregation of containers

Legend

R   Container (e.g. reefer) with electrical equipment which is not of a certified safe type.

Z   Electrical equipment which is not of a certified safe type.

X   Container not allowed when containing dangerous substances for which sufficient separation is required.

Top view
1. On deck

Top view
2. In the hold

Top view
2. In the hold

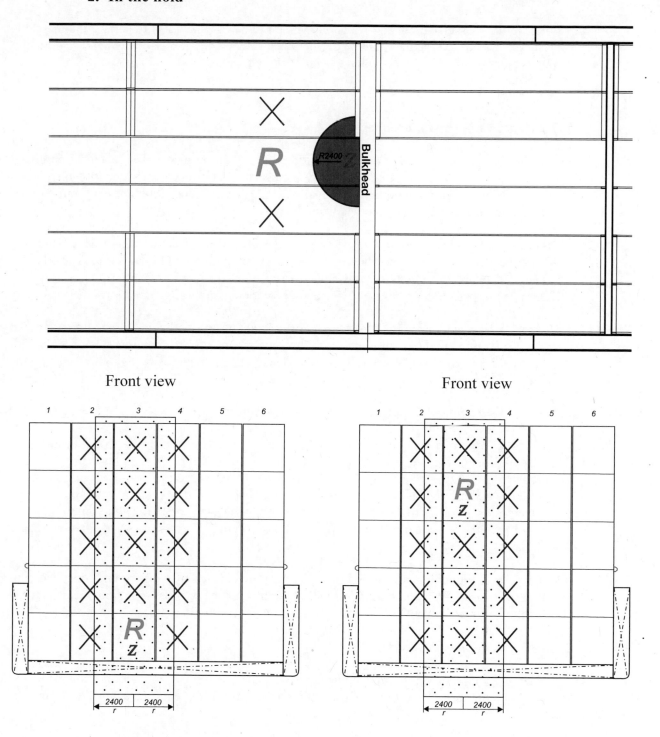

Front view

Front view

7.1.4.4.5   Electrical installations and equipment fitted on an open container may not be connected with removable electrical cables in accordance with the provisions of 9.1.0.53.5 or be used unless they are appropriate at least for use in zone 1 and they comply with the requirements for temperature class T4 and explosion group II B, or the container is loaded in a hold free of containers containing substances mentioned in 7.1.4.4.4 (b).

7.1.4.5   *Prohibition of mixed loading (seagoing vessels; inland navigation vessels carrying containers)*

For seagoing vessels and inland waterway vessels, where the latter only carry containers, the prohibition of mixed loading shall be deemed to have been met if the stowage and segregation requirements of the IMDG Code have been complied with.

7.1.4.6   *(Reserved)*

7.1.4.7   *Places of loading and unloading*

7.1.4.7.1   The dangerous goods shall be loaded or unloaded only at the places designated or approved for this purpose by the competent authority. In those places the means of evacuation mentioned in subsection 7.1.4.77 should be made available. Otherwise trans-shipment is permitted only with the authorization of the competent authority.

7.1.4.7.2   When substances or articles of Class 1 and substances of Classes 4.1 or 5.2 for which marking with three blue cones or three blue lights is prescribed in column (12) of Table A of Chapter 3.2 are on board, no goods of any kind may be loaded or unloaded except at the places designated or permitted for this purpose by the competent authority.

7.1.4.7.3   If a zone is assigned onshore at the loading or unloading station, the vessel is only authorized to stay in its immediate vicinity or within the zone if it meets the requirements of 9.1.0.12.3 (b) or (c), 9.1.0.51, 9.1.0.52.1 and 9.1.0.52.2. The competent authority may allow exceptions in individual cases.

7.1.4.8   *Time and duration of loading and unloading operations*

7.1.4.8.1   Loading and unloading operations of substances or articles of Class 1 and substances of Classes 4.1 or 5.2 for which marking with three blue cones or three blue lights is prescribed in column (12) of Table A of Chapter 3.2 shall not start without permission in writing from the competent authority. This provision also applies to loading or unloading of other goods when substances or articles of Class 1 or substances of Classes 4.1 or 5.2 for which marking with three blue cones or three blue lights is prescribed in column (12) of Table A of Chapter 3.2 are on board.

7.1.4.8.2   Loading and unloading operations of substances or articles of Class 1 and substances of Classes 4.1 or 5.2, for which marking with three blue cones or three blue lights is prescribed in column (12) of Table A of Chapter 3.2, shall be suspended in the event of a storm.

7.1.4.9   *Cargo transhipment operations*

Partial or complete cargo transhipment into another vessel without permission from the competent authority is prohibited outside a cargo transhipment place approved for this purpose.

Note: For transhipment to means of transport of another mode see 7.1.4.7.1.

7.1.4.10   *Precautions with respect to foodstuffs, other articles of consumption and animal feeds*

7.1.4.10.1   When special provision 802 is indicated for a dangerous good in column (6) of Table A of Chapter 3.2, precautions shall be taken as follows with respect to foodstuffs, other articles of consumption and animal feeds:

Packages as well as uncleaned empty packagings, including large packagings and intermediate bulk containers (IBCs), bearing labels conforming to models Nos. 6.1 or 6.2, and those bearing labels of Class 9, containing substances of Class 9, UN Nos. 2212, 2315, 2590, 3151, 3152 or 3245, shall not be stacked on or loaded in immediate proximity to packages known to contain foodstuffs, other articles of consumption or animal feeds in the same hold and at places of loading and unloading or trans-shipment.

When these packages, bearing the said labels, are loaded in immediate proximity of packages known to contain foodstuffs, other articles of consumption or animal feeds, they shall be kept apart from the latter:

(a)   by complete partitions which should be as high as the packages bearing the said labels; or

(b)   by packages not bearing labels conforming to models Nos. 6.1, 6.2 or 9 or packages bearing labels of Class 9 but not containing substances of that class, UN Nos. 2212, 2315, 2590, 3151, 3152 or 3245; or

(c)   by a space of at least 0.8 m;

unless the packages bearing said labels are provided with an additional packaging or are completely covered (e.g. by a sheeting, a fibreboard cover or other measures).

7.1.4.11   *Stowage plan*

7.1.4.11.1   The master shall enter on a stowage plan the dangerous goods stowed in the individual holds or on deck. The goods shall be described as in the transport document in accordance with 5.4.1.1.1 (a), (b), (c) and (d).

7.1.4.11.2   Where the dangerous goods are transported in containers, the number of the container shall suffice. In this case, the stowage plan shall contain as an annex a list of all containers with their numbers and the description of the goods contained therein in accordance with 5.4.1.1.1 (a), (b), (c) and (d).

7.1.4.12   *Ventilation*

7.1.4.12.1   During loading or unloading of road vehicles into or from the holds of ro-ro-vessels, there shall be not less than five changes of air per hour based upon the total volume of the empty hold.

7.1.4.12.2   On board vessels carrying dangerous goods only in containers placed in open holds, ventilators do not require to be incorporated but must be on board. Where damage of the container or release of content inside the container is suspected, the holds shall be ventilated so as to reduce the concentration of flammable gases and vapours given off by the cargo to less than 10% of the LEL or in the case of toxic gases and vapours to below national accepted exposure levels.

7.1.4.12.3   If tank-containers, portable tanks, MEGCs, tank vehicles or tank wagons are carried in closed holds, such holds shall be permanently ventilated for ensuring five air changes per hour.

7.1.4.13   *Measures to be taken before loading*

The holds and cargo areas shall be cleaned prior to loading. The holds shall be ventilated.

7.1.4.14   *Handling and stowage of the cargo*

7.1.4.14.1   The various components of the cargo shall be stowed such as to prevent them from shifting in relation to one another or to the vessel and such that no damage can be caused by other cargo.

7.1.4.14.1.1   Packages containing dangerous substances and unpackaged dangerous articles shall be secured by suitable means capable of restraining the goods (such as fastening straps, sliding slatboards, adjustable brackets) in a manner that will prevent any movement during carriage which would change the orientation of the packages or cause them to be damaged. When dangerous goods are carried with other goods (e.g. heavy machinery or crates), all goods shall be securely fixed or packed so as to prevent the release of dangerous goods. Movement of packages may also be prevented by filling any voids by the use of dunnage or by blocking and bracing. Where restraints such as banding or straps are used, these shall not be over-tightened to cause damage or deformation of the package. Flexible bulk containers shall be stowed in such way that there are no void spaces between them in the hold. If the flexible bulk containers do not completely fill the hold, adequate measures shall be taken to avoid shifting of cargo.

7.1.4.14.1.2   Packages shall not be stacked unless designed for that purpose. Where different design types of packages that have been designed for stacking are to be loaded together, consideration shall be given to their compatibility for stacking with each other. Where necessary, stacked packages shall be prevented from damaging the package below by the use of load-bearing devices. Flexible bulk containers may be stacked on each other in holds provided that the stacking height does not exceed three high. When flexible bulk containers are fitted with venting devices, the stowage of the flexible bulk containers shall not impede their function.

7.1.4.14.1.3   During loading and unloading, packages containing dangerous goods shall be protected from being damaged.

NOTE: Particular attention shall be paid to the handling of packages during their preparation for carriage, the type of vessel on which they are to be carried and to the method of loading or unloading, so that accidental damage is not caused through dragging or mishandling the packages.

7.1.4.14.1.4   When orientation arrows are required, packages and overpacks shall be oriented in accordance with such markings.

NOTE: Liquid dangerous goods shall be loaded below dry dangerous goods whenever practicable.

7.1.4.14.2   Dangerous goods shall be stowed at a distance of not less than 1 m from the accommodation, the engine rooms, the wheelhouse and any sources of heat.

When the accommodation or wheelhouse is situated above a hold, dangerous goods shall in no case be stowed beneath such accommodation or wheelhouse.

7.1.4.14.3   Packages shall be protected against heat, sunlight and the effects of the weather. This provision does not apply to vehicles, wagons, tank-containers, portable tanks, MEGCs and containers.

Where packages are not enclosed in vehicles, wagons or containers but loaded on deck, they shall be covered with tarpaulins that are not readily flammable.

The ventilation shall not be obstructed.

7.1.4.14.4   The dangerous goods shall be stowed in the holds. However, dangerous goods packed or loaded in:

–   closed containers;

–   MEGCs;

–   sheeted vehicles or sheeted wagons;

–   tank-containers or portable tanks;

–   tank vehicles or tank wagons;

may be carried on deck in the protected area.

7.1.4.14.5   Packages containing dangerous goods of Classes 3, 4.1, 4.2, 5.1 or 8 may be stowed on deck in the protected area provided that drums are used or that they are contained in containers with complete walls or vehicles or wagons with complete walls. Substances of Class 2 may be stowed on deck in the protected area, provided they are contained in cylinders.

7.1.4.14.6   For seagoing vessels, the stowage requirements set out in 7.1.4.14.1 to 7.1.4.14.5 above and 7.1.4.14.7 below shall be deemed to have been met, if the relevant stowage provisions of the IMDG Code and, in the case of carriage of dangerous goods in bulk, those set out in subsection 9.3 of the IMSBC Code have been complied with.

7.1.4.14.7   *Handling and stowage of radioactive material*

NOTE 1: *"Critical group" means a group of members of the public which is reasonably homogeneous with respect to its exposure for a given radiation source and given exposure pathway and is typical of individuals receiving the highest effective dose by the given exposure pathway from the given source.*

NOTE 2: *"Members of the public" means in a general sense, any individuals in the population except when subject to occupational or medical exposure.*

NOTE 3: *"Workers" are any persons who work, whether full time, part-time or temporarily, for an employer and who have recognized rights and duties in relation to occupational radiation protection.*

7.1.4.14.7.1   *Segregation*

7.1.4.14.7.1.1   Packages, overpacks, containers, tanks and vehicles and wagons containing radioactive material and unpackaged radioactive material shall be segregated during carriage:

(a)   from workers in regularly occupied working areas;

(i)   in accordance with Table A below; or

(ii)   by distances calculated using a dose criterion of 5 mSv in a year and conservative model parameters;

NOTE: *Workers subject to individual monitoring for the purposes of radiation protection shall not be considered for the purposes of segregation.*

(b)   from members of the critical group of the public, in areas where the public has regular access;

(i)   in accordance with Table A below; or

(ii)   by distances calculated using a dose criterion of 1 mSv in a year and conservative model parameters;

(c)   from undeveloped photographic film and mailbags;

    (i)   in accordance with Table B below; or

    (ii)   by distances calculated using a radiation exposure criterion for undeveloped photographic film due to the transport of radioactive material for 0.1 mSv per consignment of such film; and

NOTE: *Mailbags shall be assumed to contain undeveloped film and plates and therefore be separated from radioactive material in the same way.*

(d)   from other dangerous goods in accordance with 7.1.4.3.

Table A: Minimum distances between packages of category II-YELLOW or of category III-YELLOW and persons

Sum of transport indexes not more than	Exposure time per year (hours)			
	Areas where members of the public have regular access		Regularly occupied working areas	
	50	250	50	250
	Segregation distance in metres, no shielding material intervening, from:			
2	1	3	0.5	1
4	1.5	4	0.5	1.5
8	2.5	6	1.0	2.5
12	3	7.5	1.0	3
20	4	9.5	1.5	4
30	5	12	2	5
40	5.5	13.5	2.5	5.6
50	6.5	15.5	3	6.5

Table B: Minimum distances between packages of category II-YELLOW or of category III-YELLOW and packages bearing the word "FOTO", or mailbags

Total number of packages not more than		Sum of transport indexes not more than	Journey or storage duration, in hours							
Category			1	2	4	10	24	48	120	240
III-yellow	II-yellow		Minimum distances in metres							
		0.2	0.5	0.5	0.5	0.5	1	1	2	3
		0.5	0.5	0.5	0.5	1	1	2	3	5
	1	1	0.5	0.5	1	1	2	3	5	7
	2	2	0.5	1	1	1.5	3	4	7	9
	4	4	1	1	1.5	3	4	6	9	13
	8	8	1	1.5	2	4	6	8	13	18
1	10	10	1	2	3	4	7	9	14	20
2	20	20	1.5	3	4	6	9	13	20	30
3	30	30	2	3	5	7	11	16	25	35
4	40	40	3	4	5	8	13	18	30	40
5	50	50	3	4	6	9	14	20	32	45

7.1.4.14.7.1.2   Category II-YELLOW or III-YELLOW packages or overpacks shall not be carried in compartments occupied by passengers, except those exclusively reserved for couriers specially authorized to accompany such packages or overpacks.

7.1.4.14.7.1.3   No persons other than the master of the vessel or the driver of the vehicle embarked, persons who are on board for duty reasons and the other members of the crew shall be permitted in vessels carrying packages, overpacks or containers bearing category II-YELLOW or III-YELLOW labels.

7.1.4.14.7.2   *Activity limits*

The total activity in a single hold or compartment of a vessel, or in another conveyance, for carriage of LSA material or SCO articles in Type IP-1, Type IP-2, Type IP-3 or unpackaged, shall not exceed the limits shown in Table C below. For SCO-III, the limits in Table C below may be exceeded provided that the transport plan contains precautions which are to be employed during carriage to obtain an overall level of safety at least equivalent to that which would be provided if the limits had been applied.

**Table C: Conveyance activity limits for LSA material and SCO
in industrial packages or unpackaged**

Nature of material or articles	Activity limit for conveyances other than by vessel	Activity limit for a hold or compartment of a vessel
LSA-I	No limit	No limit
LSA-II and LSA-III non-combustible solids	No limit	$100A_2$
LSA-II and LSA-III combustible solids, and all liquids and gases	$100A_2$	$10A_2$
SCO	$100A_2$	$10A_2$

7.1.4.14.7.3   *Stowage during carriage and storage in transit*

7.1.4.14.7.3.1   Consignments shall be securely stowed.

7.1.4.14.7.3.2   Provided that its average surface heat flux does not exceed $15W/m^2$ and that the immediately surrounding cargo is not in bags, a package or overpack may be carried or stored among packaged general cargo without any special stowage provisions except as may be specifically required by the competent authority in an applicable approval certificate.

7.1.4.14.7.3.3   Loading of containers and accumulation of packages, overpacks and containers shall be controlled as follows:

(a)   Except under the conditions of exclusive use, and for consignments of LSA-I material, the total number of packages, overpacks and containers aboard a single conveyance shall be so limited that the total sum of the transport indexes aboard the conveyance does not exceed the values shown in Table D below;

(b)   The dose rate under routine conditions of carriage shall not exceed 2 mSv/h at any point on the external surface of vehicles, wagons or containers and 0.1 mSv/h at 2 m from the external surface of vehicles, wagons or containers, except for consignments carried under exclusive use for which the dose rate limits around the vehicles or wagons are set forth in 7.1.4.14.7.3.5 (b) and (c);

(c)   The total sum of the criticality safety indexes in a container and aboard a conveyance shall not exceed the values shown in Table E below.

Table D: Transport Index limits for containers and conveyances not under exclusive use

Type of container or conveyance	Limit on total sum of transport indexes in a container or aboard a conveyance
Small container	50
Large container	50
Vehicle or wagon	50
Vessel	50

Table E: Criticality Safety Index for containers and vehicles containing fissile material

Type of container or conveyance	Limit on total sum of criticality safety indexes	
	Not under exclusive use	Under exclusive use
Small container	50	n.a.
Large container	50	100
Vehicle or wagon	50	100
Vessel	50	100

7.1.4.14.7.3.4   Any package or overpack having either a transport index greater than 10, or any consignment having a criticality safety index greater than 50, shall be carried only under exclusive use.

7.1.4.14.7.3.5   For consignments under exclusive use in vehicles or wagons, the dose rate shall not exceed:

(a)   10 mSv/h at any point on the external surface of any package or overpack, and may only exceed 2 mSv/h provided that:

(i)   the vehicle or wagon is equipped with an enclosure which, during routine conditions of carriage, prevents the access of unauthorized persons to the interior of the enclosure;

(ii)   provisions are made to secure the package or overpack so that its position within the vehicle or wagon enclosure remains fixed during routine conditions of carriage; and

(iii)   there is no loading or unloading during the shipment;

(b)   2 mSv/h at any point on the outer services of the vehicle or wagon, including the upper and lower surfaces, or, in the case of an open vehicle or wagon, at any point on the vertical planes projected from the outer edges of the vehicle or wagon, on the upper surface of the load, and on the lower external surface of the vehicle or wagon; and

(c)   0.1 mSv/h at any point 2 m from the vertical planes represented by the outer lateral surfaces of the vehicle or wagon, or, if the load is carried in an open vehicle or wagon, at any point 2 m from the vertical planes projected from the outer edges of the vehicle or wagon.

7.1.4.14.7.3.6   Packages or overpacks having a surface dose rate greater than 2 mSv/h, unless being carried in or on a vehicle or wagon under exclusive use and unless they are not removed from the vehicle or wagon when on board the vessel shall not be transported by vessel except under special arrangement.

7.1.4.14.7.3.7   The transport of consignments by means of a special use vessel which, by virtue of its design, or by reason of its being chartered, is dedicated to the purpose of carrying radioactive material, shall be excepted from the requirements specified in 7.1.4.14.7.3.3 provided that the following conditions are met:

(a)   A radiation protection programme for the shipment shall be approved by the competent authority of the flag state of the vessel and, when requested, by the competent authority at each port of call of the transit countries;

(b)   Stowage arrangements shall be predetermined for the whole voyage including any consignments to be loaded at ports of call en route; and

(c)   The loading, carriage and unloading of the consignments shall be supervised by persons qualified in the transport of radioactive material.

7.1.4.14.7.4   *Segregation of packages containing fissile material during carriage and storage in transit*

7.1.4.14.7.4.1   Any group of packages, overpacks, and containers containing fissile material stored in transit in any one storage area shall be so limited that the total sum of the criticality safety indexes in the group does not exceed 50. Each group shall be stored so as to maintain a spacing of at least 6 m from other such groups.

7.1.4.14.7.4.2   Where the total sum of the criticality safety indexes on board a vehicle, a wagon or in a container exceeds 50, as permitted in Table E above, storage shall be such as to maintain a spacing of at least 6 m from other groups of packages, overpacks or containers containing fissile material or other vehicles or wagons carrying radioactive material. The space between such groups may be used for other dangerous goods of ADN. The carriage of other goods with consignments under exclusive use is permitted provided that the pertinent provisions have been taken by the consignor and that carriage is not prohibited under other requirements.

7.1.4.14.7.4.3   Fissile material meeting one of the provisions (a) to (f) of 2.2.7.2.3.5 shall meet the following requirements:

(a)   Only one of the provisions (a) to (f) of 2.2.7.2.3.5 is allowed per consignment;

(b)   Only one approved fissile material in packages classified in accordance with 2.2.7.2.3.5 (f) is allowed per consignment unless multiple materials are authorized in the certificate of approval;

(c)   Fissile material in packages classified in accordance with 2.2.7.2.3.5 (c) shall be carried in a consignment with no more than 45 g of fissile nuclides;

(d)   Fissile material in packages classified in accordance with 2.2.7.2.3.5 (d) shall be carried in a consignment with no more than 15 g of fissile nuclides;

(e)   Unpackaged or packaged fissile material classified in accordance with 2.2.7.2.3.5 (e) shall be carried under exclusive use on a vehicle with no more than 45 g of fissile nuclides.

7.1.4.14.7.5   *Damaged or leaking packages, contaminated packagings*

7.1.4.14.7.5.1   If it is evident that a package is damaged or leaking, or if it is suspected that the package may have leaked or been damaged, access to the package shall be restricted and a qualified person shall, as soon as possible, assess the extent of contamination and the resultant dose rate of the package. The scope of the assessment shall include the package, the vehicle, the wagon, the vessel, the adjacent loading and unloading areas, and, if necessary, all other material which has been carried in the vessel. When necessary, additional steps for the protection of people, property and the environment, in accordance with provisions established by the competent authority, shall be taken to overcome and minimize the consequences of such leakage or damage.

7.1.4.14.7.5.2   Packages damaged or leaking radioactive contents in excess of allowable limits for normal conditions of carriage may be removed to an acceptable interim location under supervision, but shall not be forwarded until repaired or reconditioned and decontaminated.

7.1.4.14.7.5.3   Vehicles, wagons, vessels and equipment used regularly for the carriage of radioactive material shall be periodically checked to determine the level of contamination. The frequency of such checks shall be related to the likelihood of contamination and the extent to which radioactive material is carried.

7.1.4.14.7.5.4   Except as provided in paragraph 7.1.4.14.7.5.6, any vessel, or equipment or part thereof which has become contaminated above the limits specified in 7.1.4.14.7.5.5 in the course of carriage of radioactive material, or which shows a dose rate in excess of 5 µSv/h at the surface, shall be decontaminated as soon as possible by a qualified person and shall not be re-used unless the following conditions are fulfilled:

(a)   The non-fixed contamination shall not exceed the limits specified in 4.1.9.1.2 of ADR;

(b)   The dose rate resulting from the fixed contamination shall not exceed 5 µSv/h at the surface.

7.1.4.14.7.5.5   For the purposes of 7.1.4.14.7.5.4, non-fixed contamination shall not exceed:

– $4\,Bq/cm^2$ for beta and gamma emitters and low toxicity alpha emitters;

– $0.4\,Bq/cm^2$ for all other alpha emitters.

These are average limits applicable to any area of $300\,cm^2$ on any part of the surface.

7.1.4.14.7.5.6   Vessels dedicated to the carriage of radioactive material under exclusive use shall be excepted from the requirements of the previous paragraph 7.1.4.14.7.5.4 solely with regard to its internal surfaces and only for as long as it remains under that specific exclusive use.

7.1.4.14.7.6   *Limitation of the effect of temperature*

7.1.4.14.7.6.1   If the temperature of the accessible outer surfaces of a Type B (U) or Type B (M) package could exceed 50 ºC in the shade, carriage is permitted only under exclusive use. As far as practicable, the surface temperature shall be limited to 85 ºC. Account may be taken of barriers or screens intended to give protection to transport workers without the barriers or screens being subject to any test.

7.1.4.14.7.6.2   If the average heat flux from the external surfaces of a Type B (U) or B (M) package could exceed $15\,W/m^2$, the special stowage requirements specified in the competent authority package design approval certificate shall be met.

7.1.4.14.7.7   *Other provisions*

If neither the consignor nor the consignee can be identified or if the consignment cannot be delivered to the consignee and the carrier has no instructions from the consignor the consignment shall be placed in a safe location and the competent authority shall be informed as soon as possible and a request made for instructions on further action.

7.1.4.15   *Measures to be taken after unloading*

7.1.4.15.1   After unloading the holds shall be inspected and cleaned if necessary. In the case of carriage in bulk, this requirement does not apply if the new cargo comprises the same goods as the previous cargo.

7.1.4.15.2   For material of Class 7 see also 7.1.4.14.7.5.

7.1.4.15.3   A cargo transport unit or hold space which has been used to carry infectious substances shall be inspected for release of the substance before re-use. If the infectious substances were released during carriage, the cargo transport unit or hold space shall be decontaminated before it is re-used. Decontamination may be achieved by any means which effectively inactivates the released infectious substance.

7.1.4.16   *Measures to be taken during loading, carriage, unloading and handling of the cargo*

The filling or emptying of receptacles, tank vehicles, tank wagons, intermediate bulk containers (IBCs), large packagings, MEGCs, portable tanks or tank-containers on board the vessel is prohibited without special permission from the competent authority.

7.1.4.17 to 7.1.4.40   *(Reserved)*

7.1.4.41   *Fire and naked light*

The use of fire or naked light is prohibited while substances or articles of Divisions 1.1, 1.2, 1.3, 1.5 or 1.6 of Class 1 are on board and the holds are open or the goods to be loaded are located at a distance of less than 50 m from the vessel.

7.1.4.42 to 7.1.4.50   *(Reserved)*

7.1.4.51   *Electrical equipment*

The use of radiotelephone or radar transmitters is not permitted while substances or articles of Divisions 1.1, 1.2, 1.3, 1.5 or 1.6 of Class 1 are being loaded or unloaded.

This shall not apply to VHF-transmitters of the vessel, in cranes or in the vicinity of the vessel, provided the power of the VHF-transmitter does not exceed 25 W and no part of its aerial is located at a distance less than 2.00 m from the substances or articles mentioned above.

7.1.4.52   *(Reserved)*

7.1.4.53   *Lighting*

If loading or unloading is performed at night or in conditions of poor visibility, effective lighting shall be provided.

If provided from the deck, it shall be effected by properly secured electric lamps which shall be positioned in such a way that they cannot be damaged.

Where these lamps are positioned on deck in zone 2, they must conform to the requirements for use in zone 2.

7.1.4.54 to 7.1.4.74   *(Reserved)*

7.1.4.75   *Risk of sparking*

All electrically continuous connections between the vessel and the shore shall be so designed that they do not present a source of ignition. If substances are carried that have in column (9) of Table A of Chapter 3.2 an entry "EX", then taking off clothes not sufficiently dissipative shall be prohibited in the protected area.

7.1.4.76   *Synthetic ropes*

During loading or unloading operations, the vessel may be moored by means of synthetic ropes only when steel cables are used to prevent the vessel from going adrift.

Steel cables sheathed in synthetic material or natural fibres are considered as equivalent when the minimum tensile strength required in accordance with the Regulations referred to in 1.1.4.6 is obtained from the steel strands.

However, during loading or unloading of containers, vessels may be moored by means of synthetic ropes.

7.1.4.77   *Possible means of evacuation in case of an emergency*

		Dry cargo bulk (vessel and barge)		Container (vessel and barge) and packaged goods
		Class		**Class**
		4.1, 4.2, 4.3	**5.1, 6.1, 7, 8, 9**	**All classes**
1	Two escape routes inside or outside the protected area in opposite directions	•	•	•
2	One escape route outside the protected area and one safe haven outside the vessel including the escape route towards it at the opposite end	•	•	•
3	One escape route outside the protected area and one safe haven on the vessel at the opposite end	•	•	•
4	One escape route outside the protected area and one life boat at the opposite end	•	•	•
5	One escape route outside the protected cargo area and one escape boat at the opposite end	•	•	•
6	One escape route inside the protected area and one escape route outside the cargo area at the opposite end	•	•	•
7	One escape route inside the protected area and one safe haven outside the vessel in the opposite direction	•	•	•
8	One escape route inside the protected area and one safe haven on the vessel in the opposite direction	•	•	•
9	One escape route inside the protected cargo area and one life boat at the opposite end	•	•	•
10	One escape route inside the protected area and one escape boat at the opposite end	•	•	•
11	One escape route inside or outside the protected cargo area and two safe havens on the vessel at opposite ends	•	•	•
12	One escape route inside or outside the protected area and two safe areas on the vessel at opposite ends	•	•	•
13	One escape route outside the protected area	•	•	•
14	One escape route inside the protected area	•	•	•
15	One or more safe havens outside the vessel, including the escape route towards it	•	•	•
16	One or more safe havens on the vessel		•	•
17	One or more escape boats	•	•	•
18	One escape boat and one evacuation boat	•	•	•
19	One or more evacuation boats		•	•

• = *Possible option.*

Based on local circumstances, competent authorities may prescribe additional requirements for the availability of means of evacuation.

7.1.4.78 to 7.1.4.99   *(Reserved)*

7.1.5   **Additional requirements concerning the operation of vessels**

7.1.5.0   *Marking*

7.1.5.0.1   Vessels carrying dangerous goods listed in Table A of Chapter 3.2 shall, in accordance with Chapter 3 of the European Code for Inland Waterways (CEVNI), display the markings prescribed in column (12) in this table.

7.1.5.0.2   Vessels carrying the dangerous goods listed in Table A of Chapter 3.2 in packages placed exclusively in containers shall display the number of blue cones or blue lights indicated in column (12) of Table A of Chapter 3.2 where:

–   three blue cones or three blue lights are required; or

–   two blue cones or two blue lights are required, a substance of Class 2 is involved or packing group I is indicated in column (4) of Table A of Chapter 3.2 and the total gross mass of these dangerous goods exceeds 30 000 kg; or

–   one blue cone or one blue light is required, a substance of Class 2 is involved or packing group I is indicated in column (4) of Table A of Chapter 3.2 and the total gross mass of these dangerous goods exceeds 130 000 kg.

7.1.5.0.3   Vessels carrying empty, uncleaned tanks, battery vehicles, battery wagons or MEGCs shall display the marking referred to in column (12) of Table A of Chapter 3.2 if these cargo transport units have contained dangerous goods for which this table prescribes marking.

7.1.5.0.4   Where more than one marking could apply to a vessel, only the marking which includes the greatest number of blue cones or blue lights shall apply, i.e. in the following order of precedence:

–   three blue cones or three blue lights; or

–   two blue cones or two blue lights; or

–   one blue cone or one blue light.

7.1.5.0.5   By derogation from paragraph 7.1.5.0.1, and in accordance with the footnotes to article 3.14 of the European Code for Inland Waterways (CEVNI), the competent authority of a Contracting Party may authorize seagoing vessels temporarily operating in an inland navigation area on the territory of this Contracting Party, the use of the day and night signals prescribed in the Recommendations on the Safe Transport of Dangerous Cargoes and Related Activities in Port Areas adopted by the Maritime Safety Committee of the International Maritime Organization (by night an all-round fixed red light and by day flag "B" of the International Code of Signals), instead of the signals prescribed in 7.1.5.0.1. Contracting Parties which have taken the initiative with respect to the derogation granted shall notify the Executive Secretary of the UNECE, who shall bring this derogation to the attention of the Administrative Committee.

7.1.5.1   *Mode of navigation*

7.1.5.1.1   The competent authorities may impose restrictions on the inclusion of vessels carrying dangerous goods in pushed conveys of large dimension.

7.1.5.1.2 When vessels carry substances or articles of Class 1, or substances of Classes 4.1 or 5.2 for which marking with three blue cones or three blue lights is prescribed in column (12) of Table A of Chapter 3.2, or material of Class 7 of UN Nos. 2912, 2913, 2915, 2916, 2917, 2919, 2977, 2978 or 3321 to 3333, the competent authority may impose restrictions on the dimensions of convoys or side-by-side formations. Nevertheless, the use of a motorized vessel giving temporary towing assistance is permitted.

7.1.5.2 *Vessels under way*

Vessels carrying substances or articles of Class 1, or substances of Classes 4.1 or 5.2 for which marking with three blue cones or three blue lights is prescribed in column (12) of Table A of Chapter 3.2, when under way shall keep not less than 50 m away from any other vessel, if possible.

7.1.5.3 *Mooring*

Vessels shall be moored securely, but in such a way that they can be released quickly in an emergency and that the electric cables are not compressed, folded or subject to tensile strain.

7.1.5.4 *Berthing*

7.1.5.4.1 The distances to be kept by vessels carrying dangerous goods at berth from other vessels shall not be less than the distance prescribed by the Regulations referred to in 1.1.4.6.

7.1.5.4.2 An expert in accordance with 8.2.1.2 shall be permanently on board berthed vessels for which marking is prescribed in column (12) of Table A of Chapter 3.2.

The competent authority may, however, exempt from this obligation those vessels which are berthed in a harbour basin or in an accepted berthing position.

7.1.5.4.3 Outside the berthing areas specifically designated by the competent authority, the distances to be kept by berthed vessels shall not be less than:

– 100 m from residential areas, civil engineering structures or storage tanks, if the vessel is required to be marked with one blue cone or one blue light in accordance with the requirements of column (12) of Table A of Chapter 3.2;

– 100 m from civil engineering structures and storage tanks and 300 m from residential areas if the vessel is required to be marked with two blue cones or two blue lights in accordance with the requirements of column (12) of Table A of Chapter 3.2;

– 500 m from residential areas, civil engineering structures and storage tanks holding gas or flammable liquids if the vessel is required to be marked with three blue cones or three blue lights in accordance with the requirements of column (12) of Table A of Chapter 3.2.

While waiting in front of locks or bridges, vessels are allowed to keep distances different from and lower than those given above. In no case shall the distance be less than 100 m.

7.1.5.4.4 The competent authority may prescribe distances lower than those given in 7.1.5.4.3 above, especially taking local conditions into account.

7.1.5.5   *Stopping of vessels*

If navigation of a vessel carrying substances and articles of Class 1 or substances of Class 4.1 or 5.2 for which marking with three blue cones or three blue lights is prescribed in column (12) of Table A of Chapter 3.2 threatens to become dangerous owing either to:

–   external factors (bad weather, unfavourable conditions of the waterway, etc.); or

–   the condition of the vessel itself (accident or incident);

the vessel shall be stopped at a suitable berthing area as far away as possible from residential areas, harbours, civil engineering structures or storage tanks for gas or flammable liquids, regardless of the provisions set out in 7.1.5.4.

The competent authority shall be notified without delay.

7.1.5.6 and 7.1.5.7   *(Reserved)*

7.1.5.8   *Reporting duty*

7.1.5.8.1   In the States where the reporting duty is in force, the master of the vessel shall provide information in accordance with paragraph 1.1.4.6.1.

7.1.5.8.2 to 7.1.5.8.4   *(Deleted)*

7.1.5.9 to 7.1.5.99   *(Reserved)*

7.1.6   **Additional requirements**

7.1.6.1 to 7.1.6.10   *(Reserved)*

7.1.6.11   *Carriage in bulk*

The following additional requirements shall be met when they are indicated in column (11) of Table A of Chapter 3.2:

CO01:   The surfaces of holds shall be coated or lined such that they are not readily flammable and not liable to impregnation by the cargo.

CO02:   Any part of the holds and of the hatchway covers which may come into contact with this substance shall consist of metal or of wood having a specific density of not less than 750 kg/m^3 (seasoned wood).

CO03:   The inner surfaces of holds shall be lined or coated so as to prevent corrosion.

ST01:   The substances shall have been stabilized in accordance with the requirements applicable to ammonium nitrate fertilizers set out in the IMSBC Code. Stabilizing shall be certified by the consignor in the transport document.

          In those States where this is required, these substances may be carried in bulk only with the approval of the competent authority.

ST02:   These substances may be carried in bulk if the results of the trough test according to subsection 38.2 of the *Manual of Tests and Criteria* show that the self-sustaining decomposition rate is not greater than 25 cm/h.

RA01: The materials may be carried in bulk provided that:

   (a)   for materials other than natural ores, carriage is under exclusive use and there is no escape of contents out of the vessel and no loss of shielding under normal conditions of transport; or

   (b)   for natural ores, carriage is under exclusive use.

RA02: The materials may be carried in bulk provided that:

   (a)   they are carried in a vessel so that, under normal conditions of transport, there is no escape of contents or loss of shielding;

   (b)   they are carried under exclusive use if the contamination on the accessible and inaccessible surfaces is greater than 4 Bq/cm^2 (10^{-4} µCi/cm^2) for beta and gamma emitters and low toxicity alpha emitters or 0.4 Bq/cm^2 (10^{-5} µCi/cm^2) for all other alpha emitters;

   (c)   measures are taken to ensure that radioactive material is not released into the vessel, if it is suspected that non-fixed contamination exists on inaccessible surfaces of more than 4 Bq/cm^2 (10^{-4} µCi/cm^2) for beta and gamma emitters and low toxicity alpha emitters or 0.4 Bq/cm^2 (10^{-5} µCi/cm^2) for all other alpha emitters.

Surface contaminated objects group (SCO-II) shall not be carried in bulk.

RA03: *Merged with RA02.*

7.1.6.12   *Ventilation*

The following additional requirements shall be met when they are indicated in column (10) of Table A of Chapter 3.2:

VE01: Holds containing these substances shall be ventilated with the ventilators operating at full power, where after measurement it has been established that the concentration of flammable gases and vapours given off by the cargo exceeds 10% of the LEL. The measurement shall be carried out immediately after loading. A control measurement shall be repeated after one hour. The results of the measurement shall be recorded in writing.

VE02: Holds containing these substances shall be ventilated with the ventilators operating at full power, where after measurement it has been established that the holds are not free from toxic gases and vapours given off by the cargo. The measurement shall be carried out immediately after loading. A control measurement shall be repeated after one hour. The results of the measurement shall be recorded in writing. Alternatively, on vessels only containing these substances in containers in open holds, the holds containing such containers may be ventilated with the ventilation operating at full power only when it is suspected that the holds are not free of toxic gases and vapours given off by the cargo. Prior to unloading, the unloader shall be informed about this suspicion.

VE03: Spaces such as holds, accommodation and engine rooms, adjacent to holds containing these substances shall be ventilated.

After unloading, holds having contained these substances shall undergo forced ventilation.

After ventilation, the concentration of flammable or toxic gases and vapours given off by the cargo in these holds shall be measured.

The results of the measurement shall be recorded in writing.

VE04 When aerosols are carried for the purposes of reprocessing or disposal under special provision 327 of Chapter 3.3, provisions of VE01 and VE02 are applied.

7.1.6.13 *Measures to be taken before loading*

The following additional requirements shall be met when they are indicated in column (11) of Table A of Chapter 3.2:

LO01: Before these substances or articles are loaded, it shall be ensured that there are no metal objects in the hold which are not an integral part of the vessel.

LO02: These substances may be loaded in bulk only if their temperature is not above 55 °C.

LO03: Before loading these substances in bulk or unpackaged, holds should be made as dry as possible.

LO04: Any loose organic material shall be removed from holds before loading these substances in bulk.

LO05: Prior to carriage of pressure receptacles it shall be ensured that the pressure has not risen due to potential hydrogen generation.

7.1.6.14 *Handling and stowage of cargo*

The following additional requirements shall be met when they are indicated in column (11) of Table A of Chapter 3.2:

HA01: These substances or articles shall be stowed at a distance of not less than 3.00 m from the accommodation, engine rooms, the wheelhouse and from any sources of heat.

HA02: These substances or articles shall be stowed at a distance of not less than 2.00 m from the vertical planes defined by the sides of the vessel.

HA03: Any friction, impact, jolting, overturning or dropping shall be prevented during handling of these substances or articles.

All packages loaded in the same hold shall be stowed and wedged as to prevent any jolting or friction during carriage.

Stacking of non-dangerous goods on top of packages containing these substances or articles is prohibited.

Where these substances or articles are loaded together with other goods in the same hold, these substances or articles shall be loaded after, and unloaded before, all the other goods.

There is no need for these substances or articles to be loaded after, and unloaded before, all others if these substances or articles are contained in containers.

While these substances or articles are being loaded or unloaded, no loading or unloading operations shall take place in the other holds and no filling or emptying of fuel tanks shall be allowed. The competent authority may, however, permit exceptions to this provision.

HA04: *Merged with HA03.*

HA05: *Merged with HA03.*

HA06: *Merged with HA03.*

HA07: It is prohibited to load or unload these substances in bulk or unpackaged if there is a danger that they may get wet because of the prevailing weather conditions.

HA08: If the packages with these substances are not contained in a container, they shall be placed on gratings and covered with waterproof tarpaulins arranged in such a way that the water drains off to the outside and the air circulation is not hindered.

HA09: If these substances are carried in bulk they shall not be loaded in the same hold together with flammable substances.

HA10: These substances shall be stowed on deck in the protected area. For seagoing vessels, the stowage requirements are deemed to be met if the provisions of the IMDG Code are complied with.

7.1.6.15   *(Reserved)*

7.1.6.16   *Measures to be taken during loading, carriage, unloading and handling of cargo*

The following additional requirements shall be met when they are indicated in column (11) of Table A of Chapter 3.2:

IN01: After loading and unloading of these substances in bulk or unpackaged and before leaving the cargo transfer site, the concentration of flammable gases and vapours given off by the cargo in the accommodation, engine rooms and adjacent holds shall be measured by the loader or unloader or by an expert according to 8.2.1.2 using a gas detector. The results of the measurement shall be recorded in writing.

Before any person enters a hold and prior to unloading, the concentration of flammable gases and vapours given off by the cargo shall be measured by the unloader of the cargo or by an expert according to 8.2.1.2. The results of the measurement shall be recorded in writing.

The hold shall not be entered or unloading started until the concentration of flammable gases and vapours given off by the cargo in the airspace above the cargo is below 50% of the LEL.

If the concentrations of flammable gases and vapours given off by the cargo is not below 50% of the LEL safety measures shall be taken immediately by the loader, the unloader or the responsible master.

IN02: If a hold contains these substances in bulk or unpackaged, the concentration of toxic gases and vapours given off by the cargo shall be measured in all other spaces of the vessel which are used by the crew at least once every eight hours with a toximetcr. The results of the measurements shall be recorded in writing.

IN03:   If a hold contains these substances in bulk or unpackaged, the master shall make sure every day by checking the hold bilge wells or pump ducts that no water has entered the hold bilges.

Water which has entered the hold bilges shall be removed immediately.

7.1.6.17 to 7.1.6.99   *(Reserved)*

7.1.7   Special provisions applicable to the carriage of self-reactive substances of Class 4.1, organic peroxides of Class 5.2 and substances stabilized by temperature control (other than self-reactive substances and organic peroxides)

7.1.7.1   All self-reactive substances, organic peroxides and polymerizing substances shall be protected from direct sunlight and all sources of heat, and placed in adequately ventilated areas.

7.1.7.2   Where a number of packages are assembled in a container or closed vehicle, the total quantity of substance, the type and number of packages and the stacking arrangement shall not create an explosion hazard.

7.1.7.3   *Temperature control provisions*

7.1.7.3.1   These provisions apply to certain self-reactive substances when required by 2.2.41.1.17, and certain organic peroxides when required by 2.2.52.1.15 and certain polymerizing substances when required by 2.2.41.1.21 or special provision 386 of Chapter 3.3 which may only be carried under conditions where the temperature is controlled.

7.1.7.3.2   These provisions also apply to the carriage of substances for which:

(a)   The proper shipping name as indicated in column (2) of Table A of Chapter 3.2 or according to 3.1.2.6 contains the word "STABILIZED"; and

(b)   The SADT or SAPT determined for the substance (with or without chemical stabilization) as offered for carriage is:

(i)   50 °C or less for single packagings and IBCs; or

(ii)   45 °C or less for tanks.

When chemical inhibition is not used to stabilize a reactive substance which may generate dangerous amounts of heat and gas, or vapour, under normal carriage conditions, this substance needs to be carried under temperature control. These provisions do not apply to substances which are stabilized by the addition of chemical inhibitors such that the SADT or the SAPT is greater than that prescribed in (b) (i) or (ii), above.

7.1.7.3.3   In addition, if a self-reactive substance or organic peroxide or a substance the proper shipping name of which contains the word "STABILIZED" and which is not normally required to be carried under temperature control is carried under conditions where the temperature may exceed 55 °C, it may require temperature control.

7.1.7.3.4   The "control temperature" is the maximum temperature at which the substance can be safely carried. It is assumed that during carriage the temperature of the immediate surroundings of the package does not exceed 55 °C and attains this value for a relatively short time only during each period of 24 hours. In the event of loss of temperature control, it may be necessary to implement emergency procedures. The "emergency temperature" is the temperature at which such procedures shall be implemented.

7.1.7.3.5   *Derivation of control and emergency temperatures*

Type of receptacle	SADT[a] /SAPT[a]	Control temperature	Emergency temperature
Single packagings and IBCs	20 °C or less	20 °C below SADT/SAPT	10 °C below SADT/SAPT
	over 20 °C to 35 °C	15 °C below SADT/SAPT	10 °C below SADT/SAPT
	over 35 °C	10 °C below SADT/SAPT	5 °C below SADT/SAPT
Tanks	≤ 45 °C	10 °C below SADT/SAPT	5 °C below SADT/SAPT

[a]   i.e. the SADT/SAPT of the substance as packed for carriage.

7.1.7.3.6   The control and emergency temperatures are derived using the table in 7.1.7.3.5 from the SADT or from the SAPT which are defined as the lowest temperatures at which self-accelerating decomposition or self-accelerating polymerization may occur with a substance in the packaging, IBC or tank as used in carriage. An SADT or SAPT shall be determined in order to decide if a substance shall be subjected to temperature control during carriage. Provisions for the determination of the SADT and SAPT are given in Part II, section 28 of the Manual of Tests and Criteria.

7.1.7.3.7   Control and emergency temperatures, where appropriate, are provided for currently assigned self-reactive substances in 2.2.41.4 and for currently assigned organic peroxide formulations in 2.2.52.4.

7.1.7.3.8   The actual carriage temperature may be lower than the control temperature but shall be selected so as to avoid dangerous separation of phases.

7.1.7.4   *Carriage under temperature control*

7.1.7.4.1   Maintenance of the prescribed temperature is an essential feature of the safe carriage of substances stabilized by temperature control. In general, there shall be:

(a)   Thorough inspection of the cargo transport unit prior to loading;

(b)   Instructions to the carrier about the operation of the refrigeration system including a list of the suppliers of coolant available en route;

(c)   Procedures to be followed in the event of loss of control;

(d)   Regular monitoring of operating temperatures; and

(e)   Provision of a back-up refrigeration system or spare parts.

7.1.7.4.2   Any control and temperature sensing devices in the refrigeration system shall be readily accessible and all electrical connections weather-proof. The temperature of air space within the cargo transport unit shall be measured by two independent sensors and the output shall be recorded so that temperature changes are readily detectable. The temperature shall be checked every four to six hours and logged. When substances having a control temperature of less than +25 °C are carried, the cargo transport unit shall be equipped with visible and audible alarms, powered independently of the refrigeration system, set to operate at or below the control temperature.

7.1.7.4.3   If during carriage the control temperature is exceeded, an alert procedure shall be initiated involving any necessary repairs to the refrigeration equipment or an increase in the cooling capacity (e.g. by adding liquid or solid refrigerants). The temperature shall also be checked frequently and preparations made for implementation of the emergency procedures. If the emergency temperature is reached, the emergency procedures shall be initiated.

7.1.7.4.4   The suitability of a particular means of temperature control for carriage depends on a number of factors. Factors to be considered include:

(a)   The control temperature(s) of the substance(s) to be carried;

(b)   The difference between the control temperature and the anticipated ambient temperature conditions;

(c)   The effectiveness of the thermal insulation;

(d)   The duration of carriage; and

(e)   Allowance of a safety margin for delays.

7.1.7.4.5   Suitable methods for preventing the control temperature being exceeded are, in order of increasing control capability:

(a)   Thermal insulation provided that the initial temperature of the substance(s) to be carried is sufficiently below the control temperature;

(b)   Thermal insulation with coolant system provided that:

(i)   An adequate quantity of non-flammable coolant (e.g. liquid nitrogen or solid carbon dioxide), allowing a reasonable margin for delay, is carried or a means of replenishment is assured;

(ii)   Liquid oxygen or air is not used as coolant;

(iii)   There is a uniform cooling effect even when most of the coolant has been consumed; and

(iv)   The need to ventilate the transport unit before entering is clearly indicated by a warning on the door(s) of the transport unit;

(c)   Thermal insulation and single mechanical refrigeration provided that for substance(s) to be carried with a flash point lower than the sum of the emergency temperature plus 5 °C explosion-proof electrical fittings, EEx IIB T3 are used within the cooling compartment to prevent ignition of flammable vapours from the substances;

(d)   Thermal insulation and combined mechanical refrigeration system with coolant system; provided that:

(i)   The two systems are independent of one another;

(ii)   The provisions in (b) and (c) are complied with;

(e)   Thermal insulation and dual mechanical refrigeration system; provided that:

(i)   Apart from the integral power supply unit, the two systems are independent of one another;

(ii)   Each system alone is capable of maintaining adequate temperature control; and

(iii)   For substance(s) to be carried with a flash point lower than the sum of the emergency temperature plus 5 °C explosion-proof electrical fittings, EEx IIB T3 are used within the cooling compartment to prevent ignition of flammable vapours from the substances.

7.1.7.4.6   The methods described in 7.1.7.4.5 (d) and (e) may be used for all organic peroxides and self-reactive substances and polymerizing substances.

The method described in 7.1.7.4.5 (c) may be used for organic peroxides and self-reactive substances of Types C, D, E and F and, when the maximum ambient temperature to be expected during carriage does not exceed the control temperature by more than 10 °C, for organic peroxides and self-reactive substances of Type B and polymerizing substances.

The method described in 7.1.7.4.5 (b) may be used for organic peroxides and self-reactive substances of Types C, D, E and F and polymerizing substances when the maximum ambient temperature to be expected during carriage does not exceed the control temperature by more than 30 °C.

The method described in 7.1.7.4.5 (a) may be used for organic peroxides and self-reactive substances of Types C, D, E and F and polymerizing substances when the maximum ambient temperature to be expected during carriage is at least 10 °C below the control temperature.

7.1.7.4.7   Where substances are required to be carried in insulated, refrigerated or mechanically-refrigerated vehicles or containers, these vehicles or containers shall satisfy the requirements of Chapter 9.6 of ADR.

7.1.7.4.8   If substances are contained in protective packagings filled with a coolant, they shall be loaded in closed or sheeted vehicles or closed or sheeted containers. If the vehicles or containers used are closed they shall be adequately ventilated. Sheeted vehicles and containers shall be fitted with sideboards and a tailboard. The sheets of these vehicles and containers shall be of an impermeable and non-combustible material.

7.1.7.5 to 7.1.9.99   *(Reserved)*

CHAPTER 7.2

TANK VESSELS

7.2.0   **General requirements**

7.2.0.1   The provisions of 7.2.0 to 7.2.5 are applicable to tank vessels.

7.2.0.2 to 7.2.0.99 *(Reserved)*

7.2.1   **Mode of carriage of goods**

7.2.1.1 to 7.2.1.20   *(Reserved)*

7.2.1.21   *Carriage in cargo tanks*

7.2.1.21.1   Substances, their assignment to the various types of tank vessels and the special conditions for their carriage in these tank vessels, are listed in Table C of Chapter 3.2.

7.2.1.21.2   Substances, which according to column (6) of Table C of Chapter 3.2, have to be carried in a tank vessel of type N, open, may also be carried in a tank vessel of type N, open, with flame-arresters; type N, closed; types C or G provided that all conditions of carriage prescribed for tank vessels of type N, open, as well as all other conditions of carriage required for these substances in Table C of Chapter 3.2 are met.

7.2.1.21.3   Substances which, according to column (6) of Table C of Chapter 3.2 have to be carried in a tank vessel of type N, open, with flame-arresters, may also be carried in tank vessels of type N, closed, and types C or G provided that all conditions of carriage prescribed for tank vessels of type N, open, with flame arresters, as well as all other conditions of carriage required for these substances in Table C of Chapter 3.2 are met.

7.2.1.21.4   Substances which, according to column (6) of Table C of Chapter 3.2 have to be carried in a tank vessel of type N, closed, may also be carried in tank vessels of type C or G provided that all conditions of carriage prescribed for tank vessels of type N, closed, as well as all other conditions of carriage required for these substances in Table C of Chapter 3.2 are met.

7.2.1.21.5   Substances which, according to column (6) of Table C of Chapter 3.2 have to be carried in tank vessels of type C may also be carried in tank vessels of type G provided that all conditions of carriage prescribed for tank vessels of type C as well as all other conditions of carriage required for these substances in Table C of Chapter 3.2 are met.

7.2.1.21.6   Oily and greasy wastes resulting from the operation of the vessel may only be carried in fire-resistant receptacles, fitted with a lid, or in cargo tanks.

7.2.1.21.7   A substance which according to column (8) of Table C of Chapter 3.2 must be carried in cargo tank type 2 (integral cargo tank), may also be carried in a cargo tank type 1 (independent cargo tank) or cargo tank type 3 (cargo tank with walls distinct from the outer hull) of the vessel type prescribed in Table C or a vessel type prescribed in 7.2.1.21.2 to 7.2.1.21.5, provided that all other conditions of carriage required for this substance by Table C of Chapter 3.2 are met.

7.2.1.21.8   A substance which according to column (8) of Table C of Chapter 3.2 must be carried in cargo tank type 3 (cargo tank with walls distinct from the outer hull), may also be carried in a cargo tank type 1 (independent cargo tank) of the vessel type prescribed in Table C or a vessel type prescribed in 7.2.1.21.2 to 7.2.1.21.5 or in a type C vessel with cargo tank type 2 (integral cargo tank), provided that at least the conditions of carriage concerning the prescribed N type are met and all other conditions of carriage required for this substance by Table C of Chapter 3.2 or 7.2.1.21.2 to 7.2.1.21.5 are met.

7.2.1.22 to 7.2.1.99   (Reserved)

7.2.2   **Requirements applicable to vessels**

7.2.2.0   *Permitted vessels*

NOTE 1: The relief pressure of the safety valves shall be indicated in the certificate of approval (see 8.6.1.3).

NOTE 2: The design pressure and the test pressure of cargo tanks shall be indicated in the certificate of the recognised classification society prescribed in 9.3.1.8.1 or 9.3.2.8.1 or 9.3.3.8.1.

NOTE 3: Where a vessel carries cargo tanks with different valve-relief pressures, the relief pressure of each tank shall be indicated in the certificate of approval and the design and test pressures of each tank shall be indicated in the certificate of the recognised classification society.

7.2.2.0.1   Dangerous substances may be carried in tank vessels of Types G, C or N in accordance with the requirements of sections 9.3.1, 9.3.2 or 9.3.3 respectively. The type of tank vessel to be used is specified in column (6) of Table C of Chapter 3.2 and in 7.2.1.21.

NOTE: The substances accepted for carriage in the individual vessel are listed in the vessel substance list to be drawn up by the recognised classification society (see 1.16.1.2.5).

7.2.2.1 to 7.2.2.4   (Reserved)

7.2.2.5   *Instructions for the use of devices and installations*

Where specific safety rules have to be complied with when using any device or installation, instructions for the use of the particular device or installation shall be readily available for consultation at appropriate places on board in the language normally spoken on board, and also, if that language is not English, French or German, in English, French or German unless agreements concluded between the countries concerned in the transport operation provide otherwise.

7.2.2.6   *Gas detection system*

When the list of substances on the vessel according to 1.16.1.2.5 contains substances for which n-Hexane is not representative, the gas detection system shall also be calibrated in addition according to the most critical LEL of the substances accepted for carriage on the vessel.

7.2.2.7 to 7.2.2.18   (Reserved)

7.2.2.19   *Pushed convoys and side-by-side formations*

7.2.2.19.1   Where at least one vessel of a convoy or side-by-side formation is required to be in possession of a certificate of approval for the carriage of dangerous goods, all vessels of such convoy or side-by-side formation shall be provided with an appropriate certificate of approval.

Vessels not carrying dangerous goods shall comply with the provisions of 7.1.2.19.

7.2.2.19.2   For the purposes of the application of this Chapter, the entire pushed convoy or side-by-side formation shall be deemed to be a single vessel.

7.2.2.19.3   When a pushed convoy or a side-by-side formation comprises a tank vessel carrying dangerous substances, vessels used for propulsion shall meet the requirements of the following paragraphs:

1.16.1.1, 1.16.1.2, 1.16.1.3, 1.16.1.4, 7.2.2.5, 8.1.4, 8.1.5, 8.1.6.1, 8.1.6.3, 8.1.7, 8.3.5, 9.3.3.0.1, 9.3.3.0.3.1, 9.3.3.0.5, 9.3.3.10.1, 9.3.3.10.4, 9.3.3.12.4, 9.3.3.12.6, 9.3.3.16.1, 9.3.3.16.2, 9.3.3.17.1 to 9.3.3.17.4, 9.3.3.31.1 to 9.3.3.31.5, 9.3.3.32.2, 9.3.3.34.1, 9.3.3.34.2, 9.3.3.40.1, (however, one single fire or ballast pump shall be sufficient), 9.3.3.40.2, 9.3.3.41, 9.3.3.51, 9.3.3.52.1 to 9.3.3.52.8, 9.3.3.71 and 9.3.3.74.

Vessels used only to move tank vessels where the list of substances on the vessel according to 1.16.1.2.5 contains only substances for which explosion protection is not required do not have to meet the requirements of 9.3.3.10.1, 9.3.3.10.4, 9.3.3.12.6, 9.3.3.51 and 9.3.3.52.1. In this case the following entry shall be made in the certificate of approval or provisional certificate of approval under number 5, permitted derogations: 'Derogation from 9.3.3.10.1, 9.3.3.10.4, 9.3.3.12.6, 9.3.3.51 and 9.3.3.52.1; the vessel may only move tank vessels where the list of substances on the vessel according to 1.16.1.2.5 contains only substances for which explosion protection is not required'.

7.2.2.19.4   During loading and unloading of substances for which explosion protection is required in column (17) of Table C of Chapter 3.2, only installations and equipment that meet the requirements of 9.3.3.53 may be used on the deck of other vessels of the convoy. This condition shall not apply to:

(a)   Installations and equipment of vessels linked fore or aft of the vessel which is being loaded or unloaded, if the tank vessel being loaded or unloaded is equipped with a protective wall at the respective end of the cargo area or located at a distance of at least 12.00 m from the boundary plane of the cargo area of the vessel being loaded or unloaded.

(b)   Installations and equipment of tank vessels coupled side-by-side with the vessel being loaded or unloaded, if such installations or equipment are positioned behind a protective wall according to 9.3.3.10.3 and the protective wall is not next to the cargo area of the vessel being loaded or unloaded, or located at a distance of at least 12.00 m from the boundary plane of the cargo area of the vessel being loaded or unloaded.

7.2.2.20   *(Reserved)*

7.2.2.21   *Safety and control equipment*

It shall be possible to interrupt loading or unloading of substances of Class 2 and substances assigned to UN Nos. 1280 and 2983 of Class 3 by means of switches installed at two locations on the vessel (fore and aft) and at two locations ashore (directly at the access to the vessel and at an appropriate distance on shore). Interruption of loading and unloading shall be effected by the means of a quick closing valve which shall be directly fitted to the flexible connecting hose between the vessel and the shore facility.

The system of disconnection shall be designed in accordance with the closed circuit principle.

7.2.2.22   *(Deleted)*

7.2.2.23 to 7.2.2.99   *(Reserved)*

7.2.3   **General service requirements**

7.2.3.1   *Access to cargo tanks, residual cargo tanks, cargo pump-rooms below deck, cofferdams, double-hull spaces, double bottoms and hold spaces; inspections*

7.2.3.1.1   The cofferdams shall be empty. They shall be inspected once a day in order to ascertain that they are dry (except for condensation water).

7.2.3.1.2   Access to the cargo tanks, residual cargo tanks, cofferdams, double-hull spaces, double bottoms and hold spaces is not permitted except for carrying out inspections or cleaning operations.

7.2.3.1.3   Access to the double-hull spaces and the double bottoms is not permitted while the vessel is under way.

7.2.3.1.4   When the concentration of flammable or toxic gases and vapours given off by the cargo or the oxygen content has to be measured before entry into cargo tanks, residual cargo tanks, cargo pump-rooms below deck, cofferdams, double-hull spaces, double bottoms or hold spaces, the results of these measurements shall be recorded in writing.

The measurement may only be effected by an expert referred to in 8.2.1.2 equipped with breathing apparatus suited to the substance carried.

Entry into these spaces is not permitted for the purpose of measuring.

7.2.3.1.5   Before any person enters cargo tanks, the residual cargo tanks, the cargo pump-rooms below deck, cofferdams, double-hull spaces, double bottoms, hold spaces or other confined spaces:

(a)   When dangerous substances of Classes 2, 3, 4.1, 6.1, 8 or 9 for which a gas detector is required in column (18) of Table C of Chapter 3.2 are carried on board the vessel, it shall be established, by means of this device that the concentration of flammable gases and vapours given off by the cargo in these cargo tanks, residual cargo tanks, cargo pump-rooms below deck, cofferdams, double-hull spaces, double bottoms, or hold spaces is not more than 50% of the LEL. For the cargo pump-rooms below deck this may be determined by means of the permanent gas detection system;

(b)   When dangerous substances of Classes 2, 3, 4.1, 6.1, 8 or 9 for which a toximeter is required in column (18) of Table C of Chapter 3.2 are carried on board the vessel, it shall be established, by means of this device that the cargo tanks, residual cargo tanks, cargo pump-rooms below deck, cofferdams, double-hull spaces, double bottoms or hold spaces do not contain concentration of toxic gases and vapours given off by the cargo which exceeds national accepted exposure levels.

In deviation of 1.1.4.6, more stringent national legislation on the entry into holds shall take precedence over the ADN.

7.2.3.1.6   Entry into empty cargo tanks, the residual cargo tanks, the cargo pump-rooms below deck, cofferdams, double-hull spaces, double bottoms, hold spaces or other confined spaces is only permitted if:

−   The concentration of flammable gases and vapours given off by the cargo in the cargo tanks, the residual cargo tanks, the cargo pump-rooms below deck, cofferdams, double-hull spaces, double bottoms, hold spaces or other confined spaces, is below 10% of the LEL, the concentration of toxic gases and vapours given off by the cargo is below national accepted exposure levels, and the percentage of oxygen is between 20 and 23,5 vol %; or

– The concentration of flammable gases and vapours given off by the cargo in the cargo tanks, the residual cargo tank, the cargo pump-rooms below deck, cofferdams, double-hull spaces, double bottoms, hold spaces or other confined spaces, is below 10% of the LEL, and the person entering the spaces wears a self-contained breathing apparatus and other necessary protective and rescue equipment, and is secured by a line. Entry into these spaces is only permitted if this operation is supervised by a second person for whom the same equipment is readily at hand. Another two persons capable of giving assistance in an emergency shall be on the vessel within calling distance. If a rescue winch has been installed, only one other person is sufficient.

In case of emergency or mechanical problems, it is allowed to enter the tank when the concentration of flammable gases and vapours given off by cargo is between 10 and 50% of the LEL. The breathing apparatus (self-contained) in use has to be designed in such a way that the causing of sparks is avoided.

In deviation of 1.1.4.6, more stringent national legislation on the entry into cargo tanks shall take precedence over the ADN.

7.2.3.2   *Cargo pump-rooms below deck*

7.2.3.2.1   When carrying dangerous substances of classes 3, 4.1, 6.1, 8 or 9, the cargo pump-rooms below deck shall be inspected daily so as to ascertain that there are no leaks. The bilges and the drip pans shall be kept free from products.

7.2.3.2.2   When the gas detection system is activated, the loading and unloading operations shall be stopped immediately. All shut-off devices shall be closed and the cargo pump-rooms shall be evacuated immediately. All entrances shall be closed. The loading or unloading operations shall not be continued except when the damage has been repaired or the fault eliminated.

7.2.3.3 to 7.2.3.5   *(Reserved)*

7.2.3.6   *Gas detection system*

The gas detection system shall be maintained and calibrated by trained and qualified personnel in accordance with the instructions of the manufacturer.

7.2.3.7   *Degassing of empty or unloaded cargo tanks and piping for loading and unloading*

7.2.3.7.0   Degassing of empty or unloaded cargo tanks and piping for loading and unloading into the atmosphere or to reception facilities is permitted under the conditions below but only if and insofar it is not prohibited on the basis of other legal requirements.

7.2.3.7.1   *Degassing of empty or unloaded cargo tanks and piping for loading and unloading into the atmosphere*

7.2.3.7.1.1   Empty or unloaded cargo tanks having previously contained dangerous substances of:

– Class 2 or Class 3, with a classification code including the letter "T" in column (3b) of Table C of Chapter 3.2;

– Class 6.1; or

– Packing group I of Class 8;

may only be degassed by an expert according to 8.2.1.2. This may be carried out only at the locations approved by the competent authority.

7.2.3.7.1.2   Where degassing of cargo tanks having previously contained the dangerous goods referred to in 7.2.3.7.1.1 above is not practicable at the locations approved for this purpose by the competent authority, degassing may be carried out while the vessel is under way, provided that:

– The requirements of the first paragraph of 7.2.3.7.1.3 are complied with; the concentration of flammable gases and vapours given off by the cargo in the vented mixture at the outlet shall, however, be not more than 10% of the LEL;

– The crew is not exposed to a concentration of gases and vapours which exceeds national accepted exposure levels;

– Any entrances or openings of spaces connected to the outside are closed; this provision does not apply to the air supply openings of the engine room and overpressure ventilation systems;

– Any member of the crew working on deck is wearing suitable protective equipment;

– It is not carried out within the area of locks including their lay-bys, under bridges or within densely populated areas.

7.2.3.7.1.3   Degassing of empty or unloaded cargo tanks having contained dangerous goods other than those referred to under 7.2.3.7.1.1, when the concentration of flammable gases and vapours given off by the cargo is 10% of the LEL or above, may be carried out while the vessel is underway or at locations approved by the competent authority by means of suitable venting equipment with the tank lids closed and by leading the gas/air mixtures through flame-arresters capable of withstanding steady burning (Explosion group / subgroup according to column (16) of Table C of Chapter 3.2). The concentration of flammable gases and vapours in the vented mixture at the outlet shall be less than 50% of the LEL. The suitable venting equipment may be used for degassing by extraction only when a flame-arrester is fitted immediately before the ventilation fan on the extraction side (Explosion group /subgroup according to column (16) of Table C of Chapter 3.2). The concentration of flammable gases and vapours shall be measured once each hour during the two first hours after the beginning of the degassing operation by forced ventilation or by extraction, by an expert referred to in 8.2.1.2. The results of these measurements shall be recorded in writing.

Degassing is, however, prohibited within the area of locks including their lay-bys, under bridges or within densely populated areas.

Degassing of empty or unloaded cargo tanks having contained dangerous goods other than those referred to in 7.2.3.7.1.1, when the concentration of gases and vapours given off by the cargo is below 10% of the LEL, is allowed, and also additional openings of the cargo tank are allowed to be opened as long as the crew is not exposed to a concentration of gases and vapour which exceeds national accepted exposure levels. Also, there is no obligation to use a flame arrester.

It is prohibited within the area of locks, including their lay-bys, under bridges or within densely populated areas.

7.2.3.7.1.4   Degassing operations shall be interrupted during a thunderstorm or when, due to unfavourable wind conditions, dangerous concentrations of flammable or toxic gases and vapours are to be expected outside the cargo area in front of the accommodation, the wheelhouse and service spaces. The critical state is reached as soon as concentrations given off by the cargo of flammable gases and vapours of more than 20% of the LEL or of toxic gases and vapours exceeding the national accepted exposure levels have been detected in those areas by measurements by means of portable measurement devices.

7.2.3.7.1.5   The marking prescribed in 7.2.5.0.1 may be withdrawn by order of the master when, after degassing of the cargo tanks, it has been ascertained, using the equipment described in column (18) of Table C of Chapter 3.2, that none of the cargo tanks contain flammable gases and vapours in concentrations of more than 20% of the LEL or contain a concentration of toxic gases and vapours which exceeds national accepted exposure levels. The result of the measurement shall be recorded in writing.

7.2.3.7.1.6   Before taking measures which could cause hazards as described in 8.3.5, all cargo tanks and pipes in the cargo area shall be made gas-free. This shall be documented in a gas-free certificate, valid on the day the works commence. The condition of being gas-free may only be declared and certified by a person approved by the competent authority.

7.2.3.7.2   *Degassing of empty or unloaded cargo tanks and piping for loading and unloading to reception facilities*

7.2.3.7.2.1   Empty or unloaded cargo tanks may only be degassed by an expert according to 8.2.1.2. If required by international or national law, it may only be carried out at the locations approved by the competent authority. Degassing to a mobile reception facility while the vessel is underway, is prohibited. Degassing to a mobile reception facility is prohibited while another vessel degasses to the same facility. Degassing to an on board mobile reception facility is prohibited.

7.2.3.7.2.2   Before the degassing operation commences, the degassing vessel shall be earthed. The master of the degassing vessel or an expert according to 8.2.1.2 mandated by him and the operator of the reception facility shall have filled in and signed a checklist confirming with 8.6.4 of ADN.

The checklist shall be printed at least in languages understood by the master or the expert and the operator of the reception facility.

If a positive response to all the questions is not possible, degassing to a reception facility is only permitted with the consent of the competent authority.

7.2.3.7.2.3   Degassing to reception facilities may be carried out by using the piping for loading and unloading or the venting piping to remove the gases and vapours from the cargo tanks while using the other piping respectively to prevent exceedance of the maximum permissible overpressure or vacuum of the cargo tanks.

Piping shall be part of a closed system or, if used to prevent exceedance of the maximum permissible vacuum in the cargo tanks, be equipped with a permanently installed or portable spring-loaded low-pressure valve, with a flame-arrester (Explosion group/subgroup according to column (16) of Table C of Chapter 3.2) if explosion protection is required (column (17) of Table C of Chapter 3.2). This low-pressure valve shall be so installed that under normal working conditions the vacuum valve is not activated. A permanently installed valve or the opening to which a portable valve is connected, must remain closed with a blind flange when the vessel is not degassing to a reception facility.

All piping connected between the degassing vessel and the reception facility shall be equipped with an appropriate flame arrester if explosion protection is required in column (17) of Table C of Chapter 3.2. The requirements for piping on board shall be: Explosion group/subgroup according to column (16) of Table C of Chapter 3.2.

7.2.3.7.2.4   It shall be possible to interrupt degassing operations by means of switches installed at two locations on the vessel (fore and aft) and at two locations at the reception facility (directly at the access to the vessel and at the location from where the reception facility is operated). Interruption of degassing shall be effected by the means of a quick closing valve which shall be directly fitted in the connection between the degassing vessel and the reception facility. The system of disconnection shall be designed in accordance with the closed circuit principle and may be integrated in the emergency shutdown system of the cargo pumps and overfill protections prescribed in 9.3.1.21.5, 9.3.2.21.5 and 9.3.3.21.5.

Degassing operations shall be interrupted during a thunderstorm.

7.2.3.7.2.5   The marking prescribed in column (19) of Table C of Chapter 3.2 may be withdrawn by order of the master when, after degassing of the cargo tanks, it has been ascertained, using the equipment described in column (18) of Table C of Chapter 3.2, that none of the cargo tanks contain flammable gases and vapours in concentrations of more than 20% of the LEL or contain a concentration of toxic gases and vapours which exceeds national accepted exposure levels. The result of the measurement shall be recorded in writing.

7.2.3.7.2.6   Before taking measures which could cause hazards as described in 8.3.5, all cargo tanks and pipes in the cargo area shall be made gas-free. This shall be documented in a gas-free certificate, valid on the day the works commence. The condition of being gas-free may only be declared and certified by a person approved by the competent authority.

7.2.3.7.3 to 7.2.3.7.6   *(Deleted)*

7.2.3.8 to 7.2.3.11   *(Reserved)*

7.2.3.12   *Ventilation*

7.2.3.12.1   While the machinery in the service spaces is operating, the extension ducts connected to the air inlets, if any, shall be in the upright position; otherwise the inlets shall be closed. This provision does not apply to air inlets of service spaces outside the cargo area, provided the inlets without extension duct are located not less than 0.50 m above the deck.

7.2.3.12.2   The ventilation of pump rooms shall be in operation:

–   at least 30 minutes before entry and during occupation;

–   during loading, unloading and degasing; and

–   after the gas detection system has been activated.

7.2.3.13 and 7.2.3.14   *(Reserved)*

7.2.3.15   *Expert on board the vessel*

When dangerous substances are carried, the responsible master shall at the same time be an expert according to 8.2.1.2. In addition this expert shall be:

–   An expert as referred to in 8.2.1.5 when dangerous goods are carried for which a type G tank vessel is prescribed in column (6) of Table C of Chapter 3.2; and

–   An expert as referred to in 8.2.1.7 when dangerous goods are carried for which a type C tank vessel is prescribed in column (6) of Table C of Chapter 3.2.

NOTE: Which master of the vessel's crew is the responsible master shall be determined and documented on board by the carrier. If there is no such determination, the requirement applies to every master.

By derogation from this, for the loading and unloading of dangerous goods in a tank barge, it is sufficient that the person who is responsible for loading and unloading and for ballasting of the tank barge has the expertise required according to 8.2.1.2.

During the carriage of goods for which a type C tank vessel is prescribed in column (6) of Table C of Chapter 3.2 and cargo tank type 1 in column (8), an expert referred to in 8.2.1.5 for carriage in type G vessels is sufficient.

7.2.3.16   All measurements on board the vessel shall be performed by an expert according to 8.2.1.2, unless provided otherwise in the Regulations annexed to ADN. The results of the measurements shall be recorded in writing in the book according to 8.1.2.1 (g).

7.2.3.17 to 7.2.3.19   *(Reserved)*

7.2.3.20   *Water ballast*

7.2.3.20.1   Cofferdams and hold spaces containing insulated cargo tanks shall not be filled with water. Double-hull spaces, double bottoms and hold spaces which do not contain insulated cargo tanks may be filled with ballast water provided:

–   this has been taken into account in the intact and damage stability calculations; and

–   the filling is not prohibited in column (20) of Table C of Chapter 3.2.

If the water in the ballast tanks and compartments leads to the vessel no longer respecting these stability criteria:

–   fixed level indicators shall be installed; or

–   the filling level of the ballast tanks and compartments shall be checked daily before departure and during operations.

In case of the existence of level indicators, ballast tanks may also be partially filled. Otherwise they shall be completely full or empty.

7.2.3.20.2   *(Deleted)*

7.2.3.21   *(Reserved)*

7.2.3.22   *Entrances to hold spaces, cargo pump-rooms below deck and cofferdams, openings of cargo tanks and residual cargo tanks; closing devices*

The cargo tanks, residual cargo tanks and entrances to cargo pump-rooms below deck, cofferdams and hold spaces shall remain closed. This requirement shall not apply to cargo pump-rooms on board oil separator and supply vessels or to the other exceptions set out in this Part.

7.2.3.23 and 7.2.3.24   *(Reserved)*

7.2.3.25   *Connections between pipes*

7.2.3.25.1   Connecting two or more of the following groups of pipes is prohibited:

(a)   piping for loading and unloading;

(b)   pipes for ballasting and draining cargo tanks, cofferdams, hold spaces, double-hull spaces and double bottoms;

(c)   pipes located outside the cargo area.

7.2.3.25.2   The provision of 7.2.3.25.1 above does not apply to removable pipe connections between cofferdam pipes and

–   piping for loading and unloading;

–   pipes located outside the cargo area while the cofferdams have to be filled with water in an emergency.

In these cases the connections shall be designed so as to prevent water from being drawn from the cargo tanks. The cofferdams shall be emptied only by means of ejectors or an independent system within the cargo area.

7.2.3.25.3   The provisions of 7.2.3.25.1 (b) and (c) above do not apply to:

–   pipes intended for ballasting and draining double-hull spaces and double bottoms which do not have a common boundary with the cargo tanks;

–   pipes intended for ballasting hold spaces where the pipes of the fire-fighting system within the cargo area are used for this purpose. Double-hull and double bottom spaces and hold spaces shall be stripped only by means of ejectors or an independent system within the cargo area.

7.2.3.26 and 7.2.3.27   *(Reserved)*

7.2.3.28   *Instruction on maximum loading temperature*

For the carriage of refrigerated substances, an instruction shall be on board mentioning the permissible maximum loading temperature, in relation to the insulation design of the cargo tanks and, if on board, the capacity of the refrigeration system.

7.2.3.29   *Lifeboats*

7.2.3.29.1   The lifeboat required in accordance with the Regulations referred to in 1.1.4.6 shall be stowed outside the cargo area. The lifeboat may, however, be stowed in the cargo area provided an easily accessible collective life-saving appliance conforming to the Regulations referred to in 1.1.4.6 is available within the accommodation areas. If the vessel substance list according to 1.16.1.2.5 contains substances for which explosion protection is required in column (17) of Table C of Chapter 3.2,

–   Outboard motors and their fuel tanks shall be carried on board only outside the cargo area; and

–   Mechanical inflation devices, outboard motors and their electrical installations shall be put into operation only outside the cargo area.

7.2.3.29.2   7.2.3.29.1 above does not apply to oil separator or supply vessels.

7.2.3.30   *(Reserved)*

7.2.3.31   *Engines*

7.2.3.31.1   The use of engines running on fuels having a flashpoint equal to or lower than 55 °C (e.g. petrol engines) is prohibited. This provision does not apply to:

– the petrol-operated outboard motors of lifeboats;

– the propulsion and auxiliary systems which meet the requirements of Chapter 30 and Annex 8, Section 1 of the European Standard laying down Technical Requirements for Inland Navigation vessels (ES-TRIN) as amended.[1]

7.2.3.31.2   The carriage of power-driven conveyances such as passenger cars and motor boats in the cargo area is prohibited.

7.2.3.32   *Oil fuel tanks*

Double bottoms with a height of at least 0.60 m may be used as oil fuel tanks, provided they have been constructed in accordance with Part 9.

7.2.3.33 to 7.2.3.40   *(Reserved)*

7.2.3.41   *Smoking, fire or naked light*

7.2.3.41.1   Smoking, including electronic cigarettes and other similar devices, fire and naked light are prohibited on board the vessel.

This prohibition shall be displayed on notice boards at appropriate places.

The prohibition on smoking does not apply in the accommodation or the wheelhouse, provided that their windows, doors, skylights and hatches are closed or the ventilation system is adjusted to guarantee an overpressure of at least 0.1 kPa.

7.2.3.41.2   Heating, cooking and refrigerating appliances shall not be fuelled with liquid fuels, liquid gas or solid fuels.

Cooking and refrigerating appliances may only be used in the accommodation and in the wheelhouse.

7.2.3.41.3   Heating appliances or boilers fuelled with liquid fuels having a flash-point above 55 °C which are installed in the engine room or in another suitable space may, however, be used.

7.2.3.42   *Cargo heating system*

7.2.3.42.1   Heating of the cargo is not permitted except where there is risk of solidification of the cargo or where the cargo, because of its viscosity, cannot be unloaded in the usual manner.

In general, a liquid shall not be heated up to a temperature above its flash-point.

Special provisions are included in column (20) of Table C of Chapter 3.2.

7.2.3.42.2   Cargo tanks containing substances which are heated during transport shall be equipped with devices for measuring the temperature of the cargo.

---

[1]   *As available on the website of the Comité Européen pour l'Élaboration de Standards dans le Domaine de Navigation Intérieure – CESNI,* https://www.cesni.eu/en/documents/es-trin/.

7.2.3.42.3 During unloading, the cargo heating system may be used provided that the space where it has been installed meets in all respects the provisions of 9.3.2.52.3 or 9.3.3.52.3.

7.2.3.42.4 The provisions of 7.2.3.42.3 above do not apply when the cargo heating system is supplied with steam from shore and only the circulation pump is in operation, as well as when the flash-point of the cargo being unloaded is not less than 60 °C.

7.2.3.43 *(Reserved)*

7.2.3.44 ***Cleaning operations***

The use of liquids having a flash-point below 55 °C for cleaning purposes is permitted only in the explosion hazardous area.

7.2.3.45 to 7.2.3.50 *(Reserved)*

7.2.3.51 ***Electrical and non-electrical installations and equipment***

7.2.3.51.1 The electrical and non-electrical installations and equipment shall be properly maintained in a faultless condition.

7.2.3.51.2 The use of movable electric cables is prohibited in the explosion hazardous area. This provision does not apply to the movable electric cables referred to in 9.3.1.53.3, 9.3.2.53.3, and 9.3.3.53.3.

Movable electric cables must undergo visual inspection each time before use. They must be installed in such a way as to ensure that they are not at risk of damage. Connectors must be located outside of the explosion danger area.

The use of electric cables to connect the power network of a vessel to a land-based power network is not permitted:

– During the loading or unloading of substances for which explosion protection is required in column (17) of Table C of Chapter 3.2; or

– When the vessel is located immediately adjacent to or within an onshore assigned zone.

7.2.3.51.3 The sockets for connecting the signal lights and gangway lighting or for submerged pumps on board oil separator vessels shall not be live except when the signal lights or the gangway lighting or the submerged pumps on board oil separator vessels are switched on.

Connecting or disconnecting shall not be possible except when the sockets are not live.

7.2.3.51.4 During a stay in the immediate vicinity of or within an onshore assigned zone, electrical and non-electrical installations and equipment not complying with the requirements of 9.3.x.51 (a), 9.3.x.51 (b), 9.3.x.51 (c) or 9.3.x.52.1 (marked in red according to 9.3.x.51 and 9.3.x.52.3) shall be switched off, cooled down to below the temperature mentioned in 9.3.x.51 (a) or 9.3.x.51 (b), or the measures mentioned in 7.2.3.51.6 shall be taken.

When the list of substances on the vessel according to 1.16.1.2.5 contains substances for which explosion protection is required in column (17) of Table C of Chapter 3.2, this provision applies also during loading and unloading and degassing during berthing.

7.2.3.51.5 When the list of substances on the vessel according to 1.16.1.2.5 contains substances for which the temperature classes T4, T5 or T6 are indicated in column (15) of Table C of Chapter 3.2, the corresponding surface temperatures within the assigned zones shall not exceed 135 °C (T4), 100 °C (T5) or 85 °C (T6), respectively.

7.2.3.51.6   7.2.3.51.4 and 7.2.3.51.5 do not apply in the accommodation, the wheelhouse or service spaces located outside the cargo area if:

(a)   The ventilation system is adjusted to guarantee an overpressure of at least 0.1 kPa; and

(b)   The gas detection system is switched on, taking measurements continuously.

7.2.3.51.7   Installations and equipment according to 7.2.3.51.4 that have been switched off during loading and unloading, degassing during berthing or a stay in the vicinity of or within an onshore assigned zone may only be switched on again:

–   Once the vessel is no longer in the vicinity of or within the onshore assigned zone; or

–   When values corresponding to 10% of the LEL of n-Hexane or 10% of the LEL of the cargo, whichever is the more critical, are reached in the wheelhouse, accommodation and service spaces located outside the cargo area.

The results of the measurements shall be recorded in writing.

7.2.3.51.8   If vessels are not able to meet the requirements of 7.2.3.51.4 and 7.2.3.51.6, they are not permitted to remain in the immediate vicinity of or within an onshore assigned zone.

7.2.3.52 to 7.2.3.99   *(Reserved)*

7.2.4   Additional requirements concerning loading, carriage, unloading and other handling of cargo

7.2.4.1   *Limitation of the quantities carried*

7.2.4.1.1   The carriage of packages in the cargo area is prohibited. This prohibition does not apply to:

–   residual cargo, washing water, cargo residues and slops contained in no more than six approved receptacles for residual products and receptacles for slops having a maximum total capacity of not more than 12 m³. The receptacles for residual products and the receptacles for slops shall be properly secured in the cargo area, be located at a minimum distance from the hull equal to one quarter of the vessel's breadth and comply with the provisions of 9.3.2.26.3 or 9.3.3.26.3 concerning them;

–   to cargo samples, up to a maximum of 30, of substances accepted for carriage in the tank vessel, where the maximum contents are 500 ml per receptacle. Receptacles shall meet the packing requirements referred to in Part 4 of ADR and shall be placed on board, at a specific point in the cargo area, such that under normal conditions of carriage they cannot break or be punctured and their contents cannot spill in the hold space. Fragile receptacles shall be suitably padded.

7.2.4.1.2   On board oil separator vessel receptacles with a maximum capacity of 2.00 m³ oily and greasy wastes resulting from the operation of vessels may be placed in the cargo area provided that these receptacles are properly secured.

7.2.4.1.3   On board supply vessels or other vessels delivering products for the operation of vessels, packages of dangerous goods and non-dangerous goods may be carried in the cargo area up to a gross quantity of 5,000 kg provided that this possibility is mentioned in the certificate of approval. The packages shall be properly secured and shall be protected against heat, sun and bad weather.

7.2.4.1.4   On board supply vessels or other vessels delivering products for the operation of vessels, the number of cargo samples referred to in 7.2.4.1.1 may be increased from 30 to a maximum of 500.

7.2.4.2   *Reception of oily and greasy wastes resulting from the operation of vessels and delivery of products for the operation of vessels*

7.2.4.2.1   The reception from inland navigation vessels of unpackaged liquid oily and greasy wastes resulting from the operation of vessels shall be ensured by suction; the reception from seagoing vessels may also be ensured by pressurization provided that:

–   the quantity to be transferred and the maximum loading rate is determined and agreed between the seagoing vessel and the inland navigation vessel;

–   if feasible, the pressure pump on the seagoing vessel can be switched off from the receiving inland navigation vessel;

–   there is permanent and continuous supervision on the operation from both vessels; and

–   communication between both vessels in ensured at all times during the operation.

7.2.4.2.2   Mooring and reception of oily and greasy wastes may not take place during the loading and unloading of substances for which protection against explosion is required in column (17) of Table C of Chapter 3.2 nor during the degasing of tank vessels. This requirement does not apply to oil separator vessels provided that the provisions for protection against explosion applicable to the dangerous substance are complied with.

7.2.4.2.3   Mooring and handing over of products for the operation of vessels shall not take place during the loading or unloading of substances for which protection against explosions is required in column (17) of Table C of Chapter 3.2 nor during the degasing of tank vessels. This requirement does not apply to supply vessels provided that the provisions for protection against explosion applicable to the dangerous substance are complied with.

7.2.4.2.4   The competent authority may issue derogations to the requirements of 7.2.4.2.1 and 7.2.4.2.2 above. During unloading it may also issue derogations to 7.2.4.2.3 above.

7.2.4.3 to 7.2.4.6   *(Reserved)*

7.2.4.7   *Places of loading and unloading*

7.2.4.7.1   Tank vessels shall be loaded or unloaded only at the places designated or approved for this purpose by the competent authority. If a zone is assigned onshore at the loading or unloading station, the vessel is only authorized to stay in its immediate vicinity or within the zone if it meets the requirements of 9.3.x.12.4 (b) or (c), 9.3.x.51, 9.3.x.52.1 and 9.3.x.52.3. The competent authority may allow exceptions in individual cases.

7.2.4.7.2   The reception from other vessels of unpackaged oily and greasy liquid wastes resulting from the operation of vessels and the handing over of products for the operation of vessels into the bunkers of other vessels shall not be taken to be loading or unloading within the meaning of 7.2.4.7.1 above or transhipment within the meaning of 7.2.4.9.

7.2.4.8   *(Reserved)*

7.2.4.9   *Cargo transfer operations*

Partial or complete cargo transfer into another vessel without permission from the competent authority is prohibited outside a cargo transfer place approved for this purpose.

NOTE 1: For transhipment to means of transport of another mode see 7.2.4.7.1.

NOTE 2: This prohibition also applies to transhipment between supply vessels.

7.2.4.10	*Checklist*

7.2.4.10.1   Loading or unloading shall start only once a checklist conforming with section 8.6.3 of ADN has been completed for the cargo in question and questions 1 to 19 of the list have been checked off with an "X". Irrelevant questions should be deleted. The list shall be completed, after the pipes intended for the handling are connected and prior to the handling, in duplicate and signed by the master or a person mandated by him and the person responsible for the handling at the shore facilities. If a positive response to all the questions is not possible, loading or unloading is only permitted with the prior consent of the competent authority.

7.2.4.10.2   The list shall conform to the model in 8.6.3.

7.2.4.10.3   The checklist shall be printed at least in languages understood by the master and the person responsible for the handling at the shore facilities.

7.2.4.10.4   The provisions of 7.2.4.10.1 to 7.2.4.10.3 above shall not apply to the reception of oily and greasy wastes by oil separator vessels nor to the handing over of products for the operation of vessels by supply vessels.

7.2.4.11	*Loading plan*

7.2.4.11.1   (*Deleted*)

7.2.4.11.2   The master shall enter on a cargo stowage plan the goods carried in the individual cargo tanks. The goods shall be described as in the transport document (information according to 5.4.1.1.2 (a) to (d)).

7.2.4.12	*Registration during the voyage*

The following particulars shall immediately be entered in the register referred to in 8.1.11:

Loading: Place of loading and loading berth, date and time, UN number or identification number of the substance, proper shipping name of the substance, the class and packing group if any;

Unloading: Place of unloading and unloading berth, date and time;

Degasing of UN No. 1203 petrol: Degasing place and facility or sector, date and time.

These particulars shall be provided for each cargo tank.

7.2.4.13	**Measures to be taken before loading**

7.2.4.13.1   When residues of the previous cargo may cause dangerous reactions with the next cargo, any such residues shall be properly removed.

Substances which react dangerously with other dangerous goods shall be separated by a cofferdam, an empty space, a pump-room, an empty cargo tank or a cargo tank loaded with a substance which does not react with the cargo.

Where an empty, uncleaned cargo tank, or a cargo tank containing residues of previous cargo of a substance liable to react dangerously with other dangerous goods, this separation is not required if the master has taken appropriate measures to avoid a dangerous reaction.

If the vessel is equipped with piping for loading and unloading below the deck passing through the cargo tanks, the mixed loading or carriage of substances likely to react dangerously with each other is prohibited.

7.2.4.13.2   Before the start of loading operations, any prescribed safety and control devices and any items of equipment shall, if possible, be checked and controlled for proper functioning.

7.2.4.13.3   Before the start of loading operations the overflow control device switch shall be connected to the shore installation.

7.2.4.14   *Cargo handling and stowage*

Dangerous goods shall be loaded in the cargo area in cargo tanks, in cargo residue tanks or in packages permitted under 7.2.4.1.1.

7.2.4.15   *Measures to be taken after unloading (stripping system)*

7.2.4.15.1   If the provisions listed in 1.1.4.6.1 foresee the application of a stripping system, the cargo tanks and the cargo piping shall be emptied by means of the stripping system in accordance with the conditions laid down in the testing procedure after each unloading operation. This provision need not be complied with if the new cargo is the same as the previous cargo or a different cargo, the carriage of which does not require a prior cleaning of the cargo tanks.

Residual cargo shall be discharged ashore by means of the equipment provided for that effect (article 7.04 Nr. 1 and appendix II model 1 of CDNI) or shall be stored in the vessel's own tank for residual products or in receptacles for residual products according to 7.2.4.1.1.

7.2.4.15.2   During the filling of the residual tanks and receptacles for residual products, released gases shall be safely evacuated. They shall only be connected to the venting piping for the time necessary to fill them.

Capacity to collect any leaking liquids shall be placed under the connections used during filling.

7.2.4.15.3   The degasing of cargo tanks and piping for loading and unloading shall be carried out in compliance with the conditions of 7.2.3.7.

7.2.4.16   *Measures to be taken during loading, carriage, unloading and handling*

7.2.4.16.1   The loading rate and the maximum operational pressure of the cargo pumps shall be determined in agreement with the personnel of the shore installation.

7.2.4.16.2   All safety or control devices required in the cargo tanks shall remain switched on. During carriage this provision is only applicable for the installations mentioned in 9.3.1.21.1 (e) and (f), 9.3.2.21.1 (e) and (f) or 9.3.3.21.1 (e) and (f).

In the event of a failure of a safety or control device, loading or unloading shall be suspended immediately.

When a cargo pump-room is located below deck, the prescribed safety and control devices in the cargo pump-room shall remain permanently switched on.

Any failure of the gas detection system shall be immediately signalled in the wheelhouse and on deck by a visual and audible warning.

7.2.4.16.3   The shut-off devices of the loading and unloading piping if available, as well as of the pipes of the stripping systems shall remain closed except during loading, unloading, stripping, cleaning or degasing operations.

7.2.4.16.4   *(Deleted)*

7.2.4.16.5   Receptacles intended for recovering possible liquid spillage shall be placed under connections to shore installations used for loading and unloading. Before coupling and after uncoupling the connections and in between if necessary, the receptacles shall be emptied. These requirements shall not apply to the carriage of substance of Class 2.

7.2.4.16.6   In case of recovery of the gas-air mixture from shore into the vessel, the pressure at the connecting-point of the vapour return piping and the venting piping shall not be more than the opening pressure of the pressure relief device/high-velocity vent valve.

7.2.4.16.7   When a tank vessel conforms to 9.3.2.22.4 (b) or 9.3.3.22.4 (b), the individual cargo tanks shall be closed off during carriage and opened during loading, unloading and degassing.

7.2.4.16.8   Persons entering the premises located in the cargo area below deck during loading or unloading shall wear the PP equipment referred to in 8.1.5 if this equipment is prescribed in column (18) of Table C of Chapter 3.2.

Persons connecting or disconnecting the loading and unloading piping or the venting piping, relieving pressure in cargo tanks, taking samples, carrying out measurements or cleaning or replacing the flame arrester plate stack (see 7.2.4.22), shall wear the PP equipment referred to in 8.1.5 if this equipment is prescribed in column (18) of Table C of Chapter 3.2; they shall also wear protective equipment A if a toximeter (TOX) is prescribed in column (18) of Table C of Chapter 3.2.

7.2.4.16.9   (a)   During loading or unloading in a closed tank vessel of substances for which an open type N vessel with a flame arrester is sufficient according to columns (6) and (7) of Table C of Chapter 3.2, the cargo tanks may be opened using the safe pressure-relief device referred to in 9.3.2.22.4 (a) or 9.3.3.22.4 (a).

(b)   During loading or unloading in a closed tank vessel of substances for which an open type N vessel is sufficient according to columns (6) and (7) of Table C of Chapter 3.2, the cargo tanks may be opened using the safe pressure-relief device referred to in 9.3.2.22.4 (a) or 9.3.3.22.4 (a) or using another suitable opening in the venting piping if any accumulation of water and its penetration into the cargo tanks is prevented and the opening is appropriately closed again after loading or unloading.

7.2.4.16.10   7.2.4.16.9 shall not apply when the cargo tanks contain gases or vapour from substances for the carriage of which a closed-type tank vessel is required in column (7) of Table C of Chapter 3.2.

7.2.4.16.11   The shut-off device referred to in 9.3.1.21.1 (g), 9.3.2.21.1 (g) or 9.3.3.21.1 (g) shall be opened only after a gastight connection for a sampling device has been made to the closed or partly closed sampling device.

7.2.4.16.12   For substances requiring protection against explosions according to column (17) of Table C of Chapter 3.2, the connection of the venting piping to the shore installation shall be such that the vessel is protected against detonations and the passage of flames from the shore (explosion group/subgroup according to column (16) of table C of Chapter 3.2). The protection of the vessel against detonations and the passage of flames from the shore is not required when the cargo tanks are inerted in accordance with 7.2.4.18.

7.2.4.16.13   For the carriage of substances of UN No. 2448, or of goods of Class 5.1 or 8, the bulwark ports, openings in the foot rail, etc., shall not be closed off. Nor shall they be closed off, during the voyage, in the event of carriage of other dangerous goods.

7.2.4.16.14   If supervision is required in column (20) of Table C of Chapter 3.2 for substances of Classes 2 or 6.1, loading and unloading shall be carried out under the supervision of a person who is not a member of the crew and has been mandated for the task by the consignor or the consignee.

7.2.4.16.15   The initial cargo throughput established in the loading instructions shall be such as to ensure that no electrostatic charge exists at the start of loading.

7.2.4.16.16   Measures to be taken before loading refrigerated liquefied gases

Unless the temperature of the cargo is controlled in accordance with 9.3.1.24.1 (a) or 9.3.1.24.1 (c) guaranteeing the use of the maximal boil-off in any service conditions, the holding time has to be determined by the master or another person on his behalf before loading and validated by the master or another person on his behalf during loading and shall be documented on board.

7.2.4.16.17   Determination of the holding time

A table, approved by the recognized classification society that certified the vessel, giving the relation between holding time and filling conditions, incorporating the parameters below shall be kept on board.

The holding time of the cargo shall be determined on the basis of the following parameters:

–   The heat transmission coefficient as defined in 9.3.1.27.9;

–   The set pressure of the safety valves;

–   The initial filling conditions (temperature of cargo during loading and degree of filling);

–   The ambient temperatures as given in 9.3.1.24.2;

–   When using the boil-off vapours, the minimum guaranteed use of the boil-off vapours (that is the amount of boil-off vapours used under any service conditions), may be taken into account.

Adequate safety margin

To leave an adequate margin to ensure safety, the holding time is at least three times the expected duration of the journey of the vessel, including the following:

–   To ensure safety for short journeys of (as expected) no more than 5 days, the minimum holding time for any vessel with refrigerated liquefied gases is 15 days.

–   For long journeys of (as expected) more than 10 days, the minimum holding time shall be 30 days, adding two days for each day the journeys takes more than 10 days.

As soon as it becomes clear that the cargo will not be unloaded within the holding time, the master shall inform the nearest emergency services according to 1.4.1.2.

7.2.4.17   *Closing of windows and doors*

7.2.4.17.1   During loading, unloading, degasing operations, or a stay in the vicinity of or within an onshore assigned zone, all entrances or openings of spaces which are accessible from the deck and all openings of spaces facing the outside shall remain closed.

This provision does not apply to:

–   air intakes of running engines;

–   ventilation inlets of engine rooms while the engines are running;

–   air intakes of the ventilation system referred to in 9.3.1.12.4, 9.3.2.12.4 or 9.3.3.12.4;

–   air intakes of air conditioning installations if these openings are fitted with a gas detection system referred to in 9.3.1.12.4, 9.3.2.12.4 or 9.3.3.12.4.

These entrances and openings may only be opened when necessary and for a short time, after the master has given his permission.

7.2.4.17.2   After the loading, unloading and degasing operations, the spaces which are accessible from the deck shall be ventilated.

7.2.4.17.3   The provisions of 7.2.4.17.1 and 7.2.4.17.2 above shall not apply to the reception of oily and greasy wastes resulting from the operation of vessels nor to the handing over of products for the operation of vessels. The provision of 7.2.4.17.1 and 7.2.4.17.2 however, shall apply to the handing over of liquefied natural gas (LNG) for the operation of vessels.

7.2.4.18   *Blanketing of the cargo and inerting*

7.2.4.18.1   In cargo tanks and the corresponding piping, inerting in the gaseous phase or blanketing of the cargo may be necessary. Inerting and blanketing of the cargo are defined as follows:

–   Inerting: cargo tanks and the corresponding piping and other spaces for which this process is prescribed in column (20) of Table C of Chapter 3.2 are filled with gases or vapours which prevent combustion, do not react with the cargo and maintain this state;

–   Blanketing of the cargo: spaces in the cargo tanks above the cargo and the corresponding piping are filled with a liquid, gas or vapour so that the cargo is separated from the air and this state is maintained.

7.2.4.18.2   For certain substances the requirements for inerting and blanketing of the cargo in cargo tanks, in the corresponding piping and in adjacent empty spaces are given in column (20) of Table C of Chapter 3.2.

7.2.4.18.3   (*Reserved*)

7.2.4.18.4   Inerting or blanketing of flammable cargoes shall be carried out in such a way as to reduce the electrostatic charge as far as possible when the inerting agent is added.

7.2.4.19   (*Deleted*)

7.2.4.20   (*Reserved*)

7.2.4.21   *Filling of cargo tanks*

7.2.4.21.1   The degree of filling given in column (11) of Table C of Chapter 3.2 or calculated in accordance with 7.2.4.21.3 for the individual cargo tank shall not be exceeded.

7.2.4.21.2   The provisions of 7.2.4.21.1 above do not apply to cargo tanks the contents of which are maintained at the filling temperature during carriage by means of heating equipment. In this case calculation of the degree of filling at the beginning of carriage and control of the temperature shall be such that, during carriage, the maximum allowable degree of filling is not exceeded.

7.2.4.21.3   For carriage of substances having a relative density higher than that stated in the certificate of approval, the maximum permissible degree of filling of the cargo tanks shall be calculated in accordance with the following formula:

maximum permissible degree of filling (%) = a * 100/b

a = relative density stated in the certificate of approval,

b = relative density of the substance.

The degree of filling given in column (11) of Table C of Chapter 3.2 shall, however, not be exceeded.

NOTE: Furthermore, the requirements concerning stability, longitudinal strength and the deepest permissible draught of the vessel shall be observed when filling the cargo tanks.

7.2.4.21.4   If the degree of filling of 97.5% is exceeded a technical installation shall be authorized to pump off the overflow. During such an operation an automatic visual alarm shall be activated on deck.

7.2.4.22   *Opening of openings of cargo tanks*

7.2.4.22.1   Opening of cargo tanks apertures shall be permitted only after the tanks have been relieved of pressure.

Pressure relief of cargo tanks is permitted only when using the device for safe pressure relief prescribed in 9.3.2.22.4 (a) and 9.3.2.22.4 (b) or 9.3.3.22.4 (a) and 9.3.3.22.4 (b). When explosion protection is required under column (17) of Table C of Chapter 3.2, the opening of cargo tank covers shall be permitted only if the cargo tanks in question have been degassed and the concentration of flammable gases in the tanks is less than 10% of the lower explosive limit of the cargo/previous cargo. The results of the measurements shall be recorded in writing. Entry into these cargo tanks is not permitted for the purpose of measuring.

7.2.4.22.2   Opening of sampling outlets is only permitted for sampling and control or cleaning of empty cargo tanks.

7.2.4.22.3   Sampling shall be permitted only if a device prescribed in column (13) of Table C of Chapter 3.2 or a device ensuring a higher level of safety is used.

Opening of sampling outlets of cargo tanks loaded with substances for which marking with one or two blue cones or one or two blue lights is prescribed in column (19) of Table C of Chapter 3.2 shall be permitted only when loading has been interrupted for not less than 10 minutes.

7.2.4.22.4   The sampling receptacles including all accessories such as ropes, etc., shall consist of electrostatically conductive material and shall, during sampling, be electrically connected to the vessel's hull.

7.2.4.22.5   Opening of the housing of the flame arresters is permitted only for the cleaning of the flame arrester plate stack or replacement by flame arrester plate stacks of the same design.

Opening is permitted only when the relevant cargo tanks are empty and the concentration of flammable gases in the cargo tank is less than 10% of the lower explosive limit of the cargo/previous cargo.

The results of the measurements shall be recorded in writing.

Cleaning and replacing of the flame arrestor plate stack shall be carried out only by trained and qualified personnel.

7.2.4.22.6 For the operations referred to in 7.2.4.22.4 and 7.2.4.22.5, only low-sparking hand tools (e.g. chromium vanadium steel screwdrivers and wrenches) shall be used.

7.2.4.22.7 The duration of opening shall be limited to the time necessary for control, cleaning, replacing the flame arrester or sampling.

7.2.4.22.8 The provisions of 7.2.4.22.1 to 7.2.4.22.7 above shall not apply to oil separator or supply vessels.

7.2.4.23 *(Reserved)*

7.2.4.24 ***Simultaneous loading and unloading***

During loading or unloading of cargo tanks, no other cargo shall be loaded or unloaded. The competent authority may grant exceptions during unloading.

7.2.4.25 ***Loading and unloading piping and venting piping***

7.2.4.25.1 Loading and unloading as well as stripping of cargo tanks shall be carried out by means of the fixed cargo piping of the vessel.

The metal fittings of the connections to the shore piping shall be electrically earthed so as to prevent the accumulation of electrostatic charges.

7.2.4.25.2 The loading and unloading piping shall not be extended by pipes or hose assemblies fore or aft beyond the cofferdams.

This requirement shall not apply to hose assemblies used for the reception of oily and greasy wastes resulting from the operation of vessels and the delivery of products for the operation of vessels.

7.2.4.25.3 *(Reserved)*

7.2.4.25.4 The liquid remaining in the piping shall be completely drained into the cargo tanks, if possible, or safely removed. This requirement shall not apply to supply vessels.

7.2.4.25.5 The gas/air mixtures released during loading operations shall be returned ashore through a vapour return piping if:

– A closed cargo tank is required according to column (7) of Table C of Chapter 3.2; or

– A closed cargo tank was required for the previous cargo in column (7) of Table C of Chapter 3.2 and before the loading the concentration of flammable gases of the previous cargo in the cargo tank is above 10% of the LEL or the cargo tank contains toxic gases, corrosive gases (packing group I or II) or gases with CMR-characteristics (Categories 1A or 1B) in a concentration above national accepted exposure levels. If these conditions are not met and the vapour return piping is not used, the measured concentrations shall be recorded in writing.

If the substance to be loaded requires explosion protection according to column (17) of Table C of Chapter 3.2, and the use of the vapour return piping is prescribed, the connection of the vapour return piping shall be designed such that the vessel is protected against detonations and the passage of flames from the shore. The protection of the vessel against detonations and the passage of flames from the shore is not required when the cargo tanks are inerted in accordance with 7.2.4.18.

7.2.4.25.6   When substances of Class 2 are carried the requirements of 7.2.4.25.4 shall be deemed to have been satisfied if the piping for loading and unloading have been purged with the cargo gas or with nitrogen.

7.2.4.25.7   For connecting or disconnecting loading or unloading piping and venting piping, only low-sparking hand tools (e.g. chromium vanadium steel screwdrivers and wrenches) shall be used.

7.2.4.26 and 7.2.4.27   *(Reserved)*

7.2.4.28   *Water-spray system*

7.2.4.28.1   If a gas or vapour water-spray system is required in column (9) of Table C of Chapter 3.2, it shall be kept ready for operation during loading, unloading and carriage. If a water-spray system is required to cool the tank-deck, it shall be kept ready for operation during the carriage.

7.2.4.28.2   When water-spraying is required in column (9) of Table C of Chapter 3.2 and the pressure of the gaseous phase in the cargo tanks may reach 80% of the relief pressure of the pressure relief devices/high-velocity vent valves, the master shall take all measures compatible with safety to prevent the pressure from reaching that value. He shall in particular activate the water-spray system.

7.2.4.28.3   If a water-spray system is required in column (9) of Table C of Chapter 3.2 and remark 23 is indicated in column (20) of Table C of Chapter 3.2, the instrument measuring the internal pressure shall activate an alarm when the internal pressure reaches 40 kPa (0.4 bar). The water-spray system shall immediately be activated and remain in operation until the internal pressure drops to 30 kPa (0.3 bar).

7.2.4.29   *Transport of refrigerated liquefied gases*

During loading or unloading the drip tray as mentioned in 9.3.1.21.11 shall be placed under the shore connection of the piping for loading and unloading in use, and a water film as mentioned in 9.3.1.21.11 shall be activated.

7.2.4.30 to 7.2.4.39   *(Reserved)*

7.2.4.40   *Fire-extinguishing arrangements*

During loading and unloading, the fire extinguishing systems, the fire main with hydrants complete with couplings and jet/spray nozzles or with couplings and hose assemblies with couplings and jet/spray nozzles shall be kept ready for operation in the cargo area on deck.

The freezing of fire-mains and hydrants shall be prevented.

7.2.4.41   *Smoking, fire or naked light*

During loading, unloading or degassing operations, fires, naked lights, and smoking are prohibited on board the vessel.

However, the provisions of 7.2.3.42.3 and 7.2.3.42.4 are applicable.

7.2.4.42   *Cargo heating system*

The maximum allowable temperature for carriage indicated in column (20) of Table C of Chapter 3.2 shall not be exceeded.

7.2.4.43 to 7.2.4.50   *(Reserved)*

7.2.4.51   *Electrical installations and equipment*

7.2.4.51.1 and 7.2.4.51.2   *(Deleted)*

7.2.4.51.3   Equipment for active cathodic corrosion protection shall be disconnected before berthing and may not be re-connected until after the departure of the vessel, at earliest.

7.2.4.52   *(Reserved)*

7.2.4.53   *Lighting*

If loading or unloading is performed at night or in conditions of poor visibility, effective lighting shall be provided. If provided from the deck, it shall be effected by properly secured electrical lighting appliances which shall be positioned in such a way that they cannot be damaged.

7.2.4.54 to 7.2.4.59   *(Reserved)*

7.2.4.60   *Special equipment*

The shower and the eye and face bath prescribed in the rules for construction shall be kept ready in all weather conditions for use during loading and unloading operations and cargo transfer operations by pumping.

7.2.4.61 to 7.2.4.73   *(Reserved)*

7.2.4.74   *(Deleted)*

7.2.4.75   *Risk of sparking*

All electrically continuous connections between the vessel and the shore shall be so designed that they do not present a source of ignition. If the vessel substance list as referred to in 1.16.1.2.5 includes substances that require anti-explosion protection in accordance with column (17) of Table C of Chapter 3.2, taking off clothes not sufficiently dissipative shall be prohibited in zone 1.

7.2.4.76   *Synthetic ropes*

During loading and unloading operations, the vessel may be moored by means of synthetic ropes only when steel cables are used to prevent the vessel from going adrift.

Steel cables sheathed in synthetic material or natural fibres are considered as equivalent when the minimum tensile strength required in accordance with the Regulations referred to in 1.1.4.6 is obtained from the steel strands.

Oil separator vessels may, however, be moored by means of appropriate synthetic ropes during the reception of oily and greasy wastes resulting from the operation of vessels, as may supply vessels and other vessels during the delivery of products for the operation of vessels.

7.2.4.77 Possible means of evacuation in case of an emergency

		Tank vessel/tank barge				
		Class				
		2, 3 (except second and third entries of UN No. 1202, packing group III, in Table C)	**3 (only for the second and third entries of UN No. 1202, packing group III, in Table C), 4.1**	**5.1, 6.1**	**8**	**9**
1	Two escape routes inside or outside the cargo area in opposite directions	•	•	•	•	•
2	One escape route outside the cargo area and one safe haven outside the vessel including the escape route towards it from the opposite end	•	•	•	•	•
3	One escape route outside the cargo area and one safe haven on the vessel at the opposite end	•	•	•**	•	•
4	One escape route outside the cargo area and one life boat at the opposite end		•		•	•
5	One escape route outside the cargo area and one escape boat at the opposite end	•	•	•	•	•
6	One escape route inside the cargo area and one escape route outside the cargo area at the opposite end	•	•	•	•	•
7	One escape route inside the cargo area and one safe haven outside the vessel in the opposite direction	•	•	•	•	•
8	One escape route inside the cargo area and one safe haven on the vessel in the opposite direction	•	•	•**	•	•
9	One escape route inside the cargo area and one life boat at the opposite end		•		•	•
10	One escape route inside the cargo area and one escape boat at the opposite end	•	•	•	•	•
11	One escape route inside or outside the cargo area and two safe havens on the vessel at opposite ends	•	•	•**	•	•
12	One escape route inside or outside the cargo area and two safe areas on the vessel at opposite ends	•	•	•**	•	•
13	One escape route outside the cargo area		•		*•	•
14	One escape route inside the cargo area		•		*•	•
15	One or more safe havens outside the vessel, including the escape route towards it	•	•	•	*•	•

• = Possible option.

* – Not accepted in case of classification codes TFC, CF or CFT.

**= Not accepted if there is a risk that oxidizing substances in combination with flammable liquids may cause an explosion.

Based on local circumstances, competent authorities may prescribe additional requirements for the availability of means of evacuation.

7.2.4.78 to 7.2.4.99   *(Reserved)*

7.2.5   Additional requirements concerning the operation of vessels

7.2.5.0   *Marking*

7.2.5.0.1   Vessels carrying dangerous goods listed in Table C of Chapter 3.2 shall display the number of blue cones or blue lights indicated in column (19) and in accordance with CEVNI. When because of the cargo carried no marking with blue cones or blue lights is prescribed but the concentration of flammable or toxic gases and vapours in the cargo tanks, given off by the last cargo for which marking was required, is higher than 20% of the LEL or exceeds the national accepted exposure levels, the number of blue cones or blue lights to be carried is determined by the last cargo for which this marking was required.

7.2.5.0.2   When more than one marking should apply to a vessel, the first of the options below shall apply:

–   two blue cones or two blue lights; or

–   one blue cone or one blue light.

7.2.5.0.3   By derogation from 7.2.5.0.1 above, and in accordance with the footnotes to article 3.14 of the CEVNI, the competent authority of a Contracting Party may authorize seagoing vessels temporarily operating in an inland navigation area on the territory of this Contracting Party, the use of the day and night signals prescribed in the Recommendations on the Safe Transport of Dangerous Cargoes and Related Activities in Port Areas adopted by the Maritime Safety Committee of the International Maritime Organization (by night an all-round fixed red light and by day flag "B" of the International Code of Signals), instead of the signals prescribed in 7.2.5.0.1. The competent authority which has taken the initiative with respect to the derogation granted shall notify the Executive Secretary of the UNECE, who shall bring this derogation to the attention of the Administrative Committee.

7.2.5.1   *Mode of navigation*

The competent authorities may impose restrictions on the inclusion of tank vessels in pushed convoys of large dimension.

7.2.5.2   *(Reserved)*

7.2.5.3   *Mooring*

Vessels shall be moored securely, but in such a way that they can be released quickly in an emergency and the electric cables and hose assemblies are not compressed, folded or subject to tensile strain.

7.2.5.4   *Berthing*

7.2.5.4.1   The distances from other vessels to be kept by berthed vessels carrying dangerous goods shall be not less than those prescribed by the Regulations referred to in 1.1.4.6.

7.2.5.4.2   An expert, as required by 7.2.3.15 shall be permanently on board berthed vessels carrying dangerous substances. The competent authority may, however, exempt from this obligation those vessels which are berthed in the harbour basin or in a permitted berthing position.

7.2.5.4.3   Outside the berthing areas specifically designated by the competent authority, the distances to be kept by berthed vessels shall not be less than:

   –   100 m   from residential areas, civil engineering structures or storage tanks, if the vessel is required to be marked with one blue cone or blue light in accordance with column (19) of Table C of Chapter 3.2;

   –   100 m   from civil engineering structures and storage tanks; and 300 m from residential areas if the vessel is required to be marked with two blue cones or two blue lights in accordance with column (19) of Table C of Chapter 3.2.

   While waiting in front of locks or bridges, vessels are allowed to keep distances less than those given above. In no case shall the distance be less than 100 m.

7.2.5.4.4   The competent authority may prescribe distances less than those given in 7.2.5.4.3 above.

7.2.5.5 to 7.2.5.7   *(Reserved)*

7.2.5.8   ***Reporting duty***

7.2.5.8.1   In the States where the reporting duty is in force, the master of the vessel shall provide information in accordance with paragraph 1.1.4.6.1.

7.2.5.8.2 to 7.2.5.8.4   *(Deleted)*

7.2.5.9 to 7.2.9.99   *(Reserved)*

PART 8

Provisions for vessel crews, equipment, operation and documentation

CHAPTER 8.1

GENERAL REQUIREMENTS APPLICABLE TO VESSELS AND EQUIPMENT

8.1.1   *(Reserved)*

8.1.2   Documents

8.1.2.1   In addition to the documents required by other regulations, the following documents shall be kept on board:

(a)   The vessel's certificate of approval referred to in 1.16.1.1 or the vessel's provisional certificate of approval referred to in 1.16.1.3 and the annex referred to in 1.16.1.4;

(b)   Transport documents referred to in 5.4.1 for all dangerous goods carried as cargo on board and, where necessary the container/vehicle packing certificate (see 5.4.2);

(c)   The instructions in writing prescribed in 5.4.3;

(d)   A copy of the ADN with the latest version of its annexed Regulations which may be a copy which can be consulted by electronic means at any time;

(e)   The inspection certificate of the insulation resistance of the electrical installations and equipment prescribed in 8.1.7.1 and the certificates prescribed in 8.1.7.2 concerning the inspection of all installations, equipment and autonomous protection systems and the conformity of the documents required in 8.1.2.2 (e) to (h) and 8.1.2.3 (r) to (v) with the circumstances on board;

(f)   A certificate concerning the inspection of the fire-extinguishing hoses prescribed in 8.1.6.1 and a certificate concerning the inspection of the special equipment prescribed in 8.1.6.3;

(g)   A book in which all required measurement results are recorded;

(h)   A copy of the relevant text of the special authorizations referred to in 1.5 if the transport operation is performed under this/these special authorization(s);

(i)   Means of identification, which include a photograph, for each crew member, in accordance with 1.10.1.4; and

(j)   *(Deleted)*

(k)   For vessels which carry hose assemblies used for loading, unloading or delivering liquefied natural gas for the operation of the vessel, the inspection certificate and the documentation of the calculated maximum load stress prescribed in 8.1.6.2.

8.1.2.2   In addition to the documents prescribed in 8.1.2.1, the following documents shall be carried on board dry cargo vessels:

(a)   The stowage plan prescribed in 7.1.4.11;

(b)   The ADN specialized knowledge certificate prescribed in 8.2.1.2;

(c)   For vessels complying with the additional requirements for double-hull vessels:

  –   a damage-control plan;

  –   the documents concerning intact stability as well as all conditions of intact stability taken into account for the damaged stability calculation in a form the master understands;

  –   the certificate of the recognized classification society (see 9.1.0.88 or 9.2.0.88);

(d)   The inspection certificates concerning the fixed fire extinguishing systems prescribed in 9.1.0.40.2.9;

(e)   A list of or a general plan indicating the fixed installations and equipment suitable for use at least in zone 1 and the installations and equipment complying with 9.1.0.51;

(f)   A list of or a general plan indicating the fixed installations and equipment which are not authorized for use during loading and unloading, during a stay near to or within an onshore assigned zone (marked in red according to 9.1.0.52.2);

(g)   A plan indicating the boundaries of the zones and the location of the electrical and non-electrical equipment installed in the relevant zones intended for use in explosion hazardous areas;

(h)   A list of the installations and equipment referred to under (g) with the following information:

  –   Installation/equipment, location, marking (explosion protection level according to IEC 60079-0, equipment category according to Directive 2014/34/EU[1] or equivalent protection level, explosion group, temperature class, type of protection, test body) in case of electrical equipment for use in zone 1 (alternatively, a copy of the certificate of conformity according to Directive 2014/34/EU[1]);

  –   Installation/equipment, location, marking (explosion protection level according to IEC 60079-0, equipment category according to Directive 2014/34/EU[1] or equivalent protection level, including explosion group and temperature class, type of protection, identification number) in case of electrical equipment for use in zone 2 and in the case of non-electrical equipment for use in zone 1 and zone 2 (alternatively, a copy of the certificate of conformity according to Directive 2014/34/EU[1]);

The documents listed in paragraphs (e) to (h) shall bear the stamp of the competent authority issuing the certificate of approval.

8.1.2.3   In addition to the documents prescribed in 8.1.2.1, the following documents shall be carried on board tank vessels:

(a)   The cargo stowage plan prescribed in 7.2.4.11.2;

(b)   The ADN specialized knowledge certificate prescribed in 8.2.1.2;

---

[1]   *Official Journal of the European Union No. L 96 of 29 March 2014, p. 309.*

(c) For vessels which have to conform to the conditions of damage-control (see 9.3.1.15, 9.3.2.15 or 9.3.3.15)

    –   a damage-control plan;

    –   the documents concerning intact stability as well as all conditions of intact stability taken into account for the damaged stability calculation in a form the master understands; the stability booklet and the proof of the loading instrument having been approved by the recognized classification society;

(d) (*Deleted*)

(e) The certificate of class issued by the recognized classification society prescribed in 9.3.1.8.1, 9.3.2.8.1 or 9.3.3.8.1;

(f) The certificates concerning the inspection of the gas detection systems and the oxygen measuring system prescribed in 8.1.6.3;

(g) The vessel substance list prescribed in 1.16.1.2.5;

(h) The inspection certificate for the hose assemblies for loading and unloading prescribed in 8.1.6.2;

(i) The instructions relating to the loading and unloading flows prescribed in 9.3.2.25.9 or 9.3.3.25.9;

(j) The inspection certificate of the cargo pump-rooms prescribed in 8.1.8;

(k) In the event of the carriage of goods having a melting point ≥ 0 °C, heating instructions;

(l) (*Deleted*)

(m) The registration document referred to in 8.1.11;

(n) For the carriage of refrigerated substances, the instruction required in 7.2.3.28;

(o) The certificate concerning the refrigeration system, prescribed in 9.3.1.27.10, 9.3.2.27.10 or 9.3.3.27.10;

(p) The inspection certificates concerning the fixed fire extinguishing systems prescribed in 9.3.1.40.2.9, 9.3.2.40.2.9 or 9.3.3.40.2.9; and

(q) When carrying refrigerated liquefied gases and the temperature is not controlled in accordance with 9.3.1.24.1 (a) and 9.3.1.24.1 (c), the determination of the holding time (7.2.4.16.16, 7.2.4.16.17 and documentation on the heat transmission coefficient);

(r) A list of or a general plan indicating the fixed installations and equipment suitable to be used at least in zone 1 and the installations and equipment complying with 9.3.x.51;

(s) A list of or a general plan indicating the fixed installations and equipment which are not authorized for use during loading and unloading, degassing or during a stay near to or within an onshore assigned zone (marked in red according to 9.3.1.52.3, 9.3.2.52.3 or 9.3.3.52.3);

(t) A plan approved by a recognized classification society indicating the boundaries of the zones and the location of the electrical and non-electrical equipment installed in the relevant zone intended to be used in explosion hazardous areas, as well as autonomous protection systems;

(u)   A list of the installations/equipment referred to under (t) and of the autonomous protection systems, with the following information:

–   Installations/equipment, location, marking (explosion protection level according to IEC 60079-0, equipment category according to Directive 2014/34/EU[1] or at least equivalent), including explosion group and temperature class, type of protection and test body, in the case of electrical equipment for use in zone 0 or zone 1 and, in the case of non-electrical equipment for use in zone 0; (alternatively, a copy of the inspection certificate, for example the declaration of conformity under Directive 2014/34/EU[1]);

–   Installation/equipment, location, marking (explosion protection level according to IEC 60079-0, equipment category according to Directive 2014/34/EU[1] or equivalent protection level, including explosion group and temperature class, type of protection, identification number) in the case of electrical equipment for use in zone 2 and in the case of non-electrical equipment for use in zone 1 and zone 2 (alternatively, a copy of the inspection certificate, for example, the certificate of conformity according to Directive 2014/34/EU[1]);

–   Self-protection system, place of installation, marking (explosion group/subgroup):

(v)   A list of or general plan indicating the fixed installations and equipment installed outside the explosion hazardous areas that may be used during loading, unloading, degassing, berthing or during a stay in the immediate vicinity of or within an onshore assigned zone, if not referred to in (r) and (u).

The documents listed in (r) to (v) shall bear the stamp of the competent authority issuing the certificate of approval.".

(w)   The certificates required under 3.2.3.1, Explanations concerning Table C, explanatory note for column (20), remark 12 subparagraphs (p) and (q), if appropriate;

(x)   The certificates required under 3.2.3.1, Explanations concerning Table C, explanatory note for column (20), remark 33 subparagraphs (i), (n) and (o), if appropriate.

8.1.2.4   The instructions in writing referred to in 5.4.3 shall be handed to the master before loading. They shall be kept readily at hand in the wheelhouse.

On board dry cargo vessels, the transport documents shall be handed to the master before loading and on board tank vessels they shall be handed to him after loading and before the journey commences.

8.1.2.5   (*Reserved*)

8.1.2.6   The presence on board of the certificate of approval is not required in the case of pusher barges which are not carrying dangerous goods, provided that the following additional particulars are indicated, in identical lettering, on the plate furnished by CEVNI:

Number of the certificate of approval: …

issued by: …

valid until: …

---

[1]   *Official Journal of the European Union No. L 96 of 29 March 2014, p. 309.*

The barge–owner shall thereafter keep the certificate of approval and the annex covered by 1.16.1.4 in his possession.

The similarity of the particulars on the plate and those contained in the certificate of approval shall be certified by a competent authority which shall affix its stamp to the plate.

8.1.2.7   The presence on board of the certificate of approval is not required in the case of dry cargo barges or tank barges carrying dangerous goods provided that the plate furnished by CEVNI is supplemented by a second metal or plastic plate reproducing by photo–optical means a copy of the entire certificate of approval. A photo–optical copy of the annex referred to in 1.16.1.4 is not required.

The barge–owner shall thereafter keep the certificate of approval and the annex referred to in 1.16.1.4 in his possession.

The similarity of the particulars on the plate and the certificate of approval shall be certified by a competent authority which shall affix its stamp to the plate.

8.1.2.8   All documents shall be on board in a language the master is able to read and understand. If that language is not English, French or German, all documents, with the exception of the copy of ADN with its annexed Regulations and those for which the Regulations include special provisions concerning languages, shall be on board also in English, French or German, unless agreements concluded between the countries concerned in the transport operation provide otherwise.

8.1.2.9   8.1.2.1 (b), 8.1.2.1 (g), 8.1.2.4 and 8.1.2.5 do not apply to oil separator vessels or supply vessels. 8.1.2.1 (c) does not apply to oil separator vessels.

8.1.3   (*Reserved*)

8.1.4   Fire-extinguishing arrangements

In addition to the fire-extinguishing appliances prescribed in the Regulations referred to in 1.1.4.6, each vessel shall be equipped with at least two additional hand fire-extinguishers having the same capacity. The fire-extinguishing agent contained in these additional hand fire-extinguishers shall be suitable for fighting fires involving the dangerous goods carried.

8.1.5   Special equipment

8.1.5.1   Insofar as the provisions of Chapter 3.2, Tables A or C require, the following equipment shall be available on board:

PP: for each member of the crew, a pair of protective goggles, a pair of protective gloves, a protective suit and a suitable pair of protective shoes (or protective boots, if necessary). On board tank vessels, protective boots are required in all cases;

EP: a suitable escape device for each person on board;

EX: a gas detector;

TOX: a toximeter appropriate for the current and previous cargo, with the accessories and instructions for its use;

A: a breathing apparatus ambient air-dependent.

8.1.5.2   For operations carried out in explosion hazardous areas or during stay in the vicinity of or within a shoreside assigned zone only low-sparking hand-tools (e.g. chromium vanadium steel screwdrivers and wrenches) shall be used.

8.1.5.3   For pushed convoys or side–by–side formations under way, it shall be sufficient, however, if the pusher tug or the vessel propelling the formation is equipped with the special equipment referred to in 8.1.5.1 above, when this is required in Chapter 3.2, Tables A or C.

8.1.6   Checking and inspection of equipment

8.1.6.1   Hand fire-extinguishers and fire-extinguishing hoses shall be inspected at least once every two years by persons authorized for this purpose by the competent authority. Proof of inspection shall be affixed to the hand fire-extinguishers. A certificate concerning the inspection of fire extinguishing hoses shall be carried on board.

8.1.6.2   Hose assemblies used for loading, unloading or delivering products for the operation of the vessel (other than liquified natural gas) and residual cargo shall comply with European standard EN 12115:2011-04 (Rubber and thermoplastics hoses and hose assemblies) or EN 13765:2010-08 (Thermoplastic multilayer (non-vulcanized) hoses and hose assemblies) or EN ISO 10380:2003-10 (Corrugated metal hoses and hose assemblies). They shall be checked and inspected in accordance with table A.1 of standard EN 12115:2011-04 or table K.1 of standard EN 13765:2010-08 or paragraph 7 of standard EN ISO 10380:2003-10 at least once a year, according to the manufacturer's instructions, by persons authorized for this purpose by the competent authority. A certificate concerning this inspection shall be carried on board.

Hose assemblies used for loading, unloading or delivering liquefied natural gas for the operation of the vessel shall comply with part 5.5.2 of ISO 20519:2017 (Ships and marine technology – Specification for bunkering of liquefied natural gas fuelled vessels) and shall be checked and inspected at least once a year according to the manufacturer's instructions. A certificate concerning this inspection and the documentation of the calculated maximum load stress shall be carried on board.

8.1.6.3   The proper functioning of the special equipment referred to in 8.1.5.1, the gas detection systems referred to in 9.3.1.12.4, 9.3.2.12.4 and 9.3.3.12.4 and the oxygen measuring system referred to in 9.3.1.17.6, 9.3.2.17.6 and 9.3.3.17.6 must be checked in accordance with the instructions of the manufacturer by persons authorized for this purpose by the manufacturer. A certificate concerning the latest inspection of the special equipment must be carried on board. The certificate must provide details of the result and date of the checks.

The gas detection systems and the oxygen measuring systems must also be inspected by a recognized classification society whenever the certificate of approval is renewed and during the third year of validity of the certificate. This inspection must include at least a general visual inspection of the installations and confirmation that the checks mentioned in the preceding sentence have been carried out.

An inspection certificate from the recognized classification society concerning the latest inspection conducted must be carried on board. All inspection certificates must provide at least the abovementioned details regarding the inspection, its results and the date on which it was conducted.

8.1.6.4   The measuring instruments prescribed in 8.1.5.1 shall be checked each time before use by the expert in accordance with the instructions for use.

8.1.6.5 and 8.1.6.6   *(Deleted)*

8.1.7   **Installations, equipment and autonomous protection systems**

8.1.7.1   *Electrical installations and equipment*

The insulation resistance of the fixed electrical installations and equipment and their earthing shall be inspected whenever the certificate of approval is renewed and, in addition, within the third year from the date of issue of the certificate of approval by a person authorized for this purpose by the competent authority.

A certificate concerning this inspection shall be carried on board.

8.1.7.2   *Installations and equipment intended for use in explosion hazardous areas, "limited explosion risk" type equipment, installations and equipment complying with 9.3.1.51, 9.3.2.51 and 9.3.3.51 and autonomous protective systems*

Such installations, equipment and autonomous protective systems and their compliance with the documents referred to in 8.1.2.2 (e) to (h) or 8.1.2.3 (r) to (v) in respect of the situation on board shall be inspected whenever the certificate of approval is renewed and, in addition, within the third year from the date of issue of the certificate of approval, by the classification society that classified the vessel or by a person authorized for this purpose by the competent authority. A certificate concerning this inspection shall be carried on board.

The marking on the installations and equipment intended for use in explosion hazardous areas showing that they are appropriate for use in explosion hazardous areas and marking on autonomous protection systems with their conditions of use should remain in place throughout the period of use on board.

The manufacturer's instruction on flame arresters or high-velocity vent valves/safety valves may require a more regular frequency of inspection.

8.1.7.3   *Repair of explosion-protected installations and equipment and autonomous protection systems*

Repair of explosion-protected installations and equipment and autonomous protection systems is permitted only by an expert from a specialized company. Following repairs, a certificate must be issued attesting to their reusability in explosion hazardous areas. The certificate must be available on board.

8.1.8   **Inspection of the cargo pump-rooms of tank vessels**

The cargo pump-room must be inspected by a recognized classification society whenever the certificate of approval is renewed and during the third year of validity of the certificate.

The inspection must include at least the following:

–   An inspection of the entire system, focusing on its state, corrosion, leaks and any unauthorized modifications;

–   A general visual inspection of the state of the gas detection system in the cargo pump-room;

–   Confirmation of the presence of the certificate referred to in 8.1.6.3 issued by the manufacturer or an authorized person.

The inspection certificates signed by the recognized classification society concerning the inspection of the cargo pump-room must be carried on board and provide at least the abovementioned details regarding the inspection, its results and the date on which it was conducted.

8.1.9 and 8.1.10   *(Deleted)*

8.1.11   **Register of operations during carriage relating to the carriage of UN 1203**

Tank vessels accepted for the carriage of UN No. 1203 petrol shall have on board a register of operations during carriage. This register may consist of other documents containing the information required. This register or these other documents shall be kept on board for not less than three months and cover at least the last three cargoes.

CHAPTER 8.2

REQUIREMENTS CONCERNING TRAINING

8.2.1   **General requirements concerning training of experts**

8.2.1.1   An expert shall not be less than 18 years of age.

8.2.1.2   An expert is a person who has a special knowledge of the ADN. Proof of this knowledge shall be furnished by means of a certificate from a competent authority or from an agency recognized by the competent authority.

This certificate shall be issued to persons who, after training, have passed a qualifying ADN examination.

8.2.1.3   The experts referred to in 8.2.1.2 shall take part in a basic training course. Training shall take place in the context of classes approved by the competent authority. The primordial objective of the training is to make the experts aware of the hazards of the carriage of dangerous goods and provide them with the necessary basic knowledge to reduce the dangers of an incident to a minimum, to enable them to take the necessary measures to ensure their own safety, general safety and the protection of the environment and to limit the consequences of the incident. This training, which shall include individual practical exercises, takes the form of a basic course; it shall cover at least the objectives referred to in 8.2.2.3.1.1 and in 8.2.2.3.1.2 or 8.2.2.3.1.3.

8.2.1.4   After five years, the certificate shall be renewed by the competent authority or by a body recognized by it if the expert furnishes proof, of successful completion of a refresher course taken in the last year prior to the expiry of the certificate, covering at least the objectives referred to in 8.2.2.3.1.1 and in 8.2.2.3.1.2 or 8.2.2.3.1.3 and comprising current new developments in particular. A refresher course shall be considered to have been successfully completed if a final written test conducted by the course organizer under 8.2.2.2 has been passed. The test can be retaken two times during the validity of the certificate. If the test is not passed after it is retaken two times then, within the period of validity of the certificate, the refresher course may be taken again.

8.2.1.5   Experts for the carriage of gases shall take part in a specialization course covering at least the objectives referred to in 8.2.2.3.3.1. Training shall take place in the context of classes approved by the competent authority. An expert certificate shall be issued to persons who, after training, have successfully passed an examination concerning the carriage of gases and have produced evidence of not less than one year's work on board a type G vessel during a period of two years prior to or following the examination.

8.2.1.6   After five years, the certificate shall be renewed by the competent authority or by a body recognized by it if the expert on the carriage of gases furnishes proof:

    –   that during the year preceding the expiry of the certificate, he has participated in a refresher course covering at least the objectives referred to in 8.2.2.3.3.1 and comprising current new developments in particular; or

    –   that during the previous two years he has performed a period of work of not less than one year on board a type G tank vessel.

8.2.1.7   Experts for the carriage of chemicals shall take part in a specialization course covering at least the objectives referred to in 8.2.2.3.3.2. Training shall take place in the context of classes approved by the competent authority. An expert certificate shall be issued to persons who, after training, have successfully passed an examination concerning the carriage of chemicals and have produced evidence of not less than one year's work on board a type C vessel during a period of two years prior to or following the examination.

8.2.1.8   After five years, the certificate shall be renewed by the competent authority or by a body recognized by it if the expert on the carriage of chemicals furnishes proof:,

–   that during the year preceding the expiry of the certificate, he has participated in a refresher course covering at least the objectives referred to in 8.2.2.3.3.2 and comprising current new developments in particular, or

–   that during the previous two years he had performed a period of work of not less than one year on board a type C tank vessel.

8.2.1.9   The document attesting training and experience in accordance with the requirements of Chapter V of the International Convention on Standards of Training, Certification and Watchkeeping for Seafarers of 7 July 1978 (STCW Convention), as amended; on liquefied gas tankers shall be equivalent to the certificate referred to in 8.2.1.5, provided it has been recognized by a competent authority. No more than five years shall have passed since the date of issue or renewal of such a document.

8.2.1.10   The document attesting training and experience in accordance with the requirements of Chapter V of the International Convention on Standards of Training, Certification and Watchkeeping for Seafarers of 7 July 1978 (STCW Convention), as amended; on chemical tankers shall be equivalent to the certificate referred to in 8.2.1.7, provided it has been recognized by a competent authority. No more than five years shall have passed since the date of issue or renewal of such a document.

8.2.1.11   *(Deleted)*

8.2.2   Special requirements for the training of experts

8.2.2.1   Theoretical knowledge and practical abilities shall be acquired as a result of training in theory and practical exercises. The theoretical knowledge shall be tested by an examination. During the refresher course exercises and tests shall ensure that the participant takes an active role in the training.

8.2.2.2   The training organizer shall ensure that training instructors have a good knowledge of the subject and shall take into account the latest developments concerning the Regulations and the requirements for training in the transport of dangerous goods. Teaching shall relate closely to practice. In accordance with the approval, the teaching syllabus shall be drawn up on the basis of the objectives referred to in 8.2.2.3.1.1 to 8.2.2.3.1.3 and in 8.2.2.3.3.1 or 8.2.2.3.3.2. Basic training and their refresher courses shall comprise individual practical exercises (see 8.2.2.3.1.1).

8.2.2.3   *Organization of training*

Initial basic training and the refresher courses shall be organized in the context of basic courses (see 8.2.2.3.1) and if necessary specialization courses (see 8.2.2.3.3). The courses referred to in 8.2.2.3.1 may comprise three variants: transport of dry cargo, transport in tank vessels and a combination of transport of dry cargo and transport in tank vessels.

8.2.2.3.1   *Basic course*

Basic course on the transport of dry cargo

Prior training: none

Knowledge: ADN in general, except Chapter 3.2, Table C, Chapters 7.2 and 9.3

Authorized for: dry cargo vessel

Training: general 8.2.2.3.1.1 and dry cargo vessels 8.2.2.3.1.2

Basic course on transport by tank vessels

Prior training: none

Knowledge: ADN in general, except Chapter 3.2, Table A, Chapters 7.1, 9.1 and 9.2

Authorized for: tank vessels for the transport of substances for which a type N tank vessel is prescribed

Training: general 8.2.2.3.1.1 and tank vessels 8.2.2.3.1.3

Basic course – combination of transport of dry cargo and transport in tank vessels

Prior training: none

Knowledge: ADN in general

Authorized for: dry cargo vessels and tank vessels for the transport of substances for which a type N tank vessel is prescribed

Training: general 8.2.2.3.1.1, dry cargo vessels 8.2.2.3.1.2 and tank vessels 8.2.2.3.1.3

8.2.2.3.1.1   The general part of the basic training course shall comprise at least the following objectives:

General:

–   Objectives and structure of ADN.

Construction and equipment:

–   Construction and equipment of vessels subject to ADN.

Measurement techniques:

–   Measurements of toxicity, oxygen content and the concentration of flammable gases.

Knowledge of products:

–   Classification and hazard characteristics of the dangerous goods.

Loading, unloading and transport:

–   Loading, unloading, general service requirements and requirements relating to transport.

Documents:

–   Documents which must be on board during transport.

Hazards and measures of prevention:

–   General safety measures.

Practical exercises:

– Practical exercises, in particular with respect to entry into spaces, use of fire-extinguishers, fire–fighting equipment and personal protective equipment as well as gas detectors, oxygen meters and toximeters.

Stability:

– parameters of relevance to stability;

– heeling moments;

– exemplary calculations;

– damage stability, intermediate states and final state of flooding;

– influence of free surfaces;

– evaluation of stability on the basis of existing stability criteria (text of Regulations);

– evaluation of intact stability with the help of the lever arm curve

– application of loading instruments;

– use of loading instruments;

– application of the stability booklet according to 9.3.13.3.

Basics of explosion protection:

– according to the definition of 'explosion protection';

– selection of appropriate devices and installations.

8.2.2.3.1.2   The "dry cargo vessels" part of the basic training course shall comprise at least the following objectives:

Construction and equipment:

– Construction and equipment of dry cargo vessels.

Treatment of holds and adjacent spaces:

– degassing, cleaning, maintenance,

– ventilation of holds and spaces outside the protected area.

Loading, unloading and transport:

– loading, unloading, general service and transport requirements,

– labelling of packages.

Documents:

– documents which must be on board during transport.

Hazards and measures of prevention:

- general safety measures,

- personal protective and safety equipment.

8.2.2.3.1.3   The "tank vessel" part of the basic training course shall comprise at least the following objectives:

Construction and equipment:

- construction and equipment of tank vessels,

- ventilation,

- loading and unloading systems.

Treatment of cargo tanks and adjacent spaces:

- degassing into the atmosphere and to reception facilities, cleaning, maintenance,

- heating and cooling of cargo,

- handling of receptacles for residual products.

Measurement and sampling techniques:

- measurements of toxicity, oxygen content and the concentration of flammable gases.

- sampling.

Loading, unloading and transport:

- loading, unloading, general service and transport requirements.

Documents:

- documents which must be on board during transport.

Hazards and measures of prevention:

- prevention and general safety measures,

- spark formation,

- personal protective and safety equipment,

- fires and fire–fighting.

Basics of explosion protection:

- according to the definition of 'explosion protection';

- selection of appropriate devices and installations.

8.2.2.3.2   *Refresher training courses*

Refresher training course on transport of dry cargo

Prior training: valid ADN "dry cargo vessels" or combined "dry cargo vessels/tank vessels" certificate

Knowledge: ADN in general, except Chapter 3.2, Table C, Chapters 7.2 and 9.3

Authorized for: dry cargo vessel

Training: general 8.2.2.3.1.1 and dry cargo vessels 8.2.2.3.1.2

Refresher training course on transport in tank vessels

Prior training: valid ADN "tank vessels" or combined "dry cargo vessels/tank vessels" certificate

Knowledge: ADN in general, except Chapter 3.2, Table A, Chapters 7.1, 9.1 and 9.2

Authorized for: tank vessels for the transport of substances for which a type N tank vessel is prescribed

Training: general 8.2.2.3.1.1 and tank vessels 8.2.2.3.1.3

Refresher training course – combination of transport of dry cargo and transport in tank vessels

Prior training: valid ADN combined "dry cargo vessels and tank vessels" certificate

Knowledge: ADN in general

Authorized for: dry cargo vessels and tank vessels for the transport of substances for which a type N tank vessel is prescribed

Training: general 8.2.2.3.1.1, dry cargo vessels 8.2.2.3.1.2 and tank vessels 8.2.2.3.1.3

8.2.2.3.3   *Specialization courses*

Specialization course on gases

Prior training: valid ADN "tank vessels" or combined "dry cargo vessels/tank vessels" certificate

Knowledge: ADN, in particular knowledge relating to loading, transport, unloading and handling of gases

Authorization for: tank vessels for the transport of substances for which a type G tank vessel is required and transport in type G of substances for which a type C is required with cargo tank design 1 required in column (7) of Table C of Chapter 3.2

Training: gases 8.2.2.3.3.1

Specialization course on chemicals

Prior training:	valid ADN "tank vessels" or combined "dry cargo vessels/tank vessels" certificate
Knowledge:	ADN, in particular knowledge relating to loading, transport, unloading and handling of chemicals
Authorized for:	tank vessels for the transport of substances for which a type C tank vessel is required
Training:	chemicals 8.2.2.3.3.2

8.2.2.3.3.1   The specialization course on gases shall comprise at least the following objectives:

Knowledge of physics and chemistry:

–   laws of gases, e.g. Boyle, Gay–Lussac and fundamental law

–   partial pressures and mixtures, e.g. definitions and simple calculations, pressure increase and gas release from cargo tanks

–   Avogadro's number and calculation of masses of ideal gas and application of the mass formula

–   mass density, relative density and volume of liquids, e.g. mass density, relative density, volume in terms of temperature increase and maximum degree of filling

–   critical pressure and temperature

–   polymerization, e.g. theoretical and practical questions, conditions of carriage

–   vaporization, condensation, e.g. definition, liquid volume and vapour volume ratio

–   mixtures, e.g. vapour pressure, composition and hazard characteristics

–   chemical bonds and formulae.

Practice:

–   flushing of cargo tanks, e.g. flushing in the event of a change of cargo, addition of air to the cargo, methods of flushing (degassing) before entering cargo tanks

–   sampling

–   danger of explosion

–   health risks

–   gas concentration measures, e.g. which apparatus to use and how to use it

–   monitoring of closed spaces and entry to these spaces

–   certificates for the status of being gas free and permitted work

–   degree of filling and over–filling

–   safety installations

–　pumps and compressors

–　handling refrigerated liquefied gases.

Emergency measures:

–　physical injury, e.g. substances on the skin, breathing in gas, assistance

–　irregularities relating to the cargo, e.g. leak in a connection, over-filling, polymerization and hazards in the vicinity of the vessel.

8.2.2.3.3.2　　The specialization course on chemicals shall comprise at least the following objectives:

Knowledge of physics and chemistry:

–　chemical products, e.g. molecules, atoms, physical state, acids, bases, oxidation

–　mass density, relative density, pressure and volume of liquids, e.g. mass density, relative density, volume and pressure in terms of temperature increase, maximum degree of filling

–　critical temperature

–　polymerization, e.g. theoretical and practical questions, conditions of carriage

–　mixtures, e.g. vapour pressure, composition and hazard characteristics

–　chemical bonds and formulae.

Practice:

–　cleaning of cargo tanks, e.g. degasing, washing, residual cargo and receptacles for residual products

–　loading and unloading, e.g. venting piping systems, rapid closing devices, effects of temperature

–　sampling

–　danger of explosion

–　health risks

–　gas concentration measures, e.g. which apparatus to use and how to use it

–　monitoring of closed spaces and entry to these spaces

–　certificates for the status of being gas free and permitted work

–　degree of filling and over–filling

–　safety installations

–　pumps and compressors.

Emergency measures:

– physical injury, e.g. contact with the cargo, breathing in gas, assistance

– irregularities relating to the cargo, e.g. leak in a connection, over–filling, polymerization and hazards in the vicinity of the vessel.

8.2.2.3.4 *Refresher courses*

Refresher course on gases

Prior training:	valid ADN "gases" and "tank vessels" certificate or combined "dry cargo/tank vessels" certificate
Knowledge:	ADN, in particular, loading, transport, unloading and handling of gases
Authorization for:	tank vessels for the transport of substances for which a type G tank vessel is required and transport in type G of substances for which a type C is required with cargo tank design 1 required in column (7) of Table C of Chapter 3.2
Training:	gases 8.2.2.3.3.1

Refresher course on chemicals

Prior training:	valid ADN "chemicals" and "tank vessels" certificate or combined "dry cargo/tank vessels" certificate
Knowledge:	ADN, in particular, loading, transport, unloading and handling of gases
Authorization for:	tank vessels for the transport of substances for which a type C tank vessel is required
Training:	chemicals 8.2.2.3.3.2

8.2.2.4 Planning of refresher and specialization courses

The following minimum periods of training shall be observed:

Basic "dry cargo vessels course"	32 lessons of 45 minutes each
Basic "tank vessels" course	32 lessons of 45 minutes each
Basic combined course	40 lessons of 45 minutes each
Specialization course on gases	16 lessons of 45 minutes each
Specialization course on chemicals	16 lessons of 45 minutes each

Each day of training may comprise not more than eight lessons.

If the theoretical training is by correspondence, equivalences to the above–mentioned lessons shall be determined. Training by correspondence shall be completed within a period of nine months.

Approximately 30% of basic training shall be devoted to practical exercises. Practical exercises shall, where possible, be undertaken during the period of theoretical training; in any event, they shall be completed not later than three months following the completion of theoretical training.

8.2.2.5   *Planning of refresher course*

The refresher course shall take place before the expiry of the deadline referred to in 8.2.1.4, 8.2.1.6 or 8.2.1.8.

The following minimum periods of training shall be observed:

Basic refresher course:

–	dry cargo vessels	16 lessons of 45 minutes each
–	tank vessels	16 lessons of 45 minutes each
–	combined dry cargo vessels and tank vessels	16 lessons of 45 minutes each

Specialization refresher course on gases	8 lessons of 45 minutes each
Specialization refresher course on chemicals	8 lessons of 45 minutes each

Each day of training may comprise not more than eight lessons.

Approximately 30% of basic training shall be devoted to practical exercises. Practical exercises shall, where possible, be undertaken during the period of theoretical training; in any event, they shall be completed not later than three months following the completion of theoretical training. The proportion of stability training in the refresher course shall amount to at least 2 lessons.

8.2.2.6   *Approval of training courses*

8.2.2.6.1   Training courses shall be approved by the competent authority.

8.2.2.6.2   Approval shall be granted only on written application.

8.2.2.6.3   Applications for approval shall be accompanied by:

(a)   the detailed course curriculum showing the course topics and the length of time to be devoted to them, as well as the teaching methods envisaged;

(b)   the roster of training instructors, listing their qualifications and the subjects to be taught by each one;

(c)   information on classrooms and teaching materials, as well as on the facilities available for practical exercises;

(d)   enrolment requirements, e.g. the number of participants;

(e)   detailed plan for final tests, including, if necessary, the infrastructure and organisation of electronic examinations in accordance with 8.2.2.7.1.7, if these are to be carried out.

8.2.2.6.4   The competent authority shall be responsible for monitoring training courses and examinations.

8.2.2.6.5   The approval comprises the following conditions, <u>inter alia</u>:

(a)   training courses shall conform to the information accompanying the application for approval;

(b)   the competent authority may send inspectors to attend training courses and examinations;

(c)   the timetables for the various training courses shall be notified in advance to the competent authority.

Approval shall be granted in writing for a limited period. It may be withdrawn in the event of failure to comply with the conditions of approval.

8.2.2.6.6   The approval document shall indicate whether the course in question is a basic training course, a specialization course or a refresher course.

8.2.2.6.7   If, after approval is granted, the training body wishes to change conditions affecting the approval, it shall seek the prior agreement of the competent authority. This provision shall apply in particular to amendments to syllabuses.

8.2.2.6.8   Training courses shall take account of the current developments in the various subjects taught. The course organizer shall be responsible for ensuring that recent developments are brought to the attention of, and properly understood by, training instructors.

8.2.2.7   *Examinations and final tests*

8.2.2.7.0   The examination shall be organized by the competent authority or by an examining body designated by the competent authority. The examining body shall not be a training provider.

The examining body shall be designated in writing. This approval may be of limited duration and should be based on the following criteria:

–   Competence of the examining body;

–   Specifications of the form of the examinations the examining body is proposing, including, if necessary, the infrastructure and organisation of electronic examinations in accordance with 8.2.2.7.1.7, if these are to be carried out;

–   Measures intended to ensure that examinations are impartial;

–   Independence of the body from all natural or legal persons employing ADN experts.

8.2.2.7.1   *Basic training courses*

8.2.2.7.1.1   After initial training an ADN basic training examination shall be taken. This examination shall be held either immediately after the training or within six months following the completion of such training.

8.2.2.7.1.2   In the examination the candidate shall furnish evidence that, in accordance with the basic training course, he has the knowledge, understanding and capabilities required of an expert on board a vessel.

8.2.2.7.1.3   The Administrative Committee shall establish a catalogue of questions comprising the objectives set out in 8.2.2.3.1.1 to 8.2.2.3.1.3 and a directive on the use of the catalogue of questions.[1] The examination questions shall be selected from this list. The candidate shall not have advance knowledge of the questions selected.

8.2.2.7.1.4   The model attached to the directive on the use of the catalogue of questions is to be used to compile the examination questions.

8.2.2.7.1.5   The examination shall be written. Candidates shall be asked 30 questions. The examination shall last 60 minutes. It is deemed to have been passed if at least 25 of the 30 questions have been answered correctly.

8.2.2.7.1.6   The competent authority or an examining body designated by the competent authority shall invigilate every examination. Any manipulation and deception shall be ruled out as far as possible. Authentication of candidates shall be ensured.

The use in the written test of documentation other than the texts of regulations on dangerous goods, CEVNI and related police regulations, is not permitted. Non–programmable pocket calculators are authorized for use during specialization courses and shall be supplied by the competent authority or by the examining body designated by the competent authority.

Examination documents (questions and answers) shall be recorded and kept as a print–out or electronically as a file.

8.2.2.7.1.7   Written examinations may be performed, in whole or in part, as electronic examinations, where the answers are recorded and evaluated using electronic data processing (EDP) processes, provided the following conditions are met:

(a)   The hardware and software shall be checked and accepted by the competent authority or by the examining body designated by the competent authority.

(b)   Electronic media may be used only if provided by the competent authority or by the examining body designated by the competent authority.

(c)   Proper technical functioning shall be ensured. Arrangements as to whether and how the examination can be continued shall be made in the case of a failure of the devices and applications. No aids shall be available on the input devices (e.g. electronic search function); the electronic data processing equipment provided shall not allow the candidates to communicate with any other device during the examination.

(d)   There shall be no means of a candidate introducing further data to the electronic media provided; the candidate may only answer the questions posed.

(e)   The final inputs of each candidate shall be logged. The determination of the results shall be transparent.

8.2.2.7.2   *Specialization course on gases and chemicals*

8.2.2.7.2.1   Candidates who are successful in the ADN basic training examination may apply for enrolment in a "gases" and/or "chemicals" specialization course, to be followed by an examination. The examination shall be based on the Administrative Committee's list of questions.

---

[1]   *Note by the secretariat: the catalogue of questions and the directive for its application are available on the website of the secretariat of the United Nations Economic Commission for Europe (http://www.unece.org/trans/danger/publi/adn/catalog_of_questions.html.*

8.2.2.7.2.2 During the examination the candidate shall furnish proof that, in accordance with the "gases" and/or "chemicals" specialization course, he has the knowledge, understanding and capabilities required of the expert on board vessels carrying gases or chemicals, respectively.

8.2.2.7.2.3 The Administrative Committee shall prepare a catalogue of questions for the examination, comprising the objectives set out in 8.2.2.3.3.1 or 8.2.2.3.3.2 and a directive on the use of the catalogue of questions.[1] The examination questions shall be selected from the list. The candidate shall not have advance knowledge of the questions selected.

8.2.2.7.2.4 The model attached to the directive on the use of the catalogue of questions is to be used to compile the examination questions.

8.2.2.7.2.5 The examination shall be written.

The candidate is to be asked 30 multiple–choice questions and one substantive question. The examination shall last a total of 150 minutes, of which 60 minutes for the multiple–choice questions and 90 minutes for the substantive questions.

The examination shall be marked out of a total of 60, of which 30 marks will go to the multiple–choice questions (one mark per question) and 30 to the substantive question (the distribution of marks is left to the appreciation of the competent authority). A total of 44 marks must be achieved to pass. However, not less than 20 marks must be obtained in each part. If the candidate obtains 44 but does not achieve 20 in one part, the part in question may be resat once.

The provisions of 8.2.2.7.1.6 and 8.2.2.7.1.7 shall apply by analogy.

8.2.2.7.3 *Refresher training course*

8.2.2.7.3.1 At the end of the refresher course in accordance with paragraph 8.2.1.4, the course organizer shall conduct a test.

8.2.2.7.3.2 The test shall be in writing. Candidates shall be asked 20 multiple–choice questions. At the end of every refresher course, a fresh question paper shall be prepared. The test shall last 40 minutes. It shall be deemed to have been passed if at least 16 of the 20 questions have been answered correctly.

8.2.2.7.3.3 The provisions of 8.2.2.7.1.2, 8.2.2.7.1.3, 8.2.2.1.7.6 and 8.2.2.1.7.7 shall apply to the administration of the tests (outside the provisions of the directive on the use of the catalogue of questions for examining authorities and bodies).

8.2.2.7.3.4 The course organizer shall deliver to successful candidates a written certificate for presentation to the competent authority under paragraph 8.2.2.8.

8.2.2.7.3.5 The course organizer shall keep test papers of candidates for five years from the date of the test.

8.2.2.8 **ADN specialized knowledge certificate**

8.2.2.8.1 The issue and renewal of the ADN specialized knowledge certificate conforming to the model in 8.6.2 shall be the responsibility of the competent authority or a body authorized by such authority.

---

[1] *Note by the secretariat: the catalogue of questions and the directive for its application are available on the website of the secretariat of the United Nations Economic Commission for Europe (http://www.unece.org/trans/danger/publi/adn/catalog_of_questions.html).*

8.2.2.8.2 The certificate's dimensions shall be in accordance with ISO/IEC 7810:2003, card size ID-1, and it shall be made of plastic. The colour shall be white, with black lettering. The certificate shall include an additional security feature such as a hologram, UV printing or engraved patterns. Its text shall be in the language(s) or in one of the languages of the State whose competent authority has issued it. If none of these languages is English, French or German, the title of the certificate, the title of item 8 and the titles on the back, and if applicable the additions under "tank vessels" or "dry cargo vessels" shall also be drawn up in English, French or German.

8.2.2.8.3 Certificates shall be issued to:

(a) candidates who have met the conditions of the second sentence of 8.2.1.2 and 8.2.1.3 (basic training course); they shall be valid for five years from the date when the examination has been passed following basic training;

(b) Candidates who meet the conditions of 8.2.1.5 or of 8.2.1.7 ("gas" or "chemicals" specialization course); in this case, a new certificate shall be issued containing certificates for the basic training and specialization courses. The new certificate to be issued shall be valid for five years from the date when the examination has been passed following basic training.

8.2.2.8.4 The certificate shall be renewed:

(a) when the proof required under 8.2.1.4 is provided (basic training); the new duration of validity shall begin on the expiry date of the previous certificate. If the test has been taken more than one year before the certificate's expiry date, it shall begin on the date of the certificate of participation in the course;

(b) when the proof required under 8.2.1.6 and 8.2.1.8 are provided ("gas" or "chemicals" specialization courses). In this case, a new certificate containing all the certificates relating to the basic training and specialization courses shall be issued. The new certificate to be issued shall have a period of validity of five years from the date of the successfully completed refresher course for basic training. When the refresher course is taken in the year before the certificate's expiry date, the new period of validity shall begin on the expiry date of the previous certificate; otherwise it shall begin on the date of the certificate of participation in the course.

8.2.2.8.5 If the refresher course for the renewal of the certificate has not been fully and successfully completed before the expiry of the period of validity of the certificate, or if the work on board a vessel for one year has not been certified during the two years preceding the certificate's expiry, a new certificate shall be issued, for which participation in a further initial basic training course and an examination in accordance with 8.2.2.7 shall be required.

8.2.2.8.6 If a new certificate is issued in accordance with 8.2.2.8.3 (b) or a certificate is renewed in accordance with 8.2.2.8.4 and the previous certificate had been issued by another authority or by a body authorized to do so by such an authority, the issuing authority or body approved by that authority that has issued the previous certificate shall be informed without delay.

8.2.2.8.7 Contracting Parties shall provide the UNECE secretariat with an example of the national model for any certificate intended for issue in accordance with this section. Contracting Parties shall also provide explanatory notes to enable the verification of conformity of certificates with the examples provided. The secretariat shall make this information available on its website.

CHAPTER 8.3

MISCELLANEOUS REQUIREMENTS TO BE COMPLIED WITH BY THE CREW OF THE VESSEL

8.3.1   **Persons authorized on board**

8.3.1.1   Unless otherwise provided for in Part 7, only the following persons are authorized to be on board:

(a)   members of the crew;

(b)   persons who, although not being members of the crew, normally live on board; and

(c)   persons who are on board for duty reasons.

8.3.1.2   The persons referred to in 8.3.1.1 (b) are not authorized to remain in the protected area of dry cargo vessels or in the cargo area of tank vessels except for short periods.

8.3.1.3   When the vessel is required to carry two blue cones or two blue lights in accordance with column (19) of Table C of Chapter 3.2, persons under 14 years of age are not permitted on board.

8.3.2   **Portable lighting apparatus**

On board, only portable lighting appliances with their own source of power are permitted in explosion hazardous areas and on deck.

In explosion hazardous areas, they shall meet at least the requirements for use in the relevant area.

8.3.3   **Admittance on board**

No unauthorized person shall be permitted on board. This prohibition shall be displayed on notice boards at appropriate places.

8.3.4   **Prohibition on smoking, fire and naked light**

Smoking, including of electronic cigarettes and similar devices, fire and naked light are prohibited on board. However, the provisions of 7.1.3.41.1 and 7.2.3.41.1 are applicable.

This prohibition shall be displayed on notice boards at appropriate places.

The prohibition does not apply in the accommodation or the wheelhouse, provided that their windows, doors, skylights and hatches are closed or the ventilation system is adjusted to guarantee an overpressure of at least 0.1 kPa.

8.3.5   **Work on board**

No work requiring the use of an open flame or electric current or liable to cause sparks may be carried out on board.

This provision does not apply:

–   to berthing operations;

–   in the service spaces outside the protected area or the cargo area, provided the doors and openings of those areas are closed for the duration of the work and the vessel is not being loaded, unloaded or degassed; or

–   when the vessel is not in the vicinity of or within an onshore assigned zone and, in the case of a tank vessel, has a certificate attesting to the totally gas-free condition of the vessel in accordance with 7.2.3.7.6 or an authorization from the competent authority or in the case of a dry cargo vessel, has a certificate attesting to the totally gas-free condition of the protected area or an authorization from the competent authority.

The use of low-sparking hand-tools (chromium vanadium steel screwdrivers and wrenches or screwdrivers and wrenches of equivalent material from the point of view of spark formation) and appropriate equipment at least for the zone concerned is permitted.

NOTE: In addition, all other applicable regulations regarding workplace safety and safety of operations must be observed.

CHAPTER 8.4

(Reserved)

CHAPTER 8.5

(Reserved)

CHAPTER 8.6

DOCUMENTS

8.6.1   **Certificate of approval**

8.6.1.1   *Model for a certificate of approval for dry cargo vessels*

1

Competent authority: ....
Space reserved for the emblem and name of the State

ADN certificate of approval No.:

1.   Name of vessel ....
2.   Official number ....
3.   Type of vessel ....
4.   Additional requirements: Vessel referred to in 7.1.2.19.1[1]
     Vessel referred to in 7.2.2.19.3[1]
     The vessel complies with the additional rules of construction referred to in 9.1.0.80 to 9.1.0.95/9.2.0.80 to 9.2.0.95[1]
     Vessel complies with the rules of construction referred to in 9.1.0.12.3 (b) or (c), 9.1.0.51 or 9.1.0.52[1]
     Ventilation system referred to in 9.1.0.12.3 (b)[1]
     in ....
     Vessel complies with the rules of construction referred to in 9.1.0.53[1]
     Stationary electrical and non-electrical installations and equipment for use in protected areas:
     Temperature classification: ....
     Explosion group: .....

5.   Permitted derogations[1]:   ....
....
....
....
....

6.   The validity of this certificate of approval expires on .... (date)

7.   The previous certificate of approval No. ....was issued on ....
by .... (competent authority)

8.   The vessel is approved for the carriage of dangerous goods based on:

     – Inspection on[1] (date).................................

     – The inspection report of a recognized classification society [1]
     (name of the classification society) .... (date).....................

     – The inspection report of a recognized inspection body [1]
     (name of the inspection body) .... (date).....................

9.   Subject to permitted equivalence:[1] ....
....
....
....

---

[1] Delete as appropriate

10.   Subject to special authorizations:[1] ....
....
....
....-448-...

11.   Issued at: .... on ....
                   (place)   (date)

12.   (Stamp)   ....
                                         (competent authority)

                                           ....
                                         (signature)

Extension of the validity of the certificate of approval

13.   The validity of this certificate is extended under Chapter 1.16 of ADN

       until ....
             (date)

14.   .... on ....
      (place)   (date)

                                         ....
15.   (Stamp)   (competent authority)

                                         ....
                                         (signature)

---

[1] Delete as appropriate

1

Competent authority: ....

Space reserved for the emblem and name of the State

ADN provisional certificate of approval No: ....

1. Name of vessel ....
2. Official number ....
3. Type of vessel ....
4. Additional requirements:

> Vessel referred to in 7.1.2.19.1[1]
> Vessel referred to in 7.2.2.19.3[1]
> The vessel complies with the additional rules of construction referred to in 9.1.0.80 to 9.1.0.95/9.2.0.80 to 9.2.0.95[1]
> Vessel complies with the rules of construction referred to in 9.1.0.12.3 (b) or (c), 9.1.0.51 or 9.1.0.52[1]
> Ventilation system referred to in 9.1.0.12.3 (b)[1]
> in ....
> Vessel complies with the rules of construction referred to in 9.1.0.53[1]
> Stationary electrical and non-electrical installations and equipment for use in protected areas:
> Temperature classification: ....
> Explosion group: .....

5. Permitted derogations[1]: ....
   ....
   ....

6. The provisional certificate of approval is valid...
   6.1   until ....[1]

   6.2   for a single journey from .... to ....[1]

7. Issued at .... on ....
   (place)   (date)

8. (Stamp)   ....
                                   (competent authority)

                                   ....
                                   (signature)

....

_____

[1] Delete as appropriate.

NOTE: *This model provisional certificate of approval may be replaced by a single certificate model combining a provisional certificate of inspection and the provisional certificate of approval, provided that this single certificate model contains the same particulars as the model above and is approved by the competent authority.*

1

Competent authority: ....

Space reserved for the emblem and name of the State

ADN certificate of approval No.:

1.   Name of vessel ....
2.   Official number ....
3.   Type of vessel ....
4.   Type of tank vessel ....
5.   Cargo tank design   1.   Pressure cargo tanks [1,2]
                                                 2.   Closed cargo tanks [1,2]
                                                 3.   Open cargo tanks with flame arresters [1,2]
                                                 4.   Open cargo tanks [1,2]

6.   Types of cargo tanks   1.   Independent cargo tanks [1,2]
                                                 2.   Integral cargo tanks [1,2]
                                                 3.   Cargo tank with walls distinct from the outer hull [1,2]
                                                   4.   Membrane tanks [1,2]

7.   Opening pressure of the pressure relief valves/high-velocity vent valves/safety valves
   .... kPa[1,2]

8.   Additional equipment:
   - Sampling device
          connection for a sampling device...........yes/no [1,2]
          sampling opening ....…. yes/no [1,2]
   - Water–spray system .... yes/no [1,2]
          Internal pressure alarm 40 kPa .... yes/no [1,2]
   - Cargo heating system:
          possibility of cargo heating from shore ..... yes/no [1,2]
          cargo heating installation on board .... yes/no [1,2]
   - Cargo refrigeration system ....…. yes/no [1,2]
   - Inerting facilities ....…................ yes/no [1,2]
   - Pump–room below deck ....…...   yes/no [1]
   - Ventilation system according to 9.3.x.12.4 (b)   yes/no [1,3]
          in ....
   - Conforms to the rules of construction referred to in 9.3.x.12.4 (b) or 9.3.x.12.4 (c),
     9.3.x.51 and 9.3.x.52   Yes/No [1,3]
   - Venting piping and heated installation   Yes/No [1,2]
   - Conforms to the rules of construction resulting from the remark(s) ... in column (20)
     of Table C of Chapter 3.2 [1,2]

9.   Stationary electrical installations and equipment:
   - Temperature class: ....…....
   - Explosion group: ....…....

10.   Autonomous protection systems:
         Explosion group/subgroup of explosion group II B: ....

11.   Loading/unloading rate: .... m^3/h [1] or see loading instructions on loading and unloading[1]

----

[1]   Delete as appropriate.
[2]   If the tanks are not all of the same type, see page 3.
[3]   For "x", note the relevant information

12.   Permitted relative density: ....

13.   Additional observations
        Vessel complies with the rules of construction referred to in 9.3.x.12, 9.3.x.51,
        9.3.x.52   Yes/No [1,3]
        ....
        ....

14.   The validity of this certificate of approval expires on .... (date)

15.   The previous certificate of approval No. .... was issued on ....
        by .... (competent authority)

16.   The vessel is approved for the carriage of the dangerous goods entered in the vessel substance
        list according to 1.16.1.2.5 based on:
        – Inspection on[1] (date)...
        – The inspection report of a recognized classification society [1]
          (name of the classification society) .... (date)...........................
        – The inspection report of a recognized inspection body [1]
          (name of the inspection body) .... (date).........................

17.   Subjected to permitted equivalence:[1]
        ....
        ....

18.   Subject to special authorizations:[1]
        ....
        ....

19.   Issued at: ....   on ....
            (place)   (date)

20.   (Stamp)   ....
                                            (competent authority)

                                     ....
                                            (signature)

Extension of the validity of the certificate of approval

21.   The validity of this certificate is extended under Chapter 1.16 of ADN

        Until ....
        (date)

22.   ....   on ....
        (place)   (date)

23.   (Stamp)   ....
                                          (competent authority)

                                     ....
                                            (signature)

---

[1] Delete as appropriate.
[3] For "x", note the relevant information

If the cargo tanks of the vessel are not all of the same type or the same design or the equipment is not the same, their type, their design and their equipment shall be indicated below:

1	Cargo tank number	1	2	3	4	5	6	7	8	9	10	11	12
2	Pressure cargo tank												
3	Closed cargo tank												
4	Open cargo tank with flame arrester												
5	Open cargo tank												
6	Independent cargo tank												
7	Integral cargo tank												
8	Cargo tank with walls distinct from the outer hull												
9	Membrane tank												
10	Opening pressure of the pressure relief device/high velocity vent valve/safety valve in kPa												
11	Connection for a sampling device												
12	Sampling opening												
13	Water–spray system												
14	Internal pressure alarm 40 kPa ……..												
15	Possibility of cargo heating from shore												
16	Cargo heating installation on board												
17	Cargo refrigeration installation												
18	Inerting facilities												
19	Venting piping and heated installation												
20	Conforms to the rules of construction resulting from the remark(s) …….. of column (20) of Table C of Chapter 3.2												

1

Competent authority: ....

Space reserved for the emblem and name of the State

ADN provisional certificate of approval No: ....

1.   Name of vessel..

2.   Official number...

3.   Type of vessel...

4.   Type of tank vessel ....

5.   Cargo tank design   1.   Pressure cargo tanks [1,2]

      2.   Closed cargo tanks [1,2]

      3.   Open cargo tanks with flame arresters [1,2]

      4.   Open cargo tanks [1,2]

6.   Types of cargo tanks   1.   Independent cargo tanks [1,2]

      2.   Integral cargo tanks [1,2]

      3.   Cargo tank with walls distinct from the outer hull [1,2]

      4.   Membrane tanks [1,2]

7.   Opening pressure of the pressure relief valves/high-velocity vent valves/
safety valves .... kPa [1,2]

8.   Additional equipment:

- Sampling device

      connection for a sampling device ....   yes/no [1,2]

      sampling opening ....   yes/no [1,2]

- Water–spray system ....   yes/no [1,2]

      Internal pressure alarm 40 kPa ....   yes/no [1,2]

- Cargo heating system:

      possibility of cargo heating from shore ....   yes/no [1,2]

      cargo heating installation on board ....   yes/no [1,2]

- Cargo refrigeration system ....   yes/no [1,2]

- Inerting facilities ....   yes/no [1,2]

- Pump–room below deck ....   yes/no [1]

- Ventilation system according to 9.3.x.12.4 (b)   yes/no [1,3]
      in...

- Conforms to the rules of construction referred to in 9.3.x.12.4 (b) or 9.3.x.12.4 (c),
      9.3.x.51 and 9.3.x.52   Yes/No [1,3]

- Venting piping and heated installation   Yes/No [1,2]

- Conforms to the rules of construction resulting from the remark(s) ... in column (20)
      of Table C of Chapter 3.2 [1,2]

9.   Stationary electrical installations and equipment:

- Temperature class: ....

- Explosion group: ....

10.   Autonomous protection systems:
      Explosion group/subgroup of explosion group II B: ....

---

[1] Delete as appropriate.

[2] If the tanks are not all of the same type, see page 3.

[3] For "x", note the relevant information.

11.   Loading/unloading rate ....   m^3/h^1 or see loading instructions^1 or see instructions on loading and unloading^1.

12.   Permitted relative density: ....

13.   Additional observations:
         Vessel complies with the rules of construction referred to in 9.3.x.12, 9.3.x.51,
         9.3.x.52   Yes/No ^{1,3}

         ....

14.   The provisional certificate of approval is valid..
         14.1   until ^{1}...

         14.2   for a single journey from ^{1}.................. to ....

15.   Issued at .... on ....
         (place)   (date)

16.   (Stamp)   ....
                                                      (competent authority)·

                                                      ....
                                                      (signature)

_____
^{1} Delete as appropriate.
^{2} If the tanks are not all of the same type, see page 3.
^{3} For "x", note the relevant information

NOTE: *This model provisional certificate of approval may be replaced by a single certificate model combining a provisional certificate of inspection and the provisional certificate of approval, provided that this single certificate model contains the same particulars as the model above and is approved by the competent authority.*

If the cargo tanks of the vessel are not all of the same type or the same design or the equipment is not the same, their type, their design and their equipment shall be indicated below:

1	Cargo tank number	1	2	3	4	5	6	7	8	9	10	11	12
2	Pressure cargo tank												
3	Closed cargo tank												
4	Open cargo tank with flame arrester												
5	Open cargo tank												
6	Independent cargo tank												
7	Integral cargo tank												
8	Cargo tank with walls distinct from the outer hull												
9	Membrane tank												
10	Opening pressure of the pressure relief device/high velocity vent valve/safety valve in kPa												
11	Connection for a sampling device												
12	Sampling opening												
13	Water–spray system												
14	Internal pressure alarm 40 kPa ……..												
15	Possibility of cargo heating from shore												
16	Cargo heating installation on board												
17	Cargo refrigeration installation												
18	Inerting facilities												
19	Venting piping and heated installation												
20	Conforms to the rules of construction resulting from the remark(s) ……. of column (20) of Table C of Chapter 3.2												

8.6.1.5 Annex to the certificate of approval and provisional certificate of approval according to 1.16.1.3.1 (a)

Annex to the certificate of approval

1. Official number ....
2. Type of vessel ....
3. Transitional provisions applicable as from

ADN certificate of approval No.:	Competent authority	Issued on	Valid until	Stamp and signature]

ADN certificate of approval No.:	Competent authority	Issued on	Valid until	Stamp and signature

8.6.2   Certificate of special knowledge of ADN according to 8.2.1.2, 8.2.1.5 or 8.2.1.7

(Recto)   (Verso)

(**) Certificate of special knowledge of ADN 1. (No. of certificate) 2. (Name) 3. (First name(s)) 4. (Born on DD/MM/YYYY) 5. (Nationality) 6. (Signature of holder) 7. (Issued by) 8. VALID UNTIL: (DD/MM/YYYY)	Photo of holder

1. (No. of certificate)

The certificate is valid for special knowledge of ADN according to: (Insert the corresponding subsection of ADN 8.2.1, if applicable with the mention "only for dry cargo vessels" or "only for tank vessels".)

**   Letter code(s) used for international navigation (CEVNI – Annex 1).

1

ADN Checklist

concerning the observance of safety provisions and the implementation of the necessary measures for loading/unloading

- **Particulars of vessel**

  …………………………………..   No. …………………………………………..

  (name of vessel)   (official number)

  …………………………………….

  (vessel type)

- **Particulars of loading or unloading operations**

  …………………………………..   …………………………………………..

  (shore loading or unloading installation)   (place)

  ……………………………………..   …………………………………………..

  (date)   (time)

- **Particulars of the cargo as indicated in the transport document**

Quantity m³	Proper shipping name***	UN Number or Identification number	Dangers* …………….	Packing Group
………………	…………………………………	………………..	……………	……………
………………	…………………………………	………………..	……………	……………
………………	…………………………………	………………..	……………	……………

- **Particulars of last cargo****

Proper shipping name ***	UN Number or Identification number	Dangers* …………….	Packing Group
……………………………………………	………………..	……………	……………
……………………………………………	………………..	……………	……………
……………………………………………	………………..	……………	……………

Dangers indicated in column (5) of Table C, as relevant (as mentioned in the transport document in accordance with 5.4.1.1.2 (c)).
** *To be filled in only if vessel is to be loaded.*
*** *The proper shipping name given in column (2) of Table C of Chapter 3.2, supplemented, when applicable, by the technical name in parenthesis.*

Loading/unloading rate (not to be filled in if vessel is to be loaded with gas or have gas unloaded)

Proper shipping name**	Cargo tank number	agreed rate of loading/unloading					
		start		half way		end	
		rate m³/h	quantity m³	rate m³/h	quantity m³	rate m³/h	quantity m³
....	....	....	....	....	....	....	....
....	....	....	....	....	....	....	....
....	....	....	....	....	....	....	....

Will the cargo piping be drained after loading or unloading by stripping or by blowing residual quantities to the shore installation/to the vessel?*

by blowing*
by stripping*

If drained by blowing, how?

....
(e.g. air, inert gas, sleeve)

.... kPa
(permissible maximum pressure in the cargo tank)

....litres
(estimated residual quantity)

Questions to the master or the person mandated by him and the person in charge at the loading/unloading place

Loading/unloading may only be started after all questions on the checklist have been checked off by "X", i.e. answered with YES and the list has been signed by both persons.

Non–applicable questions have to be deleted.

If not all questions can be answered with YES, loading/unloading is only allowed with consent of the competent authority.

---

* *Delete as appropriate.*
** *The proper shipping name given in column (2) of Table C of Chapter 3.2, supplemented, when applicable, by the technical name in parenthesis.*

	vessel	loading/ unloading place
		3
1. Is the vessel permitted to carry this cargo?	O*	O*
2. (*Reserved*)		
3. Is the vessel well moored in view of local circumstances?	O	–
4. Have suitable means in accordance with 7.2.4.77 been provided for leaving the vessel, including in cases of emergency?	O	O
5. Are the escape routes and the loading/unloading place adequately lighted?	O	O
6. Vessel/shore connection		
6.1 Is the piping for loading or unloading between vessel and shore in satisfactory condition?	–	O
Is it correctly connected?	–	O
6.2 Are all the connecting flanges fitted with suitable gaskets?	–	O
6.3 Are all the connecting bolts fitted and tightened?	O	O
6.4 Are the shoreside loading arms free to move in all directions and do the hose assemblies have enough room for easy movement?	–	O
7. Are all flanges of the connections of the piping for loading and unloading and of the venting piping not in use, correctly blanked off?	O	O
8.1 Are suitable means of collecting leakages placed under the pipe connections which are in use and are they empty??	O	O
8.2 Is a water film as mentioned in 9.3.1.21.11 activated?	O	O
9. Are the movable connecting pieces between the ballast and bilge piping on the one hand and the piping for loading and unloading on the other hand disconnected?	O	–
10. Is continuous and suitable supervision of loading/unloading ensured for the whole period of the operation?	O	O
11. Is communication between vessel and shore ensured?	O	O
12.1 For the loading of the vessel, is the venting piping, where required, or if it exists, connected with the vapour return piping?	O	O
12.2 Is it ensured that the shore installation is such that the pressure at the connecting-point of the vapour return piping and the venting piping cannot exceed the opening pressure of the pressure relief devices/high velocity vent valves (pressure at connecting point __ kPa)?	–	O*
12.3 When anti–explosion protection is required in Chapter 3.2, Table C, column (17) does the shore installation ensure that its vapour return piping is such that the vessel is protected against detonations and flame fronts from the shore.	–	O
13. Is it known what actions are to be taken in the event of an "Emergency–stop" and an "Alarm"?	O	O

* *To be filled in only if vessel is to be loaded.*

		vessel	loading/ unloading place
14.	Check on the most important operational requirements:		
	– Are the required fire extinguishing systems and appliances operational?	O	O
	– Have all valves and other closing devices been checked for correct open – or closed position?	O	O
	– Has smoking been generally prohibited?	O	O
	– Are the flame operated heating applications on board turned off?	O	–
	– Is the voltage cut off from the radar installations?	O	–
	– Are all electrical installations and equipment marked red switched off?	O	–
	– Are all windows and doors closed?	O	–
15.1	Has the starting working pressure of the vessel's cargo discharge pump been adjusted to the permissible working pressure of the shore installation? (agreed pressure __ kPa)	O	–
15.2	Has the starting working pressure of the shore pump been adjusted to the permissible working pressure of the on–board installation? (agreed pressure __ kPa)	–	O
16.	Is the liquid level alarm–installation operational?	O	–
17.	Is the following system plugged in, in working order and tested?		
	Overflow prevention device ☐ when loading ☐ when unloading	O	O
	Device for switching off the on–board pump from the shore facility (only when unloading the vessel)	O	O
18.	To be filled in only in the case of loading or unloading of substances for the carriage of which a closed cargo tank or an open cargo tank with flame arrester is required:		
	Are the cargo tank hatches and cargo tank inspection and sampling openings closed or protected by flame arresters fulfilling the requirements of column (16) of Table C of Chapter 3.2?	O	–
19.	When transporting refrigerated liquefied gases, has the holding time been determined according to 7.2.4.16.16, and is known and documented on board?	O**	O**
20	Is the loading temperature within the range of the maximum permissible temperature as prescribed in 7.2.3.28?	O**	O**

Checked, filled in and signed

for the vessel:

....

(name in capital letters)

....

(signature)

for the installation of loading and unloading:

....

(name in capital letters)

....

(signature)

** To be filled in only if the vessel is to be loaded.

Explanation

Question 3

"Well moored" means that the vessel is fastened to the pier or the cargo transfer station in such a way that, without intervention of a third person, movements of the vessel in any direction that could hamper the operation of the cargo transfer gear will be prevented. Established or predictable variations of the water–level at that location and special factors have to be taken into account.

Question 4

It must be possible to escape safely from the vessel at any time. If there is none or only one protected escape route available at the shoreside for a quick escape from the vessel in case of emergency, a suitable means of escape has to be provided on the vessel side if required in accordance with 7.2.4.77.

Question 6

A valid inspection certificate for the hose assemblies must be available on board. The material of the piping for loading and unloading must be able to withstand the expected loads and be suitable for cargo transfer of the respective substances. The piping for loading and unloading between vessel and shore must be placed so that it cannot be damaged by ordinary movements of the vessel during the loading and unloading process or by variations of the water. In addition, all flanged joints must be fitted with appropriate gaskets and sufficient bolt connections in order to exclude the possibility of leakage.

Question 10

Loading/unloading must be supervised on board and ashore so that dangers which may occur in the vicinity of piping for loading and unloading between vessel and shore can be recognized immediately. When supervision is effected by additional technical means it must be agreed between the shore installation and the vessel how it is to be ensured.

Question 11

For a safe loading/unloading operation good communications between vessel and shore are required. For this purpose telephone and radio equipment may be used only if of an explosion protected type and located within reach of the supervisor.

Question 13

Before the start of the loading/unloading operation the representative of the shore installation and the master or the person mandated by him must agree on the applicable procedure. The specific properties of the substances to be loaded/unloaded have to be taken into account.

Question 17

To prevent backflow from the shore, it is also necessary to activate the overflow prevention device on the vessel under certain circumstances when unloading. It is obligatory during loading and optional during unloading. Delete this item if it is not necessary during unloading.

1

ADN Checklist

concerning the observance of safety provisions and the implementation of the necessary measures for degassing to reception facilities

– **Particulars of vessel**

    ....   No. ....
    (name of vessel)   (official number)

    ....
    (vessel type)

– **Particulars of reception facility**

    ....
    (reception facility)   (place)

    ....
    (date)   (time)

    Reception facility approved according CDNI   ☐ Yes ☐ No

– **Particulars of the previous cargo in the tank before degassing as indicated in the transport document**

Cargo tank #	Quantity m³	Proper shipping name**	UN Number or Identification number	Dangers*	Packing Group
....	....	....	....	....	....

---

*   *Dangers indicated in column (5) of Table C, as relevant (as mentioned in the transport document in accordance with 5.4.1.1.2 (c)).*
**   *The proper shipping name given in column (2) of Table C of Chapter 3.2, supplemented, when applicable, by the technical name in parenthesis.*

Degassing rate

Proper shipping name**	Cargo tank number	agreed rate of degassing
		rate m³/h
....	....	....
....	....	....
....	....	....

Questions to the master or the person mandated by him and the person in charge at the reception facility

Degassing may only be started after all questions on the checklist have been checked off by "X", i.e. answered with YES and the list has been signed by both persons.

Non–applicable questions have to be deleted.

If not all questions can be answered with YES, degassing is only allowed with consent of the competent authority.

** *The proper shipping name given in column (2) of Table C of Chapter 3.2, supplemented, when applicable, by the technical name in parenthesis.*

		vessel	3 reception facility
1.	Is the vessel well moored in view of local circumstances?	O	–
2.	Are the pipings for degassing between vessel and reception facility in satisfactory condition?	–	O
	Are they correctly connected and are appropriate flame arresters fitted in the piping between the vessel and the reception facility?	O	O
3.	Are all flanges of the connections of the piping for loading and unloading and of the venting piping not in use, correctly blanked off?	O	O
4.	Is continuous and suitable supervision of degassing ensured for the whole period of the operation?	O	O
5.	Is communication between vessel and reception facility ensured?	O	O
6.1	Is it ensured that the reception facility is such that the pressure at the connecting point cannot exceed the opening pressure of the high–velocity vent valves (pressure at connecting point ___ kPa)?	–	O*
6.2	Is the air inlet part of a closed system or equipped with a spring-loaded low-pressure valve?	–	O**
6.3	When anti–explosion protection is required in Chapter 3.2, Table C, column (17) does the reception facility ensure that its piping is such that the vessel is protected against detonations and passage of flames from the reception facility.	–	O
7.	Is it known what actions are to be taken in the event of an "Emergency–stop" and an "Alarm"?	O	O

* *Not applicable if vacuum is used to generate air flows.*
** *Only applicable is vacuum is used to generate air flows.*

		vessel	reception facility
8.	Check on the most important operational requirements:		
	– Are the required fire extinguishing systems and appliances operational?	O	O
	– Have all valves and other closing devices been checked for correct open or closed position?	O	O
	– Has smoking been generally prohibited?	O	O
	– Are the flame operated heating applications on board turned off?	O	–
	– Is the voltage cut off from the radar installations?	O	–
	– Is all electrical equipment marked red switched off?	O	–
	– Are all windows and doors closed?	O	–
9.1	Has the pressure of the vessel's piping been adjusted to the permissible working pressure of the reception facility? (agreed pressure __ kPa)	O	–
9.2	Has the pressure of the reception facility piping been adjusted to the permissible working pressure of the on–board installation? (agreed pressure __ kPa)	–	O
10.	Are the cargo tank hatches and cargo tank inspection, gauging and sampling openings closed or protected by flame arresters in good condition?	O	–

Checked, filled in and signed

for the vessel:	for the reception facility:
....	....
(name in capital letters)	(name in capital letters)
....	....
(signature)	(signature)

Explanation

Question 1

"Well moored" means that the vessel is fastened to the pier or the reception facility in such a way that, without intervention of a third person, movements of the vessel in any direction that could hamper the degassing operation will be prevented. Established or predictable variations of the water–level at that location and special factors have to be taken into account.

Question 2

The material of the piping must be able to withstand the expected rates and be suitable for degassing. The piping between vessel and reception facility must be placed so that it cannot be damaged by ordinary movements of the vessel during the degassing process or by variations of the water.

Question 4

Degassing must be supervised on board and at the reception facility so that dangers which may occur in the vicinity of the piping between vessel and reception facility can be recognized immediately. When supervision is effected by additional technical means it must be agreed between the reception facility and the vessel how it is to be ensured.

Question 5

For a safe degassing operation good communications between vessel and shore are required. For this purpose telephone and radio equipment may be used only if of an explosion protected type and located within reach of the supervisor.

Question 7

Before the start of the degassing operation the representative of the reception facility and the master or the person mandated by him must agree on the applicable procedure. The specific properties of the substances to be degassed have to be taken into account.

PART 9

Rules for construction

CHAPTER 9.1

RULES FOR CONSTRUCTION OF DRY CARGO VESSELS

9.1.0   **Rules for construction applicable to dry cargo vessels**

Provisions of 9.1.0.0 to 9.1.0.79 apply to dry cargo vessels.

9.1.0.0   *Materials of construction*

The vessel's hull shall be constructed of shipbuilding steel or other metal, provided that this metal has at least equivalent mechanical properties and resistance to the effects of temperature and fire.

9.1.0.1   *Vessel record*

NOTE: For the purpose of this paragraph, the term "owner" has the same meaning as in 1.16.0.

The vessel record shall be retained by the owner who shall be able to provide this documentation at the request of the competent authority and the recognized classification society.

The vessel record shall be maintained and updated throughout the life of the vessel and shall be retained for 6 months after the vessel is taken out of service.

Should a change of owner occur during the life of the vessel the vessel record shall be transferred to the new owner.

Copies of the vessel record or all necessary documents shall be made available on request to the competent authority for the issuance of the certificate of approval and for the recognized classification society or inspection body for first inspection, periodic inspection, special inspection or exceptional checks.

9.1.0.2 to 9.1.0.10   (*Reserved*)

9.1.0.11   **Holds**

9.1.0.11.1   (a)   Each hold shall be bounded fore and aft by watertight metal bulkheads.

          (b)   The holds shall have no common bulkhead with the oil fuel tanks.

9.1.0.11.2   The bottom of the holds shall be such as to permit them to be cleaned and dried.

9.1.0.11.3   The hatchway covers shall be spraytight and weathertight or be covered by waterproof tarpaulins.

Tarpaulins used to cover the holds shall not readily ignite.

9.1.0.11.4   No heating appliances shall be installed in the holds.

9.1.0.12   *Ventilation*

9.1.0.12.1   It must be possible to ventilate each hold by means of two mutually independent extraction ventilators having a capacity of not less than five changes of air per hour based on the volume of the empty hold. The extraction ducts shall be positioned at the extreme ends of the hold and extend down to not more than 50 mm above the bottom. The extraction of gases and vapours through the duct shall also be ensured for carriage in bulk.

If the extraction ducts are movable they shall be suitable for the ventilator assembly and capable of being firmly fixed. Protection shall be ensured against bad weather and spray. The air intake shall be ensured during ventilation.

9.1.0.12.2   The ventilation system of a hold shall be arranged so that dangerous gases cannot penetrate into the accommodation, wheelhouse or engine rooms.

9.1.0.12.3   (a)   Ventilation shall be provided for the accommodation, wheelhouse and for service spaces;

(b)   The ventilation system in such spaces shall meet the following requirements:

(i)   The air intakes of the ventilation system shall be located as far away as possible, and not less than 6.00 m from the protected area and not less than 2.00 m above the deck;

(ii)   Overpressure of at least 0.1 kPa (0.001 bar) may be maintained in the premises;

(iii)   A breakdown alarm is integrated;

(iv)   The ventilation system, including the breakdown alarm, shall be at least of the 'limited explosion risk' type;

(v)   A gas detection system conforming to conditions 1. to 4. below is connected to the ventilation system:

1.   It is appropriate at least for use in zone 1, explosion group IIC and temperature class T6;

2.   It is equipped with sensors:

• On the suction inlets of the ventilation systems; and

• Directly below the top edge of the sill of the entrance doors;

3.   Its t90-time is lower than or equal to 4 s;

4.   Measurement shall be continuous;

(vi)   In the service spaces, the ventilation system is linked to the emergency lighting, which shall be at least of the 'limited explosion risk' type;

This emergency lighting is not necessary if the lighting installations in the service spaces are of at least the 'limited explosion risk' type;

(vii)   The suction of the ventilation system and installations and equipment that do not meet the requirements of 9.1.0.51 and 9.1.0.52.1 shall be shut down when a concentration equal to 20% of the LEL of n-Hexane is reached;

The switching-off shall be indicated in the accommodation and wheelhouse by visual and audible signals;

(viii) In the event of failure of the ventilation system or of the gas detection installations in the accommodation, installations and equipment in the accommodation that do not comply with the requirements of 9.1.0.51 and 9.1.0.52.1 shall be switched off;

The switching-off shall be indicated in the accommodation, the wheelhouse and on the deck by visual and audible signals;

(ix) In the event of failure of the ventilation system or of the gas detection installations in the wheelhouse or the service spaces, installations and equipment in those spaces that do not comply with the requirements of 9.1.0.51 and 9.1.0.52.1 shall be switched off;

The switching-off shall be indicated in the wheelhouse and on the deck by visual and audible signals. The alarm must be relayed to the accommodation automatically if it has not been switched off;

(x) Any switching-off shall take place immediately and automatically and, if necessary, shall switch on the emergency lighting;

The automatic switch-off device is set so that no automatic switching-off may occur while the vessel is under way;

(c) If there is no ventilation system or the ventilation system of a space does not comply with all the requirements set out in (b) above, any installations or equipment present in that space that may, if switched on, give rise to surface temperatures higher than those mentioned in 9.1.0.51 or that do not meet the requirements set out in 9.1.0.52.1 must be capable of being switched off.

9.1.0.12.4   Notice boards shall be fitted at the ventilation inlets indicating the conditions under which they shall be closed. All ventilation inlets of accommodation, wheelhouse and service spaces leading into the open air outside of the protected area shall be located not less than 2.00 m from the protected area.

All ventilation inlets shall be fitted with fixed devices according to 9.1.0.40.2.2 (c) enabling them to be closed rapidly. It shall be clear whether they are open or closed.

9.1.0.12.5   Ventilators including their motors used within the protected area and motors for hold ventilators which are arranged in the air flow shall fulfil at least the requirements for use in zone 1. They shall meet at least the requirements for temperature class T4 and explosion group II B.

9.1.0.12.6   The requirements of 9.1.0.12.3 (b) or (c) must be met only if the vessel is located within or in the immediate vicinity of a shoreside assigned zone.

9.1.0.13 to 9.1.0.16   (*Reserved*)

9.1.0.17   *Accommodation and service spaces*

9.1.0.17.1   The accommodation shall be separated from the holds by metal bulkheads having no openings.

9.1.0.17.2   Gastight closing appliances shall be provided for openings in the accommodation and wheelhouse facing the holds.

9.1.0.17.3   No entrances or openings of the engine rooms and service spaces shall face the protected area.

9.1.0.18 and 9.1.0.19   (*Reserved*)

9.1.0.20   *Water ballast*

The double-hull spaces and double bottoms may be arranged for being filled with water ballast.

9.1.0.21 to 9.1.0.30   *(Reserved)*

9.1.0.31   *Engines*

9.1.0.31.1   Only internal combustion engines running on fuel having a flashpoint above 55 °C are allowed. This provision does not apply to internal combustion engines which are part of propulsion and auxiliary systems. These systems shall meet the requirements of Chapter 30 and Annex 8, Section 1 of the European Standard laying down Technical Requirements for Inland Navigation vessels (ES-TRIN) as amended.[1]

9.1.0.31.2   The air vents in the engine rooms and the air intakes of the engines which do not take air in directly from the engine room shall be located not less than 2.00 m from the protected area.

9.1.0.31.3   Sparking shall not be possible in the protected area.

9.1.0.32   *Oil fuel tanks*

9.1.0.32.1   Double bottoms within the hold area may be arranged as oil fuel tanks provided their depth is not less than 0.6 m. Oil fuel pipes and openings to such tanks are not permitted in the holds.

9.1.0.32.2   The open ends of the air pipes of each oil fuel tanks shall be extended to not less than 0.50 m above the open deck. These open ends and the open ends of overflow pipes leading to the deck shall be fitted with a protective device consisting of a gauze diaphragm or a perforated plate.

9.1.0.33   *(Reserved)*

9.1.0.34   *Exhaust pipes*

9.1.0.34.1   Exhausts shall be evacuated from the vessel into the open air either upwards through an exhaust pipe or through the shell plating. The exhaust outlet shall be located not less than 2.00 m from the hatchway openings. The exhaust pipes of engines shall be arranged so that the exhausts are led away from the vessel. The exhaust pipes shall not be located within the protected area.

9.1.0.34.2   Exhaust pipes shall be provided with a device preventing the escape of sparks, e.g. spark arresters.

9.1.0.35   *Stripping installation*

The stripping pumps intended for the holds shall be located in the protected area. This requirement shall not apply when stripping is effected by eductors.

9.1.0.36 to 9.1.0.39   *(Reserved)*

---

[1]   *As available on the website of the Comité Européen pour l'Élaboration de Standards dans le Domaine de Navigation Intérieure – CESNI, https://www.cesni.eu/en/documents/es-trin/*

9.1.0.40   *Fire-extinguishing arrangements*

9.1.0.40.1   A fire-extinguishing system shall be installed on the vessel. This system shall comply with the following requirements:

–   It shall be supplied by two independent fire or ballast pumps one of which shall be ready for use at any time. These pumps and their means of propulsion and electrical equipment shall not be installed in the same space;

–   It shall be provided with a water main fitted with at least three hydrants in the protected area above deck. Three suitable and sufficiently long hoses with jet/spray nozzles having a diameter of not less than 12 mm shall be provided. Alternatively one or more of the hose assemblies may be substituted by directable jet/spray nozzles having a diameter of not less than 12 mm. It shall be possible to reach any point of the deck in the protected area simultaneously with at least two jets of water which do not emanate from the same hydrant. A spring-loaded non-return valve shall be fitted to ensure that no gases can escape through the fire-extinguishing system into the accommodation or service spaces outside the protected area;

–   The capacity of the system shall be at least sufficient for a jet of water to reach a distance of not less than the vessel's breadth from any location on board with two spray nozzles being used at the same time;

–   The water supply system shall be capable of being put into operation from the wheelhouse and from the deck;

–   Measures shall be taken to prevent the freezing of fire-mains and hydrants.

A single fire or ballast pump shall suffice on board pushed barges without their own means of propulsion.

9.1.0.40.2   In addition, the engine rooms shall be provided with a permanently fixed fire-extinguishing system meeting the following requirements:

9.1.0.40.2.1   *Extinguishing agents*

For the protection of spaces in engine rooms, boiler rooms and pump rooms, only permanently fixed fire-extinguishing systems using the following extinguishing agents are permitted:

(a) CO_2 (carbon dioxide);

(b)   HFC 227 ea (heptafluoropropane);

(c)   IG-541 (52% nitrogen, 40% argon, 8% carbon dioxide);

(d)   FK-5-1-12 (dodecafluoro 2–methylpentane–3–one);

(e)   (*Reserved*)

(f) K_2CO_3 (potassium carbonate).

Other extinguishing agents are permitted only on the basis of recommendations by the Administrative Committee.

9.1.0.40.2.2   *Ventilation, air extraction*

(a)   The combustion air required by the combustion engines which ensure propulsion should not come from spaces protected by permanently fixed fire-extinguishing systems. This requirement is not mandatory if the vessel has two independent main engine rooms with a gastight separation or if, in addition to the main engine room, there is a separate engine room installed with a bow thruster that can independently ensure propulsion in the event of a fire in the main engine room.

(b)   All forced ventilation systems in the space to be protected shall be shut down automatically as soon as the fire-extinguishing system is activated.

(c)   All openings in the space to be protected which permit air to enter or gas to escape shall be fitted with devices enabling them to be closed rapidly. It shall be clear whether they are open or closed.

(d)   Air escaping from the pressure–relief valves of the pressurised air tanks installed in the engine rooms shall be evacuated to the open air.

(e)   Overpressure or negative pressure caused by the diffusion of the extinguishing agent shall not destroy the constituent elements of the space to be protected. It shall be possible to ensure the safe equalisation of pressure.

(f)   Protected spaces shall have a facility for extracting the extinguishing agent and the combustion gases. Such facilities shall be capable of being operated from positions outside the protected rooms and which must not be made inaccessible by a fire within such spaces. If there are permanently installed extractors, it shall not be possible for these to be switched on while the fire is being extinguished.

9.1.0.40.2.3   *Fire alarm system*

The space to be protected shall be monitored by an appropriate fire alarm system. The alarm signal shall be audible in the wheelhouse, the accommodation and the space to be protected.

9.1.0.40.2.4   *Piping system*

(a)   The extinguishing agent shall be routed to and distributed in the space to be protected by means of a permanent piping system. Piping installed in the space to be protected and their fittings shall be made of steel. This shall not apply to the connecting nozzles of tanks and compensators provided that the materials used have equivalent fire–retardant properties. Piping shall be protected against corrosion both internally and externally.

(b)   The discharge nozzles shall be so arranged as to ensure the regular diffusion of the extinguishing agent. In particular, the extinguishing agent must also be effective beneath the floor.

9.1.0.40.2.5   *Triggering device*

(a)   Automatically activated fire-extinguishing systems are not permitted.

(b)   It shall be possible to activate the fire-extinguishing system from a suitable point located outside the space to be protected.

(c)   Triggering devices shall be so installed that they can be activated in the event of a fire and so that the risk of their breakdown in the event of a fire or an explosion in the space to be protected is reduced as far as possible.

Systems which are not mechanically activated shall be supplied from two energy sources independent of each other. These energy sources shall be located outside the space to be protected. The control lines located in the space to be protected shall be so designed as to remain capable of operating in the event of a fire for a minimum of 30 minutes. The electrical installations are deemed to meet this requirement if they conform to the IEC 60331–21:1999 standard.

When the triggering devices are so placed as not to be visible, the component concealing them shall carry the "Fire-fighting system" symbol, each side being not less than 10 cm in length, with the following text in red letters on a white ground:

Fire-extinguishing system

(d)   If the fire-extinguishing system is intended to protect several spaces, it shall comprise a separate and clearly–marked triggering device for each space;

(e)   The instructions shall be posted alongside all triggering devices and shall be clearly visible and indelible. The instructions shall be in a language the master can read and understand and if this language is not English, French or German, they shall be in English, French or German. They shall include information concerning:

    (i)   the activation of the fire-extinguishing system;

    (ii)   the need to ensure that all persons have left the space to be protected;

    (iii)   The correct behaviour of the crew in the event of activation and when accessing the space to be protected following activation or diffusion, in particular in respect of the possible presence of dangerous substances;

    (iv)   the correct behaviour of the crew in the event of the failure of the fire-extinguishing system to function properly.

(f)   The instructions shall mention that prior to the activation of the fire-extinguishing system, combustion engines installed in the space and aspirating air from the space to be protected, shall be shut down.

9.1.0.40.2.6   *Alarm device*

(a)   Permanently fixed fire-extinguishing systems shall be fitted with an audible and visual alarm device;

(b)   The alarm device shall be set off automatically as soon as the fire-extinguishing system is first activated. The alarm device shall function for an appropriate period of time before the extinguishing agent is released; it shall not be possible to turn it off;

(c)   Alarm signals shall be clearly visible in the spaces to be protected and their access points and be clearly audible under operating conditions corresponding to the highest possible sound level. It shall be possible to distinguish them clearly from all other sound and visual signals in the space to be protected;

(d)   Sound alarms shall also be clearly audible in adjoining spaces, with the communicating doors shut, and under operating conditions corresponding to the highest possible sound level;

(e) If the alarm device is not intrinsically protected against short circuits, broken wires and drops in voltage, it shall be possible to monitor its operation;

(f) A sign with the following text in red letters on a white ground shall be clearly posted at the entrance to any space the extinguishing agent may reach:

Warning, fire-extinguishing system!
Leave this space immediately when the ... (description) alarm is activated!

9.1.0.40.2.7 *Pressurised tanks, fittings and piping*

(a) Pressurised tanks, fittings and piping shall conform to the requirements of the competent authority or, if there are no such requirements, to those of a recognized classification society.

(b) Pressurised tanks shall be installed in accordance with the manufacturer's instructions.

(c) Pressurised tanks, fittings and piping shall not be installed in the accommodation.

(d) The temperature of cabinets and storage spaces for pressurised tanks shall not exceed 50 °C.

(e) Cabinets or storage spaces on deck shall be securely stowed and shall have vents so placed that in the event of a pressurised tank not being gastight, the escaping gas cannot penetrate into the vessel. Direct connections with other spaces are not permitted.

9.1.0.40.2.8 *Quantity of extinguishing agent*

If the quantity of extinguishing agent is intended for more than one space, the quantity of extinguishing agent available does not need to be greater than the quantity required for the largest of the spaces thus protected.

9.1.0.40.2.9 *Installation, maintenance, monitoring and documents*

(a) The mounting or modification of the system shall only be performed by a company specialised in fire-extinguishing systems. The instructions (product data sheet, safety data sheet) provided by the manufacturer of the extinguishing agent or the system shall be followed.

(b) The system shall be inspected by an expert:

(i) before being brought into service;

(ii) each time it is put back into service after activation;

(iii) after every modification or repair;

(iv) regularly, not less than every two years.

(c) During the inspection, the expert is required to check that the system conforms to the requirements of 9.1.0.40.2.

(d) The inspection shall include, as a minimum:

(i) an external inspection of the entire system;

(ii) an inspection to ensure that the piping is leakproof;

(iii) an inspection to ensure that the control and activation systems are in good working order;

(iv) an inspection of the pressure and contents of tanks;

(v) an inspection to ensure that the means of closing the space to be protected are leakproof;

(vi) an inspection of the fire alarm system;

(vii) an inspection of the alarm device.

(e) The person performing the inspection shall establish, sign and date a certificate of inspection.

(f) The number of permanently fixed fire-extinguishing systems shall be mentioned in the vessel certificate.

9.1.0.40.2.10 *Fire-extinguishing system operating with CO_2*

In addition to the requirements contained in 9.1.0.40.2.1 to 9.1.0.40.2.9, fire-extinguishing systems using CO_2 as an extinguishing agent shall conform to the following provisions:

(a) Tanks of CO_2 shall be placed in a gastight space or cabinet separated from other spaces. The doors of such storage spaces and cabinets shall open outwards; they shall be capable of being locked and shall carry on the outside the symbol "Warning: general danger," not less than 5 cm high and "CO_2" in the same colours and the same size;

(b) Storage cabinets or spaces for CO_2 tanks located below deck shall only be accessible from the outside. These spaces shall have an artificial ventilation system with extractor hoods and shall be completely independent of the other ventilation systems on board;

(c) The level of filling of CO_2 tanks shall not exceed 0.75 kg/l. The volume of depressurised CO_2 shall be taken to be 0.56 m^3/kg;

(d) The concentration of CO_2 in the space to be protected shall be not less than 40% of the gross volume of the space. This quantity shall be released within 120 seconds. It shall be possible to monitor whether diffusion is proceeding correctly;

(e) The opening of the tank valves and the control of the diffusing valve shall correspond to two different operations;

(f) The appropriate period of time mentioned in 9.1.0.40.2.6 (b) shall be not less than 20 seconds. A reliable installation shall ensure the timing of the diffusion of CO_2.

9.1.0.40.2.11 *Fire-extinguishing system operating with HFC-227 ea (heptafluoropropane)*

In addition to the requirements of 9.1.0.40.2.1 to 9.1.0.40.2.9, fire-extinguishing systems using HFC-227 ea as an extinguishing agent shall conform to the following provisions:

(a) Where there are several spaces with different gross volumes, each space shall be equipped with its own fire-extinguishing system;

(b) Every tank containing HFC-227 ea placed in the space to be protected shall be fitted with a device to prevent overpressure. This device shall ensure that the contents of the tank are safely diffused in the space to be protected if the tank is subjected to fire, when the fire-extinguishing system has not been brought into service;

(c)   Every tank shall be fitted with a device permitting control of the gas pressure;

(d)   The level of filling of tanks shall not exceed 1.15 kg/l. The specific volume of depressurised HFC-227 ea shall be taken to be 0.1374 m^3/kg;

(e)   The concentration of HFC-227 ea in the space to be protected shall be not less than 8% of the gross volume of the space. This quantity shall be released within 10 seconds;

(f)   Tanks of HFC-227 ea shall be fitted with a pressure monitoring device which triggers an audible and visual alarm in the wheelhouse in the event of an unscheduled loss of propellant gas. Where there is no wheelhouse, the alarm shall be triggered outside the space to be protected;

(g)   After discharge, the concentration in the space to be protected shall not exceed 10.5% (volume);

(h)   The fire-extinguishing system shall not comprise aluminium parts.

9.1.0.40.2.12   *Fire-extinguishing system operating with IG-541*

In addition to the requirements of 9.1.0.40.2.1 to 9.1.0.40.2.9, fire-extinguishing systems using IG-541 as an extinguishing agent shall conform to the following provisions:

(a)   Where there are several spaces with different gross volumes, every space shall be equipped with its own fire-extinguishing system;

(b)   Every tank containing IG-541 placed in the space to be protected shall be fitted with a device to prevent overpressure. This device shall ensure that the contents of the tank are safely diffused in the space to be protected if the tank is subjected to fire, when the fire-extinguishing system has not been brought into service;

(c)   Each tank shall be fitted with a device for checking the contents;

(d)   The filling pressure of the tanks shall not exceed 200 bar at a temperature of +15 °C;

(e)   The concentration of IG-541 in the space to be protected shall be not less than 44% and not more than 50% of the gross volume of the space. This quantity shall be released within 120 seconds.

9.1.0.40.2.13   *Fire-extinguishing system operating with FK-5-1-12*

In addition to the requirements of 9.1.0.40.2.1 to 9.1.0.40.2.9, fire-extinguishing systems using FK-5-1-12 as an extinguishing agent shall comply with the following provisions:

(a)   Where there are several spaces with different gross volumes, every space shall be equipped with its own fire-extinguishing system;

(b)   Every tank containing FK-5-1-12 placed in the space to be protected shall be fitted with a device to prevent overpressure. This device shall ensure that the contents of the tank are safely diffused in the space to be protected if the tank is subjected to fire, when the fire-extinguishing system has not been brought into service;

(c)   Every tank shall be fitted with a device permitting control of the gas pressure;

(d)   The level of filling of tanks shall not exceed 1.00 kg/l. The specific volume of depressurized FK-5-1-12 shall be taken to be 0.0719 m^3/kg;

(e)   The volume of FK-5-1-12 in the space to be protected shall be not less than 5.5% of the gross volume of the space. This quantity shall be released within 10 seconds;

(f)   Tanks of FK-5-1-12 shall be fitted with a pressure monitoring device which triggers an audible and visual alarm in the wheelhouse in the event of an unscheduled loss of extinguishing agent. Where there is no wheelhouse, the alarm shall be triggered outside the space to be protected;

(g)   After discharge, the concentration in the space to be protected shall not exceed 10.0%.

9.1.0.40.2.14   *(Reserved)*

9.1.0.40.2.15   *Fire-fighting systems using K_2CO_3 as the extinguishing agent*

In addition to the requirements laid down in 9.1.0.40.2.1 to 9.1.0.40.2.3, 9.1.0.40.2.5, 9.1.0.40.2.6, and 9.1.0.40.2.9, fire-fighting systems using K_2CO_3 as the extinguishing agent shall comply with the following provisions:

(a)   The fire-fighting system shall have a type-approval pursuant to Directive 2014/90/EU[2] or to MSC/Circ. 1270[3];

(b)   Each room shall be provided with its own firefighting system;

(c)   The extinguishing agent must be stored in specially provided unpressurised tanks in the room to be protected. These tanks shall be fitted in such a way that the extinguishing agent is dispensed evenly in the room. In particular the extinguishing agent shall also work underneath the deck plates;

(d)   Each tank is separately connected with the triggering device;

(e)   The quantity of dry aerosol-forming extinguishing agent relative to the room to be protected shall be at least 120 g per m^3 of the net volume of this room. This net volume is calculated according to Directive 2014/90/EU[2] or to MSC/Circ. 1270[3]. It shall be possible to supply the extinguishing agent within 120 seconds.

9.1.0.40.2.16   *Fixed fire-extinguishing system for physical protection*

In order to ensure physical protection in the engine rooms, boiler rooms and pump rooms, permanently fixed fire-extinguishing systems are accepted solely on the basis of recommendations by the Administrative Committee.

9.1.0.40.3   The two hand fire–extinguishers referred to in 8.1.4 shall be located in the protected area or in proximity to it.

9.1.0.40.4   The fire-extinguishing agent in the permanently fixed fire-extinguishing system shall be suitable and sufficient for fighting fires.

---

[2]   *Official Journal of the European Union, L 257 of 28 August 2014, p.146.*

[3]   *International Maritime Organization Circular MSC/Circ. 1270 and corrigenda — Revised Guidelines for the approval of fixed aerosol fire-extinguishing systems equivalent to fixed gas extinguishing systems, as referred to in SOLAS 1974, for machinery spaces — adopted on 4 June 2008.*

9.1.0.41   *Fire and naked light*

9.1.0.41.1   The outlets of funnels shall be located not less than 2 m from the hatchway openings. Arrangements shall be provided to prevent the escape of sparks and the entry of water.

9.1.0.41.2   Heating, cooking and refrigerating appliances shall not be fuelled with liquid fuels, liquid gas or solid fuels. The installation in the engine room or other separate space of heating appliances fuelled with liquid fuel having a flashpoint above 55 °C is, however, permitted.

Cooking and refrigerating appliances are permitted only in wheelhouses with metal floor and in the accommodation.

9.1.0.41.3   Only electric lighting appliances are permitted outside the accommodation and the wheelhouse.

9.1.0.42 to 9.1.0.50   (*Reserved*)

9.1.0.51   *Surface temperatures of electrical and non-electrical installations and equipment*

(a)   The surface temperatures of electrical and non-electrical installations and equipment as well as the outer parts of engines and their inlets and exhaust ducts shall not exceed 200 °C;

(b)   The following are exempt from the above provision:

– Accommodation, wheelhouse and service spaces where surface temperatures higher than 200 °C occur that are equipped with a ventilation system according to 9.1.0.12.3; or

– Installations and equipment which generate surface temperatures higher than 200 °C and that can be switched off. Such installations and equipment shall be marked in red;

(c)   Within the protected area, 9.1.0.53.1 applies;

(d)   The requirements of 9.1.0.51 (a) and (b) must be met only if the vessel is located within or in the immediate vicinity of a shoreside assigned zone.

9.1.0.52   *Type and location of electrical installations and equipment*

9.1.0.52.1   Electrical installations and equipment outside the protected area shall be at least of the 'limited explosion risk' type. This provision does not apply to:

(a)   Lighting installations in the accommodation and in the wheelhouse, except for switches located near to the entrances;

(b)   Mobile phones, fixed telephone installations as well as stationary and portable computers in the accommodation or the wheelhouse;

(c)   Electrical installations and equipment which, during a stay in the immediate vicinity of or within a shoreside assigned zone, are:

– Not live; or

– Installed in spaces which are equipped with a ventilation system according to 9.1.0.12.3;

(d)   Radiotelephone installations and inland AIS (automatic identification systems) stations in the accommodation and in the wheelhouse if no part of an aerial for radiotelephone installations or AIS stations is situated above or within 2.00 m from the protected area.

9.1.0.52.2   Fixed electrical installations and equipment which do not meet the requirements set out in 9.1.0.52.1 and their switches shall be marked in red. The disconnection of such equipment shall be controlled from a centralized location on board.

9.1.0.52.3   Sockets for the connection of signal lights and gangway lighting shall be solidly fitted to the vessel close to the signal mast or the gangway. Sockets intended to supply the submerged pumps, hold ventilators and containers shall be permanently fitted to the vessel in the vicinity of the hatches. The sockets shall be designed to ensure that it is only possible to connect or disconnect them when they are not live.

9.1.0.52.4   Accumulators shall be located outside the protected area.

9.1.0.52.5   Failure of the power supply for the safety and control equipment shall be immediately indicated by visual and audible signals in the wheelhouse and on the deck. The alarm must be relayed to the accommodation automatically if it has not been switched off.

9.1.0.52.6   Electrical switches, sockets and cables on deck shall be protected against mechanical damage.

9.1.0.52.7   The requirements of 9.1.0.52.1 and 9.1.0.52.2 shall be met only if the vessel is located within or in the immediate vicinity of an onshore assigned zone.

9.1.0.53   *Type and location of electrical and non-electrical installations and equipment intended for use in the protected area*

9.1.0.53.1   It shall be possible to switch off the electrical installations and equipment in the protected area by means of centrally located isolation switches except where:

–   In the holds, they are appropriate at least for use in zone 1, for temperature class T4 and explosion group II B; and

–   In the protected area on the deck, they are of the limited explosion risk type.

The corresponding electrical circuits shall have control lamps to indicate whether or not the circuits are live.

The isolation switches shall be protected against unintended operation. Submerged pumps installed or used in the holds shall be appropriate at least for use in zone 1, temperature class T4 and explosion group II B.

9.1.0.53.2   The sockets used in the protected area shall be designed so as to prevent connection or disconnection except when they are not live.

9.1.0.53.3   Except in the case of optical fibres, electrical cables within the protected area shall be armoured or placed in a metallic sheath or in protective tubes.

9.1.0.53.4   Movable electric cables are prohibited in the protected area, except electric cables for intrinsically safe electric circuits or for connecting:

(a)   Signal lights and lighting for gangways, provided the connection point (for example, the socket) is permanently fitted to the vessel close to the signal mast or gangway;

(b)   Containers;

(c)   Electrically operated hatch cover gantries;

(d) Submerged pumps;

(e) Hold ventilators;

(f) The power network on a vessel to a land-based power network; provided that:

  – The electric cables and the power supply unit conform to a valid standard (for example, EN 15869-03: 2010);

  – The power supply unit and connectors are located outside of the protected area.

Connecting and disconnecting sockets/connectors shall only be possible when they are not live.

9.1.0.53.5   For movable electrical cables permitted in accordance with 9.1.0.53.4, only rubber-sheathed electrical cables of type H07 RN-F in accordance with IEC-60245-4:2011[4] or electrical cables of at least equivalent design having conductors with a cross-section of not less than 1.5 mm^2, shall be used.

9.1.0.53.6   Non-electrical installations and equipment in the protected area which are intended for use during loading and unloading or stay in the immediate vicinity of or within a shoreside assigned zone shall meet at least the requirements for use in the area concerned. They shall meet at least the requirements for temperature class T4 and explosion group II B.

9.1.0.54 and 9.1.0.55   (*Reserved*)

9.1.0.56   (*Deleted*)

9.1.0.57 to 9.1.0.69   (*Reserved*)

9.1.0.70   *Metal wires, masts*

All metal wires passing over the holds and all masts shall be earthed, unless they are electrically bonded to the metal hull of the vessel through their installation.

9.1.0.71   *Admittance on board*

The notice boards displaying the prohibition of admittance in accordance with 8.3.3 shall be clearly legible from either side of the vessel.

9.1.0.72 and 9.1.0.73   (*Reserved*)

9.1.0.74   *Prohibition of smoking, fire and naked light*

9.1.0.74.1   The notice boards displaying the prohibition of smoking in accordance with 8.3.4 shall be clearly legible from either side of the vessel.

9.1.0.74.2   Notice boards indicating the circumstances under which the prohibition applies shall be fitted near the entrances to the spaces where smoking or the use of fire or naked light is not always prohibited.

9.1.0.74.3   Ashtrays shall be provided close to each exit of the accommodation and the wheelhouse.

9.1.0.75 to 9.1.0.79   (*Reserved*)

---

[4]   *Identical to EN 50525-2-21: 2011*

9.1.0.80   *Additional rules applicable to double-hull vessels*

The rules of 9.1.0.88 to 9.1.0.99 are applicable to double-hull vessels intended to carry dangerous goods of Classes 2, 3, 4.1, 4.2, 4.3, 5.1, 5.2, 6.1, 7, 8 or 9, except those for which label No. 1 is prescribed in column (5) of Table A of Chapter 3.2, in quantities exceeding those of 7.1.4.1.4.

9.1.0.81 to 9.1.0.87   *(Reserved)*

9.1.0.88   *Classification*

9.1.0.88.1   Double-hull vessels intended to carry dangerous goods of Classes 2, 3, 4.1, 4.2, 4.3, 5.1, 5.2, 6.1, 7, 8 or 9 except those for which label No. 1 is prescribed in column (5) of Table A of Chapter 3.2, in quantities exceeding those referred to in 7.1.4.1.4 shall be built or transformed under survey of a recognised classification society in accordance with the rules established by that classification society to its highest class. This shall be confirmed by the classification society by the issue of an appropriate certificate.

9.1.0.88.2   Continuation of class is not required.

9.1.0.88.3   Future conversions and major repairs to the hull shall be carried out under survey of this classification society.

9.1.0.89 and 9.1.0.90   *(Reserved)*

9.1.0.91   *Holds*

9.1.0.91.1   The vessel shall be built as a double-hull vessel with double-hull spaces and double bottom within the protected area.

9.1.0.91.2   The distance between the sides of the vessel and the longitudinal bulkheads of the hold shall be not less than 0.80 m. Regardless of the requirements relating to the width of walkways on deck, a reduction of this distance to 0.60 m is permitted, provided that, compared with the scantlings specified in the rules for construction published by a recognised classification society, the following reinforcements have been made:

(a)   Where the vessel's sides are constructed according to the longitudinal framing system, the frame spacing shall not exceed 0.60 m.

The longitudinals shall be supported by web frames with lightening holes similar to the floors in the double bottom and spaced not more than 1.80 m apart. These intervals may be increased if the construction is correspondingly reinforced;

(b)   Where the vessel's sides are constructed according to the transverse framing system, either:

– two longitudinal side shell stringers shall be fitted. The distance between the two stringers and between the uppermost stringer and the gangboard shall not exceed 0.80 m. The depth of the stringers shall be at least equal to that of the transverse frames and the cross-section of the face plate shall be not less than 15 cm².

The longitudinal stringers shall be supported by web frames with lightening holes similar to plate floors in the double bottom and spaced not more than 3.60 m apart. The transverse shell frames and the hold bulkhead vertical stiffeners shall be connected at the bilge by a bracket plate with a height of not less than 0.90 m and thickness equal to the thickness of the floors; or

–   web frames with lightening holes similar to the double bottom plate floors shall be arranged on each transverse frame;

(c)   The gangboards shall be supported by transverse bulkheads or cross-ties spaced not more than 32 m apart.

As an alternative to compliance with the requirements of (c) above, a proof by calculation, issued by a recognised classification society confirming that additional reinforcements have been fitted in the double-hull spaces and that the vessel's transverse strength may be regarded as satisfactory.

9.1.0.91.3   The depth of the double bottom shall be at least 0.50 m. The depth below the suction wells may, however, be locally reduced, but the space between the bottom of the suction well and the bottom of the vessel floor shall be at least 0.40 m. If spaces are between 0.40 m and 0.49 m, the surface area of the suction well shall not exceed 0.5 m^2.

The capacity of the suction wells must not exceed 0.120 m^3.

9.1.0.92   *Emergency exit*

Spaces the entrances or exits of which are partly or fully immersed in damaged condition shall be provided with an emergency exit not less than 0.10 m above the waterline. This does not apply to forepeak and afterpeak.

9.1.0.93   *Stability (general)*

9.1.0.93.1   Proof of sufficient stability shall be furnished including stability in the damaged condition.

9.1.0.93.2   The basic values for the stability calculation – the vessel's lightweight and the location of the centre of gravity – shall be determined either by means of an inclining experiment or by detailed mass and moment calculation. In the latter case the lightweight shall be checked by means of a lightweight test with a resulting difference of not more than ± 5% between the mass determined by the calculation and the displacement determined by the draught readings.

9.1.0.93.3   Proof of sufficient intact stability shall be furnished for all stages of loading and unloading and for the final loading condition.

Floatability after damage shall be proved for the most unfavourable loading condition. For this purpose calculated proof of sufficient stability shall be established for critical intermediate stages of flooding and for the final stage of flooding. Negative values of stability in intermediate stages of flooding may be accepted only if the continued range of curve of righting lever in damaged condition indicates adequate positive values of stability.

9.1.0.94   *Stability (intact)*

9.1.0.94.1   The requirements for intact stability resulting from the damaged stability calculation shall be fully complied with.

9.1.0.94.2   For the carriage of containers, proof of sufficient stability shall also be furnished in accordance with the provisions of the Regulations referred to in 1.1.4.6.

9.1.0.94.3   The most stringent of the requirements of 9.1.0.94.1 and 9.1.0.94.2 above shall prevail for the vessel.

9.1.0.95 *Stability (damaged condition)*

9.1.0.95.1 The following assumptions shall be taken into consideration for the damaged condition:

(a) The extent of side damage is as follows:

longitudinal extent:	at least 0.10 L, but not less than 5.00 m;
transverse extent:	0.59 m inboard from the vessel's side at right angles to the centreline at the level corresponding to the maximum draught;
vertical extent:	from the baseline upwards without limit;

(b) The extent of bottom damage is as follows:

longitudinal extent:	at least 0.10 L, but not less than 5.00 m;
transverse extent:	3.00 m;
vertical extent:	from the base 0.49 m upwards, the sump excepted;

(c) Any bulkheads within the damaged area shall be assumed damaged, which means that the location of bulkheads shall be chosen so as to ensure that the vessel remains afloat after the flooding of two or more adjacent compartments in the longitudinal direction.

The following provisions are applicable:

 – For bottom damage also two adjacent athwartships compartments shall be assumed as flooded;

 – The lower edge of any openings that cannot be closed watertight (e.g. doors, windows, access hatchways) shall, at the final stage of flooding, be not less than 0.10 m above the damage waterline;

 – In general, permeability shall be assumed to be 95%. Where an average permeability of less than 95% is calculated for any compartment, this calculated value may be used.

However, the following minimum values shall be used:

 – engine rooms: 85%

 – accommodation: 95%

 – double bottoms, oil fuel tanks, ballast tanks, etc.,
  depending on whether, according to their
  function, they have to be assumed as full or
  empty for the vessel floating at the maximum
  permissible draught: 0% or 95%

For the main engine room only the one–compartment standard needs to be taken into account, i.e. the end bulkheads of the engine room shall be assumed as not damaged.

9.1.0.95.2 At the stage of equilibrium (final stage of flooding) the angle of heel shall not exceed 12°. Non-watertight openings shall not be immersed before reaching the stage of equilibrium. If such openings are immersed before that stage, the corresponding spaces shall be considered as flooded for the purpose of stability calculation.

The positive range of the righting lever curve beyond the position of equilibrium shall have a righting lever of ≥ 0.05 m in association with an area under the curve of ≥ 0.0065 m.rad. The minimum values of stability shall be satisfied up to immersion of the first non-weathertight opening and in any event up to an angle of heel ≤ 27°. If non-weathertight openings are immersed before that stage, the corresponding spaces shall be considered as flooded for the purposes of stability calculation.

9.1.0.95.3   Inland navigation vessels carrying containers which have not been secured shall satisfy the following damage stability criteria:

At the stage of equilibrium (final stage of flooding) the angle of heel shall not exceed 5°. Non-watertight openings shall not be immersed before reaching the stage of equilibrium. If such openings are immersed before that stage, the corresponding spaces shall be considered as flooded for the purpose of stability calculation;

The positive range of the righting lever curve beyond the position of equilibrium shall have an area under the curve of ≥ 0.0065 m.rad. The minimum values of stability shall be satisfied up to immersion of the first non-weathertight opening and in any event up to an angle of heel ≤ 10°. If non-weathertight openings are immersed before that stage, the corresponding spaces shall be considered as flooded for the purposes of stability calculation.

9.1.0.95.4   If openings through which undamaged compartments may become additionally flooded are capable of being closed watertight, the closing devices shall be appropriately marked.

9.1.0.95.5   Where cross- or down-flooding openings are provided for reduction of unsymmetrical flooding, the time for equalisation shall not exceed 15 minutes if during the intermediate stages of flooding sufficient stability has been proved.

9.1.0.96 to 9.1.0.99   (*Reserved*)

CHAPTER 9.2

RULES FOR CONSTRUCTION APPLICABLE TO SEAGOING VESSELS WHICH COMPLY WITH THE REQUIREMENTS OF THE SOLAS 74 CONVENTION, CHAPTER II-2, REGULATION 19 OR SOLAS 74, CHAPTER II-2, REGULATION 54

9.2.0   The requirements of 9.2.0.0 to 9.2.0.79 are applicable to seagoing vessels which comply with the following requirements:

–   SOLAS 74, Chapter II-2, Regulation 19 in its amended version; or

–   SOLAS 74, Chapter II-2, Regulation 54 in its amended version in accordance with the resolutions mentioned in Chapter II-2, Regulation 1, paragraph 2.1, provided that the vessel was constructed before 1 July 2002.

Seagoing vessels which do not comply with the above–mentioned requirements of the SOLAS 74 Convention shall meet the requirements of 9.1.0.0 to 9.1.0.79.

9.2.0.0   *Materials of construction*

The vessel's hull shall be constructed of shipbuilding steel or other metal, provided that this metal has at least equivalent mechanical properties and resistance to the effects of temperature and fire.

9.2.0.1 to 9.2.0.19   (*Reserved*)

9.2.0.20   *Water ballast*

The double-hull spaces and double bottoms may be arranged for being filled with water ballast.

9.2.0.21 to 9.2.0.30   (*Reserved*)

9.2.0.31   *Engines*

9.2.0.31.1   Only internal combustion engines running on a fuel having a flashpoint above 60 °C, are allowed.

9.2.0.31.2   Ventilation inlets of the engine rooms and the air intakes of the engines which do not take air in directly from the engine room shall be located not less than 2 m from the protected area.

9.2.0.31.3   Sparking shall not be possible in the protected area.

9.2.0.32 and 9.2.0.33   (*Reserved*)

9.2.0.34   *Exhaust pipes*

9.2.0.34.1   Exhausts shall be evacuated from the vessel into the open–air either upwards through an exhaust pipe or through the shell plating. The exhaust outlet shall be located not less than 2.00 m from the hatchway openings. The exhaust pipes of engines shall be arranged so that the exhausts are led away from the vessel. The exhaust pipes shall not be located within the protected area.

9.2.0.34.2   Exhaust pipes shall be provided with a device preventing the escape of sparks, e.g. spark arresters.

9.2.0.35 to 9.2.0.40   (*Reserved*)

9.2.0.41   *Fire and naked light*

9.2.0.41.1   The outlets of funnels shall be located not less than 2.00 m from the hatchway openings. Arrangements shall be provided to prevent the escape of sparks and the entry of water.

9.2.0.41.2   Heating, cooking and refrigerating appliances shall not be fuelled with liquid fuels, liquid gas or solid fuels. The installation in the engine room or other separate space of heating appliances fuelled with liquid fuel having a flashpoint above 55 °C shall, however, be permitted.

Cooking and refrigerating appliances are permitted only in wheelhouses with metal floor and in the accommodation.

9.2.0.41.3   Only electric lighting appliances are permitted outside the accommodation and the wheelhouse.

9.2.0.42 to 9.2.0.70   (*Reserved*)

9.2.0.71   *Admittance on board*

The notice boards displaying the prohibition of admittance in accordance with 8.3.3 shall be clearly legible from either side of the vessel.

9.2.0.72 and 9.2.0.73   (*Reserved*)

9.2.0.74   *Prohibition of smoking, fire and naked light*

9.2.0.74.1   The notice boards displaying the prohibition of smoking in accordance with 8.3.4 shall be clearly legible from either side of the vessel.

9.2.0.74.2   Notice boards indicating the circumstances under which the prohibition applies shall be fitted near the entrances to the spaces where smoking or the use of fire or naked light is not always prohibited.

9.2.0.74.3   Ashtrays shall be provided close to each exit of the wheelhouse.

9.2.0.75 to 9.2.0.79   (*Reserved*)

9.2.0.80   *Additional rules applicable to double-hull seagoing vessels*

The rules of 9.2.0.88 to 9.2.0.99 are applicable to double-hull seagoing vessels intended to carry dangerous goods of Classes 2, 3, 4.1, 4.2, 4.3, 5.1, 5.2, 6.1, 7, 8 or 9, except those for which label No. 1 is prescribed in column (5) of Table A of Chapter 3.2, in quantities exceeding those of 7.1.4.1.4.

9.2.0.81 to 9.2.0.87   (*Reserved*)

9.2.0.88   *Classification*

9.2.0.88.1   Double-hull seagoing vessels intended to carry dangerous goods of Classes 2, 3, 4.1, 4.2, 4.3, 5.1, 5.2, 6.1, 7, 8 or 9 except those for which label No. 1 is prescribed in column (5) of Table A of Chapter 3.2, in quantities exceeding those referred to in 7.1.4.1.4, shall be built under survey of a recognised classification society in accordance with the rules established by that classification society to its highest class. This shall be confirmed by the classification society by the issue of an appropriate certificate.

9.2.0.88.2   The vessel's highest class shall be continued.

9.2.0.89 and 9.2.0.90   (*Reserved*)

9.2.0.91   *Holds*

9.2.0.91.1   The vessel shall be built as a double-hull vessel with double–wall spaces and double bottom within the protected area.

9.2.0.91.2   The distance between the sides of the vessel and the longitudinal bulkheads of the hold shall be not less than 0.80 m. A locally reduced distance at the vessel's ends shall be permitted, provided the smallest distance between vessel's side and the longitudinal bulkhead (measured perpendicular to the side) is not less than 0.60 m. The sufficient structural strength of the vessel (longitudinal, transverse and local strength) shall be confirmed by the certificate of class.

9.2.0.91.3   The depth of the double bottom shall be not less than 0.50 m.

The depth below the suction wells may however be locally reduced to 0.40 m, provided the suction well has a capacity of not more than 0.03 m^3.

9.2.0.92   (*Reserved*)

9.2.0.93   *Stability (general)*

9.2.0.93.1   Proof of sufficient stability shall be furnished including stability in the damaged condition.

9.2.0.93.2   The basic values for the stability calculation – the vessel's lightweight and the location of the centre of gravity – shall be determined either by means of an inclining experiment or by detailed mass and moment calculation. In the latter case the lightweight shall be checked by means of a lightweight test with a resulting difference of not more than ± 5% between the mass determined by the calculation and the displacement determined by the draught readings.

9.2.0.93.3   Proof of sufficient intact stability shall be furnished for all stages of loading and unloading and for the final loading condition.

Floatability after damage shall be proved for the most unfavourable loading condition. For this purpose calculated proof of sufficient stability shall be established for critical intermediate stages of flooding and for the final stage of flooding. Negative values of stability in intermediate stages of flooding may be accepted only if the continued range of curve of righting lever in damaged condition indicates adequate positive values of stability.

9.2.0.94   *Stability (intact)*

9.2.0.94.1   The requirements for intact stability resulting from the damaged stability calculation shall be fully complied with.

9.2.0.94.2   For the carriage of containers, additional proof of sufficient stability shall be furnished in accordance with the requirements of the Regulations referred to in 1.1.4.6.

9.2.0.94.3   The most stringent of the requirements of 9.2.0.94.1 and 9.2.0.94.2 shall prevail for the vessel.

9.2.0.94.4   For seagoing vessels the provisions of 9.2.0.94.2 above may be regarded as having been complied with if the stability conforms to Resolution A.749 (18) of the International Maritime Organization and the stability documents have been checked by the competent authority. This applies only when all containers are secured as usual on seagoing vessels and a relevant stability document has been approved by the competent authority.

9.2.0.95   *Stability (damaged condition)*

9.2.0.95.1   The following assumptions shall be taken into consideration for the damaged condition:

(a)   The extent of side damage is as follows:

longitudinal extent:	at least 0.10 L, but not less than 5.00 m;
transverse extent:	0.59 m inboard from the vessel's side at right angles to the centreline at the level corresponding to the maximum draught;
vertical extent:	from the baseline upwards without limit;

(b)   The extent of bottom damage is as follows:

longitudinal extent:	at least 0.10 L, but not less than 5.00 m;
transverse extent:	3.00 m;
vertical extent:	from the base 0.49 m upwards, the sump excepted;

(c)   Any bulkheads within the damaged area shall be assumed damaged, which means that the location of bulkheads shall be chosen so that the vessel will remain afloat after flooding of two or more adjacent compartments in the longitudinal direction.

The following provisions are applicable:

–   For bottom damage, adjacent athwartship compartments shall also be assumed as flooded;

–   The lower edge of any openings that cannot be closed watertight (e.g. doors, windows, access hatchways) shall, at the final stage of flooding, be not less than 0.10 m above the damage waterline;

–   In general, permeability shall be assumed to be 95%. Where an average permeability of less than 95% is calculated for any compartment, this calculated value may be used.

However, the following minimum values shall be used:

– engine rooms	85%
– accommodation	95%
– double bottoms, oil fuel tanks, ballast tanks, etc.,	
depending on whether according to their function,	
they have to be assumed as full or empty for the	
vessel floating at the maximum permissible draught	0% or 95%

For the main engine room only the one–compartment standard needs to be taken into account. (Consequently, the end bulkheads of the engine room shall be assumed as not damaged.)

9.2.0.95.2   At the stage of equilibrium (final stage of flooding) the angle of heel shall not exceed 12°. Non-watertight openings shall not be immersed before reaching the stage of equilibrium. If such openings are immersed before that stage, the corresponding spaces shall be considered as flooded for the purpose of stability calculation.

The positive range of the righting lever curve beyond the position of equilibrium shall have a righting lever of $\geq$ 0.05 m in association with an area under the curve of $\geq$ 0.0065 m.rad. The minimum values of stability shall be satisfied up to immersion of the first non-weathertight opening and in any event up to an angle of heel $\leq$ 27°. If non-weathertight openings are immersed before that stage, the corresponding spaces shall be considered as flooded for the purposes of stability calculation.

9.2.0.95.3   If openings through which undamaged compartments may become additionally flooded are capable of being closed watertight, the closing devices shall be appropriately marked.

9.2.0.95.4   Where cross- or down-flooding openings are provided for reduction of unsymmetrical flooding, the time for equalisation shall not exceed 15 minutes if during the intermediate stages of flooding sufficient stability has been proved.

9.2.0.96 to 9.2.0.99   (*Reserved*)

CHAPTER 9.3

RULES FOR CONSTRUCTION OF TANK VESSELS

9.3.1   **Rules for construction of type G tank vessels**

The rules for construction of 9.3.1.0 to 9.3.1.99 apply to type G tank vessels.

9.3.1.0   *Materials of construction*

9.3.1.0.1   (a)   The vessel's hull and cargo tanks shall be constructed of shipbuilding steel or other at least equivalent metal.

Independent cargo tanks and membrane tanks may also be constructed of other materials, provided these have at least equivalent mechanical strength and resistance against the effects of temperature and fire.

For membrane tanks the equivalence for resistance against the effect of temperature and fire is deemed to be proven where the materials of the membrane tanks fulfil the following requirements:

–   They withstand the range between the maximum temperature in service and 5 °C below the minimum design temperature, but not lower than -196 °C; and

–   They are fire-resistant or protected by a suitable system such as a permanent inert gas environment or provided with a fire-retardant barrier.

     (b)   Every part of the vessel including any installation and equipment which may come into contact with the cargo shall consist of materials which can neither be dangerously affected by the cargo nor cause decomposition of the cargo or react with it so as to form harmful or hazardous products. In case it has not been possible to examine this during classification and inspection of the vessel a relevant reservation shall be entered in the vessel substance list according to 1.16.1.2.5.

9.3.1.0.2   Except where explicitly permitted in 9.3.1.0.3 below or in the certificate of approval, the use of wood, aluminium alloys, plastic materials or rubber within the cargo area is prohibited.

9.3.1.0.3   The use of wood, aluminium alloys, plastic materials or rubber in the cargo area is permitted as shown in the following table:

The use of wood, aluminium alloys, plastic materials or rubber is permitted only for:	Wood	Aluminium alloys	Plastic material	Rubber (X indicates permitted)
Gangways	X	X	X	X
External ladders and passageways (gangways) *)		X	X	X
Cleaning equipment, e.g. brooms	X		X	X
Movable equipment e.g. fire extinguishers, portable gas detectors, rescue winches		X	X	X
Fenders	X		X	X
Mooring cables, fender ropes			X	
Chocking of cargo tanks which are independent of the vessel's hull and chocking of installations and equipment	X		X	

The use of wood, aluminium alloys, plastic materials or rubber is permitted only for:				(X indicates permitted)
	Wood	**Aluminium alloys**	**Plastic material**	**Rubber**
Masts and similar round timber	X	X	X	
Engine parts		X	X	
Protective covers of engines and pumps			X	
Parts of the electrical installation		X	X	
Parts of the loading and unloading installation, e.g., gaskets		X	X	X
Boxes, cabinets or other receptacles placed on the deck for storage of disposal and recovery equipment for capstans, extinguishers, fire hoses, waste, etc.		X	X	
Supports and stops of any kind	X		X	
Ventilators, including hose assemblies for ventilation		X	X	
Parts of the water spray system, the shower and the eye and face bath		X	X	
Insulation of cargo tanks and of piping for loading and unloading, gas discharge pipes and heating pipes			X	X
Coating of cargo tanks and of piping for loading and unloading		X	X	X
All kinds of gaskets (e.g. for dome or hatch covers)			X	X
Cables for electrical equipment			X	X
Mat under hose assemblies for loading and unloading piping system			X	X
Fire hoses, air hoses, hoses for cleaning the deck, etc.			X	X
Sampling equipment and bottles			X	
Photo-optical copies of the certificate of approval according to 8.1.2.6 or 8.1.2.7, and of the vessel's certificate, the measurement certificate and the Rhine navigation membership certificate		X	X	
Drip trays			X	
(*) Take account of 9.3.1.0.5, 9.3.2.0.5 or 9.3.3.0.5, as appropriate				
Aluminium gauging rods are permitted, provided that they are fitted with brass feet or protected in another way to avoid sparking.				

All permanently fitted materials in the accommodation or wheelhouse, with the exception of furniture, shall not readily ignite. They shall not evolve fumes or toxic gases in dangerous quantities, if involved in a fire.

9.3.1.0.4   The paint used in the cargo area shall not be liable to produce sparks in case of impact.

9.3.1.0.5   The use of plastic material for a vessel's boats is permitted only if the material does not readily ignite.

The use of aluminium alloys or plastic material for passageways (gangways) in the cargo area is permitted only if the material does not readily ignite or conduct electricity.

9.3.1.1   *Vessel record*

NOTE: For the purpose of this paragraph, the term "owner" has the same meaning as in 1.16.0.

The vessel record shall be retained by the owner who shall be able to provide this documentation at the request of the competent authority and the recognized classification society.

The vessel record shall be maintained and updated throughout the life of the vessel and shall be retained for 6 months after the vessel is taken out of service.

Should a change of owner occur during the life of the vessel the vessel record shall be transferred to the new owner.

Copies of the vessel record or all necessary documents shall be made available on request to the competent authority for the issuance of the certificate of approval and for the recognized classification society or inspection body for first inspection, periodic inspection, special inspection or exceptional checks.

9.3.1.2 to 9.3.1.7   (*Reserved*)

9.3.1.8   *Classification*

9.3.1.8.1   The tank vessel shall be built under the survey of a recognised classification society and be classed in its highest class.

The vessel's highest class shall be continued. This shall be confirmed by an appropriate certificate issued by the recognized classification society (certificate of class).

The certificate of class shall confirm that the vessel is in conformity with its own additionally applicable rules and regulations that are relevant for the intended use of the vessel.

The design pressure and the test pressure of cargo tanks shall be entered in the certificate.

If a vessel has cargo tanks with different valve opening pressures, the design and test pressures of each tank shall be entered in the certificate.

The recognized classification society shall draw up a vessel substance list mentioning all the dangerous goods accepted for carriage by the tank vessel (see also 1.16.1.2.5).

9.3.1.8.2 to 9.3.1.8.4   (*Deleted*)

9.3.1.9   (*Reserved*)

9.3.1.10   *Protection against the penetration of dangerous gases and the spreading of dangerous liquids*

9.3.1.10.1   The vessel shall be designed so as to prevent dangerous gases and liquids from penetrating into the accommodation, wheelhouse and service spaces. None of the windows in these spaces shall be capable of being opened unless its intended use is as an emergency exit and it is marked as such.

9.3.1.10.2 Liquid-tight protective coamings shall be fitted on deck at the height of the external bulkheads of the cargo tanks, at a maximum distance of 0.60 m from the outer cofferdam bulkheads or the hold end bulkheads. The protective coamings shall either extend over the entire width of the vessel or be fixed between the longitudinal spill coamings so as to prevent liquids from entering the forepeak and afterpeak. The height of the protective coamings and the spill coamings shall be at least 0.075 m. The protective coaming may correspond to the protection wall prescribed in 9.3.1.10.3 if the protection wall extends across the entire width of the vessel.

9.3.1.10.3 If the list of substances on the vessel according to 1.16.1.2.5 is going to include substances that require explosion protection in accordance with column (17) of Table C of Chapter 3.2, then the use of installations and equipment that are not of at least the 'limited explosion risk' type is not permitted during loading and unloading operations in parts of the deck outside the cargo area, unless those parts are protected against the entry of gases and liquids by a gas- and liquid-tight protection wall. The wall must either extend from one side of the vessel to the other or surround the areas to protect in an U-shaped form. The wall must cover the whole width of the area to protect and at least 1.00 m in the direction opposite to the cargo area (see Classification of zones diagram). The height of the wall shall be at least 1.00 m above the adjacent cargo deck area in the cargo area. The outer wall and side walls of the accommodation can be considered as a protection wall if they do not include openings and if the dimensions are complied with.

A protection wall is not required where the distance between the areas to be protected and the safety valve, the shore connections of the piping for loading and unloading, and venting piping, the compressor on deck and the opening of the closest pressure tanks is at least 12.00 m.

9.3.1.10.4 On deck, the lower edges of door-openings in the sidewalls of superstructures and the sills of hatches and ventilation openings of premises located under the deck shall have a height of not less than 0.50 m above the deck.

This requirement does not apply to access openings to double-hull spaces and double bottoms.

9.3.1.10.5 The bulwarks, foot-rails, etc., shall be provided with sufficiently large openings which are located directly above the deck.

9.3.1.11 *Hold spaces and cargo tanks*

9.3.1.11.1 (a) The maximum permissible capacity of a cargo tank shall be determined in accordance with the following table:

$L \times B \times H$ (m^3)	Maximum permissible capacity of a cargo tank (m^3)
up to 600	$L \times B \times H \times 0.3$
600 to 3 750	$180 + (L \times B \times H - 600) \times 0.0635$
> 3 750	380

Alternative constructions in accordance with 9.3.4 are permitted.

In the table above $L \times B \times H$ is the product of the main dimensions of the tank vessel in metres (according to the measurement certificate), where:

L = overall length of the hull in m;

B = extreme breadth of the hull in m;

H = shortest vertical distance between the top of the keel and the lowest point of the deck at the side of the vessel (moulded depth) within the cargo area in m;

where:

For trunk vessels, H shall be replaced by H', where H' shall be obtained from the following formula:

$$H' = H + \left(ht \times \frac{bt}{B} \times \frac{lt}{L} \right)$$

where:

ht = trunk height (distance between trunk deck and main deck measured on trunk side at L/2) in m;

bt = trunk breadth in m;

lt = trunk length in m;

(b) Pressure tanks whose ratio of length to diameter exceeds 7 are prohibited.

(c) The pressure tanks shall be designed for a cargo temperature of + 40 °C.

9.3.1.11.2 (a) In the cargo area, the hull shall be designed as follows:[1]

– as a double-hull and double bottom vessel. The internal distance between the sideplatings of the vessel and the longitudinal bulkheads shall not be less than 0.80 m, the height of the double bottom shall be not less than 0.60 m, the cargo tanks shall be supported by saddles extending between the tanks to not less than 20° below the horizontal centreline of the cargo tanks.

Refrigerated cargo tanks and cargo tanks used for the transport of refrigerated liquefied gases shall be installed only in hold spaces bounded by double-hull spaces and double–bottom. Cargo tank fastenings shall meet the requirements of a recognised classification society; or

– as a single–hull vessel with the sideplatings of the vessel between gangboard and top of floor plates provided with side stringers at regular intervals of not more than 0.60 m which are supported by web frames spaced at intervals of not more than 2.00 m. The side stringers and the web frames shall have a height of not less than 10% of the depth, however, not less than 0.30 m. The side stringers and web frames shall be fitted with a face plate made of flat steel and having a cross-section of not less that 7.5 cm² and 15 cm², respectively.

The distance between the sideplating of the vessel and the cargo tanks shall be not less than 0.80 m and between the bottom and the cargo tanks not less than 0.60 m. The depth below the suction wells may be reduced to 0.50 m.

The lateral distance between the suction well of the cargo tanks and the bottom structure shall be not less than 0.10 m.

The cargo tank supports and fastenings should extend to not less than 10° below the horizontal centreline of the cargo tanks.

---

[1] *For a different design of the hull in the cargo area, proof shall be furnished by way of calculation that in the event of a lateral collision with another vessel having a straight bow, an energy of 22 MJ can be absorbed without any rupture of the cargo tanks and the piping leading to the cargo tanks. Alternative constructions in accordance with 9.3.4 are permitted.*

(b)   The cargo tanks shall be fixed so that they cannot float.

(c)   The capacity of a suction well shall be limited to not more than 0.10 m³. For pressure cargo tanks, however, the capacity of a suction well may be of 0.20 m³.

(d)   Side–struts linking or supporting the load-bearing components of the sides of the vessel with the load-bearing components of the longitudinal walls of cargo tanks and side–struts linking the load-bearing components of the vessel's bottom with the tank-bottom are prohibited.

(e)   Cargo tanks intended to contain products at a temperature below -10°C shall be suitably insulated to ensure that the temperature of the vessel's structure does not fall below the minimum allowable material design temperature. The insulation material shall be resistant to flame spread.

9.3.1.11.3   (a)   The hold spaces shall be separated from the accommodation, engine rooms and service spaces outside the cargo area below deck by bulkheads of Class "A-60" as defined in SOLAS 74, Chapter II-2, Regulation 3. A space of not less than 0.20 m shall be provided between the cargo tanks and the end bulkheads of the hold spaces. Where the cargo tanks have plane end bulkheads this space shall be not less than 0.50 m.

(b)   The hold spaces and cargo tanks shall be capable of being inspected.

(c)   All spaces in the cargo area shall be capable of being ventilated. Means for checking their gas-free condition shall be provided.

9.3.1.11.4   The bulkheads bounding the hold spaces shall be watertight. The cargo tanks and the bulkheads bounding the cargo area shall have no openings or penetrations below deck.

The bulkhead between the engine room and the service spaces within the cargo area or between the engine room and a hold space may be fitted with penetrations provided that they conform to the requirements of 9.3.1.17.5.

9.3.1.11.5   Double-hull spaces and double bottoms in the cargo area shall be arranged for being filled with ballast water only. Double bottoms may, however, be used as oil fuel tanks, provided they comply with the requirements of 9.3.1.32.

9.3.1.11.6   (a)   A space in the cargo area below deck may be arranged as a service space, provided that the bulkhead bounding the service space extends vertically to the bottom and the bulkhead not facing the cargo area extends from one side of the vessel to the other in one frame plane. This service space shall only be accessible from the deck.

(b)   The service space shall be watertight with the exception of its access hatches and ventilation inlets.

(c)   No piping for loading or unloading shall be fitted within the service space referred to under (a) above.

Piping for loading and unloading may be fitted in the cargo pump-rooms below deck only when they conform to the provisions of 9.3.1.17.6.

9.3.1.11.7   Where service spaces are located in the cargo area under deck, they shall be arranged so as to be easily accessible and to permit persons wearing protective clothing and breathing apparatus to safely operate the service equipment contained therein. They shall be designed so as to allow injured or unconscious personnel to be removed from such spaces without difficulty, if necessary by means of fixed equipment.

9.3.1.11.8   Hold spaces and other accessible spaces within the cargo area shall be arranged so as to ensure that they may be completely inspected and cleaned in an appropriate manner. The dimensions of openings, except for those of double-hull spaces and double bottoms which do not have a wall adjoining the cargo tanks, shall be sufficient to allow a person wearing breathing apparatus to enter or leave the space without difficulty. These openings shall have a minimum cross-sectional area of 0.36 m² and a minimum side length of 0.50 m. They shall be designed so as to allow injured or unconscious persons to be removed from the bottom of such spaces without difficulties, if necessary by means of fixed equipment. In these spaces the distance between the reinforcements shall not be less than 0.50 m. In double bottoms this distance may be reduced to 0.45 m.

Cargo tanks may have circular openings with a diameter of not less than 0.68 m.

9.3.1.11.9   In case the vessel has insulated cargo tanks, the hold spaces shall only contain dry air to protect the insulation of the cargo tanks against moisture.

9.3.1.12   *Ventilation*

9.3.1.12.1   Each hold space shall have two openings the dimensions and location of which shall be such as to permit effective ventilation of any part of the hold space. If there are no such openings, it shall be possible to fill the hold spaces with inert gas or dry air.

9.3.1.12.2   Double-hull spaces and double bottoms within the cargo area which are not arranged for being filled with ballast water and cofferdams between engine rooms and pump-rooms, if they exist, shall be provided with ventilation systems.

9.3.1.12.3   (a)   A service space located within the cargo area below deck shall be provided with a ventilation system. The capacity of the fans shall be sufficient to ensure 20 complete changes of air per hour based on the volume of the service space.

The ventilation exhaust ducts shall extend down to 50 mm above the bottom of the service space. The air shall be supplied through a duct at the top of the service space.

(b)   If the list of substances on the vessel according to 1.16.1.2.5 is going to include substances that require explosion protection in accordance with column (17) of Table C of Chapter 3.2, then the air inlets shall be located not less than 2.00 m above the deck, at a distance of not less than 2.00 m from tank openings and 6.00 m from the outlets of safety valves.

The extension pipes which may be necessary may be of the hinged type.

9.3.1.12.4   (a)   Ventilation shall be provided for the accommodation, wheelhouse and service spaces.

(b)   The ventilation system in such spaces shall meet the following requirements:

(i)   The air intakes shall be located as far away as possible, and not less than 6.00 m from the cargo area and not less than 2.00 m above the deck;

(ii)   Pressure of at least 0.1 kPa (0.001 bar) may be maintained in the premises;

(iii)   A breakdown alarm is integrated;

(iv)   The ventilation system, including the breakdown alarm, shall be at least of the 'limited explosion risk' type;

(v) A gas detection system conforming to conditions 1. to 4. below is connected to the ventilation system:

1. It is appropriate at least for use in zone 1, explosion group IIC and temperature class T6;

2. It is equipped with sensors;

   • On the suction inlets of the ventilation systems; and

   • Directly below the top edge of the sill of the entrance doors;

3. Its t90 response time is lower than or equal to 4 s;

4. Measurement shall be continuous;

(vi) In the service spaces, the ventilation system is linked to the emergency lighting, which shall be at least of the 'limited explosion risk' type;

This emergency lighting is not necessary if the lighting installations in the service spaces are of at least the 'limited explosion risk' type;

(vii) The suction of the ventilation system and installations and equipment that do not meet the requirements set out in 9.3.1.51 (a) and (b) and 9.3.1.52.1 must be shut down when a concentration of 20% of LEL of n-Hexane is reached;

The switching-off shall be indicated in the accommodation and wheelhouse by visual and audible signals;

(viii) In the event of failure of the ventilation system or the gas detection installations in the accommodation, installations and equipment in the accommodation that do not meet the requirements set out in 9.3.1.51 (a) and (b) and 9.3.1.52.1 must be stopped;

The failure shall be indicated in the accommodation, the wheelhouse and on the deck by visual and audible signals;

(ix) In the event of failure of the ventilation system or the gas detection installations in the wheelhouse or service spaces, installations and equipment in those spaces that do not meet the requirements set out in 9.3.1.51 (a) and (b) and 9.3.1.52.1 must be shut down;

The failure shall be indicated in the wheelhouse and on the deck by visual and audible signals. The alarm must be relayed to the accommodation automatically if it has not been switched off;

(x) Any switching-off shall take place immediately and automatically and, if necessary, shall activate the emergency lighting;

The automatic switch-off device is set so that no automatic switching-off may occur while the vessel is under way;

(c) If there is no ventilation system or the ventilation system of a space does not comply with all the requirements set out in (b) above, any installations or equipment present in that space that may, if switched on, give rise to surface temperatures higher than those mentioned in 9.3.1.51 (a) and (b) or that do not meet the requirements set out in 9.3.1.52.1 must be capable of being switched off.

9.3.1.12.5   *(Deleted)*

9.3.1.12.6   Notice boards shall be fitted at the ventilation inlets indicating the conditions under which they shall be closed. All ventilation inlets of accommodation, wheelhouse and service spaces leading to the open air outside the cargo area shall be fitted with devices permanently fixed according to 9.3.1.40.2.2 (c), enabling them to be closed rapidly. It shall be clear whether they are open or closed.

Such ventilation inlets shall be located not less than 2.00 m from the cargo area.

Ventilation inlets of service spaces in the cargo area may be located within that area.

Ventilation inlets of service spaces in the cargo area may be located within such area.

9.3.1.13   *Stability (general)*

9.3.1.13.1   Proof of sufficient stability shall be furnished including for stability in damaged condition.

9.3.1.13.2   The basic values for the stability calculation – the vessel's lightweight and location of the centre of gravity – shall be determined either by means of an inclining experiment or by detailed mass and moment calculation. In the latter case the lightweight of the vessel shall be checked by means of a lightweight test with a tolerance limit of ± 5% between the mass determined by calculation and the displacement determined by the draught readings.

9.3.1.13.3   Proof of sufficient intact stability shall be furnished for all stages of loading and unloading and for the final loading condition for all the relative densities of the substances transported contained in the vessel substance list according to 1.16.1.2.5.

For every loading case, taking account of the actual fillings and floating position of cargo tanks, ballast tanks and compartments, drinking water and sewage tanks and tanks containing products for the operation of the vessel, the vessel shall comply with the intact and damage stability requirements.

Intermediate stages during operations shall also be taken into consideration.

The proof of sufficient stability shall be shown for every operating, loading and ballast condition in the stability booklet, to be approved by the recognized classification society, which classes the vessel. If it is unpractical to pre-calculate the operating, loading and ballast conditions, a loading instrument approved by the recognised classification society which classes the vessel shall be installed and used which contains the contents of the stability booklet.

NOTE: A stability booklet shall be worded in a form comprehensible for the responsible master and containing the following details:

General description of the vessel:

–   *General arrangement and capacity plans indicating the assigned use of compartments and spaces (cargo tanks, stores, accommodation, etc.);*

–   *A sketch indicating the position of the draught marks referring to the vessel's perpendiculars;*

–   *A scheme for ballast/bilge pumping and overflow prevention systems;*

–   *Hydrostatic curves or tables corresponding to the design trim, and, if significant trim angles are foreseen during the normal operation of the vessel, curves or tables corresponding to such range of trim are to be introduced;*

– *Cross curves or tables of stability calculated on a free trimming basis, for the ranges of displacement and trim anticipated in normal operating conditions, with an indication of the volumes which have been considered buoyant;*

– *Tank sounding tables or curves showing capacities, centres of gravity, and free surface data for all cargo tanks, ballast tanks and compartments, drinking water and sewage water tanks and tanks containing products for the operation of the vessel;*

– *Lightship data (weight and centre of gravity) resulting from an inclining test or deadweight measurement in combination with a detailed mass balance or other acceptable measures. Where the above–mentioned information is derived from a sister vessel, the reference to this sister vessel shall be clearly indicated, and a copy of the approved inclining test report relevant to this sister vessel shall be included;*

– *A copy of the approved test report shall be included in the stability booklet;*

– *Operating loading conditions with all relevant details, such as:*

  – *Lightship data, tank fillings, stores, crew and other relevant items on board (mass and centre of gravity for each item, free surface moments for liquid loads);*

  – *Draughts amidships and at perpendiculars;*

  – *Metacentric height corrected for free surfaces effect;*

  – *Righting lever values and curve;*

  – *Longitudinal bending moments and shear forces at read–out points;*

  – *Information about openings (location, type of tightness, means of closure); and*

  – *Information for the master.*

– *Calculation of the influence of ballast water on stability with information on whether fixed level gauges for ballast tanks and compartments have to be installed or the ballast tanks, or compartments shall only be completely full or completely empty when underway.*

9.3.1.13.4 Floatability after damage shall be proved for the most unfavourable loading condition. For this purpose, calculated proof of sufficient stability shall be established for critical intermediate stages of flooding and for the final stage of flooding.

9.3.1.14 *Stability (intact)*

9.3.1.14.1 The requirements for intact stability resulting from the damaged stability calculation shall be fully complied with.

9.3.1.14.2 For vessels with cargo tanks of more than 0.70 B in width, proof shall be furnished that the following stability requirements have been complied with:

(a) In the positive area of the righting lever curve up to immersion of the first non-watertight opening there shall be a righting lever (GZ) of not less than 0.10 m;

(b) The surface of the positive area of the righting lever curve up to immersion of the first non-watertight opening and in any event up to an angle of heel < 27° shall not be less than 0.024 m.rad;

(c) The metacentric height (GM) shall be not less than 0.10 m.

These conditions shall be met bearing in mind the influence of all free surfaces in tanks for all stages of loading and unloading.

9.3.1.14.3   The most stringent requirement of 9.3.1.14.1 and 9.3.1.14.2 is applicable to the vessel.

9.3.1.15   *Stability (damaged condition)*

9.3.1.15.1   The following assumptions shall be taken into consideration for the damaged condition:

(a)   The extent of side damage is as follows:

longitudinal extent:	at least 0.10 L, but not less than 5.00 m;
transverse extent:	0.79 m inboard from the vessel's side at right angles to the centreline at the level corresponding to the maximum draught, or when applicable, the distance allowed by section 9.3.4, reduced by 0.01 m;
vertical extent:	from the base line upwards without limit;

(b)   The extent of bottom damage is as follows:

longitudinal extent:	at least 0.10 L, but not less than 5.00 m;
transverse extent:	3.00 m;
vertical extent:	from the base 0.59 m upwards, the well excepted;

(c)   Any bulkheads within the damaged area shall be assumed damaged, which means that the location of bulkheads shall be chosen so as to ensure that the vessel remains afloat after the flooding of two or more adjacent compartments in the longitudinal direction.

The following provisions are applicable:

–   For bottom damage, adjacent athwartship compartments shall also be assumed as flooded;

–   The lower edge of any non-watertight openings (e.g. doors, windows, access hatchways) shall, at the final stage of flooding, be not less than 0.10 m above the damage waterline;

–   In general, permeability shall be assumed to be 95%. Where an average permeability of less than 95% is calculated for any compartment, this calculated value obtained may be used.

However, the following minimum values shall be used:

– engine rooms:	85%;
– accommodation:	95%;
– double bottoms, oil fuel tanks, ballast tanks, etc., depending on whether, according to their function, they have to be assumed as full or empty for the vessel floating at the maximum permissible draught:	0% or 95%.

For the main engine room only the one–compartment standard need be taken into account, i.e. the end bulkheads of the engine room shall be assumed as not damaged.

9.3.1.15.2   For the intermediate stage of flooding the following criteria have to be fulfilled:

GZ ≥ 0.03m

Range of positive GZ: 5°.

At the stage of equilibrium (final stage of flooding), the angle of heel shall not exceed 12°. Non-watertight openings shall not be flooded before reaching the stage of equilibrium. If such openings are immersed before that stage, the corresponding spaces shall be considered as flooded for the purpose of stability calculation.

The positive range of the righting lever curve beyond the stage of equilibrium shall have a righting level of ≥ 0.05 m in association with an area under the curve of ≥ 0.0065 m.rad. The minimum values of stability shall be satisfied up to immersion of the first non-weathertight opening and in any event up to an angle of heel ≤ 27°. If non-watertight openings are immersed before that stage, the corresponding spaces shall be considered as flooded for the purpose of stability calculation.

9.3.1.15.3   If openings through which undamaged compartments may additionally become flooded are capable of being closed watertight, the closing appliances shall be marked accordingly.

9.3.1.15.4   When cross- or down-flooding openings are provided for reduction of unsymmetrical flooding, the time for equalisation shall not exceed 15 minutes, if during the intermediate stages of flooding sufficient stability has been proved.

9.3.1.16   ***Engine rooms***

9.3.1.16.1   Internal combustion engines for the vessel's propulsion as well as internal combustion engines for auxiliary machinery shall be located outside the cargo area. Entrances and other openings of engine rooms shall be at a distance of not less than 2.00 m from the cargo area.

9.3.1.16.2   The engine room shall be accessible from the deck; the entrances shall not face the cargo area. When the doors are not located in a recess whose depth is at least equal to the door width, the hinges shall face the cargo area.

9.3.1.17   *Accommodation and service spaces*

9.3.1.17.1   Accommodation spaces and the wheelhouse shall be located outside the cargo area forward of the fore vertical plane or abaft the aft vertical plane bounding the part of the cargo area below deck. Windows of the wheelhouse which are located not less than 1.00 m above the bottom of the wheelhouse may tilt forward.

9.3.1.17.2   Entrances to spaces and openings of superstructures shall not face the cargo area. Doors opening outward and not located in a recess the depth of which is at least equal to the width of the doors shall have their hinges facing the cargo area.

9.3.1.17.3   Entrances from the deck and openings of spaces facing the weather shall be capable of being closed. The following instruction shall be displayed at the entrance of such spaces:

**Do not open during loading, unloading and degassing
without the permission of the master.
Close immediately.**

9.3.1.17.4   Entrances and windows of superstructures and accommodation spaces which can be opened as well as other openings of these spaces shall be located not less than 2.00 m from the cargo area. No wheelhouse doors and windows shall be located within 2.00 m from the cargo area, except where there is no direct connection between the wheelhouse and the accommodation.

9.3.1.17.5   (a)   Driving shafts of the bilge or ballast pumps may penetrate through the bulkhead between the service space and the engine room, provided the arrangement of the service space is in compliance with 9.3.1.11.6.

(b)   The penetration of the shaft through the bulkhead shall be gastight and shall have been approved by a recognised classification society.

(c)   The necessary operating instructions shall be displayed.

(d)   Penetrations through the bulkhead between the engine room and the service space in the cargo area, and the bulkhead between the engine room and the hold spaces may be provided for electrical cables, hydraulic lines and piping for measuring, control and alarm systems, provided that the penetrations have been approved by a recognised classification society. The penetrations shall be gastight. Penetrations through a bulkhead with an "A-60" fire protection insulation according to SOLAS 74, Chapter II-2, Regulation 3, shall have an equivalent fire protection.

(e)   Pipes may pass through the bulkhead between the engine room and the service space in the cargo area provided that these are pipes between the mechanical equipment in the engine room and the service space which do not have any openings within the service space and which are provided with shut-off devices at the bulkhead in the engine room.

(f)   Notwithstanding 9.3.1.11.4, pipes from the engine room may pass through the service space in the cargo area or a cofferdam or a hold space or a double-hull space to the outside provided that within the service space or cofferdam or hold space or double-hull space they are of the thick-walled type and have no flanges or openings.

(g)   Where a driving shaft of auxiliary machinery penetrates through a wall located above the deck the penetration shall be gastight.

9.3.1.17.6   A service space located within the cargo area below deck shall not be used as a cargo pump room for the vessel's own gas discharging system, e.g. compressors or the compressor/heat exchanger/pump combination, except where:

–   the cargo pump-room is separated from the engine room or from service spaces outside the cargo area by a cofferdam or a bulkhead with an insulation of Class "A-60" as defined in SOLAS 74, Chapter II-2, Regulation 3, or by a service space or a hold space;

–   the "A-60" bulkhead required above does not include penetrations referred to in 9.3.1.17.5 (a);

–   ventilation exhaust outlets are located not less than 6.00 m from entrances and openings of the accommodation, wheelhouse and service spaces outside the cargo area;

–   the access hatches and ventilation inlets can be closed from the outside;

–   all piping for loading and unloading (at the suction side and the delivery side) are led through the deck above the pump-room. The necessary operation of the control devices in the pump-room, starting of pumps or compressors and control of the liquid flow rate shall be effected from the deck;

–   the system is fully integrated in the gas and liquid piping system;

–   the cargo pump room is provided with a permanent oxygen detection system which automatically indicates the amount of oxygen and which actuates a visual and audible alarm when the oxygen concentration has reached 19.5% by volume. The sensors of this system shall be placed at suitable positions at the bottom and at a height of 2.00 m. Measurement shall be continuous and displayed near to the entrance. Audible and visual alarms shall be installed in the wheelhouse and in the cargo pump-room and, when the alarm is actuated, the loading and unloading system shall be shut down;

–   failure of the oxygen measuring system shall actuate a visual and audible alarm in the wheelhouse and on deck. The alarm must be relayed to the accommodation automatically if it has not been switched off;

–   the ventilation system prescribed in 9.3.1.12.3 has a capacity sufficient to ensure not less than 30 changes of air per hour based on the total volume of the service space.

If the list of substances on the vessel according to 1.16.1.2.5 is going to include substances that require explosion protection in accordance with column (17) of Table C of Chapter 3.2, then the cargo pump room shall also be provided with a permanent gas detection system which automatically indicates the presence of flammable gases and actuates a visual and audible alarm when the gas concentration has reached 20% of the LEL of the cargo or 20% of the LEL of n-Hexane, whichever gives the more critical value.

The sensors of this gas detection system shall be placed at suitable positions at the bottom and directly below the deck.

Measurement shall be continuous and displayed near to the entrance.

Audible and visual alarms shall be installed in the wheelhouse and in the cargo pump-room and, when the alarm is actuated, the loading and unloading system shall be shut down.

Any failure of the gas detection system shall be immediately signalled in the wheelhouse and on deck by a visual and audible warning. The alarm must be relayed to the accommodation automatically if it has not been switched off.

9.3.1.17.7   The following instruction shall be displayed at the entrance of the cargo pump-room:

Before entering the cargo pump-room check whether
it is free from gases and contains sufficient oxygen.
Do not open doors and entrance openings without
the permission of the master.
Leave immediately in the event of alarm.

9.3.1.18   *Inerting facilities*

9.3.1.18.1   In cases in which inerting or blanketing of the cargo is prescribed, the vessel shall be equipped with an inerting system.

The system shall be capable of keeping permanently a minimum pressure of 7 kPa (0.07 bar) in the spaces to be inerted. In addition, the inerting system shall not increase the pressure in the cargo tank to a pressure greater than that at which the pressure valve is regulated. The set pressure of the vacuum-relief valve shall be 3.5 kPa (0.035 bar).

A sufficient quantity of inert gas for loading or unloading shall be carried or produced on board if it is not possible to obtain it on shore. In addition, a sufficient quantity of inert gas to offset normal losses occurring during carriage shall be on board.

The premises to be inerted shall be equipped with connections for introducing the inert gas and monitoring systems so as to ensure the correct atmosphere on a permanent basis.

When the pressure or the concentration of inert gas in the gaseous phase falls below a given value, this monitoring system shall activate an audible and visible alarm in the wheelhouse. When the wheelhouse is unoccupied, the alarm shall also be perceptible in a location occupied by a crew member.

9.3.1.18.2   Vessels equipped with membrane tanks shall have an inerting system capable of inerting all insulation spaces of the tanks.

The system shall be capable of keeping permanently a minimum pressure above atmospheric pressure in the spaces to be inerted.

The inert gas shall be produced on board or carried in a quantity that is sufficient for the entire holding time as determined in accordance with 7.2.4.16.16 and 7.2.4.16.17. The circulation of inert gas throughout the spaces to be inerted shall be sufficient to allow for effective means of gas detection.

The spaces to be inerted shall be equipped with connections for introducing the inert gas and monitoring systems so as to ensure the required atmosphere on a permanent basis.

When the pressure, the temperature or the concentration of the inert gas falls below a given value, this monitoring system shall activate an audible and visible alarm in the wheelhouse. When the wheelhouse is unoccupied, the alarm shall also be perceptible in a location occupied by a crew member.

9.3.1.19 and 9.3.1.20   (*Reserved*)

9.3.1.21   *Safety and control installations*

9.3.1.21.1   Cargo tanks shall be provided with the following equipment:

    (a)   (*Reserved*)

    (b)   a level gauge;

(c)   a level alarm device which is activated at the latest when a degree of filling of 86% is reached;

(d)   a high level sensor for actuating the facility against overflowing at the latest when a degree of filling of 97.5% is reached;

(e)   an instrument for measuring the pressure of the gas phase in the cargo tank;

(f)   an instrument for measuring the temperature of the cargo;

(g)   a connection for a closed-type sampling device. The connection shall be fitted with a shut-off device resistant to the internal pressure at the connection.

9.3.1.21.2   When the degree of filling in per cent is determined, an error of not more than 0.5% is permitted. It shall be calculated on the basis of the total cargo tank capacity including the expansion trunk.

9.3.1.21.3   The level gauge shall allow readings from the control position of the shut-off devices of the particular cargo tank. The permissible maximum filling levels of 91%, 95% and 97%, as given in the list of substances, shall be marked on each level gauge.

Permanent reading of the overpressure and vacuum shall be possible from a location from which loading or unloading operations may be interrupted. The permissible maximum overpressure and vacuum shall be marked on each level gauge.

Readings shall be possible in all weather conditions.

9.3.1.21.4   The level alarm device shall give a visual and audible warning on board when actuated. The level alarm device shall be independent of the level gauge.

9.3.1.21.5   (a)   The high level sensor referred to in 9.3.1.21.1 (d) shall give a visual and audible alarm on board and at the same time actuate an electrical contact which in the form of a binary signal interrupts the electric current loop provided and fed by the shore facility, thus initiating measures at the shore facility against overflowing during loading operations.

The signal shall be transmitted to the shore facility via a watertight two–pin plug of a connector device in accordance with standard EN 60309–2:1999 + A1:2007 + A2:2012 for direct current of 40 to 50 volts, identification colour white, position of the nose 10 h.

The plug shall be permanently fitted to the vessel close to the shore connections of the loading and unloading piping.

The high level sensor shall also be capable of switching off the vessel's own discharging pump.

The high level sensor shall be independent of the level alarm device, but it may be connected to the level gauge.

(b)   During discharging by means of the on-board pump, it shall be possible for the shore facility to switch it off. For this purpose, an independent intrinsically safe power line, fed by the vessel, shall be switched off by the shore facility by means of an electrical contact.

It shall be possible for the binary signal of the shore facility to be transmitted via a watertight two–pole socket or a connector device in accordance with standard EN 60309-2:1999 + A1:2007 + A2:2012, for direct current of 40 to 50 volts, identification colour white, position of the nose 10 h.

This socket shall be permanently fitted to the vessel close to the shore connections of the unloading piping.

9.3.1.21.6 The visual and audible signals given by the level alarm device shall be clearly distinguishable from those of the high level sensor.

The visual alarm shall be visible at each control position on deck of the cargo tank stop valves. It shall be possible to easily check the functioning of the sensors and electric circuits or these shall be of the "failsafe" design.

9.3.1.21.7 When the pressure or the temperature exceeds a set value, the instruments for measuring the pressure and the temperature of the cargo shall activate a visual and an audible alarm in the wheelhouse. When the wheelhouse is unoccupied the alarm shall also be perceptible in a location occupied by a crew member.

When the pressure exceeds a set value during loading or unloading, the instrument for measuring the pressure shall simultaneously initiate an electrical contact which, by means of the plug referred to in 9.3.1.21.5 above, enables measures to be taken to interrupt the loading and unloading operation. When the vessel's own discharge pump is used, it shall be switched off automatically. The sensor for the alarms referred to above may be connected to the alarm installation.

9.3.1.21.8 Where the control elements of the shut-off devices of the cargo tanks are located in a control room, it shall be possible to stop the loading pumps and read the level gauges in the control room, and the visual and audible warning given by the level alarm device, the high level sensor referred to in 9.3.1.21.1 (d) and the instruments for measuring the pressure and temperature of the cargo shall be noticeable in the control room and on deck.

Satisfactory monitoring of the cargo area shall be ensured from the control room.

9.3.1.21.9 The vessel shall be so equipped that loading or unloading operations can be interrupted by means of switches, i.e. the quick closing valve located on the flexible vessel–to–shore connecting line must be capable of being closed. The switches shall be placed at two points on the vessel (fore and aft).

The interruption systems shall be designed according to the quiescent current principle.

9.3.1.21.10 When refrigerated substances are carried the opening pressure of the safety system shall be determined by the design of the cargo tanks. In the event of the transport of substances that must be carried in a refrigerated state the opening pressure of the safety system shall be not less than 25 kPa (0.25 bar) greater than the maximum pressure calculated according to 9.3.1.27.

9.3.1.21.11 On vessels certified to carry refrigerated liquefied gases the following protective measures shall be provided in the cargo area:

– Drips trays shall be installed under the shore connections of the piping for loading and unloading through which the loading and unloading operation is carried out. They must be made of materials which are able to resist the temperature of the cargo and be insulated from the deck. The drip trays shall have a sufficient volume and an overboard drain;

–   A water spray system to cover:

        1.   exposed cargo tank domes and exposed parts of cargo tanks;

        2.   exposed on–deck storage vessels for flammable or toxic products;

        3.   parts of the cargo deck area where a leakage may occur.

The capacity of the water spray system shall be such that when all spray nozzles are in operation, the outflow is of 300 litres per square meter of cargo deck area per hour. The system shall be capable of being put into operation from the wheelhouse and from the deck;

–   A water film around the shore connection of the piping for loading and unloading in use to protect the deck and the shipside in the way of the shore connection of the piping for loading and unloading in use during connecting and disconnecting the loading arm or hose. The water film shall have sufficient capacity. The system shall be capable of being put into operation from the wheelhouse and from the deck.

9.3.1.21.12   Vessels carrying refrigerated liquefied gases shall have on board, for the purpose of preventing damage to the cargo tanks during loading and the piping for loading and unloading during loading and unloading, a written instruction for pre–cooling. This instruction shall be applied before the vessel is put into operation and after long–term maintenance.

9.3.1.22   *Cargo tank openings*

9.3.1.22.1   (a)   Cargo tank openings shall be located on deck in the cargo area.

(b)   Cargo tank openings with a cross-section greater than 0.10 m^2 shall be located not less than 0.50 m above the deck.

9.3.1.22.2   Cargo tank openings shall be fitted with gastight closures which comply with the provisions of 9.3.1.23.1.

9.3.1.22.3   The exhaust outlets of the pressure relief valves shall be located not less than 2.00 m above the deck at a distance of not less than 6.00 m from the accommodation and from the service spaces located outside the cargo area. This height may be reduced when within a radius of 1.00 m round the pressure relief valve outlet there is no equipment, no work is being carried out and signs indicate the area.

9.3.1.22.4   The closing devices normally used in loading and unloading operations shall not be capable of producing sparks when operated.

9.3.1.22.5   Each tank in which refrigerated substances are carried shall be equipped with a safety system to prevent unauthorized vacuum or overpressure.

9.3.1.23   *Pressure test*

9.3.1.23.1   Cargo tanks and piping for loading and unloading shall comply with the provisions concerning pressure vessels which have been established by the competent authority or a recognised classification society for the substances carried.

9.3.1.23.2   Any cofferdams shall be subjected to initial tests before being put into service and thereafter at the prescribed intervals.

The test pressure shall be not less than 10 kPa (0.10 bar) gauge pressure.

9.3.1.23.3   The maximum intervals for the periodic tests referred to in 9.3.1.23.2 above shall be 11 years.

9.3.1.24 *Regulation of cargo pressure and temperature*

9.3.1.24.1 Unless the entire cargo system is designed to resist the full effective vapour pressure of the cargo at the upper limits of the ambient design temperatures, the pressure of the tanks shall be kept below the permissible maximum set pressure of the safety valves, by one or more of the following means:

(a) a system for the regulation of cargo tank pressure using mechanical refrigeration;

(b) a system ensuring safety in the event of the heating or increase in pressure of the cargo. The insulation or the design pressure of the cargo tank, or the combination of these two elements, shall be such as to leave an adequate margin for the operating period and the temperatures expected; in each case the system shall be deemed acceptable by a recognized classification society and shall ensure safety for a minimum time of three times the operation period;

(c) For UN No. 1972 only, a system for the regulation of cargo tank pressure whereby the boil-off vapours are utilized as fuel;

(d) other systems deemed acceptable by a recognized classification society.

9.3.1.24.2 The systems prescribed in 9.3.1.24.1 shall be constructed, installed and tested to the satisfaction of the recognized classification society. The materials used in their construction shall be compatible with the cargoes to be carried. For normal service, the upper ambient design temperature limits shall be:

air: +30 °C;
water: +20 °C.

9.3.1.24.3 The cargo storage system shall be capable of resisting the full vapour pressure of the cargo at the upper limits of the ambient design temperatures, whatever the system adopted to deal with the boil-off gas. This requirement is indicated by remark 37 in column (20) of Table C of Chapter 3.2.

9.3.1.25 *Pumps and piping*

9.3.1.25.1 Pumps, compressors and accessory loading and unloading piping shall be placed in the cargo area. Cargo pumps and compressors shall be capable of being shut down from the cargo area and, in addition, from a position outside the cargo area. Cargo pumps and compressors situated on deck shall be located not less than 6.00 m from entrances to, or openings of, the accommodation and service spaces outside the cargo area.

9.3.1.25.2 (a) Piping for loading and unloading shall be independent of any other piping of the vessel. No cargo piping shall be located below deck, except those inside the cargo tanks and in the service spaces intended for the installation of the vessel's own gas discharging system.

(b) *(Reserved)*

(c) Piping for loading and unloading shall be clearly distinguishable from other piping, e.g. by means of colour marking.

(d)   The piping for loading and unloading on deck, the venting piping with the exception of the shore connections but including the safety valves, and the valves shall be located within the longitudinal line formed by the outer boundaries of the domes and not less than one quarter of the vessel's breadth from the outer shell. This requirement does not apply to the relief pipes situated behind the safety valves. If there is, however, only one dome athwartships, these pipes and their valves shall be located at a distance not less than 2.70 m from the shell.

Where cargo tanks are placed side by side, all the connections to the domes shall be located on the inner side of the domes. The external connections may be located on the fore and aft centre line of the dome. The shut-off devices shall be located directly at the dome or as close as possible to it. The shut-off devices of the loading and unloading piping shall be duplicated, one of the devices being constituted by a quick closing valve. When the inside diameter of a shut-off device is less than 50 mm this device may be regarded as a safety device against bursts in the piping.

(e)   The shore connections shall be located not less than 6.00 m from the entrances to or openings of, the accommodation and service spaces outside the cargo area.

(f)   Each shore connection of the venting piping and shore connections of the piping for loading and unloading, through which the loading or unloading operation is carried out, shall be fitted with a shut-off device and a quick closing valve. However, each shore connection shall be fitted with a blind flange when it is not in operation.

(g)   Piping for loading and unloading, and venting piping, shall not have flexible connections fitted with sliding seals.

For transport of refrigerated liquefied gases

(h)   The piping for loading and unloading and cargo tanks shall be protected from excessive stresses due to thermal movement and from movements of the tank and hull structure.

(i)   Where necessary, piping for loading and unloading shall be thermally insulated from the adjacent hull structure to prevent the temperature of the hull falling below the design temperature of the hull material.

(j)   All piping for loading and unloading, which may be closed off at each end when containing liquid (residue), shall be provided with safety valves. These safety valves shall discharge into the cargo tanks and shall be protected against inadvertent closing.

9.3.1.25.3   *(Deleted)*

9.3.1.25.4   Every component of the piping for loading and unloading shall be electrically connected to the hull.

9.3.1.25.5   The stop valves or other shut-off devices of the piping for loading and unloading shall indicate whether they are open or shut.

9.3.1.25.6   The piping for loading and unloading shall have, at the test pressure, the required elasticity, leakproofness and resistance to pressure.

9.3.1.25.7   The piping for unloading shall be fitted with pressure gauges at the inlet and outlet of the pump.

Reading of the pressure gauges shall be possible from the control position of the vessel's own gas discharging system. The maximum permissible overpressure or vacuum shall be indicated by a measuring device.

Readings shall be possible in all weather conditions.

9.3.1.25.8   Use of the cargo piping for ballasting purposes shall not be possible.

9.3.1.25.9   *(Reserved)*

9.3.1.25.10   Compressed air generated outside the cargo area can be used in the cargo area subject to the installation of a spring-loaded non-return valve to ensure that no gases can escape from the cargo area through the compressed air system into accommodation, wheelhouse or service spaces outside the cargo area.

9.3.1.26   *(Reserved)*

9.3.1.27   ***Refrigeration system***

9.3.1.27.1   The refrigeration system referred to in 9.3.1.24.1 (a) shall be composed of one or more units capable of keeping the pressure and temperature of the cargo at the upper limits of the ambient design temperatures at the prescribed level. Unless another means of regulating cargo pressure and temperature deemed satisfactory by a recognized classification society is provided, provision shall be made for one or more stand-by units with an output at least equal to that of the largest prescribed unit. A stand-by unit shall include a compressor, its engine, its control system and all necessary accessories to enable it to operate independently of the units normally used. Provision shall be made for a stand-by heat-exchanger unless the system's normal heat-exchanger has a surplus capacity equal to at least 25% of the largest prescribed capacity. It is not necessary to make provision for separate piping.

Cargo tanks, piping and accessories shall be insulated so that, in the event of a failure of all cargo refrigeration systems, the entire cargo remains for at least 52 hours in a condition not causing the safety valves to open.

9.3.1.27.2   The security devices and the connecting lines from the refrigeration system shall be connected to the cargo tanks above the liquid phase of the cargo when the tanks are filled to their maximum permissible degree of filling. They shall remain within the gaseous phase, even if the vessel has a list up to 12 degrees.

9.3.1.27.3   When several refrigerated cargoes with a potentially dangerous chemical reaction are carried simultaneously, particular care shall be given to the refrigeration systems so as to prevent any mixing of the cargoes. For the carriage of such cargoes, separate refrigeration systems, each including the full stand-by unit referred to in 9.3.1.27.1, shall be provided for each cargo. When, however, refrigeration is ensured by an indirect or combined system and no leak in the heat exchangers can under any foreseeable circumstances lead to the mixing of cargoes, no provision need be made for separate refrigeration units for the different cargoes.

9.3.1.27.4   When several refrigerated cargoes are not soluble in each other under conditions of carriage such that their vapour pressures are added together in the event of mixing, particular care shall be given to the refrigeration systems to prevent any mixing of the cargoes.

9.3.1.27.5   When the refrigeration systems require water for cooling, a sufficient quantity shall be supplied by a pump or pumps used exclusively for the purpose. This pump or pumps shall have at least two suction pipes, leading from two water intakes, one to port, the other to starboard. Provision shall be made for a stand-by pump with a satisfactory flow; this may be a pump used for other purposes provided that its use for supplying water for cooling does not impair any other essential service.

9.3.1.27.6   The refrigeration system may take one of the following forms:

(a)   Direct system: the cargo vapours are compressed, condensed and returned to the cargo tanks. This system shall not be used for certain cargoes specified in Table C of Chapter 3.2. This requirement is indicated by remark 35 in column (20) of Table C of Chapter 3.2;

(b)   Indirect system: the cargo or the cargo vapours are cooled or condensed by means of a coolant without being compressed;

(c)   Combined system: the cargo vapours are compressed and condensed in a cargo/coolant heat-exchanger and returned to the cargo tanks. This system shall not be used for certain cargoes specified in Table C of Chapter 3.2. This requirement is indicated by remark 36 in column (20) of Table C of Chapter 3.2.

9.3.1.27.7   All primary and secondary coolant fluids shall be compatible with each other and with the cargo with which they may come into contact. Heat exchange may take place either at a distance from the cargo tank, or by using cooling coils attached to the inside or the outside of the cargo tank.

9.3.1.27.8   When the refrigeration system is installed in a separate service space, this service space shall meet the requirements of 9.3.1.17.6.

9.3.1.27.9   For all cargo systems, the heat transmission coefficient as used for the determination of the holding time (7.2.4.16.16 and 7.2.4.16.17) shall be determined by calculation. Upon completion of the vessel, the correctness of the calculation shall be checked by means of a heat balance test. The calculation and test shall be performed under supervision by the recognized classification society which classified the vessel.

The heat transmission coefficient shall be documented and kept on board. The heat transmission coefficient shall be verified at every renewal of the certificate of approval.

9.3.1.27.10   A certificate from a recognized classification society stating that 9.3.1.24.1 to 9.3.1.24.3, 9.3.1.27.1 and 9.3.1.27.4 above have been complied with shall be submitted together with the application for issue or renewal of the certificate of approval.

9.3.1.28   *Water-spray system*

When water-spraying is required in column (9) of Table C of Chapter 3.2 a water-spray system shall be installed in the cargo area on deck for the purpose of reducing gases given off by the cargo by spraying water.

The system shall be fitted with a connection device for supply from the shore. The spray nozzles shall be so installed that released gases are precipitated safely. The system shall be capable of being put into operation from the wheelhouse and from the deck. The capacity of the water-spray system shall be such that when all the spray nozzles are in operation, the outflow is of 50 litres per square metre of cargo deck area and per hour.

9.3.1.29 and 9.3.1.30   (*Reserved*)

9.3.1.31   *Engines*

9.3.1.31.1   Only internal combustion engines running on fuel with having a flashpoint above 55 °C are allowed. This provision does not apply to internal combustion engines which are part of propulsion and auxiliary systems. These systems shall meet the requirements of Chapter 30 and Annex 8, Section 1 of the European Standard laying down Technical Requirements for Inland Navigation vessels (ES-TRIN) as amended.[2]

9.3.1.31.2   Ventilation inlets of the engine room and, when the engines do not take in air directly from the engine room, the air intakes of the engines shall be located not less than 2.00 m from the cargo area.

9.3.1.31.3 and 9.3.1.31.4   *(Deleted)*

9.3.1.31.5   The ventilation in the closed engine room shall be designed so that, at an ambient temperature of 20 °C, the average temperature in the engine room does not exceed 40 °C.

9.3.1.32   *Oil fuel tanks*

9.3.1.32.1   When the vessel is fitted with hold spaces and double bottoms, double bottoms within the cargo area may be arranged as oil fuel tanks, provided their depth is not less than 0.6 m.

Oil fuel pipes and openings of such tanks are not permitted in the hold space.

9.3.1.32.2   The open ends of the air pipes of each oil fuel tanks shall extend to not less than 0.5 m above the open deck. These open ends and the open ends of overflow pipes leading to the deck shall be fitted with a protective device consisting of a gauze diaphragm or a perforated plate.

9.3.1.33   *(Reserved)*

9.3.1.34   *Exhaust pipes*

9.3.1.34.1   Exhausts shall be evacuated from the vessel into the open air either upwards through an exhaust pipe or through the shell plating. The exhaust outlet shall be located not less than 2 m from the cargo area. The exhaust pipes of engines shall be arranged so that the exhausts are led away from the vessel. The exhaust pipes shall not be located within the cargo area.

9.3.1.34.2   Exhaust pipes of engines shall be provided with a device preventing the escape of sparks, e.g. spark arresters.

9.3.1.35   *Bilge pumping and ballasting arrangements*

9.3.1.35.1   Bilge and ballast pumps for spaces within the cargo area shall be installed within such area.

This provision does not apply to:

–   double-hull spaces and double bottoms which do not have a common boundary wall with the cargo tanks;

–   cofferdams and hold spaces where ballasting is carried out using the piping of the fire-fighting system in the cargo area and bilge-pumping is performed using eductors which are installed in the cargo area.

---

[2]   *As available on the website of the Comité Européen pour l'Élaboration de Standards dans le Domaine de Navigation Intérieure – CESNI, https://www.cesni.eu/en/documents/es-trin/.*

9.3.1.35.2   Where the double bottom is used as a liquid oil fuel tank, it shall not be connected to the bilge piping system.

9.3.1.35.3   Where the ballast pump is installed in the cargo area, the standpipe and its outboard connection for suction of ballast water shall be located within the cargo area.

9.3.1.35.4   It shall be possible for an under-deck pump-room to be stripped in an emergency using a system located in the cargo area and independent of any other system. This stripping system shall be located outside the pump-room.

9.3.1.36 to 9.3.1.39   (*Reserved*)

9.3.1.40   *Fire-extinguishing arrangements*

9.3.1.40.1   A fire-extinguishing system shall be installed on the vessel.

This system shall comply with the following requirements:

–   It shall be supplied by two independent fire or ballast pumps, one of which shall be ready for use at any time. These pumps and their means of propulsion and electrical equipment shall not be installed in the same space;

–   It shall be provided with a water main fitted with at least three hydrants in the cargo area above deck. Three suitable and sufficiently long hoses with jet/spray nozzles having a diameter of not less than 12 mm shall be provided. Alternatively one or more of the hose assemblies may be substituted by directable jet/spray nozzles having a diameter of not less than 12 mm. It shall be possible to reach any point of the deck in the cargo area simultaneously with at least two jets of water which do not emanate from the same hydrant.

A spring-loaded non-return valve shall be fitted to ensure that no gases can escape through the fire-extinguishing system into the accommodation, wheelhouse or service spaces outside the cargo area;

–   The capacity of the system shall be at least sufficient for a jet of water to have a minimum reach of not less than the vessel's breadth from any location on board with two spray nozzles being used at the same time;

–   The water supply system shall be capable of being put into operation from the wheelhouse and from the deck;

–   Measures shall be taken to prevent the freezing of fire-mains and hydrants.

9.3.1.40.2   In addition the engine rooms, the cargo pump-room and all spaces containing special equipment (switchboards, compressors, etc.) for the refrigerant equipment if any, shall be provided with a permanently fixed fire-extinguishing system meeting the following requirements:

9.3.1.40.2.1   *Extinguishing agents*

For the protection of spaces in engine rooms, boiler rooms and pump rooms, only permanently fixed fire-extinguishing systems using the following extinguishing agents are permitted:

(a) CO_2 (carbon dioxide);

(b)   HFC 227 ea (heptafluoropropane);

(c)   IG-541 (52% nitrogen, 40% argon, 8% carbon dioxide);

(d)   FK-5-1-12 (dodecafluoro 2–methylpentane–3–one);

(e)   (*Reserved*)

(f) K_2CO_3 (potassium carbonate).

Other extinguishing agents are permitted only on the basis of recommendations by the Administrative Committee.

9.3.1.40.2.2   *Ventilation, air extraction*

(a)   The combustion air required by the combustion engines which ensure propulsion should not come from spaces protected by permanently fixed fire-extinguishing systems. This requirement is not mandatory if the vessel has two independent main engine rooms with a gastight separation or if, in addition to the main engine room, there is a separate engine room installed with a bow thruster that can independently ensure propulsion in the event of a fire in the main engine room.

(b)   All forced ventilation systems in the space to be protected shall be shut down automatically as soon as the fire-extinguishing system is activated.

(c)   All openings in the space to be protected which permit air to enter or gas to escape shall be fitted with devices enabling them to be closed rapidly. It shall be clear whether they are open or closed.

(d)   Air escaping from the pressure–relief valves of the pressurised air tanks installed in the engine rooms shall be evacuated to the open air.

(e)   Overpressure or negative pressure caused by the diffusion of the extinguishing agent shall not destroy the constituent elements of the space to be protected. It shall be possible to ensure the safe equalisation of pressure.

(f)   Protected spaces shall have a facility for extracting the extinguishing agent and the combustion gases. Such facilities shall be capable of being operated from positions outside the protected rooms and which must not be made inaccessible by a fire within such spaces. If there are permanently installed extractors, it shall not be possible for these to be switched on while the fire is being extinguished.

9.3.1.40.2.3   *Fire alarm system*

The space to be protected shall be monitored by an appropriate fire alarm system. The alarm signal shall be audible in the wheelhouse, the accommodation and the space to be protected.

9.3.1.40.2.4   *Piping system*

(a)   The extinguishing agent shall be routed to and distributed in the space to be protected by means of a permanent piping system. Piping installed in the space to be protected and their fittings shall be made of steel. This shall not apply to the connecting nozzles of tanks and compensators provided that the materials used have equivalent fire–retardant properties. Piping shall be protected against corrosion both internally and externally.

(b)   The discharge nozzles shall be so arranged as to ensure the regular diffusion of the extinguishing agent. In particular, the extinguishing agent must also be effective beneath the floor.

9.3.1.40.2.5   *Triggering device*

(a)   Automatically activated fire-extinguishing systems are not permitted.

(b)   It shall be possible to activate the fire-extinguishing system from a suitable point located outside the space to be protected.

(c)   Triggering devices shall be so installed that they can be activated in the event of a fire and so that the risk of their breakdown in the event of a fire or an explosion in the space to be protected is reduced as far as possible.

Systems which are not mechanically activated shall be supplied from two energy sources independent of each other. These energy sources shall be located outside the space to be protected. The control lines located in the space to be protected shall be so designed as to remain capable of operating in the event of a fire for a minimum of 30 minutes. The electrical installations are deemed to meet this requirement if they conform to the IEC 60331–21:1999 standard.

When the triggering devices are so placed as not to be visible, the component concealing them shall carry the "Fire-fighting system" symbol, each side being not less than 10 cm in length, with the following text in red letters on a white ground:

Fire-extinguishing system

(d)   If the fire-extinguishing system is intended to protect several spaces, it shall comprise a separate and clearly–marked triggering device for each space.

(e)   The instructions shall be posted alongside all triggering devices and shall be clearly visible and indelible. The instructions shall be in a language the master can read and understand and if this language is not English, French or German, they shall be in English, French or German. They shall include information concerning:

   (i)   the activation of the fire-extinguishing system;

   (ii)   the need to ensure that all persons have left the space to be protected;

   (iii)   The correct behaviour of the crew in the event of activation and when accessing the space to be protected following activation or diffusion, in particular in respect of the possible presence of dangerous substances;

   (iv)   the correct behaviour of the crew in the event of the failure of the fire-extinguishing system to function properly.

(f)   The instructions shall mention that prior to the activation of the fire-extinguishing system, combustion engines installed in the space and aspirating air from the space to be protected, shall be shut down.

9.3.1.40.2.6   *Alarm device*

(a)   Permanently fixed fire-extinguishing systems shall be fitted with an audible and visual alarm device.

(b)   The alarm device shall be set off automatically as soon as the fire-extinguishing system is first activated. The alarm device shall function for an appropriate period of time before the extinguishing agent is released; it shall not be possible to turn it off.

(c) Alarm signals shall be clearly visible in the spaces to be protected and their access points and be clearly audible under operating conditions corresponding to the highest possible sound level. It shall be possible to distinguish them clearly from all other sound and visual signals in the space to be protected.

(d) Sound alarms shall also be clearly audible in adjoining spaces, with the communicating doors shut, and under operating conditions corresponding to the highest possible sound level.

(e) If the alarm device is not intrinsically protected against short circuits, broken wires and drops in voltage, it shall be possible to monitor its operation.

(f) A sign with the following text in red letters on a white ground shall be clearly posted at the entrance to any space the extinguishing agent may reach:

Warning, fire-extinguishing system!
Leave this space immediately when the ... (description) alarm is activated!

9.3.1.40.2.7 *Pressurised tanks, fittings and piping*

(a) Pressurised tanks, fittings and piping shall conform to the requirements of the competent authority or, if there are no such requirements, to those of a recognized classification society.

(b) Pressurised tanks shall be installed in accordance with the manufacturer's instructions.

(c) Pressurised tanks, fittings and piping shall not be installed in the accommodation.

(d) The temperature of cabinets and storage spaces for pressurised tanks shall not exceed 50 °C.

(e) Cabinets or storage spaces on deck shall be securely stowed and shall have vents so placed that in the event of a pressurised tank not being gastight, the escaping gas cannot penetrate into the vessel. Direct connections with other spaces are not permitted.

9.3.1.40.2.8 *Quantity of extinguishing agent*

If the quantity of extinguishing agent is intended for more than one space, the quantity of extinguishing agent available does not need to be greater than the quantity required for the largest of the spaces thus protected.

9.3.1.40.2.9 *Installation, maintenance, monitoring and documents*

(a) The mounting or modification of the system shall only be performed by a company specialised in fire-extinguishing systems. The instructions (product data sheet, safety data sheet) provided by the manufacturer of the extinguishing agent or the system shall be followed.

(b) The system shall be inspected by an expert:

(i) before being brought into service;

(ii) each time it is put back into service after activation;

(iii) after every modification or repair;

(iv) regularly, not less than every two years.

(c)   During the inspection, the expert is required to check that the system conforms to the requirements of 9.3.1.40.2.

(d)   The inspection shall include, as a minimum:

        (i)   an external inspection of the entire system;

        (ii)   an inspection to ensure that the piping is leakproof;

        (iii)   an inspection to ensure that the control and activation systems are in good working order;

        (iv)   an inspection of the pressure and contents of tanks;

        (v)   an inspection to ensure that the means of closing the space to be protected are leakproof;

        (vi)   an inspection of the fire alarm system;

        (vii)   an inspection of the alarm device.

(e)   The person performing the inspection shall establish, sign and date a certificate of inspection.

(f)   The number of permanently fixed fire-extinguishing systems shall be mentioned in the vessel certificate.

9.3.1.40.2.10   *Fire-extinguishing system operating with CO_2*

In addition to the requirements contained in 9.3.1.40.2.1 to 9.3.1.40.2.9, fire-extinguishing systems using CO_2 as an extinguishing agent shall conform to the following provisions:

(a)   Tanks of CO_2 shall be placed in a gastight space or cabinet separated from other spaces. The doors of such storage spaces and cabinets shall open outwards; they shall be capable of being locked and shall carry on the outside the symbol "Warning: general danger", not less than 5 cm high and "CO_2" in the same colours and the same size;

(b)   Storage cabinets or spaces for CO_2 tanks located below deck shall only be accessible from the outside. These spaces shall have an artificial ventilation system with extractor hoods and shall be completely independent of the other ventilation systems on board;

(c)   The level of filling of CO_2 tanks shall not exceed 0.75 kg/l. The volume of depressurised CO_2 shall be taken to be 0.56 m^3/kg;

(d)   The concentration of CO_2 in the space to be protected shall be not less than 40% of the gross volume of the space. This quantity shall be released within 120 seconds. It shall be possible to monitor whether diffusion is proceeding correctly;

(e)   The opening of the tank valves and the control of the diffusing valve shall correspond to two different operations;

(f)   The appropriate period of time mentioned in 9.3.1.40.2.6 (b) shall be not less than 20 seconds. A reliable installation shall ensure the timing of the diffusion of CO_2.

9.3.1.40.2.11   *Fire-extinguishing system operating with HFC-227 ea (heptafluoropropane)*

In addition to the requirements of 9.3.1.40.2.1 to 9.3.1.40.2.9, fire-extinguishing systems using HFC-227 ea as an extinguishing agent shall conform to the following provisions:

(a)   Where there are several spaces with different gross volumes, each space shall be equipped with its own fire-extinguishing system;

(b)   Every tank containing HFC-227 ea placed in the space to be protected shall be fitted with a device to prevent overpressure. This device shall ensure that the contents of the tank are safely diffused in the space to be protected if the tank is subjected to fire, when the fire-extinguishing system has not been brought into service;

(c)   Every tank shall be fitted with a device permitting control of the gas pressure;

(d)   The level of filling of tanks shall not exceed 1.15 kg/l. The specific volume of depressurised HFC-227 ea shall be taken to be 0.1374 m^3/kg;

(e)   The concentration of HFC-227 ea in the space to be protected shall be not less than 8% of the gross volume of the space. This quantity shall be released within 10 seconds;

(f)   Tanks of HFC-227 ea shall be fitted with a pressure monitoring device which triggers an audible and visual alarm in the wheelhouse in the event of an unscheduled loss of propellant gas. Where there is no wheelhouse, the alarm shall be triggered outside the space to be protected;

(g)   After discharge, the concentration in the space to be protected shall not exceed 10.5% (volume);

(h)   The fire-extinguishing system shall not comprise aluminium parts.

9.3.1.40.2.12   *Fire-extinguishing system operating with IG-541*

In addition to the requirements of 9.3.1.40.2.1 to 9.3.1.40.2.9, fire-extinguishing systems using IG-541 as an extinguishing agent shall conform to the following provisions:

(a)   Where there are several spaces with different gross volumes, every space shall be equipped with its own fire-extinguishing system;

(b)   Every tank containing IG-541 placed in the space to be protected shall be fitted with a device to prevent overpressure. This device shall ensure that the contents of the tank are safely diffused in the space to be protected if the tank is subjected to fire, when the fire-extinguishing system has not been brought into service;

(c)   Each tank shall be fitted with a device for checking the contents;

(d)   The filling pressure of the tanks shall not exceed 200 bar at a temperature of +15 °C;

(e)   The concentration of IG-541 in the space to be protected shall be not less than 44% and not more than 50% of the gross volume of the space. This quantity shall be released within 120 seconds.

9.3.1.40.2.13   *Fire-extinguishing system operating with FK-5-1-12*

In addition to the requirements of 9.3.1.40.2.1 to 9.3.1.40.2.9, fire-extinguishing systems using FK-5-1-12 as an extinguishing agent shall comply with the following provisions:

(a)   Where there are several spaces with different gross volumes, every space shall be equipped with its own fire-extinguishing system;

(b)   Every tank containing FK-5-1-12 placed in the space to be protected shall be fitted with a device to prevent overpressure. This device shall ensure that the contents of the tank are safely diffused in the space to be protected if the tank is subjected to fire, when the fire-extinguishing system has not been brought into service;

(c)   Every tank shall be fitted with a device permitting control of the gas pressure;

(d)   The level of filling of tanks shall not exceed 1.00 kg/l. The specific volume of depressurized FK-5-1-12 shall be taken to be 0.0719 m^3/kg;

(e)   The volume of FK-5-1-12 in the space to be protected shall be not less than 5.5% of the gross volume of the space. This quantity shall be released within 10 seconds;

(f)   Tanks of FK-5-1-12 shall be fitted with a pressure monitoring device which triggers an audible and visual alarm in the wheelhouse in the event of an unscheduled loss of extinguishing agent. Where there is no wheelhouse, the alarm shall be triggered outside the space to be protected;

(g)   After discharge, the concentration in the space to be protected shall not exceed 10.0%.

9.3.1.40.2.14   *(Reserved)*

9.3.1.40.2.15   *Fire-fighting systems using K_2CO_3 as the extinguishing agent*

In addition to the requirements laid down in 9.3.1.40.2.1 to 9.3.1.40.2.3, 9.3.1.40.2.5, 9.3.1.40.2.6 and 9.3.1.40.2.9, fire-fighting systems using K_2CO_3 as the extinguishing agent shall comply with the following provisions:

(a)   The fire-fighting system shall have a type-approval pursuant to Directive 2014/90/EU[3] or to MSC/Circ. 1270;[4]

(b)   Each room shall be provided with its own firefighting system;

(c)   The extinguishing agent must be stored in specially provided unpressurised tanks in the room to be protected. These tanks shall be fitted in such a way that the extinguishing agent is dispensed evenly in the room. In particular the extinguishing agent shall also work underneath the deck plates;

(d)   Each tank is separately connected with the triggering device;

(e)   The quantity of dry aerosol-forming extinguishing agent relative to the room to be protected shall be at least 120 g per m^3 of the net volume of this room. This net volume is calculated according to Directive 2014/90/EU[3] or to MSC/Circ. 1270[4]. It shall be possible to supply the extinguishing agent within 120 s.

---

[3]   *Official Journal of the European Union, L 257 of 28 August 2014, p.146.*
[4]   *International Maritime Organization Circular MSC/Circ. 1270 and corrigenda — Revised Guidelines for the approval of fixed aerosol fire-extinguishing systems equivalent to fixed gas extinguishing systems, as referred to in SOLAS 1974, for machinery spaces — adopted on 4 June 2008.*

9.3.1.40.2.16 *Fixed fire-extinguishing system for physical protection*

In order to ensure physical protection in the engine rooms, boiler rooms and pump rooms, permanently fixed fire-extinguishing systems are accepted solely on the basis of recommendations by the Administrative Committee.

9.3.1.40.3 The two hand fire–extinguishers referred to in 8.1.4 shall be located in the cargo area.

9.3.1.40.4 The fire-extinguishing agent and the quantity contained in the permanently fixed fire-extinguishing system shall be suitable and sufficient for fighting fires.

9.3.1.41 *Fire and naked light*

9.3.1.41.1 The outlets of funnels shall be located not less than 2.00 m from the cargo area. Arrangements shall be provided to prevent the escape of sparks and the entry of water.

9.3.1.41.2 Heating, cooking and refrigerating appliances shall not be fuelled with liquid fuels, liquid gas or solid fuels.

The installation in the engine room or in another separate space of heating appliances fuelled with liquid fuel having a flash–point above 55 °C is, however, permitted.

Cooking and refrigerating appliances are permitted only in the accommodation.

9.3.1.41.3 Only electrical lamps are permitted.

9.3.1.42 to 9.3.1.49 *(Reserved)*

9.3.1.50 *(Deleted)*

9.3.1.51 *Surface temperatures of installations and equipment*

(a) Surface temperatures of electrical and non-electrical installations and equipment shall not exceed 200 °C.

(b) Surface temperatures of the outer parts of engines and of their air inlets and exhaust ducts shall not exceed 200 °C;

(c) If the list of substances on the vessel according to 1.16.1.2.5 is going to include substances for which the temperature classes T4, T5 or T6 are indicated in column (15) of Table C of Chapter 3.2, then the corresponding surface temperatures within the assigned zones shall not exceed 135 °C (T4), 100 °C (T5) or 85 °C (T6) respectively;

(d) (a) and (b) do not apply if the following requirements are met (see also 7.2.3.51.4):

(i) Accommodation, wheelhouse and service spaces where surface temperatures higher than those mentioned in (a) and (b) occur are equipped with a ventilation system according to 9.3.1.12.4 (b); or

(ii) Installations and equipment which generate surface temperatures higher than those set out in (a) or (b), respectively, must be capable of being shut down. Such installations and equipment shall be marked in red.

9.3.1.52   *Type and location of electrical installations and equipment*

9.3.1.52.1   Electrical installations and equipment shall be of at least the 'limited explosion risk' type.

This provision does not apply to:

(a)   Lighting installations in the accommodation and the wheelhouse, except for switches near to the entrances;

(b)   Mobile phones, fixed telephone installations, stationary and portable computers and loading instruments in the accommodation or the wheelhouse;

(c)   Electrical installations and equipment which, during a stay in the immediate vicinity of or within a shoreside assigned zone:

         (i)   Are extinguished; or

         (ii)   Are placed in premises equipped with a ventilation system according to 9.3.1.12.4;

(d)   To radiotelephone installations and inland AIS (automatic identification systems) stations in the accommodation and the wheelhouse, if no part of an aerial for radiotelephone installations or AIS stations is situated above or within 2.00 m of the cargo area.

9.3.1.52.2   In the cofferdams, double-hull spaces, double bottoms and hold spaces, only hermetically sealed echo sounding devices are allowed, the cables of which are led through thick-walled steel tubes with gastight connections up to the main deck.

9.3.1.52.3   The fixed electrical installations and equipment which do not meet the requirements set out in 9.3.1.51 (a), 9.3.1.51 (b) and 9.3.1.52.1 above and their switches shall be marked in red. The disconnection of such equipment shall be controlled from a centralized location on board.

9.3.1.52.4   Every insulated distribution network shall be fitted with an automatic device with a visual and audible alarm for checking the insulation level.

9.3.1.52.5   Only distribution systems without return connection to the hull are permitted. This provision does not apply to:

     –   Active cathodic corrosion protection;

     –   Certain limited sections of the installations situated outside the cargo area (e.g., connections of starters of diesel engines);

     –   The device for checking the insulation level referred to in 9.3.1.52.4.

9.3.1.52.6   An electric generator which is permanently driven by an engine and which does not meet the requirements of 9.3.1.52.1 above, shall be fitted with a multipolar switch capable of shutting down the generator. A notice board with the operating instructions shall be displayed near the switch.

9.3.1.52.7   Failure of the power supply for the safety and control equipment shall be immediately indicated by visual and audible signals in the wheelhouse and on the deck. The alarm must be relayed to the accommodation automatically if it has not been switched off.

9.3.1.52.8   Electrical switches, sockets and cables on deck shall be protected against mechanical damage.

9.3.1.52.9   Sockets for the connection of signal lights and gangway lighting shall be solidly fitted to the vessel close to the signal mast or the gangway. The sockets used in this area shall be designed so as to prevent connection or disconnection except when they are not live.

9.3.1.52.10   Accumulators shall be located outside the cargo area.

9.3.1.53   *Type and location of electrical and non-electrical installations and equipment intended to be used in explosion hazardous areas*

9.3.1.53.1   On board vessels covered by the classification of zones as defined in 1.2.1, electrical and non-electrical installations and equipment used in explosion hazardous areas shall meet at least the requirements for use in the area concerned.

They shall be selected on the basis of the explosion groups/subgroups and temperature classes to which the substances to be carried belong (see columns (15) and (16) of Table C of Chapter 3.2).

If the list of substances on the vessel according to 1.16.1.2.5 is going to include substances for which temperature classes T4, T5 or T6 are indicated in column (15) of Table C of Chapter 3.2, then the corresponding surface temperatures within the assigned zones shall not exceed 135 °C (T4), 100 °C (T5) or 85 °C (T6).

If the list of substances on the vessel according to 1.16.1.2.5 is going to include substances for which temperature classes T1 or T2 are indicated in column (15) of Table C of Chapter 3.2, then the corresponding surface temperatures within the assigned zones shall not exceed 200 °C.

9.3.1.53.2   Except in the case of optical fibres, electrical cables shall be armoured or placed in a metallic sheath or in protective tubes.

Electrical cables for the active cathodic protection of the shell plating shall be led through thick-walled steel tubes with gastight connections up to the main deck.

9.3.1.53.3   Movable electric cables are prohibited in the explosion danger area, except for electric cables for intrinsically safe electric circuits or for connecting:

(a)   Signal lights and lighting for gangways, provided the connection point (for example, the socket) is permanently fitted to the vessel close to the signal mast or gangway;

(b)   The power network on a vessel to a land-based power network; provided

    –   The electric cables and the power supply unit conform with a valid standard (for example, EN 15869-03: 2010);

    –   The power supply unit and connectors are located outside of the explosion danger area.

Connecting and disconnecting sockets/connectors shall only be possible when they are not live.

9.3.1.53.4   Electrical cables of intrinsically safe circuits shall be separated from other cables not intended for use in such circuits and shall be marked (they shall not be installed together in the same string of cables and they shall not be fixed by the same cable clamps).

9.3.1.53.5   For movable electrical cables permitted under 9.3.1.53.3, only sheathed cables of type H07RN-F in accordance with standard IEC 60245-4:2011[5] or electrical cables of at least equivalent design having conductors with a cross-section of not less than 1.50 mm^2 shall be used.

9.3.1.54   Earthing

9.3.1.54.1   The metal parts of electrical installations and equipment in the cargo area which are not live, as well as the protective metal tubes or metal sheaths of cables, in normal service shall be earthed, unless they are so arranged that they are automatically earthed by bonding to the metal structure of the vessel.

9.3.1.54.2   The provisions of 9.3.1.54.1 also apply to installations with a voltage of less than 50 Volts.

9.3.1.54.3   Independent cargo tanks, metal intermediate bulk containers and tank-containers shall be earthed.

9.3.1.54.4   Receptacles for residual products shall be capable of being earthed.

9.3.1.55   (*Reserved*)

9.3.1.56   (*Deleted*)

9.3.1.57 to 9.3.1.59   (*Reserved*)

9.3.1.60   Special equipment

A shower and an eye and face bath shall be provided on the vessel at a location which is directly accessible from the cargo area. The water shall meet the quality of drinking water on board.

NOTE: Additional decontamination substances for the purpose of avoiding corrosion of eyes and skin are allowed.

A connection of this special equipment with the area outside the cargo zone is accepted.

A spring-loaded non-return valve shall be fitted to ensure that no gases can escape through the shower and the eye and face bath system outside the cargo area.

9.3.1.61   (*Reserved*)

9.3.1.62   Valve for degassing to reception facilities

A permanently installed or portable spring-loaded low-pressure valve used during degassing operations to reception facilities, shall be fitted at the piping used to extract air. If the vessel's substance list, according to 1.16.1.2.5, contains substances for which explosion protection is required according to column (17) of Table C of Chapter 3.2, this valve shall be fitted with a flame arrester capable of withstanding a deflagration. When the vessel is not degassing to a reception facility, the valve shall be closed with a blind flange. The low-pressure valve shall be so installed that under other normal working conditions the vacuum valve is not activated.

NOTE: Degassing operations are part of normal working conditions.

9.3.1.63 to 9.3.1.70   (*Reserved*)

---

[5]   *Identical to EN 50525-2-21: 2011.*

9.3.1.71 *Admittance on board*

The notice boards displaying the prohibition of admittance in accordance with 8.3.3 shall be clearly legible from either side of the vessel.

9.3.1.72 and 9.3.1.73   (*Reserved*)

9.3.1.74 *Prohibition of smoking, fire or naked light*

9.3.1.74.1   The notice boards displaying the prohibition of smoking in accordance with 8.3.4 shall be clearly legible from either side of the vessel.

9.3.1.74.2   Notice boards indicating the circumstances under which the prohibition is applicable shall be fitted near the entrances to the spaces where smoking or the use of fire or naked light is not always prohibited.

9.3.1.74.3   Ashtrays shall be provided close to each exit of the accommodation and the wheelhouse.

9.3.1.75 to 9.3.1.91   (*Reserved*)

9.3.1.92 *Emergency exit*

Spaces the entrances or exits of which are likely to become partly or completely immersed in the damaged condition shall have an emergency exit which is situated not less than 0.10 m above the damage waterline. This does not apply to forepeak and afterpeak.

9.3.1.93 to 9.3.1.99   (*Reserved*)

9.3.2 **Rules for construction of type C tank vessels**

The rules for construction of 9.3.2.0 to 9.3.2.99 apply to type C tank vessels.

9.3.2.0 *Materials of construction*

9.3.2.0.1   (a)   The vessel's hull and the cargo tanks shall be constructed of shipbuilding steel or other at least equivalent metal.

The independent cargo tanks may also be constructed of other materials, provided these have at least equivalent mechanical properties and resistance against the effects of temperature and fire.

(b)   Every part of the vessel including any installation and equipment which may come into contact with the cargo shall consist of materials which can neither be dangerously affected by the cargo nor cause decomposition of the cargo or react with it so as to form harmful or hazardous products. In case it has not been possible to examine this during classification and inspection of the vessel a relevant reservation shall be entered in the vessel substance list according to 1.16.1.2.5.

(c)   Venting piping shall be protected against corrosion.

9.3.2.0.2   Except where explicitly permitted in 9.3.2.0.3 below or in the certificate of approval, the use of wood, aluminium alloys, plastic materials or rubber within the cargo area is prohibited.

9.3.2.0.3 The use of wood, aluminium alloys, plastic materials or rubber in the cargo area is permitted as shown in the following table:

The use of wood, aluminium alloys, plastic materials or rubber is permitted only for:	Wood	Aluminium alloys	Plastic material	Rubber
Gangways	X	X	X	X
External ladders and passageways (gangways) *)		X	X	X
Cleaning equipment, e.g. brooms	X		X	X
Movable equipment e.g. fire extinguishers, portable gas detectors, rescue winches		X	X	X
Fenders	X		X	X
Mooring cables, fender ropes				X
Chocking of cargo tanks which are independent of the vessel's hull and chocking of installations and equipment	X		X	
Masts and similar round timber	X	X	X	
Engine parts		X	X	
Protective covers of engines and pumps			X	
Parts of the electrical installation		X	X	
Parts of the loading and unloading installation, e.g., gaskets		X	X	X
Boxes, cabinets or other receptacles placed on the deck for storage of disposal and recovery equipment for capstans, extinguishers, fire hoses, waste, etc.		X	X	
Supports and stops of any kind	X		X	
Ventilators, including hose assemblies for ventilation		X	X	
Parts of the water spray system, the shower and the eye and face bath		X	X	
Insulation of cargo tanks and of piping for loading and unloading, gas discharge pipes and heating pipes			X	X
Coating of cargo tanks and of piping for loading and unloading		X	X	X
All kinds of gaskets (e.g. for dome or hatch covers)			X	X
Cables for electrical equipment			X	X
Mat under hose assemblies for loading and unloading piping system			X	X
Fire hoses, air hoses, hoses for cleaning the deck, etc.			X	X
Sampling equipment and bottles			X	
Photo-optical copies of the certificate of approval according to 8.1.2.6 or 8.1.2.7, and of the vessel's certificate, the measurement certificate and the Rhine navigation membership certificate		X	X	
Drip trays			X	
(*) Take account of 9.3.1.0.5, 9.3.2.0.5 or 9.3.3.0.5, as appropriate				
Aluminium gauging rods are permitted, provided that they are fitted with brass feet or protected in another way to avoid sparking.				

All permanently fitted materials in the accommodation or wheelhouse, with the exception of furniture, shall not readily ignite. They shall not evolve fumes or toxic gases in dangerous quantities, if involved in a fire.

9.3.2.0.4   The paint used in the cargo area shall not be liable to produce sparks in case of impact.

9.3.2.0.5   The use of plastic material for a vessel's boats is permitted only if the material does not readily ignite.

The use of aluminium alloys or plastic material for passageways (gangways) in the cargo area is permitted only if the material does not readily ignite or conduct electricity.

9.3.2.1   *Vessel record*

NOTE: *For the purpose of this paragraph, the term "owner" has the same meaning as in 1.16.0.*

The vessel record shall be retained by the owner who shall be able to provide this documentation at the request of the competent authority and the recognized classification society.

The vessel record shall be maintained and updated throughout the life of the vessel and shall be retained for 6 months after the vessel is taken out of service.

Should a change of owner occur during the life of the vessel the vessel record shall be transferred to the new owner.

Copies of the vessel record or all necessary documents shall be made available on request to the competent authority for the issuance of the certificate of approval and for the recognized classification society or inspection body for first inspection, periodic inspection, special inspection or exceptional checks.

9.3.2.2 to 9.3.2.7   (*Reserved*)

9.3.2.8   *Classification*

9.3.2.8.1   The tank vessel shall be built under the survey of a recognised classification society and be classed in its highest class.

The vessel's highest class shall be continued. This shall be confirmed by an appropriate certificate issued by the recognized classification society (certificate of class).

The design pressure and the test pressure of cargo tanks shall be entered in the certificate.

If a vessel has cargo tanks with different valve opening pressures, the design and test pressures of each tank shall be entered in the certificate.

The recognized classification society shall draw up a vessel substance list mentioning all the dangerous goods accepted for carriage by the tank vessel (see also 1.16.1.2.5).

9.3.2.8.2 to 9.3.2.8.4   (*Deleted*)

9.3.2.9   (*Reserved*)

9.3.2.10 *Protection against the penetration of dangerous gases and the spreading of dangerous liquids*

9.3.2.10.1 The vessel shall be designed so as to prevent dangerous gases and liquids from penetrating into the accommodation, wheelhouse and service spaces. None of the windows in these spaces shall be capable of being opened unless its intended use is as an emergency exit and it is marked as such.

9.3.2.10.2 Liquid-tight protective coamings shall be fitted on deck at the height of the external bulkheads of the cargo tanks, at a maximum distance of 0.60 m from the outer cofferdam bulkheads or the hold end bulkheads. The protective coamings shall either extend over the entire width of the vessel or be fixed between the longitudinal spill coamings so as to prevent liquids from entering the forepeak and afterpeak. The height of the protective coamings and the spill coamings shall be at least 0.075 m. The protective coaming may correspond to the protection wall prescribed in 9.3.2.10.3 if the protection wall extends across the entire width of the vessel.

9.3.2.10.3 If the list of substances on the vessel according to 1.16.1.2.5 is going to include substances that require explosion protection in accordance with column (17) of Table C of Chapter 3.2, then the use of installations and equipment that are not of at least the 'limited explosion risk' type is not permitted during loading and unloading operations in parts of the deck outside the cargo area, unless those parts are protected against the penetration of gases and liquids by a gas- and liquid-tight protection wall. The wall must either extend over the full width of the vessel or surround the areas to be protected in a U-shaped form. The wall must cover the whole width of the area to be protected and at least 1.00 m in the direction opposite to the cargo area (see Classification of zones diagram). The height of the wall shall be at least 1.00 m above the adjacent cargo deck area in the cargo area. The outer wall and side walls of the accommodation can be considered as a protection wall if they do not include openings and if the dimensions are complied with.

A protection wall is not required where the distance between the areas to be protected and the high velocity vent valve, the shore connections of the piping for loading and unloading, the compressor on deck and the opening of the closest pressure tanks is at least 12.00 m.

9.3.2.10.4 On deck, the lower edges of door-openings in the sidewalls of superstructures and the sills of hatches and ventilation openings of premises located under the deck shall have a height of not less than 0.50 m above the deck.

This requirement does not apply to access openings to double-hull spaces and double bottoms.

9.3.1.10.5 The bulwarks, foot-rails, etc., shall be provided with sufficiently large openings which are located directly above the deck.

9.3.2.11 *Hold spaces and cargo tanks*

9.3.2.11.1 (a) The maximum permissible capacity of a cargo tank shall be determined in accordance with the following table:

$L \times B \times H$ (m^3)	Maximum permissible capacity of a cargo tank (m^3)
up to 600	$L \times B \times H \times 0.3$
600 to 3 750	$180 + (L \times B \times H - 600) \times 0.0635$
> 3 750	380

Alternative constructions in accordance with 9.3.4 are permitted.

In the table above L×B×H is the product of the main dimensions of the tank vessel in metres (according to the measurement certificate), where:

L = overall length of the hull in m;

B = extreme breadth of the hull in m;

H = shortest vertical distance in m between the top of the keel and the lowest point of the deck at the side of the vessel (moulded depth) within the cargo area.

(b) The relative density of the substances to be carried shall be taken into consideration in the design of the cargo tanks. The maximum relative density shall be indicated in the certificate of approval;

(c) When the vessel is provided with pressure cargo tanks, these tanks shall be designed for a working pressure of 400 kPa (4 bar);

(d) For vessels with a length of not more than 50.00 m, the length of a cargo tank shall not exceed 10.00 m; and

For vessels with a length of more than 50.00 m, the length of a cargo tank shall not exceed 0.20 L;

This provision does not apply to vessels with independent built–in cylindrical tanks having a length to diameter ratio ≤ 7.

9.3.2.11.2 (a) In the cargo area (except cofferdams) the vessel shall be designed as a flush–deck double-hull vessel, with double-hull spaces and double bottoms, but without a trunk;

Cargo tanks independent of the vessel's hull and refrigerated cargo tanks may only be installed in a hold space which is bounded by double-hull spaces and double bottoms in accordance with 9.3.2.11.8 below. The cargo tanks shall not extend beyond the deck;

(b) The cargo tanks independent of the vessel's hull shall be fixed so that they cannot float. Refrigerated cargo tank fastenings shall meet the requirements of a recognised classification society;

(c) The capacity of a suction well shall be limited to not more than 0.10 m³;

(d) Side–struts linking or supporting the load-bearing components of the sides of the vessel with the load-bearing components of the longitudinal walls of cargo tanks and side–struts linking the load-bearing components of the vessel's bottom with the tank-bottom are prohibited;

(e) A local recess in the cargo deck, contained on all sides, with a depth greater than 0.10 m, designed to house the cargo pump, is permitted if it fulfils the following conditions:

– The recess shall not be greater than 1.00 m in depth;

– The recess shall be located not less than 6.00 m from entrances and openings to accommodation and service spaces outside the cargo area;

– The recess shall be located at a minimum distance from the side plating equal to one quarter of the vessel's breadth;

– All pipes linking the recess to the cargo tanks shall be fitted with shut-off devices fitted directly on the bulkhead;

- All the controls required for the equipment located in the recess shall be activated from the deck;

- It shall be possible to drain the recess using a system installed on deck in the cargo area and independent of any other system;

- The recess shall be provided with a level alarm device which activates the draining system and triggers a visual and audible alarm in the wheelhouse and on the deck when liquid accumulates at the bottom;

- When the recess is located above the cofferdam, the engine room bulkhead shall have an insulation of Class "A-60" as defined in SOLAS 74, Chapter II-2, Regulation 3;

- When the cargo area is fitted with a water-spray system, electrical equipment located in the recess shall be protected against infiltration of water;

- Pipes connecting the recess to the hull shall not pass through the cargo tanks;

(f)   If the list of substances on the vessel according to 1.16.1.2.5 is going to include substances that require explosion protection in accordance with column (17) of Table C of Chapter 3.2 and the recess is deeper than 0.50 m, then it shall be provided with a permanent gas detection system which automatically indicates the presence of flammable gases by means of direct-measuring sensors and actuates a visual and audible alarm when the gas concentration has reached 20% of the LEL of the cargo or 20% of the LEL of n-Hexane, whichever is the more critical value. The sensors of this system shall be placed at suitable positions at the bottom of the recess.

Measurement shall be continuous.

Visual and audible alarms shall be installed in the wheelhouse and on deck and, when the alarm is actuated, the vessel loading and unloading system shall be shut down. Failure of the gas detection system shall be immediately signalled in the wheelhouse and on deck by means of visual and audible alarms.

The alarm shall be automatically relayed to the accommodation if it has not been switched off.

9.3.2.11.3   (a)   The cargo tanks shall be separated by cofferdams of at least 0.60 m in width from the accommodation, engine rooms and service spaces outside the cargo area below deck or, if there are no such accommodation, engine rooms and service spaces, from the vessel's ends. Where the cargo tanks are installed in a hold space, a space of not less than 0.50 m shall be provided between such tanks and the end bulkheads of the hold space. In this case an end bulkhead of Class "A-60" as defined in SOLAS 74, Chapter II-2, Regulation 3, shall be deemed equivalent to a cofferdam. For pressure cargo tanks, the 0.50 m distance may be reduced to 0.20 m;

(b)   Hold spaces, cofferdams and cargo tanks shall be capable of being inspected;

(c)   All spaces in the cargo area shall be capable of being ventilated. It has to be possible to check their gas-free condition.

9.3.2.11.4   The bulkheads bounding the cargo tanks, cofferdams and hold spaces shall be watertight. The cargo tanks and the bulkheads bounding the cargo area shall have no openings or penetrations below deck.

The bulkhead between the engine room and the cofferdam or service space in the cargo area or between the engine room and a hold space may be fitted with penetrations provided that they conform to the provisions of 9.3.2.17.5.

The bulkhead between the cargo tank and the cargo pump-room below deck may be fitted with penetrations provided that they conform to the provisions of 9.3.2.17.6. The bulkheads between the cargo tanks may be fitted with penetrations provided that the loading or unloading piping are fitted with shut-off devices in the cargo tank from which they come. These shut-off devices shall be operable from the deck.

9.3.2.11.5   Double-hull spaces and double bottoms in the cargo area shall be arranged for being filled with ballast water only. Double bottoms may, however, be used as oil fuel tanks, provided they comply with the provisions of 9.3.2.32.

9.3.2.11.6   (a)   A cofferdam, the centre part of a cofferdam or another space below deck in the cargo area may be arranged as a service space, provided the bulkheads bounding the service space extend vertically to the bottom. This service space shall only be accessible from the deck;

(b)   The service space shall be watertight with the exception of its access hatches and ventilation inlets;

(c)   No piping for loading and unloading shall be fitted within the service space referred to under (a) above;

Piping for loading and unloading may be fitted in the cargo pump-rooms below deck only when they conform to the provisions of 9.3.2.17.6.

9.3.2.11.7   For double-hull construction with the cargo tanks integrated in the vessel's structure, the distance between the side wall of the vessel and the longitudinal bulkhead of the cargo tanks shall be not less than 1.00 m. A distance of 0.80 m may however be permitted, provided that, compared with the scantling requirements specified in the rules for construction of a recognised classification society, the following reinforcements have been made:

(a)   25% increase in the thickness of the deck stringer plate;

(b)   15% increase in the side plating thickness;

(c)   Arrangement of a longitudinal framing system at the vessel's side, where depth of the longitudinals shall be not less than 0.15 m and the longitudinals shall have a face plate with the cross-sectional area of at least 7.0 cm^2;

(d)   The stringer or longitudinal framing systems shall be supported by web frames, and like bottom girders fitted with lightening holes, at a maximum spacing of 1.80 m. These distances may be increased if the longitudinals are strengthened accordingly.

When a vessel is built according to the transverse framing system, a longitudinal stringer system shall be arranged instead of (c) above. The distance between the longitudinal stringers shall not exceed 0.80 m and their depth shall be not less than 0.15 m, provided they are completely welded to the frames. The cross-sectional area of the facebar or faceplate shall be not less than 7.0 cm^2 as in (c) above. Where cut-outs are arranged in the stringer at the connection with the frames, the web depth of the stringer shall be increased with the depth of cut-outs.

The mean depth of the double bottoms shall be not less than 0.70 m. It shall, however, never be less than 0.60 m.

The depth below the suction wells may be reduced to 0.50 m.

Alternative constructions in accordance with 9.3.4 are permitted.

9.3.2.11.8   When a vessel is built with cargo tanks located in a hold space or refrigerated cargo tanks, the distance between the double walls of the hold space shall be not less than 0.80 m and the depth of the double bottom shall be not less than 0.60 m.

9.3.2.11.9   Where service spaces are located in the cargo area under deck, they shall be arranged so as to be easily accessible and to permit persons wearing protective clothing and breathing apparatus to safely operate the service equipment contained therein. They shall be designed so as to allow injured or unconscious personnel to be removed from such spaces without difficulties, if necessary by means of fixed equipment.

9.3.2.11.10   Cofferdams, double-hull spaces, double bottoms, cargo tanks, hold spaces and other accessible spaces within the cargo area shall be arranged so that they may be completely inspected and cleaned in an appropriate manner. The dimensions of openings except for those of double-hull spaces and double bottoms which do not have a wall adjoining the cargo tanks shall be sufficient to allow a person wearing breathing apparatus to enter or leave the space without difficulties. These openings shall have a minimum cross-sectional area of $0.36\ m^2$ and a minimum side length of 0.50 m. They shall be designed so as to allow an injured or unconscious person to be removed from the bottom of such a space without difficulties, if necessary by means of fixed equipment. In these spaces the distance between the reinforcements shall not be less than 0.50 m. In double bottoms this distance may be reduced to 0.45 m.

Cargo tanks may have circular openings with a diameter of not less than 0.68 m.

9.3.2.12   *Ventilation*

9.3.2.12.1   Each hold space shall have two openings the dimensions and location of which shall be such as to permit effective ventilation of any part of the hold space. If there are no such openings, it shall be possible to fill the hold spaces with inert gas or dry air.

9.3.2.12.2   Double-hull spaces and double bottoms within the cargo area which are not arranged for being filled with ballast water, hold spaces and cofferdams shall be provided with ventilation systems.

9.3.2.12.3   (a)   A service space located within the cargo area below deck shall be provided with a ventilation system. The capacity of the fans shall be sufficient to ensure 20 complete changes of air per hour based on the volume of the service space.

The ventilation exhaust ducts shall extend down to 50 mm above the bottom of the service space. The air shall be supplied through a duct at the top of the service space.

(b)   If the list of substances on the vessel according to 1.16.1.2.5 is going to include substances that require explosion protection in accordance with column (17) of Table C of Chapter 3.2, then the air inlets shall be located not less than 2.00 m above the deck, at a distance of not less than 2.00 m from tank openings and 6.00 m from the outlets of safety valves.

The extension pipes which may be necessary may be of the hinged type.

9.3.2.12.4   (a)   Ventilation shall be provided for the accommodation, wheelhouse and service spaces.

(b)   The ventilation system in such spaces shall meet the following requirements:

(i)   The air intakes shall be located as far away as possible, and not less than 6.00 m from the cargo area and not less than 2.00 m above the deck;

(ii)   Pressure of at least 0.1 kPa (0.001 bar) may be maintained in the premises;

(iii)   A breakdown alarm is integrated;

(iv)   The ventilation system, including the breakdown alarm, shall be at least of the 'limited explosion risk' type;

(v)   A gas detection system conforming to conditions 1. to 4. below is connected to the ventilation system:

1.   It is appropriate at least for use in zone 1, explosion group IIC and temperature class T6;

2.   It is equipped with sensors;

–   On the suction inlets of the ventilation systems; and

–   Directly below the top edge of the sill of the entrance doors;

3.   Its t90 response time is lower than or equal to 4 s;

4.   Measurement shall be continuous;

(vi)   In the service spaces, the ventilation system is linked to the emergency lighting, which shall be at least of the 'limited explosion risk' type;

This emergency lighting is not necessary if the lighting installations in the service spaces are of at least the 'limited explosion risk' type;

(vii)   The suction of the ventilation system and installations and equipment that do not meet the requirements set out in 9.3.2.51 (a) and (b) and 9.3.2.52.1 must be shut down when a concentration of 20% of LEL of n-Hexane is reached;

The switching-off shall be indicated in the accommodation and wheelhouse by visual and audible signals;

(viii)   In the event of failure of the ventilation system or the gas detection installations in the accommodation, installations and equipment in the accommodation that do not meet the requirements set out in 9.3.2.51 (a) and (b) and 9.3.2.52.1 must be stopped;

The failure shall be indicated in the accommodation, the wheelhouse and on the deck by visual and audible signals;

(ix)   In the event of failure of the ventilation system or the gas detection installations in the wheelhouse or service spaces, installations and equipment in those spaces that do not meet the requirements set out in 9.3.2.51 (a) and (b) and 9.3.2.52.1 must be shut down;

The failure shall be indicated in the wheelhouse and on the deck by visual and audible signals. The alarm must be relayed to the accommodation automatically if it has not been switched off;

(x)   Any switching-off shall take place immediately and automatically and, if necessary, shall activate the emergency lighting;

The automatic switch-off device is set so that no automatic switching-off may occur while the vessel is under way;

(c)   If there is no ventilation system or the ventilation system of a space does not comply with all the requirements set out in (b) above, any installations or equipment present in that space that may, if switched on, give rise to surface temperatures higher than those mentioned in 9.3.2.51 (a) and (b) or that do not meet the requirements set out in 9.3.2.52.1 must be capable of being switched off.

9.3.2.12.5   *(Deleted)*

9.3.2.12.6   Notice boards shall be fitted at the ventilation inlets indicating the conditions under which they shall be closed. All ventilation inlets of accommodation, wheelhouse and service spaces leading to the open air outside the cargo area shall be fitted with devices permanently fixed according to 9.3.2.40.2.2 (c), enabling them to be closed rapidly. It shall be clear whether they are open or closed.

Such ventilation inlets shall be located not less than 2.00 m from the cargo area.

Ventilation inlets of service spaces in the cargo area may be located within that area.

9.3.2.12.7   *(Deleted)*

9.3.2.13   *Stability (general)*

9.3.2.13.1   Proof of sufficient stability shall be furnished including for stability in damaged condition.

9.3.2.13.2   The basic values for the stability calculation - the vessel's lightweight and location of the centre of gravity - shall be determined either by means of an inclining experiment or by detailed mass and moment calculation. In the latter case the lightweight of the vessel shall be checked by means of a lightweight test with a tolerance limit of $\pm$ 5% between the mass determined by calculation and the displacement determined by the draught readings.

9.3.2.13.3   Proof of sufficient intact stability shall be furnished for all stages of loading and unloading and for the final loading condition for all the relative densities of the substances transported contained in the vessel substance list according to 1.16.1.2.5.

For every loading operation, taking account of the actual fillings and floating position of cargo tanks, ballast tanks and compartments, drinking water and sewage tanks and tanks containing products for the operation of the vessel, the vessel shall comply with the intact and damage stability requirements.

Intermediate stages during operations shall also be taken into consideration.

The proof of sufficient stability shall be shown for every operating, loading and ballast condition in the stability booklet, to be approved by the recognized classification society, which classes the vessel. If it is unpractical to pre-calculate the operating, loading and ballast conditions, a loading instrument approved by the recognised classification society which classes the vessel shall be installed and used which contains the contents of the stability booklet.

NOTE: *A stability booklet shall be worded in a form comprehensible for the responsible master and containing the following details:*

General description of the vessel:

– *General arrangement and capacity plans indicating the assigned use of compartments and spaces (cargo tanks, stores, accommodation, etc.);*

– *A sketch indicating the position of the draught marks referring to the vessel's perpendiculars;*

– *A scheme for ballast/bilge pumping and overflow prevention systems;*

– *Hydrostatic curves or tables corresponding to the design trim, and, if significant trim angles are foreseen during the normal operation of the vessel, curves or tables corresponding to such range of trim are to be introduced;*

– *Cross curves or tables of stability calculated on a free trimming basis, for the ranges of displacement and trim anticipated in normal operating conditions, with an indication of the volumes which have been considered buoyant;*

– *Tank sounding tables or curves showing capacities, centres of gravity, and free surface data for all cargo tanks, ballast tanks and compartments, drinking water and sewage water tanks and tanks containing products for the operation of the vessel;*

– *Lightship data (weight and centre of gravity) resulting from an inclining test or deadweight measurement in combination with a detailed mass balance or other acceptable measures. Where the above-mentioned information is derived from a sister vessel, the reference to this sister vessel shall be clearly indicated, and a copy of the approved inclining test report relevant to this sister vessel shall be included;*

– *A copy of the approved test report shall be included in the stability booklet;*

– *Operating loading conditions with all relevant details, such as:*

    – *Lightship data, tank fillings, stores, crew and other relevant items on board (mass and centre of gravity for each item, free surface moments for liquid loads);*

    – *Draughts amidships and at perpendiculars;*

    – *Metacentric height corrected for free surfaces effect;*

    – *Righting lever values and curve;*

    – *Longitudinal bending moments and shear forces at read–out points;*

    – *Information about openings (location, type of tightness, means of closure); and*

    – *Information for the master;*

– *Calculation of the influence of ballast water on stability with information on whether fixed level gauges for ballast tanks and compartments have to be installed or whether the ballast tanks or compartments shall be completely full or completely empty when underway.*

9.3.2.13.4   Floatability after damage shall be proved for the most unfavourable loading condition. For this purpose, calculated proof of sufficient stability shall be established for critical intermediate stages of flooding and for the final stage of flooding.

9.3.2.14   *Stability (intact)*

9.3.2.14.1   The requirements for intact stability resulting from the damage stability calculation shall be fully complied with.

9.3.2.14.2   For vessels with cargo tanks of more than 0.70 B in width, proof shall be furnished that the following stability requirements have been complied with:

(a)   In the positive area of the righting lever curve up to immersion of the first non-watertight opening there shall be a righting lever (GZ) of not less than 0.10 m;

(b)   The surface of the positive area of the righting lever curve up to immersion of the first non-watertight opening and in any event up to an angle of heel $\leq 27°$ shall not be less than 0.024 m.rad;

(c)   The metacentric height (GM) shall be not less than 0.10 m.

These conditions shall be met bearing in mind the influence of all free surfaces in tanks for all stages of loading and unloading.

9.3.2.14.3   The most stringent requirement of 9.3.2.14.1 and 9.3.2.14.2 is applicable to the vessel.

9.3.2.15   *Stability (damaged condition)*

9.3.2.15.1   The following assumptions shall be taken into consideration for the damaged condition:

(a)   The extent of side damage is as follows:

longitudinal extent:	at least 0.10 L, but not less than 5.00 m;
transverse extent:	0.79 m inboard from the vessel's side at right angles to the centreline at the level corresponding to the maximum draught, or when applicable, the distance allowed by section 9.3.4, reduced by 0.01 m;
vertical extent:	from the base line upwards without limit.

(b)   The extent of bottom damage is as follows:

longitudinal extent:	at least 0.10 L, but not less than 5.00 m;
transverse extent:	3.00 m;
vertical extent:	from the base 0.59 m upwards, the sump excepted.

(c)   Any bulkheads within the damaged area shall be assumed damaged, which means that the location of bulkheads shall be chosen so as to ensure that the vessel remains afloat after the flooding of two or more adjacent compartments in the longitudinal direction.

The following provisions are applicable:

–   For bottom damage, adjacent athwartship compartments shall also be assumed as flooded;

–   The lower edge of any non-watertight openings (e.g. doors, windows, access hatchways) shall, at the final stage of flooding, be not less than 0.10 m above the damage waterline;

–   In general, permeability shall be assumed to be 95%. Where an average permeability of less than 95% is calculated for any compartment, this calculated value obtained may be used.

However, the following minimum values shall be used:

- engine rooms: 85%;

- accommodation: 95%;

- double bottoms, oil fuel tanks, ballast tanks, etc., depending on whether, according to their function, they have to be assumed as full or empty for the vessel floating at the maximum permissible draught: 0% or 95%.

For the main engine room only the one–compartment standard need be taken into account, i.e. the end bulkheads of the engine room shall be assumed as not damaged.

9.3.2.15.2   For the intermediate stage of flooding the following criteria have to be fulfilled:

GZ ≥ 0.03m
Range of positive GZ: 5°.

At the stage of equilibrium (final stage of flooding), the angle of heel shall not exceed 12°. Non-watertight openings shall not be flooded before reaching the stage of equilibrium. If such openings are immersed before that stage, the corresponding spaces shall be considered as flooded for the purpose of the stability calculation.

The positive range of the righting lever curve beyond the stage of equilibrium shall have a righting lever of ≥ 0.05 m in association with an area under the curve of ≥ 0.0065 m.rad. The minimum values of stability shall be satisfied up to immersion of the first non-watertight opening and in any event up to an angle of heel ≤ 27°. If non-watertight openings are immersed before that stage, the corresponding spaces shall be considered as flooded for the purposes of stability calculation.

9.3.2.15.3   If openings through which undamaged compartments may additionally become flooded are capable of being closed watertight, the closing appliances shall be marked accordingly.

9.3.2.15.4   Where cross- or down-flooding openings are provided for reduction of unsymmetrical flooding, the time for equalisation shall not exceed 15 minutes, if during the intermediate stages of flooding sufficient stability has been proved.

9.3.2.16 *Engine rooms*

9.3.2.16.1 Internal combustion engines for the vessel's propulsion as well as internal combustion engines for auxiliary machinery shall be located outside the cargo area. Entrances and other openings of engine rooms shall be at a distance of not less than 2.00 m from the cargo area.

9.3.2.16.2 The engine rooms shall be accessible from the deck; the entrances shall not face the cargo area. Where the doors are not located in a recess whose depth is at least equal to the door width, the hinges shall face the cargo area.

9.3.2.17 *Accommodation and service spaces*

9.3.2.17.1 Accommodation spaces and the wheelhouse shall be located outside the cargo area forward of the fore vertical plane or abaft the aft vertical plane bounding the part of the cargo area below deck. Windows of the wheelhouse which are located not less than 1.00 m above the bottom of the wheelhouse may tilt forward.

9.3.2.17.2 Entrances to spaces and openings of superstructures shall not face the cargo area. Doors opening outward and not located in a recess the depth of which is at least equal to the width of the doors shall have their hinges face the cargo area.

9.3.2.17.3 Entrances from the deck and openings of spaces facing the weather shall be capable of being closed. The following instruction shall be displayed at the entrance of such spaces:

**Do not open during loading, unloading and degassing
without the permission of the master.
Close immediately.**

9.3.2.17.4 Entrances and windows of superstructures and accommodation spaces which can be opened as well as other openings of these spaces shall be located not less than 2.00 m from the cargo area. No wheelhouse doors and windows shall be located within 2.00 m from the cargo area, except where there is no direct connection between the wheelhouse and the accommodation.

9.3.2.17.5 (a) Driving shafts of the bilge or ballast pumps in the cargo area may penetrate through the bulkhead between the service space and the engine room, provided the arrangement of the service space is in compliance with 9.3.2.11.6.

(b) The penetration of the shaft through the bulkhead shall be gastight and shall have been approved by a recognised classification society.

(c) The necessary operating instructions shall be displayed.

(d) Penetrations through the bulkhead between the engine room and the service space in the cargo area and the bulkhead between the engine room and the hold spaces may be provided for electrical cables, hydraulic and piping for measuring, control and alarm systems, provided that the penetration have been approved by a recognised classification society. The penetrations shall be gastight. Penetrations through a bulkhead of Class "A-60" as defined in SOLAS 74, Chapter II-2, Regulation 3, shall have an equivalent fire protection.

(e) Pipes may penetrate the bulkhead between the engine room and the service space in the cargo area provided that these are pipes between the mechanical equipment in the engine room and the service space which do not have any openings within the service space and which are provided with shut-off devices at the bulkhead in the engine room.

(f)   Notwithstanding 9.3.2.11.4, pipes from the engine room may pass through the service space in the cargo area or a cofferdam or a hold space or a double-hull space to the outside provided that within the service space or cofferdam or hold space or double-hull space they are of the thick-walled type and have no flanges or openings.

(g)   Where a driving shaft of auxiliary machinery penetrates through a wall located above the deck the penetration shall be gastight.

9.3.2.17.6   A service space located within the cargo area below deck shall not be used as a cargo pump-room for the loading and unloading system, except where:

–   The cargo pump-room is separated from the engine room or from service spaces outside the cargo area by a cofferdam or a bulkhead with an insulation of Class "A-60" as defined in SOLAS 74, Chapter II-2, Regulation 3, or by a service space or a hold space;

–   The "A-60" bulkhead required above does not include penetrations referred to in 9.3.2.17.5 (a);

–   Ventilation exhaust outlets are located not less than 6.00 m from entrances and openings of the accommodation, wheelhouse and service spaces outside the cargo area;

–   The access hatches and ventilation inlets can be closed from the outside;

–   All piping for loading and unloading as well as that of stripping systems is provided with shut-off devices at the pump suction side in the cargo pump-room immediately at the bulkhead. The necessary operation of the control devices in the pump-room, starting of pumps and control of the liquid flow rate shall be effected from the deck;

–   The bilge of the cargo pump-room is equipped with a gauging device for measuring the filling level which activates a visual and audible alarm in the wheelhouse when liquid is accumulating in the cargo pump-room bilge;

–   The cargo pump room is provided with a permanent oxygen detection system which automatically indicates the amount of oxygen and which actuates a visual and audible alarm when the oxygen concentration has reached 19.5% by volume. The sensors of this system shall be placed at suitable positions at the bottom and at a height of 2.00 m. Measurement shall be continuous and displayed near to the entrance. Audible and visual alarms shall be installed in the wheelhouse and in the cargo pump-room and, when the alarm is actuated, the loading and unloading system shall be shut down;

–   Failure of the oxygen measuring system shall activate a visual and audible alarm in the wheelhouse and on deck. The alarm must be relayed to the accommodation automatically if it has not been switched off;

–   The ventilation system prescribed in 9.3.2.12.3 has a capacity sufficient to ensure not less than 30 changes of air per hour based on the total volume of the service space.

If the list of substances on the vessel according to 1.16.1.2.5 is going to include substances that require explosion protection in accordance with column (17) of Table C of Chapter 3.2, then the cargo pump room shall also be provided with a permanent gas detection system which automatically indicates the presence of flammable gases and actuates a visual and audible alarm when the gas concentration has reached 20% of the LEL of the cargo or 20% of the LEL of n-Hexane, whichever gives the more critical value.

The sensors of this gas detection system shall be placed at suitable positions at the bottom and directly below the deck. Measurement shall be continuous and displayed near to the entrance.

Audible and visual alarms shall be installed in the wheelhouse and in the cargo pump-room and, when the alarm is actuated, the loading and unloading system shall be shut down.

Any failure of the gas detection system shall be immediately signalled in the wheelhouse and on deck by a visual and audible warning. The alarm must be relayed to the accommodation automatically if it has not been switched off.

9.3.2.17.7   The following instruction shall be displayed at the entrance of the cargo pump-room:

**Before entering the cargo pump-room check whether
it is free from gases and contains sufficient oxygen.
Do not open doors and entrance openings without
the permission of the master.
Leave immediately in the event of alarm.**

9.3.2.18   *Inerting facility*

In cases in which inerting or blanketing of the cargo is prescribed, the vessel shall be equipped with an inerting system.

This system shall be capable of maintaining a permanent minimum pressure of 7 kPa (0.07 bar) in the spaces to be inerted. In addition, the inerting system shall not increase the pressure in the cargo tank to a pressure greater than that at which the pressure valve is regulated. The set pressure of the vacuum-relief valve shall be 3.5 kPa (0.035 bar).

A sufficient quantity of inert gas for loading or unloading shall be carried or produced on board if it is not possible to obtain it on shore. In addition, a sufficient quantity of inert gas to offset normal losses occurring during carriage shall be on board.

The premises to be inerted shall be equipped with connections for introducing the inert gas and monitoring systems so as to ensure the correct atmosphere on a permanent basis.

When the pressure or the concentration of inert gas in the gaseous phase falls below a given value, this monitoring system shall activate an audible and visible alarm in the wheelhouse. When the wheelhouse is unoccupied, the alarm shall also be perceptible in a location occupied by a crew member.

9.3.2.19   (*Reserved*)

9.3.2.20   *Arrangement of cofferdams*

9.3.2.20.1   Cofferdams or cofferdam compartments remaining once a service space has been arranged in accordance with 9.3.2.11.6 shall be accessible through an access hatch.

9.3.2.20.2   Cofferdams shall be capable of being filled with water and emptied by means of a pump. Filling shall be effected within 30 minutes. These requirements are not applicable when the bulkhead between the engine room and the cofferdam comprises fire-protection insulation "A-60" in accordance with SOLAS 74, Chapter II-2, Regulation 3, or has been fitted out as a service space. The cofferdams shall not be fitted with inlet valves.

9.3.2.20.3   No fixed pipe shall permit connection between a cofferdam and other piping of the vessel outside the cargo area.

9.3.2.20.4   If the list of substances on the vessel according to 1.16.1.2.5 is going to include substances that require explosion protection in accordance with column (17) of Table C of Chapter 3.2 then the ventilation openings of cofferdams shall be fitted with a flame arrester capable of withstanding a deflagration. The flame arresters shall be chosen according to the explosion groups/subgroups of the substances foreseen for inclusion in the list of substances on the vessel (see column (16) of Table C of Chapter 3.2).

9.3.2.21   *Safety and control installations*

9.3.2.21.1   Cargo tanks shall be provided with the following equipment:

(a)   a mark inside the tank indicating the liquid level of 95%;

(b)   a level gauge;

(c)   a level alarm device which is activated at the latest when a degree of filling of 90% is reached;

(d)   a high level sensor for actuating the facility against overflowing at the latest when a degree of filling of 97.5% is reached;

(e)   an instrument for measuring the pressure of the vapour phase inside the cargo tank;

(f)   an instrument for measuring the temperature of the cargo, if in column (9) of Table C of Chapter 3.2, a cargo heating installation or a possibility of heating the cargo is required on board, or if a maximum temperature is indicated in column (20) of Table C of Chapter 3.2;

(g)   a connection for a closed-type or partly closed-type sampling device, and/or at least one sampling opening as required in column (13) of Table C of Chapter 3.2. The connection shall be fitted with a shut-off device resistant to the internal pressure at the connection;

If the list of substances on the vessel according to 1.16.1.2.5 is going to include substances that require explosion protection in accordance with column (17) of Table C of Chapter 3.2, then the flame arrester plate stack capable of withstanding steady burning of the sampling opening shall be selected according to the explosion groups/subgroups of the substances foreseen for inclusion in the list of substances on the vessel (see column (16) of Table C of Chapter 3.2).

9.3.2.21.2   When the degree of filling in per cent is determined, an error of not more than 0.5% is permitted. It shall be calculated on the basis of the total cargo tank capacity including the expansion trunk.

9.3.2.21.3   The level gauge shall allow readings from the control position of the shut-off devices of the particular cargo tank. The permissible maximum filling levels of 95% and 97%, as given in the list of substances, shall be marked on each level gauge.

Permanent reading of the overpressure and vacuum shall be possible from a location from which loading or unloading operations may be interrupted. The permissible maximum overpressure and vacuum shall be marked on each level gauge.

Readings shall be possible in all weather conditions.

9.3.2.21.4   The level alarm device shall give a visual and audible warning on board when actuated. The level alarm device shall be independent of the level gauge.

9.3.2.21.5   (a)   The high level sensor referred to in 9.3.2.21.1 (d) above shall give a visual and audible alarm on board and at the same time actuate an electrical contact which in the form of a binary signal interrupts the electric current loop provided and fed by the shore facility, thus initiating measures at the shore facility against overflowing during loading operations.

The signal shall be transmitted to the shore facility via a watertight two–pin plug of a connector device in accordance with standard EN 60309-2:1999 + A1:2007 + A2:2012 for direct current of 40 to 50 volts, identification colour white, position of the nose 10 h.

The plug shall be permanently fitted to the vessel close to the shore connections of the loading and unloading piping.

The high level sensor shall also be capable of switching off the vessel's own discharging pump. The high level sensor shall be independent of the level alarm device, but it may be connected to the level gauge.

(b)   During discharging by means of the on-board pump, it shall be possible for the shore facility to switch it off. For this purpose, an independent intrinsically safe power line, fed by the vessel, shall be switched off by the shore facility by means of an electrical contact.

It shall be possible for the binary signal of the shore facility to be transmitted via a watertight two–pole socket or a connector device in accordance with standard EN 60309-2:1999 + A1:2007 + A2:2012, for direct current of 40 to 50 volts, identification colour white, position of the nose 10 h.

This socket shall be permanently fitted to the vessel close to the shore connections of the unloading piping.

(c)   Vessels which may be delivering products required for operation of vessels shall be equipped with a transhipment facility compatible with European standard EN 12827:1999 and a rapid closing device enabling refuelling to be interrupted. It shall be possible to actuate this rapid closing device by means of an electrical signal from the overflow prevention system. The electrical circuits actuating the rapid closing device shall be secured according to the quiescent current principle or other appropriate error detection measures. The state of operation of electrical circuits which cannot be controlled using the quiescent current principle shall be capable of being easily checked.

It shall be possible to actuate the rapid closing device independently of the electrical signal.

The rapid closing device shall actuate a visual and audible alarm on board.

9.3.2.21.6   The visual and audible signals given by the level alarm device shall be clearly distinguishable from those of the high level sensor.

The visual alarm shall be visible at each control position on deck of the cargo tank stop valves. It shall be possible to easily check the functioning of the sensors and electric circuits or these shall be "intrinsically safe apparatus".

9.3.2.21.7   When the pressure or temperature exceeds a set value, instruments for measuring the vacuum or overpressure of the gaseous phase in the cargo tank or the temperature of the cargo shall activate a visual and audible alarm in the wheelhouse and on deck. The alarm must be relayed to the accommodation automatically if it has not been switched off.

When the pressure exceeds the set value during loading and unloading, the instrument for measuring the pressure shall, by means of the plug referred to in 9.3.2.21.5 above, immediately initiate an electrical contact which shall put into effect measures to interrupt the loading or unloading operation. When the vessel's own discharge pump is used, it shall be switched off automatically.

The instrument for measuring the overpressure or vacuum shall activate the alarm at latest when:

(a)   An overpressure equal to 1.15 times the opening pressure of the pressure relief valves/high velocity vent valves is reached; or

(b)   The lower threshold of the design pressure of the vacuum valves, but not exceeding a vacuum of 5 kPa (0.05 bar), is reached.

The maximum permissible temperature is indicated in column (20) of Table C of Chapter 3.2. The sensors for the alarms mentioned in this paragraph may be connected to the alarm device of the sensor.

When it is prescribed in column (20) of Table C of Chapter 3.2, the instrument for measuring the overpressure of the gaseous phase in the cargo tank shall actuate a visible and audible alarm in the wheelhouse when the overpressure exceeds 40 kPa (0.4 bar) during the voyage. The alarm must be relayed to the accommodation automatically if it has not been switched off. It shall be possible to read the gauges in direct proximity to the control for the water spray system.

9.3.2.21.8   Where the control elements of the shut-off devices of the cargo tanks are located in a control room, it shall be possible to stop the loading pumps and read the level gauges in the control room, and the visual and audible warning given by the level alarm device, the high level sensor referred to in 9.3.2.21.1 (d) and the instruments for measuring the pressure and temperature of the cargo shall be noticeable in the control room and on deck.

Satisfactory monitoring of the cargo area shall be ensured from the control room.

9.3.2.21.9   The vessel shall be so equipped that loading or unloading operations can be interrupted by means of switches, i.e. the quick closing valve located on the flexible vessel–to–shore connecting line must be capable of being closed. The switches shall be placed at two points on the vessel (fore and aft).

This provision applies only when prescribed in column (20) of Table C of Chapter 3.2.

The interruption system shall be designed according to the quiescent current principle.

9.3.2.21.10   When refrigerated substances are carried the opening pressure of the safety system shall be determined by the design of the cargo tanks. In the event of the transport of substances that must be carried in a refrigerated state the opening pressure of the safety system shall be not less than 25 kPa (0.25 bar) greater than the maximum pressure calculated according to 9.3.2.27.

9.3.2.22   *Cargo tank openings*

9.3.2.22.1   (a)   Cargo tank openings shall be located on deck in the cargo area.

                (b)   Cargo tank openings with a cross-section of more than 0.10 m² and openings of safety devices for preventing overpressures shall be located not less than 0.50 m above deck.

9.3.2.22.2   Cargo tank openings shall be fitted with gastight closures capable of withstanding the test pressure in accordance with 9.3.2.23.2

9.3.2.22.3   Closures which are normally used during loading or unloading operations shall not cause sparking when operated.

9.3.2.22.4   (a)   Each cargo tank or group of cargo tanks connected to a common venting piping shall be fitted with:

         –   A connection for the safe return ashore of gases expelled during loading;

         –   A safe depressurization device for the cargo tanks, on which the position of the shut-off valve indicates clearly whether it is open or shut;

         –   Safety devices for preventing unacceptable overpressures or vacuums.

                The opening pressure of the safety valves shall be permanently marked on the valves;

                The setting of the pressure relief valves shall be such that during the transport operation they do not blow off until the maximum permissible working pressure of the cargo tanks is reached;

                The gases shall be discharged upwards;

                The outlets of the pressure relief valves shall be located not less than 1.00 m above the deck and at a distance of not less than 6.00 m from the openings of accommodation, the wheelhouse and the service spaces outside the cargo area. No equipment shall be present in a circle of 1.00 m radius around the outlet of the pressure relief valve outlets. This area shall be marked as a danger zone;

                (b)   When the list of substances on the vessel according to 1.16.1.2.5 is going to include substances for which explosion protection is required in column (17) of Table C of Chapter 3.2:

         –   At the connection to each cargo tank, the venting piping and the vacuum valve shall be equipped with a flame arrester capable of withstanding a detonation; and

         –   The device for the safe depressurization of cargo tanks shall be deflagration safe and capable of withstanding steady burning;

                (c)   If the list of substances on the vessel according to 1.16.1.2.5 is going to include substances that require explosion protection in accordance with column (17) of Table C of Chapter 3.2, or for which there is a T in column (3b) of Table C of Chapter 3.2, then the pressure relief valve shall be designed as a high velocity vent valve;

                (d)   If a shut-off device is to be mounted between the venting piping and the cargo tank, it shall be placed between the cargo tank and the flame arrester, and each cargo tank shall be equipped with pressure relief valves;

(e)   The autonomous protection systems mentioned in (b) and (c) shall be chosen according to the explosion groups/subgroups of the substances foreseen for inclusion in the list of substances on the vessel (see column (16) of Table C of Chapter 3.2). The outlets of the high-velocity vent valves shall be located not less than 2.00 m above the deck and at a distance of not less than 6.00 m from the openings of the accommodations, the wheelhouse and the service spaces outside the cargo area. This height may be reduced to 1.00 m when there is no drive unit within a radius of 1.00 m around the pressure relief valve outlet. This area shall be marked as a danger zone;

If the high velocity vent valve, the vacuum valve, the flame arresters and the venting piping are required to be heatable, the devices concerned shall be suitable for the relevant temperature.

9.3.2.22.5   *Venting piping*

(a)   When two or more cargo tanks are connected to common venting piping, it is sufficient that the equipment according to 9.3.2.22.4 (safety valves to prevent unacceptable overpressures and vacuums, high velocity vent valve, vacuum valve protected against deflagrations, safe pressure relief device for cargo tanks protected against deflagrations) is installed on the joint venting piping (see also 7.2.4.16.7);

(b)   When each cargo tank is connected to its own venting piping, each cargo tank or the associated venting piping shall be equipped according to 9.3.2.22.4.

9.3.2.23   *Pressure tests*

9.3.2.23.1   The cargo tanks, residual cargo tanks, cofferdams, piping for loading and unloading shall be subjected to initial tests before being put into service and thereafter at prescribed intervals.

Where a heating system is provided inside the cargo tanks, the heating coils shall be subjected to initial tests before being put into service and thereafter at prescribed intervals.

9.3.2.23.2   The test pressure for the cargo tanks and residual cargo tanks shall be not less than 1.3 times the construction pressure. The test pressure for the cofferdams and open cargo tanks shall be not less than 10 kPa (0.10 bar) gauge pressure.

9.3.2.23.3   The test pressure for piping for loading and unloading shall be not less than 1,000 kPa (10 bar) gauge pressure.

9.3.2.23.4   The maximum intervals for the periodic tests shall be 11 years.

9.3.2.23.5   The procedure for pressure tests shall comply with the provisions established by the competent authority or a recognised classification society.

9.3.2.24   *Regulation of cargo pressure and temperature*

9.3.2.24.1   Unless the entire cargo system is designed to resist the full effective vapour pressure of the cargo at the upper limits of the ambient design temperatures, the pressure of the tanks shall be kept below the permissible maximum set pressure of the safety valves, by one or more of the following means:

(a)   a system for the regulation of cargo tank pressure using mechanical refrigeration;

(b) a system ensuring safety in the event of the heating or increase in pressure of the cargo. The insulation or the design pressure of the cargo tank, or the combination of these two elements, shall be such as to leave an adequate margin for the operating period and the temperatures expected; in each case the system shall be deemed acceptable by a recognised classification society and shall ensure safety for a minimum time of three times the operation period;

(c) other systems deemed acceptable by a recognised classification society.

9.3.2.24.2 The systems prescribed in 9.3.2.24.1 shall be constructed, installed and tested to the satisfaction of the recognised classification society. The materials used in their construction shall be compatible with the cargoes to be carried. For normal service, the upper ambient design temperature limits shall be:

air: +30 °C;
water: +20 °C.

9.3.2.24.3 The cargo storage system shall be capable of resisting the full vapour pressure of the cargo at the upper limits of the ambient design temperatures, whatever the system adopted to deal with the boil-off gas. This requirement is indicated by remark 37 in column (20) of Table C of Chapter 3.2.

9.3.2.25 *Pumps and piping*

9.3.2.25.1 Pumps, compressors and accessory loading and unloading piping shall be placed in the cargo area. Cargo pumps shall be capable of being shut down from the cargo area and, in addition, from a position outside the cargo area. Cargo pumps situated on deck shall be located not less than 6.00 m from entrances to, or openings of, the accommodation and service spaces outside the cargo area.

9.3.2.25.2 (a) Piping for loading and unloading shall be independent of any other piping of the vessel. No cargo piping shall be located below deck, except those inside the cargo tanks and inside the cargo pump-room.

(b) The piping for loading and unloading shall be arranged so that, after loading or unloading operations, the liquid remaining in these pipes may be safely removed and may flow either into the vessel's tanks or the tanks ashore.

(c) Piping for loading and unloading shall be clearly distinguishable from other piping, e.g. by means of colour marking.

(d) The piping for loading and unloading located on deck, with the exception of the shore connections, shall be located not less than a quarter of the vessel's breadth from the outer shell.

(e) The shore connections shall be located not less than 6.00 m from the entrances to, or openings of, the accommodation and service spaces outside the cargo area.

(f) Each shore connection of the venting piping and shore connections of the piping for loading and unloading, through which the loading or unloading operation is carried out, shall be fitted with a shut-off device. However, each shore connection shall be fitted with a blind flange when it is not in operation.

(g) (*Deleted*)

(h)   The flanges and stuffing boxes shall be provided with a spray protection device.

(i)   Piping for loading and unloading, and venting piping, shall not have flexible connections fitted with sliding seals.

9.3.2.25.3   *(Deleted)*

9.3.2.25.4   (a)   Every component of the piping for loading and unloading shall be electrically connected to the hull.

(b)   The piping for loading shall extend down to the bottom of the cargo tanks.

9.3.2.25.5   The stop valves or other shut-off devices of the piping for loading and unloading shall indicate whether they are open or shut.

9.3.2.25.6   The piping for loading and unloading shall have, at the test pressure, the required elasticity, leakproofness and resistance to pressure.

9.3.2.25.7   The piping for loading and unloading shall be fitted with pressure gauges at the outlet of the pumps. The permissible maximum overpressure or vacuum value shall be indicated on each measuring device. Readings shall be possible in all weather conditions.

9.3.2.25.8   (a)   When piping for loading and unloading are used for supplying the cargo tanks with washing or ballast water, the suctions of these pipes shall be located within the cargo area but outside the cargo tanks.

Pumps for tank washing systems with associated connections may be located outside the cargo area, provided the discharge side of the system is arranged in such a way that the suction is not possible through that part.

A spring-loaded non-return valve shall be provided to prevent any gases from being expelled from the cargo area through the tank washing system.

(b)   A non-return valve shall be fitted at the junction between the water suction pipe and the cargo loading pipe.

9.3.2.25.9   The permissible loading and unloading flows shall be calculated.

Calculations concern the permissible maximum loading and unloading flow for each cargo tank or each group of cargo tanks, taking into account the design of the ventilation system. These calculations shall take into consideration the fact that in the event of an unforeseen cut–off of the vapour return piping of the shore facility, the safety devices of the cargo tanks will prevent pressure in the cargo tanks from exceeding the following values:

over–pressure: 1.15 times the opening pressure of the pressure relief valve/high velocity vent valve;

vacuum pressure: not more than the design pressure, but not exceeding a vacuum of 5 kPa (0.05 bar).

The main factors to be considered are the following:

1.   Dimensions of the ventilation system of the cargo tanks;

2.   Gas formation during loading: multiply the largest loading flow by a factor of not less than 1.25;

3. Density of the vapour mixture of the cargo based on 50% volume vapour and 50% volume air;

4. Loss of pressure through ventilation pipes, valves and fittings. Account will be taken of a 30% clogging of the mesh of the flame-arrester;

5. Chocking pressure of the safety valves.

Instructions concerning the permissible maximum loading and unloading flows for each cargo tank or for each group of cargo tanks shall be carried on board.

9.3.2.25.10 Compressed air generated outside the cargo area can be used in the cargo area subject to the installation of a spring-loaded non-return valve to ensure that no gases can escape from the cargo area through the compressed air system into accommodation, wheelhouse or service spaces outside the cargo area.

9.3.2.25.11 If the vessel is carrying several dangerous substances liable to react dangerously with each other, a separate pump with its own piping for loading and unloading shall be installed for each substance. The piping shall not pass through a cargo tank containing dangerous substances with which the substance in question is liable to react.

9.3.2.26 *Residual cargo tanks and receptacles for residual products*

9.3.2.26.1 When vessels are provided with tanks for residual products or receptacles for residual products, they shall be located in the cargo area and comply with the provisions of 9.3.2.26.2 and 9.3.2.26.3. Receptacles for residual products shall be located only in the cargo area on deck and not less than a quarter of the vessel's breadth from the outer shell.

9.3.2.26.2 Tanks for residual products shall be equipped with:

– A level gauge;

– Connections, with stop valves, for pipes and hose assemblies;

– A pressure relief/vacuum valve;

The pressure relief valve shall be sized so that, during the transport operation, it does not open when in normal operation. This condition is met when the opening pressure of the valve meets the conditions required in column (10) of Table C of Chapter 3.2 for the substances to be carried.

If the list of substances on the vessel according to 1.16.1.2.5 is going to include substances that require explosion protection in accordance with column (17) of Table C of Chapter 3.2, then the vacuum valve shall be designed so as to be capable of withstanding a deflagration. The deflagration safety may also be ensured by a flame arrester.

If the list of substances on the vessel according to 1.16.1.2.5 is going to include substances that require explosion protection in accordance with column (17) of Table C of Chapter 3.2, or for which there is a T in column (3b) of Table C of Chapter 3.2, then the pressure relief valve shall be designed as a high velocity vent valve.

The pressure relief valve shall be sized so that, during the transport operation, it does not open when in normal operation. This condition is met when the opening pressure of the valve meets the conditions required in column (10) of Table C of Chapter 3.2 for the substance to be carried.

The high velocity vent valve and the deflagration safe vacuum valve shall be chosen according to the explosion groups/subgroups of the substances listed in the list of substances on the vessel (see column (16) of Table C of Chapter 3.2).

The maximum permissible capacity is 30 m^3.

9.3.2.26.3   The receptacles for residual products shall be equipped with:

–   A possibility of indicating the degree of filling;

–   Connections, with stop valves, for pipes and hose assemblies;

A connection enabling gases released during filling to be evacuated safely.

9.3.2.26.4   *(Deleted)*

9.3.2.27   *Refrigeration system*

9.3.2.27.1   The refrigeration system referred to in 9.3.2.24.1 (a) shall be composed of one or more units capable of keeping the pressure and temperature of the cargo at the upper limits of the ambient design temperatures at the prescribed level. Unless another means of regulating cargo pressure and temperature deemed satisfactory by a recognised classification society is provided, provision shall be made for one or more stand-by units with an output at least equal to that of the largest prescribed unit. A stand-by unit shall include a compressor, its engine, its control system and all necessary accessories to enable it to operate independently of the units normally used. Provision shall be made for a stand-by heat-exchanger unless the system's normal heat-exchanger has a surplus capacity equal to at least 25% of the largest prescribed capacity. It is not necessary to make provision for separate piping.

Cargo tanks, piping and accessories shall be insulated so that, in the event of a failure of all cargo refrigeration systems, the entire cargo remains for at least 52 hours in a condition not causing the safety valves to open.

9.3.2.27.2   The security devices and the connecting lines from the refrigeration system shall be connected to the cargo tanks above the liquid phase of the cargo when the tanks are filled to their maximum permissible degree of filling. They shall remain within the gaseous phase, even if the vessel has a list up to 12 degrees.

9.3.2.27.3   When several refrigerated cargoes with a potentially dangerous chemical reaction are carried simultaneously, particular care shall be given to the refrigeration systems so as to prevent any mixing of the cargoes. For the carriage of such cargoes, separate refrigeration systems, each including the full stand-by unit referred to in 9.3.2.27.1, shall be provided for each cargo. When, however, refrigeration is ensured by an indirect or combined system and no leak in the heat exchangers can under any foreseeable circumstances lead to the mixing of cargoes, no provision need be made for separate refrigeration units for the different cargoes.

9.3.2.27.4   When several refrigerated cargoes are not soluble in each other under conditions of carriage such that their vapour pressures are added together in the event of mixing, particular care shall be given to the refrigeration systems to prevent any mixing of the cargoes.

9.3.2.27.5   When the refrigeration systems require water for cooling, a sufficient quantity shall be supplied by a pump or pumps used exclusively for the purpose. This pump or pumps shall have at least two suction pipes, leading from two water intakes, one to port, the other to starboard. Provision shall be made for a stand-by pump with a satisfactory flow; this may be a pump used for other purposes provided that its use for supplying water for cooling does not impair any other essential service.

9.3.2.27.6   The refrigeration system may take one of the following forms:

(a)   Direct system: the cargo vapours are compressed, condensed and returned to the cargo tanks. This system shall not be used for certain cargoes specified in Table C of Chapter 3.2. This requirement is indicated by remark 35 in column (20) of Table C of Chapter 3.2;

(b)   Indirect system: the cargo or the cargo vapours are cooled or condensed by means of a coolant without being compressed;

(c)   Combined system: the cargo vapours are compressed and condensed in a cargo/coolant heat-exchanger and returned to the cargo tanks. This system shall not be used for certain cargoes specified in Table C of Chapter 3.2. This requirement is indicated by remark 36 in column (20) of Table C of Chapter 3.2.

9.3.2.27.7   All primary and secondary coolant fluids shall be compatible with each other and with the cargo with which they may come into contact. Heat exchange may take place either at a distance from the cargo tank, or by using cooling coils attached to the inside or the outside of the cargo tank.

9.3.2.27.8   When the refrigeration system is installed in a separate service space, this service space shall meet the requirements of 9.3.2.17.6.

9.3.2.27.9   For all cargo systems, the heat transmission coefficient as used for the determination of the holding time (7.2.4.16.16 and 7.2.4.16.17) shall be determined by calculation. Upon completion of the vessel, the correctness of the calculation shall be checked by means of a heat balance test. The calculation and test shall be performed under supervision by the recognized classification society which classified the vessel.

The heat transmission coefficient shall be documented and kept on board. The heat transmission coefficient shall be verified at every renewal of the certificate of approval.

9.3.2.27.10   A certificate from a recognised classification society stating that 9.3.2.24.1 to 9.3.2.24.3, 9.3.2.27.1 and 9.3.2.27.4 above have been complied with shall be submitted together with the application for issue or renewal of the certificate of approval.

9.3.2.28   *Water-spray system*

When water-spraying is required in column (9) of Table C of Chapter 3.2, a water-spray system shall be installed in the cargo area on deck to enable gas emissions from loading to be precipitated or to cool the tops of cargo tanks by spraying water over the whole surface so as to avoid safely the activation of the pressure relief valves/high velocity vent valves at 50 kPa (0.5 bar).

The gas precipitation system shall be fitted with a connection device for supply from a shore installation.

The spray nozzles shall be so installed that the entire cargo deck area is covered and the gases released are precipitated safely.

The system shall be capable of being put into operation from the wheelhouse and from the deck. Its capacity shall be such that when all the spray nozzles are in operation, the outflow is not less than 50 litres per square metre of deck area and per hour.

9.3.2.29 and 9.3.2.30   (*Reserved*)

9.3.2.31   *Engines*

9.3.2.31.1   Only internal combustion engines running on fuel with having a flashpoint above 55 ºC are allowed. This provision does not apply to internal combustion engines which are part of propulsion and auxiliary systems. These systems shall meet the requirements of Chapter 30 and Annex 8, Section 1 of the European Standard laying down Technical Requirements for Inland Navigation vessels (ES-TRIN) as amended.[2]

9.3.2.31.2.   Ventilation inlets of the engine room, and when the engines do not take in air directly from the engine room, air intakes of the engines shall be located not less than 2.00 m from the cargo area.

9.3.2.31.3 and 9.3.2.31.4   *(Deleted)*

9.3.2.31.5   The ventilation in the closed engine room shall be designed so that, at an ambient temperature of 20 °C, the average temperature in the engine room does not exceed 40 °C.

9.3.2.32   *Oil fuel tanks*

9.3.2.32.1   Where the vessel is provided with hold spaces, the double bottoms within these spaces may be arranged as oil fuel tanks, provided their depth is not less than 0.6 m.

Oil fuel pipes and openings of such tanks are not permitted in the hold space.

9.3.2.32.2   The open ends of the air pipes of each oil fuel tanks shall extend to not less than 0.5 m above the open deck. These open ends and the open ends of overflow pipes leading to the deck shall be fitted with a protective device consisting of a gauze diaphragm or a perforated plate.

9.3.2.33   *(Reserved)*

9.3.2.34   *Exhaust pipes*

9.3.2.34.1   Exhausts shall be evacuated from the vessel into the open air either upwards through an exhaust pipe or through the shell plating. The exhaust outlet shall be located not less than 2.00 m from the cargo area. The exhaust pipes of engines shall be arranged so that the exhausts are led away from the vessel. The exhaust pipes shall not be located within the cargo area.

9.3.2.34.2   Exhaust pipes shall be provided with a device preventing the escape of sparks, e.g. spark arresters.

9.3.2.35   *Bilge pumping and ballasting arrangements*

9.3.2.35.1   Bilge and ballast pumps for spaces within the cargo area shall be installed within such area.

This provision does not apply to:

–   double-hull spaces and double bottoms which do not have a common boundary wall with the cargo tanks;

–   cofferdams, double-hull spaces, hold spaces and double bottoms where ballasting is carried out using the piping of the fire-fighting system in the cargo area and bilge-pumping is performed using eductors which are installed in the cargo area.

---

[2]   *As available on the website of the Comité Européen pour l'Élaboration de Standards dans le Domaine de Navigation Intérieure – CESNI, https://www.cesni.eu/en/documents/es-trin/.*

9.3.2.35.2   Where the double bottom is used as a liquid oil fuel tank, it shall not be connected to the bilge piping system.

9.3.2.35.3   Where the ballast pump is installed in the cargo area, the standpipe and its outboard connection for suction of ballast water shall be located within the cargo area but outside the cargo tanks.

9.3.2.35.4   A cargo pump-room below deck shall be capable of being drained in an emergency by an installation located in the cargo area and independent from any other installation. This installation shall be provided outside the cargo pump-room.

9.3.2.36 to 9.3.2.39   (*Reserved*)

9.3.2.40   *Fire-extinguishing arrangements*

9.3.2.40.1   A fire-extinguishing system shall be installed on the vessel. This system shall comply with the following requirements:

–   It shall be supplied by two independent fire or ballast pumps, one of which shall be ready for use at any time. These pumps and their means of propulsion and electrical equipment shall not be installed in the same space;

–   It shall be provided with a water main fitted with at least three hydrants in the cargo area above deck. Three suitable and sufficiently long hoses with jet/spray nozzles having a diameter of not less than 12 mm shall be provided. Alternatively one or more of the hose assemblies may be substituted by directable jet/spray nozzles having a diameter of not less than 12 mm. It shall be possible to reach any point of the deck in the cargo area simultaneously with at least two jets of water which do not emanate from the same hydrant.

A spring-loaded non-return valve shall be fitted to ensure that no gases can escape through the fire-extinguishing system into the accommodation, wheelhouse or service spaces outside the cargo area;

–   The capacity of the system shall be at least sufficient for a jet of water to have a minimum reach of not less than the vessel's breadth from any location on board with two spray nozzles being used at the same time;

–   The water supply system shall be capable of being put into operation from the wheelhouse and from the deck;

–   Measures shall be taken to prevent the freezing of fire-mains and hydrants.

9.3.2.40.2   In addition, the engine rooms, the pump-room and all spaces containing essential equipment (switchboards, compressors, etc.) for the refrigeration equipment, if any, shall be provided with a permanently fixed fire-extinguishing system meeting the following requirements:

9.3.2.40.2.1   *Extinguishing agents*

For the protection of spaces in engine rooms, boiler rooms and pump rooms, only permanently fixed fire-extinguishing systems using the following extinguishing agents are permitted:

(a) CO_2 (carbon dioxide);

(b)   HFC 227 ea (heptafluoropropane);

(c)   IG-541 (52% nitrogen, 40% argon, 8% carbon dioxide);

(d)   FK-5-1-12 (dodecafluoro 2-methylpentane-3-one);

(e)   (*Reserved*)

(f) K_2CO_3 (potassium carbonate).

Other extinguishing agents are permitted only on the basis of recommendations by the Administrative Committee.

9.3.2.40.2.2   *Ventilation, air extraction*

(a)   The combustion air required by the combustion engines which ensure propulsion should not come from spaces protected by permanently fixed fire-extinguishing systems. This requirement is not mandatory if the vessel has two independent main engine rooms with a gastight separation or if, in addition to the main engine room, there is a separate engine room installed with a bow thruster that can independently ensure propulsion in the event of a fire in the main engine room.

(b)   All forced ventilation systems in the space to be protected shall be shut down automatically as soon as the fire-extinguishing system is activated.

(c)   All openings in the space to be protected which permit air to enter or gas to escape shall be fitted with devices enabling them to be closed rapidly. It shall be clear whether they are open or closed.

(d)   Air escaping from the pressure–relief valves of the pressurised air tanks installed in the engine rooms shall be evacuated to the open air.

(e)   Overpressure or negative pressure caused by the diffusion of the extinguishing agent shall not destroy the constituent elements of the space to be protected. It shall be possible to ensure the safe equalisation of pressure.

(f)   Protected spaces shall have a facility for extracting the extinguishing agent and the combustion gases. Such facilities shall be capable of being operated from positions outside the protected rooms and which must not be made inaccessible by a fire within such spaces. If there are permanently installed extractors, it shall not be possible for these to be switched on while the fire is being extinguished.

9.3.2.40.2.3   *Fire alarm system*

The space to be protected shall be monitored by an appropriate fire alarm system. The alarm signal shall be audible in the wheelhouse, the accommodation and the space to be protected.

9.3.2.40.2.4   *Piping system*

(a)   The extinguishing agent shall be routed to and distributed in the space to be protected by means of a permanent piping system. Piping installed in the space to be protected and their fittings shall be made of steel. This shall not apply to the connecting nozzles of tanks and compensators provided that the materials used have equivalent fire-retardant properties. Piping shall be protected against corrosion both internally and externally.

(b)   The discharge nozzles shall be so arranged as to ensure the regular diffusion of the extinguishing agent. In particular, the extinguishing agent must also be effective beneath the floor.

9.3.2.40.2.5   *Triggering device*

(a)   Automatically activated fire-extinguishing systems are not permitted.

(b)   It shall be possible to activate the fire-extinguishing system from a suitable point located outside the space to be protected.

(c)   Triggering devices shall be so installed that they can be activated in the event of a fire and so that the risk of their breakdown in the event of a fire or an explosion in the space to be protected is reduced as far as possible.

Systems which are not mechanically activated shall be supplied from two energy sources independent of each other. These energy sources shall be located outside the space to be protected. The control lines located in the space to be protected shall be so designed as to remain capable of operating in the event of a fire for a minimum of 30 minutes. The electrical installations are deemed to meet this requirement if they conform to the IEC 60331–21:1999 standard.

When the triggering devices are so placed as not to be visible, the component concealing them shall carry the "Fire-fighting system" symbol, each side being not less than 10 cm in length, with the following text in red letters on a white ground:

Fire-extinguishing system

(d)   If the fire-extinguishing system is intended to protect several spaces, it shall comprise a separate and clearly–marked triggering device for each space.

(e)   The instructions shall be posted alongside all triggering devices and shall be clearly visible and indelible. The instructions shall be in a language the master can read and understand and if this language is not English, French or German, they shall be in English, French or German. They shall include information concerning:

   (i)   the activation of the fire-extinguishing system;

   (ii)   the need to ensure that all persons have left the space to be protected;

   (iii)   The correct behaviour of the crew in the event of activation and when accessing the space to be protected following activation or diffusion, in particular in respect of the possible presence of dangerous substances;

   (iv)   the correct behaviour of the crew in the event of the failure of the fire-extinguishing system to function properly.

(f)   The instructions shall mention that prior to the activation of the fire-extinguishing system, combustion engines installed in the space and aspirating air from the space to be protected, shall be shut down.

9.3.2.40.2.6   *Alarm device*

(a)   Permanently fixed fire-extinguishing systems shall be fitted with an audible and visual alarm device.

(b)   The alarm device shall be set off automatically as soon as the fire-extinguishing system is first activated. The alarm device shall function for an appropriate period of time before the extinguishing agent is released; it shall not be possible to turn it off.

(c)   Alarm signals shall be clearly visible in the spaces to be protected and their access points and be clearly audible under operating conditions corresponding to the highest possible sound level. It shall be possible to distinguish them clearly from all other sound and visual signals in the space to be protected.

(d)   Sound alarms shall also be clearly audible in adjoining spaces, with the communicating doors shut, and under operating conditions corresponding to the highest possible sound level.

(e)   If the alarm device is not intrinsically protected against short circuits, broken wires and drops in voltage, it shall be possible to monitor its operation.

(f)   A sign with the following text in red letters on a white ground shall be clearly posted at the entrance to any space the extinguishing agent may reach:

Warning, fire-extinguishing system!
Leave this space immediately when the … (description) alarm is activated!

9.3.2.40.2.7   *Pressurised tanks, fittings and piping*

(a)   Pressurised tanks, fittings and piping shall conform to the requirements of the competent authority or, if there are no such requirements, to those of a recognized classification society.

(b)   Pressurised tanks shall be installed in accordance with the manufacturer's instructions.

(c)   Pressurised tanks, fittings and piping shall not be installed in the accommodation.

(d)   The temperature of cabinets and storage spaces for pressurised tanks shall not exceed 50 °C.

(e)   Cabinets or storage spaces on deck shall be securely stowed and shall have vents so placed that in the event of a pressurised tank not being gastight, the escaping gas cannot penetrate into the vessel. Direct connections with other spaces are not permitted.

9.3.2.40.2.8   *Quantity of extinguishing agent*

If the quantity of extinguishing agent is intended for more than one space, the quantity of extinguishing agent available does not need to be greater than the quantity required for the largest of the spaces thus protected.

9.3.2.40.2.9   *Installation, maintenance, monitoring and documents*

(a)   The mounting or modification of the system shall only be performed by a company specialised in fire-extinguishing systems. The instructions (product data sheet, safety data sheet) provided by the manufacturer of the extinguishing agent or the system shall be followed.

(b)   The system shall be inspected by an expert:

(i)   before being brought into service;

(ii)   each time it is put back into service after activation;

(iii)   after every modification or repair;

(iv)   regularly, not less than every two years.

(c)   During the inspection, the expert is required to check that the system conforms to the requirements of 9.3.2.40.2.

(d)   The inspection shall include, as a minimum:

       (i)   an external inspection of the entire system;

       (ii)   an inspection to ensure that the piping is leakproof;

       (iii)   an inspection to ensure that the control and activation systems are in good working order;

       (iv)   an inspection of the pressure and contents of tanks;

       (v)   an inspection to ensure that the means of closing the space to be protected are leakproof;

       (vi)   an inspection of the fire alarm system;

       (vii)   an inspection of the alarm device.

(e)   The person performing the inspection shall establish, sign and date a certificate of inspection.

(f)   The number of permanently fixed fire-extinguishing systems shall be mentioned in the vessel certificate.

9.3.2.40.2.10   *Fire-extinguishing system operating with CO_2*

In addition to the requirements contained in 9.3.2.40.2.1 to 9.3.2.40.2.9, fire-extinguishing systems using CO_2 as an extinguishing agent shall conform to the following provisions:

(a)   Tanks of CO_2 shall be placed in a gastight space or cabinet separated from other spaces. The doors of such storage spaces and cabinets shall open outwards; they shall be capable of being locked and shall carry on the outside the symbol "Warning: danger", not less than 5 cm high and "CO_2" in the same colours and the same size;

(b)   Storage cabinets or spaces for CO_2 tanks located below deck shall only be accessible from the outside. These spaces shall have an artificial ventilation system with extractor hoods and shall be completely independent of the other ventilation systems on board;

(c)   The level of filling of CO_2 tanks shall not exceed 0.75 kg/l. The volume of depressurised CO_2 shall be taken to be 0.56 m^3/kg;

(d)   The concentration of CO_2 in the space to be protected shall be not less than 40% of the gross volume of the space. This quantity shall be released within 120 seconds. It shall be possible to monitor whether diffusion is proceeding correctly;

(e)   The opening of the tank valves and the control of the diffusing valve shall correspond to two different operations;

(f)   The appropriate period of time mentioned in 9.3.2.40.2.6 (b) shall be not less than 20 seconds. A reliable installation shall ensure the timing of the diffusion of CO_2.

9.3.2.40.2.11   *Fire-extinguishing system operating with HFC-227 ea (heptafluoropropane)*

In addition to the requirements of 9.3.2.40.2.1 to 9.3.2.40.2.9, fire-extinguishing systems using HFC-227 ea as an extinguishing agent shall conform to the following provisions:

(a)   Where there are several spaces with different gross volumes, each space shall be equipped with its own fire-extinguishing system;

(b)   Every tank containing HFC-227 ea placed in the space to be protected shall be fitted with a device to prevent overpressure. This device shall ensure that the contents of the tank are safely diffused in the space to be protected if the tank is subjected to fire, when the fire-extinguishing system has not been brought into service;

(c)   Every tank shall be fitted with a device permitting control of the gas pressure;

(d)   The level of filling of tanks shall not exceed 1.15 kg/l. The specific volume of depressurised HFC-227 ea shall be taken to be 0.1374 m^3/kg;

(e)   The concentration of HFC-227 ea in the space to be protected shall be not less than 8% of the gross volume of the space. This quantity shall be released within 10 seconds;

(f)   Tanks of HFC-227 ea shall be fitted with a pressure monitoring device which triggers an audible and visual alarm in the wheelhouse in the event of an unscheduled loss of propellant gas. Where there is no wheelhouse, the alarm shall be triggered outside the space to be protected;

(g)   After discharge, the concentration in the space to be protected shall not exceed 10.5% (volume);

(h)   The fire-extinguishing system shall not comprise aluminium parts.

9.3.2.40.2.12   *Fire-extinguishing system operating with IG-541*

In addition to the requirements of 9.3.2.40.2.1 to 9.3.2.40.2.9, fire-extinguishing systems using IG-541 as an extinguishing agent shall conform to the following provisions:

(a)   Where there are several spaces with different gross volumes, every space shall be equipped with its own fire-extinguishing system;

(b)   Every tank containing IG-541 placed in the space to be protected shall be fitted with a device to prevent overpressure. This device shall ensure that the contents of the tank are safely diffused in the space to be protected if the tank is subjected to fire, when the fire-extinguishing system has not been brought into service;

(c)   Each tank shall be fitted with a device for checking the contents;

(d)   The filling pressure of the tanks shall not exceed 200 bar at a temperature of +15 °C;

(e)   The concentration of IG-541 in the space to be protected shall be not less than 44% and not more than 50% of the gross volume of the space. This quantity shall be released within 120 seconds.

9.3.2.40.2.13 *Fire-extinguishing system operating with FK-5-1-12*

In addition to the requirements of 9.3.2.40.2.1 to 9.3.2.40.2.9, fire-extinguishing systems using FK-5-1-12 as an extinguishing agent shall comply with the following provisions:

(a) Where there are several spaces with different gross volumes, every space shall be equipped with its own fire-extinguishing system;

(b) Every tank containing FK-5-1-12 placed in the space to be protected shall be fitted with a device to prevent overpressure. This device shall ensure that the contents of the tank are safely diffused in the space to be protected if the tank is subjected to fire, when the fire-extinguishing system has not been brought into service;

(c) Every tank shall be fitted with a device permitting control of the gas pressure;

(d) The level of filling of tanks shall not exceed 1.00 kg/l. The specific volume of depressurized FK-5-1-12 shall be taken to be 0.0719 m^3/kg;

(e) The volume of FK-5-1-12 in the space to be protected shall be not less than 5.5% of the gross volume of the space. This quantity shall be released within 10 seconds;

(f) Tanks of FK-5-1-12 shall be fitted with a pressure monitoring device which triggers an audible and visual alarm in the wheelhouse in the event of an unscheduled loss of extinguishing agent. Where there is no wheelhouse, the alarm shall be triggered outside the space to be protected;

(g) After discharge, the concentration in the space to be protected shall not exceed 10.0%.

9.3.2.40.2.14 *(Reserved)*

9.3.2.40.2.15 *Fire-fighting systems using K_2CO_3 as the extinguishing agent*

In addition to the requirements laid down in 9.3.2.40.2.1 to 9.3.2.40.2.3, 9.3.2.40.2.5, 9.3.2.40.2.6 and 9.3.2.40.2.9, fire-fighting systems using K_2CO_3 as the extinguishing agent shall comply with the following provisions:

(a) The fire-fighting system shall have a type-approval pursuant to Directive 2014/90/EU[3] or to MSC/Circ. 1270;[4]

(b) Each room shall be provided with its own firefighting system;

(c) The extinguishing agent must be stored in specially provided unpressurised tanks in the room to be protected. These tanks shall be fitted in such a way that the extinguishing agent is dispensed evenly in the room. In particular the extinguishing agent shall also work underneath the deck plates;

(d) Each tank is separately connected with the triggering device;

(e) The quantity of dry aerosol-forming extinguishing agent relative to the room to be protected shall be at least 120 g per m^3 of the net volume of this room. This net volume is calculated according to Directive 2014/90/EU[3] or to MSC/Circ. 1270[4]. It shall be possible to supply the extinguishing agent within 120 s.

---

[3]   *Official Journal of the European Union, L 257 of 28 August 2014, p.146.*
[4]   *International Maritime Organization Circular MSC/Circ. 1270 and corrigenda — Revised Guidelines for the approval of fixed aerosol fire-extinguishing systems equivalent to fixed gas extinguishing systems, as referred to in SOLAS 1974, for machinery spaces — adopted on 4 June 2008.*

9.3.2.40.2.16   *Fixed fire-extinguishing system for physical protection*

In order to ensure physical protection in the engine rooms, boiler rooms and pump rooms, permanently fixed fire-extinguishing systems are accepted solely on the basis of recommendations by the Administrative Committee.

9.3.2.40.3   The two hand fire–extinguishers referred to in 8.1.4 shall be located in the cargo area.

9.3.2.40.4   The fire-extinguishing agent and the quantity contained in the permanently fixed fire-extinguishing system shall be suitable and sufficient for fighting fires.

9.3.2.41   *Fire and naked light*

9.3.2.41.1   The outlets of funnels shall be located not less than 2.00 m from the cargo area. Arrangements shall be provided to prevent the escape of sparks and the entry of water.

9.3.2.41.2   Heating, cooking and refrigerating appliances shall not be fuelled with liquid fuels, liquid gas or solid fuels.

The installation in the engine room or in another separate space of heating appliances fuelled with liquid fuel having a flash–point above 55 °C is, however, permitted.

Cooking and refrigerating appliances are permitted only in the accommodation.

9.3.2.41.3   Only electrical lamps are permitted.

9.3.2.42   *Cargo heating system*

9.3.2.42.1   Boilers which are used for heating the cargo shall be fuelled with a liquid fuel having a flashpoint of more than 55 °C. They shall be placed either in the engine room or in another separate space below deck and outside the cargo area, which is accessible from the deck or from the engine room.

9.3.2.42.2   The cargo heating system shall be designed so that the cargo cannot penetrate into the boiler in the case of a leak in the heating coils. A cargo heating system with artificial draught shall be ignited electrically.

9.3.2.42.3   The ventilation system of the engine room shall be designed taking into account the air required for the boiler.

9.3.2.42.4   Where the cargo heating system is used during loading, unloading or degassing with a concentration given off by the cargo of 10% of the LEL or above, the service space which contains this system shall fully comply with the requirements of 9.3.2.52.1. This requirement does not apply to the inlets of the ventilation system. These inlets shall be located at a minimum distance of 2 m from the cargo area and 6 m from the openings of cargo tanks or residual cargo tanks, loading pumps situated on deck, openings of high velocity vent valves, pressure relief devices and shore connections of loading and unloading piping and must be located not less than 2 m above the deck.

The requirements of 9.3.2.52.1 are not applicable to the unloading of substances having a flash point of 60 °C or more when the temperature of the product is at least 15 K lower at the flash point.

9.3.2.43 to 9.3.2.49   (*Reserved*)

9.3.2.50   (*Deleted*)

9.3.2.51   *Surface temperatures of installations and equipment*

(a)   Surface temperatures of electrical and non-electrical installations and equipment shall not exceed 200 °C.

(b)   Surface temperatures of the outer parts of engines and of their air inlets and exhaust ducts shall not exceed 200 °C;

(c)   If the list of substances on the vessel according to 1.16.1.2.5 is going to include substances for which the temperature classes T4, T5 or T6 are indicated in column (15) of Table C of Chapter 3.2, then the corresponding surface temperatures within the assigned zones shall not exceed 135 °C (T4), 100 °C (T5) or 85 °C (T6) respectively;

(d)   (a) and (b) do not apply if the following requirements are met (see also 7.2.3.51.4):

  (i)   Accommodation, wheelhouse and service spaces where surface temperatures higher than those mentioned in (a) and (b) occur are equipped with a ventilation system according to 9.3.2.12.4 (b); or

  (ii)   Installations and equipment which generate surface temperatures higher than those set out in (a) or (b), respectively, must be capable of being shut down. Such installations and equipment shall be marked in red.

9.3.2.52   *Type and location of electrical installations and equipment*

9.3.2.52.1   Electrical installations and equipment shall be of at least the 'limited explosion risk' type.

This provision does not apply to:

(a)   Lighting installations in the accommodation and the wheelhouse, except for switches near to the entrances;

(b)   Mobile phones, fixed telephone installations, stationary and portable computers and loading instruments in the accommodation or the wheelhouse;

(c)   Electrical installations and equipment which, during a stay in the immediate vicinity of or within a shoreside assigned zone:

  (i)   Are extinguished; or

  (ii)   Are placed in premises equipped with a ventilation system according to 9.3.2.12.4;

(d)   To radiotelephone installations and inland AIS (automatic identification systems) stations in the accommodation and the wheelhouse, if no part of an aerial for radiotelephone installations or AIS stations is situated above or within 2.00 m of the cargo area.

9.3.2.52.2   In the cofferdams, double-hull spaces, double bottoms and hold spaces, only hermetically sealed echo sounding devices are allowed, the cables of which are led through thick-walled steel tubes with gastight connections up to the main deck.

9.3.2.52.3   The fixed electrical installations and equipment which do not meet the requirements set out in 9.3.2.51 (a), 9.3.2.51 (b) and 9.3.2.52.1 above and their switches shall be marked in red. The disconnection of such equipment shall be controlled from a centralized location on board.

9.3.2.52.4   Every insulated distribution network shall be fitted with an automatic device with a visual and audible alarm for checking the insulation level.

9.3.2.52.5   Only distribution systems without return connection to the hull are permitted. This provision does not apply to:

–   Active cathodic corrosion protection;

–   Certain limited sections of the installations situated outside the cargo area (e.g., connections of starters of diesel engines);

–   The device for checking the insulation level referred to in 9.3.2.52.4.

9.3.2.52.6   An electric generator which is permanently driven by an engine and which does not meet the requirements of 9.3.2.52.1 above, shall be fitted with a multipolar switch capable of shutting down the generator. A notice board with the operating instructions shall be displayed near the switch.

9.3.2.52.7   Failure of the power supply for the safety and control equipment shall be immediately indicated by visual and audible signals in the wheelhouse and on the deck. The alarm must be relayed to the accommodation automatically if it has not been switched off.

9.3.2.52.8   Electrical switches, sockets and cables on deck shall be protected against mechanical damage.

9.3.2.52.9   Sockets for the connection of signal lights and gangway lighting shall be solidly fitted to the vessel close to the signal mast or the gangway. The sockets used in this area shall be designed so as to prevent connection or disconnection except when they are not live.

9.3.2.52.10   Accumulators shall be located outside the cargo area.

9.3.2.53   *Type and location of electrical and non-electrical installations and equipment intended to be used in explosion hazardous areas*

9.3.2.53.1   On board vessels covered by the classification of zones as defined in 1.2.1, electrical and non-electrical installations and equipment used in explosion hazardous areas shall meet at least the requirements for use in the area concerned.

They shall be selected on the basis of the explosion groups/subgroups and temperature classes to which the substances to be carried belong (see columns (15) and (16) of Table C of Chapter 3.2).

If the list of substances on the vessel according to 1.16.1.2.5 is going to include substances for which temperature classes T4, T5 or T6 are indicated in column (15) of Table C of Chapter 3.2, then the corresponding surface temperatures within the assigned zones shall not exceed 135 °C (T4), 100 °C (T5) or 85 °C (T6).

If the list of substances on the vessel according to 1.16.1.2.5 is going to include substances for which temperature classes T1 or T2 are indicated in column (15) of Table C of Chapter 3.2, then the corresponding surface temperatures within the assigned zones shall not exceed 200 °C.

9.3.2.53.2   Except in the case of optical fibres, electrical cables shall be armoured or placed in a metallic sheath or in protective tubes.

Electrical cables for the active cathodic protection of the shell plating shall be led through thick-walled steel tubes with gastight connections up to the main deck.

9.3.2.53.3   Movable electric cables are prohibited in the explosion danger area, except for electric cables for intrinsically safe electric circuits or for connecting:

(a)   Signal lights and lighting for gangways, provided the connection point (for example, the socket) is permanently fitted to the vessel close to the signal mast or gangway;

(b)   The power network on a vessel to a land-based power network; provided

    –   The electric cables and the power supply unit conform with a valid standard (for example, EN 15869-03: 2010);

    –   The power supply unit and connectors are located outside of the explosion danger area.

Connecting and disconnecting sockets/connectors shall only be possible when they are not live.

9.3.2.53.4   Electrical cables of intrinsically safe circuits shall be separated from other cables not intended for use in such circuits and shall be marked (they shall not be installed together in the same string of cables and they shall not be fixed by the same cable clamps).

9.3.2.53.5   For movable electrical cables permitted under 9.3.2.53.3, only sheathed cables of type H07RN-F in accordance with standard IEC 60245-4:2011[5] or electrical cables of at least equivalent design having conductors with a cross-section of not less than 1.50 mm^2 shall be used.

9.3.2.54   *Earthing*

9.3.2.54.1   The metal parts of electrical installations and equipment in the cargo area which are not live, as well as the protective metal tubes or metal sheaths of cables, in normal service shall be earthed, unless they are so arranged that they are automatically earthed by bonding to the metal structure of the vessel.

9.3.2.54.2   The provisions of 9.3.2.54.1 also apply to installations with a voltage of less than 50 Volts.

9.3.2.54.3   Independent cargo tanks, metal intermediate bulk containers and tank-containers shall be earthed.

9.3.2.54.4   Receptacles for residual products shall be capable of being earthed.

9.3.2.55   (*Reserved*)

9.3.2.56   (*Deleted*)

9.3.2.57 to 9.3.2.59   (*Reserved*)

---

[5]   *Identical to EN 50525-2-21: 2011.*

9.3.2.60 *Special equipment*

A shower and an eye and face bath shall be provided on the vessel at a location which is directly accessible from the cargo area. The water shall meet the quality of drinking water on board.

NOTE: Additional decontamination substances for the purpose of avoiding corrosion of eyes and skin are allowed.

A connection of this special equipment with the area outside the cargo zone is accepted.

A spring-loaded non-return valve shall be fitted to ensure that no gases can escape through the shower and the eye and face bath system outside the cargo area.

9.3.2.61 (*Reserved*)

9.3.2.62 *Valve for degassing to reception facilities*

A permanently installed or portable spring-loaded low-pressure valve used during degassing operations to reception facilities, shall be fitted at the piping used to extract air. If the vessel's substance list, according to 1.16.1.2.5, contains substances for which explosion protection is required according to column (17) of Table C of Chapter 3.2, this valve shall be fitted with a flame arrester capable of withstanding a deflagration. When the vessel is not degassing to a reception facility, the valve shall be closed with a blind flange. The low-pressure valve shall be so installed that under other normal working conditions the vacuum valve is not activated.

NOTE: Degassing operations are part of normal working conditions.

9.3.2.63 to 9.3.2.70 (*Reserved*)

9.3.2.71 *Admittance on board*

The notice boards displaying the prohibition of admittance in accordance with 8.3.3 shall be clearly legible from either side of the vessel.

9.3.2.72 and 9.3.2.73 (*Reserved*)

9.3.2.74 *Prohibition of smoking, fire or naked light*

9.3.2.74.1 The notice boards displaying the prohibition of smoking in accordance with 8.3.4 shall be clearly legible from either side of the vessel.

9.3.2.74.2 Notice boards indicating the circumstances under which the prohibition is applicable shall be fitted near the entrances to the spaces where smoking or the use of fire or naked light is not always prohibited.

9.3.2.74.3 Ashtrays shall be provided close to each exit of the accommodation and the wheelhouse.

9.3.2.75 to 9.3.2.91 (*Reserved*)

9.3.2.92 *Emergency exit*

Spaces the entrances or exits of which are likely to become partly or completely immersed in the damaged condition shall have an emergency exit which is situated not less than 0.10 m above the damage waterline. This requirement does not apply to forepeak and afterpeak.

9.3.2.93 to 9.3.2.99 (*Reserved*)

9.3.3 **Rules for construction of type N tank vessels**

The rules for construction of 9.3.3.0 to 9.3.3.99 apply to type N tank vessels.

9.3.3.0 *Materials of construction*

9.3.3.0.1 (a) The vessel's hull and the cargo tanks shall be constructed of shipbuilding steel or other at least equivalent metal.

The independent cargo tanks may also be constructed of other materials, provided these have at least equivalent mechanical properties and resistance against the effects of temperature and fire.

(b) Every part of the vessel including any installation and equipment which may come into contact with the cargo shall consist of materials which can neither be dangerously affected by the cargo nor cause decomposition of the cargo or react with it so as to form harmful or hazardous products. In case it has not been possible to examine this during classification and inspection of the vessel a relevant reservation shall be entered in the vessel substance list according to 1.16.1.2.5.

(c) Inside venting piping shall be protected against corrosion.

9.3.3.0.2 Except where explicitly permitted in 9.3.3.03 below or in the certificate of approval, the use of wood, aluminium alloys, plastic materials or rubber within the cargo area is prohibited.

9.3.3.0.3 The use of wood, aluminium alloys, plastic materials or rubber in the cargo area is permitted as shown in the following table:

The use of wood, aluminium alloys, plastic materials or rubber is permitted only for:			(X indicates permitted)	
	Wood	**Aluminium alloys**	**Plastic material**	**Rubber**
Gangways	X	X	X	X
External ladders and passageways (gangways) *)		X	X	X
Cleaning equipment, e.g. brooms	X		X	X
Movable equipment e.g. fire extinguishers, portable gas detectors, rescue winches		X	X	X
Fenders	X		X	X
Mooring cables, fender ropes			X	
Chocking of cargo tanks which are independent of the vessel's hull and chocking of installations and equipment	X		X	
Masts and similar round timber	X	X	X	
Engine parts		X	X	
Protective covers of engines and pumps			X	
Parts of the electrical installation		X	X	
Parts of the loading and unloading installation, e.g., gaskets		X	X	X
Boxes, cabinets or other receptacles placed on the deck for storage of disposal and recovery equipment for capstans, extinguishers, fire hoses, waste, etc.		X	X	
Supports and stops of any kind	X		X	

The use of wood, aluminium alloys, plastic materials or rubber is permitted only for:			(X indicates permitted)	
	Wood	**Aluminium alloys**	**Plastic material**	**Rubber**
Ventilators, including hose assemblies for ventilation		X	X	
Parts of the water spray system, the shower and the eye and face bath		X	X	
Insulation of cargo tanks and of piping for loading and unloading, gas discharge pipes and heating pipes			X	X
Coating of cargo tanks and of piping for loading and unloading		X	X	X
All kinds of gaskets (e.g. for dome or hatch covers)			X	X
Cables for electrical equipment			X	X
Mat under hose assemblies for loading and unloading piping system			X	X
Fire hoses, air hoses, hoses for cleaning the deck, etc.			X	X
Sampling equipment and bottles			X	
Photo-optical copies of the certificate of approval according to 8.1.2.6 or 8.1.2.7, and of the vessel's certificate, the measurement certificate and the Rhine navigation membership certificate		X	X	
Drip trays			X	
(*) Take account of 9.3.1.0.5, 9.3.2.0.5 or 9.3.3.0.5, as appropriate				
Aluminium gauging rods are permitted, provided that they are fitted with brass feet or protected in another way to avoid sparking.				

9.3.3.0.3.1   All permanently fitted materials in the accommodation or wheelhouse, with the exception of furniture, shall not readily ignite. They shall not evolve fumes or toxic gases in dangerous quantities, if involved in a fire.

9.3.3.0.4   The paint used in the cargo area shall not be liable to produce sparks in case of impact.

9.3.3.0.5   The use of plastic material for a vessel's boats is permitted only if the material does not readily ignite.

The use of aluminium alloys or plastic material for passageways (gangways) in the cargo area is permitted only if the material does not readily ignite or conduct electricity.

9.3.3.1   **Vessel record**

NOTE: For the purpose of this paragraph, the term "owner" has the same meaning as in 1.16.0.

The vessel record shall be retained by the owner who shall be able to provide this documentation at the request of the competent authority and the recognized classification society.

The vessel record shall be maintained and updated throughout the life of the vessel and shall be retained for 6 months after the vessel is taken out of service.

Should a change of owner occur during the life of the vessel the vessel record shall be transferred to the new owner.

Copies of the vessel record or all necessary documents shall be made available on request to the competent authority for the issuance of the certificate of approval and for the recognized classification society or inspection body for first inspection, periodic inspection, special inspection or exceptional checks.

9.3.3.2 to 9.3.3.7   *(Reserved)*

9.3.3.8   ***Classification***

9.3.3.8.1   The tank vessel shall be built under the survey of a recognised classification society and be classed in its highest class.

The vessel's highest class shall be continued. This shall be confirmed by an appropriate certificate issued by the recognized classification society (certificate of class).

The design pressure and the test pressure of cargo tanks shall be entered in the certificate.

If a vessel has cargo tanks with different valve opening pressures, the design and test pressures of each tank shall be entered in the certificate.

The recognized classification society shall draw up a vessel substance list mentioning all the dangerous goods accepted for carriage by the tank vessel (see also 1.16.1.2.5).

9.3.3.8.2 to 9.3.3.8.4   *(Deleted)*

9.3.3.9   *(Reserved)*

9.3.3.10   ***Protection against the penetration of dangerous gases and the spreading of dangerous liquids***

9.3.3.10.1   The vessel shall be designed so as to prevent dangerous gases and liquids from penetrating into the accommodation, wheelhouse and service spaces. None of the windows in these spaces shall be capable of being opened unless its intended use is as an emergency exit and it is marked as such.

9.3.3.10.2   Liquid-tight protective coamings shall be fitted on deck at the height of the external bulkheads of the cargo tanks, at a maximum distance of 0.60 m from the outer cofferdam bulkheads or the hold end bulkheads. The protective coamings shall either extend over the entire width of the vessel or be fixed between the longitudinal spill coamings so as to prevent liquids from entering the forepeak and afterpeak. The height of the protective coamings and the spill coamings shall be at least 0.075 m. The protective coaming may correspond to the protection wall prescribed in 9.3.3.10.3 if the protection wall extends across the entire width of the vessel.

9.3.3.10.3   If the list of substances on the vessel according to 1.16.1.2.5 is going to include substances that require explosion protection in accordance with column (17) of Table C of Chapter 3.2, then the use of installations and equipment that are not of at least the 'limited explosion risk' type is not permitted during loading and unloading operations in parts of the deck outside the cargo area, unless those parts are protected against the penetration of gases and liquids by a gas- and liquid-tight protection wall. The wall must either extend over the full width of the vessel or surround the areas to be protected in a U-shaped form. The wall must cover the whole width of the area to be protected and at least 1.00 m in the direction opposite to the cargo area (see Classification of zones diagram). The height of the wall shall be at least 1.00 m above the adjacent cargo deck area in the cargo area. The outer wall and side walls of the accommodation can be considered as a protection wall if they do not include openings and if the dimensions are complied with.

A protection wall is not required where the distance between the areas to be protected and the high velocity vent valve, the shore connections of the piping for loading and unloading, the compressor on deck and the opening of the closest pressure tanks is at least 12.00 m.

9.3.3.10.4   On deck, the lower edges of door-openings in the sidewalls of superstructures and the sills of hatches and ventilation openings of premises located under the deck shall have a height of not less than 0.50 m above the deck.

This requirement does not apply to access openings to double-hull spaces and double bottoms.

9.3.3.10.5   The bulwarks, foot-rails, etc. shall be provided with sufficiently large openings which are located directly above the deck.

9.3.3.10.6   Open Type N vessels are only required to meet the requirements of 9.3.3.10.1 if the vessel remains in the immediate vicinity of or within a shoreside assigned zone.

9.3.3.11   *Hold spaces and cargo tanks*

9.3.3.11.1   (a)   The maximum permissible capacity of a cargo tank shall be determined in accordance with the following table:

$L \times B \times H$ (m³)	Maximum permissible capacity of a cargo tank (m³)
up to 600	$L \times B \times H \times 0.3$
600 to 3 750	$180 + (L \times B \times H - 600) \times 0.0635$
> 3 750	380

Alternative constructions in accordance with 9.3.4 are permitted.
In the table above $L \times B \times H$ is the product of the main dimensions of the tank vessel in metres (according to the measurement certificate), where:

L = overall length of the hull in m;
B = extreme breadth of the hull in m;
H = shortest vertical distance between the top of the keel and the lowest point of the deck at the side of the vessel (moulded depth) within the cargo area in m;

where:

For trunk vessels, H shall be replaced by H', where H' shall be obtained from the following formula:

$$H' = H + \left(ht \times \frac{bt}{B} \times \frac{lt}{L} \right)$$

where:

ht = trunk height (distance between trunk deck and main deck measured on trunk side at L/2) in m;
bt = trunk breadth in m;
lt = trunk length in m.

(b)   The relative density of the substances to be carried shall be taken into consideration in the design of the cargo tanks. The maximum relative density shall be indicated in the certificate of approval.

(c) When the vessel is provided with pressure tanks, these tanks shall be designed for a working pressure of 400 kPa (4 bar).

(d) For vessels with a length of not more than 50.00 m, the length of a cargo tank shall not exceed 10.00 m; and

For vessels with a length of more than 50.00 m, the length of a cargo tank shall not exceed 0.20 L.

This provision does not apply to vessels with independent built–in cylindrical tanks having a length to diameter ratio ≤ 7.

9.3.3.11.2 (a) The cargo tanks independent of the vessel's hull shall be fixed so that they cannot float.

Refrigerated cargo tank fastenings shall meet the requirements of a recognised classification society.

(b) The capacity of a suction well shall be limited to not more than 0.10 m³.

(c) *(Reserved)*

(d) Side-struts linking or supporting the load-bearing components of the sides of the vessel with the load-bearing components of the longitudinal walls of cargo tanks and side-struts linking the load-bearing components of the vessel's bottom with the tank-bottom are prohibited.

9.3.3.11.3 (a) The cargo tanks shall be separated by cofferdams of at least 0.60 m in width from the accommodation, engine rooms and service spaces outside the cargo area below deck or, if there are no such accommodation, engine room and service spaces, from the vessel's ends. Where the cargo tanks are installed in a hold space, a space of not less than 0.50 m shall be provided between such tanks and the end bulkheads of the hold space. In this case an end bulkhead of Class "A-60" as defined in SOLAS 74, Chapter II-2, Regulation 3, shall be deemed equivalent to a cofferdam. For pressure cargo tanks, the 0.50 m distance may be reduced to 0.20 m.

(b) Hold spaces, cofferdams and cargo tanks shall be capable of being inspected.

(c) All spaces in the cargo area shall be capable of being ventilated. It has to be possible to check their gas-free condition.

9.3.3.11.4 The bulkheads bounding the cargo tanks, cofferdams and hold spaces shall be watertight. The cargo tanks and the bulkheads bounding the cargo area shall have no openings or penetrations below deck.

The bulkhead between the engine room and the cofferdam or service space in the cargo area or between the engine room and a hold space may be fitted with penetrations provided that they conform to the provisions of 9.3.3.17.5.

The bulkhead between the cargo tank and the cargo pump-room below deck may be fitted with penetrations provided that they conform to the provisions of 9.3.3.17.6. The bulkheads between the cargo tanks may be fitted with penetrations provided that the loading and unloading piping are fitted with shut-off devices in the cargo tank from which they come. These pipes shall be fitted at least 0.60m above the bottom. The shut-off devices shall be capable of being activated from the deck.

9.3.3.11.5 Double-hull spaces and double bottoms in the cargo area shall be arranged for being filled with ballast water only. Double bottoms may, however, be used as oil fuel tanks, provided they comply with the provisions of 9.3.3.32.

9.3.3.11.6   (a)   A cofferdam, the centre part of a cofferdam or another space below deck in the cargo area may be arranged as a service space, provided the bulkheads bounding the service space extend vertically to the bottom. This service space shall only be accessible from the deck.

                     (b)   The service space shall be watertight with the exception of its access hatches and ventilation inlets.

                     (c)   No piping for loading and unloading shall be fitted within the service space referred to under 9.3.3.11.4 above.

                               Piping for loading and unloading may be fitted in the cargo pump-rooms below deck only when they conform to the provisions of 9.3.3.17.6.

9.3.3.11.7   Where independent cargo tanks are used, or for double-hull construction where the cargo tanks are integrated in the vessel's structure, the space between the wall of the vessel and wall of the cargo tanks shall be not less than 0.60 m.

            The space between the bottom of the vessel and the bottom of the cargo tanks shall be not less than 0.50 m. The space may be reduced to 0.40 m under the pump sumps.

            The vertical space between the suction well of a cargo tank and the bottom structures shall be not less than 0.10 m.

            When a hull is constructed in the cargo area as a double hull with independent cargo tanks located in hold spaces, the above values are applicable to the double hull. If in this case the minimum values for inspections of independent tanks referred to in 9.3.3.11.9 are not feasible, it must be possible to remove the cargo tanks easily for inspection.

9.3.3.11.8   Where service spaces are located in the cargo area under deck, they shall be arranged so as to be easily accessible and to permit persons wearing protective clothing and breathing apparatus to safely operate the service equipment contained therein. They shall be designed so as to allow injured or unconscious personnel to be removed from such spaces without difficulties, if necessary by means of fixed equipment.

9.3.3.11.9   Cofferdams, double-hull spaces, double bottoms, cargo tanks, hold spaces and other accessible spaces within the cargo area shall be arranged so that they may be completely inspected and cleaned. The dimensions of openings except for those of double-hull spaces and double bottoms which do not have a wall adjoining the cargo tanks shall be sufficient to allow a person wearing breathing apparatus to enter or leave the space without difficulties. These openings shall have a minimum cross-section of 0.36 m^2 and a minimum side length of 0.50 m. They shall be designed so as to allow injured or unconscious personnel to be removed from the bottom of such a space without difficulties, if necessary by means of fixed equipment. In these spaces the free penetration width shall not be less than 0.50 m in the sector intended for the penetration. In double bottoms this distance may be reduced to 0.45 m.

            Cargo tanks may have circular openings with a diameter of not less than 0.68 m.

9.3.3.11.10   9.3.3.11.6 (c) above does not apply to open type N.

9.3.3.12   *Ventilation*

9.3.3.12.1   Each hold space shall have two openings the dimensions and location of which shall be such as to permit effective ventilation of any part of the hold space. If there are no such openings, it shall be possible to fill the hold spaces with inert gas or dry air.

9.3.3.12.2 Double-hull spaces and double bottoms within the cargo area which are not arranged for being filled with ballast water, hold spaces and cofferdams shall be provided with ventilation systems.

9.3.3.12.3 (a) A service space located within the cargo area below deck shall be provided with a ventilation system. The capacity of the fans shall be sufficient to ensure 20 complete changes of air per hour based on the volume of the service space.

The ventilation exhaust ducts shall extend down to 50 mm above the bottom of the service space. The air shall be supplied through a duct at the top of the service space.

(b) If the list of substances on the vessel according to 1.16.1.2.5 is going to include substances that require explosion protection in accordance with column (17) of Table C of Chapter 3.2, then the air inlets shall be located not less than 2.00 m above the deck, at a distance of not less than 2.00 m from tank openings and 6.00 m from the outlets of safety valves.

The extension pipes which may be necessary may be of the hinged type.

(c) On board open Type N vessels, other suitable installations without ventilator fans shall be sufficient.

9.3.3.12.4 (a) Ventilation shall be provided for the accommodation, wheelhouse and service spaces.

(b) The ventilation system in such spaces shall meet the following requirements:

(i) The air intakes shall be located as far away as possible, and not less than 6.00 m from the cargo area and not less than 2.00 m above the deck;

(ii) Pressure of at least 0.1 kPa (0.001 bar) may be maintained in the premises;

(iii) A breakdown alarm is integrated;

(iv) The ventilation system, including the breakdown alarm, shall be at least of the 'limited explosion risk' type;

(v) A gas detection system conforming to conditions 1. to 4. below is connected to the ventilation system:

1. It is appropriate at least for use in zone 1, explosion group IIC and temperature class T6;

2. It is equipped with sensors;

   – On the suction inlets of the ventilation systems; and

   – Directly below the top edge of the sill of the entrance doors;

3. Its t90 response time is lower than or equal to 4 s;

4. Measurement shall be continuous;

(vi) In the service spaces, the ventilation system is linked to the emergency lighting, which shall be at least of the 'limited explosion risk' type;

This emergency lighting is not necessary if the lighting installations in the service spaces are of at least the 'limited explosion risk' type;

(vii) The suction of the ventilation system and installations and equipment that do not meet the requirements set out in 9.3.3.51 (a) and (b) and 9.3.3.52.1 must be shut down when a concentration of 20% of LEL of n-Hexane is reached;

The switching-off shall be indicated in the accommodation and wheelhouse by visual and audible signals;

(viii) In the event of failure of the ventilation system or the gas detection installations in the accommodation, installations and equipment in the accommodation that do not meet the requirements set out in 9.3.3.51 (a) and (b) and 9.3.3.52.1 must be stopped;

The failure shall be indicated in the accommodation, the wheelhouse and on the deck by visual and audible signals;

(ix) In the event of failure of the ventilation system or the gas detection installations in the wheelhouse or service spaces, installations and equipment in those spaces that do not meet the requirements set out in 9.3.3.51 (a) and (b) and 9.3.3.52.1 must be shut down;

The failure shall be indicated in the wheelhouse and on the deck by visual and audible signals. The alarm must be relayed to the accommodation automatically if it has not been switched off;

(x) Any switching-off shall take place immediately and automatically and, if necessary, shall activate the emergency lighting;

The automatic switch-off device is set so that no automatic switching-off may occur while the vessel is under way;

(c) If there is no ventilation system or the ventilation system of a space does not comply with all the requirements set out in (b) above, any installations or equipment present in that space that may, if switched on, give rise to surface temperatures higher than those mentioned in 9.3.3.51 (a) and (b) or that do not meet the requirements set out in 9.3.3.52.1 must be capable of being switched off.

9.3.3.12.5   *(Deleted)*

9.3.3.12.6   Notice boards shall be fitted at the ventilation inlets indicating the conditions under which they shall be closed. All ventilation inlets of accommodation, wheelhouse and service spaces leading to the open air outside the cargo area shall be fitted with devices permanently fixed according to 9.3.3.40.2.2 (c), enabling them to be closed rapidly. It shall be clear whether they are open or closed.

Such ventilation inlets shall be located not less than 2.00 m from the cargo area.

Ventilation inlets of service spaces in the cargo area may be located within that area.

9.3.3.12.7   Open Type N vessels are only required to meet the requirements of 9.3.3.12.4 (b) or (c) if the vessel remains in the immediate vicinity of or within a shoreside assigned zone.

9.3.3.12.8   9.3.3.12.6 and 9.3.3.12.7 above do not apply to open type N.

9.3.3.13   *Stability (general)*

9.3.3.13.1   Proof of sufficient stability shall be furnished. This proof is not required for single hull vessels with cargo tanks the width of which is not more than 0.70 B.

9.3.3.13.2   The basic values for the stability calculation – the vessel's lightweight and location of the centre of gravity – shall be determined either by means of an inclining experiment or by detailed mass and moment calculation. In the latter case the lightweight of the vessel shall be checked by means of a lightweight test with a tolerance limit of ± 5% between the mass determined by calculation and the displacement determined by the draught readings.

9.3.3.13.3   Proof of sufficient intact stability shall be furnished for all stages of loading and unloading and for the final loading condition for all the relative densities of the substances transported contained in the vessel substance list according to 1.16.1.2.5.

For every loading operation, taking account of the actual fillings and floating position of cargo tanks, ballast tanks and compartments, drinking water and sewage tanks and tanks containing products for the operation of the vessel, the vessel shall comply with the intact and damage stability requirements.

Intermediate stages during operations shall also be taken into consideration.

The proof of sufficient stability shall be shown for every operating, loading and ballast condition in the stability booklet, to be approved by the recognized classification society, which classes the vessel. If it is unpractical to pre-calculate the operating, loading and ballast conditions, a loading instrument approved by the recognised classification society which classes the vessel shall be installed and used which contains the contents of the stability booklet.

NOTE: A stability booklet shall be worded in a form comprehensible for the responsible master and containing the following details:

General description of the vessel:

–   *General arrangement and capacity plans indicating the assigned use of compartments and spaces (cargo tanks, stores, accommodation, etc.);*

–   *A sketch indicating the position of the draught marks referring to the vessel's perpendiculars;*

–   *A scheme for ballast/bilge pumping and overflow prevention systems;*

–   *Hydrostatic curves or tables corresponding to the design trim, and, if significant trim angles are foreseen during the normal operation of the vessel, curves or tables corresponding to such range of trim are to be introduced;*

–   *Cross curves or tables of stability calculated on a free trimming basis, for the ranges of displacement and trim anticipated in normal operating conditions, with an indication of the volumes which have been considered buoyant;*

–   *Tank sounding tables or curves showing capacities, centres of gravity, and free surface data for all cargo tanks, ballast tanks and compartments, drinking water and sewage water tanks and tanks containing products for the operation of the vessel;*

- *Lightship data (weight and centre of gravity) resulting from an inclining test or deadweight measurement in combination with a detailed mass balance or other acceptable measures. Where the above–mentioned information is derived from a sister vessel, the reference to this sister vessel shall be clearly indicated, and a copy of the approved inclining test report relevant to this sister vessel shall be included;*

- *A copy of the approved test report shall be included in the stability booklet;*

- *Operating loading conditions with all relevant details, such as:*

  - *Lightship data, tank fillings, stores, crew and other relevant items on board (mass and centre of gravity for each item, free surface moments for liquid loads);*

  - *Draughts amidships and at perpendiculars;*

  - *Metacentric height corrected for free surfaces effect;*

  - *Righting lever values and curve;*

  - *Longitudinal bending moments and shear forces at read–out points;*

  - *Information about openings (location, type of tightness, means of closure); and*

  - *Information for the master;*

- *Calculation of the influence of ballast water on stability with information on whether fixed level gauges for ballast tanks and compartments have to be installed or whether the ballast tanks or compartments shall only be completely full or completely empty when underway.*

9.3.3.13.4   Floatability after damage shall be proved for the most unfavourable loading condition. For this purpose, calculated proof of sufficient stability shall be established for critical intermediate stages of flooding and for the final stage of flooding.

9.3.3.14   *Stability (intact)*

9.3.3.14.1   For vessels with independent cargo tanks and for double-hull constructions with cargo tanks integrated in the frames of the vessel, the requirements for intact stability resulting from the damage stability calculation shall be fully complied with.

9.3.3.14.2   For vessels with cargo tanks of more than 0.70 B in width, proof shall be furnished that the following stability requirements have been complied with:

(a)   In the positive area of the righting lever curve up to immersion of the first non-watertight opening there shall be a righting lever (GZ) of not less than 0.10 m;

(b)   The surface of the positive area of the righting lever curve up to immersion of the first non-watertight opening and in any event up to an angle of heel $\leq 27°$ shall not be less than 0.024 m.rad;

(c)   The metacentric height (GM) shall be not less than 0.10 m.

These conditions shall be met bearing in mind the influence of all free surfaces in tanks for all stages of loading and unloading.

9.3.3.15   *Stability (damaged condition)*

9.3.3.15.1   For vessels with independent cargo tanks and for double-hull vessels with cargo tanks integrated in the construction of the vessel, the following assumptions shall be taken into consideration for the damaged condition:

(a)   The extent of side damage is as follows:

longitudinal extent:	at least 0.10 L, but not less than 5.00 m;
transverse extent:	0.59 m inboard from the vessel's side at right angles to the centreline at the level corresponding to the maximum draught, or when applicable, the distance allowed by section 9.3.4, reduced by 0.01 m;
vertical extent:	from the base line upwards without limit.

(b)   The extent of bottom damage is as follows:

longitudinal extent:	at least 0.10 L, but not less than 5.00 m;
transverse extent:	3.00 m;
vertical extent:	from the base 0.49 m upwards, the sump excepted.

(c)   Any bulkheads within the damaged area shall be assumed damaged, which means that the location of bulkheads shall be chosen so as to ensure that the vessel remains afloat after the flooding of two or more adjacent compartments in the longitudinal direction.

The following provisions are applicable:

–   For bottom damage, adjacent athwartship compartments shall also be assumed as flooded;

–   The lower edge of any non-watertight openings (e.g. doors, windows, access hatchways) shall, at the final stage of flooding, be not less than 0.10 m above the damage waterline;

–   In general, permeability shall be assumed to be 95%. Where an average permeability of less than 95% is calculated for any compartment, this calculated value obtained may be used.

However, the following minimum values shall be used:

– engine rooms:	85%;
– accommodation:	95%;
– double bottoms, oil fuel tanks, ballast tanks, etc., depending on whether, according to their function, they have to be assumed as full or empty for the vessel floating at the maximum permissible draught:	0% or 95%.

For the main engine room only the one–compartment standard need be taken into account, i.e. the end bulkheads of the engine room shall be assumed as not damaged.

9.3.3.15.2   For the intermediate stage of flooding the following criteria have to be fulfilled:

$GZ \geq 0.03$m

Range of positive GZ: 5°

At the stage of equilibrium (final stage of flooding), the angle of heel shall not exceed 12°. Non-watertight openings shall not be flooded before reaching the stage of equilibrium. If such openings are immersed before that stage, the corresponding spaces shall be considered as flooded for the purpose of the stability calculation.

The positive range of the righting lever curve beyond the stage of equilibrium shall have a righting lever of ≥ 0.05 m in association with an area under the curve of ≥ 0.0065 m.rad. The minimum values of stability shall be satisfied up to immersion of the first non-watertight opening and in any event up to an angle of heel $\leq 27°$. If non-watertight openings are immersed before that stage, the corresponding spaces shall be considered as flooded for the purposes of stability calculation.

9.3.3.15.3   If openings through which undamaged compartments may additionally become flooded are capable of being closed watertight, the closing appliances shall be marked accordingly.

9.3.3.15.4   Where cross- or down-flooding openings are provided for reduction of unsymmetrical flooding, the time for equalization shall not exceed 15 minutes, if during the intermediate stages of flooding sufficient stability has been proved.

9.3.3.16   *Engine rooms*

9.3.3.16.1   Internal combustion engines for the vessel's propulsion as well as internal combustion engines for auxiliary machinery shall be located outside the cargo area. Entrances and other openings of engine rooms shall be at a distance of not less than 2.00 m from the cargo area.

9.3.3.16.2   The engine rooms shall be accessible from the deck; the entrances shall not face the cargo area. Where the doors are not located in a recess whose depth is at least equal to the door width, the hinges shall face the cargo area.

9.3.3.16.3   The last sentence of 9.3.3.16.2 does not apply to oil separator or supply vessels.

9.3.3.17   *Accommodation and service spaces*

9.3.3.17.1   Accommodation spaces and the wheelhouse shall be located outside the cargo area forward of the fore vertical plane or abaft the aft vertical plane bounding the part of the cargo area below deck. Windows of the wheelhouse which are located not less than 1.00 m above the bottom of the wheelhouse may tilt forward.

9.3.3.17.2   Entrances to spaces and openings of superstructures shall not face the cargo area. Doors opening outward and not located in a recess whose depth is at least equal to the width of the doors shall have their hinges face the cargo area.

9.3.3.17.3   Entrances from the deck and openings of spaces facing the weather shall be capable of being closed. The following instruction shall be displayed at the entrance of such spaces:

Do not open during loading, unloading and degassing
without the permission of the master.
Close immediately.

9.3.3.17.4   Entrances and windows of superstructures and accommodation spaces which can be opened as well as other openings of these spaces shall be located not less than 2.00 m from the cargo area. No wheelhouse doors and windows shall be located within 2.00 m from the cargo area, except where there is no direct connection between the wheelhouse and the accommodation.

9.3.3.17.5   (a)   Driving shafts of the bilge or ballast pumps may penetrate through the bulkhead between the service space and the engine room, provided the arrangement of the service space is in compliance with 9.3.3.11.6.

(b)   The penetration of the shaft through the bulkhead shall be gastight and shall have been approved by a recognised classification society.

(c)   The necessary operating instructions shall be displayed.

(d)   Penetrations through the bulkhead between the engine room and the service space in the cargo area and the bulkhead between the engine room and the hold spaces may be provided for electrical cables, hydraulic lines and piping for measuring, control and alarm systems, provided that the penetrations have been approved by a recognised classification society. The penetrations shall be gastight. Penetrations through a bulkhead with an "A-60" fire protection insulation according to SOLAS 74, Chapter II-2, Regulation 3, shall have an equivalent fire protection.

(e)   Pipes may penetrate the bulkhead between the engine room and the service space in the cargo area provided that these are pipes between the mechanical equipment in the engine room and the service space which do not have any openings within the service space and which are provided with shut-off devices at the bulkhead in the engine room.

(f)   Notwithstanding 9.3.3.11.4, pipes from the engine room may pass through the service space in the cargo area or a cofferdam or a hold space or a double-hull space to the outside provided that within the service space or cofferdam or hold space or double-hull space they are of the thick-walled type and have no flanges or openings.

(g)   Where a driving shaft of auxiliary machinery penetrates through a wall located above the deck the penetration shall be gastight.

9.3.3.17.6   A service space located within the cargo area below deck shall not be used as a cargo pump-room for the loading and unloading system, except where:

–   The cargo pump-room is separated from the engine room or from service spaces outside the cargo area by a cofferdam or a bulkhead with an insulation of Class "A-60" as defined in SOLAS 74, Chapter II-2, Regulation 3, or by a service space or a hold space;

–   The "A-60" bulkhead required above does not include penetrations referred to in 9.3.3.17.5 (a);

–   Ventilation exhaust outlets are located not less than 6.00 m from entrances and openings of the accommodation, wheelhouse and service spaces outside the cargo area;

–   The access hatches and ventilation inlets can be closed from the outside;

–   All piping for loading and unloading as well as that of stripping systems is provided with shut-off devices at the pump suction side in the cargo pump-room immediately at the bulkhead. The necessary operation of the control devices in the pump-room, starting of pumps and control of the liquid flow rate shall be effected from the deck;

–   The bilge of the cargo pump-room is equipped with a gauging device for measuring the filling level which activates a visual and audible alarm in the wheelhouse when liquid is accumulating in the cargo pump-room bilge;

–   The cargo pump room is provided with a permanent oxygen detection system which automatically indicates the amount of oxygen and which actuates a visual and audible alarm when the oxygen concentration has reached 19.5% by volume. The sensors of this system shall be placed at suitable positions at the bottom and at a height of 2.00 m. Measurement shall be continuous and displayed near to the entrance. Audible and visual alarms shall be installed in the wheelhouse and in the cargo pump-room and, when the alarm is actuated, the loading and unloading system shall be shut down;

–   Failure of the oxygen measuring system shall activate a visual and audible alarm in the wheelhouse and on deck. The alarm must be relayed to the accommodation automatically if it has not been switched off;

–   The ventilation system prescribed in 9.3.3.12.3 has a capacity sufficient to ensure not less than 30 changes of air per hour based on the total volume of the service space.

If the list of substances on the vessel according to 1.16.1.2.5 is going to include substances that require explosion protection in accordance with column (17) of Table C of Chapter 3.2, then the cargo pump room shall also be provided with a permanent gas detection system which automatically indicates the presence of flammable gases and actuates a visual and audible alarm when the gas concentration has reached 20% of the LEL of the cargo or 20% of the LEL of n-Hexane, whichever gives the more critical value.

The sensors of this gas detection system shall be placed at suitable positions at the bottom and directly below the deck. Measurement shall be continuous and displayed near to the entrance.

Audible and visual alarms shall be installed in the wheelhouse and in the cargo pump-room and, when the alarm is actuated, the loading and unloading system shall be shut down.

Any failure of the gas detection system shall be immediately signalled in the wheelhouse and on deck by a visual and audible warning. The alarm must be relayed to the accommodation automatically if it has not been switched off.

9.3.3.17.7   The following instruction shall be displayed at the entrance of the cargo pump-room:

**Before entering the cargo pump-room check whether
it is free from gases and contains sufficient oxygen.
Do not open doors and entrance openings without
the permission of the master.
Leave immediately in the event of alarm.**

9.3.3.17.8   9.3.3.17.5 (g), 9.3.3.17.6 except for the permanent oxygen measuring system and 9.3.3.17.7 do not apply to open type N.

9.3.3.17.2, last sentence, 9.3.3.17.3, last sentence and 9.3.3.17.4 do not apply to oil separator and supply vessels.

9.3.3.18   *Inerting facility*

In cases in which inerting or blanketing of the cargo is prescribed, the vessel shall be equipped with an inerting system.

This system shall be capable of maintaining a permanent minimum pressure of 7 kPa (0.07 bar) in the spaces to be inerted. In addition, the inerting system shall not increase the pressure in the cargo tank to a pressure greater than that at which the pressure valve is regulated. The set pressure of the vacuum-relief valve shall be 3.5 kPa (0.035 bar).

A sufficient quantity of inert gas for loading or unloading shall be carried or produced on board if it is not possible to obtain it on shore. In addition, a sufficient quantity of inert gas to offset normal losses occurring during carriage shall be on board.

The premises to be inerted shall be equipped with connections for introducing the inert gas and monitoring systems so as to ensure the correct atmosphere on a permanent basis.

When the pressure or the concentration of inert gas in the gaseous phase falls below a given value, this monitoring system shall activate an audible and visible alarm in the wheelhouse. When the wheelhouse is unoccupied, the alarm shall also be perceptible in a location occupied by a crew member.

9.3.3.19   (*Reserved*)

9.3.3.20   *Arrangement of cofferdams*

9.3.3.20.1   Cofferdams or cofferdam compartments remaining once a service space has been arranged in accordance with 9.3.3.11.6 shall be accessible through an access hatch.

9.3.3.20.2   Cofferdams shall be capable of being filled with water and emptied by means of a pump. Filling shall be effected within 30 minutes. These requirements are not applicable when the bulkhead between the engine room and the cofferdam has an "A-16" fire protection insulation according to SOLAS 74, Chapter II-2, Regulation 3.

The cofferdams shall not be fitted with inlet valves.

9.3.3.20.3   No fixed pipe shall permit connection between a cofferdam and other piping of the vessel outside the cargo area.

9.3.3.20.4   If the list of substances on the vessel according to 1.16.1.2.5 is going to include substances that require explosion protection in accordance with column (17) of Table C of Chapter 3.2 then the ventilation openings of cofferdams shall be fitted with a flame arrester capable of withstanding a deflagration. The flame arresters shall be chosen according to the explosion groups/subgroups of the substances foreseen for inclusion in the list of substances on the vessel (see column (16) of Table C of Chapter 3.2).

9.3.3.20.5   9.3.3.20.2 above does not apply to oil separator and supply vessels.

9.3.3.21   *Safety and control installations*

9.3.3.21.1   Cargo tanks shall be provided with the following equipment:

(a)   a mark inside the tank indicating the liquid level of 97%;

(b)   a level gauge;

(c)   a level alarm device which is activated at the latest when a degree of filling of 90% is reached;

(d)   a high level sensor for actuating the facility against overflowing when a degree of filling of 97.5% is reached;

(e)   an instrument for measuring the pressure of the vapour phase inside the cargo tank;

(f)   an instrument for measuring the temperature of the cargo, if in column (9) of Table C of Chapter 3.2, a cargo heating installation or a possibility of heating the cargo is required on board, or if a maximum temperature is indicated in column (20) of Table C of Chapter 3.2;

(g)   A connection for a closed-type or partly closed-type sampling device, and/or at least one sampling opening as required in column (13) of Table C of Chapter 3.2. The connection shall be fitted with a shut-off device resistant to the internal pressure at the connection;

If the list of substances on the vessel according to 1.16.1.2.5 is going to include substances that require explosion protection in accordance with column (17) of Table C of Chapter 3.2, then the flame arrester plate stack capable of withstanding steady burning of the sampling opening shall be selected according to the explosion groups/subgroups of the substances foreseen for inclusion in the list of substances on the vessel (see column (16) of Table C of Chapter 3.2).

9.3.3.21.2   When the degree of filling in per cent is determined, an error of not more than 0.5% is permitted. It shall be calculated on the basis of the total cargo tank capacity including the expansion trunk.

9.3.3.21.3   The level gauge shall allow readings from the control position of the shut-off devices of the particular cargo tank. The permissible maximum filling levels of 95% and 97%, as given in the list of substances, shall be marked on each level gauge.

Permanent reading of the overpressure and vacuum shall be possible from a location from which loading or unloading operations may be interrupted. The permissible maximum overpressure and vacuum shall be marked on each level gauge.

Readings shall be possible in all weather conditions.

9.3.3.21.4   The level alarm device shall give a visual and audible warning on board when actuated. The level alarm device shall be independent of the level gauge.

9.3.3.21.5   (a)   The high level sensor referred to in 9.3.3.21.1 (d) above shall give a visual and audible alarm on board and at the same time actuate an electrical contact which in the form of a binary signal interrupts the electric current loop provided and fed by the shore facility, thus initiating measures at the shore facility against overflowing during loading operations. The signal shall be transmitted to the shore facility via a watertight two–pin plug of a connector device in accordance with standard EN 60309-2:1999 + A1:2007 + A2:2012 for direct current of 40 to 50 volts, identification colour white, position of the nose 10 h.

The plug shall be permanently fitted to the vessel close to the shore connections of the loading and unloading piping.

The high level sensor shall also be capable of switching off the vessel's own discharging pump.

The high level sensor shall be independent of the level alarm device, but it may be connected to the level gauge.

(b)   On board oil separator vessels the sensor referred to in 9.3.3.21.1 (d) shall activate a visual and audible alarm and switch off the pump used to evacuate bilge water.

(c)   Supply vessels and other vessels which may be delivering products required for operation shall be equipped with a transshipment facility compatible with European standard EN 12827:1999 and a rapid closing device enabling refuelling to be interrupted. It shall be possible to actuate this rapid closing device by means of an electrical signal from the overflow prevention system. The electrical circuits actuating the rapid closing device shall be secured according to the quiescent current principle or other appropriate error detection measures. The state of operation of electrical circuits which cannot be controlled using the quiescent current principle shall be capable of being easily checked.

It shall be possible to actuate the rapid closing device independently of the electrical signal.

The rapid closing device shall actuate a visual and an audible alarm on board.

(d)   During discharging by means of the on-board pump, it shall be possible for the shore facility to switch it off. For this purpose, an independent intrinsically safe power line, fed by the vessel, shall be switched off by the shore facility by means of an electrical contact.

It shall be possible for the binary signal of the shore facility to be transmitted via a watertight two–pole socket or a connector device in accordance with standard EN 60309-2:1999 + A1:2007 + A2:2012, for direct current of 40 to 50 volts, identification colour white, position of the nose 10 h.

This socket shall be permanently fitted to the vessel close to the shore connections of the unloading piping.

9.3.3.21.6   The visual and audible signals given by the level alarm device shall be clearly distinguishable from those of the high level sensor.

The visual alarm shall be visible at each control position on deck of the cargo tank stop valves. It shall be possible to easily check the functioning of the sensors and electric circuits or these shall be intrinsically safe apparatus.

9.3.3.21.7   When the pressure or temperature exceeds a set value, instruments for measuring the vacuum or overpressure of the gaseous phase in the cargo tank or the temperature of the cargo shall activate a visual and audible alarm in the wheelhouse and on deck. The alarm must be relayed to the accommodation automatically if it has not been switched off.

When the pressure exceeds the set value during loading and unloading, the instrument for measuring the pressure shall, by means of the plug referred to in 9.3.3.21.5 above, immediately initiate an electrical contact which shall put into effect measures to interrupt the loading or unloading operation. When the vessel's own discharge pump is used, it shall be switched off automatically.

The instrument for measuring the overpressure or vacuum shall activate the alarm at latest when:

(a)   An overpressure equal to 1.15 times the opening pressure of the pressure relief valves/high velocity vent valves is reached; or

(b)   The lower threshold of the design pressure of the vacuum valves, but not exceeding a vacuum of 5 kPa (0.05 bar), is reached.

The maximum permissible temperature is indicated in column (20) of Table C of Chapter 3.2. The sensors for the alarms mentioned in this paragraph may be connected to the alarm device of the sensor.

When it is prescribed in column (20) of Table C of Chapter 3.2, the instrument for measuring the overpressure of the gaseous phase in the cargo tank shall actuate a visible and audible alarm in the wheelhouse when the overpressure exceeds 40 kPa (0.4 bar) during the voyage. The alarm must be relayed to the accommodation automatically if it has not been switched off. It shall be possible to read the gauges in direct proximity to the control for the water spray system.

9.3.3.21.8   Where the control elements of the shut-off devices of the cargo tanks are located in a control room, it shall be possible to stop the loading pumps and read the level gauges in the control room, and the visual and audible warning given by the level alarm device, the high level sensor referred to in 9.3.3.21.1 (d) and the instruments for measuring the pressure and temperature of the cargo shall be noticeable in the control room and on deck.

Satisfactory monitoring of the cargo area shall be ensured from the control room.

9.3.3.21.9   9.3.3.21.1 (e), 9.3.3.21.7 as regards measuring the pressure, do not apply to open type N with flame-arrester and to open type N.

9.3.3.21.1 (b), (c) and (g), 9.3.3.21.3 and 9.3.3.21.4 do not apply to oil separator and supply vessels.

A flame arrester plate stack in sampling openings is not required on board open type N tank vessels.

9.3.3.21.1 (f) and 9.3.3.21.7 do not apply to supply vessels.

9.3.3.21.5 (a) does not apply to oil separator vessels.

9.3.3.21.10   When refrigerated substances are carried the opening pressure of the safety system shall be determined by the design of the cargo tanks. In the event of the transport of substances that must be carried in a refrigerated state the opening pressure of the safety system shall be not less than 25 kPa (0.25 bar) greater than the maximum pressure calculated according to 9.3.3.27.

9.3.3.22   *Cargo tank openings*

9.3.3.22.1   (a)   Cargo tank openings shall be located on deck in the cargo area.

(b)   Cargo tank openings with a cross-section of more than 0.10 m² and openings of safety devices for preventing overpressures shall be located not less than 0.50 m above deck.

9.3.3.22.2   Cargo tank openings shall be fitted with gastight closures capable of withstanding the test pressure in accordance with 9.3.3.23.2.

9.3.3.22.3   Closures which are normally used during loading or unloading operations shall not cause sparking when operated.

9.3.3.22.4   Each cargo tank or group of cargo tanks connected to a common venting piping shall be fitted with:

Open Type N:

–   Devices to prevent unacceptable overpressures or vacuums and constructed so as to prevent any accumulation of water and penetration of water into the cargo tank.

Open Type N with flame arresters:

– Devices to prevent unacceptable overpressures or vacuums, equipped with flame arresters capable of withstanding steady burning and constructed so as to prevent any accumulation of water and penetration of water into the cargo tank.

Closed Type N:

(a) A connection for the safe return ashore of gases expelled during loading;

(b) A safe depressurization device for the cargo tanks, on which the position of the shut-off valve indicates clearly whether it is open or shut;

(c) Safety valves for preventing unacceptable overpressures or vacuums;

The opening pressure of the safety valves shall be marked indelibly on the valves;

(d) If the list of substances on the vessel according to 1.16.1.2.5 is going to include substances that require explosion protection in accordance with column (17) of Table C of Chapter 3.2, then:

– At the connection to each cargo tank, the venting piping shall be equipped with a flame arrester capable of withstanding a detonation;

– The vacuum valve and the safe depressurization device for cargo tanks shall be deflagration safe. The deflagration safety may also be ensured by a flame arrester; and

– The pressure relief device shall be designed as a high velocity vent valve, with the gases discharged upwards;

The setting of the pressure relief valves shall be such that during the transport operation they do not blow off until the maximum permissible working pressure of the cargo tanks is reached;

The autonomous protection systems shall be chosen according to the explosion groups/subgroups of the substances listed in the list of substances on the vessel (see column (16) of Table C of Chapter 3.2);

If the high velocity vent valve, the vacuum valve, the flame arresters and the venting piping are required to be heatable for carriage, the safety devices concerned shall be suitable for the relevant temperature;

The opening pressure of the pressure relief valves, the vacuum valve and the high velocity vent valves shall be marked indelibly on the valves;

If a shut-off device is to be mounted between the venting piping and the cargo tank, it shall be placed between the cargo tank and the flame arrester, and each cargo tank shall be equipped with its own safety valves;

(e) The outlets of the pressure relief devices/high velocity vent valves shall be located not less than 2.00 m above the deck and at a distance of not less than 6.00 m from the openings of the accommodations, the wheelhouse and the service spaces outside the cargo area. This height may be reduced to 1.00 m when there is no equipment and no work is being carried out within a radius of 1.00 m around the pressure relief valve outlet. This area shall be marked as a danger zone.

9.3.3.22.5   *Venting piping*

(a)   When two or more cargo tanks are connected to common venting piping, it is sufficient that the equipment according to 9.3.3.22.4 (safety valves to prevent unacceptable overpressures and vacuums, high velocity vent valve, vacuum valve protected against deflagrations, safe pressure relief device for cargo tanks protected against deflagrations) is installed on the joint venting piping (see also 7.2.4.16.7);

(b)   When each cargo tank is connected to its own venting piping, each cargo tank or the associated venting piping shall be equipped according to 9.3.3.22.4.

9.3.3.22.6   9.3.3.22.2 and 9.3.3.22.5 do not apply to open type N with flame-arrester and to open type N.

9.3.3.22.3 does not apply to open type N.

9.3.3.23   *Pressure tests*

9.3.3.23.1   The cargo tanks, residual cargo tanks, cofferdams, piping for loading and unloading, with the exception of discharge hoses shall be subjected to initial tests before being put into service and thereafter at prescribed intervals.

Where a heating system is provided inside the cargo tanks, the heating coils shall be subjected to initial tests before being put into service and thereafter at prescribed intervals.

9.3.3.23.2   The test pressure for the cargo tanks and residual cargo tanks shall be not less than 1.3 times the design pressure. The test pressure for the cofferdams and open cargo tanks shall be not less than 10 kPa (0.10 bar) gauge pressure.

9.3.3.23.3   The test pressure for piping for loading and unloading shall be not less than 1,000 kPa (10 bar) gauge pressure.

9.3.3.23.4   The maximum intervals for the periodic tests shall be 11 years.

9.3.3.23.5   The procedure for pressure tests shall comply with the provisions established by the competent authority or a recognised classification society.

9.3.3.24   *Regulation of cargo pressure and temperature*

9.3.3.24.1   Unless the entire cargo system is designed to resist the full effective vapour pressure of the cargo at the upper limits of the ambient design temperatures, the pressure of the tanks shall be kept below the permissible maximum set pressure of the safety valves, by one or more of the following means:

(a)   a system for the regulation of cargo tank pressure using mechanical refrigeration;

(b)   a system ensuring safety in the event of the heating or increase in pressure of the cargo. The insulation or the design pressure of the cargo tank, or the combination of these two elements, shall be such as to leave an adequate margin for the operating period and the temperatures expected; in each case the system shall be deemed acceptable by a recognised classification society and shall ensure safety for a minimum time of three times the operation period;

(c)   other systems deemed acceptable by a recognised classification society.

9.3.3.24.2   The systems prescribed in 9.3.3.24.1 shall be constructed, installed and tested to the satisfaction of the recognised classification society. The materials used in their construction shall be compatible with the cargoes to be carried. For normal service, the upper ambient design temperature limits shall be:

    air: +30 °C;
    water: +20 °C.

9.3.3.24.3   The cargo storage system shall be capable of resisting the full vapour pressure of the cargo at the upper limits of the ambient design temperatures, whatever the system adopted to deal with the boil-off gas. This requirement is indicated by remark 37 in column (20) of Table C of Chapter 3.2.

9.3.3.25   *Pumps and piping*

9.3.3.25.1   (a)   Pumps and accessory loading and unloading piping shall be located in the cargo area;

    (b)   Cargo pumps shall be capable of being shut down from the cargo area and from a position outside the cargo area;

    (c)   Cargo pumps situated on deck shall be located not less than 6.00 m from entrances to, or openings of, the accommodation and service spaces outside the cargo area.

9.3.3.25.2   (a)   Piping for loading and unloading shall be independent of any other piping of the vessel. No cargo piping shall be located below deck, except those inside the cargo tanks and inside the cargo pump-room;

    (b)   The piping for loading and unloading shall be arranged so that, after loading or unloading operations, the liquid remaining in these pipes may be safely removed and may flow either into the vessel's cargo tanks or the tanks ashore;

    (c)   Piping for loading and unloading shall be clearly distinguishable from other piping, e.g. by means of colour marking;

    (d)   (*Reserved*)

    (e)   The shore connections shall be located not less than 6.00 m from the entrances to, or openings of, the accommodation and service spaces outside the cargo area;

    (f)   Each shore connection of the venting piping and shore connections of the piping for loading and unloading, through which the loading or unloading operation is carried out, shall be fitted with a shut-off device. However, each shore connection shall be fitted with a blind flange when it is not in operation;

    (g)   (*Deleted*)

    (h)   Piping for loading and unloading, and venting piping, shall not have flexible connections fitted with sliding seals.

9.3.3.25.3   (*Deleted*)

9.3.3.25.4   (a)   Every component of the piping for loading and unloading shall be electrically connected to the hull;

    (b)   The piping for loading shall extend down to the bottom of the cargo tanks.

9.3.3.25.5   The stop valves or other shut-off devices of the piping for loading and unloading shall indicate whether they are open or shut.

9.3.3.25.6   The piping for loading and unloading shall have, at the test pressure, the required elasticity, leakproofness and resistance to pressure.

9.3.3.25.7   The piping for loading and unloading shall be fitted with pressure gauges at the outlet of the pumps. The permissible maximum overpressure or vacuum value shall be indicated on each measuring device. Readings shall be possible in all weather conditions.

9.3.3.25.8   (a)   When piping for loading and unloading are used for supplying the cargo tanks with washing or ballast water, the suctions of these pipes shall be located within the cargo area but outside the cargo tanks;

Pumps for tank washing systems with associated connections may be located outside the cargo area, provided the discharge side of the system is arranged in such a way that suction is not possible through that part;

A spring-loaded non-return valve shall be provided to prevent any gases from being expelled from the cargo area through the tank washing system.

(b)   A non-return valve shall be fitted at the junction between the water suction pipe and the cargo loading pipe.

9.3.3.25.9   The permissible loading and unloading flows shall be calculated.

Calculations concerning the permissible maximum loading and unloading flows for each cargo tank or each group of cargo tanks, taking into account the design of the ventilation system. These calculations shall take into consideration the fact that in the event of an unforeseen cut-off of the vapour return piping of the shore facility, the safety devices of the cargo tanks will prevent pressure in the cargo tanks from exceeding the following values:

over–pressure: 1.15 times the opening pressure of the pressure relief valve/high velocity vent valve;

vacuum pressure: not more than the design pressure, but not exceeding a vacuum of 5 kPa (0.05 bar).

The main factors to be considered are the following:

1.   Dimensions of the ventilation system of the cargo tanks;

2.   Gas formation during loading: multiply the largest loading flow by a factor of not less than 1.25;

3.   Density of the vapour mixture of the cargo based on 50% volume vapour of 50% volume air;

4.   Loss of pressure through ventilation pipes, valves and fittings. Account will be taken of a 30% clogging of the mesh of the flame-arresters;

5.   Chocking pressure of the safety valves.

Instructions concerning the permissible maximum loading and unloading flows for each cargo tank or for each group of cargo tanks shall be carried on board.

9.3.3.25.10   Compressed air generated outside the cargo area can be used in the cargo area subject to the installation of a spring-loaded non-return valve to ensure that no gases can escape from the cargo area through the compressed air system into accommodation, wheelhouse or service spaces outside the cargo area.

9.3.3.25.11   If the vessel is carrying several dangerous substances liable to react dangerously with each other, a separate pump with its own piping for loading and unloading shall be installed for each substance. The piping shall not pass through a cargo tank containing dangerous substances with which the substance in question is liable to react.

9.3.3.25.12   9.3.3.25.1 (a) and (c), 9.3.3.25.2 (a), last sentence and (e) and 9.3.3.25.4 (a) do not apply to type N open unless the substance carried has corrosive properties (see column (5) of Table C of Chapter 3.2, hazard 8).

9.3.3.25.4 (b) does not apply to open type N.

9.3.3.25.2 (f), last sentence, 9.3.3.25.2 (g), 9.3.3.25.8 (a), last sentence and 9.3.3.25.10 do not apply to oil separator and supply vessels.

9.3.3.25.9 does not apply to oil separator vessels.

9.3.3.25.2 (h) does not apply to supply vessels.

9.3.3.26   *Residual cargo tanks and receptacles for residual products*

9.3.3.26.1   When vessels are provided with tanks for residual products or receptacles for residual products, they shall be located in the cargo area and comply with the provisions of 9.3.3.26.2 and 9.3.3.26.3. Receptacles for residual products shall be located only in the cargo area on deck and not less than a quarter of the vessel's breadth from the outer shell.

9.3.3.26.2   Tanks for residual products shall be equipped with:

In the case of an open system:

–   An ullage opening;

–   Connections, with stop valves, for pipes and hose assemblies;

–   A device for ensuring pressure equilibrium.

In the case of an open system with flame arrester:

–   An ullage opening;

–   Connections, with stop valves, for pipes and hose assemblies;

–   A device for ensuring pressure equilibrium, fitted with a flame arrester capable of withstanding steady burning.

In the case of a closed system:

(a)   A level indicator;

–   Connections, with stop valves, for pipes and hose assemblies;

–   A vacuum valve and a pressure relief valve;

The pressure relief valve shall be sized so that, during the transport operation, it does not open when in normal operation. This condition is met when the opening pressure of the valve meets the conditions required in column (10) of Table C of Chapter 3.2 for the substance to be carried;

(b)   If the list of substances on the vessel according to 1.16.1.2.5 is going to include substances that require explosion protection in accordance with column (17) of Table C of Chapter 3.2, then the pressure relief valve shall be a high velocity vent valve and the vacuum valve shall be deflagration safe. The deflagration safety may also be ensured by a flame arrester;

The high velocity vent valve and the deflagration safe vacuum valve shall be chosen according to the explosion groups/subgroups of the substances listed in the list of substances on the vessel (see column (16) of Table C of Chapter 3.2).

The maximum permissible capacity is 30 m^3.

9.3.3.26.3   The receptacles for residual products shall be equipped with:

–   A possibility of indicating the degree of filling;

–   Connections, with stop valves, for pipes and hose assemblies;

A connection enabling gases released during filling to be evacuated safely.

9.3.2.26.4   *(Deleted)*

9.3.3.26.5   9.3.3.26.1, 9.3.3.26.2 (final sentence) and 9.3.3.26.3 do not apply to oil separator vessels.

9.3.3.27   *Refrigeration system*

9.3.3.27.1   The refrigeration system referred to in 9.3.3.24.1 (a) shall be composed of one or more units capable of keeping the pressure and temperature of the cargo at the upper limits of the ambient design temperatures at the prescribed level. Unless another means of regulating cargo pressure and temperature deemed satisfactory by a recognised classification society is provided, provision shall be made for one or more stand-by units with an output at least equal to that of the largest prescribed unit. A stand-by unit shall include a compressor, its engine, its control system and all necessary accessories to enable it to operate independently of the units normally used. Provision shall be made for a stand-by heat-exchanger unless the system's normal heat-exchanger has a surplus capacity equal to at least 25% of the largest prescribed capacity. It is not necessary to make provision for separate piping.

Cargo tanks, piping and accessories shall be insulated so that, in the event of a failure of all cargo refrigeration systems, the entire cargo remains for at least 52 hours in a condition not causing the safety valves to open.

9.3.3.27.2   The security devices and the connecting lines from the refrigeration system shall be connected to the cargo tanks above the liquid phase of the cargo when the tanks are filled to their maximum permissible degree of filling. They shall remain within the gaseous phase, even if the vessel has a list up to 12 degrees.

9.3.3.27.3   When several refrigerated cargoes with a potentially dangerous chemical reaction are carried simultaneously, particular care shall be given to the refrigeration systems so as to prevent any mixing of the cargoes. For the carriage of such cargoes, separate refrigeration systems, each including the full stand-by unit referred to in 9.3.3.27.1, shall be provided for each cargo. When, however, refrigeration is ensured by an indirect or combined system and no leak in the heat exchangers can under any foreseeable circumstances lead to the mixing of cargoes, no provision need be made for separate refrigeration units for the different cargoes.

9.3.3.27.4   When several refrigerated cargoes are not soluble in each other under conditions of carriage such that their vapour pressures are added together in the event of mixing, particular care shall be given to the refrigeration systems to prevent any mixing of the cargoes.

9.3.3.27.5   When the refrigeration systems require water for cooling, a sufficient quantity shall be supplied by a pump or pumps used exclusively for the purpose. This pump or pumps shall have at least two suction pipes, leading from two water intakes, one to port, the other to starboard. Provision shall be made for a stand-by pump with a satisfactory flow; this may be a pump used for other purposes provided that its use for supplying water for cooling does not impair any other essential service.

9.3.3.27.6   The refrigeration system may take one of the following forms:

(a)   Direct system: the cargo vapours are compressed, condensed and returned to the cargo tanks. This system shall not be used for certain cargoes specified in Table C of Chapter 3.2. This requirement is indicated by remark 35 in column (20) of Table C of Chapter 3.2;

(b)   Indirect system: the cargo or the cargo vapours are cooled or condensed by means of a coolant without being compressed;

(c)   Combined system: the cargo vapours are compressed and condensed in a cargo/coolant heat-exchanger and returned to the cargo tanks. This system shall not be used for certain cargoes specified in Table C of Chapter 3.2. This requirement is indicated by remark 36 in column (20) of Table C of Chapter 3.2.

9.3.3.27.7   All primary and secondary coolant fluids shall be compatible with each other and with the cargo with which they may come into contact. Heat exchange may take place either at a distance from the cargo tank, or by using cooling coils attached to the inside or the outside of the cargo tank.

9.3.3.27.8   When the refrigeration system is installed in a separate service space, this service space shall meet the requirements of 9.3.3.17.6.

9.3.3.27.9   For all cargo systems, the heat transmission coefficient as used for the determination of the holding time (7.2.4.16.16 and 7.2.4.16.17) shall be determined by calculation. Upon completion of the vessel, the correctness of the calculation shall be checked by means of a heat balance test. The calculation and test shall be performed under supervision by the recognized classification society which classified the vessel.

The heat transmission coefficient shall be documented and kept on board. The heat transmission coefficient shall be verified at every renewal of the certificate of approval.

9.3.3.27.10   A certificate from a recognised classification society stating that 9.3.3.24.1 to 9.3.3.24.3, 9.3.3.27.1 and 9.3.3.27.4 above have been complied with shall be submitted together with the application for issue or renewal of the certificate of approval.

9.3.3.28   *Water-spray system*

When water-spraying is required in column (9) of Table C of Chapter 3.2, a water-spray system shall be installed in the cargo area on deck for the purpose of cooling the tops of cargo tanks by spraying water over the whole surface so as to avoid safely the activation of the pressure relief valves/high velocity vent valves at 10 kPa or as regulated.

The spray nozzles shall be so installed that the entire cargo deck area is covered and the gases released are precipitated safely.

The system shall be capable of being put into operation from the wheelhouse and from the deck. Its capacity shall be such that when all the spray nozzles are in operation, the outflow is not less than 50 litres per square metre of deck area and per hour.

9.3.3.29 and 9.3.3.30   (*Reserved*)

9.3.3.31   *Engines*

9.3.3.31.1   Only internal combustion engines running on fuel with having a flashpoint above 55 °C are allowed. This provision does not apply to internal combustion engines which are part of propulsion and auxiliary systems. These systems shall meet the requirements of Chapter 30 and Annex 8, Section 1 of the European Standard laying down Technical Requirements for Inland Navigation vessels (ES-TRIN) as amended.[2]

9.3.3.31.2   Ventilation inlets of the engine room and, when the engines do not take in air directly from the engine room, air intakes of the engines shall be located not less than 2.00 m from the cargo area.

9.3.3.31.3 and 9.3.3.31.4   *(Deleted)*

9.3.3.31.5   The ventilation in the closed engine room shall be designed so that, at an ambient temperature of 20 °C, the average temperature in the engine room does not exceed 40 °C.

9.3.3.31.6   9.3.3.31.2 above does not apply to oil separator or supply vessels.

9.3.3.32   *Oil fuel tanks*

9.3.3.32.1   Where the vessel is provided with hold spaces, the double bottoms within these spaces may be arranged as oil fuel tanks, provided their depth is not less than 0.6 m.

Oil fuel pipes and openings of such tanks are not permitted in the hold space.

9.3.3.32.2   The open ends of the air pipes of each oil fuel tanks shall extend to not less than 0.5 m above the open deck. These open ends and the open ends of overflow pipes leading to the deck shall be fitted with a protective device consisting of a gauze diaphragm or a perforated plate.

9.3.3.33   *(Reserved)*

9.3.3.34   *Exhaust pipes*

9.3.3.34.1   Exhaust shall be evacuated from the vessel into the open air either upwards through an exhaust pipe or through the shell plating. The exhaust outlet shall be located not less than 2.00 m from the cargo area. The exhaust pipes of engines shall be arranged so that the exhausts are led away from the vessel. The exhaust pipes shall not be located within the cargo area.

9.3.3.34.2   Exhaust pipes shall be provided with a device preventing the escape of sparks, e.g. spark arresters.

9.3.3.34.3   The distance prescribed in 9.3.3.34.1 above does not apply to oil separator or supply vessels.

9.3.3.35   *Bilge pumping and ballasting arrangements*

9.3.3.35.1   Bilge and ballast pumps for spaces within the cargo area shall be installed within such area.

This provision does not apply to:

–   double-hull spaces and double bottoms which do not have a common boundary wall with the cargo tanks;

---

[2]   *As available on the website of the Comité Européen pour l'Élaboration de Standards dans le Domaine de Navigation Intérieure – CESNI, https://www.cesni.eu/en/documents/es-trin/.*

– cofferdams, double-hull, double bottom and hold spaces where ballasting is carried out using the piping of the fire-fighting system in the cargo area and bilge-pumping is performed using eductors which are installed in the cargo area.

9.3.3.35.2   Where the double bottom is used as a liquid oil fuel tank, it shall not be connected to the bilge piping system.

9.3.3.35.3   Where the ballast pump is installed in the cargo area, the standpipe and its outboard connection for suction of ballast water shall be located within the cargo area but outside the cargo tanks.

9.3.3.35.4   A cargo pump-room below deck shall be capable of being drained in an emergency by an installation located in the cargo area and independent from any other installation. The installation shall be provided outside the cargo pump-room.

9.3.3.36 to 9.3.3.39   (*Reserved*)

9.3.3.40   *Fire-extinguishing arrangements*

9.3.3.40.1   A fire-extinguishing system shall be installed on the vessel. This system shall comply with the following requirements:

– It shall be supplied by two independent fire or ballast pumps, one of which shall be ready for use at any time. These pumps and their means of propulsion and electrical equipment shall not be installed in the same space;

– It shall be provided with a water main fitted with at least three hydrants in the cargo area above deck. Three suitable and sufficiently long hoses with jet/spray nozzles having a diameter of not less than 12 mm shall be provided. Alternatively one or more of the hose assemblies may be substituted by directable jet/spray nozzles having a diameter of not less than 12 mm. It shall be possible to reach any point of the deck in the cargo area simultaneously with at least two jets of water which do not emanate from the same hydrant;

A spring-loaded non-return valve shall be fitted to ensure that no gases can escape through the fire-extinguishing system into the accommodation, wheelhouse or service spaces outside the cargo area;

– The capacity of the system shall be at least sufficient for a jet of water to have a minimum reach of not less than the vessel's breadth from any location on board with two spray nozzles being used at the same time;

– The water supply system shall be capable of being put into operation from the wheelhouse and from the deck;

– Measures shall be taken to prevent the freezing of fire-mains and hydrants.

9.3.3.40.2   In addition the engine room, the pump-room and all spaces containing essential equipment (switchboards, compressors, etc.) for the refrigeration equipment, if any, shall be provided with a fixed fire-extinguishing system meeting the following requirements:

9.3.3.40.2.1   *Extinguishing agents*

For the protection of spaces in engine rooms, boiler rooms and pump rooms, only permanently fixed fire-extinguishing systems using the following extinguishing agents are permitted:

(a) CO_2 (carbon dioxide);

(b)   HFC 227 ea (heptafluoropropane);

(c)   IG-541 (52% nitrogen, 40% argon, 8% carbon dioxide);

(d)   FK-5-1-12 (dodecafluoro 2–methylpentane–3–one);

(e)   *(Reserved)*

(f) K_2CO_3 (potassium carbonate).

Other extinguishing agents are permitted only on the basis of recommendations by the Administrative Committee.

9.3.3.40.2.2   *Ventilation, air extraction*

(a)   The combustion air required by the combustion engines which ensure propulsion should not come from spaces protected by permanently fixed fire-extinguishing systems. This requirement is not mandatory if the vessel has two independent main engine rooms with a gastight separation or if, in addition to the main engine room, there is a separate engine room installed with a bow thruster that can independently ensure propulsion in the event of a fire in the main engine room;

(b)   All forced ventilation systems in the space to be protected shall be shut down automatically as soon as the fire-extinguishing system is activated;

(c)   All openings in the space to be protected which permit air to enter or gas to escape shall be fitted with devices enabling them to be closed rapidly. It shall be clear whether they are open or closed;

(d)   Air escaping from the pressure–relief valves of the pressurised air tanks installed in the engine rooms shall be evacuated to the open air;

(e)   Overpressure or negative pressure caused by the diffusion of the extinguishing agent shall not destroy the constituent elements of the space to be protected. It shall be possible to ensure the safe equalisation of pressure;

(f)   Protected spaces shall have a facility for extracting the extinguishing agent and the combustion gases. Such facilities shall be capable of being operated from positions outside the protected rooms and which must not be made inaccessible by a fire within such spaces. If there are permanently installed extractors, it shall not be possible for these to be switched on while the fire is being extinguished.

9.3.3.40.2.3   Fire alarm system

The space to be protected shall be monitored by an appropriate fire alarm system. The alarm signal shall be audible in the wheelhouse, the accommodation and the space to be protected.

9.3.3.40.2.4   *Piping system*

(a)   The extinguishing agent shall be routed to and distributed in the space to be protected by means of a permanent piping system. Piping installed in the space to be protected and their fittings shall be made of steel. This shall not apply to the connecting nozzles of tanks and compensators provided that the materials used have equivalent fire–retardant properties. Piping shall be protected against corrosion both internally and externally;

(b)   The discharge nozzles shall be so arranged as to ensure the regular diffusion of the extinguishing agent. In particular, the extinguishing agent must also be effective beneath the floor.

9.3.3.40.2.5   *Triggering device*

(a)   Automatically activated fire-extinguishing systems are not permitted;

(b)   It shall be possible to activate the fire-extinguishing system from a suitable point located outside the space to be protected;

(c)   Triggering devices shall be so installed that they can be activated in the event of a fire and so that the risk of their breakdown in the event of a fire or an explosion in the space to be protected is reduced as far as possible;

Systems which are not mechanically activated shall be supplied from two energy sources independent of each other. These energy sources shall be located outside the space to be protected. The control lines located in the space to be protected shall be so designed as to remain capable of operating in the event of a fire for a minimum of 30 minutes. The electrical installations are deemed to meet this requirement if they conform to the IEC 60331–21:1999 standard;

When the triggering devices are so placed as not to be visible, the component concealing them shall carry the "Fire-fighting system" symbol, each side being not less than 10 cm in length, with the following text in red letters on a white ground:

Fire-extinguishing system

(d)   If the fire-extinguishing system is intended to protect several spaces, it shall comprise a separate and clearly–marked triggering device for each space;

(e)   The instructions shall be posted alongside all triggering devices and shall be clearly visible and indelible. The instructions shall be in a language the master can read and understand and if this language is not English, French or German, they shall be in English, French or German. They shall include information concerning:

    (i)   the activation of the fire-extinguishing system;

    (ii)   the need to ensure that all persons have left the space to be protected;

    (iii)   the correct behaviour of the crew in the event of activation and when accessing the space to be protected following activation or diffusion, in particular in respect of the possible presence of dangerous substances;

    (iv)   the correct behaviour of the crew in the event of the failure of the fire-extinguishing system to function properly.

(f)   The instructions shall mention that prior to the activation of the fire-extinguishing system, combustion engines installed in the space and aspirating air from the space to be protected, shall be shut down.

9.3.3.40.2.6   *Alarm device*

(a)   Permanently fixed fire-extinguishing systems shall be fitted with an audible and visual alarm device;

(b)   The alarm device shall be set off automatically as soon as the fire-extinguishing system is first activated. The alarm device shall function for an appropriate period of time before the extinguishing agent is released; it shall not be possible to turn it off;

(c) Alarm signals shall be clearly visible in the spaces to be protected and their access points and be clearly audible under operating conditions corresponding to the highest possible sound level. It shall be possible to distinguish them clearly from all other sound and visual signals in the space to be protected;

(d) Sound alarms shall also be clearly audible in adjoining spaces, with the communicating doors shut, and under operating conditions corresponding to the highest possible sound level;

(e) If the alarm device is not intrinsically protected against short circuits, broken wires and drops in voltage, it shall be possible to monitor its operation;

(f) A sign with the following text in red letters on a white ground shall be clearly posted at the entrance to any space the extinguishing agent may reach:

Warning, fire-extinguishing system!
Leave this space immediately when the ... (description)
alarm is activated!

9.3.3.40.2.7 *Pressurised tanks, fittings and piping*

(a) Pressurised tanks, fittings and piping shall conform to the requirements of the competent authority or, if there are no such requirements, to those of a recognized classification society;

(b) Pressurised tanks shall be installed in accordance with the manufacturer's instructions;

(c) Pressurised tanks, fittings and piping shall not be installed in the accommodation;

(d) The temperature of cabinets and storage spaces for pressurised tanks shall not exceed 50 °C;

(e) Cabinets or storage spaces on deck shall be securely stowed and shall have vents so placed that in the event of a pressurised tank not being gastight, the escaping gas cannot penetrate into the vessel. Direct connections with other spaces are not permitted.

9.3.3.40.2.8 *Quantity of extinguishing agent*

If the quantity of extinguishing agent is intended for more than one space, the quantity of extinguishing agent available does not need to be greater than the quantity required for the largest of the spaces thus protected.

9.3.3.40.2.9 *Installation, maintenance, monitoring and documents*

(a) The mounting or modification of the system shall only be performed by a company specialised in fire-extinguishing systems. The instructions (product data sheet, safety data sheet) provided by the manufacturer of the extinguishing agent or the system shall be followed;

(b) The system shall be inspected by an expert:

(i) before being brought into service;

(ii) each time it is put back into service after activation;

(iii) after every modification or repair;

(iv) regularly, not less than every two years.

(c) During the inspection, the expert is required to check that the system conforms to the requirements of 9.3.3.40.2;

(d) The inspection shall include, as a minimum:

    (i) an external inspection of the entire system;

    (ii) an inspection to ensure that the piping is leakproof;

    (iii) an inspection to ensure that the control and activation systems are in good working order;

    (iv) an inspection of the pressure and contents of tanks;

    (v) an inspection to ensure that the means of closing the space to be protected are leakproof;

    (vi) an inspection of the fire alarm system;

    (vii) an inspection of the alarm device.

(e) The person performing the inspection shall establish, sign and date a certificate of inspection;

(f) The number of permanently fixed fire-extinguishing systems shall be mentioned in the vessel certificate.

9.3.3.40.2.10 *Fire-extinguishing system operating with CO_2*

In addition to the requirements contained in 9.3.3.40.2.1 to 9.3.3.40.2.9, fire-extinguishing systems using CO_2 as an extinguishing agent shall conform to the following provisions:

(a) Tanks of CO_2 shall be placed in a gastight space or cabinet separated from other spaces. The doors of such storage spaces and cabinets shall open outwards; they shall be capable of being locked and shall carry on the outside the symbol "Warning: danger", not less than 5 cm high and "CO_2" in the same colours and the same size;

(b) Storage cabinets or spaces for CO_2 tanks located below deck shall only be accessible from the outside. These spaces shall have an artificial ventilation system with extractor hoods and shall be completely independent of the other ventilation systems on board;

(c) The level of filling of CO_2 tanks shall not exceed 0.75 kg/l. The volume of depressurised CO_2 shall be taken to be 0.56 m^3/kg;

(d) The concentration of CO_2 in the space to be protected shall be not less than 40% of the gross volume of the space. This quantity shall be released within 120 seconds. It shall be possible to monitor whether diffusion is proceeding correctly;

(e) The opening of the tank valves and the control of the diffusing valve shall correspond to two different operations;

(f) The appropriate period of time mentioned in 9.3.3.40.2.6 (b) shall be not less than 20 seconds. A reliable installation shall ensure the timing of the diffusion of CO_2.

9.3.3.40.2.11 *Fire-extinguishing system operating with HFC-227 ea (heptafluoropropane)*

In addition to the requirements of 9.3.3.40.2.1 to 9.3.3.40.2.9, fire-extinguishing systems using HFC-227 ea as an extinguishing agent shall conform to the following provisions:

(a)   Where there are several spaces with different gross volumes, each space shall be equipped with its own fire-extinguishing system;

(b)   Every tank containing HFC-227 ea placed in the space to be protected shall be fitted with a device to prevent overpressure. This device shall ensure that the contents of the tank are safely diffused in the space to be protected if the tank is subjected to fire, when the fire-extinguishing system has not been brought into service;

(c)   Every tank shall be fitted with a device permitting control of the gas pressure;

(d)   The level of filling of tanks shall not exceed 1.15 kg/l. The specific volume of depressurised HFC-227 ea shall be taken to be 0.1374 m^3/kg;

(e)   The concentration of HFC-227 ea in the space to be protected shall be not less than 8% of the gross volume of the space. This quantity shall be released within 10 seconds;

(f)   Tanks of HFC-227 ea shall be fitted with a pressure monitoring device which triggers an audible and visual alarm in the wheelhouse in the event of an unscheduled loss of propellant gas. Where there is no wheelhouse, the alarm shall be triggered outside the space to be protected;

(g)   After discharge, the concentration in the space to be protected shall not exceed 10.5% (volume);

(h)   The fire-extinguishing system shall not comprise aluminium parts.

9.3.3.40.2.12 *Fire-extinguishing system operating with IG-541*

In addition to the requirements of 9.3.3.40.2.1 to 9.3.3.40.2.9, fire-extinguishing systems using IG-541 as an extinguishing agent shall conform to the following provisions:

(a)   Where there are several spaces with different gross volumes, every space shall be equipped with its own fire-extinguishing system;

(b)   Every tank containing IG-541 placed in the space to be protected shall be fitted with a device to prevent overpressure. This device shall ensure that the contents of the tank are safely diffused in the space to be protected if the tank is subjected to fire, when the fire-extinguishing system has not been brought into service;

(c)   Each tank shall be fitted with a device for checking the contents;

(d)   The filling pressure of the tanks shall not exceed 200 bar at a temperature of +15 °C;

(e)   The concentration of IG-541 in the space to be protected shall be not less than 44% and not more than 50% of the gross volume of the space. This quantity shall be released within 120 seconds.

9.3.3.40.2.13   *Fire-extinguishing system operating with FK-5-1-12*

In addition to the requirements of 9.3.3.40.2.1 to 9.3.3.40.2.9, fire-extinguishing systems using FK-5-1-12 as an extinguishing agent shall comply with the following provisions:

(a)   Where there are several spaces with different gross volumes, every space shall be equipped with its own fire-extinguishing system;

(b)   Every tank containing FK-5-1-12 placed in the space to be protected shall be fitted with a device to prevent overpressure. This device shall ensure that the contents of the tank are safely diffused in the space to be protected if the tank is subjected to fire, when the fire-extinguishing system has not been brought into service;

(c)   Every tank shall be fitted with a device permitting control of the gas pressure;

(d)   The level of filling of tanks shall not exceed 1.00 kg/l. The specific volume of depressurized FK-5-1-12 shall be taken to be 0.0719 m^3/kg;

(e)   The volume of FK-5-1-12 in the space to be protected shall be not less than 5.5% of the gross volume of the space. This quantity shall be released within 10 seconds;

(f)   Tanks of FK-5-1-12 shall be fitted with a pressure monitoring device which triggers an audible and visual alarm in the wheelhouse in the event of an unscheduled loss of extinguishing agent. Where there is no wheelhouse, the alarm shall be triggered outside the space to be protected;

(g)   After discharge, the concentration in the space to be protected shall not exceed 10.0%.

9.3.3.40.2.14   *(Reserved)*

9.3.3.40.2.15   *Fire-fighting systems using K_2CO_3 as the extinguishing agent*

In addition to the requirements laid down in 9.3.3.40.2.1 to 9.3.3.40.2.3, 9.3.3.40.2.5, 9.3.3.40.2.6 and 9.3.3.40.2.9, fire-fighting systems using K_2CO_3 as the extinguishing agent shall comply with the following provisions:

(a)   The fire-fighting system shall have a type-approval pursuant to Directive 2014/90/EU[3] or to MSC/Circ. 1270;[4]

(b)   Each room shall be provided with its own firefighting system;

(c)   The extinguishing agent must be stored in specially provided unpressurised tanks in the room to be protected. These tanks shall be fitted in such a way that the extinguishing agent is dispensed evenly in the room. In particular the extinguishing agent shall also work underneath the deck plates;

(d)   Each tank is separately connected with the triggering device;

---

[3]   *Official Journal of the European Union, L 257 of 28 August 2014, p.146.*
[4]   *International Maritime Organization Circular MSC/Circ. 1270 and corrigenda — Revised Guidelines for the approval of fixed aerosol fire-extinguishing systems equivalent to fixed gas extinguishing systems, as referred to in SOLAS 1974, for machinery spaces — adopted on 4 June 2008.*

(e) The quantity of dry aerosol-forming extinguishing agent relative to the room to be protected shall be at least 120 g per m^3 of the net volume of this room. This net volume is calculated according to Directive 2014/90/EU[3] or to MSC/Circ. 1270.[4] It shall be possible to supply the extinguishing agent within 120 s.

9.3.3.40.2.16 *Fixed fire-extinguishing system for physical protection*

In order to ensure physical protection in the engine rooms, boiler rooms and pump rooms, permanently fixed fire-extinguishing systems are accepted solely on the basis of recommendations by the Administrative Committee.

9.3.3.40.3 The two hand fire–extinguishers referred to in 8.1.4 shall be located in the cargo area.

9.3.3.40.4 The fire-extinguishing agent and the quantity contained in the permanently fixed fire-extinguishing system shall be suitable and sufficient for fighting fires.

9.3.3.40.5 9.3.3.40.1 and 9.3.3.40.2 above do not apply to oil separator or supply vessels.

9.3.3.41 *Fire and naked light*

9.3.3.41.1 The outlets of funnels shall be located not less than 2.00 m from the cargo area. Arrangements shall be provided to prevent the escape of sparks and the entry of water.

9.3.3.41.2 Heating, cooking and refrigerating appliances shall not be fuelled with liquid fuels, liquid gas or solid fuels.

The installation in the engine room or in another separate space of heating appliances fuelled with liquid fuel having a flashpoint above 55 °C is, however, permitted.

Cooking and refrigerating appliances are permitted only in the accommodation.

9.3.3.41.3 Only electrical lamps are permitted.

9.3.3.42 *Cargo heating system*

9.3.3.42.1 Boilers which are used for heating the cargo shall be fuelled with a liquid fuel having a flashpoint of more than 55 °C. They shall be placed either in the engine room or in another separate space below deck and outside the cargo area, which is accessible from the deck or from the engine room.

9.3.3.42.2 The cargo heating system shall be designed so that the cargo cannot penetrate into the boiler in the case of a leak in the heating coils. A cargo heating system with artificial draught shall be ignited electrically.

9.3.3.42.3 The ventilation system of the engine room shall be designed taking into account the air required for the boiler.

---

[3] *Official Journal of the European Union, L 257 of 28 August 2014, p.146.*
[4] *International Maritime Organization Circular MSC/Circ. 1270 and corrigenda — Revised Guidelines for the approval of fixed aerosol fire-extinguishing systems equivalent to fixed gas extinguishing systems, as referred to in SOLAS 1974, for machinery spaces — adopted on 4 June 2008.*

9.3.3.42.4 Where the cargo heating system is used during loading, unloading or degassing with a concentration given off by the cargo of 10% of the LEL or above, the service space which contains this system shall fully comply with the requirements of 9.3.3.52.1. This requirement does not apply to the inlets of the ventilation system. These inlets shall be located at a minimum distance of 2 m from the cargo area and 6 m from the openings of cargo tanks or residual cargo tanks, loading pumps situated on deck, openings of high-velocity vent valves, pressure relief devices and shore connections of loading and unloading piping and must be located not less than 2 m above the deck.

The requirements of 9.3.3.52.1 are not applicable to the unloading of substances having a flashpoint of 60 °C or more when the temperature of the product is at least 15 K lower at the flashpoint.

9.3.3.43 to 9.3.3.49   (Reserved)

9.3.3.50   (Deleted)

9.3.3.51   Surface temperatures of installations and equipment

(a) Surface temperatures of electrical and non-electrical installations and equipment shall not exceed 200 °C;

(b) Surface temperatures of the outer parts of engines and their air inlets and exhaust ducts shall not exceed 200 °C;

(c) If the list of substances on the vessel according to 1.16.1.2.5 is going to include substances for which the temperature classes T4, T5 or T6 are indicated in column (15) of Table C of Chapter 3.2, then the corresponding surface temperatures within the assigned zones shall not exceed 135 °C (T4), 100 °C (T5) or 85 °C (T6), respectively;

(d) (a) and (b) do not apply if the following requirements are met (see also 7.2.3.51.4):

   (i) Accommodation, wheelhouse and service spaces where surface temperatures higher than those mentioned in (a) and (b) occur are equipped with a ventilation system according to 9.3.3.12.4 (b); or

   (ii) Installations and equipment which generate surface temperatures higher than those set out in (a) or (b), respectively, must be capable of being shut down. Such installations and equipment shall be marked in red;

(e) Open Type N vessels are only required to meet the requirements of (a), (b) and (d) if the vessel remains in the immediate vicinity of or within a shoreside assigned zone.

9.3.3.52   Type and location of electrical installations and equipment

9.3.3.52.1 Electrical installations and equipment shall be of at least the 'limited explosion risk' type.

This provision does not apply to:

(a) Lighting installations in the accommodation and the wheelhouse, except for switches near to the entrances;

(b) Mobile phones, fixed telephone installations, stationary and portable computers and loading instruments in the accommodation or the wheelhouse;

(c) Electrical installations and equipment which, during a stay in the immediate vicinity of or within a shoreside assigned zone:

(i) Are extinguished; or

(ii) Are placed in premises equipped with a ventilation system according to 9.3.3.12.4;

(d) To radiotelephone installations and inland AIS (automatic identification systems) stations in the accommodation and the wheelhouse, if no part of an aerial for radiotelephone installations or AIS stations is situated above or within 2.00 m of the cargo area.

9.3.3.52.2 In the cofferdams, double-hull spaces, double bottoms and hold spaces, only hermetically sealed echo sounding devices are allowed, the cables of which are led through thick-walled steel tubes with gastight connections up to the main deck.

9.3.3.52.3 The fixed electrical installations and equipment which do not meet the requirements set out in 9.3.3.51 (a), 9.3.3.51 (b) and 9.3.3.52.1 above and their switches shall be marked in red. The disconnection of such equipment shall be controlled from a centralized location on board.

9.3.3.52.4 Every insulated distribution network shall be fitted with an automatic device with a visual and audible alarm for checking the insulation level.

9.3.3.52.5 Only distribution systems without return connection to the hull are permitted. This provision does not apply to:

– Active cathodic corrosion protection;

– Certain limited sections of the installations situated outside the cargo area (e.g., connections of starters of diesel engines);

– The device for checking the insulation level referred to in 9.3.3.52.4.

9.3.3.52.6 An electric generator which is permanently driven by an engine and which does not meet the requirements of 9.3.3.52.1 above, shall be fitted with a multipolar switch capable of shutting down the generator. A notice board with the operating instructions shall be displayed near the switch.

9.3.3.52.7 Failure of the power supply for the safety and control equipment shall be immediately indicated by visual and audible signals in the wheelhouse and on the deck. The alarm must be relayed to the accommodation automatically if it has not been switched off.

9.3.3.52.8 Electrical switches, sockets and cables on deck shall be protected against mechanical damage.

9.3.3.52.9 Sockets for the connection of signal lights and gangway lighting shall be solidly fitted to the vessel close to the signal mast or the gangway. The sockets used in this area shall be designed so as to prevent connection or disconnection except when they are not live.

9.3.3.52.10 Accumulators shall be located outside the cargo area.

9.3.3.52.11 Open Type N vessels are only required to meet the requirements of 9.3.3.52.1 and 9.3.3.52.3 if the vessel remains in the immediate vicinity of or within a shoreside assigned zone.

9.3.3.53 *Type and location of electrical and non-electrical installations and equipment intended to be used in explosion hazardous areas*

9.3.3.53.1　On board vessels covered by the classification of zones as defined in 1.2.1, electrical and non-electrical installations and equipment used in explosion hazardous areas shall meet at least the requirements for use in the area concerned.

They shall be selected on the basis of the explosion groups/subgroups and temperature classes to which the substances to be carried belong (see columns (15) and (16) of Table C of Chapter 3.2).

If the list of substances on the vessel according to 1.16.1.2.5 is going to include substances for which temperature classes T4, T5 or T6 are indicated in column (15) of Table C of Chapter 3.2, then the corresponding surface temperatures within the assigned zones shall not exceed 135 °C (T4), 100 °C (T5) or 85 °C (T6).

If the list of substances on the vessel according to 1.16.1.2.5 is going to include substances for which temperature classes T1 or T2 are indicated in column (15) of Table C of Chapter 3.2, then the corresponding surface temperatures within the assigned zones shall not exceed 200 °C.

9.3.3.53.2　Except in the case of optical fibres, electrical cables shall be armoured or placed in a metallic sheath or in protective tubes.

Electrical cables for the active cathodic protection of the shell plating shall be led through thick-walled steel tubes with gastight connections up to the main deck.

9.3.3.53.3　Movable electric cables are prohibited in the explosion danger area, except for electric cables for intrinsically safe electric circuits or for connecting:

(a)　Signal lights and lighting for gangways, provided the connection point (for example, the socket) is permanently fitted to the vessel close to the signal mast or gangway;

(b)　The power network on a vessel to a land-based power network; provided

–　　The electric cables and the power supply unit conform with a valid standard (for example, EN 15869-03: 2010);

–　　The power supply unit and connectors are located outside of the explosion danger area.

Connecting and disconnecting sockets/connectors shall only be possible when they are not live.

9.3.3.53.4　Electrical cables of intrinsically safe circuits shall be separated from other cables not intended for use in such circuits and shall be marked (they shall not be installed together in the same string of cables and they shall not be fixed by the same cable clamps).

9.3.3.53.5　For movable electrical cables permitted under 9.3.3.53.3, only sheathed cables of type H07RN-F in accordance with standard IEC 60245-4:2011[5] or electrical cables of at least equivalent design having conductors with a cross-section of not less than 1.50 mm^2 shall be used.

---

[5]　　*Identical to EN 50525-2-21: 2011.*

9.3.3.54   *Earthing*

9.3.3.54.1   The metal parts of electrical installations and equipment in the cargo area which are not live, as well as the protective metal tubes or metal sheaths of cables, in normal service shall be earthed, unless they are so arranged that they are automatically earthed by bonding to the metal structure of the vessel.

9.3.3.54.2   The provisions of 9.3.3.54.1 also apply to installations with a voltage of less than 50 Volts.

9.3.3.54.3   Independent cargo tanks, metal intermediate bulk containers and tank-containers shall be earthed.

9.3.3.54.4   Receptacles for residual products shall be capable of being earthed.

9.3.3.55   (*Reserved*)

9.3.3.56   (*Deleted*)

9.3.3.57 to 9.3.3.59   (*Reserved*)

9.3.3.60   *Special equipment*

A shower and an eye and face bath shall be provided on the vessel at a location which is directly accessible from the cargo area. The water shall meet the quality of drinking water on board.

NOTE: Additional decontamination substances for the purpose of avoiding corrosion of eyes and skin are allowed.

A connection of this special equipment with the area outside the cargo zone is accepted.

A spring-loaded non-return valve shall be fitted to ensure that no gases can escape through the shower and the eye and face bath system outside the cargo area.

9.3.3.61   9.3.3.60 above does not apply to oil separator and supply vessels.

9.3.3.62   *Valve for degassing to reception facilities*

A permanently installed or portable spring-loaded low-pressure valve used during degassing operations to reception facilities, shall be fitted at the piping used to extract air. If the vessel's substance list, according to 1.16.1.2.5, contains substances for which explosion protection is required according to column (17) of Table C of Chapter 3.2, this valve shall be fitted with a flame arrester capable of withstanding a deflagration. When the vessel is not degassing to a reception facility, the valve shall be closed with a blind flange. The low-pressure valve shall be so installed that under other normal working conditions the vacuum valve is not activated.

NOTE: Degassing operations are part of normal working conditions.

9.3.3.63 to 9.3.3.70   (*Reserved*)

9.3.3.71   *Admittance on board*

The notice boards displaying the prohibition of admittance in accordance with 8.3.3 shall be clearly legible from either side of the vessel.

9.3.3.72 and 9.3.3.73   (*Reserved*)

9.3.3.74   *Prohibition of smoking, fire or naked light*

9.3.3.74.1   The notice boards displaying the prohibition of smoking in accordance with 8.3.4 shall be clearly legible from either side of the vessel.

9.3.3.74.2   Notice boards indicating the circumstances under which the prohibition is applicable shall be fitted near the entrances to the spaces where smoking or the use of fire or naked light is not always prohibited.

9.3.3.74.3   Ashtrays shall be provided close to each exit in the accommodation and the wheelhouse.

9.3.3.75 to 9.3.3.91   *(Reserved)*

9.3.3.92   On board of tank vessels referred to in 9.3.3.11.7, spaces the entrances or exits of which are likely to become partly or completely immersed in the damaged condition shall have an emergency exit which is situated not less than 0.10 m above the damage waterline. This requirement does not apply to forepeak and afterpeak.

9.3.3.93 to 9.3.3.99   *(Reserved)*

9.3.4   **Alternative constructions**

9.3.4.1   *General*

9.3.4.1.1   The maximum permissible capacity and length of a cargo tank in accordance with 9.3.1.11.1, 9.3.2.11.1 and 9.3.3.11.1 may be exceeded and the minimum distances in accordance with 9.3.1.11.2 a) and 9.3.2.11.7 may be deviated from provided that the provisions of this section are complied with. The capacity of a cargo tank shall not exceed 1000 m^3.

9.3.4.1.2   Tank vessels whose cargo tanks exceed the maximum allowable capacity or where the distance between the side wall and the cargo tank is smaller than required, shall be protected through a more crashworthy side structure. This shall be proved by comparing the risk of a conventional construction (reference construction), complying with the ADN regulations with the risk of a crashworthy construction (alternative construction).

9.3.4.1.3   When the risk of the more crashworthy construction is equal to or lower than the risk of the conventional construction, equivalent or higher safety is proven. The equivalent or higher safety shall be proven in accordance with 9.3.4.3.

9.3.4.1.4   When a vessel is built in compliance with this section, a recognised classification society shall document the application of the calculation procedure in accordance with 9.3.4.3 and shall submit its conclusions to the competent authority for approval.

The competent authority may request additional calculations and proof.

9.3.4.1.5   The competent authority shall include this construction in the certificate of approval in accordance with 8.6.1.

9.3.4.2   *Approach*

9.3.4.2.1   The probability of cargo tank rupture due to a collision and the area around the vessel affected by the cargo outflow as a result thereof are the governing parameters. The risk is described by the following formula:

$$R = P \bullet C$$

Wherein: R risk [m²],

P probability of cargo tank rupture [ ],

C consequence (measure of damage) of cargo tank rupture [m²].

9.3.4.2.2 The probability P of cargo tank rupture depends on the probability distribution of the available collision energy represented by vessels, which the victim is likely to encounter in a collision, and the capability of the struck vessel to absorb collision energy without cargo tank rupture. A decrease of this probability can be achieved by means of a more crashworthy side structure.

The consequence C of cargo spillage resulting from cargo tank rupture is expressed as an affected area around the struck vessel.

9.3.4.2.3 The procedure according to 9.3.4.3 shows how tank rupture probabilities shall be calculated as well as how the collision energy absorbing capacity of side structure and a consequence increase shall be determined.

9.3.4.3 *Calculation procedure*

9.3.4.3.1 The calculation procedure shall follow 13 basic steps. Steps 2 through 10 shall be carried out for both the alternative design and the reference design. The following table shows the calculation of the weighted probability of cargo tank rupture:

A	B	C	D	E	F	G	H	I	J	K	L	M	N	O
							F x G			I x J			L x M	
Identify collision locations and associated weighting factors, Collision scenario I														
	Loc1	Finite element analysis	Eloc1	Calculate probability with CPDF 50%	P50%	wf 50%	Pw50%							
				Calculate probability with CPDF 66%	P66%	wf 66%	Pw66%							
				Calculate probability with CPDF 100%	P100%	wf 100%	Pw100%	+						
							sum	Ploc 1	wf loc 1	Pwloc 1				
	Loci	Finite element analysis	Eloci	Calculate probability with CPDF 50%	P50%	wf 50%	Pw50%							
				Calculate probability with CPDF 66%	P66%	wf 66%	Pw66%							
				Calculate probability with CPDF 100%	P100%	wf 100%	Pw100%	+						
							sum	Ploci	wf loci	Pwloci	+			
	Locn	Finite element analysis	Elocn	Calculate probability with CPDF 50%	P50%	wf 50%	Pw50%							
				Calculate probability with CPDF 66%	P66%	wf 66%	Pw66%							
				Calculate probability with CPDF 100%	P100%	wf 100%	Pw100%	+						
							sum	Plocn	wf locn	Pwlocn	+			
										sum	Pscenl	wfscenl	Pwscenl	
Identify collision locations and associated weighting factors, Collision scenario II														
	Loc1	Finite element analysis	Eloc1	Calculate probability with CPDF 30%	P30%	wf 30%	Pw30%							
				Calculate probability with CPDF 100%	P100%	wf 100%	Pw100%	+						
							sum	Ploc 1	wf loc 1	Pwloc 1				
	Locn	Finite element analysis	Elocn	Calculate probability with CPDF 30%	P30%	wf 30%	Pw30%							
				Calculate probability with CPDF 100%	P100%	wf 100%	Pw100%	+						
							sum	Plocn	wf locn	Pwlocn	+			
										sum	Pscenll	wfscenll	Pwscenll	+
													sum	Pw

CPDF: Cumulative probability density function

9.3.4.3.1.1   *Step 1*

Besides the alternative design, which is used for cargo tanks exceeding the maximum allowable capacity or a reduced distance between the side wall and the cargo tank as well as a more crashworthy side structure, a reference design with at least the same dimensions (length, width, depth, displacement) shall be drawn up. This reference design shall fulfil the requirements specified in section 9.3.1 (Type G), 9.3.2 (Type C) or 9.3.3 (Type N) and shall comply with the minimum requirements of a recognised classification society.

9.3.4.3.1.2   *Step 2*

9.3.4.3.1.2.1   The relevant typical collision locations i=1 through n shall be determined. The table in 9.3.4.3.1 depicts the general case where there are 'n' typical collision locations.

The number of typical collision locations depends on the vessel design. The choice of the collision locations shall be accepted by the recognised classification society.

9.3.4.3.1.2.2   Vertical collision locations

9.3.4.3.1.2.2.1   Tank vessel type C and N

9.3.4.3.1.2.2.1.1 The determination of the collision locations in the vertical direction depends on the draught differences between striking and struck vessel, which is limited by the maximum and minimum draughts of both vessels and the construction of the struck vessel. This can be depicted graphically through a rectangular area which is enclosed by the values of the maximum and minimum draught of both striking and struck vessel (see following figure).

Definition of vertical striking locations

9.3.4.3.1.2.2.1.2 Each point in this area represents a possible draught combination. T_{1max} is the maximum draught and T_{1min} is the minimum draught of the striking vessel, while T_{2max} and T_{2min} are the corresponding minimum and maximum draughts of the struck vessel. Each draught combination has an equal probability of occurrence.

9.3.4.3.1.2.2.1.3 Points on each inclined line in the figure in 9.3.4.3.1.2.2.1.1 indicate the same draught difference. Each of these lines reflects a vertical collision location. In the example in the figure in 9.3.4.3.1.2.2.1.1 three vertical collision locations are defined, depicted by three areas. Point P_1 is the point where the lower edge of the vertical part of the push barge or V–bow strikes at deck level of the struck vessel. The triangular area for collision case 1 is bordered by point P_1. This corresponds to the vertical collision location "collision at deck level". The triangular upper left area of the rectangle corresponds to the vertical collision location "collision below deck". The draught difference ΔT_i, i=1,2,3 shall be used in the collision calculations (see following figure).

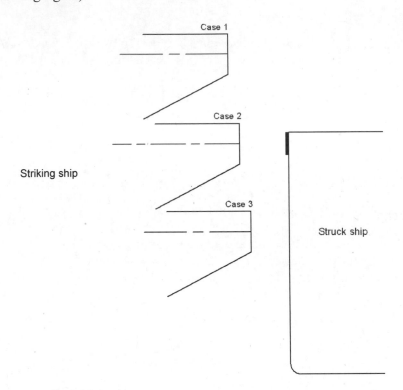

Example of vertical collision locations

9.3.4.3.1.2.2.1.4 For the calculation of the collision energies the maximum masses of both striking vessel and struck vessel must be used (highest point on each respective diagonal ΔT_i).

9.3.4.3.1.2.2.1.5 Depending on the vessel design, the recognised classification society may require additional collision locations.

9.3.4.3.1.2.2.2 *Tank vessel type G*

For a tank vessel type G a collision at half tank height shall be assumed. The recognised classification society may require additional collision locations at other heights. This shall be agreed with the recognised classification society.

9.3.4.3.1.2.3 Longitudinal collision location

9.3.4.3.1.2.3.1 Tank vessels type C and N

At least the following three typical collision locations shall be considered:

- at bulkhead,

- between webs and

- at web.

9.3.4.3.1.2.3.2   Tank vessel type G

For a tank vessel type G at least the following three typical collision locations shall be considered:

- at cargo tank end,

- between webs and

- at web.

9.3.4.3.1.2.4   Number of collision locations

9.3.4.3.1.2.4.1   Tank vessel type C and N

The combination of vertical and longitudinal collision locations in the example mentioned in 9.3.4.3.1.2.2.1.3 and 9.3.4.3.1.2.3.1 results in 3 • 3 = 9 collision locations.

9.3.4.3.1.2.4.2   Tank vessel type G

The combination of vertical and longitudinal collision locations in the example mentioned in 9.3.4.3.1.2.2.2 and 9.3.4.3.1.2.3.2 results in 1 • 3 = 3 collision locations.

9.3.4.3.1.2.4.3   Additional examinations for tank vessels type G, C and N with independent cargo tanks

As proof that the tank seatings and the buoyancy restraints do not cause any premature tank rupture, additional calculations shall be carried out. The additional collision locations for this purpose shall be agreed with the recognised classification society.

9.3.4.3.1.3   Step 3

9.3.4.3.1.3.1   For each typical collision location a weighting factor which indicates the relative probability that such a typical collision location will be struck shall be determined. In the table in 9.3.4.3.1 these factors are named $wf_{loc(i)}$ (column J). The assumptions shall be agreed with the recognised classification society.

The weighting factor for each collision location is the product of the factor for the vertical collision location by the factor for the longitudinal collision location.

9.3.4.3.1.3.2   Vertical collision locations

9.3.4.3.1.3.2.1   Tank vessel type C and N

The weighting factors for the various vertical collision locations are in each case defined by the ratio between the partial area for the corresponding collision case and the total area of the rectangle shown in the Figure in 9.3.4.3.1.2.2.1.1.

For example, for collision case 1 (see figure in 9.3.4.3.1.2.2.1.3) the weighting factor equals the ratio between the triangular lower right area of the rectangle, and the area of the rectangle between minimum and maximum draughts of striking and struck vessels.

9.3.4.3.1.3.2.2   Tank vessel type G

The weighting factor for the vertical collision location has the value 1.0, if only one collision location is assumed. When the recognised classification society requires additional collision locations, the weighting factor shall be determined analogous to the procedure for tank vessels type C and N.

9.3.4.3.1.3.3   Longitudinal collision locations

9.3.4.3.1.3.3.1   Tank vessel type C and N

The weighting factor for each longitudinal collision location is the ratio between the "calculational span length" and the tank length.

The calculational span length shall be calculated as follows:

(a)   collision on bulkhead:

0.2 • distance between web frame and bulkhead, but not larger than 450 mm,

(b)   collision on web frame:

sum of 0.2 • web frame spacing forward of the web frame, but not larger than 450 mm, and 0.2 • web frame spacing aft of the web frame, but not larger than 450 mm, and

(c)   collision between web frames:

cargo tank length minus the length "collision at bulkhead" and minus the length "collision at web frame".

9.3.4.3.1.3.3.2   Tank vessel type G

The weighting factor for each longitudinal collision location is the ratio between the "calculational span length" and the length of the hold space.

The calculational span length shall be calculated as follows:

(a)   collision at cargo tank end:

distance between bulkhead and the start of the cylindrical part of the cargo tank,

(b)   collision on web frame:

sum of 0.2 • web frame spacing forward of the web frame, but not larger than 450 mm, and 0.2 • web frame spacing aft of the web frame, but not larger than 450 mm, and

(c)   collision between web frames:

cargo tank length minus the length "collision at cargo tank end" and minus the length "collision at web frame".

9.3.4.3.1.4   *Step 4*

9.3.4.3.1.4.1   For each collision location the collision energy absorbing capacity shall be calculated. For that matter the collision energy absorbing capacity is the amount of collision energy absorbed by the vessel structure up to initial rupture of the cargo tank (see the table in 9.3.4.3.1, column D: $E_{loc(i)}$). For this purpose a finite element analysis in accordance with 9.3.4.4.2 shall be used.

These calculations shall be done for two collision scenarios according to the following table. Collision scenario I shall be analysed under the assumption of a push barge bow shape. Collision scenario II shall be analysed under the assumption of a V–shaped bow.

These bow shapes are defined in 9.3.4.4.8.

Table : Speed reduction factors for scenario I or scenario II with weighting factors

Worst case scenarios					Causes		
					Communication error and poor visibility	Technical error	Human error
					0,50	0,20	0,30
	I		Push barge–bow, striking angle 55°	0,80	0.66	0.50	1.00
	II		V–shaped–bow, striking angle 90°	0,20	0.30		1.00

9.3.4.3.1.5   *Step 5*

9.3.4.3.1.5.1   For each collision energy absorption capacity $E_{loc(i)}$, the associated probability of exceedance is to be calculated, i.e. the probability of cargo tank rupture. For this purpose, the formula for the cumulative probability density functions (CPDF) below shall be used. The appropriate coefficients shall be selected from the Table in 9.3.4.3.1.5.6 for the effective mass of the struck vessel.

$$P_{x\%} = C_1(E_{loc(i)})^3 + C_2(E_{loc(i)})^2 + C_3 E_{loc(i)} + C_4$$

with: $P_{x\%}$ probability of tank rupture,

C_{1-4} coefficients from table in 9.3.4.3.1.5.6,

$E_{loc(i)}$ collision energy absorbing capacity.

9.3.4.3.1.5.2   The effective mass shall be equal to the maximum displacement of the vessel multiplied by a factor of 1.4. Both collision scenarios (9.3.4.3.1.4.2) shall be considered.

9.3.4.3.1.5.3   In the case of collision scenario I (push barge bow at 55°), three CPDF formulas shall be used:

CPDF 50% (velocity 0.5 V_{max}),

CPDF 66% (velocity 2/3 V_{max}) and

CPDF 100% (velocity V_{max}).

9.3.4.3.1.5.4   In the case of scenario II (V–shaped bow at 90°), the following two CPDF formulas shall be used:

CPDF 30% (velocity 0.3 V_{max}) and

CPDF 100% (velocity V_{max}).

9.3.4.3.1.5.5   In the table in 9.3.4.3.1, column F, these probabilities are called *P50%*, *P66%*, *P100%* and *P30%*, *P100%* respectively.

9.3.4.3.1.5.6   Table: Coefficients for the CPDF formulas

| Effective mass of struck vessel in tonnes | velocity = 1 x V_{max} | | | | |
| | coefficients | | | | |
	C_1	C_2	C_3	C_4	range
14000	4.106E–05	–2.507E–03	9.727E–03	9.983E–01	$4<E_{loc}<39$
12000	4.609E–05	–2.761E–03	1.215E–02	9.926E–01	$4<E_{loc}<36$
10000	5.327E–05	–3.125E–03	1.569E–02	9.839E–01	$4<E_{loc}<33$
8000	6.458E–05	–3.691E–03	2.108E–02	9.715E–01	$4<E_{loc}<31$
6000	7.902E–05	–4.431E–03	2.719E–02	9.590E–01	$4<E_{loc}<27$
4500	8.823E–05	–5.152E–03	3.285E–02	9.482E–01	$4<E_{loc}<24$
3000	2.144E–05	–4.607E–03	2.921E–02	9.555E–01	$2<E_{loc}<19$
1500	– 2.071E–03	2.704E–02	–1.245E–01	1.169E+00	$2<E_{loc}<12$

| Effective mass of struck vessel in tonnes | velocity = 0.66 x V_{max} | | | | |
| | coefficients | | | | |
	C_1	C_2	C_3	C_4	range
14000	4.638E–04	–1.254E–02	2.041E–02	1.000E+00	$2<E_{loc}<17$
12000	5.377E–04	–1.427E–02	2.897E–02	9.908E–01	$2<E_{loc}<17$
10000	6.262E–04	–1.631E–02	3.849E–02	9.805E–01	$2<E_{loc}<15$
8000	7.363E–04	–1.861E–02	4.646E–02	9.729E–01	$2<E_{loc}<13$
6000	9.115E–04	–2.269E–02	6.285E–02	9.573E–01	$2<E_{loc}<12$
4500	1.071E–03	–2.705E–02	7.738E–02	9.455E–01	$1<E_{loc}<11$
3000	–1.709E–05	–1.952E–02	5.123E–02	9.682E–01	$1<E_{loc}<8$
1500	–2.479E–02	1.500E–01	–3.218E–01	1.204E+00	$1<E_{loc}<5$

| Effective mass of struck vessel in tonnes | velocity = 0.5 x V_{max} | | | | |
| | coefficients | | | | |
	C_1	C_2	C_3	C_4	range
14000	2.621E–03	–3.978E–02	3.363E–02	1.000E+00	$1<E_{loc}<10$
12000	2.947E–03	–4.404E–02	4.759E–02	9.932E–01	$1<E_{loc}<9$
10000	3.317E–03	–4.873E–02	5.843E–02	9.878E–01	$2<E_{loc}<8$
8000	3.963E–03	–5.723E–02	7.945E–02	9.739E–01	$2<E_{loc}<7$
6000	5.349E–03	–7.407E–02	1.186E–01	9.517E–01	$1<E_{loc}<6$
4500	6.303E–03	–8.713E–02	1.393E–01	9.440E–01	$1<E_{loc}<6$
3000	2.628E–03	–8.504E–02	1.447E–01	9.408E–01	$1<E_{loc}<5$
1500	–1.566E–01	5.419E–01	–6.348E–01	1.209E+00	$1<E_{loc}<3$

Effective mass of struck vessel in tonnes	velocity = 0.3 x V_{max}				
	coefficients				range
	C_1	C_2	C_3	C_4	
14000	5.628E–02	–3.081E–01	1.036E–01	9.991E–01	1<E_{loc}<3
12000	5.997E–02	–3.212E–01	1.029E–01	1.002E+00	1<E_{loc}<3
10000	7.477E–02	–3.949E–01	1.875E–01	9.816E–01	1<E_{loc}<3
8000	1.021E–02	–5.143E–01	2.983E–01	9.593E–01	1<E_{loc}<2
6000	9.145E–02	–4.814E–01	2.421E–01	9.694E–01	1<E_{loc}<2
4500	1.180E–01	–6.267E–01	3.542E–01	9.521E–01	1<E_{loc}<2
3000	7.902E–02	–7.546E–01	5.079E–01	9.218E–01	1<E_{loc}<2
1500	–1.031E+00	2.214E–01	1.891E–01	9.554E–01	0.5<E_{loc}<1

The range where the formula is valid is given in column 6. In case of an E_{loc} value below the range the probability equals $P_{x\%}$ = 1.0. In case of a value above the range $P_{x\%}$ equals 0.

9.3.4.3.1.6   *Step 6*

The weighted probabilities of cargo tank rupture $P_{wx\%}$ (table in 9.3.4.3.1, column H) shall be calculated by multiplying each cargo tank rupture probability $P_{x\%}$ (table in 9.3.4.3.1, column F) by the weighting factors $wf_{x\%}$ according to the following table:

Table: Weighting factors for each characteristic collision speed

			weighting factor
Scenario I	CPDF 50%	wf50%	0.2
	CPDF 66%	wf66%	0.5
	CPDF 100%	wf100%	0.3
Scenario II	CPDF 30%	wf30%	0.7
	CPDF 100%	wf100%	0.3

9.3.4.3.1.7   *Step 7*

The total probabilities of cargo tank rupture $P_{loc(i)}$ (table in 9.3.4.3.1, column I) resulting from 9.3.4.3.1.6 (step 6) shall be calculated as the sum of all weighted cargo tank rupture probabilities $P_{wx\%}$ (table in 9.3.4.3.1, column H) for each collision location considered.

9.3.4.3.1.8   *Step 8*

For both collision scenarios the weighted total probabilities of cargo tank rupture $P_{wloc(i)}$ shall, in each case, be calculated by multiplying the total tank probabilities of cargo tank rupture $P_{loc(i)}$ for each collision location, by the weighting factors $wf_{loc(i)}$ corresponding to the respective collision location (see 9.3.4.3.1.3 (step 3) and table in 9.3.4.3.1, column J).

9.3.4.3.1.9   *Step 9*

Through the addition of the weighted total probabilities of cargo tank rupture $P_{wloc(i)}$, the scenario specific total probabilities of cargo tank rupture P_{scenI} and P_{scenII} (table in 9.3.4.3.1, column L) shall be calculated, for each collision scenario I and II separately.

9.3.4.3.1.10   *Step 10*

Finally the weighted value of the overall total probability of cargo tank rupture P_w shall be calculated by the formula below (table in 9.3.4.3.1, column O):

$$P_w = 0.8 \cdot P_{scenI} + 0.2 \cdot P_{scenII}$$

9.3.4.3.1.11   *Step 11*

The overall total probability of cargo tank rupture P_w for the alternative design is called P_n. The overall total probability of cargo tank rupture P_w for the reference design is called P_r.

9.3.4.3.1.12   *Step 12*

9.3.4.3.1.12.1   The ratio (C_n/C_r) between the consequence (measure of damage) C_n of a cargo tank rupture of the alternative design and the consequence C_r of a cargo tank rupture of the reference design shall be determined with the following formula:

$$C_n/C_r = V_n / V_r$$

With C_n/C_r the ratio between the consequence related to the alternative design, and the consequence related to the reference design,

V_n maximum capacity of the largest cargo tank in the alternative design,

V_r maximum capacity of the largest cargo tank reference design.

9.3.4.3.1.12.2   This formula was derived for characteristic cargoes as listed in the following table.

Table: Characteristic cargoes

	UN No.	Description
Benzene	1114	Flammable liquid Packing group II Hazardous to health
Acrylonitrile Stabilised ACN	1093	Flammable liquid Packing group I Toxic, stabilised
n–Hexane	1208	Flammable liquid Packing group II
Nonane	1920	Flammable liquid Packing group III
Ammonia	1005	Toxic, corrosive gas Liquefied under pressure
Propane	1978	Flammable gas Liquefied under pressure

9.3.4.3.1.12.3   For cargo tanks with capacities between 380 m³ and 1000 m³ containing flammable, toxic and acid liquids or gases it shall be assumed that the effect increase relates linearly to the increased tank capacity (proportionality factor 1.0).

9.3.4.3.1.12.4   If substances are to be carried in tank vessels, which have been analysed according to this calculation procedure, where the proportionality factor between the total cargo tank capacity and the affected area is expected to be larger than 1.0, as assumed in the previous paragraph, the affected area shall be determined through a separate calculation. In this case the comparison as described in 9.3.4.3.1.13 (step 13) shall be carried out with this different value for the size of the affected area, t.

9.3.4.3.1.13   *Step 13*

Finally the ratio $\dfrac{P_r}{P_n}$ between the overall total probability of cargo tank rupture P_r for the reference design and the overall total probability of cargo tank rupture P_n for the alternative design shall be compared with the ratio $\dfrac{C_n}{C_r}$ between the consequence related to the alternative design, and the consequence related to the reference design.

When $\dfrac{C_n}{C_r} \leq \dfrac{P_r}{P_n}$ is fulfilled, the evidence according to 9.3.4.1.3 for the alternative design is provided.

9.3.4.4   *Determination of the collision energy absorbing capacity*

9.3.4.4.1   *General*

9.3.4.4.1.1   The determination of the collision energy absorbing capacity shall be carried out by means of a finite element analysis (FEA). The analysis shall be carried out using a customary finite element code (e.g. LS–DYNA[6], PAM–CRASH[7], ABAQUS[8] etc.) capable of dealing with both geometrical and material non–linear effects. The code shall also be able to simulate rupture realistically.

9.3.4.4.1.2   The program actually used and the level of detail of the calculations shall be agreed upon with a recognised classification society.

9.3.4.4.2   Creating the finite element models (FE models)

9.3.4.4.2.1   First of all, FE models for the more crashworthy design and one for the reference design shall be generated. Each FE model shall describe all plastic deformations relevant for all collision cases considered. The section of the cargo area to be modelled shall be agreed upon with a recognised classification society.

9.3.4.4.2.2   At both ends of the section to be modelled all three translational degrees of freedom are to be restrained. Because in most collision cases the global horizontal hull girder bending of the vessel is not of significant relevance for the evaluation of plastic deformation energy it is sufficient that only half beam of the vessel needs to be considered. In these cases the transverse displacements at the centre line (CL) shall be constrained. After generating the FE model, a trial collision calculation shall be carried out to ensure that there is no occurrence of plastic deformations near the constraint boundaries. Otherwise the FE modelled area has to be extended.

9.3.4.4.2.3   Structural areas affected during collisions shall be sufficiently finely idealized, while other parts may be modelled more coarsely. The fineness of the element mesh shall be suitable for an adequate description of local folding deformations and for determination of realistic rupture of elements.

---

[6]   LSTC, 7374 Las Positas Rd, Livermore, CA 94551, USA Tel : +1 925 245–4500.

[7]   ESI Group, 8, Rue Christophe Colomb, 75008 Paris, France
Tel: +33 (0)1 53 65 14 14, Fax: +33 (0)1 53 65 14 12, E–mail: info@esi–group.com.

[8]   SIMULIA, Rising Sun Mills, 166 Valley Street, Providence, RI 02909–2499 USA
Tel: +1 401 276–4400, Fax: +1 401 276–4408, E–mail: info@simulia.com.

9.3.4.4.2.4   The calculation of rupture initiation must be based on fracture criteria which are suitable for the elements used. The maximum element size shall be less than 200 mm in the collision areas. The ratio between the longer and the shorter shell element edge shall not exceed the value of three. The element length L for a shell element is defined as the longer length of both sides of the element. The ratio between element length and element thickness shall be larger than five. Other values shall be agreed upon with the recognised classification society.

9.3.4.4.2.5   Plate structures, such as shell, inner hull (tank shell in the case of gas tanks), webs as well as stringers can be modelled as shell elements and stiffeners as beam elements. While modelling, cut outs and manholes in collision areas shall be taken into account.

9.3.4.4.2.6   In the FE calculation the 'node on segment penalty' method shall be used for the contact option. For this purpose the following options shall be activated in the codes mentioned:

-    "contact_automatic_single_surface" in LS–DYNA,

-    "self impacting" in PAMCRASH, and

-    similar contact types in other FE–programs.

9.3.4.4.3   *Material properties*

9.3.4.4.3.1   Because of the extreme behaviour of material and structure during a collision, with both geometrical and material non–linear effects, true stress–strain relations shall be used:

$$\sigma = C \cdot \varepsilon^n,$$

where

$$n = \ln(1 + A_g),$$

$$C = R_m \cdot \left(\frac{e}{n}\right)^n,$$

Ag = the maximum uniform strain related to the ultimate tensile stress Rm and

e = the natural logarithmic constant.

9.3.4.4.3.2   The values Ag and Rm shall be determined through tensile tests.

9.3.4.4.3.3   If only the ultimate tensile stress Rm is available, for shipbuilding steel with a yield stress ReH of not more than 355 N/mm² the following approximation shall be used in order to obtain the Ag value from a known Rm [N/mm²] value:

$$A_g = \frac{1}{0.24 + 0.01395 \cdot R_m}$$

9.3.4.4.3.4   If the material properties from tensile tests are not available when starting the calculations, minimum values of A_g and R_m, as defined in the rules of the recognised classification society, shall be used instead. For shipbuilding steel with a yield stress higher than 355 N/mm² or materials other than shipbuilding steel, material properties shall be agreed upon with a recognised classification society.

| 9.3.4.4.4 | *Rupture criteria* |

| 9.3.4.4.4.1 | The first rupture of an element in a FEA is defined by the failure strain value. If the calculated strain, such as plastic effective strain, principal strain or, for shell elements, the strain in the thickness direction of this element exceeds its defined failure strain value, the element shall be deleted from the FE model and the deformation energy in this element will no longer change in the following calculation steps. |

| 9.3.4.4.4.2 | The following formula shall be used for the calculation of rupture strain: |

$$\varepsilon_f(l_e) = \varepsilon_g + \varepsilon_e \cdot \frac{t}{l_e}$$

where
ε_g = uniform strain
ε_e = necking
t = plate thickness
l_e = individual element length.

| 9.3.4.4.4.3 | The values of uniform strain and the necking for shipbuilding steel with a yield stress R_{eH} of not more than 355 N/mm² shall be taken from the following table: |

stress states	1–D	2–D
ε_g	0.079	0.056
ε_e	0.76	0.54
element type	truss beam	shell plate

| 9.3.4.4.4.4 | Other ε_g and ε_e values taken from thickness measurements of exemplary damage cases and experiments may be used in agreement with the recognised classification society. |

| 9.3.4.4.4.5 | Other rupture criteria may be accepted by the recognised classification society if proof from adequate tests is provided. |

| 9.3.4.4.4.6 | *Tank vessel type G* |

For a tank vessel type G the rupture criterion for the pressure tank shall be based on equivalent plastic strain. The value to be used while applying the rupture criterion shall be agreed upon with the recognised classification society. Equivalent plastic strains associated with compressions shall be ignored.

| 9.3.4.4.5 | Calculation of the collision energy absorbing capacity |

| 9.3.4.4.5.1 | The collision energy absorbing capacity is the summation of internal energy (energy associated with deformation of structural elements) and friction energy. |

The friction coefficient μ_c is defined as:

$$\mu_c = FD + (FS - FD) \cdot e^{-DC|v_{rel}|},$$

with FD = 0.1,
FS = 0.3,
DC = 0.01
$|v_{rel}|$ = relative friction velocity.

NOTE: *Values are default for shipbuilding steel.*

9.3.4.4.5.2 The force penetration curves resulting from the FE model calculation shall be submitted to the recognised classification society.

9.3.4.4.5.3 *Tank vessel type G*

9.3.4.4.5.3.1 In order to obtain the total energy absorbing capacity of a tank vessel type G the energy absorbed through compression of the vapour during the collision shall be calculated.

9.3.4.4.5.3.2 The energy E absorbed by the vapour shall be calculated as follows:

$$E = \frac{p_1 \cdot V_1 - p_0 \cdot V_0}{1 - \gamma}$$

with:

γ 1.4

(Note: The value 1.4 is the default value c_p/c_v with, in principle:

c_p = specific heat at constant pressure [J/(kgK)]

c_v = specific heat at constant volume [J/(kgK)])

p_0 = pressure at start of compression [Pa]

p_1 = pressure at end of compression [Pa]

V_0 = volume at start of compression [m^3]

V_1 = volume at end of compression [m^3]

9.3.4.4.6 Definition of striking vessel and striking bow

9.3.4.4.6.1 At least two types of bow shapes of the striking vessel shall be used for calculating the collision energy absorbing capacities:

–   bow shape I: push barge bow (see 9.3.4.4.8),

–   bow shape II: V–shape bow without bulb (see 9.3.4.4.8).

9.3.4.4.6.2 Because in most collision cases the bow of the striking vessel shows only slight deformations compared to the side structure of the struck vessel, a striking bow will be defined as rigid. Only for special situations, where the struck vessel has an extremely strong side structure compared to the striking bow and the structural behaviour of the struck vessel is influenced by the plastic deformation of the striking bow, the striking bow shall be considered as deformable. In this case the structure of the striking bow should also be modelled. This shall be agreed upon with the recognised classification society.

9.3.4.4.7 Assumptions for collision cases

For the collision cases the following shall be assumed:

As collision angle between striking and struck vessel 90° shall be taken in case of a V–shaped bow and 55° in case of a push barge bow; and

The struck vessel has zero speed, while the striking vessel runs into the side of the struck ship with a constant speed of 10 m/s.

The collision velocity of 10 m/s is an assumed value to be used in the FE analysis.

9.3.4.4.8 *Types of bow shapes*

9.3.4.4.8.1 Push barge bow

Characteristic dimensions shall be taken from the table below:

fr	half breadths			stem	heights		
	Knuckle 1	Knuckle 2	deck		Knuckle 1	Knuckle 2	deck
145	4.173	5.730	5.730	0.769	1.773	2.882	5.084
146	4.100	5.730	5.730	0.993	2.022	3.074	5.116
147	4.028	5.730	5.730	1.255	2.289	3.266	5.149
148	3.955	5.711	5.711	1.559	2.576	3.449	5.181
149	3.883	5.653	5.653	1.932	2.883	3.621	5.214
150	3.810	5.555	5.555	2.435	3.212	3.797	5.246
151	3.738	5.415	5.415	3.043	3.536	3.987	5.278
152	3.665	5.230	5.230	3.652	3.939	4.185	5.315
transom	3.600	4.642	4.642	4.200	4.300	4.351	5.340

The following figures are intended to provide illustration.

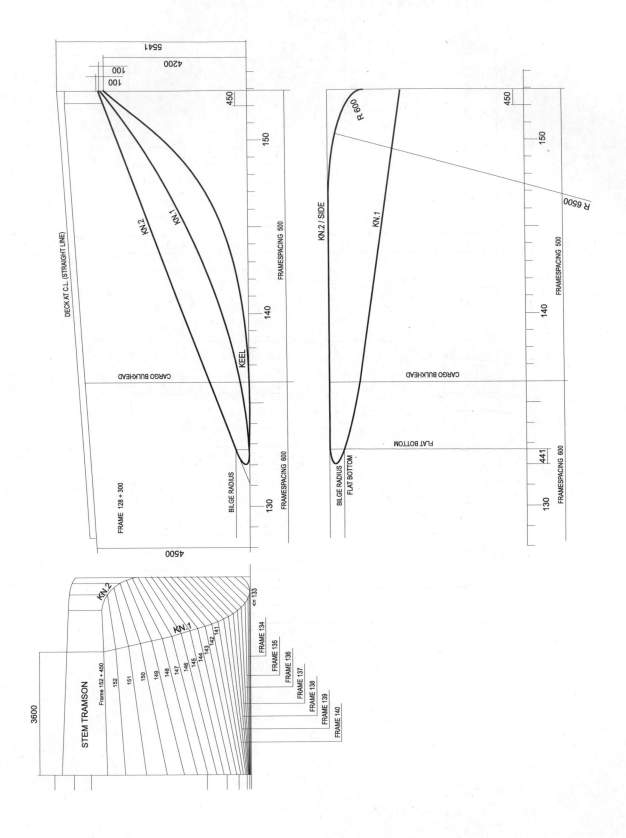

9.3.4.4.8.2   V–bow

Characteristic dimensions shall be taken from the table below:

Reference number	x	y	z
1	0.000	3.923	4.459
2	0.000	3.923	4.852
11	0.000	3.000	2.596
12	0.652	3.000	3.507
13	1.296	3.000	4.535
14	1.296	3.000	4.910
21	0.000	2.000	0.947
22	1.197	2.000	2.498
23	2.346	2.000	4.589
24	2.346	2.000	4.955
31	0.000	1.000	0.085
32	0.420	1.000	0.255
33	0.777	1.000	0.509
34	1.894	1.000	1.997
35	3.123	1.000	4.624
36	3.123	1.000	4.986
41	1.765	0.053	0.424
42	2.131	0.120	1.005
43	2.471	0.272	1.997
44	2.618	0.357	2.493
45	2.895	0.588	3.503
46	3.159	0.949	4.629
47	3.159	0.949	4.991
51	0.000	0.000	0.000
52	0.795	0.000	0.000
53	2.212	0.000	1.005
54	3.481	0.000	4.651
55	3.485	0.000	5.004

The following figures are intended to provide illustration.

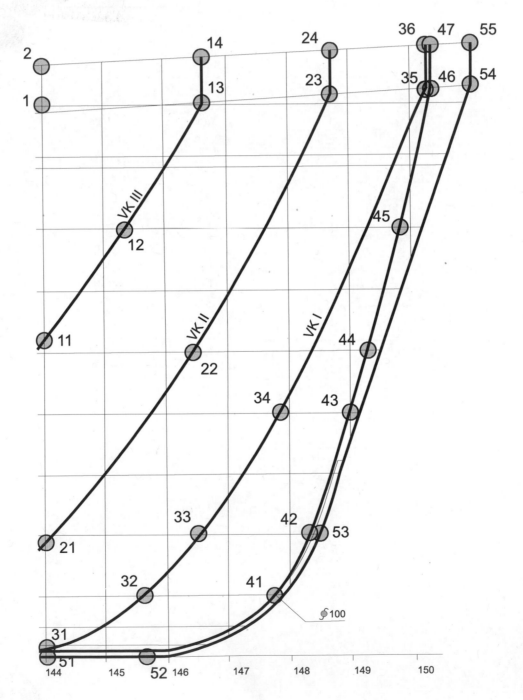

THE PATH TO POWER

MARGARET THATCHER

THE
PATH TO POWER

HarperCollins*Publishers*

ISBN 0-06-017270-3

95 96 97 98 99 HC 10 9 8 7 6 5 4 3 2 1

This book is dedicated to the memory of
KEITH JOSEPH

Contents

List of Illustrations

Acknowledgements

Writing this second volume of memoirs proved, slightly to my surprise, even more taxing than writing the first. In preparing *The Downing Street Years*, I had been able to consult a great mass of official papers which both revived and checked my memory of events. But when I turned to write the history of my early years – our family life, the first steps I took in politics, my experience as a minister and finally as Leader of the Opposition – I found that much less documentary evidence was readily available. There were, it is true, precious family papers for the Grantham years. Denis and I pooled our recollections of the fifties and sixties. Material from the Conservative Party archive and a (now sadly diminished) quantity of papers from the Department of Education supplemented this. Others allowed me to consult their papers, as I record below.

But I depended on my memoirs team to display even greater resourcefulness and powers of detection than for Volume I in the search for letters, diaries, cuttings, conference reports and all the multifarious files where little bits of modern lives are written down and stored away. All my companions in this venture were indispensable. But the most indispensable was Robin Harris, who helped me shape my thoughts, raised fruitful objections and ensured that I met a series of deadlines. John O'Sullivan parachuted in from America to polish the prose and sharpen the argument. Chris Collins ventured not only into the Conservative Party Archive but over half the country to assemble the scattered fragments of my life so as to refresh and correct my recollection. Debbie Fletcher worked unconscionably long hours, both in typing the manuscript and in looking after us, so that an accurate text was deposited in the publisher's hands. If the work was often hard, it was always great fun. And I shall miss the convivial and stimulating times we spent knocking the book into shape. I must also record my gratitude to Eddie Bell and Stuart Proffitt of Harper-Collins for encouragement and helpful suggestions.

I was fortunate to have the opportunity to discuss the turbulent and crucial years of my time as Leader of the Opposition with others who lived through them. A number of these friends also lent or gave me access to their papers. I would like to thank, in particular, the following: Sir Tim Bell, Roger Boaden, Sir Adam Butler, Lord Colnbrook, Gerald Frost, Sir George Gardiner MP, Sir John Hoskyns, Derek Howe, Sir John Lacy, Lord McAlpine, Sir Fergus Montgomery MP, Sir Peter Morrison, Sir Michael Partridge, Sir Gordon Reece, Richard Ryder MP and Caroline Ryder, Sir William Shelton, Sir Alfred Sherman, Sir John Stanley MP, Harvey Thomas, Alison Wakeham and Simon Webley.

Tessa Gaisman again helped me sort through the photographs. A number of people in Grantham kindly assisted in unearthing records of my life there: the editor and staff of the *Grantham Journal*; Jim Allen; and Lisa Budreau of Grantham Museum. In Oxford, Dr Pauline Adams gave me access to the archives of Somerville College. Dr Ann Gold helped in finding material relating to her brother, Edward Boyle. Tessa Phillips retrieved valuable material concerning Finchley. Alistair Cooke, Shirley Oxenbury and Dr Michael Maw gave me access to the archives of the Conservative Party. I am especially grateful to the Neave family for allowing me to see Airey Neave's fascinating diary and papers.

For the last section of this book I was also able to call upon a number of experts who generously gave me advice. Some of these are mentioned in acknowledgements in the course of the text. But I would like to make special reference to: Martin Howe (on Europe, Chapter 13); Professor James Q. Wilson (on social policy, Chapter 15); Sir Alan Walters, Professor Tim Congdon and Professor Patrick Minford (on the economy, Chapter 16). Valuable information was also provided by Peter Campbell (Chapter 15) and Ramesh Ponnuru (Chapter 16). The chapter on foreign affairs (Chapter 14) reflects conversations over several years with, among others, Vladimir Bukovsky, Bob Conquest, Chris Cviic, Noel Malcolm, Radek Sikorski and Professor Norman Stone. It is, however, a more than formal disclaimer when I add that the views expressed are mine alone and should not be ascribed to others.

Finally, I had the benefit of the recollections and insights of the late Lord Joseph of Portsoken. As he approached the end in hospital, Keith, though mortally weak, was still alert; characteristically, after what would be our final discussion, he asked whether I would find it useful if he recorded his views in a memorandum. Sadly, it never came. The dedication of this volume records a debt which is acknowledged but which can never be repaid.

PART ONE

CHAPTER I

A Provincial Childhood

Grantham 1925 to 1943

My first distinct memory is of traffic. I was being pushed in a pram through the town to the park on a sunny day, and I must have encountered the bustle of Grantham on the way. The occasion stays in my mind as an exciting mixture of colour, vehicles, people and thunderous noise – yet, perhaps paradoxically, the memory is a pleasant one. I must have liked this first conscious plunge into the outside world.

As for indistinct memories, most of us probably recall our earliest years as a sort of blur. Mine was an idyllic blur in which the sun was always shining through the leaves of the lime tree into our living room and someone – my mother, my sister, one of the people working in the shop – was always nearby to cuddle me or pacify me with a sweet. Family tradition has it that I was a very quiet baby, which my political opponents might have some difficulty in believing. But I had not been born into a quiet family.

Four generations of the Roberts family had been shoemakers in Northamptonshire, at that time a great centre of the shoe industry. My father, who had wanted to be a teacher, had to leave school at thirteen because the family could not afford for him to stay on. He went instead to work at Oundle, one of the better public (i.e. private) schools. Years later, when I was answering questions in the House of Commons, Eric Heffer, a left-wing Labour MP and regular sparring partner of mine, tried to pull working-class rank by mentioning that his father had been a carpenter at Oundle. He was floored when I was able to retort that mine had worked in the tuck shop there.

3

My father had a number of jobs, I think most of them in the grocery trade, until in 1913 he was offered the post of manager of a grocery store in Grantham. In later years he would say that of the fourteen shillings a week he received, twelve shillings paid for his board and lodging, one shilling he saved, and only then did he spend the remaining shilling. The First World War broke out a year later. My father, a deeply patriotic man, tried to enlist in the army no fewer than six times, but was rejected on each occasion on medical grounds. His younger brother, Edward, did enlist, and died on active service in Salonika in 1917. Few British families escaped such a bereavement, and Remembrance Day after the war was observed throughout the country both strictly and intensely.

Four years after arriving in Grantham my father met my mother, Beatrice Ethel Stephenson, through the local Methodist church. She had her own business as a dressmaker. They were married in that church in May 1917 and my sister, Muriel, was born in 1921.

My mother was quite a saver too, and by 1919 they were able to take out a mortgage to buy their own shop in North Parade. Our home was over this shop. In 1923 my father opened a second shop in Huntingtower Road – opposite the primary school which I would later attend. On 13 October 1925 I was born over the shop at North Parade.

That same year, my father expanded his business further, taking in two adjoining buildings in North Parade. Our shop and house were situated at a busy crossroads and the main railway line – Grantham was an important junction – was just a hundred yards away. We could set our clocks by the 'Flying Scotsman' as it thundered through. What I most regretted was that at this time we could not have a garden. Not until the end of the Second World War did my father buy a house with a long garden further along North Parade, on which the family had set our hearts some years previously.

Life 'over the shop' is much more than a phrase. It is something which those who have lived it know to be quite distinctive. For one thing, you are always on duty. People would knock on the door at almost any hour of the night or weekend if they ran out of bacon, sugar, butter or eggs. Everyone knew that we lived by serving the customer; it was pointless to complain – and so nobody did. These orders were, of course, on top of the regular ones. My father or his staff – we had three staff at North Parade and someone else at Huntingtower – would generally go out and collect these. But sometimes my mother would do so, and then she might take Muriel and me along too. My sister and I knew a lot of people in the town as a result.

There was, of course, no question of closing down the shop for long family holidays. We used to go to the local seaside resort, Skegness. But my father and mother had to take their holidays at different times, with my father taking a week off every year to play his favourite game, competing in the bowls tournament at Skegness. Living over the shop, children see far more of their parents than in most other walks of life. I saw my father at breakfast, lunch, high tea and supper. We had much more time to talk than some other families, for which I have always been grateful.

My father was a specialist grocer. He always aimed to supply the best-quality produce, and the shop itself suggested this. Behind the counter there were three rows of splendid mahogany spice drawers with sparkling brass handles, and on top of these stood large, black, lacquered tea canisters. One of the tasks I sometimes shared was the weighing out of tea, sugar and biscuits from the sacks and boxes in which they arrived into 1lb and 2lb bags. In a cool back room we called 'the old bake house' hung sides of bacon which had to be boned and cut up for slicing. Wonderful aromas of spices, coffee and smoked hams would waft through the house.

I was born into a home which was practical, serious and intensely religious. My father and mother were both staunch Methodists; indeed, my father was much in demand as a lay preacher in and around Grantham. He was a powerful preacher whose sermons contained a good deal of intellectual substance. But he was taken aback one day when I asked him why he put on a 'sermon voice' on these occasions. I don't think he realized that he did this. It was an unconscious homage to the biblical message, and quite different to the more prosaic tones in which he despatched council business and current affairs.

Our lives revolved around Methodism. The family went to Sunday Morning Service at 11 o'clock, but before that I would have gone to morning Sunday School. There was Sunday School again in the afternoon; later, from about the age of twelve, I played the piano for the smaller children to sing the hymns. Then my parents would usually go out again to Sunday Evening Service.

This I found somewhat too much of a good thing, and on a few occasions I remember trying to get out of going. But when I said to my father that my friends were able to go out for a walk instead and I would like to join them, he would reply: 'Never do things just because other people do them.' In fact, this was one of his favourite expressions – used when I wanted to learn dancing, or sometimes when I wanted to go to the cinema, or out for the day somewhere. Whatever I felt at the time, the sentiment stood me in good stead, as it did my father.

My father's sense of duty, however, always had its gentler side. This was not true of everyone. Life for poor people in the years before the Second World War was very difficult; and it was not much easier for those who had worked hard, accumulated a nest egg, and achieved a precarious respectability. They lived on a knife-edge and feared that if some accident hit them, or if they relaxed their standards of thrift and diligence, they might be plunged into debt and poverty. This precariousness often made otherwise good people hard and unforgiving. I remember a discussion between my father and a church-goer about the 'prodigal son' of a friend who, after running through his parents' savings, had turned up penniless and with a young family on their doorstep. The church-goer was clear: the boy was no good, would never be any good, and should be shown the door. My father's reply is vivid in my mind. No, he said. A son remained a son, and he must be greeted with all the love and warmth of his family when he turned to them. Whatever happens, you must always be able to come home.

As this suggests, my father was a man of firm principles – 'Your father always sticks to his principles,' as my mother would say – but he did not believe in applying these principles in a way which made life wretched for everyone else. He showed this in his dealings as a local councillor and later alderman with the vexed question of what could be done on the Sabbath. In those days in Grantham and in most places cinemas were closed on Sundays, but during the war – adopting a utilitarian rather than a dogmatic approach

– he supported Sunday opening because it gave the servicemen stationed near the town somewhere to go, without disturbing others who wanted a quieter, more contemplative Sabbath. At the same time he strongly (though in the end unsuccessfully) opposed the opening of the parks for the playing of games, which he felt would ruin other people's peace and quiet. He wanted to keep Sunday a special day, but he was flexible about how it should be done. For my own part, I was unpersuaded, even as a girl, of the need for these restrictions: but I can now appreciate how much this highly principled man was prepared to bend on the matter when circumstances made it sensible.

These upright qualities, which entailed a refusal to alter your convictions just because others disagreed or because you became unpopular, were instilled into me from the earliest days. In 1936, when I was eleven, I was given a special edition of *Bibby's Annual*. Joseph Bibby was a Liverpool food manufacturer who used part of his considerable self-made fortune to edit a religious magazine which was an odd combination of character building, homespun philosophy and religion; it also contained beautiful reproductions of great pictures. I was too young at the time to know that the underlying approach was Theosophist;* but the *Annual* was one of my most treasured possessions. Above all, it taught me some verses which I still use in off-the-cuff speeches because they came to embody for me so much of what I was brought up to feel.

> One ship drives East, and another drives West,
> By the self-same gale that blows;
> 'Tis the set of the sail, and not the gale,
> That determines the way she goes.
>
> ELLA WHEELER WILCOX

Or again:

> The heights by great men reached and kept
> Were not attained by sudden flight,

* Theosophy was a mixture of mysticism, Christianity and the 'wisdom of the East', sense and nonsense.

But they, while their companions slept,
Were toiling upward in the night.

HENRY WADSWORTH LONGFELLOW

Whether it was that early exposure to *Bibby's Annual* or just a natural bent, I was soon fascinated by poetry. Aged ten, I was the proud winner of a prize at the Grantham Eisteddfod for reciting poetry. (I read John Drinkwater's 'Moonlit Apples' and Walter de la Mare's 'The Travellers'.) One day soon afterwards, when I called at a door to collect an order for groceries, I was given an edition of Milton by someone who knew how much poetry meant to me: I have treasured the book ever since. In the first years of the war I would go out as part of a concert party to the surrounding villages and recite from my *Oxford Book of English Verse* – another book which even now is never far from reach. Methodism itself, of course, has, in the form of the Wesley hymns, some really fine religious poetry.

Religious life in Grantham was very active and, in the days before Christian ecumenism, competitive and fuelled by a spirit of rivalry. There were three Methodist chapels, St Wulfram's Anglican church – the sixth-highest steeple in England, according to local legend – and a Roman Catholic church just opposite our house. From a child's standpoint, the Catholics seemed to have the most light-hearted time of all. I used to envy the young Catholic girls making their first communion, dressed in white party dresses with bright ribbons, and carrying baskets of flowers. The Methodist style was much plainer, and if you wore a ribboned dress an older chapel-goer would shake his head and warn against 'the first step to Rome'.

Even without ribbons, however, Methodism was far from dour, as people are inclined to imagine today. It placed great emphasis on the social side of religion and on music, both of which gave me plenty of opportunities to enjoy life, even if it was in what might seem a rather solemn way. Our friends from church would often come in to cold supper on Sunday evenings, or we would go to them. I always enjoyed the adults' conversation, which ranged far wider than religion or happenings in Grantham to include national and international politics. And one of the unintended consequences of the temperance side of Methodism was that Methodists tended to devote more time and attention to eating. 'Keeping a good table' was a common phrase, and many of the social occasions were built around tea parties and suppers. There was also a constant round of church events, organized either to keep the young people happy or to raise funds for one purpose or other.

It was, I confess, the musical side of Methodism which I liked best. We sang special hymns on the occasion of Sunday School anniversaries. The Kesteven and Grantham Girls' School (KGGS) carol service – and the weeks of practice which preceded it – was something I always looked forward to. Our church had an exceptionally good choir. Every other year we would perform an oratorio: Handel's *Messiah*, Haydn's *Creation* or Mendelssohn's *Elijah*. We would have professionals from London to sing the more difficult solo parts. But what made an impression on me was the latent richness of musical talent which serious training and practice could develop. My family also belonged to a music society and three or four times a year there would be a chamber music concert.

We were a musical family. From the age of five my parents had me learn the piano: my mother played too. In fact, I turned out to be quite good, and I was fortunate enough to have excellent teachers and won several prizes at local music festivals. The piano on which I was taught was made by my great uncle, John Roberts, in Northampton. He also made church organs. When I was ten I visited him and was thrilled to be allowed to play one of the two he had built in a cavernous barn-like building in his garden. Sadly, at sixteen I found it necessary to stop music lessons when I was cramming for my university entrance, and I still regret that I never took the piano up again. At this time, however, it was I who played the piano at home, while my father (who had a good bass voice) and mother (a contralto) and sometimes friends sang the old favourites of an evening – 'The Holy City', 'The Lost Chord', Gilbert and Sullivan, etc.

Perhaps the biggest excitement of my early years was a visit to London when I was twelve years old. I came down by train in the charge of a friend of my mother's, arriving at King's Cross, where I was met by the Rev. Skinner and his wife, two family friends who were going to look after me. The first impact of London was overwhelming: King's Cross itself was a giant bustling cavern; the rest of the city had all the dazzle of a commercial and imperial capital. For the first time in my life I saw people from foreign countries, some in the traditional native dress of India and Africa. The sheer volume of traffic and of pedestrians was exhilarating; they seemed to generate a sort of electricity. London's buildings were impressive for another reason; begrimed with soot, they had a dark imposing magnificence which constantly reminded me that I was at the centre of the world.

I was taken by the Skinners to all the usual sites. I fed the pigeons in Trafalgar Square; I rode the Underground – a slightly forbidding experience for a child; I visited the Zoo, where I rode on an elephant and recoiled from the reptiles – an early portent of my relations with Fleet Street; I was disappointed by Oxford Street, which was much narrower than the boulevard of my imagination; made a pilgrimage to St Paul's, where John Wesley had prayed on the morning of his conversion; and of course, to the Houses of Parliament and Big Ben, which did not disappoint at all; and I went to look at Downing Street, but unlike the young Harold Wilson did not have the prescience to have my photograph taken outside No. 10.

All this was enjoyable beyond measure. But the high point was my first visit to the Catford Theatre in Lewisham where we saw Sigmund Romberg's famous musical *The Desert Song*. For three hours I lived in another world, swept away as was the heroine by the daring Red Shadow – so much so that I bought the score and played it at home, perhaps too often.

I could hardly drag myself away from London or from the Skinners, who had been such indulgent hosts. Their kindness had given me a glimpse of, in Talleyrand's words, *'la douceur de la vie'* – how sweet life could be.

Our religion was not only musical and sociable – it was also intellectually stimulating. The ministers were powerful characters with strong views. The general political tendency among Methodists and other Nonconformists in our town was somewhat to the left wing and even pacifist. Methodists in Grantham were prominent in organizing the 'Peace Ballot' of 1935, circulating a loaded questionnaire to the electorate, which was then declared overwhelmingly to have 'voted for peace'. It is not recorded how far Hitler and Mussolini were moved by this result; we had our own views about that in the Roberts household. The Peace Ballot was a foolish idea which must take some of the blame nationally for delaying the rearmament necessary to deter and ultimately defeat the dictators. On this question and others, being staunchly Conservative, we were the odd family out. Our friend the Rev. Skinner was an enthusiast for the Peace Ballot. He was the kindest and holiest man, and he married Denis and me at Wesley's Chapel in London many years later. But personal virtue is no substitute for political hard-headedness.

The sermons we heard every Sunday made a great impact on me. It was an invited Congregationalist minister, the Rev. Childe, who brought home to me the somewhat advanced notion for those days that whatever the sins of the fathers (and mothers) they must never be visited on the children. I still recall his denunciation of the Pharisaical tendency to brand children born outside marriage as 'illegitimate'. All the town knew of some children without fathers; listening to the Rev. Childe, we felt very guilty about think-ing of them as different. Times have changed. We have since removed the stigma of illegitimacy not only from the child but also from the parent – and perhaps increased the number of disadvan-taged children thereby. We still have to find some way of combining Christian charity with sensible social policy.

When war broke out and death seemed closer to everybody, the sermons became more telling. In one, just after the Battle of Britain, the preacher told us that it is 'always the few who save the many': so it was with Christ and the apostles. I was also inspired by the theme of another sermon: history showed how it was those who were born at the depths of one great crisis who would be able to cope with the next. This was proof of God's benevolent providence and a foundation for optimism about the future, however dark things now looked. The values instilled in church were faithfully reflected in my home.

So was the emphasis on hard work. In my family we were never idle – partly because idleness was a sin, partly because there was so much work to be done, and partly no doubt because we were just that sort of people. As I have mentioned, I would help whenever necessary in the shop. But I also learned from my mother just what it meant to cope with a household so that everything worked like clockwork, even though she had to spend so many hours serving behind the counter. Although we had a maid before the war – and later a cleaning lady a couple of days a week – my mother did much of the work herself, and of course there was a great deal more than in a modern home. She showed me how to iron a man's shirt in the correct way and to press embroidery without damaging it. Large flat-irons were heated over the fire and I was let in on the secret of how to give a special finish to linen by putting just enough candle wax to cover a sixpenny piece on the iron. Most unusually for those times, at my secondary school we had to study domestic science – everything from how to do laundry properly to the management of the household budget. So I was doubly equipped to lend a hand with the domestic chores. The whole house at North Parade was not just cleaned daily and weekly: a great annual spring clean was intended to get to all those parts which other cleaning could not reach. Carpets were taken up and beaten. The mahogany furniture – always good quality which my mother had bought in auction sales – was washed down with a mixture of warm water and vinegar before being repolished. Since this was also the time of the annual stocktaking in the shop, there was hardly time to draw breath.

Nothing in our house was wasted, and we always lived within our means. The worst you could say about another family was that they 'lived up to the hilt'. Because we had always been used to such a careful regime, we could cope with wartime rationing, though we used to note down the hints on the radio about the preparation of such stodgy treats as 'Lord Woolton's potato pie', an economy dish named after the wartime Minister for Food. My mother was an excellent cook and a highly organized one. Twice a week she had her big bake – bread, pastry, cakes and pies. Her home-made bread was very famous, as were her Grantham gingerbreads. Before the war there were roasts on Sunday, which became cold cuts on Monday and disappeared into rissoles on Tuesday. With wartime, however, the Sunday roast became almost meatless stew or macaroni cheese.

Small provincial towns in those days had their own networks of private charity. In the run-up to Christmas as many as 150 parcels were made up in our shop, containing tinned meat, Christmas cake and pudding, jam and tea – all purchased for poorer families by one of the strongest social and charitable institutions in Grantham, the Rotary Club. There was always something from those Thursday or Sunday bakes which was sent out to elderly folk living alone or who were sick. As grocers, we knew something about the circumstances of our customers.

Clothes were never a problem for us. My mother had been a professional seamstress and made most of what we wore. In those days there were two very good pattern services, Vogue and Butterick's; and in the sales at Grantham and Nottingham we could get the best-quality fabrics at reduced prices. So we got excellent value for money and were, by Grantham standards, rather fashionable. For my father's mayoral year, my mother made both her daughters new dresses – a blue velvet for my sister and a dark green velvet for me – and herself a black *moiré* silk gown. But in wartime the ethos of frugality was almost an obsession. Even my mother and I were taken aback by one of our friends, who told us that she never threw away her tacking cottons but re-used them: 'I consider it my duty to do so,' she said. After that, so did we. We were not Methodists for nothing.

I had less leisure time than other children. But I used to enjoy going for long walks, often on my own. Grantham lies in a little hollow surrounded by hills, unlike most of Lincolnshire which is very flat. I loved the beauty of the countryside and being alone with my thoughts in those surroundings. Sometimes I used to walk out of the town by Manthorpe Road and cut across on the north side to return down the Great North Road. I would also walk up Hall's Hill, where in wartime we were given a week off school to go and gather rose hips and blackberries. There was tobogganing there when it snowed.

I did not play much sport, though I soon learned to swim, and at school I was a somewhat erratic hockey player. At home we played the usual games, like Monopoly and Pit – a noisy game based on the Chicago Commodities Exchange. In a later visit to America I visited the Exchange; but my dabbling in commodities ended there.

It was, however, the coming of the cinema to Grantham which really brightened my life. We were fortunate in having among our customers the Campbell family who owned three cinemas in Grantham. They would sometimes invite me around to their house to play the gramophone, and I got to know their daughter Judy, later to be a successful actress who partnered Noël Coward in his wartime comedy *Present Laughter* and made famous the song 'A Nightingale Sang in Berkeley Square'. Because we knew the Campbells, the cinema was more acceptable to my parents than it might otherwise have been. They were content that I should go to 'good' films, a classification which fortunately included Fred Astaire and Ginger Rogers musicals, and the films of Alexander Korda. They rarely went with me – though on a Bank Holiday we would go together to the repertory theatre in Nottingham or to one of the big cinemas there – so usually I would be accompanied by friends of my own age. Even then, however, there were limits. Ordinarily there was a new film each week; but since some of these did not sustain enough interest to last six days, another one was shown from Thursday. Some people would go along to the second film, but that was greatly frowned on in our household.

Perhaps that was a fortunate restraint; for I was entranced with the romantic world of Hollywood. These were, after all, its Golden Years. For 9d you had a comfortable seat in the darkness while the screen showed first the trailer for forthcoming attractions, then the British Movietone News with its chirpy optimistic commentary, after that a short public service film on a theme like *Crime Does Not Pay*, and finally the Big Picture. These ran the gamut from imperialistic adventures like *The Four Feathers* and *Drum*, to sophisticated comedies like *The Women* (with every female star in the business), to the four-handkerchief weepies like Barbara Stanwyck in *Stella Dallas* or Ingrid Bergman in anything. Nor was I entirely neglecting my political education 'at the pictures'. My views on the French Revolution were gloriously confirmed by Leslie Howard and lovely Merle Oberon in *The Scarlet Pimpernel*. I saw my father's emphasis on the importance of standing up for your principles embodied by James Stewart in *Mr Smith Goes to Washington*. I rejoiced to see Soviet communism laughed out of court when Garbo, a stern Commissar, was seduced by a lady's hat in *Ninotchka*.

And my grasp of history was not made more difficult by the fact that William Pitt the Younger was played by Robert Donat and, in *Marie Walewska*, Napoleon was played by the great French charmer Charles Boyer.

I often reflect how fortunate I was to have been born in 1925 and not twenty years earlier. Until the 1930s, there was no way that a young girl living in a small English provincial town could have had access to this extraordinary range of talent, dramatic form, human emotion, sex appeal, spectacle and style. To a girl born twenty years later these offerings were commonplace and, inevitably, taken much more for granted. Grantham was a small town, but on my visits to the cinema I roamed to the most fabulous realms of the imagination. It gave me the determination to roam in reality one day.

For my parents the reality which mattered was here and now, not that of romance. Yet it was not really a dislike of pleasure which shaped their attitude. They made a very important distinction between mass- and self-made entertainment, which is just as valid in the age of constant soap operas and game shows – perhaps more so. They felt that entertainment that demanded something of you was preferable to being a passive spectator. At times I found this irksome, but I also understood the essential point.

When my mother, sister and I went on holiday together, usually to Skegness, there was always the same emphasis on being active, rather than sitting around day-dreaming. We would stay in a self-catering guesthouse, much better value than a hotel, and first thing in the morning I went out with the other children for PT exercises arranged in the public gardens. There was plenty to keep us occupied and, of course, there were buckets and spades and the beach. In the evening we would go to the variety shows and reviews, very innocent entertainments by today's standards, with comedians, jugglers, acrobats, 'old tyme' singers, ventriloquists and lots of audience participation when we joined in singing the latest hit from Henry Hall's *Guest Night*. My parents considered that such shows were perfectly acceptable, which in itself showed how attitudes changed: we would never have gone to the variety while Grandmother Stephenson, who lived with us till I was ten, was still alive.

That may make my grandmother sound rather forbidding. Again, not at all. She was a warm presence in the life of myself and my sister. Dressed in the grandmotherly style of those days – long black sateen beaded dress – she would come up to our bedrooms on warm summer evenings and tell us stories of her life as a young girl. She would also make our flesh creep with old wives' tales of how earwigs would crawl under your skin and form carbuncles. With time on her hands, she had plenty to spare for us. Her death at the age of eighty-six was the first time I had ever encountered death. As was the custom in those days, I was sent to stay with friends until the funeral was over and my grandmother's belongings had all been packed away. In fact, life is very much a day-to-day experience for a child, and I recovered reasonably quickly. But Mother and I went to tend her grave on half-day closing days. I never knew either of my grandfathers, who died before I was born, and I saw Grandmother Roberts only twice, on holidays down to Ringstead in Northamptonshire. Less stately than Grandmother Stephenson, she was a bustling, active little old lady who kept a fine garden. I remember particularly that she kept a store of Cox's orange pippins in an upstairs room from which my sister and I were invited to select the best.

My father was a great bowls player, and he smoked (which was very bad for him because of his weak chest). Otherwise, his leisure and entertainment always seemed to merge into duty. We had no alcohol in the house until he became mayor at the end of the war, and then only sherry and cherry brandy, which for some mysterious reason was considered more respectable than straight brandy, to entertain visitors. (Years of electioneering also later taught me that cherry brandy is very good for the throat.)

Like the other leading businessmen in Grantham, my father was a Rotarian. The Rotary motto, 'Service Above Self', was engraved on his heart. He spoke frequently and eloquently at Rotary functions, and we could read his speeches reported at length in the local paper. The Rotary Club was constantly engaged in fund raising for the town's different charities. My father would be involved in similar activity, not just through the church but as a councillor and in a private capacity. One such event which I used to enjoy was the League of Pity (now NSPCC) Children's Christmas party, which

I would go to in one of the party dresses beautifully made by my mother, to raise money for children who needed help.

Apart from home and church, the other centre of my life was, naturally enough, school. Here too I was very lucky. Huntingtower Road Primary School had a good reputation in the town. It had quite new buildings and excellent teachers. By the time I went there I had already been taught simple reading by my parents, and even when I was very young I enjoyed learning. Like all children, I suspect, these days remain vividly immediate for me. I remember a heart-stopping moment at the age of five when I was asked how to pronounce W-R-A-P; I got it right, but I thought 'They always give me the difficult ones.' Later, in General Knowledge, I first came across the mystery of 'proverbs'. I already had a logical and indeed somewhat literal mind – perhaps I have not changed much in this regard – and I was perplexed by the metaphorical element of phrases like 'Look before you leap'. I thought it would be far better to say 'Look before you cross' – a highly practical point given the dangerous road I must traverse on my way to school. And like other children before and after I triumphantly pointed out the contradiction between that proverb and 'He who hesitates is lost'.

It was in the top class at primary school that I first came across the work of Kipling, who died that January of 1936. I immediately became fascinated by his poems and stories and often asked my parents for a Kipling book at Christmas. His poems, themselves wonderfully accessible, gave a child access to a wider world – indeed wider worlds – of the Empire, work, English history and the animal kingdom. Like the Hollywood films later, Kipling offered glimpses into the romantic possibilities of life outside Grantham. By now I was probably reading more widely than most of my classmates, doubtless through my father's influence, and it showed on occasion. I can still recall writing an essay about Kipling and burning with childish indignation at being accused of having copied down the word 'nostalgia' from some book, whereas I had used it quite naturally and easily.

From Huntingtower Road I went on to Kesteven and Grantham Girls' School. It was in a different part of town, but what with coming home for lunch, which was more economical than the

school lunch, I still walked four miles a day back and forth. Our
uniform was saxe-blue and navy and so we were called 'the girls
in blue'. (When Camden Girls' School from London was evacuated
to Grantham for part of the war they were referred to as 'the girls
in green'.) The headmistress was Miss Williams, a petite, upright,
grey-haired lady, who had started the school as headmistress in
1910, inaugurated certain traditions such as that all girls however
academic had to take domestic science for four years, and whose
quiet authority by now dominated everything. I greatly admired
the special outfits Miss Williams used to wear on important days,
such as at the annual school fête or prize-giving, when she appeared
in beautiful silk, softly tailored, looking supremely elegant. But she
was very practical. The advice to us was never to buy a low-quality
silk when the same amount of money would purchase a very good-
quality cotton. 'Never aspire to a cheap fur coat when a well-
tailored wool coat would be a better buy.' The rule was always to
go for quality within your own income.

My teachers had a genuine sense of vocation and were highly
respected by the whole community. The school was small enough
– about 350 girls – for us to get to know them and one another,
within limits. The girls were generally from middle-class backgrounds; but that covered a fairly wide range of occupations from
town and country. My closest friend, indeed, came in daily from
a rural village about ten miles distant, where her father was a
builder. I used to stay with her family from time to time. Her
parents, no less keen than mine to add to a daughter's education,
would take us out for rural walks, identifying the wild flowers and
the species of birds and birdsongs.

I had a particularly inspiring History teacher, Miss Harding,
who gave me a taste for the subject which, unfortunately, I never
fully developed. I found myself with absolute recall remembering
her account of the Dardanelles campaign so many years later when,
as Prime Minister, I walked over the tragic battlegrounds of
Gallipoli.

But the main academic influence on me was undoubtedly Miss
Kay, who taught Chemistry, in which I decided to specialize. It
was not unusual – in an all-girls' school, at least – for a girl to
concentrate on science, even before the war. My natural enthusiasm

for the sciences was whetted by reports of breakthroughs which were occurring – for example in the splitting of the atom and the development of plastics. It was clear that a whole new scientific world was opening up. I wanted to be part of it. Moreover, as I knew that I would have to earn my own living, this seemed an exciting way to do so.

As my father had left school at the age of thirteen, he was determined to make up for this and to see that I took advantage of every educational opportunity. We would both go to hear 'Extension Lectures' from the University of Nottingham about current and international affairs, which were given in Grantham regularly. After the talk would come a lively question time in which I and many others would take part: I remember, in particular, questions from a local RAF man, Wing-Commander Millington, who later captured Chelmsford for Common Wealth – a left-wing party of middle-class protest – from the Churchill coalition in a by-election towards the end of the war.

My parents took a close interest in my schooling. Homework always had to be completed – even if that meant doing it on Sunday evening. During the war, when the Camden girls were evacuated to Grantham and a shift system was used for teaching at our school, it was necessary to put in extra hours at the weekend which were religiously performed. My father, in particular, who was an all the more avid reader for being a self-taught scholar, would discuss what we read at school. On one occasion he found that I did not know Walt Whitman's poetry; this was quickly remedied, and Whitman is still a favourite author of mine. I was also encouraged to read the classics – the Brontës, Jane Austen and, of course, Dickens: it was the latter's *A Tale of Two Cities*, with its strong political flavour, that I liked best. My father also used to subscribe to the *Hibbert Journal* – a philosophical journal. But this, though I struggled, I found heavy going.

Beyond home, church and school lay the community which was Grantham itself. We were immensely proud of our town; we knew its history and traditions; we were glad to be part of its life. Grantham was established in Saxon times, though it was the Danes who made it an important regional centre. During the twelfth century the Great North Road was re-routed to run through the town, literally putting Grantham on the map. Communications were always the town's lifeblood. In the eighteenth century the canal was cut to carry coke, coal and gravel into Grantham and corn, malt, flour and wool out of it. But the real expansion had come with the arrival of the railways in 1850.

Our town's most imposing structure I have already mentioned – the spire of St Wulfram's Church, which could be seen from all directions. But most characteristic and significant for us was the splendid Victorian Guildhall and, in front of it, the statue of Grantham's most famous son, Sir Isaac Newton. It was from here, on St Peter's Hill, that the Remembrance Day parades began to process en route to St Wulfram's. I would watch from the windows of the Guildhall Ballroom as (preceded by the Salvation Army band and the band from Ruston and Hornsby's locomotive works) the mayor, aldermen and councillors with robes and regalia, followed by Brownies, Cubs, Boys' Brigade, Boy Scouts, Girl Guides, Freemasons, Rotary, Chamber of Commerce, Working Men's Clubs, trade unions, British Legion, soldiers, airmen, the Red Cross, the St John's Ambulance and representatives of every organization which made up our rich civic life filed past. It was also on the green at St Peter's Hill that every Boxing Day we gathered to watch the pink coats of the Belvoir Hunt hold their meet (followed by the traditional tipple) and cheered them as they set off.

1935 was a quite exceptional and memorable year for the town. We celebrated King George V's Silver Jubilee along with Grantham's Centenary as a borough. Lord Brownlow, whose family (the Custs) with the Manners family (the Dukes of Rutland) were the most distinguished aristocratic patrons of the town, became mayor. The town itself was heavily decorated with blue and gold waxed streamers – our local colours – across the main streets. Different streets vied to outdo one another in the show they put on. I recall that it was the street with some of the poorest families in the worst housing, Vere Court, which was most attractively turned out. Everyone made an effort. The brass bands played throughout the day, and Grantham's own 'Carnival Band' – a rather daring innovation borrowed from the United States and called 'The Grantham Gingerbreads' – added to the gaiety of the proceedings. The schools took part in a great open-air programme and we marched in perfect formation under the watchful eye of the wife of the headmaster of the boys' grammar school to form the letters 'G-R-A-N-T-H-A-M'. And, appropriately enough, I was part of the 'M'.

My father's position as a councillor, Chairman of the Borough Finance Committee, then alderman* and finally in 1945–46 mayor meant that I heard a great deal about the town's business and knew those involved in it. Politics was a matter of civic duty and party was of secondary importance. The Labour councillors we knew were respected and friendly and, whatever the battles in the council chamber or at election time, they came to our shop and there was no partisan bitterness. My father understood that politics has limits – an insight which is all too rare among politicians. His politics would perhaps be best described as 'old-fashioned liberal'. Individual responsibility was his watchword and sound finance his passion. He was an admirer of John Stuart Mill's *On Liberty*. Like many other business people he had, as it were, been left behind by the Liberal Party's acceptance of collectivism. He stood for the council as a rate-payer's candidate. In those days, before comprehensive schools became an issue and before the general advance of Labour politics into local government, local council work was considered as properly non-partisan. But I never remember him as anything other than a staunch Conservative.

I still recall with great sorrow the day in 1952 when Labour, having won the council elections, voted my father out as an alderman. This was roundly condemned at the time for putting party above community. Nor can I forget the dignity with which he behaved. After the vote in the council chamber was taken, he rose to speak: 'It is now almost nine years since I took up these robes in honour, and now I trust in honour they are laid down.' And later, after receiving hundreds of messages from friends, allies and even old opponents, he issued a statement which said: 'Although I have toppled over I have fallen on my feet. My own feeling is that I was content to be in and I am content to be out.' Years

* Aldermen were indirectly elected council members – elected to serve a fixed term by the directly elected element in the council; a highly honoured position which has since been abolished.

later, when something not too dissimilar happened to me, and after my father was long dead, I tried to take as an example the way he left public life.

But this is to anticipate. Perhaps the main interest which my father and I shared while I was a girl was a thirst for knowledge about politics and public affairs. I suspect that we were better informed than many families. We read the *Daily Telegraph* every day, *The Methodist Recorder*, *Picture Post* and *John O'London's Weekly* every week, and when we were small we took *The Children's Newspaper*. Occasionally we read *The Times*.

And then came the day my father bought our first wireless – a Philips of the kind you sometimes now see in the less pretentious antique shops. I knew what he was planning and ran much of the way home from school in my excitement. I was not disappointed. It changed our lives. From then on it was not just Rotary, church and shop which provided the rhythm of our day: it was the radio news. And not just the news. During the war after the 9 o'clock news on Sundays there was *Postscript*, a short talk on a topical subject, often by J.B. Priestley, who had a unique gift of cloaking left-wing views as solid, down to earth, Northern homespun philosophy, and sometimes an American journalist called Quentin Reynolds who derisively referred to Hitler by one of his family names, 'Mr Schicklgruber'. There was *The Brains Trust*, an hour-long discussion of current affairs by four intellectuals, of whom the most famous was Professor C.E.M. Joad, whose answer to any question always began 'It all depends what you mean by . . .'. On Friday evenings there were commentaries by people like Norman Birkett in the series called *Encounter*. I loved the comedy *ITMA* with its still serviceable catchphrases and its cast of characters like the gloomy charlady 'Mona Lott' and her signature line 'It's being so cheerful as keeps me going.'

As for so many families, the unprecedented immediacy of radio broadcasts gave special poignancy to great events – particularly those of wartime. I recall sitting by our radio with my family at Christmas dinner and listening to the King's broadcast in 1939. We knew how he struggled to overcome his speech impediment and we knew that the broadcast was live. I found myself thinking just how miserable he must have felt, not able to enjoy his own

Christmas dinner, knowing that he would have to broadcast. I remember his slow voice reciting those famous lines:

And I said to the man who stood at the gate of the year: 'Give me a light that I may tread safely into the unknown.'
And he replied: 'Go out into the darkness and put your hand into the Hand of God. That shall be to you better than light and safer than a known way.'*

I was almost fourteen by the time war broke out, and already old enough and informed enough to understand the background to it and to follow closely the great events of the next six years. My grasp of what was happening in the political world during the thirties was less sure. But certain things I did take in. The years of the Depression – the first but not the last economic catastrophe resulting from misguided monetary policy – had less effect on Grantham itself than on the surrounding agricultural communities, and of course much less than on Northern towns dependent on heavy industry. Most of the town's factories kept going – the largest, Ruston and Hornsby, making locomotives and steam engines. We even attracted new investment, partly through my father's efforts: Aveling-Barford built a factory to make steamrollers and tractors. Our family business was also secure: people always have to eat, and our shops were well run. The real distinction in the town was between those who drew salaries for what today would be called 'white collar' employment and those who did not, with the latter being in a far more precarious position as jobs became harder to get. On my way to school I would pass a long queue waiting at the Labour Exchange, seeking work or claiming the dole. We were lucky in that none of our closest friends was unemployed, but naturally we knew people who were. We also knew – and I have never forgotten – how neatly turned out the children of those unemployed families were. Their parents were determined to make the sacrifices that were necessary for them. The spirit of self-reliance and independence was very strong in even the poorest

* From *God Knows*, by Minnie Louise Haskins.

people of the East Midlands towns. It meant that they never dropped out of the community and, because others quietly gave what they could, the community remained together. Looking back, I realize just what a decent place Grantham was.

So I did not grow up with the sense of division and conflict between classes. Even in the Depression there were many things which bound us all together. The monarchy was certainly one. And my family like most others was immensely proud of the Empire. We felt that it had brought law, good administration and order to lands which would never otherwise have known them. I had a romantic fascination for out-of-the-way countries and continents and what benefits we British could bring to them. As a child, I heard with wonder a Methodist missionary describing his work in Central America with a tribe so primitive that they had never written down their language until he did it for them. Later, I seriously considered going into the Indian Civil Service, for to me the Indian Empire represented one of Britain's greatest achievements. (I had no interest in being a civil servant in Britain.) But when I discussed it with my father he said, all too perceptively as it turned out, that by the time I was ready to join it the Indian Civil Service would probably not exist.

As for the international scene, everyone's recollections of the thirties, not least those of a child, are heavily influenced by what came later. But I recall when I was very young my parents expressing unease about the weakness of the League of Nations and its failure to come to the aid of Abyssinia when Italy invaded it in 1935. We had a deep distrust of the dictators.

We did not know much about the ideology of communism and fascism at this time. But, unlike many conservative-minded people, my father was fierce in rejecting the argument, put forward by some supporters of Franco, that fascist regimes had to be backed as the only way to defeat communists. He believed that the free society was the better alternative to both. This too was a conviction I quickly made my own. Well before war was declared, we knew just what we thought of Hitler. On the cinema newsreels I would watch with distaste and incomprehension the rallies of strutting brownshirts, so different from the gentle self-regulation of our own civic life. We also read a good deal about the barbarities and absurdities of the Nazi regime.

But none of this meant, of course, that we viewed war with the dictators as anything other than an appalling prospect, which should be avoided if possible. In our attic there was a trunk full of magazines showing, among other things, the famous picture from the Great War of a line of British soldiers blinded by mustard gas walking to the dressing station, each with a hand on the shoulder of the one in front to guide him. Hoping for the best, we prepared for the worst. As early as September 1938 – the time of Munich – my mother and I went out to buy yards of blackout material. My father was heavily involved in organizing the town's air raid precautions. As he would later say, 'ARP' stood for 'Alf Roberts' Purgatory', because it was taking up so much time that he had none to spare for other things.

The most pervasive myth about the thirties is perhaps that it was the Right rather than the Left which most enthusiastically favoured appeasement. Not just from my own experience in a highly political right-wing family, but from my recollection of how Labour actually voted against conscription even after the Germans marched into Prague, I have never been prepared to swallow this. But in any case it is important to remember that the atmosphere of the time was so strongly pacifist that the practical political options were limited.

The scale of the problem was demonstrated in the general election of 1935 – the contest in which I cut my teeth politically, at the age of ten. It will already be clear that we were a highly political family. And for all the serious sense of duty which underlay it, politics was fun. I was too young to canvass for my father during council elections, but I was put to work folding the bright red election leaflets extolling the merits of the Conservative candidate, Sir Victor Warrender. The red came off on my sticky fingers and someone said, 'There's Lady Warrender's lipstick.' I had no doubt at all about the importance of seeing Sir Victor returned. On election day itself, I was charged with the responsible task of running back and forth between the Conservative committee room and the polling station (our school) with information about who had voted. Our candidate won, though with a much reduced majority, down from 16,000 to 6,000.

I did not grasp at the time the arguments about rearmament

and the League of Nations, but this was a very tough election, fought in the teeth of opposition from the enthusiasts of the Peace Ballot and with the Abyssinian war in the background. Later, in my teens, I used to have fierce arguments with other Conservatives about whether Baldwin had culpably misled the electorate during the campaign, as was widely alleged, in not telling them the dangers the country faced. In fact, had the National Government not been returned at that election there is no possibility that rearmament would have happened faster, and it is very likely that Labour would have done less. Nor could the League have ever prevented a major war.

We had mixed feelings about the Munich Agreement of September 1938, as did many people who were opposed to appeasement. At the time, it was impossible not to be pulled in two directions. On the one hand, we knew by now a good deal about Hitler's regime and probable intentions – something brought home to my family especially by the fact that Hitler had crushed Rotary in Germany, which my father always considered one of the greatest tributes Rotary could ever be paid. Dictators, we learned, could no more tolerate Burke's 'little platoons' – the voluntary bodies which help make up civil society – than they could individual rights under the law. Dr Jauch, of German extraction and probably the town's best doctor, received a lot of information from Germany which he passed on to my father, and he in turn discussed it all with me.

I knew just what I thought of Hitler. Near our house was a fish and chip shop where I was sent to buy our Friday evening meal. Fish and chip queues were always a good forum for debate. On one occasion the topic was Hitler. Someone suggested that at least he had given Germany some self-respect and made the trains run on time. I vigorously argued the opposite, to the astonishment and doubtless irritation of my elders. The woman who ran the shop laughed and said: 'oh, she's always debating.'

My family understood particularly clearly Hitler's brutal treatment of the Jews. At school we were encouraged to have foreign penfriends. Mine was a French girl called Colette: alas, I did not keep up contact with her. But my sister, Muriel, had an Austrian Jewish penfriend called Edith. After the Anschluss in March 1938, when Hitler annexed Austria, Edith's father, a banker, wrote to mine asking whether we could take his daughter, since he very clearly foresaw the way events were leading. We had neither the time – having to run the shops – nor the money to accept such a responsibility alone; but my father won the support of the Grantham Rotarians for the idea, and Edith came to stay with each of our families in turn until she went to live with relatives in South America. She was seventeen, tall, beautiful, well-dressed, evidently from a well-to-do family, and spoke good English. She told us what it was like to live as a Jew under an anti-semitic regime. One thing Edith reported particularly stuck in my mind: the Jews, she said, were being made to scrub the streets.

We wanted to see Hitler's wickedness ended, even by war if that proved necessary. From that point of view Munich was nothing to be proud of. We knew too that by the Munich Agreement Britain had complicity in the great wrong that had been done to Czechoslovakia. When fifty years later as Prime Minister I visited Czechoslovakia I addressed the Federal Assembly in Prague and told them: 'We failed you in 1938 when a disastrous policy of appeasement allowed Hitler to extinguish your independence. Churchill was quick to repudiate the Munich Agreement, but we still remember it with shame.' British foreign policy is at its worst when it is engaged in giving away other people's territory.

But equally we all understood the lamentable state of unpreparedness in Britain and France to fight a major war, and during the Munich crisis war had seemed so close at one point that when the settlement was announced we were simply relieved not to have to fight. Also, unfortunately, some were taken in by the German propaganda and actually believed that Hitler was acting to defend the Sudeten Germans from Czech oppression. If we had gone to war at that point, moreover, we would not have been supported by all of the Dominions. It was the Germans' subsequent dismemberment of what remained of Czechoslovakia in March 1939 that finally convinced almost everyone that appeasement had been a disaster and that war would soon be necessary to defeat Hitler's ambitions. Even then, as I have pointed out, Labour voted against conscription the following month. There was strong anti-war feeling in Grantham too: many Methodists opposed the official recruiting campaign of May 1939, and right up to the outbreak of war and beyond pacifists were addressing meetings in the town.

In any case, the conflict was soon upon us. Germany invaded Poland on 1 September 1939. When Hitler refused to withdraw by 11 a.m. on Sunday 3 September in accordance with Britain's ultimatum we were waiting by the radio, desperate for the news. It was the only Sunday in my youth when I can remember not attending church. Neville Chamberlain's fateful words, relayed live from the Cabinet Room at No. 10, told us that we were at war.

It was natural at such times to ask oneself how we had come to such a pass. Each week my father would take two books out of the library, a 'serious' book for himself (and me) and a novel for my mother. As a result, I found myself reading books which girls of my age would not generally read. I soon knew what I liked – anything about politics and international affairs. I read, for instance, John Strachey's *The Coming Struggle for Power*, which had first appeared in 1932. The contents of this fashionable communist analysis, which predicted that capitalism was shortly to be super- seded by socialism, seemed to many of my generation exciting and new.

But both by instinct and upbringing I was always a 'true blue' Conservative. No matter how many left-wing books I read or left- wing commentaries I heard, I never doubted where my political loyalties lay. Such an admission is probably unfashionable. But though I had great friends in politics who suffered from attacks of doubt about where they stood and why, and though of course it would take many years before I came to understand the philosophi- cal background to what I believed, I always knew my mind. In this I can see now that I was probably unusual. For the Left were setting the political agenda throughout the thirties and forties, even though the leadership of Churchill conccaled it during the years of the war itself. This was evident from many of the books which were published at about this time. The Left had been highly successful in tarring the Right with appeasement, most notably in Victor Gollancz's Left Book Club, the so-called 'yellow books'. One in particular had enormous impact: *Guilty Men*, co-authored by

Michael Foot, which appeared under the pseudonym 'Cato' just after Dunkirk in 1940.

Robert Bruce Lockhart's best-selling *Guns or Butter?* appeared in the autumn of 1938, after Munich. Lockhart's travels through Europe led him to Austria (now Nazi-controlled after the Anschluss) and then to Germany itself at the height of Hitler's triumph. There the editor of a German national newspaper is reported as telling him that 'Germany wanted peace, but she wanted it on her own terms.' The book ends with Lockhart, woken by 'the tramp of two thousand feet in unison', looking out of his window onto a misty dawn, where 'Nazi Germany was already at work'.

A more original variation on the same theme was Douglas Reed's *Insanity Fair*. This made a deep impression on me. Reed witnessed the persecution of the Jews which accompanied the advance of Nazi influence. He described the character and mentality – alternately perverted, unbalanced and calculating – of the Nazi leaders. He analysed and blisteringly denounced that policy of appeasement by Britain and France which paved the way for Hitler's successes. Written on the eve of the Anschluss, it was powerfully prophetic.

Out of the Night by Jan Valtin – pen name for the German communist Richard Krebs – was lent to my father by our future MP Denis Kendall. It was such strong meat that my father forbade me to read it – but in vain. When he went out to meetings I would take it down from the shelf on which it was hidden and read its spine-chilling account of totalitarianism in action. It is, in truth, an unsuitable book for a girl of sixteen, full of scenes of sadistic violence whose authenticity makes them still more horrifying. The appalling treatment by the Nazis of their victims is undoubtedly the most powerful theme. But underlying it is another, just as significant. For it describes how the communists set out in cynical alliance with the Nazis to subvert the fragile democracy of Germany by violence in the late twenties and early thirties. That same alliance against democracy would, of course, be replicated in the Nazi-Soviet pact of 1939 to 1941 which destroyed Poland, the Baltic states and Finland and plunged the world into war. The book undoubtedly contributed to my growing belief that Nazism (national socialism) and communism (international socialism) were but two sides of the same coin.

A book which had a particular influence on me was the American Herbert Agar's *A Time for Greatness*, which appeared in 1944. This was a strangely powerful analysis of how the West's moral failure allowed the rise of Hitler and the war which had followed. It urged a return to Western liberal democratic values and – though I liked this less – a fair amount of left-wing social engineering. For me the important message of Agar's book was that the fight against Hitler had a significance for civilization and human destiny which exceeded the clash of national interests or spheres of influence or access to resources or any of the other – doubtless important – stuff of power politics.

Agar also wrote of the need, as part of the moral regeneration which must flow from fighting the war, to solve what he called 'the Negro problem'. I had never heard of this 'problem' at all. Although I had seen some coloured people on my visit to London, there were almost none living in Grantham. Friends of ours once invited two American servicemen – one black, one white – stationed in Grantham back to tea and had been astonished to detect tension and even hostility between them. We were equally taken aback when our friends told us about it afterwards. This sort of prejudice was simply outside our experience or imagination.

Like many other young girls in wartime, I read Barbara Cartland's *Ronald Cartland*, the life of her brother, a young, idealistic Conservative MP, who had fought appeasement all the way and who was killed at Dunkirk in 1940. In many ways her most romantic book, it was a striking testament to someone who had no doubt that the war was not only necessary but right, and whose thinking throughout his short life was 'all of a piece', something which I always admired. But the sense that the war had a moral significance which underlay the fear and suffering – or in our family's case in Grantham the material dreariness and mild deprivation – which accompanied it, was perhaps most memorably conveyed by Richard Hillary's *The Last Enemy*. The author – a young pilot – portrays the struggle which had claimed the lives of so many of his friends, and which would claim his own less than a year later, as one which was also being fought out in the human heart. It was a struggle for a better life in the sense of simple decency.

A generation which, unlike Richard Hillary, survived the war felt this kind of desire to put things right with themselves, their country and the world. As I would come to learn when dealing with my older political colleagues, no one who fought came out of it quite the same person as went in. Less frequently understood, perhaps, is that war affected deeply, if inevitably less powerfully, people like me who while old enough to understand what was happening in the conflict were not themselves in the services. Those who grow up in wartime always turn out to be a serious-minded generation. But we all see these great calamities with different eyes, and so their impact upon us is different. It never seemed to me, for example, as it apparently did to many others, that the 'lesson' of wartime was that the state must take the foremost position in our national life and summon up a spirit of collective endeavour in peace as in war.

The 'lessons' I drew were quite different. The first was that the kind of life that the people of Grantham had lived before the war *was* a decent and wholesome one, and its values were shaped by the community rather than by the government. Second, since even a cultured, developed, Christian country like Germany had fallen under Hitler's sway, civilization could never be taken for granted and had constantly to be nurtured, which meant that good people had to stand up for the things they believed in. Third, I drew the obvious political conclusion that it was appeasement of dictators which had led to the war, and that had grown out of wrong-headed but decent impulses, like the pacifism of Methodists in Grantham, as well as out of corrupt ones. One can never do without straightforward common sense in matters great as well as small. And finally I have to admit that I had the patriotic conviction that, given great leadership of the sort I heard from Winston Churchill in the radio broadcasts to which we listened, there was almost nothing that the British people could not do.

Our life in wartime Grantham – until I went up to Oxford in 1943 – must have been very similar to that of countless other families. There was always voluntary work to do of one kind or another in the Service canteens and elsewhere. Our thoughts were at the front; we devoured voraciously every item of available news; and we ourselves, though grateful for being more or less safe, knew that we were effectively sidelined. But we had our share of bombing. There were altogether twenty-one German air raids on the town, and seventy-eight people were killed. The town munitions factory – the British Manufacturing and Research Company (B.M.A.R.Co., or 'British Marcs' as we called it) – which came to the town in 1938, was an obvious target, as was the junction of the Great North Road and the Northern Railway Line – the latter within a few hundred yards of our house. My father was frequently out in the evenings on air raid duty. During air raids we would crawl under the table for shelter – we had no outside shelter for we had no garden – until the 'all clear' sounded. On one occasion, coming back from school with my friends, carrying our gas masks, we made a dive for the shelter of a large tree as someone called out that the aircraft overhead was German. After bombs fell on the town in January 1941 I asked my father if I could walk down to see the damage. He would not let me go. Twenty-two people died in that raid. We were also concerned for my sister Muriel, who was working day and night in the Orthopaedic Hospital in Birmingham: Birmingham was, of course, very badly bombed.

In fact, Grantham itself was playing a more dramatic role than I knew at the time. Bomber Command's 5 Group was based in Grantham, and it was from a large house off Harrowby Road that much of the planning was done of the bombing raids on Germany; the officers' mess was in Elm House in Elmer Street, which I used to pass walking to school. The Dambusters flew from near Grantham – my father met their commander, Squadron Leader Guy Gibson. I always felt that Bomber Harris – himself based in Grantham in the early part of the war – had not been sufficiently honoured. I would remember what Winston Churchill wrote to him at the end of the war:

> For over two years Bomber Command alone carried the war to the heart of Germany, bringing hope to the peoples of Occupied Europe and to the enemy a foretaste of the mighty power which was rising against him . . .
>
> All your operations were planned with great care and skill. They were executed in the face of desperate opposition and appalling hazards. They made a decisive contribution to

Germany's final defeat. The conduct of these operations demonstrated the fiery gallant spirit which animated your air
crews and the high sense of duty of all ranks under your
command. I believe that the massive achievements of Bomber
Command will long be remembered as an example of duty
nobly done.

    Winston S. Churchill

In Grantham, at least, politics did not stand still in the war
years. Hitler's invasion of the Soviet Union in June 1941 sharply
altered the attitudes of the Left to the war. Pacifist voices suddenly
became silent. Anglo-Soviet friendship groups sprouted. We attended,
not without some unease, Anglo-Soviet evenings held at the town
hall. It was the accounts of the suffering and bravery of the Russians
at Stalingrad in 1942–43 which had most impact on us.

Although it can now be seen that 1941 – with Hitler's attack on
Russia in June and the Japanese bombing of Pearl Harbor which
brought America into the war in December – sowed the seeds
of Germany's ultimate defeat, the news was generally bad, and
especially so in early 1942. This almost certainly contributed to
the outcome of the by-election held in Grantham on 27 February
1942, after Victor Warrender was elevated to the Lords as Lord
Bruntisfield, to become an Admiralty spokesman. Our town had
the dubious distinction of being the first to reject a government
candidate during the war. Denis Kendall stood as an Independent
against our Conservative candidate, Sir Arthur Longmore. Kendall
fought an effective populist campaign in which he skilfully used his
role as General Manager of British Marcs to stress the theme of
an all-out drive for production for the war effort and the need for
'practical' men to promote it. To our great surprise, he won by
367 votes. Then and later the Conservative Party was inclined to
complacency. A closer analysis of the limited number of by-
elections should have alerted us to the likelihood of the Socialist
landslide which materialized in 1945.

Unusually, I took little part in the campaign because I was
working very hard, preparing for examinations which I hoped
would get me into Somerville College, Oxford. In particular, my
evenings were spent cramming the Latin which was required for

the entrance exam. Our school did not teach Latin. Fortunately, our new headmistress, Miss Gillies, herself a classicist, was able to arrange Latin lessons for me from a teacher at the boys' grammar school, and to lend me her own books, including a textbook written by her father. The hard work helped keep my mind off the ever more dismal news about the war. In particular, there was a series of blows in the Far East – the loss of Malaya, the sinking of the *Prince of Wales* and *Repulse*, the fall of Hong Kong and then Singapore, the retreat through Burma and the Japanese threat to Australia. One evening in the spring of 1942 when I had gone for a walk with my father I turned and asked him when – and how – it would all end. He replied very calmly: 'We don't know how, we don't know when; but we have no doubt that we *shall* win.'

In spite of my efforts to get into Somerville, I failed to win the scholarship I wanted. It was not too surprising, for I was only seventeen, but it was something of a blow. I knew that if I was not able to go up in 1943 I would not be allowed to do more than a two-year 'wartime degree' before I was called up for national service at the age of twenty. But there was nothing I could do about it, and so at the end of August 1943 I entered the third-year sixth and became Joint Head of School. Then, suddenly, a telegram arrived offering me a place at Somerville in October. Someone else had dropped out. And so it was that I suddenly found myself faced with the exciting but daunting prospect of leaving home, almost for the first time, for a totally different world.

CHAPTER II

Gowns-woman

Oxford 1943 to 1947

Oxford does not set out to please. Freshmen arrive there for the Michaelmas term in the misty gloom of October. Monumental buildings impress initially by their size rather than their exquisite architecture. Everything is cold and strangely forbidding. Or so it seemed to me.

It had been at Somerville during bitterly cold mid-winter days that I had taken my Oxford entrance exams. But I had seen little of my future college and less still of the university as a whole before I arrived, rather homesick and apprehensive, to begin my first term. In fact, Somerville always takes people by surprise. Many incurious passers-by barely know it is there, for the kindest thing to say of its external structure is that it is unpretentious. But inside it opens up into a splendid green space onto which many rooms face. I was to live both my first and second years in college, moving from the new to the older buildings. In due course, a picture or two, a vase and finally an old armchair brought back from Grantham allowed me to feel that the rooms were in some sense mine. In my third and fourth years I shared digs with two friends in Walton Street.

Both Oxford and Somerville were strongly if indirectly affected by the war. For whatever reason, Oxford was not bombed, in spite of the presence of the motor works at Cowley which had become a centre for aircraft repair. But like everywhere else, both town and university were subject to the blackout ('dim-out' from 1944) and much affected by wartime stringencies. Stained-glass windows were boarded up. Large static water tanks – as in Somerville's East

Quad off the Woodstock Road – stood ready for use in case of fire. Most of our rations were allocated direct to the college which provided our unexciting fare in hall, though on rare occasions I would be asked out to dinner. There were a few coupons left over for jam and other things. One of the minor benefits to my health and figure of such austerities was that I ceased having sugar in my tea – though only many years later would I deny my ever-sweet tooth the pleasure of sugared coffee (not that there was over-much coffee for some time either). There were tight controls over the use of hot water. For example, there must be no more than five inches of water in the bath – a line was painted round at the right level – and of course I rigidly observed this, though coming from a family where the relationship between cleanliness and Godliness was no laughing matter. Not that we ever felt like complaining. After all, we were the lucky ones.

Moreover, though I was not the first member of my family to go to university – my cousin had gone to London – I was the first Roberts to go to Oxbridge and I knew that, however undemonstrative they might be, my parents were extremely proud of the fact. Before I went up to Oxford, I had a less clear idea of what the place would be like than did many of my contemporaries. But I regarded it as being quite simply the best, and if I was serious about getting on in life that is what I should always strive for. There was no point in lowering my sights. So, excellent as it was, particularly in the sciences, I was never tempted to opt for Nottingham, our 'local' university, even though I would have been able to live so much nearer my home, family and friends. Another aspect of Oxford which appealed to me then – and still does – is the collegiate system. Oxford is divided into colleges, though it also has some central university institutions such as the Bodleian Library. In my day, life centred on the college (where you ate and slept and received many of your tutorials) and around other institutions – church and societies – which had more or less a life of their own. As a scientist, my life probably revolved more around university institutions and facilities, such as the chemistry laboratories, than did that of students in other disciplines. Still, my experience of college life contributed to my later conviction that if you wish to bring the best out of people they should be encouraged to be part of smaller, human-scale communities rather than be left to drift on a sea of impersonality.

Perhaps the most obvious way in which wartime conditions affected the 'feel' of university life was the fact that so many of us were very young – only seventeen or just eighteen, and at that age an extra year can mean a great difference in outlook and maturity. Later, from 1944, the feel of Oxford changed again as older people, invalided out, started coming back from the services either to complete a shortened wartime degree or to begin a full degree course. They had been through so much more than we had. As Kipling wrote (in 'The Scholars') of young naval officers returning to Cambridge after the Great War to continue their studies:

Far have they steamed and much have they known, and most
would they fain forget;
But now they are come to their joyous own with all the world
in their debt.

By the time I left I found myself dealing with friends and colleagues who had seen much more of the world than I had. And I gained a great deal from the fact that Oxford at the end of the war was a place of such mixed views and experience.

I began by keeping myself to myself, for I felt shy and ill at ease in this quite new environment. I continued, as in Grantham, to take long walks on my own, around Christ Church Meadow, through the university parks and along the Cherwell or the Thames, enjoying my own company and thoughts. But I soon started to appreciate Oxford life. My first years there coincided with the end of the war; so it is perhaps not surprising that my pleasures were the slightly Nonconformist ones I had brought with me from Grantham. I was a member of a Methodist Study Group which gave and attended tea parties. My mother would send me cakes through the post and on a Saturday morning I would join the queue outside the 'cake factory' in north Oxford for an hour or so to buy the sustenance for tea that Sunday. I joined the Bach Choir, conducted by Sir Thomas Armstrong (by a nice coincidence Robert Armstrong's father), whose repertoire was wider than its name suggested. I especially remember our performance of the

St Matthew Passion in the Sheldonian Theatre, which Wren might have designed for the purpose. We also sang *Prince Igor*, Constant Lambert's *Rio Grande*, and Holst's *Hymn of Jesus*. Sometimes I went to listen rather than to sing: I heard Kathleen Ferrier in Elgar's *Dream of Gerontius*.

With the end of the war and the return of the servicemen, the pace of entertainment quickened. Eights Week was revived and I went down to the river to watch the races. It was at this time that I first went out to dances and even on occasion drank a little wine (I had previously only tasted sherry and did not like it; nor do I now). I smoked my first cigarettes. I did not like them much either, though I knew I would get the taste if I persisted. I decided not to, to save the money and buy *The Times* every day instead. I now went to my first commem ball, and like the girl in the song danced all night. I saw Chekhov and Shakespeare at the Playhouse and the New Theatre. (Christopher Fry's first plays were being performed at that time.) And I saw a wonderful OUDS (Oxford University Dramatic Society) production which was performed in a college garden and featured Kenneth Tynan, Oxford's latest dandy. I cannot remember the play, partly because it was always difficult to distinguish Ken Tynan on stage from Ken Tynan in everyday life.

I might have had a more glittering Oxford career, but I had little money to spare and would have been hard put to make ends meet if it had not been for a number of modest grants secured for me from the college at the instance of my ever-helpful tutor, the chemist Dorothy Hodgkin. I was also assisted by some educational trusts. I might have been able to supplement my income further from such sources if I had been prepared to give an undertaking to go into teaching. But I knew I had no such calling; and I did and do believe that good teachers need a vocation which most people just do not have. In fact, I did teach science for one vacation at a school in Grantham in the summer of 1944: this earned the money for that luxury in Grantham but near-necessity in Oxford – a bicycle. It was while I was teaching there that Paris was liberated. The headmaster called the school together, announced that Paris was free again and told us how the brave Resistance fighters had helped the Allies by rising up against the German occupiers.

It was a thrilling moment. The war was evidently being won; I felt somehow less guilty for not being able to play a larger part; and I shared the joy of the British people that the French Resistance had restored French honour and pride. We may have had an exaggerated view in those days of the universality of resistance – we told each other stories of how the customers of a café would tap out 'V for Victory' in morse code on their glasses when a German soldier entered the café – but we had no doubt that every true Frenchman wanted to be free.

I threw myself into intensely hard work. In Dorothy Hodgkin the college was fortunate to have a brilliant scientist and a gifted teacher, working in the comparatively new field of X-ray crystallography. Mrs Hodgkin was a Fellow of the Royal Society and later made a decisive contribution towards discovering the structure of penicillin, the first antibiotic – work for which she won the Nobel Prize in 1964. (Penicillin itself had been discovered and given its first trials in the Radcliffe Infirmary, which stands just beside Somerville, two years before I went up to Oxford.) In my fourth and final year (1946–47) I worked with a refugee German scientist, Gerhard Schmidt, under Dorothy Hodgkin's direction, on the simple protein Gramicidin B as the research project required to complete Part II of my chemistry course. Through the Cosmos Club and the Scientific Club I also came across other budding young scientists and heard many well-known scientists speak, including J.D. Bernal. His politics were very left wing, as indeed were those of many other scientists at that time. But they would never have dreamt of carrying their politics over into their professional relationships with their students.

Religion also figured large in my Oxford life. There are many tales of young people entering university and, partly through coming into contact with scepticism and partly for less wholesome reasons, losing their faith. I never felt in any danger of that. Methodism provided me with an anchor of stability and, of course, contacts and friends who looked at the world as I did. I usually attended the Wesley Memorial Church on Sundays. There was, as in Grantham, a warmth and a sober but cheerful social life which I found all the more valuable in my initially somewhat strange surroundings. The church had a very vigorous Students'

Fellowship. After Sunday Evening Service there was usually a large gathering over coffee in the minister's house, where there would be stimulating discussion of religious and other matters. Occasionally I would go to the University Church of St Mary the Virgin to listen to a particularly interesting university sermon – though that church has about it a certain 'official' formality which makes it a somewhat cold place of worship. Sometimes I would go to the college chapel, especially when I knew that Miss Helen Darbishire, who was Principal and a distinguished scholar of Milton and Wordsworth when I first went up to Somerville, was preaching.

Generally speaking, though, I did not go to Anglican churches. But oddly enough – or perhaps not so oddly when one considers the great impact he had on so many of my generation – it was the religious writing of that High Anglican C.S. Lewis which had most impact upon my intellectual religious formation. The power of his broadcasts, sermons and essays came from a combination of simple language with theological depth. Who has ever portrayed more wittily and convincingly the way in which Evil works on our human weaknesses than he did in *The Screwtape Letters*? Who has ever made more accessible the profound concepts of Natural Law than he did in *The Abolition of Man* and in the opening passages of *Mere Christianity*? I remember most clearly the impact on me of *Christian Behaviour* (republished in *Mere Christianity*, but originally appearing as radio talks). This went to the heart of the appalling disparity between the way in which we Christians behave and the ideals we profess. One of C.S. Lewis's messages was that the standards of Christianity are not just binding on the saints. As he put it:

Perfect behaviour may be as unattainable as perfect gear-changing when we drive; but it is a necessary ideal prescribed for all men by the very nature of the human machine just as perfect gear-changing is an ideal prescribed for all drivers by the very nature of cars.

Similarly, I was helped by what he wrote of the application of that sublime principle of Christian charity which seems to most of us so impossible of fulfilment. Lewis did not for a moment contest or diminish the sublimeness; but he very helpfully set out what charity is *not*.

> ... what [does] loving your neighbour as yourself [mean?] I have to love him as I love myself. Well, how exactly do I love myself? Now that I come to think of it, I have not exactly got a feeling of fondness or affection for myself, and I do not even always enjoy my own society. So apparently 'Love your neighbour' does not mean 'feel fond of him' or 'find him attractive' ... I can look at some of the things I have done with horror and loathing. So apparently I am allowed to loathe and hate some of the things my enemies do ... Consequently, Christianity does not want us to reduce by one atom the hatred we feel for cruelty and treachery ... Even while we kill and punish we must try to feel about the enemy as we feel about ourselves – to wish that he were not bad, to hope that he may, in this world or another be cured: in fact, to wish his good.

Such words had a special poignancy, of course, at this time.

The main contribution one can make as a student to one's country in peace or wartime is to study hard and effectively, not to daydream about what else one might be doing. But we all also tried to do something more directly. For my part, I would serve one or two evenings a week at the Forces canteen in Carfax. British soldiers and American airmen from the nearby bases at Upper Heyford were among our main customers. It was hot, sticky and very hard on the feet. But the work was also good fun, with plenty of company and wisecracking humour.

Reports of the D-day landings in July 1944, though, brought both apprehension and anxiety. The deadly struggle on those exposed beaches, carried on by so many of about my own age, made us deeply uneasy. For perhaps the only time I wondered whether I was right to be at Oxford.

In fact we were now within a year of the end of the war in Europe. There were still the battle of the Bulge and the tragedy of Arnhem to come. But slowly the emphasis came to be on preparing for peace. And among the peacetime activities which began to take an increasing amount of my time was politics.

Almost as soon as I came up to Oxford I had joined the Oxford University Conservative Association (OUCA), which was founded in the 1920s under the inspiration of a don at Christ Church – Keith Feiling, the historian of the Tory Party and later biographer of Neville Chamberlain. Although the national agreement to suspend party political electoral contests for the duration of the war had no direct implications for politics at the universities, in practice political life in Oxford was a good deal quieter than it had been in the 1930s. But, for all that, OUCA activities quickly became a focus for my life. In those days the Oxford Union, in which star speakers would come to debate issues of the highest importance as well as ones of unbelievable triviality, did not admit women to its membership, though I used sometimes to listen to debates. But I would never have excelled in the kind of brilliant, brittle repartee which the Union seemed to encourage. I preferred the more serious forensic style of our discussions in OUCA and of the real hustings. OUCA also provided a further network of acquaintance and often friendship. It was, indeed, an effective forum for matchmaking, as a number of my OUCA colleagues demonstrated.

Oxford politics was a nursery for talent. I made friends in university politics who, as in the novels of Anthony Powell, kept reappearing in my life as the years passed by. Much the closest was Edward Boyle who, though he moved easily in a sophisticated social and political world which I had only glimpsed, shared with me a serious interest in politics. At this time Edward, the wealthy and cultivated son of a Liberal MP, was himself a classical liberal whose views chimed in pretty well with my own provincial middle-class conservatism. Although we were later to diverge politically, we remained dear friends until his tragically early death from cancer.

William Rees-Mogg, whom I knew in my final year, was a distinguished editor of *The Times* from a very early age. I was never as close to William as I was to Edward, but one sensed that there was something formidable behind his somewhat formal exterior and that he was marked out for higher things.

Robin Day was a prominent Liberal. Like Edward he was a

leading light in the Oxford Union, and we later met as lawyers in the same chambers. One sometimes wondered what career would be open to the brilliant wits of the Union, until Robin Day invented a new one by pioneering television interviewing – after which our paths and our swords crossed frequently.

Another star was Tony Benn, at that time still rattling his full complement of syllables as the Hon. Anthony Wedgwood Benn. From start to finish he and I have rarely agreed on anything, but he was always a courteous and effective debater, an English patriot, and as time has made socialism more and more a thing of the past, even a traditional figure. But perhaps we enjoy a sympathy based on our religious roots. When Tony became President of the Union I was invited to a celebration, attended by his father Viscount Stansgate, which, true to Tony's Nonconformist principles, was teetotal.

Kenneth Harris was another leading debater, who along with Edward Boyle and Tony Benn spent several months touring the United States giving demonstration debates. He subsequently had a distinguished career in political journalism. We met again many times, notably when he wrote my biography.

As an officer in OUCA I was naturally taken up with the 1945 general election campaign. In Oxford I was busy campaigning for the city's MP Quintin Hogg until term ended, when I returned to Grantham to work for Squadron Leader Worth in his attempt to dislodge the sitting Independent Member, Denis Kendall.

In retrospect, we should all have known what to expect. By some mysterious but inexorable law, wars always seem to advance state control and those who advocate it. My husband Denis's view, which he explained to me after we were married, was that in the services people from totally different backgrounds mix in an unprecedented way and that the result is an acute twinge of social conscience and a demand for the state to step in and ameliorate social conditions. But, in any case, the Conservatives had done uniformly badly in the limited number of wartime electoral contests, and there was a general tendency for our share of the vote to fall. Nobody paid much attention to opinion polls then: but they too told the same story. As I have noted, the Left were extremely effective after Dunkirk in portraying the Conservatives as exclusively responsible for appeasement, and managed, by skilful sleight of hand, to distance Churchill from the party he led. Nor did people remember that Labour had opposed even the limited rearmament carried out by Baldwin and Chamberlain.

But there were also other influences at work. The command economy required in wartime conditions had habituated many people to an essentially socialist mentality. Within the Armed Forces it was common knowledge that left-wing intellectuals had exerted a powerful influence through the Army Education Corps, which as Nigel Birch observed was 'the only regiment with a general election among its battle honours'. At home, broadcasters like J.B. Priestley gave a comfortable yet idealistic gloss to social progress in a left-wing direction. It is also true that Conservatives, with Churchill in the lead, were so preoccupied with the urgent imperatives of war that much domestic policy, and in particular the drawing-up of the agenda for peace, fell largely to the socialists in the Coalition Government. Churchill himself would have liked to continue the National Government at least until Japan had been beaten and, in the light of the fast-growing threat from the Soviet Union, perhaps beyond then. But the Labour Party had other thoughts and understandably wished to come into its own collectivist inheritance.

In 1945, therefore, we Conservatives found ourselves confronting two serious and, as it turned out, insuperable problems. First, the Labour Party had us fighting on their ground and were always able to outbid us. Churchill had been talking about post-war 'reconstruction' for some two years, and as part of that programme Rab Butler's Education Act was on the Statute Book. Further, our manifesto committed us to the so-called 'full employment' policy of the 1944 Employment White Paper, a massive house-building programme, most of the proposals for National Insurance benefits made by the great Liberal social reformer Lord Beveridge and a comprehensive National Health Service. Moreover, we were not able effectively to take the credit (so far as this was in any case appropriate to the Conservative Party) for victory, let alone to castigate Labour for its irresponsibility and extremism, because Attlee and his colleagues had worked cheek by jowl with the Conservatives in government since 1940. In any event, the war effort had involved the whole population.

I vividly remember sitting in the student common room in Somerville listening to Churchill's famous (or notorious) election broadcast to the effect that socialism would require 'some sort of Gestapo' to enforce it, and thinking, 'He's gone too far.' However logically unassailable the connection between socialism and coercion was, in our present circumstances the line would not be credible. I knew from political argument on similar lines at an election meeting in Oxford what the riposte would be: 'Who's run the country when Mr Churchill's been away? Mr Attlee.' And such, I found, was the reaction now.

Back in Grantham, I was one of the 'warm-up' speakers for the Conservative candidate at village meetings. In those days, many more people turned out to public meetings than today, and they expected their money's worth. I would frequently be speaking at half a dozen meetings an evening. Looking back at the reports in the local newspapers of what I said at the time, there is little with which I would disagree now. Germany must be disarmed and brought to justice. There must be co-operation with America and (somewhat less realistically) with the Soviet Union. The British Empire, the most important community of peoples that the world had ever known, must never be dismembered. (Perhaps not very realistic either – but my view of Britain's imperial future was not uncommon in the aftermath of victory.) The main argument I advanced for voting Conservative was that by doing so we would keep Winston Churchill in charge of our foreign policy. And indeed perhaps if Churchill had been able to see through the July 1945 Potsdam Conference the post-war world might have looked at least a little different.

Like many other members of OUCA, I had received lessons in public speaking from Conservative Central Office's Mrs Stella Gatehouse. Her emphasis was on simplicity and clarity of expression and as little jargon as possible. In fact, at election meetings, when you never knew how long you would have to speak before the candidate arrived, a touch more long-windedness would have been very useful. Most valuable of all for me personally, however, was the experience of having to think on my feet when answering questions from a good-humoured but critical audience. I recall a point made by an elderly man at one such meeting that had a lasting effect on my views about welfare: 'Just because I've saved a little bit of money of my own, "Assistance" won't help me. If I'd spent everything, they would.' It was an early warning of the hard choices that the new Welfare State would shortly place before politicians.

Three weeks after polling day, by which time the overseas and service votes had been returned, I went to the election count at Sleaford. As we waited for the Grantham result, news trickled in of what was happening elsewhere. It was bad, and it became worse – a Labour landslide with Tory Cabinet ministers falling one after the other. Then our own candidate lost too. I was shocked and upset. I returned to Grantham to see more results coming through on the screen at the Picture House cinema. The prospect did not improve. I simply could not understand how the electorate could do this to Churchill. On my way back home I met a friend, someone who I had always thought was a staunch Conservative, and said how shocked I was by the terrible news. He was not shocked at all. In fact, he said he thought the news was rather good. Incomprehension deepened. At the time I felt that the British electorate's treatment of the man who more than anyone else secured their liberty was shameful. But was it not Edmund Burke who said: 'A perfect democracy is the most shameless thing in the world'? In retrospect, the election of the 1945–51 Labour Government seems the logical fulfilment of the collectivist spirit that came to dominate wartime Britain. It was to be about thirty-five years before this collectivism would run its course – shaping and distorting British society in the process, before it collapsed in 1979's Winter of Discontent.

At the time, it was clear to everyone that fundamental reassessment of Conservative principles and policies was required. We felt this as much in Oxford as anywhere else. It lay behind the preparation of a report of the OUCA Policy Sub-Committee which I co-authored in Michaelmas term 1945 with Michael Kinchin-Smith and Stanley Moss. The report contained no more profound insights than any other Tory undergraduate paper. And its two themes we have heard many times since – more policy research and better presentation.

There may have been some merit in this recommendation.

Perhaps the main problem as regards what we would now call the 'image' of the Conservative Party was that we seemed to have lost our way and, to the extent that our policies did have coherence, they seemed to be devised for the wealthy rather than for ordinary people. As our OUCA paper put it: 'Conservative policy has come to mean in the eyes of the public little more than a series of administrative solutions to particular problems, correlated in certain fields by a few unreasoning prejudices and the selfish interests of the moneyed classes.' The accusation was, of course, unfair. If the Conservatives had won in 1945 we would still have had a Welfare State – doubtless with less immediate public expenditure and certainly with greater scope for private and voluntary initiative. But the idea that Conservatism was simply that – conserving the interests of the status quo against change and reform – was immensely powerful at this time.

In March 1946 I became Treasurer of OUCA and later that month went as one of the Oxford representatives to the Federation of University Conservative and Unionist Associations (FUCUA) Conference at the Waldorf Hotel in London. It was my first such conference and I enjoyed it hugely. When I spoke it was in support of more involvement by people from working-class backgrounds in university Conservative politics. I felt that we had to get away from the perception of Conservatism as both stuffy and frivolous. It was not so much that I wanted a classless society, as the socialists (somewhat disingenuously) said they did, but rather that I could not see that class was important. Everyone had something unique to offer in life and their responsibility was to develop those gifts – and heroes come from all backgrounds. As I put it to the FUCUA Conference: 'We have heard all about this being the age of the common man – but do not forget the need for the uncommon man.' Or, I suppose I might have added, 'woman'.

In October 1946 I was elected President of OUCA – the third woman to hold the position. I had done my final exams that summer and was now beginning the research project which constituted the fourth and last year of the Chemistry degree, so I had a little more time to spend on politics. For example, I attended my first Conservative Party Conference, held that year in Blackpool. I was immediately entranced. So often in Grantham and in Oxford it had felt unusual to be a Conservative. Now suddenly I was with hundreds of other people who believed as I did and who shared my insatiable appetite for talking politics.

The Conference had a most extraordinary atmosphere. From my humble position as a 'representative', I had the sense that the Party leadership – with the notable exception of the Party Leader – had arrived at Blackpool prepared to reconcile itself and Conservatism to the permanence of socialism in Britain. A perceptive observer of the 1946 Conference, Bertrand de Jouvenal, wrote of our Front Bench: 'These great, intelligent thoroughbreds, trained from their earliest years to prudent administration and courteous debate, were in their hearts not far from accepting as definitive their electoral defeat in 1945.'* This was decidedly not what the rank and file wanted to hear. Indeed, there was open dissent from the floor. A request on the first day for a general debate on questions of philosophy and policy was refused by the chairman. There was a lukewarm reaction to the consensus approach of speeches from the platform, though these became notably tougher the longer the Conference went on, as Shadow ministers perceived our discontent. My instincts were with the rank and file, though I had not yet fully digested the strong intellectual case against collectivism, as I was to do in the next few years.

Back in Oxford I had organized a very full programme of speakers. Lord Dunglass (Alec Douglas-Home) urged support for Ernest Bevin's foreign policy – support we readily gave. Bob Boothby – a wonderful speaker, with great style – declaimed against the 'revolutionary totalitarian absolutism of Moscow'. David Maxwell-Fyfe, whose daughter Pamela was at Oxford at the time, attacked nationalization and urged a property-owning democracy. Peter Thorneycroft put forward what seemed the very advanced views of the 'Tory Reform' wing in a debate with the University Labour Club at the Union. Lady (Mimi) Davidson told us how it felt to be the only Conservative woman Member of the House of Commons. Anthony Eden charmed and impressed us all over sherry. Each term we had a lively debate with the other political

* *Problems of Socialist England* (1947).

clubs at the Oxford Union, particularly the Labour Club, which at the time was very left wing and included some famous names like Anthony Crosland – who even in those days could condescend to a Duchess – and Tony Benn. Generally, however, OUCA met in the Taylorian Institute on a Friday evening, entertaining the speaker to dinner beforehand at the Randolph Hotel. So it was there that I first rubbed shoulders with the great figures of the Tory Party – and, in fact, I kept in touch with many of them over the years.

Such activity, though, was insignificant as regards the overall position of the Conservative Party nationally. Looking back, one can see that there were two alternative strategies for the Party to have followed. Either it could have accommodated the collectivism of the times, though seeking to lessen its impact where possible, trying to slow down the leftward march through our institutions and to retain some scope for individual choice and free enterprise. Or it could have fought collectivism root and branch, seeking to persuade national opinion that 1945 represented a wrong turning from the country's destined path. In fact, it sought to do both. Voices were raised in favour of a radical onslaught against collectivism, but in opposition the predominant view was that pragmatism represented the best path back to government.

The Party document which came nearest to embodying the pragmatic approach was *The Industrial Charter*, which appeared in May 1947. In a sense, it was no new departure: indeed, continuity and consensus were its underlying themes. Just as the wartime 1944 Employment Policy White Paper represented a compromise with Keynesianism – combining the emphasis on counter-cyclical public spending to sustain demand and employment with more orthodox observations about efficiency, competitiveness and mobility – so *The Industrial Charter* represented a compromise between corporatism and free enterprise. *The Industrial Charter* defended economic planning, industrial 'partnership' and workers' 'consultation'; but it continued to emphasize the need for fewer controls, fewer civil servants and modestly lower taxation. And this tension continued in the Conservative Party throughout the 1950s and sixties. *The Industrial Charter* gave us all something to say, and it kept the Party united. But such documents hardly made the pulse beat faster. Nor were they important in returning the Party to power. It was, in fact, the economic failures of the Labour Government – in particular the February 1947 fuel crisis and the devaluation of sterling in 1949 – rather than Conservative Party initiatives which turned the political tide in our favour.

Documents like *The Industrial Charter* gingerly avoided the real battleground on which socialism ultimately had to be defeated. In the end, Churchill was right. Whether socialism needed a 'Gestapo' as it did in Eastern Europe and the Soviet Union, or just those banal and bureaucratic instruments of coercion, confiscatory taxation, nationalization and oppressive regulation employed in the West, ultimately depended only on the degree of socialism desired. In diminishing economic freedom, the socialists had embarked on a course which, if pursued to its ultimate destination, would mean the extinction of all freedom. I had no doubt myself about the truth of this proposition. But for some Tories it was always a difficult argument to take. The traditional economic liberalism which constituted so important a part of my political make-up – and which Edmund Burke himself embraced – was often alien and uncongenial to Conservatives from a more elevated social background. It was, after all, none other than Harold Macmillan who in 1938 proposed in his influential book *The Middle Way* to extend state control and planning over a wide range of production and services. Other Conservatives were inhospitable to theory of any kind. They took J.S. Mill's appellation 'the stupid party' as a compliment. Not surprisingly, therefore, the most powerful critique of socialist planning and the socialist state which I read at this time, and to which I have returned so often since, F.A. Hayek's *The Road to Serfdom*, is dedicated famously 'To the socialists of all parties'.

I cannot claim that I fully grasped the implications of Hayek's little masterpiece at this time. It was only in the mid-1970s, when Hayek's works were right at the top of the reading list given me by Keith Joseph, that I really came to grips with the ideas he put forward. Only then did I consider his arguments from the point of view of the kind of state Conservatives find congenial – a limited government under a rule of law – rather than from the point of view of the kind of state we must avoid – a socialist state where bureaucrats rule by discretion. At this stage it was the (to my mind) unanswerable criticisms of socialism in *The Road to Serfdom* which had an impact. Hayek saw that Nazism – national socialism – had its roots in nineteenth-century German social planning. He showed that intervention by the state in one area of the economy or society gave rise to almost irresistible pressures to extend planning further into other sectors. He alerted us to the profound, indeed revolutionary, implications of state planning for Western civilization as it had grown up over the centuries.

Nor did Hayek mince his words about the monopolistic tendencies of the planned society which professional groups and trade unions would inevitably seek to exploit. Each demand for security, whether of employment, income or social position, implied the exclusion from such benefits of those outside the particular privileged group – and would generate demands for countervailing privileges from the excluded groups. Eventually, in such a situation everyone will lose. Perhaps because he did not come from a British Conservative background and did not in fact ever consider himself a Conservative at all, Hayek had none of the inhibitions which characterized the agonized social conscience of the English upper classes when it came to speaking bluntly about such things.

Hayek was unusual and unpopular, but he was not quite alone in root and branch criticism of socialism. I also read at this time and later the polemical journalist Colm Brogan's writings. Where Hayek deployed philosophy, Brogan relied on withering irony and mordant wit. In 1943 in *Who Are 'The People'?* Brogan wrote the unthinkable – namely that it was precisely the 'progressive' Left which had created the circumstances for Hitler's rise to power and been most thoroughly duped by him. The progressives did not by and large come from, and had little real claim to represent, the 'working class'. They applied the most blatant and culpable double standards when it came to the Soviet Union. The real interest which they represented was that of a burgeoning bureaucracy determined to exploit every opportunity to increase its numbers and enlarge its power. In *Our New Masters*, which appeared in 1947, Brogan widened his attack on socialism. He refused to see the 1945 election result as anything other than a collective loss of common sense.

> [The people] have been deceived, most certainly, but they wanted to be deceived . . . they have voted against that modest expectation in life which is all that a sober public man can ever strive for. They have voted to eat their cake and have it, to save it for a rainy day and to give it away. They have voted for high wages and low production and a world of plenty. They have voted like the courtiers of King Canute who planted his seat before the encroaching waves and commanded them to retire by authority of the royal and unimpeachable will. The people are able to fill the seat with the sovereign of their own choosing. Nobody denies their right. But the tide keeps coming in.

Brogan therefore saw the disillusionment with Labour, which was already manifest at the time he wrote, as being the socialists' inevitable nemesis for raising so wildly expectations which no one – let alone they with the wrong policy prescriptions – could fulfil. As Brogan said in a classic attack: 'Wherever Sir Stafford Cripps has tried to increase wealth and happiness, grass never grows again.'

But Brogan also saw socialism as a force for disorder and disintegration, a kind of poison threatening to corrupt the whole body politic, and the Labour Party as 'a feeble and querulous thing, equally unfit to govern because of the intemperance of its mind and the childish unreality of its view of life'. They were sentiments which many of us felt, but which it generally seemed imprudent to express with quite such vigour.

The tension between these two possible approaches to resisting collectivism – gradualist and radical – would be played out throughout my time in active Conservative politics. But the specific issues which meant most to me in these early post-war years concerned foreign rather than domestic affairs.

I was in Blackpool visiting my sister (who had gone there from the Birmingham Orthopaedic Hospital) when I learned from the radio news on that fateful 6 August 1945 that an atomic bomb had been dropped on Hiroshima. It had been known for some time that we were on the eve of a breakthrough in the technology of weapons of mass destruction. My own academic study and the fascination exerted on me by issues relating to the practical application of science probably meant that I was better informed than most about the developments lying behind the manufacture of the atomic bomb. The following year I was able to read (and largely understand) the very full account contained in *Atomic Energy for Military Purposes* published by the United States. Yet – cliché as it may be – I was immediately aware on hearing the preliminary reports of Hiroshima that with the advent of the A-bomb 'somehow the world had changed'. Or as Churchill himself would put it in his majestic memoirs *The Second World War*: 'Here then was a speedy end to the Second World War, and perhaps to much else besides.'

The full scientific, strategic and political implications of the nuclear weapon would take some years to assess; moreover, like the science involved, they would continue to change and develop. But the direct human and environmental consequences of the use of atomic weapons were more quickly grasped. In the winter of 1946 I read the American journalist John Hersey's report on Hiroshima, first submitted to the *New Yorker* and subsequently published as a Penguin Special. Oddly enough, even more affecting than the accounts of the hideous injuries, the fire, the fall-out and the radiation sickness was the bitter-sweet image of weeds and wild flowers sprouting through the ashes – their growth unnaturally stimulated by radiation from the bomb.

Yet neither on that first evening reflecting on the matter in the train home from Blackpool, nor later when I read accounts and saw the pictures of the overwhelming devastation, did I have any doubt about the rightness of the decision to use the bomb. I considered it justified primarily because it would avoid the losses inevitable if Allied forces were to take by assault the main islands of Japan. The Japanese still had 2½ million men under arms. We had already seen the fanatical resistance which they had put up during the Battle of Okinawa. Only the scale of the Allies' technological military superiority, demonstrated first at Hiroshima and then at Nagasaki, could persuade the Japanese leadership that resistance was hopeless. And so one week after Hiroshima, and after a second bomb had been dropped on Nagasaki, the Japanese surrendered.

Britain had, of course, been closely involved in the development of the bomb, though because of the breakdown of Anglo-American nuclear co-operation after the war it was not till 1952 that we ourselves were able to explode one. Churchill and Truman, as we now know, were duped by Stalin at Potsdam when the American President 'broke the news' of the bomb to the Soviet leader, who knew about it already and promptly returned to Moscow to urge his own scientists to speed up their atomic programme. But the fact remains, as I used to remind the Soviets when I became Prime Minister, that the most persuasive proof of the essential benevolence of the United States was that in those few crucial years when it alone possessed the military means to enforce its will upon the world, it refrained from doing so.

If the atomic bomb raised one set of questions about Britain's role in the post-war world, the situation in India raised another. The subject retained its fascination for me. I knew that Churchill, for whom my admiration by now knew no bounds, had fought ferociously against the moves to appease nationalist opinion in India, which had been implemented in the Government of India Act of 1935. The situation in India had deteriorated sharply in the war years and it seemed highly unlikely that even the earlier prospect of Dominion status would seriously lessen the pressure for independence. This was, moreover, against the background, which we did not yet all fully understand, of a much less significant world role for Britain after the war. The two material circumstances which had allowed us to fight Hitler all but alone – the existence of huge accumulated overseas investments and the most successful and extensive empire the world had seen – had been lost or greatly diminished as the price of victory in that great struggle.

For all that, people of my age – even those committed to the links with Empire developing into a Commonwealth – took a more positive view of what was happening in India than did many of our elders. I myself read at about this time two books which emphasized the role of Britain, not just as guarantor of sound administration and humane justice in our Imperial territories, but rather as a kind of midwife for their birth, growth and maturity as responsible members of the international community. Leo Amery's *Thoughts on the Constitution* (lectures delivered at Oxford) emphasized the crucial need to ensure Imperial 'unity of thought and purpose' through free co-operation: such thinking also, for a time at least, attracted me towards ideas of Imperial Preference as a means of sustaining our community of interest. I also read Lord Elton's *Imperial Commonwealth* which saw our evolving Empire as an example of unity and co-operation:

> To have spread organized political freedom across the world; three times to have saved Europe, and twice the world as well, from a tyrant; to have ended slavery, and taught other nations to end it too; to have been so reluctant to acquire territory, and so often to have acquired it in the interests of others; to have learned wisdom from adversity and to have held a giant's power without using it like a giant . . . all this has richly earned the Empire survival hitherto, and has given it abundant titles to the gratitude of mankind . . . And it may well be that the island from which the world learned the art of freedom will yet teach it the art of unity. It may well be that her present sufferings have finally fitted Britain for that role.

In retrospect, much of this was self-deception. We could not both give independence to the colonies and continue to determine their future afterwards. At that time, however, such ideas seemed to promise a continued world role for Britain, without either the burden or the guilt of empire.

Between the spring 1946 mission of Stafford Cripps to India to seek agreement among Indians on the future of their country and the summer of 1947, when the Government finally endorsed a settlement based on partition, I followed events closely. I felt that there was much to criticize in the means, but that the ends of our policy were right and in the direction of progress for Britain, India and the wider Commonwealth. But the Labour Government and Mountbatten as Viceroy undoubtedly tried to move too fast. In a tragic sense the civil war which now broke out, in which a million people died, showed the degree to which British rule had been the guarantee of Indian unity and peace.

These thoughts, however, seemed out of place in a post-war world in which the new global institutions were the UN, the IMF and the World Bank, and in which the European colonial empires had a very limited future. Indeed, we have still not achieved a full and successful transition from a stable colonial to a stable post-colonial world. As crises like Somalia demonstrate, there are parts of Africa and Asia where order cannot be provided locally, but for which the international institutions have no remedy – certainly no remedy as effective as colonial rule was a century ago.

But the greatest transformation affecting Britain at the time – and the one which would have a great impact on my political life – was the change of the Soviet Union from comrade in arms to deadly enemy. It is important to stress how little understanding most people in the West had at this time of conditions within the USSR. True, many of the facts were available if anyone had cared to investigate and report them. But by and large and for a variety of reasons they did not. As I have described, I was never tempted to sympathize with communism. But my opposition to it was at this time more visceral than intellectual. It was much later that I thought and read more deeply about the communist system and saw precisely where its weaknesses and wickednesses lay. And it is interesting to note that when Hayek came to write a new preface to *The Road to Serfdom* in 1976 he too felt that he had 'under-stressed the significance of the experience of communism in Russia'.

So too, by and large, did the newspapers. For example, the *Daily Telegraph* gave little prominence to Stalin's purges of the 1930s, and even after the Molotov–Ribbentrop pact in August 1939 oddly interpreted the Russian invasion of eastern Poland as a sign of 'tension' with Hitler. In wartime, Anglo-Soviet friendship societies bloomed. Smiling, soft-hearted Uncle Joe, the creation as much of Western wishful thinking as of Soviet propaganda, concealed the reality of the paranoid tyrant. Douglas Hyde's *I Believed* (which appeared in 1950, and which I read) reveals the extent to which British communists infiltrated, manipulated and distorted so as subtly to shape political debate. Hyde's account shows too how the war of disinformation in Britain was as ruthlessly and directly controlled from Moscow as were the communist movements which worked in Eastern Europe alongside the advancing Red Army to impose Stalin's grip on countries whose liberties we had fought the war against Hitler to defend.

A strong case can be made to mitigate Churchill's and Britain's role in the abandonment of Central and Eastern Europe. The famous half sheet of paper on which Churchill scribbled his proposals for shared spheres of influence in the Balkans when he met Stalin in Moscow in October 1944 does indeed have a whiff of cynical *realpolitik* about it, as Churchill himself accepted when he described it as a 'naughty document'. It clearly flies in the face of the proclaimed principles of the 1941 Atlantic Charter. But it recognized the reality that the Red Army had occupied a large part of Eastern Europe – and it may have helped to preserve Greek independence. Churchill at least saw, as the Americans did not, that the precipitate withdrawal of our troops in the face of the Red Army would leave the central zone of Germany in Soviet hands and effectively remove any chance at all of our being able to influence the fate of Eastern Europe.

That said, there is a difference between recognizing reality and legitimizing it. For legitimacy tends to set injustice in concrete. So the Conservatives who abstained or voted against the Government on the issue of the Yalta Agreement of February 1945 – among them Alec Douglas-Home – were right. My own unease was transformed into opposition on hearing a powerful speech by Lord De L'Isle and Dudley to OUCA in the Taylorian. It would certainly have been difficult, and perhaps impossible, to force the Soviets to respect democracy and the right of national self-determination in the countries which they now occupied. It was understandable that weary and wounded American and British forces wanted to put the horrors of war behind them and not to risk some new conflict with their former ally. But to set a seal of approval on agreements which we knew in our hearts would not be honoured – let alone to try to force the exiled non-communist government of Poland to accept them – was wrong.

Yalta made me begin to think hard about the military aspect of the communist threat. Little by little, I was also piecing together in my own mind other features of the reality of communism. For example, I read Arthur Koestler's *Darkness at Noon* with its poignant account of a communist show trial. Unlike Valtin's description of Gestapo brutality, Koestler's book allowed me for the first time to get inside, as it were, the mentality of the communist. Even more subtly, it showed that through the eyes of the communist *himself* the communist system makes no sense. Koestler's character, Rubashov, reflects:

> The Party denied the free will of the individual – and at the same time it exacted his willing self-sacrifice. It denied his capacity to choose between two alternatives – and at the same time it demanded that he should constantly choose the right one. It denied his power to distinguish good and evil – and at the same time it spoke pathetically of guilt and treachery. The individual stood under the sign of economic fatality, a wheel in a clockwork which had been wound up for all eternity and could not be stopped or influenced – and the Party demanded that the wheel should revolt against the clockwork and change its course. There was somewhere an error in the calculation; the equation did not work out.

Years later, when as Leader of the Opposition I met Koestler, I said how powerful I had found his book. I asked him how he had been able to imagine Rubashov and his tormentors. He told me no imagination was required. They were real.

As with the whole question of the atomic bomb, so with the (alleged) theoretical basis of Marxism: the fact that I was a scientist gave me a somewhat different insight into some of the arguments. It was in fact after I left university that I read Karl Popper's *The Open Society and its Enemies*. Popper, whose analysis in many ways complemented that of Hayek, approached Marxism from the point of view of the philosopher of the natural sciences. This meant that he was ideally equipped to expose the fraudulent claim of Marxists to have discovered immutable laws of history, social development or 'progress' – laws which were comparable to the laws of natural science. It was not just that the 'inevitable' course of events which Marx had prophesied had not occurred and showed no signs of occurring. Marx and Marxists had not even understood the scientific method, let alone practised it in their analysis. Unlike the

Marxists – whether historians, economists or social scientists – who tried to 'prove' their theories by accumulating more and more facts to sustain them, 'the method of science is rather to look out for facts which may refute the theory . . . and the fact that all tests of the theory are attempted falsifications of predictions derived with its help furnishes the clue to scientific method'. The political consequences of this basic error – perhaps more properly described as basic fraud – were summed up by Popper in the dedication of his later book, *The Poverty of Historicism*: 'In memory of the countless men, women and children of all creeds or nations or races who fell victims to the fascist and communist belief in Inexorable Laws of Historical Destiny.'

With such a background of reading, it is therefore easy to imagine how I reacted to Churchill's speech of 5 March 1946 in Fulton, Missouri. It is, of course, rightly famous for its powerful warning that 'from Stettin in the Baltic to Trieste in the Adriatic an iron curtain has descended across the Continent', and that in these Russian-dominated states 'police governments' were prevailing. But no less significant in my eyes was Churchill's evocation of the special relationship between Britain and the United States, and of the idealistic 'message of the British and American peoples to mankind' which lay behind it. The ideas of liberty found their fullest development in the political traditions and institutions of our two countries. The speech is now rightly seen as extraordinarily prescient. But at the time it was bitterly criticized as warmongering hyperbole by commentators on both sides of the Atlantic. It would not be long, however, before their tone started to change, as Soviet intentions in Eastern Europe and Greece became unmistakably clear.

By the time I left Oxford with a second-class degree in Chemistry under my belt, I knew a great deal more about the world and particularly about the world of politics. My character had not changed; nor had my beliefs. But I had a clearer idea of where I stood in relation to other people, their ambitions and opinions. I had, in short, grown up. And, by that mysterious process which leads people to every kind of prominent or obscure vocation, I had discovered what I really wanted to do with my life.

Shortly before my university days came to an end I went back to Corby Glen, a village some ten miles from Grantham, to a dance. Afterwards a few of us gathered for coffee and a sandwich in the kitchen of the house where I was staying. Not unusually, I was talking about politics. Something I said, or perhaps the way I said it, prompted one of the men to remark: 'What you really want to do is to be an MP, isn't it?' Almost without thinking I said: 'Yes: that really *is* what I want to do.' I had never said it before – not even to myself. When I went to bed that night I found that I had a lot on my mind.

CHAPTER III

House Bound

Marriage, Family, Law and Politics 1947–1959

MY POLITICAL APPRENTICESHIP

If going up to Oxford is one sort of shock, coming down is quite another. I had made many like-minded friends at Oxford, I had enjoyed my adventures in chemistry and I was passionately interested in university politics. It was a wrench to leave all that behind.

The newly created Oxford University Appointments Committee, which helped new graduates to find suitable jobs, arranged several interviews for me, including one at a Northern ICI plant, I think at Billingham. We hopefuls were interviewed by several managers whose written comments were passed on to the general manager, who gave us our final interview. The remarks on me were lying on the table at the interview, and I could not resist using my faculty for reading upside down. They were both encouraging and discouraging; one manager had written: 'This young woman has much too strong a personality to work here.' In fact, I had three or four interviews with other companies and, though I was unsuccessful, I enjoyed them all. Not only was I given entry to a new world of industry, but the interviewers in those days were invariably courteous and interested in one's own hopes and ambitions. Eventually I was taken on by BX Plastics at Manningtree just outside Colchester to work in their research and development section. BX produced a full range of plastics both for industrial use and consumer use, including for films.

Very few people greatly enjoy the early stages of a new job, and in this I was no exception. It had been understood when we originally discussed the position that it would involve my being in effect Personal Assistant to the Research and Development Director. I had been looking forward to this because I thought it would allow me to get to know more of how the company as a whole operated and also to use the talents I had, over and above my knowledge of chemistry. But on my arrival it was decided that there was not enough to do in that capacity and so I found myself donning my white coat again and immersing myself in the wonderful world of plastics. The Research and Development Section had only just been created as a separate unit and its teething troubles compounded mine. But by the time Christmas 1947 was approaching I had made one or two friends and things became easier. My supervisor helped me along. The Section moved into a separate and rather pleasant house in nearby Lawford. Like many others at the company, I lived in Colchester – a town which I increasingly came to like and where I had found comfortable lodgings. A bus took us all out to Lawford every day.

And, as always with me, there was politics. I immediately joined the Conservative Association and threw myself into the usual round of Party activities. In particular, I thoroughly enjoyed what was called the ''39-'45' discussion group, where Conservatives of the war generation met to exchange views and argue about the political topics of the day. I also kept in touch, in so far as I could, with friends like Edward Boyle, who was later adopted for a Birmingham seat in the 1950 election. It was as a representative of the Oxford University Graduate Conservative Association (OUGCA) that I went to the Llandudno Conservative Party Conference in October 1948.

It had originally been intended that I should speak at the Conference, seconding an OUGCA motion deploring the abolition of university seats. At that time universities had separate representation in Parliament, and graduates had the right to vote in their universities as well as in the constituency where they lived. (I supported separate university representation, but not the principle that graduates should have more than one vote; my view was that graduates should be able to choose to vote in one or the other constituency.) It would have been my first Conference speech, but in the end the seconder chosen was a City man, because the City seats were also to be abolished.

My disappointment at this was, however, very quickly overcome and in a most unexpected way. After one of the debates, I found myself engaged in one of those speculative conversations which young people have about their future prospects. An Oxford friend, John Grant, said he supposed that one day I would like to be a Member of Parliament. 'Well, yes,' I replied, 'but there's not much hope of that. The chances of my being selected are just nil at the moment.' I might have added that with no private income of my own there was no way I could have afforded to be an MP on the salary then available. I had not even tried to get on the Party's list of approved candidates.

Later in the day, John Grant happened to be sitting next to the Chairman of the Dartford Conservative Association, John Miller. The Association was in search of a candidate. I learned afterwards that the conversation went something like this: 'I understand that you're still looking for a candidate at Dartford?' (In fact, Conservative Central Office was becoming exasperated at Dartford's failure to pick someone to fight the seat in an election that had to take place in 1950 and might be called before then.)

'That's right. Any suggestions?'

'Well, there's a young woman, Margaret Roberts, that you might look at. She's very good.'

'Oh, but Dartford is a real industrial stronghold. I don't think a woman would do at all.'

'Well, you know best of course. But why not just look at her?'

And they did. I was invited to have lunch with John Miller and his wife, Phee, and the Dartford Women's Chairman, Mrs Fletcher, on the Saturday on Llandudno Pier. Presumably, and in spite of any reservations about the suitability of a woman candidate for their seat, they liked what they saw. I certainly got on well with them. The Millers were to become close friends and I quickly developed a healthy respect for the dignified Mrs Fletcher. After lunch we walked back along the pier to the Conference Hall in good time for a place to hear Winston Churchill give the Party Leader's speech. It was the first we had seen of him that week, because in those days the Leader did not attend the Conference itself, appearing only at a final rally on the Saturday. Foreign affairs naturally dominated his speech – it was the time of the Berlin blockade and the Western airlift – and his message was sombre, telling us that only American nuclear weapons stood between Europe and communist tyranny and warning of 'what seems a remorselessly approaching third world war'.

I did not hear from Dartford until December, when I was asked to attend an interview at Palace Chambers, Bridge Street – then housing Conservative Central Office – not far from Parliament itself. With a large number of other hopefuls I turned up on the evening of Thursday 30 December for my first Selection Committee. Very few outside the political arena know just how nerve-racking such occasions are. The interviewee who is not nervous and tense is very likely to perform badly: for, as any chemist will tell you, the adrenaline needs to flow if one is to perform at one's best. I was lucky in that at Dartford there were some friendly faces around the table, and it has to be said that on such occasions there are advantages as well as disadvantages to being a young woman making her way in the political world.

I found myself short-listed, and was asked to go to Dartford itself for a further interview. Finally, I was invited to the Bull Hotel in Dartford on Monday 31 January 1949 to address the Association's Executive Committee of about fifty people. As one of five would-be candidates, I had to give a fifteen-minute speech and answer questions for a further ten minutes.

It was the questions which were more likely to cause me trouble. There was a good deal of suspicion of women candidates, particularly in what was regarded as a tough industrial seat like Dartford. This was quite definitely a man's world into which not just angels feared to tread. There was, of course, little hope of winning it for the Conservatives, though this is never a point that the prospective candidate even in a Labour seat as safe as Ebbw Vale would be advised to make. The Labour majority was an all but unscalable 20,000. But perhaps this unspoken fact turned to my favour. Why not take the risk of adopting the young Margaret Roberts? There was not much to lose, and some good publicity for the Party to gain.

The most reliable sign that a political occasion has gone well is that you have enjoyed it. I enjoyed that evening at Dartford, and the outcome justified my confidence. I was selected. Afterwards I stayed behind for drinks and something to eat with the officers of the Association. The candidate is not the only one to be overwhelmed by relief on these occasions. The selectors too can stop acting as critics and start to become friends. The happy if still slightly bewildered young candidate is deluged with advice, information and offers of help. Such friendly occasions provide at least part of the answer to that question put to all professional politicians: 'Why on earth do you do it?'

My next step was to be approved by the national Party. Usually Party approval precedes selection, but when I went to Central Office the day after to meet the Women's Chairman, Miss Marjorie Maxse, I had no difficulties. A few weeks afterwards I was invited to dinner to meet the Party Chairman Lord Woolton, his deputy J.P.L. Thomas, Miss Maxse and the Area Agent, Miss Beryl Cook. Over the next few years Marjorie Maxse and Beryl Cook proved to be strong supporters and they gave me much useful advice.

After selection comes adoption. The formal adoption meeting is the first opportunity a candidate has to impress him or herself on the rank and file of the Association. It is therefore a psychologically important occasion. It is also a chance to gain some good local publicity, for the press are invited too. Perhaps what meant most to me, however, was the presence of my father. For the first time he and I stood on the same platform to address a meeting. He recalled how his family had always been Liberal, but that now it was the Conservatives who stood for the old Liberalism. In my own speech I too took up a theme which was Gladstonian in content if not quite style (or length), urging that 'the Government should do what any good housewife would do if money was short – look at their accounts and see what's wrong'.

After the adoption meeting at the end of February I was invited back by two leading lights of the Association, Mr and Mrs Soward, to a supper party they had arranged in my honour. Their house was at the Erith end of the constituency, not far from the factory of the Atlas Preservative Company, which made paint and chemicals, where Stanley Soward was a director. His boss, the Managing

Director, had been at my adoption meeting and was one of the dinner guests: and so it was that I met Denis.

It was clear to me at once that Denis was an exceptional man. He knew at least as much about politics as I did and a good deal more about economics. His professional interest in paint and mine in plastics may seem an unromantic foundation for friendship, but it also enabled us right away to establish a joint interest in science. And as the evening wore on I discovered that his views were no-nonsense Conservatism.

After the evening was over he drove me back to London so that I could catch the midnight train to Colchester. It was not a long drive at that time of night, but long enough to find that we had still more in common. Denis is an avid reader, especially of history, biography and detective novels. He seemed to have read every article in *The Economist* and *The Banker*, and we found that we both enjoyed music – Denis with his love of opera, and me with mine of choral music.

From then on we met from time to time at constituency functions, and began to see more of each other outside the constituency. He had a certain style and dash. He had a penchant for fast cars and drove a Jaguar and, being ten years older, he simply knew more of the world than I did. At first our meetings revolved around political discussion. But as we saw more of each other, we started going to the occasional play and had dinner together. Like any couple, we had our favourite restaurants, small pasta places in Soho for normal dates, the wonderful White Tower in Fitzrovia, the Écu de France in Jermyn Street and The Ivy for special occasions. I was very flattered by Denis's attentions, but I first began to suspect he might be serious when the Christmas after my first election campaign at Dartford I received from him a charming present of a crystal powder bowl with a silver top, which I still treasure.

We might perhaps have got married sooner, but my passion for politics and his for rugby football – Saturdays were never available for a date – both got in the way. He more than made up for this, however, by being an immense help in the constituency – problems were solved in a trice and all the logistics taken care of. Indeed, the fact that he had proposed to me and that we had become engaged was one final inadvertent political service, because unbeknown to me Beryl Cook leaked the news just before election day to give my campaign a final boost.

When Denis asked me to be his wife, I thought long and hard about it. I had so much set my heart on politics that I really hadn't figured marriage in my plans. I suppose I pushed it to the back of my mind and simply assumed that it would occur of its own accord at some time in the future. I know that Denis too, because a wartime marriage had ended in divorce, only asked me to be his wife after much reflection. But the more I considered, the surer I was. There was only one possible answer. More than forty years later I know that my decision to say 'yes' was one of the best I ever made.

I had in any case been thinking of leaving BX Plastics and Colchester for some time. It was my selection for Dartford that persuaded me I had to look for a new job in London. I had told the Selection Committee that I would fight Dartford with all the energy at my disposal, and I meant it. Nor was I temperamentally inclined to do otherwise. So I began to look for a London-based job which would give me about £500 a year – not a princely sum even in those days, but one which would allow me to live comfortably if modestly. I went for several interviews, but found that they were not keen to take on someone who was hoping to leave to take up a political career. I was certainly not going either to disguise my political ambitions or agree to drop them; so I just kept on looking. Finally, I was taken on by the laboratories of J. Lyons in Hammersmith as a food research chemist. There was a stronger theoretical side to my work there, which made it more satisfying than my position at BX had been.

I moved into lodgings in the constituency. Indeed, Dartford became my home in every sense. The families I lived with fussed over me and could not have been kinder, their natural good nature undoubtedly supplemented by the fact that they were ardent Tories. The Millers also took me under their wing. After evening meetings I would regularly go back to their house to unwind over a cup of coffee. While I was still working and living in Colchester I would stay at their house at weekends. It was a cheerful household in which everyone seemed to be determined to enjoy themselves after the worst of the wartime stringencies were over. We regularly went out to political and non-political functions, and the ladies made an extra effort to wear something smart. John Miller's father – a widower – lived with the family and was a great friend to me: whenever there was a party he would send me a pink carnation as a buttonhole.

I also used to drive out to the neighbouring North Kent constituencies: the four Associations – Dartford, Bexley Heath (where Ted Heath was the candidate), Chislehurst (Pat Hornsby-Smith) and Gravesend (John Lowe) – worked closely together and had a joint President in Morris Wheeler. From time to time he would bring us all together at his large house, 'Franks', at Horton Kirby.

Of the four constituencies, Dartford at that time was by far the least winnable, and therefore doubtless in the eyes of its neighbours – though not Dartford's – the least important. But there is always good political sense in linking safe or at least winnable constituencies on the one hand with hopeless cases on the other. If an active organization can be built up in the latter there is a good chance of drawing away your opponents' party workers from the political territory you need to hold. This was one of the services which Central Office expected of us to help Ted Heath in the winnable seat of Bexley.

It was thus that I met Ted. He was already the candidate for Bexley, and Central Office asked me to speak in the constituency. By now Ted was an established figure. He had fought in the war, ending up as a Lieutenant-Colonel; his political experience went back to the late 1930s when he had supported an anti-Munich candidate in the Oxford by-election; and he had won the respect of Central Office and the four Associations. When we met I was struck by his crisp and logical approach – he always seemed to have a list of four aims, or five methods of attack. Though friendly with his constituency workers, he was always very much the man in charge, 'the candidate', or 'the Member', and this made him seem, even when at his most affable, somewhat aloof and alone.

Pat Hornsby-Smith, his next-door neighbour at Chislehurst, could not have been a greater contrast. She was a fiery, vivacious redhead and perhaps the star woman politician of the time. She had brought the Tory Conference to its feet with a rousing right-wing speech in 1946, and was always ready to lend a hand to other young colleagues: she spoke all around the country. She and I became great friends, and had long political talks at her informal supper parties.

Well before the 1950 election we were all conscious of a Conservative revival. This was less the result of fundamental rethinking within the Conservative Party than of a strong reaction both among Conservatives and in the country at large against the socialism of the Attlee Government. Aneurin Bevan's description in July 1948 of Conservatives as 'lower than vermin' gave young Tories like me a great opportunity to demonstrate their allegiance in the long English tradition of ironic self-deprecation. We went around wearing 'vermin' badges – a little blue rat. A whole hierarchy was established, so that those who recruited ten new party members wore badges identifying them as 'vile vermin'; if you recruited twenty you were 'very vile vermin'. There was a Chief Rat, who lived somewhere in Twickenham.

Of Clement Attlee, however, I was an admirer. He was a serious man and a patriot. Quite contrary to the general tendency of politicians in the 1990s, he was all substance and no show. His was a genuinely radical and reforming government. The 1945 Labour manifesto was in fact a very left-wing document. That is clearer now than it was then. Straight after the war much of the talk of planning and state control echoed wartime rhetoric, and so its full implications were not grasped. In fact, it was a root and branch assault on business, capitalism and the market. It took as its essential intellectual assumption that 'it is doubtful whether we have ever, except in war, used the whole of our productive capacity. This must be corrected.' The state was regarded as uniquely competent to judge where resources should and should not be employed in the national interest. It was not solely or even primarily on social grounds that nationalization, controls and planning were advanced, but on economic grounds. Harmful monopolies were seen as occurring only in the private sector. So nationalization of iron and steel was justified on the argument that 'only if public ownership replaces private monopoly can the industry become efficient'. Most radical of all, perhaps, was the Labour Party's attitude to land, where it was made clear that compulsory purchase by local authorities was only the beginning of a wider programme, for 'Labour believes in land nationalization and will work towards it.'

As regards the specific promises of the Labour manifesto, the Labour Government had been remarkably bold in giving them effect. No one could have questioned Labour's record in implementing socialism. Rather, it was the economic consequences of socialism – devaluation and a return of inflation – which were the obvious targets for attack. Very heavy public spending had kept the standard rate of income tax almost at wartime levels – nine shillings in the pound. Far from being dismantled, wartime controls had if anything been extended – for example rationing was extended to bread in 1946 and even potatoes a year later. It was therefore possible to fight the 1950 election campaign on precisely the kind of issues which are most dangerous for a sitting government – and ones with which I personally felt most at ease – that is, a combination of high ideological themes with more down to earth 'bread and butter' matters.

The 1950 Conservative manifesto was a cleverly crafted document which combined a devastating indictment of socialism in theory and in practice with a prudent list of specific pledges to reverse it. It stressed the effects of inflation, the evidence of economic mismanagement and waste and bureaucracy. I was particularly pleased with its robust statement on foreign affairs, which noted:

Socialism abroad has been proved to be the weakest obstacle to communism and in many countries of Eastern Europe has gone down before it. We are not prepared to regard those ancient states and nations which have already fallen beneath the Soviet yoke as lost for ever.

But Conservatives were careful not to promise an immediate end to rationing, large-scale reversal of nationalization, or anything too controversial on social security or the Health Service; and there was a positively cloying reference to the trade union 'movement', which was described as 'essential to the proper working of our economy and of our industrial life'. All of us knew that the three areas on which we were likely to be most vulnerable were unemployment (where the voters remembered the high unemployment of the thirties, but not that it had risen under the second Labour Government and fallen under the National Government), the Welfare State (which many people thought we wanted to dismantle) and alleged 'war-mongering' (where there was a danger that the Labour Government's robust line would make Churchill's Cold War rhetoric seem extreme rather than prescient, as it was). I found myself dealing with all these questions at public meetings in the course of the 1950 and 1951 campaigns.

The 1950 election campaign was the most exhausting few weeks I had ever spent. So much was new to me; and novelty always drains the stamina. Unlike today's election campaigns, we had well-attended public meetings almost every night, and so I would have to prepare my speech some time during the day. I also wrote my letters to prospective constituents. Then, most afternoons, it was a matter of doorstep canvassing and, as a little light relief, blaring out the message by megaphone. I was well supported by my family: my father came to speak and my sister to help.

Before the election Lady Williams (wife of Sir Herbert Williams, veteran tariff reformer and a Croydon MP for many years) told candidates that we should make a special effort to identify ourselves by the particular way we dressed when we were campaigning. I took this very seriously and spent my days in a tailored black suit and a hat which I bought in Bourne and Hollingsworth in Oxford Street specially for the occasion. And just to make sure I put a black and white ribbon around it with some blue inside the bow.

Quite whether these precautions were necessary is another matter. How many other twenty-four-year-old girls could be found standing on a soapbox in Erith Shopping Centre? In those days it was not often done for women candidates to canvass in factories. But I did – inside and outside. There was always a lively if sometimes noisy reception. The socialists in Dartford became quite irked until it turned out that their candidate – the sitting MP Norman Dodds – would have had the same facilities extended to him if they had thought of asking. It was only the pubs that I did not like going into, and indeed would not do so alone. Some inhibitions die hard.

I was lucky to have an opponent like Norman Dodds, a genuine and extremely chivalrous socialist of the old school. He knew that he was going to win, and he was a big enough man to give an ambitious young woman with totally different opinions a chance. Soon after I was adopted he challenged me to a debate in the hall of the local grammar school and, of course, I eagerly accepted. He and I made opening speeches, there were questions and then we each wound up our case. Each side had its own supporters, and the noise was terrific. Later in the campaign there was an equally vigorous and inconclusive re-run. What made it all such fun was that the argument was about issues and facts, not personalities. On one occasion, a national newspaper reported that Norman Dodds thought a great deal of my beauty but not a lot of my election chances – or of my brains. This perfect socialist gentleman promptly wrote to me disclaiming the statement – or at least the last part.

My own public meetings were also well attended. It was not unusual for the doors of our hall to be closed twenty minutes before the meeting was due to start because so many people were crowding in. Certainly, in those days one advantage of being a woman was that there was a basic courtesy towards us on which we could draw – something which today's feminists have largely dissipated. So, for example, on one occasion I arrived at a public meeting from another in a different part of the constituency to find the visiting speaker, the former Air Minister Lord Balfour of Inchrye, facing a minor revolution from hecklers in the audience – to such an extent indeed that the police had already been sent for. I told the organizers to cancel the request, and sure enough once I took my place on the platform and started to speak the tumult subsided and order – if not exactly harmony – was restored.

I was also fortunate in the national and indeed international publicity which my candidature received. At twenty-four, I was the youngest woman candidate fighting the 1950 campaign, and as such was an obvious subject for comment. I was asked to write on the role of women in politics. My photograph made its way into *Life* magazine, the *Illustrated London News* where it rubbed shoulders with those of the great men of politics, and even the West German press where I was described as a '*junge Dame mit Charme*' (perhaps for the last time).

The slogans, coined by me, gained in directness whatever they lacked in subtlety – 'Vote Right to Keep What's Left' and, still more to the point, 'Stop the Rot, Sack the Lot'. My speeches, even then, pulled no ideological punches. I told a meeting in the Church Hall, Lowfield Street:

> We are going into one of the biggest battles this country has ever known – a battle between two ways of life, one which leads inevitably to slavery and the other to freedom. Our opponents like to try and make you believe that Conservatism is a privilege of the few. But Conservatism conserves all that is great and best in our national heritage. What is one of the first tenets of Conservatism? It is that of national unity. We say one nation, not one class against another. You cannot build a great nation or a brotherhood of man by spreading envy or hatred.
>
> Our policy is not built on envy or hatred, but on liberty for the individual man or woman. It is not our policy to suppress success: our policy is to encourage it and encourage energy and initiative. In 1940 it was not the cry of nationalization that made this country rise up and fight totalitarianism. It was the cry for freedom and liberty.

I felt that our hard work had been worthwhile when I heard the result at the count in the local grammar school. I had cut the Labour majority by 6,000. It was in the early hours at Lord Camrose's *Daily Telegraph* party at the Savoy Hotel – to which candidates, MPs, ministers, Opposition figures and social dignitaries were in those days all invited – that I experienced the same bittersweet feeling about the national result, where the Conservatives had cut Labour's overall majority from 146 to 5 seats. But victory, as yet at least, it was not.

I should recall, however, one peculiar experience I had as candidate for Dartford. I was asked to open a Conservative fête in Orpington and was reluctantly persuaded to have my fortune told while I was there. Some fortune tellers have a preference for crystal balls. This one apparently preferred jewellery. I was told to take off my string of pearls so that they could be felt and rubbed as a source of supernatural inspiration. The message received was certainly optimistic: 'You will be great – great as Churchill.' Most politicians have a superstitious streak; even so, this struck me as quite ridiculous. Still, so much turns on luck that anything which seems to bring a little with it is more than welcome. From then on I regarded my pearls as lucky. And, all in all, they seem to have proved so.

MARRIAGE, FAMILY AND LAW

As I have said, the 1950 result was inconclusive. After the initial exhilaration dies away such results leave all concerned with a sense of anti-climax. There seemed little doubt that Labour had been fatally wounded and that the *coup de grâce* would be administered in a second general election fairly shortly. But in the meantime there was a good deal of uncertainty nationally. For me too in Dartford it was inconvenient. If I were to pursue my political career further I needed to set about finding a winnable seat. But I felt morally bound to fight the Dartford constituency again. It would be wrong to leave them to find another candidate at such short notice. Moreover, it was difficult to imagine that I would be able to make the kind of impact in a second campaign that I had in the one just concluded. I was also extremely tired and, though no one with political blood in their veins shies away from the excitement of electioneering, another campaign within a short while was not an attractive prospect.

I had also decided to move to London. With a little more money to spend from my job with J. Lyons, I had found a very small flat in St George's Square Mews, in Pimlico. Mr Soward (Senior) came down from Dartford to help me decorate it. I was able to see a good deal more of Denis and in more relaxing conditions than in the hubbub of Conservative activism in Dartford.

I also learned to drive and acquired my first car. My sister, Muriel, had a pre-war Ford Prefect which my father had bought her for £129, and I now inherited it. My Ford Prefect became well known around Dartford, where I was re-adopted, and did me excellent service until I sold it for about the same sum when I got married.

The general election came in October 1951. This time I shaved another 1,000 votes off Norman Dodds' majority and was hugely delighted to discover when all the results were in that the Conservatives now had an overall majority of seventeen.

During my time at Dartford I had continued to widen my acquaintanceship with senior figures in the Party. I had spoken as proposer of a vote of thanks to Anthony Eden (whom I had first met in Oxford) when he addressed a large and enthusiastic rally at Dartford football ground in 1949. The following year I spoke as seconder of a motion applauding the leadership of Churchill and Eden at a rally of Conservative Women at the Albert Hall, to which Churchill himself replied in vintage form. This was a great occasion for me – to meet in the flesh and talk to the leader whose words had so inspired me as I sat with my family around our wireless in Grantham. In 1950 I was appointed as representative of the Conservative Graduates to the Conservative Party's National Union Executive, which gave me my first insight into Party organization at the national level.

But it was always policy rather than organization which interested me. In my holidays I would attend courses at Swinton College,* where the Director, Reggie Northam – a man of great generosity of spirit and a friend of John Maynard Keynes, who in the 1930s had gone to South Wales to experience for himself the life of the unemployed – would instil into us that the real political battle was for 'the hearts and minds of the people'. At Swinton and at the various Conservative Political Centre (CPC) meetings in different constituencies, to which I was frequently asked to speak, I was made to think through the real implications for policy of such widely toted concepts as 'One Nation', 'the property-owning democracy' and 'the safety net' (of Social Security benefits).

The greatest social events in my diary were the Eve of (parliamentary) Session parties held by Sir Alfred Bossom, the Member for Maidstone, at his magnificent house, No. 5 Carlton Gardens.

* The Party's staff college in Yorkshire, where everyone from ordinary Party members to Cabinet ministers attended courses and discussions on policy.

Several marquees were put up, brilliantly lit and comfortably heated, in which the greatest and the not so great – like one Margaret Roberts – would mingle convivially. Sir Alfred Bossom would cheerily describe himself as the day's successor to Lady Londonderry, the great Conservative hostess of the inter-war years. You would hardly have guessed that behind his amiable and easy-going exterior was a genius who had devised the revolutionary designs of some of the first skyscrapers in New York. He was specially kind and generous to me. It was his house from which I was married, and there that our reception was held; and it was he who proposed the toast to our happiness.

I was married on a cold and foggy December day at Wesley's Chapel, City Road. It was more convenient for all concerned that the ceremony take place in London, but it was the Methodist minister from Grantham, our old friend the Rev. Skinner, who assisted the Rev. Spivey, the minister at City Road. Then all our friends – from Grantham, Dartford, Erith and London – came back to Sir Alfred Bossom's. Finally, Denis swept me off to our honeymoon in Madeira, where I quickly recovered from the bone-shaking experience of my first and last aquatic landing in a seaplane to begin my married life against the background of that lovely island.

On our return from Madeira I moved into Denis's flat in Swan Court, Flood Street in Chelsea. It was a light, sixth-floor flat with a fine view of London. It was also the first time I learned the convenience of living all on one level. As I would find again in the flat at 10 Downing Street, this makes life far easier to run. There was plenty of space – a large room which served as a sitting room and dining room, two good-sized bedrooms, another room which Denis used as a study and so on. Denis drove off to Erith every morning and would come back quite late in the evening. But I found that I had plenty to do: this was the first time I had had to keep house. We quickly made friends with our neighbours; one advantage of living in a block of flats with a lift is that you meet everyone. By the end of the month I knew most of my neighbours, some of whom were rather distinguished. Late at night there was always the possibility of hearing Dame Sybil Thorndike's unmistakable contralto booming around the courtyard as she returned from a show. During the time we were there we did a good deal of entertaining, with drinks in the evening or supper at the weekend.

To be a young married woman in comfortable circumstances must always be a delight if the marriage is a happy one, as mine was. But to be a young married woman in those circumstances in the 1950s was very heaven. I am always astonished when people refer to that period as a time of repression, dullness or conformity – the Age of Anxiety, etc. The 1950s were, in a thousand different ways, the reawakening of normal happy life after the trials of wartime and the petty indignities of post-war austerity. Rationing came to an end. Wages and salaries started to rise. Bananas, grapes and fruits I had never heard of suddenly reappeared in the shops. After the drabness of Utility clothing, fashion recovered its confidence and colour with Dior's wide skirts, strapless evening dresses, and Ascot hats. Italian restaurants popped up where boarded-up shop fronts had been before. Coffee bars, selling cappuccino, instantly christened 'frothy coffee', spread down high streets. Teenagers were invented. Ordinary homes began to accommodate fridges, Hoovers and electric washing machines. Billboards sprouted fewer Government notices and more commercial advertising ('Murray Mints, Murray Mints. Too-good-to-hurry mints'). TV aerials multiplied across the rooftops of England. Hollywood responded to the expansive mood of those years with the invention of wide-screen Cinemascope and big films to go with it, whether biblical epics like *Quo Vadis* or picturesque musicals like *South Pacific*. And people who had never thought to afford a foreign holiday discovered Spain.

It was the age of affluence, and with affluence came a relaxation of all the restrictions that had marked English life since wartime and, even beforehand, the Grantham of my youth. I cannot pretend to have liked, or even understood, all the expressions of this new popular freedom. When rock and roll was imported from America, along with names like Bill Haley and Elvis Presley, I assumed it would be a nine days' journalistic wonder. (It has never eclipsed *The Desert Song* in my affection.) The Angry Young Man and kitchen-sink drama also appeared to challenge the West End. Again, I assumed that this too would disappear in short order and, besides, I had had too much of kitchen sinks in real life to want to visit them on my night out. I little imagined that I would one day read John Osborne with approval and become a good friend of Kingsley Amis, grateful for his support in the culture wars of my administration. And as Ascot, the Derby, Henley and Wimbledon recovered their old style in those years, the gossip columnists who lived off them re-emerged from their post-war hiding places in Obituaries or Garden Notes. Reading them was a somewhat shameful taste, like gorging on liqueur chocolates. But I have to admit it was a taste few could resist. Readers made the acquaintance of new household names like Lady Docker, Aristotle Onassis and Stavros Niarchos; and Monte Carlo once again became a synonym for high life.

People felt that after all the sacrifices of the previous twenty years, they wanted to enjoy themselves, to get a little fun out of life. Although I may have been perhaps rather more serious than my contemporaries, Denis and I enjoyed ourselves quite as much as most, and more than some. We went to the theatre, we took holidays in Rome and Paris (albeit in very modest hotels), we gave parties and went to them, we had a wonderful time.

But the high point of our lives at that time was the coronation of Queen Elizabeth in June 1953. Those who had televisions – we did not – held house parties to which all their friends came to watch the great occasion. Denis and I, passionate devotees of the monarchy that we were, decided the occasion merited the extravagance of a seat in the covered stand erected in Parliament Square just opposite the entrance to Westminster Abbey. The tickets were an even wiser investment than Denis knew when he bought them, for it poured all day and most people in the audience were drenched – not to speak of those in the open carriages of the great procession. The Queen of Tonga never wore *that* dress again. Mine lived to see another day.

Pleasant though married life was in London, I still had time enough after housework to pursue a long-standing intellectual interest in the law. As with my fascination with politics, it was my father who had been responsible for stimulating this interest. Although he was not a magistrate, as Mayor of Grantham in 1945–46 my father would automatically sit on the Bench. During my university vacations I would go along with him to the Quarter Sessions (where many minor criminal offences were tried), at which an experienced lawyer would be in the chair as Recorder. On one such occasion my father and I lunched with him, a King's Counsel called Norman Winning. I was captivated by what I saw in court, but I was enthralled by Norman Winning's conversation about the theory and practice of law. At one point I blurted out: 'I wish I could be a lawyer; but all I know about is chemistry and I can't change what I'm reading at Oxford now.' But Norman Winning said that he himself had read physics for his first degree at Cambridge before changing to law as a second degree. I objected that there was no way I could afford to stay on all those extra years at university. He replied that there was another way, perfectly possible but very hard work, which was to get a job in or near London, join one of the Inns of Court and study for my law exams in the evenings. And this in 1950 is precisely what I had done. Now with Denis's support I could afford to concentrate on legal studies without taking up new employment. There was a great deal to read, and I also attended courses at the Council of Legal Education.

I had decided that what with running a home and reading for the Bar I would have to put my political ambitions on ice for some time to come. At twenty-six I could afford to do that and I told Conservative Central Office that such was my intention. But as a young woman candidate I still attracted occasional public attention. For example, in February 1952 an article of mine appeared in the *Sunday Graphic* on the position of women 'At the Dawn of the New Elizabethan Era'. I was also on the list of sought-after Party speakers and was invited to constituencies up and down the country. In any case, try as I would, my fascination for politics got the better of all contrary resolutions.

I talked it over with Denis and he said that he would support me all the way. So in June I went to see Beryl Cook at Central Office and told her: 'It's no use. I must face it. I don't like being left out of the political stream.' As I knew she would, 'Auntie Beryl' gave me her full support and referred me to John Hare, the Party Vice-Chairman for Candidates. In the kindest possible way, he told me about the pressures which membership of the House of Commons placed on family life, but I said that Denis and I had talked it through and this was something we were prepared to face. I said that I would like to have the chance of fighting a marginal or safe seat next time round. We both agreed that, given my other commitments, this should be in London itself or within a radius of thirty miles. I promptly asked to be considered for Canterbury, which was due to select a candidate. I left Central Office very pleased with the outcome – though I did not get Canterbury.

The question which John Hare had raised with me about how I would combine my home life with politics was soon to become even more sensitive. For in August 1953 the twins, Mark and Carol, put in an appearance. Late one Thursday night, some six weeks before what we still called 'the baby' was due, I began to have pains. I had seen the doctor that day and he asked me to come back on the Monday for an X-ray because there was something he wanted to check. Now Monday seemed a very long way away, and off I was immediately taken to hospital. I was given a sedative which helped me sleep through the night. Then on Friday morning the X-ray was taken and to the great surprise of all it was discovered that I was to be the mother of twins. Unfortunately, that was not the whole story. The situation required a Caesarean operation the following day. The two tiny babies – a boy and a girl – had to wait a little before they saw their father. For Denis, imagining that all was progressing smoothly, had very sensibly gone to the Oval to watch the Test Match and it proved quite impossible to contact him. On that day he received two pieces of good but equally surprising news. England won the Ashes, and he found himself the proud father of twins.

I had to stay in hospital for over a fortnight: indeed, one was expected in those days to wait three weeks before coming out. This meant that after the first few uncomfortable days of recovery I found myself with time on my hands. We had, of course, been expecting only one addition to the Thatcher household. Consequently, the first and most immediate task was to telephone all the relevant stores to order two rather than just one of everything. Oddly enough, the very depth of the relief and happiness at having brought Mark and Carol into the world made me uneasy. The pull of a mother towards her children is perhaps the strongest and most instinctive emotion we have. I was never one of those people who regarded being 'just' a mother or indeed 'just' a housewife as second best. Indeed, whenever I heard such implicit assumptions made both before and after I became Prime Minister it would make me very angry indeed. Of course, to be a mother and a housewife is a vocation of a very high kind. But I simply felt that it was not the whole of my vocation. I knew that I also wanted a career. A phrase that Irene Ward, MP for Tynemouth, and I often used was that 'while the home must always be the centre of one's life, it should not be the boundary of one's ambitions'. Indeed, I needed a career because, quite simply, that was the sort of person I was. And not just any career. I wanted one which would keep me mentally active and prepare me for the political future for which I believed I was well suited.

So it was that at the end of my first week in hospital I came to a decision. I had the application form for my Bar finals in December sent to me. I filled it in and sent off the money for the exam, knowing that this little psychological trick I was playing on myself would ensure that I plunged into legal studies on my return to Swan Court with the twins, and that I would have to organize our lives so as to allow me to be both a mother and a professional woman.

This was not, in fact, as difficult as it might sound. The flat at Swan Court was large enough, even though it was not ideal: being on the sixth floor, we had to have bars put on all the windows. Without a garden, the twins had to be taken out twice a day to Ranelagh Gardens. But this turned out to be good for them because they became used to meeting and playing with other children – though early on, when we did not know the rules, we had our ball confiscated by the Park Superintendent. Usually, however, it was the nanny, Barbara, who took Mark and Carol to the park, except at weekends when I took over. Barbara had been trained at Dr Barnardo's and turned out to be a marvellous friend to the children.

The fifties marked the start of a major change in the role of women. Until then they tended to be well into middle age when the last child of an often large family fled the nest; work within the house, without the benefit of labour-saving devices, took much longer; and home was also a more social place, visited throughout the day by a wide range of tradesmen, from the milkman to the window cleaner, each perhaps stopping off for a chat or cup of tea. Consequently, fewer women had the opportunity or felt the need to go out to work. The fifties marked the beginning of the end of

this world, and by the eighties it had changed out of recognition.
Women were younger when the children left home because families
were smaller; domestic work was lighter owing to new home appliances; and home deliveries were replaced by a weekly visit to the
mall or supermarket. And the 1980s saw yet another twist: the
trend whereby women started to remain at work in the early years
of marriage, but to leave the workforce to have children for a time
in their thirties.

These changes led to a powerful and largely middle-class lobby
for tax allowances for child care – either nannies or play groups
or, in educational disguise, nursery provision. As Prime Minister
I resisted this pressure. I did not believe that working wives, who
would presumably be bringing more money into the family anyway,
should in effect be subsidized by the taxes paid by couples where
the woman looked after the children at home and there was only
one income. This was a straightforward matter of fairness.

Of course, these general arguments were not ones which affected
my own decisions as a young mother. I was especially fortunate
in being able to rely on Denis's income to hire a nanny to look
after the children in my absences. I could combine being a good
mother with being an effective professional woman, as long as I
organized everything intelligently down to the last detail. It was
not enough to have someone in to mind the children; I had to
arrange my own time to ensure that I could spend a good deal
of it with them. As regards being a barrister after I had become
qualified, I would have a certain amount of latitude in the cases
I took on, so I could to some extent adjust my workload in line
with the demands of family. As regards politics, we lived in
London, my husband worked in the London area, Parliament
was in London – clearly, I must seek a constituency which was
also in or near London. It was only this unusual combination of
circumstances which enabled me to consider becoming an MP
while I had young children.

Not long after I had the twins, John Hare wrote to me from
Central Office:

I was delighted to hear that you had had twins. How very
clever of you. How is this going to affect your position as a

My paternal grandfather.

My paternal grandmother.

My maternal grandmother.

OPPOSITE: My father's shop in Grantham, where I grew up.

BELOW: The Boxing Day Meet of the Belvoir Hunt on St Peter's Hill, Grantham. In the background is the Congregational church and, to the right, the town hall, with the statue of Sir Isaac Newton in front of it.

ABOVE: My mother as a young woman.

BELOW: The Baptist Christmas party. I am standing behind Lady Brownlow in the centre; Lord Brownlow is on the left, seated.

ABOVE: At the house of some friends during the summer of 1935, aged ten.

RIGHT: In the garden on the same visit.

BELOW: The Rotary Club Annual Dinner in 1936, during my father's Presidential year. Standing to his left is Lord Brownlow, and my mother is four to his right.

Aged thirteen, portrait by Grantham's local photographer, Walter Lee.

LEFT: Muriel, father
mother and me, on t
day my father becam
Mayor of Grantham.

BELOW: My father a
Mayor of Grantham,
taking the salute on t
town hall steps durin;
post-war RAF parad

candidate? I have gaily been putting your name forward; if you would like me to desist, please say so.

I replied thanking him and noting:

Having unexpectedly produced twins – we had no idea there were two of them until the day they were born – I think I had better not consider a candidature for at least six months. The household needs considerable reorganization and a reliable nurse must be found before I can feel free to pursue such other activities with the necessary fervour.

So my name was, as John Hare put it, kept 'in cold storage for the time being'. It was incumbent on me to say when I would like to come onto the active list of candidates again.

My self-prescribed six months of political limbo were quickly over. I duly passed my Bar finals. I had begun by considering specializing in patent law because I thought I would be able to make use of my industrial and scientific knowledge. But it seemed that the opportunities there were very limited and so perhaps tax law would be a better bet. In any case, I would need a foundation in the criminal law first. So in December 1953 I joined Frederick Lawton's Chambers in the Inner Temple for a six months' pupillage. Fred Lawton's was a common law Chambers. He was, indeed, one of the most brilliant criminal lawyers I ever knew. He was witty, with no illusions about human nature or his own profession, extraordinarily lucid in exposition, and a kind guide to me.

In fact, I was to go through no fewer than four sets of Chambers, partly because I had to gain a grounding in several fields before I was competent to specialize in tax. So I witnessed the rhetorical fireworks of the Criminal Bar, admired the precise draftsmanship of the Chancery Bar and then delved into the details of company law. But I became increasingly confident that tax law could be my forte. It was a meeting point with my interest in politics; it offered the right mixture of theory and practical substance; and of one thing we could all be sure – there would never be a shortage of clients desperate to cut their way out of the jungle of over-complex and constantly changing tax law.

Studying, observing, discussing and eventually practising law had a profound effect on my political outlook. In this I was probably unusual. Familiarity with the law usually breeds if not contempt, at least a large measure of cynicism. For me, however, it gave a richer significance to that expression 'the rule of law' which so easily tripped off the Conservative tongue.

From my reading at university and earlier I had gained a clear idea that what distinguished free from un-free regimes was that law ruled in the first and force in the second. But what was the essence of this 'law'? By what process had it evolved? And why did it have such deep roots in Britain and, as recent history showed, such shallow ones elsewhere? The legal textbooks that I now studied were not by and large intended to provide answers to such points. But the principles of law which they expounded continually raised in my mind these questions. Similarly, as I read about the great judges of the formative periods of English law, I was increasingly fascinated by the mysterious and cumulative process by which the courts of England had laid the foundations for English freedom.

But it was A.V. Dicey whose writing – above all his classic textbook *The Law of the Constitution* – had most impact on me. It had long been fashionable to attack Dicey for his doctrinaire opposition to the new administrative state, and there are plenty of learned commentators still inclined to do so. But I found myself immediately at home with what he said – it is not perhaps without significance that though Dicey's was a great legal mind, he was at heart a classical liberal. The 'law of the constitution' was, in Dicey's words, the result of two 'guiding principles, which had been gradually worked out by the more or less conscious efforts of generations of English statesmen and lawyers'. The first of these principles was the sovereignty of Parliament. The second was the rule of law, which I will summarize briefly and inadequately as the principle that no authority is above the law of the land.* For Dicey, writing in 1885, and for me reading him some seventy years later, the rule

---

* A.V. Dicey, *Introduction to the Study of the Law of the Constitution* (8th edition, 1915), pp. 465–6.

of law still had a very English, or at least Anglo-Saxon, feel to it. It was later, through reading Hayek's masterpieces *The Constitution of Liberty* and *Law, Legislation and Liberty* that I really came to think of this principle as having wider application.

When politics is in your blood, every circumstance seems to lead you back to it. Whether pondering Dicey, poring over the intricacies of tax law or discussing current issues with other members of the Inns of Court Conservative Society, political questions insisted on taking centre stage in my imagination. So when in December 1954 I heard that there was a vacancy for the Conservative candidature in Orpington – which of course, being next to my old constituency of Dartford, I knew, and which was not too far from London – I telephoned Central Office and asked to have my name put forward. I was interviewed and placed on the short-list. Sitting just outside the selection meeting with Denis, I heard Donald Sumner, the local candidate (and Association Chairman), advancing in his speech the decisive argument that in Orpington what they really needed was 'a Member who really knows what is going on in the constituency – who knows the state of the roads in Locksbottom'. Denis and I roared with laughter. But Donald Sumner got the seat.

I was naturally disappointed by the decision, because Orpington would have been an ideal constituency for me. It seemed extremely unlikely now that a similarly suitable seat would become available before what looked liked an increasingly imminent general election. So I wrote to John Hare to say that I would now 'continue at the Bar with no further thought of a parliamentary career for many years'. Knowing me better than I knew myself perhaps, he wrote back urging me at least to reconsider if a winnable seat in Kent became available. But I was adamant, though I made it clear that I would always be available to speak in constituencies and would of course be active in the general election campaign.

Although I was in general a loyal Conservative, I had felt for some time that the Government could have moved further and faster in dismantling socialism and installing free-enterprise policies. But it had not been easy for them to persuade popular opinion – or indeed themselves – that a somewhat stronger brew would be palatable. In fact, by 1955 a good deal of modest progress had been made as regards the removal of controls and, even more modestly, returning nationalized industries to the private sector. The rationing of food had finally been brought to an end. Large steps had been taken towards restoring the convertibility of the currency. Iron and steel nationalization had been halted and a start made in selling road haulage. Above all, the proportion of GNP taken by the state had been reduced steadily in the years from 1951. And there was one development of great importance for the future: the breaking of the BBC's monopoly of broadcasting and the beginning of commercial television.

SUEZ AND AFTER

Conservative thinking about policy matters was also becoming more self-confident and more radical. This can be illustrated by a comparison between the two most influential publications produced by the Party over these years – *One Nation* (October 1950) and *Change is our Ally* (May 1954). Both were written by an overlapping group of remarkably gifted young Members of Parliament, including Enoch Powell, Angus Maude, Robert Carr and (*One Nation* only) Ted Heath and Iain Macleod. Admittedly, *One Nation* dealt with social policy which, particularly at a time when it was clear that a Conservative government would have to rein back on public expenditure, was a tricky topic. But still the relative blandness of that document – which emphasized (soundly enough, of course) Conservative commitment to a 'safety net' of benefits securing a living standard below which none must fall, and to Anthony Eden's notion of the strengthening of the weak rather than the weakening of the strong – suggested a defensive exercise and indeed a defensive mentality.

Change is our Ally is a far more exciting document which, when I re-read it in the late 1980s, I found to contain very much the same analysis as that we had adopted since I became Party Leader. It began by tracing the growth of collectivism in the British economy between the wars. It then boldly attacked the notion that the planning of the Second World War economy could appropriately be extended into peacetime. It even pointed out – what everyone knew to be true, but what for years after the war went largely unsaid – that the wartime system of planning had been inefficient, wasteful and bureaucratic, however necessary in the emergency the nation faced at the time. The follies and absurdities of the economic plan, with its detailed predictions and quantified targets, were further exposed by retrospective comparisons between the assumptions made in Lord Beveridge's unofficial study *Full Employment in a Free Society*, published in 1944, and the situation a decade later. It was all admirably commonsensical. What the authors of *Change is our Ally*, and indeed those of the following year's Conservative manifesto, did not do – and I certainly claim no credit for thinking at the time that they should have done – was to propose the root and branch dismantling of collectivism in industry or fundamental reform in the Welfare State. But in the mid–1950s the Conservative Party was at least playing with a consistent free market analysis which would, in due course and given the opportunities of government, have led to free market policies. This, however, was not how matters were to develop.

In April 1955 Churchill resigned as Prime Minister to be succeeded by Anthony Eden, and there was in quick succession a snap general election, a new Conservative Government, the débâcle of Suez and the arrival at No. 10 of Harold Macmillan, the wizard of change.

During the general election campaign of May 1955 I spoke in a number of constituencies. But for me it was generally a dull affair. Once you have been a candidate everything else palls. Moreover, there was very little doubt of the outcome on this occasion. Sure enough, the Conservatives won an overall majority of fifty-eight. But the Eden administration's political honeymoon turned out to be a short one. It quickly appeared that Rab Butler's pre-election Budget had been too loose, and there followed a much tighter emergency Budget in October, which badly damaged Butler's reputation – he was replaced as Chancellor by Harold Macmillan six months later – and seriously dented the Government's. But it was, of course, to be foreign affairs which would be Eden's real undoing.

The background to the Suez crisis of July to November 1956 has been much discussed. At the time the general feeling, at least among

Conservatives, was that Britain was a great power which should not be pushed around by Nasser's Egypt and that the latter needed to be taught a lesson, not least *pour encourager les autres*. Many of the details, for example the degree of collusion between Britain and France on the one hand and Israel on the other, were not available to the wider public at the time. To us, therefore, it appeared almost incomprehensible that first Anthony Nutting and then my old friend Edward Boyle should resign from the Government in protest at the intervention. Now their actions are more understandable, though even all these years later I could not endorse them.

The balance of interest and principle in the Suez affair is not a simple one. I had no qualms about Britain's right to respond to Nasser's illegal seizure of an international waterway – if only action had been taken quickly and decisively. Over the summer, however, we were outmanoeuvred by a clever dictator into a position where our interests could only be protected by bending our legal principles. Among the many reasons for criticizing the Anglo-French-Israeli collusion is that it was bound to tarnish our case when it became known, as it assuredly would and did. At the same time, Suez was the last occasion when the European powers might have withstood and brought down a Third World dictator who had shown no interest in international agreements, except where he could profit from them. Nasser's victory at Suez had among its fruits the overthrow of the pro-Western regime in Iraq, the Egyptian occupation of the Yemen, and the encirclement of Israel which led to the Six Day War – and the bills were still coming in when I left office.

As I came to know more about it, I drew four lessons from this sad episode. First, we should not get into a military operation unless we were determined and able to finish it. Second, we should never again find ourselves on the opposite side to the United States in a major international crisis affecting Britain's interests. Third, we should ensure that our actions were in accord with international law. And finally, he who hesitates is lost.

At the time, I fiercely supported the Suez campaign in argument. I was repelled by what seemed to me the opportunism of the Labour Party in turning against the operation after initially supporting it. Denis and I were among the thousands of readers who cancelled the *Observer* and pledged never to read it again because of its opposition to Suez. This is not to say that I had no misgivings. Even though in those days I was much less conscious of international legal niceties than I later became, I did think it slightly rum that the evening paper which I dashed across Chancery Lane in a downpour to secure blared out the headline 'Ultimatum!' Britain and France were demanding that the Egyptians and Israelis withdraw from the canal and allow an Anglo-French force to separate them and protect the waterway. It was not quite clear to me how the British could issue an ultimatum to the Egyptians to withdraw from their own territory. Still, I swallowed my hesitations and supported Eden.

Politically, the failure of the Suez operation came as a body blow. Although it took many years for the full picture to emerge, it was immediately clear that the Government had been incompetent, and that its incompetence had been exposed in the most humiliating fashion. For a Conservative government – particularly one led by someone whose reputation was founded on the conduct of foreign affairs – the outcome was particularly damaging. There was a mood of dismay bordering on despair among Conservative supporters. Denis's reaction, as an ex-officer in the Royal Artillery, was sharpened by anger that our troops had been let down when the operation was halted close to completion. As he said to me: 'You never announce a ceasefire when your troops are out on patrol.' I would remember this: politicians must never take decisions in war without full consideration of what they mean to our forces on the ground.

We also blamed harshly the conduct of the United States. Some Conservatives never forgave the Americans, and the fact that anti-Americanism lingered on in some generally right-wing circles when I was Prime Minister must be in part attributed to this. I too felt that we had been let down by our traditional ally – though at the time, of course, I did not realize that Eisenhower felt equally let down by the Anglo-French decision to launch military operations on the eve of a Presidential election in which he was running on a peace ticket. But in any case I also felt that the 'special relationship' with our transatlantic cousins had foundations too solid to be eroded by even such a crisis as Suez. Some people argued that

Suez demonstrated that the Americans were so hostile to Britain's imperial role, and were now so much a superpower, that they could not be trusted and that closer European integration was the only answer. But, as I have argued, there was an alternative – and quite contrary – conclusion. This was that British foreign policy could not long be pursued without ensuring for it the support of the United States. Indeed, in retrospect I can see that Suez was an unintended catalyst in the peaceful and necessary transfer of power from Britain to America as the ultimate upholder of Western interests and the liberal international economic system.

I was not so preoccupied with Suez as to be unconscious of the wicked ruthlessness of the Soviet Union's behaviour in crushing the Hungarian revolution in November 1956 – even under bouncy Nikita Khrushchev, who had visited Britain with his amiable wife just a few months earlier. I never imagined that communism even with a human face could somehow generate a human heart. But at the time it seemed extraordinary to me that the Soviet Union should be prepared to undo all the efforts it had made since the death of Stalin to improve its image by such a crude and barbarous affront to decency. Some years later I discussed my reaction with Bob Conquest, who was to provide me with so much wise advice when I became Leader of the Opposition and whose *The Great Terror* in the late 1960s first fully exposed the scale of Stalin's murders. He said that the classic error we all made in dealing with the Soviets was in assuming that they would behave as Westerners would in their circumstances. They were shaped by a very different and much more brutal political culture. It was my recollection of all this that led me, after Iraq attacked Iran in September 1980, to ask our Intelligence Services to look back over events like Hungary, which we had not foreseen because we had failed to penetrate the psychology of the aggressor, and draw out any conclusions for future action.

Yet there is little we could have done to prevent the Hungarian tragedy – and no way that NATO would have risked a major war for Hungary, with or without Suez. But many Hungarians thought that they had been encouraged to think otherwise, which added to their bitterness at our betrayal. I remember a Sunday newspaper interview with a Hungarian woman sheltering in a basement. She

said: 'The West will not come and help. Freedom is very selfish.'
I burned at the reproach. Whatever we were or were not in a
position to do, it seemed to me that a world divided into spheres
of influence which condemned this woman to live under communism was one which had to be changed.

After the fiasco of Suez it was clear that Anthony Eden could
not remain as Prime Minister. He fell ill during the crisis and
resigned in January 1957. There was much speculation in the
circles in which I moved as to who would succeed – in those days,
of course, Conservative Leaders 'emerged' rather than being
elected. My Conservative friends in Chambers were convinced that
Rab Butler would never be summoned by the Queen because he was
too left wing. By contrast, the Chancellor of the Exchequer at the
time of Suez, Harold Macmillan, was considered to be the right-
wing candidate. All of which shows how little we knew of the past
and present convictions of both men – particularly the brilliant,
elusive figure who was shortly to become Prime Minister.

Harold Macmillan had the strengths and weaknesses of the
consummate politician. He cultivated a languorous and almost
antediluvian style which was not – and was not intended to be –
sufficiently convincing to conceal the shrewdness behind it. He was
a man of masks. It was impossible to tell, for instance, that behind
the cynical Edwardian façade was one of the most deeply religious
souls in politics.

Harold Macmillan's great and lasting achievement was to repair
the relationship with the United States. This was the essential
condition for Britain to restore her reputation and standing. Unfortunately, he was unable to repair the damage inflicted by Suez on
the morale of the British political class – a veritable 'Suez syn-
drome'. They went from believing that Britain could do anything
to an almost neurotic belief that Britain could do nothing. This
was always a grotesque exaggeration. At that time we were a
middle-ranking diplomatic power after America and the Soviet
Union, a nuclear power, a leading member of NATO, a permanent
member of the UN Security Council and the centre of a great
Commonwealth.

Macmillan's impact on domestic affairs was mixed. Under his
leadership there was the 1957 decontrol of private sector rents –

which greatly reduced the scope of the rent control that had existed in one form or another since 1915 – a necessary, though far from popular move. Generally, however, Macmillan's leadership edged the Party in the direction of state intervention, a trend which would become much more marked after 1959.

Even at the time some developments made me uneasy. When Peter Thorneycroft, Enoch Powell and Nigel Birch – Macmillan's entire Treasury team – resigned over a £50 million increase in public expenditure in January 1958, Macmillan talked wittily of 'little local difficulties'. I felt in no position to judge the rights and wrongs of the dispute itself. But the husbanding of public money did not strike me as an ignoble cause over which to resign. The first steps away from the path of financial rectitude always make its final abandonment that much easier. And that abandonment brings its own adverse consequences. Such was the case in the years that followed.

Yet in Macmillan the Party certainly had an immensely shrewd and able politician. As early as the summer of 1957 he had understood that the living standards of ordinary people had been rising fast, and that this offered the best hope of political success. It was then that he observed that 'most of our people have never had it so good'.*

The Labour Party and the critics pounced on this as an example of Macmillan's complacency and materialism. But in fact it was true and politically potent. There was a feeling that things never *had* been better, and that this was attributable to private enterprise rather than planning. The last thing the country wanted was to return to hair-shirted austerity. So the attacks on 'Super-Mac' rebounded.

That said, the political recovery was by no means immediate. At the time of the October 1957 Party Conference – one of the very few that I did not attend – the opinion polls were showing Labour at 52 per cent and the Conservatives at 33 per cent. On top of that,

---

* Admittedly he went on, as I used to point out: 'What is beginning to worry some of us is "Is it too good to be true?" or perhaps I should say "Is it too good to last?" for, amidst all the prosperity, there is one problem that has troubled us in one way or another ever since the war. It's the problem of rising prices.'

the Liberal Party dealt us a severe blow by winning the Torrington by-election in March 1958.

It was not until the late summer of that year that the Conservatives caught up with Labour in the opinion polls. By the time of the 1959 general election the two main parties were unashamedly competing to appeal to the nation's desire for material self-advancement. The Conservative manifesto bluntly stated: 'Life's better with the Conservatives, don't let Labour ruin it.' It went on to promise a doubling of the British standard of living in a generation. As for Labour, a few days into the campaign the Party Leader Hugh Gaitskell promised that there would be no rise in income tax in spite of all the extra spending Labour planned – even in that political climate of optimism, a fatally incredible pledge.

THE FINCHLEY ROAD

Well before this I myself had re-entered the fray. In February 1956 I wrote to Donald Kaberry, the Party Vice-Chairman in charge of candidates:

> For some time now I have been feeling the temptation to return to active politics. I had intended, when I was called to the Bar, to concentrate entirely on legal work but a little experience at the Revenue Bar, and in Company matters, far from turning my attention from politics has served to draw my attention more closely to the body which is responsible for the legislation about which I have come to hold strong views.

I went to see Donald Kaberry the following month. There was no problem in my being put back on the list of candidates – this time to be considered for safe Conservative-held seats only. I was all the more delighted because I found in Donald Kaberry a constant and dependable source of wise advice and friendship – no small thing for an aspiring candidate.

I was less fortunate in the reception I received from Selection

Committees. It had begun at Orpington in 1954. It was the same at Beckenham, Hemel Hempstead and then Maidstone in 1957 and 1958. I would be short-listed for the seat, would make what was generally acknowledged to be a good speech – and then the questions, most of them having the same purpose, would begin. With my family commitments, would I have time enough for the constituency? Did I realize how much being a Member of Parliament would keep me away from home? Might it not be better to wait for a year or two before trying to get into the House? And sometimes more bluntly still: did I really think that I could fulfil my duties as a mother with young children to look after and as an MP?

I felt that Selection Committees had every right to ask me these questions. I explained our family circumstances and that I already had the help of a first-class nanny. I also used to describe how I had found it possible to be a professional woman and a mother by organizing my time properly. What I resented, however, was that beneath some of the criticism I detected a feeling that the House of Commons was not really the right place for a woman anyway. Perhaps some of the men at Selection Committees entertained this prejudice, but I found then and later that it was the women who came nearest to expressing it openly. Not for the first time the simplistic left-wing concept of 'sex discrimination' had got it all wrong.

I was hurt and disappointed by these experiences. They were, after all, an attack on me not just as a candidate but as a wife and mother. But I refused to be put off by them. I was confident that I had something to offer in politics. I knew that many others who had crossed my political path very much wanted me to get into the House. And most important of all, Denis never had any doubts. He was always there to comfort and support me.

In April 1958 I had another long talk with Donald Kaberry at Central Office. He told me about the constituencies which were likely to select soon and I, for my part, spoke frankly about the difficulties I had faced as a woman with the Selection Committees. Unfortunately, this is not one of the topics on which even the wisest male friend can give very useful counsel. But Donald Kaberry did give me advice on what to wear on these sensitive occasions –

something smart but not showy. In fact, looking me up and down, he said he thought the black coat dress with brown trim which I was wearing would be just fine. His sartorial judgement would soon be put to the test. For I now entered my name for – and in July was called to interview at – the safe Conservative seat of Finchley, North London, whose MP was retiring.

Finchley was not an area of London that I knew particularly well. But like any enthusiastic would-be candidate I set to work to find out all there was to know about it. I was determined that no one would know the Finchley equivalent of Locksbottom better than I. But one advantage of an urban seat, particularly a London seat, is that you know that the most topical issues locally will correspond very closely to the most important political issues nationally. And that is not always the case with a rural or regional seat. So, for example, rent decontrol was bound to be controversial in Finchley, as nationally. Immigration too was just starting to figure on the political landscape – it was to lead to the first Notting Hill riots just a few weeks later. The state of the economy, and which party was more likely to keep living standards rising and services improving, were bound to be at the forefront of people's minds in Finchley as elsewhere. On all of these things I knew exactly where I stood and what I would say.

I was one of a 'long list' of some 150 applicants, which contained a number of my future colleagues in the House. I was also one of those called for preliminary interview by the Constituency Selection Committee. I could tell that I had a good deal of support, which was satisfying but hardly grounds for confidence. Being the most popular person on these occasions can sometimes be less important than being the least unpopular person. If, as the weaker candidates are eliminated, all their support goes to your opponent it is quite possible to fall at the last fence – and we were barely out of the paddock.

It was arranged that the final four of us – three men and myself – should go before the Executive Council of the Association. I knew I would have a large number of friends, but I was also pretty sure that I could expect some fierce opposition; it would be a fight.

I prepared myself as best I could. I felt reasonably confident that I knew the constituency. I had no doubt that I could cope with even quite abstruse questions of economic or foreign policy, for I had voraciously read the newspapers and all the briefing I could obtain. I prepared my speech until it was word perfect, and I had mastered the technique of talking without notes. Equally important was that I should put myself in the right state of mind – confident but not too confident. I decided to obey instructions and wear the black coat dress. I saw no harm either in courting the fates: so I wore not just my lucky pearls but also a lucky brooch which had been given to me by my Conservative friends in Dartford.

There was, however, one piece of thoroughly bad luck. This was that on the date of the meeting – Monday 14 July – it was quite impossible for Denis to come with me. Indeed, so quick was the whole selection process that he knew nothing whatever about it. Every year he would go away on a foreign sales tour for a month or so, and at this point his whereabouts were only 'somewhere in Africa'. By contrast, the other candidates were accompanied by their spouses. So as I entered the packed meeting on that warm July evening and took my place beside the chairman I felt very much alone.

But as soon as I was on my feet the inhibitions fell away. As always, I quickly became too taken up with the thrust of my argument to worry too much about what other people were thinking. The applause when I sat down seemed warm and genuine. As I had expected, it was at questions that the trouble began.

Could a mother with young children really effectively represent Finchley? What about the strains on my family life? I gave my usual answers, and as usual too a section of the audience was determinedly unconvinced. And doubtless it was easier for them because poor Denis at that moment was absent. At least he did not have to hear it all. But I wished he were with me all the same.

I rejoined the other candidates and their wives, where the tension was only relieved by that over-polite inconsequential small talk which such occasions always seem to generate. Once the last of us had performed, it seemed an endless wait until one of the officers came through to tell us the result. And when he did, it was to me that he spoke. There was no time to feel relief, pleasure or even exhaustion, because it was now necessary to return to receive the congratulations of the Executive.

It was only afterwards that I knew the precise result. The first round of voting gave me thirty-five votes as against thirty-four for my nearest rival. On the second round, when the two other candidates had dropped out, I had forty-six against his forty-three. It was then expected that, for form's sake and to show that there was no ill feeling, the Executive should unanimously vote to select me as their candidate. Unfortunately, some of those who opposed my candidature had no such intentions. So I inherited an Association which I would have to unite behind me, and this would mean winning over people who had not disguised their disapproval.

But that was for tomorrow. First I must break the good news to my family back in Grantham. Denis was entirely incommunicado, blissfully unaware of what I had been through at Finchley. I had written him a letter some time before about the prospects, but he never received it. A couple of days later he was on his way from Johannesburg to Lagos via Kano in northern Nigeria. On changing planes he picked up a copy of the London *Evening Standard* which someone had left behind, and as he leafed through it he discovered the astonishing news that his wife had been selected for the safe seat of Finchley. I always seemed to be giving him surprises.

My first opportunity to impress myself on the Finchley Association as a whole was at the Adoption Meeting early the following month. This time I again appeared in a plain black outfit with a small black hat. I received what I afterwards learned was an almost embarrassingly glowing introduction from Bertie Blatch, the constituency chairman, who was to be a great patron and protector. (It was an added advantage then and later that Bertie owned the most important local newspaper, the *Finchley Press*.) As I entered the hall, I was met with warm applause. I used the occasion to speak at some length about both international and domestic affairs. I pulled out every stop. I knew that though I was the only duly selected candidate, this adoption meeting was not, as it should have been, a mere formality. There was still some die-hard opposition to my candidature, centred on one woman and her little *coterie*, who were trying to have the contest re-run. I was determined to overcome this. There were no problems in dealing with the three questions from the body of the hall. As Conservatives do on such occasions, they gave me a terrific reception. But at the end – and contrary to the newspaper report of the occasion – a few of those present refused to vote for my adoption, which was overwhelming but not (that magic word) 'unanimous'. I left the meeting knowing that I had secured my candidature and confident of the loyalty of the great majority of the Association, but aware too that some were still determined to make life as difficult as possible.

I went as far as to write to Ted Heath, then Chief Whip but previously my near neighbour in Dartford, about the problems I was having. Partly as a result of his assistance, and partly because I used my own personal contacts, I managed to attract a distinguished field of speakers to come and speak on my behalf between my adoption and election day. Iain Macleod, Keith Joseph, Peter Thorneycroft and John Boyd-Carpenter – all people around whom my future political life would soon revolve – were among them. Denis's belated but extremely welcome arrival on the scene also helped in a rather different way. Bertie Blatch gave me constant and unstinting support.

Finchley had been run with a degree of gentlemanly disengagement that was neither my style nor warranted by political realities. I intended to work and then campaign as if Finchley were a marginal seat, and I hoped and expected that others would follow my lead. From now on I was in the constituency two or three times a week and regularly went out canvassing in each of the wards, returning afterwards to get to know the Party activists over a drink in the local pub or someone's house.

By the time I arrived as candidate, there was a good deal of concern that the Liberals in Finchley were becoming strongly entrenched. They were always excellent campaigners, particularly effective in local government elections. A few years before, there had been a famous local scandal over the barring of Jews from membership of Finchley Golf Club, in which a number of local Conservatives had been involved: the Liberals never missed an opportunity to remind people of it. I simply did not understand anti-semitism myself, and I was upset that the Party should have been tainted by it. I also thought that the potential Conservative vote was not being fully mobilized because of this. So I set out to make it absolutely clear that we wanted new members, especially Jewish Conservatives, in our branch organizations. Though I did not know it at the time, I was subsequently to find some of my closest political friends and associates among Jews. What was clear was that the potential Conservative vote was not being fully exploited, and that however many feathers might be ruffled in the process it was vital to strengthen our branch organization. I also put a good deal of effort into strengthening the Young Conservative organization in the constituency: I was sure that it was by attracting energetic young people that we could most surely resist the challenge of activist Liberals. By the time the election was called in September 1959 the constituency organization was looking in better shape, and I had begun to feel very much at home.

I also felt that the Party was on course for winning the general election. There had been a large number of Tory gains in the local elections in May, and conditions looked increasingly favourable for a Conservative general election victory. In Finchley we got on with our final preparations. In fact, I was on holiday with Denis and the twins on the Isle of Wight when the general election was called, and so I hurried back to London. The campaign itself, though the issues of Suez and rent decontrol were thrown back at me, was largely about which party could better secure and manage prosperity. In the debates I held with the other candidates in the churches and synagogues of Finchley that was always the underlying question. This was favourable territory. For, as we claimed, life really was better with the Conservatives – in Finchley as elsewhere. On top of the sense of prosperity, there was an awareness that in Harold Macmillan Britain had a statesman capable of acting a distinguished role on the international stage, whether it was in the United States or the Soviet Union or Continental Europe.

My first general election polling day in Finchley in October 1959 was very much to set the pattern for the nine such polling days which would succeed it. Soon after the opening of the poll I would vote in my own home constituency – Orpington in 1959, Chelsea and Westminster in later elections – and then drive up to Finchley with Denis. I visited each of the polling stations and our committee rooms, breaking for lunch with Bertie Blatch and others in a hotel. There I rigorously paid just for my own food and drink, to avoid

the accusation of 'treating' electors, terror of which is instilled by
Conservative Central Office into all our candidates. From five
o'clock I carefully avoided visiting committee rooms, which should
all be sending out workers to summon our supporters to the polls,
just dropping into a polling station or two to show the flag. Then
at close of poll Denis and I went to the Blatches for something to
eat, visited the constituency offices to catch the latest largely anec-
dotal news, and finally attended the count – on this occasion at
Christ's College, though later all nine constituency counts would
be held at Barnet Town Hall.

At the school, I found that each of the candidates had been
allocated a room where he or she with a select band of supporters
who had tickets for the count could get something to eat and drink
and where we had access to that miracle of modern political life –
a television. The 1959 campaign had, in fact, been the first in which
television played a serious part. And it was the television results
service which now told me how the Party was faring in the country.
I divided my time between watching the growing piles of ballot
papers, candidate by candidate, on the long tables in the body of the
hall, and slipping back to my room to catch the equally satisfactory
results coming in across the country as a whole.

At about 12.30 a.m. I was told that the Finchley results were
shortly to be announced, and was asked to join the Electoral
Returning Officer with the other candidates on the platform. Perhaps some people in a safe seat when the Tories were on course
for a national victory would have been confident or even complacent. Not me. Throughout my time in politics, whether from
some sixth sense or perhaps – who knows? – from mere superstition,
I have associated such attitudes with imminent disaster. So I stood
by the side of Denis with a fixed smile and tried not to look as I
felt.

The Returning Officer began: 'Deakins, Eric Petro: thirteen
thousand, four hundred and thirty-seven.' (Labour cheers.)
'Spence, Henry Ivan: twelve thousand, seven hundred and one.'
(Liberal cheers.) And finally we reached: 'Thatcher, Margaret
Hilda: twenty-nine thousand, six hundred and ninety-seven.' I was
home and dry – and not just with plenty to spare but with a
majority of 16,260, almost 3,500 more than my predecessor. The

cheers, always more controlled from Tory than from Liberal or socialist lips, rose. I made my short speech of acceptance, thanked all my splendid helpers, received a warm hug from Denis and walked down from the platform – the elected Member for Finchley.

In an unguarded moment, shortly after I had been selected for Finchley, I had told the twins that once I became an MP they could have tea on the terrace of the House of Commons. From then on the plaintive request had been: 'Aren't you there yet, Mummy? It's taking a long time.' I had known the feeling. It had seemed so very long for me too. But I now knew that within weeks I would take my seat on the green leather benches of the House of Commons.

It was the first step.

CHAPTER IV

The Outer Circle

Backbencher and junior minister 1959–1964

A GARDEN AT LAST

By now my family and I were comfortably installed in a large-ish detached house at Farnborough in Kent. We had decided to buy 'Dormers', which we saw advertised in *Country Life*, after rent decontrol threatened to make it a good deal more expensive to continue renting our flat in Swan Court. In any event, we felt the children needed a garden to play in.

Our new house had seen better days. Though it was structurally sound, the previous owner had not been able to maintain it properly. There was no central heating, and the one and a half acres of garden were heavily overgrown. But I enjoyed setting to work to improve things. In particular I bubbled with enthusiasm for the garden. I had always wanted one, but when my parents finally moved to a house with quite a large garden – very long but narrow – I was no longer living at home. So the garden at 'Dormers' was my first real opportunity to don thick gardening gloves and rip out brambles, trundle barrows of leaf-mould from the nearby wood to improve the soil, and plant out flower beds. I read up on the requirements of azaleas, rhododendrons and dahlias. Luckily, in Bertie Blatch I had a constituency chairman who doubled as horticulturist: but for all his tips my roses never quite resembled his.

For the twins, 'Dormers' was a seventh heaven. There was the new experience of their own garden, neighbours with children and all the excitement of a wood to walk in – though not alone. The house was part of an estate, so there was no through-traffic and it was safe for the children. I eliminated right at the beginning the dreadful possibility of their falling in the pond by having it filled with earth and turned into a rose bed.

Mark and Carol were six when I became an MP, old enough to get into plenty of trouble if not firmly handled. Nor was Denis at home as much as he would have liked, since his job took him abroad a good deal. Because my parliamentary duties meant that I was not always back before the twins went to bed, I insisted on full family attendance at breakfast. We also had the advantage of the long parliamentary recess and indeed the long parliamentary weekends. But I owe a debt of gratitude to Barbara, the children's nanny at 'Dormers' until she married a local horticulturist who advised me on the garden – and to Abby who replaced her and who in due course became a close family friend. They kept the children in order and I always telephoned from the House shortly before six each evening to see that all was well and to give the children a chance to tell me that it wasn't.

I had learned from my mother the importance of making every house a home. In particular, I insisted on a warm kitchen, large enough to eat in, as its heart. Although I like somewhere to be clean and tidy, I have no taste for austerity for its own sake. A lived-in house should be both comfortable and attractively furnished – a combination which is less difficult and less expensive than is sometimes thought. Like my mother, I favoured mahogany furniture. And since nothing looks better on a dark mahogany table than silver, Denis and I started to build up a modest collection for a table service.

Antique shops used to cast a dangerous spell over me. Though keeping my sights prudently low and avoiding the grand establishments where, even in those days, price digits seemed to multiply alarmingly, I would spend spare moments from shopping or political work to see what 'finds' were on offer. Antique (or reproduction) furniture continued to be a favourite because I felt it was useful and not just attractive. When I lost a sapphire scarf pin one Sunday in Richmond Park – Denis had brought the stones back with him from a business trip in Ceylon – I used the insurance money to buy an antique piece to serve as a cocktail cabinet. Denis thought that I should have bought some more jewellery, but I was annoyed with myself: 'at least I can't lose a cocktail cabinet in Richmond Park,' I told him. And so our house gradually acquired its contents.

It did not, however, acquire many pictures. Apart from a few prints and the addition (in later years) of several drawings and portraits, Denis and I felt that good paintings – and there was no point in hanging bad ones – were just too expensive. Instead, I began to collect porcelain. Porcelain dishes on the walls and figures in display cabinets provided our rooms with plenty of colour, and somehow the purchase of individual pieces always seemed less of an extravagance. I bought my first pieces of Crown Derby at Frinton when we were visiting my sister Muriel and her husband on their farm. On one occasion after an evening's canvassing in Finchley I discovered that one of our Branch Chairmen had her own impressive little collection that showed her impeccable taste. From then on she would tell me about anything she saw that she thought I would like.

My childhood experiences in Grantham had convinced me that the best way to make a cheerful home is to ensure it is busy and active. This was not difficult. My own life was full to overflowing. Before I became an MP there had been both the law and my search for a parliamentary seat to combine with my duties as wife and mother. Once I was elected the pace was even more hectic. We had a daily help in to do most of the regular housework, but there were some things which I insisted on doing myself. Whatever time the House rose, even in the early hours of the morning, I would drive back to Farnborough so as to be ready to prepare breakfast for Denis and the family – and to grab some fruit and a cup of coffee for myself. I would then take one or both of the twins and sometimes another local child off to their schools – we had a team of mothers who shared out the duties between us. Then I would usually do some shopping before driving the forty-five minutes to Westminster where the House commenced its sitting at 2.30 p.m.

Although there were often constituency duties, the weekends provided the opportunity to sort out the house and usually to do a large bake, just as we had done at home in Grantham. In the summer months Denis and I and the children would work – or in their case play at working – in the garden. But on Saturdays in the rugby season Denis would probably be refereeing or watching a match – an arrangement which from the earliest days of our marriage had been solemnly set down in tablets of stone. Sometimes if he was refereeing an important game I would go along as well, though my concentration on the game was frequently disturbed by the less than complimentary remarks which English crowds are inclined to exchange about the conduct of referees. On Sundays we took the twins to the Family Service at the Farnborough parish church. Denis was an Anglican, but we both felt that it would be confusing for the children if we did not attend the same church. The fact that our local church was Low Church made it easier for the Methodist in me to make the transition. Anyway, John Wesley regarded himself as a member of the Church of England to his dying day. I did not feel that any great theological divide had been crossed.

Weekends, therefore, provided me with an invaluable and invigorating tonic. So did family holidays. I remembered what I had enjoyed – and not enjoyed – about my own holidays at Skegness. My conclusion was that for young children nothing beats buckets and spades and plenty of activity. So we used to take a house on the Sussex coast for a month right by the side of the beach, and there always seemed to be other families with small children nearby. Later we went regularly to a family hotel at Seaview on the Isle of Wight or rented a flat in the village. Crossing the Solent by ferry seemed a great adventure to the children who, like all twins, had a degree of (usually) playful rivalry. On the way down to the coast in the car we always passed through a place called 'Four Marks'. I was never able to answer Mark's question about who these four were. Nor could I think up a satisfactory response to Carol who thought that it was all unfair and that there should also be a 'Four Carols'. Not to be outdone, Mark pointed out that it was no less unfair that Christmas carols had no male equivalent.

In 1960 we had planned to take the children abroad for the summer holidays to Brittany. But at the last moment Mark caught chickenpox and to everyone's great disappointment the trip had to be cancelled. To compensate, still more adventurously, we decided to go skiing at Lenzerheide in Switzerland at Christmas. None of us had ever skied before, so we joined a ski club in Sloane Square and took a course in skiing from Lillywhites before we went. The holiday was a great success, and we went back to the same hotel year after year. I loved the scenery and the exercise. And I loved the hot chocolate and pastries afterwards even more.

It is a cliché, but no less true for all that, that in family life you have to take the rough with the smooth. Knowing that you have a family to turn to is a great strength in politics, but the other side is one's emotional vulnerability to their suffering. I was always worried about Mark, who at that time seemed to catch every germ that was going, including pneumonia one winter at Lenzerheide. One of the worst days of my life was when it became clear that he had appendicitis and I had to rush him to the nearby hospital. I spent so much time with him in the weeks which followed that I began to worry that Carol might feel left out. So I bought her a magnificent teddy bear which was christened Humphrey. Whatever Carol thought of her new friend, I became very attached to him, and indeed brought him with me to Downing Street. Only later did he sadly disintegrate when, dismayed by his grubby looks, I tried to wash him. '*Sic transit gloria Humphri*'.

It is hard to know whether one worries more about one's children when they are within reach or far away. I wanted the twins to be at home when they were young, though I was reconciled to their going to boarding school later. Unfortunately, the nearby day school to which Mark went had to close in 1961, and Denis persuaded me that it was best that he should go to Belmont Preparatory School. At least Belmont was just on the edge of Finchley, so I could take him out to lunch. Also I knew he was not too far away in case of emergencies. But then, of course, not to be left out, Carol decided that she wanted to go to boarding school as well, and did so two years later. The house seemed empty without them.

By now there was another emptiness in my life which could never be filled, and that was the loss of my mother, who died in 1960. She had been a great rock of family stability. She managed the household, stepped in to run the shop when necessary, entertained, supported my father in his public life and as Mayoress, did a great deal of voluntary social work for the church, displayed a series of practical domestic talents such as dressmaking and was never heard to complain. Like many people who live for others, she made possible all that her husband and daughters did. Her life had not been an easy one. Although in later years I would speak more readily of my father's political influence on me, it was from my mother that I inherited the ability to organize and combine so many different duties of an active life. Her death was a great shock, even though it had not been entirely unexpected. We were all staying with my sister's family in Essex when my mother fell ill: Denis and I drove her back to Grantham for an emergency operation. But she was never really well again, and died a few months later. Even young children have a keen sense of family grief. After my mother's funeral, my father came back to stay with us for a while at 'Dormers'. That evening when I turned back the coverlet of his bed, I found a little note from Mark on the pillow: 'Dear Grandad, I'm so sorry Granny died.' It was heartbreaking.

LAW-MAKING FOR BEGINNERS

I was very glad, however, that both my parents had seen their daughter enter the Palace of Westminster as a Member of Parliament – quite literally 'seen', because the press contained flattering photographs of me in my new hat on the way to the House. My first real contact with the Conservative Parliamentary Party was when on the day before Parliament opened I went along as a member of the 1922 Committee – the Party committee to which all Conservative backbench MPs belong – to discuss the question of the Speakership of the House. I knew only a relatively small number of the several hundred faces packed into that rumbustious, smoky committee room, but I immediately felt at home.

Everyone in those early days was immensely kind. The Chief Whip would give new Members a talk about the rules of the House and the whipping system. Old-stagers gave me useful hints about dealing with correspondence. They also told me that I should not just concentrate on the big issues like foreign affairs and finance, but also find one or two less popular topics on which I could make a mark. Another piece of good practical advice was to find myself a 'pair', which I promptly did in the form of Charlie Pannell, the

Labour MP for Leeds West.* I had met him years earlier when he lived in Erith, in my old Dartford constituency. He was exactly the sort of good-humoured, decent Labour man I liked.

The Palace of Westminster seems a bewildering labyrinth of corridors to the uninitiated. It was some time before I could find my way with ease around it. The Tea Room, the Library and the main committee rooms were all points of reference for me. There were modestly appointed rooms set apart for the twenty-five women Members – the 'Lady Members' Rooms' – where I would find a desk to work at. Neither taste nor convention suggested my entering the Smoking Room. My formidably efficient secretary, Paddi Victor Smith, had a desk in a large office with a number of other secretaries where we worked on constituency correspondence. But the heart of the House of Commons was, even more than now, the Chamber itself. Early on, I was advised that there was no substitute for hours spent there. Finance and Foreign Affairs Committee meetings might be more informative. The weekly 1922 Committee meetings might be more lively. But it was only by absorbing the atmosphere of the House until its procedures became second nature and its style of debate instinctive that one could become that most respected kind of English politician, a 'House of Commons man' (or woman).

So that is what I did. I took my pre-arranged place in the fourth row back below the gangway – where thirty-one years later I chose to sit again after I resigned as Prime Minister. The House itself was – and still is – a very masculine place. This manifested itself above all, I found, in the sheer volume of noise. I was used to university debates and questions at the general election hustings, yet my brief previous visits to the Visitors' Gallery of the House had never prepared me for this. But when I remarked on it to a colleague he just laughed and said, 'You should have heard it during Suez!' Masculinity, I soon found, however, did not degenerate into male prejudice. In different ways I had on occasion been

---

* 'Pairing' is an informal arrangement by which pairs of MPs from opposing parties agree to abstain in parliamentary votes when one or other of them wishes to be absent from the House of Commons. The arrangement does not usually apply to crucial votes.

made to feel small because I was a woman in industry, at the Bar and indeed in Tory constituency politics. But in the House of Commons we were all equals; and woe betide ministers who suggest by their demeanour or behaviour that they consider themselves more equal than the rest. I soon saw with appreciation that sincerity, logic and technical mastery of a subject could earn respect from both sides of the House. Shallowness and bluff were quickly exposed. Perhaps every generation of young men and women considers that those it once regarded as great figures had a stature lacked by their equivalents in later years. But I would certainly be hard put now to find on the backbenches the extraordinary range of experience and talents which characterized the House of Commons then. Almost whatever the subject, there would be some figure on either side of the House who would bring massive, specialized knowledge and obvious intuition to bear on it – and be listened to with respect by front and backbenches alike.

As it happens, I had very little opportunity during my first few months as an MP for the relaxed acquisition of experience of the House. With 310 other Members I had entered the Commons ballot for the introduction of Private Members' Bills. Never previously having so much as won a raffle, I was greatly astonished to find myself drawn second. Only the first few Private Members' Bills have any chance of becoming legislation, and even then the Government's attitude towards them is crucial.

I had only given the most general consideration to the topic I would choose, but I now had just a week to make up my mind, for the Bill had to be tabled by 11 November. Clearly, it must be something about which I not only felt strongly but also, preferably, in an area I already knew. I got as far as approving a draft long title for a Bill relating to appeals in contempt of court cases – one of those minor Bills which the Whips' Office keeps in reserve to pass off on unsuspecting backbenchers. But this seemed rather dry and I could not summon up much enthusiasm for it. So I thought again.

Many of us on the right of the Party – and not just on the right – were becoming very concerned about the abuse of trade union power. I had read and discussed with my lawyer friends a pamphlet on the subject produced by the Inns of Court Conservative Society the previous year. Entitled *A Giant's Strength*, it was, I understood, largely the work of a brilliant young Tory barrister called Geoffrey Howe. In particular, I was following throughout this period the lengthy and controversial case of *Rookes v Barnard*, relating to the closed shop. Rookes had resigned from his trade union which thereupon threatened his employer, the airline BOAC, with a strike if he was not dismissed from his post. BOAC promptly and pusillanimously complied and Rookes sued the trade union officials. I was outraged by the trampling of what I saw as someone's basic right to join or not to join a union. I also admired Rookes's determination and courage. I sought advice about whether I could introduce a Bill which would break or at least weaken the power of the closed shop.

But here again there were difficulties. Although younger Tories and many backbenchers were restive on the issue, the prevailing ethos in the upper ranks of the Conservative Party was still one of accommodating and appeasing the unions. It was therefore extremely unlikely that I could effect the change in the law which I wanted. The Whips made it clear to me that I would not have the Party's support. Moreover, the case itself was still undecided – and would not finally be determined until 1964. At the time that I was considering introducing a Bill the Appeal Court had ruled against Rookes, but in the end the House of Lords found against the trade union. There were, therefore, strong arguments that the law should not be changed partway through a test case. I bowed to these considerations.

The issue on which I finally alighted was also essentially one of civil liberties under threat from collectivism. As a result of an industrial dispute in the printing industry which began in July 1958, a number of Labour-controlled councils in big cities had denied normal reporting facilities to journalists working on provincial newspapers involved in the dispute. This had highlighted a loophole in the law which many councils used to conceal information from the general public about their activities. The press had a statutory right of admission only to meetings of the full council, not to its committees. By the device of resolving to go into committee, councils could therefore exclude the press from their deliberations. And besides these 'committees of the whole council' there were many other committees which were closed. Large sums of rate-payers' money could be spent – or mis-spent – without outside scrutiny. Nor did members of the public themselves have the right to attend any council or council committee meetings.

My own interest in the question stemmed partly from the fact that it had come to a head because of socialist connivance with trade union power, partly because I knew from Nottingham, not far from Grantham, what was going on, and partly because the present situation offended against my belief in accountability by government for the spending of people's money. The 1959 Conservative manifesto had contained a promise 'to make quite sure that the press have proper facilities for reporting the proceedings of local authorities'. Having read this, I imagined that a Bill to do just that would be welcome to the Government. I was again swiftly disillusioned by the Whips. Apparently, nothing more than a code of practice on the subject had been envisaged. This seemed to me extremely feeble, and so I decided to go ahead.

It quickly became clear that the objection to a measure with teeth came not from ministers at the Ministry of Housing and Local Government but rather from officials, who in turn were doubtless echoing the fierce opposition of the local authorities to any democratic check on their powers. Henry Brooke, the Cabinet minister in charge, was consistently sympathetic. Each Private Member's Bill is placed under the supervision of a junior minister who either helps or hinders its progress. My Bill was given to Sir Keith Joseph, and it was in examination of the tedious technical intricacies of the measure that I first got to know Keith.

I learned a great deal in a very short time from the experience of devising, refashioning and negotiating for my Bill. Partly because the issue had been a live one for a number of years, but partly also because of senior Members' kindness towards a new Member, I was able to rely on invaluable assistance from backbench colleagues. Sir Lionel Heald, a former Attorney General, gave me the benefit of his great legal experience. I learned from him and others the techniques of legal draftsmanship which were generally the preserve of the parliamentary draftsmen.

I also witnessed the power of pressure groups. The influence of the local authority lobby made itself felt in a hundred ways, and not only through the Labour Party. I therefore learned to play pressure group against pressure group and made the most of the help offered to me by the Newspaper Editors' Guild and other press bodies.

In the end, however, there is no substitute for one's own efforts. I wanted to get as many MPs as possible to the House on a Friday (when most MPs have returned to their constituency) for the Bill's Second Reading – this was the great hurdle. I have always believed in the impact of a personal handwritten letter – even from someone you barely know. So just before Second Reading I wrote 250 letters to Government backbenchers asking them to attend and vote for my measure.

There were other complications. I had originally envisaged waiting several months to make my maiden speech, because I had been advised first to get the feel of the House. I had had it in mind to speak on Lord Radcliffe's *Report on the Working of the Monetary System* which had appeared in the late summer – I was fascinated by the techniques of monetary policy which it outlined. But I did not have the time to prepare such a speech as well as the speech to introduce the Second Reading of my new Bill, so I decided to concentrate on the latter. That in turn faced a further obstacle. Convention dictated that a maiden speech should be a modest, uncontroversial affair, larded with appreciative references to my predecessor and my constituency. This was now impossible, because a maiden speech on the Second Reading of a Bill like mine could not have avoided controversy.

At least, though, I was not short of content. By the time I rose to deliver my speech on Friday 5 February 1960, I knew the arguments by heart. As a result, I could speak for almost half an hour without notes to hand – though not without nerves. The three women members of the Government – Pat Hornsby-Smith, Mervyn Pike and Edith Pitt – showed moral support from the front bench, and the House was very full for a Friday. I was delighted that nearly 200 Members voted, and we won handsomely. I was also genuinely moved by the comments that different MPs made to me personally – particularly Rab Butler, the Leader of the House and a master of ambiguous compliments, whose congratulations on this occasion, however, were straightforward, generous and very welcome to a new Member.

It was clear from the press next day that the speech had been a success and that I was – for the present at least – a celebrity. 'A new star was born in Parliament', thrilled the *Daily Express*. 'Fame and Margaret Thatcher made friends yesterday', shrieked the *Sunday Dispatch*. 'A triumph', observed the *Daily Telegraph* evenly. Feature articles appeared about me and my family. I was interviewed on television. The cameras came down to 'Dormers', and in an unguarded moment in answer to one of the more preposterous questions I told a journalist that 'I couldn't even consider a Cabinet post until my twins are older.' But apart from this gaffe it was roses, roses all the way.

Excessive praise? I had no doubt myself that it was. And I was slightly nervous that it might excite the jealousy of colleagues. My speech had been a competent performance, but it was not an epic.

But was it, however, a portent? Some time before the general election I had read John Buchan's *The Gap in the Curtain*. I had not thought more about it until I considered these somewhat overstated headlines. John Buchan's tale concerns a group of men, including several politicians, who spend Whitsun at a friend's house where they are enabled by another guest, a mysterious and fatally ill physicist of world renown, to glimpse the contents of a page of *The Times* one year later. Each sees something affecting his own future. One, a new Conservative MP, reads a brief obituary of himself which notes that he had delivered a brilliant maiden speech that had made him a national figure overnight. And so it turns out. The speech is outstanding, praised and admired on all sides; but after that, deprived of the self-confidence which knowledge of the future gave him, he fails totally and sinks into oblivion, waiting for the end. I shuddered slightly and reached for my lucky pearls.

But my Bill – with the significant addition that members of the general public should have the same rights as the press to attend council meetings, and with committees (apart from committees of the whole council) excluded from its provisions – duly passed into law; and, though my seven-day stardom faded somewhat, I had learned a lot and gained a good deal of confidence.

THE RIGHT LEFT PEOPLE

Life on the backbenches was always exciting – but so hectic that on one occasion, to the consternation of my male colleagues, I fainted in the Members' Dining Room. I spent as much time as I could in the House and at backbench committees. I also regularly attended the dining club of new Tory Members to which the great figures of the Party – Harold Macmillan, Rab Butler, Iain Macleod and Enoch Powell – and brilliant young Tory journalists like Peter Utley would come to speak.

The natural path to promotion and success at this time lay in the centre of politics and on the left of the Conservative Party. Above all, the up-and-coming Tory politician had to avoid being 'reactionary'. Nothing was likely to be so socially and professionally damaging as to bear that label. Conservatism at this time lacked fire. Even though what are now widely seen as the damaging moral, social and economic developments of the sixties mainly belong to the period of Labour Government after 1964, the first years of the decade also were ones of drift and cynicism, for which Conservatives must be held in large part responsible.

Indeed, Conservatives in the early sixties were living through one of their occasional phases of complacency. Macmillan's 1959 landslide and the continuous rise in affluence combined to persuade even non-partisan commentators that the Tories were now the party of 'modernization' and that Labour, with its 'cloth cap image', was in danger of being relegated to permanent opposition. Rab Butler told us at the New Members' Dining Club one evening that if the Party played its cards well, we would be in power for the next twenty-five years. In these circumstances there was little incentive for either serious forward thinking on policy or philosophical reflection. The main dispute within the Tory Party was over Iain Macleod's 'Scramble from Africa', with the old right complaining that Britain was abandoning its responsibility both to white settlers and to the African majorities of tribal farmers by giving power to rootless urban African politicians who would become dictators in short order. Time has made these fears seem prescient; in the early sixties they looked like a nostalgic hankering for an Empire that had almost passed into history. A passionate minority of Tory MPs embraced these criticisms; most of us, though, thought that Iain Macleod was applying Tory 'modernization' to colonial policy and backed him.

The odd thing is, looking back, that Conservatives in the sixties, though increasingly and obsessively worried about being out of touch with contemporary trends and fashions, were beginning to lose touch with the instincts and aspirations of ordinary conservative-minded people. This was true on issues as different as trade unions and immigration, law and order and aid to the Third World. But it was also and most directly important as regards management of the economy.

It was not so much inflation, which was zero throughout the winter of 1959–60 and did not reach 5 per cent until the summer of 1961, but rather the balance of payments that was seen as the main economic constraint on growth. And the means adopted to deal with the problems at this time – credit controls, interest rate rises, the search for international credit to sustain the pound, tax rises and, increasingly, prototype incomes policies – became all too familiar over the next fifteen years.

The rethinking that produced first 'Selsdon Man' and later Thatcherism was barely in evidence. Enoch Powell at this time was pushing through his ten-year hospital building programme – one of the largest programmes of public spending presided over by Macmillan. Only a handful of backbenchers – including the recently arrived John Biffen – were prepared to argue the case against incomes policy and for monetary control of inflation. Indeed, an unhealthy concern with inflation (as opposed to unemployment) was seen by the powers-that-be as reflecting the interests of declining sectors of British society, such as fixed-income pensioners, rather than the new and exciting 'young managers' of Conservative Central Office's imagination – at least until the fixed-income pensioners handed us a series of by-election defeats like Orpington and Middlesbrough West in the Tory heartland. These, together with the series of scandals from 1962 onwards, marked the end of the complacent period of Macmillanite Conservatism. Ahead of us lay years of defeat, opposition and (eventually) serious rethinking as Conservatives felt their way instinctively out of paternalism and into a new style of Toryism.

Although no really serious trouble in my relations with the Government and with the prevailing orthodoxy in the Conservative Party ever threatened when I was on the backbenches, I was conscious that, for all the plaudits I had received, I was not one of those young Tories who could expect to rise without trace. I had my own beliefs. I was uneasy about the general direction in which we seemed to be going. It would be wrong to suggest anything stronger than that. But for someone who believed in sound finance, the creative potential of free enterprise and social discipline, there was much to be concerned about.

The more I learned about it, the less impressed I was by our management of the economy. I listened with great care to the speeches of the Tory backbencher Nigel Birch, which were highly critical of the Government's failure to control public spending. The Government's argument was that increases could be afforded as long as the economy continued to grow. But this in turn edged us towards policies of injecting too much demand and then pulling back sharply when this produced pressures on the balance of payments or sterling. This is precisely what happened in the summer of 1961 when the Chancellor of the Exchequer Selwyn Lloyd introduced a deflationary Budget and our first incomes policy, the 'pay pause'. Another effect, of course, was to keep taxation higher than would otherwise be necessary. Chancellors of the Exchequer, wary of increases in basic income tax, laid particular importance on checking tax avoidance and evasion, repeatedly extending Inland Revenue powers to do so. Both as a tax lawyer and from my own instinctive dislike of handing more power to bureaucracies, I felt strongly on the matter and helped to write a critical report by the Inns of Court Conservative Society.

I felt even more strongly that the fashionable liberal tendencies in penal policy should be sharply reversed. So I spoke – and voted – in support of a new clause which a group of us wanted to add on to that year's Criminal Justice Bill which would have introduced birching or caning for young violent offenders. In the prevailing climate of opinion, this was a line which I knew would expose me to ridicule from the self-consciously high-minded and soft-hearted commentators. But my constituents did not see it that way, and nor did a substantial number of us on the right. Although the new clause was entirely predictably defeated, sixty-nine Tory back-benchers voted against the Government and in support of it. It was the biggest Party revolt since we came to power in 1951, and the Whips' Office were none too pleased. It was also the only occasion in my entire time in the House of Commons when I voted against the Party line.

The summer of 1961 was a more than usually interesting time in politics. I retained my close interest in foreign affairs, which were dominated by the uneasy developing relationship between Kennedy and Khrushchev, the building by the Soviets of the Berlin Wall (which the House was recalled to discuss) and, closer to home, by the beginning of negotiations for Britain to join the Common Market. There was also speculation about a reshuffle. In spite of my slightly blotted copybook, I had some reason to think that I might be a beneficiary of it. I had remained to a modest degree in the public eye, and not just with my speech on corporal punishment. I gave a press conference with Eirene White, the Labour MP for East Flint, on the lack of provision being made for the needs of pre-school children in high-rise flats, a topic of growing concern at this time when so many of these badly designed monstrosities were being erected. But the main reason why I had hopes of benefiting from the reshuffle was very simple. Pat Hornsby-Smith had decided to resign to pursue her business interests, and it was thought politically desirable to keep up the number of women in the Government. I even had more than an inkling of what my future post might be. It leaked out that there were two jobs available – one at Aviation and the other at Pensions. Much as I would have liked it, I could not see them giving Aviation in those days to a young woman.

That said, I did not try to conceal my delight when the telephone rang and I was summoned to see the Prime Minister. Harold Macmillan was camping out in some style at Admiralty House while 10 Downing Street was undergoing extensive refurbishment. I had already developed my own strong impressions of him, not just from speeches in the House and to the 1922 Committee, but also when he came to speak to our New Members' Dining Club – on which occasion he had strongly recommended Disraeli's *Sybil* and *Coningsby* as political reading. But Disraeli's style was too ornate for my taste, though I can see why it may have appealed to Harold Macmillan. It is now clear to me that Macmillan was a more complex and sensitive figure than he appeared; but appearance did seem to count for a great deal. Certainly, whether it was striking a bargain and cementing a friendship with President Kennedy, or delivering a deliciously humorous put-down to a ranting Khrushchev, Harold Macmillan was a superb representative of Britain abroad.

In both foreign and home policies Macmillan always prided himself on having a sense of history. In his attempts to establish harmony between the two superpowers, as in his fervent belief that Britain's destiny lay in Europe, he was much affected by the experience of two world wars. Indeed, as he would remind us, he was one of the few surviving members of the House who had fought in the Great War. In his preference for economic expansion over financial soundness and his long-standing belief in the virtues of planning, he was reacting against the deflation and unemployment of the 1930s which he had seen as MP for Stockton-on-Tees. It is said that when he was Chancellor of the Exchequer Treasury officials kept a tally of how many times he mentioned 'Stockton' each week. But history's lessons usually teach us what we want to learn. It was possible to take a very different view of the causes of war and of the historic achievements of capitalism. Things looked different from the perspective of Grantham than from that of Stockton.

INTO OFFICE...

I sorted out my best outfit, this time sapphire blue, to go and see the Prime Minister. The interview was short. Harold Macmillan charmingly greeted me and offered the expected appointment. I enthusiastically accepted. I wanted to begin as soon as possible and asked him how I should arrange things with the department. Characteristically, he said: 'Oh well, ring the Permanent Secretary and turn up at about 11 o'clock tomorrow morning, look around and come away. I shouldn't stay too long.'

So it was the following morning – rather before eleven – that I arrived at the pleasant Georgian house in John Adam Street, just off the Strand, which was at that time the headquarters of the Ministry of Pensions and National Insurance. In a gesture which I much appreciated – and which I myself as a Cabinet minister always emulated – John Boyd-Carpenter, my minister, was there at the front door to meet me and take me up to my new office. John was someone it was easy to like and admire for his personal kindness, grasp of detail and capacity for lucid exposition of a complex case. He was an excellent speaker and debater. All in all, a good model for a novice Parliamentary Secretary to follow. After his promotion to become Chief Secretary to the Treasury in 1962, my new minister was Niall Macpherson, who in turn made way for Richard Wood. I was very lucky in all of them. A Parliamentary Secretary's job is only as interesting and worthwhile as the senior minister makes it. I felt that they gave me every opportunity. This first day at John Adam Street was more or less a whirl of new faces and unfamiliar issues. There was little time to do more than take my bearings and receive my briefing.

On Friday (my birthday) I was given a prominent place on the platform at the Conservative Party Conference in Brighton. The cameras were once more active when I appeared at the Conference emerging, as it was remarked, from a royal blue car and wearing a royal blue dress and hat. Both my appointment and my appearance were something of a contrast to the general mood of the Conference which, like the limited reshuffle itself that had brought Iain Macleod to the Party Chairmanship, was widely seen as moving the Party in a leftward direction.

Back at the Ministry I was not at all displeased to substitute grind for glamour. The issues dealt with by what was then the Ministry of Pensions and National Insurance and is now the Department of Social Security are more technically complicated than those falling to any other branch of government, with the possible exception of the tax side of the Treasury. It was not just a matter of avoiding being caught out in the House of Commons. If one was to make any serious contribution to the development of policy one had to have mastered both the big principles and the detail. This I now set out to do.

The first step was to re-read the original Beveridge Report in which the philosophy of the post-war system of pensions and benefits was clearly set out. I was already quite well acquainted with its main aspects and I strongly approved of them. At the centre was the concept of a comprehensive 'social insurance scheme', which was intended to cover loss of earning power caused by unemployment, sickness or retirement. This would be done by a single system of benefits at subsistence level financed by flat-rate individual contributions. By the side of this there would be a system of National Assistance, financed out of general taxation, to help those who were unable to sustain themselves on National Insurance benefits, either because they had been unable to contribute, or had run out of cover. National Assistance was means tested and had been envisaged as in large part a transitional system, whose scope would diminish as pensions or personal savings rose.

It is easy in retrospect to poke fun at many of Beveridge's assumptions and predictions. He greatly underestimated the cost of his proposals, though this was partly because the post-war Labour Government introduced full rate old-age pensions immediately, without the twenty-year phasing-in period which Beveridge had envisaged. There were other problems too. The relationship, which in any individual case was always bound to be indirect, between contributions on the one hand and benefits on the other became ever more obscure as pensions were increased and as the proportion of elderly people in the population grew. Far from diminishing, National Assistance and its successors, Supplementary Benefit and Income Support, swelled to become an alarming burden on the taxpayer. Anomalies between the two notionally complementary, but in practice often contradictory, systems became a perpetual headache.

But for all that, Beveridge had sought to guard against the very problems which later governments more or less ignored and which have now returned to plague us, in particular the debilitating effects of welfare dependency and the loss of private and voluntary effort. Whatever the effects in practice, the Beveridge Report's rhetoric has what would later be considered a Thatcherite ring to it:

. . . The State should offer security for service and contribution. The State in organizing security should not stifle
incentive, opportunity, responsibility; in establishing a
national minimum, it should leave room and encouragement
for voluntary action by each individual to provide more than
that minimum for himself and his family. [Paragraph 9]
. . . The insured persons should not feel that income for idleness, however caused, can come from a bottomless purse.
[Paragraph 22]
. . . Material progress depends upon technical progress which
depends upon investment and ultimately upon savings . . . It
is important that part of the additional resources going to
wage-earners and others of limited means should be saved by
them instead of being spent forthwith. [Paragraph 376]

Much of our time at the Ministry was taken up both with coping
with the effects of and finding remedies to the difficulties which
flowed from the gap between Beveridge's original conception and
the way in which the system – and with it public expectations –
had developed. So, for example, in those days before inflation took
hold and benefits were annually up-rated to cope with it, there
were cries of disapproval when National Insurance pensions were
increased and National Assistance, which made up your income to
a certain level, was not. People also increasingly came to expect
something better than a subsistence-level pension to retire upon,
but the contribution levels or financing from general taxation which
this would require seemed prohibitive. This lay behind John Boyd-
Carpenter's idea of the 'graduated pensions' scheme, whereby the
payment of higher contributions could secure a somewhat higher
pension, and provision was made for the encouragement of private
occupational pension schemes. Another constant source of difficulty
for which we found no ultimate (affordable) answer was the 'earnings rule' whereby pensioners who worked would at a certain level
of income lose part or all of their pension payments. As I shall
explain, it was the impact of this on pensioner widows which caused
me most difficulty and not a little heart-searching.

Three other questions, which were to trouble governments for
many years to come, had also already begun to loom. There was

the issue of how to ensure decent levels of incomes for elderly pensioners who had not paid in sufficient contributions to be able to claim a full National Insurance pension. There was the continual search for greater 'selectivity' (as the jargon had it) in Social Security benefits generally – that is, concentrating them on the most needy rather than on the general broad range of benefit recipients. (In fact, as our current debates on 'targeting benefits' – in today's jargon – shows, this has proved a largely fruitless exercise.) Finally, there was the whole argument about the 'stigma' attached to National Assistance and the means test. As I frequently pointed out, this had two sides to it. On the one hand, of course, people living in real poverty ought to be encouraged to take the state help which is on offer. On the other hand, the self-respect of those people I used to refer to as 'the proud ones', who were not going to take hand-outs from anyone, was morally admirable and, as can now be seen all too clearly, a check on dependency whose removal could ultimately have devastating social consequences.

Apart from the Beveridge Report and other general briefing from the department, it was the case work – that is the investigation of particular people's problems raised in letters – which taught me most about the Social Security system. I was not prepared to sign a reply if I did not feel that I properly understood the background. Consequently, a stream of officials came in and out of my modest office to give me the benefit of their matchless knowledge of each topic. I adopted a similar approach to parliamentary questions, which would be shared out between the ministers. I was not content to know the answer or the line to take. I wanted to know why. The weekend before my first appearance at the Despatch Box to answer questions was, I fear, almost as nerve-racking for my Private Secretary as it was for me, since I was all the time on the telephone to him for explanations.

Apart from some peppery exchanges with the civil servants allocated to deal with my Private Member's Bill, it was at Pensions that I had my first professional dealings with the civil service. The Permanent Secretary of the department in practice wields a good deal more power than a junior minister. It was made clear to me early on that he was answerable only to the ministerial head of the department. The two successive Permanent Secretaries during my time at Pensions, Eric Bowyer and Clifford Jarrett, were representatives of the civil service at its best – clever, conscientious and of complete integrity. But the real experts were likely to be found further down the hierarchy. I quickly discovered that the infallible source of information on pensions was a Deputy Secretary, John Walley. Generally, the calibre of the officials I met impressed me.

Having served as a junior minister to three different ministers in the same department I was interested to see that the advice tendered to the ministers by civil servants differed, even though it was on the same topic. So I complained when both Niall Macpherson and Richard Wood received policy submissions proposing approaches that I knew had not been put to their predecessor, John Boyd-Carpenter. I remember saying afterwards: 'That's not what you advised the previous minister.' They replied that they had known that he would never accept it. I decided then and there that when I was in charge of a department I would insist on an absolutely frank assessment of all the options from any civil servants who would report to me. Arguments should be from first principles.

I also learned another lesson. There was a good deal of pressure to remove the earnings rule as regards widowed mothers. I sympathized with it strongly. Indeed, this was one of the issues upon which, as a new MP, I had publicly stated my position. I thought that if a woman who had lost her husband but still had children to support decided to try to earn a little more through going out to work she should not lose pension for doing so. Perhaps as a woman I had a clearer idea of what problems widows faced. Perhaps it was my recollection of the heartbreaking sight of a recently widowed mother eking out her tiny income buying bruised fruit at my father's shop in Grantham. But I found it almost impossible to defend the Government line against Opposition attack. I raised the matter with officials and with my minister. On one occasion, I even raised it with Alec Douglas-Home as Prime Minister when he came to speak to a group of junior ministers. But although he seemed sympathetic, I never got anywhere.

The argument from officials in the department was always that ending the earnings rule for even this most deserving group would have 'repercussions' elsewhere. And, of course, they were logically correct. But how I came to hate that word 'repercussions'.

Ministers were wrong to take such arguments at face value and
not to apply political judgement to them. It was no surprise to me
that one of the first acts of the incoming Labour Government in
1964 was to make the change for which I had been arguing, and
to get the credit too. The moral was clear to me: bureaucratic
logic is no substitute for ministerial judgement. Forget that as a
politician, and the political 'repercussions' will be on you.

My days at Pensions were full. Although I shared a ministerial
car with my colleague, the junior minister who dealt with war
pensions, I generally drove myself in from Farnborough in the
mornings. At the Ministry the day might begin with the two junior
ministers meeting John Boyd-Carpenter to discuss the larger policy
issues or the current political situation. Then there would be
batches of letters for me to sign or on which I would seek advice.
I might have a meeting about particular areas of responsibility
which my minister had given me, such as working out reciprocal
arrangements on pensions with other countries. I would have meetings with officials in preparation for papers on forward planning in
Social Security – a task which was as necessary as it was difficult.
In the afternoon a deputation from the pressure groups, which even
in those days abounded in the social services field, might arrive to
put its case to me for the correction of some alleged anomaly or
the increase of some benefit. I sometimes visited regional Social
Security offices, talking to the staff about the problems they faced
and listening to suggestions. I would dine at the House or perhaps
with political friends – an invitation to dinner with Ernest Marples,
the ebullient and original politician who made a name for himself
as Transport Minister, and his wife was always a guarantee of
superb food and fine wine, as well as jovial company. If there was
a division, I would often be in the House to vote at 10 o'clock,
before driving back home with two or three red boxes full of draft
letters and policy papers to read into the early hours.

I retained my taste for the Chamber of the Commons, developed
during my two years on the backbenches. We faced no mean opponents on the Labour benches. Dick Crossman had one of the finest
minds in politics, if also one of the most wayward, and Douglas
Houghton a formidable mastery of his brief. I liked both of them,
but I was still determined to win any argument. I enjoyed the

battle of facts and figures when our policies were under fire at Question Time and when I was speaking in debates – though sometimes I should have trod more warily. One day at the Despatch Box I was handed a civil service note giving new statistics about a point raised in the debate. 'Now,' I said triumphantly, 'I have the latest red hot figure.' The House dissolved into laughter, and it took a moment for me to realize my *double entendre*.

As luck would have it, at Pensions we were due to answer questions on the Monday immediately after the notorious Cabinet reshuffle in July 1962 which became known as 'The Night of the Long Knives'. John Boyd-Carpenter departed to become Chief Secretary to the Treasury and Niall Macpherson had not yet replaced him at Pensions. Since most of the questions on the Order Paper related to my side of the department's activities, rather than War Pensions, I would have to answer in the place of the senior minister for nearly an hour. That meant another nerve-racking weekend for me and for the officials I had to pester. The Labour Party was in rumbustious mood and Iain Macleod was the only Cabinet minister in the Chamber. But I got through, saying when asked about future policy that I would refer the matter to my minister – 'when I had one'.

. . . AND OUT AGAIN

But would the Government get through? As I was to experience myself many years later, every Cabinet reshuffle contains its own unforeseen dangers. But no difficulties I ever faced – even in 1989 – matched the appalling damage to the Government done by 'The Night of the Long Knives', in which one third of the Cabinet, including the Lord Chancellor and the Chancellor of the Exchequer, were despatched and a new generation including Reggie Maudling, Keith Joseph and Edward Boyle found themselves in the front line of politics. One of the lessons I learned from the affair was that one should try to bring in some younger people to the Government at each reshuffle so as to avoid a log-jam. But in any case the handling of the changes was badly botched by Macmillan, whose standing never really recovered.

We were already in trouble for a number of obvious – and some less obvious – reasons. Inflation had started to rise quite sharply. Incomes policy in the form of the 'pay pause' and then the 'guiding light' had been employed in an attempt to control it. Industrial disputes, especially the engineering and shipbuilding strikes, led to more days being lost due to strikes in 1962 than in any year since the General Strike of 1926. Rather than deal with the roots of the problem, which lay in trade union power, the Government moved towards corporatist deals with organized labour by setting up the National Economic Development Council (NEDC) – shortly to be supplemented by a National Incomes Commission (NIC) – so accepting a fundamentally collectivist analysis of what was wrong with Britain.

Above all, out in the country there had grown up a detectable feeling that the Conservatives had been in power too long and had lost their way. That most dangerous time for a government had arrived when most people feel, perhaps only in some vague way, that it is 'time for a change'. Later in the autumn of 1962 the Government ran into squalls of a different kind. The Vassall spy case, the flight of Philby to the Soviet Union, confirming suspicions that he had been a KGB double-agent since the 1930s, and in the summer of 1963 the Profumo scandal – all served to enmesh the Government in rumours of sleaze and incompetence. These might have been shrugged off by a government in robust health. But the significance attached to these embarrassments was the greater because of the general *malaise*.

Europe was one of the main reasons for that *malaise*. In October 1961 Ted Heath had been entrusted by Harold Macmillan with the difficult negotiations for British membership of the European Economic Community. Not least because of Ted's tenacity and dedication, most of the problems, such as what to do about Britain's agriculture and about trade links with the Commonwealth, seemed eminently soluble. Then in January 1963 General de Gaulle vetoed our entry. No great popular passions about Europe were aroused at this time in Britain. There was a general sense, which I shared, that in the past we had underrated the potential advantage to Britain of access to the Common Market, that neither the European Free Trade Association (EFTA) nor our links with the Commonwealth and the United States offered us the trading future we needed, and that the time was right for us to join the EEC. I was an active member of the European Union of Women – an organization founded in Austria in 1953 to promote European integration – and sat on its 'Judicial Panel' which debated issues relating to law and the family. But I saw the EEC as essentially a trading framework – a Common Market – and neither shared nor took very seriously the idealistic rhetoric with which 'Europe' was already being dressed in some quarters. In fact, it is now clear to me that General de Gaulle was much more perceptive than we were at this time when, to our great chagrin and near universal condemnation, he noted:

England in effect is insular, she is maritime, she is linked through her exchanges, her markets, her supply lines to the most diverse and often the most distant countries; she pursues essentially industrial and commercial activities, and only slight agricultural ones . . . In short, the nature, the structure, the very situation that are England's differ profoundly from those of the Continentals . . .

But he also said:

If the Brussels negotiations were shortly not to succeed, nothing would prevent the conclusion between the Common Market and Great Britain of an accord of association designed to safeguard exchanges, and nothing would prevent close relations between England and France from being maintained, nor the pursuit and development of their direct cooperation in all kinds of fields . . .

It is evident that if this is what de Gaulle was indeed offering, it would have been a better reflection of British interests than the terms of British membership that were eventually agreed a decade later. We may have missed the best European bus that ever came along. At the time, however, so much political capital had been invested by Harold Macmillan in the European venture that its undignified collapse deprived our foreign policy of its main current objective and contributed to the impression that the Government had lost its sense of direction.

The Labour Party had suffered a tragedy when Hugh Gaitskell died young in January 1963. Harold Wilson was elected as Leader. Though lacking the respect which Gaitskell had won, Wilson was in himself a new and deadly threat to the Government. He was a formidable parliamentary debater with a rapier wit. He knew how to flatter the press to excellent effect. He could coin the kind of ambiguous phrase to keep Labour united (e.g. 'planned growth of incomes' rather than 'incomes policy'), and he could get under Harold Macmillan's skin in a way Hugh Gaitskell never could. While Gaitskell was more of a statesman than Wilson, Wilson was an infinitely more accomplished politician.

As a result of all these factors, the Conservatives' standing in the polls fell alarmingly as the dismal course of 1963 unfolded. In July Labour were some 20 per cent ahead. In early October at the Labour Party Conference Harold Wilson's brilliant but shallow speech about the 'white heat' of scientific revolution caught the imagination of the country, or at least of the commentators. And then just a few days later – a bombshell – a resignation statement from Harold Macmillan's hospital bed was read out by Alec Douglas-Home to the Party Conference at Blackpool, which was immediately transformed into a kind of gladiatorial combat by the leadership candidates.

This made Blackpool the most exciting Tory Conference anyone has ever witnessed. There was an atmosphere of 'buzz, buzz, buzz' as the contenders – at first Rab Butler and Quintin Hogg – and their supporters manoeuvred for advantage. As a junior minister, I was very much on the outside of even the outer ring of the magic circle. But I felt that the victory was Rab's for the taking. He was a statesman of vast experience and some vision who had missed the leadership by a whisker six years before. Quintin Hogg, or as he still was and later became Lord Hailsham, had more flair and great powers of oratory, but also a reputation at that time for erratic judgement. In brief, Rab failed to grasp the opportunity which was there, making a pedestrian speech at the final rally; while Quintin grabbed and ran off with an opportunity that had never existed in the first place. So when the politicians entrained for London that Saturday, the contest was still undecided.

But the real battle for the Conservative leadership – if a military metaphor can be applied to the subtle processes by which Tory leaders at that time 'emerged' – was taking place elsewhere. The subtlest process of all was the way in which Harold Macmillan let it be known that he favoured Hogg over Butler, thus stopping any bandwagon for the latter and preparing the ground for the 'emergence' of Alec Douglas-Home. Iain Macleod was to write devastatingly in the *Spectator* about the way in which the magic circle of the Party ignored Butler and at Macmillan's behest engineered this. I admired Iain Macleod, as I did Enoch Powell, both of whom subsequently refused to serve in the new Prime Minister's Cabinet. But I did not agree with their criticisms either of the process or of the choice. I thought at the time there was something to be said for avoiding the public divisions in the Party which open elections would necessitate. I am not in general a believer in changing customs and conventions simply because rationalizing critics demand it. The way in which a Party Leader is chosen seemed to me of much less importance than whether the right person came out on top – and I thought that the right person had come out on top.

The Monday following the Conference I received a phone call from the Whips' Office to gauge my views on the leadership. I first told them that I would support Rab over Quintin, because he was simply the more qualified of the two. I was then asked my view of Alec. This opened up a possibility I had not envisaged. 'Is it constitutionally possible?' I asked. Assured that it was, I did not hesitate. I replied: 'Then I am strongly in favour of Alec.'

My only reservation, which I expressed at the time, was that there was something dubious about assuming the result of an election – Alec would have to disclaim his peerage and fight a by-election – when asking the monarch to choose a Prime Minister. But I also said that I left that question for others better qualified to consider. In retrospect, though, I would have to add one other qualification. Events in fact showed that the magic circle no longer provided the legitimacy for the men who emerged. It was a handicap to Alec as Prime Minister. By the time a new system was announced I too had come to see the need for it.

My admiration for Alec Douglas-Home was not the result of a recent conversion. When he became Foreign Secretary in June 1960 I had expressed doubts to Bettie Harvie-Anderson (MP for Renfrewshire East). I thought that there surely ought to be a suitable candidate for the post among the ministers in the Commons. Moreover, Anthony Eden had, I recalled, ostensibly refused to give the Foreign Secretaryship to Lord Salisbury on these grounds. But Betty told me that Alec was quite outstanding and deserved the job. So I decided to read the new Foreign Secretary's first speech in Hansard. It was a masterly survey of East–West relations, which emphasized the need for deterrence as well as negotiation with the Soviets and stressed the importance of our relationship with the United States. Alec now and later managed, most unusually, to combine skill in diplomacy with clarity of vision. He exhibited none of those tendencies, so characteristic of those who aspire to be Foreign Secretary, towards regarding the processes of negotiation as an end in themselves. Yet he had the charm, polish and eye for detail of the perfect negotiator.

Moreover, Alec Douglas-Home was a manifestly good man – and goodness is not to be underrated as a qualification for those considered for powerful positions. He was also in the best possible way 'classless'. You always felt that he treated you not as a category but as a person. And he actually listened – as I found when I took up with him the vexed question of the widowed mothers' allowance.

But the press were cruelly, ruthlessly and almost unanimously against him. He was easy to caricature as an out-of-touch aristocrat, a throwback to the worst sort of reactionary Toryism. Inverted snobbery was always to my mind even more distasteful than the straightforward self-important kind. By 1964 British society had entered a sick phase of liberal conformism passing as individual self-expression. Only progressive ideas and people were worthy of respect by an increasingly self-conscious and self-confident media class. And how they laughed when Alec said self-deprecatingly that he used matchsticks to work out economic concepts. What a contrast with the economic models with which the technically brilliant mind of Harold Wilson was familiar. No one stopped to question whether the weaknesses of the British economy were fundamentally simple and only superficially complex. In fact, if politicians had been compelled to use more honest language and simple illustrations to ensure that people understood their policies, we might well have avoided Britain's slither into relative decline.

For all that – in spite of the media criticism, in spite of the chaotic end of the Macmillan Government, in spite of the correct but appallingly timed abolition of Retail Price Maintenance which so offended small-business support for the Conservatives – we very nearly won the 1964 general election. This recovery was not because of any economic improvement, for inflation worsened and the balance of payments deficit yawned. Nor was it because of our 1964 manifesto, with its heavy emphasis on corporatism as the way out of the country's economic problems – territory on which the socialists were bound to be more convincing. In part it was because the closer one looked at the Labour Party's programme and its Leader, the less substantial they seemed. But mainly the credit for our political recovery should go to Alec. It is ironic that he had already been cast in the role of scapegoat for the defeat many thought inevitable.

There had been some press speculation that I might not hold Finchley. The Liberals, never reticent in talking up their chances, began predicting another Orpington. They had secured a tight grip on the old Finchley council, though in May 1964 they had done rather less well in the elections for the new Barnet borough council. The Golf Club scandal kept rumbling on. The Liberals' new, energetic candidate, John Pardoe, campaigned principally on local issues while I mainly stuck to national ones – above all, how to secure prosperity without inflation. The Party asked me to speak in a number of constituencies in and around London. I answered attacks on the Government's record on pensions and benefits at a noisy, hostile meeting of women at Bethnal Green. I wrote in an article in the *Evening Standard* on 'good housekeeping' as the test for sound policies.

But it was understood by Conservative Central Office that most of my effort should go into Finchley. It was my usual schedule of campaigning – daily canvassing, answering letters and a full programme of visits and public meetings, at which it seemed to me that not only did the numbers grow but also my support. I am always anxious on election day; but in 1964 my anxieties were, in spite of the predictions of my defeat at the start of the campaign, much greater for the Party nationally than for me in Finchley.

The results bore this out. I found myself with a majority over John Pardoe of almost 9,000. But I had seen the last of the Ministry at John Adam Street, for Labour had secured an overall majority of four seats. Thirteen years of Conservative Government were over and a period of fundamental rethinking of Conservative philosophy was about to begin – alas, not for the last time.

CHAPTER V

A World of Shadows

Opposition 1964–1970

CHANGING THE PIANIST

The Conservative Party has never been slow to shoot the pianist as a substitute for changing its tune. So it proved in the wake of our narrow 1964 election defeat. Anyone seriously thinking about the way forward for Conservatism would have started by examining whether the established tendency to fight on socialist ground with corporatist weapons had not something to do with the Party's predicament. Then and only then – after a more or less inevitable second election defeat, for there was a general sense in the country that Labour needed a larger working majority if it were to carry out its programme – would have been the time to consider a leadership change. I had hoped and indeed naively expected that the Party would soldier on under Alec Douglas-Home. I later heard that the supporters of Ted Heath and others anxious to oust Alec had been busy behind the scenes; but I never ventured into the Smoking Room and so I was unaware of these mysterious cabals until it was too late. I was stunned and upset when Alec told the 1922 Committee that he intended to stand down to make way for someone else; I was all the more distressed by his evident unhappiness. I kept on saying to people, 'Why didn't he let his supporters know? We might have been able to help.'

Reggie Maudling and Ted Heath were generally accepted as the only two figures in serious contention for the leadership, which for the first time would be decided by a ballot of MPs. Iain Macleod was considered too left wing and by many, in Lord Salisbury's jibe, as 'too clever by half'. Enoch Powell, who did indeed put his name forward, had no large following at this time. Of the two serious contenders, Reggie Maudling was thought to have the better chance. Although his performance as Chancellor of the Exchequer had incurred serious and in some ways justified criticism, there was no doubting Reggie's experience, brilliant intellect and command of the House. His main weakness, which grew more evident in later years, was a certain laziness – something which is a frequent temptation to those who know that they are naturally and effortlessly cleverer than those around them.

Ted had a very different character. He too had a very well organized mind. He was methodical, forceful and, at least on the one question which mattered to him above all others – Europe – a man of unyielding determination. As Shadow Chancellor he had the opportunity to demonstrate his capabilities in attacking the 1965 Finance Bill, which in those days was taken on the floor of the House. Ted was regarded as being somewhat to the right of Reggie, but they were both essentially centrists in Party terms. Something could be made of the different approaches they took to Europe, with Reggie regarding EFTA more favourably and Ted convinced that membership of the EEC was essential. But their attitudes to specific policies hardly affected the question of which to support.

I did not start with any particularly strong views on the matter. I knew both of them – Reggie Maudling as a neighbouring MP for Barnet and Ted Heath over a longer period when we were candidates for Kent constituencies. At this time I knew Reggie better. I liked his combination of laid-back charm and acute intellect. My acquaintanceship with Ted, though there was none of that bitter hostility which would develop in later years, had never risked developing into friendship. Although we came from not dissimilar backgrounds, neither of us having enjoyed the educational and social advantages of the traditional Tory politician, we were totally different sorts of people. Ted, of course, had fought with distinction in the war while I was a student at Somerville. He had been part of that generation which had been ineradicably affected by the rise of Nazism and fascism and the question of appeasement in the 1930s. So, of course, was I; but rather differently. Ted, to my mind, had swallowed a good deal of the fashionable interpretation of what had gone wrong in the world between the wars. For him, I imagine, as for many others who were to become passionate advocates of all things European, the evil genius of those times was nationalism. Consequently, Britain now had a duty to help create a Europe-wide structure which would supplant the nation state, provide an alternative focus for loyalties and so prevent war. For me, such grandiose visions had little appeal. I saw the principal cause of the conflict as being the appeasement of dictators – something which Ted himself had courageously opposed at Oxford – and I saw the principal victor of the conflict, whose health was itself the best guarantee of peace, as being the spirit and unity of the English-speaking world. Ted's character seemed to me in many ways admirable. But he was not charming – nor, to be fair, did he set out to be. He was probably more at ease talking to men than women. But it was not just women who found him difficult to get on with. I felt that though I had known him for years, there was a sense in which I did not know him at all. Perhaps I never would. I was not conscious at this time of any hostility, simply of a lack of human warmth. I did not either then or later regard amiability as an indispensable or even particularly important attribute of leadership. Yet, all things considered, I thought that I would vote for Reggie Maudling.

It was Keith Joseph who persuaded me to change my mind. By now Keith was a friend, not just a senior colleague whom I liked. We worked together, though with him very much as the senior partner, on pensions policy in 1964–65. Like everyone else who came to know him, I was deeply impressed by the quality of his mind and the depth of his compassion. Keith had gone into politics for the same reason that many on the left had done so – he wanted to improve the lot of ordinary people, particularly those he saw living deprived, stunted, unfulfilled lives. Many jokes would be made – and the best of them by Keith himself – about the way in which he changed his mind and reversed his policies on matters ranging from housing to health to social benefits. But the common thread was his relentless search for the right answer to the practical problems of human suffering. So I took him very seriously when he telephoned to say that while he knew I was currently intending to vote for Reggie, I should think again. Keith understood Reggie's weaknesses, and as a long-time colleague in Government and the Shadow Cabinet he had seen these weaknesses at close hand. But it was Ted's strengths that he wanted to speak about. He summed them up: 'Ted has a passion to get Britain right.' And, of course, so did Keith, and so did I.

This was decisive for me. To the disappointment and surprise of Reggie Maudling and his PPS, Neil Marten, I told them that Ted Heath would be getting my vote. Sufficient numbers thought similarly. Ted emerged with a clear majority on the first ballot, Reggie withdrawing to make a second ballot unnecessary.

I was not displeased to be given a different portfolio by the new Leader, exchanging my role as Shadow spokesman on Pensions for that of Housing and Land under my old boss, John Boyd-Carpenter. I would always regard my knowledge of the Social Security system as one of the most important aspects of what turned out to be my training to become Prime Minister. Now that we were in Opposition, however, it was not easy to oppose the large pension and benefit increases which the Labour Government was making: only later would the full financial implications of this spending spree become evident. So it was a relief to me to be moved to Housing and Land, where I was able to set about attacking with a will one of the most ideological socialist measures – the setting-up of the Land Commission, a means of achieving the socialist obsession of nationalizing development gains. It was in this role also that I first became fully acquainted with the complexities and anomalies of the rating system, whose fate seemed destined to be inextricably intertwined with mine.* One of my early tasks was to devise and explain to a sceptical Conservative Party Conference how we intended to reform domestic rates by a combination of moving some expenditure onto central government and introducing rate rebates. It was my first Conference speech. At least those who heard it would have appreciated that I grasped the problems. But it would be too much to claim that I offered any very satisfactory solutions. It was only a *succès d'estime*.

---

* See pp. 247–9; also *The Downing Street Years*, pp. 642–67.

AGAINST THE TREASURY

As was widely expected, Harold Wilson called an early snap election at the end of March 1966. The result – a Conservative rout and an overall Labour majority of ninety-seven – was equally expected. We fought an uninspiring campaign on the basis of a flimsy manifesto entitled *Action not Words*, which accurately summed up Ted's impact on politics. This was widely seen as a completion of Wilson's 1964 victory, and Ted was not blamed. I largely concentrated my efforts on Finchley and was not displeased to keep a healthy majority of 9,464, this time over the Labour Party which had beaten the Liberals into third place. But it was a depressing time. Denis knew my mood and went out to buy me an eternity ring to cheer me up.

I received a further fillip when Ted Heath made me Treasury spokesman on Tax under the Shadow Chancellor, Iain Macleod. There had been some speculation in the press that I would be promoted to the Shadow Cabinet myself. But I was not expecting it. I now know, having read Jim Prior's memoirs,* that I was indeed considered but that Ted, rather presciently, decided against it because if they got me in 'they would never get [me] out again'.

In any case, I was better placed to make an impact as Treasury spokesman outside the Shadow Cabinet than as something else within it. As a tax lawyer I already knew my way around my new brief. Although I had no formal training in economic theory, I felt naturally at ease with the concepts. I had always had strong convictions about the way in which public money should be handled. As I had found when junior minister responsible for pensions, I was lucky enough to have the sort of mind to grasp technical detail and understand quite complex figuring fairly easily. None of which meant, however, that I could afford to relax. Debating Finance Bills from Opposition, necessarily without the technical assistance available from the civil service, and relying on the help

---

* *A Balance of Power* (1986), p. 42.

of a few outside experts and colleagues in the House, is immensely demanding.

Luckily, the family's domestic arrangements permitted me to keep to my rigorous parliamentary schedule. By now, Mark and Carol were away at boarding school. Denis was still very active in business, although in 1965 he had sold the family firm to Castrol, which itself was soon bought by Burmah Oil. We felt that it would now make life much easier for us both to rent a flat in Westminster Gardens, not far from the House of Commons. We also sold our home in Farnborough and bought 'The Mount', a mock-Tudor house with a large garden in Lamberhurst, near Tunbridge Wells. One of my very few hobbies is interior decorating, and I now spent most of my free time painting and papering the bedrooms – all eight of them. But even I was defeated by the large hall and staircase and had to bring in the professionals. One reason why we bought the house was to have somewhere in the country for the children when they came back from boarding school in the holidays. But at this age they seemed to prefer staying in London with their friends. So 'The Mount' was not as much used as I would have liked. My programme of repairs and redecoration was not wasted, however: in 1972 we sold it, and out of the proceeds bought the house in Flood Street (Chelsea) which would be my home until in 1979 I moved into the flat above 10 Downing Street.

I not only felt well-suited to my new job: it was also an exciting time to begin it. The incoherence and irresponsibility of socialist economic management had become apparent. The optimistic pro-jections of George Brown's National Plan, published in September 1965, were an albatross to hang around Labour's neck, as forecasts of economic growth were not met. Labour's pre-election promises of 'no severe increases in taxation' were broken with the announce-ment in the Budget of May 1966 that a new Selective Employment Tax (SET) would be introduced, in effect a payroll tax falling particularly heavily on service industries: it was a major part of my brief to oppose it. The Labour Government's reliance on its alleged special relationship with the trade unions to secure volun-tary incomes restraint as a means of controlling inflation had already lost credibility with the failure of the Government-TUC joint *Declaration of Intent*, which had first been proclaimed amid

fanfares in December 1964. In July 1966 the 'voluntary' approach
was jettisoned. It was announced that there would be a six months'
wage freeze followed by six months of 'severe restraint'. Prices
would be frozen for a year, and a plea was made for limits to be
applied to dividends over the same period. The National Board of
Prices and Incomes, which Labour had established, was given
powers to require one month's advance notification of any price
and wage increases and powers to delay increases by Order-in-
Council for up to three months. The Government might take power
to direct that specified price and wage increases should not be
made. Fighting this policy in general and, under Iain Macleod's
leadership, opposing the 'Standstill orders' which came before the
House of Commons, were the other important aspects of my brief.

In preparing myself for my first major Commons speech in my
new role, I got out from the House of Commons Library every
Budget speech and Finance Bill since the war and read them. I
was thus able to demonstrate to a somewhat bemused Jim Callaghan, then Chancellor of the Exchequer, and Jack Diamond, his
Chief Secretary, that this was the only Budget which had failed to
make even a minor concession in the social services area. Then I
sunk my teeth into the SET. It was riddled with absurdities which I
took great pleasure in exposing. The attempt to distinguish between
manufacturing and service industries, shifting the tax burden onto
the second and handing the money back as subsidies to the first,
was a demonstrably inefficient, anomaly-ridden procedure. As I
put it in the House: 'Whatever the payroll tax is, it is thoroughly
bad administration . . . I only wish that Gilbert and Sullivan were
alive today so that we could have an opera about it.'

Our side of the House liked it. I got a good press, the *Daily
Telegraph* observing that 'it has taken a woman . . . to slam the
faces of the Government's Treasury ministers in the mud and then
stamp on them'. Iain Macleod himself wrote some generous lines
about the performance in another paper.

He did the same after my speech that autumn to the Party
Conference in Blackpool, my first real Conference success. I put a
special effort into it – though the nine hours of work I did would
have seemed culpable idleness compared with the time I took for
Conference speechwriting as Party Leader. That autumn, however,

I spoke from notes, which gives extra spontaneity and the flexibility to insert a joke or jibe on the spur of the moment. Although the debate I was answering was on taxation, the cheers came in response to what I said about the way in which the Government was undermining the rule of law by the arbitrary powers it had taken through incomes policy and tax policy. With more than a touch of hyperbole, it must be admitted, I said: 'All this is fundamentally wrong for Britain. It is a step not merely towards socialism but towards communism.' Some of the more squeamish journalists demurred. But not the new and still left-of-centre *Sun*, which noted: 'A Fiery Blonde Warns of the Road to Ruin'.

I was right to see a connection between the socialist approach to public expenditure and taxation on the one hand and to incomes policy on the other. They were both aspects of the same collectivist programme which, if taken to its ultimate conclusion, would jeopardize not just economic but political freedom as well. But what I and almost all of my colleagues at this time failed to do was to think through the full implications for our own policies. Although we wanted lower and simpler taxes on people and businesses, we were still inclined to assume – and not just for public presentation, but because we really thought it – that faster economic growth would allow us to cut taxes, as public expenditure measured as a share of GDP fell. We had some proposals to reduce public expenditure on socialist projects and waste. But we thought that we could create an atmosphere favourable to enterprise and so establish what was called a 'virtuous circle' in which higher growth allowed larger tax revenues with lower tax rates, which in turn stimulated further growth. Consequently, we were not as serious about making real public expenditure cuts as we should have been. Indeed, over the whole of this period – whether in 1956, 1966 or above all in 1976 – real cuts in public spending were only made by governments of either party under the exigent circumstances of a sterling crisis, a gilt strike or the arrival on the scene of the International Monetary Fund. This approach was only finally changed when in the run-up to the 1979 election the Conservative Opposition actually planned for public expenditure cuts because we believed in them.

Our failure in the 1960s to consider as an alternative government where we really stood on incomes policy was at least as serious.

As Iain Macleod and I demonstrated by our vigorous opposition to Labour's statutory incomes policy, we knew what we were against, but we were much less clear about what we were for. There was good reason for this, because the Shadow Cabinet itself was sharply divided. Ted Heath, true to the pragmatic, problem-solving approach which he prided himself on taking, was never able to give the lead required on this question. Probably the only member of the Shadow Cabinet who was opposed in principle to all kinds of incomes policy – voluntary or involuntary – was Enoch Powell, and he had failed to persuade his colleagues by the time I entered the Shadow Cabinet in 1967.

But Enoch was right. He had made the two intellectual leaps in economic policy which Keith Joseph and I would only make some years later. First, he had grasped that it was not the unions which caused inflation by pushing up wages, but rather the Government which did so by increasing the supply of money in the economy. Consequently, incomes policies – quite apart from their other effects of diminishing incentives, imposing distortions and leading to strikes which pitted the state against organized labour – were a supreme irrelevance to anti-inflation policy. In effect, Government was creating a problem which it then blamed on others. The only aspect of the matter which Enoch then and later failed sufficiently to grasp was the importance of the *indirect* link between trade union power and inflation. This lay in the fact that over-powerful trade unions could raise real wages well above market levels, but that in turn priced their own members out of jobs, and inflicted unemployment on both union and non-union workers alike. Governments, supremely sensitive to the length of dole queues, would then react by lowering interest rates and expanding the money supply. This would increase demand and jobs for a time, but it also increased inflation. All these effects would prompt the trade unions to ratchet up wages once more. And the whole process would start up again, from a higher level of inflation. But this could only be tackled by tightening monetary policy and by reducing the power of the unions – the first to halt inflation, the second to prevent the unions from creating unemployment. We would therefore at some point have to tackle trade union law. That said, Enoch's insight into the cause of inflation was of supreme importance.

Secondly, he had seen that the consensus economic policy nurtured another damaging delusion. This concerned the 'constraint' allegedly exercised by the current account of the balance of payments. It was in order to increase exports and reduce imports that corporatist, interventionist industrial policies were considered necessary. But the real 'constraint', which was assumed and not challenged, was that imposed by a pegged exchange rate. If sterling were allowed to float freely, as Enoch advocated, the alleged constraint of the balance of payments disappeared. And so did some of the pressure for other kinds of interventionism. As he put it in a seminal Institute of Economic Affairs pamphlet in 1967: 'The control of the international price of currencies, like every other suppression of market prices, leads to other controls, which make a mockery of the individual's freedom to trade, travel or invest.'*

True, in abandoning pegged exchange rates, one loses the anchor of the dollar (or gold). True too, a country which persists in running a large trade deficit may well be one with a weak economy which needs radical restructuring. (Though that may not always be so: a current account deficit may be evidence of large inflows of private capital into an economy which, *because of* reforms, has a high rate of return on investment.)

None of these qualifications, however, diminishes the fundamental importance of Enoch Powell's contribution. By showing that it was government monetary policy rather than wages which caused inflation, and that freely floating exchange rates would break free of the 'constraint' allegedly exercised by the current account of the balance of payments, Enoch permitted a radical revision of Conservative economic policy. He allowed us to break out of the mind-set which seemed to condemn Britain to an increasingly planned economy and society.

In October 1967 Ted made me front-bench spokesman on Fuel and Power and a member of the Shadow Cabinet. It may be that my House of Commons performances and perhaps Iain Macleod's recommendation overcame any temperamental reluctance on Ted's part. My first task was to read through all the evidence given to the inquiry about the causes of the terrible Aberfan disaster the

* *Exchange Rates and Liquidity.*

previous year, when 116 children and 28 adults were killed by a slag tip which slipped onto a Welsh mining village. Many of the parents of the victims were in the gallery for the debate, and I felt for them. Very serious criticisms had been made of the National Coal Board and as a result someone, I thought, should have resigned, though I held back from stating this conclusion with complete clarity in my first speech to the House as Shadow spokesman. What was revealed by the report made me realize how very easy it is in any large organization to assume that someone else has taken the requisite action and will assume responsibility. This is a problem which, as later tragedies have demonstrated, industrial civilization has yet to solve.

Outside the House, my main interest was in trying to find a framework for privatization of electricity generation. To this end I visited power stations and sought all the advice I could from business contacts. But it turned out to be a fruitless enterprise, and I had not come up with what I considered acceptable answers by the time my portfolio was changed again – to Transport – in October 1968. Transport was not one of the more interesting portfolios, because Parliament had just passed a major Transport Bill reorganizing the railways, nationalizing the bus companies, setting up a new National Freight Authority – in effect, implementing most of the Government's transport programme in one measure. In the brief period during which I shadowed Transport I argued our case against nationalization of the ports. But, all in all, Transport proved a brief with limited possibilities.

TED AND ENOCH

As a member of the Shadow Cabinet I attended its weekly discussions, usually on a Wednesday, in Ted's room in the House. Discussion was generally not very stimulating. We would begin by looking ahead to the parliamentary business for the week and agreeing who was to speak and on what line. There might be a paper from a colleague which he would introduce. But, doubtless because we knew that there were large divisions between us, particularly on economic policy, issues of principle were not usually openly debated. Ted was a competent chairman. On matters which really interested him, like Europe and trade union legislation, he would lead the discussion. But generally he allowed the spokesman to make the running on whatever subject was being considered.

For my part, I did not make a particularly important contribution to Shadow Cabinet. Nor was I asked to do so. For Ted and perhaps others I was principally there as the statutory woman whose main task was to explain what 'women' – Kiri Te Kanawa, Barbara Cartland, Esther Rantzen, Stella Rimington and all the rest of our uniform, undifferentiated sex – were likely to think and want on troublesome issues. I had, of course, great affection for Alec Douglas-Home, then Shadow Foreign Secretary, and got on perfectly well with most of my colleagues, but I had only three real friends around the table – Keith Joseph, Peter Thomas and Edward Boyle. And Edward by now was very much on the opposite wing of the Party from me.

The atmosphere at our meetings was certainly made more difficult by the fact that the most senior figures now had somewhat tense relations with each other. Ted was settling into the role of Party Leader with determination, but without any real or easy assurance. Reggie Maudling, Deputy Leader, had never really recovered from his unexpected defeat for the leadership. Iain Macleod was the most politically acute of us, with a special understanding of how whatever line we took would be interpreted by the press. But though a superb public orator he was in truth a rather private and reserved character. He was also growing out of sympathy with his old friend Enoch Powell, who was increasingly concerned about immigration, a topic about which Iain felt equally strongly on the other side. Undoubtedly, Enoch was our finest intellect – classicist, historian, economist and biblical scholar. In a quite different way from Iain, he was a powerful public orator and able to command the House of Commons, or indeed any audience, with his remorseless logic and controlled passion. But as regards the Shadow Cabinet, by this stage he had largely withdrawn into himself. He was disliked and probably feared by Ted Heath. He had fought and lost his battle against the chimera of incomes policy. As Defence spokesman, he had the uneasy task of attacking Labour's policy of withdrawal of British troops from east of Suez when he himself believed such withdrawal was inevitable. Above all, as a West Midlands MP witnessing the effect of large-scale immigration in his constituency he was frustrated by the Party's failure to take a tougher stance on the question.

The first modern immigration control measure had been introduced by Rab Butler in 1961. Hitherto, Commonwealth citizens had not been subject to the controls which applied to the admission of alien immigrants from foreign countries. The Commonwealth Immigrants' Act 1962, bitterly opposed by Labour and the Liberals, introduced an annual quota of employment vouchers to limit the inflow, a system subsequently tightened up by the Labour Government in 1965. During 1967 the Kenyan Government's discriminatory policies against Kenya's Asians resulted in a large inflow of immigrants into Britain. This raised awareness both of the scale and impact of past immigration and fears about its unchecked future size. There was particular worry about UK passport holders who were not connected by birth or descent with the United Kingdom. In February 1968 Jim Callaghan announced legislation to deal with this. The issue was also closely linked to the introduction of race relations legislation, which became the Race Relations Act 1968, aimed at curbing discrimination on grounds of colour. This was opposed by many on the right who saw in it a danger of making immigrants a legally privileged community which would have no incentive to integrate fully into British society.

On Monday 26 February 1968 Shadow Cabinet discussed the Government's Commonwealth Immigrants' Bill to introduce the new controls. A statement had been issued the previous week setting out the principles on which we would judge the measure. Ted Heath said that it was now up to Shadow Cabinet to decide whether the Bill came sufficiently within those terms. In fact, it did some of the things which we advocated. But it did not provide for registration of dependants, nor for appeal by those refused entry, nor for financial help for voluntary repatriation. It was decided to support the Bill, but also to move amendments where possible and appropriate. Iain Macleod, however, said that he would vote against the Bill, and he was as good as his word.

On Wednesday 10 April Shadow Cabinet discussed the other

side of the Government's policy, the Race Relations Bill. Ted again opened the discussion. He said that though the Bill itself appeared to have many faults he thought that some legal machinery would be necessary to help improve the prospects for coloured immigrants in Britain. Quintin Hogg, the Shadow Home Secretary, outlined his own views in some detail. He thought that legislation was necessary, but that we should move amendments. However, he noted that our backbenchers were very hostile to the Bill. Reggie Maudling agreed with Quintin on both points. In the discussion which followed, in which I did not participate, the main point in dispute was whether, flawed as the Bill was, to vote against it at Second Reading would be misinterpreted as racist. Shadow Cabinet's view was that the best assurance for good race relations was confidence that future numbers of immigrants would not be too great and that the existing law of the land would be upheld. In the end it was decided that a reasoned amendment would be drafted and there would be a two-line whip. Keith Joseph, Edward Boyle and Robert Carr, on the liberal wing, reserved their positions until they had seen the terms of the amendment. In the event they all supported it, though there were to be a number of abstentions by backbenchers.

On Sunday 21 April 1968 – two days before the debate – I woke up to find the front pages of the newspapers dominated by reports of a speech Enoch Powell had made in Birmingham on immigration the previous afternoon. It was strong meat, and there were some lines which had a sinister ring about them. But I strongly sympathized with the gravamen of his argument about the scale of New Commonwealth immigration into Britain. I too thought this threatened not just public order but also the way of life of some communities, themselves already beginning to be demoralized by insensitive housing policies, Social Security dependence and the onset of the 'permissive society'. I was also quite convinced that, however selective quotations from his speech may have sounded, Enoch was no racist.

At about eleven o'clock the telephone rang. It was Ted Heath. He said: 'I am ringing round all the Shadow Cabinet. I have come to the conclusion that Enoch must go.' It was more statement than enquiry. But I said that I really thought that it was better to let things cool down for the present rather than heighten the crisis.

Ted was having none of it. 'No, no,' he said. 'He absolutely must go, and most people think he must go.' In fact, I understood later that several members of the Shadow Cabinet would have resigned if Enoch had not gone.

Yet for several reasons it was a tragedy. In the short term it prevented our gaining the political credit for our policy of controlling immigration more strictly. This was an issue which crossed the political and social divide, as was demonstrated when London dockers marched in support of Enoch. Moreover, in practical terms there was very little to choose between the policies of Ted and Enoch on the matter. Although it is true that as a result of the speech the official Conservative line on immigration became more specific, essentially we all wanted strict limits on further New Commonwealth immigration and we were all prepared to support financial assistance for those who wanted to return to their country of origin.

But the longer-term consequences of Enoch's departure on this issue and under these circumstances extended far beyond immigration policy. He was free to develop a philosophical approach to a range of policies, uninhibited by the compromises of collective responsibility. This spanned both economic and foreign affairs and embraced what would come to be called 'monetarism', deregulation, denationalization, an end to regional policy, and culminated in his opposition to British membership of the Common Market. Having Enoch preaching to such effect in the wilderness carried advantages and disadvantages for those of us on the right in the Shadow Cabinet and later the Cabinet. On the one hand, he shifted the basis of the political argument to the right and so made it easier to advance sound doctrines without being accused of taking an extreme position. On the other hand, so bitter was the feud between Ted and Enoch that querying any policy advanced by the leadership was likely to be branded disloyalty. Moreover, the very fact that Enoch advanced all his positions as part of a coherent whole made it more difficult to express agreement with one or two of them. For example, the arguments against prices and incomes policies, intervention and corporatism might have been better received if they had not been associated with Enoch's views about immigration or Europe.

At this time, as it happens, other Conservatives were moving independently in the same direction, with the notable exception of Europe, and Ted gave me an opportunity to chart this way ahead. The annual Conservative Political Centre lecture is designed to give some intellectual meat to those attending the Tory Party Conference. The choice of speaker is generally reserved to the Party Leader. It was doubtless a pollster or Party adviser who suggested that it might be a good idea to have me talk about a subject which would appeal to 'women'. Luckily, I was free to choose my subject, and I decided on something more topical which might appeal to thinking people of both sexes: I spoke on 'What's Wrong With Politics?'

There is no better way to clarify your own thinking than to try to explain it clearly to someone else. I was conscious that there were great issues being discussed in politics at this time. Whatever else can be said of the sixties they were intellectually lively, even if too many of the ideas motivating change originated on the left. I took armfuls of books on philosophy, politics and history, White Papers, Hansard Society publications and speeches down to Lamberhurst. I had no one to guide or help me so I just plunged in. Like the proverbial iceberg, most of the work lay below the surface of the document I finally wrote.

I began by listing the reasons why there was so much disillusionment with politics. Some of these really consisted of the growth of a critical spirit through the effects of education and the mass media. But others were the fault of the politicians themselves. Political programmes were becoming dominated by a series of promises whose impact was all the greater because of the growth of the Welfare State. This led me on to what I considered the main cause of the public's increasing alienation from political parties – too much government. The competition between the parties to offer ever higher levels of economic growth and the belief that government itself could deliver these had provided the socialists with an opportunity massively to extend state control and intervention. This in turn caused ordinary people to feel that they had insufficient say in their own and their families' lives. The Left claimed that the answer was the creation of structures which would allow more democratic 'participation' in political decisions. But the real problem was that politics itself was intruding into far too many decisions that were properly outside its scope. Alongside the expansion of government had developed a political obsession with size – the notion that large units promoted efficiency. In fact, the opposite was true. Smaller units – small businesses, families and ultimately individuals – should once again be the focus of attention.

Apart from these general reflections, my CPC lecture also contained a section about prices and incomes policy. Although I stuck to the Shadow Cabinet line of condemning a compulsory policy while avoiding the issue of a voluntary one, I included a passage which reads:

> We now put so much emphasis on the control of incomes that we have too little regard for the essential role of government which is *the control of the money supply* and management of demand [emphasis added]. Greater attention to this role and less to the outward detailed control would have achieved more for the economy. It would mean, of course, that the government had to exercise itself some of the disciplines on expenditure it is so anxious to impose on others. It would mean that expenditure in the vast public sector would not have to be greater than the amount which could be financed out of taxation plus genuine saving.

In retrospect, it is clear to me that this summed up how far my understanding of these matters had gone – and how far it still needed to go. I had come to see that the money supply was central to any policy to control inflation. But I had not seen either that this made any kind of incomes policy irrelevant or that monetary policy itself was the way in which demand should be managed.

Partly as a result, I suspect, of the attention I received for the CPC lecture, I was asked to contribute two articles on general political philosophy to the *Daily Telegraph* early the following year. In these I developed some of the same themes. In particular, I argued the case for the ideological clash of opposing political parties as essential to the effective functioning of democracy. The pursuit of 'consensus', therefore, was fundamentally subversive of popular choice. It was wrong to talk of taking the big issues 'out of politics' or to imply that different approaches to a subject involved 'playing politics'. I applied this specifically to the question of nationalization versus free enterprise. But I could have done so on a range of other matters, not least education, which was soon to become my main political concern and where the ruthless pursuit by the socialists of comprehensivization was threatening not just Britain's schools but long-term social progress. The fraudulent appeal of consensus was a theme to which I would return again and again, both as Leader of the Opposition and as Prime Minister.

JOURNEYS TO THE FUTURE

By now (1968) the left-of-centre consensus on economic policy was being challenged and would continue to be. But the new liberal consensus on moral and social matters was not. That is to say that people in positions of influence in government, the media and universities managed to impose metropolitan liberal views on a society that was still largely conservative morally. The 1960s saw in Britain the beginning of what has become an almost complete separation between traditional Christian values and the authority of the state. Some politicians regarded this as a coherent programme. But for the great majority, myself included, it was a matter of reforms to deal with specific problems, in some cases cruel or unfair provisions.

So it was that I voted in 1966 for Leo Abse's Bill proposing that homosexual conduct in private between consenting adults over twenty-one should no longer be a criminal offence. In the same year I voted for David Steel's Bill to allow abortion if there was substantial risk that a child would suffer from such physical or mental abnormalities as to be seriously handicapped, or 'where the woman's capacity as a mother would be severely overstrained'. On both these issues I was strongly influenced by my own experience of other people's suffering. For example, when I was a barrister I had been moved by the humiliation I had seen inflicted in the dock on a man of considerable local standing who had been found engaging in homosexual conduct.

On the other hand, some aspects of the liberal agenda, even at the time, seemed to me to go too far. Divorce law reform was such a case. I had talked in my constituency surgeries to women subjected to a life of misery from their brutal husbands and for whom marriage had become a prison from which, in my view, they should be released. In these circumstances divorce might be the only answer. But if divorce became too easy it might undermine marriages simply going through a bad patch. If people can withdraw lightly from their responsibilities they are likely to be less serious about entering into the initial obligation. I was concerned about the spouse who was committed to make the marriage work and was deserted. I was also very concerned about what would become of the family of the first marriage when the man (or woman) chose to start a second family. So in 1968 I was one of the minority who voted against a Bill to make divorce far easier. Divorce would be possible where it was judged that there had been an 'irretrievable breakdown', broadly defined, in the marriage. I also supported two amendments, the first of which made available a special form of marriage that was indissoluble (except by judicial separation). The second would seek to ensure that in any conflict of interest between the legal wife and children of the first marriage and a common-law wife and her children, the former should have priority.

Similarly, I voted against Sydney Silverman's Bill to abolish the death penalty for murder in 1965. Like all the other measures listed above this was passed by Parliament, but subject to a Conservative amendment to the effect that the Act was to expire at the end of July 1970 unless Parliament determined otherwise. I then voted against the motion in December 1969 to make the Act permanent.

As I had shown in my earlier speech as a backbencher on corporal punishment, I believed that the state had not just a right but a duty to deter and punish violent crime and to protect the law-abiding public. However sparingly it is used, the power to deprive an individual of liberty, and under certain circumstances of life itself, is inseparable from the sovereignty of the state. I never had the slightest doubt that in nearly all cases the supreme deterrent would be an influence on the potential murderer. And the deterrent effect of capital punishment is at least as great on those who go armed on other criminal activities, such as robbery.

To my mind, the serious difficulty in the issue lay in the possibility of the conviction and execution of an innocent man – which has certainly happened in a small number of cases. Against these tragic cases, however, must be set the victims of convicted murderers who have been released after their sentence was served only to be convicted of murder a second time – who have certainly numbered many more. Despite all the uncertainties and complexities, for example of forensic evidence, I believe that the potential victim of the murderer deserves that highest protection which only the existence of the death penalty gives. The notion of certain particularly heinous murders as 'capital murders' (as under the 1957 Act) – a concept which now again underlies changes in the system relating to life sentences – seems to me the right model. I have consistently voted in Parliament for a return of capital punishment for such murders.

As regards abortion, homosexuality, and divorce reform it is easy to see that matters did not turn out as was intended. For most of us in Parliament – and certainly for me – the thinking underlying these changes was that they dealt with anomalies or unfairnesses which occurred in a minority of instances, or that they removed uncertainties in the law itself. Or else they were intended to recognize in law what was in any case occurring in fact. Instead, it could be argued that they have paved the way towards a more callous, selfish and irresponsible society. Reforming the law on abortion was primarily intended to stop young women being forced to have back-street abortions. It was not meant to make abortion simply another 'choice'. Yet in spite of the universal availability of artificial contraception the figures for abortion have kept on rising. Homosexual activists have moved from seeking a right of privacy to demanding social approval for the 'gay' lifestyle, equal status with the heterosexual family and even the legal right to exploit the sexual uncertainty of adolescents. Divorce law reform has contributed to – though it is by no means the only cause of – a very large increase in the incidence of marriage breakdown which has left so many children growing up without the continual care and guidance of two parents.

Knowing how matters have turned out, would I have voted differently on any of these measures? I now see that we viewed them too narrowly. As a lawyer and indeed as a politician who believed so strongly in the rule of law, I felt that the prime considerations were that the law should be enforceable and its application fair to those who might run foul of it. But laws also have a symbolic significance: they are signposts to the way society is developing – and the way the legislators of society envisage that it should develop. Moreover, taking all of the 'liberal' reforms of the 1960s together they amount to more than their individual parts. They came to be seen as providing a radically new framework within which the younger generation would be expected to behave.

Indeed, this was a period of obsessive and naive interest in 'youth'. Parents worried so much about the 'generation gap' that even teenagers began to take it seriously. A whole 'youth culture' of misunderstood Eastern mysticism, bizarre clothing and indulgence in hallucinatory drugs emerged. I found Chelsea a very different place when we moved back to London in 1970. I had mixed feelings about what was happening. There was vibrancy and talent, but this was also in large degree a world of make-believe. A perverse pride was taken in Britain about our contribution to these trends. Carnaby Street in Soho, the Beatles, the mini-skirt and the maxi-skirt were the new symbols of 'Swinging Britain'. And they did indeed prove good export earners. Harold Wilson was adept at taking maximum political credit for them. The trouble was that they concealed the real economic weaknesses which even a talented fashion industry and entrepreneurial recording companies could not counter-balance. As Desmond Donnelly remarked, 'My greatest fear is that Britain will sink giggling into the sea.'*

Although Britain gave a distinctive gloss to these trends, the affluent consumer society to which they catered was above all to be found in the United States. I had made my first visit to the USA in 1967 on one of the 'Leadership' programmes run by the American Government to bring rising young leaders from politics and business over to the US. For six weeks I travelled the length and breadth of the United States. The excitement which I felt has

---

* Desmond Donnelly was a Labour MP for almost twenty years. He resigned the Labour whip in 1968 in protest at the withdrawal from east of Suez and died a Conservative.

never really subsided. At each stop-over I was met and accommodated by friendly, open, generous people who took me into their homes and lives and showed me their cities and townships with evident pride. The high point was my visit to the NASA Space Center at Houston. I saw the astronaut training programme which would just two years later help put a man on the moon. As a living example of the 'brain drain' from which over-regulated, high-taxed Britain was suffering, I met someone from my constituency of Finchley who had gone to NASA to make full use of his talents. I saw nothing wrong with that, and indeed was glad that a British scientist was making such an important contribution. But there was no way Britain could hope to compete even in more modest areas of technology if we did not learn the lessons of an enterprise economy.

Two years after that I went on a week-long visit to the Soviet Union. I had already come up against the obstinate contempt for human rights which was so characteristic of the USSR in the case of the detention of my constituent, the lecturer Gerald Brooke, for alleged 'subversive criminal activities' (i.e. smuggling in anti-Soviet pamphlets). I repeatedly raised the case both with the Government and in the House of Commons, though to no avail. Mr Brooke had become a pawn in the game the Soviets were trying to play to have their spies, the Krogers, released to them. (Eventually an exchange took place in 1969.) One good thing which came out of my work on Gerald Brooke's behalf was that I made contact with the Anglo-Soviet Parliamentary Group. To my great surprise, when I went along to it I found MPs with equally strong anti-communist instincts as mine, but who unlike me were real experts in the field. In particular, Cyril Osborne began my education in assessing and countering Soviet tactics. It was he who before I went to the Soviet Union advised me that first of all I should not allow the Soviets to pay for my fare, and second that I should insist on visiting some churches. I took his advice. He also told me that the only way to win any respect from them was to make it clear that one was no soft touch. This entirely accorded with my own inclinations.

I travelled to Moscow with the amiable Paul Channon and his wife. We had a full schedule including not just the sights of Moscow but also Leningrad (formerly, and now once again, St Petersburg) and Stalingrad (Volgograd). But though the names might vary, the propaganda was the same. It was relentless, an endless flow of statistics proving the industrial and social superiority of the Soviet Union over the West. At least to the visitor, the sheer unimaginative humourlessness of it was an open invitation to satire. Outside an art gallery I visited there was a sculpture of a blacksmith beating a sword with a hammer. 'That represents communism,' my guide proudly observed. 'Actually, it doesn't,' I replied. 'It's from the Old Testament – "And they shall beat their swords into plough-shares, and their spears into pruning-hooks".' Collapse of stout aesthete. Methodist Sunday School has its uses. I reflected, however, that at least it was a better work of art than the usual lantern-jawed, muscle-bound Stakhanovite outside the factories.

On another occasion I was asked rhetorically whether since it must be the aim of all peoples to live together in peace and harmony, surely NATO, that symbol of Cold War hostility, could be dispensed with. 'Certainly not,' I said. 'NATO has kept the peace and we have to keep it strong.' A similar line was taken with me at Stalingrad where the local politicians complained that Coventry had severed its connections with them since the Soviet invasion of Czechoslovakia the previous year. I was not going to apologize for that either. Indeed, as sanctions went, it was hardly such as to strike terror into the Kremlin.

Yet, behind the official propaganda, the grey streets, all but empty shops and badly maintained workers' housing blocks, Russian humanity peeped out. There was no doubt about the genuineness of the tears when the older people at Leningrad and Stalingrad told me about their terrible sufferings in the War. The young people I talked to from Moscow University, though extremely cautious about what they said in the full knowledge that they were under KGB scrutiny, were clearly fascinated to learn all they could about the West. And even bureaucracy can prove human. When I visited the manager of the Moscow passenger transport system he explained to me at great length how decisions about new development had to go from committee to committee in what seemed – as I said – an endless chain of non-decision-making. I caught the eye of a young man, perhaps the chairman's assistant, standing behind him and he could not repress a broad smile.

The other abiding impression I had of Russia, which would be strengthened on my subsequent visits, was of the contrast between the exquisite cultural achievement, admittedly stemming from the old Russia but excellently conserved by the communists, on the one hand and the hardness of life for ordinary people on the other. Leningrad housed the extraordinary Hermitage collection and the Kirov Ballet, both of which I visited. And it was in Leningrad, from the window of my hotel bedroom, that at six thirty on a cold, dark morning I would see all the working mothers crossing the square with their children hanging on to them to place them all day in the state crèche whence they would be collected some twelve hours later. At Moscow airport while waiting for my delayed flight home I bought an exquisite coral-green porcelain tea service, the pride of my collection. Whenever I see it I also think of the grinding, hopeless toil which the system that produced it exacted. There could be no more poignant demonstration that communism was the regime for the privileged élite, capitalism the creed for the common man.

SELSDON WOMAN

On my return to London I was moved to the Education portfolio in the Shadow Cabinet. Edward Boyle was leaving politics to become Vice-Chancellor of the University of Leeds. There was by now a good deal of grassroots opposition at Party Conferences to what was seen as his weakness in defence of the grammar schools. Although our views had diverged, I was sorry to see him go. He was my oldest friend in politics and I knew I would miss his intellect, sensitivity and integrity. But for me this was definitely a promotion, even though, as I have since learned, I was in fact the reserve candidate, after Keith Joseph who was the first choice to succeed Edward: I got the job because Reggie Maudling refused to take over Keith's job as Trade and Industry Shadow.

I was delighted with my new role. I knew that I had risen to my present position as a result of free (or nearly free) good education, and I wanted others to have the same chance. Socialist education policies, by equalizing downwards and denying gifted children the opportunity to get on, were a major obstacle to that. I was also fascinated by the scientific side – the portfolio in those days being to shadow the Department of Education *and* Science. Moreover, I suspect that women, or at least mothers, have an instinctive interest in the education of children.

Education was by now one of the main battlegrounds of politics. Since their election in 1964 Labour had been increasingly committed to making the whole secondary school system comprehensive, and had introduced a series of measures to make local education authorities (LEAs) submit plans for such a change. (The process culminated in legislation, introduced a few months after I took over as Education Shadow.) The difficulties Edward had faced in formulating and explaining our response soon became clear to me.

The Shadow Cabinet and the Conservative Party were deeply split over the principle of selection in secondary education and, in particular, over the examination by which children were selected at the age of eleven, the 11-Plus. To over-simplify a little, it was possible to distinguish four different attitudes among Conservatives. First, there were those who had no real interest in state education in any case because they themselves and their children went to private schools. This was an important group, all too likely to be swayed by arguments of political expediency. Second, there were those who, themselves or their children, had failed to get into grammar school and had been disappointed with the education received at a secondary modern. Third, there were those Conservatives who, either because they themselves were teachers or through some other contact with the world of education, had absorbed a large dose of the fashionable egalitarian doctrines of the day. Finally, there were people like me who had been to good grammar schools, were strongly opposed to their destruction and felt no inhibitions at all about arguing for the 11-Plus.

Within the Shadow Cabinet I was aware of a broadly similar range of views. Shadow ministers in general did not want to make education a major issue in the forthcoming election. Nor was this necessarily a foolish view. Both the Party's own internal polling and published polls showed that the 11-Plus was widely unpopular and that people were at least prepared to say that they supported

comprehensive schools. Whether they would have felt the same if
they had been asked about re-organizing specific local schools on
comprehensive lines and whether, in any case, they understood
what was meant by 'comprehensivization' were of course different
matters. There was, for example, a large difference between the
full expression of the comprehensive concept, which was essentially
one of social engineering and only secondarily educational, under
which there was no streaming at all according to ability, and – on
the other hand – a school to which entry was open to all, but which
streamed by ability. In fact, as I was to point out in the Second
Reading debate of Labour's Education Bill in February 1970, it
was absurd for the socialists to attack the principle of selection,
since it would continue to apply in one way or another throughout
the system from the age of eleven. I might have added that when
you stop selecting by ability you have to select according to some
other inevitably less satisfactory criterion. In practice, this would
usually be income, because families with sufficient money would
move and buy houses in middle-class areas where a well-run school
was available for their children. Some Labour Members and many
Labour supporters understood all this well enough, and felt
betrayed by Harold Wilson's abandonment of his own personal
commitment to keep the grammar schools. When I won a surprise
victory in the Committee Stage debate, knocking out Clause 1 of
the Bill, it was because two Labour Members absented themselves.

But by the time I took on the Education portfolio, the Party's
policy group had presented its report and the policy itself was
largely established. It had two main aspects. We had decided to
concentrate on improving primary schools. And in order to defuse
as much as possible the debate about the 11-Plus, and in place of
Labour's policy of comprehensivization by coercion, we stressed
the autonomy of local education authorities in proposing the retention of grammar schools or the introduction of comprehensive
schools.

The good arguments for this programme were that improvements in the education of younger children were vital if the growing
tendency towards illiteracy and innumeracy was to be checked and,
secondly, that in practice the best way to retain grammar schools
was to fight centralization. There were, however, arguments on the

other side. There was not much point in spending large sums on nursery and primary schools and the teachers for them, if the teaching methods and attitudes were wrong. Nor, of course, were we in the long run going to be able to defend grammar schools – or, for that matter, private schools, direct grant schools and even streamed comprehensive schools – if we did not fight on grounds of principle.

Within the limits which the agreed policy and political realities allowed me, I went as far as I could. This was a good deal too far for some people, as I learned when, shortly after my appointment, I was the guest of the education correspondents at the Cumberland Hotel in London. I put the case not just for grammar schools but for secondary moderns. Those children who were not able to shine academically could in fact acquire responsibilities and respect at a separate secondary modern school, which they would never have done if in direct and continual competition and contact with the more academically gifted. I was perfectly prepared to see the 11-Plus replaced or modified by testing later in a child's career, if that was what people wanted. I knew that it was quite possible for late developers at a secondary modern to be moved to the local grammar school so that their abilities could be properly stretched. I was sure that there were too many secondary modern schools which were providing a second-rate education – but this was something which should be remedied by bringing their standards up, rather than grammar school standards down. Only two of those present at the Cumberland Hotel lunch seemed to agree. Otherwise I was met by a mixture of hostility and blank incomprehension. It was not just that they thought me wrong: they could not imagine that I could seriously believe such things. It opened my eyes to the dominance of socialist thinking among those whose task it was to provide the public with information about education.

There were still some relatively less important issues in Conservative education policy to be decided. I fought hard to have an unqualified commitment to raising the school leaving age to sixteen inserted into the manifesto, and succeeded against some doubts from the Treasury team. I also met strong opposition from Ted Heath when at our discussions at Selsdon Park in early 1970 I argued that the manifesto should endorse the proposed new independent University of Buckingham. In spite of backing from Keith

Joseph and others, I lost this battle but was at least finally permitted to make reference to the university in a speech. Quite why Ted felt so passionately against it I have never fully understood.

The Selsdon Park policy weekend at the end of January and beginning of February was a success, but not for the reasons usually given. The idea that Selsdon Park was the scene of debate which resulted in a radical rightward shift in Party policy is false. The main lines of policy had already been agreed and incorporated into a draft manifesto which we spent our time considering in detail. Our line on immigration had also been carefully spelt out. Our proposals for trade union reform had been published in *Fair Deal at Work*. On incomes policy, a rightward but somewhat confused shift was in the process of occurring. Labour had effectively abandoned its own policy. There was no need, therefore, to enter into the vexed question of whether some kind of 'voluntary' incomes policy might be pursued. But it was clear that Reggie Maudling was unhappy that we had no proposals to deal with what was still perceived as 'wage inflation'. In fact, the manifesto, in a judicious muddle, avoided either a monetarist approach or a Keynesian one and said simply: 'The main causes of rising prices are Labour's damaging policies of high taxation and devaluation. Labour's compulsory wage control was a failure and we will not repeat it.'

This in turn led us into some trouble later. During the election campaign the fallacious assertion that high taxes caused inflation inspired a briefing note from Central Office. This note allowed the Labour Party to claim subsequently that we had said that we would cut prices 'at a stroke' by means of tax cuts.

Thanks to the blanket press coverage of Selsdon Park, we seemed to be a serious alternative Government committed to long-term thinking about the policies for Britain's future. We were also helped by Harold Wilson's attack on 'Selsdon Man'. It gave us an air of down-to-earth right-wing populism which countered the somewhat aloof image conveyed by Ted. Above all, both Selsdon Park and the Conservative manifesto, *A Better Tomorrow*, contrasted favourably with the deviousness, inconsistency and horse trading which by now characterized the Wilson Government, especially since the abandonment of *In Place of Strife* under trade union pressure.*

Between our departure from Selsdon Park and the opening of the general election campaign in May, however, there was a reversal of the opinion poll standing of the two parties. At Selsdon we were in the lead and we thought we would win. In May quite suddenly we lost ground and appeared to be several points behind. Influenced by the short-term change in the polls, Harold Wilson called the election for 10 June – a mistake I never forgot when I became Prime Minister. But at the time most of us – including myself – thought that we would lose. The gloom steadily deepened. During the campaign I called in one day at the Conservative Research Department offices in Old Queen Street for some briefing material and was struck by how depressed everybody seemed.

Quite why this turnaround had occurred (or indeed how real it actually was) is hard to know. With the prospect of a general election there is always a tendency for disillusioned supporters to resume their party allegiance. But it is also true – and it is something that we would pay dearly for in Government – that we had not seriously set out to win the battle of ideas against socialism during our years in Opposition. And indeed, although we did not realize it, our rethinking of policy had not been as fundamental as it should have been.

The campaign itself was largely taken up with Labour attacks on our policies. We for our part, like any Opposition, but with more cause and opportunity than most, highlighted the long list of Labour's broken promises – 'steady industrial growth all the time', 'no stop-go measures', 'no increase in taxation', 'no increase in unemployment', 'the pound in your pocket not devalued', 'economic miracle' and many more. This was the theme I pursued in my campaign speeches. But I also used a speech to a dinner organized by the National Association of Head Teachers in Scarborough to outline our education policies.

---

* *In Place of Strife* was the – in retrospect ironically chosen – title of a Labour White Paper of 1969 which proposed a range of union reforms. The proposals had to be abandoned due to internal opposition within the Cabinet and the Labour Party, led by Jim Callaghan.

It is hard to know just what turned the tide, if indeed there was a tide against us to turn. Paradoxically perhaps, the Conservative figures who made the greatest contribution were those two fierce enemies Ted Heath and Enoch Powell. No one could describe Ted as a great communicator, not least because for the most part he paid such little attention to communication. But as the days went by he came across as a decent man, someone with integrity and a vision – albeit a somewhat technocratic one – of what he wanted for Britain. It seemed, to use Keith's words to me five years earlier, that he had 'a passion to get Britain right'. This was emphasized in Ted's powerful introduction to the manifesto in which he attacked Labour's 'cheap and trivial style of government' and 'government by gimmick' and promised 'a new style of government'. Ted's final Party Election Broadcast also showed him as an honest patriot who cared deeply about his country and wanted to serve it. Though it would not have saved him had we lost, he had fought a good campaign.

So had Enoch Powell. There had been much speculation as to whether he would endorse the Conservative leadership and programme. Attitudes towards Enoch remained sharply polarized. When he came in March to speak to my Association we were subject to strong criticism and I decided to issue a statement to the effect that: 'Those who use this country's great tradition of freedom of speech should not seek to deny that same freedom to others, especially to those who, like Mr Powell, spent their war years in distinguished service in the Forces.'

In the June campaign Enoch made three powerful speeches on the economic failure of the Labour Government, law and order, and Europe, urging people to vote Conservative. Furthermore, a bitter personal attack on Enoch by Tony Benn, linking him to fascism, probably rallied many otherwise unsympathetic voters to his standard. There is some statistical evidence that Enoch's intervention helped tip the balance in the West Midlands in a close election.

When my own result was announced to a tremendous cheer at Hendon College of Technology, it appeared that I had increased my majority to over 11,000 over Labour. Then I went down to the *Daily Telegraph* party at the Savoy, where it quite soon became clear that the opinion polls had been proved wrong and that we were on course for an overall majority.

Friday was spent in my constituency clearing up and writing the usual thank-you letters. I thought that probably Ted would have at least one woman in his Cabinet, and that since he had got used to me in the Shadow Cabinet I would be the lucky girl. On the same logic, I would probably get the Education brief.

On Saturday morning the call from the No. 10 Private Secretary came through. Ted wanted to see me. When I went in to the Cabinet Room I began by congratulating him on his victory. But not much time was spent on pleasantries. He was as ever brusque and businesslike, and he offered me the job of Education Secretary, which I accepted.

I went back to the flat at Westminster Gardens with Denis and we drove to Lamberhurst. Sadly my father was not alive to share the moment. Shortly before his death in February, I had gone up to Grantham to see him. Having always had a weak chest, he had now developed emphysema and had oxygen beside the bed. My stepmother, Cissy, whom he had married several years earlier and with whom he had been very happy, was constantly at his bedside. While I was there, friends from the church, business, local politics, the Rotary and bowling club, kept dropping in 'just to see how Alf was'. I hoped that at the end of my life I too would have so many good friends.

I understand that my father had been listening to me as a member of a panel on a radio programme just before he died. He never knew that I would become a Cabinet minister, and I am sure that he never imagined I would eventually become Prime Minister. He would have wanted these things for me because politics was so much a part of his life and because I was so much his daughter. But nor would he have considered that political power was the most important or even the most effective thing in life. In searching through my papers to assemble the material for this volume I came across some of my father's loose sermon notes slipped into the back of my sixth-form chemistry exercise book.

Men, nations, races or any particular generation cannot be saved by ordinances, power, legislation. We worry about all this, and our faith becomes weak and faltering. But all these things are as old as the human race – all these things confronted Jesus 2,000 years ago . . . This is why Jesus had to come.

My father lived these convictions to the end.

CHAPTER VI

Teacher's Pest

The Department of Education 1970–1974

FIRST IMPRESSIONS

On Monday 22 June 1970 I arrived at the Department of Education and Science (DES) in its splendid old quarters in Curzon Street (alas, in 1973 we moved to a hideous new office block at Waterloo). I was met by the Permanent Secretary, Bill (later Sir William) Pile and the outgoing Permanent Secretary, Sir Herbert Andrew. They gave me a warm greeting and showed me up to my impressive private office. It was all too easy to slip once more into the warm water of civil service respect for 'the minister', but I was very conscious that hard work lay ahead. I was generally satisfied with the ministerial team I had been allotted: one friendly, one hostile and one neutral. My old friend Lord Eccles, as Paymaster General, was responsible for the Arts. Bill Van Straubenzee, a close friend of Ted's, dealt with Higher Education. Lord Belstead answered for the department in the Lords. I was particularly pleased that David Eccles, a former Minister of Education, was available, though installed in a separate building, to give me private advice based on his knowledge of the department.

My difficulties with the department, however, were not essentially about personalities. Nor, after the first culture shock, did they stem from the opposition between my own executive style of decision-making and the more consultative style to which they were accustomed. Indeed, by the time I left I was aware that I had won a somewhat grudging respect because I knew my own mind and expected my decisions to be carried out promptly and efficiently.

The real problem was – in the widest sense – one of politics.

I do not know and did not enquire how the senior civil servants around me voted. But the ethos of the DES was self-righteously socialist. For the most part, these were people who retained an almost reflex belief in the ability of central planners and social theorists to create a better world. There was nothing cynical about this. Years after many people in the Labour Party had begun to have their doubts, the educationalists retained a sense of mission. Equality in education was not only the overriding good, irrespective of the practical effects of egalitarian policies on particular schools; it was a stepping stone to achieving equality in society, which was itself an unquestioned good. It was soon clear to me that on the whole I was not among friends.

The counter-argument would presumably be that since I was seeking to challenge the conventional wisdom in education, I could hardly complain when I met with opposition. There are, however, two considerations which must be weighed against that. First, civil servants owe ministers honest, accurate advice based on fact, rather than slanted submissions based on preconceptions that the Government (and the electorate) have rejected. Second, it is highly damaging, even judged by the narrow criteria of good and impartial administration, for a department to become as closely connected with its clients as the DES was with the teaching unions, in particular the National Union of Teachers (NUT). I saw this in the flesh quite early on when on Saturday 12 September 1970 I was deputed at the last moment, because of the Leila Khalid affair,* to deliver Ted Heath's speech at a Guildhall dinner to celebrate the centenary of the NUT. There were a large number of DES senior civil servants present and it was immediately clear to me that they and the NUT leaders were on the closest of terms. There were all those in-jokes, unstated allusions, and what is now called 'body language' which signify not just common courtesy but rather a common sympathy.

My difficulties with the civil service were compounded by the fact that we had been elected in 1970 with a set of education policies which were perhaps less clear than they appeared. During the campaign I had hammered away at seven points:

* See p. 198.

- a shift of emphasis onto primary schools
- the expansion of nursery education (which fitted in with Keith Joseph's theme of arresting the 'cycle of deprivation')
- in secondary education, the right of local education authorities to decide what was best for their areas, while warning against making 'irrevocable changes to any good school unless . . . the alternative is better'
- raising the school leaving age to sixteen
- encouraging direct grant schools and retaining private schools*
- expanding higher and further education
- holding an inquiry into teacher training

But those pledges did not reflect a clear philosophy. As I have already indicated, different people and different groups within the Conservative Party favoured very different approaches to education, in particular to secondary education and the grammar schools. On the one hand, there were some Tories who had a commitment to comprehensive education which barely distinguished them from moderate socialists. On the other, the authors of the so-called *Black Papers* on education had, to their credit, started to spell out a radically different approach, based on discipline, choice and standards (including the retention of existing grammar schools with high standards). Their case was strongly founded in well-informed criticisms of the present system. We were caught between these two opposing views. And for all our talk of coherent strategies and deliberate decision-making, this was not a government which felt any inclination to resolve fundamental contradictions. I was very conscious that in any struggle with the civil service I might not be able to count on the support of all my Cabinet colleagues.

* Direct grant schools, which included some of the most famous and successful secondary schools in Britain, entry to which was often highly competitive, were funded direct from the DES and were outside local control.

GRAMMATICALLY INCORRECT

On that first day at the department I brought with me a list of about fifteen points for action which I had written down over the weekend at Lamberhurst in an old exercise book. After enlarging upon them, I tore out the pages and gave them to Bill Pile. The most immediate action point was the withdrawal of Tony Crosland's Circular 10/65, under which local authorities were required to submit plans for reorganizing secondary education on completely comprehensive lines, and Circular 10/66, issued the following year, which withheld capital funding from local education authorities that refused to go comprehensive.

The department must have known that this was in our manifesto – they always scrutinize the Opposition parties' policies during an election campaign. But apparently they thought that the policy could be watered down, or at least its implementation postponed. I, for my part, knew that the pledge to stop pressuring local authorities to go comprehensive was of great importance to our supporters, that any delay would be taken as a sign of weakness, and that it was important to act speedily in order to end uncertainty. Consequently, even before I had given Bill Pile my fifteen points, I had told the press that I would immediately withdraw Labour's Circulars. I even indicated that this would have happened by the time of the Queen's Speech. The alarm this provoked seems to have made its way to No. 10, for I was reminded that I should have Cabinet's agreement to the policy, though of course this was only a formality.

More seriously, I had not understood that the withdrawal of one Circular requires the issue of another. This was a technicality, but it was one which those who disagreed with the policy inside and outside the department used to maximum effect. My civil servants made no secret of the fact that they considered that a Circular should contain a good deal of material setting out the department's views on its preferred shape for secondary education in the country as a whole. This might take for ever, and in any event I did not see things that way. The essence of our policy was to encourage variety and choice rather than 'plan' the system. Moreover, to the extent that it was necessary to lay down from the centre the criteria by which local authorities' reorganization proposals would be judged, this could be done now in general terms, with any further elaboration taking place later. It was immensely difficult to persuade them that I was serious. I eventually succeeded by doing an initial draft myself: they quickly decided that cooperation was the better part of valour. And in the end a very short Circular – referred to as Circular 10/70 – was issued on Tuesday 30 June in good time for the Education Debate on the Queen's Speech on Wednesday 8 July.

I now came under fierce attack from the educational establishment because I had failed to engage in the 'normal consultation' which took place before a Circular was issued. I felt no need to apologize. As I put it in my speech in the House, we had after all 'just completed the biggest consultation of all', that is a general election. But this carried little weight with those who had spent the last twenty-five years convinced that they knew best. Ted Short, Labour's Education spokesman, himself a former schoolmaster, even went so far as to suggest that, in protest, teachers should refuse to mark 11-Plus exam papers. A delegation from the NUT came to see me to complain about what I had done. Significantly, the brunt of their criticism was that I had 'resigned responsibility for giving shape to education'. If indeed that had been my responsibility, I do not think the NUT would have liked the shape I would have given it.

In fact, the policy which I now pursued was more nuanced than the caricatures it attracted – though a good deal could have been said for the positions caricatured. Circular 10/70 withdrew the relevant Labour Government Circulars and then went on: 'The Secretary of State will expect educational considerations in general, local needs and wishes in particular and the wise use of resources to be the main principles determining the local pattern.' It also made it clear that the presumption was basically against upheaval: 'where a particular pattern of organization is working well and commands general support the Secretary of State does not wish to cause further change without good reason'.

Strange though it may seem, although local education authorities had been used to sending in general plans for reorganization of all the schools under their control, neither these nor the Secretary of State's comments on them had any legal standing. The law only entered the picture when the notices were issued under Section 13 of the 1944 Education Act. This required local education authorities to give public notice – and notice to the department – of their intention to close or open a school, significantly alter its character, or change the age range of its pupils. Locally, this gave concerned parents, school governors and residents two months in which to object. Nationally, it gave me, as Secretary of State, the opportunity to intervene. It read: 'Any proposals submitted to the Secretary of State under this section may be approved by him after making such modifications therein, if any, as appear to him desirable.'

The use of these powers to protect particular good schools against sweeping reorganization was not only a departure from Labour policy; it was also a conscious departure from the line taken by Edward Boyle, who had described Section 13 as 'reserve powers'. But as a lawyer myself and as someone who believed that decisions about changing and closing schools should be sensitive to local opinion, I thought it best to base my policy on the Section 13 powers rather than on exhortation through Circulars. This may sound arbitrary, but in fact I was very conscious that my actions were subject to the scrutiny of the courts and that the grounds on which I could intervene were limited. And by the time I made my speech in the debate I was in a position to spell out more clearly how this general approach would be implemented.

My policy had a further advantage, though it was not one that it would have been politically prudent to expound. At a time when even Conservative education authorities were bitten with the bug of comprehensivization, it offered the best chance of saving good local grammar schools. The administrative disadvantage was that close scrutiny of large numbers of individual proposals meant delays in giving the department's response. Inevitably, I was attacked on the grounds that I was holding back in order to defer the closure of more grammar schools. But in this the critics were unjust. I took a close interest in speeding up the responses. It was just that we were deluged.

A further point I dealt with in that first Commons debate as

Education Secretary was the argument, constantly advanced by the proponents of wholesale comprehensivization, that it was impossible to have a 'mixed' system of both comprehensive and grammar schools. Although, in truth, this was just a more sophisticated version of the argument that the egalitarian educationalist knows best, it was superficially persuasive. It is, after all, impossible in theory to divide a given group of children between grammars and secondary moderns *and* to mix them all together in one comprehensive school. Either the children will not be selected or they will not be mixed. But this theoretical argument ignored the fact that, given a large enough 'catchment' area, it was possible to have selective schools and schools with the full range of ability in operation at the same time. As I pointed out in answer to Ted Short in the debate:

> Certainly, with a small rural area, I do not believe that it would be possible to have a comprehensive school and a grammar school, but in some of the very large urban areas it is possible, because the grammar school and direct grant school have quite different catchment areas from the comprehensive school. [Hon. Members: 'Impossible.'] It is of little avail for Hon. Gentlemen opposite to say that this is impossible, because it happens now. Some of the best comprehensive schools are in areas where there are very good selective schools.

For all the political noise which arose from this change of policy, its practical effects were limited. During the whole of my time as Education Secretary we considered some 3,600 proposals for reorganization – the great majority of them proposals for comprehensivization – of which I rejected only 325, or about 9 per cent. In the summer of 1970 it had seemed possible that many more authorities might decide to reverse or halt their plans. For example, Conservative-controlled Birmingham was one of the first education authorities to welcome Circular 10/70. A bitter fight had been carried on to save the city's thirty-six grammar schools. But in 1972 Labour took control and put forward its own plans for comprehensivization. I rejected sixty of the council's 112 proposals in June 1973, saving eighteen of the city's grammar schools.

Similarly, Richmond Council in Surrey had refused to come forward with a scheme under the Labour Government's Circular 10/65, but in September 1970 voted by a large majority to end selection. I had no choice but to give my approval to the change the following year.

Perhaps the most awkward decisions I had to make related to Barnet, which included my own constituency. The Conservative-controlled Barnet Council decided to go comprehensive in October 1970, having conducted a survey of parents in which 79 per cent apparently favoured ending selection. (In fact, other national opinion polls showed a great deal of confusion on the issue, with a majority of people favouring both comprehensive education *and* the retention of grammar schools.) There was fierce opposition to Barnet's scheme, and in January 1971 I received 5,400 letters of protest. The following month I approved a scheme which ended two grammar schools, but I saved a third on the grounds that the proposed merger would lead to an inconvenient divided-site school. In April I saved another grammar school and in June blocked two more schemes, thus saving a good secondary modern and another grammar school. The Conservative Party locally was split and I was censured by the local council. Most of the borough's secondary schools in fact went comprehensive that September. The local authority kept reformulating its plans. Christ's College and Woodhouse Grammar Schools were the main bones of contention. They were still grammar schools when I became Leader of the Opposition in 1975; they only became part of a comprehensive system (in Woodhouse's case, a sixth-form college) in 1978 after Labour's 1976 Education Act scrapped Section 13 and attempted to impose a comprehensive system from the centre on England and Wales.

In retrospect, it is clear that a near obsessive concern with educational structures characterized the 1960s and seventies. It is not that structures – either at the level of administration or at the level of schools – are unimportant. But educational theorists manifest a self-confidence which events have done nothing to justify when they claim that there is one system which in all circumstances and for all individuals is better than another. During my time at the DES

I came across this attitude above all when dealing with plans for secondary school reorganization, in the prejudice against grammar schools: they even wanted to eliminate streaming by ability within schools. I tried to convince Her Majesty's Inspectorate of Schools (HMI) that whatever their theories might suggest, they should at least recognize that there were large numbers of excellent teachers in grammar schools doing a first-class job, and that they were having the heart taken out of them by the tone of so many HMI Reports.

The view that a utopian, monolithic structure could be devised and implemented without trauma was also exploded time and again as I heard the experience of individual parents. People living in a crime-ridden council estate with a comprehensive 'community school', to which their catchment area under local authority regulation required them to send their children, were often desperate to get out. The lucky few who had a direct grant school in the vicinity might be able to do so. But some socialist local education authorities refused to take up places allocated to them at direct grant schools because they objected to independent schools on doctrinaire grounds. I had to intervene to ensure that these places were filled. But in any case only a limited number of parents and children could escape from bad conditions in this way. I found it heartbreaking to tell mothers that there was little or nothing I could do under the present system.

Only later – first with the Assisted Places Scheme and then with grant-maintained schools – could I, as Prime Minister, do something substantial to help.* Not that this situation, which continues today, is entirely satisfactory. We need to make it easier to start up new schools so as to widen parental choice. And the argument for education vouchers becomes stronger every day. They would finally bridge the gap between the independent and state sectors.

There is a further consideration which I have only come to appreciate in recent years. In defending grammar schools, Con-

---

* The Assisted Places Scheme makes public funds available for gifted children from poorer backgrounds to take up places in private schools. Grant-maintained schools are state schools which have opted to move outside local education authority control.

servatives were rightly defending an existing institution that provided a fine education for children of all backgrounds. But we were also defending a principle – namely, that the state should select children by the single criterion of ability and direct them to one of only two sorts of school – that is far more consonant with socialism and collectivism than with the spontaneous social order associated with liberalism and conservatism. State selection by ability is, after all, a form of manpower planning. And variety and excellence in education are far more securely founded, and far more politically defensible, when parental choice rather than state selection of children by ability is their justification.

Be that as it may, by the end of 1970 it was already becoming clear that there would be no swing away from comprehensive education.

SCIENCE AND TEACHER TRAINING

I arrived at the Department of Education with a strong personal interest in science, and the science responsibilities of the DES were mine alone. At that time a block sum was allocated on the advice of scientists between five research councils – covering science and engineering, medicine, agriculture, the environment and social science. But discussion of science policy was soon dominated by the Central Policy Review Staff (CPRS or 'think tank') Report which formed the basis of the White Paper of July 1972, *A Framework for Government Research and Development*. Its central recommendation was that a proportion of this money should henceforth be allocated to the relevant Government department so that it could decide the projects to be financed by its own council – the so-called 'customer-contractor' principle. Although I did not oppose the principle, I was worried that it would reduce the amount of money at the *direct* disposal of the research councils – unless there was an increase in the total science budget.

All this may seem of limited importance. And indeed in terms of overall science policy it was. That was part of the problem. Arguments about the precise relations between departments and research councils were irrelevant to the wider and crucially important question of the Government's strategic role in scientific research. Ted's view was that pure research was not really work for Government-funded research and development, though he recognized that in any research establishment there was bound to be some proportion of pure or basic research. My view was precisely the opposite. It was only years later, when I was Prime Minister, that I was able to formulate my own answer to the problem, which was that Government should concentrate on funding basic science and leave its application and development to the private sector. But I already felt deeply uneasy about any policy that threatened to starve pure science of funds.

In one particular instance, I was involved directly in supporting a large and expensive project on the frontiers of science. This was the decision to join in European plans for a giant proton accelerator, or 'atom smasher', to elucidate the ultimate structure of matter, a project from which the previous Labour Government had withdrawn in 1968. As part of the Government's early spending curbs we too had drawn back from this project, which some people considered too expensive, given its theoretical nature. But I was haunted by the knowledge that if Britain had not pressed ahead with some nuclear research even in the cash-strapped thirties, Britain and America would not have developed the atomic bomb which first secured victory in the Second World War and later protected Western Europe against Stalin. It was a vital lesson. So in September 1970 I went with Sir Brian Flowers, Chairman of the Science and Engineering Research Council, to the European Centre for Nuclear Research (CERN) near Geneva to see for myself what was envisaged and learn more about the science and its possibilities. I came back convinced that if we could ensure sound financial control the twelve-nation project was worth backing, and managed to convince my colleagues to this effect.

Generally, though, I did not feel that the Government's approach to science was radical or imaginative enough. I suspect that many scientists – and not just those with a professional axe to grind – thought so too. On Tuesday 26 June 1973 Ted held a dinner at No. 10 for British Nobel Prize winners in science – among them my old Oxford tutor, Dorothy Hodgkin. Naturally, I attended as well. For several reasons it was an illuminating occasion. Ted set the discussion against the background of Britain's entry into the European Community, which he thought historians would conclude was the greatest achievement of his administration. He presented science as something to be applied so as to allow British industry to take advantage of access to the European market. There was some support for this view, but there were also some criticisms which represented my own standpoint. Essentially, this was that government should fund pure science, rather than organizing Europe's scientists together in vast projects to make European economies technologically more competitive. Science was already international; the expansion of the European Community would not make a good deal of difference; and international science depended upon a number of people working separately in different countries. Arguably the less they were officially organized, the better the results would be. A commonsense exception to this rule was when the investment required was so costly that no one nation could afford it – hence my support for CERN.

So I was somewhat sceptical about the science policy that I as minister had to implement. But the policy never amounted to much. Science is less amenable to political direction than politicians like to think. Indeed, the history of science is in many ways more similar to the history of imaginative art than to economic history. The great scientific advances have not come from 'practical' plans for research and development but from creative scientific minds – the sort of minds which were around the dinner table that evening with Ted and me – people who by pushing outward at the frontiers of knowledge unlock the secrets of the universe. Politicians are reluctant to accept this; they want a quick technological fix and a quick pay-off into the bargain. Scientists rightly take a longer view. When Gladstone met Michael Faraday, he asked him whether his work on electricity would be of any use. 'Yes, sir,' remarked Faraday with prescience. 'One day you will tax it.'

My second area of frustration was that of teacher training. As I have already mentioned, the manifesto had committed us to set up an inquiry into it. This was one of the points which figured large on the list I handed to Bill Pile on my first day in the department. I already held strong views on the subject. It seemed to me that the large increase in the number of teachers had to some extent been at the expense of quality. Although there were continuing difficulties about finding enough student teachers wanting to go into mathematics and sciences, there was not much substance to the complaints about 'teacher shortages'. The real shortage was in the number of *good* teachers. Changing the salary structure of the profession would help by rewarding and encouraging long-serving and senior teachers, though the NUT was very wary of increased differentials. But teacher training was the key.

I wanted a serious investigation into whether trainee teachers were being taught the right subjects in the right way and at the right level. So I appointed Lord James of Rusholme, a former Headmaster of Manchester Grammar School, one of the country's great schools, as Chairman of an inquiry into teacher training. I insisted that those who served with him should work virtually full-time and that their report be completed within a year; it was duly published in January 1972. The report was workmanlike and made a number of sensible suggestions. It placed the greater emphasis I wanted on in-service training so that teachers really knew how to cope with a class full of children. Second, it proposed a new, two-year Diploma in Higher Education – for which I had also pressed – in which future teachers would study side by side with others who intended going into industry or the professions. But the fact that it confined itself to the structure rather than the curriculum content of teacher training limited its value. In effect, I got nowhere in my attempts to get the curriculum of the teacher training institutions discussed within the planned inquiry. It was still regarded as taboo for politicians to become involved in such matters. Fifteen years later the situation had not materially improved. As Prime Minister, I would still be puzzling about how to raise the quality of the teaching profession.

Still, although I was very critical of the outlook of many teacher trade unionists (who were in some cases more trade unionists than teachers), my final impression gained from my years at the DES was of the sincerity and commitment of most teachers. Sometimes teachers from the most difficult schools dealing with 'problem' children (who could usually be traced back to 'problem' parents) would come in to the department to tell me of their experience. On other occasions, I would talk to them in their schools and see something of what they had to cope with in their classrooms.

The teacher can never be a sufficient substitute for the family: yet a good teacher cannot ignore what happens to the child when he or she goes home, perhaps to be ill-treated. On one occasion, someone put the dilemma to me:

> At 4 o'clock on a Friday afternoon when the other children have gone home, one child clings to you and begs not to leave. You feel sure – but you cannot prove – that something is seriously wrong. Perhaps there is violence or neglect, or just deep unhappiness from one source or another. Do you walk the child home and tell his parents that he seems a bit off-colour; saying, of course, that he has not complained or been a nuisance; but gently enquiring if anything is wrong? You don't know whether the child may be beaten as soon as you leave. Do you alert the authorities? That may have even more traumatic consequences. Or do you do nothing and hope that it's just a temporary problem which will sort itself out? Well, Mrs Thatcher, what would *you* do?

There is no single good answer to this question. And despite our agonizings over such cases, we have still not found a solution that is right for all circumstances. We need teachers, social workers and policemen who are trained to recognize the symptoms of abuse, while remembering the commonsense reality that most parents love their children. Of the three, teachers are by far the most important because they know the child personally and see him or her almost every day. If they are to carry out this delicate and important task they can do so only if their authority is fully restored, not only over the child but also in the eyes of the parent. And when that happens, the bad parent is more likely to be held in check.

MILKING PUBLICITY

In one respect at least, the Department of Education was an excellent preparation for the premiership. I came under savage and unremitting attack that was only distantly related to my crimes.

ABOVE: The 1943 intake at Somerville College, Oxford. I am in the back row, fifth from right.

LEFT: At work as a research chemist.

ABOVE: Speaking to Conservative supporters at a fête in Dartford, summer 1950.

BELOW: On the same occasion.

ABOVE: Talking to workmen on a building site in Dartford.

BELOW: Attending a gala dinner in Dartford with Ted Heath and
Pat Hornsby-Smith.

LEFT: With Lord Woolton, Conservative Party Chairman, at the Candidates' Conference just before the 1951 general election.

BELOW: Rally at the football stadium, Dartford, attended by Anthony Eden – photographed here with Kent Conserva MPs and prospective candidates. Ted H stands between Anthony Eden and me.

RIGHT: Attending a constituency engagement in Dartford in 1951, accompanied by the Conservative agent, Mr Potts.

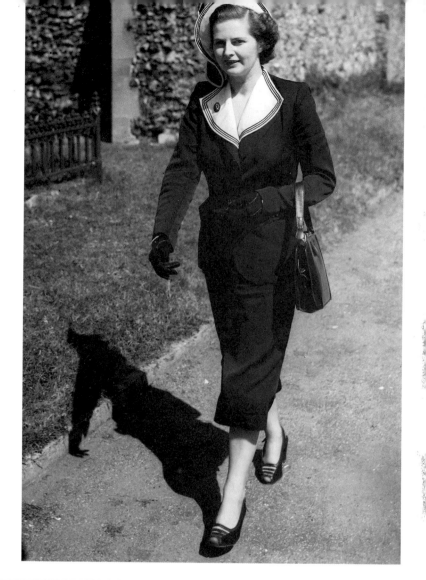

ABOVE: Attending a wedding in the black silk suit made for the 1950 Buckingham Palace garden party.

GENERAL ELECTION 1951

DARTFORD CONSTITUENCY

Polling Day
Thursday, 25th October
7 a.m.—9 p.m.

PEACE

COST OF LIVING

HOMES

FUEL

GO AND HEAR

MARGARET
ROBERTS
The Conservative Candidate

LEFT: My 1951 election address.

With Denis in Dartford, shortly after we had become engaged.

ABOVE: Visiting Versailles on our honeymoon.

BELOW: Dining out in Lisbon with a friend of Denis's.

But it did not begin like that. I have described the arguments about grammar schools and comprehensives. Yet these caused me only limited trouble, partly because many people – and not just Conservatives – agreed with me and partly because I was the bringer of good tidings in other matters. For example, I was hailed in a modest way as the saviour of the Open University. In Opposition both Iain Macleod and Edward Boyle, who thought that there were educational priorities more deserving of Government help, had committed themselves in public against it. And although its abolition was not in the manifesto, many people expected it to perish. But I was genuinely attracted to the concept of a 'University of the Airwaves', as it was often called, because I thought that it was an inexpensive way of giving wider access to higher education, because I thought that trainee teachers in particular would benefit from it, because I was alert to the opportunities offered by technology to bring the best teaching to schoolchildren and students, and above all because it gave people a second chance in life. In any case, the university was due to take its first students that autumn, and cancellation would have been both expensive and a blow to many hopes. On condition that I agreed to reduce the immediate intake of students and find other savings, my Cabinet colleagues allowed the Open University to go ahead.

There were more discussions of public expenditure that autumn of 1970. The Treasury had its little list of savings for the education budget – including charges for libraries, museums, school meals and school milk. I knew from my own experience in Grantham how vital it was to have access to books. So I persuaded the Cabinet to drop the proposed library charges, while reluctantly accepting entry charges for museums and galleries. (We kept one free day.) But pressure for more cuts was maintained, and I had to come up with a list of priority targets.

Savings on school meals and school milk were, I had to admit, an obvious candidate. There seemed no reason why families who could afford to do so should not make a larger contribution to the cost of school meals. I thought that I could defend such cuts if I could demonstrate that some of the money saved would go towards meeting the priority which we had set, namely the primary school building programme. And within the Department of Education budget it seemed logical that spending on education should come before 'welfare' spending, which should in principle fall to Keith Joseph's department, Social Services.

As for milk, there were already mixed views on health grounds about the advantage of providing it. When I was at Huntingtower Road Primary School my parents paid 2½d a week for my school milk: and there were no complaints. By 1970 very few children were so deprived that school milk was essential for their nourishment. Tony Barber, who became Chancellor in July 1970, after the death of Iain Macleod, wanted me to abolish free school milk altogether. But I was more cautious, both on political and on welfare grounds. I managed to hold the line at an increased price for school meals and the withdrawal of free milk from primary school children over the age of seven. These modest changes came with safeguards: children in need of milk for medical reasons continued to receive it until they went to secondary school. All in all, I had defended the education budget effectively.

Nor was this lost on the press. The *Daily Mail* said that I had emerged as a 'new heroine'. The *Daily Telegraph* drew attention to my plans to improve 460 of the oldest primary schools. The *Guardian* noted: 'School meals and milk were the main casualties in a remarkably light raid on the education budget. Mrs Thatcher has won her battle to preserve a high school-building programme and turn it to the replacement of old primary schools.'

It was pleasant while it lasted.

The trouble was, it didn't last long. Six months later we had to introduce a Bill to remove the legal duty for local education authorities to provide free milk and allow them discretion to make it available for a small charge. This gave Labour the parliamentary opportunity to cause havoc.

Even before that, however, the newspapers had unearthed the potential in stories about school meals. One report claimed that some local education authorities were going to charge children who brought sandwiches to school for their lunch. 'Sandwich Kids In "Fines" Storm' was how the *Sun* put it. Labour provided a parliamentary chorus. I introduced a circular to prevent the practice. But that story in turn restored attention to the increase in school meal charges. Overnight the number of children eating such meals became a politically sensitive indicator. The old arguments about the 'stigma' of means-tested benefits, which I had come to know so well as a Parliamentary Secretary in the 1960s, surfaced again. It was said that children from families poor enough to be entitled to free school meals would be humiliated when better-off classmates paid for their own. Probably unwisely, I came up with a suggestion in a television programme that this could be avoided if mothers sent dinner money to schools in envelopes. The teachers could put the change back in the envelope. A poor child entitled to free meals would bring an envelope with coins that would just be put back again by the teacher. This, of course, just added a new twist to the story.

In any case, it was not long before the great 'milk row' dwarfed debate about meals. Newspapers which had congratulated me on my success in protecting the education budget at the expense of cuts in milk and meals suddenly changed their tune. The *Guardian* described the Education (Milk) Bill as 'a vindictive measure which should never have been laid before Parliament'. The *Daily Mail* told me to 'think again'. The *Sun* demanded to know: 'Is Mrs Thatcher Human?' But it was a speaker at the Labour Party Conference who seems to have suggested to the press the catchy title 'Mrs Thatcher, milk snatcher'.

When the press discover a rich vein they naturally exhaust it. After all, editors and journalists have a living to earn, and politicians are fair game. So it seemed as if every day some variant of the theme would emerge. For example, a Labour council was discovered to be considering buying its own herd of cows to provide milk for its children. Local education authorities sought to evade the legislation by serving up milky drinks but not milk. Councils which were *not* education authorities took steps to provide free milk for children aged seven to eleven under powers contained in the Local Government Act 1963. Only in Scotland and Wales did the action of councils involve a breach of the law, and it was for my Cabinet colleagues in the Scottish and Welsh departments to deal with the consequences of that rather than for me. But there was no doubt where the blame for it all was felt to lie. The campaign against me reached something of a climax in November 1971 when the *Sun* voted me 'The Most Unpopular Woman in Britain'.

Perhaps I had been naive in thinking that doing what was

generally agreed to be best for education was likely to count in argument about the sacrifices required. The local authorities, for blatantly political reasons, were unwilling to sell milk to the children, and it was almost impossible to force them to do so. I learned a valuable lesson. I had incurred the maximum of political odium for the minimum of political benefit. I and my colleagues were caught up in battles with local authorities for months, during which we suffered constant sniping in the media, all for a saving of £9 million which could have been cut from the capital budget with scarcely a ripple. I resolved not to make the same mistake again. In future if I were to be hanged, it would be for a sheep, not a lamb, still less a cow.

By now I was hurt and upset, somewhat sadder but considerably wiser. It is probably true that a woman – even a woman who has lived a professional life in a man's world – is more emotionally vulnerable to personal abuse than most men. The image which my opponents and the press had painted of me as callously attacking the welfare of young children was one which, as someone who was never happier than in children's company, I found deeply wounding. But any politician who wants to hold high office must be prepared to go through something like this. Some are broken by it, others strengthened. Denis, always the essence of commonsense, came through magnificently. If I survived, it was due to his love and support. I later developed the habit of not poring over articles and profiles in the newspapers about myself. I came to rely instead on briefings and summaries. If what the press wrote was false, I could ignore it; and if it was true, I already knew it.

Throughout 1971 as the assault on me was being mounted over the issue of school milk, I was locked in battle within the Cabinet on public spending. It was politically vital to my argument about school meals and milk that the primary school building programme – crucial to the emphasis our policy placed on primary education generally – should go ahead as envisaged. So within the department I rejected early suggestions of compromise with the Treasury budget cutters. In a note to Bill Pile in April 1971 I laid down our last-ditch position: 'We cannot settle for less than last year in real terms.'

This was more than political realism. I felt that other colleagues, who had not delivered the painful savings I had made, had been allowed to get away with it. In return for the cuts in meals and milk I had obtained agreement on the size of the school building programme for just one year ahead. But since it takes several years to plan and build a school, the promise had implications for future years. Others had won agreement for continuing expenditure over the whole five-year period of our public expenditure planning, the so-called Public Expenditure Survey Committee (PESC) system. Moreover, my department was now offering *savings* of over £100 million on higher education to the Treasury, while huge sums were still being paid out in industrial subsidies.

I could not reach agreement with Maurice Macmillan, then Chief Secretary, and so appealed, as any Cabinet minister has a right to do, to Cabinet. But I was then irritated to learn that No. 10 had decided that I would not be allowed to put in a paper. I wrote a sharply worded letter to Ted pointing out the pressures I was under to announce the 1973/74 school building programme. The letter concluded:

> You are constantly urging us to improve departmental administration. At present I am being prevented from doing just that on the capital building side.
>
> I urgently need a good 73/74 programme which takes into account my last year's extensive cuts. The third, fourth and fifth years can be left to the PESC meetings but I hope to agree them then.
>
> I'm afraid this letter sounds terse, but you would be critical if it were long. May I see you when you return from Paris?

I won his agreement to put in my paper in June 1971 – and I got my way. At Cabinet later that month I succeeded in obtaining almost everything that I wanted for the school building programme. It was just in time to announce to the annual conference of the Association of Education Committees in Eastbourne and prompted such headlines as 'Record Programme to Improve Old Primary Schools'.

On my arrival at the DES, that really had been *the* priority for me. Because of it, as I have just explained, I had to make (or at least accept) spending decisions which made life extraordinarily difficult. I felt that in the 1970s it was wrong for schools still to have leaky roofs, primitive equipment and outside lavatories. Moreover, now that the demographic 'bulge' of primary-school-age children had more or less been accommodated – the peak was in 1973 – there was some financial leeway to improve the quality of the often very old and gloomy schools which had been kept in use.

It was, however, graphically demonstrated to me when I visited a new school in south London that there was a lot more to improving education than bricks and mortar. The teachers who showed me round were obviously members of the academic awkward squad. One of them told me that the children at this school were upset that some of their friends had to go to an old school in the neighbourhood. And indeed most of the children had clearly been well coached to support this view. But one of them spoke up, to the teachers' evident embarrassment, to challenge this, saying: 'Oh, I am not sure that's right. Before I came here I went to a school which was older than this and smaller; but it was cosier, more friendly, and we knew where we were.' As time went by, I too felt increasingly strongly about the importance of smaller schools. I also came to consider in later years that we had all of us been too interested in the 'inputs' (new buildings, expensive equipment and, above all, more and more teachers) rather than the 'outputs' (quality of teaching, levels of achievement and standards of behaviour).

Oddly, perhaps, it was not mainly by reading thoughtful analyses or arguing with perceptive critics that I gradually formed my views about what was wrong with the educational system – and the educational establishment which lived off it – but rather by practical, almost random, experience of what was actually happening in schools.

Take primary school education. Few would quarrel with the assertion that those first years of schooling are essential to a child's formation. But what were these young children actually to be taught – and how? The Plowden Report commissioned by the previous Conservative Minister of Education, Edward Boyle, and regarded by almost everyone as the last word in expert opinion, leaned strongly in favour of teaching in small groups and even one-to-one, rather than classes. I had no strong views on the matter when I arrived at the DES, and the report was well argued. But I now suspect that it sent primary schools in the wrong direction for a generation. Again, my doubts only started to surface when I visited schools and found that in reality individual children were often not being taught in a group, let alone in a class, but were largely left to their own – not necessarily very useful – devices. I saw how in large, open-plan classrooms, groups were inclined to disintegrate into a disorderly hubbub in which quieter children felt lost and even intimidated. I came back to the department and told the Ministry's architects' department not to encourage this type of open-plan school.

What I rejected right from the start was the idea, fashionable among the middle classes as much as among experts, that the best way for a child to learn was by self-discovery. This belief entailed the abandonment of the kind of education my generation had had as mere 'learning by rote'. In fact, any worthwhile education involves the teaching of knowledge, memory training, the ability to apply what one has learned and the self-discipline required for all of these. In all the frenzy of theorizing, these truths were forgotten.

STUDENT PRINCES

Whether or not the acclaim for my defence of the primary school building programme was justified, it soon faded away as a new agitation over the financing of student unions got under way. Unlike the controversy over school milk, this was largely a campaign organized by the hard Left. It was, therefore, less politically dangerous. But it was very vicious. Nor was it just directed against me. My daughter Carol, reading Law at University College, London, also had a hard time. I was thankful she was living at home.

In both Europe and the United States this was the height of the period of 'student revolution'. Looking back, it is extraordinary that so much notice should have been taken of the kindergarten Marxism and egocentric demands which characterized it. In part, it was a development of that youth cult of the 1960s whereby the young were regarded as a source of pure insight into the human condition. In response, many students accordingly expected their opinions to be treated with reverence.

Yet the student protests of the time, far from being in the vanguard of progress, were phenomena of a world which was about to pass away. The universities had been expanded too quickly in the 1960s. In many cases standards had fallen and the traditional character of the universities had been lost. Moreover, this had occurred at a time when market principles were in retreat and the assumption was near-universal that everyone had a right to a job and the state had the power to give it to them. So these rootless young people lacked both the authority which had been imposed on their predecessors in the 1950s and the discipline which the need to qualify for a good job would place on students in the eighties.

The Left had managed to gain control of many student unions, and therefore of the public money which financed them, using this position to mount campaigns of disruption which infuriated ordinary taxpayers and ratepayers and even many students who simply wanted to study. There were two aspects: first, the financing of student bodies, and second what those bodies did. On the first, the main source of money for student unions was subscriptions out of mandatory grants received from their local education authorities. Union membership was normally obligatory and the union subscription was then paid direct to the student union. As regards activities, some student unions took advantage of this to spend the revenue on partisan purposes, often in defiance of both their constitution and the wishes of their members.

In July 1971 I put proposals to the Home and Social Affairs Committee of the Cabinet (HS) for reform. I had considered setting up a Registrar of student unions, but that would have required legislation. So I limited myself to proposing something more modest. In future, the union subscription should not be included in the fees payable to colleges and universities. The student maintenance grant would be increased slightly to enable students to join particular clubs or societies on a voluntary basis. Responsibility for providing student union facilities would then be placed on each academic institution. The facilities of each union would be open to all students, whether or not they were members of the union. Besides dealing with the question of accountability for public money, these changes would also abolish the closed-shop element in student unions which I found deeply objectionable on grounds of principle. HS was not prepared to go along with my proposals immediately, but I came back to the argument, fully recognizing how controversial they would be, and gained the Committee's approval.

Bill Van Straubenzee was the minister directly responsible for dealing with consultations on the proposals. But I was the one immediately marked down as the hate-figure to be targeted for them. Student mobs hounded me wherever I went. In early November in Leeds, where I was laying a stone to mark the construction of new buildings, about 500 students tried to shout me down. Later that month 2,000 screaming students tried to prevent my presenting the designation document of the South Bank Polytechnic at the Queen Elizabeth Hall. A dozen mounted police had to protect my car. In December the student protesters found time from their studies to organize a nationwide day of protest. My effigy was burnt at various universities.

By now many of the Vice-Chancellors and college authorities were giving tacit approval to the protests. Edward Boyle even addressed a mass meeting of students at Leeds to declare his opposition to my proposals. Since these had only been put out for consultation – though 'consultation' is not the most obvious description of what had occurred – it was perfectly possible to allow tempers to cool and to delay action, which I did. The main problem was that until university authorities themselves were prepared to uphold the values of a university and exert some authority, no proposal for reform was likely to succeed. This was also the time when freedom of speech began to be denied by groups of students, who were then indulged by nervous university authorities. University intolerance was at its most violent in the early seventies. But, less visible and more institutionalized, the same censorship continues today.

TRYING, STILL TRYING...

1971 had been a crucial year for the Government and for me personally. The pressures which mounted were all the more intolerable because they were cumulative. As I shall describe, the Government's self-confidence broke in early 1972.* Somehow, although under greater strain than at any time before or since, my own held.

But a number of commentators, with varying mixtures of relish and regret, thought that I was done for. On my return after the Christmas holiday at Lamberhurst, I was able to read my fate openly discussed in the newspapers. One described me as 'The Lady Nobody Loves'. Another published a thoughtful article entitled 'Why Mrs Thatcher is so Unpopular'. But I pushed the stuff aside and concentrated on my red boxes.

In fact, it was not long before the tide – for me personally, though not for the Government – began to turn. Probably the 'milk snatcher' campaign had in any case come to the end of its natural life. The far more serious issues of 1972 were now upon us – the miners' strike and the various elements of the U-turn** – and these dwarfed the personal campaign against me. And, of course, I was evidently not going to buckle or depart – at least voluntarily. But I owe a debt of gratitude to Ted Heath as well.

Ted asked me and my officials down to Chequers on Wednesday 12 January to have a general discussion about education. I took with me an *aide-mémoire* summing up the situation and looking ahead. In spite of all the difficulties, there was only one pre-election commitment which still remained to be implemented: the expansion of nursery education. More money was needed if something substantial was to be achieved. The other area in which our supporters were disappointed was secondary school organization. There the problem was, as I put it, 'many of our own local councils are running with the comprehensive tide. The question is what sort of balance should be struck between defending existing grammar

* See p. 219.
** See pp. 213–30.

schools and leaving local education authorities free to make their own decisions?' We discussed both these points at Chequers, as well as other irritants such as school milk and student unions. Ted was clearly interested. He was keen on nursery education; he had been pressing for action on student unions; and he very reasonably asked whether we could not use educational arguments in justifying our policy on selection, rather than just resting on the arguments about local authority autonomy.

From my point of view, however, at least as important as the discussion was the fact that by inviting me down with my officials Ted implied that there was no intention to move me from Education in the foreseeable future. This was a useful, indeed – facing the problems I did – a vital reinforcement for my authority. Ted went on a few days later in the House to list my achievements. Why did he give me such strong support? Some felt that he needed a woman in the Cabinet and it was difficult to find a credible alternative candidate. But I like to think that it also showed Ted's character at its admirable best. He knew that the policies for which I had been so roundly attacked were essentially policies which I had reluctantly accepted under pressure from the Treasury and the requirements of public finance. He also knew that I had not tried to shift the blame onto others. However unreliable his adherence to particular policies, he always stood by people who did their best for him and his Government. This was one of the better reasons why his Cabinet reciprocated by remaining united behind him.

Ted's expressions of support provided me with no more than a breathing space. But it was enough. From the spring of 1972 the chilly political climate in which I had been living began noticeably to thaw. My speech to the NUT in April was well received, not just by most of the audience (which cheered me at the end) but, more importantly, by the press in general. Unusually, the proposals it contained appealed across the political spectrum. I announced an increase in the school building programme, now running at a record level. I also announced the setting-up of a committee to inquire into the teaching of reading in schools and the use of English – matters which were already the subject of widespread concern. I hinted at a further expansion of nursery education, though drawing attention to the problem of financing it. But what seized the imagination of the commentators was my criticism of giant comprehensive schools. (I elaborated on this last point at a press conference after the speech, noting that I had just rejected plans for a school for 2,700 pupils in Wiltshire.)

As I stood up to speak, there was an ill-mannered walk-out by a number of left-wing delegates. But this turned out to be an added bonus. The media not only liked the emphasis on the merits of smaller schools, but had some harsh things to say about the example given to their pupils by teachers who were not even prepared to hear the arguments. In May the same newspaper column which had described me as 'The Lady Nobody Loves' was celebrating 'The Mellowing of Margaret'. And the irony was that the theme which had struck home – my advocacy of small schools – was one which I had held to since my days as a schoolgirl in Grantham.

It was, however, the Education White Paper, published in December 1972, which restored the fortunes of our education policy. The decision to publish it stemmed from discussions of the three Programme Analysis and Review (PAR) Reports which we had prepared in the department.* The title was the result of a last-minute decision at Cabinet. *Education: A Framework for Advance* was the original suggestion but, in a change which appears in retrospect to be all too typical of these over-ambitious, high-spending years, this became *Education: A Framework for Expansion*. The White Paper set out a ten-year plan for higher spending and better provision. There were six main points to it. There was a programme for improving or replacing old secondary schools. The building programme for special schools for handicapped children would be increased. There would be a modest improvement in school staffing ratios. To help pay for this, the rate of expansion of higher education would be restrained. We published our response to the James Committee's recommendations on teacher training. But the most important aspect was the announcement of a major expansion of nursery education. This would be provided for up to 90 per cent of four-year-olds and 50 per cent of three-year-

---

* The PAR system was a characteristic innovation of the Heath Government – an ambitious attempt to review existing departmental programmes with the professed intention of radically reducing the role of Government, but with little or no effect.

olds, subject to demand, with priority being given in the early stages to deprived areas. In retrospect, the White Paper marks the high-point of the attempts by Government to overcome the problems inherent in Britain's education system by throwing money at them.

The White Paper received a disconcertingly rapturous reception. The *Daily Telegraph*, although making some criticisms about the lack of proposals for student loans or vouchers, said that the White Paper established me 'as one of our most distinguished reforming – and spending – Ministers of Education'. The *Daily Mail* described it as a 'Quiet Revolution' and commented, 'there has been nothing like it since the war'. More unsettling was the *Guardian*'s praise for a 'progressive programme' and the comment – I hoped tongue in cheek – that 'apart from not mandatorily ending 11-Plus segregation, Mrs Thatcher is more than half way towards a respectably socialist education policy'.

REALITY BITES

With the exception of some vigorous exchanges with Labour's new and highly articulate Education spokesman, Roy Hattersley, about the rate of increase of education expenditure, the early months of 1973 were as near as any at the DES to being quiet. But the consequences of the Government's fiscal and monetary policies were shortly to catch up with us. The first instalment was in May – a round of public expenditure cuts designed to cool the overheated economy. Capital spending in education, particularly the less politically sensitive area of higher education, was an obvious target. In the event, I staved off Treasury pressure and my building programmes were not cut.

But there were other problems in the DES budget. As inflationary pressures pushed up prices in the construction industry, an increasingly alarmed Treasury refused to sanction higher spending. The rest of the school building programme had to be slowed down as well. As October – the time for firm public expenditure decision-making – approached it was increasingly clear to me that public expenditure cuts were essential, and that it made political sense to agree early with Patrick Jenkin, the new Chief Secretary, on reductions in my education budget. In the event, there were cuts in the school building plans and in teacher training, and school meal prices were increased.

Nor was this the end of the search for savings. As the effects of the oil crisis and the miners' strike bit in December, Tony Barber began a frantic search for further cuts.* Capital spending is the only area in which large immediate public expenditure cuts can be made. So ministers were required to reduce their capital programmes by a fifth and their procurement of supplies and other current expenditure on goods and services by a tenth. Accordingly, I implemented further cuts in the school and higher education building programmes, including most painfully a moratorium on replacing older primary schools; for the longer term there would also be a reduction in the rate of expansion of student numbers. The reduction in the DES budget for 1974/75 was £182 million – out of £1,200 million total cuts in public spending. But I did manage for the time being to salvage the nursery school programme and also building programmes for special schools.

By now, however, my mind was fast focusing on the cataclysmic events overtaking the Government. It was not long before I would have to mount my soapbox and defend the policies I had pursued in my years at Education. I found no difficulty in doing so, for on almost every front the record was one of advance. And if the measures by which 'advance' at this time was assessed – resources committed rather than results achieved – are accepted, it was also a record of genuine improvement. Nearly 2,000 out-of-date primary schools in England and Wales were replaced or improved. There was a substantial expansion of nursery education. I pushed through the raising of the school leaving age, which the Labour Party had had to postpone. Fewer pupils were now taught in very large classes. There were more qualified teachers and more students in higher education. But too much of my time at Education had been spent arguing about structures and resources, too little in addressing the crucial issue of the *contents* of education.

* See p. 232.

Equally, it was clear by the time of the general election that both the figures and more fundamentally the approach of *A Framework for Expansion* had been by-passed by events. There was no way that a programme of universal nursery education was affordable. Schools would have to make do with leaky roofs for many more years, until declining pupil numbers and school closures allowed resources to be better used. The Robbins Report principle – that 'courses of higher education should be available for all those qualified by ability and attainment to pursue them' (paragraph 31) – would have to take second place to the demands of financial stringency.

However frustrating it was to watch the shrinkage of my cherished plans and programmes, I can now see that it was unavoidable. And it may have had the side effect of forcing us to think creatively about how to get the best value from our suddenly limited resources. In the economic sphere, the crises of 1973 to 1976 led to a deep scepticism about the value of Keynesian demand management and to a new appreciation of the classical liberal economic approach of balanced budgets, low taxes and free markets. Similarly, in education and in other areas of social policy too, the realization that remedies must be found other than increased public expenditure opened up a whole new world. Fundamental questions began to be asked about whether the education system in its present form could deliver the results expected of it. Did it not in practice largely exist for the benefit of those who ran it, rather than those who received it? Was the state – whether the DES or local education authorities – doing too much, rather than too little? What did the – often superior – results of other countries' education systems and methods have to teach us? It was becoming necessary to rethink these policies; and we were shortly to be granted plenty of time to think.

CHAPTER VII

No End of a Lesson

The Heath Government 1970–1974

GLAD CONFIDENT MORNING

Shortly before 11 o'clock on Tuesday 23 June 1970 my new ministerial car dropped me in Downing Street, where with other colleagues I ran the gauntlet of press and television outside No. 10. The hubbub in the ante-room was of enthusiasm and laughter. There was a spring in our step as we filed into the Cabinet Room where Ted Heath, with the Cabinet Secretary Sir Burke Trend beside him, awaited us. I found my place at the Cabinet table, but my mind was at least as much on the department* as on the large strategic issues before the Government. As I shall explain, it remained there – perhaps excessively so. But I felt an exhilaration which was prompted by more than the fact that this was my first ever Cabinet meeting: I felt, as I suspect we all did, that this was a decisive moment in the life of the country.

It was an impression which Ted himself did everything to justify. Speaking with the same intensity which had suffused his introduction to the manifesto on which we had just fought the election, he announced his intention of establishing a new style of administration and a fresh approach to the conduct of public business. The emphasis was to be upon deliberation and the avoidance of hasty or precipitate reactions. There was to be a clean break and a fresh start and new brooms galore.

The tone was just what we would all have expected from Ted.

* For the Department of Education and Science, see the previous chapter.

194

He had a great belief in the capacity of open-minded politicians to resolve fundamental problems if the processes and structures of government were right and advice of the right technical quality was available and properly used. This was the approach which would lie behind the decision that autumn to set up the Central Policy Review Staff under Victor Rothschild, to reconstruct the machinery of government on more 'rational' lines (including the setting up of the mammoth Department of the Environment) and the establishment of the PAR system. More generally, it inspired what turned out to be an excessive confidence in the Government's ability to shape and control events.

Inevitably, this account contains a large measure of hindsight. I was not a member of the key Economic Policy Committee (EPC) of the Cabinet, though I would sometimes attend if teachers' pay or spending on schools was an issue. More frequently, I attended Terence Higgins's sub-committee on pay when the full rigours of a detailed statutory prices and incomes policy – the policy our manifesto pledged us to avoid – were applied, and made some contributions there. And, naturally, I was not a member of Ted's inner circle where most of the big decisions originated. The role of the Cabinet itself was generally of reduced importance after the first year of the Heath Government until its very end. The full account of these years will, therefore, have to await Ted Heath's own memoirs.

This, however, is said in explanation not exculpation. As a member of the Cabinet I must take my full share of responsibility for what was done under the Government's authority. Reviewing the events of this period with the benefit of two decades' hindsight (including more than one of these as Prime Minister), I can see more clearly how Ted Heath, an honest man whose strength of character made him always formidable, whether right or wrong, took the course he did. And as time went on, he *was* wrong, not just once but repeatedly. His errors – our errors, for we went along with them – did huge harm to the Conservative Party and to the country. But it is easy to comprehend the pressures upon him.

It is also important to remember that the policies Ted pursued between the spring of 1972 and February 1974 were urged on him by most influential commentators and for much of the time enjoyed a wide measure of public support. The Nixon administration in the United States adopted a broadly similar approach, as did other European countries. There were brave and far-sighted critics who were proved right. But they were an embattled, isolated group. Although my reservations steadily grew, I was not at this stage among them.

But some of us (though never Ted, I fear) learned from these mistakes. I can well understand how after I became Leader of the Conservative Party Enoch Powell, who with a small number of other courageous Tory backbenchers had protested at successive U-turns, claimed that: 'If you are looking for somebody to pick up principles trampled in the mud, the place to look is not among the tramplers.'

But Enoch was wrong. In Rudyard Kipling's words, Keith Joseph and I had 'had no end of a lesson':

Let us admit it fairly, as a business people should;
We have had no end of a lesson; it will do us no end of good.*

In this sense, we owed our later successes to our inside knowledge and to our understanding of the earlier failures. The Heath Government showed, in particular, that socialist policies pursued by Tory politicians are if anything even more disastrous than socialist policies pursued by Labour politicians. Collectivism, without even the tincture of egalitarian idealism to redeem it, is a deeply unattractive creed.

How did it happen? I have already outlined some of the background. In spite of the acclaim for the Selsdon Park manifesto, we had thought through our policies a good deal less thoroughly than appeared. In particular that was true of our economic policy. We had no clear theory of inflation or the role of wage settlements within it. And without such a theory we drifted into the superstition that inflation was the direct result of wage increases and the power

---

* 'The Lesson' (1902). The lesson in question was the Boer War, in which Britain had suffered many military reverses.

of trade unions. So we were pushed inexorably along the path of
regulating incomes and prices.

Ted was also impatient. I share this characteristic. I am often
impatient with people. But I knew – partly of course by seeing
what happened under Ted – that, in a broader sense, patience is
required if a policy for long-term change is to work. This is especially true if, like Ted's Government in 1970 and mine in 1979, you
are committed to a non-interventionist economic policy that relies
on setting a framework rather than designing a plan. Sudden shifts
of direction, taken because the results are too long in appearing,
can have devastating effects in undermining the credibility of the
strategy. And so a government which came to power proud of its
principle and consistency left behind it, among other embarrassing
legacies, a host of quips about 'the U-turn'. Ted's own words in
his introduction to the 1970 manifesto came back to haunt him:

> Once a decision is made, once a policy is established, the
> Prime Minister and his colleagues should have the courage
> to stick to it. Nothing has done Britain more harm in the
> world than the endless backing and filling which we have seen
> in recent years.

At another level, however – the level of day-to-day human experience in government – the explanation of what happened is to be
found within the events themselves, in the forces which buffeted us
and in our reactions to them. We thought we were well enough prepared to face these. But we were not. Little by little we were blown
off course until eventually, in a fit of desperation, we tore up the map,
threw the compass overboard and, sailing under new colours but
with the same helmsman, still supremely confident of his naviga-
tional sense, set off towards unknown and rock-strewn waters.

The squalls began early. Within weeks of taking office the
Government had been forced to declare a State of Emergency* as

---

* A State of Emergency may be proclaimed by the Crown – effectively by Ministers – whenever a situation arises which threatens to deprive the community of
the essentials of life by disrupting the supply and distribution of food, water,
fuel or light, or communications. It gives Government extensive powers to make
regulations to restore these necessities. Troops may be used. If Parliament is not

a national docks strike began to bite. At the same time a Court of Inquiry was set up to find an expensive solution. Although the strike evaporated within a fortnight, it was an ambiguous triumph.

The following month the crisis was international. On Sunday 6 September terrorists from the Popular Front for the Liberation of Palestine (PFLP) hijacked four aircraft (none of them British) and demanded that they be flown to Jordan. Three of the hijacks were successful, but on the fourth – an Israeli plane *en route* to London – the hijackers were overpowered by security men. The surviving terrorist, Leila Khalid, was arrested at Heathrow.

The PFLP demanded her release, and just before Cabinet met on Wednesday 9 September they hijacked a British aircraft in order to bring more pressure to bear. The plane was flying to Beirut as we met. It was explained to Cabinet that we had already acquiesced in an American suggestion to offer the release of Leila Khalid in return for the freedom of the hostages. Over the next few weeks Cabinet discussed the question many times as negotiations ran on. Meanwhile, Jordan itself fell into a state of civil war as King Hussein fought the Palestinians for control of his country and the Syrians invaded and occupied much of the north. Ted resisted any British involvement on the King's side and was certain that we were right to negotiate with the PFLP. Though it went against the grain to release Khalid, in the end the deal was made. In due course all the hostages were released, though the hijacked aircraft were blown up by the terrorists, and King Hussein survived the events of 'Black September' – barely but triumphantly.

But by then the Government had already suffered a blow from which, perhaps, we never fully recovered. In mid-July Iain Macleod had gone into hospital for a small abdominal operation. It had been a success and he had returned to No. 11 for a few days' rest. At about midnight on Monday 20 July my telephone rang. It was Francis Pym, the Chief Whip. He said that Ted had asked him to ring round to tell us all that Iain had suffered a heart attack that evening and had just died. He was only fifty-six.

I felt the blow personally, for Iain had always been a generous

---

sitting when the proclamation is made, it must be recalled within five days. A State of Emergency expires at the end of one month, but may be extended.

and kind man for whom to work. I knew that he had given me my chance to shine and so make my way into the Shadow and then the real Cabinet. But I also immediately recognized that we had lost our shrewdest political intellect and best communicator. How Iain would have performed as Chancellor I do not know. But if one accepts, as I did and do, that the worst mistakes of economic policy derived from Ted's overruling the Treasury, it is reasonable to suppose that matters might have turned out better if Iain had lived. He was succeeded by Tony Barber, a man of considerable intellectual ability, who by and large had an unhappy time at the Treasury. The economic problems of the next few years were founded in this transition. Although Tony may have had sounder economic instincts, Iain boxed at a much higher political weight.

The Cabinet which met after Iain Macleod's death was a sombre one. Around the Cabinet table already sat nearly all of those who would be my colleagues over the next four and a half years. Their personal qualities would be severely tested. Tony Barber was an old if not particularly close friend from the Bar, an able tax lawyer, but not someone to stand up against Ted. Reggie Maudling, Home Secretary until his resignation over the Poulson affair in 1972,* was still interested in and had strong views about economic policy. By contrast, he was less than fascinated by his new brief. Technically still extremely competent, he was unlikely to oppose any shift back towards a more interventionist economic policy, which indeed he had always favoured.

Alec Douglas-Home had returned effortlessly to his old Foreign Office brief where, however, plenty of effort was soon required in giving effect to our promises made in Opposition to lift the arms embargo on South Africa and in trying to devise an affordable way of retaining a British military presence east of Suez. He was unlikely to take much part in domestic political affairs now, any more than he had in Shadow Cabinet. Quintin Hailsham had found his ideal role as Lord Chancellor, beginning a long spell in that office under Ted and then me, where he managed to combine his old sense of

---

* John Poulson was an architect convicted in 1974 of making corrupt payments to win contracts. A number of local government figures also went to gaol. Reggie Maudling had served on the board of one of Poulson's companies.

mischief and theatre with the sedate traditions of the Upper House. Peter Carrington was Defence Secretary, a post for which he was well suited and which he filled with aplomb. I knew that he was close to Ted. He doubtless became still closer when later as Party Chairman and Energy Secretary he had a crucial role in dealing with the final miners' strike which precipitated the general election of February 1974. He was one of Ted's 'inner circle'.

Keith Joseph, by contrast, though a senior Cabinet figure and someone whose views had always to be taken seriously, was certainly not part of that circle and was never, so far as I know, invited to join it. Having been appointed to be Secretary of State for Social Services, Keith's compassionate, social reforming side had become uppermost at the expense of his more conservative economic convictions, though he retained a profound distrust of corporatism in all its forms. His passion became the need to tackle the problem of the 'cycle of deprivation' which condemned successive generations to poverty. Like me, Keith had been given a high-spending 'social' department, and there was a natural opposition between what he (also like me) wanted for his own preferred programmes and the requirements of tight public expenditure control. Whether by chance or calculation, Ted had ensured that the two most economically conservative members of his Cabinet were kept well out of economic decision-making, which was left to those over whom he could wield maximum influence.

John Davies, the former Director General of the Confederation of British Industry (CBI) (who knew nothing of politics when he was summoned after Iain Macleod's death to become Minister of Technology), certainly fell into that category. John was someone I liked and indeed appointed later to a post in my Shadow Cabinet. But his warmest admirer would have been hard put to make a case for his handling of the turbulent industrial politics which would now become his responsibility. John also represented 'business', a concept which Ted, with his latent corporatism, considered had some kind of 'role' in government.

With Tony Barber and John Davies, Robert Carr was, as Employment Secretary, the third key figure responsible for economic strategy under Ted. He was a good deal senior to me and we had different views and temperaments. He was a decent, hard-working though not a colourful personality. But he had a difficult, arguably impossible, brief in trying to make the flawed Industrial Relations Act work. His reputation as a left winger in Conservative terms was less useful than some might have expected; trade unionists used to regard left-wing Conservatives not as more compassionate but merely as less candid. As Employment Secretary at the time of the first (1972) miners' strike and Home Secretary at the time of the second (1974), few people faced greater difficulties during these years.

One who did was Willie Whitelaw as, successively, Leader of the House, Northern Ireland Secretary and finally Employment Secretary at the time of the three-day week. Willie was part of the generation which had fought the war. We seemed to have little in common and neither of us, I am sure, suspected how closely our political destinies would come to be linked. Since Education was not a department requiring at this time a heavy legislative programme, our paths rarely crossed. But I was already aware of Willie as a wise, reassuring figure whose manner, voice and stature made him an excellent Leader of the House. By the end of the Government his judgement and qualities were playing a role second in significance only to Ted's own. Willie's bluff public persona, however, concealed a shrewd political intelligence and instinct for managing men.

After Iain Macleod's untimely death, Geoffrey Rippon was given responsibility for negotiating the terms of our entry into the European Economic Community. Although we had superficially similar backgrounds – both having been Presidents of OUCA and barristers – Geoffrey and I were never close. It always seemed to me that he tried to overwhelm opponents with the force of his personality rather than with the force of his argument. This may have been because Ted had given him the task of getting the best deal he could in negotiations with the EEC – and that deal was not always in our best long-term interests. This was something we were to realize more and more as time went on.

My impression was that the two members of Cabinet Ted trusted most were Jim Prior and Peter Walker. Both had proved their loyalty, Jim as Ted's PPS in Opposition, and Peter as organizer of his 1965 leadership campaign. Jim was Agriculture Minister, a post which his farming background and rubicund features helped him make his own, before becoming Deputy Chairman of the Party under Peter Carrington in April 1972. Peter Walker's thirst for the 'modernization' of British institutions must have helped draw him closer to Ted. He soon became Secretary of State for the huge new Department of the Environment, where he embarked with vigour upon the most unpopular local government reforms until my own Community Charge – and at the cost of far greater bureaucracy. Later he would go to the other conglomerate, the Department of Trade and Industry (DTI). Jim and, still more so, Peter were younger than me, but both had far more influence over the general direction of Government. Although their political views were very different from mine, I respected their loyalty to Ted and their political effectiveness.

The other members of Cabinet – Gordon Campbell at Scotland, George Jellicoe as Lord Privy Seal and Leader of the Lords, Peter Thomas, a close parliamentary neighbour and friend, as Secretary of State for Wales and Party Chairman, and Michael Noble briefly at Trade – did not figure large in discussions. I therefore found myself with just one political friend in Cabinet – Keith. Although I generally had polite and pleasant relations with my other colleagues, I knew that we were not soulmates. Doubtless they knew it too. Such things often show through more clearly in casual conversation and spontaneous reactions than in argument. What with the formidable difficulties I faced in Education, I therefore had little incentive to try to win wider strategic points in Cabinet.

Ted's mastery of the Cabinet was complete and unchallenged. He had won the 1970 election against all expectations and by means of a very personal campaign. We were aware of this and so was he. Moreover, argument from first principles was alien to his nature and disagreeable to his temperament. Until 1972–73 and the events of the U-turn, the unity of Cabinet under Ted's leadership was at least in part simply recognition that he was Prime Minister and had a right to expect support in carrying through the programme. Once the programme itself was abandoned and an exercise in corporate interventionism adopted in its stead, the atmosphere grew worse, not manifesting itself in dissent but in the occasional leaked grumble. We knew we were locked in.

A ROLLS-ROYCE POLICY

For all the difficulties which were quickly upon us that summer and autumn of 1970, such melancholy reflections were still far from our thoughts. Indeed, Ted Heath, Tony Barber, Robert Carr and John Davies set out on the course of radical reform with impressive zeal; and the rest of us in the Cabinet were enthusiastic cheer-leaders.

First, the Government embarked with a will on cutting public spending. (In fact this review was to be the only sustained Cabinet-level exercise of the kind during the entire period of 1970–74; the cuts of December 1973 would be made at speed and without detailed discussion in Cabinet.) Discussions began at the end of July. A target was agreed of £1,700 million net reduction in planned spending by 1974/75, and Ted circulated a paper on the economy to show his commitment to the strategy. The cuts were to fall most heavily on industrial spending, though as already noted I had my own departmental spending battles at Education. Investment grants were ended. The Industrial Re-organization Corporation (IRC) would be closed down. Aircraft and space projects would be subject to the closest scrutiny. Even with the reprieve of the hugely expensive Concorde project, largely on European policy grounds, it was an impressive free-market economic programme. And it made possible a tax-cutting Budget in October, which reduced the standard rate of income tax by 6d, down from 8s.3d in the pound (just over 41p), and made reductions in corporation tax to take effect at the beginning of the next financial year.

Nor was there any delay in bringing forward the other key feature of our economic programme – the Industrial Relations Bill. The framework of the Bill was already familiar: this was one of the areas of policy most thoroughly worked out in Opposition and we had published our proposals in 1968. It was to be an ambitiously comprehensive attempt to provide a new basis for industrial relations. The main principles were that collective bargaining agreements should be legally enforceable unless the parties to them agreed otherwise, and that the unions' historic immunities from civil action should be both significantly narrowed and confined to those whose rule books met certain minimum standards ('registered unions').

Cases brought under this legislation would be dealt with by a new system of industrial courts and tribunals, headed by a branch of the High Court – the National Industrial Relations Court (NIRC). The Bill also gave new powers to the Secretary of State for Employment, as a last resort when negotiation had failed, to apply to the NIRC either for an order deferring industrial action for up to sixty days – a 'cooling off' period – or for one requiring a secret ballot of the workers involved before a strike.

There was a good deal in the Bill that actively favoured trade unionism, for all the hostility it encountered on the Left. For the first time in English law there would be a legally enforceable right to belong (or not to belong) to a trade union. There would be statutory protection against unfair dismissal – again, a new principle in English law. Finally, the Bill would repeal provisions under previous legislation that made it a criminal offence for gas, water and electricity workers to strike during the lifetime of their contracts.

At the time I was a strong supporter of the Bill, although I had doubts about particular parts, such as the measure on essential services. We were all conscious that the previous Labour Government had backed off from its *In Place of Strife* proposals for trade union reform under a mixture of union and Party pressure. We were, therefore, doubly determined to make the changes required.

In retrospect, the philosophy of the Bill was muddled. It assumed that if the unions were in general confirmed in their powers they would both discipline their own members industrially, reducing wildcat strikes for instance, and use their industrial strength in a regulated and orderly fashion on the American model. But it also contained provisions to strengthen the powers of individuals against the unions. So the Bill was in part corporatist and in part libertarian.

Specifically there were four flaws. First, the Bill was full of loopholes. By refusing to sign agreements unless the employer conceded that they need not be legally binding, the unions effectively bypassed one legal sanction. They also discovered an effective tactic to stymie the Bill's ambition to transform the nature of British industrial relations – many simply de-registered and went on behaving as if they still possessed the old immunities, defying anyone damaged by their activities to bring an action, and defying the courts on the rare occasions when actions were brought.

Second, we were not clear how the Industrial Relations Act fitted into our overall economic strategy. Our movement towards a 'voluntary' incomes policy – starting with the so-called 'n–1' policy* which had begun even before the Bill was introduced – increased the occasions for disputes about pay and put the fledgling Act under huge pressures. Eventually, the Industrial Relations Act was shelved, at least tacitly, as part of the attempt to stitch up a deal with the trade unions on pay.

Third, if we were to rely so heavily on the law to improve the climate of industrial relations, we should have avoided creating so many new institutions and procedures all at once. This allowed our opponents to claim that the system was rigged against them. And when we used the new powers to impose 'cooling off' periods and strike ballots, these were promptly discredited as disputes heated up and the votes went against us.

Finally, we naively assumed that our opponents would play by the same rules as we did. In particular, we imagined that there would not be either mass opposition to laws passed by a democratically elected government or mass infringement of the criminal law, as in the miners' strike of 1972. We did not recognize that we were involved in a struggle with unscrupulous people whose principal objectives lay not in industrial relations but in politics. Had we understood this we might have embarked upon a step-by-step approach, fighting on our own territory at our own timing, as we were to do after 1979. It was later, as Leader of the Opposition, that I realized how far the extreme Left had penetrated into trade union leaderships and why that 'giant's strength', of which the Tory pamphlet had spoken in the late 1950s, was now being used in such a ruthless manner. The communists knew that they could not be returned to Parliament, so they chose to advance their cause

---

* 'n–1' was a semi-official policy that each year's pay increase should be 1 per cent less than the previous year's.

by getting into office in the trade union movement. And the fact that both the Wilson and Heath Governments had stood up to the unions and then lost increased their influence more than if we had not challenged their power in the first place.

But at this early stage we pressed ahead. The TUC was told by Robert Carr in October 1970 that the central aspects of the Industrial Relations Bill were not negotiable. The Bill was published and had its Second Reading in December. February and March 1971 saw mass protests and strikes against it. Labour used every device to fight the Bill, but in August 1971 it duly reached the Statute Book. The TUC Congress passed a resolution instructing unions to de-register. It therefore remained to be seen, when the Act came into force at the end of February 1972, what its practical effects would be – revolution, reform or business as usual. We were soon to find out.

Meanwhile other problems preoccupied us. It is sometimes suggested – and was at the time by Enoch Powell – that the Government's decision in February 1971 to take control of the aerospace division of Rolls-Royce marked the first U-turn. This is not so. Shortly before the company told the Government of the impossible financial problems it faced (as a result of the escalating cost of the contract with Lockheed to build the RB–211 engine for its Tri-star aircraft), a constituent of mine had told me that he was worried about the company. So I asked Denis to look at the figures. I arrived home late one evening to find him surrounded by six years' accounts. He told me that Rolls-Royce had been treating research and development costs as capital, rather than charging it to the profit and loss account. This spelt real trouble.

A few days later I was suddenly called to a Cabinet meeting and found Fred Corfield, the Aviation Minister, waiting in the Cabinet ante-room. 'What are you here for, Fred?' I asked. I wasn't surprised when he replied gloomily: 'Rolls-Royce.' His expression said it all. At the meeting itself we heard the full story. To the amazement of my colleagues I confirmed the analysis, based on what Denis had told me. We decided without much debate to let the company itself go into liquidation but to nationalize the aerospace division. Over the next few months there were many more complicated discussions as we renegotiated the original contract with

Lockheed, which was then itself in financial difficulties. One could argue – and people did – about the terms and the sum which needed to be provided. But I do not think any of us doubted that on defence grounds it was important to keep an indigenous aircraft engine capability. And in the long term, of course, this was one 'lame duck' which eventually found the strength to fly away again into the private sector, when I was Prime Minister.

The Rolls-Royce controversy proved to be of short duration, and it was to be a year before the serious economic U-turns – reflation, subsidies to industry, prices and incomes policy – occurred, and began the alienation of the Conservative right in Parliament and of many Tory supporters outside it. The failure of these U-turns to deliver success divided the Party still further and had other consequences. It created an inflationary boom which caused property prices to soar and encouraged a great deal of dubious financial speculation, tarnishing capitalism and, in spite of all the disclaimers, the Conservative Party with it. I shall return to the economic developments which led to all this shortly. But it is important not to underrate the impact on the Party of two non-economic issues – Europe and immigration.

FROM EMPIRE TO EUROPE

I was wholeheartedly in favour of British entry into the EEC for reasons which I have already outlined. General de Gaulle's departure from the Elysée Palace in April 1969 had transformed the prospects. His successor, Georges Pompidou, was keen to have Britain in; and, of course, no one on our side of the Channel was keener than the new Prime Minister, Ted Heath. There was never any doubt what the incoming Conservative Government's position would be; but nor was there doubt that many people across the political spectrum would oppose it. These included some of the most effective parliamentarians such as Michael Foot, Peter Shore and Enoch Powell. But the worlds of business, the media and fashionable opinion generally were strongly in favour, for a variety of high- and low-minded reasons.

Talks formally opened in Brussels at the end of October 1970, with Geoffrey Rippon reporting back to Ted and a Cabinet Committee and, on occasion, to the rest of us in full Cabinet. Twice in December we had detailed discussions of our negotiating position on the EEC budget. There was no doubt that the financial cost of entry would be high. It was estimated that the best we could hope for would be a gross British contribution of 17 per cent of total EEC expenditure, with a five-year transition, and three years of so-called 'correctives' after that (to hold it at 17 per cent). To defuse the inevitable criticism, Geoffrey Rippon also hoped to negotiate a special review provision which we could invoke at any time if the burden of our net contributions to the budget threatened to become intolerable; but he seemed to attach little significance to it, and assumed that we could reopen the question whether there was a formal review mechanism or not.

At the time Ted resolved discussion about the costs of entry by saying that no one was arguing that the burden would be so intolerable that we should break off negotiations. But this whole question of finance should have been considered more carefully. It came to dominate Britain's relations with the EEC for more than a decade afterwards, and it did not prove so easy to reopen. Though the Community made a declaration during the entry negotiations that 'should an unacceptable situation arise within the present Community or an enlarged Community, the very survival of the Community would demand that the Institutions find equitable solutions', the net British contribution quickly grew. The Labour Government of 1974–79 made no progress in reducing it. It was left to me to do so later.

Cabinet discussed the matter again in early May 1971, by which time the talks were reported to be 'deadlocked'. There were difficulties outstanding on preferential arrangements for New Zealand products (butter and lamb) and Commonwealth sugar, and shadow-boxing by the French about the role of sterling as an international currency. But the budget was still the real problem. We had an idea what deal might be on offer: promises to cut the cost of the Common Agricultural Policy and the creation of a Regional Development Fund from which Britain would benefit disproportionately. It was still not the settlement we would have wanted

– and anyway promises are not bankable – but at the time none of us foresaw how large the burden would turn out to be. Ted ended the discussion by telling us that he was planning a summit with President Pompidou in Paris to cut through the argument.

Ted spent two days talking to the French President. In view of all the past difficulties with the French, the summit was seen as a veritable triumph for him. Negotiations were completed rapidly afterwards – other than for the Common Fisheries Policy, which took years to resolve – and the terms approved by Cabinet the following month. Parliamentary approval could not be assumed, for both parties were deeply split and Labour had reversed its former support for British entry, arguing that the present terms were unacceptable. In the end, the Government decided that there would be a free vote on the Conservative side on the principle of entry. This embarrassed Labour, especially when sixty-nine Labour MPs ignored their own party whip and voted in favour, giving a majority of 112 for entry. But when it came to the terms rather than the principle of entry, the argument was far from won. The Second Reading of the European Communities Bill in February 1972 was only passed by 309 to 301, with the Liberals backing the Government and after much arm-twisting by Conservative Whips. The Bill itself was enacted in October.

The dog that barely barked at the time was the issue of sovereignty – both national and parliamentary – which as the years have gone by has assumed ever greater importance. There was some discussion of the question in Cabinet in July 1971, but only in the context of the general presentation of the case for entry in the White Paper. The resulting passages of the document – paragraphs 29–32 – can now be read in the light of events, and stand out as an extraordinary example of artful confusion to conceal fundamental issues. In particular, two sentences are masterpieces:

There is no question of any erosion of essential national sovereignty; what is proposed is a sharing and an enlargement of individual national sovereignties in the general interest.

And:

The common law will remain the basis of our legal system, and our Courts will continue to operate as they do at present.

I can claim to have had no special insight into these matters at the time. It then seemed to me, as it did to my colleagues, that the arguments about sovereignty which were advanced by Enoch Powell and others were theoretical points used as rhetorical devices.

In the debate on Clause 2 of the Bill, Geoffrey Howe, as Solicitor-General, gave what appeared to be satisfactory assurances on the matter in answer to criticisms from Derek Walker-Smith, saying that 'at the end of the day if repeal [of the European Communities Act], lock, stock and barrel, was proposed, the ultimate sovereignty of Parliament must remain intact'. Asking himself the question: 'What will happen if there is a future Act of Parliament which inadvertently, to a greater or lesser extent, may be in conflict with Community law?' Geoffrey said: 'The courts would ... try in accordance with the traditional approach to interpret Statute in accordance with our international obligations.' But what if they could not be reconciled? He went on, elliptically:

> One cannot do more than that to reconcile the inescapable and enduring sovereignty of Parliament at the end of the road with the proposition that we should give effect to our treaty obligations to provide for the precedence of Community law ... If through inadvertence any such conflict arose, that would be a matter for consideration by the Government and Parliament of the day ...*

The decision of the European Court that the Merchant Shipping Act, 1988, is in contravention of the Treaty of Rome has made it impossible to put off consideration of these matters any longer.**

It was not, however, this question which was to make the Common Market such a difficult issue for the Government. The main political error was to overplay the advantages due to come

* *Hansard*, 13 June 1972: Volume 838, columns 1319–20.
** See pp. 497–8.

from membership. As regards the Government itself, this tendency led ministers to adopt and excuse unsound policies. In order to 'equip' British industry to meet the challenges of Europe, subsidies and intervention were said to be necessary – reasoning which was endorsed in the 1972 Budget speech. Still worse, loose monetary and fiscal policies were justified on the grounds that high levels of economic growth – of the order of 5 per cent or so – were now sustainable within the new European market of some 300 million people. It was also suggested that competition from Europe would compel the trade unions to act more responsibly. As regards the general public, expectations of the benefits of membership rose – and then were sharply dashed as economic conditions deteriorated and industrial disruption worsened. Yet the White Paper had promised that 'membership of the enlarged Community will lead to much improved efficiency and productivity in British industry, with a higher rate of investment and a faster growth of real wages'.

The success of the negotiations for British entry and their ratification by Parliament also seemed to have a psychological effect on Ted Heath. His enthusiasm for Europe had already developed into a passion. As the years went by it was to become an obsession – one increasingly shared by the great and the good. The argument became less and less about what was best for Britain and more and more about the importance of being good Europeans.

There was a mood of euphoria in the Establishment. It reached a peak with the 'Fanfare for Europe' celebrations of January 1973, held to mark Britain's accession to the Common Market. After a gala performance by British and international figures at the Royal Opera House, where among many other performances our former next-door neighbour Sybil Thorndike recited Browning, Denis and I were among hundreds invited to a State Banquet at Lancaster House. I could not help but be reminded of two madrigals sung at one of Ted's Downing Street dinners a couple of years before: 'All creatures are merry, merry-minded' and, more particularly, 'Late is my rash accounting'.

The other issue which alienated many Conservative supporters, particularly in the West Midlands, was immigration. As I have suggested, Ted's and the Government's line on this was in fact extremely firm. Our Immigration Bill which received its Second

Reading in March 1971 proposed a single system of control for Commonwealth citizens and aliens, while giving free entry to 'patrials', that is those with a right of abode.* Admittedly, the pledge on grants for voluntary repatriation was effectively shelved. But then it is doubtful whether any such system would have had much impact on net immigration.

The trouble arose when in August 1972 President Idi Amin of Uganda announced the mass expulsion of Asians who had prudently held on to their British passports following independence. In September a full Cabinet was devoted to the Ugandan Asian question. In the back of our minds was the possibility that Asian UK passport holders might also now be expelled from Kenya and Tanzania. My first thoughts when I arrived at Cabinet were that we should hold fast to our manifesto commitment that there should be 'no further large-scale immigration'. But Ted opened by saying that there was no question of our refusing to admit the expelled British passport holders. The Attorney-General, Peter Rawlinson, explained that we were under an obligation in international law to accept them – regardless of domestic immigration laws. After this there could not be much argument. Later I came to feel that the decision was right on other grounds. There was just no way of evading the humanitarian duty we had – a duty that no one else would accept. I found the Asians who came to my constituency admirable, hard-working people. And this measure really did turn out to be an exception to the rule of strict immigration control, rather than the first step towards its abandonment.

My instincts, however, had accurately reflected Party feeling. There was deep disquiet about the decision. Enoch Powell spoke strongly against it at that year's Party Conference. In late November the Government was defeated as a result of a large backbench revolt on new immigration rules. Ted himself had been shaken and was convinced that public opinion would not tolerate a repetition. He set up a small group of ministers to consider legislation to

---

* Patrials were those citizens of the United Kingdom and Colonies whose parents or grandparents were born in the UK; citizens of the UK and Colonies who had been settled here for five years; any Commonwealth citizen who had a father *or* mother *or* grandparent born in the UK.

prevent another influx, but when it reported back in December – favouring not a Bill but a 'declaration' that Britain would not necessarily accept future expellees in large numbers but would consult internationally – Cabinet was divided and the idea fell. It was one of the few occasions on which the Prime Minister did not get his way.

The immigration issue itself, as we recognized in discussion in Cabinet after the Commons defeat, had been fuelled by discontent on a whole range of other issues. To understand how this had occurred it is necessary to turn back to economic matters.

REVERSING COURSE

January and February 1972 saw three events which together tried the Government's resolve and found it wanting – the miners' strike, the financial problems of Upper Clyde Shipbuilders (UCS) and the unemployment total reaching one million. It is always a shock when unemployment reaches a new high figure, especially one as dramatic as a million. Unemployment is what economists call a lagging indicator. Although we did not know it at the time, it had just peaked and was to begin a downward trend. The rise of unemployment in 1971 was in fact the consequence of Roy Jenkins' tight fiscal and monetary policies of 1969–70. Since monetary policy had already been significantly eased in 1971, largely as a result of financial decontrol, we could have sat tight and waited for it to work through in lower unemployment from 1972 onwards. In fact, Ted never bought this analysis, and he greatly underestimated the stimulating effects of removing credit controls. He felt that emergency fiscal measures were necessary to boost demand and reduce unemployment. And this conviction influenced his decisions across the board. Ironically, because it led to higher inflation whose main effects were suffered under the following Labour Government, and because inflation destroys jobs rather than preserves them, it ultimately led to higher unemployment as well.

In particular, the approach of the Government to Upper Clyde Shipbuilders flowed from fear of the consequences of higher unemployment. But because it was also seen as caving in to the threats of left-wing militants, it added a new charge against us. When we first discussed the company's problems in December 1970 the Cabinet gave a fairly robust response. It was agreed that existing Government support for the UCS Group would not be continued, though there was a lifeline: we would continue with credit guarantees so long as the management agreed to close the Clydebank yard and separate out Yarrow Shipbuilders from the rest of the group. Yarrow – an important Royal Navy supplier – seemed salvageable. But by June 1971 the UCS Group was insolvent and its liquidation was announced. There followed a protest strike on Clydeside. In July trade unionists led by militant shop stewards occupied the four UCS shipyards.

There was further discussion in Cabinet in the autumn of 1971, and the Government allowed itself to be sucked into talks with the trade unions, who it was believed might be able to influence the militant shop stewards behind the occupation. The Economic Committee of the Cabinet had agreed that money should be provided to keep open the yards while the liquidator sought a solution, but only on condition that the unions gave credible undertakings of serious negotiations on new working practices. There was strong criticism of this from some of my colleagues, rightly alert to the danger of seeming to give in on the basis of worthless undertakings. But the money was provided and negotiations went ahead.

It was the unemployment prospect rather than the prospects for shipbuilding which by now were undisguisedly foremost. In November Ted Heath affirmed in a Party Political Broadcast that the 'Government is committed completely and absolutely to expanding the economy and bringing unemployment down'. The fateful one million mark was passed on 20 January 1972. On 24 February at Cabinet we heard that the Economic Committee had agreed the previous day to provide £35 million to keep three of the four yards open. John Davies openly admitted to us that the new group had little chance of making its way commercially and that if the general level of unemployment had been lower and the economy reviving faster, he would not have recommended this course. There was tangible unease. It was pointed out that we could expect a rough reception from our supporters for the decision. But Cabinet endorsed it and at the end of February John announced the decision. It was a small but memorably inglorious episode. I discussed it all privately with Jock Bruce-Gardyne, who was scathing about the decision. He regarded it as a critical, unforgivable U-turn. I was deeply troubled.

But by now we all had other things to worry about. In framing the Industrial Relations Act we had given too much emphasis to achieving the best possible legal framework and not enough to how the attacks on our proposals were to be repelled. The same mentality prevailed as regards the threat which the National Union of Mineworkers (NUM) posed to the Government and the country. We knew, of course, that the miners and the power workers held an almost unbeatable card in pay negotiations, because they could turn off the electricity supply to industry and people. Industrial action by the power workers in December 1970 had been settled after the setting-up of a Court of Inquiry under Lord Wilberforce which recommended a large increase in February the following year. Within the NUM, however, there was a large militant faction at least as interested in bringing down the Conservative Government as in flexing industrial muscle to increase miners' earnings. The NUM held a strike ballot in October 1970 and narrowly turned down an offer from the National Coal Board (NCB). Fearing unofficial action, Cabinet authorized the NCB to offer a productivity bonus to be paid in mid–1971. The NUM again turned the offer down, following which Derek Ezra, the NCB Chairman, without consulting ministers, offered to pay the bonus at once and without strings attached to productivity. Cabinet accepted this *fait accompli*. Perhaps John Davies and other ministers continued to monitor events. If they did I heard nothing about it. Nor does what subsequently happened suggest that any monitoring was accompanied by forward thinking.

Only in early December 1971 did the issue of miners' pay surface at Cabinet, and then in what seemed a fairly casual way. The NUM's annual conference earlier that year had significantly revised the rules which provided for an official strike, so that now only a 55 per cent, as opposed to a two-thirds, majority was required. The NUM ballot, which was still going on, had, it was thought, resulted in a 59 per cent majority vote for strike action.

Yet nobody seemed too worried. We were all reassured that coal stocks were in any case high.

Such complacency proved unwarranted. At the last Cabinet before Christmas Robert Carr confirmed to us that the NUM was indeed calling a national strike to begin on 9 January 1972. There was more trouble over pay in the gas and electricity industries. And we only needed to glance outside to know that winter was closing in, with all that meant for power consumption. But there was no real discussion and we all left for the Christmas break.

There was still some suggestion over Christmas that the strike might not be solid and would be concentrated in the more militant areas. But two days after it began it was all too clear that the action was total. There was then discussion in Cabinet about whether we should use the 'cooling off' provisions of the Industrial Relations Act. But it was said to be difficult to satisfy the legal tests involved – 'cooling off' orders would only be granted by the courts if there was a serious prospect that they would facilitate a settlement, which in this case was doubtful. The possibility of using the ballot provisions of the Act remained. But there was no particular reason to think that a ballot forced on the NUM would lead to anything other than a continuation of the strike, and perhaps also a hardening of attitudes. It was an acutely uncomfortable demonstration of the fragility of the principal weapons with which the Act had equipped us. Moreover, important parts of the Act had yet to come into force, and we were also aware that there was a good deal of public sympathy with the miners.

The pressure on the Government to intervene directly to try to end the dispute now increased. Looking back, and comparing 1972 with the threatened miners' strike of 1981 and the year-long strike of 1984–85, it is extraordinary how little attention we gave to 'endurance' – the period of time we could keep the power stations and the economy running with limited or no coal supplies – and how easily Cabinet was fobbed off by assurances that coal stocks were high, without considering whether those stocks were in the right locations to be usable, i.e. actually at the power stations. The possibility of effective mass picketing, which would prevent oil and coal getting to power stations, was simply not on the agenda.

Instead, our response was to discuss the prospects for conciliation by Robert Carr and the use of 'emergency powers' which would allow us to conserve power station stocks a few weeks longer by imposing power cuts. There was a great deal of useless talk about 'keeping public opinion on our side'. But what could public opinion do to end the strike? This was one more thing I learned from the Heath years – and anyway, on the whole public opinion *wasn't* on our side. A further lesson from this period – when no fewer than five States of Emergency were called – was that for all the sense of urgency and decision that the phrase 'emergency powers' conveys they could not be relied upon to change the basic realities of an industrial dispute.

The situation steadily worsened. The crunch came on the morning of Thursday 10 February when we were all in Cabinet. A State of Emergency had been declared the previous day. By now Robert Carr was directly involved with the NCB and the NUM in trying to find a way out. But it was John Davies who dropped the bombshell. He told us that picketing had now immobilized a large part of the remaining coal stocks, and that the supplies still available might not even suffice beyond the end of the following week. Thereafter electricity output would fall to as little as 25 per cent of normal supply. Drastic power cuts were inevitable, and large parts of industry would be laid off. The Attorney-General reported that the provisions of the Industrial Relations Act against secondary boycotts, blacking of supplies and the inducement of other workers to take action resulting in the frustration of a commercial contract, would not come into force until 28 February. He thought that most of the picketing which had taken place during the strike was lawful. As regards the criminal law, some arrests had been made but, as he put it, 'the activities of pickets confronted the police with very difficult and sensitive decisions'.

This was something of an understatement. The left-wing leader of the Yorkshire miners, Arthur Scargill, who was to organize the politically motivated miners' strike I faced in 1984–85, was already busy winning his militant's spurs. In the course of Cabinet a message came through to the Home Secretary, Reggie Maudling, which he read out. The Chief Constable of Birmingham had asked that the West Midlands Gas Board's Saltley Coke Depot be closed because lorries were being prevented from entering by 7,000 'pickets' who were facing just 500 police.

There was no disguising that this was a victory for violence. To the Left it came to assume legendary proportions. To large numbers of politicians and commentators it proved that no one could hope to stand up to the miners. Police self-confidence was shattered. From now on many senior policemen put greater emphasis on maintaining 'order' than on upholding the law. In practice, that meant failing to uphold the rights of individuals against the rule of the mob – though to be fair the police lacked the equipment as much as the stomach for the action required. For me, what happened at Saltley took on no less significance than it did for the Left. I understood, as they did, that the struggle to bring trade unions properly within the rule of law would be decided not in the debating chamber of the House of Commons, nor even on the hustings, but in and around the pits and factories where intimidation had been allowed to prevail.

Ted now sounded the retreat. He appointed a Court of Inquiry under the ubiquitous Lord Wilberforce. By now the power crisis had reached such proportions that we sat in Cabinet debating whether we had time to wait for the NUM to ballot its members on ending a strike; a ballot might take over a week to organize. There was therefore no inclination to quibble when Wilberforce recommended a massive pay increase, way beyond the level allowed for in the 'n–1' voluntary pay policy already in force.

But we were stunned when the militant majority on the NUM Executive rejected the court's recommendation, demanding still more money and a ragbag of other concessions – 'a list as long as your arm', in the words of the miners' President, Joe Gormley.

Ted summoned us all together on the evening of Friday 18 February to decide what to do. The dispute simply had to be ended quickly. If we had to go an additional mile, so be it. Later that night Ted called the NUM and the NCB to No. 10 and persuaded the union to drop the demand for more money, while conceding the rest. The NUM Executive accepted, and just over a week later so did the miners in a ballot. The dispute was over. But the devastation it had inflicted on the Government and indeed on British politics as a whole lived on.

The immediate effect was to convince *bien pensant* opinion that in a country like Britain there was simply no alternative to corporatism. The *Sunday Times* leader of 20 February put the point crisply:

After the Wilberforce settlement, there is only one course for the Government to adopt if it is to derive any profit from the ruin of its wages policy. It must open formal and serious talks with the Confederation of British Industry and the Trades Union Congress to plot a way forward towards an organized policy for incomes. This will involve all sides of industry, but above all the Government itself, in the liquidation of old nostrums. But far from losing face, the Government would thereby seize the best chance to rebuild its economic policy.

Such a message found a ready hearing from shocked and bewildered ministers. The combination of the rise in unemployment, the events at Upper Clyde Shipbuilders and the Government's humiliation by the miners resulted in a fundamental reassessment of policy. I suspect that this took place in Ted's own mind first, with other ministers and the Cabinet very much second. It was not so much that he jettisoned the whole Selsdon approach, but rather that he abandoned some aspects of it, emphasized others and added a heavy dose of statism which probably appealed to his temperament and his Continental European sympathies. We had always been keen advocates of economic growth: but now we promoted growth at the expense of sound finance. We had always been in favour of industrial and technological modernization: but now we relied on government intervention rather than competition to ensure it. We had always entertained a basic confusion between a 'monetarist' and a wage-push theory of inflation: we now ignored the first and swallowed the second to such an extent that we introduced the most comprehensively regulated system of wages and prices that peacetime Britain has known.

None of this pleased me. But our inability to resist trade union power, whether exerted through irresponsible wage demands which forced companies into liquidation and workers out of jobs, or through strikes which brought the country to a halt, was now manifest. The Industrial Relations Act itself already seemed hollow: it was soon to be discredited entirely. Like most Conservatives, I was prepared to give at least a chance to a policy which retained some of the objectives we had set out in 1969/70. I was even prepared to go along with a statutory prices and incomes policy, for a time, to try to limit the damage inflicted by the arrogant misuse of trade union power. But I was wrong. State intervention in the economy is not ultimately an answer to over-mighty vested interests: for it soon comes to collude with them.

It is unusual to hold Cabinets on a Monday, and I had arranged a long-standing scientific engagement for Monday 20 March 1972, so I was not present at the Cabinet which discussed the Budget and the new Industry White Paper on that day. Both of them signalled a change in strategy, each complementing the other. The Budget was highly reflationary, comprising large cuts in income tax and purchase tax, increased pensions and social security benefits and extra investment incentives for industry. It was strongly rumoured that Tony Barber and the Treasury were very unhappy with the Budget and that it had been imposed on them by Ted. The fact that the Budget speech presented these measures as designed to help Britain meet the challenge opened up by membership of the EEC in a small way confirms this. It was openly designed to provide a large boost to demand, which it was argued would not involve a rise in inflation, in conditions of high unemployment and idle resources. Monetary policy was mentioned, but only to stress its 'flexibility'; no numerical targets for monetary growth were set.

On Wednesday 22 March John Davies published his White Paper on *Industry and Regional Development*, which was the basis for the 1972 Industry Act. Even more than the Budget, this was seen by our supporters and opponents alike as an obvious U-turn. Keith and I and probably others in the Cabinet were extremely unhappy, and some of this found its way into the press. As far as I can recall there had been no prior discussion of the White Paper in Cabinet: it was presented to the Commons in the Budget statement and its preparation within Government was subject to all the secrecy usually applied to Budget measures. From this point on I was conscious that on the Labour benches enmity had been transformed into contempt. I was not in the House at the time, but I read *The Times* report which sums up the reaction to John Davies's speech on the Bill:

> Lame ducks never looked healthier as Mr Davies, Secretary of State for Trade and Industry, opened today's debate on the Second Reading of the Industry Bill with possibly the most remarkable speech heard in the Commons during the life of the present Government. At the end, the cheers from the Labour benches and the almost total silence from Conservative MPs showed more clearly than anything the Opposition could say how complete had been the Government *volte face* on intervention in industry and on aid to the regions.

I was not, I know, the only Conservative to squirm on reading stuff like this. Should I have resigned? Perhaps so. But those of us who disliked what was happening had not yet either fully analysed the situation or worked out an alternative approach. Nor, realistically speaking, would my resignation have made a great deal of difference. I was not senior enough for it to be other than the littlest 'local difficulty'. All the more reason for me to pay tribute to people like Jock Bruce-Gardyne, John Biffen, Nick Ridley and, of course, Enoch Powell who did expose the folly of what was happening in Commons speeches and newspaper articles.

There is also a direct connection between the policies pursued from March 1972 and the very different approach of my own administration later. A brilliant, but little-known, monetary economist called Alan Walters resigned from the CPRS and delivered not only scathing criticism of the Government's approach but also accurate predictions of where it would lead.*

One more blow to the approach we adopted in 1970 had still to fall: and it was not long in coming. This was the effective destruction of the Industrial Relations Act. It had never been envisaged that the Act would result in individual trade unionists going to gaol. Of course, no legal provisions can be proof against some remote possibility of that happening if troublemakers are intent on

---

* Alan Walters became my economic adviser as Prime Minister 1981–84 and again in 1989.

martyrdom. It was a long-running dispute between employers and dockers about 'containerization' which provided the occasion for this to happen. In March 1972 the National Industrial Relations Court (NIRC) fined the Transport and General Workers' Union (TGWU) £5,000 for defying an order to grant access to Liverpool Docks. The following month the union was fined £50,000 for contempt on the matter of secondary action at the docks. The TGWU maintained that it was not responsible for the action of its shop stewards, but the NIRC ruled against this in May. Then, out of the blue, the Court of Appeal reversed these judgements and ruled that the TGWU was *not* responsible, and so the shop stewards themselves were personally liable. This was extremely disturbing, for it opened up the possibility of trade unionists going to jail. The following month three dockers involved in blacking were threatened with arrest for refusing to appear before the NIRC. 35,000 trade unionists were now on strike. At the last moment the Official Solicitor applied to the Court of Appeal to prevent the dockers' arrest. But then in July another five dockers were jailed for contempt.

The Left were merciless. Ted was shouted down in the House. Sympathetic strikes spread, involving the closure of national newspapers for five days. The TUC called a one-day general strike. On 26 July, however, the House of Lords reversed the Court of Appeal decision and confirmed that unions were accountable for the conduct of their members. The NIRC then released the five dockers.

This was more or less the end of the Industrial Relations Act, though it was not the end of trouble in the docks. A national dock strike ensued and another State of Emergency was declared. This only ended – very much on the dockers' terms – in August. In September the TUC General Congress rubbed salt into the wound by expelling thirty-two small unions which had refused, against TUC instructions, to de-register under the Act. Having shared to the full the Party's enthusiasm for the Act, I was appalled.

A U-TURN TOO FAR

In the summer of 1972 the third aspect – after reflation and industrial intervention – of the new economic approach was revealed to us. This was the pursuit of an agreement on prices and incomes through 'tripartite' talks with the CBI and the TUC. Although there had been no explicit pay policy, we had been living in a world of 'norms' since the autumn of 1970 when the 'n–1' was formulated in the hope that there would be deceleration from the 'going rate' figure in successive pay rounds. The miners' settlement had breached that policy spectacularly, but Ted drew the conclusion that we should go further rather than go back. From the summer of 1972 a far more elaborate prices and incomes policy was the aim, and more and more the centre of decision-making moved away from Cabinet and Parliament. I can only, therefore, give a partial account of the way in which matters developed. Cabinet simply received reports from Ted on what policies had effectively been decided elsewhere, though individual ministers became increasingly bogged down in the details of shifting and complicated pay negotiations. This almost obsessive interest in the minutiae of pay awards was matched by a large degree of impotence over the deals finally struck. In fact, the most important result was to distract ministers from the big economic issues and blind us with irrelevant data when we should have been looking ahead to the threats which loomed.

The period of the tripartite talks with the TUC and the CBI from early July to the end of October did not get us much further as regards the Government's aim of controlling inflation by keeping down wage demands. It did, however, move us down other slippery slopes. In exchange for the CBI's offer to secure 'voluntary' price restraint by 200 of Britain's largest firms, limiting their price increases to 5 per cent during the following year, we embarked on the costly and self-defeating policy of holding nationalized industry price increases to the same level, even though this meant that they continued to make losses. The TUC, for its part, used the role it had been accorded by the tripartite discussions to set out its own alternative economic policy. In flat contradiction to the policies we had been elected to implement, they wanted action to keep down council rents (which would sabotage our Housing Finance Act – intended to bring them closer to market levels). They urged the control of profits, dividends and prices, aimed at securing the redistribution of income and wealth (in other words the implementation of socialism), and the repeal of the Industrial Relations Act. These demands, made at the TUC Congress in September, were taken sufficiently seriously by Ted for him to agree studies of methods by which the pay of low-paid workers could be improved without entailing proportionate increases to other workers. We had, in other words, moved four-square onto the socialist ground that 'low pay' – however that might be defined – was a 'problem' which it was for government rather than the workings of the market to resolve. In fact, the Government proposed a £2 a week limit on pay increases over the following year, with the CBI agreeing maximum 4 per cent price increases over the same period and the extension of the Government's 'target' of 5 per cent economic growth.

In any case, it was not enough. The TUC was not willing – and probably not able – to deliver wage restraint. At the end of October we had a lengthy discussion of the arguments for now proceeding to a statutory policy, beginning with a pay freeze. It is an extraordinary comment on the state of mind that we had reached that, as far as I can recall, neither now nor later did anyone at Cabinet raise the objection that this was precisely the policy we had ruled out in our 1970 general election manifesto. Yet no one could accuse Ted of not being willing to go the extra mile. Only with the greatest reluctance did he accept that the TUC were unpersuadable. And so on Friday 3 November 1972 Cabinet made the fateful decision to introduce a statutory policy beginning with a ninety-day freeze of prices and incomes. No one ever spoke a truer word than Ted when he concluded by warning that we faced a troubled prospect.

The change in economic policy was accompanied by a Cabinet reshuffle. Maurice Macmillan – Harold's son – had already taken over at Employment from Robert Carr in July 1972, when the latter replaced Reggie Maudling at the Home Office. Ted now promoted his younger disciples. He sent Peter Walker to replace John Davies at the DTI and promoted Jim Prior to be Leader of the House. Geoffrey Howe, an instinctive economic liberal, was brought into the Cabinet but given the poisoned chalice of overseeing prices and incomes policy. It has been said that I was thought of for the job; if so, I can only be thankful that I wasn't asked.

For a growing number of backbenchers the new policy was a U-turn too far. When Enoch Powell asked in the House whether the Prime Minister had 'taken leave of his senses', he was publicly cold-shouldered, but many privately agreed with him. Still more significant was the fact that staunch opponents of our policy like Nick Ridley, Jock Bruce-Gardyne and John Biffen were elected to chairmanships or vice-chairmanships of important backbench committees, and Edward du Cann, on the right of the Party and a sworn opponent of Ted, became Chairman of the 1922 Committee.

As the freeze – Stage 1 – came to an end we devised Stage 2. This extended the pay and price freeze until the end of April 1973; for the remainder of 1973 workers could expect £1 a week and 4 per cent, with a maximum pay rise of £250 a year – a formula designed to favour the low-paid. A Pay Board and a Prices Commission were set up to administer the policy. Our backbench critics were more perceptive than most commentators, who considered that all this was a sensible and pragmatic response to trade union irresponsibility. In the early days it seemed that the commentators were right. A challenge to the policy by the gas workers was defeated at the end of March. The miners – as we hoped and expected after their huge increase the previous year – rejected a strike (against the advice of their Executive) in a ballot on 5 April. The number of working days lost because of strikes fell sharply. Unemployment was at its lowest since 1970. Generally, the mood in Government grew more relaxed. Ted clearly felt happier wearing his new collectivist hat than he ever had in the disguise of Selsdon.

Our sentiments should have been very different. The effects of the reflationary Budget of March 1972 and the loose financial policy it typified were now becoming apparent. The Treasury, at least, had started to worry about the economy, which was growing at a clearly unsustainable rate of well over 5 per cent. The money supply, as measured by M3 (broad money), was growing too fast – though the (narrower) M1, which the Government preferred, less so.* The March 1973 Budget did nothing to cool the overheating and was heavily distorted by the need to keep down prices and charges so as to support the 'counter-inflation policy', as the prices and incomes policy was hopefully called. In May modest public expenditure reductions were agreed. But it was too little, and far too late. Although inflation rose during the first six months of 1973, Minimum Lending Rate (MLR) was steadily cut and a temporary mortgage subsidy was introduced. The Prime Minister also ordered that preparations be made to take statutory control of the mortgage rate if the building societies failed to hold it down when the subsidy ended. These fantastic proposals only served to distract us from the need to tackle the growing problem of monetary laxity. Only in July was MLR raised from 7.5 per cent, first to 9 per cent and then to 11.5 per cent. We were actually ahead of Labour in the opinion polls in June 1973, for the first time since 1970. But in July the Liberals took Ely and Ripon from us at by-elections. Economically and politically we had, without knowing it, already begun to reap the whirlwind.

Over the summer of 1973 Ted held more talks with the TUC, seeking their agreement to Stage 3. The detailed work was done by a group of ministers chaired by Ted, and the rest of us knew little about it. Nor did I know at the time that close attention was already being given to the problem which might arise with the miners. Like most of my colleagues, I imagine, I believed that they had had their pound of flesh already and would not come back for more.

I hope, though, that I would have given a great deal more attention than anyone seems to have done to building up coal stocks against the eventuality, however remote, of another miners' strike. The miners either had to be appeased or beaten. Yet, for all its technocratic jargon, this was a government which signally lacked a sense of strategy. Ted apparently felt no need of one since, as we now know, he had held a secret meeting with Joe Gormley in the

---

* M1 comprised the total stock of money held in cash and in current and deposit accounts at a particular point in time; M3 included the whole of M1, with the addition of certain other types of bank accounts, including those held in currencies other than sterling.

garden of No. 10 and thought he had found a formula to square the miners – extra payment for 'unsocial hours'. But this proved to be a miscalculation. The miners' demands could not be accommodated within Stage 3.

In October Cabinet duly endorsed the Stage 3 White Paper. It was immensely complicated and represented the high-point – if that is the correct expression – of the Heath Government's collectivism. Pay increases were to be limited to £2.25 a week or 7 per cent with a maximum £350 per annum; there were complex provisions to pay shift workers more for 'unsocial hours', and room was made for additional payments in respect of productivity agreements and moves towards equal pay for women. In addition, there were 'threshold payments' to be made if inflation rose to specified levels – we made some rosy assumptions about future rates of inflation – and there was also money for pensioners and a new mortgage subsidy for first-time buyers. But the most significant new development – and one whose necessity ultimately demonstrated the futility of the kind of approach we were pursuing – was the provision that the Pay Board should set up an inquiry into 'relativities' between groups of workers, with the aim of accommodating grievances on this score in Stage 4. All possible eventualities, you might have thought, were catered for. But as experience of past pay policies ought to have demonstrated, you would have been wrong.

My only direct involvement in the working of this new, detailed pay policy was when I attended from time to time the relevant Cabinet Economic Sub-Committee, usually chaired by Terence Higgins, a Treasury Minister of State. Even those attracted by the concept of incomes policy on grounds of 'fairness' begin to have their doubts when they see its provisions applied to individual cases. My visits to the Higgins Committee were usually necessitated by questions of teachers' pay. But on one occasion when I found myself there with Sir William Armstrong, the Head of the civil service, it was to discuss the pay of Under-Secretaries. I knew that it was at this level in my department that the most important policy work was carried on, and I saw that with inflation running at about 10 per cent and differentials squeezed as a result of union power and government pay policy, these people needed proper motivation through a decent pay rise. Of course, the same could have been said of many groups. What struck me though was that no one doubted that this *particular* group needed a larger pay increase than pay policy allowed. And what was true for Under-Secretaries in the civil service was true for innumerable other groups throughout the economy. Our pay policy was not just absurd: far from being 'fair', it was fundamentally unjust. It was, in fact, an excellent demonstration that market forces, operating within the right framework, make for fairness, and that even beneficent state control only makes for equality.

On another sublime occasion we found ourselves debating the proper rate of pay for MPs' secretaries. This was the last straw. I said that I hadn't come into politics to make decisions like this, and that I would pay my secretary what was necessary to keep her. Other ministers agreed. But then, they knew their secretaries; they did not know the other people whose pay they were deciding.

In any case, reality soon started to break in. Two days after the announcement of Stage 3 the NUM rejected an NCB offer worth 16.5 per cent in return for a productivity agreement. The Government immediately took charge of the negotiations. (The days of our 'not intervening' had long gone.) Ted met the NUM at No. 10. But no progress was made. In early November the NUM began an overtime ban. Maurice Macmillan told us that though an early strike ballot seemed unlikely and, if held, would not give the necessary majority for a strike, an overtime ban would cut production sharply. The general feeling in Cabinet was still that the Government could not afford to acquiesce in a breach of the recently introduced pay code. Instead, we should make a special effort to demonstrate what was possible within it. The miners were not the only ones threatening trouble. The firemen, electricians and engineers were all in differing stages of dispute. It is one of the penalties of pay policy that you have to fight on too many fronts.

Similarly, it is an unavoidable weakness of the planned economy to which we were now rapidly moving that economic plans take little or no account of external events. The argument that all of us used in February 1974 (and some people continued to use long afterwards) to explain the failure of the Heath Government's economic strategy was that the quadrupling of the oil price resulting from the Arab-Israeli war of 1973 shattered our policy when it was just beginning to work. This is plainly false. Loose monetary policy had already sown the seeds of inflation, which was to surge under the incoming Labour Government. Incomes policy, which does no more than redistribute inflation through time, could do little about this. Whatever limited successes it achieved would, like those of all other incomes policies, have unwound in the form of higher demands and settlements later. Moreover, the level of economic growth, particularly for an economy still unreformed by deregulation, privatization or reductions in trade union power, was far too high to be sustainable. Public expenditure had risen too fast as well, and we were already discussing cuts before the full implications of the oil price rise were known. We had not, in fact, 'modernized' British industry as we had boasted – not least because only industry, not Government, can efficiently 'modernize' itself. Worse, by fuelling inflation and taking too many decisions out of the hands of managers and wage bargainers we had created precisely the wrong climate for industrial success.

Yet, even ignoring all of this, the basic proposition that the oil price hike was just 'bad luck' is fundamentally mistaken. It is the very fact that governments *cannot* take all relevant circumstances into account that militates against economic planning. And it is because a properly operating market economy adjusts so sensitively to every signal that it avoids those sharp dislocations when cumulative pressures break through.

Admittedly, the threatened oil embargo and oil price rises resulting from the Arab-Israeli war that autumn made things far worse. As the effects of the miners' industrial action bit deeper, the sense that we were no longer in control of events deepened. Somehow we had to break out. This made a quick general election increasingly attractive. Quite what we would have done if we had been re-elected is, of course, problematic. Perhaps Ted would have liked to go further towards a managed economy. Others would probably have liked to find a way to pay the miners their Danegeld and seek a quieter political life. Keith and I and a large part of the Parliamentary Conservative Party would have wanted to discard the corporatist and statist trappings with which the Government was now surrounded and try to get back to the free market approach from which we had allowed ourselves to be diverted in early 1972.

Indeed, quite apart from our exchanges about the shortcomings of economic policy, Keith and I had also been intensely irritated by the posture the Government took during the Arab-Israeli war. In the hope of securing favourable treatment from the oil-producing states – which were limiting oil supplies to Western nations – the Government refused to condemn the Arab states which had broken the 1967 ceasefire and we applied an arms embargo to both sides, depriving the Israelis of the spare parts they needed. The Government also refused to allow the Americans to use British bases to resupply Israel.

As MP for Finchley, I knew at first hand what the Jewish community in Britain felt about our policies. The early days of the war were particularly bad for Israel – the situation was far worse than in 1967 – and I followed the news hour by hour. There were some difficult discussions in Cabinet with Alec Douglas-Home defending the policy courteously and Ted exercising a rigid determination to control an issue which – as he saw it – would determine the success or failure of our whole economic strategy. Finally, he told us bluntly that he was having a note circulated laying down the public line ministers were expected to take.

REAPING THE WHIRLWIND

At Cabinet on Tuesday 13 November it was all gloom as the crisis accelerated on every front. Tony Barber told us that the October trade figures that day would show another large deficit. There was talk of public expenditure cuts and tax increases. (MLR was in fact raised to a record 13 per cent.) A declaration of yet another State of Emergency would have to be made. Orders would be laid restricting lighting and heating in commercial premises. There was even talk of issuing petrol coupons. What I did not know was that included in the measures were plans to stop electrical heating in schools. In fact I only heard about it on the next day's radio news. I was furious, partly because it was a politically stupid act and partly because I had not been consulted. I went in to see Tom Boardman, the Industry Minister, and after what the diplomats would describe as frank exchanges had it stopped.

The disagreement over school heating was, however, part of a wider argument which continued up to and beyond the calling of the election. Should we err on the side of stringency or of liberality when it came to deciding on measures to conserve energy? This was not something which could be settled on technical grounds alone; for we could not know how long the miners' overtime ban would last, when or whether it would escalate into a strike, or how well industry would be able to cope with power shortages. In these circumstances, it was natural to look at least as closely at the political impact. But here too there were large uncertainties. Adopting the most stringent measures would certainly help convince the general public that this was a real emergency provoked by union militancy at a time of grave international economic problems. But there was a risk that people would become angry with the restrictions, particularly any which seemed needlessly petty – such as the decision to close down television broadcasting at 10.30 at night. And then, of course, any subsequent relaxation would be met with the retort that it showed we had overreacted, doubtless for party political reasons, in the first place.

One shrewd move on Ted's part at the beginning of December was to bring Willie Whitelaw back from Northern Ireland to become Employment Secretary in place of Maurice Macmillan. Willie was both conciliatory and cunning, a combination of qualities which was particularly necessary if some way were to be found out of the struggle with the miners. The Government's hand was also strengthened by the fact that, perhaps surprisingly, the opinion polls were now showing us with a clear lead over Labour as the public reacted indignantly to the miners' actions. In these circumstances, all but the most militant trade unionists would be fearful of a confrontation precipitating a general election. Speculation on these lines soon began to grow in the press.

On Thursday 13 December Ted announced the introduction of a three-day working week to conserve energy. He also gave a broadcast that evening. This gave an impression of crisis which polarized opinion in the country. At first industrial output remained more or less the same, itself an indication of the inefficiency and overmanning of so much of British industry. But we did not know this at the time. Nor could we know how long even a three-day week would be sustainable. I found strong support among Conservatives for the measures taken. There was also understanding of the need for the £1.2 billion public spending cuts, which were announced a few days later.

At this stage we believed that we could rely on business leaders. Shortly before Christmas, Denis and I went to a party at a friend's house in Lamberhurst. There was a power cut and so night lights had been put in jam jars to guide people up the steps. There was a touch of wartime spirit about it all. The businessmen there were of one mind: 'Stand up to them. Fight it out. See them off. We can't go on like this.' It was all very heartening. For the moment.

There still seemed no honourable or satisfactory way out of the dispute itself. Negotiations with the NUM got nowhere. The Government offer of an immediate inquiry into the future of the mining industry and miners' pay if the NUM went back to work on the basis of the present offer was turned down flat. One possible opportunity was missed when Tony Barber rejected an offer by the TUC, made at the NEDC on 9 January 1974, that they would not use a larger offer to the NUM as an argument in negotiations for other settlements. Tony explained to us the next day that he considered this had been a propaganda exercise rather than a serious offer. Although Cabinet agreed afterwards that we should follow up the offer, and the TUC were invited to No. 10 for several long meetings, the damage had been done: it looked as if we were not interested. We might have done better to accept it and put the TUC on the spot. As it was, the TUC offer undoubtedly put us on the defensive. The incident taught me neither to accept nor to reject any offer until the consequences had been fully weighed.

By candlelight in the flat in Flood Street, Denis and I talked through the predicament in which the Government found itself. It was clear that many mistakes had been made, and that if and when we managed to come through the present crisis, fundamental questions would need to be asked about the Government's direction. Yet, whatever we might have done differently, there was no doubting that we now faced a struggle which had to be won. The miners, backed in varying degrees by other trade unions and the Labour Party, were flouting the law made by Parliament. The militants were clearly out to bring down the Government and to demonstrate once and for all that Britain could only be governed with the consent of the trade union movement. This was intolerable not just to me as a Conservative Cabinet minister but to millions of others who saw the fundamental liberties of the country under threat. Denis and I, our friends and most of my Party workers, felt that we now had to pick up the gauntlet and that the only way to do that was by calling and winning a general election. From now on, this was what I urged whenever I had the opportunity.

I was, though, surprised and frustrated by Ted Heath's attitude. He seemed out of touch with reality. He was still more interested in the future of Stage 3 and in the oil crisis than he was in the pressing question of the survival of the Government. Cabinet discussions concentrated on tactics and details, never the fundamental strategy. Such discussions were perhaps taking place in some other forum; but I rather doubt it. Certainly, there was a strange lack of urgency. I suspect it was because Ted was secretly desperate to avoid an election and did not seriously wish to think about the possibility of one. In the end, perhaps – as some of us speculated – because his inner circle was split on the issue, Ted finally did ask some of us in to see him, in several small groups, on Monday 14 January in his study at No. 10.

By this stage we were only days away from the deadline for calling a 7 February election – the best and most likely 'early' date. At No. 10 in our group John Davies and I did most of the talking. We both strongly urged Ted to face up to the fact that we could not have the unions flouting the law and the policies of a democratically elected Government in this way. We should have an early election and fight unashamedly on the issue of 'Who governs Britain?' Ted said very little. He seemed to have asked us in for form's sake, rather than anything else. I gathered that he did not agree, though he did not say as much. I went away feeling depressed. I still believe that if he had gone to the country earlier we would have scraped in, because we might have been able to focus the campaign on the issue of trade union power.

On Thursday 24 January Cabinet met twice. Peter Carrington,

now both Secretary of State for Energy and Party Chairman, urged some relaxation of the power restrictions. But many of us were worried about any such move, for the reasons I have outlined earlier. The second meeting of the day, held in the evening, took place after the NUM Executive had decided on a strike ballot. This more or less tipped the balance in favour of caution, though there was some minor easing of restrictions. It seemed likely to me that there would be a sufficient vote for a strike, and in this case that a general election campaign would follow.

The following Wednesday, 30 January, with the ballot still pending, an emergency Cabinet was called. Ted told us that the Pay Board's report on relativities had now been received. The question was whether we should accept the report and set up new machinery to investigate 'relativities' claims. The miners had always claimed to be demanding an improvement in their relative pay – hence their rejection of Ted's 'unsocial hours' provision, which applied to *all* shift workers. The Pay Board report might provide a basis for them to settle within the incomes policy – all the more so because it specifically endorsed the idea that changes in the relative importance of an industry due to 'external events' could also be taken into account when deciding pay. The rapidly rising price of oil was just such an 'external event'.

We felt that the Government had no choice but to set up the relativities machinery. Not to do so – having commissioned the relativities report in the first place – would make it seem as if we were actively trying to prevent a settlement with the miners. And with an election now likely we had to consider public opinion at every step.

But there were important tactical questions as to how we did this. We could demand that the TUC accept the principle of pay policy as a condition. We could require that the miners go back to work and accept the NCB's existing offer while the Pay Board undertook its inquiry. These were not unreasonable conditions in the circumstances, but they were very unlikely to be acceptable to either the TUC or the NUM.

Ted and a group of ministers had drafted a letter to the TUC and CBI that made the reference conditional on the miners accepting the existing NCB offer and returning to work. The letter invited the TUC and the CBI for talks. I suspect that Ted was less than happy with this tough draft. In his heart of hearts he wanted a settlement and up to the very last moment believed he could achieve it. But by this stage even some of his closest friends in Cabinet wanted to bring matters to a head with the miners. The split within the inner circle of the Government had already been exposed on the issue of an early election: I assumed that the same divisions existed in the group which drafted the letter.

In the end Cabinet watered down the contents of the letter, removing the condition that the miners accept the NCB offer and attaching no strings to the proposal that the TUC meet ministers for talks. The letter was published. When we met again the following day there was a general feeling that the press coverage had been good and that we had regained some of the initiative lost over the TUC offer earlier in the month. But in practice we were committed now to accepting the relativities machinery and any offer that it might come up with. There was no hiding the fact that the miners were likely to win a large increase. If we went ahead and held an election, the prospect was that we would face another Wilberforce immediately afterwards. At the time it made tactical sense. But looking back I have to believe that others were preparing the ground to buy the miners off.

An election became all but certain when, on Tuesday 5 February, we learned that 81 per cent of those voting in the NUM ballot had supported a strike. Election speculation reached fever pitch from which there was no going back. I suspect none of us was surprised when Ted told us at Cabinet two days later that he had decided to go to the country. The general election would take place on Thursday 28 February – that is, as soon as possible.

Willie proposed formally to refer the miners' claim to the Pay Board for a relativities study. He couched his argument for this course entirely in terms of its giving us something to say during the election in reply to the inevitable question: How will you solve the miners' dispute if you win? Cabinet then made the fateful decision to agree to Willie's proposal.

Because of the emergency nature of the election, I had not been involved in the early drafts of even the education section of the manifesto, which was now published within days. There was little new to say, though the record was set out. In any case, the dominant theme of the document – the need for firm and fair government at a time of crisis – was clear and stark. The main new pledge was to change the system whereby Social Security benefits were paid to strikers' families. Apart from the questions of inflation and trade union power, the mortgage rate of 11 per cent created political difficulties for us. Naturally, I was mainly questioned about education matters, as when Willie Whitelaw and I joined Robin Day on *Election Call* in the course of the campaign. But in answer to one questioner I set out my strongly held views on a coalition government: 'I think it's a false assumption that if you get a government of all the best brains, the best brains will agree what to do. You can get two experts on anything and they will not in fact agree on what the solution is . . . You have in a coalition government to drop many of your own beliefs.'

This statement was to be unexpectedly relevant to the period after the election when the Conservative leadership, licking its wounds and seeking some new vehicle to carry it back to power, was attracted by the notion of a 'Government of National Unity'. I might also have added that if you have no beliefs, or if you have already abandoned them, 'Government of National Unity' has rather more attractions.

During most of the campaign I was reasonably confident that we would win. Conservative supporters who had been alienated by the U-turns started drifting back to us. Indeed, their very frustrations at what they saw as our past weaknesses made them all the more determined to back us now that we had decided, as they saw it, to stand up to trade union militancy. Harold Wilson set out Labour's approach in the context of a 'social contract' with the unions. Those who longed for a quiet life could be expected to be seduced by that. But I felt that if we could stick to the central issue summed up by the phrase 'Who governs?' we would win the argument, and with it the election.

I felt victory – almost tangibly – slip away from us in the last week. I just could not believe it when I heard on the radio of the leak of evidence taken by the Pay Board which purported to show that the miners could have been paid more within Stage 3, with the implication that the whole general election was unnecessary.

The Government's attempts to deny this – and there did indeed turn out to have been a miscalculation – were stumbling and failed to carry conviction. We had become caught up in the complexities of pay policy and finally been strangled by them. From now on it was relentlessly downhill.

Two days later, Enoch Powell urged people to vote Labour in order to secure a referendum on the Common Market. I could understand the logic of his position, which was that membership of the Common Market had abrogated British sovereignty and that the supreme issue in politics was therefore how to restore it. But what shocked me was his manner of doing it – announcing only on the day the election was called that he would not be contesting his Wolverhampton seat and then dropping this bombshell at the end of the campaign. It seemed to me that to betray one's local supporters and constituency workers in this way was heartless. I suspect that Enoch's decision in February 1974, like his earlier intervention in 1970, had a crucial effect.

Then three days later there was another blow. Campbell Adamson, the Director General of the CBI, publicly called for the repeal of the Industrial Relations Act. It was all too typical of the way in which Britain's industrial leaders were full of bravado before battle was joined, but lacked the stomach for a fight. I must admit, though, that our own interventionist policies had hardly encouraged British businessmen and managers to accept the risks and responsibilities of freedom.

Partly because of these developments, but partly too no doubt because it was bound to be difficult to focus on just one issue for a three-week campaign, we lost our momentum. I still thought that we might possibly win, but I was aware of a slackening of enthusiasm for our cause and confusion about our objectives. I also knew from the opinion polls and soundings in my own constituency that the Liberals were posing a serious threat. So by polling day my optimism had been replaced by unease.

That sentiment grew as I heard from Finchley and elsewhere around the country of a surprisingly heavy turn-out of voters to the polls that morning. I would have liked to think that these were all angry Conservatives, coming out to demonstrate their refusal to be blackmailed by trade union power. But it seemed more likely that they were voters from the Labour-dominated council estates who had come out to teach the Tories a lesson. I was glad to be wearing a spray of blue flowers in my buttonhole instead of the usual paper rosette. They had been given me by Mark and they stayed fresh all day, helping to keep up my spirits.

The results themselves quickly showed that we had nothing to be cheerful about. We lost thirty-three seats. It would be a hung Parliament. Labour had become the largest party with 301 seats – seventeen short of a majority; we were down to 296, though with a slightly higher percentage of the vote than Labour; the Liberals had gained almost 20 per cent of the vote with fourteen seats, and smaller parties, including the Ulster Unionists, held twenty-three. My own majority in Finchley was down from 11,000 to 6,000, though some of that decline was the result of boundary changes in the constituency.

I was upset at the result. We had finally squared up to the unions and the people had not supported us. Moreover, I had enjoyed my time as Education Secretary, or most of it. I would miss the workload and the decisions, and of course the conveniences like the ministerial car: from now on I would be driving myself around once more in my Vauxhall Viva. At least the painful process of clearing out desks and cupboards full of personal belongings was largely spared me. I had never taken much personal clutter to the DES in any case and, prudently, I had brought most of what there was back home at the start of the campaign and popped into the office to sign urgent letters when in central London. I could make a more or less clean break.

On Friday afternoon we met, a tired and downcast fag-end of a Cabinet, to be asked by Ted Heath for our reactions as to what should now be done. There were a number of options. Ted could advise the Queen to send for Harold Wilson as the leader of the largest single party. Or the Government could face Parliament and see whether it could command support for its programme. Or he could try to do a deal with the smaller parties for a programme designed to cope with the nation's immediate difficulties. Having alienated the Ulster Unionists through our Northern Ireland policy, this in effect meant a deal with the Liberals – though even that would not have given us a majority. There was little doubt from the way Ted spoke that this was the course he favoured. We argued in circles about these possibilities.

My own instinctive feeling was that the party with the largest number of seats in the House of Commons was justified in expecting that they would be called to try to form a government. But Ted argued that with the Conservatives having won the largest number of votes, he was duty bound to explore the possibility of coalition. So he offered the Liberal Leader Jeremy Thorpe a place in a coalition Government and promised a Speaker's conference on electoral reform. Thorpe went away to consult his party. Although I wanted to remain Secretary of State for Education, I did not want to do so at the expense of the Conservative Party's never forming a majority government again. Yet that is what the introduction of proportional representation, which the Liberals would be demanding, might amount to. I was also conscious that this horse-trading was making us look ridiculous. The British dislike nothing more than a bad loser. It was time to go.

When we met again on Monday morning Ted gave us a full account of his discussions with the Liberals. They had in any case not been willing to go along with what Jeremy Thorpe wanted. A formal reply from him was still awaited. But it now seemed almost certain that Ted would have to tender his resignation. The final Cabinet was held at 4.45 that afternoon. By now Jeremy Thorpe's reply had been received. From what Ted said, there were clues that his mind was already turning to the idea of a National Government of all parties, something which would increasingly attract him. It did not, of course, attract me at all. In any case, the Liberals were not going to join a coalition Government with us. There was nothing more to say.

I left Downing Street, sad but with some sense of relief. I had given little thought to the future. But I knew in my heart that it was time not just for a change in government but for a change in the Conservative Party.

CHAPTER VIII

Seizing the Moment

*The October 1974 general election and the campaign
for the Tory Leadership*

THE 9½ PER CENT SOLUTION

It is never easy to go from government to opposition. But for several reasons it was particularly problematical for the Conservatives led by Ted Heath. First, of course, we had up until almost the last moment expected to win. Whatever the shortcomings of our Government's economic strategy, every department had its own policy programme stretching well into the future. This now had to be abandoned for the rigours of Opposition. Secondly, Ted himself desperately wanted to continue as Prime Minister. He had been unceremoniously ejected from 10 Downing Street and for some months had to take refuge in the flat of his old friend and PPS Tim Kitson, having no home of his own – from which years later I drew the resolution that when my time came to depart I would at least have a house to go to. Ted's passionate desire to return as Prime Minister lay behind much of the talk of coalitions and Governments of National Unity which came to disquiet the Party, though doubtless there was a measure of genuine conviction as well. Indeed, the more that the Tory Party moved away from Ted's own vision, the more he wanted to see it tamed by coalition. Thirdly, and worst of all perhaps, the poisoned legacy of our U-turns was that we had no firm principles, let alone much of a record, on which to base our arguments. And in Opposition argument is everything.

For my part, I was glad that Ted did not ask me to cover my old department at Education but gave me the Environment portfolio instead. I had learned during our previous period in Opposition in the 1960s that there are difficulties in attacking proposals many of which will have been in some stage of gestation within one's own department. Moreover, I was convinced from my own soundings in the course of the general election campaign that both rates and housing – particularly the latter – were issues which had contributed to our defeat. The task of devising and presenting sound and popular policies in these areas appealed to me.

There were rumblings about Ted's own position, though that is what they largely remained. This was partly because most of us expected an early general election to be called in order to give Labour a working majority, and it hardly seemed sensible to change leaders now. But there were other reasons as well. Ted still inspired nervousness, even fear among many of his colleagues. In a sense, even the U-turns contributed to the aura around him. For he had single-handedly and with barely a publicly expressed murmur of dissent reversed Conservative policies and had gone far, with his lieutenants, in reshaping the Conservative Party. Paradoxically too, both those committed to Ted's approach and those – like Keith and me and many on the backbenches – who thought very differently agreed that the vote-buying policies which the Labour Party was now pursuing would inevitably lead to economic collapse. Just what the political consequences of that would be was uncertain. But there were many Tory wishful thinkers who thought that it might result in the Conservative Party somehow returning to power with a 'doctor's mandate'. And Ted had no doubt of his own medical credentials.

He did not, though, make the concessions to his critics in the Party which would have been required. He might have provided effectively against future threats to his position if he had changed his approach in a number of ways. He might have shown at least some willingness to admit and learn from the Government's mistakes. He might have invited talented backbench critics to join him as Shadow spokesmen and contribute to the rethinking of policy. He might have changed the overall complexion of the Shadow Cabinet to make it more representative of parliamentary opinion.

But he did none of these things. He replaced Tony Barber – who announced that he intended to leave the Commons though he would stay on for the present in the Shadow Cabinet without portfolio – with Robert Carr, who was even more committed to the interventionist approach that had got us into so much trouble. He promoted to the Shadow Cabinet during the year those MPs like Michael Heseltine and Paul Channon who were seen as his acolytes, and were unrepresentative of backbench opinion of the time. Only John Davies and Joe Godber, neither of whom was ideologically distinct, were dropped. Above all, he set his face against any policy rethinking that would imply that his Government's economic and industrial policy had been seriously flawed. When Keith Joseph was not made Shadow Chancellor, he said he wanted no portfolio but rather to concentrate on research for new policies – something which would prove as dangerous to Ted as it was fruitful for the Party. Otherwise, these were depressing signals of 'more of the same' when the electorate had clearly demonstrated a desire for something different. Added to this, the important Steering Committee of Shadow Ministers was formed even more in Ted's image. I was not at this stage invited to join it, and of its members only Keith and perhaps Geoffrey Howe were likely to oppose Ted's wishes.

With everyone expecting another election before the end of the year – October being the favoured date – the Tory Party entered on an almost frantic search for attractive policies to be deployed in our next manifesto. These had to meet two criteria: they had to be novel, and they had to cast no doubt on the underlying correctness of the recent Conservative Government's policies. I added a third complication: as far as my area of responsibility was concerned, the new policies also had to be recognisably Conservative. Meeting all these criteria involved us in some extremely testing acrobatics.

Between the February and October 1974 elections most of my time was taken up with work on housing and the rates. I had an effective housing policy group of MPs working with me. Hugh Rossi, a friend and neighbouring MP, was a great housing expert, with experience of local government. Michael Latham and John Stanley were well versed in the building industry. The brilliant Nigel Lawson, newly elected, always had his own ideas. We also had the help of people from the building societies and construction industry. It was a lively group which I enjoyed chairing.

The political priority was clearly lower mortgage rates. The technical problem was how to achieve these without open-ended subsidy. Of course, the purist view would be that artificially controlling the price of borrowing for house purchase was bound to be counterproductive. And in this matter the purist, as so often, was right. If we had pursued a responsible economic policy there would have been no boom and bust of property prices, and rising inflation would not have driven up mortgage rates. Policies providing for sound money and the release of sufficient quantities of development land are the proper way to ensure an orderly housing market. But of course we had not pursued policies of that sort. And Labour was already embarking on a vendetta against property development. In these circumstances, holding the mortgage rate down below the level the market – or more precisely the building societies – would otherwise have set made short-term political sense. In Government we had introduced a mortgage subsidy, and there had even been talk of taking powers to control the mortgage rate. The Labour Government quickly came up with its own scheme devised by Harold Lever to make large cheap short-term loans to the building societies. Our task was to devise something more attractive.

As well as having an eye for a politically attractive policy, I had reasons of conviction for action on the mortgage rate and for the other measures we devised to help homebuyers. I had always believed in a property-owning democracy and wider home ownership. At this point too, I was acutely aware of how much the middle classes were suffering. Because of the inflation which we and the Labour Party had conspired to create, the value of people's savings had been eroded by negative real interest rates. On top of that, by 1974 house values had slumped. So had the stock market: the FT Ordinary Share index went down to 146, the lowest level for twenty years. Trade union power and left-wing socialism were in the ascendant. Tax increases were bearing down on businesses and people.

In such circumstances, it can be right to make modest temporary provision for the interests of the middle classes of a country on whom future prosperity largely depends. Moreover, it is cheaper to assist people to buy homes with a mortgage – whether by a subsidized mortgage rate, or by help with the deposit, or just by mortgage interest tax relief – than it is to build more council houses or to buy up private houses through municipalization. I used to quote the results of a Housing Research Foundation study which observed: 'On average each new council house now costs roughly £900 a year in subsidy in taxes and rates (including the subsidy from very old council houses) . . . Tax relief on an ordinary mortgage, if this be regarded as a subsidy, averages about £280 a year.'

My housing policy group met regularly on Mondays. Housing experts and representatives from the building societies gave their advice. I reported from time to time to Shadow Cabinet where, in the absence of real agreement on economic policy or much constructive thinking on anything else, attention focused heavily on my areas of responsibility. It was clear to me that Ted and others were determined to make our proposals on housing and possibly rates the centrepiece of the next election campaign, which we expected sooner rather than later. For example, at the Shadow Cabinet on Friday 3 May we had an all-day discussion of policies for the manifesto. I reported on housing and was authorized to set up a rates policy group. But this meeting was more significant for another reason. At it Keith Joseph argued at length but in vain for a broadly 'monetarist' approach to dealing with inflation.

The question of the rates was a far more difficult one than any aspect of housing policy, and I had a slightly different group to help me. There was a huge amount of technical information to master. Moreover, reform, let alone abolition, of the rates had profound implications for the relations between central and local government and for the different local authority services, particularly education. I drew on the advice of the experts – municipal treasurers proved the best source, and gave readily of their technical advice. But working as I was under tight pressure of time and close scrutiny by Ted and others who expected me to deliver something radical, popular and defensible, my task was not an easy one.

That said, I could well understand how much was at stake politically. For example, on Tuesday 21 May I met 350 protesters from Northamptonshire – one from every town and village in the county

– who were furious about rate rises of between 30 and 100 per cent. Several factors combined to raise the issue to such political prominence: there was the basic unfairness of a system which taxed a single widow at the same rate as a family with three grown-up working sons; our own rating revaluation in 1973 had led to inordinate rate rises;* and, more recently, Labour's rate support grant settlement had treated the rural shire counties particularly harshly. There was, in short, on the rates issue as on housing, a full-scale middle-class anti-socialist revolt, and it was essential that it be harnessed, not dissipated. This I was determined to do.

The housing policy group had already held its seventh meeting and our proposals were well developed by the time the rates group started work on 10 June. I knew Ted and his advisers wanted a firm promise that we would abolish the rates. But I was loath to make such a pledge until we were clear about what to put in their place. Anyway, if there was to be an autumn election, there was by now little chance of doing more than finding a sustainable line to take in the manifesto.

Meanwhile, throughout that summer of 1974 I received far more publicity than I had ever previously experienced, mainly as a result of our housing policy. Some of this was inadvertent. The interim report of the housing policy group which I circulated to Shadow Cabinet appeared on the front page of *The Times* on Monday 24 June. On the previous Friday Shadow Cabinet had spent the morning discussing the fourth draft of the manifesto. By now the main lines of my proposed housing policy were agreed. The mortgage rate would be held down to some unspecified level by cutting the composite rate of tax paid by building societies on depositors' accounts, in other words by subsidy disguised as tax relief. A grant would be given to first-time buyers saving for a deposit, though again no figure was specified. There would be a high-powered inquiry into building societies; this was an idea I modelled on the James Inquiry into teachers' training. I hoped it might produce a long-term answer to the problem of high mortgage rates and yet save us from an open-ended subsidy.

The final point related to the right of tenants to buy their council

* A property revaluation was due every five years, but was often postponed.

houses. Of all our proposals this was to prove the most far-reaching and the most popular. The February 1974 manifesto had offered council tenants the chance to buy their houses, but retained a right of appeal for the council against sale, and had not offered a discount. We all wanted to go further than this; the question was how far. Peter Walker constantly pressed for the 'Right to Buy' to be extended to council tenants at the lowest possible prices. My instinct was on the side of caution. It was not that I underrated the benefits of wider property ownership. Rather, I was wary of alienating the already hard-pressed families who had scrimped to buy a house on one of the new private estates at the market price and who had seen the mortgage rate rise and the value of their house fall. These people were the bedrock Conservative voters for whom I felt a natural sympathy. They would, I feared, strongly object to council house tenants who had made none of their sacrifices suddenly receiving what was in effect a large capital sum from the Government. We might end up losing more support than we gained. In retrospect, this argument seems both narrow and unimaginative. And it was. But there was a lot to be said politically for it in 1974 at a time when the value of people's houses had slumped so catastrophically.

In the event, we went a long way in Peter's direction. The October 1974 manifesto offered council tenants who had been in their homes for three years or more the right to buy them at a price a third below market value. If the tenant sold again within five years he would surrender part of any capital gain. Also by the time the manifesto reached its final draft we had quantified the help to be given to first-time buyers of private houses and flats. We would contribute £1 for every £2 saved for the deposit up to a given ceiling. (We ducked the question of rent decontrol.)

It was, however, the question of how low a maximum mortgage interest rate we would promise in the manifesto that caused me most trouble. Although, for the reasons I have already outlined, I had convinced myself that some kind of pledge in this area was justified, I was very aware of how the cost to the Exchequer might escalate alarmingly if inflation and interest rates kept on rising. Ted and those around him seemed to entertain no such caution. On Thursday 1 August he summoned me back from Lamberhurst for a meeting at his new house in Wilton Street with Peter Walker, Ian Gilmour and Robert Carr. I was put under great pressure to go beyond the phrase which had by now been agreed for the manifesto of pegging the mortgage rate at a 'reasonable' level. Ted and the others wanted a specific figure. I argued strongly against, but in the end I had to concede a pledge that we would hold the rate 'below 10 per cent'. Beyond that, I did not agree to a specific figure. I hoped it would be the end of the matter.

But when I was in the car on the way from London to Tonbridge on Wednesday 28 August in order to record a Party Political Broadcast the bleeper signalled that I must telephone urgently. Ted apparently wanted a word. Willie Whitelaw answered the phone and it was clear that the two of them, and doubtless others of the inner circle, were meeting. Ted came on the line. He asked me to announce on the PPB the precise figure to which we would hold down mortgages, and to take it down as low as I could. I said I could understand the psychological point about going below 10 per cent. That need could be satisfied by a figure of 9½ per cent, and in all conscience I could not take it down any further. To do so would have a touch of rashness about it. I was already worried about the cost. I did not like this tendency to pull figures out of the air for immediate political impact without proper consideration of where they would lead. So I stuck at 9½ per cent.

It was a similar story on the rates. When we had discussed the subject at our Shadow Cabinet meeting on Friday 21 June I had tried to avoid any firm pledge. I suggested that our line should be one of reform to be established on an all-party basis through a Select Committee. I was the first to admit that this was not likely to set the world on fire. But even more than housing, this was not an area in which precipitate pledges were sensible. Ted would have none of this and said I should think again. The need for something clearer was indeed demonstrated by the Commons debate on the rates a few days later. We called for fundamental reform, some interim rate relief and a provision that water charges should qualify for rate rebate. In my speech I also argued for central government having the power to cap local government spending and then for a general inquiry into the rates. But though I emerged with my reputation as a parliamentarian intact, Tony Crosland, the

Environment Secretary, arguing for an increased central government subsidy to local authorities without major reform of the system, was generally thought to have had the better of the debate. His victory was pyrrhic. For increased subsidies led not to lower rates but to higher local spending. Within a year Mr Crosland was announcing sternly: 'The party is over.'

In July Charles Bellairs at the Conservative Research Department and I worked on a draft rates section for the manifesto. We were still thinking in terms of an inquiry and an interim rate relief scheme. I went along to discuss our proposals at the Shadow Cabinet Steering Committee. I argued for the transfer of teachers' salaries – the largest item of local spending – from local government onto the Exchequer. Another possibility I raised was the replacement of rates with a system of block grants, with local authorities retaining discretion over spending but within a total set by central government. Neither of these possibilities was particularly attractive. But at least discussion revealed to those present that 'doing something' about the rates was a very different matter from knowing what to do.

On Saturday 10 August I used my speech to the Candidates' Conference at the St Stephen's Club to publicize our policies. I argued for total reform of the rating system to take into account individual ability to pay, and suggested the transfer of teachers' salaries and better interim relief as ways to achieve this. It was a good time of the year – a slack period for news – to unveil new proposals, and we gained some favourable publicity.

It seemed to me that this proved that we could fight a successful campaign *without* being more specific; indeed, looking back, I can see that we were *already* a good deal too specific because, as I was to discover fifteen years later, such measures as transferring the cost of services from local to central government do not in themselves lead to lower local authority rates.

I had hoped to have a pleasant family holiday at Lamberhurst away from the sticky heat of London and the demands of politics. It would have been the first for three years. It was not to be. The telephone kept ringing, with Ted and others urging me to give more thought to new schemes. Then I was called back for another meeting at Wilton Street on Friday 16 August. Ted, Robert Carr,

Jim Prior, Willie Whitelaw and Michael Wolff from Central Office were all there. It was soon clear what the purpose was – to bludgeon me into accepting a commitment in the manifesto to abolish the rates altogether within the lifetime of a Parliament. I argued against this for very much the same reason that I argued against the '9½ per cent' pledge on the mortgage rate. But so shell-shocked by their unexpected defeat in February were Ted and his inner circle that in their desire for re-election they were clutching at straws, or what in the jargon were described as manifesto 'nuggets'.

There were various ways to raise revenue for expenditure on local purposes. We were all uneasy about moving to a system whereby central government just provided block grants to local government. So I had told Shadow Cabinet that I thought a reformed property tax seemed to be the least painful option. But in the back of my mind I had the additional idea of supplementing the property tax with a locally collected tax on petrol. Of course, there were plenty of objections to both, but at least they were better than putting up income tax.

In any case, what mattered to my colleagues was clearly the pledge to abolish the rates, and at Wilton Street Ted insisted on it. I felt bruised and resentful to be bounced again into policies which had not been properly thought out. But I thought that if I combined caution on the details with as much presentational bravura as I could muster I could make our rates and housing policies into vote-winners for the Party. This I now concentrated my mind on doing.

It was at a press conference on the afternoon of Wednesday 28 August that I unveiled our final proposals. I delivered the package of measures – built around 9½ per cent mortgages and the abolition of the rates – without a scintilla of doubt, which as veteran *Evening Standard* reporter Robert Carvel said, 'went down with hardened reporters almost as well as the sherry' served by Central Office. We dominated the news. It was by general consent the best fillip the Party had had since losing the February election. There was even some talk of the Conservatives being back in the lead in the opinion polls, though this was over-optimistic. The Building Societies' Association welcomed the proposals for 9½ per cent mortgages but questioned my figures about the cost. In fact, as I indignantly told them, it was their sums which were wrong and they subsequently retracted. Some on the economic right were understandably critical, but among the grassroots Conservatives that we had to win back the mortgage proposal was extremely popular. So too was the pledge on the rates. The Labour Party was rattled and unusually the party-giving Tony Crosland was provoked into overreaction, describing the proposals as 'Margaret's midsummer madness'. All this publicity was good for me personally as well. Although I was not to know it at the time, this period up to and during the October 1974 election campaign allowed me to make a favourable impact on Conservatives in the country and in Parliament without which my future career would doubtless have been very different.

FIRST SECOND THOUGHTS

Although it was my responsibilities as Environment spokesman which took up most of my time and energy, from late June I had become part of another enterprise which would have profound consequences for the Conservative Party, for the country and for me. The setting-up of the Centre for Policy Studies (CPS) is really part of Keith Joseph's story rather than mine. Keith had emerged from the wreckage of the Heath Government determined on the need to rethink our policies from first principles. If this was to be done, Keith was the ideal man to do it. He had the intellect, the integrity and not least the humility required. He had a deep interest in both economic and social policy. He had long experience of government. He had an extraordinary ability to form relationships of friendship and respect with a wide range of characters with different viewpoints and backgrounds. Although he could, when he felt strongly, speak passionately and persuasively, it was as a listener that he excelled. Moreover, Keith never listened passively. He probed arguments and assertions and scribbled notes which you knew he would go home to ponder. He was so impressive because his intellectual self-confidence was the fruit of continual self-questioning. His bravery in adopting unpopular positions before a hostile audience evoked the admiration of his friends, because we all knew that he was naturally shy and even timid. He was almost too good a man for politics, except that without a few good men politics would be intolerable.

I could not have become Leader of the Opposition, or achieved what I did as Prime Minister, without Keith. But nor, it is fair to say, could Keith have achieved what he did without the Centre for Policy Studies and Alfred Sherman. Apart from the fact of their being Jewish, Alfred and Keith had little in common, and until one saw how effectively they worked together it was difficult to believe that they could cooperate at all.

I understand that Keith and Alfred first met in 1962 when Keith was Housing Minister and Alfred covered local government matters at the *Daily Telegraph*. From time to time they were in touch, and then after a discussion at the Reform Club Keith asked Alfred's thoughts about a speech draft he had with him. From then on Keith took to asking for Alfred's suggestions. During the early years of the Heath Government they had less contact, but it was during the three-day week that Keith met Alfred to discuss the Middle East, on which Alfred was something of an expert, writing for the main Hebrew-language daily in Israel.

Alfred had his own kind of brilliance. He brought his convert's zeal (as an ex-communist), his breadth of reading and his skills as a ruthless polemicist to the task of plotting out a new kind of free-market Conservatism. He was more interested, it seemed to me, in the philosophy behind policies than the policies themselves. He was better at pulling apart sloppily constructed arguments than at devising original proposals. But the force and clarity of his mind, and his complete disregard for other people's feelings or opinion of him, made him a formidable complement and contrast to Keith. Alfred helped Keith to turn the Centre for Policy Studies into the powerhouse of alternative Conservative thinking on economic and social matters.

I was not involved at the beginning, though I gathered from Keith that he was thinking hard about how to turn his Shadow Cabinet responsibilities for research on policy into constructive channels. In March Keith had won Ted's approval for the setting-up of a research unit to make comparative studies with other

European economies, particularly the so-called 'social market economy' as practised in West Germany. Ted had Adam Ridley put on the board of directors of the CPS (Adam acted as his economic adviser from within the Conservative Research Department), but otherwise Keith was left very much to his own devices. Nigel Vinson, a successful entrepreneur with strong free-enterprise convictions, was made responsible for acquiring a home for the Centre, which was found in Wilfred Street, close to Victoria. Simon Webley, who ran the British/North American Research Association, ensured that the Centre's publications never forgot the realities of industry and commerce amid the economic theories. Later in 1974 Gerry Frost, the present Director, also joined the CPS and established some administrative order out of what might have been a chaos of intellectuals. Other figures who made crucial contributions from time to time were Jock Bruce-Gardyne and Peter Utley. A further reason for the Centre's success was the dedication of secretaries and cooks who twice a week provided some of the best low-cost meals in London. (Perhaps not always low-cost: Gerry Frost once complained in a memo: 'We seem to be bent on disproving the dictum that there is no such thing as a free lunch.') Increasingly, the CPS acted as a focus for a large group of free-market thinkers, by no means all of them Conservative, who sought to change the climate of opinion and achieve wider understanding of the role of the market and the shortcomings of statism.

It was at the end of May 1974 that I first became directly involved with the CPS. Whether Keith ever considered asking any other members of the Shadow Cabinet to join him at the Centre I do not know: if he had they certainly did not accept. His was a risky, exposed position, and the fear of provoking the wrath of Ted and the derision of left-wing commentators was a powerful disincentive. But I jumped at the chance to become Keith's Vice-Chairman.

The CPS was the least bureaucratic of institutions. It could not properly be called a 'think tank' for it had none of the corporate grandeur of the prestigious American foundations which that term evokes. Alfred Sherman has caught the feel of it by saying that it was an 'animator, agent of change, and political enzyme'. The original proposed social market approach did not prove particularly fruitful and was eventually quietly forgotten, though a pamphlet called *Why Britain Needs a Social Market Economy* was published. The concept of the social market was – like other terms of foreign provenance too literally translated – bedevilled with problems. How much was it simply a matter of restating the truth that only a successful market economy can sustain social improvement? How much did it signify a market economy with a high degree of 'social protection', i.e. regulation? Even its most prominent exponent, West German Chancellor Ludwig Erhard, apparently had his doubts about the way it was being implemented in later years.

What the Centre then developed was the drive to expose the follies and self-defeating consequences of government intervention. It continued to engage the political argument in open debate at the highest intellectual level. The objective was to effect change – change in the climate of opinion and so in the limits of the 'possible'. In order to do this it had, to employ another of Alfred's phrases, to 'think the unthinkable'. It was not long before more than a few feathers began to be ruffled by that approach.

Keith had decided that he would make a series of speeches over the summer and autumn of 1974 in which he would set out the alternative analysis of what had gone wrong and what should be done. The first of these, which was also intended to attract interest among potential fund-raisers, was delivered at Upminster on Saturday 22 June. Alfred was the main draftsman. But as with all Keith's speeches – except the fateful Edgbaston speech which I shall describe shortly – he circulated endless drafts for comment. All the observations received were carefully considered and the language pared down to remove every surplus word. Keith's speeches always put rigour of analysis and exactitude of language above style, but taken as a whole they managed to be powerful rhetorical instruments as well.

The Upminster speech infuriated Ted and the Party establishment because Keith lumped in together the mistakes of Conservative and Labour Governments, talking about the 'thirty years of socialistic fashions'. The last time anyone had been bold enough to speak like this was when Hayek wrote *The Road to Serfdom* in 1944. Keith pre-empted the criticism which would inevitably be levelled at him by accepting now and later his full share of the blame for what had gone wrong. One after the other he led the sacred cows to the abattoir. He said of the frantic pursuit of economic growth: 'Growth is welcome, but we just do not know how to accelerate its pace. Perhaps faster growth, like happiness, should not be a prime target but only a by-product of other policies.'

He said bluntly that the public sector had been 'draining away the wealth created by the private sector', and challenged the value of public 'investment' in tourism and the expansion of the universities. He condemned the socialist vendetta against profits and noted the damage done by rent controls and council housing to labour mobility. Finally – and, in the eyes of the advocates of consensus, unforgivably – he talked about the 'inherent contradictions [of the] . . . mixed economy'. It was a short speech but it had a mighty impact, not least because people knew that there was more to come.

A distinctive feature of Keith's approach was that he went out of his way to avoid suggesting that malice had prompted the excessive state spending, nationalization, regulation, taxation and trade union power which had done so much harm to Britain. On the contrary, he argued, all this had occurred with the best of intentions. Perhaps in this he was over-generous, attributing his own high-mindedness to others. But the patent sincerity and charity which accompanied his devastating criticism of the politics of the last thirty years increased the effect. He returned to the same theme at Leith in August, by which time I was myself more actively involved in the CPS, attending Keith's meetings, commenting on his suggestions and preparing my own notes and papers on the areas of education and social services which I knew best.

From Keith and Alfred I learned a great deal. I renewed my reading of the seminal works of liberal economics and conservative thought. I also regularly attended lunches at the Institute of Economic Affairs where Ralph Harris, Arthur Seldon, Alan Walters and others – in other words all those who had been right when we in Government had gone so badly wrong – were busy marking out a new non-socialist economic and social path for Britain. I lunched from time to time with Professor Douglas Hague, the economist, who would later act as one of my unofficial economic advisers.

At about this time I also made the acquaintance of a polished and amusing former television producer called Gordon Reece, who was advising the Party on television appearances and who had, it seemed to me, an almost uncanny insight into that medium. In fact, by the eve of the October 1974 general election I had made a significant number of contacts with those on whom I would come to rely so heavily during my years as Party Leader.

The third of Keith's troika of policy speeches was delivered in Preston on Thursday 5 September (by which time he was Shadow Home Secretary). After some early inconclusive discussion in Shadow Cabinet of Keith's various ideas, Ted had refused the general economic re-evaluation and discussion which Keith wanted. Keith decided that he was not prepared to be either stifled or ignored, and gave notice that he was intending to make a major speech on economic policy. Ted and most of our colleagues were desperate to prevent this. Geoffrey Howe and I, as the two members of Shadow Cabinet considered most likely to be able to influence Keith, were accordingly dispatched to try to persuade him not to go ahead, or at least to tone down what he intended to say. In any case, Keith showed me an early draft. It was one of the most powerful and persuasive analyses I have ever read. I made no suggestions for changes. Nor, as far as I know, did Geoffrey. The Preston speech must still be considered as one of the very few speeches which have fundamentally affected a political generation's way of thinking.

It set out in much greater detail than ever before the monetarist approach. It began with the sombre statement: 'Inflation is threatening to destroy our society.' At most times this would have seemed hyperbole, but at this time, with inflation at 17 per cent and rising, people were obsessed with its impact on their lives. That only made more explosive Keith's admission that *successive* governments bore the responsibility for allowing it to get such a grip. He rejected the idea embraced by the Shadow Cabinet that inflation had been 'imported' and was the result of rocketing world prices. In fact, it was the result of excessive growth of the money supply. Explaining as he did that there was a time lag of 'many months, or even as much as a year or two' between loose monetary policy and rising inflation, he also implicitly – and of course accurately – blamed the Heath Government for the inflation which was now beginning to take off and which would rise to even more ruinous levels the following year. He also rejected the use of incomes policy as a means of containing it. The analysis was subtle, detailed and devastating.

> Incomes policy alone [the word 'alone' being a minor concession I suppose to the official Shadow Cabinet line] as a way to abate inflation caused by excessive money supply is like trying to stop water coming out of a leaky hose without turning off the tap; if you stop one hole it will find two others . . . But long before this year, we knew all the arguments. We had used them in Opposition in 1966–70. Why then did we try incomes policy again? I suppose that we desperately wanted to believe in it because we were so apprehensive about the alternative: sound money policies.

(Of course I too in my 1968 CPC lecture had accepted the monetarist analysis: so I felt that this applied equally to me.)

Keith then put his finger on the fundamental reason why we had embarked on our disastrous U-turns – fear of unemployment. It had been when registered unemployment rose to one million that the Heath Government's nerve broke. But Keith explained that the unemployment statistics concealed as much as they revealed because they included 'frictional unemployment' – that is, people who were temporarily out of work moving between jobs – and a large number of people who were more or less unemployable for one reason or another. Similarly, there was a large amount of fraudulent unemployment, people who were drawing benefit while earning. In fact, noted Keith, the real problem had been labour shortages, not surpluses. He said that we should be prepared to admit that control of the money supply to beat inflation would temporarily risk some increase in unemployment. But if we wanted to bring down inflation (which itself destroyed jobs, though this was an argument to which Keith and I would subsequently have to return on many occasions), monetary growth had to be curbed. Keith did not argue that if we got the money supply right, everything else would be right. He specifically said that this was not his view. But if we did *not* achieve monetary control we would never be able to achieve any of our other economic objectives.

The Preston speech had a huge impact. It was, of course, highly embarrassing for Ted and the Party establishment. Some still hoped that a combination of dire warnings about socialism, hints of a National Government and our new policies on mortgages and the rates would see us squeak back into office – an illusion fostered by the fact that on the very day of Keith's speech an opinion poll showed us two points ahead of Labour. The Preston speech blew this strategy out of the water, for it was clear that the kind of reassessment Keith was advocating was highly unlikely to occur if the Conservatives returned to government with Ted Heath as Prime Minister. Keith himself discreetly decided to spend more time at the CPS in Wilfred Street than at Westminster, where some of his colleagues were furious. For my part, I did not think that there was any serious chance of our winning the election. In the short term I was determined to fight as hard as I could for the policies which it was now my responsibility to defend. In the longer term I was convinced that we must turn the Party around towards Keith's way of thinking, preferably under Keith's leadership.

TED'S LAST THROW

The Conservative Party manifesto was published early, on Tuesday 10 September – about a week before the election was announced – because of a leak to the press. I was taken by surprise by a question on it when I was opening the Chelsea Antiques Fair. The release of the manifesto in this way was not a good start to the campaign, particularly because we had so little new to say. It was clear, however, from the course of the Shadow Cabinet two days later, that what was really worrying Ted and his circle was what Keith – and to a lesser extent I – *was* likely to say. Ted laid down the law: we must speak to the manifesto and nothing else, and any amplification of policies must be made only after discussions between the relevant spokesmen, the Party Chairman and himself. Shadow Cabinet members must concentrate particularly on their *own* subjects. No one had the slightest doubt about the target for these remarks.

I was effectively on the campaign trail even before the formal announcement the following Wednesday of a general election to take place on Thursday 10 October. On Monday I spoke in the north-west for Fergus Montgomery, my splendid PPS (a front-bencher's eyes and ears in the Commons). On Tuesday I was answering questions about our policies at a meeting of the House-builders' Federation. On Wednesday itself I gave an interview to a magazine called *Pre-Retirement Choice*: this was, as I shall explain, to come back to haunt me. On Thursday there was a further general discussion of the campaign in Shadow Cabinet. The following day Parliament was dissolved and the campaign got properly under way with MPs leaving for their constituencies.

I had never had so much exposure to the media as in this campaign. The Labour Party recognized that our housing and rates proposals were just about the only attractive ones in our manifesto, and consequently they set out to rubbish them as soon as possible. On Tuesday 24 September Tony Crosland described them as 'a pack of lies'. (This was the same press conference at which Denis Healey made his notorious claim that inflation was running at 8.4 per cent, calculating the figure on a three-month basis when the annual rate was in fact 17 per cent.) I immediately issued a statement rebutting the accusation, and in order to keep the argument going, for it would highlight our policies, I said at Finchley that evening that the cut in mortgage rates would be among the first actions of a new Conservative Government. Then, in pursuit of the same goal, and having consulted Ted and Robert Carr, the Shadow Chancellor, I announced at the morning press conference at Central Office on Friday that the mortgage rate reduction would occur 'by Christmas' if we won. The main morning papers led with the story the following day – 'Santa Thatcher' – and it was generally said that we had taken the initiative for the first time during the campaign. On the following Monday I described this on a Party Election Broadcast as a 'firm, unshakeable promise'. And the brute political fact was that, despite my reservations about the wisdom of the pledge, we would have had to honour it at almost any cost.

It was at this point that the way in which I was presenting our housing and rates policies first began to run up against the general approach Ted wanted to take in the campaign. At his insistence I had made the policies I was offering as hard and specific as possible.

But the manifesto, particularly in the opening section, deliberately conveyed the impression that the Conservatives might consider some kind of National Government and would therefore be flexible on the policies we were putting forward. The passage read:

The Conservative Party, free from dogma and free from dependence upon any single interest, is broadly based throughout the nation. It is our objective to win a clear majority in the House of Commons in this election. But we will use that majority above all to unite the nation. We will not govern in a narrow partisan spirit. *After the election we will consult and confer with the leaders of other parties and with the leaders of the great interests in the nation, in order to secure for the Government's policies the consent and support of all men and women of goodwill. We will invite people from outside the ranks of our party to join with us in overcoming Britain's difficulties.* [Emphasis added.]

These undefined people who would join the Conservatives in government might include, one presumed, some members of the right wing of the Labour Party and perhaps the Liberals. The latter had all along been openly campaigning for a coalition government. This kind of rhetoric made me deeply uneasy. It was not just that, like Disraeli's England, I did not like coalitions. In practical terms, such talk reduced the credibility of the pledges I was making in my own area. For who could tell what inter-party horse-trading might do to them?

At the Conservative press conference on Friday 2 October Ted stressed his willingness as Prime Minister to bring non-Conservatives into a government of 'all the talents' (party and talent being in this context considered synonyms). This tension between firm pledges and implied flexibilities was in danger of making nonsense of our campaign and dividing Shadow ministers.

We were now entering the last week. I still did not believe we were likely to win. The opinion polls had shown us well behind since the beginning of the campaign. But I felt that in spite of criticism in the heavyweight press my housing and rates policies had proved a political success. I also thought that we might manage to get by with the present somewhat ambiguous attitude to National Governments for the few days remaining.

On Thursday I continued when campaigning in the London areas with the vigorous defence of our housing policies and combined this with attacks on 'creeping socialism' through municipalization. In the evening I was asked to come and see Ted at Wilton Street. His advisers had apparently been urging him to go further and actually start talking about the possibility of a Coalition Government. Because I was known to be firmly against this for both strategic and tactical reasons, and because I was due to appear on the radio programme *Any Questions* in Southampton the following evening, I had been called in to have the new line spelt out to me. Ted said that he was now prepared to call for a Government of National Unity which, apparently, 'the people' wanted. I was extremely angry. He had himself, after all, insisted on making the housing and rates policies I had been advocating as specific as possible: now at almost the end of the campaign he was effectively discarding the pledges in the manifesto because that seemed to offer a better chance of his returning to Downing Street.

Why, in any case, he imagined that he himself would be a Coalition Government's likely Leader quite escaped me. Ted at this time was a divisive figure, and although he had somehow convinced himself that he represented the 'consensus', this accorded with neither his record, nor his temperament, nor indeed other people's estimation. For myself, I was not going to retreat from the policies which at his insistence I had been advocating. I went away highly disgruntled.

On *Any Questions* I conceded that if there were no clear majority, a coalition would probably be necessary. But I qualified this by saying that I myself could never sit in a government with left wingers like Michael Foot or Tony Benn. I might have added that the likelihood of Keith Joseph and my being included in a coalition of the great and the good was tiny – hardly greater in fact than Ted himself leading it.

The last few days of the campaign were dominated by all the awkward questions which talk of coalitions brings. But I stuck to my own brief, repeating the manifesto pledges sitting alongside Ted Heath at the last Conservative press conference on Tuesday

7 October. The general election result two days later suggested that in spite of the natural desire of electors to give the minority Labour Government a chance to govern effectively, there was still a good deal of distrust of them. Labour finished up with an overall majority of three, which was unlikely to see them through a full term. But the Conservative result – 277 seats compared with Labour's 319 – though it might have been worse, was hardly any kind of endorsement for our approach.

KEITH BOWS OUT

I myself had fared quite well, though my majority fell a little in Finchley. I was thought to have had a good campaign. Talk of my even possibly becoming Leader of the Party, a subject which had already excited some journalists a great deal more than it convinced me, started to grow. I felt sorry for Ted Heath personally. He had his music and a small circle of friends, but politics was his life. That year, moreover, he had suffered a series of personal blows. His yacht, *Morning Cloud*, had sunk and his godson had been among those lost. The election defeat was a further blow.

Nonetheless, I had no doubt that Ted now ought to go. He had lost three elections out of four. He himself could not change and he was too defensive of his own past record to see that a fundamental change of policies was needed. So my reluctance to confirm suggestions that I might myself become Leader had little to do with keeping Ted in his present position. It had everything to do with seeing Keith take over from him. Indeed, by the weekend I had virtually become Keith's informal campaign manager. Accordingly I discouraged speculation about my own prospects. For example, I told the London *Evening News* on Friday 11 October: 'You can cross my name off the list.'

Similarly I told the *Evening Standard* on Tuesday 15 October: 'I think it would be extremely difficult for a woman to make it to the top . . . I have always taken the view that to get to the very top one has to have experience in one of the three important posts*

* i.e. Foreign Secretary, Chancellor of the Exchequer, Home Secretary.

. . . they give you confidence in yourself and give others confidence in you.'

Then on Saturday 19 October Keith spoke at Edgbaston in Birmingham. It was not intended as part of the series of major speeches designed to alter the thinking of the Conservative Party, and perhaps for this reason had not been widely circulated among Keith's friends and advisers: certainly, I had no inkling of the text. The Edgbaston speech is generally reckoned to have destroyed Keith's leadership chances. It was the section containing the assertion that 'the balance of our population, our human stock, is threatened', and going on to lament the high and rising proportion of children being born to mothers 'least fitted to bring children into the world', having been 'pregnant in adolescence in social classes 4 and 5', which did the damage. Ironically, the most incendiary phrases came not from Keith's own mouth, but from passages taken from an article by two left-wing sociologists published by the Child Poverty Action Group. This distinction, however, was lost upon the bishops, novelists, academics, socialist politicians and commentators who rushed to denounce Keith as a mad eugenicist.

On the other hand, there was an outpouring of public support for Keith in opinion polls and five bulging mail bags. One of these letters, a sample of which was analysed by Diana Spearman in the *Spectator*, summed up the feeling. In an unlettered hand, it read simply:

> Dear Sir Joseph,
> You are dead right.

For, with the exception of those few unfortunate phrases, the speech sent out powerful messages about the decline of the family, the subversion of moral values and the dangers of the permissive society, connecting all these things with socialism and egalitarianism, and proposing the 'remoralization of Britain' as a long-term aim. It was an attempt to provide a backbone for Conservative social policy, just as Keith had started to do for economic policy. The trouble was that the only short-term answer suggested by Keith for the social problems he outlined was making contraceptives more widely available – and that tended to drive away those who might have been attracted by his larger moral message.

The Edgbaston speech was bound to be dynamite, but it might at least have been a controlled explosion. Unfortunately, that is not how it happened. The speech was due to be given on Saturday night, and so the text was issued in advance with an embargo for media use. But the *Evening Standard*, for whatever reason, broke the embargo and launched a fierce attack on Keith, distorting what he said. I read its version on Waterloo Station and my heart sank. Afterwards Keith himself did not help his cause by constantly explaining, qualifying and apologizing. The Party establishment could barely contain their glee. Keith had been found guilty of that one mortal sin in the eyes of mediocrities – he had shown 'lack of judgement', i.e. willingness to think for himself. The press camped outside his house and refused to leave him or his family alone. He had probably never experienced anything quite like it. Having been vilified as the 'milk snatcher', I felt his hurt as if it were my own. But there was nothing to do except hope that it would all die down.

Doubtless as a result of all this, Ted felt a good deal more secure. He even told us in Shadow Cabinet the following Tuesday that the election campaign had been 'quite a good containment exercise and that the mechanics had worked well'. A strange unreality pervaded our discussions. Everyone except Ted knew that the main political problem was the fact that he was still Leader. But he thought that we should now concentrate on Scotland, on how to improve our appeal to the young and on how to increase our support among working-class voters. Even on its own terms this analysis was flawed. As I was to point out two days later in an interview with Max Hastings in the *Evening Standard*, which appeared under the headline 'Mrs Thatcher and the Twilight of the Middle Classes', we should be trying to re-establish our middle-class support, for '[being middle class] has never been simply a matter of income, but a whole attitude to life, a will to take responsibility for oneself'. And I was surely not the only one present at Shadow Cabinet who felt that our recent election defeat was hardly a cause for even modest self-congratulation.

Ted was now locked in a bitter battle with the 1922 Executive. In reply to their demands for a leadership contest – and indeed for reform of the leadership election procedure – he disputed their legitimacy as representatives of the backbenches on the grounds that they had been elected during the previous Parliament and must themselves first face re-election by Tory MPs. Ted and his advisers hoped that they might be able to have his opponents thrown off the Executive and replaced by figures more amenable to him. As part of a somewhat belated attempt to win over back-benchers, Ted also proposed that extra front bench spokesmen should be appointed from among them and that officers of the Parliamentary Committees might speak from the front bench on some occasions. It was also widely rumoured that there would shortly be a reshuffle of the Shadow Cabinet.

Not for the first time, I found the press more optimistic about my prospects than I was. The *Sunday Express* and the *Observer* on 3 November ran stories that I was to be appointed Shadow Chancellor. This was a nice thought and I would have loved the job; but I regarded it as extremely unlikely that Ted would give it to me. That was more or less confirmed by stories in the *Financial Times* and the *Daily Mirror* on the Monday which said that I would get a top economic job, but not the Shadow Chancellorship. And so indeed it turned out. I was appointed Robert Carr's deputy with special responsibility for the Finance Bill and also made a member of the Steering Committee. Some of my friends were annoyed that I had not received a more important portfolio. But I knew from the years when I worked under Iain Macleod on the Finance Bill that this was a position in which I could make the most of my talents. What neither Ted nor I knew was just how important that would be over the next three months. The reshuffle as a whole demonstrated something of the weakness of Ted's political stand-ing. Edward du Cann refused to join the Shadow Cabinet, which was therefore no more attractive to the right of the Party, some of whom at least Ted needed to win over. Tim Raison and Nicholas Scott who did come in were more or less on the left and, though able, not people who carried great political weight.

The re-election of all the members of the 1922 Executive, includ-ing Edward du Cann, on the day of the reshuffle – Thursday 7 November – was bad news for Ted. A leadership contest could no longer be avoided. He wrote to Edward saying that he was now willing to discuss changes to the procedure for electing the Party

Leader. From now on it was probably in Ted's interest to have the election over as soon as possible, before any alternative candidate could put together an effective campaign.

At this time I started to attend the Economic Dining Group which Nick Ridley had formed in 1972 and which largely consisted of sound money men like John Biffen, Jock Bruce-Gardyne, John Nott and others. Above all, I buried myself in the details of my new brief. It was a challenging time to take it up, for on Tuesday 12 November Denis Healey introduced one of his quarterly Budgets. It was a panic reaction to the rapidly growing problems of industry and consisted of cuts in business taxation to the tune of £775 million (£495 million of new business taxes having been imposed only six months before) and some curbs on subsidies to nationalized industries. Ted's reply – in which, against the background of an audible gasp from Tory backbenchers, he criticized the Chancellor for allowing nationalized industry prices to rise towards market levels – did him no good at all.

My chance came the following Thursday when I spoke for the Opposition in the Budget Debate. I had done my homework and I set about contrasting the Labour Government's past statements with its present actions. Some of the speech was quite technical and detailed, as it had to be. But it was my answers to the interruptions which had the backbenchers roaring support. I was directly answering Harold Lever (without whom Labour would have been still more economically inept) when he interrupted early in my speech to put me right on views I had attributed to him. Amid a good deal of merriment, not least from Harold Lever himself, a shrewd businessman from a wealthy family, I replied: 'I always felt that I could never rival him [Lever] at the Treasury because there are four ways of acquiring money. To make it. To earn it. To marry it. And to borrow it. He seems to have experience of all four.'

At another point I was interrupted by a pompously irate Denis Healey when I quoted the *Sunday Telegraph* which reported him as saying: 'I never save. If I get any money I go out and buy something for the house.' Denis Healey was most indignant, so I was pleased to concede the point, saying (in reference to the fact that like other socialist politicians he had his own country house): 'I am delighted that we have got on record the fact that the Chancellor is a jolly good saver. I know that he believes in buying houses in good Tory areas.'

No one has ever claimed that House of Commons repartee must be subtle in order to be effective. This performance boosted the shaky morale of the Parliamentary Party and with it my reputation.

Meanwhile, Alec Douglas-Home, now returned to the Lords as Lord Home, had agreed to chair a review of the procedure for the Leadership election. On Wednesday 20 November I received a note from Geoffrey Finsberg, a neighbouring MP and friend, which said: 'If you contest the leadership you will almost certainly win – for my part I hope you will stand and I will do all I can to help.' But I still could not see any likelihood of this happening. It seemed to me that for all of the brouhaha caused by his Edgbaston speech Keith must be our candidate.

The following afternoon I was working in my room in the House, briefing myself on the Finance Bill, when the telephone rang. It was Keith to check I was there because he had something he wanted to come along and tell me. As soon as he entered, I could see it was serious. He told me: 'I am sorry, I just can't run. Ever since I made that speech the press have been outside the house. They have been merciless. Helen [his wife] can't take it and I have decided that I just can't stand.'

There was no mistaking his mood. His mind was quite made up. I was on the edge of despair. We just could not abandon the Party and the country to Ted's brand of politics. I heard myself saying: 'Look, Keith, if you're not going to stand, I will, because someone who represents our viewpoint *has* to stand.'

There was nothing more to say. My mind was already a whirl. I had no idea of my chances. I knew nothing about leadership campaigns. I just tried to put the whole thing to the back of my mind for the moment and concentrate on the Finance Bill. Somehow or other the news got out and I started to receive telephone calls and notes of support from MP friends. Late that night I went back to Flood Street and told Denis of my intention.

'You must be out of your mind,' he said. 'You haven't got a hope.' He had a point. But I never had any doubt that he would support me all the way.

The following day Fergus Montgomery telephoned me, and I told him that Keith was not going to stand but that I would. I wondered how best to break the news to Ted. Fergus thought I should see him personally. I spent the weekend at Lamberhurst retreating from the press comment and speculation which now swirled about. There was plenty to think about. The main thing was that though I had few ideas about how to proceed, I was sure my reaction to Keith had been the right one. Ted had to go, and that meant that someone had to challenge him. If he won, I was politically finished. That would be sad but bearable; there are worse places than the backbenches. And it seemed to me most unlikely that I *would* win. But I did think that by entering the race, I would draw in other stronger candidates who, even if they did not think like Keith and me, would still be open to persuasion about changing the disastrous course on which the Party was set.

I arranged to see Ted on Monday 25 November. He was at his desk in his room at the House. I need not have worried about hurting his feelings. I went in and said: 'I must tell you that I have decided to stand for the leadership.' He looked at me coldly, turned his back, shrugged his shoulders and said: 'If you must.' I slipped out of the room.

Monday was, therefore, the first day I had to face the press as a declared contender for the Tory Leadership. I was glad to be able to rely on the help and advice of Gordon Reece, who had now become a friend and who sat in on some of my early press interviews, which went quite well. It was, of course, still the fact that I was a woman that was the main topic of interest. The evening was spent in the somewhat tense and awkward circumstances of Shadow Cabinet and the Steering Committee. Looking around the table, I felt that apart from Keith I would find few supporters here. I suspect that it was only due to the fact that they considered my decision ridiculous that there was not more open hostility. No such inhibitions were evident when I attended the Conservative Board of Finance shortly afterwards. I felt like the female equivalent of 'the man who said he wanted to be Tory Leader', with enraged colonels and indignant dowagers exploding about him in one of Bateman's more excruciating cartoons.

Ted's *coterie* and, I believe, at least one Central Office figure had in any case alighted on something which they hoped would destroy me as effectively as had happened to Keith. In the interview I had given to *Pre-Retirement Choice* more than two months before I had given what I considered to be practical advice to elderly people trying to make ends meet in circumstances where food prices were rising sharply. I said that it made sense to stock up on tinned food. This was precisely the sort of advice I myself had been given as a girl. Any good housewife shops around and buys several items at a time when prices are low, rather than dashing out at the last minute to buy the same thing at a greater cost.

But to my horror the press on Wednesday 27 November was full of stories of my 'hoarding' food. Someone had clearly used this obscure interview in order to portray me as mean, selfish and above all 'bourgeois'. In its way it was cleverly done. It allowed the desired caricature to be brought out to the full. It played to the snobbery of the Conservative Party, because the unspoken implication was that this was all that could be expected of a grocer's daughter. It reminded the public of all that had been said and written about me as the 'milk snatcher' at Education.

A veritable circus of indignation was now staged. Pressure groups were prompted to complain. A deputation of housewives was said to be travelling from Birmingham to urge me to give them the tins. Food chemists gave their views about the consequences of keeping tinned food too long in the larder. Martin Redmayne, the former Chief Whip, reliable Party establishment figure and now Deputy Chairman of Harrods, appeared on television to say that 'any sort of inducement to panic buying was . . . against the public interest' – although Lord Redmayne's larder probably contained something more enticing than a few tins of salmon and corned beef. There was nothing for it but to invite the cameramen in and have them check the contents of my Flood Street larder and cupboards. This may have convinced some of the Tory hierarchy that my and my family's tastes and standards were not at all what should be expected from someone who aspired to lead their party. But it certainly showed that the 'hoarding' allegation was malicious nonsense.

Finally, in order to keep the dying story alive my opponents went too far. On Friday 29 November I was in John Cope's South

Gloucestershire constituency when my secretary, Alison Ward, telephoned to say that the radio was now broadcasting that I had been seen in a shop on the Finchley Road buying up large quantities of sugar. (There was a sugar shortage at the time.) Alison had already checked and discovered that in fact no such shop existed; in any case the family consumption of sugar was minimal. It was just a straightforward lie. A firm denial prevented its circulation in the press, and marked the effective end of this surreal campaign.

I suspect that it ultimately backfired. It demonstrated to women throughout the country how ignorant male politicians were about what constituted ordinary housekeeping. It showed many people from modest backgrounds like mine how close to the surface of the Tory grandees lay an ugly streak of contempt for those they considered voting fodder. Most seriously for my opponents, it evoked a good deal of sympathy from fair-minded Conservative MPs who could see that I had been made the target of false and silly attacks.

At the time, however, I was bitterly upset by it. Sometimes I was near to tears. Sometimes I was shaking with anger. But as I told Bill Shelton, the MP for Streatham and a friend: 'I saw how they destroyed Keith. Well, they're not going to destroy me.'

What had happened made me all the more determined to throw my hat into the ring. But there was also much talk of Edward du Cann's putting himself forward as a candidate. As Chairman of the 1922 Committee – and a man – he might reasonably be expected to command more support than me. On Thursday 5 December, with the hoarding story having more or less run its course, I was in Robert Adley's constituency of Christchurch for a Party function. He was a great du Cann supporter and told me that he thought Edward was going to stand. I said that if he did, I would have to think again about my position. We must not split the right-wing vote.

One of Edward du Cann's chief supporters, Airey Neave, the MP for Abingdon and a colleague of Edward's on the 1922 Executive, was someone whom I already knew quite well. Our paths had crossed many times. As barristers we had shared the same Chambers, and he had been a neighbour at Westminster Gardens. When I was Opposition Social Security spokesman I had helped him with his Bill to make provision for pensions for the over-eighties. We both had a strong interest in science. As Secretary of State for Education and Science I had helped persuade Airey to stay on as Chairman of the Select Committee on Science and Technology when he was thinking of resigning.

Airey was a man of contrasts. His manner was quiet yet entirely self-assured. As a writer and a war hero who escaped from Colditz there was an air of romance about him. He had seen much more of the world than most MPs, and suffered a good deal too. He had the benefit, in Diana, of a marvellous political wife who backed him loyally. He had briefly been a junior minister in the late 1950s but had to resign because of ill health, and I understand Ted had unfeelingly told him that that was the end of his career. It was difficult to pin down Airey's politics. I did not consider him ideologically a man of the right. He probably did not look at the world in those terms. We got on well and I was conscious of mutual respect, but we were not yet the close friends we were to become.

Airey had come to see me shortly after my decision to stand was known. He hoped to persuade Edward du Cann to stand, but Edward himself remained undecided. Excluded by Ted from high office, he had devoted himself to a City career he was now reluctant to give up. Until Edward decided one way or the other it was not, of course, possible for Airey to support me actively, but I knew that I could rely on his advice and he promised to stay in touch, which we did: he came to my room in the House to exchange notes on several occasions between then and the end of the year. The whole 'hoarding' episode certainly demonstrated how tough a battle I could expect. If I did finally and formally enter the lists, Airey was the sort of person it would be good to have on my side.

A new factor that weakened Ted and strengthened his potential rivals was the announcement of the Home Committee's conclusions on Tuesday 7 December. There would be annual elections for the Tory Leader, challengers needed only a proposer and a seconder to put themselves forward, and the majority required to win on the first ballot was significantly increased to 50 per cent plus 15 per cent of those eligible to vote. It was in effect an incentive to challengers, since it meant that a Leader in difficulties needed to retain the confidence of a super-majority of those voting.

Still, Christmas at Lamberhurst that year was less festive than on some other occasions. We could not even walk as much as we usually did; the weather was awful. I knew that I could expect a trying time when I returned to Westminster, whether I actually stood for the Leadership or not. Denis also had business worries because Burmah Oil had run into deep trouble. Neither of us was too confident about what the future held.

SMALL EARTHQUAKE IN WESTMINSTER

On my return to London I resolved to clarify matters as regards the leadership. I invited Airey to lunch at Flood Street to have a proper discussion. I also found waiting for me a letter from Robert Adley urging that Edward du Cann and I should sort out which of us should stand rather than split the vote. The trouble was that this was impossible until Edward knew what he wanted to do, and it was clear from a conversation with him that he remained undecided. This was still the case when Airey and I had our lunch on Thursday 9 January 1975. I told him that I thought Geoffrey Howe might support me. I also told him how impossible proper discussion was under Ted's chairmanship. Airey gave me his own account of his recent talks with Ted. It was clear to both of us that there had to be a change, and the only question was whether Edward du Cann or I was better placed to effect it. Interestingly and shrewdly, as it turned out, Airey thought that Ted's support in the Parliamentary Party was overrated.

On Wednesday 15 January Edward du Cann made it publicly known that he would not run for the leadership. The way was therefore open for me. It was now vitally necessary to have an effective campaign team.

Events began to move fast. That same afternoon I was leading for the Opposition on the Committee Stage of the Finance Bill. Fergus had just learned that he would have to go on a parliamentary visit to South Africa, though he still thought (wrongly as it turned out) that he would be back in time for the leadership first ballot. He therefore asked Bill Shelton, when they met in the

Division Lobby, to run my campaign in his absence, and Bill agreed. I was delighted when Bill told me, for I knew he was loyal and would be a skilful campaigner. Then, as I learned later, in the course of a subsequent vote Airey approached Bill and said: 'You know that I have been running Edward du Cann's campaign? Edward is withdrawing. If we could come to some agreement I will bring Edward's troops behind Margaret.' In fact, the 'agreement' simply consisted of Airey taking over the running of my campaign with Bill assisting him.

This arrangement was confirmed when Airey came up to see me in my room, and we performed a diplomatic minuet. Slightly disingenuously, he asked me who was running my campaign. Hardly less so, I replied that I didn't really have a campaign. Airey said: 'I think I had better do it for you.' I agreed with enthusiasm. I knew that this meant he would swing as many du Cann supporters as possible behind me. Suddenly much of the burden of worry I had been carrying around fell away. From now on Airey, with Bill as his chief lieutenant, went to work quietly and remorselessly on their colleagues to win me support.

When I began to make suggestions to Airey about people to contact, he told me firmly not to bother about any of that, to leave it to him and to concentrate on my work on the Finance Bill. This was good advice, not least because both in the upstairs Committee Room and on the floor of the Chamber I had every opportunity to show my paces. It was, after all, the members of the Parliamentary Conservative Party who would ultimately make the decision about the Conservative leadership, and they were just as likely to be impressed by what I said in debate as by anything else. The campaign team began as a small group of about half a dozen, though it swelled rapidly and by the second ballot had become almost too large, consisting of as many as forty or fifty. Canvassing was done with great precision, and MPs might be approached several times by different people in order to verify their allegiances. Airey and his colleagues knew that there was no short cut to this process, and day after day it went on, with Bill Shelton crossing off names and keeping the tally. From time to time Airey would report to me on the position, though with the caveats which any shrewd canvasser always adds. The campaign group would also come to Flood Street, usually on the Sunday, to discuss with me articles, speeches and other initiatives for the week.

During these early days I was encouraged by the number of backbenchers who came up to offer me their support. One of the first was Peter Morrison, later to become my PPS at Downing Street, who told me that three years earlier his father, Lord Margadale, a former Chairman of the 1922 Committee, had said of me: 'That woman will be the next leader of the Tory Party.' This may be the first recorded instance of the phrase 'that woman'.

Meanwhile, dealings with the media were suddenly becoming important. In these Gordon Reece was invaluable. Angus Maude, a journalist who combined profound insights with pithy wit and who had been unceremoniously sacked from the front bench by Ted for writing a critical article in the *Spectator* in 1966, helped me with the crucial *Daily Telegraph* article called 'My Kind of Tory Party'. (I also received useful advice from a group of *Telegraph* journalists such as Peter Utley, John O'Sullivan and Frank Johnson – and of course Alfred Sherman – who were advocates of my cause in spite of their newspaper giving Ted reluctant endorsement.) George Gardiner, who was one of the February 1974 intake of MPs, a journalist himself and as editor of *Conservative News* party to some of the Central Office gossip, also helped me with drafting. It was a lively team.

In fact, the attitude towards my candidature was tangibly changing. I spoke on Tuesday 21 January to a lunch in St Stephen's Tavern of the Guinea Club, consisting of leading national and provincial newspaper journalists. By this time as a result of the soundings Airey had taken I was actually beginning to feel that I was in with a chance. I said to them wryly at one point: 'You know, I really think you should begin to take me seriously.' They looked back in amazement, and perhaps some of them soon started to do so. For by the weekend articles had begun to appear reappraising my campaign in a different light.

Nor were my prospects harmed by another exchange in the Commons the following day with the ever-obliging Denis Healey. In bitter but obscure vein he described me as the '*La Pasionaria* of privilege'. I jotted down a reply and delivered it a few moments later with relish: 'Some Chancellors are microeconomic. Some

Chancellors are fiscal. This one is just plain cheap.' The Tory benches loved it.

With just a week to go, Airey, Keith and Bill came round to Flood Street on Sunday 26 January to discuss the latest position. The number of pledges – mine at around 120 and Ted's less than eighty – looked far too optimistic. People would need to be revisited and their intentions re-examined. Presumably the Heath campaign, in which Peter Walker and Ted's PPSs Tim Kitson and Ken Baker were the main figures, was receiving equally or even more optimistic information; but they made the mistake of believing it. Certainly, in marked contrast to Airey's public demeanour, they were loudly predicting a large victory on the first ballot.

At Flood Street it was agreed that I should address my core campaigners in Committee Room 13 on Monday night. I could not tell them anything about campaigning. They had forgotten far more about political tactics and indeed political skulduggery than I would ever know. So instead I spoke and answered questions on my vision of a Conservative society from 10.30 till midnight. It was marvellous to be able to speak from the heart about what I believed, and to feel that those crucial to my cause were listening. Apparently my audience felt the same way; several MPs told me that they had never heard any senior Tory discuss policy in such philosophical terms. Plainly it was not I alone who was dispirited by the directionless expediency of the previous few years.

The Heath camp now changed the direction of their campaign, but still failed to get to the point. Ridicule had failed. Instead, the accusation became that the sort of Conservatism I represented might appeal to the middle-class rank and file supporters of the Party, particularly in the South, but would never win over the uncommitted. My article in the *Daily Telegraph*, which appeared on Thursday 30 January, took this head-on:

I was attacked [as Education Secretary] for fighting a rearguard action in defence of 'middle-class interests'. The same accusation is levelled at me now, when I am leading Conservative opposition to the socialist Capital Transfer Tax proposals. Well, if 'middle-class values' include the encouragement of variety and individual choice, the provision of fair incentives and rewards for skill and hard work, the maintenance of effective barriers against the excessive power of the state and a belief in the wide distribution of individual *private* property, then they are certainly what I am trying to defend . . . If a Tory does not believe that private property is one of the main bulwarks of individual freedom, then he had better become a socialist and have done with it. Indeed one of the reasons for our electoral failure is that people believe too many Conservatives *have* become socialists already. Britain's progress towards socialism has been an alternation of two steps forward with half a step back . . . And why should anyone support a party that seems to have the courage of no convictions?

This theme – the return to fundamental Conservative principles and the defence of middle-class values – was enormously popular in the Party. I repeated it when speaking to my Constituency Association the following day. I rejected the idea that my candidature was representative of a faction. I emphasized that I was speaking up for all those who felt let down by recent Conservative Governments. I was also prepared to accept my share of the blame for what had gone wrong under Ted.

But [I added] I hope I have learned something from the failures and mistakes of the past and can help to plan constructively for the future . . . There is a widespread feeling in the country that the Conservative Party has not defended [Conservative] ideals explicitly and toughly enough, so that Britain is set on a course towards inevitable socialist mediocrity. That course must not only be halted, it must be reversed.

It was in an open letter to the Chairman of my constituency released on Saturday afternoon, however, that I really summed up the gravamen of the charge against Ted and his leadership. Ted was a political paradox. He combined a belief in strong leadership (especially his own) with a record of buckling under the pressure of events. He was always talking about reaching out to win over the support of people from other parties, but he had no willingness to listen to the Conservative Party. By contrast, I said that what

was required was a 'leadership that listens', adding that 'in office
. . . we allowed ourselves to become detached from many who had
given us their support and trust'.

I knew from my talks with Conservative MPs that there were
many contradictory factors which would influence their votes. Some
would support Ted simply because he was the Leader *in situ*. Many
would not dare go against him because, even after two successive
election defeats, he inspired fear that there would be no forgiveness
for mutiny. Moreover, many thought that I was inexperienced –
and as I had publicly admitted, there was more than a little truth
in that. There was also some suspicion of me as too doctrinaire
and insensitive. And then, of course, there was the rather obvious
fact that I was a woman.

As a result of these conflicting considerations, many MPs were
undecided. They wanted to be able to talk to me, to find out what
I was like and where I stood. Airey and his team would send these
Members along to see me in the room of Robin Cooke – one of our
team – in the House where, singly or in small groups, over a glass
of claret or a cup of tea, I would try to answer their points as best
I could. Ted, by contrast, preferred lunch parties of MPs where,
I suspect, there was not much straight talking – at least not from
the guests. Doubtless his campaign team marked them down as
supporters, which many were not.

The press on Monday 3 February was full of the fact that the
National Union of the Party had reported that 70 per cent of Constituency Associations favoured Ted Heath and that the great
majority of Conservative supporters agreed with them. We were
not surprised by this. The Conservative Associations, nudged by
Central Office, were understandably loyal to the existing Leader:
and the opinion poll results reflected the fact that I was a relatively
unknown quantity outside the House of Commons. But obviously
it did not help, and it certainly boosted confidence in the Heath
camp. Indeed, there was evidence of a late surge of support for
Ted among MPs. Airey's and Bill's final canvass returns suggested
that I was neck and neck with Ted, with the third candidate, the
gallant and traditionalist Hugh Fraser, picking up a few right-wing
misogynist votes. But I was told that I came over quite well on
the *World in Action* television programme that night.

On Tuesday 4 February, the day of the first ballot, I was up early to prepare Denis's breakfast and see him off to work before driving from Flood Street to the House of Commons, exhibiting what I hoped was a confident smile and a few friendly words for the press gathered outside. For me it was another day on the Finance Bill Committee, while in another House of Commons Committee Room the voting for the leadership took place. The ballot was due to close at 3.30. I went up to Airey Neave's room to await the result. Bill Shelton represented me at the count and Tim Kitson represented Ted. I believe that even after they had heard the sombre news of the outcome of that day's voting the Heath camp had hoped that the proxy votes, counted last, would see Ted through. But most of the proxies also went to me. I was trying to concentrate on anything other than the future when the door opened and Airey came in. Softly, but with a twinkle in his eye, he told me: 'It's good news. You're ahead in the poll. You've got 130 votes to Ted's 119.' Hugh Fraser had sixteen.

I could barely believe it. Although I was thirty-one votes short of the required margin to win outright on the first ballot – 50 per cent plus a lead of 15 per cent of those eligible to vote – and therefore there would have to be a second round, I was nonetheless decisively ahead. I had no doubt that if I had failed against Ted that would have been the end of me in politics. As it was, I might be Leader. Who knows? I might even be Prime Minister. I went downstairs and someone opened some champagne. But I had to keep a clear head, for I was soon back to the Finance Bill amid a certain raillery from friends and opponents alike, for the news had spread like wildfire. Later that evening I went back to Airey's flat for a council of war.

My own surprise at the result was as nothing compared to the shattering blow it had delivered to the Conservative establishment. I felt no sympathy for them. They had fought me unscrupulously all the way. But I did feel sorry for Ted, who quickly announced his decision to resign as Leader and not to contest the second ballot. Willie Whitelaw now put his name forward and immediately became the favourite. I myself thought that Willie had a very good chance of winning; and though I could not seriously imagine him changing the direction of the Party as I wished, it did please me to think that between us there would be none of the bitterness which had soured my relations with Ted. Jim Prior, John Peyton and Geoffrey Howe also entered the contest. I was a little worried about Geoffrey's candidature because he held similar views to mine and might split the right-wing vote, which in a close contest could be crucial. Hugh Fraser withdrew and urged his supporters to vote for Willie.

In fact, without knowing it, I had what the Americans call 'momentum'. I had always reckoned that a substantial number of those voting for me in the first round would only do so as a tactical way of removing Ted and putting in someone more acceptable but still close to his way of thinking, such as Willie. But in fact, far from draining away, my support actually hardened. Perhaps there was an odd sense of gratitude to me for having done what no one else dared, that is to remove from the leadership someone who quite simply made the Party unelectable. Perhaps a sufficient number of my colleagues genuinely felt that the way forward for the Party was the root and branch reconsideration that Keith and I advocated. Perhaps there was a feeling that it was 'a bit offside' for those who had failed to challenge Ted when he looked unbeatable to step in to scoop up the prize once he had lost it. There were probably also doubts about whether Willie, for all his amiable qualities, was the right man to rethink Conservatism in the face of a Labour Government with a newly militant and aggressive left wing.

Certainly, many people in the Party at Westminster and outside it were now desperately anxious to bring the whole process to a swift end. The very circumstances which had counted against me in the first ballot now assisted me as the leading candidate in the second. The *Daily Telegraph*, an important barometer of Tory grassroots feeling, swung decisively onto my side. When I talked with Willie at a dinner organized by the British-American Parliamentary Group at Lancaster House on Thursday 6 February he seemed fairly confident that he was the front-runner. The new canvass returns which Airey and his team were making strongly suggested otherwise. But I was cautious. There had been some whispers that I was secretly anti-Common Market, which it was thought might damage me. So at George Gardiner's suggestion I made a short statement of my views endorsing Europe. I also continued to see – and sometimes communicate by note with – MPs who needed reassurance on particular points.

Willie and I both attended the Young Conservative Conference at Eastbourne on Saturday 8 February. One woman on the platform was dressed in funereal black and glowering. I was rather concerned and asked her whether anything was wrong. 'Yes,' she said. 'I'm in mourning for Mr Heath.' There were few other mourners present. Willie and I were photographed as we kissed for the cameras. I remarked: 'Willie and I have been friends for years. I've done that to Willie many times and he to me. It was not that difficult for him to do it, I think.' Willie replied: 'I've kissed her often. But we have not done it on a pavement outside a hotel in Eastbourne before.' It was all good fun and the atmosphere lightened.

I used my own speech to the Conference to give a full-blooded rendering of my views. I said:

> You can get your economic policies right, and still have the kind of society none of us would wish. I believe we should judge people on merit and not on background. I believe the person who is prepared to work hardest should get the greatest rewards and keep them after tax. That we should back the workers and not the shirkers: that it is not only permissible but praiseworthy to want to benefit your own family by your own efforts.

Conservatives had not heard this sort of message for many years, and it went down well.

Airey, Keith, my other advisers and I looked at the situation after the first ballot. Our general approach was to concentrate on the electorate – the 276 Tory MPs – pointing out that I had already won a near majority of them, that I was pulling steadily away from the field and that my four rivals were fighting for second place. In these circumstances we felt that I had little to gain from debates with the other candidates. But a slight stir was created when I decided not to appear on *Panorama* with them. They went ahead without me. But this was *Hamlet* without a Princess. It merely emphasized my status as the front-runner.

And then on Tuesday the second ballot took place. Again I waited nervously in Airey's room. And again it was Airey who came to give me the news. This time it was subtly but decisively different. He smiled and said: 'You are now Leader of the Opposition.' I had obtained 146 votes to Willie's seventy-nine. The other candidates were out of the picture.*

I rapidly scribbled some thoughts in the back of my diary because I knew I would now have to go and give my first press conference as Party Leader. The first item was 'TED', because it was most important to pay tribute to his leadership.

I now had to hurry down to the Grand Committee Room, off Westminster Hall, where the press were waiting. I told them: 'To me it is like a dream that the next name in the lists after Harold Macmillan, Sir Alec Douglas-Home, Edward Heath, is Margaret Thatcher. Each has brought his own style of leadership and stamp of greatness to his task. I shall take on the work with humility and dedication.'

Then it was off for the Leader's traditional first visit to Conservative Central Office. On entering, I could not help remembering how hard some of the people there had worked to stop my becoming Leader. I shook hands with a line of Party officials, stopping to kiss Russell Lewis, the Conservative Political Centre Director who I knew had actually wanted me to win. I have no doubt there were many anxious thoughts behind the polite, smiling faces that evening. And not without reason. For though I was not interested in paying off old scores, I was already sure that changes must be made.

Then I was driven back to Bill Shelton's house in Pimlico for a celebration with my friends. Denis was there. I had tried to telephone the news through to him myself, but somehow the Press Association beat me to it. Mark learned the news while he was at work as a trainee accountant. As for Carol, she could not be disturbed until she had finished the solicitors' exam she was taking that afternoon.

Only much later that night, after I had returned from dinner with the Chief Whip, Humphrey Atkins, could all of the family

---

* Jim Prior and Geoffrey Howe had nineteen votes each and John Peyton eleven.

celebrate the good news. It was wonderful to be together. I suspect that they knew, as I did, that from this moment on our lives would never be quite the same again.

Nor would the Conservative Party, as a perceptive leader in the *Daily Telegraph* the following morning observed:

> What kind of leadership Mrs Thatcher will provide remains to be seen . . . But one thing is clear enough at this stage. Mrs Thatcher is a bonny fighter. She believes in the ethic of hard work and big rewards for success. She has risen from humble origins by effort and ability and courage. She owes nothing to inherited wealth or privilege. She ought not to suffer, therefore, from that fatal and characteristic twentieth-century Tory defect of guilt about wealth. All too often this has meant that the Tories have felt themselves to be at a moral disadvantage in the defence of capitalism against social-ism. This is one reason why Britain has travelled so far down the collectivist road. What Mrs Thatcher ought to be able to offer is the missing *moral* dimension to the Tory attack on socialism. If she does so, her accession to the leadership could mark a sea-change in the whole character of the party political debate in this country.

It was a mighty challenge. At the time I did not realize how mighty.

CHAPTER IX

A Bumpy Ride

Leader of the Opposition February 1975–March 1977

SHADOW CABINET-MAKING

My first task was to compose the Shadow Cabinet. I met Humphrey Atkins, the Chief Whip, in the Leader of the Opposition's room in the House of Commons where we had an excellent dinner prepared by his wife Maggie. Humphrey Atkins had, of course, been Ted's appointment, and occupying the position he did had not declared his support for one side or the other in the leadership contest. But he was amiable and amenable and, as Chief Whip, was possessed of the unique fund of knowledge and gossip so essential when making high political appointments. I told Humphrey that although there were some people, like Keith Joseph and Airey Neave, to whom I felt a special obligation, I did not want to make a clean sweep of the existing team. After the bitterness of the contest with Ted there had to be sufficient continuity to keep the Party together.

The more we talked, however, the clearer it became to both of us that all the other dispositions depended upon Ted. If he wished to serve under my leadership – and I had publicly committed myself to offering him the opportunity during the leadership campaign – he might decide that he wanted one of the three main Shadow posts, or possibly a post without portfolio. In fact, I privately hoped that he would not take up my offer at all. Although none of us knew how enduring his sense of injury would be, it was already hard to imagine Ted behaving like Alec Douglas-Home and fitting in as a loyal and distinguished member of his successor's team. In any case, the newspapers were saying that Ted had no intention of serving. But I had to know for myself. I had thought of going to see him that evening, but all things considered it seemed better that Humphrey should make the first approach. Having sounded Ted out and received the impression that the speculation about his intentions was accurate, Humphrey reported back to me. But I had said I would make the offer, and the following morning I was driven to Ted's house in Wilton Street to do it in person.

Tim Kitson, Ted's PPS, showed me into the downstairs study, facing onto the garden. Ted was sitting at his desk. He did not get up; and I sat down without waiting to be asked. There was no point in pleasantries. I could guess what he thought about recent events and about me. Without offering a specific post, I asked him whether he would join the Shadow Cabinet. He said no, he would stay on the backbenches. The interview was effectively at an end. For my part, I had no wish to prolong the meeting. I knew that it must be painful and probably humiliating for him. But I also knew that if I walked out of Wilton Street past the assembled press after just a few minutes, the lunchtime news would be dominated by stories of snubs and splits. Also, I had not finished my coffee. So I spun things out a little by asking his views about Labour's promised referendum on Britain's continuing membership of the European Economic Community and, in particular, whether he would lead the Conservative campaign.* Again, he said no. I had done all I decently could to keep Ted within the fold and to ensure the meeting did not end too abruptly. But only five minutes or so had elapsed when I left Ted's study. So Tim Kitson (who was equally aware of the risk of bad publicity) and I talked inconsequentially for another quarter of an hour to fill out the time before I left the house. Respecting, as I thought, Ted's confidence, I did not even tell Airey Neave, who was setting up my office, the details of what had transpired. I made it public later only in order to set the record straight.** I returned to the House of Commons and told Humphrey Atkins that Ted would indeed not be in the Shadow Cabinet.

Next, Robert Carr, who had been acting Leader of the Party

* For the referendum see pp. 330–5.
** See pp. 335–6

during the leadership campaign, wanted to see me. He had, of course, been close to Ted and was identified with the corporatist tendency in the Party. I could well understand if he did not relish the prospect of serving under me. In fact, when I saw him he made it quite clear that the only post he would accept was that of Shadow Foreign Secretary. I said that I could not promise him that. Not only was I unwilling to have my hands tied before I had properly considered the shape of the team as a whole: I was not convinced that Robert Carr would have a place in it.

By contrast, Willie Whitelaw definitely had. He had demonstrated his popularity in the leadership election. He was immensely experienced and his presence would be a reassuring guarantee to many on the backbenches that evolution rather than revolution was the order of the day. Perhaps both of us already sensed that we could form a strong political partnership, our strengths and weaknesses complementing one another's. Although I could not as yet offer him a particular portfolio, I asked Willie to be Deputy Leader of the Party, and he accepted. But his loyalty was not contingent on that; he was loyal from the first.

There was much male chauvinist hilarity – 'Give us a kiss, Maggie,' etc. – when I came into the Chamber to hear the Prime Minister, Harold Wilson, make a statement. I took my place on the front bench between Willie and Robert Carr. Jim Prior, Geoffrey Howe and John Peyton – the other defeated leadership candidates – were also there, though Ted was not. I received the wittily barbed congratulations of the Prime Minister and replied somewhat less wittily to them. Harold Wilson was at his still incomparable best in the House. As I listened, I reflected that as a new Leader of a shaken and still badly split party, and as a woman striving for dominance in this noisy, boisterous, masculine world, I could expect difficulties ahead. And so it proved.

That evening I chaired the Shadow Cabinet for the first time. The meeting had a slightly unreal atmosphere since none of those present had yet been formally reappointed, and some would not be. Quintin Hailsham congratulated me on the Shadow Cabinet's behalf and pledged their loyalty and cooperation. I felt that he at least probably meant it. I said that Willie had agreed to be Deputy Leader and that Ted had turned down my offer of a place in the

Shadow Cabinet. Willie then said that he had accepted the Deputy Leadership at once and looked forward to serving in this capacity. The formalities thus indicated a kind of armed truce between the competing views and personalities.

The following evening, I made my first appearance as Leader at the 1922 Committee meeting. My relations with the wider Parliamentary Party were much easier than with the Shadow Cabinet. As I entered, everyone rose to their feet. Edward du Cann presented me with an unsigned Valentine card (a day early) which would join the other Valentines and roses that accumulated at Flood Street. In addressing the 1922 Committee it is the Leader's mood and bearing rather than the content of a speech which matter most. But they seemed to like the message as well – namely, the need to distinguish the Conservative approach clearly from that of the socialists, to return to traditional values of independence and self-help and to challenge the assumption that the onward march of the Left was irreversible. I sat down amid much clapping, banging of desks and that curious deep braying with which the Parliamentary Conservative Party expresses its approval.

In the next few days my time was taken up in meeting journalists, discussing arrangements for my office and fulfilling long-standing constituency engagements. There were few opportunities to sit down with Humphrey and Willie to discuss Shadow Cabinet membership. In any case, I wanted the weekend to make my final decisions. But the delay encouraged speculation. According to the press a battle was under way to prevent Keith Joseph becoming Shadow Chancellor. In fact, he did not ask for the position nor did I offer it.

My Shadow Cabinet-making was smoothed by the fact that Peter Thomas and Geoffrey Rippon made it clear that they did not want to continue. That meant two more vacancies to play with. I spent Saturday and Sunday at Flood Street making and remaking the list, consulting Humphrey or Willie on particular points. On Monday I made the appointments in a series of meetings with colleagues at my room in the Commons.

Willie was the first to come in. I gave him a roving brief which included the issue of devolution – which already spelt political difficulties he, as both a former Chief Whip and a Scot representing an English seat, might be able to tackle. Then I saw Keith Joseph, whom I asked to continue with his Shadow Cabinet responsibility for policy and research. In a sense, Willie and Keith were the two key figures, one providing the political brawn and the other the policy-making brains of the team. I also felt that Keith must continue his intellectual crusade from the Centre for Policy Studies for wider understanding and acceptance of free-enterprise economics. I was under no illusion that my victory in the leadership election represented a wholesale conversion. Our ability to change Party policy, as the first step towards making changes in government, depended upon using our positions to change minds. Unfortunately, on his forays into the universities Keith was to find a readier hearing from the Militant Tendency in his avowedly left-wing audiences than he would from the cynical tendency among his colleagues.

My next visitor was Reggie Maudling. I suspect that, although he had made it clear publicly that he was willing to serve, he was as surprised as the press when I made him Shadow Foreign Secretary. Though widely praised at the time, this was not a good appointment. I had always admired Reggie's intellect and regretted that he had had to resign over the Poulson affair in 1972. Also bringing Reggie back to deal with foreign affairs appeared a convincing answer to those who had contrasted Ted's experience with my own lack of it. But it soon became clear that Reggie was not prepared to modify his own views, a problem compounded by the fact that, more broadly, he had an only thinly disguised contempt for the monetarist approach which Keith and I wanted to pursue. I would have done better to appoint someone who shared my instincts on defence and foreign policy.

Still less of a soulmate was Ian Gilmour. I suspect that when he learned that I wanted to see him he expected the worst. He had been a strong partisan of Ted, and he lacked the support or standing which might have made him politically costly to dispense with. But I valued his intelligence. I felt that he could make a useful contribution as long as he was kept out of an economic post, to which in spite of his later reputation as one of the foremost advocates of 'reflation' neither his training nor his aptitudes suited him. I asked him to be Shadow Home Secretary.

Michael Heseltine, who now came in to see me, had a much more flamboyant personality than Ian's, although they shared many of the same views. He too had long been a Heath supporter, but it had always been assumed that the cause he most strongly advocated was his own. My campaign team believed him to have been an abstainer in the first round of the leadership contest. To do Michael credit, he was always refreshingly open about his ambitions. I asked him to stay on as Shadow Industry Secretary. It was a portfolio which fascinated him and which gave full scope to his talent for Opposition, since it fell to him to fight the Labour Government's main nationalization proposals. What I did not fully grasp at this time was how ideologically committed he was to an interventionist approach in industry which I could not accept.

After a lunchtime meeting of small businessmen at the National Chamber of Trade, where I made my first public speech as Leader, I returned to my room at the House for more Shadow Cabinet carpentry. I asked Peter Carrington to stay on as Leader of the House of Lords. Again, I had no illusions about Peter's position in the Tory Party's political spectrum: he was not of my way of thinking. He had, of course, been in Ted's inner circle making the political decisions about the miners' strike and the February 1974 election. But since we lost office he had proved an extremely effective Opposition Leader in the Upper House, and as a former Defence Minister and an international businessman he had wide experience of foreign affairs. Admittedly, he was likely in Shadow Cabinet to be on the opposite side to me on economic policy. But he never allowed economic disagreements to get in the way of his more general responsibilities. He brought style, experience, wit and – politically incorrect as the thought may be – a touch of class.

Geoffrey Howe had his own droll wit. But in most other ways he was a very different politician from my other appointments that day. I would in any case have felt obliged to give Geoffrey a Shadow Cabinet post, simply because he was a candidate against me and I wished to unify the Party as much as possible. But it was a calculated gamble to make him Shadow Chancellor. I knew that as an immensely hard-working lawyer he would make the effort required to master his brief. I also knew that, in spite of his role in implementing the Heath Government's prices and incomes policy as Minister for Trade and Consumer Affairs, he had a well-deserved reputation as a believer in free-market economics. As such, he was very much a rarity in the upper ranks of the Conservative Party. Once I had decided that Keith would be better employed overseeing policy rethinking, Geoffrey seemed the best candidate. Very few who come new to such a demanding portfolio find it trouble-free. Geoffrey was to have a difficult time both trying to resolve our divisions on economic policy and in defending our case in the House. I would be put under a good deal of pressure to remove him and find someone better able to take on the Chancellor, Denis Healey. But I knew that Geoffrey's difficulties, like mine, were more the result of circumstances than lack of native talent. By the time our period in Opposition was approaching its end he had become indispensable.

After careful thought I decided to keep Jim Prior as Shadow Employment Secretary. This was rightly taken as a signal that I had no immediate plans for a fundamental reform of trade union law. Jim's suitability for the job is only understandable in the light of the Heath Government's poisoned legacy. In the 1972 Industrial Relations Act Ted had attempted the most far-reaching reforms of trade union law since 1906: its failure made Conservatives right across the Party very wary of pursuing the same course again. Moreover, after Ted had taken on the militants and lost in February 1974, the main question in the public's mind was whether *any* Conservative Government could establish a working relationship with the unions, which were now seen as having an effective veto on policy. It was Jim's strong conviction that our aim should be to establish both that we accepted the existing trade union law, with perhaps a few alterations, and that we saw the union leaders as people with whom we could deal.

Such an approach made more sense at the beginning of the period in Opposition than at the end of it. But in any case it left two important questions unanswered. First, how would we react if events demonstrated that the theoretical shortcomings of the present law, as amended by the socialists, were having malign practical effects? (The circumstances of the Grunwick dispute* and of the

* See pp. 397–403.

strikes of the winter of 1978/79 would demonstrate precisely that.) Secondly, since the trade union leaders were at least as much socialist politicians as they were workers' representatives, why should they cooperate willingly with Conservatives? There was a basic incompatibility between their economic approach and ours, and indeed between their political allegiance and ours. So how valuable would any amount of personal diplomacy between Jim and the TUC turn out to be? Probably not very. For the present, though, he was the right man in the right position.

Airey Neave had already privately told me that the only portfolio he wanted was that of Shadow Northern Ireland Secretary. His intelligence contacts, proven physical courage and shrewdness amply qualified him for this testing and largely thankless task.

The other appointments were less strategically crucial. Quintin Hailsham had no portfolio, but was in effect the Lord Chancellor in waiting. Francis Pym stayed on at Agriculture, though a few months later he had to give this up on health grounds. My old friend Patrick Jenkin I kept at Energy. Norman St John-Stevas, whom I had got to know from my days at the Department of Education and who was both a lively wit and one of my few open supporters on the second ballot of the leadership election, shadowed Education. Norman Fowler, a former journalist and a Member for the politically crucial West Midlands, came in as Shadow Social Services Secretary. I had no clear view about where precisely any of these stood in relation to the balance of opinion between left and right of the Party. But in appointing Tim Raison as Shadow Environment Secretary I knew that I was promoting someone associated with the left of centre, but who was tough-minded, thoughtful and knowledgeable about social policy in general. I believed he would be an asset. Two offers of Shadow Cabinet posts were turned down – one to John Biffen, who would in fact join later, and the other to Edward du Cann, whose early campaign team had provided the nucleus of mine. Edward stayed on as Chairman of the 1922 Committee, which was probably far more useful to me.

The next day (Tuesday) I had some less pleasant business to transact. At 10.30 Peter Walker came in. We had known each other since he had succeeded me as candidate for Dartford. But those

days were long gone and there was no personal warmth between
us. He had been one of the most effective members of Ted's inner
circle, and he opposed with vigour and eloquence the approach
which Keith and I were committed to adopt. He clearly had to go.
I found it a distasteful business breaking such news; over the years
it was one of the things I most dreaded. But at least Peter can
hardly have expected anything else. He became a consistent critic
on the backbenches.

I confirmed in a discussion with Geoffrey Rippon, who now came
into my room, that he did not wish to serve: that suited us both.
I then saw Nicholas Scott, who had shadowed Housing. He too
was on the left of the Party. The conversation was made slightly
easier by the fact that I had absorbed the Housing portfolio into
the wider Environment one. His job had been shot from under
him.

I left to last the interview with Robert Carr. I told him that I
had given the Shadow Foreign Secretary post to Reggie Maudling,
which he presumably knew already. Perhaps he had just bid too
high, or perhaps he might have been persuaded to stay in another
capacity. But I was not keen to have another strong opponent in
any position on the team. So I made it clear that I could not ask
him to be in the Shadow Cabinet. After a difficult few minutes he
left and told the press of his worries about 'those people who seem
to think [monetary policy] is some automatic mechanism'. Not too
many guesses were required about who 'those people' were.

The published Shadow Cabinet list (to which Peter Thorneycroft
as Party Chairman and Angus Maude as Chairman of the Conservative Research Department would later be added) was rightly
seen as a compromise. As such, it annoyed the left of the Party
who disliked my dropping of Robert Carr, Peter Walker and Nicholas Scott: it also disappointed the right who worried about Reggie
Maudling's return, the fact that Geoffrey and not Keith was
Shadow Chancellor and the lack of any new right-wing faces from
the backbenches. In fact, given the fragility as yet of my position
and the need to express a balance of opinion in the Shadow Cabinet
to bring the Party together, it was a relatively successful operation.
It created a Treasury team that shared my and Keith's views on
the free-market economy, shifted the balance of opinion within the

Shadow Cabinet as a whole somewhat in my direction, and yet gave grounds for loyalty to those I had retained from Ted's regime. I felt I could expect support (within limits) from such a team, but I knew I could not assume agreement – even on basic principles.

MACHINE POLITICS

It is said that when Ted Heath was offered a Junior Whip's job in 1950, he asked the advice of Lord Swinton, the Tory Party's elder statesman, as to whether he should accept it. 'Get in on the machine – at however squalid a level,' said Lord Swinton. Ted had taken this advice to heart, and I, in my still vulnerable position as head of the machine, could not afford to neglect it. So I set out to get some control of it.

Airey Neave and I decided that there would have to be changes at Conservative Central Office. Constitutionally, Central Office is the Leader of the Party's office: events during the leadership campaign had convinced me that it would be very difficult for some of those there to act in that capacity under me.

At Central Office I wanted as Chairman an effective administrator, one preferably with business connections, who would be loyal to me. I had always admired Peter Thorneycroft and in retrospect I thought that his courageous resignation on the issue of public expenditure in 1958 had signalled a wrong turning for the post-war Conservative Party. As part of that older generation which had been leading the Party when I first entered Parliament, and as chairman of several large companies, Peter seemed to me to fit the bill. But how to persuade him? It turned out that Willie Whitelaw was related to him, and Willie persuaded him to take the job. It would have taxed the energy of a much younger man, for the Party Chairman has to keep up morale even in the lowest periods, of which there would be several. Peter had the added problem that at this stage most of the Party in the country accepted my leadership only on sufferance. This would gradually change after the 1975 Party Conference. But it took a good deal longer – and some painful and controversial personnel changes – before I felt that the leading figures at Central Office had any real commitment to me. Peter gradually replaced them with loyalists; I never enquired how.

Alistair McAlpine's arrival as Party Treasurer certainly helped. The existing Treasurers, Lords Ashdown and Chelmer, told me that they had decided to resign. Airey Neave had suggested that Alistair, who had been Treasurer for 'Britain in Europe' during the referendum campaign, had the personality, energy and connections to do the job. He was right. Although a staunch Tory from a family of Tories, Alistair had to turn himself into something of a politician overnight. I told him that he would have to give up his German Mercedes for a British Jaguar and he immediately complied. But I had not prepared him for the host of minor but irritating examples of obstructive behaviour which confronted him at Central Office, nor for the great difficulties he would encounter in trying to persuade businessmen that in spite of the years of Heathite corporatism we were still a free-enterprise Party worth supporting.

Some people expected me to make even more substantial changes at the Conservative Research Department. The CRD was in theory a department of Central Office, but largely because of its geographical separateness (in Old Queen Street) and its intellectually distinguished past, it had a specially important role, particularly in Opposition. In a sense, the Centre for Policy Studies had been set up as an alternative to the Research Department. Now that I was Leader, however, the CRD and the CPS would have to work together. The Director of the Research Department, Chris Patten, I knew to be on the left of the Party. Much bitterness and rivalry had built up between the CRD and the CPS. In the eyes of many on the right it was precisely the consensus-oriented, generalist approach epitomized by the CRD which had left us directionless and – in the words of Keith Joseph – 'stranded on the middle ground'. I decided to replace Ian Gilmour with Angus Maude as Chairman of the Research Department, who would work with Keith on policy, but leave Chris Patten as Director and Adam Ridley, Ted's former economic adviser, as his deputy. These were good decisions. I came to have a high regard for the work of the department, particularly when it was fulfilling its role as Secretariat to the Shadow Cabinet rather than devising policy. Even though there were occasional squalls, the CRD moved further and further in the direction that Keith and I were taking.

Meanwhile, Airey Neave and I had to assemble a small personal staff who would run my office. The day after the leadership election result I met the secretaries who had worked for Ted. They were clearly upset, and I detected some hostility. This was quite understandable; indeed, I thought it a tribute to their loyalty. But I asked them to stay on if they felt able to, and most of them did, for a time at least. In those days the Leader of the Opposition had the present Home Secretary's office in the House. There was one large room with a small ante-room for two secretaries, and some other small rooms upstairs. There was not enough space, and as summer approached it all became very hot and airless. (It was only later in the summer of 1976 that we moved into the rather more spacious accommodation previously used as the flat of the Serjeant-at-Arms, where the secretaries I had inherited from Ted were joined by my lively and reliable constituency secretary Alison Ward.)

A flood of letters followed my becoming Leader, sometimes 800 a day. Girls would come across from Central Office to help sort out the post, but usually this was the task of my four secretaries, who sat on the floor in the main room opening envelopes and categorizing the letters. They did their best, but it was hopelessly unsystematic. Then Alistair McAlpine suggested that I ask David Wolfson to take charge of the correspondence section. Alistair thought that if David, as the man responsible for the mail-order section of Great Universal Stores, could not bring order out of this chaos no one could. In fact, both in Opposition and then at 10 Downing Street David's talents were put to a good deal wider use than sorting the mail: he gave insights into what business was thinking, provided important contacts and proved particularly adept at smoothing ruffled political feathers.

But I also needed a full-time head of my office, who had to be industrious, dependable and, with the number of speeches, articles and letters to draft, above all literate. It was my old friend and colleague, providentially translated to the editorship of the *Daily Telegraph*, Bill Deedes who suggested Richard Ryder, then working on Peterborough, the *Telegraph*'s respectable gossip column.

Richard joined me at the end of April – to begin work alongside Caroline Stephens, one of the secretaries I inherited from Ted, who would later become Caroline Ryder.

Richard Ryder ran this small office very effectively on a shoe-string. It was a happy ship, and some entertaining characters served on their way to better things. Matthew Parris, who was in charge of replying to my correspondence, showed a talent for the sketch-writing he was later to perform for *The Times* when, on the eve of the 1979 election campaign, answering an aggrieved letter from a woman rejecting our policy of selling council houses and simultaneously complaining about what was wrong with her own, he told her that she was fortunate to have been given a home paid for by the rest of us out of taxation. Like Queen Victoria, I was not amused – especially when the *Daily Mirror* published the letter at the very beginning of the campaign. But Matthew survived.

A month after Richard's arrival Gordon Reece, on secondment from EMI for a year, joined my full-time staff to help in dealing with the press and much else. Gordon was a Godsend. An ebullient former TV producer whose good humour never failed, he was able to jolly me along to accept things I would have rejected from other people. His view was that in getting my message across we must not concentrate simply on heavyweight newspapers, *The Times* and the *Daily Telegraph*, but be just as concerned about the mid-market populars, the *Daily Mail* and the *Daily Express* and – the real revolution – about the *Sun* and the *News of the World*. Moreover, he believed that even newspapers which supported the Labour Party in their editorial line would be prepared to give us fair treatment if we made a real attempt to provide them with interesting copy. He was right on both counts. The *Sun* and the *News of the World* were crucial in communicating Conservative values to traditionally non-Conservative voters. The left wing *Sunday Mirror* also gave me fair and full coverage, however critical the comments. Gordon regularly talked to the editors. But he also persuaded me that the person they really wanted to see and hear from was me. So, whatever the other demands on my diary, when Gordon said that we must have lunch with such-and-such an editor, that was the priority.

Gordon also performed another invaluable service. Every politician has to decide how much he or she is prepared to change manner and appearance for the sake of the media. It may sound grittily honourable to refuse to make any concessions, but such an attitude in a public figure is most likely to betray a lack of seriousness about winning power or even, paradoxically, the pride that apes humility. When Gordon suggested some changes in my style of hair and clothes in order to make a better impression, he was calling upon his experience in television. 'Avoid lots of jewellery near the face. Edges look good on television. Watch out for background colours which clash with your outfit.' It was quite an education.

There was also the matter of my voice. In the House of Commons one has to speak over the din to get a hearing. This is more difficult the higher the pitch of one's voice, because in increasing its volume one automatically goes up the register. This poses an obvious problem for most women. Somehow one has to learn to project the voice without shrieking. Even outside the House, when addressing an audience my voice was naturally high-pitched, which can easily become grating. I had been told about this in earlier years and had deliberately tried to lower its tone. The result, unfortunately, whatever improvement there may have been for the audience, was to give me a sore throat – an even greater problem for a regular public speaker. Gordon found me an expert who knew that the first thing to do was to get your breathing right, and then to speak not from the back of the throat but from the front of the mouth. She was a genius. Her sympathetic understanding for my difficulties, which was a great help, was only matched by that for her ailing cat. Unfortunately, the cat would sometimes fall sick just before my lesson and force its cancellation. Fortunately, I too like cats. And so we finished the course.

On one occasion Gordon took me to meet Sir Laurence Olivier to see whether he had any tips which might be useful. He was quite complimentary, telling me that I had a good gaze out to the audience, which was important, and that my voice was perfectly all right, which – no thanks to the cat – it now probably was. Above all, he understood the difference between speaking someone else's script and climbing into someone else's character, and delivering a speech reflecting one's own views and projecting one's own personality. Indeed, as a result of our conversation, I became interested in the differences as well as the similarities between the techniques of the political speaker and the actor. For example, I was later told that most stage actors would rather hear an audience's reaction without seeing the audience, buried in the gloom. But I always insisted that from any public platform I *must* be able to see as well as hear how my words were being received. I could then speed up, or slow down, or throw in what we later came to call a 'clap line' (i.e. a line which had previously got loud applause) if the speech seemed to be going over badly. So Gordon would always try to ensure that even in a darkened hall I could see the front rows of the audience when I spoke.

Getting all these things right took me several months. But all in all the general system never let me down. The real political tests of Opposition Leadership, however, still lay ahead.

SHACKLES OF THE RECENT PAST

My first real experience of the *public* aspects of being Leader of the Opposition came when I visited Scotland on Friday 21 February. From the time that I stepped off the aircraft at Edinburgh Airport, where a waggish piper played 'A man's a man for a' that', I received an enthusiastic Scottish welcome. Everywhere huge crowds turned out to see me. My planned walkabout in the centre of Edinburgh had to be abandoned altogether. Several hundred people had been expected, but 3,000 packed into the arcade of the St James's Centre near Princes Street and there were only half a dozen policemen trying in vain to hold them back. Several women fainted and others were in tears. There was a real risk of tragedy as crowds were forced against the shop windows. It was impossible to go on and I had to take refuge in a jeweller's shop, where I saw an opal (my birthstone) that I later had made into a ring. The occasion was a demonstration both to the police and to me that from now on there could be nothing amateurish about the way in which the logistics of my visits were organized.

I could always be sure of a friendly reception from grassroots Scottish Tories, whose embattled position seems to sharpen their zeal. More generally, however, the honeymoon did not last long and ordinary political life resumed with a vengeance. The opinion polls, which in February had given the Conservatives a 4 percentage point lead over Labour, showed a 2 per cent Labour lead just a month later – not statistically significant perhaps, but a check on any premature tendency to euphoria. It also soon became clear that powerful elements in the Party were out to make trouble for me. In early April Harold Macmillan and Ted Heath made speeches to a conference of Young Conservatives, warning against shifting the Conservative Party to the right. The European referendum campaign placed the focus on European issues, and this in turn gave a fillip to advocates of coalition government. All this created more difficulties for me.

My first major parliamentary performance in which I crossed swords with Harold Wilson, in a debate on the economy on Thursday 22 May, was heavily and justly criticized for not spelling out convincingly the Conservative alternative. The difficulty was that at this point we *had* no credible alternative to offer. Imprisoned by the requirement of defending the indefensible record of the Heath Government, we were unable as yet to break through to a proper free-market alternative.

Even so, however, on this and several other occasions I did not make a good speech. Leading for the Opposition in set-piece debates, one is not able to make a wide-ranging speech on the basis of a few notes, something which I was good at and liked. A front-bench speech has to be a fully prepared text, available to the press. But at the same time it has to be very different from the kind of texted speech that is appropriate to a large sympathetic audience where the only interruptions are from applause. And, of course, you need to have acquired considerable authority in the House – the sort usually accorded only to Prime Ministers, and not always to them – to get through reading a text without a barrage of barracking and interruption.

The root of all our problems, however, lay in the unresolved contradictions of policy. With Keith Joseph and Angus Maude having overall responsibility, I could have confidence that the policy-making process would now be organized along lines which I approved. But the decisive influences would never be theoretical or technical but rather personal and political. However long we argued about the rights and wrongs of public expenditure, incomes policy and industrial subsidies, some of us (probably a minority) in the Shadow Cabinet firmly believed that the free-market approach would work, while the others were equally convinced that it would not – or at least that it would only work at a political and social cost that would be unsustainable. Similarly, we were not discussing these things in a vacuum. The Labour Government in those years was producing a succession of economic packages. Each one of these forced us to define where we stood, to agree on the grounds on which we opposed their policies and to sharpen our alternative approach.

In March 1975 we discussed a paper from Keith and Angus on policy-making. They proposed involving both backbench commit-tees and sympathetic outside experts; and this was accepted. The number of policy groups continued to multiply, and some were more useful than others. They were generally chaired by the relevant front-bench spokesmen. Geoffrey Howe's Economic Reconstruction Group was the main forum for hashing over economic policy. From time to time, there would be whole-day Shadow Cabinet policy dis-cussions, which I myself would chair. The full Shadow Cabinet approved, rather than devised, policy on the basis of papers put to it by the chief Shadow spokesmen and their policy groups.

The Centre for Policy Studies and a range of outside advisers, particularly on economic matters, fed in ideas and suggestions to Keith and me (Keith also had a number of lunchtime meetings with other Shadow Cabinet colleagues on policy). And on top of all that I would sometimes advance a new policy in a speech or interview – not always to the applause of my colleagues.

As a system of decision-taking the structure had a somewhat ramshackle feel to it. But then, no amount of institutional neatness could resolve the fundamental questions we had to decide. The fact that by the time we took office in May 1979 so many of the big issues had been satisfactorily resolved, and Shadow ministers had as clear an idea of their priorities as any incoming post-war British Government, shows that in the most important sense this policy-making system 'worked'.

The foremost policy issue was how to deal with inflation, which soared to 26.9 per cent in August 1975 before beginning to fall, going below 10 per cent in January 1978. Time and again inflation registered in the opinion polls as the public's top priority for action, though often in tandem with strong support for pay policy as supposedly the only means of fighting it. But unemployment was never far behind, and one of the main attacks *we* had to face from Labour was that our policy for disinflation would result in still higher unemployment.

Discussion of how inflation was caused and cured also necessarily involved making a judgement about the Heath Government. If inflation was the result of an increase in the money supply, which takes approximately eighteen months to work through in the form of higher prices, then the prime responsibility for the high inflation during the first eighteen months or so of the Labour Government should be laid at the door of the Conservatives. If, however, the cause of high inflation was excessive wage awards after the collapse of the previous Conservative Government's incomes policy and Labour's abdication of authority to the trade unions, then political life in Opposition would be easier. We might not have any credible solutions to offer, but we could at least blame everything on the Government. This approach was likely to be particularly favoured by those of my colleagues who prided themselves on being sceptics about all kinds of economic theory. In fact, the case that the Heath Government's monetary incontinence was to blame for inflation seemed to me convincingly argued by Alan Walters, whose devastating indictment and predictions, first published in June 1972, were circulated by Keith as background for a discussion with Shadow Cabinet colleagues in March 1975. But if I had publicly accepted this it would have provoked even more trouble from Ted Heath and his supporters.

Our failure to be explicit about the overriding importance of monetary policy did, however, open up our flank to attack on incomes policy. For if wage rises were the cause of inflation, as our rhetoric in defence of the Heath years implied, then the question arose: how would we in Government be able to contain such rises? Would we do so by a statutory policy – which would not only move us towards the very interventionist approach I wanted to avoid, but would also run up against fierce trade union opposition? Or by a voluntary policy – on which Labour's traditional links with the unions and willingness to trade socialist measures to cement them put us at a political disadvantage?

The October 1974 Conservative manifesto had committed the Party to seek a voluntary policy for prices and incomes, with the qualification that it might be necessary to move to a statutory policy if voluntary support were not achieved. I could only gradually wean the Party away from this position. My task was made more difficult both by the fact that wages and prices were soaring alarmingly, and by Ted Heath and Peter Walker putting me under heavy public pressure to support successive stages of the Labour Government's incomes policy. In an interview with Robin Day in May 1975 I said that under some circumstances a pay freeze might be necessary, but not as a prelude to a permanent statutory incomes policy. Wages had, after all, been growing at some 30 per cent a year since Labour took office. But I never saw even a short wage freeze as having more than a transitional role in any realistic strategy to bring down inflation, which must be based on control of the money supply and government borrowing. In fact, there were already some early signs that the Government had woken up to the need for some financial discipline. The April 1975 Budget announced cuts in planned spending levels and raised the basic rate of income tax by two pence – to 35 per cent – in order to reduce the swelling deficit which was expected to reach £9,000 million in 1975/76.

This did not prevent the Government accepting the hugely ambitious and ill-conceived Ryder plan to rescue British Leyland with £1,400 million of taxpayers' money. Yet, however irresponsible the decision, it was the Conservative Opposition which had most difficulty in responding. BL was a crucial source of income and jobs in West Midlands seats which we had to win in order to form a government. But resources committed to an unprofitable nationalized car industry must have been diverted, through taxation or higher interest rates or inflation, from successful businesses, among other taxpayers. Keith Joseph, Michael Heseltine and I all gave non-committal reactions in public statements, but the variation in tone, particularly between Keith and Michael, was obvious to all.

If public expenditure was one aspect of the debate about counter-inflation policy, trade union power was another. On this matter, the line-up in the Shadow Cabinet over these years was slightly different from that on the question of voluntary/statutory incomes policy versus 'free collective bargaining'. Geoffrey Howe was the most consistently hawkish on trade unions. Right from the beginning, he emphasized in our discussions the need to shift the balance of power in industrial relations: indeed, I suspect that he would ideally have liked to get back to the Industrial Relations Act framework which he had devised. Keith Joseph and I shared that approach, though I remained extremely wary about committing ourselves to more changes than we could deliver. Jim Prior and most of the other Shadow Cabinet members could be found in the opposite camp.

On incomes policy, however, Geoffrey and Jim, supported by Ian Gilmour, were the strongest advocates of some kind of national understanding with the trade unions. Geoffrey's view was that we should seek to emulate the alleged successes of the West German approach of 'concerted action', whose purpose was to educate 'both sides' of industry in the realities of the state of the economy and win some kind of consent to limit wages. This did not in itself involve a renunciation of monetarism, to which Geoffrey, in contrast with Jim and Ian, was increasingly committed. But it did involve a large element of corporatism and centralized economic decision-making, to which Keith was fiercely opposed and which I too disliked.

The most convinced opponent of monetarism and all its works was Reggie Maudling who, when he put his mind to it, actually had the grasp of economics to give his arguments weight. Reggie was the most ardently committed to a statutory incomes policy. As he put it in a dissenting paper to the Shadow Cabinet in May: 'To the economic purist, no doubt, prices are only a symptom of inflation, but to us as politicians they are the real problem, because it is rising prices that are breaking the country in half.' With such divisions in our midst it is not surprising that for much of the time our economic policies were felt to lack coherence.

The difficulties I had faced in the Economic Debate on Thursday

22 May – when for these reasons I had not been able to present a coherent alternative to Government policy – persuaded me of the urgent need to sort out our position. Further public differences confirmed this. In June I spoke to the Welsh Party Conference in Aberystwyth expressing strong reservations about statutory wage controls: the same day Reggie Maudling spoke in Chislehurst implying that we might support a statutory policy. A few days later Keith made a speech casting severe doubt on the value of even a wage freeze, suggesting that it would be used as an excuse for not cutting public spending and taking the other necessary economic steps. On the same day Peter Walker called for a statutory pay policy – and was himself rebutted by Keith, who said bluntly that wage freezes did not work. Not surprisingly, Conservative splits figured large in the press. The fact that these divisions were more than replicated on the Government side was of only limited comfort.

I decided that even if we could not as yet all agree an analysis, we must at least agree to stick to a form of words that would paper over the cracks. After we had heard Denis Healey's 1 July statement foreshadowing Labour's introduction of an incomes policy based on sanctions against employers rather than unions, Shadow Cabinet met to discuss our reaction. The crucial question was whether, when it came to a vote in the House, we should support the Government, abstain or vote against. The problem was compounded by the fact that the Chancellor had only given a preliminary indication of what he intended. We would have to wait for the promised White Paper before we even knew whether the policy could properly be described as voluntary or statutory. On the other hand, we did not want to be in the position of flatly refusing support for measures to bring down inflation, even if they included a statutory policy.

Now the Chief Whip told us that there were at least thirty Tory MPs who were opposed in principle to statutory controls and would expect us to oppose them too. I summed up as best I could. Our public line at this stage must be that although the Party would always support measures it believed to be in the national interest, the Chancellor's statement was high on intentions and low on details. Moreover, he had said nothing about public expenditure cuts or about dropping policies for further nationalization, both of which were directly relevant to the control of inflation.

I found from my own soundings that Conservative opinion in the country was strongly opposed to employers having to bear the brunt of anti-inflation measures. Our supporters wanted us to be tough on Labour. The following day the Backbench Finance Committee met and Bill Shelton reported to me their concerns. While very few wanted us to vote against the Government's package outright, there was widespread anxiety lest by supporting it we would also be endorsing a continuation of the socialist programme.

At Shadow Cabinet on Monday 7 July, Jim Prior and Keith Joseph argued their conflicting cases. But the crucial question was still which Division Lobby the Party should enter, if any. By now the safest, if least glorious, course appeared to be to abstain. The risk was that such a tactic would dismay both wings of the Parliamentary Party and we could find ourselves with a three-way split.

Whatever the tactics to employ, I also needed to be clear in my own mind whether the Healey measures were a genuine step towards financial discipline or a smokescreen. So the day after the Shadow Cabinet discussion I had a working supper in my room in the House with Willie, Keith, Geoffrey, Jim and a number of economists and City experts, including people like Alan Walters, Brian Griffiths, Gordon Pepper and Sam Brittan who were in regular touch with me and on whose opinions I set a high value.* Although we would have to look at the package as a whole, especially the monetary and fiscal side, as Geoffrey said at the start of the evening, I came away feeling still less inclined to lend support to flimsy and possibly harmful proposals.

The White Paper, containing the details, was published on Friday 11 July. It was, as expected, a curate's egg, containing

---

* Alan Walters was then Cassel Professor at the London School of Economics. He left the following year for the United States to work for the World Bank. As already noted, he was my economic adviser as Prime Minister, 1981–84 and in 1989. Brian Griffiths (later Head of my Policy Unit at No. 10) was then a lecturer at the London School of Economics; he became a professor at the City University the following year. Gordon Pepper was an economic analyst at Greenwell & Co., and an expert on monetary policy. Sam Brittan then as now was Principal Economic Commentator on the *Financial Times*.

measures like cash limits which we approved but not matching these with any real public expenditure cuts. The centrepiece was a £6 limit on pay increases for the coming year. The most astonishing omission was that the Government refused to publish the draft Bill it claimed to have drawn up which would introduce statutory controls if the voluntary limits were ignored. By the time it came to a vote, backbench and Shadow Cabinet opinion favoured abstention and this was now agreed. My own speech in the debate did not go particularly well – unsurprisingly, given the protean case I had to present. That might have been awkward, but Ted bailed me out by regretting that we were not supporting the Government and then refusing to back our critical amendment.

If one good thing came out of these travails, it was that the Shadow Cabinet was pushed towards an agreed line on incomes policy. This was that the conquest of inflation required that all economic policies must be pulling in the same anti-inflationary direction, in particular public spending and monetary policy. An incomes policy might play a useful part as one of a comprehensive package of policies, but was not to be considered as an alternative to the others, and could not be expected to achieve much on its own. While hardly qualifying as an original (or even true) economic insight, this at least provided a temporary refuge.

In any case, the Government's July package was rightly judged to be insufficient to deal with the looming economic crisis. Inflation that summer reached an all-time high of 26.9 per cent.

We fled to Brittany in August for a holiday canal-cruising. For my holiday reading I took a book on British Prime Ministers. I was still away when Harold Wilson launched the incomes policy in a television broadcast asking people to give 'a year for Britain' by sticking to the £6 limit. In my absence, Willie Whitelaw replied the following evening giving this nonsense a rather warmer welcome than I could have been persuaded to do.

PROBLEMS OF OPPOSITION

In spite of the difficulties I had faced in the months since I became Leader, I approached that autumn's Party Conference in reasonably good spirits. Ted and his friends seemed likely to continue being as difficult as possible, but my foreign visits had boosted my own standing.* The Government's economic policy was in ruins. The Conservatives were 23 per cent ahead of Labour, according to a pre-Conference opinion poll. The task at Blackpool was to consolidate all this by showing that I could command the support of the Party in the country.

The Leader's speech at a Party Conference is quite unlike the Conference speeches of other front-bench spokesmen. It has to cover a sufficiently wide number of subjects to avoid the criticism that one has 'left out' some burning issue. Yet each section of the speech has to have a thematic correspondence with all the other sections. Otherwise, you finish up with what I used to call a 'Christmas tree', on which pledges and achievements are hung and where each new topic is classically announced by the mind-numbing phrase 'I now turn to . . .'. A powerful speech of the sort required to inspire the Party faithful, as well as easing the worries of the doubters, is in some ways more like a piece of poetry than prose. Not that one should be tempted to use flowery language, but rather that it is the ideas, sentiments and mood below the surface which count. Material which could easily form a clear and persuasive article may be altogether inappropriate for a speech. And although one has to scrutinize a text to ensure the removal of dangerous ambiguities, an effective speech may afterwards read almost lamely in cold print. I was to learn all these things over the next few years. But I had barely begun to grasp them when I started work on my first Leader's Conference speech in 1975.

I told my speech-writers that I was not going to make just an economic speech. The economy had gone wrong because something else had gone wrong spiritually and philosophically. The economic

* See Chapter X.

crisis was a crisis of the spirit of the nation. But when I discussed
the kind of draft I wanted with Chris Patten and others from the
Research Department, I felt they were just not getting the message
I wanted to despatch. So I sat down at home over the weekend
and wrote out sixty pages of my large handwriting. I found no
difficulty: it flowed and flowed. But was it a speech? I was reading
it all through and redrafting on Sunday morning when Woodrow
Wyatt – a former Labour MP turned entrepreneur, author, sympa-
thizer and close friend – telephoned. I told him what I was doing
and he suggested I come round to his house for supper so that he
could look at it. The experienced journalist's eye saw all that I had
not. So the two of us began to cut and shape and reorganize. By
the time I arrived in Blackpool I had the beginnings of a Conference
speech. I also found that Chris Patten and others had written new
material. We married the two and a first draft was accordingly
produced.

It was Ted who had overturned the convention that the Party
Leader only turned up at the end of the Conference, descending
from on high to deliver his speech to an adoring, servile throng. I
took this a stage further. As well as arriving early, I also, particularly on this first occasion, used every opportunity to meet the
constituency representatives, whose loyalty I knew I would have
to earn. In fact, I carried this to what the Conference organizers
considered extreme lengths by spending my time talking to people
down in the body of the hall when I was expected to be up on the
platform.

In between receptions and visits to the debates I would go in to
see how the speech-writers were proceeding. Adam Ridley helped
with the economics. Angus Maude, who like Woodrow had the
journalist's knack of making material bright and interesting simply
by reordering it, also came in from time to time. Richard Ryder was
the keeper of the text. Gordon Reece's expertise was in coaching me
on how to deliver it, seeing for example that I did not cut short
applause after a clap line by moving on too quickly – a perennial
temptation for a speaker who is inexperienced or lacks confidence.

But by Wednesday it was clear to me that none of those working
away in my suite was what in the jargon is known as a 'wordsmith'.
We had the structure, the ideas and even the foundations for some

RIGHT: Carol and Mark, aged four, in the garden at 'Dormers'.

ABOVE: On the beach at Frinton with the twins and my nephew Andrew.

INSET: My sister Muriel with Andrew.

BELOW: Carol and Mark aged five.

RIGHT: With the twins aged six.

ABOVE: At 'Dormers' in 1959.

LEFT: With the twins.

BELOW: 'The Mount', Lamberhurst, which we bought in 1965.

ABOVE: At the constituency offices in Finchley.

ABOVE: With John Boyd-Carpenter on my first day at the Ministry of Pensions, October 1961.

OPPOSITE: Walking
down Whitehall on the
day of my appointment
a junior minister.

RIGHT: Outside the
Houses of Parliament
when I was a junior
minister.

ABOVE: With friends at Seaview, Isle of Wight.

LEFT: Denis and Mark at a Belmont School cricket match.

BELOW: With Denis on a skiing holiday in Lenzerheide.

ᴠᴇ: Visit by Carol's class to the House of Commons – Carol is furthest to the right in the front row.

ᴏᴡ: Visiting a primary school as Secretary of State for Education.

ABOVE: With Ted Heath at the opening of the Conservative Party Conference in 1970.

RIGHT: With the Queen Mother at a garden party for Commonwealth exchange teachers at Lancaster House, July 1973.

BELOW: Ministerial visit to the Atomic Energy Research Establishment at Harwell in September 1973. *Left to right*: Sir William Pile, Permanent Secretary at the Department of Education; Denis; self; Walter Marshall, Director of Harwell; Airey and Diana Neave.

good jokes. But we needed someone with a feel for the words *themselves* who could make the whole text flow along. Gordon suggested that the playwright Ronnie Millar, who had drafted material in the past for Ted's broadcasts, was the man to help. So the whole text was urgently sent to Ronnie to be (what I would always later describe as) 'Ronnie-fied'. It came back transformed. More precisely, it came back a speech. Then there was more cutting and retyping throughout Thursday night. It was about 4.30 on Friday morning when the process was complete and I felt I could turn in for an hour or so's sleep.

Earlier on Thursday evening, when I was reading through the latest draft, I had been called to the telephone to speak to Willie Whitelaw. Willie told me that Ted had arrived and was staying at the same hotel (the Imperial). His suite was a couple of floors below mine. For several months a number of Ted's friends had been urging him to bury the hatchet. Willie, doubtless prompted by them, thought that this would be a perfect time for a reconciliation. He explained to me that pride was involved in these matters and Ted could not really come and see me. Would I therefore come and see him? I replied at once that of course I would. Willie said that that was 'absolutely splendid' and that he would ring me back to confirm. Meanwhile, I plunged back into the draft. About an hour and a half went by with no telephone call. Since it was now about 10 o'clock and there was still much to do on my speech, I thought that we must really get on with our 'reconciliation'. So I rang Willie and asked what was happening. I was then told that Ted had had second thoughts. The hatchet would evidently remain unburied.

The Winter Gardens is a grand popular palace in the self-confident style of the mid-Victorians when Blackpool really blossomed into a seaside resort. It has cafés, restaurants, bars, a theatre and the Empress Ballroom where the main proceedings of the Tory Conference took place. 'Ballroom' scarcely does justice to the ornate and opulent splendour of the vast hall with its high ceilings, ample balcony, gilt, stucco and red plush. It has warmth and atmosphere that seem to welcome a speaker, and I always preferred it to the cold and clinical neatness of more modern conference facilities. The climax of the Conservative Conference creates a special electricity at Blackpool. For my part, though I had had almost no sleep, I was confident of my text and resolved to put everything into its delivery.

The speech had two main purposes. First, it was to contain a conclusive indictment not just of Labour policies or even the Labour Government, but rather of the whole socialist approach which was destructive of freedom. Secondly, I would use it to spell out a Conservative vision that did not merely employ phrases like 'the free market' and 'personal independence' for form's sake, but took them seriously as the foundation of future policy. Reading it through almost twenty years later, there is nothing substantial that I would change – least of all the section about my personal creed and convictions.

> Let me give you my vision: a man's right to work as he will, to spend what he earns, to own property, to have the state as servant and not as master – these are the British inheritance . . . We must get private enterprise back on the road to recovery – not merely to give people more of their own money to spend as they choose, but to have more money to help the old and the sick and the handicapped . . . I believe that, just as each of us has an obligation to make the best of his talents, so governments have an obligation to create the framework within which we can do so . . . We can go on as we have been doing, we can continue down. Or we can stop and with a decisive act of will we can say 'Enough'.

I was relieved when, as I got into my speech, I began to be interrupted by applause and cheers. Fun is often poked at the stage-management of Conservative Conferences. But one can distinguish, if one has a mind to do so, between support which is genuine and that which is contrived. This struck me as genuine. It was also quite unlike any reception I had ever had myself and, so the commentators said, quite unlike the Conferences of recent years. I had apparently struck a chord, not so much by the way I delivered the speech as by the self-confident Conservative sentiments it expressed. The representatives on the floor were hearing their own opinions expressed from the platform and they responded with great enthusiasm. I picked up some of their excitement in turn. On both the floor and the platform there was a sense that something new was happening.

But would it play outside the Empress Ballroom? I hoped, and in my heart believed, that the *Daily Mail's* leader comment on the contents of the speech was correct: 'If this is "lurching to the right", as her critics claim, 90 per cent of the population lurched that way long ago.'

By the end of that first year as Leader of the Opposition I felt that I had found my feet. I still had difficulties adjusting to my new role in the House of Commons. But I had established a good *rapport* with the Party in Parliament and in the country. I was pleased with the way my little team in the office were working together. I only wished the Shadow Cabinet could be persuaded to do likewise.

I had also settled into a new domestic routine. Denis had officially retired from Burmah, though his other business interests kept him fully occupied. The twins, now aged twenty-two, were living very much their own lives: Carol was finishing her training as a solicitor and would take a job as a journalist in Australia in 1977; Mark was continuing his accountancy training. Flood Street remained our London home. I would entertain there or, during the week when the House was sitting, in my room at the House of Commons.

A fortnight after the Party Conference we moved into the old dower flat in Scotney Castle at Lamberhurst (we had stayed in the village after selling 'The Mount', renting a flat at Court Lodge in the interim). Our friend Thelma Cazalet-Keir, a former MP who also had a flat there, often gave lunch parties and seemed to know everyone for miles around. My old friend Edward Boyle had a house not far away. Other neighbours were the Longfords, Edward Crankshaw (the historian of the Habsburgs) and Malcolm Muggeridge. But it was around Thelma Cazalet-Keir's table that the most stimulating discussions occurred. It was a break from the intense, hothouse atmosphere of Westminster party politics. I would often come away determined to find out more about some topic or widen my reading. For example, in the course of a discussion of communism, Malcolm Muggeridge said that its whole mentality was spelt out in Dostoevsky's *The Possessed*. 'Read it,' he told me. I did, found he was right, and went on to delve more deeply into Russian thought and literature.

Our first Christmas at Scotney passed pleasantly enough. But I had no doubt that 1976 would be a testing year. Britain was in the grip of a serious economic crisis that in due course would draw the International Monetary Fund (IMF) into a direct role in running the British economy. The Labour Government was ill-equipped to deal with this, not least because it was on the verge of losing its already slim parliamentary majority. But we on the Conservative benches had difficulties in turning this situation to our advantage, notably because the trade unions were seen by people as all-powerful. So we were constantly put at a disadvantage by the question: How would *you* deal with the unions? Or more ominously: How would the unions deal with *you*?

On top of this there had been widespread criticism of the performance of the Shadow Cabinet, including of course my own, and I decided that some changes were necessary. I reshuffled the pack on 15 January 1976. Reshuffles in Opposition had strong elements of farce. The layout of the Leader of the Opposition's suite of rooms in the Commons was such that it was almost impossible to manage the entrances and exits of fortunate and unfortunate colleagues with suitable delicacy. Embarrassing encounters were inevitable. But on this occasion there was not too much blood on the carpet.

I was delighted that John Biffen was now prepared to join the Shadow Cabinet as Energy spokesman. He had been perhaps the most eloquent and effective critic on the backbenches at the time of the Heath Government U-turn and I welcomed his presence. If the promotion of John Biffen demonstrated that we were serious about correcting the corporatist mistakes of the past, so the promotion of Douglas Hurd, one of Ted's closest aides, to be Party spokesman on Europe, showed that whatever Ted himself might feel I had no grudges against those who had served him. I made Willie Shadow Home Secretary in place of Ian Gilmour, whom I moved to Defence where he proved an extremely robust and effective Shadow spokesman; if he had limited himself to that, life would have been easier for all concerned. The rest was musical chairs. Patrick Jenkin I moved sideways to Social Services, replacing

Norman Fowler who became Transport spokesman outside the Shadow Cabinet. Francis Pym returned after his illness to Agriculture.

In the remodelled Shadow Cabinet we faced three major strategic problems. The first, already mentioned, was the question, repeated mantra-like by the commentators, 'How will you get on with the trade unions if you form a government?' We urgently had to come up with a convincing answer because, as 1976 wore on, there seemed an increasing possibility of the Labour Government collapsing.

Our problem was made worse because we could not rely on many of the large industrialists prominent in the CBI, whose nerve had been badly shaken by the three-day week and the Heath Government's fall. Keith, Geoffrey, Jim and I met the CBI leaders in January 1976. We heard an extraordinary tale. CBI members would apparently be 'horrified' if we did not support the Government's incomes policy. They themselves were committed to supporting a second and possibly a third year of it. They did not like dividend controls and they were desperate to break free of price controls. This was all well and good. But it was obvious that they were not being entirely candid either with me or with themselves. Not only were their nerves shaken; in their demoralized state, they were positively attracted to wage controls – and indeed to the entire corporatist paraphernalia of the 'little neddys' (the NEDC sector working parties). These men were managers who had lost all hope of the possibility of ever really managing their companies again.

I could not go along with such defeatism. Still, I was convinced by Jim Prior's arguments that we had to show that we could, if we formed the government, achieve some sort of working relationship with the unions. I took up the theme in a speech in early February to the Young Conservatives in Scarborough, noting that 'the bigger majority we have, the more it would be obvious that many members of trade unions have voted Conservative'. It would therefore 'not be difficult to work with responsible trade union leadership'. Admittedly, this did not get us very far.

The following Friday, 13 February, we held an all-day Shadow Cabinet discussion, much of which was based on a paper by Jim Prior. This urged us both to show the electorate that the TUC was being consulted in the formation of our policies, and to show the

TUC that those policies would bring prosperity and jobs. But could this be achieved without sacrificing necessary reforms? I had my doubts, but I kept stressing that we *were* both willing and able to get on with the trade unions, using interviews and speeches in February to do so. This caused some rumbles of discontent among my supporters on the right. But it was not their opposition which finally scuttled this approach, but the failure of the TUC to respond in any meaningful way. A year after Jim's paper, in 1977, I met the leaders of the TUC privately for informal talks. The meeting itself was amicable enough, but not surprisingly there was no real meeting of minds. In any case, the Grunwick dispute and the controversy over the closed shop had by then begun to cast clouds over our relations.* Whatever the tactical benefits of the 'opening' to the trade unions in which Jim believed, it bore no worthwhile fruit. And when the Winter of Discontent came along in 1978/79, our bad relations with the TUC were a positive advantage.

Our second problem was how to use to best effect the steady shrinkage and final disappearance in April 1976 of the Government's original majority of three over all other parties combined. This was obviously a help to the Opposition, but it contained hidden difficulties. The press were inclined to exaggerate our chances of actually defeating a Government which, after all, still had a considerable margin of votes over the Conservatives. So when some measure squeaked through, our supporters in the country became depressed and resentful and looked for someone to blame.

More important, our occasional victories did not seem to lead anywhere. The Government remained insecurely in place. On Wednesday 11 February (on the first anniversary of my becoming Leader) we won a division on a motion to reduce the Industry Secretary Eric Varley's salary by £1,000 – a formal means of expressing rejection of policies. Then, in the midst of the sterling crisis of March 1976, the Government was defeated as a result of a left-wing revolt on a vote on its public expenditure plans. And, as one does on these occasions, I demanded that the Prime Minister should resign. I never imagined that he would. But the following Tuesday Harold Wilson did just that, letting me know of his

* See pp. 397–403.

decision in a note I received just before the announcement was made.

I can say little in favour of either of Harold Wilson's terms as Prime Minister. Doubtless he had principles, but they were so obscured by artful dodging that it was difficult for friends and opponents alike to decide what they might be. Yet I regretted his departure for several reasons. I had always liked him personally, I had appreciated his sense of humour, and I was aware of his many kindnesses. He was a master of Commons repartee, and I usually scored nothing better than a draw against him in the House.

This would continue to be the case with his successor, Jim Callaghan. He adopted in the House a manner that appeared avuncular, was in fact patronizing and made it hard for me to advance serious criticism of Government policy without appearing to nag. In a larger sense, Mr Callaghan in those years was a sort of moderate disguise for his left-wing party and its trade union backers. As a result, he articulated views and attitudes – on education, family policy, law and order etc. – which were never embodied in government policy. Tactically brilliant, he was strategically unsuccessful – until eventually in the Winter of Discontent the entire house of cards that was Labour moderation collapsed. Until then, however, he proved extremely talented as a party manager; he had a real feel for public opinion during the three years he was Prime Minister; and under the pressure of economic crisis, he made a brave public break with the Keynesian economics that had underpinned Government policy since the war. He was a formidable opponent.

Within weeks of Jim Callaghan's becoming Prime Minister, relations between Government and Opposition chilled to freezing point as a result of Labour chicanery on a Bill nationalizing the aircraft and shipbuilding industries. After a long campaign by one of our backbenchers, Robin Maxwell-Hyslop, the Speaker had finally ruled that the Bill was 'hybrid' and so subject to special (and time-consuming) Commons procedures. Labour announced that they would ask the House to set aside the relevant Standing Orders, effectively nullifying the Speaker's ruling. This was bad enough, but there was more to come. That night several MPs on each side were unwell and were paired. It so happened that Labour had one more sick MP than we had, and he was absent *unpaired*.

There were two divisions that evening, the second following immediately after the first. The first was tied. By precedent the Speaker cast his vote for the *status quo* and the Government lost. But this revealed to the Government Whips that they were one vote short for the next – and crucial – division. So they went out and found a Labour MP who was paired – that is he had agreed with a Tory MP that neither of them would vote that night. They pushed him into the Labour lobby, as a result of which the Government won by a single vote.

Since the Labour Party had in fact lost its majority, the temptation to do this sort of thing was obviously great. But to nationalize two great industries by a single vote, breaking agreements into the bargain, was completely unacceptable. Tempers ran high on both sides. Michael Heseltine, our Industry spokesman who had led for the Opposition in the debate and felt personally affronted, grabbed the Mace and tried to present it to the Labour benches to symbolize their breach of the conventions.* This in itself was a grave offence to the order of the House, as Michael recognized as soon as he was calmed down by Jim Prior.

Less dramatically, I called off all pairing arrangements and withdrew cooperation over Commons business, demanding that the Government hold the division again. This was designed to cause the Government maximum difficulty: not only did all their MPs – however eminent – have to turn up for important divisions, but the Government could not know how long to allow for its business, much of which passes by agreement with the Opposition. Government business slowed down to a snail's pace. This continued for almost a month until Mr Callaghan asked to see me and said somewhat huffily that we could not go on in this way. I told him that I could. In the end we agreed that the Government and Opposition Chief Whips should investigate what had happened, and when their report showed that we were in the right the Prime Minister conceded a second division on the disputed question. The Labour whips made certain that all their Members were present that night and accordingly won.

---

* The Mace – a silver gilt staff topped by an orb and cross – symbolizes the authority of the Crown delegated to the Commons. It rests on the table facing the Speaker when the House is sitting, within easy reach of the two front benches.

Against this background of ill-feeling, we decided to propose a Motion of No Confidence in the Government. Had we not done so, we would have been accused of failing to press home the attack on a Government which was resorting to chicanery because it had lost its majority. But the other side of the coin was that we would be made to look foolish if we failed, as we were very likely to do because the minority parties feared an early general election and anyway might be tempted by blandishments from the Government Whips. And, of course, this is what happened. It was not until almost three years later that the Government's lack of a majority finally brought it down.

Meanwhile, the state of the economy was worsening. In February 1976 the Government had announced spending cuts of £1,600 million for 1977/78 and £3,000 million for 1978/79 (in today's terms the equivalent of £6,000 million and £11,500 million). Impressive though this might sound, it amounted to no more than a modest cut in large planned increases. In December 1975 the International Monetary Fund had granted an application for stand-by credit to tide over Britain's finances. Even so, in March there was a full-scale sterling crisis. The pound came under heavy pressure yet again in June, and more international stand-by credit had to be obtained, repayable in six months, failing which Britain agreed to apply again to the IMF. Inflation was falling by then, but large negative interest rates, combined with the failure to make real cuts in public spending and borrowing, prevented the Government from getting to grips with its underlying financial and economic problems. The new sterling crisis in September, which would lead to the humiliating abdication of control over our economy to the IMF, was the final result of an entirely justified loss of confidence by international markets in the Labour Government's handling of the economy.

It might be expected that all of this would make an Opposition's life easier, no matter how bad it was for the country. But that was not so.

And this was our third problem. For we were expected to support the Labour Government's hesitant and belated moves to apply financial discipline. That was fair enough. But we were also under a more general pressure to be 'responsible' in dealing with the

Labour Government's self-contrived tribulations. However commendable, this inevitably cramped my attacking style.

For example, the 1976 Party Conference, held against the background of an uncontainable financial crisis, ought to have been a triumph. But it was not. All of us in Brighton were almost neurotically conscious of the need for responsibility and caution. Of course, in practice nothing I said about the Government's economic policy was likely to give the financial markets a worse opinion of it than they already had. But interest rates were raised to 15 per cent on the day before my speech. I called a Shadow Cabinet meeting at Brighton to see what our stance should be before I did the final draft. Reggie Maudling helped me rewrite the already tortured economic passages. But it was a poor text and, probably because I lacked confidence in it, I delivered it badly in the uncongenial atmosphere of a cramped temporary hall – before going next door to the overflow of the Conference and delivering an off-the-cuff speech, praised by the few journalists who heard it but which, being untexted, sank without trace.

All in all, the regular Party politics of 1976 were frustrating and inconclusive. Despite the large Tory lead in the opinion polls and the disappearing Labour majority in the Commons, the Government managed to stagger on. Our opening to the TUC ran into the sand, and with the IMF superintending economic policy, the air of extreme crisis began to subside. At a more fundamental level, however, things were looking up.

ON THE HIGH GROUND

The Right Approach, which we published on the eve of the 1976 Conference, gave a persuasive account of the new Conservatism. Indeed, it still reads well and, stylistically at least, ranks with *Change is our Ally* as one of the best-written documents produced by the post-war Conservative Party. The credit for this must go to Chris Patten and Angus Maude who, with Keith Joseph, Geoffrey Howe and Jim Prior, drafted it.

It was helped by the fact that a truce had been reached in the internal arguments about where we all stood on incomes policy. A speech by Geoffrey Howe to the Bow Group (a Conservative ginger group) in May 1976 provided an agreed 'line to take' which was broadly followed in *The Right Approach*. The document pointed out that prices and incomes policies did not offer a long-term solution to inflation, while noting that it would be unwise 'flatly and permanently' to reject the idea, and nodding favourably in the direction of the West German system of 'concerted action'. It was a fudge – but temporarily palatable.

But it was the fact that *The Right Approach* concentrated on the big general arguments, restating what differentiated our approach from that of socialism, that made it the success it was. It received a good press, not least because I and my colleagues put in considerable effort to explain it to the editors beforehand. The confident, authoritative tone of the opening sections pleasantly surprised the critics, lifting their vision above daily political infighting and the Government's obsession with ever-changing 'norms'.

The success of *The Right Approach* illustrates an important paradox about the whole of this period. For a variety of reasons, we were not a particularly successful Opposition in the ordinary sense of the word. Differences kept on emerging between us. We were usually unsuccessful in the House of Commons. We found it difficult to capitalize on the Government's mistakes. Yet on the higher plane of belief, conviction and philosophy we were extremely effective. We were winning the battle of ideas which was the necessary preliminary not just to winning the election but to winning enduring popular support for the change of direction we wanted to make.

Keith Joseph's speeches continued to put over the powerful themes he developed in the CPS. In March he delivered a speech in Harrow which took head-on the Government's claim that high public expenditure was necessary for high levels of employment. In fact, as Keith pointed out:

Government overspending is a major and continued cause of unemployment. Immediate cuts in runaway state expenditure are essential if we are to save the economy now, and eventually restore a high and stable level of employment ... Several Peters go on the dole for every Paul kept in a protected job.

Several wealth-creating private-sector Peters are thrown out of work to keep each wealth-consuming public sector Paul in make-work. The saved jobs are identifiable and concentrated: the lost jobs are anonymous and dispersed.

I wrote the introduction to the published version of Keith's Stockton Lecture, entitled *Monetarism is Not Enough*, which appeared a few months later. Since monetarism was far from accepted by most members of the Shadow Cabinet, this title was a deliberately bold way of expressing an important truth. It was 'not enough' to exert monetary control alone. That would indeed bring down inflation. But if we also failed to cut public expenditure and public borrowing, the whole burden of disinflation would then be placed on the wealth-creating private sector.

Alfred Sherman, who had assisted Keith with his Stockton Lecture, helped me draft the speech I made to the Zurich Economic Society on Monday 14 March 1977. Although delivered in Switzerland, it was aimed very much at the domestic audience. Alfred and I worked particularly hard on the text, which, in spite of the economic crisis in Britain, took an optimistic view of Britain's future, arguing that:

> The tide is beginning to turn against collectivism . . . and this turn is rooted in a revulsion against the sour fruit of socialist experience. The tide flows away from failure. But it will not automatically float us to our desired destination . . . It is up to us to give intellectual content and political direction . . . If we fail, the tide will be lost. But if it is taken, the last quarter of our century can initiate a new renaissance matching anything in our island's long and outstanding history.

It played well in Zurich to the bankers, who were joined by Carol and my friends Douglas and Eleanor Glover – Douglas had been for many years the MP for Ormskirk. But it was how it played in London that mattered. In fact, it was extremely important that I should reach out for the high ground at such a time because there were more than enough difficulties on the low ground of Westminster politics.

I have already described some of the tactical difficulties which the economic crisis now engulfing Britain presented to us. A new one now arose. There was a growing crisis of confidence in Labour, and the polls showed us more than ten points ahead. By-election victories at Walsall North and Workington with big swings to us would shortly confirm the picture. It was at this juncture that talk of a coalition began again among those Conservatives determined at all costs to snatch defeat for me from the jaws of victory.

Harold Macmillan went on television to call for a 'Government of National Unity'. Nor, it seemed, was there much doubt in his mind about who should be called back to lead it. I thought that I had better go and talk to him to see what he really thought, and it was arranged that we should meet in Maurice Macmillan's house in Catherine Place. I arrived early and waited upstairs in the sitting room. I heard Maurice's father arrive and say to him: 'Has the call come?' Maurice said: 'No, not quite.' He had to make do with me. Our meeting was pleasantly inconclusive, with Macmillan urging me not to be too critical of the Government at a time of crisis. And the only call was that eventually made to the IMF.

I now decided to make some changes of my own. Reggie Maudling's performance as Shadow Foreign Secretary had long been a source of embarrassment. He did not agree with my approach to either the economy or foreign affairs; he was increasingly unwilling to disguise his differences with me; and he was laid back.* But when I told him that he had to go, he summoned up enough energy to be quite rude. Still, out he went.

I also wanted to move Michael Heseltine out of Industry and replace him with John Biffen. When not overreacting, Michael was an effective scourge of the Government, and he was certainly passionately interested in his brief at Industry. The trouble was that his outlook was completely different from mine, and from anything recognizably Conservative. For example, in January 1976 he made a speech criticizing Labour ministers for failing to meet sufficiently often 'to agree and develop an industrial strategy for this nation'. His real criticism seemed to be that the Labour Party

* For our differences on foreign affairs, see pp. 351–3, 361.

intervened in industry and picked losers whereas he would intervene and pick winners. The notion that the state did not and could
not know who *would* win or lose, and that in intervening to back
its own judgement with taxpayers' money it was impoverishing the
economy as a whole, seemed never to have occurred to him. Again,
however, when I asked Michael to leave Industry and go to
Environment, he said that he preferred not to. I sent my PPS,
John Stanley, who knew him well, off to negotiate, and Michael
reluctantly agreed to make way for John Biffen on the understanding that he would not have to be Secretary of State for the Environment once we were in power. That settled, the rest of the changes
could now go ahead. I asked John Davies to take over from Reggie
on Foreign Affairs, where until illness tragically struck him down,
he worked hard and effectively.

It was important to have an energetic and effective front-bench
team because there seemed a growing likelihood that we might
soon be asked to become a government. On Wednesday 15
December Denis Healey introduced a further mini-Budget. He
announced deep cuts in public spending and borrowing, and targets
for the money supply (though expressed in terms of domestic credit
expansion), as part of the deal agreed with the IMF. It was, in
fact, a monetarist approach of the sort which Keith Joseph and I
believed in, and it outflanked on the right those members of my own
Shadow Cabinet who were still clinging to the outdated nostrums of
Keynesian demand management. True to the tactic of not opposing
measures necessary to deal with the crisis, we abstained in the vote
on the measures. The IMF-imposed package was a turning point,
for under the new financial discipline the economy began to
recover. But in party political terms this was a mixed blessing.
On the one hand, discontent with the Government's economic
stewardship would diminish and support was likely to swing back
towards Labour. On the other, we could now argue that
socialism as an economic doctrine was totally discredited and that
even the socialists were having to accept that reality was Conservative. The precise electoral implications of all that would
have to be seen.

The political uncertainty made everyone jittery. The Government no longer had an overall majority. No one knew how members

of the smaller parties might vote on any particular issue. It was frustrating enough even for those of us who were kept informed of the changing parliamentary arithmetic by the Whips. But it was all but incomprehensible to Conservative supporters in the country, who could not understand why we were unable to inflict a fatal defeat and bring about a general election. In fact, on Tuesday 22 February 1977 the Government was defeated on a guillotine on the Scotland and Wales Bill. The end of any immediate hope of achieving devolution in Scotland and Wales caused the Scottish and Welsh Nationalists to withdraw their support from the Government. A new parliamentary crisis – one in which the Government had ceased to have even a working majority – was upon us.

TOWARDS LIB-LABBERY

Before describing the outcome of that crisis, it is necessary to trace something of the background to the arguments about devolution, which would resurface with a vengeance later. For the devolution issue – at least until the final *dénouement* in March 1979 – had brought almost as much grief to the Conservative Party as it had to Labour.

Ted had originally committed the Conservatives to devolution at the Scottish Party Conference in May 1968, following a surge in support for the Scottish Nationalist Party (SNP) – a short-lived surge, as it turned out. Ted's 'Perth Declaration' came as a shock to most Conservatives, including those in Scotland. I was never happy with the policy and there was little enthusiasm for it among English Tories generally. But Ted pressed on. He set up a Party Committee under Alec Douglas-Home to draft a detailed plan. Alec's proposals were agreed at the Scottish Party Conference on the eve of the 1970 general election, finding their way into the manifesto. (There was no commitment for devolution in Wales.) In office between 1970–74 the devolution commitment was, however, quietly dropped. Although the Kilbrandon Royal Commission on the Constitution, which proposed an elaborate devolution scheme, reported in October 1973, our February manifesto just committed the Party to study it. Labour on the other hand committed itself to legislate.

After the general election, Ted became convinced that the Party should offer devolution to Scotland as a way of winning back lost support and appointed Alick Buchanan-Smith as Shadow Scottish Secretary with a brief to do so. At the Scottish Party Conference in May, Ted resurrected our devolution policy, promising a Scottish Development Fund financed by North Sea oil and going beyond the Home proposals in finance. This was the policy upon which we fought the October 1974 election – which, notwithstanding what was proposed on devolution, saw our support in Scotland diminish further. Indeed, for the first time ever we finished in third place in the popular vote.

Anxieties about the way in which the Party had been bounced into the new policy had never been far below the surface. There was in particular a small group of Scottish Tory MPs, including my old friend Bettie Harvie-Anderson, who began to make their views known with increasing vigour after October 1974. They saw the proposal for a Scottish Assembly as one which would threaten the Union, not consolidate it. They also saw no reason to go along with Labour Party policy, let alone try to outbid it. The Scottish party itself was deeply split, with the critics of devolution representing much grassroots opinion pitted against the left-leaning Scottish party leadership of people like Alick Buchanan-Smith, Malcolm Rifkind and George Younger.

This was the situation which I inherited as Leader. Ted had impaled the Party on an extremely painful hook from which it would be my unenviable task to set it free. As an instinctive Unionist, I disliked the devolution commitment. But I realized that so much capital had by now been invested in it that I could not change the policy immediately. Had I done so, there would have been resignations which I simply could not afford. For the moment I would have to live with the commitment.

I asked Willie Whitelaw to chair a devolution policy group. In the Shadow Cabinet we duly discussed Willie's proposals for a directly elected Assembly and agreed them, though without committing ourselves one way or the other to proportional representation.* Many of the Tory devolutionists wanted PR, fearing a future SNP victory in Scotland under the first-past-the-post electoral system and not being averse perhaps to the prospect of coalition politics, north or south of the border. On this I would not budge.

At the Scottish Party Conference in Dundee in May 1975 I repeated the commitment to a directly elected Assembly as briefly as I decently could. Talking to people at the Conference brought home more clearly than ever the fact that there were some Scottish Tories who bitterly disagreed with their leaders about the whole question. My unease grew – and so did that of other people. During the summer, English Tory MPs began to express doubts about Scottish devolution, partly because of its implications for the Union but also on sound tactical grounds. Scotland would be vastly over-represented in the Westminster Parliament if it had an Assembly as well as its present (somewhat generous) quota of MPs. Moreover, Labour was itself hopelessly divided over devolution, and it was clear that the tactical balance of advantage had swung away from proclaiming its virtues towards using it as an issue on which to embarrass the Government. I held a series of meetings with back-benchers. Their worries both echoed and increased mine. By the end of 1975 opinion on the backbenches was strongly against de-volution. At the same time Alick Buchanan-Smith and Malcolm Rifkind, getting ever more out of touch, were flirting with the idea of a separate Scottish executive. That went yet further beyond the Home proposals and took us well into Labour territory.

The Government's White Paper which proposed directly elected Assemblies for both Scotland and Wales was published in Novem-ber. But the Shadow Cabinet was deeply divided as to how to deal with it. In the run-up to the debate on the White Paper in January 1976 Alick Buchanan-Smith and Ian Gilmour pressed for mention of the Conservative commitment to an Assembly in the wording of our Amendment, while the anti-devolutionists argued that if we avoided restating the commitment, abstentions from Labour opponents of devolution might give us victory. For the present, I bowed to Alick Buchanan-Smith's line.

* For Wales there would be no such Assembly, but rather a Welsh Select Commit-tee, a strengthened Welsh (advisory) Council, and Welsh spending would be financed by block grant.

The arguments continued in 1976. Julian Amery and Maurice Macmillan proved effective leaders of the anti-devolution Tory camp. Willie devised a formula around which it was hoped the Party could unite, which I used at the Scottish Party Conference in Perth in May, repeating support for a directly elected Scottish Assembly, but making it clear that we would oppose any scheme based upon the Government's White Paper. I added, for good measure: 'I could not support an Assembly – none of us could support an Assembly – if we thought it was likely to jeopardize the Union.' The Perth speech was well received, but of course it did not resolve the Party dispute.

I now began to harden our opposition. In November, when the Bill was published, I had dinner with a constitutional lawyer, Professor Yardley of Birmingham, to discuss its details. I also saw a good deal of the constitutional scholar Nevil Johnson. The more I heard and the more closely I read the Bill, the more dangerous it appeared to the Union. It was a prescription for bureaucracy and wrangling, and the idea that it would appease those Scots who wanted independence was becoming ever more absurd. Moreover, a private poll conducted for the Party in November 1976 confirmed my suspicion of the electoral arguments for devolution. Scottish opinion was highly fragmented: the Government's devolution plans had only 22 per cent support – less than our own (26 per cent), and less even than 'no change' (23 per cent). Only 14 per cent favoured independence. A far-reaching constitutional change required much more public support than that.

In November/December 1976, with the Bill about to come before the House for Second Reading, there were four long discussions in Shadow Cabinet about whether or not to impose a three-line whip against it. Our position could be fudged no longer. In addition to the overwhelming majority of our backbenchers, most Shadow ministers were by now opposed to devolution, at least on any lines similar to those contained in the White Paper. But there was a rooted belief among its supporters that devolution was the only way of heading off independence, and even some of those who disliked it intensely were wary of appearing to be anti-Scottish or of being seen to overrule the Scottish Tory leaders. In the end, however, in a marathon meeting ending in the early hours of Thursday 2 December we decided – with a significant dissenting minority including Alick Buchanan-Smith – that we would oppose the Bill on a three-line whip.

I had no illusion that this could be done without some resignations. I wanted to minimize them, but not at the expense of failing to lance the devolution boil. The morning after the Shadow Cabinet meeting Malcolm Rifkind, George Younger, John Corrie, Hector Munro, Hamish Gray and Russell Fairgrieve (Scottish Party Chairman) came to see me, saying that Alick Buchanan-Smith must be given a special dispensation to abstain in the vote or else all six of them would resign from their front-bench posts. I could not agree to this. To my irritation, what was said at the meeting appeared in the next morning's *Financial Times*. The Tory Reform Group, which represented the left of the Party – when it was set up I had written in assumed innocence to Robert Carr, one of its founders, to ask precisely what it thought it was going to 'reform' – described us as 'set to commit electoral suicide in Scotland'. The backbenchers felt very differently. There were loud cheers when the whipping decision was announced at the 1922 Committee that evening. It was, of course, no surprise when Ted Heath popped up four days later in Glasgow to say that he himself would not vote against the Bill. Alick Buchanan-Smith duly resigned as Shadow Scottish Secretary, along with Malcolm Rifkind. Four other front benchers wanted to go, but I refused their resignations and even allowed one of them to speak against our line in the debate and vote with the Government. No Party leader could have done more. To replace Alick Buchanan-Smith I moved Teddy Taylor, whose robust patriotism and soundness had long impressed me, from Trade to become Shadow Scottish Secretary.

It is generally an unnerving experience to have to speak from the front bench when you know that the debate, and in all probability the vote, will expose divisions on your own side. But the speech I had to give on Monday 13 December at the Bill's Second Reading debate was exactly the sort of forensic operation that I enjoyed. I said as little as possible about our proposals, making only minimal reference to our residual commitment to an Assembly

in Scotland, and saying a great deal about the internal contradictions and inconsistencies of the legislation. At the end of the debate
twenty-seven Conservatives, including Ted Heath and Peter
Walker, abstained. Five voted with the Government, including
Alick Buchanan-Smith, Malcolm Rifkind and Hamish Gray. But
Labour were also divided: twenty-nine Labour MPs abstained and
ten voted with us. The forty-five-vote majority at Second Reading
thus concealed great unhappiness on the Labour side as well as
our own over the issue, which was to resurface. In the course of
the debate the Prime Minister hinted that the Government would
concede a referendum in Scotland and Wales – a commitment that
in the end proved fatal to the whole devolution enterprise.

Francis Pym had by now taken over from Willie the task of
front-bench spokesman on devolution. But he held radically different views from Teddy Taylor about how to treat the Bill, Francis
wanting to make it 'workable' and Teddy wanting to bury it. In
the end burial was its fate, as the Government's guillotine motion
was defeated by a majority of twenty-nine (with twenty-two Labour
MPs voting with us) in February 1977. Suddenly the Government
found itself deprived of Nationalist support, which in practice had
given it a working majority while devolution was in the offing.
Though Labour was to introduce new devolution legislation later
in the year, their immediate prospects were encouragingly grim.

Precisely what would happen now was far from clear. On Thursday 17 March 1977 the Government refused to contest our motion
to adjourn the House following a debate on public expenditure, for
fear of a defection of left-wing Labour MPs. I promptly described
this almost unheard-of breach of orderly procedure as 'defeat with
dishonour'. We tabled, as we had to, a Motion of No Confidence
in the Government. If it succeeded, there would be a general election. In spite of my natural caution, I thought that it would. I used
the speech I made to the Central Council at Torquay that Saturday
to put the Party on the alert for an imminent campaign.

These were days of intense manoeuvring between the parties
and their Whips. But I refused to engage in it. David Steel, the
Liberal Party Leader, had already indicated that he might be prepared to keep Labour in power if the terms and conditions were
judged right. Legislation for direct elections to the European

Assembly on a proportional representation basis, 'industrial democracy' and tax reform were the topics publicly mentioned, but no one believed that the Liberals' decision as to whether or not to support the Labour Government would be determined by secondary issues. For the Liberals there were two large questions they had to answer. Would they be blamed for keeping an unpopular Government in power? Or would they be credited with moderating its policies? I did not myself believe that they would sign up to a pact with the Government – certainly not unless there was a formal coalition with several Liberals as Cabinet ministers, which it was difficult to imagine the left of the Labour Party being prepared to tolerate.

In fact, my calculation of the political equation was broadly correct; but I left out the crucial element of vanity. Although the Lib-Lab Pact did the Liberals a good deal of harm, while doing Jim Callaghan no end of good, it did allow Liberal Party spokesmen the thrilling illusion that they were important.

After the vote on the Opposition Motion of No Confidence I was attacked in some quarters for not having been prepared to offer some kind of deal to the Liberals. But I was untempted by this beforehand and unrepentant afterwards. The undignified attempts to gain Liberal support for a minority Conservative Government after the February 1974 defeat conclusively showed the dangers. Moreover, it would be hard enough to drag the left wing of the Conservative Party and sections of the present Shadow Cabinet into supporting the measures which I knew would be required in government to set Britain right, without the burden of arrangements with the irresponsible eccentrics of the Liberal Party.

There was, of course, even less prospect of winning the support of the Nationalist parties, now that we had turned our back on devolution. The conservative-minded Ulster Unionists should have supported us. In Airey Neave and me they knew that they had strong supporters of the Union. Their demand for extra parliamentary seats at Westminster to make up for the Province's underrepresentation was likely to be supported by *any* Government, because the case on grounds of equity was so strong. But the Unionists' general resentment of the Heath Government's abolition of

Stormont – the devolved government that ran Ulster from 1920 to 1972, which they had dominated – and the personal bitterness of Enoch Powell, who was now representing South Down for the Unionists, meant that we could not in practice rely on their support.

In fact, there was very little that could be done by us to influence the vote. The minority parties would decide where they stood according to whether they thought that a general election was in their interests or not. In assessing that, each would look to the opinion polls. These suggested that a Conservative Government with an overall majority would be elected, which would greatly reduce the ability of a few disparate individuals to influence Government policy.

I was told some hours before I was due to propose the No Confidence Motion in the House that the Liberals would support the Government. I was astonished that they had signed up to such a bad deal. The pact would apparently last initially for the rest of the parliamentary session. The Liberals would not be members of the Government, but would liaise with individual ministers and send representatives to a joint consultative committee chaired by Michael Foot, the Leader of the House. The Government gave undertakings on direct elections to the European Assembly and devolution (accepting free votes on PR), promised to find time for a Liberal Bill on homelessness and agreed to limit the scope of planned legislation on local authority direct-labour organizations. It was a lacklustre shopping list. But, knowing that we were looking at certain defeat, with all the recriminations which would follow from the press and our supporters, it drained me of inspiration.

Angus Maude had helped me with the drafting of the speech. We decided to make it very short. In fact, it was too short. Moreover, it had been drafted when it seemed that we might be facing an immediate general election, so that positive statements of our policies had appeared preferable to detailed attacks on the Government's. It received the worst press of any speech I have given. Of course, if I had read out the Westminster telephone directory and we had won at the end of the day no one would have bothered. But in politics, as in life, the 'ifs' offer no consolation. As I drove back to Flood Street later that night it was not my poor reception in the House or even the Government's majority of twenty-four which most depressed me. It was the fact that after all our efforts the chance to begin turning Britain round seemed no nearer than before.

CHAPTER X

Détente or Defeat?

Foreign policy and visits 1975–1979

EUROPE

The first major political challenge I faced on becoming Leader was the referendum on Britain's membership of the European Economic Community, promised by Labour in Opposition as a way of keeping their party together. For a number of reasons I would have preferred a challenge on some other topic. Europe was very much Ted's issue. He considered that his greatest achievement was to take Britain into the EEC and, now that he had lost the leadership, it was only natural that he would engage even more passion in the cause. As had become evident during the leadership campaign, there was some suspicion that I was less enthusiastic. Compared with Ted, perhaps, that was true. But I did genuinely believe that it would be foolish to leave the Community; I thought it provided an economic bond with other Western European countries, which was of strategic significance; and above all I welcomed the larger opportunities for trade which membership gave. I did not, however, see the European issue as a touchstone for everything else. Although I thought it best for Britain to stay inside the Community and make the best we could of it, I could equally well understand others who, on balance, took a contrary view. It did not seem to me that high-flown rhetoric about Britain's European destiny, let alone European identity, was really to the point, though I had on occasion to employ a little on public platforms. For all these reasons, I was more than happy for Ted to take the leading public role on our side in the referendum campaign and for Willie to be the Conservative Vice-President of 'Britain in Europe' – the 'Yes' campaign organization which was set up in cooperation with pro-European Labour MPs and the Liberals, and of which Con O'Neill and later Roy Jenkins was President.

This arrangement had two advantages and two disadvantages. The advantages were that, though I would make some high-profile public appearances at the beginning and end of the campaign, I would have time for other things; and secondly, that the most committed Europeans of the Party would be able to throw all their energies into the front line. The two disadvantages, which perhaps I should have foreseen, were that Ted's appetite for a return to power would be whetted, and that the forces inside and outside the Conservative Party which were determined to get rid of me would seek to use the all-party coalition campaigning for a 'Yes' vote as the nucleus of a movement for a coalition of the 'centre'.

I also faced a further unexpected intellectual difficulty. The position I inherited from Ted was that of outright opposition to the whole idea of a referendum on the grounds that it was an unconstitutional and un-British practice. There was no time to change this even if I had wanted to; only a fortnight after my accession to the leadership, the Government published its Referendum White Paper. It was, moreover, a rich source of party political advantage to attack the referendum as a constitutional monstrosity devised simply to keep the Labour Cabinet together. I was, however, uneasy. First, there was the obvious practical point that if, whatever protests the Conservative Opposition made, we were to have a referendum anyway, we would soon have to take it seriously – and be seen to do so – if we wanted to secure the right result. Secondly, and only vaguely as yet, I thought that it might be necessary at some time in the future to call for a referendum when a single issue divided the nation but not the parties, making a general election an inappropriate instrument for settling it. Similarly, a Conservative Opposition might seek one if a far-left government, supported by militant trade unions, sought to challenge fundamental freedoms under the cloak of constitutional convention.

I decided to read up all there was on the subject. The idea of a referendum had quite a long pedigree in British politics. From the

1890s to the 1930s it had variously been advanced – sometimes by Conservative Leaders – in connection with Irish Home Rule, the powers of the House of Lords, and the imposition of food tariffs. In 1945 Churchill had mooted the possibility of a referendum on extending the life of Parliament until Japan was defeated. In none of these cases had a referendum in fact been held. But it was clearly wrong to treat the case for it anything other than seriously. I was particularly taken with the assertion in the revised eighth edition of Dicey's *The Law of the Constitution* that: 'The referendum is the people's veto; the nation is sovereign and may well decree that the constitution shall not be changed without the direct sanction of the nation.'

I consulted Michael Havers, shadow spokesman on legal affairs, about these arguments. His reply, which at the time seemed to me a powerful one, was that, reviewing the cases on which the Conservative Party had supported a referendum, we could say that apart from the case of food tariffs, where the Party was trying to avoid a damaging rift (as Labour was now), the issues were all constitutional. Moreover, in none had Parliament already decided the issue and in none were we risking the breaking of a treaty unilaterally. He concluded that past precedent offered no justification for a referendum on EEC membership.

I had, therefore, thought through the issue thoroughly by the time I spoke in the House in the Referendum Debate on Tuesday 11 March. It would be my maiden speech as Leader of the Opposition. In spite of the reservations I had about the case I was making, it was the kind of speech I enjoyed. The main intellectual weakness of the Government's case was the confusion about whether and how the referendum would be 'binding' on Parliament. If it was binding, then parliamentary sovereignty, which mattered a good deal to anti-Marketeers on both sides of the House, was infringed. If it was not binding, then what was its force? I did not in my speech rule out the use of referenda, but I urged that it would be necessary to consider the full constitutional implications. I rejected the argument put forward by the Government that the case of continued membership of the EEC was unique and thus a referendum was required. I said:

To use the referendum device at all is to ask the question: to what category of measure should referenda apply? Presumably the answer would be: in cases of constitutional change. But it is hard to define such a change in the British tradition because so much depends on convention and precedent.

A referendum may, however, become acceptable if given a proper constitutional foundation – that is to say, if the conditions under which it could be used were defined. But that would mean, like many other democratic countries, going as far as a written constitution or at least part of the way. The implications for parliamentary sovereignty are profound. But if our sense of constitutional rules and conventions is weakening, there may come a time when some such course should be considered.

Although there are some other passages of that speech with which I would not now agree, these assertions still seem a good starting point for consideration of the case for a referendum on, say, the Maastricht Treaty or a single European currency.* What I had not grasped at this time, though some others had, was that the conditions for a referendum which I had outlined had more or less already been met. The subordination of UK law to European Community law, which flowed from accession to the Treaty of Rome and which both successive treaty changes and the practices of Community institutions would accelerate, *did* entail a constitutional change. And we *had* gone 'at least part of the way' towards a written constitution by accepting the contents of the Treaty of Rome and a special European Court of Justice, which could strike down laws passed by Parliament which conflicted with it.

The Commons passed the proposal for a referendum by 312 votes to 248. But it was the outcome of the debate on Wednesday 9 April on the substantive issue of continued EEC membership which was a foretaste of things to come: Ayes 396, Noes 170. From now on until Thursday 5 June, the day set for the referendum, the formidable power of business, the leaderships of both parties and the wider, respectable establishment combined to extol the merits

* For further discussion of referenda see pp. 480, 501

of Community membership, to elaborate fears of job losses, to warn
of a third world war originating in intra-European conflict and
to ridicule the odd combination of Labour left-wingers and Tory
reactionaries which constituted the 'No' lobby. The 'Yes' campaign
was well organized and very well funded – not least as a result of
the efforts of Alistair McAlpine, whom I would shortly recruit to
be Conservative Party Treasurer. For all the talk of a 'great debate'
it was really a contest between David and Goliath, which Goliath
won. The substantial issues often went by default.

Most distasteful of all to me was the patent opportunism of the
Labour leadership. The 'renegotiation' of Britain's terms of entry,
which had been concluded in March at the Dublin European Council where a special 'Financial Mechanism' had been agreed to prevent Britain shouldering too heavy a financial burden, was simply
not serious: the mechanism was never triggered and so never
yielded a penny piece. Yet the booklet distributed to all households
by the Government abandoned all of the Euro-sceptical rhetoric
which Labour, particularly the Foreign Secretary Jim Callaghan,
had employed at the general election. It contained such assurances
as:

> As a result of these negotiations the Common Market's agri-
> cultural policy (known as CAP) now works more flexibly to
> the benefit of both housewives and farmers in Britain . . .
> Under the previous terms, Britain's contribution to the
> Common Market budget imposed too heavy a burden on us.
> The new terms ensure that Britain will pay a fairer share . . .
> There was a threat to employment in Britain from the move-
> ment in the Common Market towards an Economic and Mon-
> etary Union . . . This threat has been removed . . . To say that
> membership could force Britain to eat Euro-bread or drink
> Euro-beer is nonsense . . . It is the Council of Ministers, and
> not the Market's officials, who take the important decisions.

I duly launched the Conservative pro-Market campaign at the
St Ermin's Hotel, at a press conference presided over by Ted Heath,
even describing myself as 'the pupil speaking before the master'. I

spoke in my constituency and elsewhere. I contributed an article on the eve of poll to the *Daily Telegraph*. I felt that I did my share of campaigning. But others did not see it that way. There was criticism in the press – the *Sun*, for example, commenting:

> Missing: one Tory Leader. Answers to the name of Margaret Thatcher. Mysteriously disappeared from the Market Referendum Campaign eleven days ago. Has not been seen since. Will finder kindly wake her up and remind her she is failing the nation in her duty as Leader of the Opposition?

Some of this was undoubtedly being fed to the press by people who had other axes to grind at my expense. But Alistair McAlpine, a supporter soon to become a friend, was sufficiently concerned to tell Willie Whitelaw that I should take a more active role. Unfortunately, on the prearranged day for me to hold a press conference at Central Office as part of the campaign, Edward du Cann, the 1922 Committee Chairman, came out with a call for a 'No' vote in the referendum. I learned about this shortly before I had to face the press. Caught between Edward Scylla and Edward Charybdis, I had to weave and tack rather than steer directly towards Brussels.

The referendum result itself was no surprise, with 67 per cent voting 'Yes' and 33 per cent 'No'. Less predictable were the effects on the political scene as a whole. The result was a blow to the left of the Labour Party; and Harold Wilson, whose cunning tactical ploy the whole exercise had been, used it to move Tony Benn from Industry, where he had proved a political liability, to Energy where his scope for mischief was more limited. For the Conservatives, it was naturally Ted and his friends who won most of the plaudits. I myself paid tribute to him in the House. He made no response. That came later.

Soon the press was full of accounts of Ted's earlier meeting with me at Wilton Street, but given in such a way as to suggest that I had not made a serious offer to him to join the Shadow Cabinet. These stories were accompanied by suggestions that he now intended to use the position gained through the referendum campaign to make his way back – presumably at my expense – to power. Ted's ambitions were his own affair. But at least the real

facts about the Wilton Street meeting should be known. Consequently, I told them to George Hutchinson of *The Times* – not a
supporter of mine, but a journalist of great integrity – and the
account duly appeared.

No doubt Ted's hopes were buoyed up by two other things.
First, I could not fail to be aware that all sorts of well-informed
commentators were predicting that my tenure of the leadership
would not last; indeed, that I would be gone by Christmas. Secondly, the deepening economic crisis into which a combination of
the Heath Government's earlier financial irresponsibility and the
Wilson Government's present anti-enterprise policies were plung-
ing Britain might conceivably lead to that National Government
on which Ted's prospects were deemed to ride. And perhaps too,
the introduction of proportional representation might keep a cen-
trist coalition in power – and people like me out of it – permanently.

In fact, the chances of any of this happening were less than the
commentators imagined. It was not just that I had no intention of
relinquishing the leadership, nor even that Tory backbenchers were
unprepared to tolerate Ted's return. Neither was there any prospect
of a shrewd, self-assured politician like Harold Wilson stepping
aside gracefully to allow the sort of self-important figures he
despised a free hand to sort Britain's problems out. If he went he
would do so on his terms and at his timing: this of course is what
subsequently occurred.* A further aspect not widely grasped at the
time was that, for all the criticism levelled at me for my alleged
failure to beat the European drum with sufficient vigour, I emerged
from the campaign as a unifying figure for the Party. The anti-
Market Tory MPs felt no bitterness towards me. The majority of
backbenchers also felt very much as I did about Europe, viewing
it as a framework within which Britain could prosper rather than
a crusade. The issue of whether Britain should or should not be
a member of the European Community had been settled for the
foreseeable future. But the real question now was what *sort* of Community should that be? On this issue a rather different coalition of
opinions within the Conservative Party would emerge.

Two short foreign visits which I made in the course of the Euro-

* See pp. 312–13.

pean referendum campaign provided me with food for thought. At the end of April I visited Luxembourg and attended the European Assembly, which was already demanding to be termed a 'Parliament'. A lacklustre debate on some trivial issue was in progress, after which the best I could say to an eager press corps was that the institution was obviously 'very valuable' and that its members worked 'very hard'. At this time the members of the Assembly were still nominated MPs from the constituent countries. We all ought probably to have thought more carefully about whether it was right to end this system in favour of direct elections. At least under the old system there was close contact between the members of the national Parliament and members of the European Assembly; they were, indeed, the same people. The Assembly had a limited role for which full-time MEPs were unnecessary. When the latter appeared on the scene they demanded a wider role, in part in order to justify their salaries, generous expenses and existence, and this was to cause no end of problems. My main conclusion from the visit to Luxembourg, however, was that such an Assembly in which people did not speak the same language or share the same traditions illustrated the shortcomings of attempts to create artificial Europe-wide institutions. Peter Kirk, the Conservative Leader in the Assembly, who organized a reception for me in Luxembourg, was doing his best to import British parliamentary attitudes and impose some financial discipline. But it would take more than this to create a real European Parliament.

The following month I was invited to Paris as the guest of the Gaullist Party – then called the UDR, later the RPR. It was on this visit that I first met Jacques Chirac, the Prime Minister, with whom I had lunch at the Hôtel Matignon (his office and official residence), and President Valéry Giscard d'Estaing, whom I saw later at the Elysée Palace. In spite of the marked differences of character between the two – the Prime Minister's charismatic exuberance was the complete opposite of the President's chilly precision – both the Matignon and the Elysée made the same statement of the historic grandeur and national pride of France. French identity and interests would always come first in the Community or any other forum. Some people might have felt aggrieved at this, but I found it oddly reassuring: you knew where you stood.

Three different but connected developments from now on commanded my attention in Europe. First, there was the matter of the speed and extent of European integration: in particular, we had to consider the arrangements for direct elections to the European Assembly and our policy towards the European Monetary System. Secondly, there was the feeling, which I shared, that the right-of-centre parties in Europe ought to cooperate more closely, providing a kind of answer to the Socialist International. Thirdly, it was necessary to establish what Western Europe's role should be in East–West relations, particularly in the light of the Helsinki process – something which is best examined later.*

At the beginning of July Leo Tindemans, the Belgian Prime Minister, came to Britain, having been asked by the heads of Government at the Paris Summit of December 1974 to draw up a report on 'European Union'. I met him with Reggie Maudling and others in a room at the House of Commons. I had set up a committee under Reggie on which Sir Anthony Royle, a former diplomat, and others sat, to look at such matters. But I emphasized to M. Tindemans that it would be best if the Community developed organically rather than according to some pre-ordained structure. This was intended as a warning that, although I envisaged that Britain under a Conservative Government would adopt a more positive attitude to the Community than had been the case under Labour, our partners should not imagine that we were keen on grand plans imposed from the centre.

Within the Conservative Party, debate about Europe focused increasingly on direct elections. I received regular reports on Party opinion. A group of MPs led by Neil Marten argued a powerful case against having direct elections at all. A larger group of MPs reluctantly accepted that the pass had been sold and that the real question was when the elections should take place and under what electoral system. A third group was keen to create a real European Parliament to provide a check on the actions of the Council of Ministers and the Commission. Luckily, the divisions on the Government side were at least as large as on ours, and we were able to unite in blaming them for the delay in bringing the requisite

* See pp. 349–53.

legislation before the House. Equally satisfactorily, the Government proposal to use proportional representation, a gesture to sustain the Lib-Lab Pact, was soundly defeated in December 1977. Consequently, the first direct elections took place – under a first-past-the-post system – in 1979 when I was Prime Minister.

The pressure for political integration was to have its economic counterpart. The first ambitious plans for European economic and monetary union were embodied in the so-called 'Snake' set up in 1972. Britain had joined under Ted as one earnest of his iron-clad commitment to Europe; he had to pull out within six weeks. But the economic planners were only stimulated by failure, and at the end of 1978 the European Monetary System (EMS) was agreed and eight of the nine Community currencies joined. Britain alone stayed out. Her Majesty's Opposition under my leadership would have been less than human not to take advantage of this as evidence that sterling was too weak to join as a result of Labour's mismanagement of the economy. That was a fair enough tactical position, but it was more difficult to judge what a Conservative Government itself should do.

At the end of October 1978 Geoffrey Howe sent me a note outlining the case for and against joining. He felt that if we were now the Government and had committed ourselves to the right financial and economic policies, we would have been able to join. Geoffrey also believed that we needed to maintain the Party's stock of European goodwill and feared that the alternative meant 'surrendering the direction of the EEC and its policies to the Franco-German high table'. Nigel Lawson, a junior Treasury spokesman, also sent me a searching analysis at the end of October. He understood that the EMS was seen by the French and Germans as having a political objective, the next stage in the progress of European unity. He shrewdly noted that 'those who support UK membership of the EMS as part of their devotion to the EEC cause should pause to reflect whether adherence to the discipline which is its sole merit might not in practice prove so unpopular as to make support of continuing EEC membership political suicide'. Nigel's reluctant conclusion was that we should join anyway: but his 'best hope' was that the system would collapse shortly thereafter, not due to the weakness of sterling but because of pressures on other currencies, and that we could then propose some more sensible framework for European economic convergence. I was impressed by the quality of both these analyses. My thinking on this was still evolving, but I decided at this point that we should continue to adopt a positive general approach to the EMS while avoiding making any specific commitments.

The second important European theme – the closer cooperation of the right-of-centre parties – eventually led to the foundation in 1978 of the European Democratic Union (EDU). But this modestly useful organization was less significant than the political impulses which lay behind it. The mid-1970s was a time of advance by the Left, both democratic and non-democratic, in many areas and ways. Communist parties seemed to be on the verge of entering government in Mediterranean Europe. And everywhere the Left was encouraged by the feeling that history and Soviet military power were pushing the world in its direction. This was something which could only ultimately be combated and reversed by NATO decisions and under reinvigorated American leadership. In the meantime, the European Right had to fight a fierce battle on the political front.

Nowhere was it fiercer than in Portugal. Within weeks of my becoming Leader I had a long talk with Professor Diogo Freitas do Amaral, the leader of the Social Democratic Centre (CDS), the only party to the right of the ruling coalition. He was a gentle intellectual, clearly involved in politics for the highest motives. He was also, when I saw him, in deep despair. Since the overthrow of the dictatorship of Dr Caetano in April 1974, communists and other radical leftists in the army, in cahoots with the Portuguese Communist Party, had successfully manipulated their way to almost total power. This they used ruthlessly to extinguish opposition. The CDS was denied access to the media and its rallies were broken up by force. Professor do Amaral knew that under these conditions there was no hope of a successful result in the forthcoming elections. He half wondered whether it was worth his going back to Portugal at all. But we both agreed that in spite of all the difficulties he had to return and see it through. He did so. But he was fighting impossible odds. His party received less than 8 per cent of the vote. There would probably be no democracy in Portugal even now if brave men and women like Professor do Amaral had not risen up against the arrogance of the communists in northern Portugal and prevented the forcible attempt to seize the peasants' land and turn the country into a Cuban-style state. It was a frightening insight into the ambitions and methods of the Left, which were by no means confined to Portugal. Indeed, the British Labour Left, intoxicated by the prospects of a European revolution, supported the communists.

Neighbouring Spain was more fortunate, enjoying a more or less smooth transition from dictatorship after General Franco's death in November 1975. There, doubtless observing the Portuguese resistance offered to too blatant an attempt to seize power, the Spanish Communist Party from the date of its legalization in 1977 preferred to emulate its Italian and French counterparts by adopting the disguise of 'Euro-communism'. I always considered Euro-communism as a tactical ploy to be understood in very much the same way as, to take an earlier parallel, the Popular Fronts in the 1930s. It did indeed show a recognition of the force of liberal public opinion and foreshadowed the coming collapse of communism's internal self-confidence. But it did not represent any abandonment of the essential goals of Marxism-Leninism. Of course, the only 'proof' of this could be found in an assessment of the real attitudes and intentions of the Euro-communist leaderships. But in any case the *effect* of any advance by Euro-communists was to reduce the willingness and ability of the West to meet the growing Soviet threat; for it would have been unpardonably irresponsible to assume that any government in which a Communist Party shared power could be depended upon in a crisis.

I made these points wherever I went in Europe. But I did so with particular force when I addressed the West German Christian Democrat Union (CDU) Party Conference in Hanover on Tuesday 25 May 1976:

In some European countries we now see communist parties dressed in democratic clothes and speaking with soft voices. Of course, we hope that their oft-proclaimed change of heart is genuine. But every child in Europe knows the story of Little Red Riding Hood and what happened to her in her grandmother's cottage in the forest. Despite the new look of these communist parties, despite the softness of their voices, we should be on the watch for the teeth and appetite of the wolf.

It was clear to me from the uproarious applause which greeted this remark that Little Red Riding Hood had a cousin somewhere in the Black Forest.

I had been keen to visit West Germany for several reasons. It was, of course, right on the frontier of freedom in Europe at a time when the perimeter of freedom globally was steadily contracting. The West's strategy for defence depended to an important degree upon the policies of West Germany's political leaders and the will of the West German people. Konrad Adenauer and his successor Chancellors of the German Federal Republic had staunchly resisted the blandishments and threats of the Soviet Union and its East German satellite. But Willi Brandt's *Ostpolitik*, the hidden agenda of which was German reunification on Eastern terms, had shaken many assumptions. It had the unintended effects of promoting neutralist attitudes in West Germany (including in the ruling SPD) and of endorsing the legitimacy of the governments in Eastern Europe. Doubts about *Ostpolitik* and the soundness of the SPD lingered on, in spite of the robustness of Willi Brandt's successor Helmut Schmidt, who soon set about strengthening Atlantic links with his call for NATO's stationing of American intermediate-range nuclear missiles in Europe. In turn, Helmut Schmidt conceived an increasing distrust for the meanderings of US foreign policy under Jimmy Carter.

The other reason I was eager to make the trip was the importance of the CDU itself, which was, with the Conservatives, the other largest right-of-centre European party. The idea of setting up a joint organization – what became the EDU – originally came from the Austrian (Christian Democrat) People's Party leader, Alois Mock. But the Germans and ourselves were bound to be the two key elements in it. Although I was later to discover the important differences between the German Christian Democrat and British Conservative traditions, these were not nearly as great as those between Christian Democrats in countries like Italy or Belgium and ourselves. In Germany the social-market approach pioneered by Ludwig Erhard had imposed a more free-enterprise orientation than on most other Christian Democrat parties, which remained heavily confessional and usually somewhat directionless in economics.

My first visit to West Germany as Leader was from Thursday 26 June to Saturday 28 June 1975. That first Thursday evening at the British Ambassador's residence in Bonn my mind was focused, however, on what was happening back home, where the count for the Woolwich West by-election was under way. Unlike my predecessors, I had decided to campaign personally in by-elections, which carried risks but which was an advantage when things went well, as they did on this occasion, for we won the seat on a swing of 7.6 per cent. Since, as usual, the Party was strapped for cash, I was not accompanied by a press officer and, knowing this, Gordon Reece had advised me what to say and do in the event of the expected success. We agreed that I would say something on the lines of 'This is the first step on the road to the end of socialism,' and then I would make a Churchillian victory sign – all the more appropriate since I was in Germany. Gordon did not consider coaching me in the gesture itself. So when, the following day, I was asked to comment on the result I smiled and raised two fingers, unfortunately the wrong way round, which was taken by delighted cameramen as an expression of lighthearted if vulgar contempt for the Labour Party rather than satisfaction with our own success.

Later that day I had my first meeting with the socialist Chancellor Helmut Schmidt. By the end of our discussion I was concluding that he was a good deal less socialist than some members of my own Shadow Cabinet, two impressions which did not diminish as the years went by. We did, though, disagree about the role of trade unions. On the basis of German experience, Helmut Schmidt could not understand why in Britain we did not just get all the union leaders around a table and work things out sensibly. I pointed out that thanks to the reforms which the British occupying power had made in the structure of German trade unions after the war, reducing their number and making them industry-based rather than craft-based, this was a practical possibility in Bonn. In London a small stadium would be required. (My knowledge of these reforms was due to Paul Chambers, the British member of the Control Commission which had run the Western sectors of Germany during the Allied occupation: I had known him since the 1960s.) I was tempted to add that most British trade union leaders, unlike their German equivalents, were at least as interested in socialist politics as sensible wage bargaining. But I decided that could wait for another occasion.

A late lunch had been arranged for me by my CDU hosts. The three German celebrities present were Helmut Kohl, the CDU leader and Chancellor-candidate for the following year's federal elections, Kurt Biedenkopf, the CDU General Secretary and – most celebrated of all – Ludwig Erhard, the great German Finance Minister of the 1950s and sixties. I had had some discussions with Helmut Kohl earlier in the day. My first impression was that he was amiable and instinctively sound on the important issues. But neither of us spoke the other's language and our discussion tended, therefore, to be somewhat halting. For the next decade, however, we were to be broadly on the same wavelength on the East–West issues that dominated European politics. Professor Biedenkopf was a more cosmopolitan character, fluent to a fault, deeply intelligent and extraordinarily energetic. He bubbled with ideas and reflections so that I found it difficult to get a word in. He was plainly determined, as I was, that when his party returned to power it would do so with a cohesive and well thought-out programme for government. Ludwig Erhard had by this time retired from any involvement in active politics, but apparently he had heard that my politics (and economics) were sufficiently different (that is to say similar to his own) to make a discussion appealing. I was glad to discover that the former Chancellor, as well as being the architect of German prosperity, had a considerable presence and shrewdness. He asked me a number of searching questions about my economic approach, at the end of which he seemed satisfied. I felt I had performed well in an important tutorial. In their different ways these three men symbolized the considerable strengths of German Christian Democracy and I went away feeling that our two parties, both in opposition but both preparing for power, had much in common.

My reception on my next visit the following year at the CDU Conference, which I have already described, in part confirmed this.

But I could never quite adjust to the style of West German politics which I witnessed there. Successive speakers approached the microphone and, from an inch or two away, bellowed into it at great length. The technique for evoking applause appeared to be to shout at such volume that words were lost amid the crackling of overstrained loudspeakers. Neither a Conservative Party Conference, nor in all probability Conservative Central Office equipment, would have stood it.

Meanwhile, discussions between European conservative and Christian Democrat parties continued about the formation of the EDU. I tried to persuade the less enthusiastic parties, nervous of being seen as right-wing in countries where a tradition of coalition governments had blunted principled politics. In December 1976 I visited The Hague for talks with Dutch politicians – an occasion of longer-term personal importance to me because this was when I first met Ruud Lubbers, the then Economics Minister and future Prime Minister with whom in the years to come I was to strike up a mutually beneficial friendship. I also spoke to the British Chamber of Commerce there:

I am anxious that . . . there should be a closer cooperation between like-minded political parties across the Community. Of course I understand that history has put difficulties in our way . . . Nevertheless, I feel sure that as we examine our policies we will find that the common ground is much greater than we supposed at the outset.

In June 1977 I paid a flying visit to Rome. This too resulted in some valuable contacts and discussions, notably with the grand old man of Christian Democracy, Professor Amintore Fanfani, and also with one of Italy's most clever and effective Finance Ministers, Filippo Pandolfi. My visit concluded with a private audience with Pope Paul VI – my first experience of the Vatican. These are always very private occasions. With Pope Paul VI and later with Pope John Paul II I discussed Northern Ireland; and with John Paul II, whose election as Pope has always struck me as providential, I held in addition a discussion about the irreligious nature of communism and the challenge it presented to Christian statesmanship.

It is no secret that I greatly admire the role played by John Paul II in the liberation of his country, Poland, and of the other countries of Eastern Europe from the legions of communists that proved no match for his spiritual authority.

In public speeches on this visit I called for the involvement of the Italian Christian Democrats in the nascent EDU: I recognized that the word 'conservative' had a different and pejorative significance in Italy, but urged my hosts to consider instead the reality of our similar policies. I made the point in person to Aldo Moro, then the Christian Democrat party leader. He was an aloof, academic figure on the left of his party, and I did not feel he was very sympathetic to what I was saying. Alas, there was no occasion to return to the subject, for within a year Signor Moro was kidnapped and murdered.

In retrospect, I can see that the Italians were quite right in thinking that they and we saw the world very differently. Christian Democracy served a useful purpose in many European countries, where it was important for all shades of moderate opinion to combine in order to resist fascism and communism. Catholic social teaching provided a valuable framework – for Protestants as well – in societies where no strong secular centre-right political tradition existed. The trouble was that, whatever their merits as a view of life, such ideas were not in themselves sufficient to give an ideological basis for the practical policies required in the late twentieth century. This was particularly true of economic policy, where anything from full-blooded free enterprise on the one hand to corporatism on the other could be dressed up in the language of Christian Democracy. Some Christian Democrat parties, like the German CDU, have gone at least part of the way towards making up for such deficiencies by adopting free-market rhetoric (if not always free-market policies). Others, like the Italian Christian Democrats, have gone the way of all dinosaurs. Christian Democracy has also shown itself incapable of shedding light on the great question of the post-Cold War world – the long-term relationship between nation states and supra-national institutions. I conclude that however much individual Christian Democrats may command our respect and deserve our support, Conservatives have little to learn from them.

In any case, Christian Democrat and conservative parties from Austria, Denmark, Finland, Germany, Iceland, Norway, Portugal, Sweden and Britain did agree to found the European Democratic Union. I was present at the launch in Salzburg in April 1978. Among other party leaders there were Helmut Kohl and Franz Josef Strauss – the leader of the Bavarian Christian Social Union (CSU) and, after Herr Kohl's narrow defeat in the elections in October 1976, the Chancellor-candidate of the German right. The contrast between the two of them interested me. Both were very large and very German. But Herr Strauss was a mercurial intellectual, had a lively wit and was an accomplished orator. He also lacked Helmut Kohl's caution and, when pitted against Helmut Schmidt, his impulsiveness, and a not altogether deserved reputation for extremism later defeated him. It was a glittering occasion at the Klessheim Castle and the Austrians, whose brainchild the EDU was, were magnificent hosts. And for me it was also a useful platform at an important time.

As I have mentioned, the third pressing European question was the role of the countries of the Community in East–West relations. Although this issue preoccupied me from soon after my becoming Leader, I only tackled it directly on one occasion – in a speech, drafted with the help of Hugh Thomas, to the Grandes Conférences Catholiques in Brussels on Friday 23 June 1978. The theme was 'Principles of Foreign Policy', covering a wide canvas, including the need to advance democracy throughout the world so as to reduce the risk of war. But the part of the speech which received greatest attention concerned the political role of the European Community. I did not regard the EEC as merely an economic entity: it had a wider strategic purpose. As a zone of democracy, stability and prosperity adjoining Soviet-dominated Eastern Europe, it was both a showcase for the Western way of life and a magnet drawing politicians and peoples away from communism. Moreover, Western European countries should not be tempted to govern their relations with the Soviet Union and its satellites on economic grounds alone, but rather with full regard to the effects of technology transfer and cheap credits in oiling the Russian war machine.

We must see our relationships with the Soviet Union as a whole. The supply by the West of credit, grain and technology; the negotiation of different aspects of security and disarmament; Soviet and satellite activities in Africa, Asia and the Pacific are all features of one landscape. Unless we learn, as the Soviet Union has learned, to look at the landscape as a whole we shall be consistently out-manoeuvred.

In order to grasp how we had arrived at such a pass it is necessary to consider the East–West balance more generally.

EAST–WEST

One of the first foreign statesmen I met after becoming Leader was Henry Kissinger, President Gerald Ford's Secretary of State. Over the years my respect for Dr Kissinger steadily grew and – though starting from different perspectives – our analysis of international events increasingly converged. At this time, however, I was uneasy about the direction of Western policy towards the Soviet Union, of which he was acknowledged to be the impresario.

I did indeed recognize the importance of the 'opening to China' achieved under Richard Nixon in the power-play with the Soviets. It was a crucial element of victory in the Cold War to detach China permanently from the Soviet Union. As for 'linkage' – that is to recognize the links between one issue and another in bilateral relations between states, in Henry Kissinger's own words 'to create a network of incentives and penalties to produce the most favourable outcome'* – I took the view that its prospects had been undermined by President Nixon's domestic weakness induced by Watergate. But I had serious doubts about the strategy of '*détente*'.

My gut instinct was that this was one of those soothing foreign terms which conceal an ugly reality that plain English would

---

* Henry Kissinger, *Diplomacy* (New York, 1994), p. 717. This is, of course, an oversimplified description of the concept. *Diplomacy* contains a fuller, masterly account of Dr Kissinger's thinking.

expose. It was difficult to see any difference between appeasement and *détente* as it began to evolve under the conditions of American paralysis after the election of a post-Watergate Congress dominated by ultra-liberal Democrats and the collapsing position in South Vietnam. Although so many obeisances had been paid to the concept that it was not prudent to attack it directly, I came as near as I could. This was not just a reflection of my preference for plain speaking: it was also the result of my conviction that too many people in the West had been lulled into believing that their way of life was secure, when it was in fact under mortal threat.

The first condition for meeting and overcoming that threat was that the Alliance should perceive what was happening; the second and equally important condition was that we should summon up the will to change it. Even in Britain's parlous economic state we still had the resources to fight back, as part of NATO and under the leadership of the United States. But we could not assume that that would always be so. At some point decline – not just relative but absolute and not just limited to one sphere but in every sphere, economic, military, political and psychological – might become irreversible. Urgent action was required and urgency entails risks. Accordingly, my first major foreign affairs speech was a risk.

Events continued to confirm my analysis. In March the Labour Government's Defence White Paper announced sharp cuts in the defence budget, £4,700 million over the next ten years. In the same month Alexander Shelepin, previously head of the KGB and now in charge of the Soviet Union's 'trade unions', arrived in Britain as a guest of the TUC. The following month saw the fall of Saigon to the North Vietnamese communists amid scenes of chaos, adding to America's woes. Cuban 'advisers' were beginning to arrive to support the communist MPLA faction in Angola. It was, however, what I heard and read about the preparations for the Helsinki Summit that triggered my decision to speak.

The idea for Helsinki had come from the Soviets, was warmly welcomed by Chancellor Brandt's West Germany as a contribution to *Ostpolitik*, and was then accepted on to the Nixon Administration's agenda. The West wanted the Soviets to enter into talks to reduce their military superiority in Europe – Mutual Balanced

Force Reductions (MBFR) – and to respect the human rights of their subject peoples. But what did the Soviets want? This was by far the most interesting question, since even if, as the sceptics suggested, they would not honour their agreements anyway, they still would not have taken this trouble unless something important for them would result. Respectability could be the only answer. If the Soviet Union and its satellites – particularly the more potentially fragile regimes in Eastern Europe – could receive the international seal of approval they would feel more secure.

But did we want them to feel more secure? Arguably, one of the most exploitable weaknesses of totalitarian dictatorships is the paranoid insecurity which flows from the lack of consent to the regime itself and which results in inefficiency and even paralysis of decision-taking. If the Soviets felt more secure, if their new-found respectability gave them greater access to credit and technology, if they were treated with tolerant respect rather than suspicious hostility, how would they use these advantages?

That led, of course, to the further question: what was the fundamental impulse of the Soviet Union? If the Soviet leaders were reasonable people, a little hidebound perhaps but open to persuasion, not so very different from the political élites of our countries, the lessening of tension with the West would indeed lead to a more peaceful and stable world. The trouble was that no one with real knowledge of the Soviet system believed that this was so. That system was founded upon an ideology which moulded every person and institution within it according to techniques of varying sophistication and crudity. The evidence for this was the ruthlessness with which it dealt with the tiny minority who dared to challenge it. The fate of the dissidents was not just something to evoke Western compassion or outrage: it was a statement about the nature and objectives of the system which regarded them as such a threat to its existence.

But it was not necessary to listen to Alexander Solzhenitsyn to learn the truth about the Soviet Union – though, as I shall describe, his words had a powerful effect on me. One need only turn to the leaden prose of *Pravda* to establish how the Soviet leaders perceived *détente* and the Helsinki initiative which flowed from it:

Peaceful coexistence does not signify the end of the struggle between the two world social systems. The struggle will continue . . . until the complete and final victory of communism on a world scale. [*Pravda*, 22 August 1973.]

In other words, there would be no letting-up in the promotion of Soviet power and communist revolution worldwide. If such statements were a true reflection of Soviet intentions – and there was a great deal of evidence to show that they were – any weakening of external pressure on the Soviets would simply result in their having more resources and opportunities to 'bury us'.

If I was to challenge the accepted wisdom on these matters I needed expert help. But most of the experts had jumped aboard the Sovietology gravy train which ran on official patronage, conferences with 'approved' Soviet academics, visa journalism and a large dose of professional complacency. I had, however, through John O'Sullivan of the *Daily Telegraph*, heard about Robert Conquest, a British historian and fearless critic of the USSR. I asked him to help me and together we wrote the speech which I delivered on Saturday 26 July 1975 in Chelsea. The occasion itself was only arranged a few days in advance. I did not speak to Reggie Maudling or anyone else in the Shadow Cabinet about it beforehand, because I knew that all I would receive were obstruction and warnings, which would doubtless be leaked afterwards – particularly if things went wrong.

I began by setting the large military imbalance between the West and the Soviet Union against the background of the retreat of Western power. I drew particular attention to the Soviet naval build-up, describing the Soviet navy as a global force with more nuclear submarines than the rest of the world's navies put together and more surface ships than could possibly be needed to protect the USSR's coast and merchant shipping. I argued that nothing was more important to our security than the American commitment to Europe, adding that an isolationist Britain would encourage an isolationist America.

I then dealt with the imminent Helsinki Summit. I did not attack *détente* directly, indeed I called for a 'real' *détente*. But I quoted Leonid Brezhnev speaking in June 1972 to illustrate the Soviets' true intentions. Brezhnev had affirmed that peaceful coexistence 'in no way implies the possibility of relaxing the ideological struggle. On the contrary we must be prepared for this struggle to be intensified and become an even sharper form of confrontation between the systems.'

I also drew attention to the importance of human rights as a further measure of the nature of the regime with which we were dealing:

> When the Soviet leaders gaol a writer, or a priest, or a doctor or a worker for the crime of speaking freely, it is not only for humanitarian reasons that we should be concerned. For these acts reveal a country that is afraid of truth and liberty; it dare not allow its people to enjoy the freedoms we take for granted, and a nation that denies those freedoms to its own people will have few scruples in denying them to others.

Human rights would, we already knew, be the subject of far reaching verbal undertakings in the so-called 'Basket Three' of the Helsinki package – 'Cooperation in humanitarian and other fields'. But I placed no trust in the Soviets' good faith: indeed, since their whole system depended upon repression, it was difficult to see how they could comply. I suspected that for many of those present at Helsinki – and not just on the communist side – the undertakings about human rights would be regarded as uplifting rhetoric rather than clear conditions to be rigorously monitored. So I noted:

> We must work for a real relaxation of tension, but in our negotiations with the Eastern bloc we must not accept words or gestures as a substitute for genuine *détente*. No flood of words emanating from a summit conference will mean anything unless it is accompanied by some positive action by which the Soviet leaders show that their ingrained attitudes are really beginning to change.
>
> That is why we so strongly support all those European and American spokesmen, who have insisted that no serious advance towards a stable peace can be made unless some progress at least is seen in the free movement of people and of ideas.

The reaction to this speech confirmed that I was the odd woman out. The Helsinki Agreement was widely welcomed. I could imagine the shaking of wise heads at my impulsive imprudence. Reggie Maudling came round at once to see me in Flood Street to express both his anger at my delivering such a speech without consulting him and his disagreement with its content. I gave no ground. Indeed, Mr Brezhnev's evident satisfaction at what Helsinki achieved helped convince me that I must return to the subject: he described it as 'a necessary summing up of the political outcome of the Second World War'. In other words he regarded it – not least perhaps the commitment not to alter European borders except 'by peaceful means and by agreement' – as recognizing and legitimizing the Soviet hold on Eastern Europe which they had obtained by force and fraud at the end of the war.

The Helsinki Summit of 1975 is now viewed in a favourable light because the dissidents in the Soviet Union and Eastern Europe used its provisions as a programme for which to fight in their long struggle with the communist State. And indeed by making human rights a matter of treaty obligations rather than domestic law it gave the dissidents leverage which they employed to the full. Their bravery would have been of little account, however, without the subsequent Western, particularly American, renewal of resolve and defence build-up. These halted the expansion that had given Soviet communism the psychological prestige of historical inevitability, exerted an external pressure on communist regimes that diverted them from domestic repression, and gave heart to the burgeoning resistance movements against communism. This pincer movement – the revived West and the dissidents – more than countered the advantages that the Soviets received from Helsinki in the form of increased legitimacy and Western recognition. Without that, Helsinki would have been just one more step on the road to defeat.

Not surprisingly after the Helsinki speech, I was not invited to the Soviet Union, as perhaps a different Leader of the Opposition would have been. But I felt it important to deepen my knowledge of the communist system in practice. Consequently, when an invitation arrived for me to visit Romania I accepted. I already had some knowledge of that country, gained when I was Education Secretary. Improbable as it may seem, there had grown up a regular Anglo-Romanian seminar on education, held one year in Bucharest and one year in Cambridge. My Romanian opposite number, Mircea Malita, was a distinguished mathematician. Like other 'cultural' events under communism, these seminars had a largely political and diplomatic purpose. That said, there was no doubt in my mind about the cultural riches of Romania itself – not only Bucharest, known as 'the Paris of the Balkans' (still at that time spared from the later devastation inflicted on it by Ceausescu's megalomaniac building plans of the 1980s), but also the luminous painted monastery churches of Bukovina, which I visited in September 1971. Not surprisingly, the Romanians were anxious to continue to cultivate me when I became Leader of the Opposition, and for the moment this accorded with my purposes as well.

At the time of my second visit at the beginning of September 1975, Romania occupied a unique position in the communist world. Following in the footsteps of his (already disgraced) predecessor Gheorghe Dej, Nicolae Ceausescu had plotted out an independent path for Romania within the Warsaw Pact. In 1968, for example, he had visited Prague and, apparently sincerely, expressed support for the Polish reform movement and bitterly condemned the Russian suppression of it. The Western view, which I then shared, was that Romania should be accorded discreet support in the hope that its example might lead to further fragmentation in Soviet-controlled Eastern Europe. In fact, Ceausescu was playing a ruthless game in which ethnic tensions (with Hungary), East–West competition (between NATO and the Warsaw Pact) and rivalry within the communist world (between the Soviet Union and China) were exploited as seemed appropriate at any juncture.

Between the conversations I had with Ceausescu in 1971 and 1975 he had further consolidated his position. Although he had become effective leader in 1965, it was not until 1974 that he united the functions of Party Leader and Head of State and Government. From now on he was freer to indulge his political fantasies. For what we Westerners did not sufficiently grasp was that Ceausescu was a throwback both to Stalinism, whose methods he employed, and indeed to a more traditional Balkan despotism for which the promotion of his family and the flaunting of wealth and power were essential trappings. Ceausescu himself never struck me as anything out of the ordinary, just cold, rather dull, spewing forth streams of statistics and possessing that stilted formal courtesy that communists adopted as a substitute for genuine civilization. We discussed the Soviet threat and he gave me a long account, faithfully mirrored later by guides, diplomats and factory managers, of the astonishing successes of the Romanian economy. He was particularly proud of the level of 'investment' which, as a share of the national income, certainly dwarfed that of Western countries. In fact, of course, misdirected investment is a classic feature of the planned economy; it was just that Romania, whose people apart from the ruling élite lived in poverty, misdirected more than the others.

I was also shown around a scientific institute specializing in polymer research. My guide was none other than Elena Ceausescu, who had already begun to indulge a personal fantasy world which matched her husband's in absurdity, if not in human consequences: she was determined to win a Nobel Prize in chemistry for work on polymers. It subsequently emerged that she could barely have distinguished a polymer from a polygon. But behind the defences of translation and communist long-windedness she put up quite a good show.

In other ways, however, Romania did illustrate more characteristic features of the communist system. I visited a factory and heard from those in charge – I presumed they were the management – a litany of the company's achievements. 'That's very interesting,' I said, 'but could I speak to the trade union leaders here? Perhaps they may have something to add?' A look of astonishment spread across their faces. 'But that's us!' they replied. What the individual workers at the factory – or indeed the neighbours across whose houses it was belching thick brown smoke – might have commented is another matter. For, as in the fully developed socialist state, the trade unions of Romania were political not industrial institutions.

A little later I had dinner with Members of the Romanian 'Parliament'. It was explained to me that one had to be a member of an approved, i.e. reliably communist, trade union in order to stand in a parliamentary election. They showed me the list of some thirty-five such bodies. Looking down it, the 'beekeepers' union' càught my eye. The opportunity was irresistible. In grave fashion I began to interrogate them. How large was the beekeepers' bloc in Parliament? Who were its leaders? What were the factions? Was there an anti-beekeepers' faction? The evening slipped by more quickly.

A final practical lesson for me, which any Western politician or businessman visiting the Eastern bloc was well advised to learn as soon as possible, was to assume that someone was always listening. This was an inconvenience for people like me in the country for just a few days. But for the subjects of a communist state it was a kind of intellectual terror. Depriving human beings of their privacy has the intended psychological effect of making them withdrawn, introverted and incapable of the communication based on mutual trust which permits civil society. Thus communism applied sophisticated techniques in the service of a primitive ideology so as to destroy not just potential centres of opposition but rather the final enemy, human personality.

Ceausescu's Romania already reflected this in an advanced form, though for me and my party it was a matter of farce, not tragedy. I had already been told at the British Embassy how one of our diplomats, anxious to recruit a nanny for his young children and hazy about how to insert a suitable advertisement in a Romanian newspaper, decided that the simplest and most reliable method was to tell an astonished friend on the Embassy telephone of his urgent requirement. Sure enough, and without a blush, in the course of some discussion of a quite different subject a Romanian official suggested a candidate.

Richard Ryder and I were put up in the State Guest House. Interestingly, the sitting-room ceiling consisted of an open wooden grille, doubtless good for ventilation but possibly for other purposes too. I just could not make the television work when I wanted to listen to the news. Richard was no more successful. We were still struggling when a knock on the door announced the arrival of a member of the Guest House staff who helpfully put us right.

Even before this visit, I had few illusions about the oppressive nature of the regime. Whatever Western strategic interests might require, I was determined that the pressure should be kept up to improve respect for human rights, particularly when the ink was barely dry on the Helsinki Agreement. An expatriate Romanian group in Britain, knowing of my impending visit, sent me a list of five political prisoners, asking me to urge their release. I immediately agreed to do so. But somehow the Foreign Office got wind of this and sought determinedly to dissuade me on the grounds that it would alienate Ceausescu to no good purpose. A senior civil servant explained in person the deep unwisdom of my intention. I was not impressed. In Bucharest I gave the Romanians the list and said that these people were wrongly imprisoned and must be set free. I was glad to see that they subsequently were.

Undoubtedly, the most important foreign tour I made in 1975 – probably the most significant during my time as Leader of the Opposition – was to the United States in September. I already, of course, knew something of the States; and I liked and admired most of what I knew. This, however, was my first opportunity to meet all the leading political figures, and do so on something approaching equal terms. I was guaranteed plenty of media attention, if largely for the depressing reason that Britain's stock had rarely fallen lower. American newspapers, magazines and television programmes were concentrating on the precipitous decline of the British economy, the advance of trade union power, the extension of the socialist state and what was perceived to be a collapse of national self-confidence. Aside from the *schadenfreude*, also evident was a nagging worry that America, itself suffering a deep but different crisis in the wake of the fall of Vietnam and the trauma of Watergate, might suffer the same fate.*

I had discussed the situation with Norman Lamont, an early supporter whose job with Rothschilds enabled him to keep me in touch with what was going on in the City and abroad, and who had just returned from the United States where he had spoken to politicians, officials and opinion-formers. I gained the impression, which proved accurate, that the Ford Administration's confidence

---

* Typical of the coverage was an article from the *Wall Street Journal* (20 August 1975) I found in my briefing papers. It began: 'Hardly anyone needs to be told now that Great Britain is the sick country of Europe. Everywhere you look the evidence abounds.' The article described our position – falling output, runaway inflation, declining industries, a falling (and relatively low) standard of living. Its author reflected: 'It is all very curious. For Britain has not been brought to this state by defeat in war, by earthquakes, plagues, droughts or any natural disasters. Britain's undoing is its own doing. It has been brought to this by the calculated policies of its Government and by their resigned acceptance by the people.'

had started modestly to increase, which was giving them all the more opportunity to worry about what was happening in Britain. The Prime Minister, who had recently been in Washington, had done nothing to improve perceptions by claiming that all our difficulties were grossly exaggerated. Something different and more serious was expected. I resolved to provide it.

Gordon Reece flew on ahead of me to New York in order to set up the media arrangements. Just before I left London he telephoned to say that expectations of my visit were now so high that I should make the first speech I was to deliver – to the Institute of Socio-Economic Studies in New York – a blockbuster rather than, as planned, a low-key performance with the main speech coming later in Washington. This required frenzied last-minute speech-rewriting with Adam Ridley, and it showed in the text. Most of the speech struck exactly the right note. It began by taking head-on the American comments on the sorry state of contemporary Britain and treating them seriously. I then drew attention to what I called 'the progressive consensus, the doctrine that the state should be active on many fronts in promoting equality: in the provision of social welfare and in the redistribution of wealth and incomes'. There followed a detailed analysis of its effects in the form of over-taxation, the discouragement of enterprise, the squeeze on profits, the defrauding of savers by inflation and negative interest rates and the apparently inexorable growth of the public sector and public spending.

Unfortunately, tacked on to the draft and, far more seriously, to the 'final' version issued to the press by Conservative Central Office was a passage about public expenditure constraints requiring tough, painful decisions such as limiting the number of kidney machines. Kidney machines were in fact already limited in number as part of the unacknowledged rationing of health treatment under Labour. Nevertheless, a frank statement of it – particularly in the form of a throwaway line – was asking for trouble. In the helter-skelter preparations Adam and I let it through. Luckily, when Gordon in New York saw a copy of the speech he immediately understood the potential damage and removed the offending part. All press releases are subject to the usually formal qualification 'check against delivery', so he was also able to ring round Fleet

Street to tell the editors that the page in question, although part of the press release they had received from Central Office, was not being used and so should not be covered. They had sufficient respect for him to comply; and since the front page of the *Sun* had already provisionally been dominated by the headline 'Let 'em Die, Says Maggie' before it was replaced with something blander, it was a narrow escape.

In fact, the main message of the speech was given maximum attention on both sides of the Atlantic. I was promptly attacked back home by the Labour Government for running Britain down abroad. In fact, the message I was bringing to America about Britain was essentially one of hope, namely that the nation's potential was great enough to withstand even the effects of socialism. The criticism from the Foreign Secretary, Jim Callaghan, who quaintly criticized me later for putting 'argumentative passages' into my American speeches, found a faithful echo in the British Embassy where I was staying. A senior member of the Embassy staff briefed the American press against me. Gordon Reece quickly discovered what was happening, and there was a sharp exchange of letters on the subject between me and Jim Callaghan when I returned to England.

Aware of the attempt to try to cast me in this light, I used my speech to the National Press Club in Washington to point out that if the present socialist policies were abandoned, Britain had underlying strengths which would ensure its swift recovery. A shift of popular opinion against the far Left, the extent of our energy reserves and the strength of our scientific potential – shown by seventy-two Nobel Prizes, more than France, Italy, the Netherlands and Belgium put together – all justified long-term optimism.

> Now, slowly, we are finding our way. It is true that the reports about Britain still reflect a serious situation, and they are right to do so. But a change is coming over us . . . I see some signs that our people are ready to make the tough choice, to follow the harder road. We are still the same people who have fought for freedom, and won. The spirit of adventure, the inventiveness, the determination are still strands in our character.

We may suffer from a British sickness now, but our constitution is sound and we have the heart and the will to win
through.

In the course of my American visit I met the key figures in the
Ford Administration. Dr Kissinger I knew already. But this was
the first time that I had met Bill Simon, the free-market-minded
Treasury Secretary, who had jettisoned the wage and price controls
imposed under President Nixon, and the immensely experienced
James Schlesinger, the Defense Secretary, the Administration's
principal internal opponent to *détente*.

I was also received by President Ford himself. He was a large,
friendly man, unexpectedly precipitated into high office who, perhaps to his own surprise as well as that of others, had started to
relish it. He had assembled or inherited a talented team around
him and had already demonstrated to the Europeans America's
continued commitment to their security, in spite of all the
upheavals of domestic politics. He had, in fact, both the strengths
and weaknesses of what in current political parlance is described
as 'a safe pair of hands'. He was not the kind of man to challenge
accepted orthodoxies, which I increasingly believed ought to be
challenged. But he was a reassuring and steady figure who helped
America heal the self-inflicted wounds of Watergate. After a rocky
period in the wake of his pardon for Richard Nixon, his Administration's fortunes appeared to be improving, and his undeclared bid
for the Republican nomination was proceeding against a genially
effective campaign by a certain Governor Ronald Reagan. President Ford's prospects for re-election appeared good. I came away
hoping that he would succeed.

I found on my return to London that the coverage given to my
American tour had transformed my political standing. Even the
Labour Party's simulated outrage helped. For the more attention
was paid to my arguments, the more seriously they were taken. I
was soon conscious also of a change of attitude within the upper
echelons of the Conservative Party. People who had regarded my
accession to the leadership as an irritating but temporary fluke had
to think again. Not only was I evidently being treated seriously by
some of the most powerful figures in the free world; the warnings

I had given in my Helsinki speech looked ever less eccentric and more prescient.

In late September the Cubans, acting as Soviet surrogates, began to pour troops into Angola. In December the US Senate overturned President Ford's policy of providing assistance to the anti-communist forces there and resistance to the MPLA collapsed. I thought and read more about these things over Christmas and decided that I would make a further speech.

On this occasion I stuck to the conventions and told Reggie Maudling of my decision. It was perhaps a testimony to his unease at the prospect that Reggie went so far as to offer me a draft. Unfortunately, this would not do. As Denis might have said, 'It was so weak it wouldn't pull the skin off a rice pudding.' Bob Conquest had now departed for the more politically conducive Hoover Institution in California, so I asked Robert Moss to help me. The editor of *The Economist*'s Foreign Report, an expert on security and strategic matters, one of the founders of the National Association for Freedom set up to combat overweening trade union power, and destined to be a best-selling novelist, Robert turned out to be an ideal choice.

The speech which I delivered on Monday 19 January at Kensington Town Hall covered similar ground to the previous year's Chelsea speech, but concentrated more on defence and contained even stronger language about the Soviet menace. It accused the Labour Government of 'dismantling our defence at a moment when the strategic threat to Britain and her allies from an expansionist power is graver than at any moment since the end of the last war'. It also offered an analysis of Soviet intentions different from that of the proponents of *détente*.

Russia is ruled by a dictatorship of patient, far-sighted men who are rapidly making their country the foremost naval and military power in the world. They are not doing this solely for the sake of self-defence. A huge, largely land-locked country like Russia does not need to build the most powerful navy in the world just to guard its own frontiers. No. The Russians are bent on world dominance, and they are rapidly acquiring the means to become the most powerful imperial nation the world has seen. The men in the Soviet Politburo do not have to worry about the ebb and flow of public opinion. They put guns before butter, while we put just about everything before guns.

I warned of the imbalance between NATO and Warsaw Pact forces in Central Europe, where the latter outnumbered us by 150,000 men, nearly 10,000 tanks and 2,600 aircraft. But I emphasized that the West's defence could not be ensured in Europe alone: NATO's supply lines had also to be protected. This meant that we could not ignore what Soviet-backed forces were doing in Angola. In any case, if they were allowed their way there, they might well conclude that they could repeat the performance elsewhere.

The reaction to the speech, particularly in the more thoughtful sections of the British press, was much more favourable than to the Chelsea speech. The *Daily Telegraph* entitled its editorial comment 'The Truth About Russia'. *The Times* admitted that 'there has been complacency in the West'. Nor was the Soviet reaction long in coming. The Soviet Embassy wrote a letter to Reggie Maudling, and the Ambassador called on the Foreign Office to protest in person. A stream of crude invective flowed from the different Soviet propaganda organs. But it was some apparatchik in the office of *Red Star*, the Red Army newspaper, his imagination surpassing his judgement, who coined the description of me as 'The Iron Lady'.

It is one of the few defences which free societies have against totalitarian propaganda that totalitarians are inclined to see the Western mind as a mirror image of their own. They are consequently capable from time to time of the most grotesque misjudgements. This was one of them. When Gordon Reece read on the Press Association tapes what *Red Star* had said he was ecstatic and rushed into my office to tell me about it. I quickly saw that they had inadvertently put me on a pedestal as their strongest European opponent. They never did me a greater favour.

A few days later I visited the British Army on the Rhine, where my Kensington speech ensured me a warm reception. I was photographed driving a tank, which did me no harm at all at home either. What the outside world did not know was that in the course of this visit my career almost ended even more dramatically than it was to in November 1990.

Cranley Onslow, one of the Party's Defence spokesmen, Richard Ryder and I were shown aboard an elderly two-engine propeller-driven transport aircraft to fly from the British base at Rheindalen to Oerlinghausen where we were to stay the night. (The plan had been to fly by helicopter, but the weather was not good enough.) Shortly after take-off I took my draft speech out of my briefcase and started to work on it. Some time later I became conscious of an irregularity in the noisy drumming of the engines. It was cold in the cabin. Outside there was thick freezing fog, and looking more closely I could see ice forming on the wings. At this point one of the crew came back to say that there was a problem and we would have to return to Rheindalen. I could sense from his manner that it was serious and I pressed to know exactly what the trouble was. It turned out that with the fog so thick the pilot could not be sure of his bearings. There was more. We were apparently now flying blind through a range of mountains. This was why the pilot had kept our speed to the minimum, slowing until the aircraft threatened to stall, in the hope that the fog might break and he could see his way out of trouble. Worse still, the instrument measuring our air speed had failed. I stopped working on the speech and put it away carefully in my briefcase, leaned back, closed my eyes and thought about matters even more important than politics. Somehow, we managed to get back to Rheindalen. I was never more relieved to feel tarmac under my feet.

If my feet were on the ground metaphysically as well, this was in part because I had followed closely the speeches and writings of Alexander Solzhenitsyn since he was exiled from the Soviet Union in 1974. But the first time I saw and heard him speak was in an interview he gave to Michael Charlton on the BBC television programme *Panorama* in March 1976. It made a deep impression on me; I subsequently kept the transcript amid the bundle of papers I regularly referred to when in need of inspiration.

The predominant Western view at the time was that in the end the Soviet system would, by a process of 'convergence', turn into something not very different from Western society, which would itself evolve in the direction of social democracy. Solzhenitsyn challenged this complacency. The real question, according to him, was not whether and how the Soviet system would change, but rather whether the West itself could survive. This was not because of the strengths of communism but rather because of the weakness and cowardice of Western leaders. Until a few years before the cause of the dissidents in the USSR had been making real if slow headway. But now the Western nations had allowed the balance to shift dramatically against freedom. Solzhenitsyn's criticism of the Helsinki process made my own, which had caused such controversy the previous year, pale into banality. Solzhenitsyn asked:

> How do you explain that over the last few months there has been hardly any news coming out of the Soviet Union of the continuing persecution of dissidents? If you will forgive me, I will answer this myself. The journalists have bowed to the spirit of Helsinki. I know for a fact that Western journalists in Moscow, who have been given the right of freer movement, in return for this, and because of the spirit of Helsinki, no longer accept information about new persecutions of dissidents in the Soviet Union. What does the spirit of Helsinki and the spirit of *détente* mean for us within the Soviet Union? The strengthening of totalitarianism.

As I have noted, the revival of Western morale and defence preparedness altered this entire equation. But Solzhenitsyn's words are an interesting testimony to the corrosive effect of Helsinki under conditions of *détente*.

Now, however, the election of Jimmy Carter as President of the United States at the end of 1976 brought to the White House a man who put human rights at the top of his foreign policy agenda. One could at least be sure that he would not make the mistake of his predecessor, who had refused to meet Solzhenitsyn for fear of offending the Soviet Union.

President Carter was soon to be tested. In January 1977 the text of 'Charter 77', the manifesto of the Czech dissidents, was smuggled into West Germany and published. The following month Jimmy Carter wrote personally to Professor Andrei Sakharov, the Soviet nuclear scientist and leading dissident. This change of tone was reassuring.

But I soon became worried about two other aspects of the Carter Administration's approach to foreign policy. First, human rights issues were treated without reference to broader political and strategic considerations, and indeed with some moral naivete. Even the most idealistic proponent of a policy inspired by moral considerations has to be practical. There were many regimes which abused human rights – for example, some military governments in Latin America and the Middle East – but which may have been less oppressive than the totalitarian alternative.

Moreover, the primary duty a free country owes, not just to itself but to countries which are unfree, is to survive. So there is no need to apologize for supporting an unsavoury regime which temporarily serves larger Western interests, although we should always use our influence to ameliorate its worst abuses. Unfortunately, muddled thinking and divisions within the Carter Administration prevented it from pursuing such a balanced approach. As we shall see, the Carter stress on human rights in Iran helped to undermine the Shah and to replace him with the far more oppressive, and anti-Western, regime of the Ayatollah Khomeini. As Pascal points out, the first principle of morality is thinking clearly. And in this case failing to think clearly produced a markedly worse result for both human rights and Western interests.

My second criticism was that human rights policy cannot stand on its own, for the simple reason that rights have ultimately to be defended by force. In the circumstances of the 1970s, this required the United States to be militarily strong enough to resist and reverse the threat to world freedom posed by the Soviet Union. Yet President Carter had a passionate commitment to disarmament, demonstrated both by his early cancellation of the B1 strategic bomber and the renewed impetus he gave to SALT II (Strategic Arms Limitation Talks), which President Ford had initiated with the Soviets. Ironically, therefore, President Carter found that he could only take action to improve human rights against countries linked to the West, not against countries that were hostile and strong enough to ignore him.

As for the SALT II negotiations, it was possible to argue about the particular formulae, but the really important strategic fact was that the Soviet Union had in recent years been arming far faster than the Americans. Any mere 'arms limitation' agreement was bound to stabilize the military balance in such a way as to recognize this. Only deep arms *cuts* on the one hand, or a renewed drive for stronger American defences on the other, could reverse it. If, however, neither of these was a real possibility in the prevailing state of public opinion, then something on the broad lines of a SALT agreement was to the West's advantage, since it would at least halt the Soviets' advance. Either way, the United States had already lost its nuclear superiority at a time when the West had long since abandoned any attempt to keep up with the Warsaw Pact in conventional weapons. Crude as such calculations inevitably are, the scale of the change is shown by the following table:

US and Soviet strategic nuclear forces

		1966	1976
USA	ICBM	904	1,054
	SLBM	592	656
	LRB	630	387
USSR	ICBM	292	1,527
	SLBM	107	845
	LRB	155	135

ICBM: Intercontinental ballistic missiles
SLBM: Submarine-launched ballistic missiles
LRB: Long-range bombers

Source: *The Military Balance, 1976/77*, p. 75

Indeed, the position would further worsen as the Soviets produced their Backfire Bombers, multiplied their nuclear submarines and started to deploy SS20 nuclear missiles focused on Western Europe.

These facts and figures were available to anyone who was interested, which far too few journalists were. But did they actually *underestimate* the danger? I had followed closely the accounts given by Major-General George Keegan, recently retired as Chief of the

US Air Force Intelligence, of Soviet research into charged particle beams, which might provide a technology that would revolutionize defence assumptions by providing a far more effective shield against ballistic missiles. The Carter Administration belittled this threat, and only when President Reagan launched his Strategic Defence Initiative were the dangers properly understood and countervailing action taken. As early as March 1977, however, the magazine *Aviation Week and Space Technology* published observations by General Keegan on the dimensions of the overall Soviet threat. He argued that the Americans had consistently underestimated the scale of Soviet military strength and preparedness, coming to the devastating conclusion that 'the Soviet Union today has a capability to initiate, wage, survive and emerge from a global conflict with far greater effectiveness than the United States and its allies'. It would take the invasion of Afghanistan, two years later, before most Western politicians began to think in these terms.

When I visited the United States again in September 1977, the Carter Administration was still enjoying its political honeymoon. President Carter had brought a new informal style to the White House which appeared to accord with the mood of the times. Although there was unease about some of his appointments, this was largely put down to Washington resentment against outsiders. In Cyrus Vance, his Secretary of State, and Zbigniew Brzezinski, his National Security Adviser, he had two remarkable assistants, whose differences of outlook were not yet apparent.

I had met Jimmy Carter himself in London in May when he attended the G7 Summit. In spite of my growing doubts about his foreign policy, I liked him and looked forward to meeting him again. At our discussion in the White House the President was most keen to explain and justify his recently launched initiative for a comprehensive nuclear test ban. Although he had clearly mastered the details and was a persuasive advocate, I was not convinced. Believing as I did in the vital importance of a credible nuclear deterrent, and knowing that nuclear weapons had to be tested in order to be credible, I could not go along with the policy.

Equally, I was unable to agree with President Carter, or indeed Cyrus Vance and Andrew Young, the US Ambassador to the United Nations, on their preferred approach to settling the

Rhodesian question. The Americans were insisting that the Rhodesian security forces be dismantled. But I knew that would never be acceptable to the white population – who still enjoyed military superiority over the 'armed struggle' – without some real guarantee of peace. The Americans were also toying with the idea of imposing sanctions against South Africa, which seemed to me equally ill-judged considering that they needed to have the South African Government on their side if they were to persuade Ian Smith to compromise.*

At least on this occasion I did not have to contend with hostile briefing from the Embassy, which was ironic considering that the new Ambassador, Peter Jay, was Jim Callaghan's son-in-law. There had been loud accusations of nepotism when this appointment had been announced. But I liked and admired Peter Jay personally. His understanding of monetary economics would have made him a welcome recruit to the Shadow Cabinet. Even so, I have to confess that I took a certain mischievous pleasure in quoting an extract from Jim Callaghan's speech to the previous year's Labour Party Conference as the introduction to my own speech to the British-American Chamber of Commerce. In it the Labour Prime Minister had said:

> We used to think that you could just spend your way out of a recession and increase employment by cutting taxes and boosting government spending. I tell you, in all candour, that this option no longer exists, and that in so far as it ever did exist it only worked by injecting bigger doses of inflation into the economy followed by higher levels of unemployment as the next step.

It was an open secret that this uncharacteristically sound passage had been drafted by none other than Peter Jay.

In fact, the only embarrassment I faced during my American trip resulted from an open disagreement between Jim Prior and Keith Joseph about Lord Scarman's report on the Grunwick affair and about the right policy towards the closed shop. Members of

* For further discussion of the issue of Rhodesia see pp. 417–18.

the press corps were more interested in this than the results of my discussions in Washington, and I had to issue two statements to try to calm the waters. But the important matters of substance could only be sorted out on my return.

Meanwhile, uncertainties about the direction of American policy and the extent of Soviet ambitions had increasingly focused attention on those countries which were balanced uneasily between the two blocs. Of these, Yugoslavia had a special significance. Since Marshal Tito's break with Stalin in 1948, Yugoslavia had been in an anomalous but important position. After horrendous early repression and mass murder, Tito and his comrades had become somewhat more liberal because circumstances forced them to look to the West for financial support and security. This gradually moved Yugoslavia in a pseudo-capitalist and quasi-liberal direction. There might have been even more progress of this kind if Tito's every move had not been greeted with fawning admiration by a particular kind of British socialist. In fact, his real talent was as an illusionist. He persuaded both East and West, and perhaps even a section of Yugoslav opinion, that the country was an important player in the great international game. The high point of this was the formation under Tito's inspiration of the so-called 'Non-Aligned' Movement of Third World countries.

By the mid 1970s the country's economic problems were growing. The Yugoslavs had financed a consumer boom on the back of Western credit. A kind of chaotic semi-capitalism masquerading as 'self-management' had evolved. Living standards were higher than in other communist countries, partly because of remittances from Yugoslav workers overseas; but, correspondingly, the implications for the regime if living standards had to fall might be even more serious.

The fragility of Yugoslavia was both symbolized by and depended upon the state of Tito's own health. It was an open question whether the Soviets would try to reassert control in the chaos which was widely expected to follow his death. At eighty-five, he was still in control of events, but ailing. I had wanted to visit Yugoslavia for some time, but my visit was twice postponed because Tito was not well enough to receive me.

On a bitter early December day in 1977, however, in the

company of Sir Fitzroy Maclean, a comrade in arms and old friend
of the Yugoslav President from the Second World War, I arrived
in Belgrade. My first duty was to climb the 150 steps up to the
huge war memorial on the top of Mount Avala to lay a wreath. I
did not have a warm coat with me and so by the time we descended
I was chilled to the marrow. The general political reception,
though, was warm enough, not just from the politicians but even
from the communist newspapers.

As 'the Iron Lady', I was seen as someone who understood the
fact that the Yugoslavs lived every day under the shadow of possible
Soviet intervention. Paradoxically, this was one of the main considerations which kept the country together. Only with the end of
the Cold War could the nations of Yugoslavia achieve real self-
determination. An illustration of this is that the President of the
National Assembly who hosted lunch for me, Kiro Gligorov, is
now the President of the newly independent if embattled state of
Macedonia.

Fitzroy Maclean and I visited Tito at his Belgrade home. His
was a powerful personality, retaining some of the outward panache
of his flamboyant partisan past, but leaving no doubt about the
inner steel that explained his post-war dominance. We discussed
and broadly agreed about the Soviet threat. The looming question
of his legacy did not figure in our talks. Perhaps he had already
concluded, for all the elaborate constitutional safeguards, that it
would indeed be the *déluge*.

Before I departed for Yugoslavia, Alfred Sherman had asked me
to raise with Tito the case of Milovan Djilas, Tito's former friend
and colleague and for many years most insistent domestic critic.
Djilas had been one of a number of political prisoners recently
freed but was, I understood, the object of continuing harassment.
It seemed likely that he would soon disappear back into prison. I
decided on a shot across Tito's bows. I said with studied innocence
how pleased I was that Djilas had been released. Tito glowered.

'Yes, he's out,' the President said, 'but he's up to his old tricks.
And if he goes on upsetting our constitution he will go straight
back to gaol.'

'Well,' I replied, 'a man like Djilas will do you far more harm
in prison than out of it.'

Fitzroy Maclean chipped in, 'She's right, you know.'

Tito gave me a hard look. There was a pause in the conversation before he turned to other matters. As far as I know, Djilas stayed out of gaol – only to suffer more harassment for his independent thinking under the brutal regime of Serbian President Slobodan Milosevic.

From the end of 1977 until the June 1979 general election I found no major reason to reverse the judgements or revise the analysis I had made as a result of my reading and discussions on foreign policy. British, European and American opinion steadily hardened against further compromises with the Soviet Union. The Soviets themselves displayed less and less caution in dealing with internal dissent or planning foreign adventure. By now the Horn of Africa had attracted Soviet ambitions: Colonel Mengistu, ruler of Ethiopia and a Soviet puppet, embarked on a long war with Somalia. In April 1978 Soviet disinformation achieved a major success in forcing President Carter to announce deferment of the production of the neutron bomb, which might have contributed to maintaining the military balance in Europe. The following month the Soviet dissident Yuri Orlov, who had set up the Helsinki Group to monitor the Helsinki accords, was sentenced to seven years in prison. In July the dissidents Anatol Sharansky and Alexander Ginsburg were sentenced respectively to thirteen and eight years in prison and labour camps for 'anti-Soviet agitation'. For any friend of freedom it was a time of heartbreak. And out of office there was little I could do to change it.

In fact, though I did not know it at the time, three developments were opening up the long-term prospect of turning back the Soviet advance. The first, paradoxically, was that they had become too arrogant. It is a natural and often fatal trait of the totalitarian to despise opponents. The Soviets believed that the failure of Western politicians signified that Western peoples were resigned to defeat. A little more subtlety and forethought might have secured the Soviet leaders far greater gains. As it was, particularly through the invasion of Afghanistan in 1979, they provoked a Western reaction which finally destroyed the Soviet Union itself.

The second development was the election in September 1978 of a Polish Pope. John Paul II would fire a revolution in Eastern Europe which shook the Soviet Empire to its core.

Finally, there was the emergence of Ronald Reagan as a serious contender for the American Presidency. I had met Governor Reagan shortly after my becoming Conservative Leader in 1975. Even before then, I knew something about him because Denis had returned home one evening in the late 1960s full of praise for a remarkable speech Ronald Reagan had just delivered at the Institute of Directors. I read the text myself and quickly saw what Denis meant. When we met in person I was immediately won over by his charm, sense of humour and directness. In the succeeding years I read his speeches, advocating tax cuts as the root to wealth creation and stronger defences as an alternative to *détente*. I also read many of his fortnightly broadcasts to the people of California, which his Press Secretary sent over regularly for me. I agreed with them all. In November 1978 we met again in my room in the House of Commons.

In the early years Ronald Reagan had been dismissed by much of the American political élite, though not by the American electorate, as a right-wing maverick who could not be taken seriously. (I had heard that before somewhere.) Now he was seen by many thoughtful Republicans as their best ticket back to the White House. Whatever Ronald Reagan had gained in experience, he had not done so at the expense of his beliefs. I found them stronger than ever. When he left my study I reflected on how different things might look if such a man were President of the United States. But in November 1978 such a prospect seemed a long way off.

THE MIDDLE EAST

The hard-fought Yom Kippur War of 1973, in which Egypt and Syria attacked Israel, changed the way in which Western countries regarded the Middle East. First, cuts in oil production, the huge hike in its price and selective embargoes against oil-producing countries friendly to Israel, imposed by the OPEC cartel of Arab oil producers, damaged the Western economies and caused enormous alarm. The dependence of Western living standards on unpredictable Middle Eastern politics could not have been more effectively demonstrated. Secondly, although the Israeli counter-attack had crossed the Suez Canal and driven Syrian forces to within twenty-five miles of Damascus, the Egyptians and Syrians had fought better than they had in 1967 and the Soviets had threatened to send troops in a 'peacekeeping' role. Thirdly, the United States responded by taking the leading part in bringing about disengagement between Israel and the Arab forces. From now on, American diplomacy, beginning with Dr Kissinger and carried on by President Carter, was the prime external force in the search for a Middle Eastern settlement.

For states like Syria, Egypt and Jordan, and for the PLO itself, life became more complicated, though more hopeful. Each had its own priorities, none of which could realistically be achieved by force of arms in the foreseeable future. Those who proved most cooperative in seeking an agreement with Israel were likely to receive the added bonus of American assistance for their economies, which the heavy demands of preparedness for war, combined with strong doses of socialism, had weakened. In such circumstances natural rivalries previously submerged or at least concealed by commitment to the 'Arab cause' came to the surface. Such was the Middle Eastern background to the visit I made to Egypt and Syria in January and to Israel in March 1976.

But there was also a tricky domestic political background. British politicians were in Middle Eastern eyes sharply divided between supporters of Israel on the one hand and supporters of the Arab states and the Palestinians on the other. Within the Shadow Cabinet, I was probably in a minority in feeling strong ties of respect and admiration for both Israel and the traditional regimes of the Arab world. Most of my colleagues were traditional Tory 'Arabists', although among the younger members of the Parliamentary Party there was considerable support for Israel, based in part upon her fearless pursuit of national self-interest. Jewish groups in Britain scrutinized closely everything the parties said about the Arab-Israeli conflict. Hence, when Reggie Maudling, in a Commons debate in November 1975, appeared to call for British recognition of the PLO and the creation of a Palestinian state, this threatened to open Party divisions and I was bombarded by complaints.

I decided to spell out our policy clearly to a meeting of Jewish ex-servicemen in Finchley. This was that the Conservative Party believed that any Middle East settlement must be based upon UN Security Council Resolution 242, which itself stressed two fundamental requirements: the 'withdrawal of Israeli armed forces from territories occupied in the recent conflict' (i.e. the 1967 Six Day War); and recognition of the right of every state in the area 'to live in peace within secure and recognized boundaries free from threats or acts of force'. I added that we condemned terrorism in whatever form and whatever cause it purported to serve.

For me at least, this position was not just a form of words designed to let us off the hook. I did *both* believe that Israel must be assured of its security and that the Palestinians had to be treated with respect, which at that time we saw in the context of a confederation with Jordan. Nor were these objectives incompatible. Although in the light of its history Israel understandably wanted defendable borders, there could be no lasting peace without a solution of the Palestinian problem. And both for the Palestinians and the Arab states which in varying degrees supported them the best starting-point was to recognize by deeds as well as words that Israel was there to stay. The flurry over Reggie's speech, however, confirmed the complexity and diplomatic perils of the visit on which I embarked.

I arrived in Cairo on Wednesday 7 January 1976 and dined that evening with President and Madame Sadat. I had first met him briefly in London only two months earlier. Before dinner we had a long talk. I found him a powerful and direct personality who had a strong grasp of the power relations of the Western world. Sadat still had to play a shrewd diplomatic game, balancing America and the Soviet Union. Having dramatically ejected Soviet advisers in 1972, he had received Soviet support during the 1973 war, but was now inclined once more to look to the United States. Just two months after my visit, Egypt formally abrogated its 1971 Friendship Treaty with the Soviet Union.

In our conversations, he claimed to be reasonably satisfied with the state of the Egyptian economy: at this time there were still some expectations that the destruction of Beirut as a financial centre might indirectly benefit Cairo, and he was hoping for help from the Gulf states. But I thought it significant that the President lamented the amount of money which had gone into paying for war which might have been used for the peaceful development of Egypt. He told me that he was 'very tired', and I suspected this was said as much on behalf of Egypt as on his own account. He felt that he had a good relationship with President Ford, which perhaps intimated the way his mind was turning. Indeed, he gave the impression that Egypt would remain neutral unless forced into another war. There were also telltale signs in his conversation of Egypt's well-known rivalry with Syria. He told me that that country was providing arms to both sides in the Lebanese civil war and added that the Syrian Ba'athist Party was hated throughout the Arab world. I formed the impression that Sadat was a formidable man, capable of great boldness, who was contemplating a major departure in his country's foreign relations; I could not foresee, however, just how dramatic that change would be. Less than two years later he was to make his historic visit to Jerusalem, which led to Israel's peace treaty with Egypt.

Sightseeing during my short stay in Egypt was a diplomatic necessity as well as a pleasure. But even this contained risks. Having climbed the great Cheops Pyramid, and still a little breathless, I came down to find a small group of cameramen, journalists and officials standing beside a camel. The camel driver's name was Ibrahim and the camel was called 'Jack Hulbert', perhaps so named by an English Tommy after the popular long-jawed British comedian of the 1930s and forties. He was, it seems, a distinguished beast, and had been ridden on a previous visit by Alec Douglas-Home when Foreign Secretary. Everyone seemed to assume that I would follow suit. The possibilities flashed across my mind, not just getting on but staying on. I firmly declined. Ibrahim claimed to be most offended. If Jack Hulbert was good enough for Sir Alec, why not for Mrs Thatcher? I caught a gleam in the driver's eye and suggested that paying double the fare for *no* camel ride might suit both of us. With a great show of reluctance he agreed. And so the newspaper photographs in Britain showed me being welcomed by President Sadat, rather than in some less dignified posture.

On Friday afternoon I flew to Damascus. President Assad had recently marked the fifth anniversary of the military *coup* which brought him to power by a judicious air-drop of gifts in Damascus and large pay rises for civil servants and the army. He was already a proven survivor in a country where previous heads of state had never served for more than two or three years. A member of the Alawite minority, presiding over a government containing people from a wide variety of religions, tribes and political affiliations, Assad had demonstrated a high level of political cunning to attain and hold power. His Ba'athist Party was itself an odd mixture of elements derived from both socialism and Islam, but founded in the 1940s under the slogan of 'one Arab nation with an eternal mission'. Assad had developed to a fine art that particular mixture of radicalism, pragmatism and ruthlessness which success in the violent, turbulent world of Middle Eastern politics required. He was considered the most anti-Western leader in the region and was held responsible not just for many of the difficulties in the Arab-Israeli peace process but also for engineering the destruction of Lebanon. Western policy's main error, which unfortunately continued for many years, was to underrate him and to exclude him from talks. But he made it easier to do this because of his subservience to the Soviet Union and his support for international terrorism.

Syria was a tightly controlled police state. Romanian-style eavesdropping was clearly the order of the day at the official Guest House in which we stayed. On our arrival, Gordon Reece and I went up to our rooms to wash and change. But Gordon found that he had no towels in the bathroom and so knocked on my door and asked to borrow one. I had barely gone to fetch it when a maid scurried up to hand him his own.

That evening our hosts would have found their guests' private conversation more interesting. The Syrians had without warning invited me to a secret meeting with the PLO the following day. I was not going to agree to this. I would not meet them formally at all, still less in secret, because the PLO had refused to renounce terrorism. But I agreed, indeed welcomed, the opportunity to pay a visit to a Palestinian refugee camp and it was arranged that I would be taken to one on the outskirts of Damascus.

The following day began with a long, bumpy ride to Qunaitra, the last town on the Syrian side of the Golan Heights. It had been demolished by the Israeli army when they withdrew in 1974. They were even alleged to have desecrated graves, and the whole town was now a showcase for the evils of Zionism. I was told that there was only one inhabitant now, an old lady who had refused to leave and had lived through the occupation. Predictably, I bumped into her on my way round.

We stopped at the Palestinian camp on our return journey to Damascus. 'Camp' turned out to be something of a misnomer. It was an enormous settlement with roads, tents, social halls, shops, hospitals and schools. I was shown one school, where the children were assembled in a large hall, being addressed by a woman teacher with great earnestness. I imagined that this was some kind of prayer assembly and asked my guide what the woman was saying. The answer came: 'She is reminding these children that they are privileged to be at this school because at least one of their parents has been killed by a Jew.' Now I understood why it was named the 'School of the Martyrs'.

That evening after my return I had dinner with the President at his comfortable but modest house. He was obviously highly intelligent and knew precisely what he wanted. Though I was impressed, there was little meeting of minds. We talked about a draft Security Council Resolution which the Arab countries intended to put forward on the Palestinian question. It seemed to me that there was everything to be said for framing this responsibly so as not to attract the American veto. But of course I could not know quite what the Syrian President's objectives in this matter really were: given Syria's general stance of opposition to peace talks with Israel, he might well have been happier to have a strong pro-Palestinian Resolution vetoed than a weaker one passed. In any case, it was plain at that time that the Lebanese civil war was his real preoccupation, as he insisted again and again that Syria would never tolerate the partition of Lebanon. I was not surprised a few months later when Syrian troops intervened there in force. But I felt, oddly enough, that we had struck up some kind of relationship of mutual respect. He walked with me to the garden gate and jokingly asked whether I had been woken up early by the muezzin from the nearby mosque. 'No,' I said. 'I am up even before the Mullahs.'

I had sought to be the perfect diplomat in both Egypt and Syria, but questions were put to me at my final press conference in Damascus which I felt required greater directness. Members of the Arab press corps pressed me on Britain's attitude towards the PLO, demanding to know why we did not recognize it. Fresh from my visit to the camp, I set out the balanced policy described above, but I roundly condemned the PLO for its reliance on terrorism and said that you could not have peace between nations unless on the basis of law rather than violence. Their protestations at this provoked me to remind them that they themselves would not be free to ask questions if they did not benefit from some kind of rule of law. I also said that I disagreed fundamentally with the anti-Zionist Resolution, which described Zionism as a form of racism and racial discrimination, passed by the UN General Assembly. One journalist pointedly reminded me that Jewish groups in Palestine had also committed terrorist acts. I was fully aware of that. Any English person of my age remembers only too well the hanging of two Liverpool sergeants and the booby-trapping of their bodies by Irgun in July 1947. But one act of terrorism does not justify another. Some people at the time thought this plain speaking was something of a diplomatic gaffe. That would not have mattered to me, because I felt strongly about the principle. But in fact it would shortly stand me in good stead.

In March I made my third visit to Israel. One of my early meetings was with the former Prime Minister, Golda Meir, whom I had first met when she was in office. I had developed the greatest respect for her and, perhaps as another woman in politics, I particularly understood that strange blend of hardness and softness which made her alternately motherly and commanding. She was deeply pessimistic about the prospects for peace and was particularly apprehensive about the Syrians. But she warmly congratulated me on what she described as my bravery in criticizing Palestinian terrorism in Damascus. She also strongly approved of my speeches on the Soviet threat, which she flatteringly linked with Solzhenitsyn's statements. In her view the West was not nearly tough enough.

I found that my remarks about the PLO had made a similar impression on the other Israeli politicians to whom I spoke. Now and on later visits as Prime Minister, the fact that I had not flinched from condemning terrorism and had consistently defended Israel's right to a secure existence allowed me to speak frankly, but as a friend, to the Israelis. In my discussions with Mrs Meir and later with the Foreign Minister Yigal Allon, the Defence Minister Shimon Peres and the Prime Minister Yitzhak Rabin, I relayed my impressions gained from Egypt and Syria that Arab leaders were now thinking along lines which made a settlement possible. I also sought to persuade my hosts to consider not just Israel's security – which I fully recognized must be their prime objective – but also the long-term need to reach a settlement with moderate Arab regimes. But the politicians I spoke to were generally pessimistic, particularly Prime Minister Rabin, who seemed at this time to have little understanding of the difficulties Arabs faced in dealing with their people's desire to see justice for the Palestinians.

As always, however, I found much to admire in Israel – the commitment to democracy in a region where it was otherwise unknown, the sacrifices people were prepared to make for their country and the energies which had put the huge sums received from America and the Jewish diaspora to productive use: they really had made the desert bloom. One institution, however, which never appealed to me was the kibbutz. I visited one for lunch close to the Golan Heights. Living in a kibbutz in such areas was partly a requirement of security, partly a matter of economics. For me, however, it was also a rather unnerving and unnatural collectivist social experiment. I admired people who could choose such a life but would never have wanted to be one of them. Not so my daughter Carol. As a teenager with some left-wing leanings she had told Denis and me that she wanted to spend some time in a kibbutz. We were concerned about this, but we knew of one which seemed suitable and finally agreed. Life there was extremely hard and conditions rudimentary. One of Carol's tasks was to inoculate young chickens. She would take them from one box, inject them and drop them in another. Unfortunately, every now and then a fighter plane would roar over, the chicks would jump up and get mixed together. Carol returned with an unromantic view of the tasks of the farm labourer. Moreover, as Denis remarked to me later, she may not have been very good at inoculating the chickens, but she was certainly inoculated against socialism.

I was taken up on the Golan Heights by an Israeli general – a professor in civilian life. I was impressed by the balance and moderation of his opinions. At one point he told me that where we stood was not Israeli land, but rather held in trust against the day when there was a secure settlement. He was a considerate man, and seeing that I was shivering in the cold wind which swept across the mountains he lent me his flak jacket. I was photographed in this and there followed furious Syrian objections. And so my first major Middle Eastern foray ended amid the endemic misunderstandings of the region.

In retrospect, my visit to the Middle East occurred at an important time of transition between the 1973 Arab-Israeli war and the 1978–79 American-brokered Egyptian-Israeli peace settlement. Although the Camp David Agreements ultimately failed to solve the deeper problems, they were a remarkable tribute to the principal participants – Jimmy Carter, Menachem Begin and Anwar Sadat. At the time I became Prime Minister they still seemed to form the best basis for progress. In fact, however, the rise of armed, aggressive Islamic fundamentalism, principally financed by and focused on Iran, was to upset all such calculations.

I was one of the last senior Western politicians to visit Iran while the Shah was still in power. The troubles had already begun. There were riots in Tabriz in February 1978 against the Shah's programme of Westernizing reforms, which the Mullahs described as impious attacks on Islam and which, alas, ordinary people often experienced as the forced disruption of their traditional ways of life. As the disturbances increased, the Carter Administration vacillated in its attitude to the Shah. At times, it would offer him support as a bastion of Western influence in a strategically important part of the world; at others it would denounce his human rights record and demand the introduction of liberal reforms. What this recommendation failed to bear in mind was well summed up by the Shah himself: 'I will behave like the King of Sweden when my subjects behave like Swedes.' In any event, the Carter Administration's blowing hot and cold only served to undermine the Shah and encourage his opponents – a fact not lost among America's potential allies in the Middle East.

For my part, I had no doubt about the strategic importance of Iran for the West. Moreover, although by most definitions only peripheral to the Middle East, Iran, as subsequent events were to demonstrate, had a large potential influence in the region. In any case, I admired the Shah personally and believed that his policy of modernization along Western lines was ultimately the right one. In retrospect, I can see that its success depended upon its being carried out more gradually and taking into account the customs and mores of his people. But it was certainly preferable to the retreat into fundamentalism and medieval economics which have reduced the standard of living of the Iranian people and forced the regime to distract them with political and religious adventurism abroad.

All this was in the future, however, when I arrived in Tehran on the evening of Friday 28 April to be met by Tony Parsons, our Ambassador there. I found Iran to be, on the surface, a bustling, prosperous, Western-style country. There were plenty of new cars in the crowded streets. Shops sold luxury goods to sophisticated, well-dressed women. Moreover, the consumer society was underpinned not just by oil but by new industrial investment, as at the ultra-modern Iran National Automobile works which I visited.

Tony briefed me on the situation. Not only was he on good personal terms with the Shah himself: he had a vast detailed knowledge of what was happening throughout the country. At this time the accepted wisdom was that the main threat to the Shah's strongly pro-Western regime came from the communist-backed opposition, the Tudeh. Judging from his public pronouncements, even the Shah himself seemed to believe this. But Tony Parsons had perceived that the Mullahs and their supporters were also a threat. That turned out to be all too true. Tony is, however, candid enough to admit in his own account that he thought the army would be capable of holding the situation. That turned out to be all too false. But none of us foresaw how quickly the Shah's position would crumble.

On Saturday morning I was received at the palace by the

Minister of the Court, Amir Abbas Hoveyda. Hoveyda was an urbane and distinguished man, who was later executed by the Ayatollah's regime after a show trial which I saw on television.

When I met the Shah he began by expressing concern about the recent communist-backed *coup* in Afghanistan: he said he had expected one eventually, but that it had occurred ten years earlier than he envisaged. He talked repeatedly of Iran as being in the front line against communism. He gave no hint of resentment against his wavering Western backers, though he had reason to feel it. Not only was there the uncertainty about the Americans' commitment to him, but the Iranians also maintained that the Persian-language BBC World Service reports consisted largely of propaganda against the Government. I went away impressed by his grasp of world affairs. But, of course, no amount of such wisdom is proof against the kind of subversion which he was facing at home.

The Shah was a handsome man, with somewhat gaunt features which I later understood were the early signs of the cancer that would kill him. There was nothing in his manner to suggest he believed that time was running out. It was ominous perhaps that when he went to inspect his troops he travelled by helicopter: I was told that nowadays he always travelled that way rather than through the streets because of the threat of attack. I also noticed that on my visit to Isfahan, to see the ancient mosques, my personal security was particularly tight.

On reflection, my impressions of Iran seem to have something of the quality of those paintings in which the French nobility on the eve of the Revolution disport themselves amid contrived pastoral scenes. Within a year, the Shah would have fled the country, the Ayatollah Khomeini would have returned, an Islamic Republic would have been proclaimed, and bloodshed and terror would prevail. Yet here I was, invited to admire the glorious trappings of the Peacock Throne, to wonder at the spectacular crown jewels, to be enthralled by the illuminated grandeur of the ruins of Persepolis.

Could the Shah have been saved? If the Americans had been more robust, if the French had insisted that the Ayatollah refrain from political activity in Iran as a condition of asylum in Paris, if the Shah had appeased moderate Islamic opinion, perhaps things could have turned out differently. As it is, the forces unleashed by the Iranian revolution are still unchecked and represent one of the greatest threats to international peace and stability.

ASIA AND THE FAR EAST

Between the autumn of 1976 and the spring of 1977 I visited no fewer than eight states in Asia and the Far East. This provided me with a range of contacts and a fund of experience which would prove useful when I was Prime Minister. Inevitably, though, since so many countries were fitted into such a short time – among them Pakistan, India, Singapore, New Zealand, Australia and China – I received only a series of political snapshots which would have to be supplemented by wider reading and discussion.

As I reflected later on what I had learned, however, it seemed to me that two general themes stood out. First, in varying degrees and from different standpoints, countries throughout the region were becoming more alert to the extension of Soviet power and influence: this would be sharply reinforced in 1979 by the Russian invasion of Afghanistan. Secondly, it was still an open question as to how China, Japan and possibly India would arrange a new Asian balance of power. In each case, the rise to dominance was distracted at least as much by self-created obstacles as by external circumstances. The years 1976–77, therefore, were ones full of interest for an apprentice Western statesman. And, in spite of criticisms in the British press for spending too much time away from home, I never regretted making these visits.

On Sunday 5 September 1976, very early in the morning, I arrived in Pakistan at Rawalpindi. The following evening I was entertained by Prime Minister Bhutto. He was the best kind of host, never allowing his left-wing views to get in the way of a first-class dinner and serious but amusing conversation. Gordon Reece accompanied me and Mr Bhutto's daughter, Benazir, and some of her friends were present too. Prime Minister Bhutto and I had both been to Oxford and had trained as barristers at Lincoln's Inn.

Mr Bhutto had been an indifferent Prime Minister in difficult circumstances. He helped Pakistan achieve some self-respect after the previous military regime had lost Bangladesh in its disastrous war with India; Pakistan's relations with its powerful neighbour were now on a better footing. But he failed to tackle seriously the country's deeply rooted economic difficulties. Like many other Third World socialist leaders of the period, he tried to escape from domestic economic problems by calling for a 'just' new international economic order, which was shorthand for larger transfers of foreign aid from the West. Indeed, he had backed a Third World initiative for this purpose.

Though I expressed my views politely, I was known to be a critic of this kind of international socialism. It was somewhat to the surprise of his civil servants, therefore, that we immediately struck up a *rapport*. I even found him remarkably understanding – in private at least – about the need to curb Pakistani immigration into Britain.

Mr Bhutto's ideas of a new international economic order eventually foundered in the 1980s, when the Third World began to understand that free-market economics were the key to prosperity. Long before then, however, he had been overthrown by a military *coup*. Perhaps, like the Shah, he had become too detached from the religious and cultural values of his own people.

No one may ever know the whole truth about his overthrow, trial and subsequent execution. As Prime Minister I intervened in vain with his successor to spare his life. But the military was determined. So it was a strange feeling when I subsequently met President Zia-Ul-Haq at Tito's funeral in 1980. He was much more pro-Western than his predecessor, but I had also expected to meet a cold, even brutal, figure. Instead, I found him polished and he made every effort to be friendly. When my son Mark was lost for days in the North African desert in January 1982, General Zia was one of the first to telephone personally to express his concern. And under his rule Pakistan was to prove exceptionally generous to the millions of Afghan refugees driven out by the Soviet occupation.

At the time of my visit, however, Pakistan was enjoying better relations with its neighbours, including India. Indeed, by now the Indian Prime Minister, Mrs Indira Gandhi, and her Government were almost exclusively concerned with domestic problems. The first half of 1975 had seen a massive campaign of opposition against her, leading to the proclamation in June of a State of Emergency, the banning of some political parties, the suspension of fundamental human rights, severe censorship and the arrest of thousands of opponents, including some thirty Indian MPs. At the time I arrived there was a kind of eerie calm. The economy was doing quite well after several bad years, though there were disagreements about whether this was as a result of government policy or of good harvests. But it was not, of course, possible to know the real conditions of the country without a free press; even parliamentary speeches were subject to censorship.

Still, I felt no inhibitions about making my planned visit. India's ambivalent relationship with the Soviet Union, its strategic significance, as well as the traditional links with Britain which provided huge sums of overseas aid, marked out India as of special importance to me. I did, however, insist that there should be no censorship of my press conferences and that I should be able to meet representatives of the opposition. No objection was made and both conditions were fulfilled. As a consequence, I found myself with a larger British press entourage than usual on these trips, partly because some British papers sent in reporters who would otherwise have been subject to the emergency censorship regulations. They wrote not only about my visit, but about the condition of India more generally, including the sterilization campaign.

I lunched with Indira Gandhi in her own modest home, where she insisted on seeing that her guests were all looked after and clearing away the plates while discussing matters of high politics. Both her sons, Sanjay and Rajiv, were present, although it was the former who had most to say for himself. He had, indeed, allegedly been responsible for many of the abuses such as forced sterilization and compulsory rehousing which had provoked such bitter opposition. But in spite of everything I found myself liking Mrs Gandhi herself. Perhaps I naturally sympathized with a woman politician faced with the huge strains and difficulties of governing a country as vast as India. But, in spite of a long self-justificatory account she gave me of why the State of Emergency had been necessary, I could not approve of her Government's methods. She had taken a wrong turning and was to discover the fact at her party's devastating election defeat in 1977.

From India I flew to Singapore for a brief stopover on my way to New Zealand and Australia. Prime Minister Lee Kuan Yew was an old friend from my days as Education Secretary. He and I thought similarly about education. He was a great believer in selection and could never understand why even a socialist wanted to destroy the grammar schools. And the schools and education in Singapore reflected this. More significantly, he was the most important Asian statesman of his generation, an achievement all the more remarkable for being based on the small state of Singapore. He had his own kind of democracy to be sure, but his strong commitment to free-market capitalism had done wonders for the tiny island which he governed. For me, the success of Singapore demonstrated how, given the right economic framework favourable to enterprise, living standards could be transformed. Not surprisingly, Professor Milton Friedman saw in economies like that of Singapore a model which the West should follow. Of course, Lee Kuan Yew enjoyed the advantage of the Chinese people's cultural predisposition to trading and commerce: the spirit of entrepreneurship comes more easily to some peoples than to others. But I found in my discussions with him now that what really united us was common concern about the advance of Soviet influence throughout the region, which was being exerted through naval deployments disguised as trade or fishing. I was to find myself often relying on Lee Kuan Yew's wise advice and vast knowledge of world politics in my time as Prime Minister.

From Singapore I went on to New Zealand. It was my second visit and I felt very much at home. Robert Muldoon had recently won a general election. He was a mixed grill of a politician: robust and no-nonsense in manner, but surprisingly confused in economic and political philosophy, and accordingly much more interventionist than the Labour Government which succeeded him eight years later. He was something of a bruiser alongside Malcolm Fraser, the tall rancher who in 1975 had become Prime Minister of Australia after the Governor-General, Sir John Kerr, had controversially dismissed Gough Whitlam, the previous Labor Prime Minister. Although I was pleased to see a right-wing government in power in Australia as in New Zealand, I never struck up any real friendship with Malcolm Fraser. Our views and attitudes were too different.

Neither Bob Muldoon nor Malcolm Fraser was committed to the reforms required to create an effective free-enterprise economy. They were both shaped by political cultures which for almost all of this century had been built upon protectionist economics and an advanced welfare state. Ironically, within a decade the Labour Party began to dismantle radically these statist institutions in both countries. But it may be that when I arrived in 1976 public opinion had not yet shifted sufficiently to make this practical politics. I suspected this might be true when I delivered a speech to the Australian Liberal Party (the equivalent of the British Conservative Party) Federal Council in Canberra. I included in my speech some of the more philosophical assertions which I always inserted in such speeches in Britain. Indeed, I was extra keen to do so because I had been reading into the small hours Solzhenitsyn's novel *The First Circle*, which I bought at the airport, and which made me reflect on the complex relationship between freedom and democracy. The applause at the end was far from deafening, and from the subsequent comments it became clear to me that conservative-minded audiences in Australia were not used to this sort of unapologetic conservatism.

Another straw in the wind was provided by my visit to Broken Hill, an outback town dominated and largely owned by the miners' union. The union leaders were delighted and rather surprised to see me. They informed me proudly that no one could live or work in the town without belonging to the union. A bar in the town which had recently challenged the rule had simply been boycotted and forced to close down. My guides were completely unabashed, indeed perversely pleased, about this blatant infraction of liberty. I could not help wondering whether I had had an insight into Britain's future.

One memory I treasure from this Australian visit was my only meeting with Sir Robert Menzies, Prime Minister for many years and a great friend of Britain. He was ailing and could no longer walk, but one saw immediately the power and strength of character of Australia's leading statesman and former member of Churchill's

Imperial War Cabinet, though less of the sarcastic wit that had made him a famous political pugilist. I was flattered when he revealed that he had read most of my recent speeches, especially those warning against renewed aggression by the Soviet Union. I was reminded not for the last time that the political generation that had come to maturity when the British Empire was still a world power retained a global perspective that its more parochial successors lacked. When I found myself complimented by this remarkable man it strengthened me in my conviction that I was right and that the *détente* establishment was wrong.

I had the same kind of encouraging confirmation from a very different source in April the following year (1977) when I visited China. I was already much better known to the Chinese than they were to me. They had relished my Helsinki and Kensington speeches and regarded me as a valued recruit in opposition to what they described as Soviet 'hegemonism'. My daughter Carol came too: she had decided to start her career in Australia and I had persuaded her to travel out via China. It was fun having her with me and she was a great antidote to too much official solemnity. There were two others in the party – one of my PPSs, John Stanley, and Douglas Hurd, who had served on the staff of our Embassy in Peking and had a vast store of knowledge and anecdote about China. Douglas christened us 'the Gang of Four'.

I was greeted at Peking Airport by the Chinese Foreign Minister, Huang Hua, before being driven into Peking itself. It was the middle of the dry season – hot and dusty, with so much static that I had been warned not to bring silk dresses. That evening I was guest of honour at a banquet in one of the side halls of the Great Hall of the People. A Chinese orchestra played a succession of Western old favourites, including the inevitable 'Greensleeves'. I had more or less mastered the advanced use of chopsticks, but I still found some Chinese delicacies unappealing. On this occasion, I allowed the sea slugs and fish bellies to pass me by. The Chinese habit, which I was glad to see the British journalists present appreciated, of drinking innumerable toasts of Mao-Tai, a strong grain spirit, posed a more hazardous social problem. Fortunately, however, I gathered that women were permitted to sip rather than down the lethal spirit.

The anti-Soviet rhetoric of Vice-Premier Li Hsien-nien was equally strong. He described the Soviets as 'sharpening their swords on the sly and stepping up their arms expansion and war preparations'. After this, my own comments about the need for strong defence sounded almost pacifist. This first banquet set one of the themes which was to continue throughout the visit – a fierce verbal assault by the Chinese against the Soviet Union. The following morning's meeting with various local politicians provided the second theme – a scathing denunciation of the misdeeds of the real 'Gang of Four' headed by Mao's widow. Mao had died in September the previous year, and the disgrace and imprisonment of his widow and the three other radicals the following month dominated the political scene.

Again and again I heard almost identical speeches made on these themes. This itself was significant. The Chinese knew that they had been weakened by the Cultural Revolution at the very time that the Soviets were embarking on an expansion of their influence. In spite of the apparent smiling self-assurance of those I met, there was also an underlying insecurity: would they be purged next, or would the Gang of Four return and wreak revenge? Two days before my arrival official ceremonies to mourn past leaders – 'The Day of the Dead' – were cancelled in case demonstrations in favour of the ousted leaders were made under the guise of demonstrations mourning Mao.

It was unclear how many supporters the disgraced radicals still had. Deng Xiao Ping, the symbol of opposition to the Cultural Revolution, though released from prison, was still in internal exile. Official posters showed the late Mao Tse Tung saying to China's present supreme leader, Hua Guo Feng 'With you in charge my heart is at ease.' The Government had allowed people to put up their own posters expressing their views, though only in permitted places and within limits. In fact, though there seemed to be general agreement that the bad old days must not return, no one was quite sure as yet what would succeed them.

The most important talks I had were, naturally, with Chairman Hua Guo Feng. An enamel spittoon was placed between our two chairs, but neither of us, I am glad to say, had occasion to use it. The talks concentrated on the international situation and we found ourselves in broad agreement. The Chinese wanted to see Britain and Western Europe support the United States in balancing Soviet power. There was even a touch of humour, when Chairman Hua complimented me on my energy when visiting the Great Wall of China.

'He who cannot climb to the top of the Great Wall of China is no true man,' he said.

I ventured to correct this thought of Chairman Mao: 'I prefer no true *leader*.'

I came away feeling that Hua's position in China was probably secure, and indeed he survived long enough to be one of my first official visitors as Prime Minister. Although in the end he was too closely identified with the old regime and was ousted in 1981, the policies of anti-Sovietism and allowing a measure of free enterprise were not only continued, but intensified.

After three days I flew south to the city of Soochow, a beautiful historic city of parks and gardens, famed for its cuisine which featured the ancient art of carving vegetables. It was good to get out of the heat and bustle of Peking. Thousands of people turned out to greet me in the tree-lined streets. I saw women making silk portraits of Mao, fed the ducks and wandered in the appropriately named Garden of the Futility of Politics. But the peaceful and contemplative atmosphere was deceiving. That evening as we left a banquet given by the Soochow City Revolutionary Committee some photograph displays caught my eye and we left our guides for a moment to look at them. The pictures showed the denunciation of a former local official. A crowd was 'cross-examining' him – catcalling and spitting at the terrified man. The guides quickly bustled us away.

From Soochow I flew to Hangchow, the scene of riots during the Cultural Revolution and full-scale fighting the previous year. Perhaps I was invited there to show to the outside world how thoroughly peace had been restored. It was certainly peaceful enough boating there on the West Lake, where Mao had had a country villa.

From Hangchow I went by train to Shanghai. My first appointment was a visit to a university. Before I left for China two disillusioned former communists who had spent some time in that country had come to see me. They told me that everything I saw on my trip would be specially set up and quite unrepresentative of reality. By chance I was able to put this to the test. I knew that some British students were on an exchange programme at the university. I asked about them and one duly appeared. Everywhere we went the floors were swept and the furniture brightly polished. The university library displayed copies of *The Economist* and even *Hansard*. It all seemed too good to be true. And of course it was. I suddenly asked my companion to show me the dormitory in which she lived, and so I left the beaten track. The dormitory was highly uncomfortable and extremely dirty. So were the other rooms. My companion had sheets only because they had been sent from home. She washed them herself. She had never seen a copy of *The Economist* in the library before.

In appearance, Shanghai was the most Western of the cities I visited: our party was taken up the river by boat and we were all very struck by the Western-style buildings of the old International Settlement, looking much as they must have done when the Japanese invasion effectively ended the colonial concessions in 1941. But the atmosphere in the city was disturbing and alien. There were microphones in the trees blaring out political messages. Shanghai had been the home of three members of the 'Gang of Four', but the new regime had been able to establish its authority there with surprising ease. I had lunch with the new mayor who was busy rooting out political opponents; he spoke with a bland ruthlessness. When I raised the question of dissidents he said: 'We try to show them the error of their ways.' I remembered the photographs of Soochow.

Through all the excesses of the Cultural Revolution – which included the burning of the British Embassy library, with its irreplaceable collection of Chinese books and manuscripts – some of the greatest treasures had been quietly preserved. My interest in Chinese drawings led me to ask to visit the city museum and gallery. The scrolls and hangings I was shown were too fragile to be on view in sunlight and I saw them in a darkened room. There was also ancient porcelain, which had a special appeal to me, and metalwork. After all the upheavals of Maoism something of the essential China had survived.

AFTERTHOUGHTS

As I read these pages, I notice with some disquiet that I seem to have established amicable relations with a number of rulers whose record on human rights will not bear too close an examination. Indeed, if I had been the Leader of the Opposition in some of these countries, I might not have retained my life, let alone my liberty. How, then, did I contrive to be on reasonably good terms with them?

A number of explanations suggest themselves. The first, and most obvious, is that I was a visiting statesman with a fair prospect of exercising political power in my own country within a few years. They therefore put themselves out to deal with, and even be pleasant towards, me. I was under no illusion about that. Equally, I saw that it was my duty to establish terms on which British interests could, then or later, be protected and advanced. Since they were the rulers of their countries, they were the people with whom I had to deal. Also I can see that certain distinctions can and should be maintained: namely, that rulers with blood on their hands should be treated correctly but no more, while democratic statesmen should be eligible for those additional marks of regard, from an honorary knighthood to an official dinner at Downing Street, which Britain has within her gift. Even so, I am not so naive as to think that this would greatly alter the conduct of authoritarian regimes.

My second consideration is that I was able, on some occasions, to obtain the release or emigration of political prisoners as a sort of *quid pro quo* for my visit. Those released were never as many as I would have liked; but even a handful was better than none. And every prisoner freed meant hope for ten more. Indeed, it told all those remaining that we had not forgotten them.

Third, we must remember that vice, like virtue, comes in many varieties. It is an odd reflection on human nature that a ruler might order the murder of a political opponent in the morning and yet carry out a pledge he had made in a treaty in the afternoon. Some of those with whom I supped with a long spoon nonetheless kept the promises they had made to Britain and, in one instance, materially helped another country to resist and overcome aggression and occupation.

Finally, international relations is a matter of second-best alternatives rather than the ideal. Even if it had been within my power to replace one ruler with another – which it never was – I would rarely have been able to replace a bad one with a better, and often it would have been with a worse. Those, for instance, who rejoiced in the fall of the Shah must reconcile themselves today to the sad truth that the regime of the Mullahs is more oppressive to its own citizens, and abroad promotes terrorism and subversion, where the Shah was a pillar of stability, if in the end a shaky one.

States tend to act upon their own interests rather than the interests of the peoples of other countries. That is all the more reason for people in democratic countries to pressurize not only foreign governments which suppress human rights, but also their own governments to make improvements in human rights one aim of Western diplomacy. I may sometimes have resented this second sort of criticism of my own actions in power; not long afterwards, however, I was usually glad to have had my elbow jogged.

CHAPTER XI

Apprenticeship for Power

Leader of the Opposition March 1977 to March 1979

A PLEASANT INTERLUDE

The Lib-Lab Pact did none of the things subsequently claimed for it by its exponents. It did not halt, let alone reverse, the advance of socialism: indeed, it kept the Labour Government in office and enabled it to complete the nationalization of the aircraft and ship-building industries. Nor was it responsible for the frail but real economic recovery which gradually improved the Labour Party's political standing in 1977/78: that was the result of the financial measures imposed by the IMF several months before the Pact was agreed. It did not help Mr Callaghan to marginalize and defeat the Left; indeed, the Left emerged strong enough to take over the Labour Party within a few years.

The real benefits were quite different and completely un-intended. First, the fact that the Liberal Party demonstrated the closeness of its approach to that of Labour gave a salutary warning to potential Conservatives who, for whatever reason, flirted with the idea of voting Liberal as a more civilized alternative to social-ism. The Pact therefore hardened our support. Secondly, I can see now that in March 1977 we were not yet ready to form the kind of government which could have achieved a long-term shift away from the policies which had led to Britain's decline. Neither the Shadow Cabinet, nor the Parliamentary Party, nor in all prob-ability the electorate, would have been prepared to take the neces-sary but unpalatable medicine, because they had not witnessed how far the disease had spread. It took the strikes of the winter of

1978/79 to change all that. Finally, the Government's survival was a real, if well disguised, blessing for me. I benefited greatly from the next two gruelling years as Leader of the Opposition. I learned more about how to achieve what I wanted, even though I always felt in a minority in the Shadow Cabinet. Although I had both good and bad days, I also became a more effective debater, public speaker and campaigner, all of which would stand me in good stead as Prime Minister. Above all, perhaps, I had the opportunity to demonstrate both to myself and to others that I had that elusive 'instinct' for what ordinary people feel – a quality which, I suspect, one is simply born with or not, but which is sharpened and burnished through adversity.

My disappointment with my speech in the No Confidence debate on Wednesday 23 March 1977 was quickly dispelled by a succession of good news. Politicians sagely remark, when questioned on such matters, that they take little notice of opinion polls; but political life is a great deal easier when they are substantially in your favour. It was quickly apparent that the public did not like the deal which had been stitched up between the Labour and Liberal Parties. The polls showed the Conservatives fifteen to twenty percentage points in the lead over Labour and registered a sharp drop in approval for the Liberals. My speech attacking Denis Healey's Budget the week after the No Confidence debate reassured the Parliamentary Party: I spoke from rapidly scribbled notes, reaching through the statistical smokescreen to draw out the contradictions which lay behind it. Then the following day we won Birmingham Stechford – Roy Jenkins's old seat – with a swing of 17.4 per cent. Having watched the result on television at Flood Street, I put out a statement, rubbing in the salt, saying: 'We are the people's party now.'

On my return from my visit to the Far East in April, I plunged into campaigning at two more by-elections – first in the Nottinghamshire mining seat of Ashfield and then in the Humberside fishing port of Grimsby. In normal times both would have been safe seats for Labour. I was told that we probably would not win Ashfield but that Grimsby was within our grasp. Talking to voters – over fish and chips in Ashfield and haddock and poached egg in Grimsby – I had a rather different impression. Although we had two good candidates, it was the misfortune of our man in Grimsby, who worked in the fishing industry, to follow in the footsteps of the late Tony Crosland. It was clear that even Conservative voters had appreciated having a rather grand socialist to represent them and would have liked someone similar. In fact, I was right. We won at Ashfield, overturning a Government majority of nearly 23,000, and narrowly failed to take Grimsby, where the voters chose the nearest thing to a grand socialist, the television personality Austin Mitchell. Just a week later we secured large gains in the Metropolitan and County Council elections, recapturing the GLC (Greater London Council) – an important prize which would give us an opportunity, so important to any Opposition, to demonstrate at a local level some of the policies, such as the sale of council houses, which we intended to pursue nationally.

This was a good time for me as well as for the Party. I felt able to alter some policies which I had inherited and to set out my own views more clearly on others. I took advantage of the Scottish Party Conference in May effectively to jettison the commitment to devolution, which passed off remarkably quietly.

Then, delivering the Iain Macleod Memorial Lecture in July, I sought to explain how my own personal philosophy fitted in with the Conservative tradition, and indeed with that religious view of the world which is an essential aspect of Toryism. I always put a special effort into such speeches because I regarded it as crucial to show that Conservatives need feel no unease or inhibitions about taking on their opponents on moral just as on practical grounds.

Later that month, before the House rose for the summer recess, I had a good day speaking in the Economic Debate. It was one of those days when every hostile intervention seems designed to trigger a pungent retort. Somewhat to my own surprise, I found myself knocking down opponents like ducks in a shooting gallery. As one friendly journalist wrote: 'Margaret Thatcher's one-woman massacre of both the Government and the Liberals could not have come at a better time.' The press was, for now at least, full of pleasantly flattering discussion of my qualities and prospects. Still more flattering was the reaction of the Labour benches to my next major appearance: total silence intended to disconcert.

But just as the political reality was never as bad as it seemed at the time of the agreement of the Lib-Lab Pact, so we were now in truth facing far more serious problems than even the commentators understood. Our popularity largely reflected widespread reaction against the Government's manifest failures. Now that some order was being restored to the public finances, which would bring inflation and interest rates down, we would be under more pressure to spell out our own alternative. We would have to win on more than a doctor's mandate. We would have to set out clearly and persuasively an alternative analysis and set of policies. For my part, I was keen to do just that. But I knew that on such central questions as trade union power, incomes policy and public spending there was still no agreement in Shadow Cabinet between the minority of us who fundamentally rejected the approach pursued between 1970 and 1974 and the majority who more or less wished to continue it. All of the damaging divisions which plagued us over these years, and which we desperately tried to minimize by agreeing on 'lines to take', stemmed from that basic problem. Ultimately, it was not one which was amenable to the techniques of political management, only to the infinitely more difficult process of clarifying thoughts and changing minds.

GRUNWICK

So it was that what came to be known as the 'Grunwick affair' burst onto the political scene. This was a clear case of the outrageous abuse of trade union power. Paradoxically, it proved almost as politically damaging to us, whom the unions regarded with undisguised hostility, as to the Labour Party, who were their friends and sometime clients.

Grunwick was a medium-sized photographic processing and printing business in north-west London run by a dynamic Anglo-Indian entrepreneur, George Ward, with a largely immigrant workforce. A dispute in the summer of 1976 resulted in a walkout of a number of workers and their subsequent dismissal. This then escalated into a contest between the management and the APEX trade

union, which had subsequently signed up the dismissed workers
and demanded 'recognition'. That would have given the union the
right to negotiate on behalf of its members working for the company. APEX consequently demanded the reinstatement of those
who had been dismissed.

For its part, Grunwick established in the courts that the dis-
missals had been perfectly legal – even under Labour's new union
legislation, which the unions had virtually written themselves.
None of those who had been dismissed could be taken back under
existing law unless *all* were taken back, and in a number of cases
there was simply too much bad blood. Grunwick argued too that
the behaviour of APEX in other firms suggested that it was out to
impose a closed shop. Finally, secret ballots conducted by MORI
and Gallup showed that the great majority of the Grunwick workforce – over 80 per cent – did not want to join APEX, or any other
union.

A left-wing coalition emerged to support APEX and punish
Grunwick. Every part of the socialist world was represented: the
local Brent Trades Council, trade union leaders and 'flying pickets',
the Socialist Workers Party, and leading members of the Labour
Party itself, among them Cabinet ministers Shirley Williams and
Fred Mulley, and the Minister for Sport, Denis Howell, who dusted
off their donkey jackets and joined the Grunwick picket line for a
short time, a couple of weeks before the picketing turned violent.
Someone called it 'the Ascot of the Left'.

The National Association for Freedom (NAFF), took up the case
of George Ward as part of its campaign against abuses of individual
freedom resulting from overweening trade union power. NAFF had
been launched in December 1975, shortly after the IRA's murder
of someone who would have been one of its leading lights – Ross
McWhirter, whom I had known (along with his twin brother
Norris) from Orpington days.* NAFF's Chairman was Bill De
L'Isle and Dudley, the war hero and the MP who had spoken to
us at Oxford attacking Yalta when I was an undergraduate.** The

* His death had a particular significance for me, quite apart from the loss of a
courageous friend: within days I was assigned a team of personal detectives who
have been with me ever since.
** See p. 57.

organization quickly become nationally known through its support for three British railwaymen, dismissed for refusing to join a union, who successfully took their case to the European Court of Human Rights. It fought (but eventually lost) an equally prominent action to prevent British Post Office unions boycotting mail to South Africa. I gave NAFF as much support as I could, though a number of my colleagues regarded it with deep distaste and made public criticisms of its activities. Without NAFF, Grunwick would almost certainly have gone under. When the postal union illegally blacked Grunwick's outgoing mail, which contained the developed films on which the firm's business depended, NAFF volunteers smuggled it through the pickets, distributed it around Britain, and discreetly posted it in thousands of pillarboxes.

The mass picketing began at the end of June 1977 and continued day after day with terrifying scenes of mob violence, injuries to police and pickets. At times thousands of demonstrators crowded the narrow suburban streets around the Grunwick factory in north-west London, to waylay the coaches laid on by the firm to bring their employees through. So I asked my PPS, Adam Butler, and Jim Prior's number two, Barney Hayhoe, to join the employees on one of their morning coach journeys through the hail of missiles and abuse. Adam reported back to me on the fear – and the courage – of the people he had been with.

During this period a strange reticence gripped the Government. The Shadow Cabinet organized a number of Private Notice Questions to force ministers to declare their position on the violence. We issued a statement demanding that the Prime Minister state categorically that the police had the Government's backing in carrying out their duties. But as I wrote to John Gouriet, one of NAFF's directors, at the time: 'we feel that the scenes of wild violence portrayed on television plus the wild charges and allegations being thrown about in certain quarters, are enough in themselves to put most of the public on the side of right and are doing more than hours of argument'.

Although the scenes outside the factory seemed to symbolize the consequences of giving trade unions virtually unlimited immunity in civil law, it was in fact the criminal law against violence and intimidation which was being breached. No matter how many new legal provisions might be desirable, the first duty of the authorities was to uphold the existing law. All the more so because the violence at Grunwick was part of a wider challenge posed by the far Left to the rule of law; and no one quite knew how far that challenge would ultimately go. The attitude of Sam Silkin, the Attorney-General, to law-breaking by trade unions had been revealed as at best ambiguous in the case raised by NAFF in January 1977, when two Post Office unions banned telephone calls, mail and telegrams to South Africa.* Later he would coin a memorable phrase which summed up the Labour Government's shifty attitude to the law and individual rights, when he described certain sorts of picketing as 'lawful intimidation'.**

It was also at this time that a new shamelessness on the part of the Left became apparent. Until the early 1970s, Transport House banned members of certain 'proscribed organizations' on the far Left from being members of the Labour Party. The lifting of this ban, long sought by the Left, was a very significant landmark in Labour's drift to extremism. Hard-left Labour MPs saw less reason to conceal their links with communist organizations. The warmth of fraternal relations between trade union leaders and socialist politicians on the one hand and the Soviet bloc on the other was undisguised. High-ranking Soviet visitors were received by both the TUC and the Labour Party. Trotskyist organizations, such as the Militant Tendency, began to gain a grip on Labour Party constituencies. There was an almost tangible sense that, whatever the IMF or Prime Minister Jim Callaghan might think, it was the extreme Left whose programme represented Labour's future, and that whether the tactics employed to achieve it were violent or peaceful was the only question at issue. In such an atmosphere,

---

* The Attorney-General attempted unsuccessfully to stop NAFF applying for an injunction to prevent the boycott, claiming that he alone had discretion to decide on applications for injunctions from private citizens without standing in the action. The Court of Appeal found in favour of NAFF, but on appeal to the House of Lords the Attorney's view was upheld.

** *Hansard*, Vol. 961, cc.712–15, 25 January 1979. Asked whether withdrawal of a union card could constitute intimidation within the meaning of the law, the Attorney-General replied: 'The answer . . . must be that it depends on whether the intimidation is of a lawful character.'

the scenes at Grunwick suggested – and not only to the Left itself – that perhaps the revolution had begun.

As well as the assault on the rule of law and the advance of the extreme Left, however, Grunwick also came to symbolize the closed shop. This was because NAFF, which defended Grunwick's cause, was also vigorously campaigning against the closed shop. Also APEX clearly wished to coerce Grunwick's employees, probably with a view ultimately to achieving a closed shop in the industry. More broadly, the closed shop represented a secure redoubt of trade union power from which further assaults on liberty could be mounted.

Yet, for all that, Grunwick was not limited to the closed shop; it was about the sheer power of the unions. Appalled as I was by what was happening at Grunwick, I did not believe that the time was yet ripe to depart from the cautious line about trade union reform (which I had agreed with Jim Prior) in order to mount a radical attack on the closed shop. We had to consider a much wider raft of questions, ranging from the unions' immunity under civil law, to violence and intimidation which only escaped the criminal law because they came under the guise of lawful picketing. Until we had begun to solve some of these problems, we could not effectively outlaw the closed shop. The Prior line, which we had evolved when opposing elements of the Labour Government's Trade Union and Labour Relations Acts, was to widen the safeguards and improve the compensation for workers who lost their jobs as a result of the closed shop, without trying to ban it as such. (It was widely argued that it would in practice continue to exist as a result of covert understandings between employers and trade unions, whatever we did; moreover, some groups of employers actually favoured the closed shop because it made their lives easier since they could rely on the trade union to discipline the workforce.) And this was the ground on which we uneasily stood.*

Jim Prior, himself, stood rather more easily than I did. For him,

* In fact, it was not until 1990 that we passed legislation to end the closed shop, making it unlawful to deny people a job because they are, or are not, members of a union, though we had already significantly tightened the law on the closed shop in earlier legislation.

I suspect, it was a practical question rather than a moral one: the important thing was to be realistic and accept that the trade unions could not be tamed by law. Any reform would need their cooperation. By contrast, Keith Joseph was an unswerving opponent of what he saw as a breach of human rights resulting from collectivist bullying. Jim's and Keith's opposing views, expressed in public statements on the Scarman Report on the Grunwick dispute, brought all this out into the open. I have described earlier the problems this caused me on my American visit.* At the time, I thought that Keith's criticisms of Lord Scarman were too sharp, though the Scarman Report itself was anything but a judicial document and had no legal force. Moreover Jim, not Keith, was the spokesman on these matters. Either I sacked Jim, or I moved him (neither of which I could afford to do), or I had to go along with his approach.

That was what I did. In retrospect, Jim and I were wrong and Keith was right. What the whole affair demonstrated was that our careful avoidance of any kind of commitment to changing the law on industrial relations, though it might make sense in normal times, would be weak and unsustainable in a crisis. But I took the decision to support Jim in part because, as yet, the climate was still not right to try to harden our policy. Within the Shadow Cabinet the great majority of my colleagues would not have gone along with me. But some time soon the nettle would have to be grasped.

In reflecting on all this, I came back to the idea of a referendum. On my return from America I knew that I would be pressed hard by Brian Walden, who was making his début as interviewer on the television programme *Weekend World*, on what a Conservative Government would do if it were faced with an all-out confrontation with the trade unions. I had to have a convincing answer: and there was not much hope that any amount of discussion within Shadow Cabinet would arrive at one. So on the programme I argued that although such a confrontation was unlikely, yet if such an emergency was reached, then a referendum might be necessary. The suggestion was well received both in the press and – most significantly in the light of the stories of splits and conflicts – got

* See pp. 368–9.

public backing from both wings of the Party. (It helped perhaps that Jim was expecting a rough ride at the Conservative Party Conference over the closed shop.) I set up a Party Committee under Nick Edwards to report on referenda and their possible uses. But, of course, though the suggestion of a referendum bought us vital time, it was not in itself an answer to the problem of trade union power. Assuming that we won a referendum, so demonstrating that the general public backed the Government against the militants, it would still be necessary to frame the measures to reduce trade union power. And so far we had not seriously considered what those measures should be.

EDGING AWAY FROM INCOMES POLICY

The argument about trade union power remained linked to that about incomes policies. At this time the Government's own incomes policy was looking increasingly fragile. No formal policy could be agreed with the unions after the end of the second year of 'restraint', though the TUC exhorted its members not to seek more than one increase in the next twelve months and the Chancellor of the Exchequer pleaded for settlements to be below 10 per cent (backed as before with the threat of sanctions against employers who paid more). But, of course, whatever difficulties the Labour Government had in agreeing incomes policy with the trade unions were likely to pale into insignificance by comparison with ours. Unfortunately, we were committed to produce a document on economic policy, including incomes policy, before the 1977 Party Conference. David Howell, an able journalist of monetarist persuasions and also a front-bench spokesman, was the principal draftsman. And Geoffrey Howe, remorselessly seeking some kind of consensus between the conflicting views in his Economic Reconstruction Group, had by now become thoroughly convinced of the merits of German-style 'concerted action' within some kind of economic forum.

I could see trouble coming down the track and I expressed my unease about all of this. Geoffrey tried to convince me of the system's merits by sending me a paper on how the Germans did it, but I wrote back: 'This paper frightens me to death even more. We really must avoid some of this terrible jargon. Also we should recognize that the German talking shop works because it consists of Germans.'

Work on the document continued, but among the front-bench economic spokesmen rather than the Shadow Cabinet. By contrast with the Grunwick/closed shop issue, Keith, who shared my misgivings about the 'forum', was prepared to compromise more than I would have done. And in the end, the document appeared under the signatures of Keith, Geoffrey, Jim Prior, David Howell and Angus Maude; it was not formally endorsed by the Shadow Cabinet.

I never felt much affection for *The Right Approach to the Economy*. Unlike *The Right Approach* of 1976, it made little impact either on the outside world or on the policy we would pursue as a Government. I was careful to ensure that 'concerted action' – apart from within the limited framework of the NEDC – never saw the light of day.

So it was that we more or less successfully papered over the policy cracks up to the 1977 Party Conference at Blackpool. The Conference itself taught me an important lesson which Party managers in general find it hard to accept. On the face of it, the Blackpool Conference was a success. Colleagues generally stuck to the agreed lines on controversial issues. Embarrassing splits were avoided. Somewhat in the same spirit was my own speech. It contained many good lines but, for all the spit and polish, it was essentially a rollicking attack on Labour that lacked positive substance. Although the immediate reception was good, it was soon clear that it left the large questions about our policies unanswered; and I was not satisfied with it. My instincts proved correct. Having entered the Conference season several points ahead of Labour in the opinion polls, we finished it running neck and neck. A 'good' Conference never avoids rows at the expense of issues.

In any case, January 1978 saw the spotlight turn back onto just those difficult, important issues which the Party managers considered best avoided. Geoffrey Howe, speaking in Swindon, delivered a sharp and comprehensive attack on the role of trade unions in Britain and was met by a barrage of abuse from the union leaders and scarcely concealed irritation from some colleagues. I agreed with Geoffrey and strongly defended him in public. But I was still basically sticking with the Prior line and so I dissuaded him from making a second such speech, noting on the draft: 'Geoffrey: this is not your subject. Why go on with it? The press will crucify you for this.'

Oddly enough, just a few days later I found myself on the receiving end of almost equally sharp criticism. I had determined to use a speech to a conference of Scottish industrialists in Glasgow to break away from the qualification and obfuscation into which I felt we had been manoeuvred over incomes policy. I said:

> The counterpart of the withdrawal of government from interference in prices and profits in the private sector which both we and you want to see, is inevitably the withdrawal of government from interference in wage bargaining. There can be no selective return to personal responsibility.

This was attacked by, among others, *The Economist* under the timid headline: 'Mrs Thatcher Takes the Tories into Dangerous Water'.

A kind of torpid socialism had become the conventional wisdom of Britain in those years. But as the old order started to break up, it was increasingly difficult for anyone with the responsibility to think ahead to avoid challenging the prevailing orthodoxy. The succession of crises – economic, fiscal and industrial – under Labour constantly invited us to think thoughts and propose policies that deviated from both the conventional wisdom represented by *Economist* economists and the agreed line represented by Jim Prior – which as it happens usually amounted to the same thing.

IMMIGRATION

I was soon to offend against Party political wisdom still more fundamentally. Ever since Enoch Powell's Birmingham speech in April 1968 it had been the mark of civilized high-mindedness among right-of-centre politicians to avoid speaking about immigration and race at all, and if that did not prove possible, then to do so in terms borrowed from the left of the political spectrum, relishing the 'multi-cultural', 'multi-racial' nature of modern British society. This whole approach glossed over the real problems that immigration sometimes caused and dismissed the anxieties of those who were directly affected as 'racist'. I had never been prepared to go along with it. It seemed both dishonest and snobbish.

Nothing is more colour-blind than the capitalism in which I placed my faith for Britain's revival. It was part of my credo that individuals were worthy of respect *as individuals*, not as members of classes or races; the whole purpose of the political and economic system I favoured was to liberate the talents of those individuals for the benefit of society. I felt no sympathy for rabble rousers, like the National Front, who sought to exploit race. I found it deeply significant that such groups, both now and in the past, were just as much socialist as they were nationalist. All collectivism is always conducive to oppression: it is only the victims who differ.

At the same time, large-scale New Commonwealth immigration over the years had transformed large areas of Britain in a way which the indigenous population found hard to accept. It is one thing for a well-heeled politician to preach the merits of tolerance on a public platform before returning to a comfortable home in a tranquil road in one of the more respectable suburbs, where house prices ensure him the exclusiveness of apartheid without the stigma. It is quite another for poorer people, who cannot afford to move, to watch their neighbourhoods changing and the value of their house falling. Those in such a situation need to be reassured rather than patronized. Nor, as I knew from talking to immigrants in my own constituency, was it just white families who were deeply worried. Those immigrants who had already come here and wanted to be accepted as full members of the community knew that continuing large-scale immigration would provoke a reaction of which they might be victims. The failure to articulate the sentiments of ordinary people like these had left the way open to the extremists. And, of course, the very success of those extremists was something which the Left in all its varieties could turn to its advantage. No matter how much the socialists mismanaged the economy, cut Britain's defences or failed to uphold law and order, they were at least able to guarantee a sympathetic hearing by condemning their opponents as bigots. For the Left has never been slow to exploit the problems it creates.

Policy work on immigration had been proceeding under Willie Whitelaw's direction for some time by January 1978. But it had not progressed very far – certainly not as far as many of our supporters, vocal at Party Conferences, wished. This was only partly because Willie himself was instinctively liberal-minded on Home Office matters. The problem was that it was very difficult to see what scope existed to cut down on present and potential future immigration.

Roy Jenkins had changed the immigration rules to allow in male fiancés for the purpose of marriage to UK citizens, a provision which had been much abused. Illegal immigration, about whose size one could only speculate, had in effect been encouraged by amnesties. It had become normal practice for those who entered Britain after 1 January 1973 for a 'temporary' stay to be accepted later for settlement on removal of the time limit and their dependants also admitted. Work permits were not sufficiently tightly restricted. There was much uncertainty both about the accuracy of the immigration figures and, above all, about the number of potential immigrants and their dependants who had a right to come to Britain. There was, therefore, scope for action in these areas, but that scope was limited. For there were a number of commitments upon which we could not honourably or humanely renege – in particular, to UK passport holders in East Africa and (under the Conservative Government's 1971 Immigration Act) to the dependants of those immigrants who were ordinarily resident in the UK on 1 January 1973.

Closing loopholes, tightening up administration and some new controls on primary and secondary immigration – all of these offered opportunities to reduce the inflow. But I knew that the single most important contribution we could make to good race relations was to reduce the uncertainties about the future. It was fear of the unknown rather than the awkwardnesses of the present which threatened danger. Willie Whitelaw shared that basic analysis, which is why he had pledged us at the 1976 Party Conference 'to follow a policy which is clearly designed to work towards the end of immigration as we have seen it in these post-war years'.

Although I had not planned any specific announcement on immigration, I was not surprised when I was asked in an interview on *World in Action* about the subject. I had been giving it a good deal of thought, having indeed expressed myself strongly in other interviews. Nor, for the reasons that I have outlined, did I feel any inhibitions about doing so. I said:

> People are really rather afraid that this country might be rather swamped by people with a different culture . . . So, if you want good race relations you have got to allay people's fears on numbers . . . We do have to hold out the prospect of an end to immigration, except, of course, for compassionate cases. Therefore we have got to look at the numbers who have a right to come in . . . Everyone who is here must be treated equally under the law and that, I think, is why quite a lot of them too are fearful that their position might be put in jeopardy, or people might be hostile to them, unless we cut down the incoming numbers.

Even I was taken aback by the reaction to these extremely mild remarks. What it quickly showed was the degree to which politicians had become isolated from people's real worries. I was denounced as 'appallingly irresponsible' by David Steel, the Liberal Party Leader, who later added for good measure that my remarks were 'really quite wicked'. Denis Healey spoke of my 'cold-blooded calculation in stirring up the muddy waters of racial prejudice . . . to spread fear and hatred among peaceful communities'. The Home Secretary, Merlyn Rees, accused me of 'making respectable racial hatred'. The bishops joined in. Fifteen years later, this reaction to ideas which were later embodied in legislation and are all but universally accepted seems hysterical.

Even at the time, the reaction in the country, undoubtedly sharpened by the exaggerated rhetoric of critics who imagined they had finally sunk me, was completely different. Before my interview, the opinion polls showed us level-pegging with Labour. Afterwards, they showed the Conservatives with an eleven-point lead. This unintended effect of a spontaneous reply to an interviewer's question had important political consequences. Whatever Willie in his heart of hearts and my other colleagues felt about it, it provided a large and welcome boost at an extremely difficult time. It also sharpened up the discussion within Shadow Cabinet of our proposals. Within weeks we had a comprehensive and agreed approach which satisfied all but the diehard advocates of repatriation and which would see us through the general election.*

The whole affair was a demonstration that I must trust my own judgement on crucial matters, rather than necessarily hope to persuade my colleagues in advance; for I could expect that somewhere out in the country there would be a following and perhaps a majority for me.

THE NON-ELECTION OF 1978

Quite apart from the immigration issue, 1978 had all the makings of a politically difficult year for the Opposition. As a result of the financial measures introduced under pressure from the IMF, the economic situation improved. In January 1978 inflation fell below 10 per cent for the first time since 1974 and it continued to fall. Unemployment was also falling gradually from its peak in August 1977; although there were sharp increases during the summer of 1978, 1.36 million were registered unemployed by that December, 120,000 fewer than the year before. We succeeded, with support from the Liberals, in forcing a cut of one penny in the basic rate of income tax: but that in itself would probably reduce the gloom about the economy which had played such an important part in

---

* Our manifesto pledged us to introduce a British Nationality Act defining British citizenship and the right to abode, to set up a register of dependants from Commonwealth countries who had the right of settlement under existing legislation (whose numbers were uncertain) and to establish a quota system to restrict the rate of entry for settlement from non-EC countries. In the event, only the first of these measures was passed into law. During the 1980s primary immigration – the admission of heads of household in their own right – fell significantly, diminishing the number of future dependants with a right of settlement and reducing the overall total below 50,000 in most years, compared to 82,000 in 1975 and 69,000 in 1979.

Labour's unpopularity and which had worked to our advantage.

Our assumption was that Jim Callaghan hoped to coast along on these gradual improvements towards an election in the autumn on a platform of 'safety first'. One large obstacle in his way was that the Liberals now recognized that the Lib-Lab Pact had been politically disastrous for them. But their anxiety to bring it to an end was modified by their reluctance to face the electoral consequences of having sustained Labour in power at all. As for the opinion polls, Labour had drawn almost level with us by the summer and though we pulled away from them in August/September, during October and November (after a difficult Conservative Conference) they were around 5 per cent ahead, with the Liberals not even in double figures.

In these circumstances, I commissioned work on a draft manifesto. It was drawn together by Chris Patten and the Research Department on the basis of Shadow spokesmen's drafts. When I read it in July I was unimpressed. The large, simple themes had become obscured by lists of costly promises designed to appeal to interest groups. I said that the next draft must put the main emphasis on a few central objectives, like tax cuts and strengthening the country's internal and external defences. The fulfilment of all other spending pledges was conditional on meeting these pledges first. In truth, I was disagreeably reminded of what little real progress in analysis or policy we had made in Opposition over the last three years. If we continued thinking in these terms, how would we ever manage to turn the country round?

More encouraging, however, was the change which had come over the Party's publicity. Gordon Reece had returned to become Director of Publicity at Central Office. It was through Gordon that Tim Bell and Saatchi & Saatchi were made responsible for the Party's advertising. This was a significant departure in our political communications. But I needed no persuading that it was right to obtain the best professionals in their field to put across our message. There was no question of the advertising agency devising what that message was, of course. But politicians should resist the temptation to consider themselves experts in fields where they have no experience. I would frequently reject suggestions for advertising on grounds of taste or sense, but I left the creative work to them. From the first, I found Tim Bell, the Saatchi executive who handled our account, easy to work with: like Gordon, he had a feel for politics and a sense of fun. When I first met Tim I laid down the basis on which we would always cooperate, saying: 'Politicians usually have a lot of toes and you must be frightfully careful not to tread on them. I, however, have no toes – and you will tell me the truth.' Of course, I was not always so self-restrained in practice.

Saatchis put new life into the tired format of Party Political Broadcasts. There were the inevitable accusations of frivolity or over-simplification. But PPBs should not be judged on the basis of the comments of the Party faithful, but rather by whether the casual, unpolitical viewer actually chooses to watch them, rather than turning to another channel, and whether he gains a sympathetic impression. On this score, the change was a great improvement.

Most significant, however – and even more important than the work done for the 1979 general election campaign itself – was the 'Labour Isn't Working' poster campaign in the summer of 1978. Tim, Gordon and Ronnie Millar came down to Scotney on a Saturday in June 1978 to get my agreement for a campaign on this theme. Again, it would break new ground. Unemployment, which would be depicted both by the wording and by a picture of a dole queue, though it had risen to almost 1.5 million, was traditionally a 'Labour issue'. That is to say, it was a topic which we would not normally make a campaign priority because, like the Welfare State, it was one where the Labour Party was generally regarded as stronger than us. The poster would also break with the notion that in party propaganda you should not mention your opponent directly. Saatchis, however, understood – and convinced me – that political advertising of the sort proposed could ignore such considerations. It was designed to undermine confidence in our political opponents, and so it should limit itself to a simple, negative message.

Generally, Governments do well during the summer recess because the political temperature drops. The planned campaign would keep it high and doubtless provoke strong reactions. So after much discussion I agreed that the campaign should go ahead.

As expected, it evoked a response. Denis Healey launched a

bombardment. But the more it was condemned by the Labour Party, the greater publicity it got. Simply in order to explain what the controversy was about, the newspapers had to print pictures of the poster, thus multiplying the effect. So successful was it that a further series was developed on other topics, on each of which Labour was 'not working'. Partly as a result of all this, we came through to the autumn of 1978 in better political shape than might have been expected – and in August-September we were strengthening. That in turn may have been of some significance, insofar as it affected the Prime Minister's decision on whether to call an election.

Only Jim Callaghan can say precisely why he did not call a general election that autumn. Certainly, I expected that he would, particularly after his speech to the TUC Conference which ended improbably with him bursting into song: 'There was I, waiting at the church . . .' – a teasing refusal to tell them what he was going to do. Then, just two days later, on Thursday 7 September while I was on a visit to Birmingham, the news was telephoned through to me from Downing Street that in the Prime Ministerial broadcast that evening, which we knew was booked, Jim Callaghan would announce that there would not in fact be an election.

The advance warning was given in confidence, which I respected. In fact, we did not even inform the Central Office team. It was an odd feeling, knowing as I did that there would be no immediate campaign, yet receiving the excited good wishes of supporters unaware of this fact. At one factory, opposite a skill training centre I was visiting, the workforce turned out, waving and shouting 'Good luck, Maggie.' I had to complete my schedule as stoically and inscrutably as possible, while considering the right response.

I shared the general sense of anti-climax which the Prime Minister's announcement caused. But I knew that others, who had been working night and day to place the Party on a war footing in what had every sign of being a closely contested struggle, would feel the let-down even more. Later that night I telephoned through to Tim Bell to see how he and Gordon Reece had taken it. In fact, the two of them had restored their spirits over champagne in a West End restaurant and I had clearly woken Tim from the sleep of the just. I was asking where I could find Gordon when suddenly he said,

'My God, I've been burgled.' And so he had. He had managed to
get to bed without noticing.

I gave my reactions the following evening in the slot given to the
Leader of the Opposition to reply to a Prime Ministerial broadcast.
Ironically, in the light of what subsequently happened, the Prime
Minister had sought to justify his refusal to seek a new mandate
by arguing that a general election would do nothing to make the
situation easier in the forthcoming winter. I replied:

> Well, some of us look further ahead than this winter. We don't
> believe that Britain has to grind on in bottom gear. The longer
> he puts things off, the worse they will become, and the worse
> they become the longer it will take to put them right. But I
> believe they can be put right, once we've a government that
> has confidence. The confidence of the people and confidence
> in the people. A government with authority at home, and with
> authority abroad.

Would we have won a general election in the autumn of 1978?
I believe that we might have scraped in with a small overall majority. But it would only have needed one or two mistakes in our
campaign to have lost. And even if we had just won, what would
have happened next? The Labour Government's pay policy was
now clearly coming apart. The TUC had voted against a renewal
of the Social Contract – and the following month's Labour Party
Conference would vote to reject all pay restraint – so even that fig
leaf would be removed. A strike of Ford car workers already looked
impossible to settle within the Government's 5 per cent 'pay norm'.
The distortions and frustrations of several years of prices and
incomes policy were unwinding, as they had under the Heath
Government, amid bitterness and upheaval.

If we had been faced with that over the winter of 1978/79 it
might have broken us, as it finally broke the Labour Government.
First, I would have had to insist that all the talk about 'norms'
and 'limits' should be dropped immediately. For reasons I shall
explain, that would have been very unpopular and perhaps
unacceptable to most of the Shadow Cabinet. Secondly, even
had we tried to use cash limits in the public sector and market

disciplines in the private sector, rather than some kind of pay policy, there would have been a high risk of damaging strikes. Rather than giving us a mandate to curb trade union power, as they would in the following year, these would probably only have confirmed in the public mind the impression left by the three-day week in 1974 that Conservative Governments meant provoking and losing confrontations with the trade unions. Appalling as the scenes of the winter of 1978/79 turned out to be, without them and without their exposure of the true nature of socialism, it would have been far more difficult to achieve what was done in the 1980s.

But in any case, we could afford to wait. Although I cannot claim to have foreseen what followed, I was convinced that the Labour Party's basic approach was unsustainable. In exchange for agreement with the trade union leaders on pay limits, the Labour Government had pursued policies which extended state control of the economy, reduced the scope for individual enterprise and increased trade union power. At some point such a strategy would collapse. The trade union leaders and the left of the Labour Party would find their power so strengthened that they would no longer have an interest in delivering pay restraint. Nor would union members respond to calls for sacrifice in pursuit of policies that had plainly failed. The effects of socialist policies on the overall performance of the economy would be that Britain would lag further and further behind its competitors on productivity and living standards. Beyond a certain point this could no longer be concealed from the general public – nor from the foreign-exchange markets and foreign investors. Assuming that the basic structures of a free political and economic system were still operating, socialism must then break down. And that, of course, is exactly what happened that winter.

SPLITS AND REBELLIONS

The Conservative Party Conference at Brighton was always likely to be difficult. Most of those present had expected that it would never take place because of the supposedly imminent general election campaign and felt cheated of that victory. The opinion polls showed us falling behind Labour. Above all, the controversy over the Government's rapidly disintegrating pay policy focused even more attention on our approach, and that was itself threatened with disintegration.

A couple of weeks before the Conference Jim Prior had unwisely made remarks in a radio interview which seemed to offer Conservative backing for the Government's 5 per cent policy, and not only made clear his support for the principle of a statutory incomes policy but actually revealed that he thought a Conservative Government would be forced to introduce one: 'I think that may well happen under certain circumstances.' In my own interviews, I tried to shift the emphasis back towards the link between pay, profits and output and away from norms. Although I made it clear that I was not supporting the Ford strike, I equally blamed the Government's 5 per cent pay norm for what was happening and said that a statutory policy was not a practical possibility. I was widely interpreted as having called for a return to free collective bargaining, an interpretation I did not seek to deny.

Ted Heath now intervened on the other side. Speaking in the Conference economic debate, while I watched from the platform, he warned of the risks of dogmatism and said of the Government's 5 per cent policy: 'It is not yet clear to what extent it has broken down. But if it has broken down, there is nothing here for gloating, nothing for joy. We should grieve for our country.' Geoffrey Howe made a strong closing speech, handling Ted's intervention with aplomb and saying that a future Conservative Government would return to 'realistic, responsible collective bargaining, free from government interference'. But later that evening Ted appeared on television and went further. He warned that 'free collective bargaining produces massive inflation', and when asked if the Conservative Party should support the Government's pay policy at a general election, he replied: 'If the Prime Minister says he is going to the country and expresses the view that we cannot have another roaring inflation or another free-for-all, I would say I agree with that.'

This was a thinly veiled threat. An open split between the two of us during the general election would cause enormous damage.

The question of Ted's role during an election had long worried the Party, and Peter Thorneycroft had met him quietly to discuss his plans earlier in the year. Humphrey Atkins had also received messages from several MPs close to Ted who told him that he was proving amenable to an approach to help. Arrangements were made to liaise with his office during the campaign. Ted's intervention had blown all that out of the water.

Moreover, in substance Ted's view seemed to me entirely misconceived. There was no point in backing a policy which was beyond repair, even if it had been beneficial (which, in anything except the very short term, it was not). Moreover, although opposition to centrally imposed pay policies meant that we would find ourselves with strange bedfellows, including the more extreme trade union militants, the revolt against centralization and egalitarianism was basically healthy. As Conservatives, we should not frown on people being well rewarded for using sharp wits or strong arms to produce what the customer wanted. Of course, when such an approach was described, even by those allegedly on our own side, as being opportunist – and when it was accompanied by open disagreements as now between Shadow Ministers like Jim Prior and Keith Joseph – it was difficult to have the analysis taken seriously. But in fact it was an essential part of my political strategy to appeal directly to those who had not traditionally voted Conservative, but who now wanted more opportunities for themselves and their families. So I addressed much of my Conference speech directly to trade unionists.

> You want higher wages, better pensions, shorter hours, more government spending, more investment, more – more – more – more. But where is this 'more' to come from? There is no more. There can be, but there will not be, unless we all produce it. You can no more separate pay from output than you can separate two blades of a pair of scissors and still have a sharp cutting edge. And here, let me say plainly to trade union leaders, you are often your own worst enemies. Why isn't there more? Because too often restrictive practices rob you of the one thing you have to sell – your productivity.
>
> Restrictive practices are encrusted like barnacles on our

industrial life. They have been there for almost a century. They were designed to protect you from being exploited, but they have become the chief obstacle to your prosperity . . . I understand your fears. You're afraid that producing more goods with fewer people will mean fewer jobs, and those fears are naturally stronger at a time of high unemployment. But you're wrong. The right way to attack unemployment is to produce more goods more cheaply, and then more people can afford to buy them . . .

We shall do all that a government can to rebuild a free and prosperous Britain. We believe in realistic, responsible, collective bargaining, free from government interference. Labour does not. We believe in encouraging competition, free enterprise, and profits in firms large and small. Labour does not. We believe in making substantial cuts in the tax on your pay packet. Labour does not. We will create conditions in which the value of the money you earn and the money you save can be protected.

Over the next six months this strategy would be successful. But in the short term it was a liability, because the Party was not united on it and because opinion polls suggested that the public wanted us to support the Government against the unions. And not surprisingly we found ourselves at the end of the Conference season five and a half percentage points behind the Labour Party.

The removal of the prospect of an immediate election, after everyone's nerves had been screwed up to fight one, led to a breakdown in the ordinary disciplines in both parties. In the Labour Party this focused on economics. With us, it boiled over on Rhodesia, first at the Party Conference and then in the House of Commons.

Within the Shadow Cabinet it was Peter Carrington who argued most strongly against accepting an amendment in the Rhodesian debate at the Party Conference which would commit us to lifting sanctions. Peter's line was that although sanctions were largely futile, in the eyes of the Patriotic Front lifting them would constitute *de facto* recognition of the so-called 'internal settlement' earlier that year, by which Ian Smith had brought into the Rhodesian

Government moderate black parties whose claim to represent the black majority was questioned. Peter argued that it would put us in an extremely weak position in trying to bring together the various parties to the Rhodesian dispute when we had already taken sides in this way. John Davies, who had to defend this contorted and unpopular line, did so in a rambling speech in which he was thrown by loud heckling. He looked exhausted and I could see when he sat down that he was in great distress, rubbing his head. I leaned across and asked him what was wrong: he told me that he had a splitting headache and had not slept for three days. I did not like the sound of this and told him that he must immediately go back to London to have a brain scan. He protested at first but finally agreed, being taken back in my car. There it was discovered that he had a malignant brain tumour, from which tragically he died a few months later.

Events at the debate at the Conference fuelled feeling within the Parliamentary Party. Reggie Maudling was one of a formidable team of backbenchers opposed to the Shadow Cabinet line of abstaining on the Commons order renewing sanctions. I did not like this line overmuch myself and, other things being equal, would have joined them in the 'No' lobby. But it was better to have a full-scale backbench revolt than to lose members of the Shadow Cabinet at this delicate juncture. In the end 114 Conservatives rebelled against the whip, including two junior spokesmen who accordingly left the front bench – the largest Conservative rebellion since 1945.

A few days later I reshuffled the Shadow Cabinet – moving in Francis Pym to replace John Davies, bringing back John Biffen to take responsibility for small businesses, and appointing Mark Carlisle to replace Norman St John-Stevas at Education, with Norman becoming Shadow Leader of the House. With an election so close at hand, I kept the various factions more or less in place.

I also did a little before the end of the year to still the embarrassing arguments about pay policy. When we failed to win the Berwick and East Lothian by-election in late October several backbench friends publicly blamed Ted Heath's Blackpool intervention. I went on ITN and – with perhaps an excess of charity – exonerated him. And in the weeks following the Conference I temporarily bowed to the clamourings of a group of colleagues led by Peter Thorneycroft who urged me to reaffirm the line we had taken on pay policy in *The Right Approach to the Economy*. I spoke to this effect at Paddington in the week before Christmas.

So a difficult year approached its end. We were behind in the polls and seemed all too willing to behave like a permanent Opposition rather than a potential Government, a failing on which the actual Government readily capitalized. When we successfully defeated the Government's attempts to impose sanctions on Ford for paying its workers more than the 5 per cent norm in the Commons, the Prime Minister was able to paint a picture of a responsible minority administration being prevented from defending the national interest by Conservative opportunism. And when the following day there was a debate on a Vote of Confidence the Government survived by ten votes – and I made a particularly poor speech.

It was true that we had made some progress towards converting the Party and public opinion in the direction I knew was required. Events too had contributed – the scenes at Grunwick and the failure of the 'Social Contract' deal with the unions, particularly. With Labour's pay policy in ruins, the fact that we were keeping open the option of introducing a pay policy of our own troubled me less than it once had. What mattered far more was that our programme lacked the clear commitment to changes, particularly in trade union law, which I believed were necessary. In that respect, at least, we still had a long way to go.

LABOUR'S NEMESIS

But Labour's time was running out. Jim Callaghan had been dealt a bad hand by history and Harold Wilson in 1976. Like a brilliant poker player, he had employed skill, gamesmanship and simple bluff to spin out his defeat as long as possible on the chance that an ace or two might suddenly appear from up his sleeve. As 1978 became 1979, however, a succession of deuces tumbled forth. On Tuesday 12 December trade unions representing National Health Service and local authority workers rejected the 5 per cent pay limit and announced that they would strike in the New Year. At the end of December the elements conspired to create more trouble, with heavy snow, gales and floods. On Wednesday 3 January the TGWU called the lorry drivers out on strike in pursuit of a 25 per cent pay rise. Some two million workers faced being laid off. Hospital patients, including terminally ill cancer patients, were denied treatment. Gravediggers went on strike in Liverpool. Refuse piled up in Leicester Square. With Government compliance, trade union shop stewards dispensed permits to allow lorry drivers to transport 'essential' goods across picket lines. In short, Britain ground to a halt. What was more damaging even than this to the Labour Government, however, was that it had handed over the running of the country to local committees of trade unionists.

Would we be able to grasp the opportunities this provided? That might depend in part on an operation which had been proceeding in fits and starts, under conditions of the greatest secrecy, since the summer of 1977 and which went under the umbrella title of 'Stepping Stones'. It was the brainchild of John Hoskyns, an able ex-soldier who had set up one of the first computer software companies, which he had built up and then sold to concentrate on public affairs. John had been in contact with Keith Joseph at the Centre for Policy Studies for some time before we were introduced. Together with his colleague Norman Strauss, he had a refreshingly if sometimes irritatingly undisguised scorn for the *ad hoc* nature of political decision-making in general and the decision-making of the Shadow Cabinet in particular. The two of them argued that we could never succeed unless we fitted all our policies into a single strategy in which we worked out in advance the order in which actions had to be taken – hence the title. The first time I heard all this I was not very impressed. We met over Sunday lunch at Flood Street and the session ended by my remarking on the fact that they had eaten a whole joint of roast beef and I wasn't sure what I had gained from it all. Alfred Sherman, who was with us, quipped that next time they would bring sandwiches.

But under different circumstances, when long-term thinking was concerned, I came to appreciate the depth and quality of John Hoskyns' analysis. Ironically, in the light of events, the paper which he and Norman Strauss prepared in the autumn of 1977, whose title 'Stepping Stones' came to apply to the framework of discussions which followed, was about persuasion as much as about policy. Its theme was that union reform was at the centre of what we wanted to do; without it the rest of our programme for national recovery would be blocked. But that programme could only be implemented by a Conservative Government that had *won the argument*. Winning the next election, even by a large majority, would not be enough if the only basis for it was dissatisfaction with Labour's performance in office since 1974. Therefore, far from avoiding the union issue – as so many of my colleagues wanted – we should seek to open up debate. Moreover, this debate was not something to fear: the unions were an increasing liability to Labour and correspondingly a political asset to us. With intelligence and courage we could turn on its head the inhibiting and often defeatist talk about 'confrontation'.

I was warming to this analysis and said as much when (along with Keith Joseph, Angus Maude and Willie Whitelaw) I met its authors over drinks and supper at the House of Commons at the end of November 1977. To follow up the report I set up a Stepping Stones Steering Group which met in January 1978, and proposed that small groups of Shadow Ministers and outsiders with relevant knowledge should plan ways to advance the strategy through speeches, pamphlets, articles and so on. There would also be a 'Policy Search' group of some of the more solid Shadows, Keith Joseph, David Howell, Nigel Lawson and Norman Lamont, working alongside John Hoskyns and Norman Strauss, to seek new policy initiatives in line with the overall Stepping Stones theme.

But before this work could begin, sceptical and hostile colleagues had to be faced. I held a meeting of the Leader's Steering Committee at the end of January at which we argued ourselves to a standstill. Colleagues vied with each other in praising the Stepping Stones paper, but then warning against doing anything to follow it up – a well-known technique of evasion. We should avoid being 'too insensitive or controversial' (Francis Pym). We were 'against appeasement and confrontation but there had to be a third way' (John Peyton). Peter Thorneycroft, Ian Gilmour and Jim Prior all expressed degrees of doubt. John Davies said frankly that 'if we told the truth about the unions we should certainly lose the election'.

Chris Patten had submitted a paper to the meeting showing deep suspicion of Stepping Stones. Essentially, Chris favoured what he would doubtless consider a pragmatic rather than an ideological approach to Opposition. But I supported the view of the authors of Stepping Stones that it would take more than tactics to transform Britain. The majority at the meeting grasped at the straw provided by Chris's paper and expressed a nonsensical desire to unify the Patten-Hoskyns approach, to which I had to bow. Effectively they wanted to kill Stepping Stones, but that I would not allow.

It took a month to get Stepping Stones back on track and even then Chris Patten's work was to go on 'in parallel' and opponents of the whole approach, notably Jim Prior and Ian Gilmour, were in control of several of the most important 'Theme Teams'. John Hoskyns had hoped to persuade Jim Prior to break new ground on the union question but Jim's promised Stepping Stones speech, when it finally came, was no advance. Though some useful ideas (and some not so good) emerged from the Policy Search group, the crucial question of pay policy was excluded from its remit and by the end of summer 1978 the whole Stepping Stones initiative seemed to have come to a halt. Nor had it had any impact on manifesto work: had we fought an October general election the manifesto would have included no significant measures on union reform.*

What rejuvenated the Stepping Stones initiative was the collapse of the Government's 5 per cent pay policy that autumn. Immediately after the Labour Conference rejected the policy, Keith Joseph came to see Willie Whitelaw and me, expressing his disappointment that we had not got on further. At various times people had suggested that the only way forward was to shift Jim Prior, but now there was obviously an opportunity to move on without taking such a strong step. Accordingly, I arranged another meeting of the Stepping Stones Steering Group for mid-November.

At this and at a later meeting, however, Jim was still able to block proposals for a vigorous campaign on the union question that winter. Peter Thorneycroft gave him strong support. Peter had never been a friend of Stepping Stones: at one point he actually

* See pp. 435–8 for a discussion of the 1978 manifesto drafts.

suggested that every copy of the Stepping Stones report should be recalled to Central Office and burned. Even though Party opinion had begun to shift in my direction, no amount of discussion between Shadow ministers, advisers and MPs would have sufficed to persuade the Shadow Cabinet of the need to think seriously about trade union reform, had it not been for the industrial chaos of the 'Winter of Discontent'.

Even then they would require a lead. This was an area in which we had made little or no advance since 1975. As Shadow Employment spokesman, Jim Prior had been well placed to veto the development of new policy on union reform. Although just before Christmas 1978 we managed to persuade him to accept an extension of our policy of providing state funds for unions voluntarily holding secret ballots – we would offer cash to cover the cost of pre-strike ballots as well as union elections – this really amounted to very little. Indeed, to the average voter our policy on secret ballots would have been hard to distinguish from Labour's: in November 1978 the Prime Minister was offering to legislate on secret ballots if the unions wanted it.

In December Keith Joseph had tried to reopen the question of benefits paid to strikers' families. I had agreed to the summoning of a new Policy Group to consider this question, but when it met Jim Prior's opposition had prevented any progress.

I spent Christmas and New Year anxiously and reflectively at Scotney, watching the crisis build up. As it had at Christmas 1974, the bad weather discouraged us from our usual walks, and besides I had plenty to do. I read through the various Policy Group papers on union questions and I had brought down a bulging file of briefing from the press and interested outsiders. I spent many hours studying a textbook on industrial relations law and went back to the original Acts of Parliament, reading through the most important legislation since 1906. Every time I turned on the radio or the television the news was worse. I came back to London determined on one thing: the time had come to toughen our policy on union reform.

There was no difficulty in finding a platform. I had agreed before Christmas to be interviewed on Sunday 14 January by Brian Walden on *Weekend World*; the date was brought forward a week to

7 January. When I came back to London in the New Year, I saw Alfred Sherman, Gordon Reece and a few other close advisers to continue my briefing. The industrial situation was changing so fast that it was becoming more and more difficult to keep up to date, but over the next few weeks having the very latest facts to hand gave me vital advantages.

On Wednesday 3 January Jim Prior intervened to prevent a change in policy. Interviewed by Robin Day on radio, he firmly rejected compulsory strike ballots ('not something that you can make compulsory in any way'), rejected legislation on strikers' benefits, and commented on the closed shop: 'we want to take this quite quietly . . . it is better in these matters to play a quiet game rather than to shout too much'. Asked what he thought of recent criticism of the trade union leadership by David Howell and Michael Heseltine, he said: 'I don't think they are being fair to trade union leaders who at the moment are trying to give good advice to the rank and file, and the rank and file is quite often rejecting it.'

On *Weekend World* I struck rather a different note. 'Every power implies responsibility, every liberty a duty. The unions have [had] tremendous power over the years . . . [And] this is what the debate has got to be about – how unions use their power. I'm a parliamentarian, I am not in Parliament to enable them to have a licence to inflict harm, damage and injury on others and be immune from the law, and if I see it happening, then I've got to take action.'

Although I was careful not to commit us firmly to individual measures before they had received proper consideration, I ran through with Brian Walden a shopping list of possible changes, which naturally moved them higher on the agenda than some of my colleagues really wanted. I reaffirmed Jim Prior's announcement that we would make funds available for secret ballots before strikes as well as for union elections. But I hinted at compulsion if needed, holding out the possibility of legislation to refuse Social Security benefits unless there had been a strike ballot. I also mentioned the possibility of restricting strikes in essential services, announced that we would subject short-term Social Security benefits to taxation and made the case for a right of appeal to the courts for people excluded from a union, who faced losing their jobs where there was a closed shop.

On television the following day Jim Prior replied to my interview. He said that nothing had been agreed between us on Social Security benefits for strikers and that he was against compulsory secret ballots. Thankfully, others reacted more positively. I had broken ranks. People could see that I was going to fight. Offers of support, information and new ideas began to flow into my office.

Most significantly, I received a request for a meeting from a former Deputy Leader of the Labour Party, Lord George-Brown, who came to my office at the Commons on Wednesday 10 January and who on the following Saturday drove down to Scotney for a further conversation with me. George Brown had more knowledge and experience of the labour movement – that is, the unions as well as the party – than almost any of its current leadership. He had resigned from the party in 1976 (sitting as an independent in the Lords) and had become an increasingly hostile critic of the power of the unions, writing effectively in the press. He told me how the hard Left had risen to positions of influence and power within some of Britain's most important unions. He showed me that the immunities conferred by legislation since 1906 were being used with a new ruthlessness, and made an unanswerable case for a fundamental change in the law.

The strong support that I received for what I said in my *Weekend World* interview was in marked contrast to the reaction to Jim Callaghan's remarks on his arrival back three days later from the Guadeloupe summit. His absence from the country at such a critical time had itself been politically damaging, helping to strengthen the impression that the Government was paralysed in the face of the strikes. The press coverage of the summit itself had not helped him; the sight of the Prime Minister sitting with the other leaders in the Caribbean sun, all casually dressed, was a dangerous contrast to events at home. But the final disaster was the impression he left with the press when he flew into Heathrow. Although he never did use those precise words – 'Crisis? What Crisis?' – the myth faithfully represented his attempt to play down the scale of the problem. His image of unflappability and competence was never restored.

I reflected later on why Jim Callaghan, the most canny of politicians, stumbled into such an error. Partly, no doubt, it was
tiredness as a result of the transatlantic flight. That taught me a
lesson I never forgot: do not make public statements on arriving
back in the country after any lengthy absence or long journey.
Yet the misjudgement also had deeper roots. Indeed, I always
considered it a kind of nemesis. Jim Callaghan had based his
whole political career on alliance with the trade union leaders.
For him, if not for the country, it had been a winning formula. Now that the unions could no longer be appeased, he had
no other policy in his locker. This alone can explain his helpless
reaction to the crisis which overwhelmed him. The Government
could not even decide whether to declare a State of Emergency.
Although I had seen when a member of Ted Heath's Cabinet
that this was likely to be of limited effectiveness, the Government's alternative of trying to reach voluntary agreement with
the trade unions to limit the effects of the picketing was obviously
futile.

What should be our next move? Parliament was due to return
on Monday 15 January. I wrote to the Prime Minister demanding
a full statement and a debate on the industrial situation. We had
a slot already arranged for a PPB on Wednesday 17 January and
work began on a script.

The preparations I made for my speech in the debate were perhaps the most thorough I had ever made for an appearance in the
Commons. I had allowed others to prepare a text for my speech
in the last Confidence debate, a few months before: it had not been
a success and I had resolved afterwards that on occasions of such
importance I would not do this again. I did not want a written
text in any case – I always spoke better from notes. I worked on
this speech as if it were a tax brief, amassing my sources, marking
them up with coloured pens, and drafting carefully a few pages of
handwritten notes which would show me instantly the structure of
my speech when I glanced down at them on the despatch box.
Front- and backbench colleagues came in to help, some with information about their constituencies, others – particularly Ian Percival
and Leon Brittan – to assist on points of law. Sympathetic firms
affected by the strikes sent telexes giving their latest news; the CBI

was producing a daily briefing; Denis passed on a good deal that he heard; and we all scanned the press.

My original idea had been to make a hard-hitting but essentially conventional speech from the Opposition benches – hammering the Government and demanding that they change course. But at Scotney over the weekend of 13–14 January and on Monday back in London several people urged a different approach. Peter Utley and Peter Thorneycroft sent me suggestions for a speech offering support for the Government if it was prepared to introduce the kind of legislative changes necessary to break the union stranglehold. Ronnie Millar and Chris Patten – working on the PPB script – were urging the same idea.

My own immediate inclination was to avoid offers of co-operation, for several reasons. First, unlike the more coalition-minded of my colleagues, I believed that the job of Oppositions is generally to oppose. We had a fundamentally different approach from that of the Government and our main duty was to explain it and persuade the country of its merits. Secondly, it was dangerous to make an offer of cooperation without having thought through clearly in advance whether we actually wanted it accepted or not. Probably nothing which went to the heart of the problem would – or indeed could – be accepted by Jim Callaghan's Government. There was, therefore, a risk that in order to make a credible offer of support, we would have to set our sights too low as regards measures of reform. And if the Government then *did* accept the offer, we would have thrown away, for the time being at least, the opportunity of forcing it out of office. Moreover, reforms in trade union law alone would not suffice to deal with Britain's underlying economic problems: that would need a much more comprehensive strategy to which the socialists could never agree.

That evening – Monday 15 January – I called a Steering Committee meeting. Most of my senior colleagues favoured the idea of a conditional offer and by this stage I had come round to the idea myself. Reforms were essential; and if the Government were prepared to introduce the necessary measures, how could we oppose them? By offering help we enhanced our moral authority. I believed – as did most of the supporters of the idea – that the offer should be set at a level which, though abundantly justified by events, would be unlikely to be accepted by the Government. This was a difficult matter to judge in detail: the Labour Party might just be persuaded to agree to the negotiation of no-strike agreements in essential services, the payment by the taxpayer of the cost of secret ballots in trade unions and even a code of practice to end secondary picketing – though the last was doubtful. Equally, I was clear that if the Government did accept, we were honour-bound to keep our side of the bargain. For me, however, there was an additional and very important consideration. By agreeing to offer cooperation with the Government on selected measures, Jim Prior and his supporters would find it impossible to refuse support to those same measures if and when a Conservative Government introduced them.

The upshot was that the Steering Committee agreed that the Government could rely on Conservative support if it took firmer action on picketing (to get essential supplies moving), legislated to outlaw secondary picketing and to encourage secret ballots for union elections, and if it made efforts to negotiate non-strike agreements in essential industries. Events are a powerful advocate.

I opened the debate the following day. I began by describing the crisis. Transport of goods by road was widely disrupted, in many cases due to secondary picketing of firms and operators not involved in the actual disputes. British Rail had issued a brief statement: 'There are no trains today.' The CBI had reported that many firms were being strangled, due to shortage of materials and inability to move finished goods. There was trouble at the ports, adding to the problems of exporters. At least 125,000 people had been laid off already and the figure was expected to reach a million by the end of the week. The food industry, in particular, was in a shambolic state, with growing shortages of basic supplies like edible oils, yeast, salt and sugar. And all this on top of a winter of strikes – strikes by tanker drivers, bakers, staff at old people's homes and hospitals; strikes in the press and broadcasting, airports and car plants; a strike of gravediggers.

I pulled no punches in the speech. I made the point put to me by George Brown that the unions had been falling more and more under the control of left-wing militancy. I reminded the arch-moderate Shirley Williams that she had joined the Grunwick picket line. I made the conditional offer of support agreed in the Steering Committee, and I also made it a condition of cooperation that the Government should act on the closed shop; I felt too strongly on this subject not to include it.

The Prime Minister spoke next. He began his reply in a surprising way:

> I congratulate the Right Honourable lady on a most effective parliamentary performance. It was in the best manner of our debates and the style in which it was delivered was one of which the Right Honourable lady can be proud.

It was a good start. But all that the Prime Minister then had to offer in the body of his speech were further concessions to the unions – exemptions from the 5 per cent pay limit, tighter price controls and extension of the principle of 'comparability', under which public sector workers could expect more money. All these were intended as inducements to the unions to sign up to a new pay policy. But he signally failed to address what everyone except the far Left considered the main problem, excessive trade union power.

To my offer the Prime Minister made no direct reply. He had clearly been wrong-footed. The question now was whether I should repeat the offer the following evening in our Party Political Broadcast – or limit myself to attacking the Government's paralysis and pledging that a Conservative Government would reform trade union law.

I was still uneasy, and toughened the script when I saw it the following day. But after all, the offer had already been made, and the higher the profile we gave it, the more tightly it would bind reluctant colleagues and the more public support we would gain. So we went ahead, filming it in my room at the House of Commons. Again, the Government made no direct reply.

In any case, by now the whole political atmosphere had been transformed. From trailing the Labour Party by several percentage points in the opinion polls before my interview with Brian Walden, we had now opened up a twenty-point lead. From being a liability, our perceived willingness to take on the trade union militants had become an advantage. Within the Shadow Cabinet, the opposition from people like Jim Prior and Ian Gilmour to the approach which Keith Joseph, Geoffrey Howe and I wanted was effectively silenced – for the time being at least. Personally, I was conscious that in some strange way I was instinctively speaking and feeling in harmony with the great majority of the population. Such moments are as unforgettable as they are rare. They must be seized to change history.

THE FALL OF THE GOVERNMENT

But now Banquo's ghost came back to haunt the Labour Government. Devolution, which they had embraced solely as a means of staying in power with support from the Scottish and Welsh Nationalists, returned to grimace and gibber at Jim Callaghan at his lowest point. Following the defeat of the Scotland and Wales Bill in early 1977 Labour had reintroduced devolution legislation in the form of separate Bills for Scotland and Wales, with provision for referenda in each country before they came into effect. Backbench dissent on their own side led to the passage of a number of amendments, including the crucial additional requirement that a minimum of 40 per cent of those eligible to vote had to support devolution in each case. Although I had not publicly campaigned for a 'No' vote in the referenda in Scotland and Wales, that was the result I wanted. When the vote took place on 1 March 1979 in Scotland a bare majority of those voting was in favour – well below the required 40 per cent of the total electorate – and in Wales a large majority of those who voted rejected the proposal. For the moment, devolution was dead: I did not mourn it.

From this point on it seemed likely, though not certain, that the Government would be unable to continue in office; but the circumstances under which a general election would occur were far from predictable. The Prime Minister sought desperately to spin out discussion about devolution rather than go ahead immediately with the repeal of the Devolution Acts. But his potential allies were preparing to desert. The SNP now had no reason to keep Labour in office and wanted an early confidence motion. The Liberals were keen on an early election, even though their standing in the opinion polls was weak; this was principally in order to avoid the embarrassment of the forthcoming trial of their former Leader, Jeremy Thorpe, on a charge of conspiracy to murder, of which he was later acquitted. Admittedly, the Welsh Nationalists, who were more of a socialist party than their Scottish equivalents, might still be persuadable.

That meant that the Northern Irish MPs – ten Ulster Unionists, one member of the Social Democratic and Liberal Party (SDLP) and one Independent Republican – were likely to be decisive. Gerry Fitt, the SDLP Member, had been alienated from the Government by their attempts to court the Ulster Unionists with additional seats for the Province. Frank Maguire, the Independent Republican, was entirely unpredictable. A majority of the Ulster Unionists had been prepared to keep the Government in office until the legislation increasing the representation of Northern Ireland had passed through Parliament: but this it had done by 15 March. There was now much public talk of Unionist demands for a gas pipeline to link the Province to the natural gas network on the mainland and the strengthening of local government powers in Northern Ireland as the price of their support for either of the two parties. Airey Neave, who had by now established close personal links with a number of the Unionists, was responsible for the discussions on our side.

Many of our backbenchers wanted an early confidence motion, but initially the Shadow Cabinet held its fire. One reason was that we would need the support of anti-devolution Labour MPs to make absolutely sure that the order repealing the Devolution Acts went through; we did not quite trust the Government on this question. Moreover, unlike previous occasions when there had seemed a possibility of bringing down the Government in a vote in the House of Commons, we were extremely reluctant to put down a Motion of No Confidence until we were assured of its likely success. A Government victory would strengthen it at a bad time. When we considered the matter at Shadow Cabinet on Wednesday 21 March we decided, indeed, that we would not move such a motion unless the SNP, the Liberals and, if possible, the Welsh Nationalists gave

firm assurances of support. But there was still no question, as far
as I was concerned, of doing deals which would tie my hands in
government.

On Thursday 22 March the Prime Minister made a last effort
to keep devolution alive and win over the SNP, making a parliamentary statement offering yet more talks and following it with a
Prime Ministerial broadcast that evening. He never had any real
chance of success, and when assurances of SNP and Liberal support
for our motion seemed to be forthcoming – though there was none
from the Welsh Nationalists – I agreed that it should be tabled,
which was done a little before 7 p.m. The Conservative Whips now
went all out to persuade the minority parties to see that their
less reliable members actually joined us in the lobbies. Equally
important, of course, was ensuring that there was a full turn-out
of Conservative MPs. Luckily, none was seriously ill – though one
Member's car overturned on the motorway as he was driving down
and another insisted on voting for us though he had been shattered
by the death of his wife the previous day.

Oddly enough, the most intractable problem that evening was
caused by the strike of catering staff at the Palace of Westminster.
Not even the most blood-curdling threats by the Whips could prevent Tory MPs drifting off to their clubs or to the Savoy for something to eat. Willie Whitelaw and I dined in the Chief Whip's office
with Humphrey Atkins and his colleagues off the contents of two
large hampers brought back by Spencer Le Marchant and Tony
Berry from Fortnums. But I could not summon up much appetite.
The opening speeches of the debate itself had gone, I felt, more or
less as expected – neither was a triumph of oratory. But sitting
around our improvised supper table, Willie, Humphrey and I knew
that the result, on which so much hung, was too close to call.
Perhaps because they really felt that way, or perhaps because they
did not want to raise my spirits to have them dashed by the narrow-
est of defeats, I had the impression that they thought the Government would somehow manage once again to survive. In my heart
of hearts, I thought so too.

Then we returned to the Chamber to hear the closing speeches.
Michael Foot's for the Government was one of the outstanding
performances of a gifted House of Commons orator. But it would

take more than rhetoric to persuade the unpredictable Members upon whose decisions the outcome depended.

Amid clamour and confusion we began to file into the lobbies. Having voted, I returned to my place by the side of Willie, Francis and Humphrey and waited to learn our fate. Humphrey had sought to ensure that I had some advance notice of the result. He asked John Stradling Thomas, one of the senior Whips, to go through our lobby very quickly and then stand at the exit of the other one. For some reason, not just when they are in a minority, Conservative MPs go through the lobby more quickly than the Labour Party. As soon as we were all through, the message as to what our numbers were would be given to John Stradling Thomas, who meanwhile was listening to the other (Government) lobby being counted out. As soon as they had finished, he would know whether we had won or not. If we had *not* won he would come back, and just stand next to the Speaker's chair. If we *had* won, he would put up a finger so that Humphrey could tell me. Only later was I let into the secret code. I just saw John Stradling Thomas return – and then Humphrey leaned across to me and with a stage whisper said: 'We've won!'

The announced figures bore it out. 'Ayes, 311. Noes, 310.' So at last I had my chance, my only chance. I must seize it with both hands.*

* I described some of the subsequent events in *The Downing Street Years*, pp. 3–4.

AIREY

Two days later I was attending a function in my constituency – a fund-raising event organized by Motability, which provided disabled people with special cars at a modest price. I was to make the presentation. My mind was at least half on the Party Election Broadcast I was due to make that evening, when Derek Howe approached me to say: 'I think you ought to know that a bomb has gone off in the precincts of the House of Commons, in the garage they think. At least one person has been very seriously injured, but we don't know who.'

A hundred possibilities – though not the correct one – went through my mind as we drove down to the BBC studios in Portland Place. When I got there, and before I went in to be made up, one of the producers took me aside into a private room and told me who it was. It was Airey Neave. He was critically injured. The Irish National Liberation Army – a breakaway faction from the IRA – had placed a bomb under his car and it had exploded when he drove up the ramp from the House of Commons car park. It was very unlikely that he would survive – indeed, by the time I heard the news he may well have been dead. There was no way I could bring myself to broadcast after that. I telephoned the Prime Minister and explained. I felt only stunned. The full grief would come later. With it came also anger that this man – my friend – who had shrugged off so much danger in his life should be murdered by someone worse than a common criminal.

ABOVE: Working at Flood Street during the leadership campaign.

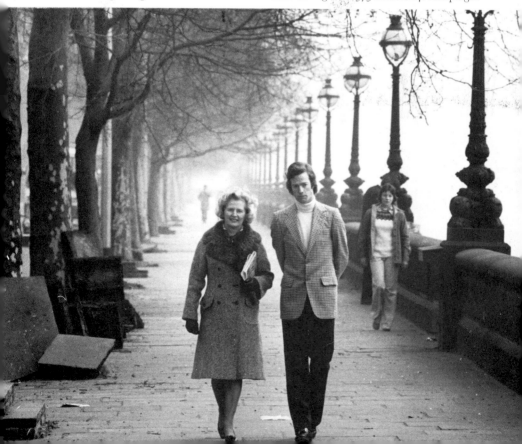

LEFT: Showing the press the contents of
my larder – at the height of the 'hoarding'
episode, November 1974.

BELOW: Walking along the Embankment with Mark during the 1975 leadership campaign.

ABOVE: Meeting the press at Conservative Central Office, 11 February 1975, the day I became Leader of the Conservative Party.

ABOVE: Outside the Europa Hotel on the day of the Party rally endorsing me as Leader. *Left to right*: Quintin Hailsham, Norman Fowler, Geoffrey Howe, Reggie Maudling, Willie Whitelaw, Sally Oppenheim.

RIGHT: The State Opening of Parliament in 1976.

ABOVE: The Shadow Cabinet in November 1976. *Left to right*: Nick Edwards, Airey Neave, Teddy Taylor, Peter Carrington, Willie Whitelaw, self, Keith Joseph, Angus Maude, Francis Pym, Patrick Jenkin, Tom King, Humphrey Atkins, Norman St John-Stevas, Michael Havers, John Nott, Jim Prior, Peter Thorneycroft, Geoffrey Howe, Quintin Hailsham, John Davies, Ian Gilmour, Michael Heseltine.

BELOW: Launch of *The Right Approach* at Conservative Central Office, October 1976. *Left to right*: Keith Joseph, Angus Maude, self, Peter Carrington, Geoffrey Howe, Peter Thorneycroft.

LEFT: On the Great Wall of China during my visit in 1977. *Left to right*: Jo Stanley, Ambassador Youde, self, Car a Chinese official, Douglas Hurd.

ABOVE: Introducing Carol to Chairm Hua during the same visit.

ABOVE: Visit to Pakistan, accompanied by John Davies (left).

RIGHT: Visit to a mine at Broken Hill in Australia in 1976. Behind Denis is Adam Butler.

ABOVE: With three former Conservative Prime Ministers at the Speaker's dinner for the Queen's Silver Jubilee in 1977 – Alec Douglas-Home, Harold Macmillan, Ted Heath.

BELOW: Meeting with Ronald Reagan at the House of Commons in November 1978.

ABOVE: Visiting the 2000th GLC council house purchasers in south London in 1978.

LEFT: Talking to a stallholder in Battersea, February 1978. On my left is my old friend Monty Modlyn, the radio presenter.

RIGHT: Photo opportunity with a GPO worker in Mill Hill – GLC elections, 1977.

ABOVE: Visit to the Thames Barrier at Woolwich during its construction in 1979. On the right is Horace Cutler, Conservative Leader of the GLC.

BELOW: Photographed just before my first *Weekend World* interview with Brian Walden, 2 September 1977.

ABOVE: With Denis at
Scotney Castle in 1975.

RIGHT: With Denis at 'The Blue
Review' in Blackpool during the
1977 Party Conference.

CHAPTER XII

Just One Chance . . .

The 1979 general election campaign

DEFINING THE THEME

As I have already described, I was far from enthusiastic about the first manifesto draft of 1978: it was too long, diffuse and chock-full of costly (but uncosted) spending commitments. The revised draft in August was better. But it was still not adequate. This was no reflection on Chris Patten and Angus Maude who drafted it, but rather on the rest of us who had not been able to agree clear and coherent policies in some crucial areas, particularly the trade unions.

I have also described how I decided to seize the initiative in January 1979. Between the summer of 1978 and the dissolution of Parliament in March 1979 outside events, above all that winter's strikes, allowed me to shift our policies in the direction I wanted. The balance of opinion in the Shadow Cabinet, following rather than leading opinion in the country, was now that we could and should obtain a mandate to clip the wings of the trade union militants. Similarly – though I was to be less successful in dispensing with this unwelcome aspect of my political inheritance – the collapse of Labour's pay policy made it easier to argue that the whole approach of prices and incomes controls, both 'voluntary' and statutory, should be abandoned. Above all, I was sure that there had been over the winter a sea-change and that our manifesto had to catch that tide.

Before Angus and Chris got to work I sent them a note.

I think the existing [autumn 1978] draft will have to be radically changed consequent upon recent events and our much more robust union policy. But the general approach of the limited objective first (i.e. tax cuts etc. to encourage wealth creation) remains. In my view the average person and a lot of non-average as well wants 'tax cuts and order'.

A comparison between the manifesto draft of August 1978 and the final text published in April 1979 illustrates both the extent and the limits of the changes which – in varying combinations – Keith Joseph, Geoffrey Howe, my advisers and I secured. The passage on trade unions, of course, was the real test. In 1978 I was prepared to go along with almost everything that Jim Prior suggested, including the promise that we would be 'even-handed in our approach to industrial problems', that we would 'not undertake any sweeping changes in the law of industrial relations' and that instead we would 'seek to promote an era of continuity and constructive reform'. The 1979 text was significantly different. Now we promised to strike 'a fair balance between the rights and duties of the trade union movement'. Furthermore, we challenged directly the idea that the law had no useful role to play in this area: 'Labour claim that industrial relations in Britain cannot be improved by changing the law. We disagree. If the law can be used to confer privileges it can and should also be used to establish obligations.'

I had disliked both the tone and the intellectual confusion which characterized Jim Prior's suggested manifesto passages on the general role of trade unions in the spring of 1978. But I objected still more strongly to Jim's suggestions on the closed shop. Although Jim wanted us to say that we were 'opposed to the closed shop in principle', he wanted to add that 'experience has shown that a number of managements and unions consider it a convenient method of conducting their negotiations'. The contrast in the same sentence between the requirements of 'principle' and 'convenience' struck me as particularly distasteful. There are, of course, many freedoms which it would be 'convenient' for powerful groups to suppress: but most of us reckon that 'principle' requires that those freedoms should be defended. Jim also wanted us to promise a 'code of practice' which would regulate the closed shop. If the code

of practice was not honoured 'it could result (as at present) in
workers losing their livelihood without compensation or redress
from either employer or union. In this event we would be prepared
to legislate to protect their rights'.

Even in 1978 I had felt that we could do better than this. I had
insisted that there must be a right of appeal to the courts if someone
was unfairly excluded or expelled from their union. But in 1979
we went significantly further by dropping the formula about the
closed shop being objectionable but inevitable and making a clear
commitment to change the law. Existing employees and 'those with
personal conviction' (a weasel phrase but still unavoidable in the
circumstances) 'must be adequately protected, and if they lose their
jobs as a result of the closed shop they must be entitled to adequate
compensation'. The manifesto also promised an enquiry into the
coercive recruitment practices of the SLADE printing union.*
Additionally we made it clear that the code of practice would have
statutory force.

But the main change of substance related to picketing. In 1978
I had gone along with what Jim Prior wanted, which was not very
much: 'In consultation with all parties, we must find acceptable
means to regulate the conduct of picketing. The strict arrangements
adopted by the NUM in February 1974 could provide a sensible
basis for this.'

There was no mention even of a code of practice, let alone legislation. It was also, in retrospect, not particularly wise to remind
voters directly of the occasion when the previous Conservative
Government had been broken by the miners' strike. Thankfully,
the shocking scenes of the Winter of Discontent ensured that this
feeble approach was now out of touch with reality and people's
expectations. We now promised to make secondary picketing
unlawful and to review trade union immunities. Moreover, there
was the clear suggestion that we would be prepared to take further

---

* See *The Downing Street Years*, p. 102n. The report showed that SLADE had been
using its strength in the printing industry to recruit among freelance artists,
photographic studios and advertising agencies by threatening to 'black' the printing of their work unless they joined the union. The report's conclusion was that
the union had acted 'without any regard whatever to the feelings, interests, or
welfare of the prospective recruits'.

legislative steps if these proved necessary: 'We shall also make any further changes that are necessary so that a citizen's right to work and to go about his or her lawful business free from intimidation or obstruction is guaranteed.'

Two other new provisions were inserted between the 1978 and 1979 texts: one was the promise to 'seek to conclude no-strike agreements in a few essential services' (which in fact came to nothing), and the other to 'ensure that unions bear their fair share of the cost of supporting those of their members who are on strike', which we later implemented. Together with the limited proposals to ease the effects of the closed shop and equally modest proposals to finance postal ballots for union elections and other important issues, these constituted our package of trade union reform. I was very happy with it: indeed, it would turn out that I was far more confident not just in its practicality but also its popularity than some of my colleagues.

By contrast with my victory over the position on trade unions, I scored no better than a draw on incomes policy. On this question, of course, I could not place my usual reliance on Geoffrey Howe who had developed a fatal attraction for the so-called 'forum'. In 1978 I had argued that we should be clearer about our intention to break away from incomes policies, suggesting that instead of asserting (as proposed) that 'the return to flexibility will take time, but it cannot be postponed for ever', the last phrase should be replaced by 'but it must start without delay'. And I did not even win this small point.

In 1979 the manifesto contained, indeed, a somewhat more explicit allusion to the 'forum', even mentioning the German model. But this I could live with. Of more practical importance, there was a strongly worded promise to avoid incomes policies in the private sector: 'Pay bargaining in the private sector should be left to the companies and workers concerned. At the end of the day, no one should or can protect them from the results of the agreements they make.'

That left one particularly thorny aspect of incomes policy to be grasped in the public sector. The Prime Minister's offer in January 1979 of new machinery to establish 'comparability' between the public and private sectors led to the setting up of a commission under Professor Hugh Clegg to take evidence and make recommendations which, of course, the Government committed itself to honour – after the election. Inevitably, when the election campaign began we were pressed to define our attitude. The question, in effect, was whether we would agree to pick up the bill (size unknown) for Labour's efforts to buy off the public sector unions.

Our policy for public sector pay had always been based on the strict application of cash limits. Geoffrey Howe and I did our best to stick to that, but there was intense pressure from colleagues and the Party, frankly concerned not to lose vital votes. And so finally we yielded and pledged ourselves to implement Professor Clegg's recommendations. It was an expensive but unavoidable commitment.*

In general, however, I was happy with the manifesto, both as regards contents and style. It contained a coherent philosophy and a limited number of clearly defined pledges. And it passed the most important final test, namely that at no stage in the campaign did we have to modify or retreat from it.

I was to fight three general elections as Leader of the Conservative Party; and each one was different. The 1983 campaign was perhaps the easiest; the 1987 campaign was certainly the most emotionally fraught; but the general election of 1979 was the most challenging both for me and the Party. I never had any illusion that if we lost or even if we failed to win an overall majority I would be given another chance. I accepted this fact and was even prepared to speak about it openly. Personally, I had little doubt that it was also a watershed for the Conservative Party and for Britain.

Unlike some Conservatives, I did not believe that the taming of the Left of the Labour Party would prove anything other than temporary if Labour won an overall majority. The Left knew what it wanted and was prepared to bide its time so as to obtain it. I never put any faith in the resolve or abilities of the 'centre'. I agreed with Keith Joseph that the 'centre' ground of politics had moved steadily leftwards, and I attributed this principally to the lack of moral courage of those who prided themselves upon being

---

* See *The Downing Street Years*, pp. 32, 44–5.

'moderates'. Time and again these people had been prepared to compromise and adjust their positions; and, as a result, socialism had continued its onward march through our institutions. This march, I believed, had more or less reached its point of no return. So many people and so many vested interests were by now significantly dependent on the state – for employment in the public sector, for Social Security benefits, for health care, education and housing – that economic freedom had begun to pose an almost unacceptable risk to their living standards. And, when that finally happened, political freedom – for example the freedom to join or not to join a union or the freedom to have controversial views and still be entitled to teach in a state school or work in a government department – would be the next victim. Moreover, the advance of communism abroad and the retreat of the West before it was helping to sap the morale of those who wished to oppose collectivism at home.

The 1979 campaign was also different in a number of other ways. It was the first time that the Conservative Party had ever fought so clearly on the theme that it was 'time for a change'. Implicit in this approach was that Britain had been in retreat for much more than the years since 1974; the 1970–74 Conservative Government, however bravely it had started out, had been part of that retreat. I therefore believed that we should be bold in explaining precisely what had gone wrong and why radical action was required to put it right. I was soon to be aware, however, that this was not how Peter Thorneycroft and Central Office in general saw things. Their belief was that we should at all costs avoid 'gaffes', which meant in practice almost anything controversial – in particular, attacks on trade union power – in the belief that the Labour Party was already sufficiently discredited to lose the election. In fact, with a few concessions, I insisted on doing it my way. But this led to tensions.

It also led to an odd reversal of roles between Government and Opposition. From the very beginning of their campaign, Labour more or less ignored their own manifesto – with the exception of vote-buying promises like free television licences for pensioners – and offered only limited excuses for their record. Instead, they concentrated on attacking real and alleged Conservative policies. Jim Callaghan largely discarded his image of avuncular *bonhomie* and led an extremely effective but wholly negative campaign. This was carried on at three levels. First, the media were fed with a daily diet of scare stories – ranging from the doubling of Value Added Tax to large cuts in the National Health Service – which would allegedly occur if we were elected. Secondly, doubt was cast on the credibility of our promises, particularly the pledge to cut income tax. Thirdly, there was an attempt to portray me as a dangerous right-wing ideologue, unsuited to the complex and demanding tasks of the premiership. Labour's strategy presented us with a fundamental dilemma. Should we reply to their attacks? Or should we stick to our own message and our own ground? We only ever partly solved this dilemma.

ORGANIZING THE CAMPAIGN

The fact that we had been expecting an election for so long before it was actually called had given us plenty of time to make preparations. For the first time, the Party hired a campaign bus which was fitted up as a mobile office in which we would travel from one campaign stop to another. In overall charge on the bus was David Wolfson – who stood in for John Stanley after John fell down the steps in Bristol on our first day out, slipped a disc and was rushed off to hospital where he spent the whole campaign. Derek Howe was my Press Officer on the 'battle bus', while David Boddy was the second Press Officer travelling with the press in a second bus. Roger Boaden was responsible for ensuring that we knew where we were going and what to do when we got there – a taxing task on occasions. My old friend and now Deputy Chairman of the Party, Janet (Lady) Young, travelled with us to keep in touch with the Chairman's office. Michael Dobbs, the future author of lurid tales of political skulduggery, was given the role of travelling librarian, accompanied by a bulging collection of sources for facts and figures I might need in answer to questions at my whistle-stops. Harvey Thomas travelled ahead of us, making the arrangements for my speeches and preparing the rallies. And three long-suffering secretaries – Tessa Jardine Paterson, Caroline Stephens and Sally

James – coped with the almost impossible task of typing my speech drafts as the bus wound and bumped its way over country roads.

The lack of word processors, faxes or photocopiers made life much more complicated than it would be in later elections. We did have a radio telephone, but it was not really satisfactory; for example, on one occasion the driver reversed the bus and knocked the aerial off. So whenever we arrived at a Conservative office there would be a mad rush to telephone through changes to speech texts to Conservative Central Office, while someone else on another line would receive an account of the day's events in London.

To allow me to cover more ground, I spent several nights away from London on tour. But I found this unsatisfactory and did not repeat it in future campaigns. It is easy to get – or at least feel – out of touch in an election campaign when you are away from London; it is also possible for other people to substitute their judgement for yours on crucial matters. Neither is acceptable in a life or death election. Usually, however, I would return late in the evening to Flood Street where secretaries would come in to serve up hot meals for me and my speech-writing team – John Hoskyns, Peter Utley, Hugh Thomas, Alfred Sherman and sometimes Ronnie Millar. Frozen cooked foods were our staple diet on weekdays. At the weekends we sampled the modestly exotic flavours of Duck à l'Orange and Sole Véronique. While we were speech-writing, Denis would be upstairs glued to the television, listening to reports on the campaign. I knew that Labour politicians were implanting some particularly hostile barb when I heard Denis yelling 'Rubbish!' – or worse.

It is always difficult to coordinate the different aspects of an election campaign. The best-laid plans unravel and in no time at all the morning press conferences are concentrating on one message, the Party Leader's speeches a second, Shadow ministers a third, and briefing for candidates something else again. In spite of the serious difference I had with Peter Thorneycroft over tactics, Peter and the team which worked with him were extremely capable: moreover their abilities complemented one another. Peter himself stayed in London throughout the campaign, chairing a tactical committee at Central Office which at times seemed to be in almost permanent session. He was always shrewd and massively authoritative. Alistair McAlpine's extraordinary abilities as a fund raiser ensured that the Party was never prevented from taking the initiatives we wanted by lack of cash. Significantly, there had been a large increase in the smaller subscriptions from business. This reflected the fact that businessmen understood that the Conservative Party was again the party of free enterprise: it also meant that we were not dependent on just a few large donors. Tony Garner, always cheerful, optimistic and dapper, was the Chief Agent in charge of the campaign organization in the country. Gordon Reece, now back at Central Office as Director of Publicity, had made us all face up to the rigorous demands of the media – emphasizing the importance of the tabloid newspapers and of having our best film coverage and press releases available in good time for the early evening news. By now, I had learned a lot from Gordon about what to do (and not to do) to come over properly on the television screen. At least there was not much reason to worry about possible colour clashes. Conservative campaigning has its own version of Henry Ford's dictum: you can wear any colour you like as long as it's blue. And for most of the time in my case it was navy blue.

A huge amount of information flows in and out of Conservative Central Office at election time: what comes in has to be analysed for significance and what goes out has to be checked for accuracy. Those responsible are some of the unsung heroes of the political battle. Keith Britto, Central Office's number-cruncher and opinion poll expert, would struggle manfully with the contradictory psephological material with which we were deluged during the campaign. While Chris Patten was fighting a seat in Bath, Adam Ridley kept the Research Department working at fever pitch. Michael Portillo, from CRD, briefed me for my morning press conferences – a task in which he demonstrated not just his grasp of facts, figures and arguments, but also an instinctive shrewdness in suggesting their deployment. One of my impressions of the campaign was that Michael was a young man who would – and deserved to – go far.

Two important tactical questions had to be addressed before the campaign got under way. The first was whether I should agree to take part in televised debates with Jim Callaghan. Discussions had been going on with the broadcasters since the summer of 1978 when the BBC (on behalf of both networks) had approached my office and the Prime Minister's simultaneously. Attempts to arrange such debates in previous elections had broken down because of the difficulty of involving the minor parties, which insisted on a presence. Neither Labour nor we would accept that. But this time – July 1978 – the broadcasters were prepared to go ahead with a two-party format regardless of what the minor parties thought. Accordingly we gave the proposal serious consideration, though at the time we did not know the Prime Minister's position. No final decision was taken because the election expected that autumn did not materialize, but influenced by Peter Thorneycroft and Gordon Reece – who were both strongly opposed – I was inclined to say no.

Shortly before the actual campaign began, ITV revived the idea, proposing two debates on successive Sundays at the end of the campaign with Brian Walden as chairman. This time I was inclined to accept. It was not just that I had always been a natural debater; I believed that Jim Callaghan was greatly overrated and I wanted the chance to expose that fact. He had built his career on giving the trade unions whatever they wanted. So I felt that he was to blame, in a uniquely personal way, for the scenes of the winter of 1978/79. Chris Patten also favoured my taking on the Prime Minister. Moreover, there was a new factor in the situation: the Prime Minister publicly accepted the ITV proposal. And I did not like the idea of beginning an election campaign on a defensive note by refusing to debate.

There were, however, still powerful arguments on the other side which persuaded Gordon Reece, Peter Thorneycroft and Willie Whitelaw to argue against. When the possibility had first been mooted, we were neck-and-neck with the Labour Party in the opinion polls. But by the time the decision had to be made we had a substantial lead of probably 10 per cent. This meant that we might hope to win *without* the risks of a televised confrontation. And those risks were certainly large. I might make a mistake which it would be hard to obliterate. Jim Callaghan was usually a polished performer on television and he would certainly have no hesitation in using his authority and experience to patronize me. The fact that in the early tentative discussions we learned that he would wish to have the first debate on foreign affairs, where he would be able to deploy all those strengths, caused me to reconsider my earlier enthusiasm.

Moreover, the Liberals were to be offered a *quid pro quo*: a long interview with David Steel on the Friday before polling day. My advisers and I were in full agreement that the most serious danger to us would be a last-minute upsurge of Liberal support – all the easier to imagine since they had just taken the Liverpool Edgehill seat from Labour at a by-election and were busily seeking, as Liberals always do, to exaggerate the 'momentum' this had given them. I had no wish to give the Liberal Leader any more political exposure than necessary.

So I was persuaded to turn down the invitation to debate. It was not worth the risks. In any case, as I wrote in my published reply to ITV's invitation: 'Personally, I believe that issues and policies decide elections, not personalities. We should stick to that approach. We are not electing a president, we are choosing a government.' It was the right decision and the criticism it provoked in some quarters quickly dissipated.

The other tactical question concerned the morning press conferences. Gordon Reece would have liked to dispense with these altogether. In terms of media impact, he was right. Very rarely did anything which happened at the press conference – other perhaps than egregious slip-ups, which were thankfully absent during this campaign – make its way into the day's main news. But the morning press conference does provide the press with opportunities to ask awkward questions, and this in turn provides an opportunity for politicians to show what they are made of. The morning press conferences are therefore an opportunity to win the respect of seasoned journalists whose judgement will influence the coverage they give throughout the campaign.

A further complication on this occasion was that neither we nor the Labour Party were prepared to surrender the convenient 9.30 a.m. slot to the other. Consequently, our press conference in Central Office was held at the same time as Labour's in Transport House across the square. A posse of journalists would arrive in the already overcrowded and overheated Central Office conference room to ask questions on the basis of allegations and attacks made by Jim Callaghan, Denis Healey or Shirley Williams at the beginning of the Labour press conference. A final element of chaos was contributed by the new 'ENG' ('electronic news-gathering') cameras. Though ridiculously unwieldy by present-day standards, they greatly increased the flexibility and extent of television coverage. But the number of cameramen also increased. And the shoulder-held television cameras with their trailing cables both at Central Office and at locations along the route of my tour were a constant threat to life and limb.

For some reason, the Conservative Party always starts campaigning later and builds up more slowly than the Labour Party. Labour on this occasion, however, had an even freer run than usual between the Dissolution and the launch of our manifesto on Wednesday 11 April – largely because the political colleagues to whom I left the public appearances and statements were not very effective. This was, indeed, a difficulty throughout the campaign. With the exception of Michael Heseltine, always relishing a headline, they seemed to behave more like ministers-in-waiting than politicians – which meant, of course, that they risked waiting a good deal longer than they expected. It also ensured that even more of the focus was on me, which even I felt was a mixed blessing. In all campaigns there should ideally be a balance of tones and personalities.

Labour used this period to some effect in order to begin attacking policies which we had not yet published. But the trade union leaders managed, before they were muzzled by Labour Party managers, to play into our hands by adopting tones reminiscent of the Winter of Discontent. Sid Weighell, leader of the National Union of Railwaymen, threatened that with free collective bargaining and a Conservative Government, he would 'say to the lads, come on, get your snouts into the trough'. Bill Keays, leader of the print union SOGAT, promised 'confrontation' if the country was 'foolish enough to elect the Tory Party'. David Basnett, leader of the General and Municipal Workers, also predicted industrial conflict. It was the same old tune which had played well for Labour in the past, but which was out of harmony with what voters were now prepared to tolerate.

Nor had I been entirely silent. On Thursday 5 April I had addressed the candidates (including Conservative MPs standing for re-election) at a meeting at Central Hall, Westminster. This was not my – or probably anyone else's – favourite place for a public meeting, since it was then rather drab and characterless. There was a special difficulty this year because the candidates expected to hear from me the main themes of a manifesto which was still unpublished. I had to give them some idea of what was coming without revealing the details. So I concentrated heavily on income tax cuts to give greater incentives for wealth-creation and on the need for trade union reform. An audience composed entirely of speakers is not the easiest to address. But their enthusiasm confirmed my instinct that we had chosen the right battleground.

THE FIRST WEEK – D–21 to D–14

On Wednesday 11 April the manifesto itself was launched at the first Conservative press conference which I chaired, joined by Willie Whitelaw, Keith Joseph, Geoffrey Howe, Peter Carrington, Jim Prior, Humphrey Atkins, Peter Thorneycroft and Angus Maude. The manifesto's tone was modest and practical and Chris Patten and Angus Maude had dressed our ideas in language which was simple and jargon-free.*

It went down well in the following day's press. But the heat at the hugely overcrowded press conference itself was almost

---

* Our proposals were distilled into five tasks:

1 To restore the health of our economic and social life, by controlling inflation and striking a fair balance between the rights and duties of the trade union movement.
2 To restore incentives so that hard work pays, success is rewarded and genuine new jobs are created in an expanding economy.
3 To uphold Parliament and the rule of law.
4 To support family life, by helping people to become home-owners, raising the standards of their children's education, and concentrating welfare services on the effective support of the old, the sick, the disabled and those who are in real need.
5 To strengthen Britain's defences and work with our allies to protect our interests in an increasingly threatening world.

unbearable. And my perspiring male colleagues clad in their thick worsted suits suffered worse than I did.

The following day was Maundy Thursday. Because Easter fell during the campaign, four days of electioneering were lost. So my first day of serious campaigning was on Monday 16 April – what in the election agents' jargon was D–17. ('D-day' of course was polling day itself.) We had decided to begin in Wales. Having flown down from Gatwick, I met the election battle bus at Swansea Airport, visited an NHS hospital and went on to the local Conservative Club, where I was to give regional television and radio interviews. I was aware of a fair amount of background noise at the club. But I only learned afterwards that a huge row, which finished up with fisticuffs, had arisen when the club authorities had tried to keep women reporters out of those rooms reserved for male members only.

Then I went on to Cardiff for the first of the major rallies of the campaign. It was an appropriate place to start. This was very much the heart of enemy territory since Mr Callaghan's constituency was Cardiff South East. So it was a good thing that Cardiff City Hall had a pleasant feel, the right acoustics and an enthusiastic audience. I also had an extremely powerful speech to deliver. It was an uncompromising statement of how socialism had debilitated Britain and of the need for a fundamental change of direction – though not towards some experiment with utopia but rather back to principles from which we had mistakenly departed.

> . . . In politics, I've learned something you in Wales are born knowing: if you've got a message, preach it. I am a conviction politician. The Old Testament prophets didn't merely say: 'Brothers, I want consensus.' They said: 'This is my faith and vision. This is what I passionately believe. If you believe it too, then come with me.' Tonight I say to you just that. Away with the recent bleak and dismal past. Away with defeatism. Under the twin banners, choice and freedom, a new and exciting future beckons the British people.

The audience loved it and so did I. But my cunning adversary, Jim Callaghan, successfully used it to awaken all of the old fears in the Tory Party establishment about the unnerving figure leading them in an uncomfortable, unfamiliar direction. The Prime Minister subsequently claimed that in my speech I had moved the Conservative Party to the right and that this opened the centre ground for him. Appropriately enough, the main speaker at the Conservative press conference that morning was Reg Prentice, former Labour Cabinet minister and now Conservative Party candidate, who with other 'converts' from socialism was living proof that it was Labour which had shifted leftwards. But in any case I agreed with Keith Joseph that it was the 'common ground', not the 'middle ground', on which we must stake our case. From now on a gap opened up between the way in which Central Office wished to campaign and the direction I insisted on taking.

Such problems were not, however, immediately evident to me. Tuesday morning's newspapers carried a report of an NOP poll suggesting that our lead was just 6 per cent, but compared with earlier NOP polls it did not suggest any narrowing of the gap. (Throughout the campaign the opinion polls were to give very different pictures of the balance of party support, ranging from the most exiguous of Tory leads – in one case a slight Labour lead – to an improbably overwhelming Tory landslide.) I felt it was an effective day's campaigning, beginning in Bristol where I visited the Kleeneze brush factory to use every possible photo-opportunity to demonstrate my intention of 'sweeping away the cobwebs', 'applying a new broom' etc.

Also in Bristol I was on the receiving end of the *Election Call* programme hosted by Robin Day. There is always an element of risk on these occasions. A well-briefed caller can expose gaps in a politician's understanding which most political opponents never could. Moreover, judging the correct reaction is always more difficult when you cannot see the person to whom you are talking over the telephone. But I felt that this *Election Call* went particularly well, because the points raised with me were on the precise questions to which we had the most convincing answers – the need for tax cuts, controlling inflation, cutting back on government borrowing and encouraging small businesses. Of course, there were critical points too. I always felt that the key to dealing with these was to admit what had gone wrong and say clearly why a future Conservative

Government would put it right. So on this occasion I agreed that the previous Conservative Government was indeed responsible for an increase in bureaucracy in the health service, and said how we were going to reverse it.

On the way back from Bristol, taking the new Intercity 125 high-speed train, I stopped off in West Country constituencies and had my photo taken with the candidates, including Chris Patten on the station platform at Bath. The day finished with my addressing a meeting at Gravesend. Since Central Office was telling me that our support among pensioners was shaky I wrote out a press release reminding voters of the record of Conservative Governments on this point.

The following day (Wednesday 18 April), after the morning press conference, I set off to campaign in East Anglia and the East Midlands. First stop was my bid for the agricultural vote. This consisted of a discussion of cattle feed with a friendly farmer, carefully navigating my way across a field full of cows (I had forgotten my boots) and then cradling a calf in my arms for the benefit of the cameras and, I hoped, the wider public. I had no experience with calves and I was not certain of the right technique. With cameramen from five continents present, Denis, ever realistic, warned that 'If we're not careful, we'll have a dead calf on our hands.' But it survived my attentions and those of the photographers. Fortunately, perhaps, the calf was not able to give an interview.

THE SECOND WEEK – D–14 to D–7

By now (Thursday 19 April) much agonizing had taken place back in London about the implications of my Cardiff speech for the 'positioning' of the Party and our campaign. Peter Thorneycroft had persuaded himself that we had made a strategic error which should not be repeated. And since nothing that Central Office or my colleagues did seemed to get much publicity, he decided to involve himself in the drafting of my speeches. Oblivious to all this, I spent that Thursday morning visiting a Leicester textile factory, where I put my childhood training to good effect by stitching overall pockets amid a chaotic crowd of journalists and an astonished workforce.

It was, however, just before the bus arrived at the Cadbury factory in Bournville that I learned that Peter Thorneycroft was insisting that a strong passage on trade unions, drafted by Paul Johnson, one of Britain's leading journalists, an historian and a convert from socialism, should be removed from that evening's speech in Birmingham – the second major rally of the campaign. Peter thought it too provocative. He had also apparently intervened to stop Keith Joseph speaking on the same subject. I did not agree with Peter's assessment. But being away from London I felt insufficiently sure of my judgement to substitute it for his. So I angrily tore out the relevant pages of my draft speech and inserted some more innocuous passages. I contented myself with the knowledge that the last section of the speech, with which I had been helped by Peter Carrington, contained some extremely strong stuff on defence and foreign affairs, deliberately adopting the tone and some of the language of my earlier Kensington Town Hall speech.

But I was not in the best of humour as our coach drew up in front of the factory. I had specifically said that I did not want a formal reception committee, but rather to go straight in and talk to individual managers and workers. Now I saw two long lines of people in white hats and coats. I could not for the moment see the camera crews but I had no doubt that they were waiting somewhere to take suitable shots of this ludicrous scene. I stayed on the bus for a minute or two to regain my cool. It was only then that I realized that I knew the faces of what I had assumed to be the factory staff. It was the pressmen who, doubtless informed of my earlier instructions, had dressed up in white overalls as a joke. As I left the bus they held up their cameras as a kind of arch beneath which I entered the factory. They were so carried away with their joke that they forgot to take any photographs; but they helped me see the funny side of campaigning, for which I suspect we were all grateful.

Having sewn pockets in the morning, I suppose it was only natural that I should find myself sorting chocolates in the afternoon. It was a tricky, demanding task – the sort which gives the lie to the loosely-used expression 'unskilled work'. It was many years since I myself had worked in a factory, but I saw that some traditions do not change. One girl who was shortly getting married had all her wedding presents laid out on a table close to the production line for her friends to see. After my chocolate-packing was over, we all discussed them at rather greater length than my programme allowed. In the end I was bustled away, for we had to get to the Midland Hotel in Birmingham. As a chocolate addict, I never thought I would lose my appetite for them. But somehow that clinging smell of vanilla put me off them for the rest of the campaign.

The Birmingham speech, for all the trouble its preparation had caused, was a great success – not just the passages on East-West relations and the communist threat, but also those on law and order, on which I pledged to 'place a barrier of steel' against the socialist path to lawlessness. Afterwards we drove back to London where the following day's (Friday 20 April) constituency visits would take place.

Saturday 21 April was a day of regular campaigning which began at a factory producing highly sophisticated electrical components in Milton Keynes. I was excited by the technology, about which I had been thoroughly briefed, and soon found myself giving a detailed exposition of it to a group of slightly bemused pressmen. I was then wired up and tested on a heart monitoring machine. With all the dials pointing in the right direction I was shown to be in good working order: 'Solid as a rock,' as I remarked – something which also reflected my judgement about how our campaign as a whole was going. For one of the oddest characteristics of the 1979 general election campaign was the wide and growing difference of perceptions between those of us who were out in the field and those who were back at the centre. Of course, politicians, like everyone else, are susceptible to self-delusion. But, far more than in 1983 and 1987 when security considerations loomed so large, I was confident that I *did* have a real sense of what the electorate felt and that their hearts were with us. I was also convinced that this change had come about largely because of the events of the winter of 1978/79 and that therefore undue caution on the issue of trade union power was bad tactics.

But it was clear from discussion at the strategy meeting I held in Flood Street on Sunday 22 April that not everyone saw matters this way. Although the opinion polls were still varied – one showing a 20 per cent and another a 5.5 per cent Conservative lead – there had not been much movement during the campaign. Peter Thorneycroft's view was that we should more or less carry on as we were. As he put it in a paper for that Sunday's meeting: 'We should not embark on any high-risk initiatives. We are in the lead.' This seemed to me fair enough as far as it went. But it begged two questions. First, had we not gained our lead in the first place by taking some quite high-risk initiatives, such as my interventions in the Winter of Discontent? Secondly, what now constituted a 'high risk'? Measures to curb union power? Or the absence of them? In any case, one of the greatest dangers in a campaign where you have started out with a significant lead is complacency. Exciting the voters, as long as it is not on some issue on which they disagree with you, is an indispensable part of winning elections.

My campaigning that week would take me to the North of England, before going on to Scotland. After the Monday morning press conference, I flew to Newcastle where the photo-opportunity was at a tea factory. Tasting the sludgy concoctions, undiluted and unmasked by milk and sugar, had something of the same effect on my tea drinking as did the Bournville factory on my consumption of chocolates.

Outside the factory a crowd had gathered, among which was a large, formidable woman who was pouring out a torrent of abuse in my direction. The police advised me to stay away. But I felt that if she had something to say she had better do so to my face rather than my back, and so I walked over to talk to her. I took her arm and told her quietly just to say what was wrong. Her manner changed completely. She had the usual grumbles and worries. But the real cause of her anger was a conviction that politicians were just not people who listened. I tried to answer as best I could and we parted amicably. As I walked away I heard her unmistakable tones telling a friend: 'I told you she wasn't half so bad.' My experience of campaigning over the years is that there are very few irredeemably hostile electors. It is one of the tragedies of the terrorist threat that politicians nowadays have so few opportunities to convince themselves of that fact.

Tuesday, too, was very much a traditional-style campaigning day, with four walkabouts, including a visit to the Sowerby candidate, Donald Thompson's butcher's shop, and to a supermarket – after which the usual piles of purchases were taken back on the battle bus. On the steps of the Conservative Party offices in Halifax I was photographed in the drizzle holding up two shopping bags – a blue bag which contained the food which could have been bought for £1 in 1974 and a half-filled red bag which contained all that £1 would buy in Labour Britain in 1979. And if this was better politics than economics it was no worse for that. Among the no-nonsense Yorkshire people it went down well.

Back in London that evening I was interviewed by Denis Tuohy for *TV Eye*. This was the most hostile interview of the campaign. But it allowed me to give a vigorous defence of our proposals for trade union reform. And on this, whatever Central Office might think, I was not going to backtrack. I reaffirmed my determination to deal with the trade union militants. I also pointed out just what was implied by the suggestion that a Conservative Government would be faced with an all-out battle with the trade unions.

> Let's come to the nub of the matter. What you are saying is that the trade union leaders are saying that the whole of this general election is a hollow mockery and a sham. If you are right, and that is what they *are* saying, then I am going to ask for the biggest majority any country has ever given any government, and I am going to ask for the biggest majority from the twelve million members of trade unions. I don't think you are right.

I was especially severe with the Labour Party's suggestion that discussion with the trade unions, the so-called 'Concordat', was a better way of dealing with union power than were changes in the law.

> You know, it would have been very, very strange if Lord Shaftesbury, the great Tory reformer, looking at conditions

which he saw in the mills and the factories decades ago, had said: I'll do it by a voluntary concordat with the mill owners. Do you think he would have got it? Of course he wouldn't. He said: There are some things which we must do *by law*.

After the Wednesday 25 April morning press conference and radio interviews I had lunch at Central Office before flying to Edinburgh in the afternoon. I was beginning to become tired of the standard speech I made to audiences around the country, which drew heavily on the texts prepared for Cardiff and Birmingham with extra pieces slotted in that would go out as press releases. As a result, I performed inadvisably radical surgery on the material I took with me to Scotland. Just minutes before I was due to speak, I was on my knees in the Caledonian Hotel applying scissors and Sellotape to a speech which spread from one wall to the other and back again. Tessa Jardine Paterson frantically typed up each page of the speech, which was handed out, more or less as I delivered it, at Leith Town Hall. At least it was fresh – even to me. At the end I inserted one of my favourite quotations from Kipling:

> So when the world is asleep, and there seems no hope of her
>   waking
> Out of some long, bad dream that makes her mutter and moan,
> Suddenly, all men arise to the noise of fetters breaking,
> And everyone smiles at his neighbour and tells him his soul is
>   his own!*

It was a marvellous audience, and from the first few cheers my spirits lifted and I gave of my best.

We went on to the hotel at Glasgow Airport to have a late supper and then turn in before another day of Scottish campaigning. I was buoyed up with that special excitement which comes of knowing you have given a good speech. Although the opinion polls suggested that Labour might be closing on us, the gap was still a healthy one and my instincts were that we were winning the argument. Labour's campaign had a distinctly tired feel about it.

---

* 'The Dawn Wind'.

They reiterated so frequently the theme that Tory policies could not work, or would work only at the cost of draconian cuts in public services, that they slipped imperceptibly into arguing that nothing could work, and that Britain's problems were in essence insoluble. This put Labour in conflict with the people's basic instinct that improvement *is* possible and ought to be pursued. We represented that instinct – indeed Labour was giving us a monopoly on it. I felt that things were going well.

Denis, Carol and Ronnie Millar were with me at the hotel and we exchanged gossip and jokes. Janet Young was also travelling with us and had slipped out during the meal. She now returned with a serious expression to tell me that Peter Thorneycroft – or 'the Chairman' as she insisted on calling him – felt that things were not too good politically and that Ted Heath should appear on the next Party Election Broadcast.

I exploded. It was about as clear a demonstration of lack of confidence in me as could be imagined. If Peter Thorneycroft and Central Office had not yet understood that what we were fighting for was a reversal not just of the Wilson-Callaghan approach but of the Heath Government's approach they had understood nothing. I told Janet Young that if she and Peter thought that then I might as well pack up. Ted had lost three elections out of four and had nothing to say about an election fought on this kind of manifesto. To invite him to deliver a Party Political for us was tantamount to accepting defeat for the kind of policies I was advancing.

It was perhaps unfair of me to blame Janet in part for conveying Peter's message. But this was the closest I came in the campaign to being really upset. I told her that I would not even hear of it. She conveyed a doubtless censored version of my response to 'the Chairman' and, still seething, I went to bed.

THE THIRD WEEK – D–7 to D-Day

Thursday morning's Glasgow press conference was an unremarkable affair. The journalists did not seem to have much to say for themselves and I still felt out of sorts. Later in the morning

I had a rather difficult interview with a Scottish television interviewer who was believed to be a Conservative supporter and, as sometimes happens, wished to prove the opposite by being particularly hostile. But from then on the day looked up. We visited a creamery in Aberdeen where I sampled some of the finest butter I have ever tasted – and was astonished to learn that it was all being produced not for consumption but to go into EEC intervention storage. It was my first meeting with the butter mountain.

Then it was on to the harbour at Buckie and a fish factory, where the irrepressibly high spirits and good humour of the people worked wonders on me. I addressed an early-evening meeting at Elgin Town Hall and then the coach drove us on to Lossiemouth to board the plane which would take us back to London. All along the way to Lossiemouth Airport the road was lined with people waving and we had to keep stopping to receive flowers and presents. Here was more proof that we were among friends.

It can well be imagined that there was some unseasonal frost in the April air when I came for my briefing at Central Office before the Friday morning press conference. I was also rather too sharp with a journalist at it on the subject of the impact of technology on employment. Then a television interviewer, whom I had been told would be sympathetic, turned out to be very much the opposite. It was that point in an election campaign when everybody's nerves have become frayed with tiredness. And the pressure was still building. I knew I had further important media interviews, the last PEB to record and big speeches at Bolton and the final Conservative Trade Unionists' rally. Moreover, the opinion polls now seemed to suggest that our lead was being eroded. The Central Office view was that it had fallen from about 10 per cent to about 6 per cent. Unfortunately, there was no reason to give any more credence to the internal Party opinion polling – which was on the optimistic side of the median – than to other polls. I had to cancel my visit to the Fulham constituency that afternoon in order to work on the PEB text and the CTU speech. But someone told the press that the real cause was that my voice was failing, which was used to paint an exaggerated picture of a 'battle-worn Maggie' trying to stop the election slipping away. In fact, my voice was in remarkably good order – but I now had to risk real strain by raising it so as to convince interviewers and audiences that my larynx was alive and well.

Saturday morning's *Daily Express* carried a MORI poll showing our lead down to just 3 per cent. There was evidence of a mild case of the jitters affecting Conservative Central Office. Peter Thorneycroft wrote to candidates saying: 'Whatever happens, I ask for no complacency and no despair.' It was not a very encouraging message and perhaps indicated all too accurately the feeling of its author and his advisers that the way to win elections was by doing nothing wrong rather than by doing something right. For myself, I publicly shrugged off the polls, noting that: 'Always as you get up to an election the lead narrows.' In fact, I had decided that by far the best course now was to shut the opinion polls out of my mind and put every ounce of remaining energy into the decisive final days of the campaign. I had a good morning of campaigning in London, including my own Finchley constituency, returning home to Flood Street in the afternoon for discussion of the Election Broadcast.

Sunday 29 April would be crucial. The opinion polls were all over the place. I ignored them. I had my hair done in the morning and then after lunch was driven to the Wembley Conference Centre for the Conservative Trade Unionists' rally. Harvey Thomas, drawing on his experience of Billy Graham's evangelical rallies, had pulled out every stop. A galaxy of actors and comedians livened up the proceedings. Ignoring previous instructions from perhaps over-serious Party officials concerned about the dignity of 'the next Prime Minister', Harvey played the campaign song 'Hello Maggie' when I entered. And dignity certainly went by the board as everyone joined in. I had never known anything quite like it – though compared with Harvey's extravaganzas of future years this came to seem quite tame.

The speech itself was short and sharp. And the reception was terrific. Then I went on to Saatchi & Saatchi to record the final Election Broadcast. From four o'clock in the afternoon Gordon, Ronnie, Tim and I worked and reworked the text. Then there was an apparently endless succession of 'takes', each of which – until the final one – seemed not quite right to at least one of us. At last, well after midnight, we were satisfied.

The main event of my campaign on Monday was the *Granada 500* programme, when each of the three party leaders was questioned by an audience from what was deemed to be the most representative seat in the country, Bolton East. (For many years Bolton East had been won by the party which formed the next government, but in 1979, dazzled perhaps by national attention, the electors got it wrong.) I enjoyed these occasions, feeling more at ease than when interviewed on a one-to-one basis. Somehow the fact that these were 'real' people with real worries helped me to relax. Judging by the 'clapometer' reading I won the contest.

But the following (Tuesday) morning there was a further opinion poll by NOP which showed Labour 0.7 per cent ahead. There was only one real question on people's lips at that morning's press conference: how would I react to the poll? I just brushed it aside, saying that I hoped it would stir Conservative Party supporters to go out and vote on the day. Not only did this line serve me at a difficult moment: I suspect it was a correct judgement. For if anything really threatened our victory it was complacency, and from this moment there was no chance of that. I went on to campaign in the North-West, finishing up, of course, by addressing a rally in Bolton, where the comedian Ken Dodd appeared on stage with a blue feather-duster to greet me. After Ken Dodd's message from Knotty Ash – which he made sound a pretty true blue constituency – any speech would have seemed over-serious. But there was only one real message for this stage of the campaign, which was that those who wished to throw the Labour Party out of government must not fritter their votes away on minor parties, but rather vote Conservative.

Moreover, the same message had to be repeated insistently until polling day. It was my theme at the final press conference on Wednesday (2 May). I returned to it as I went around the London constituencies, finishing up at the Woodhouse School in Finchley – where I had to push my way through protesting feminists chanting: 'We want women's rights not a right-wing woman.' As I drove back to Flood Street I felt the tiredness flow over me. I had had my chance and had taken it. It was oddly satisfying to know that whatever happened now was out of my hands. For the first time in many nights Denis and I had a full six hours' sleep.

I woke on election day to learn from the radio news that all of that morning's opinion polls showed the Conservatives with a lead ranging from 2 per cent to 8 per cent. Denis and I went out to vote at 9 o'clock in Chelsea before driving on to Finchley, where, as was my wont, I toured the committee rooms followed by photographers. I went back to Flood Street for a light supper and to try to have some rest before what I knew would be a long evening. At the Finchley count in Barnet Town Hall, where I arrived shortly after midnight, I kept out of the way in a side room, equipped with a television and supplied with coffee and sandwiches, where I could listen to the results as they came in. Roger Boaden was with me, supplementing the television reports with early information telephoned through from Central Office. I kept a running tally, referring to the detailed briefing which Keith Britto had prepared for me. The first few results suggested that we had won, though among them was the upsetting news that Teddy Taylor had lost Glasgow Cathcart. The projections of our majority steadily began to mount. Local councillors, my Constituency Chairman and his wife, my agent and others came in and out looking more and more cheerful. But I deliberately suppressed any inclinations to premature euphoria: calculation, superstition and above all the knowledge that it is easiest to cope with bad news when you are not expecting good entered into this. In the end, however, not even I could remain non-committal. It was clear to everyone by the time I went out to hear the results of my own count that we would form the next Government.

The events of the early hours of Friday – the welcoming clamour of supporters at the count, the visit to Central Office, the warmth and relief of brief relaxation with my family – are no more than blurred recollections. That afternoon's visit to Buckingham Palace to receive authority to form a government and my subsequent arrival at Downing Street I have described elsewhere.*

The scale of the victory took everyone – or almost everyone –

* *The Downing Street Years*, pp. 17–19.

by surprise. It was not just that we had won an election: we had also won a new kind of mandate for change. As the psephologists and commentators mulled over the detailed results, the pattern of our success bore this out. We had won a majority of forty-three seats over all other parties. The 5.6 per cent national swing from Labour to the Conservatives was the largest achieved by either – and our 7 per cent lead over Labour was also the largest – since 1945.

Equally significant, the biggest swing to us was among the skilled workers; and over a third of that lead had apparently built up during the campaign. These were precisely the people we had to win over from their often lifelong socialist allegiances. They were confronted in a particularly acute form by the fundamental dilemma which faced Britain as a whole: whether to accept an ever greater role for government in the life of the nation, or to break free in a new direction. For these people, above all, it was a severely practical matter of choosing whether to rely on the comforting security of state provision or to make the sacrifices required to win a better life for themselves and their families. They had now decided to take the risk (for it was a risk) of voting for what I offered – for what in a certain sense I knew that I now personified. I would always try to keep faith with them.

PART TWO

Beginning Again

On 28 November 1990, as I left 10 Downing Street for the last time eleven years, six months and twenty-four days after I first set foot there as Prime Minister, I was tormented by a whirl of conflicting and confused thoughts and emotions. I had passed from the well-lit world of public life where I had lived so long into . . . what? Yet, though I may have leapt – or been pushed – into the dark, I was not in free fall. I had my family and my health. I also found that there was an abundance of friends to give me moral and practical help.

Alistair McAlpine lent me his house in Great College Street, close to the Palace of Westminster, to serve as a temporary office. When Denis, Mark and I arrived there, I found a little sitting room for me to work in. John Whittingdale, who had been my Political Secretary as Prime Minister, and several other old and new faces were waiting to greet me. As for our own house, which Denis and I had bought in Dulwich partly as an investment and partly to provide for emergencies (though we had hardly foreseen this one), neither of us really wanted to keep it. It was too far from Westminster and somehow in spite of all that had happened we both assumed that whatever else I was to do, 'retirement' was not an option. I wanted and probably needed to earn a living. In any case, I would have gone mad without work.

It took some time before we found somewhere suitable to live; to begin with we were lent a lovely flat in Eaton Square by Mrs Henry Ford. But finding work to do was certainly no problem. There were countless letters to write in answer to messages of

commiseration, which had deeply moved me. Some of my correspondents were in despair. I, myself, was merely depressed.

I was fortunately distracted by immediate personal matters.
Christmas was less than a month away, and my departure from
Downing Street meant that all my plans for Christmas at Chequers
had to be cancelled. I needed to book a hotel for our Christmas
party (my own house was stacked high with packing cases from
eleven and a half years at Downing Street and Chequers), re-invite
my guests now cheated of Chequers, order a new set of non-Prime
Ministerial Christmas cards, and see that all the bills were paid.

Nonetheless, the later effect of my departure from Downing
Street was to leave time heavy on my hands. Throughout my deliberately busy life I had been able to find solace for personal disappointments by forgetting the past and taking up some new
venture. Work was my secret elixir. Now I would have to adjust
to a different pace. It was difficult to begin with.

I am not by nature either introspective or retrospective: I always
prefer to look forward. I feel easiest dealing with immediate practical problems, and (within reason) the harder the better. Now there
was far more opportunity for reflection than I had enjoyed – if that
is the word – either as Leader of the Opposition or as Prime Minister. And, painful as it was, perhaps for the first time I felt an inner
need to ponder on what I had made of my life and the opportunities
I had been given, and on the significance of events.

At first, my involuntary 'retreat' was dominated by dark
thoughts. I was still able to read in the press a series of obituary-
style assessments of the 'Thatcher years'. And it was no surprise
to discover in some newspapers a very different account of the
record of my time as Prime Minister than I remembered or thought
accurate. It was clear to me from the start that this must be put
right by giving my own account in my memoirs – after all, I had
made enough public jokes about writing them, and there was no
shortage of interest. And one thing that records do not do is 'speak
for themselves', however much politicians may wish they did. Yet
I did not see this so much as a means of self-justification – that
was essentially between me, my conscience and the Almighty.
Rather, and increasingly, I wanted to give encouragement to those
who thought and felt as I did, the next generation of political

leaders and perhaps even the ones after that, to keep their gaze fixed on the right stars.

In one sense, I had been politically marooned. Yet, as the weeks went by, I was pleasantly surprised to discover that my little island was no more deserted intellectually than socially. I found myself in the company not just of concerned friends but of like-minded academics, journalists and members of the younger generation of politicians, in fact those whose ideas and convictions were well placed to influence the future. I came to see that on leaving Downing Street I had, however disagreeably and unwillingly, broken out of the kind of self-imposed exile which high office brings. For years, I had had to deal with and work through politicians and civil servants who, with a few remarkable exceptions, by and large did not agree with me and shared little of my fundamental approach. They had dutifully done their part – and some beyond duty. But the inevitable loneliness of power had been exacerbated in my case by the fact that I so often had to act as a lone opponent of the processes and attitudes of government itself – the Government I myself headed. I was often portrayed as an outsider who by some odd mixture of circumstances had stepped inside and stayed there for eleven and a half years; in my case the portrayal was not inaccurate.

Now I was outside again. But it was a different 'outside' than I remembered. I found that by contrast with those difficult days as Leader of the Opposition which I have described earlier in this book, nearly all the cleverest conservatives, those who had something to say and much to offer, were of my way of thinking. The revolution – of privatization, deregulation, tax-cutting, wider ownership, restoring self-reliance, building ladders out of poverty, strengthening our defences, securing the Atlantic alliance, restoring the country's morale and standing – which had been so laboriously achieved inside Government had to some extent obscured from me the extent of the intellectual revolution which had occurred outside it. From time to time, for example at my annual visits to the Centre for Policy Studies, I had seen something of what was happening. But I had not grasped its full measure. And as I now came to have misgivings about some Government policies, I correspondingly placed greater hope in those outside Government who still carried on the battle of ideas. Moreover, this had its pleasant and practical side. For I never lacked stimulating conversation; and when I needed help with a speech or article or briefing on some abstruse subject there was a small army of enthusiastic and expert volunteers to provide it.

I had a similar experience abroad, where my speech tours increasingly took me. To begin with, I was received as a former Prime Minister and spent much of my time with people I had known in office. But at the top of international politics the faces change quickly. Former contacts are a diminishing source of capital. What I really enjoyed and found intellectually bracing was when I was received not just for the office I had held – or even what others considered I had achieved – but for what in some more general sense I 'represented'. I suppose I might have expected this in the United States, the seat of radical modern conservative thinking and almost my second home. But when I talked to politicians, businessmen and intellectuals from the newly liberated democracies of Central and Eastern Europe, to West Europeans who shared my concerns about Maastricht, to political and business leaders of Asian and Pacific countries whose economies were racing ahead by making full-blooded capitalism work, to those who were rapidly turning Latin American countries around from being Third World failures to First World dynamos, I found the same thing. I was simultaneously chairing and participating in a sort of revolving seminar. They wanted to hear all that they could from me; and I found myself learning much from them.

Of course, I was equally aware of the setbacks – of weakening links between America and Europe, of former communists slipping back into power in the officially 'post-communist' world, and of the horrors of the Balkan tragedy which Western weakness allowed and encouraged and which streams of Slovenes, Croats, Bosnians and democratically-minded Serbs came in to describe to me. Yet, I felt from the way in which I was received by my hosts abroad (as well as the way in which I seemed to fall on my feet at home) that the basic themes I had preached and sought to practise over the years were as relevant and potent as ever. It was not that the world had turned away from my kind of conservatism, but rather that conservatives themselves in some countries had temporarily lost confidence in themselves and their message. The foreign visits were tiring. But I decided that while I had the strength – and so far there seems plenty – I would strive to influence the thinking of peoples, if no longer the actions of governments. And I hoped that when I could no longer fulfil that role myself my Foundation would do so for me.

Sadly, as I have suggested, all this has become increasingly necessary. It is hard to imagine as I write these words that the West so recently secured a great victory over communist tyranny, and free-enterprise economics a decisive triumph over socialism. The mood in the West now seems to oscillate between bravado, cynicism and fear. There are problems at home. In most Western countries public spending on social entitlement programmes is leading to swollen deficits and higher taxes. There are problems abroad. Western defences are being run down and the resolve to use them is dwindling. There is deep confusion about the future of Europe and Britain's place in it. The 'special relationship' with the United States has been allowed to cool to near freezing point. The West has failed to give the democrats in the post-communist world the support they needed; their place is being taken by too many dubious figures. First by our inaction, now by our weakness, we are encouraging the Russians to believe that they will only receive the respect and attention of the West if they behave like the old Soviet Union. In the former Yugoslavia aggression has been allowed to pay. And disarray grows in NATO, because it has destroyed an empire and not yet found a new role. Not that everything is bad. The world is a freer, if not necessarily safer, place than during the Cold War. But that most important element of political success is missing – a sense of purpose.

Of course, I would say that, wouldn't I? Perhaps. But others who often criticized me in Government are saying it too. In the pages which follow – on Europe, the wider international scene, social policy and the economy – I offer some thoughts about putting these things right. It is now, however, for others to take the action required.

CHAPTER XIII

Bruges or Brussels?

Policy towards Europe

NARROW INTERNATIONALISM

Once a politician is given a public image by the media, it is almost impossible for him to shed it. At every important stage of his career, it steps between him and the public so that people seem to see and hear not the man himself but the invented personality to which he has been reduced.

My public image was on the whole not a disadvantageous one; I was 'the Iron Lady', 'Battling Maggie', 'Attila the Hen', etc. Since these generally gave opponents the impression I was a hard nut to crack, I was glad to be so portrayed even though no real person could be so single-mindedly tough. In one respect, however, I suffered: whenever the topic of Europe arose, I was usually depicted as a narrow, nostalgic nationalist who could not bear to see the feudal trappings of Britain's *ancien régime* crumble into dust like Miss Havisham's wedding cake, when the sunlight of Europe's rational modernity was turned upon them. I was 'isolated', 'backward-looking', 'rooted in the past', 'clinging to the wreckage of Empire', and 'obsessed with the outdated notion of sovereignty'. And virtually all my statements on Europe were read in that light.

In fact, of the three underlying reasons for my scepticism about European federalism, the most important was that the European Union was an obstacle to fruitful *internationalism*. (The other two were that Britain showed that established and 'satisfied' nationalisms were the best building-blocks for international cooperation; and that, as I argue elsewhere in this chapter, democracy cannot function in a federal superstate where the multiplicity of languages makes democratic debate and democratic accountability mere slogans.) The European federalists are in fact 'narrow internationalists', 'little Europeans' who consistently place the interests of the Community above the common interests of the wider international community. The EU came near to sabotaging the GATT; it has sparked a series of trade disputes across the Atlantic; it has prolonged the instability of Central and Eastern Europe by maintaining absurdly high trade barriers on their infant export industries; and it threatens to divide NATO with premature and militarily incomprehensible plans to establish a 'European pillar' or 'European defence identity'. And most of these obstructive initiatives make no sense in their own terms; they are launched solely in order to bring nearer the day when 'Europe' will be a fully-fledged state with its own flag, anthem, army, parliament, government, currency and, eventually one supposes, people.

I am not alone in warning that this could stimulate both the US and Japan to safeguard themselves by forming similar protectionist empires. The world might then drift towards an Orwellian future of Oceania, Eurasia and Eastasia – three mercantilist world empires on increasingly hostile terms. In the process the post-war international institutions which have served us well, like NATO and GATT, would be weakened, pushed aside and eventually made irrelevant. That prospect is still alive and should worry us.

If we look ahead still further to the end of the twenty-first century, however, an even more alarming (because more unstable) future is on the cards. Consider the number of medium-to-large states in the world that now stand poised on the edge of a free-market revolution: India, China, Brazil, possibly Russia. Add to these the present economic great powers: the USA, Japan, the European Union (or, with only a slight amendment of the scenario, a Franco-German 'fast lane' bloc). What we are possibly looking at in 2095 is an unstable world in which there are more than half a dozen 'great powers', all with their own clients, all vulnerable if they stand alone, all capable of increasing their power and influence if they form the right kind of alliance, and all engaged willy-nilly in perpetual diplomatic manoeuvres to ensure that their relative positions improve rather than deteriorate. In other words, 2095 might look like 1914 played on a somewhat larger stage.

Whether your favourite nightmare is Orwell's tripartite division of the spoils, or this vision of 1914 revisited, the key to avoiding it is the same. Neither need come to pass if the Atlantic Alliance remains, in essence, America as the dominant power surrounded by allies which, in their own long-term interest, generally follow its lead. Such are the realities of population, resources, technology and capital that if America remains the dominant partner in a united West, then the West can continue to be the dominant power in the world as a whole. And since collective security can only really be provided if there is a superpower of last resort, the rest of the world (apart from 'rogue states' and terrorist groups) would generally support, or at least acquiesce in, such an international structure.

Britain's role in such a structure would, I believe, be a disproportionately influential one. That is not, however, my principal reason for supporting it. My reason is that such a world best meets the needs of international peace and collective prosperity. It would also be a liberal world – politically, economically and culturally – and far more so than a world dominated by either Asian or Eurasian blocs, remarkable though their achievements have been in history and in recent years.

Let me stress again, however, that it will not come to pass unless America is persuaded to remain the dominant European power militarily and economically. That means we must ensure that American troops remain in Europe for the foreseeable future, and in particular for the next few years when budgetary pressures will tempt the US to withdraw. In these circumstances, the EU's creeping tendency to establish itself as a separate 'third force' risks alienating America and sending the legions home. The stakes are high. And to divide the West and move closer to permanent world instability in order that Europe may enjoy a modest increase in status as one independent superpower among seven or eight seems to me the most mischievous and irresponsible form of nationalism.

TOWARDS MAASTRICHT

One of the few things I still regret about the timing of my departure from Downing Street was that it prevented my coming to grips with the rapidly changing scene in Europe.* In the autumn of 1990 the groundwork was being laid for what would be the Maastricht Treaty, designed to set in place the framework for a federal United States of Europe. I had fought many battles within the European Community since becoming Prime Minister, but I had never before faced one of this scale and importance.

It had, of course, been increasingly clear to me that the European Commission and a number of heads of government held a quite different view from mine about the purpose and direction of the Community. It was as a warning against the way in which statism, protectionism and federalism were advancing relentlessly that I delivered the Bruges speech in 1988. At Bruges I had argued against attempts to fit nations 'into some sort of identikit European personality', calling instead for 'willing and active cooperation between independent sovereign states [as] the best way to build a successful European Community'.

From then on I had been ever more preoccupied with the need to spell out and win domestic and foreign support for an alternative vision. It was by no means an impossible task, but the difficulties were legion. Within the Conservative Party there was a large minority of irreconcilable Euro-enthusiasts, willing to welcome almost anything stamped as made in Brussels. The Single European Act, contrary to my intentions and my understanding of formal undertakings given at the time, had provided new scope for the European Commission and the European Court to press forward in the direction of centralization. For their own different reasons, both France and Germany – and the Franco-German axis was dominant – were keen to move in the same direction. In the United States the Administration had made a crucial error of judgement in believing

---

* I have described the arguments about Europe, which formed the background to my stepping down as Prime Minister, in *The Downing Street Years*.

that promotion of a united Europe led by Germany would best secure America's interests – though the experience of the Gulf War undoubtedly caused President Bush to question such assumptions.

In spite of all this, I remained confident that given singleness of purpose and strength of will the Bruges alternative could be made to prevail – for three long-term influences favoured it. First, the need to accommodate the newly liberated countries of Eastern Europe created difficulties for the narrow Europeanism of the federalists which their high-tax, high-regulation, high-subsidy system could not ultimately meet. Secondly, global economic changes, which dramatically widened horizons in finance and business, would reduce the relative importance of the European Community itself. Thirdly, not just in Britain but increasingly in other European countries, the popular mood was moving away from remote bureaucracies and towards recovering historically rooted local and national identities. It might take a decade. But this, I felt, was a cause with a future.

In my final speech to the House of Commons as Prime Minister on Thursday 22 November 1990 I taunted the Labour Party with its studied ambiguity on the large issues:

> They will not tell us where they stand. Do they want a single currency? Are they prepared to defend the rights of this United Kingdom Parliament? For them it is all compromise, sweep it under the carpet, leave it for another day, in the hope that the people of Britain will not notice what is happening to them, how the powers are gradually slipping away.

I was not at that point to know, and indeed I would not have wanted to imagine, that precisely the same would soon be said of the Conservative Government led by my successor. I knew that John Major was likely to seek some kind of compromise with the majority of heads of government who wanted political and economic union. That had become clear from our exchanges when John was Chancellor.* Moreover, I could well understand that after the bitter arguments over Europe which preceded my resignation he

* See *The Downing Street Years*, pp. 724–46.

would want to bind up wounds in the Party. But I was not prepared for the speed with which the position I had adopted would be entirely reversed.

In December the Foreign Secretary, Douglas Hurd, publicly advocated a distinctive European defence role through the Western European Union (WEU), which I had always distrusted, aware that others, particularly the French, would like to use it as an alternative to a NATO inevitably dominated by America. Then in March 1991 the Prime Minister announced in Bonn that Britain's place was 'at the very heart of Europe'. This seemed to me a plain impossibility in more than merely the geographical sense, since our traditions and interests diverged sharply in many areas from those of our Continental neighbours. For instance, in trade generally, and in agricultural trade in particular, Britain is both more open and more dependent on countries outside Europe than are our European partners.

I wanted to avoid appearing to undermine my successor. I knew that his position was still fragile and I wanted him to succeed. I had faced sufficient difficulties from Ted Heath not to wish to inflict similar ones. As a result and paradoxically, I found myself even more constrained in what I was able to say after my resignation than before it. But I could not in good conscience stay silent when the whole future direction of Britain, even its status as a sovereign state, was at issue. So although I had the gravest misgivings about the reported shape of the draft treaties being discussed by heads of government, I sought to be positive, setting out in public the kind of Europe I wanted, while giving the Government the benefit of the doubt for as long as possible.

In March 1991 I made my first major public speech since leaving office – in Washington at a meeting arranged by several American conservative think-tanks. I steered clear of the more sensitive areas for British domestic politics and concentrated on the European Community's geo-political role.

A democratic Europe of nation states could be a force for liberty, enterprise and open trade. But, if creating a United States of Europe overrides these goals, the new Europe will be one of subsidy and protection.

The European Community does indeed have a political mission. It is to anchor new and vulnerable democracies more securely to freedom and to the West. This is what happened after the end of authoritarian rule in Spain, Portugal and Greece. So the offer of full Community membership must be open to the countries of Eastern and Central Europe just as soon as democracy and the free market have taken root. In the meantime, we must strengthen links of trade, investment and culture.

It was, of course, particularly apposite to make these points in the United States which had, more or less consistently over the years, been pressing Britain towards closer integration in Europe. That approach was based on a double illusion: first, the assumption that a politically united Europe would be friendly towards the United States, relieving her of some or all of the burden of defence. In fact, the most committed European federalists quite consciously seek to move away from America, to create another superpower that would be the equal of the US and, because it would have distinct interests, eventually its rival in world affairs. This has already had practical effects. The growing protectionism of Europe provoked a series of trade skirmishes across the Atlantic even when the Cold War restrained such rivalry. Since the collapse of communism, and the draw-down of American troops in Europe, disputes over trade have become more serious, as in the US–EU row over GATT. And almost every expression of the European Community's foreign policy-making, from the 1980 Venice Declaration on the Middle East* to the Community's early and futile interventions in the Yugoslav war, have been designed to distinguish Europe from the United States, sometimes expressly so. Over time, such disputes are bound to erode the cultural and diplomatic sympathies that have hitherto underpinned Atlantic defence cooperation. At the same time, these disputes are the inevitable results of the development of a united Europe along federalist lines.

The second false assumption made by US policy-makers was that such a European superstate, moulded from separate nations,

---

* See *The Downing Street Years*, pp. 90–1.

separate cultures and separate languages, could be 'democratic' in
the American (and full) sense of the word. I answered this point
directly in my Washington speech.

> The false political mission which some would set for the Euro-
> pean Community is to turn it into a ... United States of
> Europe: a Europe in which individual nations each with its
> own living democracy would be subordinated within an arti-
> ficial federal structure which is inevitably bureaucratic. A
> Community lacking a common language can have no public
> opinion to which the bureaucrats are accountable.

Since the British Government's stance, rhetorically at least, was
similarly hostile to a United States of Europe, these were, in domestic political terms, easier points to make than criticisms of economic and monetary union, where the Government's position
appeared far less clear. Indeed, actions were already speaking
louder than words ever could. In 1991 it was clear that economic
policy was now principally determined by the parity of sterling
with the Deutschmark, rather than by considerations of domestic
monetary policy. At the same time the Exchange Rate Mechanism
(ERM) was being used as a vehicle towards economic and monetary union, which was quite contrary to what I at least had intended
on entry. Nor was this impression diminished by anything that the
authorities had to say on the matter; the possibility of currency
realignment was dismissed, and indeed it became Government
policy that Britain should move to the narrow (+ or −) 2.25 per
cent band rather than the present 6 per cent.

Yet I was conscious that in criticizing what was now occurring,
I was bound to open myself up to criticism. Just as defenders of
the Maastricht Treaty maintained that it was I who had sold the
pass in signing the Single European Act, and that they were merely
dotting 'i's and crossing 't's, so those who were now forcing the
British economy into the straitjacket of a politically determined
exchange rate claimed that I had no right to criticize this, since I
had taken sterling into the ERM. I knew that I had good answers
to both these charges. The Maastricht framework which now
looked like emerging *was* fundamentally different from the − in

practice unsatisfactory – arrangements reached as a result of negotiation on the Single European Act. The ERM *was* being used for a purpose of which I not only disapproved but which I had made clear within Government I would never implement.* Equally, these arguments were not likely to deter the critics.

So, speaking to the Economic Club of New York on Tuesday 18 June 1991, I put my argument against managed exchange rates both in an international context and in terms which frankly admitted the mistakes which my own Government had made.

With the Louvre and Plaza Agreements in the mid-1980s, we sought to put the objective of greater stability of international exchange rates *above* that of the control of inflation.** In Britain, we compounded this error when in 1987–88 we tried to shadow the Deutschmark. Again, the objective of a stable exchange rate was pursued at the expense of monetary discipline. These policies led to falls in interest rates to artificial and unsustainable levels, which in turn prompted excessive monetary and credit growth. That produced the inflation with which we are all too familiar, and which is the underlying cause of the present recession.*** 'Experience,' said Oscar Wilde, 'is the name we give to our mistakes.' And the conclusion to be drawn from our experience in both the 1970s and the 1980s is that governments should commit themselves to price stability – which can only be achieved by reduced monetary growth – and leave it to companies and individuals in the marketplace to calculate the various other risks in the business of wealth creation.

Targeting exchange rates injects excessive monetary pres-

---

* *The Downing Street Years*, p. 723.

** The Plaza Agreement (March 1985) was an attempt by international finance ministers and central bank governors to bring down the value of the dollar. The markets proved all too obliging. The Louvre Agreement (February 1987) was concluded in the hope of checking the dollar's fall and bringing about a wider stabilization of currencies – paving the way for Nigel Lawson's shadowing of the Deutschmark, which began the following month.

*** In saying this I was bending over backwards to be obliging to the Government, which in fact was unnecessarily worsening the recession by a monetary overkill resulting from an obsession with the exchange rate.

sure when central bankers 'guesstimate' the wrong rate and, like fine-tuning, can produce wild swings towards inflation or deflation when the rate is either undervalued or overvalued, as East Germany is currently discovering. When that happens, the 'stability' that makes fixed exchange rates superficially attractive to businessmen is either abandoned in dramatic devaluation or maintained at the cost of far more damaging instabilities like rapid inflation and higher interest rates. In the ERM Britain is fortunate to have a margin of 6 per cent to accommodate variations in the exchange rate.

In general, however, I recall the words of Karl-Otto Pöhl, former President of the Bundesbank: 'Interest rates should be set according to domestic monetary conditions and the exchange rate should be left to go where it will.' To which I will add: if you fix the exchange rate, then interest rates and domestic monetary conditions go where *they* will. And finance ministers are left like innocent bystanders at the scene of an accident.

It is fair to say that this analysis was not much appreciated by the Government. But some fifteen months later it was proved to be all too correct. Yet the reaction to my interventions confirmed just how difficult it was to tread the narrow line between general support for the Government and vigorous disagreement on a central aspect of what was emerging as Government policy.

One could just about get away with such a strategy outside Westminster. But it is one of the strengths of the House of Commons that speakers are pressed in debate to reveal their true opinions; and, beyond a certain point, I had neither the intention, nor, after all those years of speaking my mind, probably even the ability to dissemble. The impossibility of the situation was brought home to me by the House of Commons Debate on the European Community on Wednesday 20 November 1991. In my speech, which would in fact be my last in the House, I supported the Government's motion, attacked the Labour Party's policy on a single currency and dealt with the criticisms levelled against me for signing the Single European Act. But I went on to question whether any 'opt-out' for sterling from a single European currency would be worth much in practice, bearing in mind that the Maastricht Treaty would still require us to sign up to the goal of a single currency and the institutions designed to prepare the way for it. Repeating an idea which I had floated in interviews during my leadership election campaign almost exactly a year earlier, I called for a referendum if there was a decision to abandon the right to issue the pound sterling. This, however, was something which the Government refused to promise.

Events now moved swiftly and, as far as I was concerned, in the wrong direction. Although for some time it would prove difficult even for Members of Parliament, let alone members of the general public, to obtain the full text of the Maastricht Treaty, its provisions were agreed and the Prime Minister made his statement on it on Wednesday 11 December. Those who knew me well also knew that I could not ultimately go along with Maastricht. I could never have signed such a treaty. There were well-meaning and increasingly desperate attempts to persuade me that I could and should remain silent. I would dearly have liked to comply.

An embarrassing little occasion the day after the Prime Minister's statement illustrated how far wishful thinking would go. I was delighted that John Major was able to come to Denis's and my fortieth wedding anniversary party at Claridge's on Thursday evening. We chatted amiably about everything other than what was on our minds. But when I went out of the hotel to see the Prime Minister to his car I was faced by a whole battery of cameras and asked how I felt about his performance at the Maastricht Council. I replied that I thought he had done 'brilliantly'. And I did indeed believe that as a political operation designed to present his approach in the best possible light he had shown great skill. But naturally my remark was taken as signifying agreement with the Maastricht Treaty itself. As I read the newspapers the following day I resolved that there could be no more misunderstandings of this sort, however painful for all concerned the consequences might be.

THE MAASTRICHT TREATY

Article A of the Maastricht Treaty – viewed superficially at least – nicely combines the two alternative views of Maastricht's purpose and effect.

By this Treaty, the High Contracting Parties establish among themselves a European Union, hereinafter called 'the Union'. This Treaty marks a new stage in the process of creating an ever closer union among the peoples of Europe, in which decisions are taken as closely as possible to the citizen.

The phrase 'ever closer union' is repeated from the original Treaty of Rome, though it is worth noting that in the Rome Treaty it was in the Preamble. Maastricht elevated it for the first time into the substantive treaty text as part of the Treaty's objectives clauses. But, in any case, the concept of a 'Union' is clearly a major extension of that – 'a new stage', in fact. Moreover, Article B sets out clearly the objectives of this Union, including 'the establishment of economic and monetary union, ultimately including a single currency', 'to assert its identity on the international scene, in particular through the implementation of a common foreign and security policy including the eventual framing of a common defence policy, which might in time lead to a common defence', and the 'introduction of a citizenship of the Union'. Understandably, therefore, Chancellor Kohl has commented:

In Maastricht we laid the foundation-stone for the completion of the European Union. The European Union Treaty introduces a new and decisive stage in the process of European union which within a few years will lead to the creation of what the founder fathers of modern Europe dreamed of following the last war: the United States of Europe.*

* Speech to the Bertelsmann Foundation, 3 April 1992.

On the other hand, the phrase 'in which decisions are taken as closely as possible to the citizen', combined with the removal at British insistence of the phrase 'federal goal' from the earlier draft Treaty, gave the British Government a pretext for claiming that Maastricht actually devolved power from the centre to individual governments responsible to national parliaments. The flurry of interest in 'subsidiarity' similarly stemmed from the British Government's desire to give the impression that Maastricht was a liberalizing rather than centralizing measure. Indeed, a new Article 3b was inserted by Maastricht into the Treaty of Rome:

> In areas which do not fall within its exclusive competence, the Community shall take action, in accordance with the principle of subsidiarity, only if and insofar as the objectives of the proposed action cannot be sufficiently achieved by the Member States and can, therefore, by reason of the scale or effects of the proposed action, be better achieved by the Community.

This wording has rightly been described by a former President of the European Court of Justice as 'gobbledygook'. The past behaviour of the European Commission gives no reason to believe that it would constrain that body's activities. Initially, the Commission itself determines whether the matter is something to be devolved under the subsidiarity rule. It is extremely unlikely that the rule would be enforceable in the European Court of Justice to any practical extent. In any case, it would not apply to those areas which *do* fall within the Community's 'exclusive competence', thus ruling out its application to wide areas of Community law such as most of the internal market measures and many social provisions. Anyone who reads the Treaty closely and intelligently will see that Chancellor Kohl's interpretation of it is a great deal more accurate than the British Government's. And that, perhaps, is why it was initially made so difficult to gain access to the full text of Maastricht and why generalities and slogans were the preferred means of its exposition.

In fact, the attempt to portray Maastricht as the opposite of what it was met with only limited success. Anti-federalist Conservative MPs supported it only insofar as they felt it necessary to support the Prime Minister. The real argument therefore came to centre on the 'opt-outs' which Britain obtained. In practical terms, the best that could be said for Maastricht was that not all of it applied to us. Unfortunately, it is not at all clear how effective these exemptions will prove to be either in law or in practice.

It will be recalled that when John Major and I had been discussing the tactics required to resist pressure towards economic and monetary union in the summer of 1990, I had been quite prepared for the other eleven Governments to negotiate a *separate* treaty for Economic and Monetary Union (EMU). Under this, Germany and France would finish up paying all the regional subventions which the poorer countries would insist upon if they were going to lose their ability to compete on the basis of a currency that reflected their economic performance. I also thought that the Germans' anxiety about the weakening of their anti-inflation policies, entailed by moves towards a single currency and away from the Deutschmark, could be exploited in negotiations. Above all, we must be prepared to use our veto – and be known to be prepared – if we were to bring our Community partners up against the harsh realities which would make them think twice.* Precisely how matters would have gone if this strategy had been pursued is, of course, now impossible to say. But there was no practical reason to worry about our being 'isolated', despite the hysterical incantations to that effect. We could have continued benefiting from the Single Market under the existing Treaty arrangements – while still having to tolerate the CAP and the incursions of the European Court. The only *Götterdämmerung* was in the frenzied imaginations of panic-stricken Tory MPs.

The problem with John Major's alternative approach was that although it initially won plaudits, it left the fundamental problems unresolved. Under it, we would effectively abandon our attempts to win support for our alternative vision of the Community, going along with a new European framework which did not suit us, while relying on special exemptions which ultimately depended on the goodwill and fair dealing of people and institutions whose purposes

---

* See *The Downing Street Years*, pp. 724–5.

were radically different from ours. Arguably, the changed approach actually made our position worse by accepting important points of principle about the Union's future direction, for example by acceptance of the general objectives set out in Articles A and B, which will make it more difficult for Britain to argue for its own conception of Europe in the future.

As it turned out, Britain succeeded in negotiating two special 'opt-outs'. The first exempted Britain from the regulations on workplace and trade union rights contained in the 'Social Chapter', and the second allowed us to opt out of the third and final stage of monetary union. The Government was absolutely right to resist the social provisions, which would have increased business costs, reduced flexibility and competitiveness and destroyed jobs. But this exemption relates only to new provisions and not to other directives on social policy under the Treaty of Rome amended by the Single European Act. These still offer a means of imposing the high social costs of Germany and France on Britain by the back door. A particularly important example, which has indeed become a test case, is the June 1993 'working time' directive, which laid down a maximum forty-eight-hour week. This was introduced as a 'health and safety' measure under Article 118a to which qualified majority voting applies. The Government has mounted a legal challenge in the European Court. But the directives – whether on maternity leave or part-time employment – continue to flow. All of these measures would have one main effect – and arguably also have one main objective – namely, reducing the flexibility and competitiveness of British industry, to bring us into line with Europe.

Moreover, there is no doubt that the French, in particular, will do everything in their power to prevent transfers of investment and jobs to Britain because of our lower social costs. This was illustrated by the outraged French reaction to the decision by Hoover-Europe to transfer production of vacuum cleaners from Dijon to Cambuslang near Glasgow because, as the President of Hoover-Europe explained, in Scotland total remuneration costs were 37 per cent lower than in France. A large part of that difference reflects the cost of social benefits required by French law. What Britain regards as a desirable policy of keeping the burden of regulations and costs on business down the French denounce as 'social dumping'. In these circumstances, the pressure on Britain to accept regulations which will damage business will continue and intensify.

Similarly, the 'opt-out' on monetary union is less than meets the eye. It has only given us the right to opt out of the third stage of monetary union, not the first or second stages. The precise degree to which the first two stages of the process limit Britain's economic freedom in practice is debatable, though on any view it is considerable. Member states are required to 'regard their economic policies as a matter of common concern'; guidelines on economic policy are to be established by the Commission and the Council of Ministers, and member states are then to be monitored for compliance with those guidelines through a system called 'multilateral surveillance'. The Commission has acquired a power to monitor the public sector deficits of member states and to initiate procedures against the member state if it considers such a deficit to be 'excessive'. During the second stage of monetary union, member states must prepare their central banks for independence (as Britain has already begun to do) and adopt and adhere to a 'multi-annual convergence programme' designed to align currencies for eventual monetary union.

Finally, each member state is required to 'treat its exchange rate policy as a matter of common interest'. There is a danger that this will be interpreted by other member states and by the European institutions as imposing an obligation on Britain to rejoin the ERM and again to subordinate its monetary policy to the maintenance of an external parity. Although the effective shattering of the ERM in 1992/93 makes the future course of convergence towards EMU less predictable than at the time of the signing of Maastricht, the widened 15 per cent ERM bands are likely to be interpreted as being 'normal fluctuation margins' for the purposes of the Treaty's so-called 'convergence criteria'. This would permit an inner core of member states to proceed to the full currency union of Stage 3 with only limited slippage to the original timetable. And the basic problem with the British right to opt out of Stage 3 remains. Once an inner core had entered Stage 3 and formed an ECU currency bloc, Britain would come under strong political (and ultimately legal) pressure to maintain the pound's parity against the ECU in accordance with its continuing Stage 2 obligations, and so to follow ECU interest rates. And if some member states enter into full monetary union, Britain would have no seat on the European Central Bank Board which sets the interest rates we would be expected to follow. In these circumstances the temptation for Britain to go the whole hog and move to the third stage of monetary union would be very great. The Maastricht Treaty makes it clear that Stage 3 is 'irreversible', which means that we would, at least under Community law, have no right subsequently to withdraw and issue sterling again. That would be a fundamental and crucial loss of sovereignty and would mark a decisive step towards Britain's submergence in a European superstate.

The argument that this will never happen because the break-up of the ERM demonstrated the folly of fixed exchange rates in a turbulent world overlooks two important considerations. First, the history of the acceleration of moves towards federalism in Europe demonstrates that the federalists are not to be dissuaded by circumstances from pursuing their project: indeed, each blow to it only confirms them in their desire to move further and faster towards an irrevocable conclusion. Secondly, it would be possible to avoid much of the instability caused by speculative flows across the exchanges which caused the break-up of the ERM by moving directly to locked currencies and EMU. Of course, the consequences for the weaker national economies would be even more disastrous than they were as a result of overvalued currencies in the ERM. Large regional variations in economic activity, industrial decline and soaring unemployment on the periphery would follow in due course and these in turn would prompt heavy migration across frontiers.

But we would be brave to the point of foolhardiness to imagine that such consequences would necessarily lead to the abandonment of the venture. For such a favourable outcome would depend upon the health and responsibility of democratic institutions in Europe. But national political institutions are losing their powers to centralized European ones on which there is no real democratic check. In any case, it is an abdication of political leadership to expect hostile circumstances over which one has no control to relieve one of the responsibility of pursuing policies in the nation's long-term interest.

My dismay about Maastricht reflected my concern about its

effects internationally almost as much as the risks it posed to Britain. Although in the Bruges speech in 1988 I spoke about the distinctive strengths of British traditions and institutions, I was equally concerned about the effects on other European countries and on the outside world. Ultimately, of course, it is up to the Germans, French, Italians and others what kind of economic and political relations they want with each other. But anyone who does not sound the alarm on seeing great nations in headlong pursuit of disastrous goals is grossly irresponsible – and indeed a bad European.

It makes no sense for Germany to abandon the Deutschmark; nor for France to settle down permanently to playing second fiddle to its dominant eastern neighbour; nor for Italy to be distracted from the task of domestic political reform by looking to the European Union for solutions; nor for Spain, Portugal, Greece and Ireland to rely on subsidies from Germany in exchange for abandoning the opportunity to make the best of their lower labour costs; nor for the Scandinavian countries to export their high social costs to other European countries rather than cutting them back. As for the former communist countries of Central and Eastern Europe, how can they be expected to live with the high-cost regimes which the monetary and social policies of the Community would place upon them? It is difficult to see them being anything other than distant, poor relations of a Delors-style European Union. For the members of the Union, therefore, such a policy offers economic decline. For its neighbours it offers instability. For the rest of the world it provides a momentum towards protectionism.

For a treaty which threatens so much harm to all concerned, Maastricht has not even had the promised effect of uniting the Conservative Party. Indeed, it split the Conservative Party in Parliament and in the country, undermining confidence in the Government's sense of direction. Because the strategy of which it was a part rested essentially upon proving to our partners that Britain wished to be 'at the heart of Europe', it led directly to the unnecessarily deep recession caused by trying to maintain an unsustainable parity for sterling within the ERM. The humiliating circumstances of our departure added to the political damage to the Conservative Party. And all of the fundamental problems will surface again as we approach the 1996 Inter-Governmental Conference.

I could foresee enough of this in November 1991, even before the full details of Maastricht were known, to understand that I would have to oppose it root and branch. For the reasons I have already outlined, this was bound to be more embarrassing for all concerned if I remained in the House of Commons. Moreover, it seemed likely that the result of the general election, whenever it came, was likely to be a reduction in the large majority we had obtained in 1987. This would make it more difficult for me to speak and vote as I wanted. In any case, although I had taken the same seat on the backbenches that I had occupied some twenty-five years earlier – and I had enjoyed my time as a young backbencher – I now felt ill at ease. The enjoyment of the backbenches comes from being able to speak out freely. This, however, I knew would never again be possible. My every word would be judged in terms of support for or opposition to John Major. I would inhibit him just by my presence, and that in turn would inhibit me. So I decided to stand down as Member of Parliament for Finchley and accept a life peerage.

My mixed emotions about this were compensated by the happiness I felt in Denis's baronetcy. With the Conservative victory in the April 1992 general election, a result achieved in equal measure as a result of my record, John Major's admirable grit and the Labour Party's egregious errors, I felt newly liberated to continue the argument about Europe's future.

ANOTHER EUROPE

The Bill to implement the Maastricht Treaty was announced in the first Queen's Speech of the new Parliament. Ten days later, on Friday 15 May, I was due to speak in The Hague. My speech-writing team and I wrestled to include within one framework all the main elements of the alternative to a Maastricht-style Europe. I deliberately intended it as Bruges Mark II. Of course, I could not expect that it would have the same impact; after all, I was no longer a head of government. But for that very reason I hoped that the ideas could be developed more provocatively and would help to alert the more open-minded members of Europe's political élite to new possibilities.*

I began by likening the architecture of the Berlaymont building in Brussels – the home of the European Commission which was due to be demolished – to the political architecture of the European Community, 'infused with the spirit of yesterday's future'. Circumstances had so changed since the foundation of the Community that major rethinking was required. Looking back at its origins and development, I distinguished between two different economic traditions – those of liberalism and socialism. The time had now come when Europe had to choose between these two approaches. Maastricht's federalism was essentially the child of socialist thinking. It involved a degree of centralized control which the wider Europe created by the fall of communism made outdated. In fact, what was involved, I argued, was:

. . . a central intellectual mistake. [It was] assumed that the model for future government was that of a centralized bureaucracy that would collect information upwards, make decisions at the top, and then issue orders downwards. And what seemed the wisdom of the ages in 1945 was in fact a primitive fallacy. Hierarchical bureaucracy may be a suitable method of organizing a small business that is exposed to fierce external competition – but it is a recipe for stagnation and inefficiency in almost every other context.

. . The larger Europe grows, the more diverse must be the forms of cooperation it requires. Instead of a centralized bureaucracy, the model should be a market – not only a market of individuals and companies, but also a market in which the players are governments. Thus governments would compete with each other for foreign investments, top management and high earners through lower taxes and less regulation. Such a market would impose a fiscal discipline on governments because they would not want to drive away

* For the full text of the speech see Appendix 1, pp. 609–25.

expertise and business. It would also help to establish which fiscal and regulatory policies produced the best overall economic results. No wonder socialists don't like it. To make such a market work, of course, national governments must retain most of their existing powers in social and economic affairs. Since these governments are closer and accountable to their voters, it is doubly desirable that we should keep power at the national level.

On the basis of this analysis, I argued for two specific changes. The first conclusion I drew was that there was no reason why every new European initiative should require the participation of all Community members. If Europe did move into new areas, it must do so under separate treaties which clearly defined the powers which had been surrendered:

> We should aim at a multi-track Europe in which *ad hoc* groups of different states – such as the Schengen Group* – forge varying levels of cooperation and integration on a case-by-case basis. Such a structure would lack graph-paper neatness. But it would accommodate the diversity of post-communist Europe.

Second, far from giving the European Commission more power, it should have less. In fact, it was not needed in its present form and it should cease to be legislative in any sense; rather it should become an administrative body, not initiating policy but carrying it out.

Still more outrageously, I mentioned the issue which was on everyone's mind and no one's agenda in Europe, 'the German Question'. I expressed admiration for the German achievement and, indeed, agreement with several distinctive German policies, for example on monetary matters and on recognizing Slovenia and Croatia. But I argued that we had to face up to the fact that

---

* The Schengen Treaty has been signed and implemented by nine members of the European Union, providing for the removal of border controls between participating states.

the power of a reunited Germany was a problem. The Germans themselves realized this; it explained, for instance, why Chancellor Kohl and the German political establishment were so anxious for their country to be 'anchored' in Europe and restrained by institutions of federal decision-making. Tying the German Gulliver down within a federal European Community was no answer, however, because Germany's preponderance within it was so great that federalism itself augmented German power rather than contained it. In place of this vision, we had to return to the politics of the balance of power which would ensure that individual nation states, like Britain and France, would be able to act as a counterweight to Germany if it pursued policies which were against our interests. Meanwhile – and this was perhaps the most important element in any modern balance of power politics – the American military presence in Europe was a guarantee against any European power being tempted to assert its interests beyond a certain point.

This frank analysis was condemned in some quarters as anti-German. In fact, it was nothing of the sort. It was my firm conviction that it would be in Germany's interests as much as those of her neighbours for the realities of power politics to be reflected in diplomatic relations, rather than concealed behind a veil of federalist political correctness. Germany is a rich and powerful country in which there is much to admire. But because of its size, geographical location and history, it presents a problem. The Germans discuss this problem quite freely and responsibly (even if I happen to disagree with the particular solution they have found for it). There is no reason why we should not do the same.

As I had in Opposition all those years earlier, I found it easier to express even these controversial points about international relations abroad than at home. My every word in Britain was scrutinized for possibilities of misrepresentation. I was always conscious of the feeling, with which I could sympathize, that John Major should be left free to lead the Party and the country in his own way.

I made my maiden speech in the House of Lords in a debate on the UK Presidency of the European Community in July 1992. It was a slightly strange experience and I realized that it would take some time before I became used to the style of the Upper House, where formal courtesy and diplomatic consensus are so much more evident than anything that could be called lively debate. On this occasion, I was able to point to what I described as 'the very sharp change in attitudes' brought about by the Maastricht Treaty in Europe. The Danes had just voted in a referendum to reject the Treaty. Opinion in Germany had hardened against a single currency. The French were to hold their own referendum. Backbench Tory MPs had started to articulate the anti-Maastricht sentiments which were becoming more evident in their own constituencies.

But it was not until the autumn that events demolished far more effectively than I ever could the credibility of the European federalist project in the eyes of all but its most enthusiastic advocates. As 1992 progressed, the ERM came under increasing strain and the consequences of an overvalued exchange rate for Britain and other countries became more serious. Finally, on Wednesday 16 September, after an estimated £11,000 million pounds of reserves had been frittered away in a vain attempt to frustrate the intentions of the money markets, and after real interest rates reached a disastrous 8.4 per cent (with 11.4 per cent in prospect for the following day), sterling was withdrawn from the ERM. Panic was palpably in the air. Politicians and journalists behaved as if the Four Horsemen of the Apocalypse had just charged through the Bank of England. Government ministers sought to shift the blame for the crisis onto the Bundesbank. Commentators, unconvinced by this ploy, tried to shift it back onto the Government.

By a nice coincidence, I was due to address a CNN financial conference in Washington on the Saturday following the Wednesday ('black' or 'white', according to taste) on which Britain had left the ERM. I was staying at the British Embassy in Washington, working on my speech when the news came through. My original draft had to be abandoned, and my schedule of speaking engagements was so heavy that I found myself starting almost from scratch on the Friday evening. I worked through the night in a room down the corridor from where the Chancellor of the Exchequer, Norman Lamont, in town for the IMF Conference, was fast asleep. At least I heard no singing from the bath. He may have guessed what I was going to say:

It was not the collapse of the British Government's policy, but the policy itself which was the problem. It may be embarrassing to go back on a pledge to defend a particular exchange rate come hell or high water. But if the pledge was misguided in the first place, the act of breaking it should provoke a round of applause, not condemnation . . . Nor would I myself search for scapegoats – either inside or outside Britain. What we have to do is to learn the lessons of what has happened. The first and general lesson is that if you try to buck the market, the market will buck you. The state is not there to gamble with the nation's savings. Consequently, intervention in the exchange markets should be embarked upon with the greatest caution and within clearly understood limits. The second lesson is that the ERM in its present form, and with its present purpose, is a grave obstacle to economic progress. I do not myself believe that sterling should re-enter it and I have yet to be convinced that other currencies benefit from its combination of rigidity and fragility . . .

Since countries differ in their level of economic development and potential, their fiscal policies and their rates of inflation, the most flexible and realistic method of economic adjustment is a system of floating exchange rates. Each country can then order its monetary policy to suit its domestic conditions – and then there is no need for any ministerial shouting across the exchanges . . .

It is high time to make as complete a reversal of policy on Maastricht as has been done on the ERM. And of course the connection is very close, economically and politically. If the divergence between different European economies is so great that even the ERM cannot contain them, how would those economies react to a single European currency? The answer is that there would be chaos and resentment of the sort which would make the difficulties of recent days pale by comparison.

The Washington audience greeted this speech very warmly and the reaction even in the British media was favourable, if divergent at points: 'Mag-nanimous' said the *Sunday Express*, 'Maggie Gets

Her Revenge' said the *Mail on Sunday*. 'An elegant I told you so' said the BBC, splitting the difference.

But partly for reasons of injured pride and partly because so much political capital had been invested in the Maastricht project, the Government refused to rule out sterling's return to the ERM. At the time this refusal did not seem too significant. The circumstances of our departure from it convinced most Conservative MPs, a large majority of public opinion and, significantly, most of the financial world that pegged exchange rates were deeply damaging. It seemed that events themselves had ruled out a return to the ERM and therefore a formal undertaking was not needed. Almost overnight I found that the attitude towards my viewpoint had changed. I was 'right after all'. Unfortunately, by then the damage had been done – not least to the standing of the Government and the Conservative Party.

Appropriately enough, the pursuit of a policy towards Europe designed to comply with foreign rather than with domestic expectations had now led us into the extraordinary situation whereby the controversial Maastricht Bill's fate was itself determined by foreigners. Although the Irish, the Danes and the French were permitted referenda, the demand for one was consistently refused by the British Government. Yet it was made clear that if the French voted against Maastricht in their referendum, the Bill would not go ahead in Parliament. I had discreetly done what I could to encourage the anti-Maastricht campaign in France. I found it enormously encouraging that the three main right-of-centre opponents of Maastricht – Philippe de Villiers, Philippe Séguin and Charles Pasqua – were clearly among the most dynamic and charismatic French politicians, and that in spite of media bias their campaign quickly struck a chord with the immensely patriotic ordinary people of France. In the end, however, it was not quite enough, and by 50.95 per cent to 49.05 per cent the vote went in favour of Maastricht. And so if 269,706 French voters had voted against rather than for, Britain would never have implemented the Maastricht Treaty.

The European involvement in the agonies of ex-Yugoslavia provided in its way as devastating a commentary on Maastricht as did the collapse of the ERM. It will be recalled that Article B of the Maastricht Treaty envisaged a common European foreign and security policy leading to a common defence policy and perhaps common defence. A strengthened role for the Western European Union (WEU) was envisaged and a start on 'common defence' was made with the Franco-German 'Eurocorps'. And it was immediately realized, not least by the framers of Maastricht, that the crisis in ex-Yugoslavia on Europe's south-eastern border would be a crucial, indeed decisive, test of these aspirations. As Jacques Poos, Foreign Minister of Luxembourg, then heading the 'troika' of European foreign ministers responsible for directing the common foreign policy, graphically put it, this was 'the hour of Europe'. Setting out with his Dutch and Italian colleagues to mediate, he went on: 'If one problem can be solved by the Europeans, it is the Yugoslav problem. This is a European country and it is not up to the Americans. It is not up to anyone else.'*

Nor was it merely that the Europeans proved incapable of grasping, let alone altering, the realities of the war of aggression which Serbia and the communist-dominated Yugoslav national army were waging; Community diplomacy actually made the situation worse. The Community continued to support a policy of keeping Yugoslavia together long after it had become clear that what effectively amounted to a Serb *coup* against federal Yugoslav institutions had occurred. The Community 'monitors' became sucked into the complications of war and failed to denounce the aggressors clearly. Even when the Yugoslav army withdrew from Croatia it was allowed to station its heavily armed forces in Bosnia, the obvious next target for aggression. When an exasperated Germany finally insisted that Slovenia and Croatia be recognized at the start of 1992, against the wishes of most other Community members, the last nail was hammered into the coffin of an effective European foreign policy – let alone a common defence policy – based on consensus.

---

* Quoted in Mark Almond, *Europe's Backyard War* (London, 1994), p. 32.

A NEW BEGINNING

Not only have the economic and political aspirations of Maastricht
been discredited: a Government which started with a small but
satisfactory working majority has come perilously near on more
than one occasion to being forced into a general election as a result
of divisions on the issue on the Conservative benches. Since the
Maastricht Bill became law in the summer of 1993, an attempt has
been made to bridge divisions with a return to the rhetoric of
Euro-scepticism. The trouble is that rhetoric is not enough. We
now have to have a clearer strategic objective and a cleverer tactical
game plan than for Maastricht.

The essential starting-point for this is to weigh up honestly and
objectively our negotiating strengths and weaknesses. We should
not be under any illusion that we are 'winning the argument' in
Europe. It is deeply unpersuasive to say at one and the same time
that one subscribes to the objectives of one's partners, while trying
to change them. In any case, argument is of little importance in
European Community decision-making. While France, Germany
and a sufficient number of other Community members remain
intent on federalism, expositions of the virtues of the alternative
are, for immediate practical purposes, wasted effort. This situation
will not necessarily last for ever. But it would be altogether unrealistic to assume that the balance will alter between now and 1996.

It is equally necessary to learn from experience. Ever since
Britain joined the EEC we have seen European institutions, supported by other European governments, placing a systematically
different interpretation on texts than those which we accepted.
From 'ever closer union' in the Treaty of Rome, to 'economic and
monetary union' endorsed as the official objective at the Paris European Council in October 1972,* to the Single European Act where
the new majority voting provisions intended solely to implement

---

* My concern with this wording led to my having it glossed with the phrase
'cooperation in economic and monetary policy' in the text of the Single European
Act.

the Single Market were used by the Commission to extend its regulatory powers, our experience has been the same. Vague declarations, which we assumed at the time had no practical implication, are subsequently cited to justify the extension of Community powers into fresh areas of national life. Consequently, in judging whether further verbal concessions to federalism should be made in the Maastricht negotiations, we had no excuse for naivete about the extent to which they would be exploited and indeed twisted. Maastricht was a treaty too far. Even without Maastricht, moreover, it would have been necessary to revise some aspects of earlier agreements, going right back to the Treaty of Rome, if the unwelcome momentum was to be resisted.

This is especially relevant to the activities of the European Court of Justice. Most of us, including myself, paid insufficient regard to the issue of sovereignty in consideration of the case for joining the EEC at the beginning of the 1970s. There was, of course, a basic intellectual confusion, when phrases about 'pooling sovereignty' were used, resting on what Noel Malcolm has described as the failure 'to make any distinction between power and authority'.*

But beyond that there was a failure to grasp the true nature of the European Court and the relationship which would emerge between British law and Community law. The latter is directly applied through the courts of member states which, in the event of a conflict, are bound to give Community law, as interpreted by the European Court, precedence over domestic law. This was demonstrated by the *Factortame* case, brought against Britain by Spanish fishermen who had found a legal loophole by which they could register their ships in Britain and make use of British fishing quotas, thus thwarting the intentions of the Common Fisheries Policy. In 1988 Parliament passed a Merchant Shipping Act to close the loophole, but the subsequent litigation went against the British Government and resulted in the suspension and ultimate

* Noel Malcolm, *Sense on Sovereignty* (Centre for Policy Studies, November 1991), p. 10: 'The central fault is that they fail to make any distinction between power and authority. That distinction is the basis of all legal understanding: if you do not have the concept of authority as something different from mere power, then you cannot have the concept of law as anything other than the mere application of force.'

setting aside of the Act by the British courts, following reference of the case to the European Court.

What makes this legal situation all the more significant is that the European Court is a far from impartial interpreter of the treaties and Community laws. It makes no bones about being a force for European integration. Its opportunities for extending the powers of Community institutions are still greater under Maastricht. Above all, it will be for the Court to decide on the reality of the opt-outs on monetary union and the Social Chapter which the Prime Minister obtained for Britain. Its past attitudes and activities give little cause for comfort.

Against all these difficulties, however, Britain has even more important negotiating strengths, as long as we are prepared to use them to the full. The first and most important is our trading position and opportunities. Our trade balance with the Community has been consistently in deficit. Not that there is anything wrong with that in itself. But it does establish that other EC members have a clear interest in continuing trading with us and so puts into perspective the exaggerated fear that if we do not comply with their wishes, they will find ways to cut us off from their markets.

In addition, the European Community's relative importance as regards both world trade and Britain's global trading opportunities is diminishing and will continue to diminish. Our politicians should become less concerned with European markets, whose most dramatic expansion has probably now been achieved, and more interested in the new opportunities emerging in the Far East, Latin America and the North American Free Trade Area. The disposition of Britain's massive portfolio of overseas assets – over £1,300 billion in 1993 – provides an insight into the judgement of the private sector on this question: over 80 per cent are held in countries outside the EC, and the proportion in the emerging markets is expanding vigorously. The share of our total trade with countries outside the EC, and particularly with the Pacific Rim, is increasing and will continue to do so.

Moreover, although some of the investment which comes to Britain doubtless does so because we are within the European Community, investment will also increasingly go elsewhere than to

Europe because of the EU's regulatory inflexibilities and high social costs. Both by tradition and because of the pre-eminent position of the City of London as an international financial centre, Britain is naturally a global rather than a Continental trading country. But we need to retain the right to hold down our industrial costs if we are to compete successfully in the new global market. None of this is to say that we should lightly pick quarrels with our European neighbours. But it does suggest that we must stop speaking as if Britain's economic future primarily depended upon proving ourselves to be 'good Europeans'.

Secondly, it is also important to recognize the important non-economic strengths Britain possesses, which give us a special weight in European negotiations. In spite of the present chill in relations between the US Administration and the British Government, the 'special relationship', depending as it does upon shared experience, traditions and sentiments, is still an important underlying reality. My own experience of Anglo-American relations in the run-up to the Gulf War convinces me that, whatever the calculations of officials in the US State Department or the British Foreign Office, when serious work has to be done we all know that the US can rely only upon a handful of well-established nation states with a global outlook and a willingness to uphold international order. That means, principally, ourselves and the French; and the French, though they played a gallant part in the Gulf War, have generally been suspicious of American-led ventures. The Anglo-American relationship is itself, of course, closely linked to the unchallenged predominance of English as the language of the twenty-first century. There are, therefore, good strategic reasons for shrewd Continental European statesmen to wish to keep a mutually satisfactory, or at least tolerable, relationship with us.

Finally, our partners should not assume that we will always want to sign an agreement in the end. Although we prefer cooperation, we should be quite prepared to be very un-cooperative indeed. If there are attempts to steamroller us into further steps towards federalism, or indeed if our demands for revision of existing arrangements which have worked against us are ignored, we must be prepared to exercise our veto and resolutely use all avenues of non-cooperation open to us under the existing treaties. We have reached the point at which a Gaullist mantle may fall fittingly on Anglo-Saxon shoulders.

Years of fighting for Britain's interests at successive European Councils, not least at my final Rome Council in October 1990, caution me against believing that it will be simple, let alone easy, to achieve a successful outcome in 1996. The pressures will be applied in different ways and from different quarters well in advance. The proposals from the German CDU in September 1994 for a 'hard core' of European states committed to monetary union demonstrate that the process of softening up has already begun – though, as I shall suggest, the concept of a 'two tier' Europe should certainly not be dismissed out of hand. In the detailed negotiations it will be important to combine tactics and toughness in order to achieve the best outcome for Britain. But even at this stage it is important to spell out just what such an outcome would be.

All but a small minority of convinced Euro-federalists recognized that Britain's entry to the European Economic Community involved a balance of advantages and disadvantages. Although strategic considerations were not without weight when the frontier of communism cut through the centre of Europe, this balance was essentially economic, as the EEC's name suggests. On the one hand, we gained unhindered access to a large Western European market which we envisaged would develop both as our economies grew and as policies of internal free trade prevailed. On the other side of the ledger, we would be large net contributors to the Community budget which reflected the disproportionate costs of the Common Agricultural Policy. We were aware that France's inclination towards subsidies and protection threatened to push the EEC in the wrong direction; but we blithely thought that these could be restrained and perhaps reversed. More seriously, we did not foresee the impulse towards centralized decision-making as a result of the ambitions of the Commission, nor the spread of interventionist social regulation from Brussels, nor the scale of the challenge to parliamentary sovereignty and to the law of the United Kingdom. How can the balance of advantage be tilted back in Britain's interests?

The initial step requires only the bare minimum of consultation or negotiation with our European partners and should not be delayed. It is not good enough to say that the issue of whether we are prepared to abandon the pound sterling and sign up to a single European currency is simply one for the future. To make such a decision at any time would be to take the heart out of democracy by removing (in theory at least 'irreversibly') the central aspects of economic policy from the control of the British Government. Certainly, such a far-reaching decision should not be contemplated without a referendum. Still better, if the Government were now to declare against a single currency, that would both reassure the public and demonstrate our principled dissent from the federalist objectives of most other European governments. Similarly, it should be made clear that there is no question of sterling's return to the ERM or any successor system. To make such statements now would both lead the rest of the Community to take us more seriously and increase the pressure for other governments to reveal their hands to their electorates. It would also do no end of good in restoring support for the Conservative Party.

It is also necessary to clarify our attitude towards the project of a 'two tier' Europe in which the inner bloc embraces economic and monetary union, a high degree of social regulation and common foreign, security and defence policies. The immediate reaction in Britain to this project was hostile, but for a variety of sometimes confused and even mutually contradictory reasons. Some critics view it as a further unacceptable step towards a federal Europe whose agenda is dominated by the Franco-German axis. But others oppose it because they hanker after Britain being part of that 'hard core', for example on defence matters. In neither internal nor external European relations, however, is it in our interests to subordinate our autonomy further; in fact the reverse. There should certainly be no question of placing our defence decision-making under European control. The proper – indeed the only militarily practicable – international framework for this is NATO.

But the new situation also provides us with an opportunity. It is essential to make clear that if we were to permit amendments to the existing treaty framework which would allow the proposed development to go ahead, then our own interests would have to be accommodated. If there were an attempt to construct such a 'hard core' without respecting our fundamental views and interests, then we should be fully justified in pursuing every measure of obstruction and disruption open to us. An absolutely essential requirement would be to ensure that the 'hard core' countries were not able to impose on other members their own priorities on questions, like the operation of the Single Market, where their interests might well turn out to be different from ours. The price of our agreement to changes which those countries seek might further include the unbundling of a number of provisions in existing treaties which work to our disadvantage and, incidentally, to that of other member states.

An obvious priority involves addressing Britain's financial contributions to the European Union. In any case, it is difficult to see how the present Common Agricultural Policy (CAP) could continue if the Central and Eastern European countries where agriculture remains of considerable importance are admitted to full membership, as is eminently desirable. The CAP is not only a financial drain; it also significantly increases food prices above general international levels and so increases labour and business costs. It would be open for debate what, if anything, should be put in its place to support British farming. Similarly, the so-called 'Cohesion Fund' designed to compensate the weaker economies for the financial and monetary rigours envisaged by Maastricht should be another target for revision.

Secondly, we should try to reverse the growing protectionism of the European Community, which almost derailed the GATT round, and significantly reduced its scope, and which costs Britain wealth and jobs. Unfortunately, the protectionist mentality is only likely to grow as increased costs, resulting from Community social policy and lack of labour market flexibility, reduce the ability of industries in Europe to compete successfully. Yet the European Union can afford such protectionism less than ever because of the shift of advantage from Europe to the Americas. This has been well observed by Professor Patrick Messerlin:

Until recently, the US had no serious alternatives to a trade policy based on GATT disciplines . . . The situation will be reversed in the decades to come. The US – with South American countries opening their borders and boosting their growth

– will enjoy the relaxation that regional opportunities can offer. By contrast, the EU has exhausted its capacity to expand regional trade in a significant way for a long time to come. The EU – bordered on its southern and eastern flanks by countries unconvinced of the gains from freer trade, or too small to bring substantial benefits to the EU – will be in the same position, in this respect, as the US in the 1950s and 1960s.

The EU has only one route left. It must move the GATT from the periphery to the centre of its trade policies.*

If this does not happen – and worse if, as I have suggested, it moves further towards protectionism – Britain will be the worst affected. That is why it is so important that we should work to establish special arrangements between the European Community and the North American Free Trade Area.

What we need here is something like a North *Atlantic* Free Trade Area, which would incorporate the emerging market democracies of Central and Eastern Europe as well as the EU itself. It would have a number of important economic and political benefits. First, it would provide unimpeded access for Britain and other European countries to the rapidly expanding markets of the Americas. All the same arguments used to justify our entry into the EEC in the early 1970s and then the creation of the Single Market in the mid to late 1980s – namely the expansion of trade opportunities – apply here. Secondly, by involving the Americans, with their tradition of free enterprise and open trade, in the new transatlantic trading framework we would shift the balance away from the Continental European emphasis on subsidies and protection – to Britain's advantage. Within such a grouping we would be less likely to be a lone voice for free markets. Thirdly, the establishment of closer economic relations between Europe and America would help underpin NATO, whose *raison d'être* has been called into question by the end of the Cold War. A North Atlantic Free Trade Area

* Patrick Messerlin, 'Why such Blindness? European Union Trade Policy at the Crossroads', in *Trade Policy Review* (Centre for Policy Studies, September 1994) p. 46.

would help create the conditions for a continued American commitment to Europe's defence, while reassuring other European countries concerned about the predominance of Germany. Finally, the new Free Trade Area would be the most powerful – but also the most liberal – bloc within the GATT. As such, it would be able to insist that the global trend was towards free trade rather than protectionism. Britain is well placed to argue on both sides of the Atlantic for such an approach; moreover, our particular interests and identity as an outward-looking, open trading nation with a traditional commitment to strong links with America would be well served by it.

Finally, in planning the route to 1996 we cannot continue to ignore the erosion of our parliamentary sovereignty. As Lord Denning has said:

No longer is European law an incoming tide flowing up the estuaries of England. It is now like a tidal wave bringing down our sea walls and flowing inland over our fields and houses – to the dismay of all.

How precisely the British Constitution – which is what is ultimately at stake – can be protected against this 'tidal wave' needs now to be considered. Certainly, it can only be done by the explicit exercise of parliamentary sovereignty; moreover, the sooner the initiative is wrested from the European Court so as to clarify British judicial thinking, the better. There is a strong case for amending the 1972 European Communities Act to establish the ultimate supremacy of Parliament over all Community law, making clear that Parliament can *by express provision* override Community law.

Britain would not be alone among Community countries in protecting the ultimate supremacy of its domestic law. Germany, for example, does not acknowledge the power of Community law to override its constitutional law, as the Federal Constitutional Court made clear in the Maastricht Treaty case. France likewise maintains the ultimate supremacy of its constitutional law, and its *conseil d'état* evolved doctrines and procedures which limit the practical application of Community law in cases where the interests of the French state so require.*

We in Britain should also set out rules relating to conflicts between Community law and Acts of Parliament which unintentionally arise (as in the *Factortame* case), and establish a procedure whereby an Act unintentionally in conflict with Community law can be suspended by Order in Council where necessary rather than by the courts, so discouraging the drift in court decisions and judicial thinking towards narrowing the scope of parliamentary sovereignty. There should be a reserve list of protected matters where Parliament alone can legislate, to include our constitutional arrangements and defence. Finally, we should take reserve powers, exercisable by Order in Council, to enable us in the last resort to prevent specific Community laws and decisions taking effect in the United Kingdom.** These various powers would, one imagines, be used very sparingly; but their very existence would act as a disincentive to European encroachments. But the debate about how rather than whether such actions should be taken is overdue.

It is not possible to predict precisely where this process of negotiation would end. Whether Britain would be part of an outer tier Community membership, whether we would have some kind of association agreement similar to that enjoyed for years by the European Free Trade Area (EFTA) countries, and later by the European Economic Area (EEA) countries, or whether the European Union would be transmuted into a series of bilateral or multilateral agreements between countries under new treaties in some version of 'variable geometry' – all of these are possibilities.

In any case, it is not the form but the substance which is important. What is clear is that a point has been reached – indeed it was reached even before Maastricht – at which the objectives and

* For example, in the Cohn-Bendit case (1978), 1 CMLR 543, where the *conseil d'état* simply disregarded previous decisions of the European Court of Justice, decided that Community law could not be invoked in this case affecting public order, and quashed a decision of the lower court to refer the case to the European Court of Justice.
** I am indebted to Martin Howe both for these suggestions, made in his pamphlet *Europe and the Constitution After Maastricht* (Society of Conservative Lawyers, June 1992), and for other helpful and stimulating suggestions which have influenced my thinking on these matters.

perceived interests of the different members of the Community
radically differ. A clear understanding that this is so and that our
strategy for 1996 must be planned accordingly is the essential foundation for success.

Nor do I believe that such an approach is incompatible with the
long-term interests of other European countries. If it is allowed to
continue on its present course the European Union will fail at all
levels. It will exclude the post-communist countries of Central and
Eastern Europe by imposing conditions for entry which they will
not be able to fulfil. It will condemn the south European countries
to debilitating dependency on hand-outs from German taxpayers.
It will be a force for protectionism and instability in the wider
world.

If the Franco-German bloc decides to go ahead with the re-
creation of a modern equivalent of the Carolingian Empire, that is
its choice. The consequences will almost certainly be traumatic. In
a world of re-awakened nationalism it is hard to imagine French-
men accepting in perpetuity their country's relegation to being a
German satellite – any more than it is easy to conceive German
taxpayers providing ever greater subsidies for failing regions of
foreign countries, as well as housing, health and other benefits
for immigrants driven by economic necessity across Germany's
borders, and losing the assurance of the Deutschmark to boot. All
this against the background of a shrinking share of world trade
and wealth, as investment and jobs moved away from Europe. At
some point, the electorates of those countries will rebel against
policies which condemn them to economic disruption, rule by
remote bureaucracies and the loss of independence.

There is only a limited amount that Britain can do alone to
prevent these unwelcome developments. But it is not inappropriate
to quote the aspiration of Pitt the Younger to the effect that Britain
'has saved herself by her exertions, and will . . . save Europe by
her example'. In the meantime, the best service which can be done
by those committed to the ideals I set out at Bruges – of freely
cooperating nation states which relish free enterprise and welcome
free trade – is to gather together all those politicians, jurists, economists, writers and commentators from the different European
states to relaunch a movement for transatlantic cooperation includ-

ing a wider Europe and the Americas. As I urged at the end of the
Bruges speech:

Let us have a Europe which plays its full part in the wider
world, which looks outward not inward, and which preserves
that Atlantic community – that Europe on both sides of the
Atlantic – which is our noblest inheritance and our greatest
strength.

CHAPTER XIV

New World Disorder

Foreign policy and defence

EUPHORIA PUNCTURED

By contrast with European Community affairs, the overall path of events in foreign policy at the time I left office continued initially much as I would have wished. That may seem strange, even callous, in view of the fact that preparations were under way for a war in the Gulf whose exact course we could not predict. Yet I was convinced that the action taken was both right and necessary and that the West or, as we tactfully preferred to describe it, 'the international community', would prevail over Saddam Hussein and reverse Iraq's aggression against Kuwait. Moreover, the crisis had led to a re-establishment of that vital 'special relationship' between the United States and Britain which I regarded as central to my approach.

Of greater long-term importance, however, was the end of the Cold War, or again more precisely if less tactfully, the defeat of Soviet communism in that great conflict, without which indeed the relatively smooth passage of events in the Gulf would have been impossible. I had unsuccessfully resisted the reunification of Germany. But the course of events which led to the landslide victory of Solidarity in the Polish elections of June 1989, the fall of the Berlin Wall that November, the overthrow of the Ceausescus in Romania in December, the election of Vaclav Havel as President of a free Czechoslovakia in the same month, and the victory of non-communists in elections in Hungary in April 1990 – these I regarded as tangible and profoundly welcome results of the policies which Ronald Reagan and I had pursued unremittingly through the 1980s. And I had no doubt that the momentum was sufficient for the process to continue, for the time being at least. Where that would leave Central and Eastern Europe and the Soviet Union it was as yet impossible precisely to say. I knew enough of the complex history of these regions to understand that the risks of ethnic strife and possible attempts to change borders were real. At least the rejuvenated Conference on Security and Cooperation in Europe (CSCE), the result of the Helsinki process, could provide, we then thought, a useful diplomatic framework for resolving disputes. Events have, however, disappointed us.

I had seen for myself in Ukraine how strongly the nationalist tide was flowing against the old Soviet Union.* As I told Jacques Delors at the outset of that final European Council I attended, I did not believe that it was for West Europeans to pronounce upon the future shape of the Soviet Union or its successors – that was for the democratic choice of the peoples concerned.** But the fact that I did not believe we could see into the future, let alone be confident in shaping it, did not diminish my satisfaction at the changes which were taking place. Millions of subjects of the Soviet Empire and its client states who had been deprived of their basic rights were now living in free democracies. And these new democracies had abandoned their aggressive military alliance, armed with nuclear weapons, against the West. These were great human and security gains. Neither then nor later did I feel any nostalgia for the diplomatically simpler but deadly dangerous Cold War era.

The increasing preoccupation of a weakened, fitfully reforming Soviet Union with its own huge internal problems enabled other regional conflicts to be resolved. The ending of Soviet-backed subversion in Africa meant that reformers in South Africa had a new opportunity to reach agreement about that country's future. In fact, whether it was in Africa or the Middle East, in Central or South America, in the Indian sub-continent or in Indo-China, the end of the Soviet pursuit of a long-term strategy of global dominance opened the way for progress. Suppressed desires for political

* I have described this visit in *The Downing Street Years*, pp. 806–7.
** *The Downing Street Years*, p. 767.

and economic freedom were brought to bear on corrupt and oppressive regimes which could no longer argue for support from Moscow (or indeed from Washington) lest they go over to the other side.

An old world order – a bi-polar world divided between the Soviet Union and the West and their respective allies – had passed away. But had a new world order been born? Certainly, there was a temptation in the immediate aftermath of the collapse of communism to believe so. And statements welcoming it can be quoted from across the political spectrum. In retrospect, however, it can be seen that two quite different visions obtained. My own view of it was a *Pax Americana* in the camouflage of United Nations Resolutions. This would require strong US leadership, the staunch support of allies, and a clear strategic concept that distinguished between real threats to Western interests and international order on the one hand, and local disputes with limited consequences on the other. I still think that this prudent approach could have created a durable international order without open-ended obligations. Unfortunately, it became confused with a more messianic, and consequently less practical, concept of a world order based on universal action through multilateral agencies untainted by strategic self-interest. This is, of course, a more idealistic vision; but as Macaulay remarked: 'An acre in Middlesex is worth a principality in Utopia.'

Even in the days after the Gulf War when euphoria about the possibilities of the New World Order was at its height, I was left feeling uneasy. I suspected that too much faith was being put in high-flown international declarations and too little attention paid to the means of enforcing them. Oddly enough, it was in preparing for my visit to South Africa in May 1991 that I started to read more deeply about the ill-starred League of Nations, one of whose principal architects was the South African Jan Smuts. The rhetoric of that time struck me as uncannily like that which I was now hearing. Similarly, Smuts' own conclusion, when the League had failed to take action against the dictators and so prepared the way for the Second World War, struck me as equally damning of the kind of collective security upon which the future of post-Cold War stability and freedom was supposed to be based: 'What was everybody's business in the end proved to be nobody's business. Each one looked to the other to take the lead, and the aggressors got away with it.'

Of course, it could be argued that the situation now was different. After all, Saddam Hussein had not 'got away with it' – though he did 'get away'. But I thought it of vital importance to understand why this had been achieved. It was because, contrary to the experience of the League of Nations, America had asserted herself as the international superpower it was her destiny to be, and self-confident and well-armed nation states such as Britain and France had acted in support, that success was obtained in the Gulf. Yet there were all too many commentators and politicians prepared to deduce quite the opposite – namely that the United Nations should *itself* become a supra-national force, with the authority and the resources to intervene at will, and that nation states should accordingly abandon their sovereignty. The UN's ambitions to become a world government would only, if encouraged, lead to world disorder. But with much subtlety and to considerable effect, left-liberal opinion in the West was able, with the naive collaboration of many conservatives, to turn the circumstances arising from the end of the Cold War to its own advantage.

I spoke out against these trends in a speech to UN Ambassadors in New York in September 1991. I defended the 'new nationalism' which was apparent among the constituent peoples of the Soviet Union and Central and Eastern Europe. This was itself, I argued, a reaction against the tyranny of communism; most of those who embraced it were convinced democrats; and, to the extent that there was a risk of excesses, these should be seen as proof that attempts to suppress national identity were both bound to fail and would result in even stronger national passions when they eventually did fail. That had important implications for the future of the UN.

True internationalism will always consist of cooperation *between* nations: that's what the word means. And similarly, the United Nations, which embodies the highest aspirations of internationalism, reminds us by its very name of its true purpose. The starting-point for all your deliberations is that you represent *nations*. Your often elusive goal is that they should be united in some common purpose. But unity of *purpose* – not union – is the objective.

In fact, by the time I spoke in New York it was already becoming apparent that all was not well with the New World Order. I was deeply concerned about the West's failure to see what was at stake in the former Yugoslavia, where Slovenia's and Croatia's bids for freedom from the oppressive impoverishment of communism were being challenged by armed force. For me, rights of national self-determination and self-defence (indeed human rights more generally) lay at the heart of any just international order – and, at least as important, of any stable international order. Stability is a conservative value in foreign policy: anyone who doubts that should be given a one-way ticket to Mogadishu. But stability should not be used as an excuse for upholding a *status quo* that is itself inherently unstable because it suppresses social forces that cannot ultimately be contained.

It is perhaps significant that on each of the three occasions when I felt compelled, since leaving office, to intervene publicly on the subject of foreign affairs (other than as regards Europe), it has been my conviction that *both* moral and practical considerations required a change of approach. The first was when in April 1991 I was moved by what I heard from Kurdish women, who came to beg me to speak out in order to gain relief for their compatriots bearing the brunt of Saddam Hussein's merciless attacks. Parliament was in recess and there was no minister available to see them. I am glad to say that – doubtless coincidentally – action was subsequently taken at least to set up safe havens.

The second occasion was when, on the occasion of the *coup* in the Soviet Union in August 1991, I was dismayed by the willingness of some Western leaders apparently to 'wait and see' whether the *coup* leaders were successful, rather than give full moral support to the resistance gathered around Boris Yeltsin at the Russian White House. So, as soon as I had checked what had happened, I held a press conference outside my Great College Street office and went on to give a succession of interviews.

I said that it was quite clear that what had happened in Moscow was unconstitutional and that the Russian people should now take their lead from Boris Yeltsin as the leading democratically elected politician. In this new and dangerous situation our own planned defence cuts must not now go ahead. But I warned against assuming that the *coup* would be successful. The Soviet people had now developed a taste for democracy and would be reluctant to lose it. They should protect democracy by acting as the peoples of Central and Eastern Europe had done – by taking to the streets and making their views known.

The following morning it was already starting to become clear that my optimism that the *coup* would not succeed was being borne out by events. The news was of huge protest rallies in Leningrad and Moscow. I thought it was worth trying to speak directly by telephone to Mr Gorbachev who, according to the *coup* leaders, had had to step down 'for reasons of health'. But I was hardly surprised when the Soviet Ambassador told me this was impossible. I had assumed that telephone contact would have been cut off by the KGB – though in this I soon learned I had overestimated the *coup* leaders' competence. Later in the day the Conservative MEP Lord Bethell, a great expert on Russian matters, contacted my office to say that he had with him Mrs Galina Staravoitova, an adviser to Mr Yeltsin on a visit to London. I immediately asked them to come in and brief me. I related how I had failed to make contact with President Gorbachev. Mrs Staravoitova then asked me whether I would like to speak to Mr Yeltsin instead. After searching through her handbag, she came up with the number for the direct line to his office in the Parliament building and after several failed attempts – to my astonishment – I was put through.

Mr Yeltsin and I spoke for some time, with Lord Bethell translating. It was clear that the outlook from the besieged White House was grim but also that Mr Yeltsin and his supporters were in good heart. He asked me if I would chair a commission of doctors to investigate the truth about Mr Gorbachev's allegedly poor health, which had every appearance of a classic Soviet diplomatic illness. Of course I agreed, and the rest of the day was spent in cooperation with the Foreign Office and the Department of Health trying to compile a suitable list of distinguished doctors. Luckily, it proved unnecessary, for the *coup* by now was crumbling fast.

I was duly denounced in the press by British Government 'sources' for my call to the Russians to come out into the streets to stop the *coup*, and for my call to our politicians to stop Western defence cuts. But I had no regrets. Democracy has to be fought for and if necessary died for; and indeed three brave young men did die for it. Their sacrifice is remembered by Russians today.

But the issue on which my view and that of the Western foreign policy establishments differed most was Bosnia. What seemed to me so tragic was that, like anyone else who had bothered to follow events – and I was regularly briefed both by British experts and by others from the region – I could see the preparations for Serbia's war of aggression against Bosnia being made. The West's feeble and unprincipled response to the earlier war against Croatia made it almost inevitable. Indeed, with Western acquiescence the Yugoslav army was able to withdraw its heavy armour from Croatia into Bosnia.

I was working on Volume I of my memoirs with my advisers in Switzerland in August 1992 when I learned that Bosnian Vice-President Ejup Ganić wanted to see me: he was desperately trying to summon help from abroad for Bosnia, having slipped out of Sarajevo.

Because of the privations of Sarajevo, I had laid out a substantial afternoon tea for our meeting. To my surprise he refused all food as he gave me a thorough briefing on the political and military situation. But when I went into my study to telephone the Foreign Office to arrange a meeting for him, my colleagues again pressed him to eat something – whereupon he wolfed down several sandwiches at a go. He then explained to them that, having lived in an underground bunker for months with little to eat, he had not trusted himself to eat politely in front of me.

What he told me confirmed all that I had heard and read, and I now decided that it was my moral duty to act. I would take the highest-profile initiative I could, but focusing on the United States – for after many fruitless conversations with the Foreign Office I despaired of a hearing in Britain. In the *New York Times* and on American television I sought to awaken the conscience of the West by arguing that by doing nothing we were acting as accomplices. But I also covered the strict practicalities.

It is argued by some that nothing can be done by the West unless we are prepared to risk permanent involvement in a Vietnam- or Lebanon-style conflict and potentially high Western casualties. That is partly alarmism, partly an excuse for inertia. There is a vast difference between a full-scale land invasion like Desert Storm, and a range of military interventions from halting the arms embargo on Bosnia, through supplying arms to Bosnian forces, to direct strikes on military targets and communications.

Even if the West passes by on the other side, we cannot expect that others will do so. There is increasing alarm in Turkey and the Muslim world. More massacres of Muslims in Bosnia, terrible in themselves, would also risk the conflict spreading.

Serbia has no powerful outside backers, such as the Soviet Union in the past. It has up to now been encouraged by Western inaction, not least by explicit statements that force would not be used. A clear threat of military action would force Serbia into contemplating an end to its aggression. Serbia should be given an ultimatum to comply with certain Western demands:

- Cessation of Serbia's economic support for the war in Bosnia, to be monitored by international observers placed on the Serb-Bosnian border.
- Recognition of Bosnia's independence and territorial integrity by Belgrade and renunciation of territorial claims against it.
- Guarantees of access from Serbia and Bosnia for humanitarian teams.
- Agreement to the demilitarization of Bosnia within a broader demilitarization agreement for the whole region.
- Promise of cooperation with the return of refugees to Bosnia.

If those demands (which should be accompanied by a deadline) are not met, military retaliation should follow, including aerial bombardment of bridges on the Drina linking Bosnia with Serbia, of military convoys, of gun positions around Sarajevo and Goražde, and of military stores and other installations useful in the war. It should also be made clear that while this is not a war against the Serbian people, even installations on the Serbian side of the border may be attacked if they play an important role in the war . . .

Serbia will not listen unless forced to listen. Only the prospect of resistance and defeat will lead to the rise of a more democratic and peaceful leadership. Waiting until the conflict burns itself out will be not only dishonourable but also very costly: refugees, terrorism, Balkan wars drawing in other countries, and worse.*

For a short while it looked as if the argument might be won. I believe that within the White House, the State Department and the Pentagon there was some genuine reassessment of strategy. But then the military and foreign policy establishments recovered sufficiently to offer any number of reasons why large-scale intervention by ground troops (which I had never suggested) was too risky, why the arms embargo on Bosnia must stay (which ensured that the victims were deprived of self-defence) and why air strikes would not be effective (possibly true on their own, but plainly false if conducted in support of well-armed Bosnian forces as a means of altering the military balance).

Since the summer of 1992 there has been some movement in the direction I urged, but too little and far too late. Very limited air strikes under absurd restraints have occurred, but always against the background of protestations of the reluctance of the UN and NATO to go further. As a result of American pressure, there is some possibility of the arms embargo on Bosnia being lifted – but not before the moderate Muslim leadership had been forced into dangerously close reliance on Islamic powers such as Iran in the absence of Western help. Above all, whereas in August 1992 there was no official Russian involvement, the Russian government has now become a major player in the deadly game, thus raising the

* *New York Times*, 6 August 1992. Copyright © 1992 by The New York Times Company. Reprinted by permission.

stakes in precisely the way I feared. Finally, British troops and the other forces in the United Nations Protection Force (UNPROFOR) are stationed in vulnerable situations in Bosnia, potential hostages to the Serbs if the West does at last become serious. The shameful failure in Bosnia has not only diminished our credibility and moral stature: it has now precipitated the most serious breach in NATO since Suez.

It is, though, important to regard the Bosnian fiasco as a symptom and not just a cause. There was an almost unreal quality about much discussion of international affairs over the whole of this period which was characterized by the rise and fall of the concept of a 'New World Order'. The foreign policy thinkers were still engaging in arguments about whether 'history' (in the Hegelian sense) had 'ended' – whether we had reached, in the words of Francis Fukuyama's stimulating essay, 'the end point of mankind's ideological evolution and the universalization of Western liberal democracy as the final form of government'.*

In contrast to Mr Fukuyama's thesis has been the later prediction by Samuel Huntington that international politics will henceforth be dominated by a 'clash of civilizations' with the 'world [being] shaped in large measure by the interactions among seven or eight major civilizations . . . [in which] the most important conflicts of the future will occur along the cultural fault lines separating these civilizations from one another'.**

The sense of unreality was emphasized by the contrast between these ambitious concepts of the intellectuals on the one hand and the hesitancy of the practitioners on the other. It was increasingly clear that the end of the Cold War – and only two years passed between the fall of the Berlin Wall and the official obsequies over

---

* Francis Fukuyama, 'The End of History?', *The National Interest*, Summer 1989. In the many subsequent debates it was sometimes forgotten that Mr Fukuyama had qualified his provocative assertion as follows: 'This is not to say that there will no longer be events to fill the pages of *Foreign Affairs*'s yearly summaries of international relations, for the victory of liberalism has occurred primarily in the realm of ideas or consciousness and is as yet incomplete in the real or material world. But there are powerful reasons for believing that it is the ideal that will govern the material world *in the long run.*'
** Samuel P. Huntington, 'The Clash of Civilisations?', *Foreign Affairs*, Summer 1993.

the Soviet Union – had left Western politicians disoriented. It was not simply that security structures, above all NATO, and defence strategies had to be rethought. It was the whole justification, purpose and direction of foreign policy itself which seemed at issue.

PRINCIPLES OF CONSERVATIVE
FOREIGN POLICY

Bismarck once remarked that asking him to pay attention to political principles while conducting foreign policy was like asking him to walk through a dense forest with a twelve-foot pole between his teeth. And this view is supported by some conservative theorists who ask us to consult only the national interest when formulating foreign policy. In fact, the apparent logic of their approach dissolves upon examination. How do we recognize our vital interests? How best can we pursue them once identified? Do they include freedom and democracy in other countries? How do you persuade your own citizens, or other governments, to join in the pursuit of your chosen course? To what extent is some structure of international order also a specific national interest? And if it is, what degree of sacrifice should we make for it? These and similar questions cannot be answered without reference to principles.

For me, the conservative approach to international affairs rests on five tenets, which in different degrees and combinations can be applied to the challenges we face.

The first of these is that collective security can be upheld only if it is guaranteed by a single power or an enduring alliance which is strong enough to dwarf challenges from other powers. In our present world, this means that America must remain the single superpower. This will not be achieved without cost, which American taxpayers alone should not be expected to bear. Nor will it be without friction: Russia and in due course emerging great powers like China, India, Japan, Brazil – not to mention the hypersensitive Europeans – will all resent this. But for the sake of peace and stability it is overwhelmingly the least bad option.

The fact that the United States cannot maintain this dominant status alone over time, as other countries emerge more fully as world powers, does not negate this point – although it does amend it. In the first place, there is a time lag. Military superiority does not automatically go to the most advanced economic power, particularly when, as now, it is military technology – where the United States excels – rather than simply the volume of resources committed to defence, which is critical. In any case, it is important not to underrate the economic potential of the United States, as the prospect of a vast free trading zone embracing not just North but South America as well opens up.*

Still, America will need dependable allies, willing to share – and share fully – the burden of world leadership, if it is to be prolonged into the twenty-second century. Exactly how this might be achieved – by investing NATO with proper burden-sharing arrangements, especially for out-of-area operations, and underpinning it economically with an Atlantic Free Trade Area – is perhaps the most important topic for us to discuss over the next decade. But, whatever institutional form this burden-sharing takes, and however the burden is distributed between America and Europe, world leadership will still entail heavy obligations. They will nonetheless have compensating advantages: in particular, international arrangements and the decisions of global institutions will tend to reflect American, and by extension Western, interests. Indeed, unless this is so, democratic electorates, especially in the United States, will simply not be prepared to pay the price.

My second tenet is that in foreign policy we should recognize the value of the balance of power in regional contexts. This is an important qualification to the first assertion, regarding America's global role. The operation of regional balances of power will help to reduce the number of occasions when American-led interventions are necessary. When, in pursuit of its own interests, a state allies with other states to counter and contain a regional power which threatens to become dominant, a generally beneficial equilibrium is achieved: and the temptations and opportunities for misbehaviour open to the most powerful state are reduced. It was, of course,

* See p. 583.

British policy for many years to promote such a balance of power within Europe; and, as I have explained, this still makes sense when a major, if unstated, objective of policy should be the containment of German power.*

American policy-makers have generally rejected the balance of power principle – partly because of America's own overwhelming strength, and partly because idealism and ideology have seemed so important and the balance of power was seen by Wilsonians as amoral. More generally, the competitive jockeying for dominance has been held responsible for a succession of wars – above all the First World War. And a powerful contemporary argument has been that in a world where possession of nuclear weapons makes the risk of all war unacceptable, the tensions resulting from operation of the balance of power cannot be afforded.

These arguments are not without merit. But the US State Department has had almost fifty years of operating in world politics in ways that have tempered the principles of Woodrow Wilson with the realities of local power balances, from the Middle East to the Indian sub-continent. Secondly, as long as there is one ultimate superpower which, if necessary, can determine the outcome of regional disputes, then there are limits set on the competition between states. And the fact that the US is, in nuclear terms, more powerful than any other state, enhances its ability to set these limits. It is under these conditions that the balance of power is a force for good.

Arguably, the most important area in which the balance of power – supplemented by a sufficiently strong American presence – can help resolve future problems is in Asia and the Far East. The sometimes hysterical discussion of the 'threat' posed by Japan to the American and European economies leaves out two considerations. We are extraordinarily lucky that, both for historical reasons and because it is protected by the American nuclear umbrella, Japan does not wish to be a military as well as an economic superpower. And there are three Asia-Pacific powers which either have, or will shortly have, nuclear weapons: China, Russia and India.

The precise size and growth-rate of the Chinese economy is

* See pp. 490–1.

disputed; since China's prosperity is occurring largely in spite, rather than because, of decisions made in Beijing, probably not even the Chinese know the truth. But that the potential is huge, that it is being ever more effectively exploited by the industrious Chinese people (and the wider Chinese diaspora) and that China is building up its defences while the rest of us are running ours down – these things *are* known.

Russia, preoccupied with its internal economic and political problems, will nevertheless strive to remain a Pacific power. Given its nuclear armoury and mineral wealth, the Bear cannot be counted out. And it has quarrels with China over borders and resources that might yet be destabilizing.

India is large enough and, as long as present policies and trends continue, will in due course become wealthy enough to emerge as a major regional power. This is something the West should welcome and encourage: for example, if it is felt that the UN Security Council should be enlarged – and there is much to be said for leaving well alone – India is a strong candidate for inclusion. For all its religious and ethnic problems, India is a democracy with an established rule of law. In the old pattern determined by the Cold War, India was under the influence of the Soviet Union. This must not now blind us to the fact that she is the Asian power with which it will prove easiest to do business.

So, in the Asia-Pacific region, there will be a balance of power between three large nuclear states and one state enjoying the nuclear protection of the US. Any one of these powers is likely to meet opposition from the others if it attempts to expand its territory or sphere of influence. And in addition to providing nuclear security for Japan, the US is also available to throw its nuclear and conventional weight into the scales if any local power seems likely to upset this balance. The US already performs a similar balancing act conventionally on behalf of smaller Asian states like South Korea, Taiwan and the Philippines. This serves as a demonstration to the larger powers that they should not risk drawing America into a conflict between them. That is all the more reason why the US must now secure a favourable outcome in its dispute with North Korea over the North's nuclear programme.

NATIONS, NATION STATES
AND NATIONALISMS

The third tenet is that nationhood, nation states and national sovereignty are the best foundations for a stable international system. Superficially, that is a paradox. Is it not true that nationalism has disrupted European peace in two world wars? In fact, in most important senses the answer is 'no'. The instability of multinational empires was the background to the First World War, and transnational secular religions like communism and Nazism gave rise to the Second. And in both wars only strong nation states were able to resist and to defeat aggression.

But in any case there is no point in arguing that a world without nations – and the loyalties, frictions and institutions they generate – would be desirable, since for the foreseeable future such a world is a plain impossibility. Politics, as conservatives recognize, is about making the best of the world which exists, not in vainly devising blueprints for what it cannot become. Admittedly, xenophobic prejudice can result in concentration camps, torture and ethnic cleansing. But such crimes are usually the result of suppressed and distorted nationalisms or, in our own day, of nationalisms hijacked by communists. They are no reason why we should not be proud of our own country nor why we should disapprove if others are proud of theirs. The Mafia is based on the institution of the family; but that does not mean that the family is a pernicious institution.

For the conservative, of course, the nation (like the family) has also a profound and positive social value; around its traditions and symbolism individuals with conflicting interests can be encouraged to cooperate and make sacrifices for the common good. Nationhood provides us with that most essential psychological anchor against the disorientating storms of change – an identity which gives us a sense of continuous existence. Consequently the man who shrugs off his nationality, like the man who discards his family background or (as G.K. Chesterton famously observed) who abandons his religious faith, is a potential danger to society for he is apt to become the victim of every half-baked ideology or passion he encounters.

Some nationalisms, it is true, are disagreeable and even dangerous because some nations have committed historic crimes. Even then it is questionable whether a nation which has deliberately turned its back on its entire past is any more reliable a neighbour than one which dwells on it. A more mature response is to discover in one's history those noble episodes and themes on which a more decent and open sense of nationhood can be built. Otherwise, it is the unbalanced revolutionaries who are left to take up the national cause.

Even the artificial states, which take in different nations with different languages and traditions, pay a kind of involuntary tribute to the power of nationhood by seeking to forge a *new* national identity. This was tried in the Soviet Union and in Yugoslavia; it is now being attempted in the European Union. Such enterprises cannot work, and generally break down amid acrimony and mutual hatred. But their very artificiality often inspires the ideologues to extremes of doctrinaire chauvinism, alternately ruthless and ridiculous, from Stalin's mass deportation of peoples to the promotion of a European version of *Dallas*.

It is therefore wrong to argue, as diplomats are still prone to do, that striving to keep large multinational, multicultural states together by all possible means makes for stability. It is, of course, quite possible that several distinct peoples will live within the frontiers of a single state for a variety of reasons – security, economic resources, geography, or lack of any alternative. Developing a liberal political and economic system is the best way to persuade them to do this, as Switzerland's extraordinarily decentralized structure illustrates. But in the artificially constructed states – founded on an ideology (like the Soviet Union) or a mixture of diplomatic convenience and fear of greedy neighbours (like Yugoslavia) – it is all too likely that centralized power and the use of force will be relied upon to keep the unit together. And this – again as with the USSR and Yugoslavia – only increases national fervour and the aspiration to national independence on the part of the component peoples.

So while it is not inevitable that nation states should everywhere succeed multinational states – for example, the Kurds seem unlikely for many years to gain statehood because of the number of other states this would adversely affect – that is bound to be the trend. Or at least it will be the trend as long as the two other current trends, those towards democracy and open trading, themselves continue.

Both of these make for the emergence and viability of smaller units. Democracy is the political system that most comfortably fits the nation state. It requires a common language if it is to function really effectively – and this the nation state provides. Once established in a multinational state, moreover, democracy fosters the drive towards national self-determination. That helps explain why most multinational states are not democracies or, if they are, are perennially disturbed by linguistic and cultural disputes, as in Canada and Belgium. Similarly, free trade means that political boundaries need not be co-terminous with economic boundaries. We can thus combine political decentralization with economies of scale. As Adam Smith pointed out two hundred years ago: 'Were all nations to follow the liberal system of free exportation and free importation, the different states into which a great continent was divided would so far resemble the different provinces of a great empire.'

There are two main practical arguments advanced against regarding the nation state as the basis of the international political system. The first is that the concept of the 'nation' is something which makes little or no sense outside Europe, because it is itself rooted in and a construct of a long and distinctive European history. This has some force. It is clear, for example, that nationhood has to be understood in a somewhat different way in the Middle East or Far East or Africa – or even in North and South America – from in Europe. In some cases religion, in other cases tribe, and in still others 'culture' (as Samuel Huntington has argued) will shape and mould identity. Moreover, nations can slowly emerge as, for example, in India. And they can equally disintegrate and die.

But the failure of attempts to ignore national identity when putting together diplomatically convenient artificial states or dividing a nation into several states on ideological grounds is a common feature of our times in *every* continent. In Europe Yugoslavia was destined to fail, and even Czechoslovakia, where the tension between the constituent nations was not as great, has now been peacefully dissolved. In Africa, the Central African Federation was assembled from Northern Rhodesia, Southern Rhodesia and Nyasaland; the Sudan was put together ignoring the ethnic and religious differences between the majority Arab and Nubian population of the north and the Nilotic and Bantu people of the south; and Nigeria was created out of three constituent peoples, the Hausa, the Ibo and the Yoruba. Each of these has been riven with difficulties. In the Middle East, attempts to create a unified Arab state based on an Arab nationalism that owed too much to socialism and not enough to Islam have always come to nothing. In the Far East the division of Vietnam was ultimately unsustainable as, in all probability, is the division of Korea. By contrast, in every continent it is the states which most closely correspond to national identities – and are thus able to mobilize them – which are likely to prove the most successful: that is true from Britain and France in Western Europe, to Poland, Hungary and the Czech Republic in Central and Eastern Europe, to Egypt and Iran in the Middle East, to Japan in the Far East. Not that a sense of national identity is necessarily *enough* to ensure peace, prosperity and stability: but *without* it states will be faced with even more serious – and perhaps terminal – difficulties.

The second and perhaps the most frequent practical argument deployed against making nation states and nationalism the basis of our international political system is the problem of ethnic minorities. But in arguing for nation states I am not suggesting that it is possible, or even desirable, to seek to ensure that frontiers correspond exactly to boundaries of nationhood, let alone, of course, implying that national minorities or other groups should be shifted from one area to another to make politicians' lives simpler. In a well governed, reasonably prosperous state in which individual rights and, where appropriate, local autonomies are respected, there is no reason why national minorities should suffer oppression or have a destabilizing effect. And international conventions and bodies like the Council of Europe could ensure this.

Western politicians are all too inclined to believe that the experience of the post-communist states of Central and Eastern Europe and the Soviet Union demonstrates that nationalism is inherently dangerous. A closer investigation suggests the opposite. Yugoslavia is *not* the rule but the exception. For example, Hungary, apart from a small minority of extreme nationalists, has learned to accept the territorial losses of seventy years ago under which some two million Hungarians live in Romania, 600,000 in Slovakia, 400,000 in Yugoslavia and 200,000 in Ukraine. The Hungarians understandably insist on fair treatment for their diaspora. But they are a sufficiently mature democracy to understand that the principle of 'all Hungarians in one state' would lead to catastrophe.*

Similarly, although there are forces in Russia which would like to exploit the situation of the twenty-five million Russians living outside Russia in states which were once part of the Soviet Union, so far this has been a matter of rhetoric rather than reality. Although the Russian minorities certainly face some problems, it seems unlikely that most of them feel sufficiently threatened to wish to destroy the states of which they are now part: indeed, in many cases they voted for the independence of those states from the USSR.**

To what extent does the case of the breakaway Chechen Republic and the ensuing crisis cast doubt on the principle of nationhood as a sound basis for stable order? The Chechens certainly have solid claims to self-determination: they are a nation with their own language and religion and have long striven for independence since being forcibly absorbed within the Russian Empire in the last century. The argument that the West should overlook – or even support – the brutal military action taken to crush Chechnya in order to keep Russia together and Mr Yeltsin in the Kremlin is deeply flawed. It is not for us to determine the shape of Russia; states cannot ultimately be kept together by force, they have to create the conditions for national and regional minorities to stay within them; and when the West overlooks the abuses of human rights and breach of international (CSCE) treaty obligations which have occurred, we undermine the forces of democracy in Russia, not assist them. There is, of course, no neat democratic solution to the

---

* See Jonathan Sunley's pamphlet *Hungary: The Triumph of Compromise*, Institute for European Defence and Strategic Studies, 1993.
** These issues are examined by Neil Melvin in *Forging the New Russian Nation*, The Royal Institute of International Affairs, Discussion Paper 50, 1994.

problems which plague the sprawling entity that is Russia. But its component peoples have the right to be treated with respect – even if, as is alleged of the Chechens, some of their members are involved in criminal activities. And if ultimately the Chechens wish to go their own way, Russia will gain nothing by seeking to prevent their doing so.

Of course, as with Chechnya, the history of past struggles influences the present. It is not my purpose to suggest that all nationalisms are good, let alone safe. But much is blamed on them which is attributable to other problems – in general, primitive political cultures retarded by communism and, in particular, lack of respect for human rights and democracy. Moreover, the record of supranationalisms is at least as mixed as that of nationalisms proper and their potential far more dangerous.

ADVANCING FREEDOM

This brings me to my fourth suggested tenet of a conservative foreign policy, which is that we should persistently seek to advance freedom, democracy and human rights across the world. The reasons why are, above all, practical. Democracies do not by and large make wars upon each other. Regimes which respect human rights at home are more likely to forswear aggression abroad. In practice, even the most cynical practitioner of *realpolitik* judges the threat from different quarters not only according to military technology but also according to the nature of the regime. It is, for example, at least as much because North Korea is a totalitarian dictatorship as because it apparently possesses a nuclear capability that its behaviour has rightly caused so much concern. The values of freedom give even culturally different countries a common understanding of the need for restraint, compromise and respect. That is why it is an essential part of foreign policy to encourage them.

The so-called Reagan doctrine, which Ronald Reagan developed in a speech to both Houses of Parliament in 1982, demonstrated just how potent a weapon in international politics human rights could be. His view was that we should fight the battle of ideas for freedom against communism throughout the world and refuse to accept the permanent exclusion of the captive nations from the benefits of freedom.*

This unashamedly philosophical approach and the armed strength supporting it transformed the political world. President Reagan undermined the Soviet Union at home by giving hope to its citizens, directly assisted rebellions against illegitimate communist regimes in Afghanistan and Nicaragua, and facilitated the peaceful transition to democracy in Latin American countries and the Philippines. Of course, previous American governments had extolled human rights, and President Carter had even declared that they were the 'soul' of US foreign policy. Where President Reagan went beyond these, however, was in making the Soviets the principal target of his human rights campaign, and in moving from rhetorical to material support for anti-communist guerrillas in countries where communist regimes had not securely established themselves. The result was a decisive advance for freedom in the world.

In this instance, human rights and wider American purposes were in complete harmony. But do human rights have an independent value in foreign policy? There are two classic attacks on the idea that they do. The conservative critique is that a human rights policy amounts to a dangerous intrusion on the sovereignty of other countries; and the liberal thesis is that it is flawed because based upon an inadequate conception of human rights.

Of the conservative view, one can say that it is a partial truth that we should take into account in formulating policy. Societies plainly differ in their social and economic development, their religious traditions, their political consciousness. Where a fledgling democratic movement really exists, we can foster and encourage it – and to a limited degree protect it against government suppression by protests, public diplomacy, and similar measures. Where there is no such popular movement locally (or where it is limited to a few Western-educated intellectuals in the capital), we cannot implant democracy from outside. However, although we must necessarily pick and choose the cases where Western influence can usefully

---

* See *The Downing Street Years*, p. 258.

accelerate a peaceful transition to democratic ways, some abuses of human rights, notably torture, are so flagrant, so egregious, and so offensive by any national or cultural standard, that we will always be justified in opposing and deterring them. The main question in such cases is how best to do so – by economic pressure, or by speeches and motions in international forums, or by quiet diplomacy. In any event, a conservative human rights policy, applied as it must be with prudence and discrimination, will always fall short of a crusade.

The liberal criticism is that Western human rights policy, by concentrating on such 'procedural' rights as freedom of speech or freedom from arbitrary arrest, neglects the more important 'substantive' rights such as freedom from hunger or the right to a decent education. The international documents to which appeal is generally made on questions of human rights themselves illustrate this drift of thinking. For example, the Universal Declaration of Human Rights (1948) not only affirms, as I would, that everyone has the right to life, liberty, equality before the law, property and so on: it also affirms the 'right' to an adequate standard of living and education and to social security – which are plainly in a quite different category. Other subsequent documents go even further. The International Covenant on Economic, Social and Cultural Rights (1966) includes the 'right to work', the right to the 'continuous improvement of living conditions', the right to be 'free from hunger' and 'the right of everyone to the enjoyment of the highest attainable standard of physical and mental health'.

Of course, as soon as we discuss freedom in terms of rights rather than duties, classical liberalism slips easily into soft socialism with all kinds of 'rights' being claimed with little regard for the cost or even the possibility of fulfilling them. These 'rights', to the extent that they are even theoretically attainable, can in practice only be fulfilled if the state coerces *other* individuals by regulations, controls and taxes. By this point one has, in fact, moved the whole distance from liberalism to socialism. Moreover, by granting outside bodies the power to intervene on almost the whole of domestic social and economic policy, the liberal human rights approach does not so much intrude upon national sovereignty as abolish it outright.

If then advancing human rights as traditionally defined is a legitimate aim of foreign policy, what in general is the best way to achieve it? We are fortunate that in the post-Cold War world, new opportunities for freedom have opened up. As the revolution in the technology of communications, the opening of world markets and the opportunities for greater mobility of capital and people all put authoritarian rulers under greater pressure, it will be increasingly hard for them to resist pressures to liberalize their regimes. This, in fact, is why in seeking to advance democracy and human rights, high regard must be paid to the wider impact of economic freedom.

Even countries which maintain a fairly free economy – with a sound currency, limited government intervention, low taxes, private property and mobility of labour – but which for a time experience authoritarian rule, as for example did Chile under General Pinochet, find relatively few difficulties in developing political freedoms later. But, as the experience of Russia shows, without a framework of law, an understanding of the limits of government, private property and a living tradition of enterprise, it is extremely difficult in these conditions to build democratic institutions. Recognizing this, the conservative – as opposed to the liberal-left – enthusiast for human rights will not make the mistake of underrating the progress towards the goal of political freedom which the growth of market capitalism brings with it.

It is this consideration, quite apart from my concerns for the long-term future of Hong Kong, which has led me to oppose linking human rights issues in China with trade issues. We need consistently to press the Chinese to end human rights abuses and to observe civilized standards in their dealings with Tibet, the Christian churches, and dissidents if China is to enjoy the full practical benefits which a relationship of respect brings with it. But it would be counter-productive to slow down the rate of progress towards an open, free economy by seeking to cut China off from trade, investment and outside influence, since these are roads to freedom.

Having said all of which, I would note that policy in regard to human rights is a great deal more complicated in theory than it is in practice. Politicians and diplomats generally know by instinct the cases in which Western influence can be usefully exercised and how best to exercise it. I must add, however, that they sometimes need a kick from public opinion.

STRONG DEFENCE

These four principles have one thing, above all, in common: they can only be given effect by a fifth principle of strong defence. The same arguments which Ronald Reagan and I used during the 1980s still apply. Defence spending is an investment in peace because it is not armaments of themselves which cause wars: wars arise because potential aggressors believe they have sufficient military superiority to succeed in their aggression. Such investment has to go on year after year, even when threats seem vague or remote, because high-technology defence programmes only yield results over a lengthy period. And the only 'peace dividend' we have a right to expect from victory in the Cold War is peace itself – rather than the opportunity to spend more on welfare benefits and the dependency culture.

Admittedly, it was right that Western countries should re-examine their defence spending as a result of the dramatic changes which flowed from the fall of communist Eastern Europe, the ending of the Warsaw Pact and finally the disintegration of the Soviet Union. But I now believe that the plans for reduced spending which were announced when I was Prime Minister as *Options for Change* went too far; subsequent announcements have, of course, gone further still. Personally, I did not share all the optimism which characterized political discussion of defence at that time. But I did overestimate the rate of likely progress in turning the Soviet Union (or Russia) into an 'ordinary country', a stable liberal democracy which posed no special threat to the West.

We cannot know whether Russia will ultimately go in the direction of democracy and free enterprise. If Russia were to embark on a course of restoring the old Soviet Union as a new Russian Empire this could not happen peacefully. Nor could it leave Russian relations with the West unchanged. In any event, it would clearly be against our strategic interests if Russian power were once again to move close to the heart of Europe. Similarly, Russia's commitment of scarce resources to any such imperial strategy would inevitably mean abandonment of the continuing tasks of economic reform and political liberalism. We could thus expect both external and internal policies to revert towards those of the old USSR. And Russia is still a formidable military power.

Already, the various crises and disarray which affected the countries of the former Soviet Union have resulted in a large outflow of advanced weaponry, which was then eagerly acquired by other rogue powers, further increasing the threats we face. Clearly, the West must maintain its defences.

Since 1989/90 it has not been possible to base our defence calculations almost exclusively on assessment of the threat from just one direction – the USSR and the Warsaw Pact. That necessarily makes the task a good deal more complicated. In such circumstances, the temptations are great for politicians to try to balance the different lobbies rather than to take a long-term strategic view of likely threats and the required response. A further difficulty has been that it is not just Britain but also the United States, France, Germany and Italy which have been cutting back. Those in a position to know now claim that even if we had the front-line equipment to intervene where required, there would be big problems in supporting and supplying it. Combined with the unsatisfactory outcomes of UN-authorized interventions, these cutbacks have given the impression of a weakness of resolve and commitment.

Another element of uncertainty has concerned the future role of NATO. As I have suggested, it was right and necessary for this to be re-assessed. In particular, the *political* impact of NATO as a force for stabilization and strengthening transatlantic links had to be more fully exploited and developed. This has not, however, occurred as I envisaged. In particular, partly as a result of federalist impulses in Europe and partly as a result of different approaches over Bosnia, NATO is no longer satisfactorily fulfilling the crucial task of sustaining American commitment to Europe's defence. Indeed, NATO itself has been seriously undermined.

NATO should also have welcomed the Central European countries – Poland, Hungary, the Czech Republic and Slovakia – into full membership, as they requested. Combined with the European Community's slow and hesitant approach to bringing those countries in as full EC members, NATO's decision has come as a blow to the pro-Western democratic forces in the region. *Partnership for*

Peace, which treats a country like Poland as having the same relationship with the West as, say, a member state of the former Soviet Union like Kazakhstan, only serves to confuse the degree of commitment NATO is making. The fact that NATO has allowed Russia – or more precisely the anti-Western influences in Russia – to determine its decisions on this matter is all the more serious. It does Moscow's democrats no good to bend in this way, because it suggests that those who threaten are more likely to be listened to than those who cooperate.

Expanding NATO would be more than a military move. It would confirm the independent and 'European' status of the Central European states. Even countries, like Ukraine and probably the Baltic states, which would not (initially at least) be on the right side of the 'line' that NATO would draw on its eastern border, have now lost out. It has been well argued that 'merely having NATO close at hand . . . would affect the political psychology in the belt of states between the Baltic and the Black Seas, imparting more confidence to their liberal political forces'.* All these developments would have tended to put European peace on a much sounder footing.

They are all the more desirable because the Gulf War demonstrated something which I had already believed necessary – namely that NATO forces must be able to operate 'out of area'.** The range of potential serious threats is now truly global. That does not mean that NATO forces should be deployed whenever some local crisis in a far-flung country occurs. But it does mean that major regional threats must concern us. Some potentially serious risks are already apparent.

And where there is a clear case of aggression and our interests are involved, military interventions, whether under UN, NATO or other auspices, should be strong, swift and effective. Objectives must be clear, risks weighed and as far as possible countered and the resources deployed sufficient. Of course, every international

---

* William E. Odom, 'Strategic Realignment in Europe – NATO's Obligation to the East', in *NATO – The Case for Enlargement*, Institute for European Defence and Strategic Studies, 1993.
** I had spoken to this effect at the North Atlantic Council in Turnberry in June 1990. See *The Downing Street Years*, p. 812.

crisis is different. Rules have to be adapted to circumstances. But the temptations to guard against are always the same – namely, ill-thought-out goals, too much reliance on total consensus before action, and the use of insufficient force.

Unfortunately, in their different ways all the major military interventions carried out under UN authority since the end of the Cold War have suffered from some or all of these problems. The Gulf War left Saddam Hussein in power with sufficient weapons and resources to terrorize the Kurds and the Marsh Arabs and continue to test the international community's resolve. This crucial misjudgement was principally the result of a lack of clarity about objectives and excessive emphasis given to the search for international agreement rather than victory. But at least Desert Storm was effective in ensuring that Iraq yielded up Kuwait.

As I have suggested earlier, in spite of the personal qualities and, on occasion, the heroism of some of those involved, little can be said in praise of the international intervention in the former Yugoslavia. The justification for intervention was at least as clear as in the case of Saddam Hussein's invasion of Kuwait. A well-armed aggressor – Serbia initially acting under the institutional guise of Yugoslavia – attacked first Slovenia, then Croatia and finally Bosnia. But what should have been a clear policy of arming the victim and assisting him with air strikes on military targets was distorted into a peacekeeping and humanitarian venture.

This policy was an illusion. There was no peace to keep. Hence the humanitarian force would either fail to aid the victims or come into conflict with the aggressors. A Western diplomacy that forswore effective military action had no real power to force an aggressor to negotiate seriously, and an arms embargo, impartially applied, meant in effect intervening on the side of a well-armed aggressor against an ill-armed victim. In fact, there is hardly a moral principle or a practical rule which has not been broken in handling this crisis: it should at least provide the next generation of statesmen with a case study of what not to do.

Was it shame at events in Bosnia and Croatia which prompted the UN, under American leadership, to intervene in Somalia in December 1992? No one could criticize the humane impulse to step in and relieve the appalling suffering created by – what was in this case accurately described as – civil war. But insufficient attention was given to the political and military problems involved. It soon became clear that the humanitarian effort could not enjoy long-term success without a return to civil order. But there seemed no internal force able to supply this.

Hence, the intervention created its own painful choice: either the UN would make Somalia into a colony and spend decades engaged in 'nation-building', or the UN forces would withdraw in due course and Somalia revert to its prior anarchy. In the former case, since the Americans have no taste for imperial ventures, the UN would have to vest any new trusteeship either in a local power like the Egyptians or in a former colonial power, presumably in this case the Italians. If this is unlikely to happen – and it is – then the job of feeding the hungry and helping the sick must in future be left to civilian aid agencies and private charities. Military intervention without an attainable purpose creates as many problems as it solves.

The combined effect of interventions in Bosnia, Somalia and, indeed, Rwanda has been to shake the self-confidence of key Western powers and to tarnish the reputation of the UN. Yet a dangerous trend is increasingly evident: over the last few years, culminating in the latest intervention in Haiti in September 1994, the Security Council seems prepared to widen the legal basis for intervention. We are seeing, in fact, that classically dangerous combination – a growing disproportion between theoretical claims and practical means. All this may have further unwelcome consequences in the longer term.

If there is now a threat approaching the gravity of the Cold War, it is that of Islamic fundamentalism. The concern of policy-makers is certainly justified. The implications for Europe, the Middle East and Russia alike if more moderate or secular Muslim countries should fall under Islamic extremist regimes are indeed serious.

But it is one thing to estimate a danger, quite another to know how best to overcome it. The West has in the past disastrously misjudged the political potential of Islam. It has been well observed that: 'The two Middle East countries most torn apart by violence and civil strife since the mid-1970s were among those previously regarded as the most stable, modernized, and Western-oriented –

Lebanon and Iran.'* There is a risk that in discussing 'fundamentalism' we will come to regard conservative-minded Muslim countries as inevitable hotbeds of Islamic revolution. Yet the success of
Islamic parties does not always reflect the religious commitment
of their supporters; rather, it reflects the fact that communism is
now discredited, leaving Islamic oppositions to benefit from discontent with the incompetence and corruption of existing governments.
In fact, the umbrella of 'fundamentalism' shelters a range of distinct
and often mutually opposed phenomena, from Gulf and Lebanese
Shiites with links to Iran, to the Sunni Muslim Brotherhood of
Egypt, to the mish-mash of elements woven together in Colonel
Qaddafi's 'Third Way' – quite apart from many pious Muslims
who are only 'fundamentalist' in that they are seeking a return to
austere Islamic practice.

Within the Islamic world, Iran has, of course, a special position.
It has acquired – and continues to acquire – weapons of mass
destruction from Russia, Ukraine, China, North Korea and elsewhere. It has moved into nuclear research. It has close links with
terrorist organizations and seems to feel no inhibitions about
intervening to achieve its objectives from Lebanon to Argentina.
And in addition to these material threats, Iran is the standard-
bearer of a kind of Islam that is both revolutionary and traditional
and that puts it at odds with most Arab rulers. Like Revolutionary
France, Iran is the bearer of what Burke called an 'armed doctrine'.
The international community has no ideal way of dealing with this
phenomenon. But the best available model seems that of containment.

Otherwise, the tensions between Islam on the one hand and
modern, Western liberalism on the other will ultimately have to
be worked out by Muslims themselves. The West, for its part, must
respect the values, traditions and beliefs of Islam – while insisting
that basic human rights should be honoured and aggressive policies
forsworn.

I have set out what I consider the tenets of a conservative foreign
policy should be. But there is really no substitute for commonsense.

* J.L. Esposito, *Islam and Politics* (New York, 1991), p. 244.

In my years as Prime Minister I was always convinced that aggression must not be allowed to pay. If it did, automatically the threat to our peace and security would increase. I also reckoned that would-be aggressors are a great deal more rational than most people imagine. They ask themselves whether those of us likely to oppose them have the weapons to do so, the means of deploying those weapons sufficiently quickly, and above all the resolve. So we must make our resolve plain.

And finally, there was what I came to call Thatcher's law: 'No matter how well prepared you are, the unexpected happens.' How you cope then remains, of course, the real test.

CHAPTER XV

Virtue's Rewards

*Policies to strengthen the family, curb welfare dependency
and reduce crime*

A CONTINUING DEBATE

Social issues usually loom larger in political debate when economic
problems, particularly the problem of inflation, are less of a worry.
Low inflation and rapid economic growth were the background to
the preoccupation with the environment, urban renewal and the
Health Service which dominated politics after the 1987 general
election. Low inflation and resumed economic growth in 1994 have
had the same effect.

There are, however, three differences between the two periods.
First, whatever the economic future holds, it seems unlikely that
the arguments about social policy (which have opened up on both
sides of the Atlantic) will peter out inconclusively, because too
many raw nerves have already been struck. Secondly, in contrast
to the years 1987 to 1989, these debates are now taking place
on the traditional conservative territory of law and order, welfare
dependency and the family. Thirdly, there is a new understanding
of the *economic* consequences of crime, unchecked expenditure on
welfare benefits and family breakdown. Company executives are
unwilling to move to areas of high crime and delinquent schools.
The explosion of spending on one-parent families forces Social
Security budgets – and ultimately taxes – inexorably upwards.
Above all, there are fears that the growing welfare dependency
will demotivate and demoralize young men and women on whose
contributions in the workforce industrial expansion and advance

depend. Even hard-nosed men of the world, more interested in growth rates than crime rates, are having to take social policy seriously.

It is, therefore, the more surprising that with a few notable exceptions, political leaders have been reluctant to frame policies based on the remarkably similar analyses of academics and commentators; partly, perhaps, because those who have tentatively sought to do so have incurred instant vilification on both sides of the Atlantic. Vice-President Quayle and Peter Lilley were similarly pilloried for saying things which are now generally agreed to be commonsense: namely that the growth of single parenthood is bad for the children growing up without a father, and imposes heavy costs on society. Yet as long ago as 1987, for example, Michael Novak and several other distinguished scholars of different viewpoints agreed a number of challenging conclusions in a publication called *The New Consensus on Family and Welfare*. Among these were: 'money alone will not cure poverty; internalized values are also needed' and 'the national ethos must encourage self-reliance and responsibility'.

Talking honestly and intelligently about such matters has been obstructed – in slightly different ways – on both sides of the Atlantic by a combination of prejudice and vested interest.

Most senior politicians and professionals in the areas of penology and social work rightly feel some measure of responsibility for the liberal policies pursued since the 1960s, and are understandably reluctant to confess their failure. Or if they do make such an admission it is generally qualified by the suggestion that although present approaches may not work, nothing else will work better. This is, of course, a strange justification for a hugely costly and vastly complex system operated at the taxpayer's expense. Secondly, there is an understandable human reluctance on the part of comfortably-placed politicians to adopt a social analysis that places some of the responsibility for their condition upon the poor themselves – in the jargon, 'blaming the victim'. This reluctance is especially marked, again understandably, when the poor in question are drawn disproportionately from racial minorities. Paradoxically, however, policies which shrink from placing the responsibility where it belongs help to create more victims.

If this is not always recognized, it is because the forces of 'political correctness' also muddy the waters, particularly in America, but covertly and increasingly in Europe. If, for instance, a disproportionately large number of black people are in prison, that is automatically taken as proof of racism in the criminal justice system, and policies that require more incarceration become suspect. If the traditional nuclear family is seen as an institution which enslaves women, policies discouraging single parenthood are unlikely to find favour. Only two conditions can allow such powerful obstructions to be overcome. The first, which is increasingly evident, is the refusal of the general public to tolerate the personal, social and financial cost of continuing as we are. The second is to gain wider understanding of what has been happening and why.

CRIME *HAS* RISEN

The starting-point for all such discussion must be the rise in crime. For many years Home Office orthodoxy was to deny or at least to minimize it. Attention was, instead, focused on the 'fear of crime' which, on the basis of the incidence of recorded offences, was shown to be exaggerated, particularly among such victim groups as the elderly. The unspoken implication was that if commentators talked less about crime, unnecessary fears would subside and the public would feel safer on the streets and in their homes. Within the constraints on government applied by a free society, systematic propaganda of this sort is largely impossible and so rather less is now heard of this patronizing argument. Rightly so, for the only way to diminish fear of crime is to diminish the threat of crime. Where the threat is real – and where the potential victim is frail – fear is a rational and prudent response.

A second and more substantial point which has been made is that the figures for recorded crime suggest a larger increase than has in fact occurred. At first glance, the Home Office British Crime Surveys (BCS) carried out in 1982, 1984, 1988 and most recently 1992, lend some substance to this. The BCS asks 10,000 people directly about their experience as victims of crime, whereas the official crime figures depend upon the number of crimes reported to the police. The recorded crime figures nearly doubled between 1981 and 1991; but the BCS suggests a lower rise of about 50 per cent. The inference is that the willingness to report crime to the police has increased. Particularly in the case of crimes like sexual assault, where police treatment of victims has become much more sympathetic, this is easily explainable. It also suggests a degree of confidence in the police to which the latter's critics rarely draw attention.

What must also be borne in mind, on the other side of the argument, is that victim surveys undercount the real number of violent offences, particularly when violence occurs within the family. On violent crime, therefore, we cannot be certain which of the two sets of figures is more accurate (though both point to a large increase, differing only in the matter of degree). As for other crimes, the sharp increase in recorded burglaries since 1987 is supported by the Survey. All in all, therefore, the BCS does not cast serious doubt on the *fact* of a large increase in real crime in recent years. But, it is not only the level – or more precisely the rate – of crime from year to year which bothers the general public; it is the long-term trend. That has been dramatically upwards. The figures for recorded crime – which are of course subject to some changes in recording practice over such a long period but which form the only continuous series – paint a very clear picture. And the fact that such a picture conforms closely to popular received wisdom makes it all the more convincing.

During the last half of the nineteenth century there was a marked fall in the crime rate, both as regards property and violent crime. The crime rate – that is the number of criminal offences per 100,000 of the population – did not increase substantially until the late 1950s. It then rose ever faster. The crime rate is now ten times that of 1955 and sixty times that of 1900.

Although of scant comfort, the explosion of crime since the 1960s is not just a British phenomenon. In the United States between the mid-1960s and 1990 the crime rate trebled and the rate of violent crimes quadrupled. The United States – more specifically life in America's big cities – is still more violent than in Britain and Europe. Partly this reflects the number of guns on the streets (as opposed to in American homes, where the evidence is that they probably deter burglary); partly it reflects the number of murders and attacks associated with drug dealing. With these important exceptions, however, the picture is similar on both sides of the Atlantic. Property crime rates are now at comparable levels throughout the West. And we in Britain have to rid ourselves of the complacent assumption that we are immune from the trends we deplore in the United States because of our allegedly gentler, more communitarian culture. For example, in 1981 the rate of burglary in Britain was half that of the United States; in 1987 it equalled it; it is now higher.*

It is possible to quibble about the legitimacy of comparing statistics, both between periods and between countries. But the fact of what has happened in Western society over the last thirty years cannot be denied. Nor should its significance.**

Theorists and practical men alike have generally agreed that the primary purpose of the state is to maintain order. It is highly desirable that order should be upheld under law and that law should respect rights. But unless the state has the will and capacity to ensure order, not only bad but eventually good people will flout its authority. The law-abiding are demoralized when they see criminals getting away with it. Citizens and local communities tend to turn inwards, away from national institutions, losing confidence in the law-enforcement authorities and relying on degrees of vigilantism to protect themselves, their families and their neighbourhoods. And once that process of disintegration goes beyond a certain point it is all but impossible to reverse. This is the deeper reason why governments in Western countries should be concerned about the trends of rising crime and violence.

---

* I am grateful to Professor James Q. Wilson for drawing this and a number of other points in this chapter to my attention.
** Although I refer to the rising crime and connected problems as a 'Western' phenomenon, I do so in full recognition that a virulent crime wave has afflicted the post-communist world. This is largely a matter of infection spread from the West which the post-communist states, lacking effective police forces and the institutions of civil society, Burke's 'little platoons', have been unable to combat. By contrast, in the homogeneous and strongly group-oriented Japanese society, which in this regard is thoroughly un-Western, crime is remarkably low.

THE GROWTH OF WELFARE DEPENDENCY

If the sharp rise in crime over the last three decades is one starting-point for social policy, the barely less dramatic onset of welfare dependency is another. (I shall suggest some connections later.) Since 1949, when the British Welfare State was effectively established, public spending on social security has risen seven times (in real terms), up from under 5 per cent of GDP to about 12 per cent now; it constitutes almost a third of total public expenditure. This real increase continued when I was Prime Minister, and since. Of course, to lump together contributory and non-contributory, universal and means-tested benefits – retirement pensions, housing benefit and Income Support for single parents – is somewhat misleading.

But these crude figures show two important points.

First, insofar as the share of public expenditure and GDP taken by a particular programme reflects the importance collectively attributed to it, British society (or at least British government) is asserting that Social Security is not only more important than other programmes – its relative importance is actually increasing. The Social Security budget is twice as large as the next largest, that is spending on health. More significantly, perhaps, it is six times as large as the budget for law and order.

Secondly, in spite of the large general increase in prosperity over the last forty years, there are more people making larger demands on the taxpayer to sustain their or their families' living standards than ever before. Against this, it has been argued that in spite of the economic advance since 1979 'the poor have got poorer'. The latest official *Households Below Average Income* (HBAI) statistics suggested that *after* housing costs were taken into account the income of the bottom decile of the population between 1979 and 1991-92 fell by 17 per cent. But before housing costs it remained *constant*. And even without that gloss the figures are so misleading as to be materially false. 'Incomes' in this series of statistics do not reflect the real resources available to this group; in particular, they are not the same as living standards. Only about half of the group (excluding pensioners) were on income-related Social Security benefits. Many of this group who said they were earning nothing actually spent above the average for the population as a whole. And 70 per cent of those with 'zero incomes' before housing costs (according to the HBAI statistics) were in the top half of the nation's spenders.

It is anyway probably wrong even to think of these people as a 'group'. Its composition is constantly changing, as people's circumstances change. So the figures provide no evidence that particular people's incomes have dropped; and there is a great deal of evidence to suggest that their standard of living has risen. Most significantly, ownership of consumer durables – fridges, washing machines, central heating, telephones, videos and so on – in this group has increased dramatically. Given these facts, the crude picture painted of 'the poor getting poorer' is just not credible. By contrast, it is reasonable to conclude that the Social Security budget encourages anti-social behaviour, including dependency, and needs serious reform.

As in the field of crime, so in that of welfare dependency it is largely American scholars who have asked the boldest and most important questions. Charles Murray's pioneering study, *Losing Ground – American Social Policy 1950–1980*, has demonstrated how benignly-intended Federal Government policies in the United States aimed at reducing poverty have actually had the perverse effect of increasing it in recent years. In making it less worthwhile to work, and less troublesome and more financially advantageous to have children outside marriage, while reducing the penalties for crime and weakening the sanctions against school misbehaviour and truanting, government has changed the rules of the game. Those with the shortest time-horizons and the least self-discipline or support from their families have responded all too readily to this new framework and have begun to form what Mr Murray and others have described as an 'underclass'. In subsequent surveys of the British scene he has detected a similar development here, with its attendant signs of increased illegitimacy and crime rates.

In the 'dependency' debate most attention has focused on the impact of the tax and Social Security systems on families and the hidden encouragement to single parenthood. But ensuring that young men have the motivation, skills and opportunity for work is equally important. Here in Britain since 1979 we sought to ensure this in several ways. We felt that a period of subsidized idleness would be the worse start in life for these young people and a bad example for their fellows. So a two-year training scheme is guaranteed for every sixteen- and seventeen-year-old school-leaver who is without a job and not in full-time education; and simply going on to benefit is not generally a permitted option. The Restart programme, introduced in 1986, focuses on those who have been unemployed for more than two years and is mandatory for benefit recipients who do not take up the other employment and training options. Those undertaking the courses who do not seriously look for work, moreover, may have their benefits reduced. Incentives to work will be further strengthened by the new Jobseeker's Allowance which further tightens the rules on the conditions for receiving benefit.

It is generally necessary to reinforce offers of assistance with the threat of sanctions in cases of non-compliance in order to prevent people opting out of work while drawing benefit. They may do this for several reasons – because of low morale, or because they consider it is not sufficiently worthwhile to work, or because casual employment in the black economy pays better. Furthermore, if we want to make real jobs available to people starting out, we must forswear minimum wage laws or any other regulations which destroy low-paid and less skilled employment.

We shall, however, never devise or implement the right policy programmes to keep people out of welfare dependency if we entertain wrong assumptions about 'the poor'. It is again an American scholar, Gertrude Himmelfarb, who has done most to investigate the historical background to our current ideas about poverty.* From at least Elizabethan times, a distinction had been drawn, both in popular understanding and in administrative action to relieve poverty, between the 'deserving' and the 'undeserving' poor. And although softened and attenuated, not least because people understood the disruptive stresses of urbanization, such a

---

* See Gertrude Himmelfarb, *The Idea of Poverty: England in the Early Industrial Age* (London and Boston, 1984).

distinction continued to be made, even though the safety net of benefits widened and deepened. Indeed, for anyone who remembers the pre-war period in Britain the notion that 'the poor' constituted one identifiable, homogeneous group would have seemed quite unrealistic.

In Grantham and in similar towns up and down the country, we understood that there were some families where the bread-winner had fallen on hard times and who were going through great difficulties but who would never accept charity – even what they saw as charity from the state – being determined at all costs to keep up their respectability. 'I keep myself to myself and I've never taken a penny piece from anyone' would be the way many a digni-fied pensioner would express it. Taken to the extreme, this sense of independence could certainly lead to suffering. Neighbours would tactfully do what they could. Unfortunately, however, some indi-vidual cases of proud hardship are the counterpart of avoiding welfare dependency.

By contrast, there were others – and I came across this far more once I moved to London – for whom independence and respect-ability were of little consequence, who willingly accepted depen-dence on the state and who were unwilling to make the extra effort to improve their own lot or give their children a better start.

The fact that status in society accrued to the first of these groups and stigma to the second meant that social pressures were generally benign in the sense that people who fell, as most of us do, some-where between the two were more likely to find a job and provide for themselves and their families. Set down like this, such an approach may seem harsh. But a society that encourages such virtues as effort, thrift, independence and family obligation will tend to produce people who have greater self-esteem, and are thus happier (as well as not being a burden to others), than the people living in a society which has encouraged them to feel useless, demoralized and frustrated. Even if that were not the case, the state and society must be just as well as compassionate. To treat those who make an effort in the same way as those who do not is unjust; and not only does such injustice demoralize those who are benefiting from it, it also foments resentment among those who are not.

At some point in this century, which it is difficult now to distinguish precisely, too many Western policy-makers began to talk and act as if it were 'the system' rather than individuals – or even luck – which was the cause of poverty. We fell into the trap of considering poverty – and there is no need here to enter onto the minefield of distinctions between relative and absolute poverty – as a 'problem' created by economic policy which the redistribution of wealth and income could 'solve' by various ingenious methods. We kept on returning to the idea that poverty was a cause rather than a result of various kinds of irresponsible or deviant behaviour.

Most of those who spoke in these terms did so for the highest of motives. No one's motives were higher than Keith Joseph's, whose speech of June 1972 to the Pre-school Playgroups Association when he was Social Services Secretary constituted the most sophisticated version of this approach. Drawing on recent research, Keith suggested that a 'cycle of deprivation' was at work in which 'the problems of one generation appear to reproduce themselves in the next'. In this Keith was breaking important new ground in drawing attention to the way in which 'bad parenting' has an impact not just on the children of those parents, but on *their* children. But Keith did not question whether the state by its welfare policies was acting as a third bad parent by sapping personal responsibility and self-help. Indeed, he advocated, alongside initiatives to promote better parenting and more family planning, that the government should intervene by way of different benefits and a possible tax credit scheme. When a clear analytical thinker like Keith gets the analysis right and the prescription wrong (as he later accepted), it is indeed a good illustration of the way in which on both sides of the Atlantic both right- and left-wing governments created the conditions for our present problems. Right wingers concentrated on 'targeted' benefits, which went to those whose behaviour was most likely to be adversely affected by them; left wingers increased the global burden of Social Security benefits, which hard-pressed and even 'poor' taxpayers then had to meet.

Much less research on welfare dependency has been done in Britain. But knowing what we do of the size and rate of increase in our Social Security spending, and seeing what has occurred in the United States, we should expect to see some similarly unintended

consequences of government social policy here. And indeed we do
– which leads on to the third development, the weakening of the
traditional family.

FAMILY MISFORTUNES

The family is clearly in some sort of crisis: the question is what.
There are those who claim that the family is changing rather than
weakening. At one extreme some of these people view *any* household
unit, such as cohabiting homosexuals, as a 'family' deserving the
same degree of social recognition and respect as a married couple
with children. Rather more would argue that an unmarried couple
living together in a 'stable' relationship, who may or may not have
children and may or may not in due course get married, should be
so treated. Still more, doubtless, would regard serial monogamy,
couples who marry and divorce lightly, as simply an 'alternative
lifestyle' (divorce rates have risen rapidly in Britain as elsewhere
in the West since divorce laws were reformed in the 1960s). And
happily there is still the traditional family of dad, mum, youngsters
and relatives.

As is frequently the case with profound social change, it is much
easier to distinguish specific more or less disturbing features than
the way in which they will react together. It is, for example, possible
that we are seeing a long-term demographic change with large and
undesirable consequences. The fall in the birth rate and the
increase in life expectancy, which is a general feature of our time
and by no means one limited to or most evident in Britain, will
result in a smaller working population sustaining a larger elderly
one. People of sixty-five today are generally fitter, healthier and
more capable of remaining in work – indeed younger – than their
counterparts of fifty years ago. Many of them, possibly most, would
prefer to carry on working and resent enforced retirement. Eventually new social arrangements will have to reflect this, among them
a raising of the retirement pension age. Until that happens, the
fact that in Britain retirement pensions and other benefits are not
'funded', but rather financed on a 'pay as you go' basis, means

that the burden on those in work will at some point be significantly increased. It is a matter of speculation how they will react.

Most public attention to changes in the demographic structure has, however, focused on the case of the teenage single parent. Understandably so, for this 'lifestyle' is an exceptionally irresponsible one, which both levies heavy costs on the taxpayer and imposes severe disadvantages on children growing up in conditions of relative poverty and without a father's guidance.

Moreover, it is a problem that is getting worse. The number of one-parent families with dependent children as a proportion of all families with dependent children in Britain has approximately doubled since 1976. Of course, this group includes widows, divorced and deserted single mothers – and fathers – as well as the group which is the main focus of this discussion, the never-marrieds. It goes without saying that although the circumstances of these different one-parent families are superficially similar, they arise from very different causes and, as we shall see, require very different responses. To over-simplify greatly, widows with children require financial help; the never-marrieds need that – plus a change of outlook too.

That said, the number of single parents, though growing, actually understates the problem. Very often single mothers are concentrated either in a particular area or a particular ethnic minority. In these circumstances, complacent talk about relying on grandparents or the 'extended family' is quite unrealistic. For there may be no older married men in the narrower local community at all. Not only in such circumstances do children grow up without the guidance of a father: there are no involved, responsible men around to protect those who are vulnerable, exercise informal social control or provide examples of responsible fatherhood. Graffiti, drug trafficking, vandalism and youth gangs are the result and the police find it impossible to cope. There is also the financial cost. Of the 1.3 million single parents in Britain nearly 1 million depend on benefits, costing the tax payer £6.6 billion a year.

Charles Murray regards the dramatic rise in the rate of illegitimacy as a crucial predictive indicator of problems to come. Over the last ten years the proportion of births outside marriage has more than doubled, reaching one in every three live births. Never in Britain's recorded history has there been anything like it. It cannot be explained solely by urbanization – the catch-all explanation or excuse for most behavioural deterioration – because in Victorian Britain, which saw the most sweeping change in that direction, the illegitimacy rate, like the crime rate, actually fell. The attempt is sometimes made to minimize the significance of this change by noting that three quarters of today's births outside marriage are registered by both natural parents. This is supposed to demonstrate that the child has been born into a stable home. But a young child needs above all the total confidence that both his parents will *always* be there. If the mother and father do not have sufficient commitment to each other to enter into marriage, it would hardly be surprising if the child doubts their own commitment to him. And children are much quicker on the uptake than many adults understand.

As with crime and welfare dependency, so with family structures. Policy-making must be firmly based on analysis of what we know to be the facts. These do not show that everywhere the family is in retreat, or that most young men are criminals or that all those on means-tested benefits have accepted the culture of welfare dependency. Contrary to what the liberal-left would like to think, most children still grow up in a traditional family; most people marry; and most of these have children. In fact, no amount of philosophy, theology or social theory can provide stronger support for the argument that the family is the natural and fundamental unit of society than its resilience in the adverse climate of opinion and perverse financial incentives of the last thirty years. But this is no ground for complacency.

Changes in behaviour which may be limited and containable within society as a whole may have dangerous and dramatic effects when localized in small communities. It is far from clear that a capitalist economy and a free society can continue to function if substantial minorities flout the moral, legal and administrative rules and conventions under which everyone else operates. What is clear is that at present we are moving rapidly in the wrong direction.

A CYCLE OF CRIMINALITY

We could argue indefinitely about the precise relationship between crime, dependency and family breakdown: this is an area in which more research will be valuable. But there is now little doubt in the minds of most professionals – and none, I suspect, in the minds of the rest of us – that such a connection exists and is of the highest importance.

Take the large and important subject of juvenile delinquency as an example. The reduction of juvenile crime is not only of obvious importance in any strategy to reduce crime as a whole: it is also crucial to halt a budding career of crime in its tracks before it leads to serious and repeated offences. Discussions of the 'causes' of crime, both juvenile and adult, often end up in a cul-de-sac of generalities. The tendency to evil in human nature and the multiple opportunities for its expression are part of our ordinary experience. We can, indeed, do something about reducing the opportunities, by crime-prevention techniques such as 'Neighbourhood Watch'. But in a world of greater mobility (where miscreants can more easily achieve anonymity and make their escape) and greater prosperity (where there is more to steal), the results of such strategies are bound to be limited. Moreover, although crime prevention may reduce the amount of 'opportunist' crime, it is only likely to displace the crime committed by determined habitual criminals from one area to another. Consequently, attention is increasingly focused on crime prevention at the level of the individual – the actual or potential delinquent – rather than on the physical environment in which a crime takes place.

Research carried out in both the United States and Britain has illuminated the connection between crime, the dependency culture and family breakdown.* British research suggests that juvenile

* I am grateful to Professor Gary McDowell, Director of the Institute of United States Studies at London University, for letting me draw upon the proceedings of the Institute's conference on juvenile crime, *Juvenile Justice and the Limits of Social Policy*, held in May 1994. I would not, however, wish to suggest that the experts who presented papers at that conference would necessarily agree with my conclusions.

delinquency is associated with low intelligence, impulsiveness and troublemaking at school. As regards background, common factors appeared to be low income and poor housing. The parents of these troublesome children were inclined to administer erratic discipline and poor supervision, in short either not to care or to care impulsively or ineffectually. They may well be separated or divorced or teenage mothers and have criminal convictions in the family. The small proportion of boys who became persistent offenders, continuing into adulthood, and who constitute the real criminal menace, apparently showed the same characteristics but generally in a more extreme form.

Of course, this analysis does not seek crudely to 'prove' the 'causes' of crime. Rather, its purpose is to allow tendencies to delinquency to be predicted and – far more difficult – acted upon at an early age. But it is clearly also entirely compatible with the view that both dependency (which I suggest is more relevant than 'poverty') and family upbringing are crucial to any understanding of what has happened in the last thirty years to the crime rate.

The evidence of research from the United States is still clearer. A US Department of Health and Human Services study of 1988, which surveyed the families of more than 60,000 children all over the country, found that children who were living with a never-married or divorced mother were, at anything other than the highest income level, substantially more disposed to troublesomeness at school, and emotional and behavioural problems. The latest quinquennial survey of prison inmates by the Federal Bureau of Justice showed that two thirds of chronic violent offenders and a half of *all* inmates had come from a background other than a two-parent family; and 37 per cent of all inmates came from a foster home or child-care institution. More than half of the chronic violent criminals reported that an immediate family member had served some time in prison. Keith Joseph's 'cycle of deprivation' thus becomes a 'cycle of criminality'. The evidence about violent chronic offenders is particularly significant, because no group is perceived by the public as more of a threat.

In a free society there are limits to what government should seek to do to change people's behaviour, particularly the behaviour of families. It is in considerable part because the state *has* intervened, on the basis of necessarily inadequate information and without proper consideration for the long-term consequences, that we are faced with so many intractable problems. But it is not only compatible with but essential to a free society to create a cultural, financial and legal framework which upholds, not undermines, the attitudes and institutions on which freedom rests.

What then is to be done? Aiming at improvement rather than utopia, and without wishing to deny that there are other initiatives which the fertile minds of social scientists and policy-makers might usefully devise, I propose the following four-fold approach.

VIRTUES TO COMBAT VICES

The first, most important and most difficult area is the moral and cultural ethos. A functioning free society cannot be value-free. Down through the ages the most profound thinkers have recognized this. For me, Edmund Burke sums it up with a clarity and sweep no one else has managed:

> Men are qualified for civil liberty in exact proportion to their disposition to put moral chains upon their own appetites; in proportion as their love of justice is above their rapacity; in proportion as their soundness and sobriety of understanding is above their vanity and presumption; in proportion as they are more disposed to listen to the counsels of the wise and the good, in preference to the flattery of knaves. Society cannot exist unless a controlling power upon will and appetite be placed somewhere, and the less of it there is within, the more there must be without. It is ordained in the eternal constitution of things, that men of intemperate minds cannot be free. Their passions forge their fetters.*

Similarly, although those who framed the American Constitution chose to rely on ambition countering ambition, rather than the

* 'Letter to a Member of the National Assembly' (1791), *Reflections on the Revolution in France and Other Essays*, Everyman edition, pp. 281–2.

virtues, to preserve liberty, the fathers of the early Republic were well aware that virtue could make a significant difference. As the great patriotic American hymn puts it:

> Confirm thy soul in self-control
> Thy liberty in law.

The character of the citizen both reflects and is reflected by the character of the state. This is an encouraging fact, for it reassures us – as it reassured me in the late 1970s – that if a people is better than its government a change of administration can release undetected talents and open up undreamt-of possibilities. But it is also a warning. For even a well established system of free government is vulnerable to any profound changes in the outlook and mentality of the populace in general and the political class in particular. Character, both individual and collective, is of course formed in many ways: it develops within the family, school, church, at work and in our leisure hours. Traditionally, the good and useful habitual characteristics which are the outcome of this process have been called the 'virtues'. Although these virtues are by definition always good, their usefulness depends on the requirements of the situation. So, for example, some of the virtues extolled by Jesus in the Sermon on the Mount, though they will help get us to Heaven, may be of less practical use in our business or civic lives. Consequently, when we urge a return to those traditional virtues – for example, thrift, self-discipline, responsibility, pride in and obligation to one's community, what are sometimes called the 'Victorian virtues' – we are not necessarily suggesting that only mass re-evangelization will pull Western society together. After all, it was the ultra-humanistic ancient Greeks who originally identified the key or 'cardinal' virtues of temperance, fortitude, practical wisdom and justice in the first place.

That said, I find it difficult to imagine that anything other than Christianity is likely to resupply most people in the West with the virtues necessary to remoralize society in the very practical ways which the solution of many present problems requires. Although I have always resisted the argument that a Christian has to be a Conservative, I have never lost my conviction that there is a deep

and providential harmony between the kind of political economy
I favour and the insights of Christianity.

I tried to explain this connection in a speech at the church of
St Lawrence Jewry in the City of London in March 1978.

Freedom will destroy itself if it is not exercised within some
sort of moral framework, some body of shared beliefs, some
spiritual heritage transmitted through the Church, the family
and the school. It will also destroy itself if it has no purpose.
There is a well-known prayer which refers to God's service as
'perfect freedom'. My wish for the people of this country is
that we shall be 'free to serve' . . .

It appears to me that there are two very general and seem-
ingly conflicting ideas about society which come down to us
from the New Testament. There is that great Christian doctrine that we are all members one of another, expressed in
the concept of the Church on Earth as the Body of Christ.
From this we learn our inter-dependence, and the great truth
that we do not achieve happiness or salvation in isolation from
each other but as members of society.

That is one of the great Christian truths which has influenced our political thinking; but there is also another, that
we are all responsible moral beings with a choice between
good and evil, beings who are infinitely precious in the eyes of
their Creator. You might almost say that the whole of political
wisdom consists in getting these two ideas in the right relationship to each other.

I do not generally hold with politicians preaching sermons,
though since so many clerics preach politics there seems no room
in this regard for restrictive practices. So from time to time I did
return to this theme. Ten years later in May 1988 I addressed the
General Assembly of the Church of Scotland in similar vein. To the
disquiet of some of those present, I emphasized that Christianity
provided no special blessing for collectivism.

[We] must not profess Christianity and go to Church simply
because we want social reforms and benefits or a better

standard of living – but because we accept the sanctity of life, the responsibility that comes with freedom and the supreme sacrifice of Christ . . .

Near the end of my time as Prime Minister, I became increasingly conscious of and interested in the relationship between Christianity and economic and social policy. In Michael Alison, my former PPS, and Brian Griffiths, the head of my Policy Unit, I found two committed Christians as fascinated by these matters as I was. The discussions I had and the papers produced for them formed the basis of the book of essays *Christianity and Conservatism* to which I contributed an introduction and which appeared in 1990 shortly before I left Downing Street.

Not long ago it might have seemed unrealistic, to say the least, to envisage the return of an intellectual and moral climate conducive to the practice of the traditional virtues. Now, however, such matters are at the forefront of much serious debate about social problems.* Furthermore, at least some Church leaders, the people on whom much of the task of reshaping attitudes must depend, are having second thoughts about the beneficent effects of state provision and intervention. For example, Pope John Paul II in his Encyclical *Centesimus Annus* notes:

> By intervening directly and depriving society of its responsibility, the Social Assistance State leads to a loss of human energies and an inordinate increase of public agencies, which are dominated more by bureaucratic ways of thinking than by concern for serving their clients, and which are accompanied by an enormous increase in spending. In fact, it would appear that needs are best understood and satisfied by people who are closest to them and who act as neighbours to those in need.

Rome never seemed so close to Grantham.

The outcome of today's 'culture wars', as they have been called

---

* I am grateful to the contributors to a *National Review Institute* Conference, which I chaired in December 1993, on this theme for their insights.

in the United States, is still in doubt. As with so many other developments, the conflict of ideas and attitudes, which shows no sign of abating on the other side of the Atlantic, is bound to spill over into Britain and Europe. And with good reason. For it is as necessary for conservatives to win the battle of ideas in social as in economic policy.

Without this the likelihood of even limited initiatives succeeding is remote. But there must be such initiatives in the other three areas of social action – crime, welfare dependency and family break-up – with which I began.

CUTTING CRIME

When we turn to our second area, crime, recognizing the scale of the problem is an essential start. But rejecting the counsel of despair that 'nothing works' is almost as important. Since 1979 there have been large increases in the resources available to combat crime, including 16,700 more police officers and twenty new prisons. Yet far too often, critics of conservative criminal justice policy are allowed to get away with the argument that since crime has continued to rise, in spite of large increases in police numbers and prison capacities, some other unspecified but more liberal approach should be tried. This is, of course, a *non sequitur* – unless the critics are seriously arguing (and hardly any even of them would go so far) that extra police numbers and more prison facilities either have no effect or actually result in increased numbers of criminal offences. It is far more likely that crime would have risen still higher if these extra resources had not been provided.

The limited evidence available, supported by common sense, suggests that most professional criminals make recognizably rational calculations, weighing the likelihood of being caught and the length and discomfort of the sentence on the one hand against the perceived benefits (material and psychological) of crime on the other.* It would have to be shown conclusively that this was not

* James Q. Wilson, *Thinking About Crime* (New York, 1983), pp. 117–24.

the case before the traditional penal approach and remedies were abandoned. Moreover, Ernest Van Den Haag, a criminological expert in the United States, has made the following persuasive and significant observation:

> Whenever the risks of punishment fall, the crime rate rises. The rise in crime since the 1960s is a response to the decline in the risks criminals run, to the rise of their prospective net profit. Crime now pays for many more people than before. Between 1962 and 1979 the likelihood of a serious crime leading to arrest fell by nearly half. The likelihood of an arrest leading to conviction fell more. The likelihood of a serious crime leading to imprisonment fell altogether by 80 per cent . . . Per 1,000 serious crimes there were ninety people in prison in 1960, but only thirty in 1990.

As he concludes: 'one may wonder why crime rates did not rise more'.*

I would not wish to suggest that more police, stiffer sentences and increased prison places are the whole of the answer to increased crime. There are certainly modest but real benefits to be derived from both more effective crime prevention and better-targeted policing. But the fact remains that the most direct way to act against crime is to make life as difficult as possible for the potential and actual criminal. This cannot be done cheaply. Increasing the number of police officers on patrol, providing the most up-to-date technology to assist detection, building and refurbishing prisons are bound to require continuing real increases in spending on law and order services.

Law and order *is* a social service. Crime and the fear which the threat of crime induces can paralyse whole communities, keep lonely and vulnerable elderly people shut up in their homes, scar young lives and raise to cult status the swaggering violent bully who achieves predatory control over the streets. I suspect that there would be more support and less criticism than today's political leaders imagine for a large shift of resources from Social Security

* Ernest Van Den Haag, 'How to Cut Crime', *National Review*, 30 May 1994.

benefits to law and order – as long as rhetoric about getting tough on crime was matched by practice.

CURBING WELFARE DEPENDENCY

Third, as with formulating an effective conservative approach to crime, so with welfare dependency. We have both to combine forgotten traditional insights with modern techniques and up-to-date research. In an earlier chapter I have described the system inspired by the Beveridge Report and its merits.* Beveridge argued for a safety net of universal benefits largely based on and funded by social insurance, with means-tested benefits providing the remainder. The scale and complexity of Social Security nowadays means that a 'return to Beveridge' is hardly practical. We can, however, apply the perspective of Beveridge to our present difficulties. First, his Report made the assumption that if the state intervened too much it would reduce the willingness of individuals to provide for themselves – he was a great believer in thrift and the insurance principle. And enlarging the possibilities for *individuals* to insure themselves against sickness and old age is highly desirable today. Second, he was extremely conscious of the need to see the large extension of benefits he proposed soundly financed. Third, Beveridge described his objective as being the elimination of 'five giants on the road of reconstruction': 'Want ... Disease, Ignorance, Squalor and Idleness'. It is significant that his giants are moral, not just material; they reflect behaviour and not just circumstances. Reassuringly, we find that such an analysis fits in very well with the conclusions reached by American writers on welfare policy today.

If it is the financial burden of welfare spending which is the main concern, universal rather than means-tested benefits may be the main target for savings. If the wider 'dependency culture' is the focus, we are likely to be more wary of means-tested benefits, since they reduce the incentive to seek work and practise thrift.

* See pp. 121–2.

Nor will we be concerned with Social Security and tax only. Some means-tested financial benefits may also make recipients eligible for linked in-kind benefits such as free prescriptions, free school meals and cold-weather payments. If the recipient were to lose the original benefit, therefore, he would automatically be compelled to lose others, often a considerable financial sacrifice.

Moreover, a welfare recipient is likely to find himself and his family experiencing the most run-down local authority housing and the worst local authority schools in a disorderly and crime-ridden environment. The terrible paradox of the dependency culture is, therefore, that it offers people very considerable financial incentives to lead lives of idleness, squalor and despair. And we should especially honour those brave people who make the effort. But it is up to government to help them by removing, or at the very least scaling down, the temptations.

Some piecemeal measures to erode the dependency culture have already been taken. The 1988 introduction of Family Credit, paid to working families on low incomes, was an important step in dealing with the worst effects of the 'unemployment trap' (where people are better off out of work) and the 'poverty trap' (in which people lose benefit as their income increases). Alongside the Youth Training and Restart programmes, already mentioned, this has helped alleviate some of the problems of welfare dependency. It has dissuaded people who are fit and of working age from dropping out of the workforce. Whether it would be worth developing further initiatives such as Workfare is an open question. In principle, those who are ready to make heavy demands on society should be equally ready to fulfil some obligations to it. But US experience suggests that Workfare can be both expensive and frustrated in practice by bureaucratic obstruction. In these circumstances, probably the most important task is simply to curb public spending in general and welfare spending in particular, while reducing regulation and taxes, so as to make it more worthwhile to work and earn.

SHORING UP THE FAMILY

Our fourth objective, strengthening the family, must begin with the treatment of single parenthood in general and the never-married mother in particular. It is important not simply to concentrate on the financial cost of single parenthood. Even more worrying is the effect on all concerned, above all the child, but also the mother and (absent) father too. It is possible to give a good upbringing to one or more children alone, but the dice is loaded heavily against. A girl who has become pregnant and left the parental home – either deliberately in order to get a council flat or because of silliness which went wrong – is suddenly confronted with the demanding, draining task of looking after a baby. And, particularly if the baby is a young boy growing up without a father, the problems are likely if anything to get worse. Of course, some find the inner resources to cope; some are lucky enough to find the right professional or voluntary help. But human nature being what it is, even the instinctive love of a mother for her child is likely to be swamped by depression and difficulties. Nor, incidentally, is it just mother and child who suffer. It is the serious commitment of marriage, particularly marriage and children, which is the making of many young men. Perhaps for the first time in their lives they have to raise their sights and consider their responsibilities to others and the longer-term prospects which will allow those responsibilities to be fulfilled. Without such demands, they often find that the only way they can express their masculinity is through the life of the street, through crime and through getting other young women pregnant. This pattern of behaviour is most clear in the American 'underclass'; but traces of it can be seen in other classes and other countries.

Although, as I have suggested, the moral and cultural climate is of overarching if unquantifiable importance, the benefit and local authority housing allocation systems themselves have created the conditions for increasing single parenthood.* The argument is sometimes advanced that, given all of the difficulties likely to ensue in subsequent years, no one would make the rational calculation to become pregnant simply in order to receive housing and benefits. But this is in fact an over-simplification of any one person's rational calculation. There may, for example, be many prior or contributory reasons for taking the decision – misunderstandings with parents, paradoxically a desire for 'independence' and, of course, all of the instincts since the apple was eaten in Eden. The provision of cheap (even free) housing and of social benefits removes disincentives and penalties which might otherwise have deterred. The fact that this short-term calculation leads for the most part to long-term unhappiness does not mean that calculation is absent or irrelevant. It merely means that the calculator has a short time-horizon.

How best can we deal with this? We must first distinguish between the widow and the divorced wife with children on the one hand, and the never-married single parent on the other. Whatever benefits are available to single parents must be paid to the widow or ex-wife in whatever family circumstances she finds herself, as now. The never-married single parent would, however, receive the same benefits under certain conditions: very broadly, if she remains living with her parents or, alternatively, in some sort of supervised accommodation provided by a voluntary or charitable body with other single parents under firm but friendly guidance. In such an environment, young mothers could be helped to become effective parents, young children could be cared for under proper conditions for part of the day if the mother went out to work, and undesirable outside influences could be kept at bay. Together with quicker and better procedures for adoption, this approach would safeguard the interests of the child, discourage reckless single parenthood and still meet society's obligations to women and their children who, for whatever reason, are in need and distress.

Of course, strengthening the traditional family involves more than altering the position of never-married mothers. The very large

---

* In January 1994 the Government announced a limited but welcome tightening of the rules on local authority housing allocation to help tackle the problem of queue-jumping by single parents.

ABOVE: The workers' bus at Grunwick.

BELOW: The Winter of Discontent, 1978-79. Rubbish piling up in the street during the refuse collectors' strike.

ABOVE: Illustrating what inflation had done in five years.

LEFT: Gordon Reece.

BELOW: With Keith Joseph.

ABOVE: The first day out on the 'battle bus', with John Stanley and Caroline Stephens.

ABOVE: At a morning press conference during the 1979 general election campaign, with Barney Hayhoe and Jim Prior.

ABOVE: With Denis and Carol on a flight during the general election campaign.

ABOVE: Talking to the press on a return flight to London during the general election campaign. Standing behind me is Derek Howe, my press officer.

RIGHT: Carol returns from Australia during the campaign: meeting the press outside 19 Flood Street.

ABOVE: On a walkabout in Huddersfield during the campaign.

BELOW: On the campaign trail – with the press bus stuck in the mud.

ABOVE: Carrying the calf.

LEFT: Sampling tea at a tea factory during the campaign.

BELOW: The CTU rally at Wembley on the last Sunday of the campaign.

ABOVE: Polling day, 3 May 1979 – outside Woodhouse School in Finchley with the family and Party workers.

BELOW: Returning to Central Office from the count in the early hours of Friday 4 May.

Coming to Central Office on Friday 4 May (mid-morning) to await
the call from Buckingham Palace.

increase in the rate of divorce is also a clear threat to the family. Some divorced women have savings, a substantial marital home and a reasonable income and are consequently well able to provide financially for children. But large numbers receive little or no maintenance and have had to rely on the state. The new Child Support Agency's attempt to enforce decent levels of provision for an abandoned family, although the Agency's approach clearly has shortcomings (now being remedied), is a response to the scale of the problem.

In the circumstances of divorce, as in the case of never-married mothers, the children are disadvantaged. But the main disadvantage to such children is the trauma of family break-up itself and the emotional turmoil involved in subsequent conflicts of loyalty between two separated parents. I have always accepted that in some circumstances the best option for all concerned is to end a bad marriage, particularly one where there is serious violence. But all too often the comfortable notion of a 'clean break' for the sake of the children conceals a large amount of adult selfishness. Recent research confirms that divorce itself is bad for children, leading to lower educational achievement, and worse employment and emotional prospects; nor do these consequences just apply to the children of poor parents.*

It would be difficult to reverse the reforms of the 1960s, which in nearly all Western countries made divorce easier. But it is reasonable, knowing what we now do about the trend towards early marriage break-up and the effects on children, to reconsider the whole question. Divorce does not just concern two individuals; the stability of other people's marriages is affected too. That should certainly count against the Law Commission's proposals to remove considerations of 'fault' from divorce altogether. We ought also to consider whether a clear distinction should be made between divorce where there are no children or the children have grown up, and divorce where dependent children are involved. 'Putting the children first' and keeping the home together will sometimes require 'putting off the divorce'.

---

* This research is summarized in a Centre for Policy Studies pamphlet, *Divorce Dissent*, by Ruth Deech (1994).

Strengthening the family means more than fending off the most obvious threats to it. If we are serious about the family as the fundamental unit of society, that has implications for economic policy too. It should, for example, be reflected in the tax system. It used to be axiomatic that tax should take into account family commitments. That principle was displaced when tax allowances were abolished and universal Child Benefit, paid at a flat rate, was substituted. Child Benefit at least pays partial tribute to the principle of taking responsibility. But I believe that child tax allowances should be reintroduced as part of a fair and effective system of child support.

Equally, it is vital that, taken together, other tax changes do not squeeze the traditional family further. And unfortunately this is now occurring. Mortgage tax relief has been substantially reduced. A 3 per cent tax has been placed on insurance, which obviously bears heavily on home owners. The value of the married couple's tax allowance has been cut by failing to correct it for inflation. To encourage the traditional family means more tax relief and not less.

Modern Western society has proved more successful than any of its predecessors. It has created political and legal institutions which have extended personal freedom, generated economic ideas and structures which promote prosperity, and given birth to a bewildering array of cultural achievements. Indeed, with only limited accommodation to local traditions and conditions it has ceased in any geographically meaningful sense to be 'Western' at all, having penetrated almost every country on every continent. But such large and imposing structures require good foundations: and these are always ultimately moral and social, not material. The task which confronts us now – to keep those foundations well shored up against the tremors and pressures which threaten – is as demanding as any we have ever tackled.

CHAPTER XVI

Promoting the Free-Enterprise Revolution

Economic policy

BEHIND ECONOMICS

Economics is too important just to be left to the economists. It is no reflection upon the economist's expertise or integrity to suggest that his approach will reflect the non-economic values which make him the person he is. John Maynard Keynes famously remarked that: 'Practical men, who believe themselves to be quite exempt from any intellectual influences, are usually the slaves of some defunct economist.'

But extant economists are no less the slaves of outside influences. That was true of Keynes himself – a member of the 'Bloomsbury' set whose rejection of the Victorian virtues in their own behaviour was subtly but surely echoed in the abandonment of the classical liberal rules and restraints in economics with which 'Keynesianism' became synonymous.

So too my own views on economics flowed from personal experience of the world in which I grew up. My 'Bloomsbury' was Grantham – Methodism, the grocer's shop, Rotary and all the serious, sober virtues cultivated and esteemed in that environment. Doubtless, there are a hundred ways of coming to convictions about economics, as there are to convictions about politics or religion. But for me, experience of life in the Roberts household was the decisive influence.

For the truth is that families and governments have a great

deal more in common than most politicians and economists like to
accept. Although the consequences of flouting fundamental rules
are somewhat different for states than for households, they are still
ruinous – indeed, more ruinous in the case of states because they
have the power to bring whole nations down with them.

Nor was it only an understanding of what government could *not*
do that my upbringing and early experience left with me. I also
gained a sympathetic insight into what I would later come to think
of as 'capitalism' or the 'free-enterprise system'. Whereas for my
(usually somewhat older) political contemporaries it was the
alleged failure of that system in the Great Depression that convinced them that something better had to be found, for me the
reality of business in our shop and in the bustling centre of Grantham demonstrated the opposite. For them capitalism was alien
and harsh: for me it was familiar and creative. I was able to see
that it was satisfying customers that allowed my father to increase
the number of people he employed. I knew that it was international
trade which brought tea, coffee, sugar and spices to those who
frequented our shop. And, more than that, I experienced that
business, as can be seen in any marketplace anywhere, was a lively,
human, social and sociable reality: in fact, though serious it was
also fun. There is no better course for understanding free-market
economics than life in a corner shop. What I learned in Grantham
ensured that abstract criticisms I would hear of capitalism came
up against the reality of my own experience: I was thus inoculated
against the conventional economic wisdom of post-war Britain.

Primarily under the influence of Keynes, but also of socialism,
the emphasis during these years was on the ability of government
to improve economic conditions by direct and constant intervention. It was held that the state, if its huge powers were directed
in an enlightened manner, could break free of the constraints and
limits which applied to the lives of individuals, families or
businesses. In particular, whereas a household which spent beyond
its income was on the road to ruin, this was (according to the new
economics) for states the path to prosperity and full employment.
Of course, matters were never expressed quite so crudely. Government deficits, for example, were intended to be 'counter-cyclical'
– that is to compensate for the effects of recession – rather than

open-ended. Lip-service was paid to the need to avoid setting welfare benefits at levels which discouraged work. But behind all this was an almost universally held view that government spending was both morally and practically preferable to private spending, because it was directed to higher and more rationally established objectives. Before I ever read a page of Milton Friedman or Alan Walters, I just knew that these assertions could not be true. Thrift was a virtue and profligacy a vice; and the world would not make sense if the laws of human behaviour could be suspended by political fiat. Perhaps the single greatest change which occurred over the years in which I was Leader of the Opposition and then Prime Minister was that the great majority of policy-makers (and even economists) came round to the view which I held.

There is now a general understanding that the effect of increasing government borrowing is to raise interest rates higher than they would otherwise be. This is particularly so if it is expected that the larger deficit will raise future money supply growth and so inflation. In this way, allowing budget deficits to swell arrests rather than accelerates economic growth. The 1981 Budget, which I have described elsewhere, was based on understanding of that truth.* The 364 economists who published a statement attacking the strategy we adopted had no doubt that it represented a direct challenge to the prevailing orthodoxy. The challenge succeeded. Economic recovery was heralded by figures in the summer of 1981 and confirmed by others in the following quarter; by 1983 economic conditions were so buoyant that, along with reaction to the successful outcome of the Falklands War, they ensured me my smoothest general election victory.

As with government borrowing, so with inflation. After decades during which governments fine-tuned the economy on the assumption that there was a 'trade-off' between inflation and unemployment – the so-called Phillips Curve – it is now widely agreed that in the long run it is micro-economic changes, affecting the structure of the economy – for example, deregulation – rather than macroeconomic manipulation, which determines the number of jobs. And hardly anyone now professes to believe that 'some' inflation is

* See *The Downing Street Years*, pp. 132–9.

economically desirable. For whereas in the past governments thought they were sufficiently clever and wage bargainers sufficiently stupid for the former to reduce the latter's real remuneration by inflation, we now know that the boot has for years been on the other foot. Not only was future inflation discounted by wage bargainers – they frequently overestimated it and increased their demands accordingly. As a result, competitiveness was worsened, not assisted, by the so-called 'money illusion'. Worse still, those inflationary expectations are immensely difficult to remove from the system, which is why the benefits of low inflation take many years fully to come through.

The great advantage I had over many of my contemporaries in politics was that whereas they had first to be persuaded of the theoretical advantages of monetarism, free trade and deregulation, the technical arguments and insights were so completely in harmony with my fundamental instincts and early experience that I was much more easily convinced – and my convictions helped me to convince others.

BRITAIN IN THE 1980s

As Prime Minister between 1979 and 1990 I had the opportunity to put these convictions into effect in economic policy – and I was fortunate to have three extremely able Chancellors of the Exchequer, Geoffrey Howe, Nigel Lawson and John Major, to assist me. We intended policy in the 1980s to be directed towards fundamentally different goals from those of most of the post-war era. We believed that since jobs (in a free society) did not depend on government but upon satisfying customers, there was no point in setting targets for 'full' employment. Instead, government should create the right framework of sound money, low taxes, light regulation and flexible markets (including labour markets) to allow prosperity and employment to grow.

As for government finances, there was, it is true, some limited continuity with the period before 1979. The Labour Chancellor Denis Healey's £6 billion real cut in public spending between

1976/77 and 1977/78, and the terms of the agreement with the IMF in December 1976 which marked the first overt use of monetary targets to guide policy, were significant steps towards the kind of approach in which I believed. But they were implemented from necessity rather than conviction and would have been jettisoned at the first available opportunity. Indeed, that jettisoning had already begun, as public spending was allowed to rise again in Labour's final year. Moreover, the sound elements of policy pursued under IMF tutelage were not combined with the other crucial, complementary aspects – substantial cuts in marginal income tax rates, reform of trade union law, privatization and deregulation. They were, therefore, only half the remedy, for the vital ingredient of promoting enterprise was missing.

I came into 10 Downing Street with an overall conception of how to put Britain's economy right, rather than a detailed plan: progress in different areas would depend on circumstances, both economic and political. For example, the priority in our first Budget was cuts in income tax – both because marginal rates, particularly on those with higher incomes, had become a deterrent to work and an incentive to migrate, and because we had made such a firm pledge in our manifesto. But when political and economic imperatives pointed in opposing directions it was the economic requirements which came first – as when we put up personal taxes in order to control the deficit and beat inflation in that unpopular but crucial 1981 Budget.

The economic strategy had four complementary elements. First, in time and in importance, was the fight against inflation. Inflation had become deeply rooted in the British political and economic system and in British psychology. It had risen to successively higher peaks in the post-war years and had, as I have described, come perilously close to hyper-inflation in 1975. As a result, it was all the more difficult to eliminate. Only a sustained policy to reduce monetary growth and change expectations would suffice. So from 1980 onwards monetary policy, supported by a fiscal policy which reduced government borrowing, was conducted within the framework of a Medium Term Financial Strategy (MTFS). Like any strategy worth the name it had to adapt to circumstances. When, for example, problems arose with one particular monetary aggregate as a measure of monetary policy, it was necessary to look to others as well. Again, like any strategy, it did not of itself remove the risk of error. But it limited the scope for such errors and, as it was adhered to in passing years and in spite of difficulties, it gained a credibility which itself inspired wider economic confidence. Between 1981 and 1986, when the MTFS was most consistently at the heart of policy, inflation was brought down from a high point of 21.9 per cent (May 1980) to a low of 2.4 per cent (summer 1986). During the mid-1980s it averaged around 5 per cent, until the shadowing of the Deutschmark in 1987–88, to which I was opposed, set off a sharp increase.* It rose rapidly until it peaked at 10.9 per cent in October 1990. It had begun to fall the month I left office, and it came down rapidly during 1991, by which time the high interest rates of 1988–90 had brought monetary growth under control once more. The assessment of domestic monetary conditions remained the final determinant of policy on inflation until I left office.

A month beforehand, however, the MTFS was supplemented by sterling's membership of the Exchange Rate Mechanism of the EMS. This was intended to demonstrate to the financial markets that our commitment to low inflation was unshakeable. But then maintenance of a parity within the ERM became an end in itself, as the ERM became both a more rigid system and a conveyor belt towards a single currency. This led to a monetary overkill which certainly brought inflation down very rapidly, but at the price of inflicting an unduly severe recession in the British economy. In the end, the policy proved unsustainable and Britain had to leave the ERM.

Since then the Government has pursued a prudent policy to keep down inflation by a return to a sort of domestic monetarism. This is a tribute to the importance which the Government rightly gives to getting as near as possible to price stability. The need now is to re-establish a credible framework much on the lines of the original MTFS, which will be a permanent damper on inflationary expectations. That should not involve sterling's rejoining even a reformed ERM, since the markets know full well that what you have left

* See *The Downing Street Years*, pp. 699–707.

once you can leave again. Nor should it entail giving new autonomy to the Bank of England. Ultimately, it is politicians who must be accountable for economic policy. But they have to learn from the mistakes of the past, so that they and their successors are not condemned to repeat them.

The second priority in the 1980s was to bring Britain's public finances under control. In 1975/76 public sector borrowing as a share of GDP had reached 9.25 per cent. Under the impact of the IMF measures, the Labour Government reined it back, though it had started to grow again by the time of the 1979 election when it was over 5 per cent of GDP at the high point of the economic cycle. The 1981 Budget established a firm grip on public borrowing, which never loosened while I was Prime Minister. Between 1987/88 and 1990/91 we actually repaid £27,000 million of debt, reducing government debt as a proportion of national income to a level not seen since before the First World War. As for public spending, though the deep recession of 1980/81 pushed it up as more people became unemployed and government revenues fell, we reversed the previous long-term trend. Public spending as a share of GDP fell steadily between 1982/83 and 1988/89, when it reached a low point of 39.25 per cent. In 1989/90 and 1990/91 the proportion crept back up by 1 per cent, to 40.25 per cent – partly because of a massive overspend by local authorities (which knew that they could put the blame on the Community Charge), partly to ease the way for the NHS reforms introduced in 1990, and partly because the economy was moving into recession. Over the whole period, however, public spending as a share of GDP fell from 42.6 per cent in 1979 to 40.25 per cent in 1990.

The firm grip on public expenditure over these years also allowed tax cuts. Geoffrey Howe's 1979 Budget cut the basic rate of income tax from 33 per cent to 30 per cent, shifting the balance from direct to indirect tax. The top rates of income tax were cut from 83 per cent to 60 per cent and from 98 per cent to 75 per cent on investment income. Nigel Lawson's 1984 Budget made the fundamental changes in corporate taxation, cutting both capital allowances and corporation tax rates so as to encourage more efficient use of business investment. Nigel's 1988 Budget completed the programme of income tax reduction, bringing down the higher rate to 40 per cent (for savings income as well as earnings) and the basic

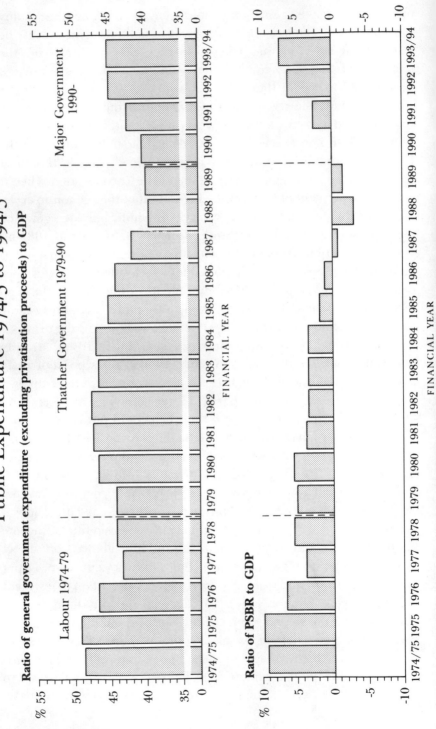

Public Expenditure 1974/5 to 1994/5

rate to 25 per cent. Sound public finances and low marginal tax rates were the goals in the 1980s: and they were achieved. Shortly after I left office, decisions were taken which led to large increases in public expenditure: in particular, the uprating of Child Benefit and extra money for the NHS, transport and local authorities. Combined with the recession, deepened as a result of sterling's overvaluation in the ERM, this increase in public expenditure has also led to a succession of large budget deficits – peaking in 1993/94 at £45,000 million, over 7 per cent of GDP – and tax increases amounting to over 2 per cent of GDP. Clearly, the sooner both of these can be reversed the better: that will require keeping a stronger hold on public spending and judicious use of the most useful monosyllable in a Prime Minister's vocabulary, 'no'.

Some of the ground won in the 1980s has been ceded to the spending lobbies, but the significance of that decade's rigorous public expenditure control has not diminished. Because we controlled public expenditure effectively in the 1980s – particularly by linking the basic retirement pension and other long-term benefits to prices rather than incomes and by scaling back the State Earnings Related Pension Scheme (SERPS) – Britain already enjoys an advantage over other European countries which failed to take such action, as the table below shows.

Government spending as a percentage of GDP – present and projected

	1993	1994	1995	1996
Britain	43.5%	43.2%	42.1%	40.9%
Germany	49.4%	48.9%	48.6%	47.2%
France	54.8%	55.3%	54.3%	53.4%
Italy	56.2%	56.0%	55.1%	54.0%
Denmark	63.1%	62.8%	61.9%	60.9%
Sweden	71.8%	67.4%	67.3%	66.6%
USA	34.5%	33.6%	33.6%	33.7%
Japan	34.0%	35.3%	36.0%	36.5%

Source: OECD *Economic Outlook*, December 1994: Annex Table 27.
Figures for 1994–96 are projections.

The potential advantage for Britain will indeed become greater as the years go by. Other European countries generally have much more adverse demographic trends, with a rapidly increasing proportion of elderly people being supported by a smaller workforce. They will be faced with the necessity of large increases in taxation. Professor Tim Congdon has argued that as a result of these trends 'in the late 1990s the tax burden could be 15 per cent to 20 per cent lower in the UK than in the rest of the European Community'.* Lower taxes, combined with a more favourable regulatory climate for business, will reinforce Britain's position as the dominant location for inward investment into Europe.

The third element of our economic strategy in the 1980s was to promote private enterprise and ownership. I wanted to shift the balance away from the state for both economic and political reasons. Privatization had a crucial role to play in this. In 1979 the only specific pledges of denationalization were those of the aerospace and shipbuilding industries and the sale of shares in the National Freight Corporation. But we got bolder and we learned as we went along. One by one, state-owned industries were brought into better financial shape and, in an improving economic climate, were prepared for privatization. By the time of the 1983 election, the list of candidates for privatization had lengthened to include British Telecom, British Airways, Rolls-Royce, parts of British Steel, British Leyland and the airports. After British Telecom, other utilities were privatized with differing structures and regulatory systems – gas, water and electricity. By the time that I left office the state-owned sector of industry had shrunk by 60 per cent and, largely as a result of the wider share ownership schemes which accompanied privatization, about a quarter of the population owned shares. I had set out to recreate a predominantly free-enterprise economy and to encourage a capital-owning society: I felt I had gone a long way, further even than I expected, in achieving both.

Finally – and, of course, cutting marginal tax rates and privatization were also a part of this – there was a wide-ranging programme of structural reforms to make markets work more efficiently, what

* *Gerrard and National Monthly Economic Review*, April 1991.

has been called a 'supply side revolution'.* From 1980 we pursued a 'step-by-step' programme of trade union reform, of which the 1982 Employment Act which reduced trade union immunities was the most crucial. The outcome of the 1984–85 miners' strike effectively cemented the new order in which jobs had to depend upon satisfying customers rather than wielding collective power to extort subsidies. There was a corresponding improvement in industrial relations. In 1990, my last year as Prime Minister, the number of industrial stoppages was the lowest in any year since 1935. Trade union reform was supplemented by Norman Fowler's 1988 reforms of Social Security to make it more worthwhile to work by reducing the so-called 'poverty trap'. Wages Councils which used to set minimum pay rates that priced people, particularly the young, out of work were reformed to exclude those under twenty-one, and have since been abolished. When I was first Leader of the Opposition the great debate in economic policy was between proponents of incomes policy and 'free collective bargaining'. By the end of my time in office incomes policy, with all its cumbersome distortions, had been laid to rest and wage bargaining was far less 'collective'. The proportion of the labour force in trade unions had fallen from 50 per cent to 35 per cent, an important cause (and indicator) of greater labour market flexibility.

But, of course, our reforms to make markets work better were not confined to the labour market: they touched every market. We abolished exchange controls, and controls on prices, incomes and dividends. We promoted greater competition in financial services. We reduced controls over private rented housing to encourage supply, and gave public-sector tenants the right to buy their homes at large discounts. Further measures to promote competition – and so improve value for money and widen choice – in the public sector were made in education, the NHS and local government.**

Our objectives – bringing down inflation, controlling the public finances with its concomitant of tax cuts, privatization and supply

---

* Patrick Minford, *The Supply Side Revolution in Britain*, Institute of Economic Affairs, 1991. I have also described this more fully myself in *The Downing Street Years*, pp. 668–87.
** See *The Downing Street Years*, pp. 589–617.

side reforms – were in varying degrees achieved. Moreover, each was valuable in its own right, not least as part of reducing the role of the state and giving people more control over their own lives. But how far can it be said that the economic programme I pursued in the 1980s fundamentally improved the performance of the British economy? There is a large body of persuasive evidence, which is still accumulating, to suggest that it did.*

Productivity is the key. Countries with sustainably improving living standards are countries whose labour and capital are productively employed. Countries which fail to achieve high rates of productivity, although they may – and should – take some of the strain on their exchange rates, cannot in the long term enjoy high living standards. This is borne out by Britain's experience. Before the Second World War there emerged a major productivity gap between us and the United States. Europe also rapidly overtook us in the 1950s and 1960s. And our performance in the 1970s was by far the worst of any leading industrial nation.

But the 1980s marked a major change. US Bureau of Labor Statistics figures for output per hour in manufacturing show UK productivity growth since 1979 to be faster than that of any other major industrial country, and particularly so since 1985. There is good reason to think that the long-term prospect for productivity growth has been permanently improved and that we have not just seen a one-off, 'catch-up' effect. Although the productivity growth was particularly dramatic in manufacturing, it occurred in services too. Output per worker in the UK non-oil economy as a whole grew by 1.7 per cent a year between 1979 and 1989 (that is over the economic cycle), compared with 0.6 per cent a year between 1973 and 1979.

A range of other evidence also suggests that the policies of the 1980s have resulted in structural changes in the British economy which, as long as they are not reversed by wrong policies, will put

* One of the best summaries of the evidence is that of N.F.R. Crafts, 'Reversing Relative Economic Decline? The 1980s in Historical Perspective', *Oxford Review of Economic Policy*, Volume 7, No. 3, 1991.

International Productivity Growth

Output per hour in manufacturing, 1979–93 (1979 = 100)

	1979	1985	1989	1993
UK	100.0	127.1	151.1	174.8
US	100.0	112.4	126.3	141.7
Germany	100.0	112.9	119.7	130.6
Japan	100.0	126.1	152.3	168.5
Italy	100.0	134.3	147.1	175.9
France	100.0	120.1	139.5	146.8
Holland	100.0	127.8	138.3	144.0
Denmark	100.0	113.0	113.7	122.6
Norway	100.0	118.7	128.9	138.4
Sweden	100.0	119.4	129.5	156.0
Canada	100.0	115.4	115.6	126.9

Productivity growth, 1973–93

	1973–79	1979–85	1985–89	1989–93
UK	6.3%	27.1%	18.9%	15.7%
US	NA	12.4%	12.4%	12.2%
Germany	28.1%	12.9%	6.0%	9.1%
Japan	39.3%	26.1%	20.7%	10.7%
Italy	39.7%	34.3%	9.6%	19.6%
France	28.9%	20.1%	16.2%	5.3%
Holland	38.1%	27.8%	8.3%	4.1%
Denmark	27.8%	13.0%	0.6%	7.9%
Norway	13.1%	18.7%	8.5%	7.4%
Sweden	16.9%	19.4%	8.5%	20.4%
Canada	12.9%	15.4%	0.2%	9.8%

Source: US Department of Labor, Bureau of Labor Statistics,
August 1994.

us in good shape in the year 2000.* One measure of an economy's success – and of course the most politically sensitive one as well – is its capacity to create new businesses and new jobs. Although the immediate effect of an increase in productivity may be to shed jobs, productivity growth is essential to enabling businesses to compete and so to providing secure, well-paid employment. So it is no surprise that the number of people in jobs rose by 1.5 million in the 1980s. It is also significant that the peak in long-term unemployment reached at the end of 1992 was more than a quarter of a million lower than its peak in the last economic cycle.

In Britain, as a result of our long-standing commitment to deregulation, we are also less badly affected than our neighbours by the European disease of controls, high taxes and corporatism which has aborted jobs that would otherwise have occurred. It would, though, be highly damaging if a future government were to sign up to the Maastricht Social Chapter, let alone move back towards minimum-wage regulations which would condemn us to Euro-sclerosis when what we need is American-style flexibility.

Along with inflation, industrial efficiency and job creation, the final significant criterion of economic performance is, of course, economic growth. That too confirms the overall picture of improvement. To reach a fair judgement one has, naturally, to try to allow for the effects of the economic cycle. When we do this, we can see that whereas Britain's non-oil GDP grew at less than 1 per cent a year between 1973 and 1979 (compared with an EEC average of 2.5 per cent), it grew at 2.25 per cent a year in the 1980s. This was contrary to the international trend: the OECD area as a whole experienced no improvement in performance in the 1980s.

It is important to restate such facts about the 1980s – and not just to get the record straight. Undervaluing what occurred then may well lead governments to turn to alternative approaches which are in fact reruns of the disastrous prescriptions of the 1970s.

There is a parallel with the United States. There the attempt by leading Republicans to distance themselves from the Reagan

---

* For example, the *Treasury Bulletin* (Winter 1991/92, Vol. 3, Issue 1) shows the remarkable improvement in the productivity and finances of the nine largest (once-) nationalized industries over the period.

years gave the opportunity to the Democrats in 1992 to claim the centre ground and successfully fight an election on the theme that it was 'time for a change'. Only now has the Republican Party perceived that it is by developing rather than detracting from 'Reaganism' that success will be achieved. The economic record of the 1980s in both our countries – low inflation, more growth, more job creation, rising living standards, lower marginal tax rates – shows what works; and the 1970s show equally conclusively what does not.*

WHY THE WEST?

But of course the prescriptions of free-enterprise economics cannot be properly understood, let alone effectively applied, in a vacuum. They depend heavily for their success upon political and – as I have described elsewhere – social conditions.** Precisely why modern Western civilization uniquely gave rise to the sustained growth of prosperity which has transformed lives and prospects over the last quarter of a millennium is fertile ground for debate. The Marxist explanation is now clearly discredited: economic growth is not simply a mechanical result of combining capital and labour. Nor can economic progress simply be ascribed to advances in science or technology, which are not just engines of growth but are also themselves stimulated by cultural and other conditions. Just as significant, in fact, is the way in which science and technology are valued and exploited – and this is something which does indeed mark out modern Western civilization. The Chinese, for example, invented gunpowder and the mariner's compass, but unlike the West they did not use them to build a maritime empire. The Tibetans discovered turbine movement, but were happy to use it for their prayer wheels. The Byzantines invented clockwork, but employed it as part of court ceremony to raise the emperor above

* For a full and persuasive defence of the Reagan record against the criticisms made of it, see *National Review*, 31 August 1992.
** See pp. 538–9.

visiting ambassadors.* But cultural/religious conditions do not offer a total explanation. The moral significance attached by Christianity to the responsible individual was undoubtedly an important element in the distinctive Western growth of liberal political and economic institutions, but its impact has clearly been very different in the Orthodox East. The Protestant Reformation and the values of Nonconformity also probably played a part – but this does not explain the growth of medieval banking and commerce or the rise of Venice. And, of course, any 'explanation' which overlooks the role of the Jews in the growth of capitalism would be no explanation at all.

But two special factors do stand out as of crucial importance – and not just as parts of a wider historical explanation, but also as pointers to future policy. The first is the growth over the centuries of a rule of law, which provided the confidence necessary for entrepreneurship, banking and trade to develop. This clearly has important implications for the strategies being pursued now to establish free-enterprise systems in the former communist states. The second vital condition was the fact that in the crucial period 'Europe comprised a system of divided and, hence, competing powers and jurisdictions'.** As a result, no single government was in a position to pursue policies which frustrated the impulses of economic (or indeed political and religious) freedom without fear of loss of resources. Although the difficulties and cost might be considerable, talented individuals could ultimately take their skills and their money to some other more welcoming state. Today also competition between governments and their differing legal, fiscal and regulatory systems remains a check on the scope for abusing power and thus for impoverishing societies. There is an obvious lesson for those who now wish to submerge European nation states in a United States of Europe where a centralized bureaucracy, by harmonizing regulations, allows no enterprise to escape its clutches.

* Hugh Trevor-Roper, *The Rise of Christian Europe* (1965), pp. 23–4.
** Ralph Raico, 'The Theory of Economic Development and "The European Miracle" ', in *The Collapse of Development Planning*, ed. Peter Boettke (New York University, 1994), p. 41.

LATIN AMERICA

Within the broad framework of 'the West' there have, of course, grown up different kinds of political economy. A particularly instructive case is that of Latin America, because two different and opposing models have been tried. The first, which the economist Hernando de Soto has described as 'mercantilism', has the longer and less glorious tradition. Originating with the Spanish and Portuguese colonial administrations, subsequently perpetuated by corrupt authoritarian regimes of Left and Right, and then all too frequently sustained by international bodies promoting 'development economics', it was based on centralized economic power wielded in the interests of powerful individuals and groups and protected against foreign competition. It bears the main responsibility for the fact that Latin American countries have not enjoyed the advancing prosperity of North America. Mr de Soto's pioneering study of economic conditions in Lima, Peru, showed that as a result of corrupt, unpredictable over-regulation it was now the so-called 'black economy' which was operating to sustain the needs of the people for housing, markets and transport.*

Most Latin American countries had to spend much of the 1980s paying off debts incurred in order to finance the misdirected policies of the 1970s. But, with Chile leading the way, followed by Mexico, Argentina, Brazil and now Peru, there has been a fundamental change of direction away from 'mercantilism' and towards limited government, sounder finances, privatization and deregulation. Significantly too, this new direction apparent in Latin America, like the successful Asia-Pacific economies, has occurred often in spite of rather than because of advice and assistance from international institutions.

Chile, of course, because of the international hostility directed towards General Pinochet's regime, was forced to take unilateral action to restore its economic fortunes by applying liberal economic

* Hernando de Soto, *The Other Path* (London, 1989).

prescriptions. These have subsequently continued under democracy. Monetary growth was curtailed to bring down hyperinflation; tariffs against imports were cut; foreign investment was welcomed; privatization was promoted (350 state companies have been sold) – even to the extent of bringing privatization to bear on the social security system. The beneficial results have been widely felt. Export-led growth has been consistently strong. Moreover, Chile's economy is better balanced and more diversified and so more able to withstand adverse conditions: almost complete reliance on copper exports has given way to the export of computer software, wine, fish, fruit and vegetables, to such an extent that the European Community is clamouring to keep Chile's products out. It is a remarkable transformation and a dramatic demonstration of how liberal economics makes the difference.

Mexico's experience is similar. For decades the quasi-authoritarian corporatist regime kept Mexicans poor. At the time of the 'North-South' Summit, which I attended at Cancún in 1981, Mexico was still determinedly misdirecting investment into large capital projects, hiding behind tariff barriers and pursuing redistributive social policies. It was, indeed, a highly appropriate location for the Third World rhetoric of which so much was then heard. But the country I since visited in 1994 had, under President Salinas, undergone a huge and welcome change. Inflation had been brought down, the public finances were in order, tariffs had been cut, trade union powers had been curbed and 996 of the original 1,155 state-owned companies had been sold, merged or closed down – including the sale of eighteen state banks, representing the largest mergers and acquisition process ever executed in the financial services sector anywhere in the world. The recent Mexican currency crisis, which had ripple effects both within and beyond Mexico, was the result not of these reforms but of a traditional pre-election monetary splurge. When this ran up against the constraint of Mexico's pegged exchange rate there was a flight of capital and the peso collapsed. What this experience establishes is that micro-economic reforms need sound money and orthodox finance if they are to be securely established.

At the time of my second visit in 1994, however, Mexico was on the verge of concluding its agreement on a North American Free Trade Area (NAFTA) with the United States. Such an initiative would have been unthinkable in earlier years when anti-American feeling and protectionist leanings were dominant. The NAFTA initiative has a wider significance. In the past, regional trade agreements in Latin America were generally a means of closing borders to wider international trade competition: nowadays, as with the Andean Group (Venezuela, Colombia, Ecuador, Peru and Bolivia), the Central American Common Market and the southern grouping of Mercosur (Brazil, Argentina, Paraguay and Uruguay), they are seen by the participants as vehicles for freer trade.

Whatever the Argentineans thought about it at the time, defeat in the Falklands War provided a shock which brought first democracy and more recently, under President Menem, the economic benefits of free-market policies. Inflation has been brought down. A far-reaching privatization programme has been undertaken. Subsidies, regulation and tariffs have all been cut. Economic growth has sharply accelerated.

Brazil – the world's fifth largest and sixth most populous state, with enormous natural resources – undoubtedly has the greatest potential. Even when in the past fundamentally unsound policies were pursued, its growth rate testified to this. A serious start has now been made with policies to curb inflation and government borrowing and to promote privatization – though there is much still to do in order to limit the worst excesses of over-government and its concomitant corruption. Economic optimism tempered with political caution is also the appropriate reaction to events in Peru. Free-market economic policies are beginning to yield results, with a successful privatization programme and strong economic growth; but political stability will be necessary if the full benefits of free-enterprise economics are to overcome the legacy of 'mercantilism'.

THE ASIA–PACIFIC REGION

The most successful economies in the world are in the Asia-Pacific region. They have the highest growth rates with output doubling every ten years, and savings ratios running at over 30 per cent of GDP which provide ample resources for investment. It is, of course, necessary to distinguish between systems, cultures and states. For example, Japan's emphasis on decision-making by consensus, its social orderliness, its intricately interlocked financial and industrial complex and its relatively underdeveloped distribution system distinguish it from the classic model of Western capitalist economy. South Korea's economy is similarly dominated by industrial conglomerates with close relationships with government.

But the picture is by no means uniform throughout the Asia-Pacific region. The rapid economic advance in China, though triggered by government decisions at the end of the 1970s to allow first in agriculture and then more generally the rise of a *de facto* private sector, is now advancing with a momentum of its own and independent of central government. Not only is its course unplanned: its final destination is unpredictable. Indeed, the Chinese people have shown themselves to be uniquely entrepreneurial throughout the region – as witness the success of Singapore, Malaysia and Taiwan. In Hong Kong Chinese flair operates within a British framework of political and financial institutions. With only six million people, Hong Kong's lightly regulated and free-trading economy has the eighth largest share of world trade.

Yet, for all the differences between them, the Asia-Pacific economies have certain characteristics in common. Government spending, borrowing and taxation as a share of GDP are low. They are unencumbered with swollen welfare states. Workforces are highly motivated, efficient and increasingly well rewarded – the caricature of Asia-Pacific economic success achieved on the back of low wages rather than high productivity becomes ever less representative of reality. Even the relatively more regimented systems of Japan and South Korea are a far cry from the mildest socialism: government forswears social engineering, is keen that success be rewarded and values the role of small, independent business. As with the evolution of modern Western capitalism, cultural factors play an important part: but the fundamentals of economic success are the same.

The case of India, on the edge of the region and an emerging great power in its own right, is also instructive. Britain's legacy to India was mixed. Among the benefits were a rule of law, a tradition of honest administration, a common language and, of course, an established democratic system. Corresponding disadvantages, however, were excessive bureaucracy, an overmanned state sector and LSE/Oxbridge socialism, which influenced two generations of indigenous politicians. Policies of wealth redistribution, industrial planning, subsidies, price and exchange controls, monopolies, import licensing and almost insurmountably high tariffs had the same result as in other countries and continents – poverty. The first steps away from this self-destructive economic regime began with agricultural reforms in the late sixties. They continued intermittently under Rajiv Gandhi. But it was only the jolt from the economic crisis of 1991 – and the appointment of Narasimha Rao as Prime Minister and Manmohan Singh as Finance Minister – which set India firmly on the right road. Tariffs have now been cut sharply and are due to fall further. Foreign exchange controls have been liberalized. Foreign investment is encouraged – and foreign firms are taking full advantage of the opportunities. With the removal of controls on farm prices, grain production has increased and farmers can begin to afford up-to-date equipment. A new, self-confident middle class is emerging. India's economy is growing strongly.

A similar economic experiment has been taking place at the other edge of the Asia-Pacific region. Australia and New Zealand were infected by socialism à l'anglaise long before India. Public (often monopoly) ownership and effective trade union control over the labour market went further in Australia. But in New Zealand too 'socialism without doctrines' had become the dominant slogan even before the First World War.* Both countries were able temporarily to withstand the debilitating effects of collectivist policies

* N.R. Evans, 'Antipodean Economics: Up from Down Under', *National Review*, 29 August 1994.

pursued by both left- and right-wing governments because of their ability to export commodities, in particular minerals and agricultural products, with which they were endowed. But by the early 1980s the extent of relative economic decline was apparent to all: a new course was required.

In Australia a Labor Government removed many financial controls and, most important, abandoned protectionism, though for political reasons the excessive controls on the labour market remained. This limited opening-up of the Australian economy to competitive pressures reversed the spiral of decline as regards economic growth; but the fact that this was not accompanied by measures to free up the labour market has kept unemployment relatively high.

New Zealand, first under the Labour Government's Finance Minister, Roger Douglas, and subsequently under the National Party Government's Finance Minister, Ruth Richardson, has gone much further – and the results have been that much better. Financial controls were lifted, import restrictions abolished, tariffs lowered, foreign competition in services welcomed, unemployment benefits reduced, income tax cut and the emphasis shifted to indirect taxes. Also – and crucially – unlike Australia, the labour market has been freed up. The result has been annual growth at over 4 per cent, more new jobs, falling unemployment and very low inflation, while productivity has increased and business is investing. The traditional similarities between New Zealand and Britain make the former's success – achieved by following the same general policies as I implemented in Britain in the 1980s – of particular significance.

THE AFRICAN PROBLEM

Even more than Latin America or India, African countries have suffered from misdirected economic policies associated with the collectivist concepts of 'development planning'.* But, as elsewhere

---

* George B.N. Ayittey, 'The Failure of Development Planning in Africa', in *The Collapse of Development Planning*, ed. Peter Boettke (New York University, 1994).

in the Third World, the same implicit reason (or, depending on one's point of view, excuse) for believing that the laws of economics can be defied with impunity is consistently advanced, namely that Africa is somehow 'different'. A wide range of arguments was used to justify this – general underdevelopment, lack of local investment capital, over-dependence on a single commodity, the encouragement of 'infant industries' or, even more dangerous in its quasi-racist implications, the 'special' character of the African himself and his culture. It is, of course, true that cultural factors have played a role in Africa's problems, particularly when departing colonial governments took insufficient heed of tribal and religious differences in putting together African states.* But, as Peter Bauer, above all, points out, experience in Africa (and elsewhere) shows two things. First, if two peoples live under the same regime of liberal capitalism, one will usually out-perform the other; but if one people lives under two regimes – capitalism and collectivism – that portion living under capitalism will out-perform its cousins. A commonsense conclusion is to choose the (capitalist) regime that makes everyone better off, even it if also allows some relative inequalities between ethnic groups with different cultural aptitudes. So anyone who understands the consequences of abandoning the tried and tested model of limited government, a rule of law and free markets can also understand why the post-colonial economic performance of African states is so abysmal.

And abysmal it certainly is. Per capita output in Africa actually declined during the 1970s and 1980s and, as a result, Africa is poorer than in 1960. Yet Africans in the 1980s received per capita a larger share of development aid from the West than anyone else. Price controls imposed on agricultural products in order to subsidize urban élites undermined agriculture, as did the confiscatory policies associated with export marketing boards and brutal forced collectivization of farms. Foreign imports and investment were discouraged. Mountains of international debt were accumulated in order to construct ill-conceived prestige projects. Finally, over-centralized power had the inevitable result of turning government in many African countries into a giant kleptocracy. As a result of

---

* See p. 525.

this catalogue of failure, there is a tendency to give up on Africa. This must be resisted. In any case, Western countries should recall that the record of institutions like the World Bank and the contribution of those Western development economists who prompted such follies hardly inspire pride.

Moreover, closer examination of the realities of African economies challenges some preconceptions. Take South Africa, for example. In terms of mineral wealth, economic development and institutional sophistication it is outstanding. So far, the worst fears about a breakdown of order have not been realized, for which the country's leading political figures deserve great credit. But it does South Africa no good at all to minimize the economic problems or to suggest that large inflows of foreign investment are likely to overcome them. There has been too much state direction of investment and too little competition. Industrial conglomerates have been immune to the beneficial threat of takeovers. The powerful general trade union COSATU has pushed up real wages, which in industry are about the same as in Taiwan, rather more than in Korea and about double those in Brazil. Not surprisingly in such circumstances, investment has gone into labour-saving equipment; and unemployment – with its resultant poverty – is very high. Unfortunately, socialist rhetoric and unrealistic expectations fuelled by the less responsible members of the ANC in the election campaigns will make these problems more difficult to solve. But the way forward is still to apply the same prescriptions as we would for any other over-collectivized economy – keeping down inflation and taxation, curbing public spending, cutting back regulations, promoting competition and avoiding protectionism. The only way to pay for the improved education and better living standards which the black population of South Africa need is to achieve the right conditions for wealth creation. Alas, there is no alternative – and no short cut.

Other states' experience confirms that free-enterprise economics can be just as effective a source of progress in Africa as elsewhere. A quiet revolution has been taking place in East Africa – so quiet that its lessons may not be learned.* Traditionally, Kenya, the

* I am grateful to Peter Anwyl-Harris and GT Management plc for much of the following information.

most industrialized and economically advanced East African country, was the exception to the generality of mis-government in the region. But now Uganda, Zambia and Tanzania – all previously impoverished by incompetent and corrupt regimes – are moving ahead fast. Uganda has curbed its inflation, turned a budget deficit into a surplus, all but abolished exchange controls, welcomed foreign investment, privatized the agricultural marketing boards which had wreaked such damage on cotton and coffee production, and now plans to establish a stock market. Zambia, though its privatization programme is only proceeding slowly, has made major progress in bringing down inflation and has opened a stock exchange. Tanzania has reduced tariffs, ended price controls and has a vigorous privatization programme. Of course political instability still risks jeopardizing economic progress in many of these countries. But economic progress also itself creates the conditions for stable democratic government. And one of the most effective ways of entrenching liberal political systems in that continent is to promote liberal economics.

CENTRAL AND EASTERN EUROPE

Perhaps the most decisive test of the creative potential of capitalism has been its application in the ex-communist countries of Central and Eastern Europe and the former Soviet Union. For a number of reasons, Russia and the other states of the former USSR are in a separate category from the other new democracies of Central and Eastern Europe. (The Baltic states, because of their history and traditional Western orientation, must though be regarded as closer to the latter than the former: and the striking success of their economic reforms emphasizes that.) Although Russia enjoyed swift capitalist growth in the half-century between the end of serfdom and the First World War, there was only a very limited period – essentially after the 1905 Revolution – in which liberal institutions and attitudes could take root. Communism extinguished these memories and also destroyed the still small middle class who were capitalism's hope. Seventy years after the Bolshevik Revolution, communist economic planning has bequeathed its own legacy of misdirected investment, wrongly located factories and power plants, ossified technology, ex-bureaucrats posing as industrial managers, an unmotivated workforce and ecological catastrophe.

More should have been done – and earlier – to help Russia, Ukraine and other ex-Soviet states to build free-enterprise economies. In particular, we should have been prepared to provide backing for a currency board to bring some stability to the Russian rouble. The Russian people rightly had no trust in their government's ability to provide a stable currency. The only solution was to take it out of the government's hands, introduce a 'hard rouble' and set it firmly in the institution of a currency board similar to that which we set up in Hong Kong in 1983.* The currency board, preferably buttressed by representatives of the IMF or the Federal Reserve Board, would always exchange hard rouble currency for US dollar notes at a fixed rate of exchange. History shows that such transparent systems work, even under the most trying circumstances. To make this feasible Russia needed sufficient dollar reserves to give over 100 per cent backing to the hard rouble notes; the West could have found no more worthy form of aid than to have provided such backing.

The secret of successful economic reform is always to ensure that all of the components work together, because then the process of adjustment is easier. On these grounds, some now criticize the Russian reformers of 1992 for freeing prices before breaking up the state-owned monopolies which dominated the economy. But at least price liberalization brought goods into the shops at a time when there was talk of Muscovites simply not having enough to eat. In any case, a far-reaching privatization programme using the voucher method pioneered in Czechoslovakia has since transferred large swathes of industry to the private sector. More than 70 per cent of Russian workers are now in the private sector. True, uncertainty about property rights, excessive bureaucratic regulation, high taxes and widespread corruption are still major problems, deterring foreign investment and driving enterprise into the mafia-controlled black economy. But, for all that, the most gloomy prog-

* This is described in *The Downing Street Years*, pp. 489–90.

nostications seem unjustified. Unreliable figures for the decline in production are more than balanced by others suggesting large increases in private consumption – which is in any case precisely the re-orientation which transformation from a production-led to a consumer-driven economy requires. And unpleasant as many of its manifestations may be in a situation where the law is not properly administered or upheld, no one visiting Russia today could claim that its people are failing to respond to the opportunities for entrepreneurship. In fact, the most important message which Westerners must impart in Russia now is that fully fledged capitalism *requires* a rule of law. Without that, private ownership in Russia will lack legitimacy and therefore stability.

The economic challenges facing the ex-communist states of Central Europe, though formidable, are of a lesser dimension. East Germany, of course, was able to merge with the most economically powerful state in Europe. Hungary had already advanced some way towards a Western-style economy in the last years of communist rule. It is, though, significant that the two most striking success stories – Poland and, still more so, the Czech Republic – occurred where governments took the boldest and earliest decisions to move from socialism to capitalism.

Poland's great advantage was that the communists had largely failed to collectivize agriculture. Communism thus failed to gain total control of the economy – just as in the face of resistance from the Catholic Church it failed to gain total control of society. Communist attempts at economic reform, however, failed: indeed, their most significant legacy was hyper-inflation. The architect of the successful reforms achieved during the Solidarity-led Government, Leszek Balcerowicz, deliberately chose a radical course – the simultaneous introduction of measures to eliminate price controls, tighten monetary policy, cut the budget deficit and remove almost all restrictions on international trade. Inflation fell dramatically. New small businesses started up. Goods flowed into the shops – certainly, at prices which people found difficult to afford, but much of the alleged drop in living standards was a statistical fiction, since previously Poles had faced crippling shortages.* Subsequently, a

---

* These reforms are well described by Jeffrey Sachs in *Poland's Jump to the Market Economy* (London, 1994).

programme of privatization added the final element to the reforms. The private sector now comprises 55 per cent of the economy. Success has not been unalloyed, however. Budget deficits under the burden of unchecked welfare spending seem likely to continue. The privatization programme appears to have slowed since the Left gained power in 1993. Partly in response to the European Community's failure to open up its markets sufficiently to Polish produce, there has been a tendency for Polish tariffs to rise once more.* On balance, however, the successes of reform far outweigh the failures: to such an extent that Poland's economy in 1993 and 1994 grew by some 4 per cent and looks likely to repeat the performance in 1995. Nor should the Right's defeat in the 1993 elections necessarily be attributed to popular discontent at the reform process itself. The fragmentation of the anti-socialist vote among small competing parties under a system of proportional representation (adopted thoughtlessly by most of the new democracies) must bear most of the blame.

The success of economic reform in the Czech Republic is also notable – as is the contrast with Slovakia, which has deliberately retained a more socialist orientation. The Czechs, of course, inherited a tradition of industrial success which not even forty years of communism could extinguish. Before the Second World War Czechoslovakia was one of the world's most advanced economies with an income per head equal to France. Moreover, the Czech reformers, unlike their Polish equivalents, did not inherit hyperinflation; nor were they inhibited by the necessity to seek communist support for the reform measures. Under the determined leadership of Vaclav Klaus, first as Finance Minister and since as Prime Minister, a radical strategy was adopted with no concessions made to demands for a 'third way' between capitalism and socialism. Price controls were removed, subsidies cut back, public spending sharply reduced and the currency made convertible for trade purposes. A pioneering scheme of mass privatization through vouchers has transformed the pattern of ownership, with 80 per cent of Czech assets now in private hands. After the traumas of change,

---

* Marek Matraszek, *Poland: The Politics of Restoration*, Institute for European Defence and Strategic Studies, 1994.

economic growth (at 2.5 per cent in 1994) has begun on a sound footing and, in spite of the shake-out of labour from old inefficient industries, unemployment (at 4 per cent in 1994) is low. Unlike in Poland and Hungary, those who pushed through the necessary economic reforms have in the Czech Republic also reaped the political rewards – which itself is the best guarantee that those reforms will continue.

Yet it is perhaps the example of the smallest and poorest of the former Eastern bloc countries, Albania, which best illustrates the creative potential of uninhibited capitalism. Indeed, what has happened since the fall of communism gives a quite new understanding of Schumpeter's description of capitalism as a process of 'creative destruction'. Albania had lived in a time warp, cut off from political or economic contact with the outside world, without decent communications, burdened by hopelessly outdated industries, its agriculture totally collectivized, the landscape dotted with bunkers built by its paranoid rulers. The only way forward was to start again from scratch; and this is what happened. A sudden huge emigration, though presenting immediate problems for Albania's neighbours, has since resulted in a substantial inflow of remittances which, with overseas aid, allowed the beginnings of a consumer society. Small businesses mushroomed everywhere. Everything which could be salvaged from the collective farms and the bunkers was dismantled and used in new private farms which sprung up and which – the government having abolished price controls – were soon able to feed the population. Albania is now achieving what almost everyone considered impossible: its economic growth has been in double digits for two years running – though, of course, from a very low level. Foreign investment is taking advantage of low wage costs, lack of regulation and the country's mineral wealth and potential for tourism.

The different rates of economic progress, therefore, in the former communist states bears out my central thesis – namely that although political, social and cultural factors are not without importance, the free-enterprise formula works whenever and wherever it is applied. Moreover, its application is crucial to the entrenchment of democracy too. As a recent survey of public opinion in ten ex-communist countries shows, in nearly every case nostalgia for the old communist regime is associated with failure to make a rapid transition to a free economy.*

TWO MODELS –
THE UNITED STATES AND GERMANY

The economic reformers of Central and Eastern Europe naturally sought to study the most successful models of the capitalist system which they intended to recreate. Many of them looked to Britain, particularly in order to learn techniques of privatization, though these have had to be adapted to different circumstances. But it was the examples of the United States and Germany which have had most influence.

There are significant differences between the American and European versions of capitalism. The American traditionally emphasizes the need for limited government, light regulation, low taxes and maximum labour-market flexibility. Its success has been shown above all in the ability to create new jobs, in which it is consistently more successful than Europe. Since the 1960s employment has grown on average by only 0.3 per cent a year in the EEC, compared with 1.8 per cent a year in the USA; moreover, in the US, by contrast with Europe, most of the jobs were created in the private sector. Over 40 per cent of the unemployed in the EC have been out of work for over a year, compared with 10 per cent in the USA.

The European model – in particular the German version – has, however, recently attracted much sympathetic consideration by policy-makers in the American administration who favour an interventionist approach to training, industrial policy and managed trade. It is, therefore, particularly important to understand the weaknesses as well as the undoubted strengths of the European system as exemplified by Germany. For if the world's greatest example and exponent of liberal capitalism were to turn away from

* This survey, part of the study *New Democracies Barometer III*, is reproduced in the magazine *Business Central Europe*, October 1994, p. 80.

it in either internal or external economic policies that would have momentous implications for the free-enterprise system generally.

West Germany's emergence as the major European economic power in the post-war years was rightly described as an 'economic miracle'. A combination of very low inflation and high productivity characterizes the German success. This reflects both the character of the German people and the policies pursued by the German government, particularly in the 1950s and 1960s when the emphasis of the 'social market' approach was on 'market' rather than 'social'. The 1970s and 1980s saw something of a reversal in that balance with a growth of state intervention and joint decision-making (*Mitbestimmung*) by unions and management. There was also a large increase in the tax and regulatory burdens on employers which, it has been suggested, now approach 100 per cent of wages. Although the German economic performance has been impressively consistent, under both these burdens and the shock of a not very well managed enlargement to take in the ex-communist East, some of the characteristics of German capitalism which made for past successes are already leading to serious problems – problems that threaten to get worse. Industrial consensus has degenerated into a more rigid corporatism, which reduces the ability of German industry to adapt flexibly to challenges from Asia and Central Europe. This applies both at the level of individual German companies and in sectors. Significantly, German employers agreed to raise East German wages to West German levels by 1994, which attempt proved deeply damaging – and ultimately practically impossible. But such a decision was only possible in an economy where centralization of wage bargaining was the accepted norm.

Moreover, the German workforce today has the shortest working hours and longest holidays of any country. Asia-Pacific industrial competitors with wage costs per hour a sixth of Germany's are an increasing challenge. And Germany is relatively more reliant on manufacturing industry than most advanced economies.

It is thus an open question how long present prosperity can last under these conditions. The temptation will grow for Germany to follow France in pressing the European Community in the direction of protectionism. But that would be self-defeating, since protectionism reduces the incentive for efficiency at home while stimulating it overseas.* It should be added that this analysis is by no means 'anti-German'. Indeed, the more corporatist model of capitalism which Germany has come to represent only works as well as it does because of the remarkable qualities of the Germans.

THE TEMPTATION OF 'STABILITY'

The attraction which the more regulated German model of capitalism offers is not solely the result of Germany's own impressive economic performance. It also stems from that perpetual desire for security and stability which tempts policy-makers to abandon the risky unpredictability of free markets for the misleading reassurance of planned order. This explains the present tendency to argue for state intervention in industry long after the economic theories justifying it are discredited. It also explains two other current preoccupations – first, the search for a new framework of stable currencies policed by international institutions on the lines of Bretton Woods, and secondly the argument that full-blooded protectionism offers the only hope of withstanding the disruptive competition of new low-cost producers. Each of these viewpoints is advanced by distinguished advocates – in the first case Paul Volcker's Bretton Woods Commission, in the second Sir James Goldsmith.

The pursuit of exchange-rate stability has done great damage during my political lifetime. Nigel Lawson's shadowing of the Deutschmark between March 1987 and March 1988 undermined my own Government's anti-inflation policy. Subsequently, the pursuit of rigid parities within the Exchange Rate Mechanism of the European Monetary System plunged Britain and other European countries into an unnecessarily deep recession. But in any case, as Professor Milton Friedman has pointed out, the experience of pegged exchange rates under the Bretton Woods system devised in 1944, which finally collapsed in 1971, hardly justifies the plaudits it sometimes receives.** In fact, it only worked as intended for

---

* See p. 599.
** Milton Friedman, 'Out of Bretton Woods: Free-Floating Anxiety', *National Review*, 12 September 1994.

eight years – from 1959 to 1967 – and even those years were not free from exchange-rate changes. Moreover, the inflation of the 1970s actually began in the last few years of the Bretton Woods system. Its final breakdown reflected both that inflation and the unwillingness of sovereign states to subordinate their interests to an exchange-rate rigidity which transmitted the inflation or deflation of other economies to their own. All experience has shown that attempts to peg exchange rates do not in fact increase stability – or, except in the very short term, confidence; they simply ensure that adjustments take place against a background of economic crisis and political discord. Talk of 'recreating Bretton Woods' is nostalgia which we cannot afford – and indeed we cannot even achieve. As Sir Samuel Brittan, a distinguished former supporter of the ERM has recently written: 'Fixed, but adjustable, (pegged) exchange rates of the Bretton Woods or ERM types are probably no longer a realistic option; and a straight choice has to be made between floating and a full monetary union with partner countries.' For reasons I advance elsewhere, my choice is firmly for floating rates. Sir Samuel will probably plump for the other option – but we both realize that there is no stopping at the halfway house.

I have more sympathy with the analysis of the international economic scene offered by Sir James Goldsmith.* Sir James is right to draw attention to the challenge posed to high-cost, over-regulated European industry by foreign competition, which he sees as inevitably leading to falling real wages and soaring unemployment – unless we erect protectionist barriers around the advanced economies of Europe. Research suggests that competition from the emerging markets has indeed begun to depress real wages and in Continental Europe is also raising unemployment.** These are real problems with which we must deal.

But the benefits of free trade do not depend upon participating countries having similar cultural or institutional arrangements, nor on their having the same economic potential. The mutual benefit comes from exploiting the comparative advantages enjoyed by

---

* See Sir James Goldsmith's powerfully argued book *The Trap* (London, 1994).
** I am grateful to Professor Patrick Minford for drawing my attention to this research, which he has conducted.

different countries. And Sir James probably exaggerates the immediacy and scale of what he calls 'a completely new type of competition' from four billion people who are coming into the world economy. The figure of four billion seems to include the entire population of the world outside the developed countries, men, women and children. Not all of these are coming on to the world economy any time soon, and the economic potential of the low-paid workers in China and the former Soviet bloc who are competing with us is very varied.

Of course, the experience of the Asian 'four tigers' suggests that some at least of these newly-industrializing countries will enjoy a very rapid rise in industrial skills and living standards. But two consequences will flow from that: they will cease to be low-wage competition, and they will increasingly provide a market for the exports of other nations, including Western nations. Competition will once again work for the benefit of all.

It could be, admittedly, that the West, even while prospering in absolute terms, might fall behind these new competitors in relative terms. That would be no great tragedy; but in any case for several reasons it is unlikely to happen. The most important one is that, the more advanced an economy, the smaller labour costs are as a proportion of total costs – especially in manufacturing industry where the developed world is allegedly most vulnerable. (This is one beneficial result of the automation revolution, which poses problems in other respects.) And in both advanced manufacturing industry and in services, where the West also has a relative advantage, investment in human capital tends to be disproportionately important. Here, again, the West scores, since our unskilled labour tends to be more skilled than their unskilled labour – not to mention that developed countries produce many more scientists, technicians, engineers, economists, accountants, bankers and other professionals at the very highest level. Indeed, many of their ablest competitors in developing countries emigrate to Western countries when they are allowed to do so.

None of which is to say that the developed world will not fall behind the Pacific Rim countries if it continues to pursue policies which neglect or positively waste the talent available to us. Sir James himself argues vigorously, and I heartily concur, that well-intentioned policies of indiscriminate welfare 'reduce the self-reliance of citizens and of their families by converting them into dependants of the state'. We are in danger in Britain and other European countries of following the example of the United States and creating a large permanent 'underclass' living off a combination of crime, welfare and the black economy. Such policies are increasingly under fire from informed opinion, but they are so entrenched politically and supported so stubbornly by special-interest lobbies that only the cold wind of economic reality will persuade us to reform them.

Sir James's prescription – tariffs and quotas to protect European Union industries – would actually be a temporary barrier against this reality. It would reassure both management and workers that they need not significantly improve their efficiency, and government that it need not cut excessive benefits and regulations. At the same time, it would stimulate our Asian and other competitors to cut costs and improve their products precisely in order to leap over the barriers we had raised. A decade later we would be worse off as a result. Again, that is not to deny that there are real problems with which we have to deal. But to the extent that the jobs of unskilled workers in Western countries are jeopardized by low-cost competition, this requires still greater labour-market flexibility, well-directed training and retraining programmes and targeted help for the living standards of the poorest households of the sort given by Family Credit at present.

One must also ask why the dividing line between allegedly beneficial and non-beneficial trade should coincide with the external frontiers of the European Union. Within the Union itself there are large differences of development, of potential and of labour costs. The logical end of Sir James's argument would be national, or even regional and sub-regional tariffs: yet it was precisely because such impediments to trade were removed that the conditions were created for the Industrial Revolution on which our prosperity was originally based. Tariffs and quotas have other undesirable consequences. As Brian Hindley points out, they discriminate against exporting industries by pushing up the exchange rate.* They also

* Brian Hindley, *The Goldsmith Fallacy*, Centre for Policy Studies, December 1994, p. 27.

run the risk of provoking retaliatory action by other countries. And they contribute to international tensions to the extent that at a certain point it may be worthwhile for a poor (but militarily strong) power excluded from markets to break its way into them by force.

Welcoming as I do Sir James Goldsmith's intervention in the debate about the future of Europe and agreeing with his support for sovereign nation states, I also find it ironic that he should be prepared to allow central European Union institutions so much power over trade and industrial policy. The decisions about which industries to protect or not are precisely those for which politicians and bureaucrats must be held tightly accountable. Such policies of discrimination encourage patronage, corruption and abuse of power. They would certainly be exploited to the full by the federalists of whom Sir James is rightly suspicious, and they have a long record of failure. So I disagree. But Sir James has forced me and other conservative free traders to re-examine our arguments in the vastly changed circumstances of the post-communist global economy.

This century has seen an unprecedented political and economic experiment. The centrally controlled model has been tried in various forms – ranging from the totalitarianism of communism and Nazism, through various brands of social democracy or democratic socialism, to an un-ideological technocratic corporatism. So has the decentralized liberal model – most notably in Britain and the United States in the 1980s. The balance sheet of the century which can now be drawn up conveys one irresistible message: whether judged on political, social or economic grounds, collectivism has failed. By contrast, the application of classical liberal principles has transformed countries and continents for the good.

The tragedy is, of course, that this great experiment was unnecessary. State monopoly and the command economy could never in the end mobilize human talent and energy. And nor could their milder coercive equivalents.

It would be nice to believe that these lessons had now been fully absorbed, that mankind will avoid these terrible errors in the future, and that in economic policy at least we will stick firmly to principles which experience has shown to be valid. Unfortunately, as one of our greatest poets reminds us:

As it will be in the future, it was at the birth of Man –
There are only four things certain since Social Progress began:
That the Dog returns to his Vomit and the Sow returns to her
    Mire,
And the burnt Fool's bandaged finger goes wabbling back to
    the Fire;
And that after this is accomplished, and the brave new world
    begins
When all men are paid for existing and no man must pay for
    his sins,
As surely as Water will wet us, as surely as Fire will burn,
The Gods of the Copybook Headings with terror and slaughter
    return!*

* Rudyard Kipling, 'The Gods of the Copybook Headings' (1919).

Epilogue

In May 1993 I visited Warsaw as guest of honour at the reopening of the historic Bristol Hotel. It was, in its way, a significant occasion. The Bristol had been one of the great hotels of Europe. Opened in 1901, owned by a company whose principal shareholder was the pianist and Polish President Paderewski, famous for the highest standards of cuisine and elegance in the elegant society of pre-1914 Europe, the Bristol had fallen on evil days when Poland itself fell on evil days under first Nazism and then communism. It had closed its doors in the early eighties. Now it had been restored to its full splendour with the help of a British company, and I had the great pleasure of reopening it. One felt that it was another sign that a high style of life was returning to its natural home in Central Europe. I also formally opened the Warsaw offices of my Foundation which I hope will help to entrench democracy and the free economy in the post-communist world.

But my visit was memorable for a far deeper reason. It coincided with the fiftieth anniversary of the Warsaw Ghetto uprising. That Saturday afternoon I walked the perimeter of the now razed quarter with the oldest survivor of the uprising as my guide, after which I was taken to see still photographs of the Nazi destruction of the city's Jewish community. It was a harrowing experience, especially so when I reflected that these terrible events had happened in my own lifetime when I was a young student enjoying Oxford.

The following morning I attended mass at the Church of the Holy Cross. The atmosphere was one of intense devotion and the ceremony elaborate, both very different from the restrained piety of Anglican services and the resolutely simple Methodism of Grantham. Every nook and cranny was packed. And the choral singing of unfamiliar Polish hymns was all the more uplifting because I could not understand the verses: it forced me to try to imagine from the music what the congregation was asking of God. Foreign though much of this experience was, it also gave me the comforting feeling that I was one soul among many in a fellowship of believers that crossed nations and denominations.

When the priest rose to give the sermon, however, I had a sense that I had suddenly become the focus of attention. Heads turned and people smiled at me. As the priest began, someone translated his words. He recalled how during the dark years of communism – that second totalitarian affliction suffered by the Poles – they had been aware of voices from the outside world offering hope of a different and better life. The voices were many, often eloquent, and all were welcome to a people starved so long of truth as well as of freedom. But Poles had come to identify with one voice in particular – my own. Even when that voice had been relayed through the distorting loudspeaker of Soviet propaganda, they had heard through the distortions the message of truth and hope. Well, communism had fallen and a new democratic order had replaced it. But they had not fully felt the change, not truly believed in its reality, until today when they finally saw me in their own church.

The priest finished his sermon and the service continued. But the kindness of priest and parishioners had not been exhausted. At the end of mass I was invited to stand in front of the altar. When I did so, lines of children presented me with little bouquets of flowers while their mothers and fathers applauded.

I had always believed, during the long struggle with the Soviet Union, that my firmest allies were the ordinary people of the Eastern bloc. Although real differences divide people from different nations and cultures, our basic needs and aspirations are very similar: a good job, a loving family, a better life for our children, a country in which a man can call his soul his own. I knew, simply *knew*, that communism and socialism either denied or corrupted these aspirations, and so the people living under them would always be in a state of rebellion. My friends in exile from Eastern Europe had assured me this was so. The popular revolutions of 1989 and

1991 confirmed it. Until the people in the Church of the Holy Cross treated me as a dear friend to whom something was owed, however, I had not really known. Now, all the general propositions favouring freedom I had either imbibed at my father's knee or acquired by candle-end reading of Burke and Hayek were suddenly embodied in the worshippers and their children and illuminated by their smiles.

A reader who has survived through both volumes of these memoirs to this point will have read the record of a busy, productive and, on the whole, happy life. I hope it will carry on being all three for some time yet. But the very act of writing memoirs has forced me not only to be more introspective than I like, but even to look at my life as some sort of completed work, as if the publisher's deadline had a higher significance. So what is the best epitaph that a living politician can reasonably aspire to? The question answers itself – dustily. But a fair verdict must begin with asking what is the most that any human being can achieve in life.

We are told on good authority that all human achievement is built on sand. Both our triumphs and our tragedies are transient. We cannot foresee, let alone determine, the future. The most that we can achieve in our private lives is to hand on better prospects to our children; it is up to them to build on those prospects. Similarly, as Prime Minister, the most I could aspire too was to hand on to my successor a better country than the one I had inherited in 1979's Winter of Discontent. I worked hard to do so and, along with some disappointments, I can claim many successes. By 1990, the British people were freer, more prosperous, less torn by civil strife, and enjoying better prospects for world peace than at any time since the First World War. But there are no final victories in politics. Will these gains prove permanent? Will they be reversed? Will they be overwhelmed by new issues or clouds which now are no bigger than a man's hand?

Naturally, such questions interest me. I have at least an average share of vanity. But they cannot be answered except in the most general (and gloomy) way: they are human achievements and therefore built on sand.

That gloom must, however, be qualified in two respects. In the first place, great political battles change the direction of history.

Subsequent conflicts may sometimes seem to reverse the outcome. But in fact they take place on a different battleground, one permanently altered by the earlier victories. So the final *status quo* may incorporate many of the features the latest victors originally opposed. Eventually, a Labour government may come to power in Britain. If it does, however, it is unlikely to nationalize the industries privatized in the 1980s, nor restore the 98 per cent top tax rates of 1979, nor reverse all the trade union reforms, let alone implement the proposals contained in the Labour election manifesto of 1983. In some Central European countries, the former communists *have* regained power (under various shades of false colours); but they show no signs of restoring the command economy or the police state, let alone reviving the Warsaw Pact. What Ronald Reagan and I achieved in the 1980s may well undergo future transformations that neither of us would find congenial. But it will never be transformed into exactly what we fought.

My second qualification is that our experiences, being in the past, are beyond amendment. Like a life that is ended, they can never be altered – for either good or ill. The young Jews killed in the Warsaw Ghetto uprising will never finish their education, raise families, serve their community, shape their own lives. The Soviet Union lasted for seventy-four years; for hundreds of millions of people that period was the whole of their reality. They lived and died under oppression. Equally, for those who lived to see the 'velvet revolution' of 1989 or the aborted 1991 Soviet *coup*, the regaining of freedom is an experience that can never be taken from them. Almost every citizen of the Eastern bloc can recount some happy experience that flowed ultimately from the West's firm resistance to communism: liberation from the Gulag, recovery of his family's property, a reunion with family members across the old Iron Curtain, leaving the collective to start his own farm, the luxury of criticizing once-omnipotent political bosses, the first exercise of consumer choice in buying something better than a Trabant, being able to go to church without fearing that it will mean demotion at work or loss of a university place.

The people of Britain lived in a free society before 1979 and therefore never suffered the oppression that was everyday life under communism. But after 1979 they enjoyed a self-fulfilment that the

rolling-back of socialism and the expansion of freedom made possible. Some were no longer prevented by union power from doing
the best work of which they were capable; some were able for the
first time to buy a home, or a private pension, or shares in a
privatized company – a nest egg to leave their children; some found
that a good private school or a private hospital bed was no longer
a privilege of the rich – they could buy it too; some exercised their
new prosperity by sharing it with others in the upsurge of charitable
giving in the 1980s; and all enjoyed the greater freedom and control
over their own lives which cuts in income tax extended. A future
government might curb the reforms which made these new lives
possible – whether in the East or the West. But it could never
remove the lived experience of freedom or the knowledge that such
freedom is possible under the sun. As a character says in the film
Ninotchka when the heroine in Moscow receives a letter censored
with heavy black lines from greeting to signature: 'They can't
censor our memories.'

Of course, no human mind, nor indeed any conceivable computer, can calculate the sum total of these experiences in terms of
happiness, achievement and virtue, nor indeed of their opposites.
It follows therefore that the full accounting of how my political
work affected the lives of others is something we will only know on
Judgement Day. It is an awesome and unsettling thought. But it
comforts me to think that when I stand up to hear the verdict, I
will at least have the people of the Church of the Holy Cross in
court as character witnesses.

Speech by Rt Hon Mrs Margaret Thatcher OM FRS to
the Global Panel in The Hague, Friday 15 May 1992

EUROPE'S POLITICAL ARCHITECTURE

Mr Chairman,

We are fortunate to be meeting in The Hague, a beautiful city kept
beautiful by a country which values its architectural heritage. Goethe
described architecture as 'frozen music'. And in a city like this it is
not hard to imagine the grand symphonic melodies that might be
released if we could defrost the Town Hall and the great urban squares.

Architecture tells us a lot about ourselves, about our idea of God,
about our relationship with our fellow men, and about our vision of
Man's destiny.

The great medieval cathedrals gave us an exalted spiritual view of
Man's place in a universe governed by an all-loving and all-seeing
Creator.

The Age of Reason pictured civilized man in a neat, geometrically
ordered landscape dotted with neo-classical structures at regular intervals – with no more than one small folly to each estate.

And in our own day, the vision of New European Man walking
purposefully towards the Common Agricultural Policy was exquisitely
realized in the Berlaymont building in Brussels.

What music would Goethe hear if he could look upon the Berlaymont, perhaps while acting as an adviser to the Commissioner responsible for developing a policy for European culture (which has
languished so long without one)?

And what a climax of discord and disharmony! For the Berlaymont
– its halls lined with cancer-causing asbestos – is to be pulled down.

Look at the architecture of the last fifty years – in particular, at the
architecture that went beyond the modern to the futuristic. It was
certainly very dramatic, but the one thing it no longer expresses is the
Future. What it expresses is yesterday's vision of the future – one
captured by the poet John Betjeman in 1945:

I have a vision of the future, chum.
The workers' flats, in fields of soya beans,
Tower up like silver pencils, score on score.

But the Berlaymont school of architecture is a convenient symbol
for the political architecture of the European Community. For it too
is infused with the spirit of 'yesterday's future'.

Mr Chairman, the European Community we have today was created
in very different circumstances to deal with very different problems.
It was built upon very different assumptions about where the world
was heading. And it embodied political ideas and economic theories
that in the light of recent history we have to question. Today I want
to do exactly that. In particular, I shall try to answer three questions.

First, how can we best deal with the imbalance in Europe created
by the reunification and revival of Germany?

Second, how can we reform European institutions so that they
provide for the diversity of post-communist Europe and be truly
democratic?

Third, how can we ensure that the new Europe contributes to –
rather than undermines – the world's economic prosperity and political
stability?

Our answers to these questions can no longer be bound by the
conventional collectivist wisdom of the 1940s and fifties. That is yesterday's future. We must draw on the ideas of liberty, democracy, free
markets and nationhood that have swept the world in the last decade.

THE BEGINNING OF THE COMMUNITY

It was Winston Churchill who, with characteristic magnanimity in
1946, with his Zurich speech, argued that Germany should be rehabili-
tated through what he called 'European Union' as 'an association
between France and Germany' which would 'assume direction'. This
could not be done overnight, and it took American leadership. In
1947, after travelling through Europe in that terrible winter when
everything froze over, George Marshall, the then Secretary of State,
promoted the idea of American help. Marshall Aid was administered
by institutions set up *ad hoc* – it had to be, if only because most
European states did not have adequate machinery, the Greek delegate
being found one day simply making up figures for his country's needs
– and I expect there were others besides.

The initial impetus was for European recovery. It owed much to simple American good-heartedness. It owed something to commercial calculation: the prosperity of Europe, in free-trade conditions, would also be the prosperity of America. But the main thing was the threat from Stalin. Eastern Europe had shown how demoralized peoples could not resist cunningly executed communist takeovers, and Marshall Aid was intended to set Western Europe back on its feet. It was a prodigious success.

But we have found, again and again, that institutions devised for one set of problems become obstacles to solving the next set – even that they become problems in their own right. The Common Agricultural Policy is an example. As originally devised, it had a modest aim that was not unreasonable.

Yet we all know that the CAP is now an expensive headache, and one quite likely to derail the Uruguay Round. Because of agricultural protection we stop food imports from the poorer countries. They themselves are nowadays vehement supporters of market principles: it is from the Cairns Group of developing countries that you hear demands for free trade. Yet in the industrialized part of the world, the taxpayer and the consumer stump up $270 billion in subsidies and higher costs; and the World Bank has calculated that, if the tariff and other barriers were cut by half, then the poorer countries would gain at once, in exports, $50 billion. In case you might think that these sentiments are somehow anti-European, I should say that they come from an editorial in the economic section of the *Frankfurter Allgemeine Zeitung* of 4 May.

Here we have a prime example of yesterday's solutions becoming tomorrow's problems. You could extend this through the European institutions as a whole. They were meant to solve post-war problems, and did so in many ways extremely well. Western Europe did unite against the Soviet threat, and, with Anglo-American precepts, became free and very prosperous. That prosperity, denied to the peoples of Eastern Europe and Russia, in the end caused demoralization among their rulers, and revolt from below. We are now in a quite different set of circumstances, with the Cold War over.

Looking at European institutions today, I am reminded of a remark made about political parties in the French Third Republic. Some of them had names which reflected radical republican origins from the 1870s, but years later they had become conservative. These radical names, ran the remark, were like the light reaching Earth from stars that were long extinct. Equally with the end of the Cold War we have to look again at the shape of Europe and its institutions.

THE GERMAN QUESTION

Mr Chairman, let me turn first to the new situation created by the reunification of Germany. And let me say that if I were a German today, I would be proud – proud but also worried. I would be proud of the magnificent achievement of rebuilding my country, entrenching democracy and assuming the undoubtedly preponderant position in Europe. But I would also be worried about the European Community and its direction. The German taxpayer pays dearly for his place in Europe. Britain and Germany have a strong joint interest in ensuring that the other Community countries pay their fair share of the cost – and control the Community's spending more enthusiastically – without leaving us to carry so much of the burden.

Germany is well equipped to encourage such financial prudence. Indeed I would trust the Bundesbank more than any other European central bank to keep down inflation – because the Germans have none-too-distant memories of the total chaos and political extremism which hyper-inflation brings. The Germans are, therefore, right to be increasingly worried about the terms they agreed for economic and monetary union. Were I a German, I would prefer the Bundesbank to provide our modern equivalent of the gold standard rather than any committee of European central bankers.

But there is an understandable reluctance on the part of Bonn to defend its views and interests so straightforwardly. For years the Germans have been led to believe by their neighbours that their respectability depends on their subordinating their national interest to the joint decisions of the Community. It is better that that pretence be stopped. A reunited Germany can't and won't subordinate its national interests in economic or in foreign policy to those of the Community indefinitely. And sometimes Germany will be right when the rest are wrong, as it was over the recognition of Croatia and Slovenia. Indeed, if the Federal Republic had led the way in recognizing these countries earlier, Serbian aggression might have been deterred and much bloodshed prevented. Whether rightly or wrongly exercised, however, Germany's new pre-eminence is a fact. We will all be better off if we recognize that modern democratic Germany has come of age.

Nevertheless Germany's power is a problem – as much for the Germans as for the rest of Europe. Germany is too large to be just another player in the European game, but not large enough to establish unquestioned supremacy over its neighbours. And the history of Europe since 1870 has largely been concerned with finding the right structure to contain Germany.

It has been Germany's immediate neighbours, the French, who have seen this most clearly. Both Briand in 1929 and Schuman after the Second World War proposed structures of economic union to achieve this. Briand's proposal was made just at the moment when the rise of the Nazis made such a visionary scheme impossible and it failed. But Schuman's vision of a European Community was realized because of an almost unique constellation of favourable circumstances. The Soviet threat made European cooperation imperative. Germany was itself divided. Other Western nations sought German participation in the defence of Western Europe. West Germany needed the respectability that NATO and the Community could give. And American presence in, and leadership of, Europe reduced the fears of Germany's neighbours.

With the collapse of the Soviet Union and reunification of Germany, the entire position has changed. A new Europe of some thirty states has come into being, the problem of German power has again surfaced and statesmen have been scrambling to produce a solution to it. At first France hoped that the post-war Franco-German partnership, with France as the senior partner, would continue. Chancellor Kohl's separate and successful negotiations with Mr Gorbachev quickly showed this to be an illusion.

The next response of France and other European countries was to seek to tie down the German Gulliver within the joint decision-making of the European Community. Again, however, this quickly proved to be an illusion. Germany's preponderance within the Community is such that no major decision can really be taken against German wishes. In these circumstances, the Community augments German power rather than containing it.

Let me illustrate this point with two examples where I agree with the German position. The first, as I have mentioned, was the German decision to recognize Croatia and Slovenia which compelled the rest of Europe to follow suit. The second is the refusal of the Bundesbank to pursue imprudent financial policies at the urging of some of the countries of the G7. However much I may sympathize with these policies, the blunt fact is that Germany has followed its own interests rather than the advice of its neighbours, who have then been compelled to adjust their own stance.

THE BALANCE OF POWER

What follows from this is that German power will be best accommodated in a looser Europe in which individual nation states retain their
freedom of action. If Germany or any other power then pursues a
policy to which other countries object, it will automatically invite a
coalition against itself. And the resulting solution will reflect the relative weight of the adversaries. A common foreign policy, however, is
liable to express the interests of the largest single actor. And a serious
dispute between EC member states locked into a common foreign
policy would precipitate a crisis affecting everything covered by the
Community.

The general paradox here is that attempts at cooperation that are
too ambitious are likely to create conflict. We will have more harmoni-
ous relationships between the states of Europe if they continue to have
room to make their own decisions and to follow their own interests –
as happened in the Gulf War.

But it would be idle to deny that such a balance of power – for that
is what I have been describing – has sometimes broken down and led
to war. And Europe on its own, however organized, will still find
the question of German power insoluble. Europe has really enjoyed
stability only since America became a European power.

The third response therefore is to keep an American presence in
Europe. American power is so substantial that it dwarfs the power of
any other single European country. It reassured the rest of Europe in
the face of Soviet power until yesterday; and it provides similar comfort
against the rise of Germany today – as the Germans themselves
appreciate.

Why aren't we worried about the abuse of American power? It is
difficult to be anxious about a power so little inclined to throw its
weight around that our principal worry is that American troops will
go home.

And there's the rub. There is pressure from isolationist opinion in
the USA to withdraw from Europe. It is both provoked and encouraged by similar thinking in the Community which is protectionist in
economics and 'little European' in strategy. In trade, in the GATT
negotiations, in NATO's restructuring, we need to pursue policies that
will persuade America to remain a European power.

EUROPE FREE AND DEMOCRATIC

If America is required to keep Europe secure, what is required to keep Europe free and democratic?

When the founders of the European Community drew up the Treaty of Rome, they incorporated features from two quite different economic traditions. From liberalism they took free trade, free markets and competition. From socialism (in guises as various as social Catholicism and corporatism) they took regulation and intervention. And for thirty years – up to the signing of the Single European Act – these two traditions were in a state of perpetual but unacknowledged tension.

Now – with the Commission exploiting the Single European Act to accumulate powers of greater direction and regulation – Europe is reaching the point at which it must choose between these two approaches. Is it to be a tightly regulated, centralized bureaucratic federal state, imposing uniform standards throughout the Continent? Or is it to be a loose-knit, decentralized free-market Europe of sovereign states, based upon competition between different national systems of tax and regulation within a free-trade area?

The federalists at least seem to be clear. The Maastricht Treaty met the Commission's requirement for a 'single institutional framework' for the Community. Yet, before the ink was even dry on the Treaty, it was reported that the President of the European Commission was seeking more money and more powers for the Commission which would become the Executive of the Community – in other words a European Government. There would seem to be no doubt about the direction in which the European federalists are now anxious to proceed – towards a federal Europe.

Nor is there any mystery about the urgency with which they press the federalist cause. Even though they may wish to defer the 'enlargement' of the Community with the accession of Eastern Europe, they realize it is impossible. A half-Europe imposed by Soviet tyranny was one thing; a half-Europe imposed by Brussels would be a moral catastrophe, depriving the Community of its European legitimacy.

The Commission knows it will have to admit many new members in the next few decades. But it hopes to construct a centralized superstate in advance – and irrevocably – so that the new members will have to apply for entry on federalist terms.

And it's just not on.

Imagine a European Community of thirty nations, ranging in their economic productivity from Germany to Ukraine, and in their political stability from Britain to Poland

– all governed from Brussels;

– all enforcing the same conditions at work;

– all having the same worker rights as the German unions;

– all subject to the same interest rates, monetary, fiscal and economic policies;

– all agreeing on a common foreign and defence policy;

– and all accepting the authority of an Executive and a remote foreign parliament over '80 per cent of economic and social legislation'.

Mr Chairman, such a body is an even more utopian enterprise than the Tower of Babel. For at least the builders of Babel all spoke the same language when they *began*. They were, you might say, *communautaire*.

Mr Chairman, the thinking behind the Commission's proposals is essentially the thinking of 'yesterday's tomorrow'. It was how the best minds of Europe saw the future in the ruins after the Second World War.

But they made a central intellectual mistake. They assumed that the model for future government was that of a centralized bureaucracy that would collect information upwards, make decisions at the top, and then issue orders downwards. And what seemed the wisdom of the ages in 1945 was in fact a primitive fallacy. Hierarchical bureaucracy may be a suitable method of organizing a small business that is exposed to fierce external competition – but it is a recipe for stagnation and inefficiency in almost every other context.

Yet it is precisely this model of remote, centralized, bureaucratic organization that the European Commission and its federalist supporters seek to impose on a Community which they acknowledge may soon contain many more countries of widely differing levels of political and economic development, and speaking more than fifteen languages. '*C'est magnifique, mais ce n'est pas la politique.*'

The larger Europe grows, the more diverse must be the forms of cooperation it requires. Instead of a centralized bureaucracy, the model should be a market – not only a market of individuals and companies, but also a market in which the players are governments.

Thus governments would compete with each other for foreign investments, top management and high earners through lower taxes and less regulation. Such a market would impose a fiscal discipline on governments because they would not want to drive away expertise and business. It would also help to establish which fiscal and regulatory policies produced the best overall economic results. No wonder socialists don't like it.

To make such a market work, of course, national governments must retain most of their existing powers in social and economic affairs. Since these governments are closer and accountable to their voters, it is doubly desirable that we should keep power at the national level.

THE ROLE OF THE COMMISSION

Mr Chairman, in 1996, when the arrangements agreed at Maastricht are due to be reviewed, and probably a good deal earlier, the Community should move in exactly the opposite direction to that proposed by the European federalists.

A Community of sovereign states committed to voluntary cooperation, a lightly regulated free market and international free trade does not need a Commission in its present form. The government of the Community – to the extent that this term is appropriate – is the Council of Ministers, consisting of representatives of democratically elected national governments. The work of the Commission should cease to be legislative in any sense. It should be an administrative body, like any professional civil service, and it should not initiate policy, but rather carry it out. In doing this it should be subject to the scrutiny of the European Parliament acting on the model of Commons Select Committees. In that way, whatever collective policies or regulations are required would emerge from deliberation between democratic governments, accountable to their national parliaments, rather than being imposed by a bureaucracy with its own agenda.

COOPERATION IN EUROPE

But need this always be done in the same 'single institutional framework'? New problems arise all the time. Will these always require the same level and type of cooperation in the same institutions? I doubt it. We need a greater flexibility than the structures of the European Community have allowed until very recently.

A single institutional framework of its nature tends to place too much power with the central authorities. It is a good thing that a Common Foreign Policy will continue to be carried on under a separate treaty and will neither be subject to the European Court nor permit the Commission to fire off initiatives at will. If 'Europe' moves into new areas, it must do so under separate treaties which clearly define the powers which have been surrendered.

And why need every new European initiative require the participation of all members of the Community? It will sometimes be the case – especially after enlargement – that only some Community members will want to move forward to another stage of integration.

Here I pay tribute to John Major's achievement in persuading the other eleven Community heads of government that they could move ahead to a Social Chapter, but not within the Treaty and without Britain's participation. It sets a vital precedent. For an enlarged Community can only function if we build in flexibility of that kind.

We should aim at a multi-track Europe in which *ad hoc* groups of different states – such as the Schengen Group – forge varying levels of cooperation and integration on a case-by-case basis. Such a structure would lack graph-paper neatness. But it would accommodate the diversity of post-communist Europe.

THE EUROPEAN PARLIAMENT

Supporters of federalism argue, no doubt sincerely, that we can accommodate this diversity by giving more powers to the European Parliament. But democracy requires more than that.

To have a genuine European democracy you would need a Europe-wide public opinion based on a single language; Europe-wide political parties with a common programme understood similarly in all member states; a Europe-wide political debate in which political and economic concepts and words had the same agreed meaning everywhere.

We would be in the same position as the unwieldy Habsburg Empire's parliament.

THE HABSBURG PARLIAMENT

That parliament was a notorious failure. There were dozens of political parties, and nearly a dozen peoples were represented – Germans, Italians, Czechs, Poles and so on. For the government to get anything through – for instance, in 1889 a modest increase in the number of conscripts – took ages, as all the various interests had to be propitiated.

When one or other was not satisfied, its spokesmen resorted to obstruction – lengthy speeches in Russian, banging of desk-lids, throwing of
ink-wells and on one occasion the blowing of a cavalry trumpet by
the Professor of Jurisprudence at the German University of Prague.
Measures could not be passed, and budgets could only be produced
by decree. The longest-lasting Prime Minister, Count Taaffe,
remarked that his highest ambition in politics was the achievement of
supportable dissatisfaction on all sides – not a bad description of what
the European Community risks becoming.

And because of the irresponsibility of parliaments, the Habsburg
Monarchy could really only be ruled by bureaucrats. It took twenty-
five signatures for a tax payment to be validated; one in four people
in employment worked for the state in some form or another, even in
1914; and so many resources went to all of this that not much was
left for defence: even the military bands had to be cut back, Radetzky
March and all. Of course it was a tremendous period in cultural terms
both in Vienna and in Budapest. We in England have done mightily
well by the emigration, often forced, to our shores of so many talented
people from Central Europe. But the fact is that they had to leave
their native lands because political life became impossible.

This example could be multiplied again and again. Belgium and
Holland, which have so much in common, split apart in 1831. Sweden
and Norway, which have even more in common, split apart in 1905.
It does seem simply to be a straightforward rule in modern times that
countries which contain two languages, even if they are very similar,
must in the end divide, unless the one language absorbs the other. It
would be agreeable to think that we could all go back to the world of
the Middle Ages, when the educated classes spoke Latin and the rulers
communicated in grunts. But we cannot. Unless we are dealing with
international cooperation and alliances freely entered into, we create
artificial structures which become the problem that they were meant
to address. The League of Nations, when the Second World War
broke out, resolved to ignore the fact and to discuss, instead, the
standardization of level-crossings.

A FEDERAL EUROPE

Mr Chairman, I am sometimes tempted to think that the new Europe
which the Commission and Euro-federalists are creating is equally
ill-equipped to satisfy the needs of its members and the wishes of their

peoples. It is, indeed, a Europe which combines all the most striking failures of our age.

The day of the artificially constructed megastate has gone. So the Euro-federalists are now desperately scurrying to build one.

The Swedish-style welfare state has failed – even in Sweden. So the Euro-statists press ahead with their Social Chapter.

Large-scale immigration has in France and Germany already encouraged the growth of extremist parties. So the European Commission is pressing us to remove frontier controls.

If the European Community proceeds in the direction which the majority of member-state governments and the Commission seem to want, they will create a structure which brings insecurity, unemployment, national resentment and ethnic conflict.

Insecurity – because Europe's protectionism will strain and possibly sever that link with the United States on which the security of the Continent ultimately depends.

Unemployment – because the pursuit of policies of regulation will increase costs, and price European workers out of jobs.

National resentment – because a single currency and a single centralized economic policy, which will come with it, will leave the electorate of a country angry and powerless to change its conditions.

Ethnic conflict – because not only will the wealthy European countries be faced with waves of immigration from the south and from the east. Also within Europe itself, the effect of a single currency and regulation of wages and social costs will have one of two consequences. Either there will have to be a massive transfer of money from one country to another, which will not in practice be affordable. Or there will be massive migration from the less successful to the more successful countries.

Yet if the future we are being offered contains so very many risks and so few real benefits, why, it may be asked, is it proving all but irresistible ?

The answer is simple. It is that in almost every European country there has been a refusal to debate the issues which really matter. And little can matter more than whether the ancient, historic nations of Europe are to have their political institutions and their very identities transformed by stealth into something neither wished nor understood by their electorates. Yet so much is it the touchstone of respectability to accept this ever-closer union, now interpreted as a federal destiny, that to question is to invite affected disbelief or even ridicule. This silent understanding – this Euro-snobbism – between politicians, bureaucracies, academics, journalists and businessmen is destructive of honest debate.

So John Major deserves high praise for ensuring at Maastricht that we would not have either a single currency or the absurd provisions of the Social Chapter forced upon us: our industry, workforce, and national prosperity will benefit as a result. Indeed, as long as we in Britain now firmly control our spending and reduce our deficit, we will be poised to surge ahead in Europe. For our taxes are low; our inflation is down; our debt is manageable; our reduced regulations are favourable to business.

We take comfort from the fact that both our Prime Minister and our Foreign Secretary have spoken out sharply against the forces of bureaucracy and federalism.

THE CHOICE

Our choice is clear. Either we exercise democratic control of Europe through cooperation between national governments and parliaments which have legitimacy, experience and closeness to the people. Or we transfer decisions to a remote multilingual parliament, accountable to no real European public opinion and thus increasingly subordinate to a powerful bureaucracy. No amount of misleading language about pooling sovereignty can change that.

EUROPE AND THE WIDER WORLD

Mr Chairman, in world affairs for most of this century Europe has offered problems, not solutions. The founders of the European Community were consciously trying to change that. Democracy and prosperity in Europe were to be an example to other peoples in other continents. Sometimes this view took an over-ambitious turn with talk of Europe as a third force brokering between two superpowers of East and West. This approach was always based upon a disastrous illusion – that Western Europe could at some future date dispense with the military defence offered by the United States.

Now that the forces of communism have retreated and the threat which Soviet tanks and missiles levelled at the heart of Europe has gone, there is a risk that the old tendency towards decoupling Europe from the United States may again emerge. This is something against which Europeans themselves must guard – and of which the United States must be aware.

This risk could become reality in several ways.

TRADE

First, there is the question of trade. It is a terrible indictment of the complacency which characterizes the modern post-Cold War world that we have allowed the present GATT round to be stalled for so long. Free trade is the greatest force for prosperity and peaceful cooperation.

It does no good to the Western alliance when Europe and the United States come to regard each other as hostile interests. In practice, whatever the theory may be, economic disputes do sour political relations. Agricultural subsidies and tariffs lie at the heart of the dispute, which will not go away unless we in Europe decide that the Common Agricultural Policy has to be fundamentally changed. That will go far to determine what kind of Europe we are building.

For, as I have said before, I would like to see the European Community – embracing the former communist countries to its east – agree to develop an Atlantic Free Trade Area with the United States. That would be a means of pressing for more open multilateral trade throughout the world. Europe must seek to move the world away from competing regional trade blocs – not promote them. In such a trading arrangement, Britain would have a vital role bridging that Atlantic divide – just as Germany should provide Europe with a bridge to the east and to the countries of the former Soviet Union.

EASTERN EUROPE

Secondly, we must modify and modernize our defence. The dangers on Europe's eastern border have receded. But let us not forget that on the credibility of NATO's military strength all our wider objectives depend – reassurance for the post-communist countries, stability in Europe, transatlantic political cooperation.

Communism may have been vanquished. But all too often the communists themselves have not. The chameleon qualities of the comrades have never been more clearly demonstrated than in their emergence as democratic socialists and varieties of nationalist in the countries of Central and Eastern Europe. From the powerful positions they retain in the bureaucracy, security apparatus and the armed forces, from their places in not-really-privatized enterprises, they are able to obstruct, undermine and plunder.

The systems of proportional representation which so many of these countries have adopted have allowed these tactics to succeed all the more, leading to weak governments and a bewildering multiplicity of parties. All this risks bringing democracy into discredit. If Eastern European countries which retain some links with a pre-communist past, and have some sort of middle class on which to draw, falter on the path to reform, how will the leaders of the countries of the former Soviet Union dare to proceed further upon it?

We can help by allowing them free access to our markets. I am delighted that Association agreements have been signed between the European Community and several of these countries. I would like speedy action to include the others in similar arrangements. But ten years is too long to wait before the restrictions on trade are removed. And I would like to see these countries offered full membership of the European Community rapidly.

Above all we must offer these countries greater security. Russian troops are still stationed on Polish territory. Moreover, it is understandable that the Central and Eastern European countries are alarmed at what conflict in the old USSR and the old Yugoslavia may portend. Although I recognize that the North Atlantic Cooperation Council has been formed with a view to this, I still feel that the European ex-communist countries are entitled to that greater degree of reassurance which a separate closer relationship with NATO would bring.

SECURITY

But, Mr Chairman, most of the threats to Europe's and the West's interests no longer come from this continent. I believe – and I have been urging this on NATO members since 1990 – that the Americans and Europeans ought to be able to deploy our forces under NATO outside the area for which the present North Atlantic Treaty allows. It is impossible to know where the danger may next come. But two considerations should make us alive to real risks to our security.

First, the break-up of the Soviet Union has led to large numbers of advanced weapons becoming available to would-be purchasers at knockdown prices: it would be foolish to imagine that these will not, some of them, fall into the worst possible hands.

Second, Europe cannot ignore its dependence for oil on the Middle East. Saddam Hussein is still in power. Fundamentalism is as strong as ever. Old scores are still unsettled. We must beware. And we must widen our ability to defend our interests and be prepared to act when necessary.

THE COMMUNITY'S WIDER ROLE

Finally, the European Community must come to recognize its place in what is called the New World Order.

The ending of the Cold War has meant that the international institutions created in the post-war years – the UN, the IMF, the World Bank, the GATT – can work much more effectively. This means that the role for the Community is inevitably circumscribed. Within Europe, a wider role for NATO and the CSCE should also be reflected in more modest ambitions for the Community's diplomacy. In Yugoslavia, the Community has shown itself incapable of dealing effectively with security questions. Outside Europe, GATT with its mandate to reduce trade barriers should be the body that establishes the rules of the game in trade. The Community must learn to live within those rules. All in all, the Community must be prepared to fit in with the new internationalism, not supplant it.

CONCLUSION

Mr Chairman, I end as I began – with architecture. The Hague is a splendid capital, and how much we should admire the Dutch for keeping it together so well, as they have done with so many other of their towns. The Mauritshuis is a testimony to the genius which they showed. It was here, and in Amsterdam, that so much of the modern world was invented in the long Dutch fight for freedom.

Dutch architecture has its own unmistakable elegance and durability – it was copied all around the north European world, from Wick in northern Scotland to Tallinn in Estonia. Some architecture does last. Other architecture does not. Let us make sure that we build a Europe as splendid and lasting as the Mauritshuis, rather than one as shabby and ephemeral as the Berlaymont.

Political Chronology
1955–1979

1955

5 April   Churchill resigned as Prime Minister; succeeded by
               Eden

26 May   General election: Conservative majority sixty

1956

26 July   Nasser nationalized the Suez Canal

29 October   Israel invaded Sinai

30 October   Joint Anglo-French ultimatum to Egypt and Israel;
               Soviet troops invaded Hungary

5 November   British and French landings at Port Said;
               intervention aborted two days later under US
               pressure

1957

9 January   Eden resigned as Prime Minister; Macmillan
               succeeded him

25 March   Treaty of Rome signed, establishing EEC

25 July   Macmillan: 'Most of our people have never had it
               so good'

19 September   Thorneycroft increased Bank Rate from 5 to 7 per
               cent

1958

6 January   Treasury Ministers (Thorneycroft, Powell and
               Birch) resigned from the Government over public

expenditure plans; Macmillan left the following day
for a Commonwealth tour, describing the
resignations as 'little local difficulties'

3 July   Credit squeeze relaxed

31 August   Notting Hill and Nottingham riots

1959

7 April   Budget: 9d reduction in income tax

8 October   General election: Conservative majority 100; MT
                  first elected MP for Finchley

28 November   Gaitskell called for reform of Clause IV of Labour's
                  constitution – forced to retreat the following year

1960

3 February   Macmillan in South Africa: 'a wind of change is
                  blowing through the continent'

5 February   MT's maiden speech

February-October Parliamentary passage of MT's Public Bodies
                  (Admission of the Press to Meetings) Bill

25 July   Deflationary emergency Budget; 'Pay Pause' for
                  Government employees

31 July   Macmillan announced beginning of negotiations for
                  Britain to join EEC

13 August   East Germany sealed the border with West Berlin;
                  Berlin Wall begun

9 October   Reshuffle: MT appointed to her first Government
                  post – Parliamentary Secretary, Ministry of
                  Pensions and National Insurance

1962

14 March   Orpington by-election: Liberals took Conservative
                  seat, overturning a majority of 14,760

13 July   'Night of the Long Knives' – seven of twenty-one
                  Cabinet ministers fired by Macmillan

October   Cuban missile crisis

November   Vassall affair

21 December	US agreement to sell Britain Polaris

1963

14 January	De Gaulle rejected first British application to join the EEC
14 February	Harold Wilson elected Labour Leader following death of Hugh Gaitskell
4 June	Profumo resigned
1 July	Philby named as 'the third man'
10 October	Macmillan resigned as Prime Minister during Conservative Party Conference in Blackpool
19 October	Douglas-Home became Prime Minister; Iain Macleod and Enoch Powell refused office

1964

July	Legislation enacted to abolish Resale Price Maintenance
15 October	General election: Labour won a majority of four; Wilson became Prime Minister
28 October	MT became Opposition spokesman on Pensions
November	Sterling crisis

1965

24 January	Churchill died, aged ninety
12 July	Crosland's circular 10/65 on comprehensive schools: LEAs to submit plans within a year to reorganize on comprehensive lines; Government's aim declared to be 'the complete elimination of selection and separatism in secondary education'
22 July	Douglas-Home resigned as Conservative Leader; Heath elected to succeed him, defeating Maudling and Powell
16 September	Labour's National Plan published
5 October	Reshuffle of Opposition spokesmen: MT moved to Shadow Housing and Land
8 November	Abolition of capital punishment

11 November	Rhodesia: Unilateral Declaration of Independence (UDI)

1966

31 March	General election: Labour returned with an overall majority of ninety-seven
19 April	Reshuffle of Opposition spokesmen: MT appointed Iain Macleod's deputy, shadowing the Treasury
3 May	Budget introduced Selective Employment Tax (SET)
May–July	Seamen's strike
15 June	Abortion Bill passed Second Reading
July	Sterling crisis; deflation; wage freeze to be followed by a prices and incomes policy
5 July	Sexual Offences Bill (legalizing homosexuality) passed Second Reading
12 October	MT spoke against SET at the Conservative Conference
10 November	Labour announced Britain to make a second application to join the EEC

1967

11 April	Massive Conservative gains in local government elections
10 October	Heath moved MT to Shadow Fuel and Power, with a place in the Shadow Cabinet
18 November	Devaluation of sterling by 14 per cent ($2.80 to $2.40)
27 November	Britain's second EEC application vetoed by France
29 November	Jenkins replaced Callaghan as Chancellor of the Exchequer; Callaghan succeeded Jenkins as Home Secretary

1968

22 February	Callaghan announced emergency legislation to curb immigration of Asians expelled from Kenya; Shadow Cabinet divided

17 March	Grosvenor Square riot – violent demonstration against Vietnam War
19 March	Budget increased indirect taxes by almost £900 million – austerity under Jenkins
20 April	Enoch Powell's 'River Tiber' speech in Birmingham; Heath dismissed him from the Shadow Cabinet the following day
10 October	MT gave her CPC lecture *What's Wrong With Politics?*
14 November	MT moved by Heath to Shadow Transport

1969

17 January	Barbara Castle introduced *In Place of Strife* – Labour's proposals to reform industrial relations law; opposition from within the Labour Party, led by Callaghan, forced their withdrawal in June
14 August	British troops deployed on the streets of Londonderry
21 October	MT appointed Opposition spokesman on Education in succession to Edward Boyle

1970

30 January– 1 February	Selsdon Park Conference – Shadow Cabinet discussion of Conservative policy for next manifesto
18 June	General election: Conservatives won majority of thirty-one; Heath became Prime Minister; MT appointed Secretary of State for Education and Science
30 June	MT issued Circular 10/70, withdrawing Labour's comprehensive education Circulars
20 July	Iain Macleod died suddenly
6–30 September	Leila Khalid affair
27 October	Budget – ending free school milk for children over seven; increasing school meal charges; Open University reprieved

1971

4 February	Nationalization of Rolls-Royce
5 August	Industrial Relations Bill became law
28 October	House of Commons on a free vote approved terms of entry to EEC

1972

9 January	Miners went on strike
20 January	Unemployment total passed one million
10 February	Mass picketing closed Saltley Coke Depot
19 February	Government conceded miners' demands to end the strike
29 February	Government announced U-turn on Upper Clyde Shipbuilders
March	Government began search for voluntary pay policy in talks with TUC and CBI
21 March	Budget – reflation began in earnest
22 March	Industry White Paper published
24 March	Suspension of Northern Ireland Parliament at Stormont; direct rule began
June–July	Industrial Relations Act badly damaged following court decisions leading to arrest of pickets in docks dispute
23 June	Sterling floated after only six weeks' membership of the European currency 'snake'
Summer-autumn	'Tripartite talks' between Government, TUC and CBI – Government attempted to negotiate a voluntary pay policy
2 November	Collapse of 'Tripartite talks'
6 November	Heath announced Stage 1 of statutory pay policy
6 December	MT's White Paper *Education: A Framework for Expansion*

1973

1 January	Britain joined EEC
17 January	Heath announced Stage 2 of statutory pay policy

16 March	End of Bretton Woods system – all major currencies floated
May	Heath/Barber boom at its height; Budget reduced spending plans
6–24 October	Yom Kippur War; oil prices dramatically increased
8 October	Heath announced Stage 3
12 November	Miners began overtime ban, sharply cutting coal production
2 December	Reshuffle – Whitelaw became Employment Secretary
13 December	Heath announced three-day week
17 December	Emergency Budget cuts £1,200 million from expenditure plans

1974

9 January	NEDC meeting at which TUC suggested miners could be treated as a special case within Government pay policy
5 February	Miners voted to strike from 10 February
7 February	General election called for 28 February
21 February	Relativities Board leak suggesting that miners' claim could have been accommodated within Stage 3
23 February	Enoch Powell announced that he would vote Labour
28 February	General election: no single party won a majority; Labour won the largest number of seats
1–3 March	Heath attempted to form a coalition with the Liberals
4 March	Heath resigned following Liberal rejection of his proposals; Wilson became Prime Minister, leading a minority Labour Government
11 March	Heath formed his Shadow Cabinet, giving MT responsibility for the Environment
May	Centre for Policy Studies (CPS) founded
22 June	Keith Joseph's speech at Upminster
28 August	MT announced Conservative pledge to abolish

	domestic rates and hold down mortgage interest rates to maximum of 9½ per cent
5 September	Keith Joseph's speech at Preston
10 October	General election: Labour majority of three
14 October	1922 Committee executive urged Heath to call a leadership election
19 October	Keith Joseph's speech at Edgbaston
7 November	Heath reshuffled Shadow Cabinet; MT became Robert Carr's assistant spokesman on Treasury questions
14 November	Heath told 1922 that he would set up a committee to review leadership election procedure
21 November	Keith Joseph told MT that he would not stand for the leadership against Heath; MT told him she would
November– December	'Hoarding' story run against MT in the press
17 December	Leadership election review reported

1975

15 January	Airey Neave took over the organization of MT's leadership campaign, Edward du Cann having decided not to stand
4 February	Leadership election first ballot: MT 130, Heath 119, Hugh Fraser 16; Heath resigned as leader
11 February	Leadership election second ballot: MT elected leader
12 February	MT called on Heath at Wilton Street; Heath refused to serve in the Shadow Cabinet
18 February	Shadow Cabinet complete: Maudling, Foreign Affairs; Howe, Treasury; Joseph, Policy and Research; Thorneycroft, Chairman
5 June	EEC referendum
July	£6 a week quasi-statutory pay policy introduced; unemployment passed one million

1976

2 March	Sterling fell below $2
16 March	Wilson announced his resignation; Callaghan elected Labour Leader on 5 April
7 April	Government lost its majority
5 May	Stage 2 of pay policy agreed between Government and TUC
10 May	Thorpe resigned as Liberal Leader over the Scott affair; Grimond interim Leader; Steel elected on 7 July
7 June	Sterling under pressure – $5,300 million standby credit made available to UK for three months
28 September	Healey forced to turn back from the airport as sterling fell to $1.63; spoke at the Labour Conference on 30 September
4 October	*The Right Approach* published
1 November	IMF team arrived in UK
19 November	MT reshuffled Shadow Cabinet, dismissing Maudling and replacing him with John Davies
1 December	Shadow Cabinet decision to oppose the Scotland and Wales Bill; Buchanan-Smith and Rifkind resigned
15 December	Healey's mini-Budget and IMF Letter of Intent

1977

22 February	Government defeated on Scotland and Wales Bill guillotine – Bill effectively lost; prospect that Government would fall
23 March	'Lib-Lab Pact' saved the Government
16 June	Government defeated over Rooker-Wise-Lawson amendments – tax allowances linked to RPI
24 June	Grunwick dispute: mass picketing began
18 September	MT interviewed by Brian Walden suggested referendum if a future Conservative Government met the kind of trade union challenge Heath faced in 1974
8 October	*The Right Approach to the Economy* published

| *16 November* | Scotland Bill and Wales Bill successfully guillotined |

1978

25 January	Scotland Bill Committee – 'Cunningham amendment': 40 per cent hurdle for devolution in referendum
30 January	MT on television referred to people's fears that they would be 'rather swamped' by immigration
3 March	Rhodesia: 'internal settlement' – Muzorewa and others to join Ian Smith's government
25 May	Steel announced end of Lib-Lab Pact after current parliamentary session
21 July	Incomes policy White Paper: Stage 3 – 5 per cent guideline for wage increases
Summer	'Labour Isn't Working' – Saatchi & Saatchi's first campaign for the Conservative Party
7 September	Callaghan announced there would be no autumn election
21 September	Ford strike (ended 2 November): breached 5 per cent pay norm
11 October	Heath spoke in favour of Stage 3 at the Conservative Party Conference
8 November	114 Conservatives rebelled against leadership decision to abstain on motion to renew Rhodesian sanctions

1979

3 January	Lorry drivers strike for 25 per cent pay claim: 'Winter of Discontent' reaching its height
7 January	MT interviewed on *Weekend World*; suggested possible union reforms
14 January	MT offered to cooperate in legislation on secondary picketing and no-strike agreements for essential services; Government made no direct reply but eased its pay guidelines and lorry-drivers' strike settled locally over the following three weeks
1 March	Scotland and Wales devolution referenda

28 March	Government defeated on Motion of Confidence 311–310, forcing general election
30 March	Airey Neave murdered by INLA bomb
3 May	General election
4 May	MT became Prime Minister

Shadow Cabinet
1975–79

February 1975

MT	Leader
WHITELAW	Deputy Leader and Devolution
JOSEPH	Policy and Research
PYM	Agriculture
OPPENHEIM	Consumer Affairs and Prices
YOUNGER	Defence
GILMOUR	Home Affairs
PEYTON	House of Commons
ST JOHN-STEVAS	Education and Arts
PRIOR	Employment
JENKIN	Energy
RAISON	Environment
MAUDLING	Foreign and Commonwealth
HESELTINE	Industry
NEAVE	Northern Ireland
BUCHANAN-SMITH	Scotland
FOWLER	Social Services
HOWE	Treasury
EDWARDS	Wales
CARRINGTON	House of Lords
HAILSHAM	Without portfolio
THORNEYCROFT	Party Chairman
MAUDE	Deputy Chairman and CRD Chairman
ATKINS	Chief Whip (ex officio)

January 1976 – reshuffle

Biffen joined Shadow Cabinet from the backbenches as Energy spokesman.

Jenkin moved from Energy to Social Services, replacing Fowler who became spokesman for Transport outside the Shadow Cabinet.

Whitelaw replaced Gilmour as Shadow Home Secretary.

Gilmour replaced Younger at Defence.

Pym returned at Agriculture (had been absent through illness since April 1975); Jopling resumed his role as Agriculture No. 2.

MT	Leader
WHITELAW	Dep. Leader, Devolution, Home Affairs
JOSEPH	Policy and Research
PYM	Agriculture
OPPENHEIM	Consumer Affairs and Prices
GILMOUR	Defence
PEYTON	House of Commons
ST JOHN-STEVAS	Education and Arts
PRIOR	Employment
BIFFEN	Energy
RAISON	Environment
MAUDLING	Foreign and Commonwealth
HESELTINE	Industry
NEAVE	Northern Ireland
BUCHANAN-SMITH	Scotland
JENKIN	Social Services
HOWE	Treasury
EDWARDS	Wales
CARRINGTON	House of Lords
HAILSHAM	Without portfolio
THORNEYCROFT	Chairman
MAUDE	Deputy Chairman and CRD Chairman
ATKINS	Chief Whip (ex officio)

November 1976 – reshuffle

MT dismissed Maudling; replaced him with John Davies.

Heseltine moved to Environment and replaced at Industry by John Biffen.

Tom King joined the Shadow Cabinet as Energy spokesman.

Teddy Taylor joined the Shadow Cabinet as Trade spokesman.

Pym took over devolution and House of Commons.

Peyton replaced Pym shadowing Agriculture.

MT	Leader
WHITELAW	Deputy Leader and Home Affairs
JOSEPH	Policy and Research
PEYTON	Agriculture
OPPENHEIM	Consumer Affairs and Prices
GILMOUR	Defence
PYM	Devolution and House of Commons
ST JOHN-STEVAS	Education and Arts
PRIOR	Employment
KING	Energy
HESELTINE	Environment
DAVIES	Foreign and Commonwealth
BIFFEN	Industry
NEAVE	Northern Ireland
BUCHANAN-SMITH	Scotland
JENKIN	Social Services
TAYLOR	Trade
HOWE	Treasury
EDWARDS	Wales
CARRINGTON	House of Lords
HAILSHAM	Without portfolio
THORNEYCROFT	Chairman
MAUDE	Deputy Chairman and CRD Chairman
ATKINS	Chief Whip (ex officio)

December 1976 – Buchanan-Smith resignation

Taylor replaced Buchanan-Smith as Scottish Shadow.
   John Nott entered the Shadow Cabinet to replace Taylor shadowing Trade.

February 1977 – Biffen resignation

Biffen resigned. Keith Joseph replaced him as Industry spokesman, remaining responsible for Policy and Research.

November 1978 – reshuffle

Francis Pym formally replaced John Davies as Conservative Foreign Affairs spokesman.

Biffen returned to the Shadow Cabinet with responsibility for Small Businesses.

Carlisle replaced St John-Stevas as Education spokesman.

St John-Stevas replaced Pym as Shadow Leader of the House of Commons.

MT	Leader
WHITELAW	Deputy Leader and Home Affairs
JOSEPH	Industry, Policy and Research
PEYTON	Agriculture
OPPENHEIM	Consumer Affairs and Prices
GILMOUR	Defence
ST JOHN-STEVAS	Devolution and House of Commons
CARLISLE	Education and Arts
PRIOR	Employment
KING	Energy
HESELTINE	Environment
PYM	Foreign and Commonwealth
BIFFEN	Small Businesses
NEAVE	Northern Ireland
TAYLOR	Scotland
JENKIN	Social Services
NOTT	Trade
HOWE	Treasury
EDWARDS	Wales
CARRINGTON	House of Lords
HAILSHAM	Without portfolio
THORNEYCROFT	Chairman
MAUDE	Deputy Chairman and CRD Chairman
ATKINS	Chief Whip (ex officio)

Index